CONWAY'S
ALL THE WORLD'S FIGHTING SHIPS 1947-1982

PART I:
THE WESTERN POWERS

NAVAL INSTITUTE PRESS

Editor

ROBERT GARDINER

Contributors

NORMAN FRIEDMAN (USA)

JOHN JORDAN (Belgium, France, Netherlands)

GERHARD KOOP (West Germany – translated by Erwin Sieche)

HUGH LYON (Greece, Italy, Portugal, Turkey)

ANTONY PRESTON (Canada, United Kingdom, Australia, New Zealand)

ROBERT L SCHEINA (Japan)

IAN STURTON (Spain)

KARL-ERIK WESTERLUND (Denmark, Norway)

Line drawings

By Przemysław Budzbon (with the assistance of Marek Twardowski)

Book design

By Dave Mills

Copy editing

By Michael Boxall

First published in 1983 by Conway Maritime Press Ltd,
24 Bride Lane, Fleet Street, London EC4Y 8DR
Reprinted 1985

Published and distributed in the United States of America
and Canada by the Naval Institute Press,
Annapolis, Maryland 21402

Library of Congress Catalog Card No. 82-42936
ISBN 0-87021-418-9 (Volume 1)
ISBN 0-87021-919-7 (Volume 2)
ISBN 0-87021-923-5 (2 volume set)

Manufactured in the United Kingdom

Contents

Foreword

This volume is the third of a series begun by *Conway's All the World's Fighting Ships 1860-1905* and continues where the previous volume (1922–1946) left off, taking the coverage down to the end of 1982. As with the 1922–1946 volume, information on the warships of this period would appear to be readily available, so it is worth explaining the particular aims of this book.

Since the Second World War there has been both a technical and a political revolution in naval affairs. To take the latter first, the growth of the Soviet Navy, and the setting up of many new naval forces following European decolonisation, has produced a significant shift in the traditional balance of seapower. Although many of these newly independent nations may be considered non-aligned, the most important political development since 1945 has been the advent of the Cold War and the polarisation of the world's major nations into two mutually antagonistic power blocs. In this atmosphere of suspicion and secrecy it has been extremely difficult to obtain reliable information on naval matters. Indeed, it is now recognised that even before the War much of the official data published – even on the part of the Western democracies – was deliberately misleading, and nowadays this problem is even more acute. The naval yearbooks, which are the principal sources of information about modern warships, are particularly vulnerable in this direction since they have to concentrate on the very latest developments, where there is often little or no reliable information. Full details may emerge some years later, but the annuals have little incentive to publish what is then old news.

Much the same situation applies to the postwar technological revolution. Warships have changed radically since 1945, but a surprising number of developments are deeply rooted in postwar responses to the lessons of the 1939–45 war at sea. Furthermore, the first (and in some cases even the second) generation of postwar warships have gone out of service and consequently security has been relaxed. Therefore, it is now possible to give an accurate and reasonably detailed account of the vitally important fifteen or so years after the war. This in turn gives the intelligent observer considerable insight into the developments of the last twenty years.

The primary aim of this book, therefore, is to provide a coherent overview of the postwar naval revolution, using newly released information wherever possible. This is evident in the introductory essays to each country, which cover the political and economic background, but can also be seen in the notes on individual ship classes, where the emphasis is on the rationale of the design rather than a straightforward description of the ship's features. For similar reasons, important projects or cancelled designs are included wherever they throw light on a particular navy's line of development.

SCOPE

It was originally intended that, like its predecessors, the 1947–1982 volume would be published as a single volume, but in order to give more detailed coverage an increased extent was necessary. When considered with the general economic situation, this indicated that division into two parts would be a sensible move. The first part contains the navies of NATO and certain other pro-Western naval powers (Australia, New Zealand and Japan); Part II (to be published later in 1983) covers the Warsaw Pact and the remainder of the world, and includes the index for both parts. This division is entirely a matter of convenience, and does not imply a judgement on the political stance of any country outside the major alliances.

In terms of coverage, this volume follows the pattern of its predecessors, concentrating specifically on *fighting ships*. Ideally, fleet support and replenishment units should have been covered in deference to their enhanced postwar importance, but shortage of space made this impossible. Therefore, only a few auxiliaries with specific combat value have been included, and non-naval maritime forces (coast guard, army, police or fishery protection services) have been omitted unless they enjoy a close relationship (like the US Coast Guard does) with the national navy. Otherwise, the coverage is both broad and deep, extending down to minor patrol and landing craft in even the smallest navies.

ORGANISATION

This will be familiar to readers of previous volumes, and follows a standard order for each country: a general introduction, followed by a statement of fleet strength in 1947, then the post-1947 classes in type and chronological order. However, since the war the traditional typology has become confused, so this volume has adopted six basic type-divisions – Major Surface Ships (aircraft carriers, cruisers, destroyers and frigates), Submarines, Amphibious Warfare Vessels, Small Surface Combatants (corvettes to patrol craft), Mine Warfare Vessels and Miscellaneous. The ships of each navy are presented in this order, but within the main divisions classes are grouped in a manner approximating to the traditional hierarchy (carriers before cruisers, cruisers before destroyers, etc) with the oldest classes first. The names of the classes in the headings to the tables are followed by a description *in italics*, but these are not necessarily official descriptions of ship-types.

The data given in each table follows the style of the earlier volumes, with the addition of an entry for Sensors. This gives the designations of the main radar and sonar sets, and in some cases, fire control systems; ECM and ESM gear has been omitted since it is virtually impossible to give a succinct description of their components or what they actually do.

The remaining data is largely self-explanatory, except for the following points:

1. Where two tonnages and speeds are quoted for submarines, the first applies to the surface condition and the second as submerged.
2. Gun armament is given in the traditional form, namely: number of barrels – size of gun/calibre (number of mountings × number of barrels per mount). For example, '6–3in/70 (3 × 2)' means six 70-calibre 3in guns disposed in three twin mountings. For missiles, where the number of independent systems is the significant factor, it is the number of launchers which is quoted: for example, '2 Sea Sparrow SAM (2 × 8)' means that each of the two launchers has eight tubes, and there are not sixteen individual systems.

In order not to duplicate information, the basic details of all purchased or transferred warships are given under the country of origin, and this also applies to warships built for export where the design originated with the navy of the shipbuilding country concerned. Only variations from the standard type are noted in the data tables for each recipient navy. For this reason, such classes are referred to in terms of the original design – for example, as 'ex-US *Adjutant* class minesweepers' where transferred, or as 'US *Adjutant* type minesweepers' when built specifically for export. Similarly, for all transferred classes the date of acquisition is quoted in the building table, the original construction dates being available under the country of origin.

ILLUSTRATIONS

Classes of frigate-size and upward are usually represented by both a photograph and a line drawing; wherever possible these are complementary, representing either sister ships, or the same vessel before and after alteration. The emphasis on appearance changes is carried into the captions for both types of illustration, which are dated wherever and as accurately as possible.

The line drawings, which were specially commissioned for this book, are mostly reproduced to 1/1250 scale. A few very large ships are reproduced to 1/1750 scale to allow them to fit horizontally onto a page, and a few small ships are reproduced at 1/750 scale, so that a reasonable degree of detail could be included. All exceptions to the standard 1/1250 scale are clearly marked.

ACKNOWLEDGEMENTS

For help with photographs we are indebted to the following individuals and organisations; Dr S Cioglia, Norman Friedman, Ross Gillett, Pierre Hervieux, Gerhard Koop, MG Photographic, MoD, Jacques Navarret, Len Pierce (Vosper-Thornycroft), Antony Preston, Robert Scheina, Ian Sturton, Clive Taylor and Karl-Erik Westerland.

NOTE

As always we welcome 'alterations and additions' to information in this book. All correspondence on this subject should be directed to Conway Maritime Press Ltd, 24 Bride Lane, Fleet Street, London EC4Y 8DR, Great Britain.

Robert Gardiner

Abbreviations

The following glossary covers most of the abbreviations and technical terms used in this book, but it does not include abbreviations in common use nor designations for machinery, equipment and electronics or companies usually known by their initials. A separate list of the now widely used US ship designations follows the glossary. See also the Introductions to France, The Netherlands, United Kingdom and USA for lists of electronics and specific codenames.

AA(W), anti-aircraft (warfare)
ABC, atomic, bacteriological and chemical (warfare). See also NBC
AC, alternating current
AD, aircraft direction (British); air defence
(Weapon) Alfa, US automatic ASW rocket
'A's & 'A's, alterations and additions (British)
ASCAC, ASW Classification and Analysis Centre (US)
ASM, air-to-surface missile
ASMD, anti-ship missile defence (US)
ASROC, Anti-Submarine Rocket (US)
ASR, air-sea rescue; Admiralty Standard Range (diesels)
ASW, anti-submarine warfare; anti-submarine weapon
AUWE, Admiralty Underwater Weapons Establishment
aux, auxiliary
Avgas, aviation fuel
AWACS, Airborne Warning and Control Systems

BATRAL, *bâtiments de transport legers* (French LSMs)
BDC, *bâtiments de débarquement de chars* (French LSTs)
bhp, brake horse power
(B) PDMS, (basic) point defence missile system
BU, broken up
BuShips, Bureau of Ships (US)

c, circa
cal, calibre
CIC, combat information centre
CIWS, close-in weapon system
CMS, coastal minesweeper (British)
CNO, chief of naval operations

Co, company
CODAG, combined diesel and gas
CODOG, combined diesel or gas
COGAG, combined gas and gas
COGOG, combined gas or gas
comm, commissioned
comp, completed
COSAG, combined steam and gas
CP, controllable pitch (propellers)
CTOL, conventional take-off and landing
cwt, hundredweight
cyl, cylinder(s)

DASH, Drone Anti-Submarine Helicopter
DC, depth charge; direct current
DCT, depth charge thrower
DD, drydock
DELEX, Destroyer Life Extension Programme (Canadian)
D/F, direction-finder (-finding)
DBM, German Navy League
DP, dual purpose
DTCN, *Direction Technique des Constructions Navales* (French)
DUKW, amphibious wheeled vehicle
DYd, dockyard

ECM, electronic countermeasures
EDA, *engins de débarquement ateliers* (French landing craft)
EDATS, extra deep armed team (mine) sweeping
EDIC, *engins de débarquement infanterie et chars* (French LCTs)
EEC, European Economic Community
EEZ, exclusive economic zone
ESM, electronic support measures
ext, extreme

FAA, Fleet Air Arm (British)
FCS, fire control system
fd, flight deck
FFDS, folding fin discarding sabot
FFO, furnace fuel oil
FIS, Frontier Inspection Service (German)
FRAM, Fleet Rehabilitation And Modernisation (US)
FPB, fast patrol boat (British)
ft, foot;feet
fwd, forward
FY, fiscal year (US)

gal, gallon(s)
GB, Great Britain
GIUK, Greenland-Iceland-United Kingdom
GMSA, German Mine Sweeping Administration
GP (MG), general purpose (machine gun)
GRP, glass reinforced plastic
GUPPY, Greater Underwater Propulsive Power (US)

HA, high angle
HDML, harbour defence motor launch (British)
H/F, high frequency
HF/DF, high frequency direction-finding
HP, high pressure
hp, horsepower
HS, harbour service
HUK, hunter-killer group (US)

I, Island
IFF, Identification Friend or Foe
ihp, indicated horsepower
IMS, inshore minesweeper (British)
in, inch(es)
Ind, industry
IoW, Isle of Wight

JMSDF, Japanese Maritime Self Defence Force

K-gun, type of (US) DCT
km, kilometre(s)
kt(s), knot(s)
kW, kilowatt(s)

LAMPS, Light Airborne Multi-Purpose System (US)
LP, low pressure
LRMP, long-range maritime patrol (aircraft)
LRO, Long-Range Objectives group (US)
LSU, Labour Service Unit (Germany)

m, metre(s)
max, maximum
MCM(V), mine countermeasures (vessel)
MDAP, Mutual Defense Assistance Program (US)
M/F, medium frequency
MG, machine gun
MGB, motor gunboat (British)
MIRV, multiple independently targetted re-entry vehicle
Mk, Mark
ML, motor launch (British)
mm, millimetre(s)
Mod, model
Mousetrap, ASW rocket (US)
MSA, Maritime Safety Agency (Japan)
MSBS, French designation for SLBM
MSDF, see JMSDF
MSTS, Maritime Sea Transportation Service (US)
MTB, motor torpedo-boat (British)

NATO, North Atlantic Treaty Organisation
NBC(D), nuclear, bateriological and chemical (defence)
NECPA, National Emergency Command Post Afloat (US)
nm, nautical mile(s)
no, number
NSRDC, Naval Ship Research and Development Centre (US)
NTDS, Naval Tactical Data System (US)
NYd, Navy Yard (US; actually known as Naval Shipyards from 1950s)

oa, overall
OPV, offshore patrol vessel (British)

PDMS, point defence missile system
pdr, pounder
PIRAZ, Positive Identification and Radar Advisory Zone (USA)
pp, between perpendiculars
psi, pounds per square inch
PUFFS, passive underwater fire control feasibility study (US submarine sonar system)

QF, quick-firing (British)

RA, rear admiral
RAF, Royal Air Force
RAM, Rolling Airframe Missile (US)
RAN, Royal Australian Navy
RARDE, Royal Artillery Research and Development Establishment
RAT, Rocket Assisted Torpedo (US)
RC, radio control
RCN, Royal Canadian Navy
R&D, research and development
RF, rapid fire (US)
R(F)L, rocket (flare) launcher
RN, Royal Navy
RPC, remote power control
rpm, revolutions per minute

SAM, surface-to-air missile
SAN, South African Navy
SATNAV, satellite navigation (US)
SB, shipbuilders; shipbuilding
SCOT, satellite communication terminal (British)
SDML, seaward defence motor launch (British)
shp, shaft horsepower
SLBM, submarine launched ballistic missile
SLEP, Service Life Extension Programme (US)
SNLE, French term for SSBN
SOSUS, Sound Surveillance System (US)
SSM, surface-to-surface missile
STAAG, Stabilised Tachymetric Anti-Aircraft Gun (British)
std, standard
STOVL, short take-off, vertical landing
STWS, Ship's Torpedo Weapon System (British)
S Yd, shipyard
SUBROC, submarine fired ASW rocket (US)

t, ton(s)
TACAN, Tactical Air Navigation aid (US)
TACTASS, Tactical Tower Array Surveillance System (US)
TCD, *transports de chalands de débarquement* (French LSDs)
TFCC, Tactical Flag Command Centre (US)
TRIP, Tartar Reliability Improvement Programme (US)
TS, training ship
TT, torpedo tube(s)

UHF, ultra high frequency
UNREP, underway replenishment (US)
US(N), United States (Navy)

VA, vice admiral
VCNS, Vice Chief of the Naval Staff
VDS, variable depth sonar
VLF, very low frequency
VLS, vertical launch system
VSTOL, vertical/short take-off and landing
VTE, vertical triple expansion
VTOL, vertical take-off and landing
VSRAD, Very Short Range Air Defence System (Dutch)

WEU, Western European Union
Wks, Works
wl, waterline
W/T, wireless telegraphy (obsolete British term for radio)

Y-ARD, Yarrow-Admiralty Research and Development organisation
Y-gun, type of DCT (US)

3-D, three-dimensional

US SHIP DESIGNATIONS

These consist of letter codes representing basic ship types with additional letters (usually added on the end) to further define the sub-types. The main types are listed (together with untypical designations) followed by the most common suffixes. A few of the rarer designations will be found under the relevant classes in the US section.

A. Ship types

AE, ammunition ship
AFS, combat stores ship
AGC, later LCC (*qv*)
AGMR, major communications relay ship
AGSS, auxiliary submarine
AKA, later LKA (*qv*)
AO, fleet oiler
AOE, fast combat support ship
AMS, later MSC (*qv*)
APA, later LPA (*qv*)

BYMS, YMS (*qv*) built for Britain

CA, heavy cruiser
CG, missile cruiser (ex-frigate)
CL, light cruiser
CPIC, coastal patrol and interdiction craft
CSGN, strike cruiser
CV, aircraft carrier
CVA, attack aircraft carrier
CVS, ASW support carrier
CVV, medium aircraft carrier

DD, fleet destroyer
DDE, fleet destroyer converted to escort destroyer
DE, destroyer escort
DL, destroyer leader (frigate)
DSRV, deep submergence rescue vehicle

FF, frigate

LCA, landing craft, assault
LCAC, landing craft, air cushion
LCC, amphibious command ship
LCM, landing craft, mechanised
LCP(L), landing craft, personnel (large)
LCT, landing craft, tank
LCU, landing craft, utility
LCVP, landing craft, vehicle and personnel
LFS, fire support ship

LHA, amphibious assault ship
LHD, amphibious assault ship, dock
LKA, amphibious cargo ship
LPA, amphibious personnel transport
LPD, amphibious transport, dock
LPH, amphibious helicopter carrier
LSD, landing ship, dock

MCM, mine countermeasures vessel
MHC, coastal minehunter
MSB, minesweeping boat
MSC, coastal minesweeper
MSD, drone minesweeper
MSI, inshore minesweeper
MSL, minesweeping launch
MSO, ocean minesweeper

PC, patrol craft
PCH, hydrofoil patrol craft
PF, patrol frigate
PG, patrol gunboat
PHM, missile firing hydrofoil
PT, torpedo boat
PTF, fast patrol boat

SC, submarine chaser
SCS, sea control ship
SS, submarine
SST, training submarine

VSS, VSTOL support ship

WHEC, Coast Guard high endurance cutter
WMEC, Coast Guard medium endurance cutter

YMS, later MSC (*qv*)

B. Principal suffixes

G, guided missile firing
N, nuclear powered
B, ballistic missile firing
K, ASW hunter-killer
R, radar-picket
X, experimental, or characteristics undecided

Belgium

Wielingen on trials – the first major warship designed and built in Belgium
Official

At the end of the Second World War the Belgian Navy was left with only two vessels of any consequence, both of which had been recovered from the Germans. Neither was in particularly good mechanical condition; *Artevelde* was incapable of proceding to sea under her own power, and *Jan Breydel*, despite her extensive conversion while in German hands, was 30 years old. An ex-US Navy patrol frigate was added in 1947, but only with the transfer of six ex-British ocean minesweepers of the *Algerine* class between 1949 and 1953 did the postwar Belgian Navy acquire a meaningful operational capability. Membership of NATO was soon to bring an expanded role, and a corresponding increase in the size of Belgium's naval forces. Operating in conjunction with the fleets of other NATO powers of northwest Europe, these forces were to be responsible for the security of maritime communications in the North Sea, the Channel and the Western Approaches. A large programme of mine countermeasures vessels was financed by the United States under the Mutual Defense Aid Program (MDAP). By 1960 no less than 47 such vessels were in service with the Belgian Navy, served by two converted logistics support ships. At about the same time, the four remaining *Algerine* type ocean minesweepers – which now included two ex-Canadian units recently transferred – were allocated to more general patrol duties.

The fleet structure built up by 1960 remained basically unaltered during the next two decades, and was reinforced by the replacement of the logistics support vessels by two purpose-built units completed 1966–67, and the replacement of the *Algerine*s by the small frigates of the E 71 type, sophisticated modern vessels which represented a considerable achievement by the small Belgian shipbuilding industry.

By the late 1970s the wooden minesweepers built during the 1950s were in urgent need of replacement. The larger MSOs of the US *Agile* type had all undergone conversion as minehunters during the mid-1970s, but many of the smaller MSCs of the *Adjutant* type had been transferred to other countries and the remainder were being steadily discarded. France and the Netherlands, who were in a similar position and had similar operational requirements, joined with Belgium in the 'Tripartite Minehunter Project'. Under the final agreement the Belgian Navy was to built ten units in the first instance, with a possible follow-on order for five more. Construction of the Belgian ships has been delayed by problems in setting up the shipbuilding consortium, and it is now becoming clear that some of the elderly MCM vessels will retire before their replacements enter service.

BASES
The main base of the Belgian Navy has traditionally been that of

Oostende, and the latter has served as the centre of operations for the major mine countermeasures vessels since the 1950s. At present it is the base of the single active MSO squadron, and the reserve MSC squadron. One active MSI squadron and a further reserve squadron are based at Kallo. A third base, at Nieuwpoort, was closed in 1976. Since 1966 a new main base has been under construction at Zeebrugge, for completion in 1985. The new frigates of the E 71 class and the logistics support vessels *Godetia* and *Zinnia* are currently based there. Naval aviation is based at Koksijde.

FLEET STRENGTH 1947

FRIGATES

Name	Launched	Disp (standard)	Fate
JAN BREYDEL (ex-*Barbara*, ex-*Zinnia*)	Aug 15	1200t	BU 1952
ARTEVELDE (ex-*K 4*, ex-*Lorelei*, ex-*Artevelde*)	Aug 40	1640t	BU 1954
LUITENANT TER ZEE VICTOR BILLET (ex-*PF 57*, *Sheboygan*)	31.7.43	1430t	Stricken 1957

Jan Breydel (formerly *Zinnia*) was an ex-British 'Flower' class sloop employed as a fishery protection vessel until captured by the Germans in 1940. She was subsequently rebuilt at the Cockerill Yard, Antwerp, and emerged with a typical German profile and an armament of 3–105mm (3×1), 8–37mm (4×2) and 12–20mm (6×2) guns).

Artevelde which, originally, was to have replaced her in the fishery protection role, was seized while on the slipway at the Cockerill Yard in 1940, and was subsequently fitted out in similar fashion to *Zinnia* by Wilton-Fijenoord. She had an armament of 3–105mm (3×1), 4–37mm (2×2) and 10–20mm (2×4, 1×2).

Neither ship was in very good mechanical condition when they reverted to Belgian control at the end of the War. *Artevelde*, which could not even procede to sea under her own power, never had her machinery repaired, and became a stationary training ship. Both vessels were stricken in the early 1950s after some modifications to their armament.

Victor Billet was an ex-US Navy patrol frigate of the *Tacoma* class acquired in 1947. Until 1950 she operated as part of the International North Atlantic Weather Organisation. She was subsequently transferred to fishery protection duties and became a stationary training ship in the mid-1950s.

1

BELGIUM

MAJOR SURFACE SHIPS

Wielingen as completed

Although a replacement plan for the *Escorteurs Côtiers* of the *Algerine* type was submitted by the Belgian Navy in 1964, it was not unitl 1969 that detailed studies based on staff requirements were undertaken. Despite the limited size and capabilities of the Belgian shipbuilding industry, the Government made procurement conditional on Belgian participation in the design and construction of the new vessels. Costs were to be kept to a minimum by providing only those features which were essential to the escort mission in the North Sea/Channel area. A further requirement was that only weapon systems currently in service or being evaluated by other NATO navies should be considered. Particular stress was laid on seaworthiness, watertight integrity, and on automation in data collection, decision-making, and the operation and maintenance of machinery.

In view of the particularly close associations between Belgium, France and the Netherlands, it was not unnatural that the latter two countries should provide assistance in certain areas of the design, and that weapon systems operational with their two navies should be adopted for the Belgian ships. French manufac-

WIELINGEN (E 71) class *frigates*

Displacement:	1880t light; 2283t full load
Dimensions:	338ft pp, 349ft oa × 40ft × 17ft
	103.0m, 106.4m × 12.3m × 5.3m
Machinery:	2-shaft CODOG: 1 Olympus TM3B gas turbine, 28,000shp = 28kts, plus 2 Cockerill Co240 V12 diesels, 6000bhp = 20kts. Range 4500nm at 18kts
Armament:	4 MM38 Exocet SSM (4×1), 1 NATO Sea Sparrow SAM (1×8), 1–100mm, 2 Corvus, 1–375mm ASW mortar (1×6), 2 TT (L5 torpedoes)
Sensors:	Radar DA-05, WM-25; sonar SQS-505A
Complement:	160

No	Name	Builder	Laid down	Launched	Comp	Fate
F 910	WIELINGEN	Boëlwerf, Temse	5.3.74	30.3.76	20.1.78	Extant 1982
F 911	WESTDIEP	Cockerill, Hoboken	2.9.74	8.12.75	20.1.78	Extant 1982
F 912	WANDELAAR	Boëlwerf, Temse	5.3.75	21.6.77	27.10.78	Extant 1982
F 913	WESTHINDER	Cockerill, Hoboken	8.12.75	31.1.77	27.10.78	Extant 1982

turers provided the anti-submarine mortars and torpedo tubes, the single 100mm mounting, the Exocet missiles, the passive radar search system (ELCOS 1) and the optical sight. The Dutch provided the air search and fire control radars, and the SEWACO 4 tactical data system. The Canadian sonar and NATO Sea Sparrow missile system have also been adopted for the Dutch 'Standard' frigate, and the main Olympus gas turbine is in service with both the French and the Netherlands navies. Under the terms

of the contract the Belgian shipyards were responsible for the commercial equipment, including the hull, the propulsion machinery and the auxiliary machinery, whereas the installation and testing of the military equipment was the responsibility of the Belgian Navy.

The action information centre and its associated computer room are between decks, and the ships can be divided into two independent gas-tight citadels for NBC close-down. All machinery can be remotely controlled

from a central control station at main deck level. Twin Vosper fin-stabilisers combine with exceptionally high freeboard to provide a high standard of seaworthiness. A single large compensated rudder similar to that employed in modern French and Dutch construction is fitted. It is intended to install a close-in weapons system similar to that under consideration by the Netherlands Navy for the 'Standard' frigate at a future date.

MINE WARFARE VESSELS

Ex-British ALGERINE class *ocean minesweepers*

Displacement:	1040t standard; 1335t full load
Dimensions:	213ft pp, 225ft oa × 36ft × 10ft 6in
	65.0m, 68.6m × 10.8m × 3.2m
Machinery:	2-shaft geared steam turbines (triple expansion in ex-Canadian vessels), 2000shp = 16kts. Range 4000nm at 10kts
Armament:	1–102mm (4in), 4–40mm (4×1) (except ex-Canadian vessels), 8–20mm (4×2); 4 DCT
Complement:	101

No	Name	Builder	Acquired	Fate
Ex-British				
M 900	ADRIEN DE GERLACHE (ex-*Liberty*)	Harland & Wolff	1949	Stricken 1969
M 901	GEORGES LECOINTE (i, ex-*Cadmus*)	Harland & Wolff	1950	Stricken 1959
M 902	JAN VAN HAVERBEKE (ex-*Ready*)	Harland & Wolff	1951	Stricken 1960
M 903	A F DUFOUR (i, ex-*Fancy*)	Blyth SB & DD Co	1951	Hulked 1959
M 904	DE BROUWER (ex-*Spanker*)	Harland & Wolff	25.2.53	Stricken 1966
M 905	DE MOOR (ex-*Rosario*)	Harland & Wolff	13.1.53	Stricken 1969
Ex-Canadian				
F 901	GEORGES LECOINTE (ii,ex-*Wallaceburg*)	Port Arthur SB, Ontario	31.7.59	Stricken 1969
F 903	A F DUFOUR (ii, ex-*Winnipeg*)	Port Arthur SB, Ontario	7.8.59	Stricken 1966

These ships were formerly ocean minesweepers of the *Algerine* class, launched in 1942–44. The six ex-Royal Navy vessels were transferred between 1949 and 1953. Their size made them well-suited to general patrol duties in addition to their minesweeping role. In the mid-1950s *De Brouwer* and *De Moor* were tropicalised for service in African waters and by the late 1950s all six ships had been reclassified *Drageurs-escorteurs* (minesweeping escorts). Three of the class paid off 1959–60, and a fourth, *Adrien de Gerlache* became a logistics vessel (*bâtiment logistique*). Her armament was reduced to two 40mm and she was given the number A 954. At the same time two ex-Canadian vessels of the same class were acquired, and took over the names *Lecointe* and *Dufour*. The Canadian ships differed from the ex-RN units in having reciprocating engines; they were fitted with 20mm twin AA guns, but these were quickly replaced by 40mm singles. Following the transfer of the Canadian vessels the class were redesignated *Escorteurs Côtiers* (coastal escorts) and were given 'F' numbers (*De Brouwer* became F 904 and *De Moor* F 905). A F *Dufour* and *De Brouwer* paid off in 1966, and the remaining pair had the single 102mm replaced by a single 40mm before they followed in 1969.

US AGILE type *ocean minesweepers*

Displacement:	720t standard; 780t full load
Dimensions:	165ft pp, 172ft oa × 36ft × 10ft
	50.3m, 52.4m × 11.0m × 3.2m
Machinery:	2 shafts, 2 General Motors 8-268A diesels, 1600bhp = 14kts. Range 3000nm at 10kts
Armament:	1–40mm
Complement:	72

Breydel Dec 1973   C & S Taylor

No	Name	Builder	Acquired	Fate
M 902	VAN HAVERBEKE (ex-*MSO 522*)	Peterson, Wisconsin	9.12.60	Extant 1982
M 903	A F DUFOUR (iii, ex-*Lagen*, ex-*MSO 498*)	Bellingham, Washington	14.4.66	Extant 1982
M 904	DE BROUWER (ii, ex-*Nansen*, ex-*MSO 499*)	Bellingham, Washington	14.4.66	Extant 1982
M 906	BREYDEL (ex-*AM 504*)	Tacoma, Washington	15.2.56	Extant 1982
M 907	ARTEVELDE (ex-*AM 503*)	Tacoma, Washington	15.12.55	Extant 1982
M 908	GEORGES TRUFFAUT (ex-*AM 515*)	Tampa SB	12.10.56	Extant 1982
M 909	FRANCOIS BOUESSE (ex-*AM 516*)	Tampa SB	25.1.57	Extant 1982

These wooden-hulled ocean minesweepers of the *Agile* class were built in the USA and transferred under MDAP shortly after completion. M 903, M 904 and M 907 were launched in 1954, M 906 and M 908 in 1955, M 909 in 1956, and M 902 (*Van Haverbeke*) in 1959; she was transferred in 1960 and took the name and number of a unit of the *Gerlache* class which had just been stricken.

In 1966 two further units, originally launched in 1954, were acquired from Norway; formerly named *Lagen* and *Nansen*, they were renamed *A F Dufour* (M 903) and *De Brouwer* (M 904) respectively, thereby replacing two vessels of the *Gerlache* class which were retired in the same year. In 1972 *Artevelde* was converted to a diving vessel. Conventional sweep gear was removed and in 1974 a Siebe Gorman decompression chamber was fitted. The remaining six units were converted to minehunters 1973–76; a General Electric SQQ-14 sonar was fitted and the single 40mm removed. The latter has been replaced on some ships by a 12.7mm twin mounting. All seven ships are expected to remain in service until replaced by the new minehunters of the 'Tripartite' type.

US ADJUTANT type *coastal minesweepers*

Displacement:	330t standard; 390t full load
Dimensions:	138ft pp, 144ft oa × 27ft × 8ft *42.0m, 44.0m × 8.3m × 2.6m*
Machinery:	2 shafts, 2 General Motors diesels, 880bhp = 13.5kts. Range 2700nm at 10.5kts
Armament:	2–20mm (1×2)
Complement:	40

Class:
Henry B Nevins, NY – *Lier* (M 912), *Sint Niklaas* (M 918), *Diksmuide* (M 920)
Quincy Adams, Mass – *Diest* (M 910), *Maaseick* (M 913)
Hodgdon Bros, Maine – *Eeklo* (M 911), *Roeselaere* (M 914), *Arlon* (M 915), *Bastogne* (M 916), *Charleroi* (M 917), *Hervé* (M 921), *Malmédy* (M 922), *Verviers* (M 934), *Veurne* (M 935)
Consolidated SB, NY – *Sint Truiden* (M 919), *Blankenberge* (M 923), *Laroche* (M 924)
Hiltebrant DD, NY – *De Panne* (M 925)
Boël & Zonen, Temse – *Mechelen* (M 926), *Spa* (M 927), *Stavelot* (M 928), *Heist* (M 929)
Béliard, Ostend – *Rochefort* (M 930), *Knokke* (M 931), *Nieuwpoort* (M 932), *Koksijde* (M 933)

All 26 of these wooden-hulled coastal minesweepers of the *Adjutant* class were financed under MDAP. The first 16 were built in the USA and transferred

1953–55. Eight more were completed by Belgian yards 1954–55, and a further two US-built vessels were added in 1956. The Belgian-built vessels were fitted out with machinery and armament from the USA.

In 1966 M 914–16 were transferred to Norway in return for two *Agile* type MSOs. At the same time *Mechelen* became an ocean research ship (A 962). Fifteen further units were returned to the USA in 1969 and were subsequently transferred to other navies: M 910–13, M 917, M 918, M 920 and M 925 to Taiwan, and M 919, M 921–24 to Greece. Those vessels which remained in service with the Belgian Navy had the original 20mm twin mounting replaced by a 40mm single at about this time. *Veurne* and *Verviers* were converted to minehunters with a Plessey Type 193 sonar and Voith-Schneider propellers in 1969 and 1972 respectively. The former was subsequently used for survey work. In 1977 *Spa* became an ammuniton ship (A 963) and *Heist* a degaussing ship (A 964). *Knokke* was stricken in 1976 and *Stavelot* in 1979. The remaining five ships, including the two minehunters, were placed in 'Special Reserve' in 1981.

Verviers Dec 1973   C & S Taylor

HERSTAL class *inshore minesweepers*

Displacement:	160t standard; 190t full load
Dimensions:	107ft pp, 113ft oa × 22ft × 7ft *32.5m, 34.5m × 6.7m × 2.1m*
Machinery:	2 shafts, 2 Fiat-Mercedes Benz MB 820 diesels, 1260bhp = 15kts. Range 2300nm at 10kts
Armament:	2–20mm (1×2)
Complement:	17

Class:
Temse (M 470), *Hasselt* (M 471), *Kortrijk* (M 472), *Lokeren* (M 473), *Turnhout* (M 474), *Tongeren* (M 475), *Merksem* (M 476), *Oudenaerde* (M 477), *Herstal* (M 478), *Huy* (M 479), *Seraing* (M 480), *Tournai* (M 481), *Vise* (M 482), *Ougrée* (M 473), *Dinant* (M 484), *Andenne* (M 485).

These inshore minesweepers were derived from the British 'Ham' class. All were built in Belgium by Mercantile Marineyard at Kruibeke, eight (M478–85) under MDAP and the remainder under Belgian Navy estimates. Four were launched in 1956, eight in 1957 and the last four in 1958. Designed to sweep the Schelde River, they were fitted for acoustic, magnetic and mechanical sweeping to a depth of 4.5–10m.

In the late 1960s the 20mm twin mounting began to be replaced by a new 12.7mm twin mounting. Two ships, *Temse* and *Tournai*, were transferred via the USA to South Korea in 1970. At the same time, *Herstal* was transferred to survey duties. In the late 1970s *Hasselt*, *Kortrijk* and *Huy* were modified as ready duty ships; all sweep gear was removed and replaced by a deckhouse, pollution clean-up gear and special cranes mounted on the stern.

3

'Tripartite' design
NB 1/750 scale

'TRIPARTITE' class *minehunters*

Displacement:	510t standard; 544t full load
Dimensions:	155ft pp, 161ft oa × 29ft × 8ft
	47.1m, 49.1m × 8.9m × 2.5m
Machinery:	1 shaft, 1 Werkspoor RUB215 V12 diesel, 2280bhp = 15kts; twin active rudders and bow thruster = 7kts. Range 3000nm at 12kts
Armament:	1–20mm
Sensors:	DUBM-21A
Complement:	22–45

The 'Tripartite' minehunter is a collaborative venture between the French, Belgian and Netherlands Navies. Belgium plans to build ten units initially, with a possible follow-on order for five. The class will replace the ocean and coastal minesweepers built during the 1950s. Belgian companies are responsible for the minehunting propulsion system, which consists of ACEC active rudders driven by gas turbines, and the electrical generating plant. Construction of the class has been delayed by problems in forming the Polyship consortium, which eventually had to be dissolved. The first ten units were reordered in early 1981 from Béliard; the hulls are to be launched at Ostend and fitted out by Béliard Mercantile at Antwerp. For further details about the design see French section.

MISCELLANEOUS

KAMINA *support ship*

Displacement:	3900t standard; 5750t full load
Dimensions:	345ft pp, 374ft oa × 48ft × 18ft
	105.0m, 114.0m × 14.6m × 5.5m
Machinery:	1 shaft, 1 Blohm & Voss diesel, 3600bhp = 15kts. Range 10,000nm at 15kts
Armament:	2–76mm (2×1), 4–40mm (4×1), 5–20mm (5×1)
Complement:	175

No	Name	Builder	Acquired	Fate
AP 907	KAMINA (ex-*Royal Harold*, ex-*Herman von Wissmann*)	Cockerill, Hoboken	1950	Stricken 1967

One of two mercantile vessels ordered from the Cockerill Yard for Poland and laid down prior to the Second World War, this ship was launched on 26.12.1940 and completed as the depot ship *Herman von Wissmann* and was employed as a support ship for U-boats in Norway. She was seized by the British in 1945, and was subsequently transferred to the Belgian Navy in 1950. She was employed as a troop transport throughout the 1950s; her original armament was replaced and there was accommodation for 800 troops. In 1962 she was reclassified as a logistics support and training vessel, and was renumbered A 957. Cable reels replaced the after gun mountings, the armament being reduced to 1–76mm, 1–40mm and 2–20mm.

GODETIA *support ship*

Displacement:	1700t light; 2500t full load
Dimensions:	288ft wl, 301ft oa × 46ft × 11ft 6in
	87.9m, 91.8m × 14m × 3.5m
Machinery:	2 shafts, 4 ACEC-MAN diesels, 500bhp = 19kts. Range 8700nm at 12kts
Armament:	4–40mm (2×2)
Complement:	100

No	Name	Builder	Launched	Fate
A 960	GODETIA	Boëlwerf, Temse	7.12.65	Extant 1982

Designed, like her half-sister *Zinnia*, primarily as a command and logistics support ship for mine countermeasures vessels, *Godetia* also doubles as a royal yacht. The ship can be protected against radioactive fallout by closed-circuit ventilation, and has space for a laboratory and accommodation for oceanographic research personnel. She has passive tank stabilisation and controllable-pitch propellers.

A central hold is served by a single crane for the transfer of supplies to smaller vessels. As completed, *Godetia* had 40mm twin mountings fore and aft, but in the late 1960s the after mounting was removed to make room for two reels for minesweeping cables. At the same time a landing platform for a light liaison helicopter was fitted aft as a continuation of the first superstructure deck. In a second major refit 1979–80 the foremost cable reel was replaced by a new deckhouse, and a 40mm single and four 12.7mm twin mountings were fitted in place of the original armament.

Zinnia 1975

ZINNIA *support ship*

Displacement:	1705t light; 2685t full load
Dimensions:	309ft wl, 326ft oa × 50ft × 12ft
	94.2m, 99.5m × 15.2m × 3.6m
Machinery:	1 shaft, 2 Cockerill-Ougrée V12 TR 240 CO diesels, 5000bhp = 20kts. Range 14000nm at 12.5kts
Armament:	3–40mm (3×1), Alouette II helicopter
Complement:	123

No	Name	Builder	Launched	Fate
A 961	ZINNIA	Cockerill, Hoboken	6.5.67	Extant 1982

Developed from *Godetia*, *Zinnia* incorporated a number of modifications. The bridge structure was set farther aft, allowing a second supply hold and crane to be accommodated in the bow section. She was also given a telescoping hangar and a landing platform on the stern, enabling her to operate an Alouette II (now III) liaison helicopter. Two cable reels were fitted on the after deckhouse from completion. Fin stabilisers were adopted in preference to the liquid anti-roll system installed in her half-sister.

Godetia and *Zinnia* replaced the war-built logistics vessels *Adrien de Gerlache* and *Kamina*, which were both retired from service in the late 1960s. In peacetime both ships are employed in the fishery protection role.

Canada

In 1947 the Royal Canadian Navy was the most sophisticated of the British Commonwealth navies, with an aircraft carrier and two cruisers as well as a large and seasoned force of destroyers, frigates and fleet minesweepers. In addition to providing 40 per cent of the escort forces engaged in the Battle of the Atlantic, the Canadians had also built a very large numbers of warships, ranging from 'Tribal' class destroyers to *Algerine* class minesweepers.

During the postwar years the RCN was forced to surrender much of its broader capability in order to retain high capability in the most essential roles. The cruisers proved expensive to run and demanded skilled manpower, so they were not replaced. For a while fixed-wing aviation was maintained with the single carrier *Magnificent*, but her successor was reduced to purely anti-submarine duties. As with most small navies, the cost of maintaining even that level of sophistication proved too expensive, and *Bonaventure* was not replaced.

Although the RCN remained strongly influenced by Royal Navy ideas on ship design, the experience of the Second World War dictated a growing reliance on the United States for electronics. Thus British-pattern equipment was very soon replaced by off-the-shelf purchases or Canadian-made variants.

The RCN has concentrated its efforts on anti-submarine warfare, and made no effort to retain fixed-wing aviation when the *Bonaventure* had to be scrapped. It was the first navy to explore the possibilities of using large helicopters from frigates and destroyers, operating S-55s from the modernised 'River' class in the 1950s and the S-61 Sea King from the *St Laurent* type DDHs. From this concept stemmed the first all-Canadian design, the very large and capable DDH-280 or *Iroquois* class helicopter-carrying destroyers. These ships have a number of unusual features, including provision for two Sea Kings with their associated Canadian-designed Bear Trap recovery system, and are among the best ASW ships afloat, but they were expensive. A Parliamentary inquiry concluded that the programme had run out of control and the decision was taken that no more major warships be designed 'in house'.

The result of this decision has been a protracted search to find a design suitable for the patrol frigate programme, replacements for the DDEs and DDHs built in the 1950s. At the time of writing the choice has narrowed to two consortia, whose proposals are currently being defined. Financial restrictions prohibit a replacement of the frigate force on a one-for-one basis, so a modernisation scheme called the 'Destroyer Life Extension Programme' (DELEX) was approved in August 1980. At a total cost of 107 million Canadian dollars the proposals envisage hull and machinery overhauls, new navigational radar, underwater telephones, the Automated Data Link Processing System, improved UHF communications and the Mk 12 IFF system. The more modern ships will receive additional modifications, depending on their life expectancy.

The RCN operates submarines, partly to back up the ASW effort, but primarily to provide high-level training for the surface ASW forces. In addition there is a large Coast Guard which mans icebreakers, hydrographic survey ships and patrol craft. Throughout the years a number of warships have served in this and in the maritime wing of the Royal Canadian Mounted Police.

FLEET STRENGTH 1947

AIRCRAFT CARRIER

Name	Launched	Disp (deep load)	Fate
Colossus class			
WARRIOR (ex-*Brave*)	20.5.44	18,300t	Returned to RN 1948

On her completion in March 1946, *Warrior* was transferred from the RN, and was returned when *Magnificent* was ready in 1948.

CRUISERS

Name	Launched	Disp (deep load)	Fate
Fiji class			
UGANDA	7.8.41	11,090t	BU 1961
Swiftsure class			
ONTARIO (ex-*Minotaur*)	29.7.43	11,480t	BU 1960

Apart from being 'winterised' with added insulation and steam heating for weapons and deck-fixtures, and the addition of USN-pattern search radar, *Uganda* remained largely unaltered. She was not renamed *Quebec* until 14.1.52 and was employed in training at Halifax.

Ontario differed from her sister *Swiftsure* in having Mk 6 fire control, like HMS *Superb*. As *Quebec* (ex-*Uganda*) she received USN-pattern search radar and was 'winterised'. She spent most of her time as a training ship at Esquimalt, BC.

DESTROYERS

Name	Fate	Name	Fate
'Tribal' class: launched 1941–46, 2745t deep load			
HAIDA	Preserved 1964	CAYUGA	BU 1964
HURON	BU 1965	MICMAC	BU 1964
IROQUOIS	BU 1966	NOOTKA	BU 1964
ATHABASKAN	BU 1969		
'Cr' class: launched 1944, 2535t deep load			
CRESCENT	Type 15 (see notes)	CRUSADER	BU 1965
Valentine class: launched 1943, 2545t deep load			
ALGONQUIN (ex-*Valentine*, ex-*Kempenfelt*)	Type 15	SIOUX (ex-*Vixen*)	BU 1965

'Tribal' class

When the war ended, *Nootka*, *Micmac*, *Cayuga* and *Athabaskan* were still fitting out and so they incorporated several changes dictated by wartime experience. *Nootka* and *Micmac* retained 4.7in guns, but omitted the DCT; in place of the pompom aft, *Nootka* had two twin 40mm Mk 5 side by side. *Cayuga* and *Athabaskan* received four twin 4in/45 Mk 16 and a Mk 6 director, with twin 40mm Mk 5 as in *Nootka*. Between 1946 and 1951 all seven underwent piecemeal modernisation, with 4.7in replaced by twin 4in, some with USN-pattern Mk 63 radar-assisted fire control. Squid DC mortars were added on the quarterdeck, and single and twin 40mm Bofors replaced the light AA.

In 1951 the class was taken in hand for full modernisation, the last ship being recommissioned in 1955. Starting with *Micmac*, the armament and fire control

CANADA

were modernised, with two RN-pattern twin 4in Mk 16 forward, a USN-pattern twin 3in/50 in 'X' position and two Squid triple DC mortars on the quarterdeck. A short aluminium lattice mast replaced the previous one, and the funnels were fitted with prominent caps. *Cayuga* and *Athabaskan* retained their Mk 6 director, but the rest had a modified version of the USN Mk 63 system, with radar trackers on each 4in gunshield, and were given a stripped Mk III(W) director for surface fire. *Cayuga* and *Athabaskan* had a fibre-glass shield fitted to the 3in guns. *Haida* was preserved as a museum at Toronto, where she remains today, the last 'Tribal'.

As modernised the ships' particulars were:

Displacement: 2200t normal; 2500t deep load
Armament: 4-4in/45 Mk 16 (2×2), 2-3in/50 Mk 22 (1×2), 4-40mm/60 Boffins (4×1) (*Cayuga*, *Athabaskan* Mk 7), 4–21in TT, 2 Squid ASW mortars
Sensors: Radar Type 275 (2 ships), SPS-10, SPS-6, Type 293, Type 262; sonar Types 170, 174
Complement: 240

'Cr' and Valentine classes
Crescent and *Algonquin* were given Type 15 conversions to frigates, and re-classified as 'destroyer escorts' in 1952 (see under Major Surface Ships). *Sioux* and *Crusader* were similarly re-rated, although they remained unconverted; some partial updating of their ASW equipment was the only modernisation carried out.

FRIGATES

Name	Fate	Name	Fate
'River' class: launched 1942–44, 2180t deep load			
NEW GLASGOW	Sold 1967	LA HULLOISE	BU 1966
NEW WATERFORD	BU 1968	LANARK	BU 1966
OUTREMONT	BU 1966	LAUZON (ex-*Glace Bay*)	Sold 1963
ST CATHERINE'S	Weather ship 1950	PENETANG (ex-*Rouyn*)	To Norway 1956
SWANSEA	BU 1968	PRESTONIAN (ex-*Beauharnois*)	To Norway 1956
ANTIGONISH	Sold 1967	STE THERESE	Sold 1967
BEACON HILL	Sold 1968	STETTLER	Sold 1967
BUCKINGHAM (ex-*Royal Mount*)	BU 1966	STONETOWN	Weather ship 1950
CAP DE LA MADELEINE	BU 1966	SUSSEXVALE (ex-*Valdorian*)	Sold 1967
FORT ERIE (ex-*La Tuque*)	BU 1966	TORONTO (ex-*Gifford*)	To Norway 1956
INCHARRON	Sold 1966	VICTORIAVILLE	Stricken 1974
JONQUIERE	Sold 1967		

'River' class
Most of the later vessels differed from the original 'River' class design in having twin 4in Mk 16 AA guns in 'B' position. In 1951–53 *Prestonian* underwent complete rebuilding to enhance her ASW capabilities. This involved extending the forecastle deck right aft, raising the funnel and providing a much larger and higher bridge. The original generating machinery (three steam and one diesel generator) was changed to two steam and two diesel generators, with much greater capacity, and a more powerful sonar was installed. The conversion was successful, and 20 more ships were converted by the end of 1958 (all except *St Catherine's* and *Stonetown*, which became weather ships). As reconstructed the particulars were:

Displacement: 1570t standard; 2360t full load
Dimensions: 310ft 4in oa × 36ft 8in × 16ft full load (aft)
91.8m × 11.2m × 4.9m
Machinery: 2-shaft VTE, 2 Admiralty 3-drum boilers, 5500ihp = 20kts. Oil 720t
Armament: 2–4in Mk 16 AA (1×2), 2–40mm/60 Mk 5 AA (1×2), 4–40mm/60 Mk 9 (4×), 2 Squid ASW mortars
Sensors: USN-pattern SPQ-2, TDY-1 ECM gear
Complement: 140

In 1956 *Buckingham* was fitted with a helicopter landing deck aft to test the feasibility of operating a large Whirlwind HO4S ASW helicopter; these trials were successful and paved the way for the even bigger SH-3A Sea King in later ships. Foreign transfers comprised *Penetang*, *Toronto* and *Prestonian* (Norwegian *Draug*, *Garm* and *Troll*, 1956); *Victoriaville* became the diving tender *Granby* in 1968.

MINESWEEPERS

Name	Fate	Name	Fate
Bangor class			
BROCKVILLE	BU 1961	GODERICH	Sold 1959
DIGBY	BU	KENORA	To Turkey 1957
GRANBY	BU 1961	KENTVILLE	To Turkey 1957
LACHINE	To RCMP 1950	MAHONE	To Turkey 1958
MELVILLE	To RCMP 1950	MALPEQUE	Sold 1959
NORANDA	To RCMP 1950	MEDICINE HAT	To Turkey 1959
TRANSCONA	To RCMP 1950	MILLTOWN	Sold 1959
TROIS RIVIERES	To RCMP 1950	MINAS	BU 1959
TRURO	To RCMP 1950	NIPIGON	To Turkey 1959
BLAIRMORE	To Turkey 1950	PORT HOPE	Sold 1959
CHIGNECTO	BU 1957	RED DEER	Sold 1959
FORT WILLIAM	To Turkey 1957	SARNIA	To Turkey 1957
GANANOQUE	Sold 1959	SWIFT CURRENT	To Turkey 1958
GEORGIAN	Sold 1959	WESTMOUNT	To Turkey 1958
Algerine class			
FORT FRANCIS	Survey ship 1949	ROCKCLIFFE	BU 1960
KAPUSKASING	Survey ship 1959	SAULTE STE MARIE	BU 1959
NEW LISKEARD	Survey ship 1959	WALLACEBURG	To Belgium 1959
OSHAWA	Survey ship *Portage* 1958	WINNIPEG	To Belgium 1959
PORTAGE	BU 1960	DRUMMONDVILLE	Sold 1958

Bangor class
All these were officially stricken, but were re-acquired from the Crown Assets Disposal Corporation in 1952. *Brockville*, *Digby*, *Granby*, *Lachine*, *Melville*, *Noranda*, *Transcona* and *Truro* were transferred to the Marine Section of the Royal Canadian Mounted Police in 1950 and renamed *Macleod*, *Perry*, *Colonel White*, *Starnes*, *Cygnus*, *Irvine*, *French*, *MacBrien* and *Herchmer*. In 1951 *Macleod*, *Perry* and *Colonel White* were returned to the RCN and assumed their former names. All were re-designated coastal escorts (FSE) in 1953. At the end of 1957 ten were sold to Turkey: *Blairmore*, *Fort William*, *Kenora*, *Kentville*, *Mahone*, *Medicine Hat*, *Nipigon*, *Sarnia*, *Swift Current* and *Westmount*, renamed *Beycoz*, *Bodrum*, *Bandirma*, *Bartin*, *Beylerbeyi*, *Biga*, *Bafra*, *Buyukdere*, *Bozcaada* and *Bornova*. A Hedgehog spigot mortar replaced the 12pdr gun in most.

Algerine class
Re-rated as coastal escorts (FSE) in 1953. *New Liskeard* and *Kapuskasing* were lent to the Department of Mines and Technical Surveys. In 1959 *Wallaceburg* and *Winnipeg* were sold to Belgium and renamed *Georges Lecointe* and *A F Dufour*, replacing ex-RN sisters of the same names.

There were also the 'Flower' class corvette *Sackville* (minelayer 1956 – see main entry below) and the 'Isles' class minelaying trawler *Whitethroat* (survey ship 1960).

PENNANT NUMBERS
Pennant numbers carried by the principal ships in this section were as follows:

Cruisers

CCL 31	UGANDA	CCL 32	ONTARIO

Destroyers

DDE 215	HAIDA	DDE 213	NOOTKA
DDE 216	HURON	DDE 219	ATHABASKAN
DDE 217	IROQUOIS	DDE 225	SIOUX
DDE 218	CAYUGA	DDE 228	CRUSADER
DDE 214	MICMAC		

Frigates

FFE 315	NEW GLASGOW	FFE 318	JONQUIERE
FFE 304	NEW WATERFORD	FFE 305	LA HULLOISE
FFE 310	OUTREMONT	FFE 321	LANARK
FFE 324	ST CATHERINE'S	FFE 322	LAUZON
FFE 306	SWANSEA	FFE 307	PENETANG
FFE 301	ANTIGONISH	FFE 316	PRESTONIAN
FFE 303	BEACON HILL	FFE 309	STE TERESE
FFE 314	BUCKINGHAM	FFE 311	STETTLER
FFE 317	CAP DE LA MADELEINE	FFE 302	STONETOWN
		FFE 313	SUSSEXVALE
FFE 312	FORT ERIE	FFE 319	TORONTO
FFE 308	INCHARRON	FFE 320	VICTORIAVILLE
Minesweepers			
FSE 180– 199	BANGOR class	FSE 168– 177	ALGERINE class

MAJOR SURFACE SHIPS

Laid down on 29.7.43 and launched 16.11.44, *Magnificent* was returned to the RN in June 1957 and was put into reserve for eight years before being sold for scrapping. While in the RCN she was designated CVL 21 and had the number '21' painted at each end of the flight deck. In 1954 she was reclassified as RML 21 and served mainly as a ferry carrier and transport. Various USN radars replaced the British sets, but she was otherwise similar.

Ex-British MAJESTIC class *aircraft carrier*

Particulars: As Australian *Sydney*

No	Name	Builder	Acquired	Fate
CVL 21	MAGNIFICENT	Harland & Wolff	21.5.48	Returned 14.6.57

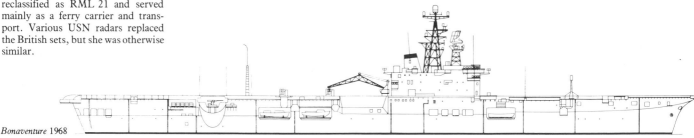

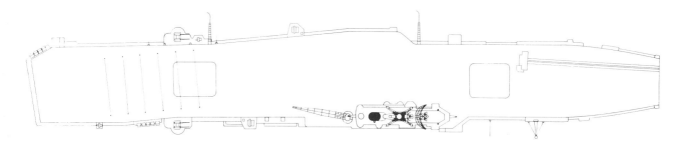

Bonaventure 1968

Laid down on 27.11.43 and launched on 27.2.45, the former *Powerful* was modernised between 1952 and 1957 and sold to the Royal Canadian Navy as HMCS *Bonaventure* (RML 22). She was completed with an angled deck, but aircraft, radar and armament were supplied from the United States. Although similar to her sisters she had a distinctive appearance, with a tall lattice mast, a raked funnel and a big sponson for her twin 3in AA guns.

The original air group consisted of 16 F-2H Banshee fighters and 8 S-2F Tracker ASW aircraft, but it was subsequently changed to an entirely ASW mission with 8 Trackers and 13 HO4S-3 Whirlwind helicopters, and in time the Whirlwinds gave way to CHSS-2 Sea King helicopters. During her 1966–67 modernisation the ship was given new radars and improved accommodation and aircraft handling, and the two forward 3in gun mountings were removed to save weight. The new radars were the Dutch Signaal type.

The ship's designation changed twice, to RRSM 22 in 1957, then to CVL 22, and she carried the number '22' for deck recognition. She was paid off in April 1970 and was laid up for disposal.

Ex-British MAJESTIC class *aircraft carrier*

Displacement:	16,000t standard; 20,000t full load
Dimensions:	704ft oa × 128ft max × 25ft
	214.6m × 39.0m × 7.6m
Machinery:	2-shaft geared steam turbines, 4 Admiralty boilers, 40,000shp = 24.5kts. Oil 3200t
Armour:	Mantlets over magazines
Armament:	8–3in/50 Mk 33 (4×2), 4–3pdr saluting, 21–24 aircraft
Complement:	1370

No	Name	Builder	Acquired	Fate
CVL 22	BONAVENTURE (ex-*Powerful*)	Harland & Wolff	17.1.57	Stricken 1970

Bonaventure 12.4.57
RCN

CANADA

Both these ships were given a Canadian variant of the British Type 15 frigate conversion. It followed the same lines but with a much bigger square bridge and American electronics. *Algonquin* had an RN-pattern twin 4in gun mounting aft and a USN-pattern twin 3in/50 forward, whereas *Crescent* had the twin 4in forward and the 3in aft. Both ships also had two single 40mm Boffin abreast of the funnel, and *Crescent* had a prominent cap to her funnel. Conversion was undertaken at Esquimalt DYd in 1952–56.

ALGONQUIN class *destroyer escorts*

Particulars: As British *Rapid* class

No	Name	Yard	Reconstructed	Fate
DDE 224	ALGONQUIN (ex-*Valentine*, ex-*Kempenfelt*)	Esquimalt Dyd	1952-56	BU 1971
DDE 226	CRESCENT	Esquimalt Dyd	1952-56	BU 1971

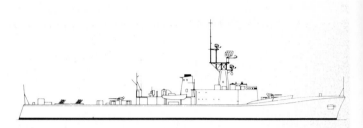

Ottawa 1957

In the late 1940s there was a pressing NATO requirement for anti-submarine vessels, and funds were voted for seven destroyer escorts or frigates for the RCN. The British *Whitby* design was still on the drawing-board, and as the USN had nothing which met the exacting RCN Staff Requirement it was decided to design a new class of ship in Canada. Using the services of the Montreal naval architects, German & Milne, and under the direction of a senior constructor, Rowland Baker, seconded from the Director of Naval Construction, work started in 1949. Baker produced a design basically similar to the *Whitby*, but incorporating several ideas of his own. The machinery was identical with the British ships and *St Laurent*'s was in fact imported from the UK, but electronics and electrical gear were of American and Canadian design. To flatter Canadian susceptibilities, Baker was careful to make the appearance as different as possible from the *Whitby*, but the ship which resulted was virtually a Type 12 specification (albeit with a different hull form) translated by a different design team.

In 1961–66 all seven were modernised, with variable-depth sonar (VDS) on the stern, one Limbo Mk 10 mortar removed and a helicopter platform added. The funnel was replaced by twin uptakes to allow a hangar to be fitted between, and the two 40mm guns were removed. Thereafter they were rated as helicopter-carrying destroyers (DDH) and shipped one CHSS-2 Sea King. *St Laurent* was laid up in 1974 but not sold until 1979; on 12.1.80 she foundered in tow to the breakers. *Skeena*, *Ottawa* and *Fraser* were given major overhauls in 1977–79; the 'Destroyer Life Extension' (DELEX) refit was applied to *Saguenay*, *Margaree* and *Assiniboine* in 1980, and to the other three in 1981. They are expected to decommission between 1987 and 1990.

ST LAURENT class *destroyer escorts*

Displacement:	2000t normal; 2600t deep load
Dimensions:	371ft wl, 366ft oa × 42ft × 13ft 2in
	113.1m, 111.6m × 12.8m × 4.2m
Machinery:	2-shaft English-Electric geared steam turbines, 2 Babcock & Wilcox boilers, 30,000ship = 28kts
Armament:	4–3in/50 DP (2×2), 2–40mm/60 Boffin (2×1), 2 Limbo Mk 10 ASW mortars
Sensors:	Radar SPS-12, SPS-10, SPG-48; sonar SQS-501, SQS-502, SQS-503, SQS-504
Complement:	290

No	Name	Builder	Laid down	Launched	Comp	Fate
DDE 205	ST LAURENT	Canadian Vickers	22.11.50	30.11.51	29.10.55	Lost 12.1.80
DDE 206	SAGUENAY	Halifax SYd	4.4.51	30.7.53	15.12.56	Extant 1982
DDE 207	SKEENA	Burrard, Vancouver	1.6.51	19.8.52	30.3.57	Extant 1982
DDE 229	OTTAWA	Canadian Vickers	8.6.51	29.4.53	10.11.56	Extant 1982
DDE 230	MARGAREE	Halifax SYd	12.9.51	29.3.56	5.10.57	Extant 1982
DDE 233	FRASER	Burrard, Vancouver	11.12.51	19.2.53	28.6.57	Extant 1982
DDE 234	ASSINIBOINE	Marine Ind Sorel	19.5.52	12.2.54	16.8.56	Extant 1982

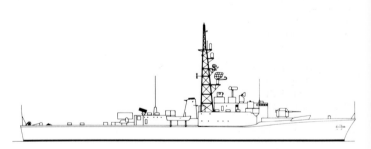

Gatineau 1972

Developed from the original *St Laurent* class and ordered in 1952. On the same hull it was possible to mount the British twin 3in/70 Mk 6 as designed for the previous class, but a USN-pattern twin 3in/Mk 22 was retained aft.

Four ships – *Restigouche*, *Gatineau*, *Kootenay* and *Terra Nova* – were modernised in 1966–73, with VDS on the stern and an ASROC anti-submarine missile launcher aft. This necessitated the removal of one Limbo Mk 10 mortar and the 3in Mk 22 twin mounting, and a new lattice foremast was stepped. *Chaudière*, *Columbia* and *St Croix* paid off into reserve in 1974, but in 1979 *St Croix* was reduced to harbour service at Halifax. The remaining four are scheduled to receive the DELEX modernisation (as in *Annapolis* class) – *Gatineau* in 1983, *Kootenay* in 1984, *Terra Nova* in 1985 and *Restigouche* in 1986.

RESTIGOUCHE class *destroyers*

Displacement:	As *St Laurent* class
Dimensions:	As *St Laurent* class
Machinery:	As *St Laurent* class
Armament:	2–3in/70 Mk 6 DP (2×2), 2–3in/50 Mk 22 DP (1×2), 2 Limbo Mk 10 ASW mortars, 2–40mm Boffin (2×1)
Sensors:	Radars SPS-12, SPS-10, Sperry Mk 2, SPG-48; sonars SQS-501, SQS-503
Complement:	290

No	Name	Builder	Laid down	Launched	Comp	Fate
DDE 257	RESTIGOUCHE	Canadian Vickers	15.7.53	22.11.54	7.6.58	Extant 1982
DDE 236	GATINEAU	Davie SB, Lauzon	30.4.53	3.6.57	17.2.59	Extant 1982
DDE 258	KOOTENAY	Burrard, Vancouver	21.8.52	15.6.54	7.3.59	Extant 1982
DDE 259	TERRA NOVA	Victoria Machinery	11.6.53	21.6.55	6.6.59	Extant 1982
DDE 235	CHAUDIERE	Halifax SYd	30.7.53	13.11.57	14.11.59	Laid up 1982
DDE 260	COLUMBIA	Burrard, Vancouver	11.6.53	1.11.56	7.11.59	Laid up 1982
DDE 256	ST CROIX	Marine Industries, Sorel	15.10.54	17.11.57	4.10.58	TS 1974

Saguenay 6.13.62   USN

Colombia as completed   Navarret Collection

Four more 'repeat *Restigouches*' were ordered in 1957, but the opportunity was taken to improve habitability and provide better pre-wetting and better bridge and weatherdeck fittings to cope with extreme cold. Originally they were rated as DDs, like the *Restigouche* class, but they carry DDE pennant numbers. They all mount 2 triple 12.75in Mk 32 launchers for ASW torpedoes, and in *Yukon* and *Qu'Appelle* the British 3in/70 mount forward has been replaced with a US 3in/50. DELEX refits (SQS-505 in lieu of SQS-503 and new navigational radar) were due to begin in 1982 for *Qu'Appelle*, 1983 for *Yukon*, 1984 for *Saskatchewan* and 1985 for *Mackenzie*.

MACKENZIE class *destroyers*

Particulars: As *Restigouche* class

No	Name	Builder	Laid down	Launched	Comp	Fate
DDE 261 MACKENZIE		Canadian Vickers	15.12.58	25.5.61	6.10.62	Extant 1982
DDE 262 SASKATCHEWAN		Victoria Machinery	16.7.59	1.2.61	16.2.63	Extant 1982
DDE 263 YUKON		Burrard, Vancouver	25.10.59	27.7.61	25.5.63	Extant 1982
DDE 264 QU'APPELLE		Davie SB, Lauzon	14.1.60	2.5.62	14.9.63	Extant 1982

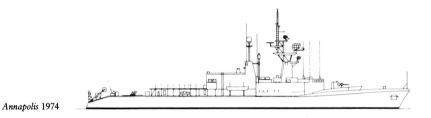

Annapolis 1974

The final development of the original *St Laurent* ordered in 1959 incorporated all the improvements approved for the earlier ships, particularly the Sea King helicopter deck and hangar. Because of the extra topweight the lighter USN-pattern 3in/50 Mk 33 was reintroduced in place of the British-pattern Mk 6. Both ships were modernised in 1977–1979 and are now rated as DDHs. Further modernisations under the DELEX programme are scheduled to commence in 1982 (*Nipigon*) and 1984. New radar, ECM, fire control and sonar are planned along with a vertically launched Sea Sparrow SAM system.

ANNAPOLIS class *helicopter destroyers*

Displacement:	2400t normal; 3000t deep load
Dimensions:	As *St Laurent* class
Machinery:	As *St Laurent* class
Armament:	2–3in/50 Mk 33 DP (1×2), 6–12.75in Mk 32 TT (2×3), 1 Limbo Mk 10 ASW mortar, 1 helicopter
Sensors:	Radar SPS-12, SPS-10, Sperry Mk 2, Mk 48; sonar SQS-503, SQS-504, SQS-501
Complement:	228

No	Name	Builder	Laid down	Launched	Comp	Fate
DDE 265 ANNAPOLIS		Halifax SYd	Jul 60	27.4.63	19.12.64	Extant 1982
DDE 266 NIPIGON		Marine Industries, Sorel	Apr 60	10.12.61	30.5.64	Extant 1982

Annapolis Oct 1977   C & S Taylor

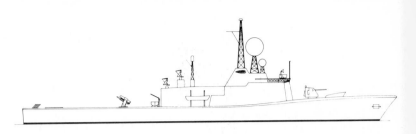

'Tribal' class design 1960

Eight large general-purpose frigates were announced in 1960; they were to be given 'Tribal' names, but in 1963 the project was cancelled before orders had been placed. The design remained in being, however, and was developed into the *Iroquois* class DDHs (see below).

'TRIBAL' class *missile frigates*

Displacement:	As *Iroquois* class
Dimensions:	As *Iroquois* class
Machinery:	2-shaft geared steam turbines, 36,000shp = 30kts
Armament:	1–5in/54 Mk 42, 1 Tartar RIM-24 SAM system, ASW TT
Complement:	As *Iroquois* class

Huron 1977

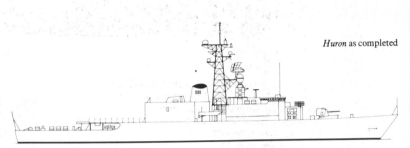

Huron as completed

Ordered in 1968 as a revised design on the same hull as the cancelled general-purpose frigates of 1963 (see above). The design allowed for two big helicopters (CHSS-2) to enhance their ASW capabilities, and they are still among the best equipped escorts in the world. The 5in gun is Italian, the radars Dutch.

IROQUOIS class *helicopter destroyers*

Displacement:	3551t normal; 4700t deep load
Dimensions:	398ft wl, 423ft oa × 50ft × 14ft 6in *121.3m, 128.9m × 15.2m × 4.4m*
Machinery:	2-shaft gas turbines, 2 Mk FT 4A2 Pratt & Whitney gas turbines, 50,000shp = 29kts
Armament:	1–5in/54 DP, 2 Sea Sparrow SAM (2×4), 1 Limbo Mk 10 ASW mortar, 6–12.75in Mk 32 TT (2×3), 2 helicopters
Sensors:	Radars SPS-502, SPQ-2D, M-22, LW-02; sonars SQS-505, SQS-504, SQS-501
Complement:	285

No	Name	Builder	Laid down	Launched	Comp	Fate
DDH 280	IROQUOIS	Marine Industries, Sorel	15.1.69	28.11.70	29.7.72	Extant 1982
DDH 281	HURON	Marine Industries, Sorel	15.1.69	3.4.71	16.12.72	Extant 1982
DDH 282	ATHABASKAN	Davie SB, Lauzon	1.6.69	27.11.70	30.11.72	Extant 1982
DDH 283	ALGONQUIN	Davie SB, Lauzon	1.9.69	23.4.71	30.9.73	Extant 1982

The decision to order 6 ships of a projected 20-vessel programme was taken on 22.12.77, but lengthy delays have afflicted the programme and in 1982 the contracts for these ships had still to be placed. Therefore the above details are still provisional. The 3in gun is the OTO Melara compact; the Sea Sparrow is a vertical launch system with 24 missiles; and the helicopters will probably be Sea Kings.

New DDH type *helicopter destroyers*

Displacement:	3398t deep load
Dimensions:	440ft oa, 410ft pp × 48ft 3in × 14ft 2½in *134.0m, 125.0m × 14.7m × 4.33m*
Machinery:	2-shaft GE LM 2500 gas turbines, 50,000shp = 29kts. Range 4500nm at 20kts
Armament:	1–3in/62, 8 Harpoon SSM (2×4), 2 Sea Sparrow SAM (2×8), 4–12.75 Mk 32 TT (2×2), 2 helicopters
Sensors:	Radar 1629C, SPS-49, 1030, WM-25; sonar SQS-505, SQR-18A
Complement:	226

SUBMARINES

An ex-USN *Balao* class (ex-radar picket) fleet submarine, launched 18.6.43, on loan to the RCN for two (extended to five) years for ASW training at Esquimalt, BC, and commissioned there on 11.5.61. In May 1966 the loan was extended indefinitely, but she was returned on 2.10.69 for disposal.

Ex-US BALAO class *submarines*

Particulars:	As US *Balao* class

No	Name	Builder	Acquired	Fate
SS 71	GRILSE (ex-*Burrfish*, SSR 312)	Electric Boat	May 61	Returned to USN 1969

Ex-USN *Tench* class (Fleet Snorkel conversion) launched 1.10.44 and bought to replace *Grilse*. Commissioned at Esquimalt 2.12.68 and returned to USN for scrapping 31.12.74.

Ex-US TENCH class *submarines*

Particulars:	As US *Tench* class

No	Name	Builder	Acquired	Fate
SS 75	RAINBOW (ex-*Argonaut*, SS 475)	Portsmouth N Yd	Dec 68	Returned to USN 1974

Identical with British *Oberon* class, but armed with Mk 37-C ASW torpedoes, not anti-ship weapons (22 carried). *Ojibwa* began 'submarine Operational Update Programme' (SOUP) in 1980, with *Onandaga* scheduled for 1983 and *Okanagan* in 1984. This involves a new fire control system (Singer-Librascope Mk 1 mod O), completely revised sonar arrangements (Krupp-Atlas CSU3-41 with enlarged bow dome for the pas-

British OBERON type *submarines*

Particulars:	As British *Oberon* class					
No	Name	Builder	Laid down	Launched	Comp	Fate
SS 72	OJIBWA (ex-*Onyx*)	Chatham DYd	Sep 62	29.2.64	23.9.65	Extant 1982
SS 73	ONANDAGA	Chatham DYd	June 64	25.9.65	22.6.67	Extant 1982
SS 74	OKANAGAN	Chatham DYd	Mar 65	17.9.66	22.6.68	Extant 1982

sive array and the active transducer in the fin; Type 2007 to be retained), and US Mk 48 torpedoes and Sub-Harpoon missiles.

MINE WARFARE VESSELS

SACKVILLE *minelayer*

Displacement:	1085t normal; 1350t deep load
Dimensions:	205ft oa × 33ft 2in × 14ft 6in
	62.5m × 10.1m × 4.4m
Machinery:	1-shaft VTE, 2 boilers, 2750ihp = 16.5kts. Oil 230t
Armament:	None
Complement:	38

The only 'Flower' class corvette retained in Canadian service, *Sackville* was laid up until 1953–56 when she was converted to a minelayer (AN 113) for laying 'loops' or controlled minefields. She was lent to the Naval Research Laboratory for oceanographic work and finally in 1964 was designated AGOR 113 when converted for survey work.

(For illustration see under France)

GASPE ('BAY') class *coastal minesweepers*

Displacement:	390t normal; 412t deep load
Dimensions:	140ft pp, 152ft oa × 28ft × 8ft 6in max
	42.7m, 46.3m × 8.5m × 2.6m
Machinery:	2 shafts, 2 GM 12cyl diesels, 2400bhp = 15kts. Oil 52t
Armament:	1–40mm/60 Mk 7
Complement:	40

No	Name	Builder	Launched	Fate
MCB 143	GASPE	Davie SB	12.11.51	To Turkey 1958
MCB 144	CHALEUR (i)	Fort Arthur	21.6.52	To France 1954
MCB 145	FUNDY (ii)	St John Dry Dock	Apr 53	To France 1954
MCB 146	COMOX	Victoria Machinery	24.4.52	To Turkey 1958
MCB 147	COWICHAN (i)	Davie SB	12.11.51	To France 1954
MCB 148	UNGAVA	Davie SB	20.5.53	To Turkey 1958
MCB 149	QUINTE	Port Arthur	8.8.53	Sold 1966
MCB 150	MIRAMICHI (i)	St John Dry Dock	Oct 52	To France 1954
MCB 151	FORTUNE	Victoria Machinery	14.4.53	Sold 1966
MCB 152	JAMES BAY	Canadian Yarrow	12.3.53	Sold 1966
MCB 153	THUNDER (i)	Canadian Vickers	17.7.52	To France 1954
MCB 154	RESOLUTE	Kingston SYd	20.6.53	Sold 1966
MCB 156	CHIGNECTO (i)	Marine Industries	21.6.52	To France 1954
MCB 157	TRINITY	Davie SB	31.7.53	To Turkey 1958
MCB 159	FUNDY (ii)	Davie SB	14.6.56	Extant 1982
MCB 160	CHIGNECTO (ii)	Davie SB	17.11.56	Extant 1982
MCB 161	THUNDER (ii)	Port Arthur	27.10.56	Extant 1982
MCB 162	COWICHAN (ii)	Canadian Yarrow	26.2.57	Extant 1982
MCB 163	MIRAMICHI (ii)	Victoria Machinery	22.2.57	Extant 1982
MCB 164	CHALEUR (ii)	Marine Industries	11.5.57	Extant 1982

Four coastal minesweepers (AMC, later MCB) were ordered in 1950, followed by ten more in 1951; they were based closely on the British 'Ton' class, with wood planking and aluminium framing. In 1954 *Chignecto, Chaleur, Fundy, Miramichi, Cowichan* and *Thunder* were sold to France and renamed *La Bayonnaise, La Dieppoise, La Dunkerquoise, La Lorientaise, La Malouine* and *La Paimpolaise*; six replacements were built for them. In 1958 four more, *Ungava, Trinity, Comox* and *Gaspe*, were sold to Turkey and renamed *Tekirdag, Terme, Tirebolu* and *Trabzon*. Designation was changed from AMC to MCB in 1954; in 1972 the six survivors were redesignated small patrol escorts (PFL) and in 1982 were being used for training with PB pennant numbers.

MISCELLANEOUS

BRAS D'OR *experimental hydrofoil*

Displacement:	180t normal; 237.5t deep load
Dimensions:	150ft 10in oa × 21ft 6in × 15ft (hull depth)
	46.0m × 6.5m × 4.6m
Machinery:	2 shafts, 2 Pratt & Whitney FT4A gas turbines, 2000shp = 15kts
Armament:	(Designed) 12–12.75in Mk 32 TT (4×3)
Complement:	17

Name	Builder	Launched	Fate
BRAS D'OR	Marine Industries, Sorel	July 68	Extant 1982

This vessel was jointly funded by the Canadian and British governments and designed by De Havilland (Canada). She ran a series of trials in 1969–71, but although moderately successful she was expensive to operate and was laid up in 1971. She remains (in 1982) at Halifax Dockyard, Nova Scotia, in a state of preservation, but is unlikely to be recommissioned.

'BIRD' class *submarine chasers*

Displacement:	66t full load
Dimensions:	92ft × 17ft × 5ft 4in
	30.2m × 5.6m × 1.7m
Machinery:	2-shaft diesels, 1200bhp = 14kts
Armament:	1–20mm, Hedgehog, DCs
Complement:	21

Class: *Loon* (PCS 780), *Cormorant* (PCS 781), *Blue Heron* (PCS 782), *Mallard* (PCS 783)

Built in 1955, of wood and aluminium, they were designed for harbour patrol and ASW training. *Blue Heron* was transferred to the Marine Section of the Royal Canadian Mounted Police in 1956, and the remaining three were paid off on 23.5.1963.

BLUETHROAT *loop-layer*

Displacement:	785t normal; 870t deep load
Dimensions:	150ft 8in pp, 157ft oa × 33ft × 10ft
	45.9m, 47.8m × 10m × 3m
Machinery:	2-shaft diesel: 1200bhp = 13kts
Armament:	None
Complement:	25

Ordered in 1951 as a loop-layer and completed in 1955. Redesignated AGOR 114 in 1964 and converted for survey duties.

Denmark

In the 1930s the majority of the Danish people and at least two political parties were in agreement that military defence of the country was unfeasible. The role of the armed forces was relegated to that of border watch and the troops were ordered to offer no resistance when the Germans invaded on 9 April 1940. Officially, Denmark was now under German 'protection', but the Danish Government was forced to 'lend' six of the most modern torpedo-boats to Germany, and more such loans were expected. Resistance and sabotage increased and by 1943 relations between the Danes and the occupiers had deteriorated. On 29 August the Germans launched a 'coup' and the occupation became official. As had been planned, the Danish Navy scuttled most of her ships, but a few small boats escaped to neutral Sweden. When the war ended, the Danish Navy had ceased to exist. A number of German warships was allotted to Denmark as war reparations, and she received other vessels, chiefly from Britain, on loan.

With Norway, Denmark became a member of NATO and gradually enlarged her navy with ships built at Copenhagen Navy Yard and various civilian yards, and with vessels lend-leased from the USA. Together with the new German Republic, Denmark found herself responsible for the protection of the narrow waters of the Baltic – a role which laid heavy emphasis on motor torpedo-boats, submarines, minelayers and minesweepers. Some frigates and corvettes have been built, and various patrol boats for use off Greenland. In 1982, the Danish Navy's strength was approximately in accordance with NATO's requirements, but like that of most European countries, the Danish economy and political situation set obstacles in the way of the increased defence expenditure urged by NATO.

FLEET STRENGTH 1947

FRIGATES

Name	Launched	Disp	Fate
British 'River' class			
HOLGER DANSKE (ex-*Monnow*)	4.12.43	1445t	Stricken 1959
NIELS EBBESEN (ex-*Annan*)	29.12.43	1445t	Stricken 1963

Both purchased 1945 and became TS.

CORVETTE

Name	Launched	Disp	Fate
THETIS (ex-*Geranium*)	23.4.40	898t	Stricken 1963

Purchased from Britain 1945

TORPEDO-BOATS

Name	Launched	Disp	Fate
HAVKATTEN	1919	108t	Stricken Nov 48
Ex-German T 4	1938	962t	BU 1950
Ex-German T 19	18.12.41	853t	BU 1951
Najaden class			
HUITFELDT (ex-*Nymfen*)	22.6.43	782t	Stricken 1966
WILLEMOES (ex-*Najaden*)	17.3.43	782t	Stricken 1966

SUBMARINES

Name	Launched	Disp	Fate
Havmanden class			
HAVMANDEN	19.6.37	340t	Discarded 1949–50
HAVRUEN	6.11.37	340t	Discarded 1949–50
HAVKALEN	3.3.38	340t	Discarded 1949–50
HAVHESTEN	11.7.40	340t	Discarded 1949–50
Ex-British 'U' class			
SPRINGEREN (ex-Polish *Dzik*, ex-*P 52*)	11.10.42	540t	Returned Oct 57, BU
STOREN (ex-*Vulpine*)	28.12.43	545t	Returned Jan 59, BU
SAELEN (ex-French *Morse*, ex-*Vortex*)	19.8.44	545t	Returned Jan 58, BU

All the *Havmanden* class were scuttled 29.8.43, but were salvaged. The 'U' class boats were chartered from the Royal Navy at the end of the war; they were originally known by their pennant numbers only, as *U 1*, *U 2* and *U 3* respectively.

Lindormen c 1965   Royal Danish Navy

MINELAYERS

Name	Launched	Disp	Fate
LINDORMEN	30.3.40	614t	Stricken 1969
LAALAND	1941	350t	Stricken 1974
LOUGEN	1941	350t	Stricken 1974

They later wore the NATO pennant numbers (in the above order) N 39, N 40 and N 41.

Huitfeldt c 1963   Royal Danish Navy

MINESWEEPERS

Name	Launched	Disp	Fate
NARHVALEN (ex-*TB*)	1917	110t	Stricken 1949
Söbjörnen class (classified as patrol boats 1957)			
SOHESTEN	30.4.42	274t	Stricken 1962
SOHUNDEN	16.5.42	274t	Stricken 1959
SOLOVEN	3.12.42	274t	Stricken 1959
SORIDDEREN	11.4.42	274t	Stricken 1962
MS 1 class			
MS 1 SORTE SARA	1941	70t	Stricken 1956
MS 2 ASKO	1941	70t	Stricken 1971
MS 3 BAAGO	1941	70t	Stricken 1968
MS 5 ENO	1941	70t	Stricken 1971
MS 6 FANO	1941	70t	Stricken 1960
MS 7 HJORTO	1941	70t	Stricken 1968
MS 8 LYO	1941	70t	Stricken 1971
MS 9 MANO	1941	70t	Stricken 1971
MS 10 STRYNO	1941	70t	Stricken 1956

In 1957 the six remaining boats were reclassified as patrol boats. Other small minesweepers were: ex-German *MR 26* (1938, 100t, stricken 1949); ex-German *MR 152*, MR 150 *Asnæs*, MR 155 *Bognæs*, MR 156 *Dyrnæs*, MR 157 *Egenæs*, MR 160, MR 167 *Helgenæs*, MR 168 *Lynæs*, MR 170, MR 173, MR 174 *Rinkenæs*, MR 175, MR 176, MR 214 (1940–43, 130t, stricken 1950–57); ex-German *MR 226*, MR 229, MR 230 *Stigsnæs*, MR 233, MR 236 *Trellenæs*, MR 242 *Vornæs* (1943, 150t, stricken 1950–57); *ME 26, ME 32, ME 36, ME 83, ME 84, ME 86, ME 152–157, ME 160, ME 173, ME 263, ME 307* (*c*1940–42, 240t, on loan from RN, 10 returned 1948, remaining 6 in 1950); *ME 1016, ME 1038, ME 1042, ME 1044* (1943–44, 360t, on loan from RN, returned 1950); *MSK 1 Aalholm*, MSK 2 *Birkholm*, MSK 3 *Ertholm* (1944–45, 70t, later patrol boats, stricken 1973, 1970 and 1976 respectively); *MSK 4 Fyrholm*, MSK 5 *Græsholm*, MSK 6 *Lindholm* (1945, 68t, later patrol boats, stricken 1970, 1968 and 1974 respectively); *ML 1 Graadyb*, ML 2 *Klördyb*, ML 3 *Vejdyb* 1945, 21t, stricken 1956, 1969 and 1969 respectively).

*Stigsnaes c*1955   Royal Danish Navy

PATROL BOATS

Name	Launched	Disp	Fate
HEIMDAL	1.2.35	705t	Stricken 1961
TERNEN	1937	82t	Stricken 1957
FREJA	23.12.38	332t	Stricken 1968

Ternen was designed for use off Greenland. *Heimdal* and *Freja* carried NATO pennant numbers A 542 and A 541 respectively.

ICEBREAKERS

Name	Launched	Disp	Fate
MJOLNER	1890	515t	Stricken 1958
ISBJORN	1923	1675t	Stricken 1969
LILLEBJORN	1926	1000t	Stricken 1975
STOREBJORN	1931	2540t	Stricken 1976

MAJOR SURFACE SHIPS

British 'Hunt' Type 2 escort destroyers, originally launched in 1941. Initially lent for 4 years, extended for further 4 years. Laid down 10.2.41, 12.6.40 and 7.6.40 respectively; completed 14.4.42, 11.12.41 and 18.10.41 respectively. Reconstructed 1953–54, and then carried 6–4in (3×2), 3–40mm (3×1), 2 DCT.

Ex-British 'HUNT' class *frigates*

Particulars:	As British 'Hunt' Type 2			

No	Name	Builder	Acquired	Fate
F 341	ESBERN SNARE (ex-*Blackmore*)	Stephen	1953	Stricken 1966
F 342	ROLF KRAKE (ex-*Calpe*)	Swan Hunter	1953	To Britain 1963
F 343	VALDEMAR SEJR (ex-*Exmoor*)	Swan Hunter	1953	Stricken Feb 1962

Hvidbornen 1974

Officially rated as 'inspection vessels'. Ordered 1960–61. Specially designed and equipped for fishery protection in Greenland, Faroe and North Sea waters. Originally carried an Alouette III helicopter; now replaced with Lynx. *Ingolf* is disarmed. Plans for a replacement class are expected in 1984.

HVIDBJORNEN class *frigates*

Displacement:	1345t standard; 1650t full load
Dimensions:	219ft 8in pp, 238ft 2in oa × 38ft × 16ft 67.0m, 72.0m × 11.5m × 5.0m
Machinery:	1 shaft, 4 General Motors diesels, 6400bhp = 18kts. Range 6000nm at 13kts
Armament:	1–3in DP, DCT, 1 helicopter
Sensors:	Radar CWS-1, NWS-1; sonar MS-26
Complement:	85

No	Name	Builder	Laid down	Launched	Comp	Fate
F 348	HVIDBJORNEN	Aarhus Flydedok	4.6.61	23.11.61	15.12.62	Extant 1982
F 349	VAEDDEREN	Aalborg	30.10.61	6.4.62	19.3.63	Extant 1982
F 350	INGOLF	Svendborg	5.12.61	27.7.61	27.7.63	Survey duties 1982
F 351	FYLLA	Aalborg	27.6.62	18.12.62	10.7.63	Extant 1982

Officially rated as 'inspection vessel' (fishery protection). Modified *Hvidbjörnen* class, specially designed and equipped for Greenland service. Alouette III helicopter will be replaced by Lynx.

BESKYTTEREN *frigate*

Displacement:	1540t standard; 1970t full load
Dimensions:	239ft 6in wl, 244ft oa × 41ft × 14ft 9in
	73.0m, 74.4m × 12.5m × 4.5m
Machinery:	1 shaft, 3 Burmeister & Wain Alpha diesels, 7440bhp = 18kts. Range 4500nm at 16kts, 6000nm at 13kts
Armament:	1–3in DP, 1 helicopter
Sensors:	Radar CWS-2, NWS-1, NWS-2; sonar MS-26
Complement:	60

No	Name	Builder	Laid down	Launched	Comp	Fate
F 340	BESKYTTEREN	Aalborg	15.12.74	27.5.75	27.2.76	Extant 1982

Herluf Trolle 1977

Indigenous Danish design, but built with US 'Offshore' funds. The original triple TT mounting was replaced by 2 twin sided amidships, and the Terne ASW missile provided for in the design was never fitted. Modernised 1976–78, when the 'B' 5in twin mount and TTs were replaced by Harpoon SSM launchers (2×4), a Sea Sparrow SAM launcher (1×8) and 6–342mm TT (2×3) for Swedish wire-guided ASW torpedoes installed.

PEDER SKRAM class *frigates*

Displacement:	2200t standard; 2720t full load
Dimensions:	354ft 3in pp, 396ft 5in oa × 39ft 5in × 14ft 1in deep
	108.0m, 112.6m × 12.0m × 4.3m
Machinery:	2-shaft CODOG: 1 MTU 20 V 956 diesel, 4800bhp = 18kts; General Electric LM 2500 gas turbine, 18,400shp = 28kts. Range 800nm at 28kts or 2500nm at 18kts
	GG4A-3 gas turbines, 37,000shp = 28kts (44,000shp = 32kts max)
Armament:	4–5in/38 (2×2), 4–40mm Bofors (4×1), 3–21in (533mm) TT (1×3), DC
Sensors:	Radar CWS-2, CWS-3, NWS-1, NWS-2, M-66, Mk 91; sonar MS-26
Complement:	200

No	Name	Builder	Laid down	Launched	Comp	Fate
F 352	PEDER SKRAM	Helsingör	25.9.64	20.5.65	30.6.66	Extant 1982
F 353	HERLUF TROLLE	Helsingör	18.12.64	4.9.65	16.4.67	Extant 1982

*Herluf Trolle c*1970   Ambrose Greenway

Niels Juel as completed   Royal Danish Navy   *Bellona* as completed   Royal Danish Navy

All vessels built as part of MDAP; sisters of the Italian *Albatros* class. Originally classified as submarine chasers, from 1954 they were referred to as corvettes, although they carry a frigate's pennant number.

BELLONA class *corvettes*

Displacement:	800t standard; 900t full load
Dimensions:	250ft 4in wl, 259ft 2in oa × 31ft 9in × 9ft 10in deep
	76.3m, 79.0m × 9.6m × 3.0m
Machinery:	2 shafts, 2 Ansaldo Fiat 409T diesels, 4400bhp = 20kts. Range 3000nm at 18kts
Armament:	2–3in (2×1), 1–40mm, 2 Hedgehogs, 4 DCTs
Sensors:	Radar NWS-1, CWS-1; sonar QCU-2
Complement:	109

No	Name	Builder	Laid down	Launched	Comp	Fate
F 344	BELLONA	Navalmeccanicia, Castellammare	1954	9.1.55	31.1.57	Stricken 1981
F 345	DIANA	Cantiere del Tirreno, Riva Trigoso	1953	19.12.54	30.7.55	Stricken 1974
F 346	FLORA	Cantiere del Tirreno, Riva Trigoso	1953	25.6.55	28.8.56	Stricken 1978
F 347	TRITON	Cantiere Navali di Taranto	1953	12.9.54	10.8.55	Stricken 1981

Olfert Fischer as completed

Contracted 5.12.75. An interesting design incorporating equipment from many countries – the 76mm gun is Italian (OTO Melara compact), missile systems and gas turbines are American, the electronics are British and Dutch, etc. The design originally provided for an ASW torpedo system, but so far the ships are confined to DCs for ASW; chaff launchers have still to be fitted and only 4 Harpoon are carried, the NATO Sea Sparrow has no reloads. The gas turbine has a maximum output of 26,000shp = 30kts for short periods.

NIELS JUEL class *corvettes*

Displacement:	1190t standard; 1320t full load
Dimensions:	262ft 6in pp, 275ft 6in oa × 33ft 9in × 13ft deep
	80.0m, 84.0 × 10.3m × 4.0m
Machinery:	2-shaft CODOG: 1 MTU 20 V 956 diesel, 4800bhp = 18kts; 1 General Electric LM 2500 gas turbine, 18,400shp = 28kts. Range 800nm at 28kts or 2500nm at 18kts
Armament:	1–76mm, 8 Harpoon SSM (2×4), 1 Sea Sparrow SAM system (1×8), DCs
Sensors:	Radar AWS-5, Skanter 009, Phillips 3cm, 9LV-200, 1 Mk 91 Mod 1; sonar MS-26
Complement:	90

No	Name	Builder	Laid down	Launched	Comp	Fate
F 354	NIELS JUEL	Aalborg	20.10.76	17.2.78	3.1.79	Extant 1982
F 355	OLFERT FISCHER	Aalborg	29.11.78	10.5.79	29.2.80	Extant 1982
F 356	PETER TORDENSKJOLD	Aalborg	5.12.79	30.4.80	30.3.81	Extant 1982

SUBMARINES

Delfinen 1960

NB 1/750 scale

First Danish-designed submarines built since the war. *Springeren* was built with US 'Offshore' funds. Plans for a replacement class are expected in 1984.

DELFINEN class *submarines*

Displacement:	595t standard; 643t submerged
Dimensions:	178ft 10in × 15ft 5in × 13ft
	54.5m × 4.7m × 4.0m
Machinery:	2-shaft Burmeister & Wain 12cyl V-diesels plus Brown-Boveri electric motors, 1200bhp/1200shp = 15kts/15kts. Range 4000nm at 8kts
Armament:	4–21in TT (bow)
Sensors:	Sonar, active and passive types
Complement:	33

No	Name	Builder	Laid down	Launched	Comp	Fate
S 326	DELFINEN	Copenhagen N Yd	1.7.54	4.5.56	16.9.58	Extant 1982
S 327	SPAEKHUGGEREN	Copenhagen N Yd	1.12.54	20.2.57	27.6.59	Extant 1982
S 328	TUMLEREN	Copenhagen N Yd	22.5.56	22.5.58	15.1.60	Extant 1982
S 329	SPRINGEREN	Copenhagen N Yd	3.1.61	26.4.63	22.10.64	Extant 1982

DENMARK

Licence-built boats of German Type 205 (West German *U 4*), modified for Danish needs. Denmark is considering building 6 submarines of the German/Norwegian Type 210 to replace all her older submarines.

NARHVALEN class *submarines*

Displacement:	370t standard; 500t submerged
Dimensions:	146ft × 15ft 4in × 12ft 6in
	44.5m × 4.6m × 3.8m
Machinery:	1 shaft, 2 Mercedes-Benz diesels, 2 electric motors, 1500bhp/1500shp = 12/17kts
Armament:	8–21in TT (bow)
Sensors:	Sonar; active and passive types
Complement:	22

No	Name	Builder	Laid down	Launched	Comp	Fate
S 320	NARHVALEN	Copenhagen N Yd	16.2.65	10.9.68	27.2.70	Extant 1982
S 321	NORDKAPEREN	Copenhagen N Yd	20.1.66	18.12.69	22.12.70	Extant 1982

SMALL SURFACE COMBATANTS

Buhl 1954

BILLE class *torpedo-boats*

Displacement:	392t standard; 400t full load
Dimensions:	210ft × 21ft 1in × 7ft 6in
	64.0m × 6.4m × 2.3m
Machinery:	2-shaft Danish Atlas geared steam turbines, 6900shp = 29kts
Armament:	3–40mm, 2–20mm, 2 DCT, 6–456mm TT (2×3), mines
Complement:	65

No	Name	Builder	Launched	Fate
T 11	BILLE	Copenhagen N Yd	21.9.46	Stricken 1960
T 12	BUHL	Copenhagen N Yd	10.9.47	Stricken 1960
T 13	HAMMER	Copenhagen N Yd	23.6.48	Stricken 1960
T 14	HOLM	Copenhagen N Yd	5.2.48	Stricken 1960
T 15	KRABBE	Copenhagen N Yd	27.6.46	Stricken 1960
T 16	KRIEGER	Copenhagen N Yd	4.5.46	Stricken 1960

Planned 1942, drawings and material ready at armistice 1945. 1952 reclassified as patrol boats with pennant numbers P 570–P 575. 1953–55 rebuilt, TTs exchanged for ASW weapons.

Flyvefisken as completed   Royal Danish Navy

(For illustration see under Germany in 1922–46 volume)

Ex-German S-BOAT type *torpedo-boats*

Displacement:	112–121t standard
Dimensions:	107ft 4in, 114ft 5in × 17ft 5in × 5ft 1in
	32.7m, 34.9m × 5.3m × 1.7m
Machinery:	3 shafts, 3 Daimler-Benz 20cyl 4-stroke diesels, 7500bhp = 39/42kts. Range 700/750nm at 30/35kts. Oil 17t
Armament:	1–37mm, 3–20mm, 2 MG, 2–21in TT
Complement:	24/40

Class:

T 51 (ex-*S 316*), *T 52* (ex-*S 107*), *T 53* (ex-*S 216*), *T 54* (ex-*S 133*), *T 55* (ex-*S 206*), *T 56* (ex-*S 127*), *T 57* (ex-*S 305*), *T 58* (ex-*S 79*), *T 59* (ex-*S 197*), *T 60* (ex-*S 97*), *T 61* (ex-*S 207*), *T 62* (ex-*S 68*)

These 12 ex-German *Schnellboote* were purchased 1947 and 1948, also ex-*S 15* and ex-*S 122* in 1947 for 'cannibalising' with spare parts to the other 12. In 1951 6 boats were transferred from Norway: *Lyn* (ex-*S 64*) *Brand* ex-*S 10*), *Storm* (ex-*S 85*), *Blink* (ex-*S 302*), *Tross* (ex-*S 117*), *Kjekk* (ex-*S 195*). In 1951 all 18 boats received new pennant numbers and names in the following order: P 551 *Glenten*, P 552 *Gribben*, P 553 *Havörnen*, P 554 *Hærfuglen*, P 555 *Högen*, P 556 *Isfuglen*, P 557 *Jagtfalken*, P 558 *Musvaagen*, P 559 *Raagen*, P 560 *Ravnen*, P 561 *Skaden*, P 562 *Stormfuglen*, P 563 *Taarnfalken*, P 564 *Tranen*, P 565 *Falken*, P 566 *Hejren*, P 567 *Lommen*, P 568 *Viben*. The gun armament was later reduced to 1–40mm, 1–20mm. *Hæfuglen* stricken 1955, *Högen*, *Isfuglen* and *Musvaagen* 1956, *Havörnen*, *Raagen* and *Taarnfalken* 1957, *Glenten*, *Gribben*, *Skaden*, *Falken* and *Lommen* 1961, *Jagtfalken*, *Ravnen*, *Stormfuglen* and *Tranen* 1963, *Hejren* and *Viben* 1965.

FLYVEFISKEN class *torpedo-boats*

Displacement:	110t standard
Dimensions:	118ft 2in, 120ft 2in × 18ft × 5ft 11in
	36.0m, 36.6m × 5.5m × 1.8m
Machinery:	3-shaft Mercedes-Benz diesels, 7500bhp = 40kts
Armament:	1–40mm, 1–20mm, 2–533mm TT
Complement:	23

Class:

Flyvefisken (P 500), *Hajen* (P 501), *Havkatten* (P 502), *Laxen* (P 503), *Makrelen* (P 504), *Sværdfisken* (P 505)

All built at Copenhagen N Yd. Voted 1952, laid down 1953, launched 1954–55. Development of German S-boat type. All stricken 1974 and scrapped 1976.

FALKEN class *torpedo-boats*

Displacement:	119t standard
Dimensions:	118ft × 17ft 10in × 6ft
	36.0m5.4m × 1.8m
Machinery:	3 shafts, MTU diesels, 9000bhp = 40kts
Armament:	1–40mm, 1–20mm, 4–533mm TT (4×1)
Sensors:	Radar NWS-1
Complement:	22

Class:

Falken (P 506), *Glenten* (P 507), *Gribben* (P 508), *Högen* (P 509)

Laid down, launched, commissioned respectively 1.11.60, 19.12.61, 4.10.62 – 3.1.61, 15.3.62, 15.12.62 – 15.5.61, 18.7.62, 26.4.63 – 1.9.61, 4.10.62, 6.6.63. All built at Copenhagen N Yd as part of US Military Aid Programme. All stricken 1978–79.

Glenten c1970   Royal Danish Navy

SOLOVEN class *torpedo-boats*

Displacement:	100t standard; 120t full load
Dimensions:	96ft 2in, 99ft 2in ×26ft 3in × 8ft 3in
	29.3m, 30.2m × 8.0m × 2.5m
Machinery:	3-shaft CODOG: 3 Bristol Proteus gas turbines, 12,750shp = 50kts; 2 GM 6V 71 diesels (on outer shafts), ?bhp = 10kts
Armament:	2–40mm (2×1), 4–533mm TT (4×1), mines
Sensors:	Radar NWS-1
Complement:	21

Class:

Söloven (P 510), *Söridderen* (P 511), *Söbjornen* (P 512), *Söhesten* (P 513), *Söhunden* (P 514), *Söulven* (P 515)

Laid down, launched, commissioned respectively 27.8.62, 19.4.63, 12.2.65 – 4.10.62, 22.8.63, 10.2.65 – 9.7.63, 19.8.64, Sept 65 – 5.9.63, 31.3.65, June 66 – 18.8.64, 12.1.66, Dec 66 – 30.3.65, 27.4.66, Mar 67. The design is a combination of British *Brave* type hull form and *Ferocity* style construction. *Söloven* and *Söridderen* built at Vosper, Portsmouth, remaining 4 at Copenhagen N Yd. A pair of TT was removed when the after gun was given an enclosed shield. Four boats will be modernised and the other two will be stricken.

Sehested as completed
NB 1/750 scale

WILLEMOES class *fast attack craft*

Displacement:	240t standard; 260t full load
Dimensions:	144ft 5in, 151ft ×24ft 4in × 7ft 3in
	44.0m, 46.0m × 7.4m × 2.2m
Machinery:	3-shaft CODOG: 3 Rolls-Royce Proteus 52M-544 gas turbines, 12,750shp = 40kts; 3 GM V 71 diesels for cruising, 800bhp = 12kts
Armament:	1–76mm/62, 2–533mm TT (2×1), 4 Harpoon SSM (2×2), 6 RFL, mines
Sensors:	Radar NWS-3, 9LV-200
Complement:	24

No	Name	Builder	Comp	Fate
P 540	BILLE	Fredrikshavn Vaerft	June 76	Extant 1982
P 541	BREDAL	Fredrikshavn Vaerft	21.7.77	Extant 1982
P 542	HAMMER	Fredrikshavn Vaerft	1.4.77	Extant 1982
P 543	HUITFELDT	Fredrikshavn Vaerft	15.6.77	Extant 1982
P 544	KRIEGER	Fredrikshavn Vaerft	22.9.77	Extant 1982
P 545	NORBY	Fredrikshavn Vaerft	22.11.77	Extant 1982
P 546	RODSTEEN	Fredrikshavn Vaerft	16.2.78	Extant 1982
P 547	SEHESTED	Fredrikshavn Vaerft	Mar 78	Extant 1982
P 548	SUENSON	Fredrikshavn Vaerft	June 78	Extant 1982
P 549	WILLEMOES	Fredrikshavn Vaerft	7.10.76	Extant 1982

Based on Swedish *Spica II* class. Armament variations include: 8 Harpoon, no TT; or 4 TT, no Harpoon. First order for 4 boats, then 8 and finally 10. *Willemoes*, the prototype boat was completed in the latter arrangement. *Bille* was the first series production boat and was modified following the *Willemoes* trials. Three CP propellers are fitted, and normal endurance is 36 hours. The gun is the OTO Melara Compact, and 20 mines can be carried in lieu of TT and missiles.

Söridderen on trials   Vosper Thornycroft

Rodsteen as completed

*Nymphen c*1970

DAPHNE class *patrol boats*

Displacement:	150t standard; 170t full load
Dimensions:	121ft 5in × 22ft 4in × 8ft 6in
	37.0m × 6.8m × 2.6m
Machinery:	3 shafts, 2 12cyl Maybach diesels, plus 1 Foden FD-6 diesel for cruising, 2600/100bhp = 20kts
Armament:	1–40mm, 2 ASW rocket launchers, 2 DCT, mines
Sensors:	Radar NWS-3; sonar MS-26
Complement:	23

Class:

Daphne (P 530), *Dryaden* (P 531), *Havmanden* (P 532), *Havfruen* (P 533), *Najaden* (P 534), *Nymfen* (P 535), *Neptun* (P 536), *Ran* (P 537), *Rota* (P 538)

Built at Copenhagen N Yd, laid down 1959–62, launched 1960–64, commissioned 1961–65. *Daphne*, *Najaden* and *Neptun* are now (1982) disarmed; *Havmanden* was stricken in 1979.

MINE WARFARE VESSELS

BESKYTTEREN class *minelayers*

Displacement:	753t standard; 1095t full load
Dimensions:	203ft 6in oa × 34ft 2in × 8ft 6in
	62.0m × 10.4m ×2.6m
Machinery:	2 shafts, 2 diesels, 2800bhp = 13kts. Range 2500nm at 12kts
Armament:	8–40mm (4×2), mines
Complement:	70

No	Name	Builder	Acquired	Fate
N 50	BESKYTTEREN	Charleston N Yd	1954	Stricken 1966
N 51	VINDHUNDEN	Charleston N Yd	1954	Stricken 1966

Ex-US *LSM 390* and *LSM 392* originally built in 1944–45, reconstructed as minelayers in USA. *Beskytteren* transferred 8.6.54.

Lindormen 1979

Royal Danish Navy

Langeland 1971
NB 1/750 scale

LANGELAND *minelayer*

Displacement:	310t standard; 330t full load
Dimensions:	134ft 6in pp, 144ft 4in × 23ft 8½in × 7ft 3in *41.0m, 44.0m × 7.2m × 2.2m*
Machinery:	2 shafts, 2 Burmeister & Wain diesels, 770bhp = 12kts
Armament:	2–40mm (2×1), 2–20mm, mines
Complement:	37

No	Name	Builder	Launched	Fate
N 42	LANGELAND	Copenhagen N Yd	17.5.50	In reserve 1982

Commissioned 1951. Layer of controlled minefields.

FALSTER class *minelayers*

Displacement:	1800t standard; 1900t full load
Dimensions:	238ft pp, 252ft 6in oa × 41ft × 13ft *73.0m, 77.0m × 12.5m × 4.0m*
Machinery:	2 shafts, 2 GM 16–56703 diesels, 4800bhp = 17kts
Armament:	4–3in (2×2), 400 mines
Sensors:	Radar CWS-2, NWS-2, NWS-3, M-46
Complement:	120

No	Name	Builder	Launched	Fate
N 80	FALSTER	Nakskov	19.9.62	Extant 1982
N 81	FYEN	Fredrikshavn	3.10.62	Extant 1982
N 82	MOEN	Fredrikshavn	6.3.63	Extant 1982
N 83	SJAELLAND	Nakskov	14.6.63	Extant 1982

First two ordered 1960, remainder 1962, commissioned 1963 and 1964 respectively. Of a special NATO design, 'Scandinavian' type of minelayer. *Fyen* also acts as a training ship for midshipmen, and *Sjælland* as a depot ship for submarines and torpedo-boats. The 3in gun is the US Mk 33.

LINDORMEN class *minelayers*

Displacement:	420t standard; 570t full load
Dimensions:	145ft 4in pp, 147ft 8in oa × 26ft 3in × 8ft 3in *44.3m, 45.0m × 8.0m × 2.5m*
Machinery:	2 shafts, 2 Wichmann diesels, 4200bhp = 14kts
Armament:	2–20mm (2×1), 60 mines
Sensors:	Radar NWS-3
Complement:	27

No	Name	Builder	Launched	Fate
N 43	LINDORMEN	Svendborg	9.9.77	Extant 1982
N 44	LOSSEN	Svendborg	11.11.77	Extant 1982

Laid down 20.1.77 and 22.6.77 respectively. Commissioned 26.10.77 and 30.1.78 respectively. Primarily layers of controlled minefields but *Lossen* also submarine depot ship.

Ex-US AMS/MSC type *coastal minesweepers*

Particulars:	As US *Bluebird* class

Class:

Aarösund (M 571 ex-*AMS 127*), *Alssund* (M 572 ex-*AMS 128*), *Egernsund* (M 573 ex-*AMS 129*), *Grönsund* (M 574 ex-*AMS 256*), *Guldborgsund* (M 575 ex-*AMS 257*), *Omösund* (M 576 ex-*AMS 221*), *Ulvsund* (M 577 ex-*AMS 263*), *Vilsund* (M 578 ex-*AMS 264*)

NATO coastal minesweepers of type MSC 60 (ex-US *AMS 60*), built in USA, launched 1954–55, commissioned 1955–56, transferred to Denmark respectively 24.1.55, 5.4.55, 3.8.55, 21.9.56, 11.11.56, 20.6.56, 20.9.56 and 15.11.56. *Guldborgsund* acts as a surveying vessel. *Aarösund* and *Omösund* were stricken in 1982, the remaining vessels will be modernised to extend their active service.

ASVIG class *inshore minesweepers*

Displacement:	180t standard; 200t full load
Dimensions:	106ft 8in pp, 116ft 2in × 23ft 8in × 5ft 5in *32.5m, 35.4m × 7.2m × 1.70m*
Machinery:	2 shafts, 2 diesels, 1100bhp = 14kts
Armament:	1–20mm
Complement:	14

Class:

Asvig (M 579), *Mosvig* (M 580), *Sandvig* (M 581), *Sælvig* (M 582)

Laid down, launched, commissioned respectively 22.4.59, 11.5.60, 6.9.61 (*Asvig*); 22.4.59, 14.9.60, 25.10.61 (*Mosvig*); 11.5.60, 1.3.61, 1.2.62 (*Sandvig*); 14.9.60, 14.7.61, 30.4.62 (*Saelvig*). Built at Copenhagen N Yd. All stricken 1977.

Falster c 1970

Royal Danish Navy

Agpa 1978; typical of the many small trawler-like patrol craft maintained by the Danish Navy

Royal Danish Navy

MISCELLANEOUS

FISHERY PROTECTION VESSELS

Since 1945 Denmark has built a number of trawler-type vessels for fishery patrols in Greenland and Faroes waters. They are not true warships, but since they are operated by the Danish Navy, their principal characteristics are listed below. All were extant in 1982 unless otherwise noted.

Skarven (Y 382), *Teisten* (Y 383) – 125t; 82ft × 20ft 9in × 10ft, *25.0m × 6.3m × 3.0m*; 1 Alfa diesel, 180bhp = 9kts; 1–20mm; launched 1951; *Skarven* grounded 7.5.66 and was stricken; *Teisten* stricken 1978.

Maagen (Y 384), *Mallemukken* (Y 385) – 190t full load; 88ft × 23ft × 10ft, *27.0m × 7.0m × 3.0m*; 1 diesel, 385bhp = 11kts; 2–20mm; launched 1960.

Barsö (Y 300), *Drejö* (Y 301), *Romsö* (Y 302), *Samsö* (Y 303), *Thurö* (Y 304), *Vejrö* (Y 305), *Farö* (Y 306), *Læsö* (Y 307), *Römö* (Y 308) – 155t standard; 84ft × 20ft × 10ft, *25.6m × 6.0m × 3.0m*; 1 diesel, 385bhp = 11kts; 2–20mm; launched 1969 (first 6), 1973 (last 3).

Agdlek (Y 386), *Agpa* (Y 387), *Tulugaq* (Y 388) + 1 unnamed (projected) – 390t full load; 103ft × 26ft × 19ft, *31.4m × 8.0m × 5.8m*; 1 B & W diesel, 800bhp = 12kts, 2–20mm; launched 1974 (except *Tulugaq* 1978).

There are also large numbers of small patrol boats: *Y 375*, *Y 376* – 12t, 26kts, 1 MG, built 1974; *Y 377–Y 379*, 7.5t, 26kts, 1 MG, built 1974–75; and about 40 inshore patrol craft manned by the Home Guard and numbered between *MHV 1* and *MHV 95*. They were built from the mid-1950s onwards.

The Ministry of Fisheries operates the new patrol vessel *Havörnen*, built to the British 'Osprey' design by Fredrikshavn Vaerft in 1979 – 3680t; 164 × 34ft × 9ft, *50.0m × 10.5m × 2.8m*; 2 diesels, 4640bhp; 1 helicopter. She is built to mercantile specifications, and is unarmed, but is included because the 'Osprey' design has been promoted as a possible warship.

The Danish Navy also has the use of 4 icebreakers operated by the Ministry of Trade and Shipping. They are *Elbjörn* (893t standard, 12kts, launched in 1932); *Danbjörn* and *Isbjörn* (3425t standard, 17kts, launched in 1966 and 1969); and *Thorbjörn* (1500t standard, 16kts, launched 1980). They are employed by the Navy for survey work during the summer months.

DANNEBROG *Royal Yacht*

Displacement:	1130t standard
Dimensions:	246ft × 35ft 9in × 12ft 2in
	75.0 × 10.9 × 3.7m
Machinery:	2 shafts, 2 diesels, 1800bhp = 14kts
Armament:	2–37mm
Complement:	57

Built at Copenhagen N Yd, launched and commissioned 1931. 1979–80 refitted, new machinery. Pennant number A 540.

France

At the end of the Second World War little remained of the powerful fleet which France had built during the 1930s. Two battleships – one incomplete – and a handful of cruisers, contre-torpilleurs and submarines had escaped the German occupation in 1940. Most had fled to North Africa and had later rejoined the Allied forces, seeing heavy service in all theatres especially during the latter part of the war. The remainder of the French fleet, including most of the élite Force de Raid, had been scuttled at Toulon in 1942.

France therefore found herself bereft of a fleet that could satisfy her traditional maritime status, her extensive naval infra-structure, and the demands of a far-flung empire which she was in the process of retrieving from the Allies and from the Japanese. Industry had been crippled by the war and the economy was in ruins. Consequently France was unable either to construct or to finance a new fleet in the immediate postwar period.

Inevitably, recourse was made to her British and American allies, who not only provided war-built ships surplus to their own requirements, but were particularly generous as regards the allocation of German and Italian prizes. Many of the latter were modern, powerful vessels which had seen little war service and were in excellent condition. By 1947 the Marine Nationale looked quite respectable – at least on paper.

Logistics and maintenance, however, soon became a nightmare. Gun calibres included 155mm (French), 152mm (French), 150mm (German), 138.6mm (French), 135mm (Italian), 127mm (German), 120mm (Italian), 105mm (German), 102mm (British), 100mm (French), 90mm (French), 88mm (German), 76mm (US), 75mm (French), 40mm (US), 37mm (French/German/Italian), 20mm (various), 13.2mm (French) and the British 2pdr. Propulsion machinery caused similar problems. Attempts were made to rationalise weaponry by the adoption of a German-pattern 105mm mounting to replace the British 4in and the Italian 135mm, and the standardisation of light AA guns around the 40mm and 20mm favoured by the British and Americans. But this hastily assembled 'fleet' could clearly do little more than tide the French over until such time as a new navy could be constructed, and the 1950s saw a steady procession of ex-German and ex-Italian units to the breakers' yards. They served their purpose, nevertheless, and the ex-German submarines proved of particular value as experimental vessels, exercising considerable influence on postwar submarine construction.

THE NEEDS OF THE EMPIRE

After the war France was anxious to re-establish herself as an imperial power. She clung tenaciously to her possessions in the Far East in the face of a growing wave of nationalism in that region. The result was the protracted conflict in Indo-China, in which the Navy played a considerable part. US-built patrol craft were purchased for use around the coast and in the rivers and estuaries, and there were successive deployments by the carriers Dixmude and Arromanches, and later by the Bois Belleau and Lafayette.

The acquisition of these two ex-American carriers on a long-term loan was largely due to the problems experienced in sustaining a French carrier presence off Indo-China. They brought with them newer and more effective aircraft – Hellcats, Helldivers, Corsairs and Avengers – to replace the ageing Seafires and Dauntlesses, and enabled the former escort carrier Dixmude to be relegated from frontline duties.

Once the usefulness of carriers as an instrument for the projection of French maritime power was established they quickly became the central element of the fleet, and the two big battleships – one of which was completed at great expense in the early postwar years – went into an early retirement. Jean Bart was present at Suez but only as a fire support ship, while the main Anglo-French naval presence was a five-carrier task force which included Lafayette and Arromanches.

NATO

In 1949 France became a founder-member of NATO. Apart from national security needs there were many advantages accruing from membership of the alliance. During the immediate postwar period much of the French fleet was of British or American construction, and not only were there clear benefits in continuing this association from a logistics point of view, but France was now given access to the latest thinking as regards naval strategy and tactics and to state-of-the-art technology. There were also to be extensive financial benefits from the American-funded Mutual Defense Assistance Program (MDAP).

Commitments to French national status as an imperial power on the one hand, and to the security of the North Atlantic on the other, made demands of a different nature on the Marine Nationale. In the first postwar review a naval statute established a requirement for (a) 400,000t of escorts, patrol vessels, minesweepers and small craft for NATO; and (b) 360,000t of carriers, submarines and amphibious vessels for national requirements. Financial and technological difficulties resulted in the failure of the French Parliament to commit itself to the programme, but the project was saved by allied aid amounting to 40 per cent of the NATO commitment. Between 1951 and 1957 30,000t was laid down per year.

In order to conform to the new thinking, the prewar system of classification – croiseur léger, contre-torpilleur, torpilleur, aviso de 1ère/2ème classe – was abandoned. The allocation of all destroyer/frigate-sized ships to the protection of the carriers (in the national defence role) or of the convoy (in the NATO role) led to the adoption of the term escorteur, to which the word rapide would be added for a vessel capable of fleet speed, together with a sub-classification to indicate ASW or AA protection as the primary role of the ship. In 1951 this system of classification was in its turn abandoned in favour of '1st class escort' (30kts plus) and '2nd class escort'. This appears to have provided inadequate differentiation of the ship's mission, and the classification system was changed again in 1953 and 1955. The Surcouf and Le Corse classes, both authorised in 1949, were the prototypes of the new escorts and underwent all these changes in classification while building:

Blue Water navy: *Isère* refuels the carrier *Clemenceau* and the escort *La Bourdonnais*   Navarret Collection

Surcouf (T 47)
(AAW – carrier escort)
1949: *Escorteur Rapide Anti-Aérien*
1951: *Escorteur de 1ère classe*
1953: *Escorteur Rapide*
1955: *Escorteur d'Escadre* (fleet escort)
Le Corse (E 50)
(ASW – convoy escort)
1949: *Escorteur Rapide Anti-Sous-marin*
1951: *Escorteur de 2ème classe*
1953: *Escorteur*
1955: *Escorteur Rapide*

Other vessels were modified to fit in with these new concepts. The former light cruiser *De Grasse*, which had been laid down prewar and launched in 1946, was redesigned as an anti-aircraft cruiser, and fitted with the same combination of 127mm and 57mm guns as the *Surcouf* class. She and her near-sister, *Colbert*, laid down in 1953, were to provide command facilities and AA protection at the centre of a carrier task force. The two former Italian light cruisers of the *Attilio Regolo* class were rebuilt 1951–54 and rearmed on the lines of the new AAW escorts; they would later serve as flotilla leaders for the latter.

Curiously, the prewar organisation of destroyer-sized ships into three-ship *divisions* persisted and is still in existence today. There was also a continuing need for the colonial sloop, designed to patrol alone on colonial stations – hence the *Escorteur d'Union Française* designation conferred on the frigates of the *Commandant Rivière* class built in the late 1950s.

Submarines continued to be divided into 1st class (1200t standard) and 2nd class (600t) boats, although a new element was a small 'hunter-killer' submarine (*Aréthuse* class) designed to prevent enemy submarines from disrupting French mercantile traffic in the Mediterranean.

After a number of false starts the new carriers and amphibious units on which France's ability to project her maritime power was to be centred were authorised. The loan or purchase of British and American vessels in the immediate postwar period had given the *Marine Nationale* a breathing-space in which to acquire the necessary operating experience and technical expertise to ensure that the designs were in line with the latest developments elsewhere.

Finally, with the help of American financial aid, large numbers of mine countermeasures and patrol craft were acquired to provide France's contribution to the security of the seaports of Western Europe.

A CHANGE OF POLICY

When General de Gaulle came to power in 1958 he expressed immediate dissatisfaction with France's position in the NATO command structure, and in particular with what he regarded as inadequate representation in the AFMED command, to which the bulk of the fleet was allocated. His claims received an unsympathetic hearing from the Americans, who were anxious not to upset their other allies, and in March 1959 France duly informed the North Atlantic Council that the French Mediterranean Fleet would henceforth remain under national control. From this moment on the withdrawal of French forces from the NATO command structure was a continuous process: the remaining naval units were withdrawn from the Channel and Atlantic commands, the land and air forces followed in 1966, and finally in 1969 notice was served on all NATO HQs and other installations on French soil.

The political aspirations of De Gaulle produced far-reaching changes in French military strategy and consequently in the structure of the fleet itself. The desire to create a foreign policy independent of Washington and Moscow brought with it a complete reorientation of defence priorities. At the beginning of the 1960s De Gaulle defined these as: 'To deter – to intervene – to defend'. France could no longer live under the protection of the American nuclear umbrella. Immediately plans were put in hand to develop a submarine-based *Force de Dissuasion* similar in concept to Polaris.

France already possessed a considerable intervention capability based on three carriers and a new generation of amphibious units and colonial sloops, and this capability would be maintained and improved through modernisation.

'Defence' now came third in the list of priorities, and in view of the limited finance available now that the Marshall Plan was at an end would continue to rely heavily on the ships procured during the 1950s.

In size and capability the French SSBN force was to be similar to that of the British Royal Navy. The British, however, acquired Polaris 'on the cheap' from their American allies; they paid no development costs, had unrestricted access to American technological expertise in the design of the submarines, and were permitted to use the firing ranges off the coast of Florida for tests and trials. France, on the other hand, had to begin from scratch: missiles and warheads had to be developed and tested, firing ranges constructed. The United States had refused to supply France with enriched uranium or with a reactor. The design of a French pressurised water-cooled reactor was therefore undertaken in collaboration with the CEA – the civilian atomic energy authority; because the Americans would supply enriched uranium only for land experimental use, a nuclear propulsion plant was built ashore at Cadaraché and tested to simulate typical SSBN patrols.

Caissons were built for test-firings of the missiles. In 1967 this role was taken on by a specially constructed submarine, *Gymnote*, fitted with the same guidance and inertial navigation system as the new SSBNs (SNLE in French parlance). The first missile was launched at sea at the Landes Trials Centre at the end of 1968. Observations of the missile's flight were made by the *Henri Poincaré*, a former Italian tanker rebuilt at Brest 1964–67 and equipped with long-range tracking antennae for monitoring the re-entry phase, accompanied by three *escorteurs rapides* specially converted for the purpose.

Simultaneously nuclear warheads were being tested at the Experimental Centre as Mururoa Island in the Pacific, the tests being supervised by a whole fleet of ships including the cruiser *De Grasse* – partially disarmed and fitted as a command ship – and the two new landing ships *Orage* and *Ouragan*.

The cost of all this was enormous. In 1965, when the SNLE programme was in full swing, the only other ships under construction or on order for the *Marine Nationale* were the two *frégates* of the *Suffren* class, two submarines of the *Daphné* class, and the landing ship *Orage*. These would be the only major vessels outside the SNLE programme completed during the second half of the decade. Not a single unit in the former NATO category – convoy escorts, MCM vessels, patrol craft – was built.

THE 'PLAN BLEU'

In 1969 De Gaulle retired from French political life; there was, however, to be no significant change in foreign policy. Nobody in the ruling Gaullist Party was prepared to engineer a *rapprochement* with the United States and thereby throw into question the independence of France's position in world affairs. In June 1970 the new Premier, Michel Debré, reaffirmed: 'We shall either have a national defence or no defence at all'. The development of the French sea-based nuclear deterrent force continued to take priority over all other naval commitments.

In some quarters of the *Marine Nationale*, however, concern was beginning to be voiced regarding the state of France's conventional naval forces. The large surface fleet built up during the 1950s was now ageing fast, despite extensive mid-life conversions to many of the large fleet escorts, and few replacements were being built. Successive five-year plans, vulnerable as they were to piecemeal deletions and postponements when money was short, had failed to deliver the goods. Inevitably recourse was made to a massive long-term building plan, in which the future size and structure of the fleet was strictly determined. The *Plan Bleu*, as it was to be known, was formulated in 1972, and provided for the following fleet structure by 1985: 5 SNLE, 2 aircraft carriers, 2 helicopter carriers, 30 *frégates/corvettes*, 5 replenishment tankers, 20 SSK/SSN, 50 LRMP aircraft, 2 assault ships, LCU, LST, etc, 35 *avisos*, 30 FPB, 36 MHC/MSC and 85,000t logistics support and maintenance ships.

The objectives of the naval policy which this fleet was intended to sustain were: (a) the maintenance of an effective sea-based nuclear deterrent force; (b) the ability of the fleet to operate on the high seas; (c) a defence capability for the French maritime approaches; and (d) a defence capability for French overseas territories.

The first three categories parallel exactly De Gaulle's 'to deter – to intervene – to defend'. The fourth, however, marked an interesting modification of previous policy in that it established the need for a French naval *presence* (as opposed to a distant intervention capability) in the overseas territories. French interest in these territories appeared to have ended during the 1960s following the withdrawal from South-East Asia and from the colonies in North Africa. The 1970s, however, have seen a steady build-up of French naval forces in the Indian Ocean – now for the first time a focal point in world affairs – and the basing of ships at Djibouti, Mayotte and La Réunion. It was to provide such a presence that the new *avisos* of the A 69 class – designed for coastal ASW and patrol – and the FPBs were included in the programme. By 1980 the French Indian Ocean squadron regularly numbered 20 ships.

The *Plan Bleu* decreed an increase in the carrier force from three to four ships, and plans were already in hand for the additional vessel, an ASW/assault helicopter carrier. The old fleet escorts of the T 47/53/56 classes were to be replaced by a scaled-down version of the *Tourville* (F 67) design, the C 70 *corvette*. The latter class would be built in two versions, one specialising in ASW and the other armed with surface-to-air missiles.

Finally, French confidence in her growing technological expertise was expressed in the intention to build nuclear attack submarines to replace the conventional boats built in the 1950s. The new design, when it finally emerged, was for a smaller boat than any in service with the other major naval powers.

French naval plans have an unhappy record, and the *Plan Bleu* appears to be no exception. In June 1977 one of the four carriers, eight of the *avisos* and eight of the submarines were deleted from the plan.

A shortage of money, due in part to the world economic situation, but also to the continuing massive investment in the SNLE prog-

ramme, has caused further postponements. Construction of the nuclear helicopter carrier designed in the mid-1970s now appears to have been postponed until the end of the 1980s. Of the projected 30 *frégates* and *corvettes* only ten will be in service by 1985, and they are currently being ordered at the rate of only one per year; perhaps half the original number of *avisos* will be in service by that date; the nuclear attack boats are coming along slowly; and the FPB programme has been halved.

Ambitious plans are currently being circulated for the replacement of the carriers *Foch* and *Clemenceau* by nuclear-powered vessels by the 1990s, but no mention is yet being made of suitable aircraft.

BUILDERS AND BASES

The prewar network of bases continued largely unaltered well into the 1950s. Private shipbuilders continued to be responsible for a significant proportion of naval construction. The next decade, however, was one of increasing rationalisation, specialisation and centralisation. The *Direction Technique des Constructions Navales* (DTCN) was set up to co-ordinate all aspects of design and construction. From now on all ships for the *Marine Nationale* would be built at the three naval dockyards on the west coast. The construction of all submarines, nuclear and conventional, was concentrated at Cherbourg, while Brest and Lorient built surface ships.

A new specialised facility was built on Ile Longue in the Brest roadstead for the operational needs of the SNLE force (known as FOST – the *Force Océanique Stratégique*). The main naval base at Brest is also the home of the Atlantic Squadron, comprising most of the major surface units of the Atlantic Fleet, and is the HQ of the *2ème Préfecture Maritime*. Lorient, which is also in *Prémar Deux*, is the base of the attack submarines (ESMAT – the *Escadrille des Sous-Marins de l'Atlantique*), which are maintained in hardened shelters built by the Germans during the Second World War. From nearby Lann-Bihoué three squadrons of long-range maritime patrol aircraft fly patrols over the Atlantic.

Cherbourg, the HQ of the *1ère Préfecture Maritime*, is the base of the Channel Fleet, consisting largely of mine countermeasures craft.

Toulon remains the only French naval base of any size in the Mediterranean. It is the HQ of the *3ème Préfecture Maritime* and accommodates the entire Mediterranean Fleet, to which the main striking force based on the carriers *Foch* and *Clemenceau* was added in 1975. A further two squadrons of LRMP aircraft operate over the Mediterranean from Nîmes-Garons.

MAJOR RADARS OF FRENCH MANUFACTURE

Designation	Description	In Service
DRBV-20A	Medium-range air search	1954
DRBV-22A	Medium-range air search	1956
DRBV-20C	Long-range air search	1961
DRBV-23B/C	Long-range air search	1961
DRBV26	Long-range air search	1974
DRBV-11	Air/surface search	1954
DRBV-13	Search and tracking	1973
DRBV-50	Low-altitude surface search	1961
DRBV-51	Low-altitude search and target-designation	1976
DRBI-10	Height-finder	1957
DRBI-23	3-D air search/tracking	1967
DRBJ-11	3-D air search/tracking	1985?
DRBR-51 A/B	Tracker/illuminator for Masurca	1967
DRBC-31	57mm fire control	1952
DRBC-32 A/B	100mm fire control	1962
DRBC-32C/D/E	100mm fire control	1972

FLEET STRENGTH 1947

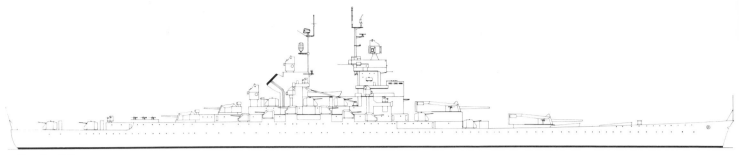

Jean Bart 1958

BATTLESHIPS

Name	Launched	Disp (std)	Fate
RICHELIEU	17.1.39	38,500t	Hulked 1959, BU 1964
JEAN BART	6.3.40	42,800t	Stricken Jan 60

Richelieu remained largely unaltered, except for the removal of some of the smaller AA weapons, until placed in reserve in 1956. *Jean Bart*, which was incomplete and had been heavily damaged at Casablanca, was transferred to Brest for completion. Work was delayed because of economic difficulties and, but for the strength of public opinion, construction would probably have been abandoned. The first sea trials took place in January 1949, but the new AA armament was not installed until the winter of 1951–52. As finally completed *Jean Bart* carried 24–100mm in twin turrets, disposed symmetrically in four groups on either side of the superstructure. There were six of the new 57mm twin mountings amidships, with four abreast 'B' turret and a further four on the quarterdeck. Modifications were made to the turret mast, and the latest search and fire control radars fitted. To compensate for the increase in topweight *Jean Bart* was fitted with a tear-shaped torpedo bulge which increased beam to 33.5m. She was present as a fire support ship at Suez in 1956, but was subsequently used as an accommodation ship at Toulon.

AIRCRAFT CARRIER

Name	Launched	Disp (std)	Fate
DIXMUDE (ex-*Biter*)	18.12.40	12,850t	Hulked 1960

Transferred from Britain in 1945, *Dixmude* saw active service off Indo-China in 1947, flying SBD Dauntless dive-bombers. In 1949 she was relegated to the role of aviation transport and served as such until 1960, when she replaced the *Jules Verne* as base ship for the amphibious forces at St Mandrier.

CRUISERS

Name	Launched	Disp (std)	Fate
SUFFREN	3.5.27	9940t	Stricken 1962
JEANNE D'ARC	14.2.30	6500t	Stricken 1964
EMILE BERTIN	9.5.33	5890t	BU 1959
La Galissonnière class			
GLOIRE	28.9.35	7600t	Stricken 1958
MONTCALM	26.10.35	7600t	Stricken 1961
GEORGES LEYGUES	24.3.36	7600t	Stricken 1959
Le Fantasque class			
X 01 LE TERRIBLE	29.11.33	2570t	Stricken 1961
X 02 LE MALIN	17.8.33	2570t	Stricken 1963
X 03 LE FANTASQUE	15.3.34	2570t	Stricken 1957
X 04 LE TRIOMPHANT	16.4.34	2570t	Stricken 1954

Suffren was the only surviving French heavy cruiser to see active service in the immediate postwar period. She served in the Far East before paying off into reserve in 1949. The older cruisers *Duquesne* and *Tourville* were used only for training and were hulked in 1950.

Of the prewar light cruisers, *Gloire*, *Montcalm* and *Georges Leygues*, all had active postwar careers until their disposal in the late 1950s. *Emile Bertin* became a sea-going gunnery ship in 1947 and was placed in reserve in 1952. The older light cruiser *Duguay Trouin* was used as a depot ship until her disposal in 1952. *Jeanne d'Arc* continued to serve as a school ship until 1964, when she was replaced by the new helicopter carrier of the same name.

The four survivors of the *Le Fantasque* class of *contre-torpilleurs* were redesignated light cruisers and saw extensive service, especially in the Far East during the early 1950s. Even by this time they could sustain a maximum speed of 35kts. *Le Triomphant* was broken up earlier than the others and cannibalised for spares. *Le Malin* was hulked in 1956 and the following year *Le Terrible* became a school ship.

DESTROYERS AND TORPEDO-BOATS

No	Name	Launched	Disp	Fate
T 05	TIGRE	2.8.24	2130t	BU 1954
T 06	ALBATROS	28.6.30	2440t	Stricken 1957
Ex-German vessels				
T 01	MARCEAU (ex-*Z 31*)	15.5.41	2660t	Stricken 1958
T 02	HOCHE (ex-*Z 25*)	16.3.40	2660t	Stricken 1958
T 03	KLEBER (ex-*Riedl*)	22.4.36	2310t	BU 1958
T 04	DESAIX (ex-*Jacobi*)	24.3.36	2310t	BU 1951
T 07	ALSACIEN (ex-*T 23*)	Nov 41	1100t	Stricken 1954
T 08	LORRAIN (ex-*T 28*)	Nov 42	1100t	Stricken 1959
T 09	DOMPAIRE (ex-*T 14*)	1939	850t	Stricken 1951
T 10	BIR HAKEIM (ex-*T 11*)	1.3.39	850t	Stricken 1951
T 11	BACCARAT (ex-*T 20*)	Oct 41	850t	Stricken 1951

Five ex-German destroyers and six torpedo-boats were transferred to the *Marine Nationale* in 946. Of the large 'Narvik'-type vessels, *Z 39* was in such bad condition that she was cannibalised to provide spares for the other two units, renamed *Hoche* and *Marceau*. The former was in reserve 1949–51 and was then refitted and served as an ASW trials ship from 1953 until 1956. Her armament at this time consisted of three single 150mm, 8–40mm (8×1) and six 550mm torpedo tubes (2×3) of the same model as that installed in the *T 47* class. *Marceau* underwent a refit 1948–50 during which US radar was installed and the AA armament was altered to 8–40mm (8×1). She saw active service until 1953, when she was placed in reserve.

Desaix was refitted 1946–47 and had US radar installed. She then served as a weapons trials ship until 1949. Her sister *Kléber* was refitted 1948–51, when US radar and 6–40mm were installed. She served until 1953 when she was placed in reserve. Of the large torpedo-boats, *T 35* was dismantled for spares. *Lorrain* was refitting until 1949, and was then used for ASW training at Toulon; *Alsacien* was similarly employed until 1952, when she was placed in reserve.

All the larger units except *Desaix* were given NATO 'D' numbers in 1951, but the three smaller torpedo-boats were disposed of before the new system of classification came into existence.

The former *contre-torpilleurs Tigre* and *Albatros* were employed as sea-going tenders, the latter being assigned to the gunnery school. *Albatros* had her forward boilers and funnels removed, speed being reduced to 24kts.

SUBMARINES

No	Name	Launched	Disp	Fate
S 01	ARCHIMEDE	6.9.30	1380t	Sold for BU 1952
S 02	LE GLORIEUX	29.11.32	1380t	BU 1952
S 03	CASABIANCA	2.2.35	1380t	Sold for BU 1952
S 04	LE CENTAURE	14.10.32	1380t	Sold for BU 1952
S 05	JUNON	15.9.35	600t	Sold for BU 1954
S 06	IRIS	23.9.34	600t	Sold for BU 1950
S 07	RUBIS	30.9.31	760t	Stricken 1949
Ex-German submarines				
S 08	MILLE (ex-*U 471*)	6.3.43	770t	Stricken 1963
S 09	LAUBIE (ex-*U 766*)	Apr 43	770t	Stricken 1961
S 10	BLAISON (ex-*U 123*)	2.3.44	1050t	Stricken 1957
S 11	BOUAN (ex-*U 510*)	4.9.41	1050t	BU 1958
S 12	ROLAND MORILLOT (ex-*U 2518*)	4.10.44	1620t	Stricken 1968

By 1947 only four submarines of the prewar *1500-tonne* ocean-going type, two of the '2nd class' *600-tonne* type, and the minelaying submarine *Rubis* remained. With the transfer of the ex-German boats even these few were quickly paid off, with the exception of *Le Glorieux* and *Junon*, the latter being employed for training.

In 1946 France received six U-boats, two from the UK and four that had been seized in French ports. *Blaison* was a Type IXB, *Bouan* a Type IXC. A second Type IXB, *U 129*, was broken up and cannibalised for spares. *Millé* and *Laubie* were both Type VIIC boats. The fifth boat, a small Type XXIII (*U 2326*), was lost accidentally in 1946. The sixth, *Roland Morillot*, was a Type XXI, and was to have a considerable influence on subsequent French construction. At first received on loan from the Royal Navy, then transferred, this boat was used extensively as a trials vessel until her disposal in the late 1960s. All the ex-German boats except *Bouan* needed repairs before entering service. Guns were removed and all received a snorkel. In the early 1950s *Bouan* was given a new streamlined fin.

Besides the larger U-boats, four Type XXVII (*Seehund*) midget submarines fell into French hands at the end of the war. Nos *74, 90, 107* and *365* became *S 621–24* respectively. They underwent extensive testing at Toulon, and provided the inspiration for a French 30t design. Two units (*Q 224–25*) were to have been built under the 1956–57 programmes but the orders did not materialise. Two of the German midgets were stricken in 1954 and the other pair in 1959.

FRIGATES

No	Name	Launched	Disp	Fate
Ex-American frigates				
F 01	ALGERIEN (ex-*DE 107*)	27.11.43	1300t	Stricken 1965
F 02	SENEGALAIS (ex-*DE 106*)	11.11.43	1300t	Stricken 1965
F 03	SOMALI (ex-*DE 111*)	12.2.44	1300t	Disarmed 1956
F 04	HOVA (ex-*DE 110*)	22.1.44	1300t	Stricken 1960
F 05	MAROCAIN (ex-*DE 109*)	1.1.44	1300t	Stricken 1960
F 06	TUNISIEN (ex-*DE 108*)	17.12.43	1300t	Stricken 1960
Ex-British frigates				
F 07	L'AVENTURE (ex-*Braid*)	30.11.43	1400t	Stricken 1961
F 08	LA SURPRISE (ex-*Torridge*)	16.8.43	1400t	To Morocco 1964
F 09	L'ESCARMOUCHE (ex-*Frome*)	1.6.43	1400t	Stricken 1961
F 10	CROIX DE LORRAINE (ex-*Strule*)	8.3.43	1400t	Stricken 1961
F 11	TONKINOIS (ex-*Moyola*)	27.8.42	1400t	Stricken 1961
F 12	LA DECOUVERTE (ex-*Windrush*)	18.6.43	1400t	BU 1959

The six ex-British frigates of the 'River' class were purchased 1943–44. The original 4in mountings were replaced postwar by two single 105mm mountings. In 1953 *Tonkinois* was renamed *La Confiance*; *L'Escarmouche* was renamed *L'Ailette*.

The six ex-American DEs were purchased in 1944. Eight further units were transferred 1950–52 (see under Major Surface Ships). *Algérien* was later renamed *Oise*, and *Sénégalais* was renamed *Yser*. In 1956 *Somali* was disarmed and became an experimental vessel. She was renumbered A 607, and in 1968 was renamed *Arago*.

AVISOS

No	Name	Launched	Disp	Fate
1st class				
A 01	LA GRANDIERE	Jun 39	1970t	Sold for BU 1959
A 02	DUMONT D'URVILLE	21.3.31	1970t	Sold for BU 1938
A 03	SAVORGNAN DE BRAZZA	18.6.31	1770t	Sold for BU 1957
2nd class				
A 05	BISSON	6.3.46	660t	Stricken 1964
A 06	COMMANDANT DE PIMODAN	1941	660t	Stricken 1966
A 07	COMMANDANT AMIOT D'INVILLE	1941	660t	Stricken 1965
A 08	GAZELLE	17.6.39	650t	Sold for BU 1961
A 09	ANNAMITE	17.6.39	650t	To Morocco 1961
A 10	CHEVREUIL	17.6.39	650t	To Tunisia 1959
A 11	COMMANDANT BORY	26.1.39	630t	Sold for BU 1953
A 12	COMMANDANT DELAGE	25.2.39	630t	Sold for BU 1960
A 13	LA MOQUEUSE	21.1.40	630t	BU 1965
A 14	LA GRACIEUSE	30.11.39	630t	BU 1958
A 15	COMMANDANT DOMINE	2.5.39	630t	BU 1960
A 16	LA CAPRICIEUSE	19.4.39	630t	BU 1964
A 17	COMMANDANT DUBOC	16.1.38	630t	BU 1963
A 18	LA BOUDEUSE	Sep 39	630t	Sold for BU 1958
A 19	ELAN	27.7.38	630t	Sold for BU 1958
Avisos Hydrographiques				
A 32	LA PEROUSE (ex-*Sans Peur*)	1940	1370t	Stricken 1969
A 33	BEAUTEMPS-BEAUPRE (ex-*Sans Souci*)	1940	1370t	Stricken 1969

The three large 1st class *avisos* served largely unaltered until the late 1950s. The more numerous 2nd class *avisos* of the *Elan* and *Annamite* classes ended the war with two main guns of 90mm, 100mm or British 4in (102mm) calibre, a single 40mm and four or six 20mm. The main calibre was standardised around the single 105mm mounting in the early postwar years. Many ships were fitted with two initially, but by the mid-1950s only a single mounting was carried. The construction of the seventh vessel of the *Annamite* class, the *Commandant Ducuing*, was abandoned in 1948. Several of the small *avisos* saw service in Indo-China. In 1957 *Gazelle* became a training ship.

MINESWEEPERS

No	Name	Fate	No	Name	Fate
Ex-German minesweepers (launched 1937–41, 685t)					
A 20	AILETTE (ex-*M 24*)	To W Germany 1963	A 26	BELFORT (ex-*M 205*)	To W Germany 1963
A 21	ANCRE (ex-*M 252*)	BU 1955	A 27	PERONNE (ex-*M 251*)	BU 1950
A 22	SOMME (ex-*M 9*)	BU 1955	A 28	VIMY (ex-*M 253*)	To W Germany 1963
A 23	MEUSE (ex-*M 28*)	Stricken 1953	A 29	BAPAUME (ex-*M 35*)	BU 1950
A 24	OISE (ex-*M 38*)	BU 1955	A 30	LAFFAUX (ex-*M 81*)	To W Germany 1963
A 25	YSER (ex-*M 85*)	To FRG 1963	A 31	CRAONNE (ex-*M 202*)	BU 1950
Ex-German minesweepers (launched 1942, 543t)					
	SUIPPE (ex-*M432*)	BU 1953		AISNE (ex-*M 452*)	BU 1949
	MARNE (ex-*M 442*)	BU 1953			

In addition to the above, the German minesweepers *M 4, M 12, M 21, M 275, M 277, M 404, M 408, M 434, M 454, M 475, M 476* and *M 495* were transferred to France, but none saw active service and they were broken up by 1949. The remaining units were reclassified *avisos de 2ème classe* and were employed as training and patrol vessels.

There were also 30 small wooden ex-American minesweepers of the YMS type. Names were:

Amarante, Anémone, Armoise, Asphodèle, Aubépine, Balsamine, Basilic, Belladone, Campanule, Capucine, Clématite, Dahlia, Digitale, Genêt, Gentiane, Géranium, Glycine, Héliotrope, Hortensia, Jasmin, Jonquille, Lotus, Marjolaine, Myosotis, Perce-neige, Pétunia, Pimprenelle, Primevère, Tiare and *Zinnia*.

In the immediate postwar period they carried the pennant numbers D 01–30. *Zinnia* was renamed *Lotus* and *Pétunia* became *Tiare*. Ten continued in service into the 1960s.

SUBMARINE-CHASERS

Thirty 280t sub-chasers of the American PC type were acquired in 1944 and designated *escorteurs*:

L'Attentif, Carabinier, Cavalier, Cimeterre, Coutelas, Dague, Dragon, L'Effronté, L'Emporté, L'Eveillé, Fantassin, Franc-tireur, Goumier, Grenadier, Hussard, L'Indiscret, Javelot, Lancier, Lansquenet, Légionnaire, Mameluk, Le Résolu, Pique, Le Rusé, Sabre, Spahi, Tirailleur, Le Vigilant, Le Volontaire and *Voltigeur*. Three more, *Hué, Luang-Prabang* and *Pnom-Penh* were purchased postwar for service in Indo-China. There were also 49 SC type wooden sub-chasers of 95t.

NATO PENNANT NUMBERS

Carried from 1950 onwards by ships in this section:

Destroyers			
D 601	MARCEAU	D 610	LE FANTASQUE
D 602	HOCHE	D 611	LE TERRIBLE
D 603	KLEBER	D 612	LE MALIN
D 604	ALSACIEN	D 613	LE TRIOMPHANT
D 605	LORRAIN		

Submarines			
S 605	JUNON	S 611	BLAISON
S 609	MILLE	S 612	BOUAN
S 610	LAUBIE	S 613	ROLAND MORILLOT

Frigates			
F 701	ALGERIEN	F 736	GAZELLE
F 702	SENEGALAIS	F 737	BISSON
F 703	SOMALI	F 738	COMMANDANT AMYOT D'INVILLE
F 704	HOVA	F 739	COMMANDANT DE PIMODAN
F 705	MAROCAIN	F 740	COMMANDANT BORY
F 706	TUNISIEN	F 741	COMMANDANT DELAGE
F 707	L'AVENTURE	F 742	COMMANDANT DOMINE

F 708	LA SURPRISE	F 743	COMMANDANT DUBOC	M 604	YSER	M 652	ZINNIA
F 709	L'ESCARMOUCHE	F 744	LA BOUDEUSE	M 605	AILETTE	M 653	BALSAMINE
F 710	CROIX DE LORRAINE	F 745	LA CAPRICIEUSE	M 606	BELFORT	M 654	CAPUCINE
F 711	TONKINOIS	F 746	LA GRACIEUSE	M 607	LAFFAUX	M 655	DIGITALE
F 712	LA DECOUVERTE	F 747	LA MOQUEUSE	M 608	VIMY	M 656	MARJOLAINE
F 731	LA GRANDIERE	F 748	ELAN	M 609	MARNE	M 657	AUBEPINE
F 732	DUMONT D'URVILLE	F 750	LA PEROUSE	M 610	SUIPPE	M 658	BELLADONE
F 733	SAVORGNAN DE	F 751	BEAUTEMPS BEAUPRE	M 641	AMARANTE	M 659	HORTENSIA
	BRAZZA			M 642	ARMOISE	M 660	JONQUILLE
F 734	ANNAMITE	F 752	AMIRAL MOUCHEZ	M 643	ASPHODELE	M 661	CAMPANULE
F 735	CHEVREUIL			M 644	BASILIC	M 662	HELIOTROPE
				M 645	DAHLIA	M 663	JASMIN
Minesweepers				M 646	PETUNIA	M 664	PERCE-NEIGE
M 601	MEUSE	M 649	PIMPRENELLE	M 647	CLEMATITE	M 665	ANEMONE
M 602	OISE	M 650	PRIMEVERE	M 648	GENTIANE	M 666	GERANIUM
M 603	SOMME	M 651	GENET				

MAJOR SURFACE SHIPS

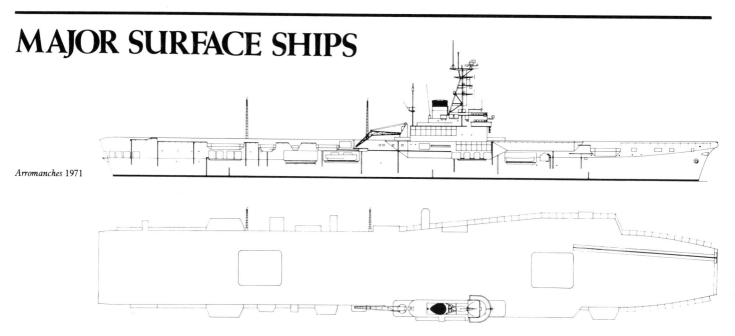

Arromanches 1971

Transferred from Britain in 1946 for a five-year loan period, *Arromanches* was purchased outright when the loan expired in 1951. By this time she had already made two deployments to Indo-China, flying SBD Dauntless dive-bombers and Seafire Mk XV fighters on the first occasion, and Helldivers and Hellcats on the second. Two further deployments followed before the collapse of the French military position in 1954. She then operated in the Mediterranean where she participated in the Suez operation in 1956, flying Corsairs and Avengers.

In 1957–58 *Arromanches* underwent a major modernisation in which she received a 4° angled flight deck and a mirror landing sight. The single catapult was removed, as was the entire AA armament, and she was fitted with a DRBV-22A air search radar. The angled deck added 6ft (1.8m) to the overall beam.

After this first modernisation *Arromanches* became a training carrier, operating the new Alizé ASW aircraft in addition to the Fouga CM175M Zéphyr, a naval version of the Magister trainer. She thus helped to build up an adequate supply of trained pilots for the jet squadrons which would operate from *Clemenceau* and *Foch*.

In 1962 *Arromanches* embarked a squadron of HSS–1 helicopters and took on the assault role in addition to the training role. After a further major refit in 1968 she was redesignated a helicopter carrier, with multiple missions including the intervention and ASW roles, the fast operational trans-

Ex-British COLOSSUS class *aircraft carrier*

Displacement:	14,000t standard; 17,900t full load
Dimensions:	630ft pp, 693ft oa × 80ft wl, 112ft fd × 23ft
	192.0m, 211.2m × 24.5m, 34.2m × 7.2m
Machinery:	2-shaft Parsons geared steam turbines, 4 boilers, 40,000shp = 25kts. Range 12,000nm at 14.6kts
Armament:	24-2pdr (6×4), 19–40mm (19×1), 24 aircraft. See notes
Complement:	824 (1400 with aircrew)

No	Name	Builder	Acquired	Fate
R 95	ARROMANCHES (ex-*Colossus*)	Vickers-Armstrong, Tyne	1946	Stricken 1974

port role, and training. She retained these missions until withdrawn from service in 1974, at which time it was envisaged that her place would be

taken by a new purpose-built helicopter carrier (see PH 75).

Arromanches 12.6.48

CPL

PA 28 design

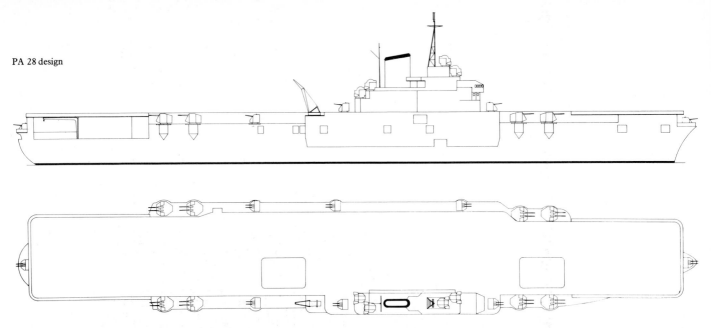

Designs for future carriers had continued throughout the Occupation and in August 1947 the construction of a new carrier, designated PA 28, was approved. She was to be named *Clemenceau* and would be laid down at Brest.

Of similar size and configuration to the light fleet carriers built by the Royal Navy during the 1940s, PA 28 was unusual in that while the flight deck was the strength deck – as in contemporary British construction – the ends of the ship were open like those of US carriers.

As in the prewar *Joffre* design, the large hangar, 164m × 24m, was offset to port. Hangar and flight deck were served by two lifts, each 15m × 10m with a capacity of 12t, and these were placed forward and aft of the island and offset in such a way as to place them on the starboard edge of the hangar itself. This permitted aircraft movement to port of the after lift, enabling the hangar to be extended farther aft without interruption. Seven arrester wires were to be fitted aft, and the PA 28 is credited with two catapults (although it is difficult to see how a second would have been accommodated on the axial flight deck, given the position of the forward lift). The propulsion system was similar to that installed in the *Volta* class *contre-torpilleurs*, resulting in a

PA 28 *aircraft carrier*

Displacement:	15,700t standard; 20,000t full load
Dimensions:	705ft pp, 755ft oa × 83ft wl, 118ft fd × 21ft
	215.0m, 230.0m × 25.4m, 36.0m × 6.5m
Machinery:	2-shaft Parsons geared steam turbines, 4 boilers, 105,000shp = 32kts
Armament:	16–100mm (8×2), 16–57mm (8×2), 45 aircraft
Complement:	1800

No	Name	Builder	Laid down	Launched	Comp	Fate
–	CLEMENCEAU	Arsenal de Brest	–	–	–	Project abandoned 1950

7kt advantage over the British light fleet carriers.

The projected AA armament was exceptionally powerful: a pair of 100mm twin mountings disposed in each quadrant, three 57mm twin mountings on either side amidships, and a further two 57mm mountings on the open ends of the ship. The 57mm mounting was of a new design which was to see service in all major French surface ships of the 1950s. Four large fire control directors were mounted on the island.

Clemenceau was to have carried a new generation of aircraft. It was planned to accommodate 22 large twin-engined torpedo-bombers of the NC1070 type then under development and five SE582 fighters (a naval version of the land-based SE580) in the hangar. A further 22 SE582 fight-

ers were to be suspended from the hangar roof.

Following intense debate concerning the military value of aircraft carriers, the PA 28 project was abandoned in 1950 and none of the carrier aircraft under development went beyond the prototype stage.

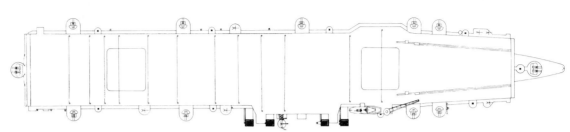

Lafayette 1959

In 1950 the USS *Langley* was obtained from the United States as part of MDAP, and she was delivered the following year as the *Lafayette*. In 1953 she was joined by the *Belleau Wood*, which was secured on a five-year loan and renamed *Bois Belleau*. Both carriers initially operated Hellcats, Helldivers and Avengers purchased from the United States in 1950–53.

Lafayette served off Indo-China in 1953, to be replaced in 1954 by her sister-ship. Both underwent refits on their return to France, at which time the single catapult was replaced and a tall lattice mast added forward of the second pair of funnels topped by a DRBV-22A air search radar. In a later refit (1958–59) *Lafayette* received a DRBI-10 height-finder in place of the US antenna which previously occupied the foremast.

From the mid-1950s both ships operated F 4 Corsairs and were based at Toulon. *Lafayette* took part in the Suez operation in 1956. In 1960 *Bois Belleau* was employed as an aircraft transport between France and the United States before being returned to the US Navy.

Ex-US INDEPENDENCE class *aircraft carriers*

Displacement:	11,000t standard; 15,800t full load
Dimensions:	600ft wl, 623ft oa × 72ft wl, 104ft fd × 24ft
	182.9m, 189.7m × 21.9m, 31.7m × 7.2m
Machinery:	4-shaft geared steam turbines, 4 boilers, 100,000shp = 32kts. Range 11,000nm at 15kts
Armament:	26–40mm (2×4, 9×2), 6–20mm (3×2), 26 aircraft
Sensors:	Radar SK-2, SP
Complement:	1400

No	Name	Builder	Acquired	Fate
R 96	LAFAYETTE (ex-*Langley*)	New York SB	1950	Returned USA 1963
R 97	BOIS BELLEAU (ex-*Belleau Wood*)	New York SB	1953	Returned USA 1960

Clemenceau c 1970　　　　　　　　　　　　　　　　　　　　　　Navarret Collection

Clemenceau 1976
NB 1/1750 scale

Clemenceau, allocated the project number PA 54, was the first carrier designed as such to be completed in France. Considerably larger than PA 28, she was designed to incorporate all the advances made in carrier aviation during the early 1950s. A fully angled flight deck was provided, together with a mirror landing sight and an altogether more comprehensive outfit of air search and tracking radars.

The length/displacement ratio is exceptional. The flight deck measures 165.5m × 29.5m and is angled at 8° to the ship's axis. The forward lift, 17m × 13m, is forward of the island and offset to starboard. The after lift, 16m × 11m, was positioned on the deck-edge in order to clear the angled flight deck and to increase hangar space. Both lifts had a designed capacity of 15t, which has since been increased to 20t. The hangar, as in previous French designs, is offset to port, and has an overall length of 180m (of which 152m are usable) and a width of 22–24m, with 7m clearance overhead. Two 52m Mitchell-Brown steam catapults are fitted. In the original design both would have been located forward, but one was moved to the angled deck in order to create a deck parking area to starboard. The catapults can accept aircraft weights of up to 20t and can produce a speed of 140kts with a 30kt wind-over-deck.

Armour was provided for the flight deck (45mm) with an armoured box 30mm–50mm over the machinery and other vital parts.

The two-shaft propulsion system is remarkable for a ship of this size; the figure of 63,000shp per shaft has been surpassed only by the 'super carriers' of the US Navy.

Originally *Clemenceau* was to have been armed with twelve 57mm twin mountings, but these were subsequently replaced by the new single 100mm, and the ship was finally completed with only eight 100mm single mountings.

A capacity of up to 60 aircraft was contemplated, but by 1960 this figure had fallen to 40 – a reflection of the increased size and weight of the new jets. A new generation of aircraft was specially designed to operate from the new carriers. Two flights of Etendard IVM ground support fighters (into which were incorporated a handful of IVP tactical reconnaissance/tanker aircraft) were embarked, together with a flight of Alizé turboprop ASW aircraft. As a temporary measure the ships operated the Aquilon (Sea

CLEMENCEAU class *aircraft carriers*

Displacement:	22,000t standard; 32,780t full load
Dimensions:	781ft pp, 870ft oa × 104ft wl, 168ft fd × 28ft 238.0m, 265.0m × 31.7m, 51.2m × 8.6m
Machinery:	2-shaft Parsons geared steam turbines, 6 boilers, 126,000shp = 32kts. Range 7500nm at 18 kts
Armament:	8–100mm (8×1), 40 aircraft
Sensors:	Radar DRBV-20C, DRBV-23B, DRBV-50, DRBI-10, 2 DRBC-32, 2 DRBC-31, NRBA-50; sonar SQS-503
Complement:	1338

No	Name	Builder	Laid down	Launched	Comp	Fate
R 98	CLEMENCEAU	Arsenal de Brest	Nov 55	21.12.57	22.11.61	Extant 1982
R 99	FOCH	Penhoët Loire/ Arsenal de Brest	Feb 57	28.7.60	15.7.63	Extant 1982

Venom) interceptor, but in 1963 42 F-8E Crusaders were purchased, and a flight of these was attached to each carrier after minor modifications in 1966. Helicopters, first of American and then of French origin, were operated for plane-guard duties and later for ASW. The Étendard IV was replaced by the Super Étendard in the late 1970s, but the small size and light construction of the ships has made it difficult to find a suitable replacement for the Crusader.

Foch had the distinction of being launched twice: once in July 1959 by Chantiers de l'Atlantique, who built the hull up to hangar deck level together with the propulsion machinery, and again in July 1960 by Arsenal de Brest, where the ship was fitted out. She was completed with bulges, which proved so successful that they were fitted to *Clemenceau* during her 1966 refit.

Fire control for the 100mm is performed by DRBC-32A and DRBC-31D radars in *Clemenceau*, and by DRBC-32C and DRBC-31C radars in *Foch*. In 1978 *Clemenceau* was fitted with a SENIT-2 tactical data system removed from the destroyer *Jauréguiberry*. *Foch* was taken in hand in 1980 at Toulon for similar modifications, the SENIT-2 system being that removed from *Tartu*.

The aviation fuel tanks in *Clemenceau* hold 1200m³ of JP-5 and 400m³ of avgas, whereas the figures for *Foch* are 1800m³ and 109m³ respectively.

Both carriers served initially in the Mediterranean. In 1966 they were transferred to the Atlantic but they returned to the Mediterranean in 1975. Since that time only one ship has been kept in full commission, the other serving as an ASW carrier with a reduced complement.

It is envisaged that *Clemenceau* and *Foch* will eventually be replaced by two nuclear-powered carriers of similar size and configuration. Provisional details released suggest a displacement of 32,000–35,000t full load, a maximum speed of 28kts, and a complement of 35–40 aircraft (including combat aircraft and ASW helicopters). They will have an angled deck, two aircraft lifts and two catapults. The first will be laid down at Brest in 1990.

*Jeanne d'Arc c*1970

Navarret Collection

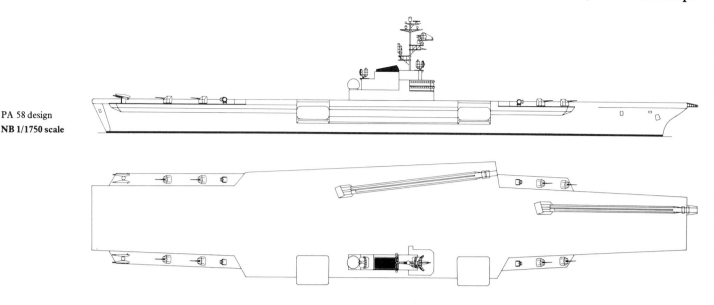

PA 58 design
NB 1/1750 scale

In 1958, while *Clemenceau* and *Foch* were still under construction, a third carrier was approved. The PA 58 design was larger and heavier, and although it bore a superficial resemblance to PA 54, was clearly influenced by the new 'super carriers' built by the US Navy. The shape of the flight deck, which was given considerable overhang on either side amidships, enabled the island to be positioned farther outboard. Parking space amidships was thereby increased, and the 200m hangar was positioned centrally. Two deck-edge lifts, each 17m × 14m, were sited forward and aft of the island to starboard. The length of the catapults was increased to about 75m so that larger aircraft could be handled. They were, however, positioned in the same way as those on *Clemenceau* so that there was a clear

PA 58 *aircraft carrier*

Displacement:	35,000t standard; 45,000t full load
Dimensions:	860ft pp, 939ft oa × 112ft wl, 190ft fd
	262.0m, 286.0m × 34.0m, 58.0m
Machinery:	4-shaft geared steam turbines, 200,000shp = 33kts
Armament:	2 Masurca SAM (2×2), 8–100mm (8×1)
Complement:	?

separation between flying operations, which were confined to the port side of the ship, and parking and handling operations. The angled deck measured 192m and was angled at 8° as on *Clemenceau*.

The significant increase in power needed to sustain fleet speed led to a corresponding increase in the number of shafts from two to four. Protection of flight deck and machinery was on a similar pattern to *Clemenceau*, but the

thickness of the armour was slightly increased.

The eight single 100mm of *Clemenceau* were to be retained but, in addition, it was planned to fit a twin launcher for the new Masurca SAMs on either side of the flight deck aft (*cf* the US Navy's *Kitty Hawk*).

In addition to Alizé ASW aircraft and Étendard fighter-bombers, PA 58 was to operate Mirage IVM heavy strike aircraft. The latter, under

development for the Navy since 1956, had a length of 19m, a wing-span of 12m, and a take-off weight of 20t.

PA 58, possibly to be named *Verdun*, was delayed by financial problems, and the Defence Staff considered a smaller design, derived from *Clemenceau*, in which the after guns would have been replaced by Masurca before the project was finally abandoned in 1961.

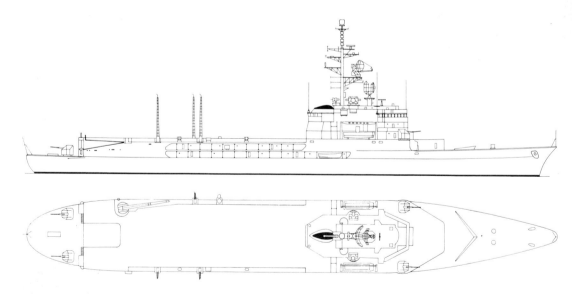

La Resolue as completed

In the mid-1950s the need arose to replace the old training cruiser *Jeanne d'Arc*. Various proposals were considered, including the use of a flotilla of *avisos escorteurs*, but in 1956 it was decided to construct a specialised helicopter cruiser which in wartime could be employed for ASW operations, for amphibious assault, or as a troop transport capable of lifting a battalion of 700 men.

The resulting PH 57 design adopted a hull form based on that of the anti-aircraft cruiser *Colbert*. A conventional cruiser superstructure

JEANNE D'ARC *helicopter carrier*

Displacement:	10,000t standard; 12,365t full load
Dimensions:	564ft pp, 597ft oa × 73ft wl, 79ft fd × 24ft
	172.0m, 182.0m × 22.0m, 24.0m × 7.3m
Machinery:	2-shaft Rateau-Bretagne geared steam turbines, 4 boilers, 40,000shp = 26.5kts. Range 6000nm at 15kts
Armament:	4–100mm (4×1), 4–8 helicopters. See notes
Sensors:	Radar DRBV-22D, DRBV-50, DRBI-10, 3 DRBC-32A; sonar SQS-503
Complement:	617 (inc 183 officer cadets)

No	Name	Builder	Laid down	Launched	Comp	Fate
R 97	JEANNE D'ARC (ex-*La Résolue*)	Arsenal de Brest	7.7.60	30.9.61	30.6.64	Extant 1982

FRANCE

forward accommodated all command and control facilities, together with the boiler uptakes, while the after part of the ship was dominated by a helicopter deck 62m × 21m beneath which were located the hangar and aviation facilities. The ship was named *La Résolue* as a temporary measure, adopting the name *Jeanne d'Arc* when her predecessor was withdrawn from service in 1964.

High speed was not a tactical requirement, so the size of the propulsion machinery was considerably reduced compared with *Colbert*. There are two main machinery spaces, each with two boilers and a turbine, separated by a single bulkhead. After the ship's sea trials, the funnel had to be heightened in order to clear the bridge structure.

Initially it was planned to fit four 100mm single mountings around the superstructure with a further two on the stern, controlled by three directors, but the two mountings abreast the superstructure were deleted.

Electronic equipment is similar to that aboard *Clemenceau*. Sonar was provided, and the ship was to have carried a quadruple 375mm ASW mortar on the forecastle, but this was never fitted. It was also planned to replace the mortar by a Masurca SAM launcher at a later date, but this plan, too, was abandoned. In 1974, however, six MM38 Exocet launchers were installed forward of the bridge, and *Jeanne d'Arc* may be fitted with Crotale in the near future. It is planned to instal a SENIT-2 action information system at the next refit (1982–83).

The bridge structure, in addition to the navigation bridge, contains an action information centre, a control centre for amphibious landing operations and, at the after end, a helicopter control bridge.

Hangar and flight deck are served by a single centreline lift with a capacity of 12t. Originally this was to have projected from the after end of the flight deck, but during construction it was decided to enclose it by extending the hangar structure aft in order to provide repair and inspection workshops and handling rooms for aircraft ordnance.

The hangar can accommodate four Super Frelon helicopters, which were introduced into service at about the same time as *Jeanne d'Arc* and can serve in both the ASW and assault roles. In wartime, hangar space could be doubled by removing some of the officer cadet accommodation, allowing a further four helicopters to be embarked. Five helicopter spots are marked on the flight deck, and there is sufficient space for two simultaneous take-offs. In peacetime, *Jeanne d'Arc* has tended to operate smaller helicopters such as the HSS-1, the Alouette III and the Lynx.

Following her commissioning *Jeanne d'Arc* carried the President of France across the Atlantic on a visit to the West Indies. Since that time she has served as flagship of the training squadron, being accompanied by the *aviso escorteur Victor Schoelcher* until 1973, when the latter was replaced by the destroyer *Forbin*. The squadron leaves Brest every autumn for a six-month cruise taking in the Atlantic, the Mediterranean, and sometimes the Indian Ocean and the Pacific.

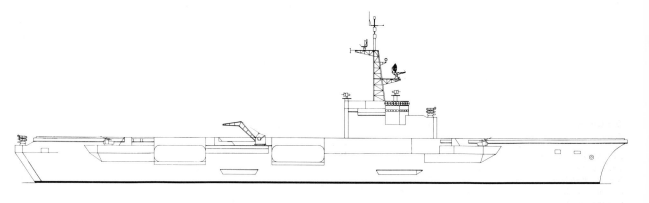

PH 75 design

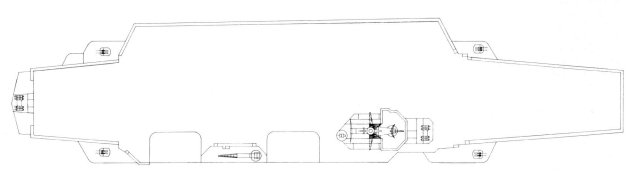

In 1970, with *Arromanches* fast approaching the end of her active life, studies were undertaken to provide for a replacement. A number of possible designs were produced, all of which shared the 55,000shp steam plant of the F 67 frigates, a through deck for helicopters, and a uniform armament of four 100mm mountings.

The first three versions displaced 20,000–22,000t, had a waterline length between 187m and 200m and a beam of 28m, with a maximum speed of 27kts. The first two versions incorporated a docking well aft, 40–50m long and 14m wide. The docking well of the first variant could accommodate four LCMs (26t), while that of the second variant, which was longer and higher, could accommodate two LCMs and two CTMs (56t). (The LCM has a cargo capacity of 30t, and the CTM of 90t, and both can carry a light or medium tank). The flight deck configuration of the first variant was clearly influenced by the US Navy's *Iwo Jima* class; the deck itself was rounded off at its forward edge, and side lifts were staggered to port and starboard. In the second variant the flight deck had a broad centre section not unlike that of the US Navy's

PH 75 *helicopter carrier*

Displacement:	16,400t standard; 18,400t full load
Dimensions:	682ft oa × 87ft wl, 157ft fd × 21ft
	208.0m × 26.4m, 46.0m × 6.5m
Machinery:	2-shaft nuclear: 1 CAS-230 reactor, 2 turbo-reduction-condenser groups, 65,000shp = 28kts; 2 AGO standby diesels
Armament:	2 Crotale SAM (2×8), 2–100mm (2×1), 2 Sagaie, 10–25 helicopters
Sensors:	Radar DRBV-26, DRBV-51, DRBC-32; sonar DUBA-25
Complement:	890 (+1000 troops)

A model of the PH 75 design   ECPA

CVAs, with lifts on either side of the island to starboard incorporated into the overhang. A similar arrangement was adopted in the third variant, which dispensed altogether with the docking well.

These first three variants all had a hangar of about 90m length with a capacity of 8 Super Frelons and 18 Lynx. There was accommodation for 600 men and their equipment, together with light vehicles.

The fourth variant was a smaller vessel, 170m × 25m, with a displacement of 15,000t, and a consequent increase in speed to 28.5kts. Flight deck configuration was similar to that of *Clemenceau*, with a centreline lift forward and a sidelift to starboard, aft of the island. Helicopter capacity was reduced to seven Super Frelons and 16 Lynx, and troop capacity to 450 men.

In the event none of these designs was proceeded with, but they served as the basis of an even more ambitious project, PH 75. Similar in conception, size and configuration to the third variant of the 1970 designs, PH 75 was to have nuclear propulsion to give her unlimited range for distant intervention. Like *Jeanne d'Arc*, she would be able to assume the ASW role as an alternative to that of amphibious assault, and was also designed for disaster relief. She was, therefore, given extensive hospital facilities consisting of three main wards, an X-ray ward, an intensive care ward, an infectious diseases ward, two dental surgeries and a laboratory.

In the intervention role she would carry a special landing force of units from the *Forces Terrestres d'Intervention* (FTI) and their supporting air units (CAFI), plus a Helicopter Movement Command Centre. 1000 troops could be accommodated in designated quarters, with a further 500 in supplementary spaces in the hangar.

The ship would embark Super Frelon and Lynx helicopters in the ASW role, or Puma helicopters for the assault mission. Hangar dimensions were 84m × 21m × 6.5m and there were two sidelifts each with a capacity of 15t. There was one fixed and one mobile crane, and extensive helicopter support facilities including workshops, munitions-handling rooms, magazines, and fuel tanks for 1000m³ of aviation fuel.

PH 75 was to be fitted as a command ship, with an action information centre, a communications centre, an ASW centre and an amphibious operations centre. She would carry 1250t of FFO for refuelling escorting warships. As with other French nuclear-powered vessels there were emergency diesel propulsion units capable of powering the ship for 3000nm at 18kts.

PH 75 was originally intended to complete in 1981, but financial problems delayed construction, and the design has been successively redesignated PA 75, PA 78, PA 82, and now PA 88. The change in classification from 'PH' (*Porte-Hélicoptères*) to 'PA' (*Porte-Aéronefs*) indicates an intention to provide for the embarkation of VTOL aircraft. It now seems likely, however, that if this ship is built at all it will be as a replacement for *Jeanne d'Arc*, and that she will not be completed before 1990.

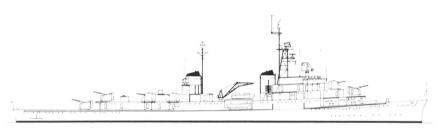

Guichen 1955

Acquired under the Peace Treaty of 1948, these two cruisers of the *Attilio Regolo* class had seen so little service that it was decided that they should undergo an extensive conversion to fit them as fast ASW/AA cruisers. They were converted 1951–54 at La Seyne Dockyard and re-rated *escorteurs d'escadre* – the same classification as the T 47 class destroyers; details in the table are as reconstructed. The original armament was completely removed. German-pattern 105mm twin mountings were fitted forward and aft, with one of the new 57mm twin mountings in 'B' position, and a further four 57mm mountings grouped around the after deckhouse. The main fire control director was located above the bridge and the secondary director aft. Four triple banks of ASW torpedo tubes were fitted at upper deck level forward of the bridge, and a short lattice foremast carried DRBV-11 and DRBV-20A surface and air search antennae.

Ex-Italian ATTILIO REGOLO class *cruisers*

Displacement:	3680t standard; 5500t full load
Dimensions:	455ft pp, 466ft oa × 47ft × 13ft
	138.7m, 142.2m × 14.4m × 4.1m
Machinery:	2-shaft Belluzzo geared steam turbines, 4 boilers, 110,000shp = 39kts. Range 3600nm at 18kts
Armament:	6–105mm (3×2), 10–57mm (5×2), 12–550mm TT (4×3)
Sensors:	Radar DRBV-20A, DRBV-11, DRBC-31
Complement:	353

No	Name	Builder	Acquired	Fate
D 606 CHATEAURENAULT (ex-*Attilio Regolo*)		OTO, Leghorn	1948	Stricken 1962
D 607 GUICHEN (ex-*Scipione Africano*)		OTO, Leghorn	1948	Stricken 1961

With the completion of the new *escorteurs d'escadre* of the T 47 and T 53 classes, *Châteaurenault* and *Guichen* were fitted out in the late 1950s as command ships and flotilla leaders, the after 105mm mounting and two banks of torpedo tubes being removed to provide extra accommodation.

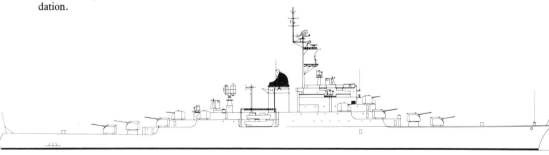

De Grasse 1961

De Grasse had been laid down at Lorient in 1938 as a conventional light cruiser armed with nine 6in (152mm) guns. Construction had been interrupted by the war and was not resumed until it ended. The hull was duly launched in 1946, but construction was again suspended to enable studies to be made of a new AA armament. It was finally decided to complete the ship as an anti-aircraft cruiser. Construction was resumed in January 1951. Completion was delayed when the ship sank in June

DE GRASSE *cruiser*

Displacement:	9380t standard; 11,545t full load
Dimensions:	592ft pp, 618ft oa × 61ft × 18ft
	180.5m, 188.3m × 18.6m × 5.5m
Machinery:	2-shaft Rateau-Bretagne geared steam turbines, 4 boilers, 110,000shp = 33kts
Armament:	16–127mm (8×2), 20–57mm (10×2)
Sensors:	Radar DRBV-22A, DRBV-11, DRBI-10, 4 DRBC-31
Complement:	950 (983 as flagship)

No	Name	Builder	Laid down	Launched	Comp	Fate
C 610	DE GRASSE	Arsenal de Lorient	Nov 38	11.8.46	3.9.56	Stricken 1973

FRANCE

1954 after she had been floated out with her sea-cocks open.

The armament selected was based on the twin 127mm and twin 57mm weapons which were to constitute the main armament of the new fleet escorts of the T 47 class. The mountings were disposed in a symmetrical pattern forward and aft, with the 127mm at upper deck and 01 deck levels and the 57mm grouped around the superstructure. Fire control arrangements were exceptionally complete: no fewer than four directors for the 127mm mountings were provided, disposed in a lozenge arrangement, and each was paired with a smaller 57mm director. All guns were radar-controlled with stabilised gunlayers for automatic tracking. Six 550mm torpedo tubes in two triple banks were also to have been fitted, but were dropped from the final plans.

De Grasse was equipped as a command ship with the ability to exercise radar control over air strikes. Besides the air and surface search radars carried on her foremast she was fitted with the new DRBI-10 height-finding radar.

De Grasse after 1966 — Navarret Collection

The machinery grouping and single funnel of the original design was retained. The main structural alterations involved lengthening and reshaping the original transom stern and the redesign of the bridge structure. When completed *De Grasse* had a standard displacement 1400t greater than envisaged in the 1938 plans. Possibly too much was attempted, as the innermost four 57mm mountings, together with the two main fire control directors abreast the bridge structure were removed in a refit in 1962.

At the same time the original DRBV-11 radar was replaced by a DRBV-20A.

In 1966 *De Grasse* underwent major reconstruction to equip her as flagship of the Pacific Experimental Centre. The signal department was considerably enlarged and a tall lattice mast carrying communications aerials was fitted aft. The after pair of 127mm mountings and all 57mm mountings, together with all directors except the main director above the bridge, were removed. The two air search radars

were replaced by a single more powerful model, DRBV-23, and the ship was given protection against fall-out. These modifications resulted in a lower standard displacement (9000t), and the complement was reduced to 560 with accommodation for 120 engineers and technicians. *De Grasse* served in her new role until stricken in 1973.

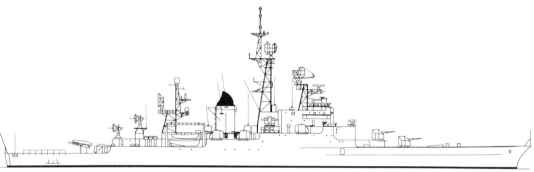

Colbert 1973 (SAM conversion)

Developed from the *De Grasse*, *Colbert* incorporated a number of modifications, including a shortened transom stern, an increase in beam, a knuckle in the hull forward, and a new system of protection (50mm deck; 50mm–80mm belt). These changes appear to have improved stability, as *Colbert* retained her full designed armament until she was rebuilt in 1970. A reduction in installed horsepower was accompanied by the adoption of higher-pressure boilers, which contributed to a lower displacement. The propulsion machinery was in two compartments separated by an 18m watertight bulkhead; each compartment contained two boilers and a turbine. The funnel was moved farther aft to clear the bridge structure, and a lattice mast

Colbert 1972 — Navarret Collection

COLBERT *cruiser*

Displacement:	8500t standard; 11,300t full load
Dimensions:	593ft oa × 66ft × 25ft
	180.8m × 20.2m × 7.7m
Machinery:	2-shaft CEM Parsons geared steam turbines, 4 boilers, 86,000shp = 31.5kts. Range 4000nm at 25kts
Armament:	16–127mm (8×2), 20–57mm (10×2)
Sensors:	Radar DRBV-20A, DRBV-22A, DRBI-10, 4 DRBC-31
Complement:	977

No	Name	Builder	Laid down	Launched	Comp	Fate
C 611	COLBERT	Arsenal de Brest	Dec 53	24.3.56	5.5.59	Extant 1982

was stepped immediately forward of it.

Like *De Grasse*, *Colbert* was equipped as a fleet command ship, but in addition there was provision for her use as a fast transport, with accom-

modation for 2400 men and their equipment. The adoption of a transom stern allowed for a helicopter landing pad aft.

Armament and fire control as completed were identical with *De Grasse*,

although early drawings show an extra pair of 57mm mountings on the stern. Provision was made in the original design for eventual missile conversion. The large planar DRBV-20C air search radar was not ready in time and, as a temporary measure, *Colbert* was fitted with the older 'A' model, which she carried until her 1962–63 refit.

From April 1970 until October 1972 *Colbert* underwent a major refit to equip her with guided missiles for fleet air defence. The original refit plan involved the suppression of all 127mm and 57mm mountings in favour of Masurca surface-to-air missiles and six single 100mm guns, but financial difficulties led to the retention of three 57mm mountings on either beam in place of four of the 100mm guns, resulting in a saving of 80 million francs from the original estimate of 350 million. The new main armament, therefore, consists of two 100mm single mountings forward, together with a DRBC-32C fire control director, and a twin Masurca

launcher aft with two DRBR-51 tracker/illuminators. Two of the original DRBC-31 directors were retained abreast the after end of the bridge structure to serve the remaining 57mm mountings. Forward of the bridge, bedplates were installed for four MM38 Exocet SSMs. Two Syllex are also carried. The bridge structure

These four ex-Italian destroyers, launched 1936-41, were acquired under the Peace Treaty of 1948. They remained largely unaltered until their disposal, and saw little active service.

was rebuilt and major modifications made to the electronics suite, which now comprises DRBV-20C, DRBV-23C, DRBV-50, DRBI-10, DRBR-51 (2), DRBC-32C and DRBC-31 (2). Electrical power was increased to 5000kW and air-conditioning provided throughout the ship. Complement was reduced to 560. Since con-

version, the original Masurca Mk 2 Mod 2 beam-riding missiles have been replaced by the Mod 3 semi-active homer, and there are plans to fit Crotale in the near future. The installation of a SENIT-1 action information system enables *Colbert* to exercise control of the air and surface situation at the centre of a widely dispersed

formation. She has served as Flagship of the Mediterranean Fleet since her conversion.

(For illustration see under Italy in 1922–46 volume)

Ex-Italian ORIANI/'SOLDATI' class *destroyers*

Displacement:	1690t (*D'Estaing* 1675t) standard; 2530t (*D'Estaing* 2254t) full load
Dimensions:	333ft pp, 350ft oa × 34ft × 12ft
	101.6m, 106.7m × 10.2m × 3.4
Machinery:	2-shaft Parsons (*Gravière*–Belluzo) geared steam turbines, 3 boilers, 48,000shp = 36kts. Range 2350nm at 14kts
Armament:	*Gravière*: 5–120mm (2×2, 1×1), 12–20mm (6×2), 6–533mm TT (2×3); *Duperré, Duchaffault*: 4–120mm (2×2), 2/3–37mm (2/3×1), 8–20mm (4×2), 3–533mm TT (1×3); *D'Estaing*: 4–120mm (2×2), 4–37mm (4×1), 6–20mm (3×2), 3–533mm TT (1×3)
Complement:	157

No	Name	Builder	Acquired	Fate
T 13	DUPERRE (ex-*Velite*)	OTO, Leghorn	1948	Stricken 1961
T 14	DUCHAFFAULT (ex-*Legionario*)	OTO, Leghorn	1948	Stricken 1956
T 12	JURIEN DE LA GRAVIERE (ex-*Mitragliere*)	CNR, Ancona	1948	Stricken 1956
T 15	D'ESTAING (ex-*Oriani*)	OTO, Leghorn	1948	Stricken 1954

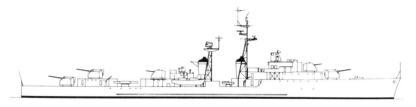

Vauquelin as completed

Larger than other contemporary European destroyers, the T 47 class, authorised 1949–52, were clearly in direct line of succession to French prewar construction. In mission, layout, and in the calibre adopted for their main armament, they bear a particularly close resemblance to the *Le Hardi* class.

From the outset, the T 47 was designed to give AAW protection to the new carriers and other fleet units. A 127mm (5in) calibre was adopted for the main armament to enable the ships to use standard US ammunition, and this was backed up by a heavy secondary battery of 57mm twin AA mountings of a new pattern. The inclusion of a heavy AA battery in addition to the dual-purpose main armament was a response to the weakness of French prewar-built ships in this respect, and was also responsible for the increase in length compared with *Le Hardi*.

In the original plans little provision was made for ASW operations beyond the traditional depth-charge racks. A single quadruple bank of 550mm anti-ship torpedo tubes was to be mounted on the centreline between the after groups of 127mm and 57mm mountings. After considering the American Hedgehog and the British Squid it was finally decided to fit the ship with four triple banks of tubes, mounted along the deck edge on either side, of which the forward pair would fire L3 anti-submarine homing torpedoes and the after pair either L3 ASW or K2 anti-ship torpedoes. Immediately aft of each bank of ASW tubes was a ready-use locker containing three reloads. Hull sonars of French design were fitted.

Dupetit Thouars 1971
(Tartar conversion)

Maille Brézé 1971
(ASW conversion)

SURCOUF (T 47) class *destroyers*

Displacement:	2750t standard; 3740t full load
Dimensions:	422ft oa × 42ft × 18ft
	128.6m × 12.7m × 5.4m
Machinery:	2-shaft Rateau geared steam turbines, 4 boilers, 63,000shp = 34kts. Range 5000nm at 18kts
Armament:	6–127mm (3×2), 6–57mm (3×2), 4–20mm (4×1), 12–550mm TT (4×3; 6 K2/L3 torpedoes)
Sensors:	Radar DRBV-20A, DRBV-11, DRBC-31; sonar DUBV-24, DUBA-1
Complement:	347

No	Name	Builder	Laid down	Launched	Comp	Fate
D 621	SURCOUF	Arsenal de Lorient	Jul 51	3.10.53	1.11.55	BU 1971
D 622	KERSAINT	Arsenal de Lorient	Nov 51	3.10.53	20.3.56	Extant 1982
D 623	CASSARD	A C Bretagne	Nov 51	12.5.53	14.4.56	Stricken 1976
D 624	BOUVET	Arsenal de Lorient	Jun 52	3.10.53	13.5.56	Stricken 1982
D 625	DUPETIT-THOUARS	Arsenal de Brest	Mar 52	4.2.54	15.9.56	Extant 1982
D 626	CHEVALIER PAUL	F C de la Gironde	Feb 52	28.7.53	22.12.56	Stricken 1975
D 627	MAILLE-BREZE	Arsenal de Lorient	Oct 53	26.9.54	4.5.57	Extant 1982
D 628	VAUQUELIN	Arsenal de Lorient	Mar 1953	26.9.54	3.11.56	Extant 1982
D 629	D'ESTREES	Arsenal de Brest	May 53	27.11.54	19.3.57	Extant 1982
D 630	DU CHAYLA	Arsenal de Brest	Jul 53	27.11.54	4.6.57	Extant 1982
D 631	CASABIANCA	A C Bretagne	Oct 53	13.11.54	4.5.57	Extant 1982
D 632	GUEPRATTE	F C de la Gironde	Aug 53	9.11.54	6.6.57	Extant 1982

FRANCE

In recognition of the increased threat from the air the T 47 was to carry a new generation of French radars. Initially it was intended to fit the ships with a tall British-pattern lattice mast carrying the DRBV-20A air search antenna, but in the event twin tripods with lattice supports were fitted, the second of which carried a DRBV-11 surface/air search radar. A single director was fitted for the main armament, with a second director aft for the 57mm.

As the new fleet escorts were designed to operate in company with the carriers and were not expected to engage in independent operations against hostile surface units, high speed was a less important consideration than it was for the smaller *Le Hardi*. Installed horsepower therefore showed little increase over the smaller *Le Hardi*. The hull was entirely welded and light alloy was used extensively in the upperworks to reduce top-weight. The ships were assembled using 84 prefabricated sections.

In the early 1960s *Surcouf*, *Cassard* and *Chevalier Paul* had their forward 57mm mounting removed to allow the bridge to be extended, and became command ships, replacing the two former Italian light cruisers in that role. In 1962 *Cassard* was fitted experimentally with a helicopter deck.

Vauquelin (ASW conversion)

Navarret Collection

Tartar conversions

Between 1962 and 1965 *Dupetit-Thouars*, *Kersaint*, *Bouvet* and *Du Chayla* were rearmed with the American Tartar missile system. A single Mk 13 launcher replaced the after pair of 127mm mountings, the twin SPG-51 tracker-illuminators being mounted on a raised deckhouse between the after pair of 57mm mountings. The forward 127mm mounting was replaced by a sextuple 375mm Bofors ASW mortar, allowing the DRBC-31 director to be moved to the bridge top in place of the main fire control director. Only the forward (ASW) torpedo tubes were retained. The masts and funnels were heightened and an SPS-39A 3-D antenna fitted in place of the DRBV-11 atop the mainmast.

From 1968 onwards the Tartar conversions were updated: an SPS-39B radar (with the planar SPA-72 antenna) replaced the 'A' model, and a SENIT-2 action information centre was installed in the after end of the bridge structure. In 1979 *Dupetit-Thouars* and *Du Chayla* had their original air search radar replaced by a DRBV-22A. Complement was reduced to 277

ASW conversions

Following the experimental installation of a bow sonar and VDS on *D'Estrées* in the early 1960s the remaining five ships underwent an extensive ASW conversion 1968–70 involving replacement of their entire armament and sensor outfit. Many of the systems had already seen service on *La Galissonière*. A single Malafon ASW missile launcher was installed aft with its magazine immediately forward of it. Single 100mm mountings (Mod 1953) controlled by a

ings (Mod 1953) controlled by a DRBC-32A director were fitted forward and aft, and a sextuple 375mm Bofors ASW mortar mounted in 'B' position. As with the Tartar conversions, only the forward set of tubes was retained. A DRBV-22A air search antenna replaced the original model atop the single tripod foremast, with a DRBV-50 air/surface radar below it; DUBV-23 and DUBV-43 sonars were fitted. The installation of a new bow sonar involved a reshaped clipper bow with a stem anchor, increasing overall length to 132.5m. Surprisingly no SENIT system is fitted. Damage control was updated and air conditioning was extended to all living spaces for a reduced ship's complement of 260.

Maille Brézé and *Casabianca* are fitted with TACAN, and in 1977 *D'Estrées* had British SCOT terminals fitted atop the bridge structure.

Forbin 1959

The T 53 design was a follow-on from the T 47. Five ships were authorised in 1953; the sixth was completed to a revised design.

The main difference compared with the T 47 was an increased capability for tracking and controlling aircraft. The air search radar – an improved model – was moved to the mainmast so that a DRBI-10 height-finder could be installed on the foremast. ASW capability was increased by the addition of a 375mm Bofors ASW mortar aft; the forward banks of ASW tubes were deleted in compensation.

In 1967 *Duperré* was disarmed and became a trials ship (pennant no A 633) for a large variable-depth sonar. In 1972–74 she underwent an extensive ASW conversion. Although in appearance she resembles the ASW conversions of the T 47 class, there are a number of important differences. Instead of Malafon, a hangar and flight deck for a WG13 Lynx were installed aft, the helicopter recovery

DUPERRE (T 53) class *destroyers*

Displacement:	As T 47
Dimensions:	As T 47
Machinery:	As T 47
Armament:	6–127mm (3×2), 6–57mm (3×2), 2/4–20mm (2/4×1), 1–375mm Bofors ASW mortar (1×6), 6–550mm TT (2×3; K2 or L3 torpedoes)
Sensors:	Radar DRBV-22A, DRBI-10, DRBC-31; sonar DUBV-24, DUBA-1
Complement:	346

No	Name	Builder	Laid down	Launched	Comp	Fate
D 633	DUPERRE	Arsenal de Lorient	Nov 54	2.7.55	8.10.57	Extant 1982
D 634	LA BOURDONNAIS	Arsenal de Brest	Aug 54	15.10.55	Mar 58	Stricken 1977
D 635	FORBIN	Arsenal de Brest	Aug 54	15.10.55	1.2.58	Stricken 1981
D 636	TARTU	A C Bretagne	Nov 54	2.12.55	5.2.58	Stricken 1980
D 637	JAUREGUIBERRY	F C de la Gironde	Sep 54	5.11.55	Jul 58	Stricken 1977

system being a simpler version of that in the F 67 and C 70 classes. Because of the space taken up by the hangar only a single 100mm (Mod 68) was fitted forward; four single MM38 Exocet launchers were installed abreast the forefunnel, and Syllex chaff dispensers abreast the hangar.

Radars and sonars are identical with those of the T 47 ASW type. All the original torpedo tubes were removed, but two catapults for eight L5 torpedoes were installed immediately aft of the bridge structure. The ship's complement was reduced to 272. The

DRBC-32E fire control was not installed until the late 1970s.

The rebuilt bridge structure houses command spaces and a SENIT-2 action information system. *Duperré* served as Flagship of the Atlantic Fleet until she ran aground in 1978. Because of the extent of her modernisation it was decided to repair her using parts from her sister-ship *Jauréguiberry*.

Between 1969 and 1971 *Tartu*, *La Bourdonnais* and *Jauréguiberry* received a SENIT-2 action information centre, and TACAN aerials were added to the foremast. In 1973 *Forbin* had her forward 57mm and after 127mm mountings removed and a flight deck fitted aft. She then served alongside *Jeanne d'Arc* as a school ship until her demise in 1981.

Forbin after 1973

ECPA

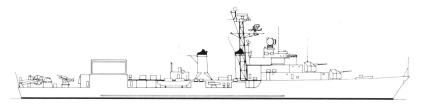

La Galissonnière 1976

LA GALISSONNIERE (T 56) *destroyer*

Displacement:	As T 47
Dimensions:	As T 47 except length 436ft
	132.8m
Machinery:	As T 47
Armament:	2–100mm (2×1), 1 Malafon ASW (13 missiles), 6–550mm TT (2 × 3; 12 L3 torpedoes), 1–305mm ASW mortar (1×4); 1 helicopter
Sensors:	Radar DRBV-22A, DRBV-50, DRBC-32A; sonar DUBV-23, DUBV-43 VDS
Complement:	333

No	Name	Builder	Laid down	Launched	Comp	Fate
D 638	LA GALISSONNIERE	Arsenal de Lorient	Nov 58	12.3.60	Jul 62	Extant 1982

Of the same basic design as the T 47/53 series, *La Galissonnière* was completed as an experimental vessel fitted with an entire new generation of weapons and sensors. Orginally it was intended that she should be armed with three of the new automatic 100mm DP mountings and 2–30mm AA, but the design was recast to incorporate the Malafon ASW missile launcher, and her armament as completed leaned heavily towards anti-submarine warfare. She therefore provided the necessary experience for the design of a new generation of ASW fleet escorts.

La Galissonnière was the first French escort to operate a helicopter. In order to make the most economical use of deck space, the top of the Malafon magazine formed the centre of the flight deck and a collapsible hangar was fitted above it, the sides folding down to provide additional width. This arrangement proved less than satisfactory and was not repeated in subsequent ships equipped with helicopters. The first helicopter operated was an Alouette II; this was later replaced by an Alouette III.

Immediately forward of the helicopter deck a quadruple 305mm ASW mortar was fitted. Only the forward banks of tubes were retained from the original design. A new generation of sonars was fitted and both the bow and the stern of the ship had to be reshaped to accommodate them,

La Galissonnière as completed

Navarret Collection

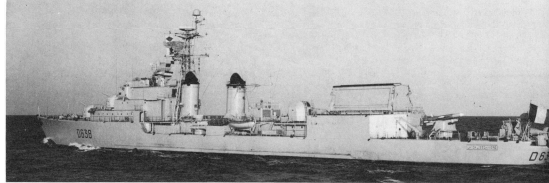

resulting in an increase in length. The low-frequency DUBV-23 bow sonar and DUBV-43 VDS are a matching pair with the same basic characteristics, and after trials aboard *La Galissonnière* were adopted as the standard sonar fit of all subsequent ASW construction.

In the late 1960s, following the completion of weapon and sonar trials, *La Galissonnière* was incorporated into the active fleet and became a squadron leader. The 305mm mortar was removed. She served in the Mediterranean until 1981 when she was transferred to the Atlantic.

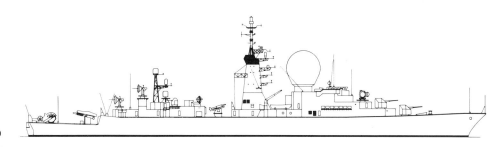

Suffren 1970

SUFFREN (FLE 60) class *guided missile destroyers*

Displacement:	5090t standard; 6090t full load
Dismensions:	486ft pp, 517ft oa × 51ft × 20ft
	148.0m, 157.6m × 15.5m × 6.1
Machinery:	2-shaft Rateau geared steam turbines, 4 boilers, 72,500shp = 34kts. Range 5100nm at 18kts
Armament:	1 Masurca SAM (1×2; 48 missiles), 2–100mm (2×1), 2–30mm (2×1), 1 Malafon ASW (13 missiles), 4 TT (4 × 1; 10 L5 torpedoes)
Sensors:	Radar DRBI-23, DRBV-50, DRBR-51, DRBC-32A; sonar DUBV-23, DUBV-43 VDS
Complement:	355

No	Name	Builder	Laid down	Launched	Comp	Fate
D 602	SUFFREN	Arsenal de Brest	Dec 62	15.5.65	Jul 67	Extant 1982
D 603	DUQUESNE	Arsenal de Lorient	Nov 64	12.2.66	Apr 70	Extant 1982

Classified first as cruisers and subsequently as *Frégates*, the *Suffren* class was designed to give AA and ASW protection to France's new carriers. Three ships were initially projected, with more to follow later, but in the event only two were laid down. They were the first French ships designed from the outset to carry surface-to-air missiles, and they marked a major step towards France's independence of other NATO navies (and in particular the US Navy) in that their weapons and sensors were almost exclusively of French origin.

In their architecture, too, they signified a radical departure from previous practice. The forecastle deck is carried well aft and is angled up at the break in line with the reload angle of the twin-arm launcher. There is a distinctive depressed clipper bow designed to keep the ship's anchors clear of the bow sonar dome while at

the same time allowing the forward guns to fire at low angles of elevation. The stern is a low and angular transom in which a well has been cut for a variable-depth sonar. A single large rudder of the semi-balanced type is fitted, and there are no fewer than three pairs of non-retractable stabilisers controlled by two central gyroscopes, ensuring a very steady missile platform. A further distinctive feature is the tall central 'mack', isolated from both the bridge and the after structure. Particular attention

was paid to the resistance of the ships to atomic blast, and there were major improvements in habitability. The *Suffren* class established a pattern for subsequent French surface ships, and also influenced the hull design of the Dutch 'Standard' class frigates.

Suffren before Exocet was fitted   Navarret Collection

The distinctive radome, unique to this class, contains the DRBI-23 3-D air search radar which feeds tracking data into a SENIT-1 action information system based on three computers. SENIT-1 has a digital link with Masurca and also controls ASW operations. The main ASW weapons and sensors themselves are those which ran trials aboard *La Galissonnière*. The magazine for Malafon is in the after deckhouse. The ASW torpedoes, however, are launched not from trainable tubes but from four catapults within the deckhouse between the mack and the bridge structure.

In the early 1970s two Syllex chaff launchers were fitted abreast the radome. In 1976–77 *Duquesne* had four MM38 Exocet launchers installed on the roof of the after deckhouse, and the single 30mm guns were replaced by single 20mm mountings, with an additional pair being fitted abreast the fire control director forward. The launchers were angled inboard to obviate the need for blast deflectors. *Suffren* underwent similar modification in 1979–80. Both ships now carry the Masurca Mod 3 semi-active missile in place of the original beam-rider.

When first completed *Suffren* and *Duquesne* served in the Atlantic Fleet, but in 1975 they were transferred to the Mediterranean along with the carriers.

Aconit 1977

Aconit was to have been the first of a class of five ASW corvettes. In appearance she closely resembles the AAW frigates of the *Suffren* class, with a prominent radome above the bridge structure and a single funnel surmounted by a tall pole mast for ECM antennae. The weapon systems are basically those which ran trials on *La Galissonnière*, although there are significant improvements in layout. The Malafon launcher is amidships and the magazine is inside the after deckhouse. The latter also contains two catapults for L5 homing torpedoes, together with cradles for a further six reloads. The 305mm mortar is forward of the bridge and is muzzle-loaded from a small glacis.

The distinctive DRBV-13 multi-mode pulse-doppler radar is unique to *Aconit*. It provides search and tracking capabilities for a SENIT-3 action information system (specially designed for this class), but the absence of a major AAW system to take full advantage of it may be the reason for its abandonment in subsequent ASW units.

The propulsion system is unusual for a ship of this size in that, like the US Navy's *Knox* class escorts, it employs only two boilers and a single shaft. This has resulted in an unusually compact machinery layout, but the experiment has not been repeated in later classes, suggesting that the French Navy was not happy with the single screw, or with the significant reduction in speed. Dissatisfaction

ACONIT (C 65) *destroyer*

Displacement:	3500t standard; 3800t full load
Dimensions:	417 ft oa × 44ft × 19ft
	127.0m × 13.4m × 5.8m
Machinery:	1-shaft Rateau geared steam turbine, 2 boilers, 28,650shp = 27kts. Range 5000nm at 15kts
Armament:	2–100mm (2×1), 1 Malafon ASW (13 missiles), 1–305mm ASW mortar (1×4), 2 TT (4 × 1; 8 L5 torpedoes), 2 Syllex
Sensors:	Radar DRBV-13, DRBV-22A, DRBC-32B; sonar DUBV-23, DUBV-43 VDS
Complement:	228

No	Name	Builder	Laid down	Launched	Comp	Fate
F 703	ACONIT	Arsenal de Lorient	Jan 67	7.3.70	30.3.73	Extant 1982

with the propulsion system plus the emergence of the helicopter as a primary anti-submarine weapon caused the remaining ships to be redesigned; they became the C 67 class.

Since completion *Aconit* has served in the Atlantic. In 1975 her pennant number was changed to D 609, although she retained the 'corvette' designation. In 1983 it is planned to

replace the 305mm ASW mortar by four MM40 Exocet launchers, and the DRBV-13 radar by a new model designated DRBV-15.

Aconit before 1975   Navarret Collection

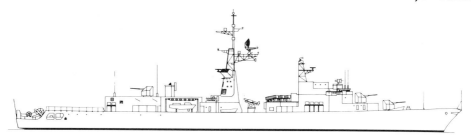

Tourville 1974

The C 67 design was a modification of *Aconit*. The principal differences were a doubling-up of installed horsepower to give a two-shaft propulsion system and an increase of 4kts in speed, and the addition of a helicopter hangar and flight deck aft. The latter modification was largely responsible for the significant increase in size. Initially the ships were given the same 'corvette' designation as *Aconit* and allocated the pennant numbers F 604, F 605 and F 606 but in 1971, when only two ships had been laid down, they were reclassified *frégates* and the project relabelled F 67.

As originally conceived *Tourville* was to have received the same sensor outfit as *Aconit*. While the ships were under construction, however, it was decided to fit the new long-range DRBV-26 air search radar, and the complex DRBV-13 was replaced by a DRBV-51 target-designation radar (*Tourville* received a DRBV-50 antenna as a temporary measure). The fire control director was updated to the lightweight 'D model. Data was co-ordinated (as in *Aconit*) by a SENIT-3 action information system.

In contrast with previous ships armed with Malafon the magazine is located in a deckhouse which extends from the after end of the bridge structure and which, from the outset, was designed to accommodate six Exocet SSMs

Tourville and *Duguay-Trouin* were completed with a third 100mm mounting atop the hangar, but it was decided to replace this by a Crotale PDMS at an early stage. The mount-

TOURVILLE (F 67) class *guided missile destroyers*

Displacement:	4850t standard; 5745t full load
Dimensions:	466ft pp, 501ft oa × 50ft × 19ft *142.0m, 152.5m × 15.3m × 5.7m*
Machinery:	2-shaft Rateau geared steam turbines, 4 boilers, 54,400shp = 31kts. Range 5000nm at 18kts
Armament:	6 MM38 Exocet SSM, 1 Crotale SAM (1×8; 26 missiles), 1 Malafon ASW (13 missiles), 2–100mm (2×1), 2–20mm (2×1), 2 TT (2×1; 8 L5 torpedoes), 2 helicopters, 2 Syllex
Sensors:	Radar DRBV-26, DRBV-51B, DRBC-32D; sonar DUBV-23, DUBV-43 VDS
Complement:	303

No	Name	Builder	Laid down	Launched	Comp	Fate
D 610	TOURVILLE	Arsenal de Lorient	16.3.70	13.5.72	21.6.74	Extant 1982
D 611	DUGUAY-TROUIN	Arsenal de Lorient	Nov 71	1.6.73	17.9.75	Extant 1982
D 612	DE GRASSE	Arsenal de Lorient	1972	30.11.74	1.10.77	Extant 1982

ing was removed from *Duguay-Trouin* within two years of her completion, while *De Grasse* was completed with only the two forward guns in place. In early 1979 *Duguay-Trouin* received the first production model of Crotale, and the associated DRBV-51 was moved to a higher position atop the mainmast. *Tourville* was similarly modified in 1980, with *De Grasse* following in 1981.

These were the first French ships of destroyer size designed from the outset to carry helicopters (the WG13 Lynx), and facilities for handling and maintenance are exceptionally complete. The large double hangar, which can accommodate two helicopters side by side, is served by a rail guidance system known as SPHEX, and in the centre of the landing area there is a grille for use with the Harpoon securing device. Two pairs of stabilisers contribute to a very steady platform, and there is a second navigation radar

provided specifically for helicopter control located on a short tripod mast on the low quarterdeck. *De Grasse* has a special modification which enables her to burn distillate fuel, and it is intended to convert *Tourville* at her Crotale refit.

Since completion all three ships have served in the Atlantic Squadron, and in 1978 *De Grasse* took over from *Duperré* as flagship of the Atlantic Fleet.

De Grasse as completed   Navarret Collection

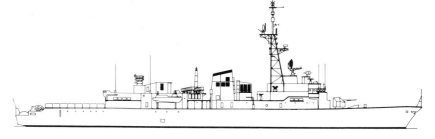

Georges Leygues as completed

Designed to replace the T 47 and T 53 class destroyers, the C 70 class is sub-divided into two groups, one specialising in ASW and the other in air defence.

ASW version
The first six ships laid down belong to the ASW sub-type, which incorporates many of the features of the ASW frigates of the F 67 type, but on a reduced displacement. They have adopted the full-width double hangar of the F 67 and have identical helicopter handling facilities. They also carry the same outfit of sensors, although the SENIT-4 action information system, based on more advanced computers with all-French components, has replaced SENIT-3. One of the two forward guns was lost because of the

GEORGES LEYGUES (C 70 ASW) class *guided missile destroyers*

Displacement:	3830t standard; 4200t full load
Dimensions:	423ft pp, 456ft oa × 46ft × 18ft *129.0m, 139.1m × 14.0m × 5.5m*
Machinery:	2-shaft CODOG: 2 Olympus RM–3B gas turbines, 52,000shp = 30kts; 2 SEMT-Pielstick 16 PA 6 diesels, 10,400bhp = 21kts. Range 9500nm at 17kts
Armament:	4 MM38 Exocet (4–8 MM40 from D 642 onwards), 1 Crotale SAM (1×8; 26 missiles), 1–100mm, 2–20mm (2×1), 2 TT (2×1; 8 L5 torpedoes), 2 helicopters, 2 Syllex
Sensors:	Radar DRBV-26, DRBV-51C, DRBC-32D; sonar DUBV-23, DUBV-43 VDS
Complement:	226 (250 max)

No	Name	Builder	Laid down	Launched	Comp	Fate
D 640	GEORGES LEYGUES	Arsenal de Brest	16.9.74	17.12.76	10.12.79	Extant 1982
D 641	DUPLEIX	Arsenal de Brest	17.10.75	2.12.78	16.6.81	Extant 1982
D 642	MONTCALM	Arsenal de Brest	5.12.75	31.5.80	28.5.82	Extant 1982
D 643	JEAN DE VIENNE	Arsenal de Brest	26.10.79	7.11.81		Building
D 644		Arsenal de Brest	19.11.81			Building
D 645		Arsenal de Brest	12.2.82			Building

FRANCE

reduction in length, however, and the Malafon launcher amidships had to be abandoned because of the adoption of gas turbine main propulsion machinery, which required large air intakes and exhaust uptakes amidships.

Although the adoption of gas turbines was undoubtedly influenced by developments in the Royal Navy and the Royal Netherlands Navy, only the Olympus half of the Olympus/Tyne COGOG package adopted by the latter navies was acceptable to the French, as it was felt that the Tyne lacked sufficient power for running astern, especially in the tropics, and was also expensive to run at cruising speed. A combined gas and gas (COGAG) turbine arrangement was considered, but there was no suitable turbine in the middle range (ie 12–13,000shp). SEMT-Pielstick diesels yielding an extra 25 per cent horsepower were therefore adopted in place of the Tyne and coupled with the Olympus main turbines in a CODOG arrangement.

On completion *Georges Leygues* was fitted with the second prototype Crotale launcher (the first was fitted in the trials ship *Ile d'Oléron*). In addition to the 8 missiles in the launcher itself, 18 reloads are stored in the deckhouse forward of the launcher. They are hoisted through a hatch in the sloping deckhead and loaded by hand. The missiles can be fired either from the ship's command centre or from an FC compartment beneath the launcher.

The Dagaie chaff dispenser system will be fitted in the near future. The 5th and 6th units will also have the EBTF passive towed array at present undergoing trials aboard the old escort *L'Agenais* in addition to the standard pair of active sonars.

AAW version

Although of the same basic design as *Georges Leygues* the AAW version incorporates a number of major changes. While the hull form, bridge structure and many of the major above-water sensors are identical, the fundamental difference in role is reflected in the replacement of the helicopter hangar by an American Mk 13 launcher (removed from the ageing T 47 destroyers) for Standard SM-1MR missiles with associated SPG-51C tracker/illuminators. The DUBV-23 bow sonar has been replaced by the austere DUBA-25 model fitted in the A 69 'avisos', and the associated VDS has been eliminated, enabling the helicopter deck to be extended over the stern. In the original plans a second 100mm would have been mounted just for-

Georges Leygues as completed

Navarret Collection

C 70 (AAW) design

(C 70 AAW) class *guided missile destroyers*

Displacement:	4000t standard; 4340t full load
Dimensions:	As C 70 ASW
Machinery:	2 shafts, 4 SEMT-Pielstick 18 PA 6 diesels, 42,300shp = 29.6kts. Range 8200nm at 17kts
Armament:	8 MM40 Exocet SSM, 1 Standard SAM (40 SM-1 missiles), 2–100mm (2×1), 2–20mm (2×1), 2 TT (2×1; 8 L5 torpedoes), 2 Sagaie, 2 Dagaie
Sensors:	Radar DRBJ-11, DRBV-26, 2 SPG-51C, DRBC-32D; sonar DUBA-25
Complement:	241

No	Name	Builder	Laid down	Launched	Comp	Fate
D 646		Arsenal de Brest	Sep 82			Building
D 647		Arsenal de Brest				On order
D 648		Arsenal de Brest				On order

ward of the helicopter landing pad and there would have been no helicopter maintenance facilities, but it is now envisaged that a simple helicopter 'shed' for a Dauphin helicopter armed with AS-15 anti-ship missiles will be fitted in place of the 100mm mounting, with a short-range SATCP surface-to-air missile launcher on either side.

The other major difference is amidships, where the abandonment of the CODOG arrangement of the *Georges Leygues* in favour of an all-diesel propulsion system has resulted in major changes in layout. Diesels were

chosen because of the problems of siting delicate equipment such as the new DRBJ-11 3-D radar and SATCOM terminals amidships where they would have been affected by the hot exhaust gases emitted by the gas turbines. The SEMT-Pielstick 18 PA is a fast diesel of a new design with double supercharging. Developments in flexible engine mountings have reduced the advantages of gas turbines as regards noise emission, which is in any case a less critical factor in a ship designed for air defence.

A novel arrangement has been adopted for the MM40 SSMs, which

are housed in a 'box' structure amidships. The reduced dimensions of the missile canisters has made it possible to double the number carried. Dagaie and Sagaie launchers for chaff and infra-red decoys will be fitted in place of Syllex. A SENIT-6 action information system will be installed.

Construction has been delayed by changes made in the original design and the first ship will not now be complete before 1987.

This ex-Italian colonial sloop was reclassified *aviso de 1ère classe* on her acquisition under the Peace Treaty of 1948. In the 1950s she became F 730.

(For illustration see under Italy in 1922–46 volume)

FRANCIS GARNIER *aviso*

Displacement:	2165t standard; 3068t full load
Dimensions:	285ft pp, 318ft oa × 44ft × 15ft
	87.0m, 96.9m × 13.3m × 4.7m
Machinery:	2 shafts, 2 Fiat diesels plus diesel-electric drive, 7800bhp + 1300hp = 20kts. Range 5000nm at 15kts
Armament:	4–120mm (2×2), 4–37mm (2×2), 4–20mm (2×2)
Complement:	234

No	Name	Builder	Acquired	Fate
A 04	FRANCIS GARNIER (ex-*Eritrea*)	CCM	1948	Stricken 1966

Acquired under MDAP, six of these ships were transferred in 1950, with *Malgache* and *Arabe* following in 1952. At first designated *torpilleurs d'escorte*, they became *escorteurs de 2ème classe* in 1951, *escorteurs* in 1953 and finally *avisos* in 1964. In the mid-1960s *Malgache* had her ASW weapons removed and became command ship of the amphibious training centre in place of *Dixmude*.

(For illustration see under United States in 1922–46 volume)

Ex-US CANNON class *destroyer escorts*

Armament:	3–76mm (3×1), 2–40mm (1×2), 8 to 12–20mm, 1 Hedgehog, 8 DCTs
Complement:	150
Other particulars:	AS US *Cannon* class (DET type)

No	Name	Builder	Acquired	Fate
F 717	ARABE (ex-DE 183)	Federal, Newark	1952	Stricken 1960
F 718	KABYLE (ex-DE 185)	Federal, Newark	1950	Stricken 1966
F 719	BAMBARA (ex-DE 186)	Federal, Newark	1950	Stricken 1966
F 720	SAKALAVE (ex-DE 194)	Federal, Newark	1950	Stricken 1960
F 721	TOUAREG (ex-DE 747)	Western Pipe & Steel, San Pedro	1950	Stricken 1966
F 722	SOUDANAIS (ex-DE 763)	Tampa SB	1950	Stricken 1966
F 723	BERBERE (ex-DE 113)	Dravo, Wilmington	1950	Stricken 1960
F 724	MALGACHE (ex-DE 190)	Federal, Newark	1952	Stricken 1969

Le Corse as completed

The E 50 class was designed to produce sea-going convoy escort vessels with a large radius of action. They were the first French ships to be built specifically for convoy escort. Although clearly influenced by the latest American thinking (they were of similar size to the contemporary *Dealey* class DEs, with which they shared an American-style flush-decked hull form with a transom stern), they were entirely of French design. Two were authorised under the 1949 Programme, and the second pair in 1950. The first three ships were financed under MDAP.

The original ASW armament comprised four triple banks of ASW torpedo tubes, all mounted forward at 01 deck level. Immediately behind each bank was a ready-use locker carrying three more reloads, the torpedoes being transferred tail-first into the muzzle of the tubes. Initial drawings show a German-pattern single 105mm gun aft, with two of the new 57mm AA mountings in 'B' and 'X' positions. In the event, however, the 105mm was replaced by a third 57mm mounting for a homogeneous AA battery. There was a fire control position forward of the bridge with a director aft above the second mounting. As with the T 47 destroyers, initial drawings show a single tall lattice foremast on the British pattern, topped by a DRBV-20A air search radar, but a tall tripod with lattice supports was eventually adopted. *Le Bordelais* was completed with a modified Strombos-Velensi funnel cap.

It was decided at a late stage to fit one of the new sextuple Bofors ASW mortars, but the only position available – immediately forward of the DRBC-31 director – was not ideal because of its poor arcs fore and aft. This defect was corrected in the E 52 class.

The designed maximum speed was 26kts, but this was exceeded by an average of 3kts on trials. In convoy escort operations the E 50s were expected to maintain 14kts for maximum fuel economy.

LE CORSE (E 50) class *frigates*

Displacement:	1250t standard; 1702t full load
Dimensions:	312ft pp, 327ft oa × 34ft × 14ft
	95.1m, 99.7m × 10.3m × 4.3m
Machinery:	2-shaft Rateau geared steam turbines, 2 boilers, 20,000shp = 28kts. Range 4000nm at 15kts
Armament:	6–57mm (3×2), 2–20mm (2×1), 1–375mm ASW mortar (1×6), 2 DC mortars, 1 DC rack, 12 TT (4×3; 24 K2/L3 torpedoes)
Sensors:	Radar DRBV-20A, DRBC-31; sonar DUBV-1, DUBA-1
Complement:	174

No	Name	Builder	Laid down	Launched	Comp	Fate
F 761	LE CORSE	Arsenal de Lorient	Oct 51	5.8.52	15.4.55	Stricken 1975
F 762	LE BRESTOIS	Arsenal de Lorient	Nov 51	16.8.52	19.1.56	Stricken 1975
F 763	LE BOULONNAIS	A C de la Loire	Mar 52	12.5.53	5.8.55	Stricken 1977
F 764	LE BORDELAIS	F C de la Méditerranée	May 52	11.7.53	7.4.55	Stricken 1975

In the early 1960s *Le Brestois* had a single 100mm fitted in place of her after 57mm mounting for experimental purposes and a DRBV-32A fire control director replaced the Bofors ASW mortar. At the same time the foremast was modified on the pattern of the latter E 52s, and a DRBV-22A antenna replaced the DRBV-20A. The other three vessels were placed in reserve in 1964–66 but were later re-activated.

Le Vendéen (date unknown)

ECPA

Le Bourguignon as completed

L'Alsacien as completed

E 52 was a follow-on design from the E 50 incorporating a number of improvements. The first seven units, ordered in 1952, were financed under MDAP. The remaining ships were paid for by France; two were ordered in 1953, two in 1954 and three in 1955.

The major difference in layout compared to E 50 was the transfer of the ASW tubes, together with their ready-use lockers, from 01 deck forward to the upper deck amidships. Besides reducing topweight this had the effect of freeing the forward position for the sextuple ASW mortar with a consequent improvement in arcs.

The first vessels completed had a similar radar fit to E 50, but later units were fitted from the start with the new DRBV-22A air search radar, which was carried at a lower level than the DRBV-20A. All ships were later brought up to the same standard.

In place of the tiered bridge structure of the earlier ships, *L'Agenais* and *Le Béarnais* were given a large single block extending well forward, the fire control position being relocated on top.

The last three ships of the class incorporated a number of important modifications, and were known as the Type E 52B. The 57mm mounting in 'X' position was replaced by a large quadruple 305mm ASW mortar of a new design. The sextuple ASW mortar was deleted and the forward 57mm mounting moved into its place to improve arcs. Reload magazines for the ASW torpedoes were removed, suggesting that the early vessels of the E 50 and E 52 classes may have suffered from stability problems. The E 52B class units had the larger bridge structure introduced by the previous

LE NORMAND (E 52) class *frigates*

Displacement:	As E 50
Dimensions:	As E 50
Machinery:	As E 50 but Parsons turbines in some. Range 4500nm at 15kts
Armament:	As E 50 except E 52B Type (*L'Alsacien, Le Provençal, Le Vendéen*) 4–57mm (2×2), 2–20mm (2×1), 1–305mm ASW mortar (1×4), 2 DC mortars, 1 DC rack, 12 TT (4×3; 12 K2/L3 torpedoes)
Sensors:	Radar DRBV-22A, DRBC-31; sonar DUBV-24 (*Le Savoyard, Le Breton, Le Basque* DUBV-1), DUBA-1
Complement:	175

No	Name	Builder	Laid down	Launched	Comp	Fate
F 765	LE NORMAND	F C de la Méditerranée	Jul 53	13.2.54	3.11.56	Stricken 1980
F 766	LE PICARD	A C de la Loire	Nov 53	31.5.54	20.9.56	Stricken 1979
F 767	LE GASCON	A C de la Loire	Feb 54	23.10.54	29.3.57	Stricken 1977
F 768	LE LORRAIN	F C de la Méditerranée	Feb 54	19.6.54	1.1.57	Stricken 1976
F 769	LE BOURGUIGNON	Penhoët	Jan 54	28.1.56	11.7.57	Stricken 1976
F 770	LE CHAMPENOIS	A C de la Loire	May 54	12.3.55	1.6.57	Stricken 1975
F 771	LE SAVOYARD	F C de la Méditerranée	Nov 53	7.5.55	14.6.56	Stricken 1980
F 772	LE BRETON	Arsenal de Lorient	Jun 54	2.4.55	20.8.57	Stricken 1977
F 773	LE BASQUE	Arsenal de Lorient	Dec 54	25.2.56	18.10.57	Stricken 1980
F 774	L'AGENAIS	Arsenal de Lorient	Aug 55	23.6.56	14.5.58	Trials ship 1979
F 775	LE BEARNAIS	Arsenal de Lorient	Dec 55	23.6.56	18.10.58	Stricken 1980
F 776	L'ALSACIEN	Arsenal de Lorient	Jul 56	26.1.57	27.8.60	Stricken 1981
F 777	LE PROVENÇAL	Arsenal de Lorient	Feb 57	5.10.57	6.11.59	Stricken 1980
F 778	LE VENDEEN	F C de la Méditerranée	Mar 57	27.7.57	1.10.60	Trials ship May 81

two ships and in addition had the Strombos-Velensi funnel cap. Two further vessels of this type were included in the 1957 naval estimates but were cancelled due to financial problems.

In the mid-1960s *Le Savoyard, Le Breton* and *Le Basque* were assigned to the Naval Group of Trials and Measurements and were involved in initial testing of the MSBS missile. The latter two ships had their bridge structure modified on the pattern of the later ships of the class, and all

three had tracking equipment installed in place of the third 57mm mounting. In the late 1970s *Le Basque* was fitted with FC equipment aft for trials of the OTOMAT missile. *L'Agenais* had a VDS fitted in place of her after 57mm mounting and became trials ship (A 784) for a linear passive sonar (Flute ETBF). In 1981 *Le Vendéen* was also reclassified as a trials ship (A 778) and had a fixed 500mm TT installed on her stern.

E 54 Type
In 1954 plans were drawn up for a new class of austere convoy escorts. Dimensions were 89.0m × 9.5m on a displacement of 1000t standard. ASW armament was to be on a par with the E 50, but AA armament was restricted to four 40mm. The first three ships were to have been laid down at Lorient but the design was not proceeded with.

Commandant Rivière 1961

In 1955, following the abandonment of the E 54 design, the first ship of a new class of escorts was ordered. The *Commandant Rivière* was a dual-purpose design intended to perform the traditional role of a colonial *aviso* in peacetime and the NATO role of convoy escort in wartime. At first christened *escorteur d'Union Française* she was redesignated *aviso escorteur* in 1959. A further six units were ordered in 1956 and the final two in 1957.

Three 100mm guns were fitted, with the provision that the third could be replaced by a helicopter deck. The DRBC-32A fire control director was located above the after two mounts. Two single 30mm AA of a new design were fitted amidships. The 305mm ASW mortar in 'B' position, which reloads from a small glacis forward of the mounting, can fire a special shore bombardment round. Only two triple banks of ASW tubes are fitted and

COMMANDANT RIVIERE class *frigates*

Displacement:	1750t (*Balny* 1650t) standard; 2250 (*Balny* 1950t) full load
Dimensions:	322ft pp, 338ft oa × 38ft × 14ft 98.0m, 103.0m × 11.5m × 4.3m
Machinery:	2 shafts, 4 SEMT-Pielstick 12cyl diesels (except *Balny, Bory*; see notes), 16,000bhp = 25kts. Range 4500nm at 15kts
Armament:	3–100mm (3×1), 2–30mm (2×1), 1–305mm ASW mortar (1×4), 6 TT (2×3; K2/L3 torpedoes)
Sensors:	Radar DRBV-22A, DRBV-50, DRBC-32A; sonar DUBA-3, SQS-17
Complement:	180 (plus 80 commandos)

No	Name	Builder	Laid down	Launched	Comp	Fate
F 733	COMMANDANT RIVIERE	Arsenal de Lorient	Apr 57	Oct 58	Dec 62	Extant 1982
F 725	VICTOR SCHOELCHER	Arsenal de Lorient	Oct 57	Oct 58	Dec 62	Extant 1982
F 726	COMMANDANT BORY	Arsenal de Lorient	May 58	Oct 58	Mar 64	Extant 1982
F 727	AMIRAL CHARNER	Arsenal de Lorient	Nov 58	Mar 60	Dec 62	Extant 1982
F 728	DOUDART DE LAGREE	Arsenal de Lorient	Mar 60	Apr 61	Mar 63	Extant 1982
F 729	BALNY	Arsenal de Lorient	Mar 59	Apr 61	Mar 63	Extant 1982
F 740	COMMANDANT BOURDAIS	Arsenal de Lorient	Mar 59	Apr 61	Mar 63	Extant 1982
F 748	PROTET	Arsenal de Lorient	Sep 61	Dec 62	May 64	Extant 1982
F 749	ENSEIGNE DE VAISSEAU HENRY	Arsenal de Lorient	Sep 62	Dec 63	Jan 65	Extant 1982

there is no provision for reloading. A flag officer and staff or an 80-man commando team can be accommodated, and two 9m LCPs, each with a capacity of 25 men, are carried on davits.

Because of the requirement for long range and fuel economy, a two-shaft diesel installation was adopted. The class is credited with excellent manoeuvrability and a small turning circle (160m at 20kts). *Commandant Bory* was fitted with Sigma free-piston generators driving gas turbines, but these were removed in 1974–75 and replaced by the standard diesel installation. *Balny* underwent a more fundamental modification which delayed her completion until 1970: she was fitted with an experimental CODAG plant comprising a Turbomeca M38 gas turbine (a modified Atar aero-engine downrated from 16,700 to 11,800hp) and two 1800bhp AGO V16 diesels for cruising. The single controllable-pitch propeller is 3.6m in diameter and is 1m below the keel. The compactness of the plant allows more fuel to be carried, with a consequent increase in range.

In 1973 *Commandant Bourdais* and *Enseigne de Vaisseau Henry* had the

Commandant Rivière as completed

third gun replaced by a helicopter deck. *Amiral Charner* followed in 1974. Other units were to have undergone the same modification, but the scheme was abandoned in favour of the removal of the second gun and its replacement by four MM38 Exocet launchers. Helicopter platforms were removed and the third mounting replaced. By 1979 all except *Balny*, which has a longer deckhouse aft than her sisters, had been converted. A number of ships have also had their DRBV-50 radar replaced by a DRBN-32 navigation radar. The 30mm AA guns are being replaced by single 40mm mounts.

Designed to operate in a variety of climates, the *avisos escorteurs* have seen extensive service in all parts of the world. They operate singly, not in divisions or squadrons. *Commandant Bourdais* commissioned as a fishery protection vessel off Newfoundland and Greenland; others have served in the West Indies, the Indian Ocean and the Far East; *Victor Schoelcher* served as a training ship alongside *Jeanne d'Arc* until replaced by *Forbin* in 1973. *Doudart de Lagrée* took on this role in 1981.

Four similar vessels were built for Portugal during the 1960s.

D'Estienne D'Orves 1975

D'ESTIENNE D'ORVES (A 69) class *corvettes*

Displacement:	950t standard; 1250t full load
Dimensions:	249ft pp, 262ft oa × 34ft × 10ft
	76.0m, 80.0m × 10.3m × 3.0m
Machinery:	2 shafts, 2 SEMT-Pielstick PC 2V diesels, 11,000bhp = 24kts. Range 4500nm at 15kts
Armament:	1–100mm, 2–20mm (2×1), 2 MM38 Exocet, 1–375mm ASW mortar (1×6), 4 TT (4×1; 4 L3/L5 torpedoes)
Sensors:	Radar DRBV-51, DRBC-32E; sonar DUBA-25
Complement:	79

No	Name	Builder	Laid down	Launched	Comp	Fate
F 781	D'ESTIENNE D'ORVES	Arsenal de Lorient	1.9.72	1.6.73	10.9.76	Extant 1982
F 782	AMYOT D'INVILLE	Arsenal de Lorient	1.9.73	30.11.74	13.10.76	Extant 1982
F 783	DROGOU	Arsenal de Lorient	1.10.73	30.11.74	30.9.76	Extant 1982
F 784	DETROYAT	Arsenal de Lorient	15.12.74	31.1.76	4.5.77	Extant 1982
F 785	JEAN MOULIN	Arsenal de Lorient	15.1.75	31.1.76	11.5.77	Extant 1982
F 786	QUARTIER-MAITRE ANQUETIL	Arsenal de Lorient	1.8.75	7.8.76	4.2.78	Extant 1982
F 787	COMMANDANT DE PIMODAN	Arsenal de Lorient	1.9.75	7.8.76	20.5.78	Extant 1982
F 788	SECOND-MAITRE LE BIHAN	Arsenal de Lorient	1.11.76	13.8.77	11.7.79	Extant 1982
F 789	LIEUTENANT DE VAISSEAU LE HENAFF	Arsenal de Lorient	Mar 77	17.3.79	13.2.80	Extant 1982
F 790	LIEUTENANT DE VAISSEAU LAVALLEE	Arsenal de Lorient	Oct 77	20.5.79	9.10.80	Extant 1982
F 791	COMMANDANT L'HERMINIER	Arsenal de Lorient	Dec 77	7.3.81	13.12.81	Extant 1982
F 792	PREMIER-MAITRE L'HER	Arsenal de Lorient	Jul 78	26.6.79		Building
F 793	COMMANDANT BLAISON	Arsenal de Lorient	Sep 78	7.3.81		Building
F 794	ENSEIGNE DE VAISSEAU JACOUBET	Arsenal de Lorient	Apr 79	28.9.81		Building
F 795	COMMANDANT DUCUING	Arsenal de Lorient	1.10.80	28.9.81		Building
F 796	COMMANDANT BIROT	Arsenal de Lorient	23.3.81			Building
F 797		Arsenal de Lorient	12.10.81			Building

Ordered as replacements for the series of *escorteurs* built during the 1950s, the *avisos* of the A 69 class illustrate the changes in French maritime philosophy which had taken place by the late 1960s. They are austere vessels designed for coastal (not ocean) ASW and for patrol on colonial stations. The first pair was authorised in 1971, and the remainder ordered at the rate of three per year between 1972 and 1975.

The *aviso* role demanded a dual-purpose gun, good endurance and manoeuvrability. Since endurance was a more important consideration than speed, a two-shaft diesel installation with CP propellers was adopted, producing a maximum speed of about 23.5kts. The two diesels are mounted side by side in a single engine room, and are controlled from a separate acoustically insulated and air-conditioned machinery control room immediately aft of the engine room itself. The electrical generating plant, consisting of two groups of diesel-alternators each of 320kW and one of 200kW, is located in compartments on either side of the main engine room.

ASW capability is strictly limited. The austere high-frequency DUBA-25, the transducer for which is retractable but housed in a fixed dome, is designed for acquisition and attack in coastal waters down to 220m. The magazine for the 375mm mortar is below the after deckhouse and contains 30 reloads, the rounds being hoisted by a hydraulic lift. The mortar itself is remote-controlled from the operations centre. Inside the deckhouse itself are four catapults for ASM torpedoes angled at 30° to the centreline on a forward bearing; no reloads are carried. It was intended to modify *Blaison* and *Jacoubet* to carry a Dauphin helicopter. A hangar and flight deck were to have been provided and stabilisers fitted, but the scheme was abandoned.

Originally the class was to have been sub-divided into two groups, designated A 69 and A 70 respectively. Ships belonging to the latter group would be fitted to fire Exocet. In the event bedplates for Exocet were fitted to all ships, but the missiles themselves are carried only by ships on overseas duty. Later units will be fitted to carry four MM40 missiles. Target designation is performed by a variant of the DRBV-51 radar. Fire control for the single 100mm is performed by a DRBC-32E in combination with a semi-analogue, semi-digital computer. There is also an optical sight.

Early ships of the class experienced problems with exhaust gases, and from *Jean Moulin* onwards funnels were heightened, the modification

D'Estienne D'Orves as completed   ECPA

being extended to all ships on refitting. L'Herminier and later ships have 12 PA 6BTC diesels, giving an increase in power to 14,400bhp.

The ruggedness, simplicity and cheapness of the class has appealed to a number of foreign buyers. In 1976 the original Le Hénaff and L'Herminier were purchased by South Africa while under construction, but following the UN arms embargo on that country they were transferred to Argentina in September 1978. They were replaced by two vessels carrying the same name and pennant number.

SUBMARINES

In 1951 four demilitarised 'S' class submarines were lent by the Royal Navy for ASW training. All had their torpedo tubes closed off and two, Saphir and Sultane, had a modified hull form and streamlined fin, giving them an increase in speed of 3kts when dived. Sibylle was accidentally lost near Toulon on 23 September 1952. The initial loan period of four years was extended for the other three.

(For illustration see under Great Britain in 1922–46 volume)

SAPHIR class *training submarines*

Displacement:	715t standard; 990t submerged
Dimensions:	217ft oa × 24ft × 14ft
	66.1m × 7.2m × 4.2m
Machinery:	2 shafts, 2 8cyl Admiralty diesels plus 2 electric motors, 1900bhp/1300shp = 14.5kts/9kts. Range 6000nm at 10kts
Armament:	See notes
Complement:	44

No	Name	Builder	Acquired	Fate
S 616	SAPHIR (ex-*Satyr*)	Scotts	1951	Returned UK 1961
S 614	SULTANE (ex-*Statesman*)	Cammell Laird	1951	Returned UK 1959
S 615	SIRENE (ex-*Spiteful*)	Scotts	1951	Returned UK 1958
S 614	SIBYLLE (ex-*Sportsman*)	Chatham DYd	1951	Lost 23.9.52

L'Artemis 1955

Five submarines of the Aurore type remained uncompleted – and relatively undamaged – at the end of the Second World War. La Créole, which had been towed to the UK at the time of the occupation, was put back on the slipway at Le Havre and launched a second time (on 8 May 1946). She and two of her sisters, L'Astrée amd L'Africaine, were completed to a modified design, with a German-model 88mm gun mounted in the forward end of an enlarged fin, and two 20mm AA at its after end. There were 10 torpedo tubes in place of the original nine. As well as the four internal bow tubes and two stern tubes there were pairs of external tubes forward and aft of the fin.

L'Artémis and L'Andromède, whose construction was less advanced, were redesigned to give faster diving and a higher submerged speed (10.3kts) and were given a fin incorporating a snorkel similar to that of the US 'Guppies'. The completion of L'Artémis was delayed in order to incorporate new fire control equipment destined for the Narval class. La Créole was fitted with a snorkel at the same time as the later two boats.

LA CREOLE class *patrol submarines*

Displacement:	970t surfaced; 1250t submerged
Dimensions:	241ft oa × 21ft × 14ft
	73.5m × 6.5m × 4.2m
Machinery:	2 shafts, 2 Sulzer (L'Africaine Schneider) diesels plus 2 electric motors, 3000bhp/1400shp = 15.5kts/9.3kts. Range 8800nm at 10kts. See notes
Armament:	10–550mm TT (4 bow, 4 amidships, 2 stern); La Créole, L'Africaine, L'Astrée also 1–88mm, 2–20mm (2×1)
Complement:	62

No	Name	Builder	Laid down	Launched	Comp	Fate
S 606	LA CREOLE	A C Augustin-Normand	Dec 37	8.4.40	1949	Stricken 1961
S 607	L'AFRICAINE	A C de la Seine-Maritime	Dec 37	7.12.46	Oct 49	Stricken 1963
S 608	L'ASTREE	A C Dubigeon	Nov 38	3.5.46	Apr 49	Stricken 1965
S 601	L'ANDROMEDE	A C Dubigeon	Nov 38	17.11.49	Apr 53	Stricken 1965
S 603	L'ARTEMIS	A C Augustin-Normand/ A C Dubigeon	May 39	28.6.42	Feb 54	Stricken 1967

L'Artemis as completed   Navarret Collection

Requin 1976

In 1947 the STCAN was asked to produce plans for a new class of submarine of 1200 tonnes standard. Requirements included a speed of over 16kts submerged and a range of 15,000nm with snorkel. Long range was the overriding consideration because the continued existence of a French empire demanded the ability to make a lengthy transit and still be able to undertake a patrol of 7–14 days.

In drawing up the plans the constructors leaned heavily on experience with the ex-German Type XXI boat *Roland Morillot* and the two reconstructed 1500t boats of French origin (*L'Andromède* and *L'Artémis*). In addition Dinechin, who was responsible for the basic design, visited the USA in order to make a detailed study of current US Navy thinking.

The result was an improved Type XXI, almost identical in dimensions and displacement but with superior performance. Comparisons with the prewar boats are even more striking; *Narval* had twice the diving depth and 8kts more speed. Two boats were ordered in 1949, two in 1950, and the final pair in 1954.

Problems were experienced in developing a high-tensile steel capable of resisting pressures at the 200m maximum diving depth, and the increased pressures also necessitated many changes in other areas, notably more efficacious emergency blowing systems. An exceptionally strong all-welded double hull was adopted. Hull-form, propellers, rudder and diving planes were all the subject of intensive studies. The Cherbourg-built boats were assembled in prefabricated sections each 7m × 10m – the first French submarines constructed by this method.

The action information and fire control centre was based on that developed in *L'Artémis*, as was the fin with its raised section aft. The latest detection equipment was fitted. In addition to the six bow tubes, two tubes were fitted aft outside the pressure hull; 14 torpedoes were carried.

NARVAL class *patrol submarines*

Displacement:	1635t standard; 1910t submerged	
Dimensions	257ft oa × 26ft × 17ft	
	78.4m × 7.8m × 5.2m	
Machinery:	2 shafts, 2 Schneider 7cyl diesels plus 2 electric motors, 4400bhp/5000shp = 16kts/18kts. Range 15,000nm at 8kts	
Armament:	8–550mm TT (6 bow, 2 stern)	
Sensors:	Sonar DUUA-1	
Complement:	63	

No	Name	Builder	Laid down	Launched	Comp	Fate
S 631	NARVAL	Arsenal de Cherbourg	Oct 51	11.12.54	1.12.57	Extant 1982
S 632	MARSOUIN	Arsenal de Cherbourg	Nov 51	21.5.55	1.10.57	Extant 1982
S 633	DAUPHIN	Arsenal de Cherbourg	Jan 52	12.9.55	1.8.58	Extant 1982
S 634	REQUIN	Arsenal de Cherbourg	Feb 52	3.12.55	1.8.58	Extant 1982
S 637	ESPADON	A C Augustin-Normand	Dec 55	15.9.58	2.4.60	Extant 1982
S 638	MORSE	A C de la Seine-Maritime	Feb 56	10.12.58	2.5.60	Extant 1982

Problems were experienced in finding a suitable diesel, as few French engineering firms were willing to undertake a series of only twelve engines. Schneider 2-stroke diesels were chosen in preference to 2/4-stroke Sulzer and 4-stroke MAN diesels. When fast diesels later became available it was decided to replace the machinery by a diesel-electric installation. Three SEMT-Pielstick PA 4 12cyl diesels, each rated at 750bhp, replaced the Schneider units. New electric motors each of 2500hp were installed, and to these were added a pair of electric cruise motors each of 40hp. All six boats were taken in hand from 1965 onwards, and besides the replacement of the propulsion system major improvements were made to the weapon and detection equipment. The two stern tubes were removed and the number of torpedoes carried was increased to 20. The fin was rebuilt.

When first completed the *Narval* class were subjected to extensive tri-

Marsouin as completed

als. In 1958 *Dauphin* established a record of 42 days snorkelling. Only the propulsion system proved less than satisfactory. But the reconstruction 1965–70 was a complete success. *Marsouin* had a serious fire on 4.8.78

but was subsequently repaired. The *Narval* class are at present based in the Atlantic, and will be replaced by the new nuclear-powered attack boats.

Aréthuse 1971

NB 1/750 scale

From their earliest conception the *Aréthuse* class were designated *sous-marins de chasse*. They were, therefore, the world's first hunter-killer submarines designed as such, and marked a significant departure from the ocean-going *Narval* class. Designed specifically for the Mediterranean, they were to be based at Mers-el-Kebir to prevent enemy submarines infiltrating the extensive mercantile traffic between metropolitan France and the colonies in North Africa.

The staff requirements demanded a 100 per cent submarine with a small silhouette and excellent manoeuvrability. They also specified the ability to dive deep and fast, to carry out operations at snorkel depth, and to maintain high speed for an hour when

ARETHUSE class *attack submarines*

Displacement:	543t surfaced; 669t submerged	
Dimensions:	163ft oa × 19ft × 13ft	
	49.6m × 5.8m × 4.0m	
Machinery:	1 shaft, 2 SEMT-Pielstick 12cyl diesels plus 1 electric motor, 1060bhp/1300shp = 12.5kts/16kts	
Armament:	4–550mm TT (bow)	
Sensors:	Sonar DUUA-1	
Complement:	2	

No	Name	Builder	Laid down	Launched	Comp	Fate
S 635	ARETHUSE	Arsenal de Cherbourg	Mar 55	9.11.57	23.10.58	Stricken Apr 79
S 636	ARGONAUTE	Arsenal de Cherbourg	Mar 55	29.6.57	11.2.59	Extant 1982
S 639	AMAZONE	Arsenal de Cherbourg	Dec 55	3.4.58	1.7.59	Stricken Jul 80
S 640	ARIANE	Arsenal de Cherbourg	Dec 55	12.9.58	16.3.60	Stricken Mar 81

FRANCE

dived. Advanced sensors were to provide data for a well-equipped action information centre.

Although in conception the *Aréthuse* class was clearly influenced by the German Type XXIII design, they were bigger boats with higher submerged speed and a heavier torpedo armament – four tubes plus four reloads.

They were the first French submarines to adopt diesel-electric propulsion. Two groups of electrogenerators producing 337kW drive a single large electric motor of 1300hp. The generators and auxiliaries have spring suspension, while the electric motor is coupled directly to the shaft.

This has resulted in near-silent operation.

All four boats have served in the Mediterranean since completion.

Arethuse as completed
Navarret Collection

Doris 1975
NB 1/750 scale

In 1952, only a year after the first moves were made towards the design of the small hunter-killer submarines of the *Aréthuse* class, plans were requested from the STCAN for a *sous-marin torpilleur de 2ème classe*. In conception, therefore, the *Daphné* was a 2nd-class ocean-going submarine to complement the larger *Narval* class.

Many of the staff requirements – excellent manoeuvrability, low noise, small crew and ease of maintenance – were similar to those laid down for the *Aréthuse*. Because of the different role envisaged, however, speed was to be sacrificed to diving depth and armament. Only 13kts dived was required (in the event, maximum speed exceeded this figure), with 7kts snorkelling and silent operation at 6kts while submerged. At least six tubes were specified, and these were disposed in similar fashion to those of *Narval*, with two tubes outside the pressure hull aft for use against ASW escorts. After further discussions, however, it was finally decided to incorporate no fewer than eight tubes in the bow, and an extra pair of tubes were worked in aft, which eliminated reloads and thus reduced the demands made on the crew. Further reductions in complement were effected by the adoption of a maintenance system based as far as possible on modular replacement.

A conventional double-hull construction was adopted. Half of the accommodation is forward of the fin with the remainder aft. Beneath the fin itself is the operations centre, with the batteries on the deck below. The machinery compartments are just aft

DAPHNE class *patrol submarines*

Displacement:	869t surfaced; 1043t submerged
Dimensions:	190ft oa × 22ft × 15ft
	57.8m × 6.8m × 4.6m
Machinery:	2 shafts, 2 SEMT-Pielstick diesels plus 1 electric motor, 1300bhp/1600shp = 13.5kts/16kts. Range 4500nm at 5kts
Armament:	12–550mm TT (8 bow, 4 stern)
Sensors:	Sonar DUUA-1
Complement:	45

No	Name	Builder	Laid down	Launched	Comp	Fate
S 641	DAPHNE	A C Dubigeon	Mar 58	20.6.59	1.6.64	Extant 1982
S 642	DIANE	A C Dubigeon	Jul 58	4.10.60	20.6.64	Extant 1982
S 643	DORIS	Arsenal de Cherbourg	Sep 58	14.5.60	26.8.64	Extant 1982
S 644	EURYDICE	Arsenal de Cherbourg	Jul 59	19.6.60	Sep 64	Lost 4.3.70
S 645	FLORE	Arsenal de Cherbourg	Sep 58	21.12.60	21.5.64	Extant 1982
S 646	GALATEE	Arsenal de Cherbourg	Sep 58	22.9.61	25.7.64	Extant 1982
S 647	MINERVE	A C Dubigeon	May 58	31.5.61	10.6.64	Lost 27.1.68
S 648	JUNON	Arsenal de Cherbourg	Jul 61	11.5.64	25.2.66	Extant 1982
S 649	VENUS	Arsenal de Cherbourg	Aug 61	24.9.64	1.1.66	Extant 1982
S 650	PSYCHE	Arsenal de Brest	May 65	28.6.69	7.6.70	Extant 1982
S 651	SIRENE	Arsenal de Brest	May 65	28.6.69	3.9.70	Extant 1982

of the fin on two deck levels, the auxiliaries being above the propulsion machinery. A single large vertical rudder is fitted, and diving planes are mounted just above it as well as on the hull forward, giving the boats excellent manoeuvrability.

Despite their relatively short range the *Daphné* class were designed to operate in the same theatres as the *Narval* class. As part of the staff requirements it was laid down that they should be capable of taking on fuel at sea. The bulk of the class, nevertheless, has served in the Mediterranean since completion, only the last pair being based at Lorient with the *Narval* class.

Besides the eleven units built for the *Marine Nationale* (three ordered 1955; four in 1956; two in 1960, and two in 1964), ten have been built in France for Portugal (4), Pakistan (3) and South Africa (3), and a further four have been built under licence in Spanish shipyards. The only shadow over their success has been the accidental loss of *Minerve* and *Eurydice* within two years while operating in the Western Mediterranean.

Electronics and weapons were modernised from 1971 onwards, when a DUUA-2A sonar was fitted. A number of boats were given a prominent new sonar dome atop the hull casing forward.

In 1954 studies were made of a torpedo-armed nuclear-powered submarine; the boat was even laid down at Cherbourg in 1956 as hull No Q 244. A surface displacement of 4000t on a length of 120m was projected. The inability of the French to produce enriched uranium at this time meant, however, that a heavy-water reactor using unrefined uranium was the only possible propulsion plant. This proved too heavy and construction was halted in 1958. Negotiations with the Americans for

GYMNOTE *ballistic missile submarine*

Displacement:	3000t surfaced; 3250t submerged
Dimensions:	276ft oa × 35ft × 25ft
	84.0m × 10.6m × 7.6m
Machinery:	2 shafts, 4 SEMT-Pielstick diesels plus 2 electric motors, ?/2600shp = 11kts/10kts
Armament:	4 SLBM tubes
Complement:	78

No	Name	Builder	Laid down	Launched	Comp	Fate
S 655	GYMNOTE	Arsenal de Cherbourg	17.3.63	17.3.64	17.10.66	Extant 1982

the purchase of a reactor failed, and even the purchase of enriched uranium was refused except for land experimental use. The project was abandoned, therefore, in 1959.

With the decision to develop an independent sea-based deterrent force, it was decided to complete the hull (now designated Q 251) as an experimental submarine for the testing of the new ballistic missiles. A prominent casing aft of the fin houses four tubes. *Gymnote* was also fitted with the prototype guidance and inertial navigation system intended for *Le Redoutable*. She launched her first

M-1 missile at the end of 1968 at the Landes Trials Centre. She has since conducted trials for the other missiles in the series, and in 1977–79 underwent a refit in which the missile tubes were enlarged to accommodate the new M-4 missile due to enter service in 1985.

Gymnote as completed
Navarret Collection

Le Redoutable 1973

LE REDOUTABLE class *ballistic missile submarines*

Displacement:	7500t surfaced; 9000t submerged
Dimensions:	420ft oa × 35ft × 33ft
	128.0m × 10.6m × 10.0m
Machinery:	1-shaft nuclear: 1 pressurised water-cooled reactor, 2 turbines plus 2 turbo-alternators, 1 electric motor, 15,000shp = 20kts/25kts. Aux diesel 2670bhp
Armament:	16 SLBM tubes, 4–550mm TT (bow). See notes
Sensors:	Sonar DUUV-23, DUUX-2
Complement:	135

No	Name	Builder	Laid down	Launched	Comp	Fate
S 611	LE REDOUTABLE	Arsenal de Cherbourg	30.3.64	29.3.67	1.12.71	Extant 1982
S 612	LE TERRIBLE	Arsenal de Cherbourg	24.6.67	12.12.69	1.1.73	Extant 1982
S 610	LE FOUDROYANT	Arsenal de Cherbourg	12.12.69	4.12.71	6.7.74	Extant 1982
S 613	L'INDOMPTABLE	Arsenal de Cherbourg	4.12.71	17.8.74	23.12.76	Extant 1982
S 614	LE TONNANT	Arsenal de Cherbourg	Oct 74	17.9.77	3.4.80	Extant 1982
S 615	L'INFLEXIBLE	Arsenal de Cherbourg	27.3.80	23.6.82		Building

Owing to the political circumstances in which the *Force de Dissuasion* was conceived (see Introduction), no American assistance in the design and construction of the SNLEs was forthcoming. The first reactor constructed, the PAT 1, was produced in collaboration with the CEA (the French Atomic Energy Authority) and tested extensively ashore at Cadaraché. Simultaneously development of the missiles took place, the first MSBS being launched from the experimental submarine *Gymnote* at the Landes Trials Centre at the end of 1968.

Construction of the submarines posed a number of technical problems such as the development of high-tensile steel to cope with the increase in diving depth (up to 300m), the adaption of the hull to nuclear propulsion, and the development of suitable steering mechanisms. The cylindrical hull was constructed using prefabricated all-welded sections each of 200t. There is a prominent casing aft of the fin which houses the missile tubes.

In addition to the main propulsion machinery there is an emergency diesel capable of bringing the submarine home in the event of a failure in the nuclear plant; it has a range of about 5000nm. The diving planes are on the fin, as in US boats. Four tor-

pedo tubes are fitted forward, a total of 18 torpedoes being carried. The submarine's position can be accurately determined by reference to three inertial navigation centres (CIN) ashore, and there is a periscope for celestial navigation.

The first MSBS was the M-1, an 18t two-stage missile of similar length and diameter to the US Poseidon, but carrying only a single 500-kiloton warhead and with a range of only 2500km. The M-1 missile was installed in the first two boats, but was then superseded by the 3000km M-2, which went into service aboard the third boat, *Le Foudroyant*. From 1976 onwards, both the M-1 and the M-2

began to be replaced by the M-20, which has a 1-megaton thermonuclear warhead and an upgraded re-entry vehicle system. The M-20 was first deployed in *L'Indomptable*, but has now been retrofitted to the earlier boats. After 1985 all except *Le Redoutable* will be modified to carry the M-4, which will have longer range (4000km) and carry six or seven MIRVs each of 150kilotons. It is similar in length to the earlier missiles but of greater diameter.

Because of the time-span over which the submarines have been constructed there are some variations in equipment. *L'Indomptable* and *Le Tonnant* have a metallic reactor core in place of the oxide cores of earlier boats. *L'Inflexible*, the sixth boat, will be an intermediate design between *Le Redoutable* and a new class planned for the 1990s.

The *Force de Dissuasion* is based at Ile Longue in the Brest roadstead. The submarines undertake patrols of two months (three months maximum) duration. Each has a Blue and Gold (*Bleu/Ambre*) crew on the American pattern.

Le Redoutable as completed
Navarret Collection

FRANCE

Agosta 1977

Although they have the same nominal displacement (1200t standard) as the earlier *Narval* class ocean-going boats, the *Agostas* differ fundamentally in conception and, on the technical side, illustrate the considerable advances made in submarine design since the early 1950s.

Range was no longer such a crucial factor for the *Marine Nationale* by 1970, so size and fuel capacity were reduced compared with the *Narval*. The value of silence, diving depth and underwater speed had, on the other hand, increased.

The new boats were of the familiar double-hulled construction, the space between the two hulls being used for ballast, fuel tanks, auxiliary tanks and for the sensing heads of most of the acoustic equipment. The outer shell is cylindrical, graduating to an oval form forward to accommodate the sensors; the profile is more streamlined than that of earlier French submarines. All deck fittings retract into recesses in the outer hull to ensure a clean water-flow. Cruciform tail surfaces were adopted.

The torpedo tubes and handling rooms are all forward. Next comes the computer-based attack centre directly beneath the fin, which is well forward compared to the earlier boats. All accommodation is aft of the fin. The batteries are below the attack centre and the accommodation compartments. The entire after section is

AGOSTA class *attack submarines*

Displacement:	1450t surfaced; 1725t submerged
Dimensions:	222ft oa × 22ft × 18ft
	67.6m × 6.8m × 5.5m
Machinery:	1 shaft, 2 SEMT-Pielstick 16 PA diesels plus electric motors, 3600bhp/4600shp = 12kts/20kts max. See notes
Armament:	4–550mm TT (bow)
Sensors:	Sonar DUUA-2, DSUV-2, DUUX-2
Complement:	54

No	Name	Builder	Laid down	Launched	Comp	Fate
S 620	AGOSTA	Arsenal de Cherbourg	1.11.72	19.10.74	28.7.77	Extant 1982
S 621	BEVEZIERS	Arsenal de Cherbourg	17.5.73	14.6.75	27.9.77	Extant 1982
S 622	LA PRAYA	Arsenal de Cherbourg	1974	15.5.76	9.3.78	Extant 1982
S 623	OUESSANT	Arsenal de Cherbourg	1974	23.10.76	27.7.78	Extant 1982

occupied by the machinery: first the auxiliary machinery, then the two diesel generators, then the electric motors and gearing. In addition to the main motor there is a small 32hp cruise motor for silent operations, capable of driving the submarine at 3.5kts. On main motors the *Agostas* can sustain a submerged speed of 17.5kts, the maximum speed of 20.5kts being available for 10 minutes during an emergency. Snorkelling is possible at speeds of up to 10kts.

The reduction to only four torpedo tubes was made possible by the high

hit probability of modern wire-guided torpedoes; a total of 16 are carried. The tubes themselves are of a new type in which a pneumatic ram is employed to discharge the torpedo, enabling firing to take place at any speed and depth. 550mm or 533mm torpedoes can be fired.

The DUUA-2 sonar fitted forward and aft is the same mode! installed in the refitted *Daphné* class. In addition, the *Agostas* are equipped with passive sonar, passive ECM, a crown of 36 hydrophones (DSUV) providing a bearing on an enemy's noise emission,

and a passive acoustic telemeter to provide range.

Their small size, speed, manoeuvrability and capability for silent operations make them well suited to the hunter-killer role. All four boats have served in the Mediterranean since completion. Two units of the same class ordered for South Africa were transferred while building to Pakistan, and four have been built under licence in Spain. The design has influenced that of the new nuclear attack submarines.

Rubis design

RUBIS (SNA 72) class *nuclear attack submarines*

In 1964 a high-performance *sous-marin nucléaire de chasse* was authorised. It was reported to be named *Rubis*, and was credited with a displacement of 4000t and an armament of four torpedo tubes. The order was cancelled in 1968, the year in which construction was due to begin, and a statement was made to the effect that SSNs would be included in the new programme.

When the new design materialised it was for a smaller submarine than any SSN in service with the other major navies. In hull form and overall layout SNA 72 resembles the *Agosta*, with which it shares identical fire control, torpedo-launching and detection systems.

The reduction in size was made possible by the development of a compact, integrated reactor-exchanger driving two turbo-alternators. Besides the main electric motor there is a small emergency motor powered by a diesel generator capable of driving the boat for 50nm. The greater depth of the hull compared to the *Agostas* has allowed three decks to be worked in beneath and immediately aft of the fin. Much of the accommodation is on the deck beneath the attack centre to allow for the extra space needed in the after part

Displacement:	2385t surfaced; 2670t submerged
Dimensions:	237ft oa × 25ft × 23ft
	72.1m × 7.6m × 6.9m
Machinery:	1-shaft nuclear: 48MW integrated reactor-exchanger driving two turbo-alternators plus 1 main electric motor = 25kts (sub), 1 emergency electric motor powered by a diesel generator
Armament:	4–550mm TT (bow; 14 torpedoes)
Sensors:	Sonar DUUA-2, DUUX-2, DSUV .2
Complement:	66

No	Name	Builder	Laid down	Launched	Comp	Fate
S 601	RUBIS (ex-*Provence*)	Arsenal de Cherbourg	11.12.76	7.7.79	Jul 82	Extant 1982
S 602	SAPHIR (ex-*Bretagne*)	Arsenal de Cherbourg	1.9.79	1.9.81		Building
S 603	(ex-*Bourgogne*)	Arsenal de Cherbourg	21.9.81			Building
S 604		Arsenal de Cherbourg	Dec 82			Building
S 605						Ordered

of the boat for the propulsion plant. The lower deck accommodates the depth-regulation ballast tanks, the pumps and compressors, and the batteries.

The forward diving planes have been moved to the fin. The submarines will also be able to fire the new SM39 anti-ship missile when it comes into service in 1985. The fifth boat will be of an improved type. Two

squadrons are envisaged: one at Brest, the other at Toulon. The first boat was renamed in December 1980.

AMPHIBIOUS WARFARE VESSELS

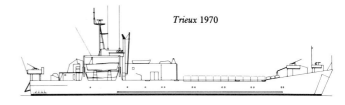

Trieux 1970

(For illustration see under United States in 1922–46 volume)

Ex-US LST type *tank landing ships*

Displacement:	1625t standard; 4080t full load
Dimensions:	316ft wl, 328ft oa × 50ft × 10ft *96.3m, 100.0m × 15.2m × 3.0m*
Machinery:	2 shafts, 2 diesels, 1800bhp = 11kts. Range 24,000nm at 9kts
Armament:	8–40mm (2×2, 4×1), 12–20mm
Complement:	111 (+163 troops)

Class:
Laïta (L 9001, ex-*LST 177*), *Orne* (L 9002, ex-*LST 508*), *Vire* (L 9003, ex-*LST 347*), *Rance* (L 9004, ex-*LST 223*), *Odet* (L 9005, ex-*LST 815*), *Chéliff* (L 9006, ex-*LST 874*), *Adour* (L 9007, ex-*LST 860*), *Golo* (L 9008, ex-*LST 973*).

A number of ex-American LSTs were transferred to the *Marine Nationale* 1949–51. *Adour* was badly damaged in the early 1950s, but was raised and subsequently became an accommodation ship. Five units were disposed of 1957–62; *Laïta* became a depot ship in 1962, and *Odet* and *Chéliff* continued in service until 1969–70.

(For illustration see under United States in 1922–46 volume)

FOUDRE (ex-US) type *dock landing ship*

Displacement:	4500t standard; 7930t full load
Dimensions:	454ft pp, 458ft oa × 72ft × 16ft *138.4m, 139.5m × 22.0m × 4.8m*
Machinery:	2-shaft geared steam turbines, 2 boilers, 7400shp = 17kts. Range 7400nm at 15 kts
Armament:	1–105mm, 2–120mm mortars, 4–40mm (2×2), 4–20mm (4×1)
Complement:	212

Built by Newport News as *LSD 12* (launched 29.12.43) and serving in the Royal Navy as *Oceanway*, this vessel was returned to the USA in 1947, and was subsequently transferred to France under MDAP in 1952. As first completed she carried a single 3in (76mm) DP gun, 4–2pdr (1×4) and 16–20mm (16×1), but she was completely re-armed by the French. The docking well could accommodate two LCT(3) landing craft. She gave the *Marine Nationale* much-needed experience in amphibious operations and influenced the design of the *Ouragan* class TCDs. She was stricken in 1969.

ISSOLE *landing craft*

Displacement:	600t full load
Dimensions:	161ft oa × 23ft × 7ft *48.7m × 7.0m × 2.1m*
Machinery:	2 shafts, 2 diesels, 100bhp = 12kts
Armament:	None

Issole (L 9097) was built at Toulon 1957–58. The design was an adaptation of a mercantile coaster, with bow doors and a ramp. In the early 1970s she became a coastal transport and was given the pennant number A 734. She was stricken in 1979.

TRIEUX class *tank landing ships*

Displacement:	1750t standard; 4225t full load
Dimensions:	327ft pp, 335ft oa × 51ft × 11ft *96.6m, 102.1m × 15.5m × 3.2m*
Machinery:	2 shafts, 2 SEMT-Pielstick diesels, 2000bhp = 11kts. Range 18,500nm at 10kts
Armament:	1–120mm mortar, 3–40mm (3×1); *Trieux, Blavet* 2–40mm (2×1), 2–20mm (2×1)
Complement:	85 (+170 troops)

No	Name	Builder	Launched	Fate
L 9007	TRIEUX	A C de Bretagne	6.12.58	Extant 1982
L 9003	ARGENS	A C de Bretagne	7.4.59	Extant 1982
L 9009	BLAVET	A C de Bretagne	15.1.60	Extant 1982
L 9008	DIVES	A C de la Seine-Maritime	29.6.60	Extant 1982
L 9004	BIDASSOA	A C de la Seine-Maritime	30.12.60	Extant 1982

Derived from the US Navy's LST, of which several were operated by the *Marine Nationale* in the postwar period, the *Trieux* class were designated BDC (*Bâtiments de débarquement de chars*). They carry four LCVPs beneath davits on each side of the superstructure. There is fixed accommodation for a maximum of 329 troops, and a further 320 can be carried over short distances. In the logistics role they can carry 1000t of freight, 400t of fresh water and 270t of diesel fuel. MacGregor-type loading hatches are fitted.

In the late 1960s *Blavet* and *Trieux* were fitted with a hangar for two Alouette helicopters immediately forward of the bridge. They have since served on distant colonial stations as logistics ships, *Blavet* being based in French Polynesia in the Pacific. *Bidassoa* is allocated to the amphibious training centre at Lorient.

EDIC/EDA type *landing craft*

Displacement:	250t standard; 670t full load
Dimensions:	194ft oa × 39ft × 4ft min *59.0m × 12.0m × 1.3m*
Machinery:	2 shafts, 2 MGO diesels, 1000bhp = 8kts. Range 1800nm at 8kts
Armament:	2–20mm (2×1)
Complement:	16

The EDIC (*Engins de Débarquement Infanterie Chars*) were built in two groups. *L 9091–96* were launched in 1958 and *L 9070–74* in 1967–69. They are conventional landing craft with a capacity of 11 trucks or 5 LVTs. In between the two groups four EDA (*Engins de Débarquement Ateliers*) were constructed. Launched in 1964 and numbered *L 9081–84*, these were basically the same design, but were specially fitted as repair and logistic support craft. The first two were designated 'auxiliary repair ships' (BAA), the third 'auxiliary electronics ship' (BAE) and the fourth 'auxiliary electrical stores ship' (BAME). Displacement for the EDA is 310t standard and 685t full load. The AA guns were suppressed. *L 9082–83* later reverted to the conventional LCT role. *L 9095* was transferred to Senegal in 1974, *L 9071* and *L 9081* were stricken in 1976–77, and *L 9082* and *L 9092* in 1981. Builders were C N Franco-Belges (9), Toulon DYd (3), La Perrière (2) and Lorient (1).

Millot Collection

L 9091 as completed

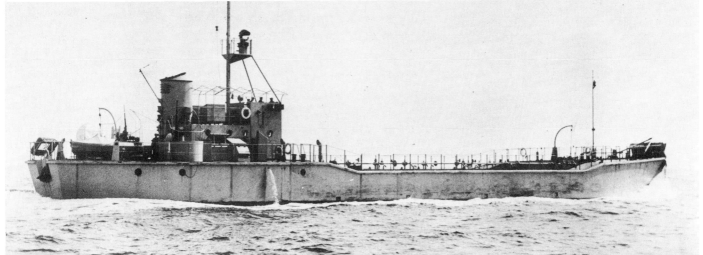

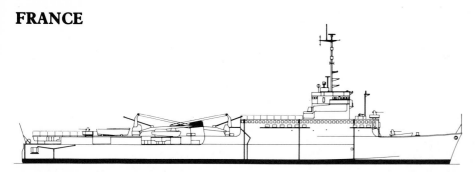

Ouragan 1975

OURAGAN class *dock landing ships*

Displacement:	5800t standard; 8500t full load
Dimensions:	474ft pp, 489ft oa × 71ft × 15ft min
	144.5m, 149.0m × 21.5m × 4.6m
Machinery:	2 shafts, 2 SEMT-Pielstick diesels, 8640bhp = 17kts. Range 8000nm at 15kts
Armament:	2–120mm mortars, 4–40mm (4×1) *Ouragan* only
Sensors:	Sonar SQS-17 (*Ouragan*)
Complement:	207 (*Orage* 201)

No	Name	Builder	Launched	Fate
L 9021	OURAGAN	Arsenal de Brest	9.11.63	Extant 1982
L 9022	ORAGE	Arsenal de Brest	22.4.67	Extant 1982

Designated TCD (*transports de chalands de débarquement*) these two vessels were designed with a dual function in mind. They can lift a full commando and its support troops and put them ashore using helicopters; and they can put ashore personnel, tanks, vehicles and supplies using landing craft. While the design was clearly influenced by the American LSD concept, an increase in flexibility was obtained, particularly with regard to the operation of helicopters and the accommodation of vehicles, by the use of removable sections of deck both externally and internally.

The docking well is 120m long, and floods to a depth of 3m. The stern gate measures 14m × 5.5m. Two EDICs, each with a capacity of 11 light tanks, or 18 LCM(6)s can be accommodated. Movement of the water control sluices and valves is automatic, using pumps controlled from a central command post. A temporary deck 90m long in 15 sections can be laid out to increase the stowage space for vehicles or cargo, but the well is then reduced to half its original size. In the logistics role, 1500t of equipment can be carried, the cargo being handled by two 35t cranes mounted above the docking well. Alternative loads include 18 Super Frelons, 80 Alouettes, 120 AMX-13 tanks, 84 DUKWs, 340 jeeps or twelve 50t barges.

Instead of the conventional LSD superstructure there is a small island to starboard which accommodates the navigation bridge and a combined centre for directing amphibious and helicopter operations. The main helicopter deck can handle either three Super Frelon troop-carrying helicopters or ten Alouettes. A further Super Frelon or three Alouettes can be operated from a removable deck in six sections which covers the after part of the well for 36m. A total of 349 troops can be transported (470 over short distances), and three LCVPs are carried topsides.

The TCDs were intended to serve as repair and maintenance ships on distant deployments. They can dock a 400t ship and are equipped with hull and machinery repair shops, and electrical and ordnance workshops. *Ouragan* was laid down in June 1962 and completed in January 1965; her sister was laid down in June 1966 and completed in March 1968. On completion *Orage* was assigned to the Pacific Experimental Centre. The guns, sonar, surgical compartments and inboard removable decks were therefore not installed at the first fitting-out. Great attention was paid to the provision of decontamination areas.

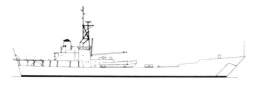

Francis Garnier 1975

CHAMPLAIN class *landing ships*

Displacement:	750t standard; 1330t full load
Dimensions:	223ft pp, 262ft oa × 43ft × 8ft
	68.0m, × 80.0m × 13.0m × 2.4m
Machinery:	2 shafts, 2 SACM V-12 diesels, 1800bhp = 16kts. Range 4500nm at 13kts
Armament:	2–40mm (2×1), 2–81mm mortars
Sensors:	Sonar 2 hull-mounted
Complement:	47 (+180 troops)

No	Name	Builder	Launched	Fate
L 9030	CHAMPLAIN	Arsenal de Brest	17.11.73	Extant 1982
L 9031	FRANCIS GARNIER	Arsenal de Brest	17.11.73	Extant 1982

Both these ships were laid down in 1973 and completed in 1974. Two further vessels are on order from Chantiers de Normandie and a fifth is planned; others have been built for Morocco. They are designated BATRAL (*bâtiments de transport leger*).

Designed for overseas service, they carry a landing company (*guépard*) consisting of five officers, 133 men, six jeeps and six lorries. The BATRAL is a classical small landing ship design with bow doors and storage for tanks and other vehicles above and below decks. One LCVP and one LCPS are carried on the upper deck; they are handled by a 10t derrick. A maximum load of 330t can be carried, and cargo can be transferred ashore either by a hydraulic crane or via the bow ramp. Controllable-pitch propellers are fitted. The designed armament was not installed at completion.

SMALL SURFACE COMBATANTS

Le Fougueux 1955
NB 1/750 scale

LE FOUGUEUX class *submarine-chasers*

Displacement:	325t standard; 400t full load
Dimensions:	174ft oa × 24ft × 10ft
	53.1m × 7.3m × 3.1m
Machinery:	2 shafts, 4 SEMT-Pielstick fast diesels, 3240bhp = 19kts. Range 3000nm at 12kts
Armament:	2–40mm (2×1), 2–20mm (2×1), 1–120mm ASW mortar, 2 DCT, 1 DC rack (*Le Fougueux, L'Opiniâtre, L'Agile* 1 Hedgehog, 4 DCT, 2 DC racks)
Sensors:	Sonar QCU-2
Complement:	62

No	Name	Builder	Launched	Fate
P 630	L'INTREPIDE	CMN, Cherbourg	12.12.58	Stricken 1977
P 635	L'ARDENT	A C Augustin-Normand	17.7.58	Stricken 1980
P 637	L'ETOURDI	F C de la Méditerranée	5.2.58	Stricken 1978
P 638	L'EFFRONTE	A C Augustin-Normand	27.1.59	Stricken 1978
P 639	LE FRONDEUR	CMN, Cherbourg	26.2.59	Stricken 1977
P 640	LE FRINGANT	F C de la Méditerranée	6.2.59	Stricken 1982
P 641	LE FOUGUEUX	A C Doubigeon	31.5.54	Stricken 1975
P 642	L'OPINIATRE	F C de la Méditerranée	4.5.54	Stricken 1975
P 643	L'AGILE	A C Provence	26.6.54	Stricken 1975
P 644	L'ADROIT	Arsenal de Lorient	6.9.58	Stricken 1979
P 645	L'ALERTE	Arsenal de Lorient	5.10.57	Stricken 1979
P 646	L'ATTENTIF	Arsenal de Lorient	10.7.58	Stricken 1978
P 647	L'ENJOUE	Arsenal de Lorient	5.10.57	Stricken 1978
P 648	LE HARDI	CMN, Cherbourg	17.9.58	Stricken 1977

The first three ships were funded under MDAP. The other eleven vessels were purchased by France: five were authorised in 1955 and six in 1956. Other similar units were built for Yugoslavia, Tunisia, Portugal and Ethiopia.

After the first three ships changes were made in the shape of the bridge structure and in the armament. *L'Intrépide* had a single torpedo tube fitted above the stern.

La Combattante c 1974

Navarret Collection

LA COMBATTANTE *patrol boat*

Displacement:	180t standard; 202t full load
Dimensions:	148ft × 24ft × 7ft *45.0m × 7.4m × 2.5m*
Machinery:	2 shafts, 2 SEMT-Pielstick 16 PA 2 diesels, 3200bhp = 23kts. Range 2000nm at 12kts
Armament:	4 SS11 SSM (1×4), 1–40mm
Complement:	25

Authorised in 1960, *La Combattante* (P 730) was to have been the prototype of a new class of *patrouilleurs garde-côtes*. She was built by CMN Cherbourg and launched on 20.6.63. Construction is of laminated wood and plastic, giving a low magnetic signature. She conducted trials of the Exocet missile and served as the basis for a whole series of FPBs built for export.

A second 40mm mounting was added aft in the 1970s, but was replaced by a launcher for 14 flares before *La Combattante* left for the Indian Ocean in 1975. She can carry a group of 80 men and their equipment for a short passage.

In 1978–79 the original diesels were replaced by the new PA 4 VG DS engine. The latter has a very high power/mass ratio, and employs two-stage supercharging and a variable-geometry precombustion chamber. Power has been increased to 4000bhp. Following sea trials, *La Combattante* departed for further trials in the Pacific.

Pertuisane 1980
NB 1/750 scale

TRIDENT class *patrol boats*

Displacement:	115t standard; 145t full load
Dimensions:	126ft pp, 134ft oa × 19ft × 5ft *38.5m, 40.7m × 5.9m × 1.6m*
Machinery:	2 shafts, 2 AGO 195 V12 diesels, 4,400bhp = 28kts. Range 1500nm at 15kts
Armament:	6 SS12 SSM (6×1), 1–40mm, 1–12.7mm
Complement:	19

Class (no, builder, launched):
Trident (P 670, Auroux, Arcachon, 31.5.75), *Glaive* (P 671, Auroux, Arcachon, 27.8.76) *Epée* (P 672, CMN Cherbourg, 31.3.76), *Pertuisane* (P 673, CMN, Cherbourg, 2.6.76).

The *patrouilleurs* of the *Trident* ('PATRA') class have as their mission the surveillance and control of territorial waters. They were to be the lead boats for a class of 30 projected under the *Plan Bleu*, 16 of which were to serve overseas. However, only four have been completed.

They have an all-welded steel hull compartmented by nine watertight bulkheads designed to preserve sufficient buoyancy with two adjacent compartments flooded. The superstructure is of light alloy and there is air-conditioning throughout. Machinery and fire control is exercised from the wheelhouse, and there is a guidance turret beneath a cupola aft of the wheelhouse to provide the gyroscopic sight with a clear view of the horizon. An inflatable dinghy is carried aft.

The *Trident* class has proved much too small for its intended tasks and the succeeding class shows a significant increase in displacement. All were in service in 1982.

RAPIERE class *patrol boats*

Displacement:	320t
Dimensions:	164ft pp × 23ft × 6ft *50.0m × 7.0m × 1.9m*
Machinery:	2 shafts, 2 SEMT-Pielstick 18 PA 4 200 diesels, 9000bhp = 28.5kts. Range 2500nm at 15kts
Armament:	2 MM38 Exocet SSM, 1–40mm, 2–20mm

These six patrol boats ('super PATRA' type) are part of the 1977–81 building programme. Those on overseas service will be fitted with Exocet launchers. They will be built by SFCN Villeneuve la Garenne.

MINE WARFARE VESSELS

(For illustration see under United States)

US AGILE type *ocean minesweepers*

Particulars:	As US *Agile* class

Class:
Bellingham Shipyards, Washington – *Alençon* (M 612), *Autun* (M 622), *Berlaimont* (M 620), *Berneval* (M 613), *Bir Hacheim* (M 614), *Cantho* (M 615), *Dompaire* (M 616), *Garigliano* (M 617), *Mytho* (M 618), *Origny* (M 621), *Vinh Long* (M 619).
Tacoma Boatbuilding, Washington – *Baccarat* (M 623).
Peterson Builders, Wisconsin – *Narvik* (M 611), *Colmar* (M 624), *Ouistreham* (M 610).

In 1952 the USA agreed to transfer 15 new ocean minesweepers of the *Agile* class to the *Marine Nationale* under MDAP. Launched 1953–54 and transferred 1954–57, they have wooden hulls and diesels of non-magnetic stainless steel alloy. *Autun, Baccarat, Berlaimont, Colmar, Narvik, Origny* and *Ouistreham* have taller funnels than the other ships.

Origny was modified 1961–62 as an ocean research vessel and was renumbered A 640. *Mytho* became a tender in 1965. *Narvik* (A 769) was converted in 1976 for trials of the AP4 sweep and a lenticular sonar. *Autun* and *Colmar* were stricken 1978, and *Bir Hacheim* was returned to the USA in 1970 and subsequently transferred to Uruguay.

Cantho, Dompaire, Garigliano, Mytho and *Vinh Long* were converted to minehunters 1975–79. They received a new block bridge structure, the PAP-104 minehunting vehicle and a bow thruster. The remaining five units were due to undergo a similar conversion but this was abandoned owing to budgetary restrictions, and they were fitted only with the DUBM-41 side-scan sonar.

49

Eglantine c1960   Navarret Collection

US ADJUTANT type *coastal minesweepers*

Particulars: As US *Adjutant* class

Class:
Harbor Boat Building, California – *Aconit* (M 640), *Azalée* (M 668), *Camélia* (M 671).
Frank L Sample, Maine – *Acacia* (M 638), *Acanthe* (M 639), *Ajonc* (M 667).
Stephen Bros, California – *Bégonia* (M 669), *Coquelicot* (M 673), *Giroflée* (M 677), *Laurier* (M 681), *Magnolia* (M 685), *Glaïeul* (M 678), *Pavot* (M 631), *Pivoine* (M 633), *Réséda* (M 635).
Tacoma Boatbuilding, Washington – *Lobélia* (M 684), *Muguet* (M 688), *Eglantine* (M 675), *Glycine* (M 679), *Liseron* (M 683), *Mimosa* (M 687), *Chrysanthème* (M 672), *Gardénia* (M 676), *Jacinthe* (M 680).
National Steel & SB, San Diego – *Lilas* (M 682), *Marguerite* (M 686), *Cyclamen* (M 674).
Pacific Boatbuilding, Tacoma, Washington – *Bleuet* (M 670).
South Coast Co, Newport Beach, California – *Pervenche* (M 632), *Renoncule* (M 634).

In 1952 the USA agreed to allocate 36 coastal minesweepers of the *Adjutant* class to the *Marine Nationale* under MDAP. Thirty were delivered 1953–54, but of the remaining six, four were returned to the USA after their delivery to Indo-China (two were subsequently transferred to Japan) and two were re-allocated to Spain.

They are constructed of wood and non-magnetic alloys. *Eglantine*, *Lobélia* and *Pivoine* became tenders in 1965. In 1968 *Jacinthe* was modified as a minelayer and renumbered A 680; minesweeping gear and winches have been removed, an additional deck extends from the bridge aft, and two cathead drums and two wire leads have been fitted from this deck to the stern. *Marguerite*, *Pavot* and *Renoncule* were returned to the USA 1969–70 and subse-

quently transferred to Uruguay and Turkey; *Bégonia* and *Glaïeul* were returned in 1974. *Coquelicot* and *Aconit* (renamed *Marjolaine* 1967) were transferred to Tunisia in 1973 and 1977 respectively. In 1974 *Ajonc* became a training vessel for divers and was renumbered A 701. Three further vessels, *Gardénia* (A 711), *Liseron* (A 723), and *Magnolia* (A 770) became base ships for mine demolition teams. *Giroflée*, *Bleuet* and *Chrysanthème* were stricken in 1977, the latter two being cannibalised for spares. *Pervenche*, *Camélia* and *Laurier* followed in 1980, *Acanthe*, *Lilas*, *Muguet*, *Mimosa* and *Lobélia* in 1981, and *Jacinthe* in 1982.

Ex-Canadian 'BAY' class *coastal minesweepers*

Particulars: As Canadian 'Bay' class

Class:
St John DD – *La Dunkerquoise* (M 726, ex-*Fundy*), *La Lorientaise* (M 731, ex-*Miramchi*)
Port Arthur SB – *La Dieppoise* (M 730, ex-*Chaleur*)
Canadian Vickers – *La Paimpolaise* (M 729, ex-*Thunder*)
Marine Industries – *La Bayonnaise* (M 728, ex-*Chignecto*)
Davie SB – *La Malouine* (M 727, ex-*Cowichan*)

These six coastal minesweepers of the Canadian 'Bay' class were launched 1951–53 and transferred to France in 1954 under MDAP. They have wooden hulls with aluminium frames and decks. In the early 1960s they were modified for service as colonial patrol boats. Sweep gear was removed, air conditioning installed, and they were renumbered P 653, P 652, P 655, P 657, P 654 and P 651 respectively. *La Bayonnaise* and *La Malouine* were stricken in 1976 and 1977 respectively. The other four units are stationed in the Pacific.

British 'HAM' class *inshore minesweepers*

Particulars: As British 'Ham' class

Class:
White, IOW – *Tulipe* (M 771), *Oeillet* (M 774), *Pâquerette* (M 775)
Blackmore, Bideford – *Hortensia* (M 783), *Jasmin* (M 776)
Harris, Appledore – *Violette* (M 773)
McLean, Renfrew – *Capucine* (M 782), *Pétunia* (M 789)
Taylor, Shoreham – *Armoise* (M 772)
Brooke Marine – *Aubépine* (M 781), *Myosotis* (M 788)
Fairlie Yacht Co – *Jonquille* (M 787)
McGiver – *Géranium* (M 784)
Vosper, Gosport – *Hibiscus* (M 785)
Taylor, Chertsey – *Dahlia* (M 786)

Built by shipyards in the UK, these inshore minesweepers of the 'Ham' class were transferred 1954–55 under MDAP. In the mid-1970s all ships of the class were reclassified as auxiliary or patrol craft. *Myosotis* became a diving tender (A 710), while *Hibiscus*, *Dahlia*, *Tulipe*, *Capucine*, *Oeillet*, *Hortensia*, *Armoise* and *Pâquerette* were allocated the numbers A 735–42. *Jasmin* (P 661), *Violette* (P 788), *Géranium* (P 784) and *Jonquille* (P 787) became patrol boats of the *Gendarmerie Maritime* at Lorient, La Pallice, Cherbourg and Toulon respectively. *Pâquerette* (P 789) was similarly fitted in 1976 and allocated to Toulon. *Pétunia* became a buoy tender (*patrouilleur baliseur*) and was given the number P 662. *Armoise* and *Aubépine* were stricken during the 1970s.

Navarret Collection

Sirius (left) and *La Bayonnais*

Vega 1954
NB 1/750 scale

SIRIUS class *coastal minesweepers*

Displacement:	365t standard; 424t full load
Dimensions:	140ft pp, 152ft oa × 28ft × 8ft
	42.7m, 46.4m × 8.6m × 2.5m
Machinery:	2 shafts, SIGMA free piston generators and Alsthom or Rateau-Bretagne gas turbines, 2000hp = 15kts; 1 diesel-electric aux engine, 500hp. Range 3000nm at 10kts
Armament:	1–40mm, 1 or 2–20mm (1 or 2×1)
Complement:	38

No	Name	Builder	Launched	Fate
M 701	SIRIUS	Arsenal de Cherbourg	6.10.52	Stricken 1972–74?
M 702	RIGEL	Arsenal de Cherbourg	13.5.53	Stricken 1972–74?
M 703	ANTARES	Arsenal de Cherbourg	21.1.54	Stricken 1978
M 704	ALGOL	A C Augustin-Normand	15.4.53	Stricken 1977
M 705	ALDEBARAN	A C Augustin-Normand	27.6.53	Stricken 1972–74?
M 706	REGULUS	Penhoët	18.11.52	Stricken 1972–74?
M 707	VEGA	Penhoët	14.1.53	Stricken 1979
M 708	CASTOR	A C Augustin-Normand	19.11.53	Stricken 1972–74?
M 709	POLLUX	A C Augustin-Normand	16.7.54	Returned USA 1970
M 710	PEGASE	A C Augustin-Normand	21.6.56	Stricken 1975
M 734	CROIX DU SUD	A C de la Seine-Maritime	13.6.56	To Seychelles 1979
M 735	ETOILE POLAIRE	A C de la Seine-Maritime	5.3.57	Stricken 1981
M 736	ALTAIR	Arsenal de Cherbourg	27.3.54	Stricken 1981
M 737	CAPRICORNE	Arsenal de Cherbourg	8.8.56	Extant 1982
M 740	CASSIOPEE	Penhoët	16.11.53	Stricken 1977
M 741	ERIDAN	Penhoët	18.5.54	Stricken 1980
M 742	ORION	A C de la Seine-Maritime	20.11.53	Returned USA 1970
M 743	SAGITTAIRE	A C de la Seine-Maritime	12.1.55	Stricken 1980
M 744	ACHERNAR	CMN, Cherbourg	12.8.54	Returned USA 1971
M 745	PROCYON	CMN, Cherbourg	12.12.54	Returned USA 1970
M 746	ARCTURUS	CNF	12.3.54	Stricken 1981
M 747	BETELGEUSE	CNF	12.7.54	Stricken 1981
M 748	PERSEE	CMN, Cherbourg	23.5.55	Stricken 1972–74?
M 749	PHENIX	CMN, Cherbourg	23.5.55	Extant 1982
M 750	BELLATRIX	A C Augustin-Normand	21.7.55	Stricken 1975
M 751	DENEBOLA	CMN, Cherbourg	12.7.56	Stricken 1975
M 752	CENTAURE	Penhoët	8.3.55	Returned USA 1971
M 753	FORMALHAUT	Penhoët	24.4.55	Returned USA 1970
M 754	CANOPUS	A C Augustin-Normand	31.12.53	Extant 1982
M 755	CAPELLA	CMN, Cherbourg	6.9.55	Extant 1982
M 756	CEPHEE	CMN, Cherbourg	3.1.56	Extant 1982
M 757	VERSEAU	CMN, Cherbourg	26.4.56	Extant 1982
M 758	ARIES	Penhoët	13.3.56	To Morocco 1974
M 759	LYRE	Penhoët	3.5.56	Stricken 1981

Of the 34 French minesweepers completed belonging to this group, 28 were funded under MDAP. Three further vessels were built for Yugoslavia. They have the same general characteristics as the British 'Ton' class and the design was developed in close collaboration with Thornycroft and the Royal Navy, but there were differences in the construction of the hull. The latter is of laminated wood and aluminium, producing a strong, rigid, light body; the keel and stern are of heavy wood. They were fitted with mechanical, magnetic and acoustic sweep gear. *Capricorne* was given greater degaussing treatment than the other ships. *Croix du Sud, Etoile Polaire, Arcturus, Bételgeuse, Phénix, Canopus, Capella, Céephée, Verseau, Aries* and *Lyre* are fitted with SEMT-Pielstick diesels instead of gas turbines.

In 1960 *Altair, Arcturus* and *Croix du Sud* became station ships in the West Indies and were renumbered P 656, P 650 and P 658 respectively; all sweep gear was removed. Six further units were reclassified as patrol boats in 1973 and modified for fishery protection and surveillance duties: *Canopus, Etoile Polaire, Véga, Antarès, Eridan* and *Sagittaire* became P 659, P 660, P 707, P 703, P 741 and P7 43 respectively. Six ships were returned to the USA 1970–71. In 1977 *Lyre* and *Véga* were placed in reserve; at the same time *Bételgeuse* became a trials ship for the DUBM-41 side-scan sonar and was renumbered A 474, and *Sagittaire* and *Aldébaran* (ex-*Eridan*) were allocated to the Missile Test Centre.

MERCURE *coastal minesweeper*

Displacement:	365t standard; 400t full load
Dimensions:	146ft oa × 27ft × 8ft 6in
	44.4m × 8.3m × 4.0m
Machinery:	2 shafts, 2 MTU diesels, 4000bhp = 15kts. Range 3000nm at 15kts
Armament:	2–20mm (1×2)
Complement:	48

Known as Type DB1, *Mercure* was to be the first of a new class of French coastal minesweeper based on the ex-American MSCs of the *Acacia* class. She was ordered from CMN, Cherbourg, under MDAP and launched on 21.2.57. Six further units were later built for the Federal German Navy.

The hull is of laminated wood assembled or glued under heavy pressure, with anti-magnetic longitudinal metal bonding. The navigation bridge is of light alloy. All propulsion and generating machinery is flexibly mounted for shock resistance, and during sweep operations the ship's engines can be operated from a small cabin just beneath the upper deck.

The original diesels did not meet expectations and *Mercure* spent a number of years in reserve. Finally funds were allocated for modification as a fishery protection vessel at Cherbourg Dockyard. The original shafts and the Ka-Me-Wa CP propellers were retained, but MGO 2500 diesels replaced the original German units. Fuel tanks were enlarged to give a radius of 6200nm at 10kts. The sweep gear was removed and a new deckhouse containing medical facilities was installed aft. Thirty days' provisions are carried. She has been renumbered P 765, and replaced *Le Fringant* in this role in 1981.

Mercure as completed   Navarret Collection

Clio as completed

CIRCE class *minehunters*

Displacement:	460t standard; 510t full load
Dimensions:	153ft pp, 167ft oa × 29ft × 8ft
	46.5m, 50.9m × 8.9m × 2.5m
Machinery:	1 shaft, 1 MTU diesel, 1800bhp = 15kts; twin active rudders (7kts). Range 3000nm at 12kts
Armament:	1–20mm
Sensors:	Sonar DUBM-20A
Complement:	48

No	Name	Builder	Launched	Fate
M 712	CYBELE	CMN, Cherbourg	2.3.72	Extant 1982
M 713	CALLIOPE	CMN, Cherbourg	21.11.71	Extant 1982
M 714	CLIO	CMN, Cherbourg	21.10.71	Extant 1982
M 715	CIRCE	CMN, Cherbourg	15.12.70	Extant 1982
M 716	CERES	CMN, Cherbourg	2.6.72	Extant 1982

The world's first purpose-built minehunters, the *Circé* class were designed around the DUBM-20A minehunting sonar and the PAP 104 anti-mine vehicle.

FRANCE

The latter is a small (2.7m) unmanned submersible which carries an explosive charge. When the sonar detects a suspected mine on the seabed one of the two PAPs is lowered over the side by a large hydraulic winch mounted on the centreline. The PAP is then guided towards the contact by remote control via a cable which can be paid out to a maximum range of 500m. A camera mounted in the nose of the PAP enables the mine to be positively identified and the PAP then deposits its 100kg charge nearby and retires. The charge is detonated by an ultrasonic signal. The system can detect and destroy mines laid as deep as 60m. Six divers with Gemini dinghies are also carried and there is a decompression chamber on the quarterdeck. There is none of the usual sweep gear. The sonar and operations control room are housed in the superstructure forward of the bridge.

A low magnetic signature and silent operation were stressed in the design requirements. As insufficient experience with GRP had been acquired it was

decided that the hull should be of sandwich construction, with blocks of wood and foam inside an outer and inner skin of wood. The outer skin was coated with a film of GRP to ease maintenance. The deckhead and superstructure are a composite of wood and glass-resin.

There are two independent propulsion systems, one specifically for mine-hunting operations. Apart from the single screw for the main propulsion diesel, there are two special rudders each with a small screw-propeller mounted at its base, energised by a 260hp electric motor for a maximum speed of 7kts. Exceptional manoeuvrability and quietness of operation are thereby obtained. All propulsion machinery can be operated either from the bridge or from a soundproof control room located above the main deck.

The *Circé* class provided the necessary technical and operational experience for the 'Tripartite' minehunter, and the PAP system has been purchased by a number of other NATO navies.

Eridan on trials

Navarret Collection

ERIDAN class *minehunters*

Displacement:	510t standard; 544t full load
Dimensions:	155ft pp, 161ft oa × 29ft × 8ft *47.1m, 49.1m × 8.9m × 2.5m*
Machinery:	1 shaft, 1 Werkspoor RUB 215 V12 diesel, 2280bhp = 15kts; twin active rudders and bow thruster (7kts). Range 3000nm at 12kts
Armament:	1–20mm
Sensors:	Sonar DUBM-21A
Complement:	22–45

No	Name	Builder	Launched	Fate
M 641	ERIDAN	Arsenal de Lorient	7.3.81	In service 28.11.1981
M 642	CASSIOPEE	Arsenal de Lorient	26.9.81	Building
M 643	ANDROMEDE	Arsenal de Lorient	22.5.82	Building
M 644		Arsenal de Lorient	30.7.81	Building
M 645				Building
M 646				Building
M 647				On order
M 648				On order
M 649				Projected
M 650				Projected

Eridan is the first of a projected fifteen French minehunters of the 'Tripartite' design, which is a collaborative effort between the French, Dutch and Belgian Navies. Under the terms of the agreement each country builds its own GRP hulls to a standard design; the French are responsible for the minehunting gear and electronics, the Dutch for the main propulsion system and the Belgians for the minehunting propulsion system and the electrical generating plant.

Because of the growing shortage of wood suitable for marine hull construction, the possibility of using a glass weave/polyester resin (GRP) compound had been under investigation since the 1950s at Cherbourg. The hull, decks and partitions of the new minehunters are formed by a single GRP skin 20–40mm thick, stiffened by trapezoid-section formers, the hull/former connections being reinforced by fibreglass pins. A total of 180t of GRP will be used in the construction of *Eridan*. The hull is moulded in a steel shell.

The propulsion system is the one pioneered by the *Circé* class with the addition of a pair of bow-thrusters for increased manoeuvrability. The electric motors for the 'active rudders' and bow-thrusters are driven by a group of three Astazou IVB gas turbine alternators, each of 150kW. A fourth diesel-drive alternator of 160kW supplies the ship with power at cruise speed or while moored. The main shaft drives a five-bladed CP propeller, enabling the blades to be 'feathered' when the auxiliary (minehunting) propulsion system is in use. The main propulsion machinery is controlled from the bridge, but the auxiliary system can be controlled from either the bridge or the operations room.

The DUBM-21A minehunting sonar is a smaller, more advanced model than the 20A which equips the *Circé* class, and can detect and classify ground and moored mines to a depth of 80m. It is retracted into a well in the hull for cruising. The French vessels will have a position for a second sonar control centre on the upper deck aft to provide facilities for a DUBM-41B towed side-scan sonar.

Two PAP 104 mine destructors and six divers with Geminis are carried. There is a magazine for 27 explosive charges. Light mechanical sweep gear is fitted.

Greece

In 1947 the Civil War which had split the country since 1944 was nearing its end, though it did not actually cease until 1949. It left a country already ruined by the German occupation even worse off. The Navy had succeeded in retaining its identity throughout the Second World War, but it had been almost completely re-equipped with ships on loan from Britain. In 1947, however, America took over from Britain as the supporter of the Greek Governments, and the Truman Doctrine, which announced that America would support the non-communist countries in south-west Europe, meant that large quantities of US arms, including warships, were supplied to Greece from the late 1940s. The first new ships to be ordered for the Greek Navy since the 1930s were the *Tjeld* type MTBs, ordered from Norway in 1965.

PROBLEMS WITH TURKEY

Since the wars of independence the traditional Greek enemy has been Turkey, and despite both countries joining NATO in 1952, little has changed. The Greek islands off the Turkish mainland in the Aegean have been a traditional source of quarrels, intensified by the search for oil and minerals on the continental shelf in the 1970s. Greece claims a continuous EEZ from the Greek mainland to the islands off Turkey, while Turkey claims that large areas of the Aegean belong to her Exclusive Economic Zone (EEZ).

An even greater source of discord than the Aegean has been Cyprus. From the beginnings of the EOKA struggle for independence against the British, Greece favoured '*Enosis*', or union with Greece, while Turkey held out for the independence of Cyprus. The formation of the Republic of Cyprus in 1960 did nothing to solve the problem, and open civil war in Cyprus between the Greek and Turkish populations led to intervention by the armed forces of both countries.

The intercession of the UN separated Greece and Turkey before open warfare could break out, but when Turkey invaded Cyprus in 1974 and Greece was prevented from intervening, she left NATO. The decision to withdraw was influenced by the association of NATO, and in particular the United States, with the military 'Colonels' regime which ruled Greece from 1967 until it was toppled in November 1973. Greece retained some ties with NATO, and eventually rejoined in 1981, though it is possible that she may withdraw again because of disputes with Turkey.

THE GREEK NAVY

The main determinant of the strength of the Greek Navy has been the strength of the Turkish Navy. Both countries acquired considerable numbers of wartime ex-USN destroyers, but the main strength of the Greek fleet lies in its force of modern German-designed medium-sized submarines and missile and torpedo armed patrol boats. The restricted waters of the Aegean offer ideal opportunities for the latter, and the many narrow channels and islands explain the large numbers of small minelayers, minesweepers and amphibious vessels. Greece has gradually been developing its own warship building industry, which has built quite sophisticated vessels, until now, with foreign assistance. The most urgent need now is to replace the larger ships which are becoming almost impossible to maintain. To do this Greece has adopted the

Dutch 'Standard' frigate, the *Kortenaer* class. The first two have been taken from those already building for the Dutch Navy, but Greece intends to build more in her own shipyards. The main problem is the weak Greek economy, which cannot support a large building programme. There is also a shortage of skilled manpower, which has not improved much since the early 1960s, when the cruiser *Helle* was discarded mainly because she absorbed almost all the trained ratings that were needed to operate the destroyers and frigates. In the 1950s the Greek Navy was almost entirely dependent on the Americans, but in the late 1960s a large amount of aid was received from West Germany. Since then Greece has tried to diversify its arms procurement policy so as not to be too dependent on the United States, which was one reason for choosing the *Kortenaer*s rather than the American *Perry*s. Even so, Greece still receives a great deal from the United States, which maintains a large base at Suda Bay in Crete as well as surveillance and communications centres.

SPECIAL NOTE

In the following tables, in the ship names
A = *Antipliarchos*
I = *Ipopliarchos*
P = *Plotarchos*

FLEET STRENGTH 1947

CRUISERS

Name	Launched	Disp (full load)	Fate
GIORGIOS AVEROFF	Mar 1910	9956t	Discarded 1951

Averoff was not finally taken out of service until the ex-Italian cruiser *Helle* was commissioned. *Averoff* is now a national monument and is moored at Poros.

DESTROYERS

Name	Launched	Disp	Fate
'*B*' class			
SALAMIS (ex-*Boreas*)	18.7.30	1360t	Discarded 1951
'*E*' class			
NAVARINON (ex-*Echo*)	16.2.34	1375t	Discarded 1956

Salamis was the ex-British 'B' class destroyer *Boreas*. She was on loan to the Greek Navy from 1944–51, and was scrapped in Apr 52. *Navarinon* was the ex-British 'E' class destroyer *Echo*, on loan from 1944–56. She was scrapped in Apr 56.

GREECE

FRIGATES

Name	Launched	Disp	Fate
'Hunt' Type 2			
AEGEON	5.8.41	1050t	Discarded 12.12.59
(ex-*Lauderdale*)			
KRITI (ex-*Hursley*)	25.7.41	1050t	Discarded 12.12.59
THEMISTOCLES	29.1.42	1050t	Discarded 12.12.59
(ex-*Bramham*)			
'Hunt' Type 3			
ADRIAS	30.4.42	1087t	Discarded 1963
(ex-*Tanatside*)			
HASTINGS	22.11.41	1087t	Discarded 1963
(ex-*Catterick*)			
KANARIS	18.12.41	1087t	Discarded 12.12.59
(ex-*Hatherleigh*)			
MIAOULIS	13.4.42	1087t	Discarded 1960
(ex-*Modbury*)			
PINDOS	5.11.41	1087t	Discarded 1960
(ex-*Bolebroke*)			
'Flower' class			
APOSTOLIS	19.8.40	1020t	Discarded 1961
(ex-*Hyacinth*)			
KRIEZIS	23.5.40	1020t	Discarded 1952
(ex-*Coreopsis*)			
SAKHTOURIS	4.6.40	1020t	Discarded 1952
(ex-*Peony*)			
TOMPAZIS	28.7.41	1020t	Discarded 1952
(ex-*Tamarisk*)			

The ex-British 'Hunt' Types 2 and 3 were originally rated as escort destroyers; they were later reclassified as frigates. Of the 'Hunt' Type 2, *Kriti* and *Themistocles* were lent by the British in 1943, and *Aegeon* was lent in 1946. The 'Hunt' Type 3 *Kanaris*, *Miaoulis* and *Pindos* were lent in 1942 and *Adrias* and *Hastings* in 1946. *Hastings* was named after a British officer who had fought in the Greek War of Independence. The ex-British 'Flower' class were originally rated as corvettes, but were later reclassified as frigates. *Tompazis* had been modified with a long forecastle, but the rest retained their original short forecastles. All four were lent by Britain in 1943. A further 'Flower' class, *St Lykoudis*, ex-mercantile *Chania*, ex-*Nasturtium*, ex-French *La Paimpolaise*, was sold to Greece as the merchantman *Chania* in 1948. She was later purchased by the Greek Navy and renamed *St Lykoudis*, and was employed as an unarmed lighthouse tender until she was discarded in 1976.

SUBMARINES

Name	Launched	Disp	Fate
'U' class (2nd Series)			
AMFITRITI	20.1.43	545/740t	Discarded 1952
(ex-*Untiring*)			
XIFIAS	24.11.42	545/740t	Discarded 1952
(ex-*Upstart*)			
'V' class			
ARGONAFTIS	23.5.44	545/740t	Discarded 1958
(ex-*Virulent*)			
DELFIN	20.7.44	545/740t	Discarded 1957
(ex-*Vengeful*)			
PIPINOS (ex-*Veldt*)	19.7.43	545/740t	Discarded 1957
TRIAINA	20.6.44	545/740t	Discarded 1958
(ex-*Volatile*)			

The ex-British 'U' class submarines *Amfitriti* and *Xifias* were both lent to Greece by Britain in 1945. Their hulks were expended as targets in July 57. The ex-British 'V' class submarine *Pipinos* was lent in 1943. *Delfin* was lent in 1944 and *Argonaftis* and *Triaina* in 1946.

PATROL VESSEL

Name	Launched	Disp	Fate
PC type			
VASSILEFS GEORGIOS II	1942	280t	Discarded *c* 1960
(ex-*PC 622*)			

The ex-USN PC boat *Vassilefs Georgios II* was transferred to Greece under lease-lend in June 44.

MINESWEEPERS

Name	Fate	Name	Fate
BYMS type: launched 1942–45, 215t			
AFROESSA	Discarded 1973	SIMI	Discarded 1966
(ex-*BYMS 2185*)		(ex-*BYMS 2190*)	
ITHAKI	Discarded 1966	ZAKYNTHOS	Discarded 1973
(ex-*BYMS 2240*)		(ex-*BYMS 2209*)	
KALYMNOS	Discarded 1973	AURA	Discarded 1967
(ex-*BYMS 2033*)		(ex-*BYMS 2054*)	
KARTERIA	Discarded 1973	ANDROMEDA	Discarded 1967
(ex-*BYMS 2065*)		(ex-*BYMS 2261*)	
KEFALLINIA	Discarded 1966	KLEIO	Discarded 1967
(ex-*BYMS 2171*)		(ex-*BYMS 2152*)	
KERKYRA	Discarded *c*1960	LAMBADIAS	Discarded 1968
(ex-*BYMS 2172*)		(ex-*BYMS 2182*)	
LEFKAS	Discarded 1966	PIGASSOS	Discarded 1968
(ex-*BYMS 2086*)		(ex-*BYMS 2221*)	
LEROS	Discarded 1966	PROKYON	Discarded 1968
(ex-*BYMS 2186*)		(ex-*BYMS 2076*)	
PAPALOS	Discarded 1973	THALIA	Discarded 1967
(ex-*BYMS 2066*)		(ex-*BYMS 2252*)	
PATMOS	Discarded 1966	ARIADNE	Discarded *c*1975
(ex-*BYMS 2229*)		(ex-*BYMS 2058*)	
PAXI	Discarded 1972	VEGAS	Discarded *c*1975
(ex-*BYMS 2056*)		(ex-*BYMS 2058*)	
SALAMINIA	Discarded *c*1960		
(ex-*BYMS 2067*)			

MMS type: launched 1940–44, 165t. All discarded *c*1960

ANDROS (ex-*MMS 310*)	MIKONOS (ex-*MMS 5*)
ARGYROKASTRON (ex-*MMS 58*)	SYROS (ex-*MMS 313*)
CHIMARA (ex-*MMS 1*)	TEPELENI (ex-*MMS 46*)
KORYTSA (ex-*MMS 53*)	TINOS (ex-*MMS 144*)

BYMS type

These ex-British BYMS were transferred to Greece prior to 1947. *Afroessa* to *Zakynthos* were used as coastal minesweepers, *Aura* to *Thalia* as coastal patrol boats and *Ariadne* and *Vegas* as coastal survey craft.

MMS type

Ex-British inshore minesweepers transferred to the Greek Navy prior to 1947.

PATROL CRAFT

Name	Name
Fairmile B type: launched 1942–44, 73t. All discarded *c*1960	
DOLIANA (ex-*ML 840*)	KARPENISSI (ex-*ML 867*)
DRAMA (ex-*ML 341*)	KASSOS (ex-*ML 554*)
ELEFTERON (ex-*ML 478*)	KASTELORIZON (ex-*ML 840*)
HALKI (ex-*ML 578*)	KOS (ex-*ML 565*)
KALAMBAKA (ex-*ML 483*)	NISSIROS (ex-*ML 864*)
KARPATHOS (ex-*ML 561*)	TILOS (ex-*ML 569*)
HDML type: launched 1940–44, 54t. All discarded *c*1960	
BIZANI (ex-*HDML 1221*)	KARIA (ex-*HDML 1307*)
DAVLIA (ex-*HDML 1032*)	KASRTAKI (ex-*HDML 1375*)
DISTRATON (ex-*HDML 1292*)	KLISSOURA (ex-*HDML 1149*)
FARSALA (ex-*HDML 1252*)	PORTARIA (ex-*HDML 1051*)

The ex-British MLs and HDMLs were all transferred prior to 1947.

LANDING SHIPS

Name	Fate	Name	Fate
LST 1–510 class			
CHIOS (ex-*LST 31*)	Discarded 1977	SAMOS (ex-*LST 35*)	Discarded 1977
LEMNOS (ex-*LST 36*)	Discarded 1977		

These three ex-USN *LST 1–510* class tank landing ships were transferred to the Greek Navy under lease-lend in 1944.

PENNANT NUMBERS

Although allocated NATO numbers Greek warships usually wear their own totally separate pennants. Since these national numbers are the ones that are usually painted up, they are quoted in the tables following. However, even these were occasionally altered.

MAJOR SURFACE SHIPS

Originally launched in 1935, *Eugenio di Savoia* was transferred to Greece under the terms of the Italian Peace Treaty to compensate Greece for the sinking of the previous *Helle* in 1940 by an Italian submarine. *Helle* was finally delivered to Greece in 1951, but she absorbed most of the skilled technicians that were needed to run the smaller Greek warships so she saw little service. She was the Greek flagship between 1951–64.

(For illustration see under Italy in 1922–46 volume)

Ex-Italian DUCA D'AOSTA class *cruiser*

Particulars: As Italian *Duca D'Aosta* class

No	Name	Builder	Acquired	Fate
C 94	HELLE (ex-*Eugenio di Savoia*)	Ansaldo	1951	Discarded 1964

Doxa and *Niki* were built as USN *Gleaves* class destroyers. *Doxa* was transferred on 21.5.51 and *Niki* in Apr 51. They were given a refit in 1962 when the 6–20mm were removed, as were the 5–21in (533mm) TT (1×5). A tripod foremast replaced the original polemast.

(For illustration see under United States in 1922–46 volume)

Ex-US GLEAVES class *destroyers*

Particulars: As US *Gleaves* class

No	Name	Builder	Acquired	Fate
20	DOXA (ex-*Ludlow*)	Bath Iron Wks	21.5.51	Discarded 1972
65	NIKI (ex-*Eberle*)	Bath Iron Wks	Apr 51	Discarded 1972

These were all built 1942–43 as USN *Fletcher* class destroyers. *Sfendoni* was transferred on loan to Greece under MDAP on 21.8.59, *Aspis*, *Lonchi* and *Velos* on 15.9.59, and *Navarinon* and *Thyella* on 27.9.62. All the loans were renewed in Mar 70 and all six were purchased on 25.4.77. *Navarinon* and *Thyella* had 5–5in (127mm) (5×1), 10–40mm (2×4, 1×2) and no TT; the rest have 4–5in (127mm) (4×1), 6–3in (76mm) (2×3) and 5–21in (533mm) TT (1×5) and 6–324mm (12.75in) Mk 32 ASW TT (2×3). Ex-West German *Fletcher* class *Z 1*, ex-USS *Anthony*, was acquired for spares in 1979 after being used as a target. Further units have since been acquired for spares from the same source: ex-*Z 4* in 1981, and ex-*Z 5* in Feb 82. Ex-*Z 2* and ex-*Z 3* have 2–533mm ASW TT in lieu of the Mk 32 and are equipped for minelaying.

Ex-US FLETCHER class *destroyers*

Particulars: As US *Fletcher* class

No	Name	Builder	Acquired	Fate
06	ASPIS (ex-*Conner*)	Boston N Yd	15.9.59	Extant 1982
56	LONCHI (ex-*Hall*)	Boston N Yd	15.9.59	Extant 1982
63	NAVARINON (ex-*Brown*)	Bethlehem, San Pedro	27.9.62	Stricken 1981
85	SFENDONI (ex-*Aulick*)	Consolidated, Orange	21.8.59	Extant 1982
28	THYELLA (ex-*Bradford*)	Bethlehem, San Pedro	27.9.62	Stricken 1981
16	VELOS (ex-*Charette*)	Boston N Yd	15.9.59	Extant 1982
65	NEARCHOS (ex-*Z 3*, ex-*Wadsworth*)	Bath Iron Wks	30.10.80	To Logistics Command 18.9.81
42	KIMON (ex-*Z 2*, ex-*Ringold*)	Federal SB	18.9.81	Extant 1982

Kimon (as German Z 2 in 1977)

(For illustration see under United States in 1922–46 volume)

Miaoulis was built 1943–44 as a USN *Allen M Sumner* class destroyer, and received a FRAM II modernisation in the 1960s. She was transferred to Greece on 16.7.71, and operated an Alouette III helicopter from the DASH flight deck.

Ex-US ALLEN M SUMNER class *destroyers*

Particulars: As US *Allen M Sumner* class (FRAM II type)

No	Name	Builder	Acquired	Fate
D 211	MIAOULIS (ex-*Ingraham*)	Federal, Kearney	16.7.71	Extant 1982

Kreizis (as US *Corry*)

All were built 1944–46 as USN *Gearing* class destroyers. *Themistocles* was given a FRAM II radar picket modernisation in the 1960s. She was transferred on 30.1.71 and given a small refit in 1976–77 when a hangar and flight deck for an Alouette III helicopter were fitted in lieu of her radar picket facilities. She now has 4–30mm Emerlec AA (2×2) in place of the single 20mm. The rest were given FRAM I modernisations in the 1960s. *Kanaris* was transferred on 1.7.72, *Kountouriotis* on 10.7.73 (purchased 11.7.78), *Sachtouris* on 4.12.73 (purchased 11.7.78) and *Toumbazis* was purchased on 17.3.77. These have been fitted with 1–3in (76mm) OTO Melara compact gun on the helicopter flight deck aft, with Orion fire control radar and 1–40mm forward, as well as other modifications. Ex-*Corry* and ex-*Dyess* will probably be

ex-US GEARING class *destroyers*

Particulars: As US *Gearing* class (FRAM I and FRAM II types)

No	Name	Builder	Acquired	Fate
212	KANARIS (ex-*Stickell*)	Consolidated, Orange	1.7.72	Extant 1982
213	KOUNTOURIOTIS (ex-*Rupertus*)	Bethlehem, Quincy	10.7.73	Extant 1982
214	SACHTOURIS (ex-*Arnold J Isbell*)	Bethlehem, Staten I	4.12.73	Extant 1982
210	THEMISTOCLES (ex-*Frank Knox*)	Bath Iron Wks	30.1.71	Extant 1982
215	TOUMBAZIS (ex-*Gurke*)	Todd-Pacific, Seattle	17.3.77	Extant 1982
216	APOSTOLIS (ex-*Myles C Fox*)	Bath Iron Wks	2.8.80	Extant 1982
217	KREIZIS (ex-*Corry*)	Consolidated, Orange	8.7.81	Extant 1982
?	(ex-*Dyess*)	Consolidated, Orange	8.7.81	Exact status unknown 1982

similarly refitted. US *Charles P Cecil*, another *Gearing*, was purchased 2.8.80 for cannibalisation to keep the other ships of the class operational.

(For illustration see under United States in 1922–46 volume)

Ex-US CANNON class *destroyer escorts*

Particulars: As US *Cannon* class (DET type)

No	Name	Builder	Acquired	Fate
01	AETOS (ex-*Slater*)	Tampa SB	15.3.51	Extant 1982
31	HIERAX (ex-*Ebert*)	Tampa SB	15.3.51	Extant 1982
54	LEON (ex-*Eldridge*)	Federal, Newark	15.1.51	Extant 1982
67	PANTHIR (ex-*Garfield Thomas*)	Federal, Newark	15.1.51	Extant 1982

All four were built 1943–44 as US DET type destroyer escorts, but were later reclassified as frigates. *Leon* and *Panthir* were transferred to Greece under MDAP on 15.1.51 and *Aetos* and *Hierax* on 15.3.51. Their 3–21in (533mm) TT (1×3) have been removed, and they have been fitted with 6–324mm (12.75in) Mk 32 ASW TT (2×3). This class is well overdue for replacement.

(For illustration see under West Germany)

Ex-West German RHEIN class *frigate/support ships*

Particulars: See West German *Rhein* class

No	Name	Builder	Acquired	Fate
03	AEGEON (ex-*Weser*)	Elsflether Werft	6.7.76	Extant 1982

The West German depot ship *Weser* was transferred to Greece on 6.7.76 and renamed *Aegeon*. These *Rhein* class depot ships were designed to be used as frigates if necessary, and were armed accordingly. Because of the Greek Navy's pressing shortage of major modern warships, *Aegeon* has therefore been used as a frigate, as well as acting as a support ship for the missile patrol boats and MTBs.

(For illustration see under Netherlands)

Dutch 'STANDARD' type *frigates*

Particulars: As Netherlands *Kortenaer* class

No	Name	Builder	Laid down	Launched	Comp	Fate
F 450	HELLE (ex-*Pieter Florisz*)	Royal Scheldt	July 77	15.12.79	10.10.81	Extant 1982
F 451	LIMNOS (ex-*Witte De With*)	Royal Scheldt	13.6.78	27.10.79	late 1982	Building 1982

Greece finally decided to re-equip its Navy with the Dutch 'Standard' frigate – the *Kortenaer* class. The first was ordered in 1980 and the second on 7.7.81. In order to ensure rapid delivery, the sixth and seventh ships building for the Dutch Navy were purchased, and replacements will be built for the Dutch Navy. The Greek ships are being fitted with a longer hangar to operate an Italian-built A/B 212 helicopter and have their NATO Sea Sparrow missiles replaced by the

Italian Aspide version. The Harpoon SSM launchers have been deleted. Greece has the option to build more of this class at Skaramanga in Greece, with Dutch assistance, and will do so if she can afford them.

SUBMARINES

Both these boats were built 1942–43 as USN *Gato* class submarines, and fitted with a streamlined fin postwar. *Poseidon* was transferred on loan under MDAP to Greece on 8.8.57 and *Amfitriti* on 21.4.58. *Poseidon* was purchased in Apr 76 for spares to keep the remaining ex-US Second World War submarines operational.

(For illustration see under United States)

Ex-US GATO class *submarines*

Particulars: As US *Gato* class

No	Name	Builder	Acquired	Fate
S 78	AMFITRITI (ex-*Jack*)	Electric Boat	21.4.58	Discarded *c*1972
S 09	POSEIDON (ex-*Lapon*)	Electric Boat	8.8.57	Stricken 1976

Triaina was built 1943–44 as a US *Balao* class submarine, and was given a streamlined fin postwar. She was transferred to Greece on loan under MDAP on 26.2.65, and was purchased in Apr 76. She is no longer operational, being used for alongside training.

(For illustration see under United States)

Ex-US BALAO class *submarine*

Particulars: As US *Balao* class (Fleet Snorkel type)

No	Name	Builder	Acquired	Fate
S 86	TRIAINA (ex-*Scabbardfish*)	Portsmouth N Yd	26.2.65	TS 1982

This submarine was built 1943–44 as a US *Balao* class boat and modernised in the early 1950s to the GUPPY IIA configuration. *Papanikolis* was purchased on 26.7.72 and is mainly used for training, but can be used operationally if necessary.

(For illustration see under United States)

Ex-US BALAO class *submarine*

Particulars: As US *Balao* class (GUPPY IIA type)

No	Name	Builder	Acquired	Fate
S 114	PAPANIKOLIS (ex-*Hardhead*)	Manitowoc	26.7.72	Extant 1982

This boat was built 1945–46 as a US *Tench* class submarine. She was first converted to GUPPY II configuration in the early 1950s, then to GUPPY III in 1961–62. Greece purchased her on 29.10.73. *Katsonis* is now mainly used for training, though she can be used operationally if required.

(For illustration see under United States)

Ex-US TENCH class *submarine*

Particulars: As US *Tench* class (GUPPY III type)

No	Name	Builder	Acquired	Fate
S 115	KATSONIS (ex-*Remora*)	Portsmouth N Yd	29.10.73	Extant 1982

Greece was the first country to adopt the German-designed and -built Type 209 single-hulled submarine, which has since been purchased by Turkey and many South American navies. She can dive to more than 650ft (200m), and has a powerful battery of torpedo tubes (plus reload torpedoes) and a comparatively small crew. The second group, ordered in 1975–76, have a longer hull to give more internal volume. The first group had proved to be rather too cramped to take all the equipment, electronics and crew. The Type 209s have replaced almost all the old Second World War American submarines.

GLAVKOS class *submarines*

Displacement:	1105t/1230t (2nd group 1180t/1300t) normal
Dimensions:	178ft 6in (2nd group 183ft 5in) oa × 20ft 4in × 17ft 11in *54.4m (55.9m) × 6.2m × 5.5m*
Machinery:	1 shaft, 4 MTU diesels plus 1 Siemens electric motor, 2250bhp/3600shp= 11kts/21kts. Range 25nm/230nm/400nm at 20kts/8kts/4kts submerged
Armament:	8–533mm TT (bow; 14 torpedoes)
Sensors:	Radar ?; sonar?
Complement:	31

No	Name	Builder	Laid down	Launched	Comp	Fate
First group						
S 110	GLAVKOS	Howaldswerke, Kiel	1.9.68	15.9.70	5.11.71	Extant 1982
S 111	NEREUS	Howaldswerke, Kiel	15.1.69	7.6.71	10.2.72	Extant 1982
S 112	TRITON	Howaldswerke, Kiel	1.6.69	19.10.71	23.11.72	Extant 1982
S 113	PROTEUS	Howaldswerke, Kiel	1.10.69	1.2.72	8.8.72	Extant 1982
Second group						
S 116	POSEIDON	Howaldswerke, Kiel	15.4.76	21.3.78	22.3.79	Extant 1982
S 117	AMFITRITI	Howaldswerke, Kiel	14.9.76	14.6.78	14.8.79	Extant 1982
S 118	OKEANOS	Howaldswerke, Kiel	1.10.76	16.11.78	15.11.79	Extant 1982
S 119	PONTOS	Howaldswerke, Kiel	15.1.77	22.3.79	29.4.80	Extant 1982

Glavkos as completed
Official

AMPHIBIOUS WARFARE VESSELS

(For illustration see under countries of origin in this and 1922–46 volume)

Ex-US LSD type *dock landing ships*

| Particulars: | | AS US LSD type | | |

No	Name	Builder	Acquired	Fate
L 153	NAFKRATOUSSA (ex-*Hyperion*)	Newport News	1953	Discarded 1971
L 153	NAFKRATOUSSA (ex-*Fort Mandan*)	Boston N Yd	1971	Extant 1982

The first ex-USN LSD to be acquired, *Hyperion* (LSD 9, built 1943), was taken over by the Greek Navy in 1953 and acted as the HQ Ship for the Greek amphibious forces. She was replaced in 1971 by ex-US *Fort Mandan* (LSD 21, built 1945), also renamed *Nafkratoussa*, which had received a FRAM I modernisation. She has recently had an SPS-6 radar added.

Ex-British LST (3) type *tank landing ships*

| Particulars: | As British LST (3) type |

Class:
Axios, Strymon, Alfios, Acheloos, Pinios, Aliakmon
    Six ex-British LST (3)s were transferred to the Greek Navy in 1947. *Axios* (ex-*LST 3007*) and *Strymon* (ex-*LST 3502*) were returned in June 62. *Alfios* (ex-*LST 3020*) was returned in Aug 63, *Acheloos* (ex-*LST 3503*) was discarded in 1964 and *Pinios* (L 104) ex-*LST 3506* and *Aliakmon* (L 171) ex-*LST 3002* in 1968–69.

Ex-US LSM 1 class *medium landing ships* s

| Particulars: | As US LSM 1 class |

Class:
I Grigoropoulos (L 161), *I Tournas* (L 162), *I Daniolos* (L 163), *I Roussen* (L 164), *I Krystalidis* (L 165), *I Merlin* (I 166)
    Six ex-USN *LSM 1* class LSMs were transferred by the USN to Greece in 1958. *I Merlin* (ex-*LSM 557*) and *I Krystalidis* (ex-*LSM 541*) on 30.10.58 and *I Daniolos* (ex-*LSM 227*), *I Grigoropoulos* (ex-*LSM 45*), *I Roussen* (ex-*LSM 399*) and *I Tournas* (ex-*LSM 102*) on 3.11.58. *I Merlin* was sunk in collision with a supertanker on 15.11.72, but the remainder were in service in 1982.

Ex-US LST 1 class *tank landing ships*

| Particulars: | As US LST type (*LST 1–510* group) |

Class:
Lesbos (L 172), *Rodos* (L 157), *Syros* (L 144)
    Three ex-USN *1–510* type LSTs were transferred to Greece in the 1960s to add to the three transferred under lease-lend in 1944. They were *Lesbos* (ex-*Boone County*, ex-*LST 389*), and *Rodos* (ex-*Bowman County*, ex-*LST 391*) transferred on 9.8.60, and *Syros* (ex-*LST 325*) transferred on 29.5.64. They were added to the three LSTs of this type transferred under lease-lend in 1944. *Lesbos*, *Rodos* and *Syros* were in service in 1982.

Ex-US LST 511 class *tank landing ships*

| Particulars: | As US LST type (*LST 511–1152* group) |

Class:
Ikaria (L 154), *Kriti* (L 171)
    Ikaria (ex-*Potter County*, ex-*LST 1086*) was transferred from the USN to Greece on 9.8.60. *Kriti* (ex-*Page County*, ex-*LST 1076*) was transferred in Mar 71 and purchased by Greece on 11.7.78. Both were in service 1982.

Ex-US TERREBONNE PARISH class *tank landing ships*

| Particulars: | As US *Terrebonne Parish* class |

Class:
Inouse (L 104), *Kos* (L 116)
    Two ex-USN *Terrebonne Parish* class LSTs *Inouse* (ex-*Terrell County*, ex-*LST 1157*) and *Kos* (ex-*Whitefield County*, ex-*LST 1169*), were purchased by Greece on 17.3.77. Both were built in 1953, and they were modernised in Greece after purchase. Both were in service in 1982. The transfer of two more was projected, but came to nothing.

Ex-British LCT (4) type *tank landing craft*

| Particulars: | As British LCT (4) type |

Twelve ex-British LCTs of the LCT (4) type were acquired by Greece from Britain in 1946. *Amorgas* (ex-*LCT 1301*), *Anafi* (ex-*LCT 1293*), *Kandados* (ex-*LCT 587*), *Kithera* (ex-*LCT 1198*), *Malakassi* (ex-*LCT 619*), *Milos* (ex-*LCT 1300*), *Palaiochori* (ex-*LCT 620*), *Serifos* (ex-*LCT 1227*), *Sofades* (ex-*LCT 594*), *Thira* (ex-*LCT 1297*), *Vraghni* (ex-*LCT 607*) and one other were all discarded (most to Greek commercial interests) prior to 1968. *Kithera* and *Milos* have been re-acquired by the Greek Navy.

Ex-US LCU 501 class *utility landing craft*

| Particulars: | As US *LCU 501* class |

Class:
Kassos (L 145), *Karpathos* (L 146), *Kimolos* (L 147), *Kea* (L 148), *Kithnos* (L 149), *Sifnos* (L 150), *Skopelos* (L 151), *Skiathos* (L 152)
    Eight ex-US *LCU 501* class (ex-LCT (6) originally built in 1944) were acquired between 1959 and 1962. *Skopelos* (ex-*LCU 852*) and *Skiathos* (ex-*LCU 827*) were transferred in 1959; *Kea* (ex-*LCU 1229*), *Kithnos* (ex-*LCU 763*), and *Sifnos* (ex-*LCU 677*) were transferred in 1961; *Kassos* (ex-*LCU 1382*), *Karpathos* (ex-*LCU 1379*) and *Kimolos* (ex-*LCU 971*) were transferred in 1962. *Kithnos* and *Skiathos* were discarded in 1975, the remainder were in service in 1982.

OTHER LANDING CRAFT

LCM
13 LCM were transferred from the USN prior to 1965.

LCA
13 ex-British LCA were on loan from 1947 to the early 1960s.

LCVP
34 ex-USN LCVP were transferred for use with the LSTs.

LCP
14 LCP have been built in Greece from 1977.

SMALL SURFACE COMBATANTS

(For illustration see under countries of origin in this and 1922–46 volume)

Ex-British ALGERINE class *corvettes*

| Particulars: | | As British *Algerine* class | | |

No	Name	Builder	Acquired	Fate
M 12	ARMATOLOS (ex-*Aries*)	Toronto Shipyard	1947	Discarded 1977
M 58	MACHITIS (ex-*Postillion*)	Redfern	1947	Discarded 1976
M 64	NAVMACHOS (ex-*Lightfoot*)	Redfern	1947	Discarded 1976
M 74	POLEMISTIS (ex-*Gozo*)	Redfern	1947	Discarded 1977
M 76	PYRPOLITIS (ex-*Arcturus*)	Redfern	1947	Discarded 1977

These five corvettes were built 1942–43 as British *Algerine* class fleet minesweepers in Canada for the USN, and supplied to the RN under lease-lend. All were transferred to Greece in 1947. By the late 1960s they were being used mainly as transports; *Armatolos* was also employed as a lighthouse tender. *Machitis* was disarmed as a training ship, *Polemistis* was also used for training and *Pyrpolitis* was a command ship for amphibious operations.

Ex-US PGM 9 class *patrol vessels*

| Particulars: | As US *PGM 9* class (ex-PC type) |

Class:
A Laskos (P 53), *A Pezopoulos* (P 75), *P Meletopoulos* (P 57), *P Arsanoglou* (P 14), *P Chadzikonstandis* (P 96), *P Blessas* (P 61)
    Six ex-USN *PGM 9* class patrol vessels, originally built in 1943–44, were acquired from the USA in Aug 47. All six had been launched in 1943–44. In 1963 all except *P Blessas* were fitted with a Hedgehog ASW mortar, and 2–40mm (2×1) were removed. *P Blessas* (ex-*PGM 28*) was discarded in 1963, *A Laskos* (ex-*PGM 16*) and *P Meletopoulos* (ex-*PGM 22*) in 1971, *A Pezopoulos* (ex-*PGM 21*) in 1977 and *P Arsanoglou* (ex-*PGM 25*) and *P Chadzikonstandis* (ex-*PGM 29*) in 1979.

Ex-US LSSL type *patrol vessels*

Particulars:	As US LSSL type

Class:

P Maridakis (P 94), *P Vlachavas* (P 95)

Two ex-USN LSSL type patrol vessels, both built in the USA in 1945, were transferred to Greece: *P Maridakis* (ex-*LSSL 65*) in June 58 and *P Vlachavas* (ex-LSSL 45) on 12.8.57. Both were discarded in 1976.

Norwegian TJELD type *motor torpedo-boats*

Particulars:	As Norwegian *Tjeld* class

Class:

Andromeda (P 21), *Iniohos* (P 22), *Kastor* (P 23), *Kykonos* (P 24), *Pigassos* (P 25), *Toxotis* (P 26)

An order for six MTBs was placed with Mandal, Norway in 1965. These were identical with the Norwegian *Tjeld* (improved *Nasty*) class except that they have 2–40mm (2×1) in place of the Norwegian boats' 1–40mm and 1–20mm. All were delivered in 1967. *Iniohos* was discarded in 1972, but the rest were all in service in 1982, renumbered P 196–P 200 respectively. These were the first new warships to be built for Greece since the 1930s.

British BRAVE type *motor torpedo-boat*

Particulars:	See West German *Strahl*

Class:

Astrapi (P 20)

The West German MTB *Strahl*, built to the British *Brave* class design and launched by Vosper on 10.1.62, was transferred to Greece and renamed *Astrapi* in Apr 67. She was refitted by Vosper in 1968 and discarded in 1979.

British FEROCITY type *motor torpedo-boat*

Particulars:	See West German *Pfeil*

Class:

Aiolos (P 19)

The West German MTB *Pfeil*, launched on 26.10.61 and built to the British *Ferocity* design by Vosper, was purchased by Greece in Apr 67 and renamed *Aiolos*. She was refitted by Vosper in 1968 and discarded in 1976.

Ex-West German SILBERMOWE class *motor torpedo-boats*

Particulars:	See West German *Silbermöwe* class

Class:

Delphin (P 15), *Drakon* (P 16), *Polikos* (P 17), *Polidefkis* (P 18), *Foinix* (P 27)

Five West German *Silbermöwe* class MTBs, built 1951–56, were transferred to Greece on 17.12.68. *Delfin* (ex-*Sturmöwe*), *Drakon* ex-*Silbermöwe*), *Foinix* (ex-*Eismöwe*), *Polikos* (ex-*Raubmöwe*) and *Polidefkis* (ex-*Wildschwan*) were all discarded in 1974.

Astrapi (as the German *Strahl* in 1962)

Ex-West German JAGUAR class *motor torpedo-boats*

Particulars:	See West German *Jaguar* class

Class:

Hesperos (P 196), *Kataigis* (P 197), *Kentauros* (P 198), *Kyklon* (P 199), *Laiaps* (P 228), *Scorpios* (P 229), *Tyfon* (P 230)

Seven ex-West German *Jaguar* class MTBs have been commissioned in the Greek Navy. *Hesperos* (ex-*Seeadler*) was transferred on 24.3.77, *Kataigis* (ex-*Falke*) on 12.12.76, *Kentauros* (ex-*Habicht*) on 22.5.77, *Kyklon* (ex-*Greif*) on 12.12.76, *Laiaps* (ex-*Kondor*) on 24.3.77, *Scorpios* (ex-*Kormoran*) on 22.5.77 and *Tyfon* (ex-*Geier*) on 12.12.76. In addition, ex-*Albatros*, ex-*Bussard* and ex-*Sperber* were transferred in 1976–77 to provide spares for the operational boats. All the active boats were refitted before being transferred. During 1980 all were renumbered P 50–P 56 in the above order. *Kataigis* was discarded late in 1981.

KELEFSTIS STAMOU class *fast attack craft*

Displacement:	80t standard; 115t full load
Dimensions:	105ft oa × 19ft × 5ft 4in
	32.0m × 5.8m × 1.6m
Machinery:	2 shafts, 2 MTU diesels, 2700shp= 30kts. Range 1500nm at 15kts
Armament:	4 SS 12 SSM (4×1), 1–40mm, 1–20mm
Sensors:	Radar ?
Complement:	17

Class:

Diopos Antoniou (P 29), *Kelefstis Stamou* (P 28)

Built by CN de l'Esterel 1974–75 for Cyprus, but the Cypriot Government was not allowed to take delivery of them (this was at the time of the Turkish invasion of Cyprus), so they were taken over by the Greek Navy instead. They have wooden hulls, and can be armed with 2–20mm (2×1) in place of 1–40mm and 1–20mm. Renumbered P 287 and P 288 respectively in 1980.

Ipopliarchos Konidis as completed

NB 1/750 scale

French 'LA COMBATTANTE II' type *fast attack craft*

Displacement:	234t standard; 255t full load
Dimensions:	154ft 3in oa × 23ft 4in × 8ft 3in
	47.0m × 7.1m × 2.5m
Machinery:	4 shafts, 4 MTU diesels, 12,000bhp= 36.5kts. Range 8500nm at 25kts
Armament:	4 MM38 Exocet SSM (4×1), 4–35mm (2×2), 2–21in (533mm) TT (2×1)
Sensors:	Radar Thomson types Pollux, Triton
Complement:	40

Class:

A Anninos (P 14), *I Arliotis* (P 15), *I Konidis* (P 16), *I Batsis* (P 17)

Four steel-hulled 'La Combattante II' type missile patrol boats similar to the Israeli *Saar* class were ordered in 1969. They were built by CM de Normandie at Cherbourg, and it was originally intended to build six more in Greece, but the more capable 'La Combattante III' type were built instead. *A Anninos* (ex-*Navsithoi*) was launched on 8.9.71, *I Arliotis* (ex-*Evniki*) on 26.4.71, *I Batsis* (ex-*Kalypso*) on 26.1.71 and *I Konidis* (ex-*Kymothoi*) on 20.12.71. They were completed in 1971–72 and renamed in 1973. They were originally numbered (in the above order) P 55, P 56, P 53 and P 54.

Antipliarchos Laskos as completed   Official

French 'LA COMBATTANTE III' type *fast attack craft*

Displacement:	359t standard; 425t (2nd group 429t) full load
Dimensions:	184ft × 26ft 3in × 8ft 3in 56.2m × 7.9m × 2.5m
Machinery:	4 shafts, 4 MTU diesels, 18,000bhp (2nd group 15,000bhp)= 36.5kts (32.5kts). Range 700nm/2000nm at 32kts/15kts
Armament:	4 MM38 Exocet SSM (4×1) (2nd group 6 Penguin SSM, 6×1), 2–76mm/62 (2×1), 4–30mm (2×2), 2–533mm TT (2×1)
Sensors:	Radar Thomson types Castor, Pollux, Triton (2nd group TM-1226, D-1280)
Complement:	42

Class:
1st group – *A Laskos* (P 50), *A Blessas* (P 51), *A Troupakis* (P 52), *A Mykonios* (P 54); 2nd group – *Simeoforos Kavaloudis* (P 24), *A Kostakos* (P 25), *I Deyiannis* (P 26), *Simeoforos Xenos* (P 27), *Simeoforos Simitzopoulos* (P 28), *Simeoforos Starakis* (P 29)

Save for the armament these closely resemble the 'La Combattante III' type large missile patrol boats in other navies including Israel's. The first group of four boats, *P Blessas* (launched 10.11.76), *A Laskos* (launched 6.7.76), *I Mykonios* (launched 5.5.77) and *I Troupakis* (launched 6.1.77) were ordered in Sep 74 and all built by CM de Normandie at Cherbourg. They have four MM38 Exocet SSMs. The SST–4 torpedoes are wire-guided, and the 3in (76mm) is an OTO Melara compact. The second group of six boats were ordered from the Hellenic Shipyard at Skaramanga in Greece, and are being built under French supervision. *Simeoforos Kavaloudis* was launched on 10.11.79 and completed on 14.7.80. The remainder were completed (in the above order) on 9.9.80, Dec 80, 24.3.81, June 81 and 12.10.81. They were ordered in 1978 and have Penguin 2 SSM in place of Exocet, and less expensive machinery and electronics.

COASTAL PATROL BOATS
The following small patrol craft are also in service:
KFK class – *Arhikelefstis Maliopoulis* (ex-*W 8*), *Arhikelefstis Stassis* ex-*W 2*), *Anemos* (ex-*W ?*)

German MFV type patrol boats of the Second World War, transferred from the West German Navy in 1969 (*Anemos*) and 30.8.75 (the other two). *Anemos* (discarded *c*1975) and *Maliopoulis* were used as survey craft.
Dilos class – *Dilos* (P 267), *Lindos* (P 269), *Knossos* (P 268)

An 86t design by Abeking & Rasmussen, used by the Greek Navy for air sea rescue, built 1977–81. More have been built for the Customs and Coast Guard. They were built by the Hellenic Shipyard, Skaramanga, and were launched 1977–81.

N I Goulandris class – *N I Goulandris I* (P 289), *N I Goulandris II* (P 290)

Coastal patrol boats of 39t, armed with 2–20mm, designed by the German firm of Abeking & Rasmussen, built in Greece 1975–77 and paid for by the Greek shipowner whose name they carry.

E Panagopoulos class – *E Panagopoulos I* (P 61)

As with the previous class, named after a prominent shipowner. Numbers II and III are under construction.

MINE WARFARE VESSELS

Ex-US MMC type *coastal minelayers*

Particulars:	As US MMC type (ex-*LSM 1* class)

Class:
Aktion (N 04), *Amvrakia* (N 05)

Aktion (ex-*MMC 6*, ex-*LSM 301*) and *Amvrakia* (ex-*MMC 7*, ex-*LSM 303*) were built in the USA in 1943–45 as *LSM 1* class medium landing ships. They were completely rebuilt as MMC prior to being transferred to Greece on 1.12.53. The armament consists of 8–40mm (4×2), 6–20mm (6×1) and 100–130 mines, handled by a pair of derricks fore and aft. Both were in service in 1982.

Ex-US ADJUTANT class *coastal minesweepers*

Particulars:	As US *Adjutant* class

Class:
Atalanti (M 202), *Antiopi* (M 205), *Faedra* (M 206), *Thalia* (M 210), *Niovi* (M 254)

Five USN *Adjutant* class coastal minesweepers, originally built in the USA for Belgium under MDAP, were subsequently returned by Belgium to the USA and re-transferred to Greece. *Atalanti* (ex-Belgian *St Truiden*) and *Antiopi* (ex-Belgian *Herve*) were transferred to Greece on 29.7.69 and *Faedra* (ex-Belgian *Malmedy*), *Niovi* (ex-Belgian *Laroche*) and *Thalia* (ex-Belgian *Blankenberge*) were transferred to Greece on 26.9.69. These all have a small funnel and open bridge. All were in service in 1982.

US FALCON class *coastal minesweepers*

Particulars:	As US *Falcon* class (MSC 294 type)

Class:
Aedon (M 248), *Klio* (M 213 ex-*Argo*), *Aigli* (M 246), *Alkyon* (M 211), *Avra* (M 214), *Dafni* (M 267), *Kichli* (M 241), *Kissa* (M 242), *Pleias* (M 240)

All were built by Peterson, and have an enclosed bridge and a large, prominent funnel. Both this and the previous class have wooden hulls.

Iceland

Although a member of NATO, Iceland has no navy. However, there is a coast guard service which is mainly employed in fishery protection and offshore patrol duties. Although its patrol craft were regularly referred to as 'gunboats' during the 1975-76 'Cod War' with the UK, they have only a nominal armament (usually 1–57mm gun). In wartime they would presumably join NATO forces and so are listed below:

Aegir, 1929, 507t, 14kts, BU 1968
Saebjorg, 1937, 98t, 10kts, stricken Aug 65
Gautur (ex-*Odinn*), 1938, 72t, 11kts, stricken 1.1.63
Hermadur, 1947, 208t, 13kts, foundered 17.7.59

Maria Julia, 1950, 138t, 11.5kts, sold 1969
*Thor**, 1951, 920t, 17kts
Albert, 1956, 200t, 12kts
*Odinn**, 1959, 1000t, 18kts
Arvakur, 1962, 716t, 12kts
*Aegir**, 1968, 1150t, 19kts
Baldur, 1974, 740t, 15kts
*Tyr**, 1974, 1150t, 19kts

Unless otherwise noted all vessels were in service in 1982.
* have sonar, helicopter deck and hangar.

Italy

The end of the Second World War found Italy with a sadly reduced Navy, and the Peace Treaty between her and the Allied powers signed on 10.2.47 diminished it still further. The treaty stipulated that the standard tonnage of warships (excluding the battleships *Andrea Doria*, and *Caio Duilio* and auxiliaries) must not exceed 67,000t, and personnel were limited to 22,500 officers and men. Italy was prohibited from building, acquiring or possessing any battleship (other than *Doria* and *Duilio*), aircraft carrier, submarine, MTB or assault craft, and the Navy might not buy or begin construction of any warship before 1.1.50, except to replace a vessel accidently lost.

This meant that the Italian Navy had to divest itself of all the prohibited classes of warship plus others, including battleships, cruisers, destroyers, submarines, corvettes, minesweepers and MTBs, which were required by certain of the Allied powers as compensation for war losses. With Allied connivance some of the treaty prohibitions were evaded; several submarines, for example, although still being used for ASW training, were reclassified as battery-charging vessels, and all MTBs simply had their TTs removed. The net result, however, remained catastrophic.

On 4.4.49, however, Italy became a member of NATO at its inception, and soon began to receive large amounts of American military aid, particularly under the Mutual Defense Assistance Program (MDAP), which paid for many of the ships that the Italian Navy acquired in the 1950s. There was a five year programme from 1.1.50 to provide a modern Navy, combined with an urgent rebuilding programme of the surviving wartime vessels. This first programme, which provided for the conversion of the 'Capitani Romani' and the building of the *Impetuosos*, *Canopos*, *Albatroses*, plus smaller craft was a great success, and was the only postwar programme to be completed in its entirety. Restrictions on the possession of submarines and MTBs were removed in 1952, and the existing craft were rearmed and new ones began to be planned.

By 1955, the personnel of the Italian Navy had crept up to 38,000 officers and men, and more sophisticated vessels began to be acquired, including guided missile destroyers and, in the 1957–58 Programme, the two *Doria* class helicopter cruisers, the first of their kind in the world. The 1959–60 Programme even included a nuclear submarine, based on the design of the USS *Skipjack*, but it proved too ambitious and expensive, and the idea had been dropped by the mid-1960s. Another change took place in the late 1950s, with the presence of the US 6th Fleet in large numbers in the Mediterranean, and from being a national force the Italian Navy began to take part in the task of providing ASW protection to the 6th Fleet as well. Since the Second World War, the Italian Navy has had a very close relationship with the USN, providing it with escorts and a base at Naples, and obtaining weapons systems and electronic equipment in return.

FINANCIAL LIMITATIONS

From 1947–82 the major problem for the Italian Navy has been posed not by external enemies – with the exception of minor fishing wars with Libya and Tunisia there have been hardly any naval operations – but by shortage of money. Almost every major building programme has been either postponed or partly cancelled because of lack of funds. Despite Italy's being a founder-member of the EEC, her economy has always been precarious throughout this period, and lack of indigenous oil and other raw materials has made it particularly so since the early 1970s. Examples of planned building that have been completely cut include a second *Veneto* and, more recently, a 6000t LPD which was to have doubled as a training ship to replace *San Giorgio*. This has meant that ships built in the first postwar building programme in the early 1950s are still theoretically in front-line service, even though the *Impetuosos* and *Albatroses*, for example, are no longer credible as effective fighting ships. A determined attempt was made in the Naval Law of 1975 to provide an adequate programme of replacements over a 10-year period, but parts of this have already been postponed for a shorter (*eg* the last two *Maestrales*) or longer (*eg* the second two *Audaces*) time because of lack of money.

WARSHIP DESIGN

In general, the Italian Navy has followed the path of gradual improvement to proved designs and concepts. The best examples are the run of destroyers, with a clearly marked progression from the *Impetuosos* to the *Audaces*, and the frigates, from the *Canopos* to the *Maestrales*. Most of the problems and mistakes have stemmed from financial difficulties, with the consequent endeavour to pack too much into too small a hull. Thus the *Dorias*, though not entirely unsuccessful, were too small, whereas their more successful descendant, *Veneto*, puts only a few more systems into a much larger hull.

Perhaps the most ambitious attempt to pack a quart into a pint pot was the reconstruction of the wartime cruiser *Garibaldi*. Although the (larger) USN Terrier CLGs were *planned* to have Polaris ICBM tubes, *Garibaldi* actually had them. Another, though related, reason for ing too much into too small a hull is the wish to produce an enticing design for third-world navies. Such ships are undoubtedly impressive from the point of view of the number of weapons systems carried, but they are not suited to a NATO navy operating in a very sophisticated electronics environment at all times of the year. This was the problem encountered by the Italian Navy when they were ordered to buy the *Lupos*, and it is to their credit that they created the *Maestrales* from it, which are very well suited to the Italian Navy's needs.

THE PRESENT

Despite Italy's economic problems, the Navy has a small but well balanced force of efficient ships. Many are over age, but the recent building programme is rapidly modernising the major ship force, and the older vessels are being refitted with improved electronics and some new weapons including Otomat SSMs. This is going some way to overcoming the existing bias in favour of AA and ASW systems, which *was* necessary because these were the most likely threats, but which left some major units virtually defenceless against the rapidly growing surface forces of potential enemies in the Mediterranean. The overall size of the Italian Navy is gradually increasing, partly as a result of the British withdrawal from Malta in the early 1970s which left a considerable gap. (Indeed, by 1976 only America and Italy were contributing ships to Allied Forces Southern Europe.) Total personnel in 1980 (including naval infantry) was 41,900 – the largest it has been since the Second World War.

FLEET STRENGTH 1947
(including ships transferred under the terms of the Peace Treaty)

BATTLESHIPS

Name	Launched	Disp (full load)	Fate
Cavour class			
GIULIO CESARE	15.10.11	29,032t	To USSR 15.12.48
Doria class			
ANDREA DORIA	30.3.13	28,882t	Discarded 1.11.56
CAIO DUILIO	24.4.13	29,391t	Discarded 15.6.56
Littorio class			
ITALIA (ex-*Littorio*)	22.8.37	45,236t	Discarded 1.6.48
VITTORIO VENETO	22.7.37	45,029t	Discarded 1.2.48

Cavour class
Cesare (reconstructed between Oct 33–Oct 37) was assigned to the USSR as war reparations as *Z 11*. The Russians renamed her *Novorossiisk*, and she was probably mined and sunk at Sevastopol on 29.10.55 (See USSR section).

Doria class
Doria (rebuilt between 8.4.37–26.10.40) and *Duilio* (rebuilt between 1.4.37–15.7.40) were both used as training ships postwar except for a period in 1947–49 when *Duilio* was the flagship of the C in C of the Italian Navy. *Doria* was laid up in reserve from June 53, followed by *Duilio*. Both were scrapped between 1957–61.

Littorio class
Italia and *Veneto* were returned to Italy in 1946. *Italia* was assigned to the USA and *Veneto* to the UK as War Reparations. They were ordered to be scrapped and were broken up between 1948–55 (*Italia*) and 1948–51 (*Veneto*).

San Giorgio c 1960   Navarret Collection

Giuseppe Garibaldi c 1965   Navarret Collection

CRUISERS

Name	Launched	Disp (full load)	Fate
Cadorna class			
LUIGI CADORNA	30.9.31	7001t	Discarded 1.5.51
Montecuccoli class			
RAIMONDO MONTECUCCOLI (C 552)	2.8.34	8853t	Discarded 1.6.64
Duca D'Aosta class			
EMANUELE FILBERTO DUCA D'AOSTA	22.4.34	10,374t	To USSR 2.3.49
EUGENIO DI SAVOIA	16.3.35	10,672t	To Greece 1.7.51
Abruzzi class			
LUIGI DI SAVOIA DUCA DEGLI ABRUZZI (C 550)	21.4.36	11,575t	Discarded 1.4.61
GIUSEPPE GARIBALDI (C 551)	21.4.36	11,117t	Discarded Jan 72
'Capitani Romani' class			
GIULIO GERMANICO	26.7.41	5334t	Renamed *San Marco* (D 563), discarded 1971
POMPEO MAGNO	24.8.41	5334t	Renamed *San Giorgio* (D 562), discarded 1980
SCIPIONE AFRICANO	12.1.41	5334t	To France 15.8.48
ATTILIO REGOLO	28.8.40	5334t	To France 15.8.48

Cadorna class
Cadorna was employed for a short period as a training ship, but was laid up in reserve before 1950.

Montecuccoli class
When she was converted to a cadet training ship between 1947–mid-1949, the 152mm/53 twin turret in 'B' position was removed as was the 100mm/47 twin mounting in 'Q' position. Her light AA armament became 8–40mm (4×2) and 4–20mm (4×1). She was also fitted with radar. Two boilers were removed during the refit, so that she developed 75,000shp giving a maximum speed of 29kts. She was replaced as cadet training ship by *San Giorgio*.

Duca D'Aosta class
Both these ships were transferred to foreign navies as war reparations. *Aosta* went to the USSR and was renamed *Stalingrad*. She was later renamed *Kerch* and was discarded in the late 1950s. *Savoia* was transferred to Greece and was renamed *Helle*. She was discarded in 1964.

Abruzzi class
These two ships formed the backbone of the Italian Navy during the 1950s. Both were rebuilt between 1950–53. The secondary armament was reduced to 4–100mm/47 (2×2) and the light AA guns altered to 24–40mm (4×4, 4×2). Two of the eight boilers were removed, reducing the power to 85,000shp and the maximum sea speed to 29kts. The bridge was rebuilt and American radar added. *Abruzzi* was discarded in 1961 without being rebuilt further, but *Garibaldi* (C 551) was completely reconstructed between 1957–62 in a manner similar to, but more extensive than, the US Terrier CLG conversions. She was completely gutted and her original armament removed. A new bridge and upperworks were installed together with a single trunked funnel with a prominent cowl (raised in 1963). 'A' and 'B' 152mm/55 gun turrets were replaced by two 135mm/45 twin mountings. The AA gun armament consisted of 8–76mm/62 single mountings arranged four each side of the bridge and funnel. 'X' turret was replaced by a twin Terrier Mk 10 SAM launcher, and 'Y' turret by four Polaris ICBM launching tubes (although she test-fired Polaris, she never carried them on an operational patrol). The machinery was reconditioned, and she could make 30kts on 100,000shp. She was fitted with new radar, including two SPG-51. After she recommissioned in Nov 72 she was used as the fleet flagship until replaced by *Vittorio Veneto*. When she finally re-entered service, the carrying of Polaris in surface ships had gone out of fashion, and it was intended to refit her as an ASW command ship but the money was never made available.

'Capitani Romani' class
Germanico had been scuttled on 29.8.43 before she was completed, but she was salvaged in 1947. Both she and *Magno* were rebuilt between 1951–55 with American weapons and radar. Their existing armament was replaced by 6–126mm/38 (3×2) in 'A', 'X' and 'Y' positions and 20–40mm AA. In 'B' position they had an Italian Menon triple ASW mortar. They were renamed *San Marco* and *San Giorgio* respectively and were recommissioned in 1956. In 1957 they were re-rated from cruisers to scouts and in 1958 from scouts to destroyer leaders. They then carried the number D 562 (*San Giorgio*) and D 563. *San Marco* was scrapped in this condition, but *San Giorgio* was completely rebuilt as

a cadet training ship between 1963–65. She was fitted with CODAG machinery (2 Tosi Metrovick G 6 gas turbines, each of 7500shp, and 4 Fiat-Tosi diesels each of 4000bhp) on two shafts, giving a maximum speed on diesels alone of 20kts and combined of 28kts. She had new funnels, the second being set much farther aft, and was given accommodation for 130 cadets. 'X' position 127mm/38 mount was replaced by a single 76mm/62 and two more single 76mm/62 were fitted amidships, all the 40mm being removed. Two triple 324mm TT were also added. Her current radar fit consists of an SPS-6 and SPQ-2, a Mk 25 and three Orion 3s. She has an SQS-11 sonar. *San Giorgio* was replaced by the refitted *Caio Duilio* in 1980 and will be deleted.

Africano and *Regolo* were transferred to France as war reparations and were renamed *Guichen* and *Châteaurenault* respectively. They were discarded in 1961 and 1962 respectively.

DESTROYERS

Name	Launched	Disp (full load)	Fate
'Navigatori' class			
NICOLOSO DA RECCO	5.1.30	2580t	Discarded 15.7.54
Maestrale class			
GRECALE (D 552)	17.6.34	2207t	Discarded 31.5.64
Oriani class			
ALFREDO ORIANI	30.7.36	2254t	To France 8.8.48
'Soldati' class (1st group)			
ARTIGLIERE (ex-*Camicia Nera*)	8.8.37	2250t	To USSR 21.2.49
CARABINIERE (D 551)	23.7.38	2250t	Discarded 18.1.65
FUCILIERE	31.7.38	2250t	To USSR 17.1.50
GRANATIERE (D 550)	24.4.38	2250t	Discarded 1.7.58
(2nd group)			
LEGIONARIO	16.4.41	2500t	To France 15.8.48
MITRAGLIERE	28.9.41	2500t	To France 15.7.48
VELITE	31.8.41	2500t	To France 24.7.48

'Navigatori' class
By 1950 *Recco's* best sea speed was 28kts. She was scrapped without being rebuilt.

Maestrale class
In 1949 *Grecale* was fitted with a British destroyer-type bridge and a lattice mast, and was given new radars. She had a light AA armament of 3–37mm guns. She was converted to a fast ASW escort in 1952–53. Her TT were removed and her light AA guns were replaced by 6–40mm. She was re-rated as a frigate on 10.4.57. In 1959–60 she was rebuilt as a command ship. All her armament except for 2–40mm was landed and she was given a CIC and extensive communications equipment and extra accommodation to enable her to act as the fleet flagship until *Garibaldi* re-entered service.

Oriani class
Oriani was transferred to France as war reparations and was renamed *D'Estaing*. She was discarded in 1954.

'Soldati' class (1st group)
Artigliere and *Fuciliere* were transferred to the USSR as war reparations as *Z 12* and *Z 20* respectively. They were discarded in the late 1950s.
Carabiniere and *Granatiere* (D 551 and D 552 respectively) were rebuilt as fast ASW escorts in 1953–54. Their TT were removed and their light AA armament was replaced by 6–40mm. They were subsequently re-rated as frigates. *Carabiniere* was used as a trials ship for the Menon ASW mortar and was later used to test new Italian naval weapons. She was again re-rated as an auxiliary experimental ship (A 5314) after 1960.

(2nd group)
Legionario, *Mitragliere* and *Velite* were transferred to France as war reparations and renamed *Duchaffault*, *Jurien de la Gravière* and *Duperré* respectively. They were discarded in 1954, 1956 and 1961 respectively.

TORPEDO-BOATS

Name	Launched	Disp (full load)	Fate
Pilo class			
GIUSEPPE CESARE ABBA	25.5.15	885t	Discarded 1.9.58
ANTONIO MOSTO	20.5.15	885t	Discarded 15.12.58
ROSOLINO PILO	24.3.15	885t	Discarded 1.10.54
La Masa class			
GIACINTO CARINI	7.11.17	837t	Discarded 31.12.58
NICOLA FABRIZI	8.7.18	837t	Discarded 1.2.57
Curtatone class			
MONZAMBANO	6.8.23	925t	Discarded 1.2.57
Spica class			
CASSIOPEA (F 553)	22.11.36	995t	Discarded 31.10.59
SAGITTARIO (F 557)	21.6.36	985t	Discarded 1.7.64

Name	Launched	Disp (full load)	Fate
SIRIO (S 554)	14.11.35	985t	Discarded 31.10.59
ARETUSA (F 556)	6.2.38	1030t	Discarded 1.8.58
CALLIOPE (F 551)	16.4.38	1030t	Discarded 1.8.58
CLIO (F 555)	3.4.38	1030t	Discarded 31.10.59
LIBRA (F 552)	3.10.38	1030t	Discarded 1.4.64
Pegaso class			
ORIONE (F 554)	21.4.37	1575t	Discarded 1.1.65
ORSA (F 558)	21.3.37	1575t	Discarded 1.7.64
Ciclone class			
ALISEO	20.9.42	1625t	To Yugoslavia 3.5.49
ANIMOSO	15.4.42	1625t	To USSR 16.3.49
ARDIMENTOSO	27.6.42		To USSR 28.2.49
FORTUNALE	18.4.42	1625t	To USSR 1.3.49
INDOMITO	6.7.43	1625t	To Yugoslavia 28.4.49
Ariete class			
ARIETE	6.3.43	1110t	To Yugoslavia 30.4.49
BALESTRA	4.10.47	1110t	To Yugoslavia 1948

Pilo class
These ships were built as destroyers but reclassified as torpedo-boats on 1.10.29. *Pilo* was scrapped without having been modified, but *Abba* and *Mosto* were converted to fast minesweepers in 1953–54. Their armament was altered to 1–102mm and 2/4–20mm AA guns, and they were given radar.

La Masa class
They were reclassified from destroyers to torpedo-boats on 1.10.29. Both were converted to fast minesweepers in 1952–54. *Carini* was armed with 2–102mm (2×1) and 2–20mm, *Fabrizi* had only 1–102mm. Both were fitted with radar. *Fabrizi* was scrapped after being discarded but *Carini* was used as a training hulk, and renumbered GM 517.

Curtatone class
Monzambano was scrapped without having been rebuilt.

Spica class
(*Climene* group) *Cassiopea* was modernised as a fast corvette in 1950–52. Her TT were removed, and a Hedgehog added. (*Perseo* group) *Sirio* was rebuilt as a fast corvette in 1951–52. Her TT were removed, a Hedgehog added and only one 100mm/47. By 1958 the 100mm/47 had been replaced by 2–40mm (2×1). *Sagittario* was converted to an armament trials ship (F 557) in 1952–53, and was equipped with a variety of weapons. (*Alcione* group) *Aretusa* and *Calliope* were converted to fast corvettes in 1952–53, *Clio* in 1951–52 and *Libra* in 1950–52. Their TT and one 100mm/47 gun were removed and a Hedgehog and new radar were fitted. By 1958 the remaining 100mm/47 had been replaced by 2–40mm (2×1).

Pegaso class
Orione was rebuilt as a fast corvette in 1953–54 and *Orsa* in 1954–55. As with the other conversions, a Hedgehog and new radar was fitted and the aft 100mm/47 gun and the TT were removed. In about 1958 the other 100mm/47 gun was also removed.

Ciclone class
Aliseo and *Indomito* were transferred to Yugoslavia as war reparations and renamed *Biokovo* and *Triglav* respectively. *Animoso*, *Ardimentoso* and *Fortunale* were transferred as war reparations to the USSR as *Z 16*, *Z 19* and *Z 17* respectively.

Ariete class
Ariete was transferred to Yugoslavia as war reparations and renamed *Durmitor*. *Balestra* was captured by the Germans on her slip and renamed *TA 47*. She was taken over and completed by the Yugoslavs and renamed *Ucka*. Their sister *Fionda* was also captured by the Germans on her slip (and renamed *TA 46*). She was taken over by the Yugoslavs, but although they renamed her *Valebit* and started to complete her, she had been very badly damaged by the Germans at the retreat and proved to be not worth completing.

SUBMARINES

Name	Launched	Disp (surface)	Fate
'H' class			
H 1	16.10.16	355t	Discarded 23.3.47
H 2	19.10.16	355t	Discarded 23.3.47
H 4	17.4.17	355t	Discarded 23.3.47
Glauco class			
OTARIA (ex-*Espadarte*)	20.3.35	1054t	Discarded 1.2.48

Name	Launched	Disp (surface)	Fate
Foca class			
ATROPO	20.11.38	1305t	Discarded 23.3.47
ZOEA	5.12.37	1305t	Discarded 23.3.47
Marcello class			
DANDOLO	20.11.37	1043t	Discarded 23.3.47
Brin class			
BRIN	3.4.38	1000t	Discarded 1.2.48
Cagni class			
AMMIRAGLIO CAGNI	20.7.40	1653t	Discarded 1.2.48
Romolo class			
R 3	7.9.46	2155t	BU *c*1947
R 4	30.9.46	2155t	BU *c*1947
R 7	21.10.43	2155t	BU *c*1947
R 8	28.12.43	2155t	BU *c*1947
R 9	27.2.44	2155t	BU *c*1947
R 10	12.7.44	2155t	BU *c*1947
R 11	6.8.44	2155t	Discarded 1947
R 12	29.9.44	2155t	Discarded 1947
Mameli class			
GIOVANNI DA PROCIDA	1.4.28	810t	Discarded 1.2.48
GOFFREDO MAMELI (ex-*Masaniello*)	9.12.26	810t	Discarded 1.2.48
TITO SPERI	25.5.28	810t	Discarded 1.2.48
Pisani class			
VETTOR PISANI	24.11.27	866t	Discarded 23.3.47
Bandiera class			
FRATELLI BANDIERA	7.2.29	925t	Discarded 1.2.48
LUCIANO MANARA	5.10.29	925t	Discarded 1.2.48
CIRO MENOTTI	29.12.29	925t	Discarded 1.2.48
Squalo class			
SQUALO	15.1.30	920t	Discarded 1.2.48
Bragadin class			
MARCANTONIO BRAGADIN	21.7.29	965t	Discarded 1.2.48
FILIPPO CORRIDONI	30.3.30	965t	Discarded 1.2.49
Settembrini class			
RUGGIERO SETTIMO	29.3.31	938t	Discarded 23.3.47
Argonauta class			
JALEA	15.6.32	650t	Discarded 1.2.48
Sirena class			
GALATEA	5.10.33	680t	Discarded 1.2.48
Perla class			
DIASPRO	5.7.36	680t	Discarded 1.2.48
ONICE	15.6.36	680t	Discarded 23.3.47
PERLA	3.5.36	680t	Captured 9.7.42, became Greek *Matrozos*
TURCHESE	19.7.36	680t	Discarded 1.2.48
Adua class			
ALAGI	15.11.36	680t	Discarded 23.5.47
Acciaio class			
BRONZO	28.9.41	697t	Captured 12.7.43, became French *Narval*
GIADA (ex-*PV 2*, ex-*Giada*) (S 501)	10.7.41	697t	Discarded 1.1.66
NICHELIO	12.4.42	697t	To USSR 7.2.49
PLATINO	1.6.41	697t	Discarded 1.2.48
Flutto class (Type I)			
MAREA	10.12.42	930t	To USSR Feb 49
NAUTILO	12.4.42	930t	Became Yugoslav *Sava*
VORTICE (ex-*PV 1*, ex-*Vortice*) (S 502)	23.2.43	930t	Discarded 1.8.67
(Type II)			
PIETRO CALVI (ex-*UIT 7*, ex-*Bario*) (S 503)	23.1.44	913t	Discarded Jan 72
CM class			
CM 1	5.9.43	90t	Discarded 1.2.48
CM 2	Apr 45	90t	Museum exhibit 1951
CB class			
CB 8	1.8.43	42t	BU 1948
CB 9	1.8.43	42t	BU 1948
CB 10	1.8.43	42t	BU 1948
CB 11	24.8.43	42t	BU 1948
CB 12	24.8.43	42t	BU 1948
CB 19	1943	42t	BU 1947
CB 20	1943	42t	To Yugoslavia ?
CB 22	1943	42t	Museum exhibit 1951

Pietro Calvi 1962

By 1947 most Italian submarines were in poor condition or totally obsolete or both, and these boats were discarded in March 1947. The Peace Treaty prohibited Italy from building or commissioning any submarines, so almost all the remainder were disposed of in February 1948. Only the USSR took submarines as war reparations, the *Acciaio* class boat *Nichelio* being transferred as the *Z 14*, and the *Flutto* class *Marea* as the *Z 13*. *Nautilo* of the same class was salvaged by the Yugoslavs and renamed *Sava*.

No *Romolo* class submarines saw service in the postwar Italian Navy, but the two incomplete boats R 11 and R 12, which had been scuttled in 1945, were salvaged in 1946 and used as oil hulks for more than 20 years. Two small submarines, *CM 2* and *CB 22*, became permanent museum exhibits in 1951.

Only two Italian submarines remained in service, the *Acciaio* class *Giada* and *Flutto* class *Vortice* (S 502). These were used as training boats, but evaded the terms of the Peace Treaty by being classed as battery-chargers with their names changed to *PV 2* and *PV 1* respectively. The 'no submarines' clause expired in 1952, and they were returned to the navy list on 1.3.51 (*Giada*) and 1.1.52 (*Vortice*), resuming their original names. Between 1951–53 both were rebuilt as training boats with no gun and a streamlined fin.

The incomplete *Bario* of the *Flutto* (Type II) class, which had been scuttled in 1945, was salvaged in the same year. She was rebuilt between 1957–61, being relaunched on 21.6.59, and she entered service on 16.12.61. She differed very considerably from her half-sister *Vortice*, having a new teardrop bow and stern, with only one shaft. As rebuilt her data was:

Displacement: 905t/1107t
Dimensions: 216ft 6in oa ×23ft ×13ft 3in (*66.0m × 7.0m × 4.0m*)
Machinery: 1-shaft, 2 MAN diesels plus 3 electric motors, 2700bhp/?shp = 14kts/14kts
Armament: 4–533mm TT (4×1)
Complement: 60

She was renamed *Pietro Calvi* (S 503) in March 1961, and was effectively a new submarine with a greatly improved underwater performance.

COLONIAL SLOOP

Name	Launched	Disp (full load)	Fate
ERITREA	28.9.36	3068t	To France 12.2.48

She was transferred to France as war reparations and renamed *Francis Garnier*. She was discarded in 1960.

CORVETTES

Name	Launched	Disp (full load)	Fate
Gabbiano class			
APE (F 567)	22.11.42	660t	Discarded 1965
BAIONETTA (ex-*Partigiana*) (F 578)	5.10.42	660t	Discarded Jan 72
BOMBARDA (ex-*UJ 206*, ex-*Bombarda*) (F 549)	31.8.42	660t	Discarded 1976–77
CHIMERA (F 569)	30.1.43	660t	Discarded 1976–77
CORMORANO (F 575)	20.9.42	660t	Discarded Jan 72
CRISALIDE (F 547)	8.12.47	660t	Discarded Jan 72
DANAIDE (F 563)	21.10.42	660t	Discarded 1968
DRIADE (F 568)	7.10.42	660t	Discarded 1966
FARFALLA (F 548)	4.1.48	660t	Discarded Jan 72
FENICE (F 577)	1.3.43	660t	Discarded 1.10.65
FLORA (F 572)	1.12.42	660t	Discarded *c*1970
FOLAGA (F 576)	14.11.42	660t	Discarded 1965
GABBIANO (F 571)	23.6.42	660t	Discarded Jan 72
GRU (F 566)	23.12.42	660t	Discarded *c*1970
IBIS (F 561)	12.12.42	660t	Discarded Jan 72
MINERVA (F 562)	5.11.42	660t	Discarded *c*1970
PELLICANO (F 574)	12.2.43	660t	Discarded *c*1970
POMONA (F 573)	18.11.42	660t	Discarded 1965
SCIMITARRA (F 564)	16.9.42	660t	Discarded Jan 72
SFINGE (F 579)	9.1.43	660t	Discarded 1976–77
SIBILLA (F 565)	10.3.43	660t	Discarded Jan 72
URANIA (F 570)	21.4.43	660t	Discarded Jan 72
Algerine class			
ALABARDA (ex-*Eritrea*, ex-*Ammiraglio Magnahi*, ex-*Larne*) (F 560)	2.9.43	1252t	Discarded 1965

The *Gabbiano* class were numerically the largest Italian ship class to survive the war. Three, *Bombarda*, *Crisalide* and *Farfalla*, were scuttled incomplete by the Germans in April 1945 and completed postwar. All were fitted with a new navigation bridge, and all were rearmed with 2–, 3– or 4–40mm. Eight were used as training ships and also had 2–450mm TT (2×1). All except *Cormorano* had a Hedgehog ASW mortar. Some also retained 1–100mm gun. *Ape* was later converted to a commando and frogmen transport, and the other members of the class that lasted into the 1970s were used to carry targets.

The ex-British *Algerine* class ocean minesweeper was acquired by Italy in 1946 as the *Ammiraglio Magnahi*, and was rated as a colonial sloop. She was later re-rated as a corvette, then as a frigate and finally as a coastal escort vessel. She was renamed *Eritrea* in 1948 and *Alabarda* in 1951. In Italian service she was armed with 1–100mm/47 and 4–37mm, but in 1957 she was rearmed with 4–40mm. After 1957 she was used as a support ship for MTBs.

GUNBOAT

Name	Launched	Disp (full load)	Fate
Bafile class			
ERNESTO GIOVANNINI	11.3.22	206t	Discarded 1.12.50

Designed as a small minelayer but used as patrol boat

MINESWEEPERS

Name	Fate	Name	Fate
'RD 6' type: launched 1916, 193t			
RD 6	To Yugoslavia 19.8.47		
'RD 16' type: launched 1917–18, 197–198t			
RD 16	To Yugoslavia 25.8.48	RD 27	To Yugoslavia 27.8.48
RD 21	To Yugoslavia 25.8.48	RD 28	To Yugoslavia 14.9.48
RD 25	To Yugoslavia 1948	RD 29	To Yugoslavia 14.9.48
'RD 32' type: launched 1919, 179t			
RD 32	Discarded 30.6.56	RD 34	Discarded 30.6.56
'RD 40' type: launched 1919, 200t			
RD 40	Discarded 15.4.56	RD 41	Discarded 1.1.53
Azalea class: launched 1942–43, 215t			
AZALEA (ex-*BYMS 2142*, ex-*YMS 142*)	Discarded 1966	MAGNOLIA (ex-*BYMS 2206*, ex-*USS 206*)	Discarded 1966
BEGONIA (ex-*BYMS 2173*, ex-*YMS 173*)	to Customs Apr 1966	ORCHIDA (ex-*BYMS 2137*, ex-*YMS 137*)	Discarded 1966
DALIA (ex-*BYMS 2141*, ex-*YMS 141*)	to Customs Apr 66	PRIMULA (ex-*BYMS 2278*, ex-*YMS 278*)	Discarded 1966
FIORDALISO (ex-*BYMS 2277*, ex-*YMS 277*)	Discarded 1966	TULIPANO (ex-*BYMS 2194*, ex-*YMS 194*)	Discarded 1966
GARDANIA (ex-*BYMS 2150*, ex-*YMS 150*)	Discarded 1966	VERBENA (ex-*BYMS 2280*, ex-*YMS 280*)	Discarded 1966
GLADIOLO (ex-*BYMS ?* ex-*YMS ?*)	Discarded 1966		
Anemone class: launched 1942, 207t			
ANEMONE (ex-*BYMS 2009*, ex-*YMS 9*)	Discarded 1966	MUGHETTO (ex-*BYMS 2023*, ex-*YMS 23*)	Discarded 1966
BIANCOSPINO (ex-*BYMS 2012*, ex-*YMS 12*)	Discarded 1966	NARCISCO (ex-*BYMS 2024*, ex-*YMS 24*)	Discarded 1966
GERANIO (ex-*BYMS 2014*, ex-*YMS 14*)	Discarded 1966	OLEANDRO (ex-*BYMS 2027*, ex-*YMS 27*)	Discarded 1966
Dance class: launched 1940–41, 530t			
DR 307 (ex-*Minuet*)	Discarded 1962	DR 312 (ex-*Gavotte*)	Discarded 1962
DR 308 (ex-*Twostep* ex-*Tarantella*)	Discarded 1962	DR 316 (ex-*Hornpipe*)	Discarded 1962
Shakespearian class: launched 1941, 545t			
DR 310 (ex-*Othello*)	Discarded 1962		

Name	Fate	Name	Fate
Isles class: launched 1940–43, 545t			
DR 301 (ex-*Burra*)	Discarded 1962	DR 309 (ex-*Grain*)	Discarded 1962
DR 302 (ex-*Cumbrae*)	Discarded 1962	DR 311 (ex-*Mousa*)	Discarded 1962
DR 303 (ex-*Unst*)	Discarded 1962	DR 313 (ex-*Foula*)	Discarded 1962
DR 304 (ex-*Staffa*)	Discarded 1962	DR 314 (ex-*Ensay*)	Discarded 1962
DR 305 (ex-*Filla*)	Discarded 1962	DR 315 (ex-*Stroma*)	Discarded 1962
DR 306 (ex-*Egilsay*)	Discarded 1962		
'DV' class: launched 1944–45, 110t			
DV 401 (ex-*DV 111*)	Discarded 1957	DV 409 (ex-*DV 116*)	Survey ship c1960
DV 402 (ex-*DV 112*)	Discarded 1959	DV 411 (ex-*DV 121*)	Discarded 1959
DV 403 (ex-*DV 113*)	Discarded 1959	DV 412 (ex-*DV 122*)	Discarded 1959
DV 404 (ex-*DV 115*)	Discarded 1959	DV 413 (ex-*DV 123*)	Discarded 1959
DV 405 (ex-*DV 131*)	Discarded 1957	DV 414 (ex-*DV 124*)	Discarded 1959
DV 406 (ex-*DV 132*)	Discarded 1957	DV 415 (ex-*DV 125*)	Discarded 1957
DV 407 (ex-*DV 134*)	Discarded 1957	DV 133	Discarded 1953
DV 408 (ex-*DV 114*)	Survey ship c1960	DV 135	Discarded 1953

The first seven went to Yugoslavia as war reparations and were renamed *ML 301–307*. The remainder served in the Italian Navy until they were scrapped.

The *Azalea* and *Anemone* class coastal minesweepers were USN YMS that had been transferred to the British Navy during the Second World War. They were acquired by the Italian Navy in Apr 47. The main difference between the two classes was that the *Azalea*s had one funnel and the *Anemone*s had two. They were allocated the pennant numbers M 5400–M 5416. Some ships of both classes had their 76mm gun replaced by a 20mm gun in 1956. The almost identical *Dance*, *Shakespearian* and *Isles* class trawlers were transferred from the British to the Italian Navy between January and March 1946. The Italians classified them as minesweepers, and gave them the pennant numbers M 5301–M 5316. In 1956 they all had their 76mm gun replaced by a 20mm, giving them an armament of 3–20mm (3×1). In 1962 they were removed from the active list and reclassified as general purpose auxiliaries. The 'DV' class coastal minesweepers were reclassified as motor patrol boats in c1955 and used for coastal patrols. Some were refitted with lattice masts, *DV 408* and *DV 409* were disarmed in c1960 and used as survey vessels. They were discarded in c1967.

LIGHT CRAFT

Name	Fate	Name	Fate
MAS 430 class: launched 1930, 14t			
MAS 433	Discarded 1.8.49	MAS 434	Discarded 1.8.49
MAS 438 class: launched 1934–35, 40t			
ME 38 (ex-*AS 25* ex-*MAS 438*)	Discarded 1.7.50	ME 41 (ex-*AS 28* ex-*MAS 441*)	Discarded 1.6.50
ME 40 (ex-*AS 27* ex-*MAS 440*)	To USSR 6.7.49		
MAS 501 class: launched 1936–37, 21.5t			
MAS 1 (ex-*MEB 1* ex-*MAS 510*)	Discarded 28.6.50	MAS 3 (ex-*MEB 3* ex-*MAS 520*)	Discarded 1.7.50
MAS 2 (ex-*MEB 2* ex-*MAS 514*)	Discarded 1.7.50	NE 109 (ex-*MAS 4* ex-*MEB 4* ex-*MAS 521*)	Discarded 1.7.50
MAS 516	To USSR 6.7.49	MAS MT 523 (ex-*MAS 523*)	Discarded 1949
MAS 519	To USSR 6.7.49	MAS 9 (ex-*MEB 9* ex-*MAS 525*)	Discarded 1950
MAS 526 class: launched 1939, 25.2t			
MAS 5 (ex-*MEB 5* ex-*MAS 538*)	Discarded 1.7.50	MAS 6 (ex-*MEB 6* ex-*MAS MT 545* ex-*MAS 545*)	Discarded 1.7.50
MAS 543	To France 26.9.49	MAS 7 (ex-*MEB 7* ex-*MAS 547*)	To Customs 1.7.50
MAS 555 class: launched 1941, 28t			
MAS 8 (ex-*MEB 8* ex-*MAS 562*)	Discarded 1.7.50		
MS First series: launched 1942, 62.4t			
MS 471 (ex-*MS 611* ex-*MV 611* ex-*MS11*)	Discarded 1.5.65	MS 473 (ex-*MS 613* ex-*MV 613* ex-*MS 31*)	Discarded 1975

Name	Fate	Name	Fate
MS 472 (ex-*MS 612* ex-*MV 612* ex-*MS 24*)	Discarded 1974	MS 35	To France 15.12.48
MS Second series: launched 1942–43, 67t			
MS 52	To USSR 18.5.49	MS 65	To USSR 6.7.49
MS 53	To USSR 18.5.49	MS 483 (ex-*MS 617* ex-*MV 617* ex-*MS 72*)	Discarded 1.3.63
MS 474 (ex-*MS 614* ex-*MV 614* ex-*MS 54*)	Discarded 1978	MS 484 (ex-*MS 618* ex-*MV 618* ex-*MS 73*)	Discarded 1.3.63
MS 481 (ex-*MS 615* ex-*MV 615* ex-*MS 55*)	Discarded 1978	MS 475 (ex-*MS 619* ex-*MV 619* ex-*MS 74*)	Discarded 1965
MS 482 (ex-*MS 616* ex-*MV 616* ex-*MS 56*)	Discarded 1.3.63	MS 75	To USSR 6.7.49
MS 61	To USSR 6.7.49		
VAS First series: launched 1942, 68t			
VAS 711 (ex-*VAS 201*)	Discarded 1953	VAS 493 (ex-*VAS 714* ex-*VAS 218*)	Discarded 1957
VAS 491 (ex-*VAS 712* ex-*VAS 204*)	Discarded 1957	VAS 715 (ex-*VAS 222*)	Discarded 1953
VAS 716 (ex-*VAS 205*)	Discarded 1953	VAS 494 (ex-*VAS 721* ex-*VAS 224*)	Discarded 1953
VAS 492 (ex-*VAS 713* ex-*VAS 211*)	Discarded 1953	? (ex-*VAS 228*)	Discarded ? 1953

Name	Fate	Name	Fate
VAS Second series: launched 1942–43, 68t			
VAS 495 (ex-*VAS 722* ex-*VAS 233*)	Discarded 1953	VAS 497 (ex-*VAS 726* ex-*RA 266* ex-*VAS 241*)	Discarded 1957
VAS 723 (ex-*VAS 235*)	Discarded 1953	VAS 245	To USSR 30.6.49
VAS 496 (ex-*VAS 724* ex-*VAS 237*)	Discarded 1957	VAS 246	Burnt out 21.8.47
VAS 725 (ex-*RA 265* ex-*VAS 240*)	Discarded 1953	VAS 248	To USSR 1949

Under the terms of the Peace Treaty the torpedo launching gear had to be removed from all Italian torpedo-boats. They were reclassified as Motovedette (MV) and rearmed with 2–6×20mm guns. All the small torpedo-boats (MAS) were either transferred to foreign navies as war reparations or discarded by the end of 1950, though many remained in use for a number of years as harbour craft. Those large torpedo-boats (MS) that were not transfered as war reparations, however, were refitted with TT in 1952–53. *MS 472* and *473* were rebuilt as convertible MTB/MGB in 1960 and *MS 474* and *481* were similarly rebuilt in 1961. They were given new machinery developing a total of 4500bhp = 33kts. As MGBs they were armed with 2–40mm (2×1) and as MTBs 1–40mm and 2–450mm TT. They could also carry mines. The VAS (anti-submarine) boats that were not transferred as war reparations were used mainly as coastal minesweepers.

MISCELLANEOUS

In 1947 the Italian Navy possessed a number of ex-Allied and ex-Axis landing craft. Of the ten ex-German (Italian-built) and four ex-Italian MFP-D class landing craft in service in 1947, nine remained in 1981. All ten ex-British LCT(3) are still in service, though three are now lighthouse tenders and seven are repair craft.

MAJOR SURFACE SHIPS

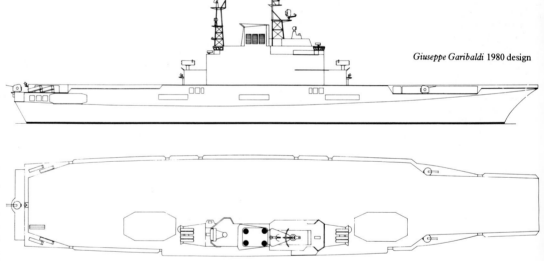

Giuseppe Garibaldi 1980 design

She was originally envisaged as a replacement for the two *Doria* class helicopter cruisers. The final arrangement was recast several times following a protracted series of design studies, and she may well be further altered before completion. She is intended to operate chiefly as part of a task force, but it is also intended that she be able to operate independently if necessary, hence the large armament. Her basic function will be to provide ASW protection for other warships and merchant convoys, but it is also intended that she carry command and control facilities for both naval and air forces (she will be equipped as a flagship) and to carry up to 600 troops for short periods.

Only 10–12 aircraft can be carried in the hangar, but she will operate up to 18 large ASW helicopters from her 570ft 5in × 68ft 11in (173.8m × 21m) flight deck. It would also be possible to operate a mix of ASW helicopters and V/STOL aircraft. *Garibaldi* has two pairs of stabilisers to make the operation of helicopters as easy as possible, and the two lifts are both well to starboard, out of the way of the flight deck. Her maintenance facilities are intended to be able to keep the smaller escorts' helicopters operational as well as her own. The hangar has a clear height of 19ft 4in (5.9m) so that it can take helicopters up to the size of the CH 47 Chinook. The Teseo launchers for Otomat Mk 2 will have 2 reloads.

The four Fiat-built GM LM 2500 gas turbines are coupled in pairs to each shaft in a COGAG arrangement. The fuel will be sufficient to give a radius of 7000nm at 20kts. *Garibaldi's* hull and island have been designed so that it will be relatively simple to fit new equipment when it has been developed, and adequate room has been left to accommodate it. This will be a great advantage if the Italians succeed in exporting the design to other navies. It is planned for *Garibaldi* to enter service in 1984 after being launched at the end of 1982, but she may well be delayed considerably by financial restraints.

GIUSEPPE GARIBALDI *aircraft carrier*

Displacement:	10,100t standard; 13,250t full load
Dimensions:	536ft 7in wl, 587ft 3in oa × 76ft 8in wl, 99ft 9in ext × 21ft 10in max
	163.5m, 179.0m × 23.4m, 30.4m × 6.7m
Machinery:	2 shafts, 4 LM 2500 gas turbines, 80,000shp = 30kts. Range 7000nm at 20kts
Armament:	6 Otomat SSM (6×1), 2 Albatros SAM (2×8), 6–40mm/70 (3×2), 6–324mm TT (2×3), 18 aircraft. See notes
Sensors:	Radar RAN-3L, RAT-31, RAN-10S, MM/SPS-702, RTN-20X; sonar SQS-23
Complement:	825

No	Name	Builder	Laid down	Launched	Comp	Fate
C 551	GIUSEPPE GARIBALDI	Italcantieri, Monfalcone	26.3.81	–	–	Building

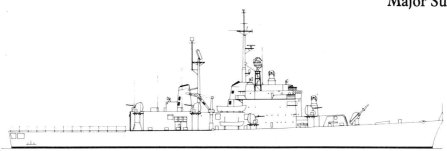

Andrea Doria 1978

Both ships were ordered under the 1957–58 new construction programme. They were designed to carry Terrier SAMs and three Sea King ASW helicopters to provide long range AA and ASW protection to task groups and convoys. An enlarged version of the *Impavido* class destroyer design was used, with a considerably increased beam to allow a hangar and a 98ft 6in × 52ft 6in (30m × 16m) flight deck to be worked in aft. In practice they proved to be too small to operate Sea Kings, so they carry four smaller ASW helicopters instead. The flight deck is cantilevered out at the extreme stern to provide more operating space, but even so both it and the hangar are extremely cramped. They were designed for service in the Mediterranean, where their relatively low freeboard is relatively unimportant, but in service they have proved to be too small to operate helicopters in all weathers. Despite stabilisers, the hull moves too much, and in any case experience with them showed that a greater number of helicopters need to be carried by one ship to make a truly effective ASW screen.

The *Doria* class introduced the Italian practice of surrounding the superstructure with single 3in (76mm)/62 AA guns to provide an adequate AA protection on all sides. *Duilio* was modernised between 1976–78 with new electronics and Standard SM-1ER SAMs (40 missiles) in place of the Terriers. *Doria* was similarly modernised between 1979–80 except that a new tactical data system (SADOC) was fitted along with Otomat SSMs and an Albatros SAM system. *Duilio* was refitted 1979–80 as a midshipmen's training ship to replace *San Giorgio* and now carries 6–76mm guns. Both are due to be replaced by *Garibaldi* in the mid–1980s.

DORIA class *helicopter cruisers*

Displacement:	5000t standard; 6500t full load
Dimensions:	472ft 7in pp, 489ft 9in oa × 56ft 5in × 16ft 5in
	144.0m, 149.3m × 17.3m × 5.0m
Machinery:	2-shaft geared steam turbines, 4 Foster Wheeler boilers, 60,000shp = 30kts. Range 5000nm at 17kts
Armament:	1 Terrier SAM (1×2), 8–76mm/62 (8×1), 6–324mm TT (2×3), 4 helicopters. See notes
Sensors:	Radar SPS-40, SPS-52 (*Doria* SPS-76B), SPQ-2, SPG-55C (*Duilio* SPG-55A), RTN-10X; sonar SQS-23 (*Duilio* SQS-39)
Complement:	485

No	Name	Builder	Laid down	Launched	Comp	Fate
C 553	ANDREA DORIA	CNR, Riva Trigoso	11.5.58	27.2.63	23.2.64	Extant 1982
C 554	CAIO DUILIO	Castellammare	16.5.58	22.12.62	30.11.64	Extant 1982

Caio Duilio as completed   Navarret Collection

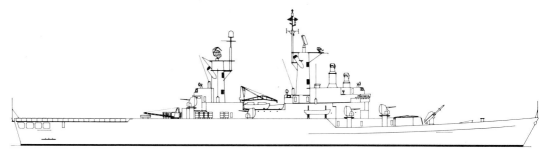

Vittorio Veneto 1974

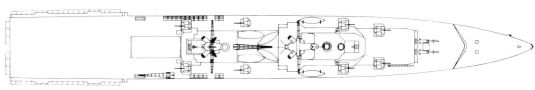

A third *Doria* was planned, but by the time *Veneto* was ordered it had already been realised that the *Doria*s were too small, so after the design had been altered several times the resulting ship was half as large again. This allowed a raised flight deck to be fitted aft with a hangar underneath. The 131ft 3in × 60ft 8in (40.0m × 18.5m) flight deck can operate up to nine A/B 204 or 212 ASW helicopters, or six of the larger SH-3Ds. The extra space forward allowed a Mk 20 Aster SAM/ASW launcher to be mounted in place of the

VITTORIO VENETO *helicopter cruiser*

Displacement:	7500t standard; 8850t full load
Dimensions:	560ft pp, 589ft 3in oa × 63ft 7in × 19ft 9in
	170.6m, 179.6m × 19.4m × 6.0m
Machinery:	2-shaft geared steam turbines, 4 Foster Wheeler boilers, 73,000shp = 30.5kts. Range 5000nm at 17kts
Armament:	1 Terrier/ASROC SAM/ASW (1×2), 8–76mm/62 (8×1), 6–324mm TT (2×3), 9 helicopters. See notes
Sensors:	Radar SPS-40, SPS-52, SPQ-2B, SPG-55B, RTN-10X; sonar SQS-23
Complement:	550

No	Name	Builder	Laid down	Launched	Comp	Fate
C 550	VITTORIO VENETO	Castellammare	10.6.65	5.2.67	12.7.69	Extant 1982

Doria's Mk 10 SAM launcher. This meant that *Veneto* could fire ASROC ASMs as well as Terrier SAMs (a total of 40–60 missiles), giving the ship itself a long-range ASW armament. *Veneto* is now being refitted (during 1981–83) with ER Standard SAMs, 4 Teseo launchers for Otomat SSMs and two Dardo systems with 3–40mm/70 Breda guns. She retains the *Doria*s' lozenge arrangement for the 3in (76mm)/62 AA guns, but has 'Macks' in place of separate masts and funnels to give even more room compared with the earlier ships.

Veneto has two sets of stabilisers, and is much more effective as an ASW

helicopter carrier than the *Doria*s. Even so, her ability to operate and maintain a large enough number of helicopters to create an adequate ASW screen as well as maintain the helicopters of the rest of the task force is not so great as it should be. A still larger ship is really needed, and this is the genesis of the *Garibaldi*. In addition, *Veneto*, like all other ships with a flight deck aft, cannot operate STOVL aircraft, which need an uninterrupted flight deck for their takeoff run. *Veneto* took over from the previous *Garibaldi* as fleet flagship, and will hand over this function to the new *Garibaldi* when she is commissioned.

Vittorio Veneto as completed   Navarret Collection

Artigliere was the ex-USN *Benson* class destroyer USS *Woodworth* and *Aviere* was the ex-USN *Gleaves* class destroyer USS *Nicholson*. *Aviere* could be distinguished from her half-sister by having round funnels, a higher bridge and no shield on 'X' 5in (127mm) gun mounting. Both were transferred to the Italian Navy under MDAP on 11.6.51. They had their 5–21in (533mm) TT (1×5) removed. When they were replaced by the ex-*Fletcher* class *Fante* and *Geniere*, *Artigliere* was discarded straight away, but *Aviere*

(For illustration see under United States in 1922–46 volume)

Ex-US BENSON/GLEAVES class *destroyers*

Particulars: As US *Benson/Gleaves* class

No	Name	Builder	Acquired	Fate
D 553 ARTIGLIERE (ex-*Woodworth*)		Bethlehem	11.6.51	Discarded 1971
D 554 AVIERE (ex-*Nicholson*)		Boston NY	11.6.51	Sunk as target 1975

was converted to an experimental ship in 1970. She was first used to develop the OTO Melara lightweight

127mm/54 (5in; mounted in 'B' position) and 76mm/62 (3in in 'X' position), and then the Albatros SAM.

(For illustration see under United States in 1922–46 volume)

The two ex-USN *Fletcher* class destroyers were transferred to Italy on 2.7.69 (*Fante*) and on 7.1.70 (*Geniere*). Originally built in 1943, both had been modernised in the early 1960s with an improved ASW armament and electronics. They filled in the gap between the phasing out of *Artigliere* and *Aviere* and the introduction of the new Italian-built *Audace* class.

Ex-US FLETCHER class *destroyers*

Particulars: As US *Fletcher* class

No	Name	Builder	Acquired	Fate
D 561 FANTE (ex-*Walker*)		Bath Iron Wks	2.7.64	Discarded 1977
D 555 GENIERE (ex-*Pritchett*)		Tacoma	7.1.70	Discarded 1975

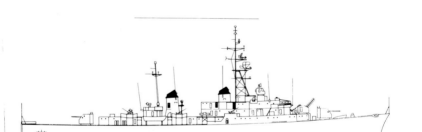

Impetuoso c 1978

These two ships were ordered in Feb 50, and were the first postwar Italian destroyers. They combined a smaller version of the 'Capitani Romani' cruiser hull with American weapons and equipment, and concentrated on AA and ASW armament. The result was two large and powerful destroyers, admirably fitted to the needs of the Italian Navy. In the early 1960s consideration was given to a large-scale reconstruction giving them a single Tartar SAM launcher aft as in the *Impavido*s, but this was rejected in favour of a minor updating in the

IMPETUOSO class *destroyers*

Displacement:	2775t standard; 3810t full load
Dimensions:	405ft pp, 418ft 9in oa × 43ft 2in × 14ft 9in
	123.4m, 127.6m × 13.2m × 4.5m
Machinery:	2-shaft geared steam turbines, 4 Foster Wheeler boilers, 65,000shp = 34kts. Range 3000nm at 16kts
Armament:	4–5in (127mm)/38 (2×2), 16–40mm/56 (2×4, 4×2) 1 triple ASW mortar, 6-324mm TT
Sensors:	Radar SPS-6, SPQ-2, SPG-34, Mk 25; sonar SQS-11
Complement:	315

No	Name	Builder	Laid down	Launched	Comp	Fate
D 558	IMPETUOSO	CNR, Riva Trigoso	7.5.52	16.9.56	25.1.58	Extant 1982
D 559	INDOMITO	Ansaldo	24.4.52	9.8.55	23.2.58	Extant 1982

mid-1970s, with modernised electronics and Mk 32 12.75in (324mm) ASW TT in place of 2–21in (533mm) fixed ASW TT. The *Impetuoso*s are now obsolescent and urgently need to be replaced, but the extra two *Audace* class that were to have done this have not yet been built, so the *Impetuoso*s will remain in service until the mid-1980s. *Impetuoso* can be distinguished from *Indomito* by her longer forward superstructure. She is now used mainly for training, and *Indomito* went into reserve in November 1981.

Impetuoso c 1975   Navarret Collection

Impavido 1976

The *Impavido*s are slightly enlarged *Impetuoso*s with a single Tartar SAM launcher aft in place of the twin 5in (127mm)/38, and a more modern AA gun armament. Somewhat surprisingly they retain the obsolescent 5in (127mm)/38 twin mount forward. *Impavido* was ordered in 1957 and *Intrepido* in 1959. They were modernised in the mid-1970s (*Intrepido* in 1974–75 and *Impavido* in 1976–77 with a new fire control and ESM and SM-1 Standard missiles (about 40) for the Mk 13 SAM launcher in place of Tartar. This gives them some SSM capability, but they may also be fitted with Otomat SSMs. There is a helicopter pad right aft, and they are fitted with stabilisers, but they do not have a hangar.

IMPAVIDO class *destroyers*

Displacement:	3201t standard; 3990t full load
Dimensions:	430ft 11in oa × 44ft 9in × 14ft 6in
	131.3m × 13.7m × 4.4m
Machinery:	2-shaft geared steam turbines, 4 Foster Wheeler boilers, 70,000shp = 33kts. Range 3300nm/1500nm at 20kts/30kts
Armament:	1 Tartar SAM, 2–5in (127mm)/38 (1×2), 4–76mm/62 (4×1), 6–324mm TT (2×3)
Sensors:	Radar SPS-12, SPS-52, SPQ-2, SPG-51, RTN-10X; sonar SQS-23
Complement:	340

No	Name	Builder	Laid down	Launched	Comp	Fate
D 570	IMPAVIDO	CNR, Riva Trigosa	10.6.57	25.5.62	16.11.63	Extant 1982
D 571	INTREPIDO	Ansaldo	16.5.59	21.10.62	28.7.64	Extant 1982

Impavido 1970   Navarret Collection

The *Audace* class used an enlarged version of the *Impavido*s' hull, with increased freeboard, but they have a vastly improved armament. There is a very well arranged gun and missile armament giving all-round medium and short-range AA protection, and there is a large hangar and flight deck aft capable of operating and maintaining two A/B 212 or one SH-3D ASW helicopters. By using modern lightweight weapons systems and mounting the Mk 13 SAM launcher above the hangar *Audace* improves over the abilities of the 10 year older *Andrea Doria* in almost every respect except numbers of helicopters carried on a consequently smaller hull. *Audace* and *Ardito* will soon be fitted with Otomat to give them full SSM capability. At present they have to rely on the

AUDACE class *destroyers*

Displacement:	3600t standard; 4400t full load
Dimensions:	448ft 3in oa × 47ft 3in × 15ft 1in
	136.6m × 14.4m × 4.6m
Machinery:	2-shaft geared steam turbines, 4 Foster Wheeler boilers, 73,000shp = 33kts. Range 3000nm at 20kts
Armament:	1 Tartar SAM, 2–127mm/54 (2×1), 4–76mm/62 (4×1), 4–533mm TT (4×1), 6–324mm TT (2×3), 2 helicopters
Sensors:	Radar SPS-12, SPS-52, SPQ-2, SPG-51B, RTN-10X; sonar CWE-610
Complement:	380

No	Name	Builder	Laid down	Launched	Comp	Fate
D 551	AUDACE	CNR, Riva Trigosa	27.4.68	2.10.71	16.11.72	Extant 1982
D 550	ARDITO	Castellammare	19.7.68	27.11.71	5.12.72	Extant 1982

SM-1 Standard's secondary SSM function. About 40 missiles are carried. The four TT for the long-range 21in (533mm) wire-guided TT are at the stern. This class have excellent habitability and seaworthiness, and is a very effective design, but the use of steam turbines in these modern vessels is surprising. Two improved *Audace*s with gas turbines and diesels were to have been built to replace the *Impetuoso* class destroyers, but laying down has been postponed until 1982 because of shortage of money.

Ardito 1977   C & S Taylor

(For illustration see under United States in 1922–46 volume)

Originally built in 1943, all three were transferred from the USN to the Italian Navy in 1951. In 1956, they were rebuilt with a pentapod foremast in place of the former pole mast. *Altair* was blown up as a target in 1971.

Ex-US CANNON class *frigates*

Particulars:	As US *Cannon* class (DET type)			

No	Name	Builder	Acquired	Fate
F 590	ALDEBARAN (ex-*Thornhill*)	Federal, Newark	10.1.51	Discarded 1976
F 591	ALTAIR (ex-*Gandy*)	Tampa	10.1.51	Discarded 1971
F 592	ANDROMEDA (ex-*Wesson*)	Federal, Newark	10.1.51	Discarded 1970

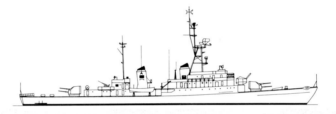

Castore 1961

CANOPO class *frigates*

Displacement:	1807t standard; 2250t full load
Dimensions:	306ft 3in pp, 338ft 4in oa × 39ft 4in × 12ft 6in
	93.3m, 103.1m × 12m × 3.8m
Machinery:	2-shaft geared steam turbines, 2 Foster Wheeler boilers, 22,000shp = 26kts. Range 3000nm at 20kts
Armament:	3–76mm/62 (3×1), 1 Menon ASW mortar (1×3), 6–324mm TT (2×3). See notes
Sensors:	Radar SPS-6, SPQ-2, RTN-10; sonar SQS-11
Complement:	207

These were designed as escort destroyers rather than as frigates, and they use a reduced version of the *Impetuoso* class hull. They utilized a large amount of American equipment, and *Castore* and *Cigno* were built under MDAP. When they first went into service they were armed with 4–3in (76mm)/62 (2×2) in 'A' and 'Y' positions, 4–40mm/70 (2×2) on each side of 'X' position, 1 ASW mortar (1×3) in 'B' position and 2–21in (533mm) fixed TT (2×1). The 3in (76mm) mountings were of unusual design, with one barrel above rather than alongside the other. *Castore* was rebuilt between 1966–67 with a single 3in (76mm) replacing the twin mountings and the 40mm, and with new electronics and Mk 32 ASW TT. The remaining ships were rebuilt subsequently. All four will be replaced by

No	Name	Builder	Laid down	Launched	Comp	Fate
F 531	CANOPO	CNT	15.5.52	20.2.55	1.4.59	Stricken 1981
F 533	CASTORE	CNT	14.3.55	8.7.56	14.7.57	Decommissioned 30.11.80; stricken
F 554	CENTAURO	Ansaldo	31.5.52	4.4.54	5.5.57	Extant 1982
F 555	CIGNO	CNT	10.2.54	20.3.55	7.3.57	Extant 1982

Maestrale class frigates as they come into service; the remaining two are expected to decommission in 1982–83.

Luigi Rizzo 1962

BERGAMINI class *frigates*

Displacement:	1410t standard; 1650t full load
Dimensions:	283ft 11in pp, 308ft 4in oa × 37ft 3in × 10ft 2in
	86.5m, 94.0m × 11.4m × 3.1m
Machinery:	2 shafts, 4 diesels, 16,000bhp = 25kts. Range 3000nm at 18kts
Armament:	2–76mm/62 (2×1), 1 Menon ASW mortar, 6–324mm TT (2×3), 1 helicopter. See notes
Sensors:	Radar SPS-12, SPQ-2, RTN-10; sonar SQS-40
Complement:	163

The *Bergamini*s were designed to be the smallest-sized ship capable of operating an ASW helicopter. As originally built, too much was attempted on too small a displacement, and they were a disappointment. Their original armament consisted of 3–3in (76mm)/62 in 'A', 'B' and 'Y' positions, with a helicopter platform and telescopic hangar for an Augusta/Bell A/B 47 helicopter at the aft end of the superstructure. The funnel was incorporated in the mast, and the ASW mortar was behind 'B' gun mounting. Despite stabilisers, both the helicopter and the pad were too small to allow useful work to be done,

No	Name	Builder	Laid down	Launched	Comp	Fate
F 593	CARLO BERGAMINI	CRDA	19.7.59	16.6.60	23.6.62	Stricken 1981
F 594	VIRGILIO FASAN	Castellammare	6.3.60	9.10.60	10.10.62	Extant 1982
F 595	CARLO MARGOTTINI	Castellammare	26.5.57	12.6.60	5.5.62	Extant 1982
F 596	LUIGI RIZZO	Castellammare	26.5.57	6.3.60	15.12.61	Stricken 30.11.80

so 'Y' mounting was replaced by a greatly expanded pad, and the telescopic hangar was enlarged to take an Augusta/Bell A/B 204 ASW helicopter. *Margotti* was modified in 1968, *Fasan* in 1969, *Bergamini* in 1970 and *Rizzo* in 1971. The A/B 204 has since been replaced by an A/B 212. As rebuilt they are much more efficient as ASW escorts, but they have no AA or surface fire astern.

The *Bergamini*s' hull is a smaller variant of the *Canopo*s', but the *Bergamini*s have high-speed diesels rather than geared steam turbines. *Bergamini* and *Rizzo* have Tosi diesels, *Fasan* and *Margottini* have Fiat. When they first came out, the *Bergamini*s were classed as fast corvettes, but they were subsequently re-rated as frigates. They will be replaced by *Maestrale*s, and the last are expected to be withdrawn from service in 1982–83.

Carlo Bergamini as completed

Navarret Collection

Alpino as completed

The *Alpino*s were originally intended to be more powerful *Canopo*s, and were given suitable names, but the design was recast several times between 1960–62. The final result was really an enlarged *Bergamini* with an adequate AA and ASW armament and CODAG machinery to give the necessary extra speed to deal with fast modern submarines, and so the names were changed. The general arrangement is almost identical with the *Bergamini*s, except that the problem of astern fire has been (expensively) solved by fitting single 3in (76mm)/62 guns on each side abreast the funnel and the hangar. The hangar is now fixed, which eases maintenance, and is big enough to take the two A/B 204 (now A/B 212) ASW helicopters which can be operated from the larger flight deck. There is a VDS at the stern. The *Alpino*s are the first major Italian warships to be powered by gas turbines, and their machinery consists of a Tosi-Metrovick gas turbine and two Tosi diesels coupled to each shaft. Cruising speed using diesels alone is up to 22kts. There were originally intended to be four in the class, but the second pair were never laid down because of financial problems.

ALPINO class *frigates*

Displacement:	2000t standard; 2700t full load
Dimensions:	349ft 2in pp, 371ft 10in oa × 43ft × 12ft 4in
	106.4m, 113.3m × 13.1m × 3.8m
Machinery:	2-shaft CODAG: 2 gas turbines plus 4 diesels, 15,000shp + 16,800bhp = 29kts. Range 3500nm at 18kts
Armament:	6–76mm/62 (6×1), 1 Menon ASW mortar, 6–324mm TT (2×3), 2 helicopters
Sensors:	Radar SPS-12, SPQ-2, RTN-30X, RTN-10X; sonar SQS-43, SQA-10 VDS
Complement:	263

No	Name	Builder	Laid down	Launched	Comp	Fate
F 580	ALPINO (ex-*Circe*)	CNR, Riva Trigoso	27.2.63	10.6.67	14.1.68	Extant 1982
F 581	CARABINIERE (ex-*Climene*)	CNR, Riva Trigoso	9.1.65	30.9.67	28.4.68	Extant 1982

Carabiniere about 1970

USN

Orsa as completed

S Cioglia

71

Lupo as completed

The design of the *Lupo* class has been optimised for foreign sales rather than for the requirements of the Italian Navy, and its performance suffers accordingly. Surface armament has been emphasised at the expense of ASW, and the large number of weapons systems and powerful machinery to give the required very high speed mean that there is very little room left for the crew despite its small size consequent on extensive automation. The Italian Navy normally operates its *Lupo*s with four rather than eight SSMs and one rather than two helicopters (only one helicopter can fit into the telescopic hangar though there is room for two to operate if the hangar is folded back). The hull is a narrower version of the *Alpino*'s, and CODOG machinery (GE/Fiat LM 2500 gas turbines and GMT diesels) gives the required high speed. Cruising speed on diesels is about 20kts. All were built by Cantieri Navali Riuniti, *Orsa* at Muggiano and the rest at Riva Trigosa.

The *Maestrale* is basically a 10 per cent stretched *Lupo* with fewer weapons systems and a greater emphasis on ASW to suit the needs of the Italian Navy. Unlike the *Lupo*, it can fight all its armament efficiently, and there is room in the larger hull to increase the habitability to more acceptable standards. The slight loss of speed in calm water is balanced by increased seaworthiness, and there is a fixed hangar and flight deck so that the two ASW helicopters can be operated and maintained. The SAM system is the Italian Aspide rather than the American Mk 29 NATO Sea Sparrow. Unlike the *Lupo*, the *Maestrale* fulfils the Italian Navy's requirements, and is being built in quantity to replace the early postwar frigates. The last two ships, *Espero* and *Zeffiro*, were ordered in 1977 with the first six and then cancelled because of shortage of money, but they were reordered in Oct 80. All are being constructed at CNR's Riva Trigoso yard, except *Grecale* which was built at Muggiano.

LUPO class *frigates*

Displacement:	2208t standard; 2500t full load
Dimensions:	347ft 10in pp, 370ft 2in oa × 39ft 4in × 12ft
	106.0m, 112.8m × 12.0m × 3.7m
Machinery:	2-shaft CODOG: 2 gas turbines, 50,000shp = 35kts, plus 2 diesels, 8490bhp = 20.5kts. Range 4350nm at 16kts on diesels
Armament:	8 Otomat SSM (8×1), 1–127mm/54, 1 Sea Sparrow SAM (1×8), 4–40mm/70 (2×2), 6–324mm TT (2×3), 1 helicopter
Sensors:	Radar RAN-10S, RAN-11, SPQ-2, RTN-10X, RTN-20; sonar DE-1160B
Complement:	185

No	Name	Builder	Laid down	Launched	Comp	Fate
F 564	LUPO	CNR	11.10.74	29.7.76	12.9.77	Extant 1982
F 565	SAGITTARIO	CNR	4.2.76	22.6.77	18.11.78	Extant 1982
F 566	PERSEO	CNR	28.2.77	12.7.78	3.8.79	Extant 1982
F 567	ORSA	CNR	1.8.77	1.3.79	13.2.80	Extant 1982

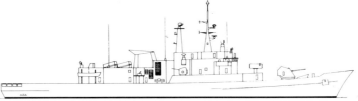

Maestrale as completed

MAESTRALE class *frigates*

Displacement:	2990t standard; 3250t full load
Dimensions:	374ft 2in pp, 402ft 9in oa × 42ft 9in × 27ft 5in
	114.0m, 122.7m × 12.9m × 8.4m
Machinery:	2-shaft CODOG: 2 Fiat LM 2500 gas turbines, 50,000shp = 33kts, or 2 diesels, 11,000bhp = 21kts. Range 6000nm at 16kts
Armament:	4 Otomat SSM (4×1), 1–127mm/54, 1 Albatros SAM (1×4), 4–40mm/70 (2×2), 2–533mm TT (2×1), 6–324mm TT (2×3), 2 helicopters
Sensors:	Radar RAN-10S, SPQ-2D, RTN-30X, RTN-20X; sonar DE-1164, DE-1164 VDS
Complement:	232

No	Name	Builder	Laid down	Launched	Comp	Fate
F 570	MAESTRALE	CNR	8.3.78	2.2.81	Feb 1982	Extant 1982
F 571	GRECALE	CNR	21.3.79	12.9.81	Aug 1982	Extant 1982
F 572	LIBECCIO	CNR	1.8.79	7.9.81	June 1982	Extant 1982
F 573	SCIROCCO	CNR	26.2.80	–	–	Building
F 574	ALISEO	CNR	10.8.80	–	–	Building
F 575	EURO	CNR	15.4.81	?	–	Building
F 576	ESPERO	CNR	–	–	–	Ordered
F 577	ZEFFIRO	CNR	–	–	–	Ordered

Maestrale as completed
CNR

SUBMARINES

These two *Gato* class submarines originally built in 1942–43, both underwent the austere 'Fleet Snorkel' type of GUPPY modernisation in 1953–54. Ex-USS *Dace* was transferred on 15.12.54 and renamed *Leonardo da Vinci* and ex-USS Barb was transferred on 31.1.55 and renamed *Enrico Tazzoli*. They were originally lent for five years, but in 1959 this was extended by another five years and it was later extended again. They formed the backbone of the Italian

(For illustration see under United States)

Ex-US GATO class *submarines*

Particulars:	As US *Gato* class (Fleet Snorkel type)			
No	**Name**	**Builder**	**Acquired**	**Fate**
S 510	LEONARDO DA VINCI (ex-*Dace*)	Electric Boat	15.12.54	Discarded 1973
S 511	ENRICO TAZZOLI (ex-*Barb*)	Electric Boat	31.1.55	Discarded 1973

submarine force in the late 1950s and early 1960s.

Ex-USS *Lizardfish* was transferred on 9.1.60 and renamed *Evangelista Torricelli*, ex-USS *Capitaine* was transferred on 5.3.66 and renamed *Alfredo Cappellini* and ex-USS *Besugo* was transferred on 31.3.66 and renamed *Francesco Morosini*. These wartime-built ex-USN *Balao* class submarines were still fitted with a 3in (76mm) gun, but this was later removed. By the early 1970s *Torricelli* was no longer operational and was used for training and experiments.

(For illustration see under United States in 1922–46 volume)

Ex-US BALAO class *submarines*

Particulars:	As US *Balao* class			
No	**Name**	**Builder**	**Acquired**	**Fate**
S 507	ALFREDO CAPPELLINI (ex-*Capitaine*)	Electric Boat	5.3.66	Discarded 1977
S 512	EVANGELISTA TORICELLI (ex-*Lizardfish*)	Manitowoc SB	9.1.60	Discarded 1976
S 514	FRANCESCO MOROSINI (ex-*Besugo*)	Electric Boat	31.3.66	Discarded 15.11.75

These ex-USN *Balao* class submarines, originally built in 1944–46, had been given the GUPPY II modernisation in 1952–54 and the very extensive GUPPY III modernisation in 1961–63.

(For illustration see under United States)

Ex-US BALAO class *submarines*

Particulars:	As US *Balao* class (GUPPY III type)			
No	**Name**	**Builder**	**Acquired**	**Fate**
S 502	GIANFRANCO GAZZANA PRIAROGGIA (ex-*Pickerel*)	Boston N Yd	18.8.72	Stricken 1981
S 501	PRIMO LONGOBARDO (ex-*Volador*)	Portsmouth N Yd	18.8.72	Stricken 31.1.80

These two ex-USN *Tang* class submarines, like the GUPPY III conversions, are equipped with the prominent three fins of the BQR-2 passive sonar to suit them to the hunter-killer role. Despite their age they are well equipped and remain formidable opponents.

(For illustration see under United States)

Ex-US TANG class *submarines*

Particulars:	As US *Tang* class			
No	**Name**	**Builder**	**Acquired**	**Fate**
S 515	LIVIO PIOMARTA (ex-*Trigger*)	Electric Boat	10.7.73	Extant 1982
S 516	ROMEO ROMEI (ex-*Harder*)	Electric Boat	20.2.74	Extant 1982

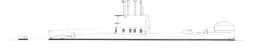

Enrico Toti as completed
NB 1/750 scale

The *Toti*s were the first postwar Italian submarines to be built, and their design was changed several times before it was completed. They are small hunter-killers roughly comparable with the German Type 206. Their great manoeuvrability is ideally suited to the restricted waters of the central Mediterranean, but their small size brings penalties including a very limited number of reload torpedoes (possibly 2). They have diesel-electric propulsion with two Fiat/MB 820 diesels.

TOTI class *attack submarines*

Displacement:	535t/591t normal (surfaced/submerged)
Dimensions:	151ft 8in oa × 15ft 5in × 13ft 1in *46.2m × 4.7m × 4m*
Machinery:	1 shaft, 2 diesels plus 1 electric motor, 2200hp = 14/20kts. Range 3000nm at 5kts (surfaced)
Armament:	4–533mm TT (bow)
Sensors:	Radar RM-20/SMG; sonar JP-64
Complement:	26

No	Name	Builder	Laid down	Launched	Comp	Fate
S 505	ATTILIO BAGNOLINI	CRDA	15.4.65	26.8.67	16.6.68	Extant 1982
S 506	ENRICO TOTI	CRDA	15.4.65	12.3.67	22.1.68	Extant 1982
S 513	ENRICO DANDOLO	CRDA	10.3.67	16.12.67	25.9.68	Extant 1982
S 514	LAZZARO MOCENIGO	CRDA	12.6.67	20.4.68	11.1.69	Extant 1982

Attilio Bagnolini c1970

Nazario Sauro as completed

This class was delayed by both financial and technical problems. *Sauro* and *Cossato* were originally ordered in 1967, but budget difficulties caused them to be cancelled and they were not reordered until 1972. Their completion was then delayed because their batteries did not work properly, and different batteries had to be purchased from Sweden. The first two did not commission until March 1980. They are considerably larger than the preceding *Totis*, but are correspondingly more capable. As well as many extra sensors they can carry 6 reload torpedoes to the *Totis*' 2. Like the *Totis* the *Sauros* are very manoeuvrable. They are identifiable by the diving planes on their fins. Two further units were requested in the 1981 budget.

SAURO class *attack submarines*

Displacement:	1456t/1641t normal (surfaced/submerged)
Dimensions:	209ft 7in oa × 22ft 5in × 18ft 9in
	63.9m × 6.8m × 5.7m
Machinery:	1 shaft, 3 diesels plus 1 electric motor, 3210bhp/3650shp = 12/20kts. Range 7000nm (surfaced)
Armament:	6–533mm TT (bow)
Sensors:	Radar RM-20/SMG; sonar IPD-70, Velox M-5
Complement:	45

No	Name	Builder	Laid down	Launched	Comp	Fate
S 518	NAZARIO SAURO	CRDA	15.7.74	9.10.76	1.1.80	Extant 1982
S 519	CARLO FECIA DI COSSATO	CRDA	15.11.75	16.11.77	5.11.79	Extant 1982
S 520	LEONARDO DA VINCI	CRDA	8.6.78	12.10.79	1981	Extant 1982
S 521	GUGLIELMO MARCONI	CRDA	23.10.79	20.9.80	Feb 82	Extant 1982

AMPHIBIOUS WARFARE VESSELS

QUARTO class *landing ships*

Displacement:	764t standard; 980t full load
Dimensions:	226ft 6in oa × 31ft 4in × 5ft 11in
	69.0m × 9.6m × 1.8m
Machinery:	3 shafts, 3 diesels, 2300bhp = 13kts
Armament:	4–40mm (2×2). See notes
Sensors:	Radar SPQ-2, RAN-3L
Complement:	?

Class:
Quarto, Marsala, Capera
Built at Taranto and launched on 18.3.67, *Quarto* was intended to be the first of a large class of landing ship, intermediate in size between LSTs and LSMs. Her trials, however, were extremely unsuccessful – the bluff bow causing problems with both speed and seaworthiness. Her sisters, *Marsala* (laid down on 18.3.67) and *Capera*, were therefore cancelled, *Marsala*'s incomplete hull being used as a pontoon, and two further vessels that had been projected, *Lombardo* and *Piemonte*, were dropped from the building programme. *Quarto* (A 5314) has since been used as a weapons trial ship, being used for sea trials of the Otomat SSM. The 40mm guns have been removed.

(For illustration see under United States)

Ex-US DE SOTO COUNTY class *landing ships*

Particulars: As US *De Soto County* class

Following the failure of the *Quarto* class landing ships, two *De Soto County* class LSTs were acquired from the USN. Both were transferred in July 72; ex-USS *York County* (launched at Newport News on 5.9.57) was renamed *Caorle* (L 9891) and ex-USS *De Soto County* (launched at Boston NYd on 28.2.57) was renamed *Grado* (L 9890). Both were purchased outright in 1981 and were extant in 1982.

A new amphibious warfare ship of 6000t was requested in the 1980 Budget. A smaller version of the US *Raleigh* class, the ship is to double as a training vessel.

Ex-US LCM type *landing craft*

Particulars: As US LCM(3) and LCM(6) type

Twenty ex-USN LCM (3) and LCM (6) numbered between MTM 9901 and MTM 9929, were transferred to the Italian Navy in 1952–53. One was discarded in 1967 and one in 1980, but the remainder were extant in 1982.

Ex-US LCVP type *landing craft*

Particulars: As US LCVP Type

Thirty LCVP were transferred from the USN to the Italian Navy between 1952–72. Twenty-two have since been discarded. A further twenty-eight have been built in Italy. The whole class was numbered in the MTP 9703–MTP 9754 range.

(For illustration see under United States in 1922–46 volume)

Ex-US LSSL type *gunboats*

Particulars: As US LSSL type

Class:
Alano (L 9851), *Bracco* (L 9852), *Mastino* (L 9853), *Molosso* (L 9854), *Segugio* (L 9855), *Spinone* (L 9856)
Six ex-USN LSSL were transferred to Italy under MDAP on 25.7.51. They were renamed *Alano* (ex-*LSSL 34*), *Bracco* (ex-*LSSL 38*), *Mastino* (ex-*LSSL 62*), *Molosso* (ex-*LSSL 63*), *Segugio* (ex-*LSSL 64*) and *Spinone* (ex-*LSSL 118*). They were rated as support gunboats in the Italian Navy. All were discarded between 1969–71.

SMALL SURFACE COMBATANTS

Ex-British 'FLOWER' class *corvette*

| Particulars: | As British 'Modified Flower' class |

No	Name	Builder	Acquired	Fate
A 5307	STAFFETTA (ex-*Elbano*, ex-*Prudent*, ex-*Privet*)	Morton	1949	Discarded 1970

She was built in 1942 as the British 'Modified Flower' class corvette (later frigate) *Privet*, and was transferred to the USN as *Prudent* (PG 96) in 1943. After the Second World War she was returned to the RN and was transferred to Italy as the *Elbano* in 1949. She was renamed *Staffetta* in 1951. In 1953 she was converted to a hydrographic survey ship, armed with 2–20mm (2×1).

Albatros 1974

ALBATROS class *corvettes*

Displacement:	800t standard; 950t full load
Dimensions:	228ft pp, 250ft 5in oa × 31ft 8in × 9ft 2in *69.5m, 76.3m × 9.7m × 2.8m*
Machinery:	2 shafts, 2 Fiat diesels, 5200bhp = 19kts. Range 5000nm at 18kts
Armament:	2–40mm/70 (2×1), 2 Hedgehog ASW mortars (2×1), 6–324mm TT (2×3). See notes
Sensors:	Radar SPQ-2; sonar QCU-2
Complement:	110

No	Name	Builder	Launched	Fate
F 542	AQUILA (ex-*Lynx*)	Breda Marghera	31.7.54	Extant 1982
F 543	ALBATROS	Castellammare	18.7.54	Extant 1982
F 544	ALCIONE	Castellammare	19.9.54	Extant 1982
F 545	AIRONE	Castellammare	21.11.54	Extant 1982

Eight ships of this type were built in Italy in the early 1950s under MDAP funding. The Italian Navy were given three (*Albatros* class), four went to Denmark (*Triton* class) and one (*Lynx*) went to the Dutch Navy. *Lynx* was ceded to the Italian Navy on 18.10.61 and was renamed *Aquila*. The Italian *Albatros* class were originally armed with 2–3in (76mm)/61 (2×1), 2–40mm/70 (2×1) and 2 Hedgehog ASW mortars. All four ships had the existing gun armament removed in 1963 – the 3in (76mm) being replaced by 40mm/70 – and their ASW armament was supplemented by 2 Mk 32 triple ASW TT.

When they were first built the *Albatros* class were already too slow and unsophisticated to be much good at hunting submarines and they are now totally unsuited to a combat role. They are mainly used as fishery protection vessels. Their replacement is well overdue, and all are expected to decommission in 1982–83.

Albatros as completed   Navarret Collection

Pietro de Cristofaro 1966

DE CRISTOFARO class *corvettes*

Displacement:	850t standard; 1020t full load
Dimensions:	246ft 2in pp, 263ft 3in oa × 32ft 10in × 8ft 3in *75.0m, 80.2m × 10.0m × 2.5m*
Machinery:	2 shafts, 2 diesels, 8400bhp = 23kts. Range 4000nm at 16kts
Armament:	2–76mm/62 (2×1), 1 Menon ASW mortar, 6–12.75in (324mm) TT (2×3)
Sensors:	Radar SPQ-2, RTN-10; sonar SQS-36, SQS-36 VDS
Complement:	131

No	Name	Builder	Launched	Fate
F 540	PIETRO DE CRISTOFARO	CNR, Riva Trigoso	29.5.65	Extant 1982
F 541	UMBERTO GROSSO	Ansaldo	12.12.64	Extant 1982
F 546	LICIO VISINTINI	CRDA	30.5.65	Extant 1982
F 550	SALVATORE TODARO	Ansaldo	24.10.64	Extant 1982

The *De Cristofaro* class are enlarged and improved versions of the *Albatros*, with a raised forecastle to improve seakeeping and give extra accommodation. The extra tonnage has enabled them to retain their original armament, unlike the earlier vessels. The ASW equipment is considerably better, with a longer-ranged ASW mortar and a VDS. Despite their extra size and slightly better speed, however, they are still really too small and too slow for ASW, and like the earlier ships are overdue for replacement.

De Cristofaro, *Grosso* and *Todaro* have Fiat high-speed diesels, but *Visintini* has Tosi machinery.

Pietro de Cristofaro during trials period   Navarret Collection

VEDETTA *patrol boat*

| Particulars: | As US PC type |

She was built at Brest as *PC 1616* under MDAP for Germany, and was launched on 30.9.54. However, she was delivered instead to Ethiopia in 1957 as *Belay Deress*. She was too sophisticated for the fledgling Ethiopian Navy, so she was again transferred under MDAP to Italy. She was delivered on 3.2.59 and was renamed *Vedetta* (F 597). After refitting she was classed as a corvette, and was mainly used as a fishery protection vessel until being discarded in 1977.

FULMINE *patrol boat*

Displacement:	300t standard; 340t full load
Dimensions:	154ft pp, 163ft oa × 21ft 8in × 7ft *46.9m, 49.7m × 6.6m × 2.1m*
Machinery:	2 shafts, 4 diesels, 9000shp = 30kts.
Armament:	1–76mm/62, 2–40mm/56 (1×2), 2–450mm TT (2×1). See notes
Complement:	60

Fulmine was ordered in 1952 from CRDA as *VAS 470*. She was launched on 14.11.55 and completed in 1956. She was designed as a submarine-chaser and was classed as a corvette. The initial armament consisted of 2–40mm/56 (1×2), 2–450mm (17.75in) torpedoes with launchers (2×1), a Hedgehog Mk 10 ASW mortar and 2 DCT. She was used as a leader for the torpedo-boat flotilla, and was renamed *Sentinella* (F 598). In 1965 she was reclassified as a gunboat and renamed *Fulmine*. In 1967 a 76mm/62 (3in) was mounted in place of the Hedgehog forward. She was discarded in c1970.

Folgore c 1970   Navarret Collection

(For illustration see under United States in 1922–46 volume)

Ex-US ELCO VOSPER type *motor torpedo-boats*

Particulars:	As US Elco Vosper type

Class: *SIS 811–SIS 814, SIS 821–SIS 824, SIS 831–SIS 834*

Twelve ex-USN Vosper type MTBs were acquired by the Italian Navy in 1948 and reconstructed between 1949–52. They were later renumbered *MS 461–64, 421–24* and *431–34* respectively. All were armed with 5–20mm/65 and 2–450mm (17.75in) torpedoes (2×1) in launchers. *MS 421, 423–4* and *434* were discarded in 1958, *MS 433, 461* and *464* in 1959, *MS· 422, 462* and *463* in 1960 and *MS 431, 432* in 1961.

(For illustration see under United States in 1922–46 volume)

Ex-US HIGGINS type *torpedo-boats*

Particulars:	As US Higgins type

Class:
GIS 841–GIS 844, GIS 851–GIS 854

Eight ex-USN Higgins type PT Boats were acquired in March 1948 and refitted between 1949–53. In the mid-1950s they were renumbered *MS 441–44* and *451–54* respectively. *MS 854* was discarded in 1959. They were armed with 1–40mm/56, 2– or 3–20mm (2 or 3×1) and 2–450mm (17.75in) torpedoes on launchers (2×1). In the early 1960s they were reconstructed with SPS-21 radar and ASM/185/CRM petrol engines in place of the original Packards. Their maximum speed after reconstruction was 34kts. *MS 444* was discarded in 1966 and in the same year *MS 442, 451* and *452* were transferred to the Customs. *MS 441* and *453* had their armament reduced to 2–20mm (2×1) forward and were used for frogmen support. *MS 441, 443* and *453* were still in service in 1981.

(For illustration see under Germany in 1922–46 volume)

Ex-German S-BOAT type *motor gunboat*

Particulars:	As German *S 701* group

Class:
MS 621

An ex-German *S 701* series S-Boat, which had been converted to the merchant ship *Toros*, was purchased by the Italian Navy and refitted in 1953–54. She was rearmed with 2–40mm/56 (2×1) and 2–21in (533mm) TT (2×1), and was numbered *MS 621*. She was later renumbered *MC 485* and was discarded in 1965.

FOLGORE *patrol boat*

Displacement:	160t standard; 190t full load
Dimensions:	129ft 4in × 19ft × 5ft 7in
	39.4m × 5.8m × 1.7m
Machinery:	4 shafts, 4 diesels, 10,000bhp = 36kts
Armament:	2–40mm (2×1), 2–533mm TT
Complement:	39

Class:
Folgore (P 490)

She was authorised in 1950 and built at CRDA. Her original number was *MC 490*, but she was later renamed *Folgore*. The design was a convertible MGB/MTB and she could carry up to 4–533mm (21in) TT in launchers (4×1). *Folgore* had a very rapid acceleration from cruising speed to full speed. She was discarded in 1977.

LAMPO class *patrol boats*

Displacement:	170t standard; 196t full load
Dimensions:	141ft 2in oa × 20ft 8in × 4ft 11in
	43.0m × 6.3m × 1.5m
Machinery:	3-shaft CODAG: 1 Metrovick gas turbine plus 2 MTU 518D diesels, 4500shp + 7200bhp = 39kts
Armament:	3–40mm/70 (3×1). See notes
Sensors:	Radar 3ST7-250
Complement:	33

Class:
Lampo (P 491), *Baleno* (P 492)

The *Lampo* class are improved versions of *Folgore*. They were designed as convertible boats, with 2– or 3–40mm/70 (2× or 3×1) as MGBs, and 1–40mm/70 and 4–17.7in (450mm) torpedoes in launchers (4×1) or 2–40mm/70 (2×1) and 2–21in (533mm) torpedoes (2×1) as MTBs. They were the first Italian warships to have gas turbines. *Lampo* (P 491, ex-*MC 491*) was built at Taranto and launched on 22.11.60. *Baleno* (P 492, ex-*MC 492*) was also built at Taranto and was launched on 10.5.64. She was modified in 1967–69. Both had their original Fiat diesels replaced by MTU diesels in 1975. Both were extant in 1982. Two further vessels of this type, *MC 493* and *MC 494* were projected, but were abandoned in favour of the improved *Freccia*s.

Freccia 1967
NB 1/750 scale

FRECCIA class *patrol boats*

Displacement:	175t standard; 205t full load
Dimensions:	151ft 4in oa × 23ft 8in × 5ft 1in
	46.1m × 23.6m × 5.1m
Machinery:	3-shaft CODAG: 1 Proteus gas turbine plus 2 Fiat diesels, 4250shp + 7600bhp = 40kts. Range 800nm at 27kts
Armament:	3–40mm/70 (3×1). See notes
Sensors:	Radar RTN-150 (*Saetta* only)
Complement:	37

Class:

The *Freccia*s are enlarged and improved *Lampo*s, with a Proteus gas turbine in place of the *Lampo*s' Metrovick. Unlike the *Lampo*s, they retain their Fiat diesels. Four *Freccia*s were ordered. *Freccia* (P 493, ex-*MC 590*), built at CNR, Riva Trigoso, was launched on 9.1.65. *Saetta* (P 494, ex-*MC 591*) built by CRDA, was launched on 11.4.65. *Dardo*, ex-*MC 592* was laid down on 10.5.64 at Taranto, but she was not completed, and *Strale*, ex-*MC 593* was never started.

They are designed to be convertible, in one day, to an MGB (2– or 3–40mm/70 (2× or 3×1), an MTB (1–40mm/70, 4–21in (533mm) torpedoes on launchers, 4×1) or a fast minelayer (1–40mm/70, 8 mines). They can also carry missiles, and *Saetta* has been used for trials with the Sea Killer SSM. They can be distinguished from the earlier boats by their raised forecastles. Both were extant in 1982.

SPARVIERO class *guided missile hydrofoils*

Displacement:	62.5t full load
Dimensions:	Foilborne: 75ft 4in oa × 39ft 7in (foils) × 4ft 9in
	23.0m × 12.1m × 1.5m
	Hullborne: 80ft 7in oa × 23ft (hull) × 6ft 2in
	24.6m × 7.0m × 1.9m
Machinery:	Foilborne: 1 Proteus gas turbine via waterjet, 4500shp = 50kts
	Hullborne: 1 shaft, 1 diesel, 180bhp = 8kts. Range 400nm/1200nm at 45kts/8kts
Armament:	2 Otomat SSM (2×1), 1–76mm/62
Sensors:	Radar 3RM-7, RTN-10X
Complement:	10

Class:
Sparviero (P 420), *Nibbio* (P 421), *Falcone* (P 422), *Astore* (P 423), *Grifone* (P 424), *Gheppio* (P 425), *Condore* (P 426)

Development of conventional Italian patrol boats ceased in 1964 when a consortium of the Italian Government's research branch, Carlo Rodriguez – which built commercial hydrofoils – and the American firm of Boeing, which was building its first jetfoil, came into existence. This consortium, Alinave, designed a small hydrofoil for the Italian Navy based on Boeing's *Tucumcari*. The prototype, *Sparviero* (P 420), was built between 1971–74, but no more were built until 1977. Six more are being completed between 1980–83. *Sparviero* has a single-cell launcher whereas the later boats use the Teseo system.

They utilise the Boeing jetfoil system, with one foil forward and two aft. Foilborne power comes from a Proteus gas turbine driving a waterjet, while hullborne power consists of a GM diesel. The boats are built entirely of aluminium. They have a short range and very restricted armament, which is acceptable for the enclosed waters around Italy, but explains why no other country has adopted this design.

MINE WARFARE VESSELS

DAINO class *minesweepers*

Particulars:	As German 1940 type and 1943 type minesweepers

Class:

Antilope, Gazzella, Daino (M 5537–M 5539)

Three ex-German coal-burning minesweepers were purchased by Italy on 20.7.49. *B 1* ex-*M 328*, launched on 12.6.43 was of the 1940 type and was slightly smaller than the other two. She was assigned to the USN in 1947 under the terms of the Peace Treaty. *B 2* ex-*M 803*, launched on 19.10.44, and *B 3* ex-*M 801*, launched on 9.9.44, were both of the 1943 type and were assigned to the USN in 1945. They were originally classed as auxiliary ships, but were converted to oil burning, reclassified as patrol ships and armed with 1–3.9in/47 (100mm) aft, and 3–40mm/56 (3×1), plus a DCT. *B 1* was renamed *Antilope*, *B 2* was renamed *Daino* and *B 3* was renamed *Gazzella*. *Daino* was later fitted with a Hedgehog ASW mortar. They were reclassified as minesweepers in 1954 and as coastal escorts in June 56 with various changes of pennant numbers. *Antilope* was discarded in 1958, and *Daino* and *Gazzella* were reclassified as corvettes in 1959. In 1960 *Daino* was converted to a survey ship and *Gazzella* to a cadet training ship. Both were discarded in 1966.

Ex-US AGRESSIVE class *ocean minesweepers*

Particulars:	As US *Agile/Agressive* class

Class:

Salmone (M 5430), *Sgombro* (M 5432), *Squalo* (M 5433), *Storione* (M 5434)

Four ex-USN *Agressive* class ocean minesweepers were transferred under MDAP to the Italian Navy while under construction in 1956–57. *Salmone* (ex-*MSO 507*) was transferred in June 56, *Sgombro* (ex-*MSO 517*) was transferred in June 57, as was *Squalo* (ex-*MSO 518*). *Storione* (ex-*MSO 506*) was transferred in Feb 56. All were extant in 1982.

Ex-US ADJUTANT/AGAVE classes *coastal minesweepers*

Particulars:	As US *Adjutant* class

Seventeen ex-USN *Adjutant* class minesweepers were transferred to Italy while the class was under construction in 1953–54. *Abete* (ex-*AMS 72*), *Acacia* ex-*AMS 73*), *Betulla* (ex-*AMS 74*), *Castragno* (ex-*AMS 75*), *Cedro* (ex-*AMS 76*), *Ciliego* (ex-*AMS 79*), *Faggio* (ex-*AMS 80*), *Frassino* (ex-*AMS 81*), *Gelso* (ex-*AMS 82*), *Larice* (ex-*AMS 88*), *Noce* (ex-*AMS 89*), *Olmo* (ex-*AMS 90*), *Ontano* (ex-*AMS 133*), *Pino* (ex-*AMS 134*), *Pioppo* (ex-*AMS 135*), *Platano* (ex-*AMS 136*) and *Quercia* (ex-*AMS 137*) all have wooden hulls, as does *Mandorlo* (ex-*Salice*, ex-*MSC 280*) transferred from the USN on 16.12.60. *Mandorlo* (*M 5519*) differs from the earlier 17 (numbered M 5501–M 5517 in the above order) by having a modified bridge and funnel.

The 19 otherwise identical *Agave* class, *Agave, Alloro, Edera, Gaggia, Gelsomino, Giaggiolo, Glicine, Loto, Mirto, Timo, Trifoglio, Vischio, Bambu, Ebano, Mango, Mogano, Palma, Rovere* and *Sandalo* (M 5531–M 5542, M 5521–M 5527) were all built in Italian yards, with composite wood and alloy hulls, from 1955–57.

Pioppo of the *Adjutant* class and *Mirto* of the *Agave* class have been converted to survey ships. Following the successful use of *Mandorlo* as a minehunter, 6 more ships of both classes have been converted to minehunters since 1978. *Acacia, Betulla* and *Ciliego* of the *Adjutant* class and *Rovere* of the *Agave* class were scrapped in 1974, *Abete* of the *Adjutant* class was scrapped in 1977, *Faggio, Ontano, Pino, Gaggia* and *Glicine* were scrapped in 1980; *Queria* and *Trifoglio* were stricken in 1981 and four more were due for disposal.

(For illustration see under United Kingdom)

ARAGOSTA class *inshore minesweepers*

Particulars:	As British 'Ham' class

Twenty NATO 'Ham' class inshore minesweepers were constructed in Italian yards between 1955–57. They are similar to the British 'Ham' class. Although they were fitted to mount 1–20mm, none has carried it in service. They were built under MDAP. *Arsella* (M 5451), *Attina* (M 5453), *Calamaro* (M 5454), *Conchiglia* (M 5455), *Dromia* (M 5456), *Ostrica* (M 5460), *Paguro* (M 5461), *Seppia* (M 5467), *Tellina* (M 5468) and *Totano* (M 5469) were discarded in

Sparviero as completed
S Cioglia

1974. *Gambero* (M 5457), *Pinna* (M 5462), *Scampo* (M 5466), *Grancio* (M 5458) and *Riccio* (M 5465) were stricken in 1979–80. *Aragosta* (M 5450), *Astice* (M 5452), *Mitilo* (M 5459), *Polipo* (M 5463, ex-*Polpo*) and *Porpora* (M 5464) were extant in 1982 though they are likely to be scrapped soon. *Aragosta* has a large deckhouse aft and is a support ship for frogmen.

Lerici class design
NB 1/750 scale

LERICI class *minesweepers/minehunters*

Displacement:	485t standard; 502t full load
Dimensions:	149ft 4in pp, 164ft oa × 31ft 4in × 8ft 7in *45.5m, 50.0m × 9.6m × 2.6m*
Machinery:	1 shaft, 1 GMT 230B diesel, 1840bhp = 15kts, or 2 hydraulic thrusters, 470hp = 7kts. See notes. Range 2500nm at 12kts
Armament:	1–20mm
Sensors:	Radar 3ST7; sonar SQQ-14 VDS
Complement:	40

Four *Lerici* class minesweepers/minehunters were ordered in April 1978. *Lerici* (M 5550) commissioned in Dec 80, *Sapri* (M 5551) and *Milazzo* (M 5552) in 1982 and *Vieste* (M 5553) will commission during 1983. Six more (*Alghero, Crotone, Gaeta, Numana, Termoli* and *Viareggio*) are projected. They have GRP hulls, and are fitted with two PAP 104 robot minehunters as well as an Oropesa wire sweep and VDS. Minehunting and sweeping is done at up to 7kts using the hydraulic thrusters.

MISCELLANEOUS

(For illustration see under United States in 1922–46 volume)

Ex-US KENNETH WHITING class *support ship*

Particulars:	As US *Kenneth Whiting* class

The ex-US seaplane tender *St George* (AU 16) was transferred on 11.12.68 and was converted to a support ship for special forces named *Andrea Bafile* (L 9871). In 1982 she was in reserve at Taranto.

Ex-US BARNEGAT class *support ship*

Particulars:	As US *Barnegat* class

The USN MTB tender *Oyster Bay* (laid down as a *Barnegat* class seaplane tender), was purchased by the Italian Navy under MDAP on 23.10.57. She was renamed *Pietro Cavezzale* (A 5301) and has been used as a frogmen support ship and for miscellaneous duties. Extant in 1982.

Netherlands

The havoc wrought on the Netherlands Navy and its supporting defence industries by the Second World War was considerable. Most of the naval units still under construction at the time of the German occupation in May 1940 had been scuttled or completed for the German Navy; a few had escaped to Britain, where many items of equipment – especially armament and fire control – had to be installed, modified or replaced, either because the ships had left without them or because those already fitted were incompatible with available munitions. A number of older vessels also fled to Britain, where they saw heavy war service, while the bulk of the powerful East Indies Squadron had been destroyed by the Japanese in the early months of 1942. Some of the older ships which served in the European theatre and proved difficult to maintain had been replaced by British construction.

As if this were not enough, the Germans, in the face of the irresistible advance of the Allied armies through northern France and Belgium in September 1944, had embarked on the systematic destruction of the installations in the Dutch seaports and shipbuilding yards in the western part of the country. Practically all the tools of these yards were dismantled and taken to Germany, together with all the items of equipment the Germans could lay hands on. Ships were scuttled in the narrow waterways and harbour entrances: the incomplete hull of the cruiser *De Zeven Provincien*, for example, was launched at Schiedam with the intention of using it for this purpose.

RECONSTRUCTION

The necessity of reconstructing the Royal Netherlands Navy in the face of a European political situation which was still far from stable was immediately recognised, and the Naval Staff accordingly drew up a new Fleet Plan which aimed at the construction of a new fleet combining the latest theories of naval warfare with the practical lessons learned from the participation of Dutch naval units in the Second World War and the losses experienced.

By 1950 authorisation had been given for the purchase of a light fleet carrier from Britain, for the completion of the two large cruisers of the *Provincien* class, and for the construction of twelve large ASW destroyers and four submarines. Until these ships could be completed the Netherlands Navy would use its motley collection of prewar Dutch-built and wartime British-built vessels to build up the expertise of its seamen, particularly in the new specialisation constituted by ASW operations. Further submarines and escorts were acquired on loan from Britain and the USA for this purpose.

The difficulties inherent in the implementation of the Fleet Plan were two-fold: the lack of experience in designing and building ships as a result of the German occupation had taken its toll of the design teams of the Netherlands United Shipbuilding Bureaux, and the near-total destruction of the Dutch defence industries caused inevitable delays in the construction and fitting out of the vessels. In particular, the decision to develop a home-based electronics industry capable of supplying all the necessary radars and fire control systems resulted in a number of ships being completed with empty mast platforms. The problems involved in designing a ship on the basis of predicted antenna dimensions and weights supplied by HSA while the radars concerned were still at the development stage will be self-evident to the reader. Nevertheless, the decision to develop a Dutch defence electronics

industry rather than rely on the purchase of US or RN equipment has been a great success for the Dutch, not only in terms of the quality of the equipment produced, but also because of foreign sales.

The design problems involved in the reconstruction of the Netherlands Navy during the immediate postwar period were eased by close collaboration with British constructors, who provided particular assistance in the revision of the plans of the *Provincien* class cruisers, and whose hand can also be seen in the hull form and layout of the *Holland* class destroyers.

NATO

The abandonment of colonial commitments in the Far East, and membership of NATO in 1949 confirmed the reorientation of Dutch naval strategy towards the European theatre in general, and anti-submarine warfare in particular. The mission of the Royal Netherlands Navy could now be divided into two clear areas of responsibility. The Navy would provide blue-water units to NATO's East Atlantic command for open-ocean ASW, and would, in addition, have a major responsibility for the defence of shipping and harbours in the North Sea against submarines, aircraft and mines. The new fleet units under construction were therefore organised into squadrons of ASW destroyers with a cruiser or carrier flagship to serve as hunting groups. The single carrier, *Karel Doorman*, was modernised and had her air complement changed from that of a conventional attack carrier to that of an ASW carrier on the American model.

For the North Sea role, small diesel-powered frigates were acquired from the United States and large numbers of minesweepers were built both in US and Dutch yards. Many of these ships were funded under the Mutual Defense Assistance Program (MDAP).

By the end of the 1950s this naval programme was complete, and most of the prewar and war-built ships had been stricken or returned.

The formulation of the new Fleet Plan was accompanied by a decision to develop Den Helder as the principal base of the Royal Netherlands Navy. This was a gigantic task because all existing naval installations there had been damaged or destroyed by Allied or German air attacks, and the prewar harbour, even if restored, was totally inadequate for the envisaged fleet. A new harbour was therefore constructed in typical Dutch fashion, using the mudflats east of the existing port to form a large central basin with finger piers of varying sizes projecting from its sides. The old harbour, which now lay to the west, was closed off at its southern end and land was provided for various new installations.

All the large ocean-going units and submarines were to be based on Den Helder under the Commander Netherlands Task Group, while the smaller patrol craft and minesweepers would be divided among Amsterdam, Rotterdam and Flushing.

During the 1960s the structure of the Navy remained basically unchanged. The British *Leander* design was adopted to provide replacements for the American DEs purchased in 1950; an ocean-going combat support ship, the *Poolster*, was built for operations in the Eastern Atlantic; and the carrier *Karel Doorman*, badly damaged by a boiler fire in 1968, was sold to Argentina and replaced by eight French Atlantique long-range maritime patrol aircraft.

A NEW PLAN

With the bulk of the 1950s-built fleet fast approaching the age at which replacements would become necessary, a review of Netherlands defence requirements resulted in a report which appeared in 1972. This recommended that the Navy should consist of three ASW task groups, each comprising a guided missile flagship, six ASW frigates and a combat support ship, all with embarked helicopters. Two of these groups would operate in the Eastern Atlantic and the other, together with an independent frigate division, would be allocated to Channel Command. The ASW hunting groups would be backed up by a submarine squadron and two dozen LRMP aircraft. Many of the older minesweepers would be returned or disposed of, while others would be converted minehunters. For work off the Dutch coast there were to be two MCM groups of 12 ships, each consisting of an HQ ship, some hunters, and coastal and inshore minesweepers; a third smaller group would be provided for operations in the North Sea.

By 1974 a change of government and a deteriorating economic situation led to some modifications to the plan. The two Atlantic task groups, each with a *Tromp* class destroyer, six 'Standard' class frigates and a combat support ship, remained intact, but the third group, with the six *Van Speijk*s, would have a smaller guided missile flagship (an AAW version of the 'Standard') and would operate without a support ship. Small reductions in the MCM and LRMP force levels were agreed and new construction was to be slowed.

In 1981 the plan was further modified when two of the 'Standard' class frigates were purchased by Greece. In view of the increased aerial threat in the Eastlant, Channel and North Sea areas it was decided that the two replacements ordered would be Air Defence versions of the 'Standard', and that the original Standard AD – the 13th ship – would be replaced by a fifth unit of the new 'M' class frigates designed to operate in the North Sea.

MAJOR RADARS OF NETHERLANDS MANUFACTURE

Designation	Description	In service
SPS-01	3-D air search/tracking	1975
LW-01	Long-range air search	1956
LW-02/03	Long-range air search	1956
LW-08	Long-range air search	1978
DA-01/02	Medium-range air/surface search	1956
DA-05	Medium-range air/surface search	1979
VI-01	Nodding height-finder	1956
ZW-01	Surface search/navigation	1954
ZW-06	Surface search/navigation	1978
M25	152mm fire control	1953
M45	120mm (and below) fire control	1953
WM25	120mm (and below)/PDMS fire control	1975
VM40	STIR tracker/illuminator	1978

FLEET STRENGTH 1947

AIRCRAFT CARRIER

Name	Launched	Disp	Fate
KAREL DOORMAN (ex-*Nairana*)	20.5.43	13,825t	Returned RN 1948

Acquired on loan in 1946, this vessel was returned to the Royal Navy in 1948, her place being taken by the former HMS *Venerable* (see under Major Surface Ships).

CRUISERS

Name	Launched	Disp	Fate
JACOB VAN HEEMSKERCK	16.9.39	4150t	Stricken 1958
TROMP	24.5.37	4200t	Stricken 1958

After several years of active service these two cruisers became accommodation ships and were renumbered A 879 and A 878 respectively.

DESTROYERS

No	Name	Launched	Disp	Fate
J 1	BANCKERT (ex-*Quilliam*)	29.11.41	1750t	Stricken 1957
J 2	EVERTSEN (ex-*Scourge*)	8.12.42	1796t	Stricken 1962
J 3	VAN GALEN (ex-*Noble*)	17.4.41	1760t	Stricken 1957
J 4	PIET HEIN (ex-*Serapis*)	25.3.43	1796t	BU 1961
J 5	TJERK HIDDES (ex-*Nonpareil*)	25.6.41	1760t	To Indonesia 1951
J 6	KORTENAER (ex-*Scorpion*, ex-*Sentinel*)	26.8.42	1796t	Stricken 1962
HX 4	MARNIX (ex-*Garland*)	24.10.35	1335t	Stricken 1964

Tjerk Hiddes and *Van Galen* were transferred in 1942, and the other war-built destroyers in 1945–46. *Evertsen*, *Kortenaer* and *Piet Hein* were reconstructed as fast frigates at the Rijkswerf Willemsoord 1957–58, when they were fitted with a helicopter platform aft. *Marnix* was transferred from the Royal Navy in 1947. Following a refit 1948–49 she became an ASW training ship.

SUBMARINES

No	Name	Launched	Disp	Fate
–	O 21	21.10.39	962t	BU 1958
–	O 23	5.12.39	962t	BU 1949
–	O 24	18.3.40	962t	Stricken 1956
–	O 27 (ex-*UD 5*)	26.9.41	962t	Stricken 1959
O 28	TIJGERHAAI (ex-*Tarn*)	29.11.44	1320t	Stricken 1966
O 29	ZWAARDVIS (ex-*Talent*)	17.7.43	1320t	Stricken 1963

From the mid-1950s the surviving three Dutch-built boats were all used for training. *Zwaardvis*, transferred in 1943, and *Tijgerhaai*, transferred 1945, were fitted with a snorkel and had a sonar dome between the bow tubes. Two further 'T' class boats were acquired on loan in 1948 (see below).

FRIGATE

No	Name	Launched	Disp	Fate
JO 1	JOHAN MAURITS VAN NASSAU (ex-*Ribble*)	23.4.43	1463t	BU 1960

Johan Maurits Van Nassau was transferred in 1943. She served postwar as an ASW and gunnery training ship. She had single 105mm mountings in place of the British 4in guns.

GUNBOATS

No	Name	Launched	Disp	Fate
N 3	VAN KINSBERGEN	5.1.39	2095t	Stricken 1959
N 5	VAN SPEIJK (ex-*K 3*)	22.3.41	1365t	BU 1960
N 1	FLORES	24.10.35	1734t	Depot ship 1955

Van Speijk had been completed by the Germans during the war. In 1953 she was re-engined with diesels from the submarine *O 23*, resulting in a 3kt increase in speed. She became an accommodation ship and was renumbered A 877. *Van Kinsbergen* was laid up in 1945, and in 1951–52 was renamed, the original 4–120mm being replaced by two single German-pattern 105mm. In 1955 she became a depot ship.

NETHERLANDS

MINELAYER

No	Name	Launched	Disp	Fate
	WILLEM VAN DER ZAAN	15.12.38	1267t	Stricken 1963

Willem Van Der Zaan was reclassified as a frigate in 1953. In 1961 she became an accommodation and repair ship for minesweepers at Flushing and was renumbered A 880. The former minelayer *Jan Van Brakel* was converted to a survey ship at Soerabaya in 1950 and renumbered A 906.

CORVETTES

Name	Launched	Disp	Fate
TERNATE (ex-*Kalgoorlie*)	7.8.41	790t	Stricken 1958
BATJAN (ex-*Lismore*)	10.8.41	790t	Stricken 1958
BOEROE (ex-*Toowoomba*)	26.3.41	790t	Stricken 1958
CERAM (ex-*Burnie*)	1941	790t	Stricken 1958
AMBAN (ex-*Cairns*)	5.7.41	790t	To Indonesia 1950
BANDA (ex-*Wollongong*)	5.7.41	790t	To Indonesia 1950
MOROTAI (ex-*Ipswich*)	1942	790t	To Indonesia 1949
TIDORE (ex-*Tamworth*)	14.3.42	790t	To Indonesia 1949

These eight Australian *Bathurst* class minesweepers were acquired in 1946 and served as patrol ships in the Far East, four being transferred to Indonesia. In the early 1950s the single 4in gun was replaced by a 105mm mounting.

MINESWEEPERS

Seven ex-British wooden MMS of 255t (launched 1943–44) were operated until disposed of 1949–52: *Duiveland* (MV 13), *Overflakkee* (MV 14), *Schokland* (MV 15), *Tholen* (MV 16), *Voorne* (MV 17), *Wieringen* (MV 19) and *Ijselmonde* (MV 20). *Duiveland* and *Ijselmonde* were transferred to Indonesia. The remainder were broken up.

There were also ten BYMS type vessels of 223t: *Borndiep, Deurloo, Hollandsch Diep, Marsdiep, Oosterschelde, Texelstroom, Vliestroom, Volkerak, Westerschelde* and *Zuiderdiep*. They were numbered from MV 34 to MV 43 respectively (changed in 1950 to NATO numbers M 831–840). In the late 1950s *Zuiderdiep, Borndiep, Marsdiep, Deurloo* and *Vliestroom* became diving vessels and were renumbered A 904–906, A 921 and A 922 respectively. The unconverted ships were disposed of in 1958 and the diving vessels followed in 1962.

Eight MMS type minesweepers (219t) were operated until 1958 (except *Vlieland*, sunk New Guinea 1951): *Ameland, Beveland, Marken II, Putten, Rozenburg, Terschelling, Texel* and *Vlieland*. They were initially numbered MV 5–12, and were subsequently given the NATO numbers M 861–867. Four prewar Netherlands-built minesweepers (460t, launched 1936–37) were employed as patrol and gate vessels: *Abraham Crijnsson, Abraham Van Der Hulst, Jan Van Gelder* and *Pieter Florisz*. Initially numbered MV 1–4, they were subsequently given the numbers A 925–928. They were stricken in 1962.

NATO PENNANT NUMBERS
Carried from 1950 onwards by ships in this section:

Cruiser
C 803	JACOB VAN HEEMSKERCK	C 804	TROMP

Destroyers
D 801	BANCKERT	D 805	PIET HEIN
D 802	EVERTSEN	D 806	TJERK HIDDES
D 803	VAN GALEN	D 807	MARNIX
D 804	KORTENAER		

Submarines
S 801	O 21	S 812	TIJGERHAAI
S 804	O 24	S 814	ZWAARDVIS
S 807	O 27		

Frigates
F 802	JOHAN MAURITS VAN NASSAU	F 814	BOEROE
F 803	FLORES	F 815	CERAM
F 804	VAN KINSBERGEN	F 816	TERNATE
F 805	VAN SPEIJK	F 824	WILLEM VAN DER ZAAN
F 813	BATJAN		

MAJOR SURFACE SHIPS

Laid down on 3.12.42, launched on 30.12.43 and completed on 17.1.45, the British light fleet carrier *Venerable* was purchased in 1948 and given the same name as the former escort carrier she replaced. In her early years she operated Sea Fury FB 11 fighter-bombers and Firefly Mk 4/5 ASW aircraft purchased from the UK; 23 Sea Fury FB 51s were later built in the Netherlands under licence.

In the early 1950s the Dutch decided that the excellent condition of the hull and machinery justified a full modernisation to incorporate the latest developments in carrier aviation. This was duly undertaken by Wilton-Fijenoord, the refit lasting from 1955 until 1958. A heavier, modified, angled flight deck, 165.8m

KAREL DOORMAN *aircraft carrier*

Displacement:	(all details 1958) 15,892t standard; 19,896t full load
Dimensions:	630ft pp, 693ft oa × 80ft wl, 121ft fd × 25ft *192.0m, 211.3m × 24.4m, 37.0m × 7.6m*
Machinery:	2-shaft Parsons geared steam turbines, 4 boilers, 40,00shp = 23.5kts. Range 12,000nm at 14kts
Armament:	12–40mm (12×1), 21 aircraft. See notes
Sensors:	Radar LW-01, LW-02, DA-01, 2 VI-01, ZW-01
Complement:	1462

No	Name	Builder	Acquired	Fate
R 81	KAREL DOORMAN (ex-*Venerable*)	Cammell Laird	1948	To Argentina 1969

long, was fitted, together with a mirror landing sight and a new steam catapult to port forward; a new type of arrester gear was installed. The island superstructure was completely redesigned to incorporate the new generation of Dutch radars. A tall funnel, of similar configuration to that of the cruisers and the new destroyers, carried an LW-02 air search antenna, while an even taller quadruped lattice mast carrying a long-range LW-01 air search and a DA-01 combined air/surface search radar replaced the former tripod. Atop either end of the island was a VI-01 'nodding' height-finder, and the sensor fit was completed by a ZW-01 navigation radar above the bridge. The original AA armament of six quadruple pompoms and single 40mm was removed and replaced by 12 single 40mm mountings, two of which occupied each quadrant with the remaining two pairs at either end of the island. Soon after the ship recommissioned, however, the port forward pair was removed to clear the end of the angled deck. A number of major internal compartments were

Karel Doorman in early 1950s

Navarret Collection

redesigned, and the main and auxiliary machinery received a complete overhaul.

After modernisation *Karel Doorman* operated a squadron of Sea Hawk FGA 6 jet fighters and a squadron of

TBM-3 Avengers. These were replaced in the early 1960s by eight S2F-1 Tracker ASW aircraft and six HSS-IN Seabat helicopters, the ship becoming the centre of a submarine hunter-killer group.

In 1965–66 *Karel Doorman* was reboilered with units removed from the uncompleted British carrier *Leviathan* of the same class. She was badly damaged by a boiler-room fire on 29.4.68, and was subsequently

sold to Argentina, being first refitted by Wilton-Fijenoord. In this refit she also received the turbines from *Leviathan*.

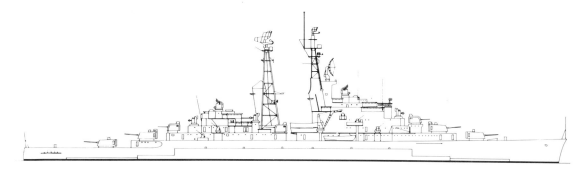

De Ruyter 1960

The hulls of the two *Provincien* class cruisers – an enlargement of the pre-war *De Ruyter* design – were still intact at the end of the Second World War, although little work had been done on them during the German occupation. *De Zeven Provincien* (which had been given an 'Atlantic' bow with more pronounced rake and flare, on the instructions of the German Navy), had been launched with a view to using her to block the port of Rotterdam, while *Eendragt* was still on the stocks. All of the equipment intended for the ships had been removed by the Germans; much of this was in any case obsolete, so construction was postponed until 1947 when completely new plans were drawn up with the aid of the British.

The armament was revised to take account of the increased threat from the air. Eight 152mm DP guns with an elevation of 60°, partly manufactured by Wilton-Fijenoord under licence from Bofors, replaced the former battery of ten 150mm. The new weapons had a rate of fire of 15 rounds per minute and were fully automatic and radar-controlled, as was the new secondary battery of twin-mounted 57mm guns in quick-revolving triaxially stabilised turrets. Eight Bofors 40mm/70 in single mounts and a 103mm flare launcher were later added.

War experience favoured the abandonment of the original layout of the propulsion machinery – three boiler rooms followed by three engine rooms – in favour of the unit system. The whole plant was therefore divided into two independent units each consisting of a boiler room and an engine room.

These two major modifications resulted in considerable changes in the internal layout of the ships because of the different arrangement of magazines, hoists, and boiler trunking. The adoption of the unit system for the propulsion machinery also necessitated a second funnel, while the need to accommodate an action information centre, new fire control stations, navigational aids and air and surface search antennae resulted in major changes in the bridge structure – which doubled in size – and the provision of two large tripod masts. In order to preserve deck space the forefunnel trunking was incorporated into the bridge structure and the foremast built around it, and the mainmast was rebuilt around the second funnel fol-

DE RUYTER class *cruisers*

Displacement:	9529t standard; 11,850t full load
Dimensions:	591ft pp, 615ft (*De Zeven Provincien* 609ft) oa × 57ft × 22ft
	182.4m, 187.3m (185.7m) × 17.3m × 6.7m
Machinery:	2-shaft De Schelde-Parsons geared steam turbines, 4 boilers, 85,000shp = 32kts
Armament:	8–152mm (4×2), 8–57mm (4×2), 8–40mm (8×1). See notes
Sensors:	Radar LW-01, DA-01, VI-01, ZW-01, 2 M25, 2 M45. See notes
Complement:	926

No	Name	Builder	Laid down	Launched	Comp	Fate
C 801	DE RUYTER (ex-*De Zeven Provincien*)	Wilton-Fijenoord	5.9.39	24.12.44	18.11.53	To Peru 1973
C 802	DE ZEVEN PROVINCIEN (ex-*Eendragt*, ex-*Kijkduin*)	Rotterdam DD	19.5.39	22.8.50	17.12.53	To Peru 1976

lowing sea trials. Welding was used wherever practicable and aluminium alloy employed extensively in order to keep topweight within limits. In spite of this the ships turned out over 1000t heavier than the original design, while retaining the same dimensions.

Other modifications made as a result of war experience included the dispersal of the electric generators (AC replacing DC), the dispersal of living quarters, and the incorporation of the latest damage-control techniques. The elimination of scuttles and the accompanying need for more ventilation and air-conditioning placed additional demands on electrical generating capacity, which had to be greatly increased. On completion the two ships, which by now had been renamed, conducted their trials in Arctic and Equatorial waters respectively.

It was planned to fit both ships with Terrier for operations in the northeast Atlantic, but the cost of reconstruction was considerable, and it was felt that the remaining useful life of *De Ruyter* was too short to justify the expense involved. The conversion of *De Zeven Provincien* involved plating up the main deck to the forecastle deck aft because of the extra depth needed to accommodate the missile magazine rings; small openings in the stern were needed for line handling. The after 152mm and 57mm mountings and the forward 40mm mountings were removed; armament as reconstructed was thus 1 Terrier Mk 10 SAM launcher (40 missiles), 4–152mm (2×2), 6–57mm (3×2) and 4–40mm (4×1). A new mainmast carrying the 3-D SPS-39 antenna was sited aft of the second funnel, the LW-01 air search antenna being

relocated on the forward edge of the funnel itself. ZW-01 was retained, as were one each of the two M25 and M45 sets, and two SPG-55s were fitted for missile guidance. In a later modification (1971–72), the obsolescent VI-01 height-finder was removed and the DA-01 scanner relocated in its place in order to reduce topweight. The original SPS-39 scanner was replaced by an AN/SPA-72 planar antenna, and Corvus chaff dispensers were added at 01 level abreast the bridge.

Both cruisers served as squadron flagships throughout their careers, being succeeded in that role by the *Tromp* class missile destroyers. The Terrier installation on *De Zeven Provincien* had to be removed and returned to the USA when she was sold to Peru.

De Zeven Provincien after Terrier SAM conversion

Holland as completed

HOLLAND class *destroyers*

Displacement:	2215t standard; 2765t full load
Dimensions:	361ft pp, 371ft oa × 37ft × 17ft 109.9m, 113.1m × 11.4m × 5.1m
Machinery:	2-shaft Werkspoor-Parsons geared steam turbines, 4 boilers, 45,000shp = 32kts. Range 4000nm at 18kts
Armament:	4–120mm (2×2), 1–40mm, 2–375mm ASW mortars (2×4), 2 DC racks
Sensors:	Radar LW-02, DA-01, ZW-01, M45; sonar Types 170B, 162
Complement:	247

No	Name	Builder	Laid down	Launched	Comp	Fate
D 808	HOLLAND	Rotterdam DD	21.4.50	11.4.53	31.12.54	To Peru 1978
D 809	ZEELAND	Royal Scheldt	12.1.51	27.6.53	1.3.55	Stricken 1979
D 810	NOORD BRABANT	Royal Scheldt	1.3.51	28.11.53	1.6.55	Scrapped following collision 1974
D 811	GELDERLAND	Wilton-Fijenoord	10.3.51	19.9.53	17.8.55	Hulked 1973

Specifically designed for ocean ASW operations, the *Holland* class were the first European fleet destroyers to be completed without anti-ship torpedoes. They were required to protect task forces or convoys against submarine attack, to hunt submarines either singly or in ASW hunter-killer groups, to assist in the air defence of task forces or convoys, and to defend them against attack by light surface forces. To equip them for the latter two roles they were to carry a heavy dual-purpose armament; the 120mm Bofors twin mounting chosen was fully automatic and radar-controlled, capable of 45 rounds per minute and with an elevation from −10° to +85°. Additional back-up in the anti-air role was to be provided by five 57mm, while a number of ASW mortars (including the British Squid) were considered before the adoption of the 4-barrelled Bofors 375mm.

Six ships were ordered in 1948 for completion in 1952, and six more in 1950 for completion 1953–55, but it proved impossible to meet these dates largely because of the damage caused to the Dutch defence industries by the war. In order to speed construction the first four units were built using

equipment salvaged from destroyers of the *Isaac Sweers* class and stored away in sheds during the German occupation. The other eight units then became a separate sub-group (see below).

The *Holland* class were fitted with propulsion machinery which had been designed for much smaller destroyers, and this imposed some restrictions on size and maximum speed compared with their successors. Two of the sets of turbines had been built prewar for the uncompleted units of the *Isaac Sweers* class, while a further two similar sets had been ordered by the Germans. In spite of this, 40.3kts were achieved on trials, albeit without a number of important items of equipment on board.

The hull form is reminiscent of contemporary British destroyers. Unusually, for ships of their size, side armour as well as deck protection was incorporated in order to reduce vulnerability to near-misses from aerial bombing, and great attention was paid to watertight subdivision. The high-tensile A52 steel which had been proved so successful in prewar vessels was used for plating and all structural work. In order to reduce topweight, aluminium alloy was used wherever possible, the entire after deckhouse being so constructed. Electric welding was used throughout – the most extensive use to date of this technique by Netherlands shipyards.

Wind tunnel tests on a forefunnel enclosed in a quadruped lattice mast led to the adoption of a common funnel design for the destroyers, the two cruisers and the *Karel Doorman* (on refit). The air search radars under development were not ready at the time of completion of the *Holland* class, and all four ships were initially fitted with a pole mainmast. This was changed to a short lattice structure in 1955, but the DA-01 and LW-02 antennae were not fitted until 1957–58. The extra topweight involved may have been responsible for the reduction of the light AA armament to a single 40mm fitted forward of the second funnel.

In the late 1950s it was proposed that the after 120mm be replaced by guided missiles, but the conversion never materialised and the ships continued in service without any major modification until disposed of in the mid-1970s. The 120mm mountings from *Gelderland* were installed in the new *Tromp* class.

Holland c1960

Navarret Collection

Friesland as completed

FRIESLAND class *destroyers*

Displacement:	2497t standard; 3070t full load
Dimensions:	370ft pp, 381ft oa × 38ft × 17ft 112.8m, 116.0m × 11.7m × 5.2m
Machinery:	2-shaft Werkspoor geared steam turbines, 4 boilers, 60,000shp = 36kts. Range 4000nm at 18kts
Armament:	4–120mm (2×2), 6–40mm (6×1), 2–375mm ASW mortars (2×4), 2 DC racks
Sensors:	Radar LW-02, DA-01, ZW-01, M45; sonar Types 170B, 162
Complement:	284

The major difference between the *Friesland* class and their predecessors lay in the increased size and power of their propulsion machinery, which was identical with that of the US *Gearing* class; 42.8kts were attained on trials. The increase in length and displacement enabled them to carry a heavier battery of light AA guns: four single 40mm were grouped around a built-up after structure carrying the lattice mainmast, and a further two were fitted forward of the bridge.

In 1960 *Utrecht* was fitted with eight 533mm anti-submarine torpedo tubes, four on each side of the upper deck. *Overijssel* followed in 1961, but the project was dropped – as was a similar one in the Royal Navy – because of new developments in ASW, and the tubes were removed.

No	Name	Builder	Laid down	Launched	Comp	Fate
D 812	FRIESLAND	Amsterdam	17.12.51	21.2.53	22.3.56	Stricken 1979
D 813	GRONINGEN	Amsterdam	21.2.52	9.1.54	12.9.56	To Peru 1980
D 814	LIMBURG	Royal Scheldt	28.11.53	5.9.55	31.10.56	To Peru 1980
D 815	OVERIJSSEL	Wilton-Fijenoord	15.10.53	8.8.55	4.10.57	Stricken 1982
D 816	DRENTHE	Amsterdam	9.1.54	26.3.55	1.8.57	To Peru 1981
D 817	UTRECHT	Royal Scheldt	15.2.54	2.6.56	1.10.57	To Peru 1980
D 818	ROTTERDAM	Rotterdam DD	7.1.54	26.1.56	28.2.57	To Peru 1981
D 819	AMSTERDAM	Amsterdam	26.3.55	25.8.56	10.4.58	To Peru 1980

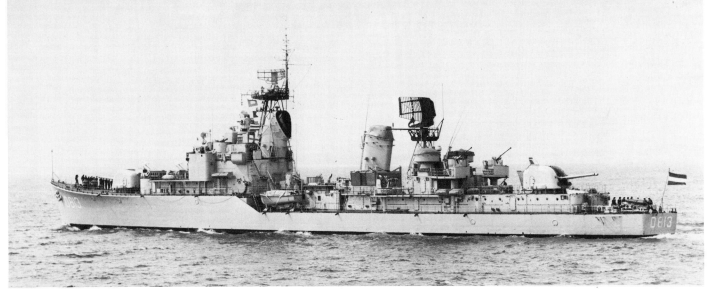

Groningen 1980   C & S Taylor

The two forward 40mm were removed in the mid-1960s, and the fire control radar for the remaining 40mm in 1977–78. In the early 1970s the British sonars originally fitted were replaced by a CWE-610 – the same model fitted in the *Tromp* class frigates.

From their completion the *Friesland* and *Holland* classes constituted the backbone of the ASW hunting groups and they have now been replaced in that role by the 'Standard' frigates.

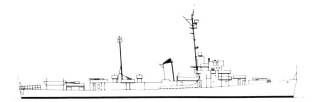

De Zeeuw 1966

These ex-American DEs of the *Cannon* class were purchased with MDAP funds in 1950; the first four were delivered in 1950 and the last pair in 1951. *Van Ewijck, Dubois, De Zeeuw* and *Van Zijll* retained their triple bank of torpedo tubes when transferred, but these, together with most of the 20mm AA, were later removed. All six ships were returned to the US Navy in December 1967 for scrapping.

Ex-US CANNON class *destroyer escorts*

Armament: 3–3in (3×1), 6–40mm (3×2), 8 to 10–20mm (8 to 10×1), 1 Hedgehog, 4 DCT, 2 DC racks, 3–21in TT (1×3) except *Van Amstel, De Bitter*

Other particulars: As US *Cannon* class (DET type)

No	Name	Builder	Acquired	Fate
F 806	VAN AMSTEL (ex-*Burrows*)	Dravo, Wilmington	1950	Returned USA Dec 67, BU
F 807	DE BITTER (ex-*Rhinehart*)	Federal, Newark	1950	Returned USA Dec 67, BU
F 808	VAN EWIJCK (ex-*Gustafson*)	Federal, Newark	1950	Returned USA Dec 67, BU
F 809	DUBOIS (ex-*O'Neill*)	Federal, Newark	1950	Returned USA Dec 67, BU
F 810	DE ZEEUW (ex-*Eisner*)	Federal, Newark	1951	Returned USA Dec 67, BU
F 811	VAN ZIJLL (ex-*Stern*)	Federal, Newark	1951	Returned USA Dec 67, BU

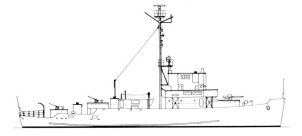

Vos 1970

NB 1/750 scale

The six 'Roofdier' class frigates were all built in the USA with MDAP funds. They were designed to escort slow coastal convoys in Channel and North Sea areas and are operated as a single squadron by the RNethN.

They are slow, lively ships fitted with Second World War-pattern anti-aircraft weapons and detection equipment. They have proved useful for a number of peacetime tasks, especially fishery protection, and some will probably be retained into the 1980s, when a start will be made on their replacements, the 'M' class frigates. Many of the 20mm AA guns were removed during the 1970s.

'ROOFDIER' class *frigates*

Displacement:	808t standard; 975t full load
Dimensions:	180ft pp, 185ft oa × 33ft × 10ft *54.9m, 56.2m × 10.0m × 2.9m*
Machinery:	2 shafts, 2 General Motors 12–567 ATL diesels, 1600bhp = 15kts. Range 4300nm at 10kts
Armament:	1–3in, 6 or 4–40mm (6×1; *Panter, Jaguar* 4×1), 8–20mm, 1 Hedgehog, 2 (*Panter, Jaguar* 4) DCT
Sensors:	Sonar QCU-2
Complement:	96

No	Name	Builder	Laid down	Launched	Comp	Fate
F 817	WOLF	Avondale	15.11.52	2.1.54	26.3.54	Extant 1982
F 818	FRET	General SB	18.12.52	30.7.53	4.5.54	Extant 1982
F 819	HERMELIJN	General SB	2.3.53	6.3.54	5.8.54	Extant 1982
F 820	VOS	General SB	3.8.52	1.5.54	2.12.54	Extant 1982
F 821	PANTER	Avondale	1.12.52	30.1.54	11.6.54	Extant 1982
F 822	JAGUAR	Avondale	10.12.52	20.3.54	11.6.54	Extant 1982

NETHERLANDS

Built under MDAP, the frigate *Lynx* was similar to the Italian *Albatros* and Danish *Triton* classes. She served for only five years in the RNethN before being transferred to Italy in 1961. For further details see under *Albatros* class (Italy).

LYNX *frigate*

Displacement:	800t standard; 950t full load
Dimensions:	228ft pp, 250ft 5in oa × 31ft 8in × 9ft
	69.5m, 76.3m × 9.7m × 2.8m
Machinery:	2 shafts, 2 Fiat diesels, 5200bhp = 19kts. Range 2400nm at 18kts
Armament:	2–3in (2×1), 2–40mm (1×2), 2 Hedgehogs, 2 DCT
Sensors:	Sonar QCU-2
Complement:	109

No	Name	Builder	Laid down	Launched	Comp	Fate
F 823	LYNX	Breda Marghera	Jul 53	31.7.54	2.10.56	To Italy Oct 61

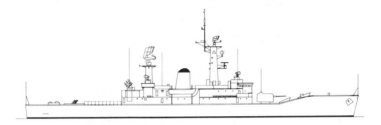

Van Speijk 1971

Built to replace the elderly DEs of the *Van Amstel* class, the *Van Speijk*s were an adaptation of the British *Leander* class. In order to facilitate rapid construction few changes were made in the basic design, and even the armament of the British ships was adopted in its entirety, thus adding the 114mm gun to the 120mm standard in other Dutch vessels. The stipulation that as much equipment of Dutch manufacture as possible be incorporated led to a number of changes in other areas, in particular the search radars and fire control systems, which were provided by HSA. The size advantage of the small M44 director provided for Seacat over the British model enabled a second launcher to be worked in on the hangar roof.

Four ships were ordered in 1962, with the other two following in 1964. They were the first Dutch escorts to operate helicopters, and on completion were quickly integrated into the ASW squadrons alongside the *Holland* and *Friesland* classes.

Plans were drawn up in 1974 for an extensive mid-life modernisation which aimed at improving the ships' operational efficiency and making

VAN SPEIJK class *frigates*

Displacement:	2200t standard; 2850t full load
Dimensions:	360ft wl, 372ft oa × 41ft × 18ft
	109.7m, 113.4m × 12.5m × 5.8m
Machinery:	2-shaft Werkspoor-English Electric geared steam turbines, 2 boilers, 30,000shp = 28.5kts. Range 4500nm at 12kts
Armament:	2–4.5in (1×2), 2 Seacat SAM (2×4), 1 helicopter, 1 ASW mortar Mk 10 (1×3). See notes
Sensors:	Radar LW-03, DA-02, M45, M44; sonar Types 170B, 162. See notes
Complement:	251

No	Name	Builder	Laid down	Launched	Comp	Fate
F 802	VAN SPEIJK	Amsterdam	1.10.63	5.3.65	14.2.67	Extant 1982
F 803	VAN GALEN	Royal Scheldt	25.7.63	19.6.65	1.3.67	Extant 1982
F 804	TJERK HIDDES	Amsterdam	1.6.64	17.12.65	16.8.67	Extant 1982
F 805	VAN NES	Royal Scheldt	25.7.63	26.3.66	9.8.67	Extant 1982
F 814	ISAAC SWEERS	Amsterdam	5.5.65	10.3.67	15.5.68	Extant 1982
F 815	EVERTSEN	Royal Scheldt	6.7.65	18.6.66	21.12.67	Extant 1982

them compatible with the new generation of frigates coming into service. Major changes in armament were the first priority, and as far as possible systems installed in the 'Standard' frigates were adopted. The 114mm twin mounting was replaced by an OTO-Melara 76mm compact gun, and Harpoon canisters were added between the funnel and the mainmast

Triple Mk 32 ASW tubes (2×3) were placed abreast the mainmast (in later conversions they were moved to the upper deck), and the hangar was extended aft to accommodate the new Lynx helicopter, the well for the Limbo mortar well being plated over to form part of the flight deck. Seacat was retained, and 2 Corvus chaff launchers were installed.

The operations room was completely rebuilt and a SEWACO-V data and weapons control system installed. The DA-02 search radar atop the foremast was replaced by a DA-05, and communications facilities were improved. The British sonars were replaced by the same US-manufactured model fitted in the *Tromp* class frigates. The full sensor outfit now consisted of LW-03, DA-05, M45 (1), M44 (2), CWE-610 and PDE-700.

Significant reductions in the complement of the ships (to 231) were achieved by increased automation of the propulsion machinery. Boiler-regulating equipment was adopted which automates fuel-spraying and enables a constant steam temperature to be maintained with greater ease. The reduction in complement enabled improvements to be made in accommodation and messing facilities.

Van Speijk was reconstructed at Den Helder Royal Dockyard 1976–78, *Van Galen* 1977–79, *Van Nes* 1978–80 and *Tjerk Hiddes* 1978–81, while *Evertsen* and *Isaac Sweers* were taken in hand in 1979 and 1980 respectively.

When the refit programme has been completed the ships will form one of the three ASW groups and will be allocated to the Channel Approaches.

Isaac Sweers 1979   C & S Taylor

Tromp as completed

C & S Taylor

Tromp 1975

TROMP class *guided missile frigates*

Displacement:	4308t standard; 5400t full load
Dimensions:	430ft pp, 453ft oa × 49ft × 15ft
	131.0m, 138.2m × 14.8m × 4.6m
Machinery:	2-shaft COGOG: 2 TM 3B Olympus gas turbines, 44,000shp = 28kts, plus 2 RM 1A Tyne gas turbines, 8200shp = 18kts. Range 5000nm at 18kts
Armament:	1 Mk 13 SAM launcher (40 SM-1 missiles), 1 NATO Sea Sparrow SAM (1×8), 2–120mm (1×2), 2 Corvus, 8 Harpoon SSM (2×4), 6 Mk 32 TT (3×2), helicopter
Sensors:	Radar SPS-01, WM-25, SPG-51C; sonar CWE-610, Type 162
Complement:	306

No	Name	Builder	Laid down	Launched	Comp	Fate
F 801	TROMP	Royal Scheldt	4.8.71	4.6.73	3.10.75	Extant 1982
F 802	DE RUYTER	Royal Scheldt	22.12.71	9.3.74	3.6.76	Extant 1982

Following discussions about how best to replace the cruisers *De Ruyter* and *De Zeven Provincien* it was decided in 1964 to build a limited number of guided missile frigates. Staff requirements demanded that they be able to give protection to a task force or convoy against aircraft and guided weapons. They would have a secondary ASW and anti-ship capability, and would have sophisticated command facilities to enable them to serve as flagships.

Beacause they were designed to operate in the Eastern Atlantic good sea-keeping qualities were essential. The solution adopted was a hull form with high freeboard, beam being increased to compensate, and non-retractable fin stabilisers. The great hull depth allows for a weather deck and a main deck running the entire length of the ship, plus two lower decks. This in turn provides the necessary space for an extensive electronics outfit and improved habitability. The construction of the hull and the superstructure below the radome is of steel, the remaining upperworks being of sea-water resistant aluminium alloy.

Initially the ships were to have had steam propulsion, but eventually gas turbines were adopted to reduce crew numbers. The COGOG system chosen is the same as that installed in contemporary British vessels, but with gearing designed and supplied by the shipbuilders. The Olympus main turbines were down-rated to improve gas-generator life and ease maintenance. The Netherlands Navy

was not entirely happy with the cruising power supplied by the Tynes, and it is envisaged that the latter will be replaced during the ships' half-life refit. The machinery arrangement has the Olympus turbines inside the forward pair of diesel generators in the first machinery room, the cruise turbines and gearing in the second machinery room, and a further pair of diesel generators in a third auxiliary machinery room. The main gearboxes and the fuel and lubricating pumps are designed as watertight units, enabling the main or cruise engines to be used in the event of one of the machinery rooms being flooded. The entire ship's electrical requirements can be supplied by only two of the 1000kW generators, allowing maintenance on a third with the fourth available for standby. Twin spade rudders are fitted, each with its own electro-hydraulic steering gear. The

rudders are electrically synchronised but can be operated independently.

Stringent noise and shock requirements were laid down. The cruise turbines and intake/uptake systems are resiliently mounted; the Olympus turbines are mounted on pneumatic-hydraulic constant-positioning mounting systems; and the diesel generators are on double-mounting systems with noise-absorbent hoods. Silencers in the uptakes and intakes further reduce transmitted noise. The entire machinery installation is controlled and monitored from a highly-automated machinery control room, situated near the operations room to ensure good communications. A new system of ventilation and air-conditioning allows individual control over all living and electronic spaces, and the ships are designed for complete NBC close-down.

Originally they were to have been

fitted with the Sea Dart SAM in return for British adoption of the large HSA 3-D radar in the new generation of carriers and the Type 82 escorts. This agreement fell through, however, when the Dutch decided in favour of the smaller, American Tartar system. The 120mm mountings were removed from the old destroyer *Gelderland*; modifications were made, including the provision of full automation. Control of all weapons and the co-ordination of data is performed by a SEWACO-1 system based on DAISY-1 computers and display sub-systems using equipment of predominently Dutch manufacture.

Since completion *Tromp* and *De Ruyter* have served in their intended role as flagships of two of the ASW hunting groups.

85

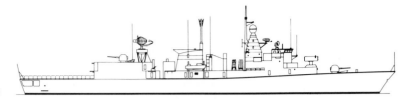

Kortenaer 1978

KORTENAER ('STANDARD') class *guided missile frigates*

Displacement:	3000t standard; 3750t full load
Dimensions:	400ft pp, 427ft oa × 47ft × 14ft
	121.8m, 130.2m × 14.4m × 4.4m
Machinery:	2-shaft COGOG: 2 Olympus TM 3B gas turbines, 51,600shp = 30kts, plus 2 Tyne TM 1C gas turbines, 9800shp = 20kts. Range 4000nm at 20kts
Armament:	(ASW version) 1 NATO Sea Sparrow SAM (1×8), 1–76mm 1–40mm (except *Kortenaer* and *Callenburg* 2–76mm), 8 Harpoon SSM (2×4), 4–324mm Mk 32 TT, 2 Corvus, 2 helicopters
	(AD version) 1 Mk 13 SAM launcher (40 SM-1 missiles), 1 Sea Sparrow SAM (8×1), 1–76mm 1–30mm VSRAD, 8 Harpoon SSM (2×4), 4–324mm Mk 32 TT
Sensors:	Radar (ASW) LW-08, WM-25, STIR, ZW-06; (AD) LW-08?, SPS-52?, SPG-51, WM-25, ZW-06; sonar SQS-505
Complement:	176 (200 max)

No	Name	Builder	Laid down	Launched	Comp	Fate
F 807	KORTENAER	Royal Scheldt	8.4.75	18.12.76	26.10.78	Extant 1982
F 808	CALLENBURGH	Royal Scheldt	30.6.75	26.3.77	26.7.79	Extant 1982
F 809	VAN KINSBERGEN	Royal Scheldt	2.9.75	16.4.77	24.4.80	Extant 1982
F 810	BANCKERT	Royal Scheldt	25.2.76	30.9.78	29.10.80	Extant 1982
F 811	PIET HEIN	Royal Scheldt	28.4.77	3.6.78	14.4.81	Extant 1982
F 812	PIETER FLORISZ (i)	Royal Scheldt	1.7.77	15.12.79		To Greece
F 813	WITTE DE WITH (i)	Royal Scheldt	13.6.78	27.10.79		To Greece
F 816	ABRAHAM CRIJNSSON	Royal Scheldt	25.10.78	16.5.81		Building
F 823	PHILIPS VAN ALMONDE	Wilton-Fijenoord	3.10.77	11.8.79	2.12.81	Extant 1982
F 824	BLOYS VAN TRESLONG	Wilton-Fijenoord	27.4.78	15.11.80		Building
F 825	JAN VAN BRAKEL	Royal Scheldt	16.11.79	16.5.81		Building
F 826	PIETER FLORISZ (ii), (ex-*Willem van der Zaan*)	Royal Scheldt	15.1.80	8.5.82		Building
Air Defence version						
F 812	JACOB VAN HEEMSKERCK	Royal Scheldt	21.1.81			Building
F 813	WITTE DE WITH (ii)	Royal Scheldt	15.12.81			Building

In the late 1960s the Dutch began to think about replacements for the twelve ASW destroyers of the *Holland* and *Friesland* classes. At first a modified *Van Speijk* was proposed, armed with a twin 120mm, SSMs, a PDMS and ASW torpedo tubes. It was rejected because of its limited cruising range and the lack of space for mid-life conversion. An attempt was then made to find sufficient common ground with the Royal Navy to share at least a hull with the projected Type 22, but this, too, proved impossible. Finally the American FFG 7 and French C 70 designs were also examined, but failed to meet requirements.

The Dutch therefore produced their own 'Standard' design – so-called because it was planned to build ASW and AAW versions on a standard, common hull, and because it conformed to the NATO requirements for ocean escorts. The close contacts with other NATO navies pursued in the early stages of the design are reflected in the adoption of a hull form similar to that of contemporary French construction, with continuous upper and main decks, a single rudder of the semi-balanced type, and a clipper bow with 'negative' sheer. The desire for good performance in a seaway resulted in a length/beam ratio less favourable than is generally accepted, and careful design was necessary to ensure that the ships met speed requirements. The hull is, in fact, finer forward than in the Standard's French counterparts, giving the ships a cigar shape.

The propulsion system and machinery layout is identical with that installed in *Tromp*, except that the power of both the Olympus and the Tyne cruise turbines was increased, giving higher maximum and cruise speeds. All machinery is spring-mounted to reduce noise and shock. As in *Tromp*, a single pair of fin stabilisers is fitted. A centralised technical control room contains panels for the propulsion machinery, for electrical supply and for NBCD. Only 4–6 men are needed on watch, while the total engine room complement is only 29. As with *Tromp*, the ship can be completely fought and navigated from the operations room, which is fitted with a SEWACO-III action data system. On the main deck there is a central passageway running the entire length of the ship, and personnel spaces are grouped in such a way as to minimise traffic.

The weapon fit reflects the ship's tasks, defined as the defence of a task force or convoy against submarines and missile-armed aircraft. The weapons systems were selected with a view to furthering standardisation within NATO. Only one WG 13 Lynx helicopter will be carried in peacetime, but two can be operated and maintained. The TT fire MU 46 torpedoes.

Eight ships were ordered in 1974, with a further four in 1976. A joint agreement was reached in 1975 for the construction of similar vessels for the Federal German Navy. Iran also expressed the intention of ordering further units from European yards and having them fitted with American weapons and sensors, but the order was cancelled when the Shah fell from power.

Air Defence (AD) version
Following the decision to build only two ships of the *Tromp* class it was envisaged that a special Air Defence version of the 'Standard' would be built to provide a third flagship for the ASW groups. This unit would have been the 13th hull. In 1980 and 1981, however, two 'Standard' class frigates were sold to Greece, and these were taken from the Navy's production line in order to speed delivery. It was subsequently decided that both replacement vessels would be of the Air Defence type, and that the 13th unit would be cancelled in favour of a fifth frigate of the projected 'M' class. The essential difference between the AD version and the original ASW design is the substitution of a Mk 13 Tartar launcher and SPG-51 tracker/illuminators for the double helicopter hangar. The Sea Sparrow SAM will employ a vertical launch system.

Kortenaer as completed   Official

'M' class design

The 'M' (for 'multi-purpose') class was designed to provide replacements for the six ships of the 'Roofdier' class. Whereas the latter were small, low-performance coastal frigates, however, the 'M' class are large, sophisticated vessels capable of ocean operations. They are required to cooperate with, and if necessary replace, 'Standard' class frigates in the ocean escort groups.

They have many features in common with the larger 'Standards'; their hull-form, although fuller forward, is based on the same formula of two continuous decks, and they have a clipper bow with 'negative' sheer and an open quarterdeck beneath the helicopter landing pad. A single pair of stabilisers is fitted abreast the bridge structure.

The layout of the propulsion and auxiliary machinery is similar to that of the 'Standard', although only a single Olympus main turbine will be installed, resulting in a slight reduction in maximum speed. More significant is the adoption of diesels for the cruise machinery, enabling the funnel to be faired into the helicopter hangar because of the elimination of the after set of air intakes and shifting

'M' class *guided missile frigates*

Displacement:	1900t light; 2650t full load
Dimensions:	344ft pp, 367ft oa × 45ft × 18ft max *105.0m, 111.8m × 13.8m × 5.8m*
Machinery:	2-shaft CODOG: 1 TM 3B Olympus gas turbine, 28,560shp = 28kts, plus 2 SEMT-Pielstick diesels, 8,450bhp = 19–20kts. Range 4000nm at 19kts
Armament:	NATO Sea Sparrow SAM (1×8 or VLS, see notes), 1–76mm, 1–30mm VSRAD, 8 Harpoon SSM (2×4), 4–324mm Mk 32 TT, 2 Corvus, 1 helicopter
Sensors:	Radar DA-08, WM-25, ZW-06; sonar PHS-36
Complement:	100

the 'balance' of the ship aft. This has resulted in shorter shaft runs and consequent weight economies. The choice of diesels was influenced by new developments in flexible engine mountings and in the construction of the engines themselves, reducing noise emission to that of a gas turbine. A speed of 15kts can be attained with a single diesel on line, and 19–20kts with two. Initially a single shaft with a single rudder was envisaged, but this was abandoned in favour of a more conventional two-shaft arrangement.

All machinery is controlled from the machinery control centre, which has automatic monitoring equipment. Automation allied to unit replacement maintenance technique is such that a crew of only 80–100 will be possible.

There is considerable commonality of weapons and sensors with the 'Standard' to enable training requirements to be reduced and to facilitate logistical back-up. Tactical data coordination and weapons control is performed by a similar SEWACO installation using the same family of DAISY computers. The PHS-36 bow sonar is of Dutch design and manufacture. It is not yet clear whether the ship will have the customary 8-cell launcher for Sea Sparrow or whether the latter missile will be fired from vertical launch tubes fitted abreast the funnel.

The ships are specially fitted for the North Sea role. Four Gemini-type dinghies are stacked to starboard of the single hangar, to be used for boarding ships and oil rigs, and for Royal Marine landing operations. There is accommodation for a detachment of 30 marines in the forward superstructure. A single helicopter was considered acceptable because of the likely proximity to friendly bases of the ship's primary operating areas.

It was originally envisaged that the 'M' class would consist of four units, but a fifth was added in 1981 as a replacement for the 13th (Air Defence) unit of the 'Standard' class. Construction is scheduled to commence in 1983.

SUBMARINES

These two ex-British 'T' class boats, launched on 27.6.42 and 21.8.44 respectively, were lent to the Netherlands from 1948 until 1953. They were unmodified save for the fitting of a snorkel.

Ex-British 'T' class *submarines*

Particulars:	As British 'T' class (1940–42 programmes)			
No	**Name**	**Builder**	**Acquired**	**Fate**
S 811	DOLFIJN (ex-*Taurus*)	Vickers-Armstrong, Barrow	1948	Returned RN 1953
S 813	ZEEHOND (ex-*Tapir*)	Vickers-Armstrong, Barrow	1948	Returned RN 1953

(For illustration see under United States)

These two submarines were former *Balao* class boats acquired on loan from the US Navy, initially for a period of five years. The loan period was later extended to ten years and then to fifteen. They were specially modified prior to their transfer to a GUPPY IA configuration. This involved the streamlining of the hull form and fin, in which a snorkel was incorporated, and the installation of improved batteries for a higher submerged speed.

Walrus (launched 20.2.44) and *Zeeleeuw* (9.1.44) were extensively employed as ASW targets from the time of their transfer in 1953 until their disposal in 1970–71.

Ex-US BALAO class *submarines*

Displacement:	1830t surface; 2440t submerged
Dimensions:	307ft oa × 27ft × 17ft *93.6m × 8.2m × 5.2m*
Machinery:	2 shafts, 4 2-stroke diesels plus electric motors, 6500bhp/4600shp = 17kts/5kts. Range 12,000nm at 10kts
Armament:	10–21in TT (6 bow, 4 stern; 24 torpedoes)
Complement:	79

No	**Name**	**Builder**	**Acquired**	**Fate**
S 802	WALRUS (ex-*Icefish*)	Manitowoc SB	1953	Returned USN 1971, BU
S 803	ZEELEEUW (ex-*Hawkbill*)	Manitowoc SB	1953	Returned USN 1970, BU

Dolfijn as completed   Navarret Collection

Potvis 1976

As part of the postwar Fleet Plan, the construction of four new submarines was proposed and approved in 1949. These were to be of a novel triple-hulled design originally conceived by M F Gunning, who had been appointed Chief Naval Constructor at the Netherlands Naval HQ set up in London in 1940. He had proposed the idea as a solution to the problem of supplying Malta, and model experiments were carried out during the war in the Admiralty Experimental Basin at Haslar.

Three cylinders are arranged in a triangular shape within a pressure-tight steel hull. The upper cylinder accommodates the crew, navigation equipment and armament, while the lower two house the propulsion machinery and batteries. The machinery is therefore divided into two independent units, each consisting of a 12cyl diesel, an electric motor, a 168-cell battery and a shaft. A single conventional rudder is fitted. The lower cylinders are shorter than the upper one, resulting in a hull which tapers fore and aft. The upper cylinder contains the fire control and machinery control centres, located directly beneath the large fin,

DOLFIJN (ii) class *submarines*

Displacement:	1494ft surfaced; 1826t submerged
Dimensions:	261ft oa × 26ft × 16ft
	79.5m × 7.9m × 4.9m
Machinery:	2 shafts, 2 MAN 12cyl diesels plus 2 electric motors, 3100bhp/4400hp = 14.5kts/17kts
Armament:	8–533mm TT (4 bow, 4 stern)
Sensors:	Radar Type 1001, sonar ?
Complement:	64

No	Name	Builder	Laid down	Launched	Comp	Fate
S 808	DOLFIJN	Rotterdam DD	30.12.54	20.5.59	16.12.60	Extant 1982
S 809	ZEEHOND	Rotterdam DD	30.12.54	20.2.60	16.3.61	Extant 1982
S 804	POTVIS	Wilton-Fijenoord	17.9.62	12.1.65	2.11.65	Extant 1982
S 805	TONIJN	Wilton-Fijenoord	27.11.62	14.6.65	24.2.66	Extant 1982

accommodation for the crew on each side, and two sets of four tubes with torpedo-handling rooms at each end of the boat.

The advantages of the triple-hull form include greater stability (because the heavy items such as machinery and batteries are located in the lower cylinders), better distribution of space, easier prefabrication, the safe storage of fuel between the three hulls, and greater diving depth.

Two submarines were ordered while the detailed drawings were still

in preparation, but the order for the second pair was cancelled and construction was postponed while the possibility of nuclear propulsion was examined. Adoption of the latter would undoubtedly have demanded a complete recasting of the design because of the space needed for the reactors themselves and for the vertical movement of the control rods. In the event the complexity and cost proved prohibitive, and in 1962 the original order was reinstated. The later two boats had a number of mod-

ifications, but modernisation of the first pair in the late 1960s brought them up to the same standard. All boats now have the HSA M8 fire control system.

In the early 1970s, *Zeehond* had a new sonar fitted in a dome atop the hull casing. *Tonijn* and *Potvis* had their main engines replaced by SEMT-Pielstick PA 4 units in 1978–79. The other pair will not be modernised and will be replaced by the new *Walrus* class boats.

Zwaardvis as completed

With the loan period of the two ex-American *Walrus* class boats due to expire in 1968 the construction of two diesel-electric submarines was approved in 1964. Simultaneously the construction of the first Dutch nuclear-powered submarine was announced, but although the project was approved the following year it was abandoned in 1968 on grounds of cost.

The *Zwaardvis* class departed from the triple-hull construction of the *Dolfijn* class in favour of the high-speed teardrop hull form of the latest American submarines. They were based on the *Barbel* class, with which they share almost identical dimensions and displacement, while the hull form itself is closer to that of the experimental *Albacore*.

The interior layout is divided into three sections. The forward section accommodates the sonars, torpedo tubes and handling room. Amidships there are three decks: the upper one houses the operational spaces and some accommodation, while the middle and lower decks are for accommodation and the batteries respectively.

ZWAARDVIS class *attack submarines*

Displacement:	2350ft surfaced; 2640t submerged
Dimensions:	219ft oa × 28ft × 22ft
	66.9m × 8.4m × 6.6m
Machinery:	1 shaft, 3 Werkspoor diesels, plus 1 main electric motor, ?bhp/5000shp = 13kts/20kts.
Armament:	6–533mm TT (bow, 20 torpedoes)
Sensors:	Radar Type 1001, sonar ?
Complement:	67

No	Name	Builder	Laid down	Launched	Comp	Fate
S 806	ZWAARDVIS	Rotterdam DD	14.7.66	2.7.70	18.8.72	Extant 1982
S 807	TIJGERHAAI	Rotterdam DD	14.7.66	25.5.71	20.10.72	Extant 1982

The after section houses the machinery; three diesel generators in line abreast coupled to a single shaft, with a single electric motor behind them. All machinery is mounted on a false deck with spring suspension to make the vessel as quiet as possible. Cross-shaped rudders were adopted, similar to those on *Barbel* and contemporary SSNs.

Experience with the *Barbel* class, which had their diving planes moved from the conventional bow position to the forward end of the fin in the early

1960s, had established that a submarine of this size would not have a tendency to break the surface if so fitted. The advantages of fin-mounted diving planes – greater manoeuvrability at low speeds and near the surface, and less noise interference with sonars – were considered sufficient to justify their adoption by the Dutch boats.

As much Netherlands-manufactured equipment as possible was incorporated. The HSA M8 fire control system, which uses a digital computer, permits simultaneous

launching of two torpedoes, one of which may be wire-guided. Twenty torpedoes are carried.

Since completion the *Zwaardvis* class have been deployed, together with the four *Dolfijn* class boats, in the East Atlantic, where they have frequently operated with the submarine squadrons of the British Royal Navy. They have proved to be particularly successful boats, capable of near-silent operations, and it is intended to bring them up to the same standard as the *Walrus* (ii) class in the mid-1980s.

Intended to replace the ageing *Dolfijn* class, two boats were ordered in 1979 for completion 1983–84, with another pair to follow two years later. Nuclear propulsion was again considered but rejected on financial and technological grounds. An attempt to reach agreement with the British for a joint design once again failed – in spite of almost identical requirements – and the Dutch opted in favour of an improved *Zwaardvis* design.

The tasks of the new submarines are stated to be surveillance, attacks against submarines or surface ships with torpedoes or missiles, special operations, and joint operations in support of Netherlands or NATO task forces. Staff requirements stipulated high submerged speed, sustainable using a discreet snorkel; high manoeuvrability in the vertical and horizontal planes; deep-diving capability; the ability to undertake operations in all climates; a reduction in self-generated noise by using machinery and hull insulation; comprehensive safety and shock protection devices to improve survivability; good maintenance facilities for machinery, equipment and weapons; and a reduction in manning levels together with higher standards of crew accommodation.

WALRUS (ii) class *attack submarines*

Displacement:	2365t surfaced; 2700t submerged
Dimensions:	222ft oa × 28ft × 23ft
	67.0m × 8.4m × 7.0m
Machinery:	1 shaft, 3 SEMT-Pielstick 12 PA 4V diesels plus 1 main electric motor, ?bhp/5500shp = 12kts/20kts
Armament:	6–533mm TT (bow)
Sensors:	Radar Type 1001; sonar Thomson-CSF
Complement:	49

No	Name	Builder	Laid down	Launched	Comp	Fate
S 802	WALRUS	Rotterdam DD	11.10.79	–	–	Building
S 803	ZEELEEUW	Rotterdam DD	24.9.81			Building
		Rotterdam DD				Projected
		Rotterdam DD				Projected

An increase in diving depth has been achieved by the use of MAREL high-tensile steel, together with the necessary intercooling systems, duplex hull valves, a non-pressurised fuel system, a 'wet' exhaust system, sophisticated hydraulics and additional emergency blowing systems.

Draught has been reduced by the adoption of 'X'-shaped rudders similar to those fitted experimentally to the American *Albacore* in 1961. Micro-processor control of rudders and diving planes will give very fine control of the boat's movements at all speeds and depths.

Werkspoor, who supplied the diesels for *Zwaardvis*, had taken that engine out of production, but suitable diesels similar to those adopted for generating electrical power in the 'Standard' class frigate were purchased from SEMT-Pielstick. All electronic components, including the main electric motors, are of Dutch manufacture. The control gear is designed to give uniform speed continuity between 1.5kts and full speed.

Manpower has been reduced by 18 by the adoption of a single control room containing the machinery control and surveillance consoles and an attack centre with a SEWACO data and weapons control system based on two main computers and seven multi-purpose display consoles (GYPSY system).

The waterslug tubes can fire either Mk 37/Mk 48 torpedoes (20 carried) or Sub-Harpoon. The Thomson-CSF medium-frequency attack sonar has a passive capability as well as a wide-band active mode, and passive range-finding and passive long-range sonar are to be fitted. The submarines will also have SATNAV equipment.

MINE WARFARE VESSELS

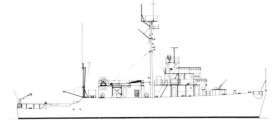
Onversaagd 1968
NB 1/750 scale

Ex-US ADJUTANT class *coastal minesweepers*

Particulars:	As US *Adjutant* class

Class:
Tampa Marine, Florida – *Beemster* (M 845), *Bedum* (M 847), *Borculo* (M 849), *Borne* (M 850), *Breukelen* (M 852)
Broward Marine, Florida – *Bolsward* (M 846), *Beilen* (M 848), *Brummen* (M 851), *Blaricum* (M 853)
G W Kneass Co, San Francisco – *Breskens* (M 855), *Boxtel* (M 857), *Brouwershaven* (M 858)
Puget Sound Navy Yard – *Brielele* (M 854), *Bruinisse* (M 856)

These fourteen coastal minesweepers of the *Adjutant* class were transferred 1953–54 under MDAP. They were constructed of wood and non-metallic alloys.

Bolsward, Breukelen and *Bruinisse* were returned to the USA in 1972. *Brummen* and *Brouwershaven* were stricken in 1974, and the remainder in 1975.

Ex-US AGILE class *ocean minesweepers*

Particulars:	As US *Agile* class

Class:
Astoria Marine Construction Co – *Onversaagd* (M 884), *Onbevreesd* (M 885), *Onvervaard* (M 888)
Peterson, Wisconsin – *Onverschrokken* (M 886), *Onvermoeid* (M 887), *Onverdrotten* (M 889)

These six *Agile* class ocean minesweepers were transferred 1954–55 under MDAP. They have wooden hulls, and diesels of non-magnetic stainless steel alloy.

In 1966 they were transferred to escort duties and renumbered A 854–59. Two years later *Onbevreesd, Onvervaard* and *Onverdrotten* became MCM Group Command and Support Ships. In 1972 *Onverschrokken* became a torpedo trials ship and was renamed *Mercuur*. *Onvermoeid* was returned to the USA in 1972, and after being refitted provisionally as a hydrographic ship *Onversaagd* was sold in 1979.

Beemster c 1960   Navarret Collection

NETHERLANDS

Dokkum 1971
NB 1/750 scale

DOKKUM class *coastal minesweepers*

Displacement:	373t standard; 417t full load
Dimensions:	153ft oa × 29ft × 8ft
	46.6m × 8.8m × 2.3m
Machinery:	2 shafts, 2 Fijenoord MAN or Werkspoor diesels, 2500bhp = 14kts
Armament:	2–40mm (2×1)
Complement:	38

No	Name	Builder	Launched	Fate
M 801	DOKKUM	Wilton-Fijenoord	12.10.54	Extant 1982
M 802	HOOGEZAND	Werf Gusto, Schiedam	22.3.55	Extant 1982
M 806	ROERMOND	Wilton-Fijenoord	13.8.55	Extant 1982
M 809	NAALDWIJK	Werf de Noord	1.2.55	Extant 1982
M 810	ABCOUDE	Werf Gusto, Schiedam	2.9.55	Extant 1982
M 812	DRACHTEN	Niestern SU	24.3.55	Extant 1982
M 813	OMMEN	J & K Smit, Kinderdijk	5.4.55	Extant 1982
M 815	GIETHORN	L K Smit & Zn, Kinderdijk	30.3.55	Extant 1982
M 817	VENLO	Arnhemse SM	21.5.55	Extant 1982
M 818	DRUNEN	Werf Gusto, Schiedam	24.3.56	Extant 1982
M 820	WOERDEN	Haarlemse SM	28.11.56	Extant 1982
M 823	NAARDEN	Wilton-Fijenoord	27.1.56	Extant 1982
M 827	HOOGEVEEN	Werf de Noord	8.5.56	Extant 1982
M 828	STAPHORST	Werf Gusto, Schiedam	21.7.56	Extant 1982
M 830	SITTARD	Niestern SU	26.4.56	Extant 1982
M 841	GEMERT	J & K Smit, Kinderdijk	13.3.56	Extant 1982
M 842	VEERE	L K Smit & Zn, Kinderdijk	9.2.56	Extant 1982
M 844	RHENEN	Arnhemse SM	31.5.56	Extant 1982
Wildervank sub-group				
M 803	WILDERVANK	De Vries Lentsch	24.2.55	Stricken 1974
M 804	STEENWIJK	Haarlemse SM	1955	Stricken 1970
M 805	GIETEN	De Haan & Oerlemans	1955	Stricken 1970
M 807	WAALWIJK	Verschure, Amsterdam	6.4.55	Stricken 1975
M 808	AXEL	De Groot & Van Vliet	5.3.55	To Oman 1974
M 811	AALSMER	Gebr Pot Bolnes	23.4.55	To Oman 1974
M 814	MEPPEL	Haarlemse SM	19.7.56	Stricken 1974
M 816	LOCHEM	E J Smit & Zn, Westerbrock	1955	Stricken 1970
M 819	GOES	De Vries Lentsch	23.3.56	Stricken 1974
M 822	LEERSUM	De Haan & Oerlemans	11.8.56	Stricken 1975
M 824	SNEEK	Verschure, Amsterdam	1956	Stricken 1970
M 826	GRIJPSKERK	De Groot & Van Vliet	10.3.56	Harbour training 1973
M 829	ELST	Gebr Pot Bolnes	21.3.56	To Ethiopia 1971
M 843	LISSE	E J Smit & Zn, Westerbrock	1956	Stricken 1970

The *Dokkum* class was based on the British 'Ton' class, 18 vessels being financed under MDAP, and a further 14 – known as the *Wildervank* sub-group – being purchased by the Netherlands. Construction was similar to that of the British vessels. The 14 units of the *Wildervank* sub-group had Werkspoor diesels in place of the Fijenoord units on the *Dokkum*s.
  Waalwijk, *Woerden*, *Leersum*, *Lisse* and *Rhenen* were fitted as diving vessels 1962–65, and *Roermond* followed in 1968. Complement was reduced to 32. *Dokkum* and *Drunen* were refitted as minehunters 1968–70 when a British Type 193 minehunting sonar was installed. *Veere* followed 1970–71 and *Staphorst* 1972–73. Following these conversions, two minehunters and two diving vessels were assigned to each of the 1st and 3rd MCM flotillas. The highly automated minehunters have the ARNAS system, which displays dropped marker buoys on a radar screen.

All 14 vessels of the *Wildervank* class were disposed of between 1970 and 1975. The remaining 11 minesweepers and diving vessels underwent modernisation from 1977 onwards, but they are due to be replaced by the minehunters of the *Alkmaar* class.

VAN STRAELEN class *inshore minesweepers*

Displacement:	151t light; 171t full load
Dimensions:	109ft oa × 22ft × 6ft
	33.1m × 6.7m × 1.8m
Machinery:	2 shafts, 2 Werkspoor diesels, 1100bhp = 13kts
Armament:	1–20mm
Complement:	12

No	Name	Builder	Launched	Fate
M 868	ABLAS	Werf de Noord	26.9.59	Extant 1982
M 869	BUSSEMAKER	De Vries Lentsch	27.2.60	Extant 1982
M 870	LACOMBLE	Arnhemse SM	6.2.60	Extant 1982
M 871	VAN HAMEL	De Vries Lentsch	28.5.60	Extant 1982
M 872	VAN STRAELEN	Arnhemse SM	17.5.60	Extant 1982
M 873	VAN MOPPES	Werf de Noord	10.5.60	Extant 1982
M 874	CHOMPFF	Werf de Noord	10.5.60	Extant 1982
M 875	VAN WELL GROENEVELD	Arnhemse SM	1.10.60	Extant 1982
M 876	SCHUILING	De Vries Lentsch	30.6.60	Extant 1982
M 877	VAN VERSENDAAL	Werf de Noord	Aug 61	Extant 1982
M 878	VAN DER WELL	De Vries Lentsch	May 61	Extant 1982
M 879	VAN'T HOFF	Werf de Noord	15.3.61	Extant 1982
M 880	MAHU	Werf de Noord	15.3.61	Extant 1982
M 881	STAVERMAN	De Vries Lentsch	Jul 61	Extant 1982
M 882	HOUTEPEN	Arnhemse SM	Jun 61	Extant 1982
M 883	ZOMER	Arnhemse SM	4.3.61	Extant 1982

Eight of these inshore minesweepers were funded under MDAP and the remaining eight were purchased by the Netherlands. Although similar in size, conception and construction to the British 'Ham' class, they are strictly a national design, and can be distinguished from other European inshore minesweepers by the configuration of their funnel and mast.

Houtepen as completed   Navarret Collection

ALKMAAR class *minehunters*

Displacement:	510t standard; 544t full load
Dimensions:	155ft pp, 161ft oa × 29ft × 8ft
	47.1m, 49.1m × 8.9m × 2.5m
Machinery:	1 Werkspoor RUB 215 V12 diesel on one shaft with CP screw, 2,280bhp = 15kts, plus twin active rudders and bow thruster driven by 3 Astazou IVB gas turbine alternators = 7kts. Range 3000nm at 12kts
Armament:	1–20mm
Sensors:	Sonar DUBM–21A
Complement:	22–45

No	Name	Builder	Launched	Fate
M 850	ALKMAAR	Van der Giessen	18.5.82	Building
M 851	DELFZIJL	De Noord, Alblasserdam		Building
M 852	DORDRECHT	De Noord, Alblasserdam		Building
M 853	HAARLEM	De Noord, Alblasserdam		Building
M 854	HARLINGEN	De Noord, Alblasserdam		Building
M 855	HELLEVOITSLUIS	De Noord, Alblasserdam		Ordered
M 856	MAASSLUIS	De Noord, Alblasserdam		Ordered
M 857	MAKKUM	De Noord, Alblasserdam		Ordered
M 858	MIDDELBURG	De Noord, Alblasserdam		Projected
M 859	SCHEVENINGEN	De Noord, Alblasserdam		Projected
M 860	SCHIEDAM	De Noord, Alblasserdam		Projected
M 861	URK	De Noord, Alblasserdam		Projected
M 862	ZIERKZEE (ex-*Veere*)	De Noord, Alblasserdam		Projected
M 863	VLAARDINGEN	De Noord, Alblasserdam		Projected
M 864	WILLEMSTAD	De Noord, Alblasserdam		Projected

The 'tripartite' minehunter is under construction for the French, Belgian and Royal Netherlands Navies, the Dutch planning to order 15 units of the *Alkmaar* class to replace the *Dokkum* class built during the 1950s. *Alkmaar* was laid down on 15.12.78, *Delfzijl* on 29.5.80, and the next three during 1981.

The Dutch are responsible for the main propulsion system, which has undergone extensive testing following the determination of acoustic performance specifications at the Netherlands Ship Model Basin. The Werkspoor supercharged diesel, the reduction gearing, the Lips CP propeller, the machinery control and the air-conditioning system are all of Netherlands manufacture.

For further details see under France.

MISCELLANEOUS

Balder 1961
NB 1/750 scale

BALDER class *submarine-chasers*

Displacement:	149t standard; 225t full load
Dimensions:	115ft pp, 119ft oa × 20ft × 6ft
	35.0m, 36.3m × 6.2m × 1.9m
Machinery:	2 shafts, 2 diesels, 1050bhp = 15.5kts. Range 1000nm at 13kts
Armament:	1–40mm, 3–20mm (3×1), 2 DCT, Mousetrap
Complement:	27

Class:
Balder (P 802), *Bulgia* (P 803), *Freyr* (P 804), *Hadda* (P 805), *Hefring* (P 806).

The five small vessels of the *Balder* class were built in the Netherlands under MDAP. They were laid down at the Rijkswerf Willemsoord (Den Helder) 1953–54, the first three were placed in reserve in 1975.

Norway

When the Second World War ended Norway had a larger and more modern navy than she had had in April 1940, when the Germans invaded. Only a few units escaped to Britain, but the Norwegian government in exile built up a new navy, mostly of ships borrowed or purchased from Great Britain and Canada. Some of these were returned to the Royal Navy in 1945. In 1947 the Norwegian Navy consisted of: 6 destroyers (1 incomplete), 4 torpedo boats, 5 submarines, 2 frigates, 3 corvettes and 2 fishery protection vessels, 1 coastal minelayer, 10 minesweepers , 1 submarine-chaser, 10 motor torpedo-boats and 3 motor launches.

During the immediate post-war years, Norway, like all the European countries, had difficulty finding money for defence measures. The Navy had received a number of German warships in 1945: 4 submarines, 9 motor torpedo-boats and some minesweepers, but all these vessels were in bad condition and were soon scrapped. In 1951, the USA delivered 10 motor torpedo-boats.

The first step to building a new navy was taken in 1950 with the ordering of motor torpedo-boats from a domestic yard. Thereafter Norway constructed, launched and commissioned series of ships and boats for the Navy, built at naval and private yards, in cooperation with other NATO navies and with help from the United States under the Mutual Defense Assistance Program.

The proliferation of offshore establishments in the North Sea oilfields has brought an increased need of defensive patrols, which is very much in Norway's – and NATO's – interest.

During the 1980s a series of new 'offshore protection ships' (frigates) were constructed, launcheed and commissioned. A series of missile, torpedo- and gun-boats are being built at domestic yards, and the submarine fleet will be renewed with cooperation from the Federal German Republic.

FLEET STRENGTH 1947

DESTROYERS

Name	Launched	Disp (standard)	Fate
Bergen class			
BERGEN (ex-*Cromwell*) (D 304)	6.8.45	1710t	Stricken 1.1.67
OSLO (ex-*Crown*) (D 303)	19.12.45	1710t	Stricken 1966, BU
STAVANGER (ex-*Crystal*) (D 306)	12.2.45	1786t	Stricken 1.1.67, BU
TRONDHEIM (ex-*Croziers*) (D 305)	19.9.44	1786t	Stricken 1.5.67
Stord class			
STORD (ex-*Success*) (D 300)	3.4.43	1796t	Stricken 1959, BU
Aalesund class			
AALESUND	1941	1220t	Scrapped 1950
Odin class			
ODIN (F 302)	17.1.39	632t	Stricken 1959
TOR (F 303)	9.9.39	632t	Stricken 1959
BALDER (F 304)	11.10.39	632t	Stricken 1959
Sleipner class			
SLEIPNER (F 300)	7.6.36	597t	Stricken 1956
GYLLER (F 301)	7.7.38	597t	Stricken 1959

Bergen class
In Norwegian service from respectively, 6.8.45, 19.12.45, 6.8.45 and 19.9.45.

Stord class
In Norwegian service from 3.4.43. *Stord*'s sister-ship *Svenner* (ex-*Shark*) was sunk by a German S-boat off Normandy 6.6.44.

Aalesund class
Two sister-ships, laid down in April 1939, were both captured by the Germans on 9 April 1940, and were renumbered *ZN 4* and *ZN 5*. The hull of the second was broken up. *Aalesund* was never completed; her construction was abandoned in 1950.

Odin class
Improved *Sleipner* class. *Odin* surrendered to the Germans at Marvika naval depot, Kristiansand on 11.4.40, and was renamed *Panther*. *Tor* and *Balder* were completed by the Germans and renamed *Tiger* and *Leopard*. All three were retro-ceded in May 1945 and converted to frigates 1954, 1954 and 1952 respectively.

Sleipner class
Sleipner was the largest Norwegian warship to get to Britain in April 1940. *Gyller* surrendered at Kristiansand on 11.4.40 and was renamed *Löwe*. Both were retro-ceded in May 1945. *Gyller* was converted to a frigate in 1957. Her sister-ship *Aeger* was bombed on 9.4.40 at Hundvaagöy, Stavanger, and wrecked.

FRIGATES

Name	Launched	Disp (standard)	Fate
ARENDAL (ex-*Badsworth*) (F 310)	17.3.41	1317t	Stricken 1.5.61
NARVIK (ex-*Glaisdale*) (F 309)	5.1.42	1230t	Stricken 1.5.61, BU

These two *Hunt* class escort destroyers, *Badsworth* (Type 2) and *Glaisdale* (Type 3) were purchased by Norway in 1946. Wore 'D' pennant numbers until 1956.

CORVETTES

Name	Launched	Disp (standard)	Fate
Andenes class			
ANDENES (ex-*Acanthus*)	26.5.41	925t	Stricken 1956
NORDKYN (ex-*Buttercup*)	10.4.41	925t	Stricken 1956
SOROY (ex-*Eglantine*)	11.6.41	925t	Stricken 1956
Nordkapp class			
NORDKAPP	18.8.37	243t	Stricken 1956, later fishing vessel
SENJA	25.8.37	243t	Stricken 1956, later fishing vessel

Andenes class
These British 'Flower' class corvettes were transferred to the Norwegian flag during the war. Other British corvettes transferred were: *Montbretia*, sunk 1942; *Rose*, sunk 1944; *Potentilla*, returned to the RN in 1944; *Tunsberg* (ex-*Shrewsbury Castle*), mined 1944.

Nordkapp class
Rated as fishery protection vessels. *Nordkapp* escaped to Britain in April 1940. *Senja* was captued by the Germans on 9.4.40, and was used as a patrol vessel, re-named *Löwe*, later *H 2*, *DW*, *V 6735* and *V 6315*, retro-ceded 1945.

SUBMARINES

Name	Launched	Disp (standard)	Fate
Ula class			
ULA (ex-*Varne*) (S 300)	22.6.43	630t	Stricken Jul 64
UTSTEIN (ex-*Venturer*) (S 302)	4.5.43	545t	Stricken Jan 64
UTVÆR (ex-*Viking*) (S 303)	5.5.43	545t	Stricken Dec 64
UTSIRA (ex-*Variance*) (S 301)	22.5.44	545t	Stricken Dec 62
UTHAUG (ex-*Votary*) (S 304)	21.8.44	545t	Stricken Oct 65

Uthaug 1957

British 'U' class, purchased from Great Britain, modernised in 1955–56, with external streamlining, snorkel and sonar dome.

MINELAYER

Name	Launched	Disp (standard)	Fate
LAUGEN	Oct 17	335t	Scrapped 1948

Captured by the Germans April 1940, designated *NN 05*, later *M 22*, retroceded May 1945.

MINESWEEPERS

Name	Fate	Name	Fate
Glomma class: launched 1940, 590t			
GLOMMA (ex-*Bangor*)	Stricken 1.12.61	TANA (ex-*Blackpool*)	Stricken 1.5.61
Orkla class: launched 1943–45, 350t			
ORKLA (ex-*MMS 1085*)	Stricken 1964	VEFSNA (ex-*MMS 1086*)	Stricken 1962
Alta class: launched 1944–45, 232t			
VINSTRA (ex-*NYMS 247*)	Stricken 1959	BEGNA (ex-*NYMS 381*)	Stricken 1961
GAULA (ex-*NYMS 305*)	Stricken 26.6.63	RANA (ex-*NYMS 406*)	Stricken Mar 62
DRIVA (ex-*NYMS 377*)	Stricken 1961	VORMA (ex-*NYMS 480*)	Stricken 1959
ALTA (ex-*NYMS 379*)	Stricken 1959		
Otra class: launched 1939, 335t			
OTRA	Stricken Apr 63	RAUMA	Stricken Apr 63

Glomma class
British *Bangor* class diesel-engined minesweepers, purchased in 1946.

Orkla class
British MMS type, purchased in June 1946. From 1951 they were used as X-ray ships for torpedo-boat testing.

Alta class
US YMS type, transferred under Lease-Lend in 1945.

Otra class
Captured by the Germans on 9.9.40 and renamed *Togo* and *Kamerun*. Retroceded in May 1945. They were also used as coastal minelayers. Four ex-whalecatchers, *Penang*, *Polarnacht*, *Rotger* and *Sölöven*, were also used as minesweepers in 1947.

SUBMARINE CHASER

Name	Launched	Disp	Fate
KONG HAAKON VII (ex-*PC 457*)	29.4.42	280t	Stricken 1974

Used as a fishery protection vessel from c 1950; TS 1953.

MOTOR TORPEDO-BOATS

Faulk (ex-*MTB 704*), *Hauk* (ex-*MTB 711*), *Jo* (ex-*MTB 713*), *Lom* (ex-*MTB 719*), *Ravn* (ex-*MTB 720*), *Skarv* (ex-*MTB 721*), *Stegg* (ex-*MTB 722*), *Teist* (ex-*MTB 723*), *Tjeld* (ex-*MTB 716*). All ex-British Fairmile 'D' type MTBs, launched 1944, 128t. *Hauk* was lost by fire on 23.11.48, *Jo* was stricken in 1958, the remaining seven were stricken in 1959.

MOTOR LAUNCHES

ML 125, *ML 213*, *ML 573*. All ex-British MLs, stricken in 1947.

NATO PENNANT NUMBERS
Carried from 1950 by ships in commission. Numbers for major ships are quoted after the name in the above tables, but the following were also allocated.

Minesweepers			
M 309	GLOMMA		
M 319	DRIVA	M 318	GAULA
M 310	TANA	M 320	ALTA
M 313	ORKLA	M 322	BEGNA
M 314	VEFSNA	M 330	RANA
M 317	VINSTRA	M 321	VORMA

Minelayers			
N 33	RAUMA	N 34	OTRA

Motor torpedo-boats			
P 343	FAULK	P 347	LOM
P 344	RAVN	P 348	TEIST
P 345	STEGG	P 349	JO
P 346	SKARV	P 350	TJELD

MAJOR SURFACE SHIPS

Taken over at the end of 1952 on a 4-year loan, but bought outright in July 1956, when the pennant numbers were changed from 'D' to 'F'. They had been refitted in 1954 with a lattice mast and 2 Squid ASW mortars in place of 'X' twin 4in, the armament then consisting of 4–4in (2×2), 4–40mm.

Originally Canadian 'River' type, modernised for ASW in 1953–54. Lent to Norway in 1956 and purchased outright in 1959. *Garm* was converted to a depot ship for MTBs in 1964 and renamed *Valkyrien*, and *Troll* to a depot ship for submarines in 1965 and renamed *Horten*. They were given the pennant numbers A 535 and A 530.

Ex-British 'HUNT' (type 2) class *escort destroyers*

Particulars:	As British 'Hunt' Type 2			
No	**Name**	**Builder**	**Acquired**	**Fate**
F 311	TROMSO (ex-*Beaufort*)	Yarrow	end 1952	Stricken 1965
F 312	HAUGESUND (ex-*Zetland*)	Cammell Laird	end 1952	Stricken 1965

Ex-Canadian 'RIVER' class *frigates*

Particulars:	As Canadian 'River' class			
No	**Name**	**Builder**	**Acquired**	**Fate**
F 313	DRAUG (ex-*Penetang*)	Davie SB	25.1.56	BU 1966
F 314	TROLL (ex-*Prestonian*)	Davie SB	Mar 56	Stricken 1972
F 315	GARM (ex-*Toronto*)	Davie SB	Mar 56	Stricken 1977

NORWAY

Bergen 1975

Built under a five-year naval programme voted in 1960, half the cost being carried by the United States. Based on the design of US *Dealey* class destroyer-escorts, but with many modifications, including increased freeboard forward to suit sea conditions off the Norwegian coast. They were modernised in the late 1970s, when the SSM, SAM and TT systems were installed. The guns are US Mk 33s, the Sea Sparrow launcher a US Mk 29, with a Mk 91 mod O radar director. The electronics are of mixed origin, the search radar being French, the Decca TM–1226 navigation set British, and the HSA M 22 tactical and fire control radar being Dutch.

OSLO class *frigates*

Displacement:	1450t standard; 1760t full load
Dimensions:	308ft pp, 318ft oa × 36ft 7in × 17ft 4in
	93.9m, 96.6m × 11.2m × 5.3m
Machinery:	1-shaft STAL-de Laval double reduction geared turbines, 2 Babcock & Wilcox boilers, 20,000shp = 25kts. Range 4500nm at 15kts
Armament:	6 Penguin SSM(2×3), 1 NATO Sea Sparrow SAM (1×8; 24 missiles), 4–3in/50 (2×2), 1 Terne III ASW (1×6), 6–324mm Mk 32 TT (2×3)
Sensors:	Radar DRBU–22, TM–1226, M22; sonar Terne Mk III attack, SQS–36
Complement:	150

No	Name	Builder	Laid down	Launched	Comp	Fate
F 300	OSLO	Horten N Yd	1963	17.1.64	29.1.66	Extant 1982
F 301	BERGEN	Horten N Yd	1964	23.8.65	15.6.67	Extant 1982
F 302	TRONDHEIM	Horten N Yd	1963	4.9.64	2.6.66	Extant 1982
F 303	STAVANGER	Horten N Yd	1965	4.2.66	1.12.67	Extant 1982
F 304	NARVIK	Horten N Yd	1964	8.1.65	30.11.66	Extant 1982

Stavanger 1979   C & S Taylor

SUBMARINES

German VIIC type U-boats, originally launched in 1943. They were transferred in 1950 from Great Britain.

Ex-German TYPE VIIC *submarines*

Particulars:	As German Type VIIC

No	Name	Builder	Acquired	Fate
S 309	KAURA (ex-*U 995*)	Blohm & Voss, Hamburg	1950	Stricken Jan 63
S 307	KYA (ex-*U 926*)	Neptun-Werft, Rostock	1950	Stricken Mar 64
S 308	KINN (ex-*U 1202*)	Schichau, Danzig	1950	Stricken 1.6.61

German XXIII type U-boat, originally launched in January 1945. Turned over to Norway in 1950 by Great Britain.

Ex-German TYPE XXIII *submarine*

Particulars: As German Type XXIII

No	Name	Builder	Acquired	Fate
–	KNERTER (ex-*U 4706*)	Germaniawerft, Kiel	1950	Stricken 1953

Voted July 1959 under a five-year programme, with half the cost being paid by United States. Based on the German Type 207, but with a stronger hull for deeper diving, and revised equipment. They can fire the US Mk 37 wire-guided torpedo. For training purposes the German *U 4* of the same design was lent 1962–64 for the building period and under the Norwegian flag she carried the name *Kobben* and pennant number S 310. *Svenner*, equipped for officer training, has a second periscope and is 1m longer.

KOBBEN class *submarines*

Displacement: 370t standard; 530t submerged
Dimensions: 149ft oa × 15ft × 14ft
 45.4m × 4.6m × 4.3m
Machinery: 1 shaft, 2 Maybach diesels plus 1 electric motor, 2400bhp/1200shp = 10kts/17kts
Armament: 8–533mm (21in) TT (bow; 8 torpedoes)
Complement: 18

No	Name	Builder	Laid down	Launched	Comp	Fate
S 315	KAURA	Nordseewerke, Emden	1961	16.10.64	5.2.65	Extant 1982
S 316	KINN	Nordseewerke, Emden	1960	30.11.63	8.4.64	Extant 1982
S 317	KYA	Nordseewerke, Emden	1961	20.2.64	15.6.64	Extant 1982
S 318	KOBBEN	Nordseewerke, Emden	1961	25.4.64	17.8.64	Extant 1982
S 319	KUNNA	Nordseewerke, Emden	1961	16.7.64	1.10.64	Extant 1982
S 300	ULA	Nordseewerke, Emden	1962	19.12.64	7.5.65	Extant 1982
S 301	UTSIRA	Nordseewerke, Emden	1963	11.3.65	1.7.65	Extant 1982
S 302	UTSTEIN	Nordseewerke, Emden	1962	19.5.65	9.9.65	Extant 1982
S 303	UTVAER	Nordseewerke, Emden	1962	30.6.65	1.12.65	Extant 1982
S 304	UTHAUG	Nordseewerke, Emden	1962	8.10.65	16.2.66	Extant 1982
S 305	SKLINNA	Nordseewerke, Emden	1963	21.1.66	17.8.66	Extant 1982
S 306	SKOLPEN	Nordseewerke, Emden	1963	24.3.66	17.8.66	Extant 1982
S 307	STADT	Nordseewerke, Emden	1963	10.6.66	15.11.66	Extant 1982
S 308	STORD	Nordseewerke, Emden	1964	2.9.66	9.2.67	Extant 1982
S 309	SVENNER	Nordseewerke, Emden	1965	27.1.67	1.7.67	Extant 1982

A new type of submarine to be built in the late 1980s to replace the *Kobben*s has been under discussion since 1981. A design contract was placed with IKL of Lübeck, and a contract for six boats (with an option on two more) was signed with Thyssen Nordseewerke on 30.9.82. Known in Norway as the P 6071 type, the first boat is expected to enter service in Feb 89, with the rest following at 6-month intervals.

TYPE 211 *submarines*

Displacement: 1600t
Dimensions: 196ft 10in oa × 17ft 4in
 60.0m × 5.3m
Machinery: 1 shaft, 2 diesels plus 1 electric motor = ?
Armament: 8–533mm (21in) TT
Complement: 18–20

Svenner as completed   Royal Norwegian Navy

AMPHIBIOUS WARFARE VESSELS

Ex-US LCU type *utility landing craft*

Particulars: As US *LCU 1466* class

In 1958 US *LCU 1478* was transferred to Norway as *Tjeldsund* (A 30). The vessel was completed in 1953, originally intended to be rebuilt as a minelayer but this was not carried out. Stricken 1975.

KVALSUND class *utility landing craft*

Displacement:	569t standard; 590t full load
Dimensions:	164ft × 33ft 6in × 5ft 10in
	50.0m × 10.2m × 1.8m
Machinery:	2 shafts, 2 Maybach diesels, 1350bhp = 11.5kts
Armament:	2–20mm (2×1)
Complement:	10

Class:
Kvalsund (L 4500, ex-A 31) *Raftsund* (L 4501, ex-A 32)
    Built by Hjöivold, Kristiansand in 1970. Can carry 5 tanks and 80–180 troops; rails for 120 mines. Both extant 1982.

REINOYSUND class *utility landing craft*

Displacement:	560t standard; 596t full load
Dimensions:	167ft 4in wl, 171ft oa × 34ft × 6ft
	51.0m, 52.1m × 10.3m × 1.8m
Machinery:	2 shafts, 2 Maybach diesels, 1350bhp = 11.5kts
Armament:	3–20mm (3×1), 2–12.7mm MG
Complement:	10

Class:
Reinöysund (L 4502, ex-A 33), *Söröysund* (L 4503, ex-A 34), *Maursund* (L 4504, ex-A 35), *Rotsund* (L 4505, ex-A 36), *Borgsund* (L 4506, ex-A 37).
    Built at Mjellem & Karlsen, Bergen, launched 1970–72, commissioned 1972–73. Modified version of *Kvalsund* class, with similar capabilities. All extant 1982.

Rotsund as completed   Royal Norwegian Navy

SMALL SURFACE COMBATANTS

Sleipner 1966

SLEIPNER class *corvettes*

Displacement:	600t standard; 780t full load
Dimensions:	227ft 4in × 26ft × 7ft 10in
	69.3m × 7.9m × 2.4m
Machinery:	2 shafts, 4 Maybach diesels 8800bhp = 22kts
Armament:	1–3in, 1–40mm AA, 1 Terne III ASW system, 6–324mm Mk 32 TT (3×2), 1 DC rack
Sensors:	Radar Decca 202, TM–1226; sonar Terne Mk III attack, SQS–36
Complement:	63

No	Name	Builder	Launched	Fate
P 950	SLEIPNER	Nylands Verksteder	9.11.63	Extant 1982
P 951	AEGER	Akers, Abers, Oslo	24.9.65	Extant 1982

In 1959 the decision was taken to build five of this class, but three were cancelled. *Sleipner* was laid down 1963 and completed 29.4.1965. *Aeger* (originally named *Balder*) was laid down 1964 and completed 31.3.1967. Both were specially equipped as submarine chasers in 1972 when the ASW TT were fitted; later renumbered F 310 and F 311. The 3in gun is a US Mk 34, and the original Mk 63 fire control system has been replaced with two Swedish TVT–300 optronic systems. Both vessels are now mainly used for training.

VADSO *corvette*

Displacement:	631t normal; 900t full load
Dimensions:	169ft 4in × 29ft 6in × 18ft
	51.0m × 9.0m × 5.5m
Machinery:	1 shaft, 1 MAK 8BM451 diesel, 1400bhp= 12kts. Range 15,000nm at 12kts
Armament:	1–40mm, 1 DC rack
Sensors:	Radar – navigational only
Complement:	20

Vadsö (P 340), built at Stord Verft as a whaler, launched 1951, purchased and rebuilt 1976. Extant 1982.

Storm as completed   Royal Norwegian Navy

Ex-US SC type *patrol boats*

Armament:	1–40mm (originally 1–6pdr), 4–20mm, 2 MG
Other particulars:	As US SC type

Class:

Hessa (ex-*SC 683*), *Hitra* (ex-*SC 718*), *Vigra* (ex-*SC 1061*)

Transferred in 1947 from USA. Pennant numbers were P 391, P 392, P 393 respectively. Stricken 1959.

Ex-German S-BOAT type *fast attack craft*

Armament:	1–40mm, 3–20mm, 2–533mm (21in) TT
Other particulars:	As German S-boats (*S 38* and *S 100* groups)

Class:

Kvikk (ex-*S 98*), *Lyn* ex-*S 64*), *Rapp* (ex-*S 174*), *Snar* (ex-*S 210*), *Storm* (ex-*S 85*), *Tross* (ex-*S 117*)

Launched 1943, 1941, 1944, 1944, 1942 and 1942 respectively. All taken over in 1947; *Storm*, *Tross* and *Lyn*, were handed over to Denmark in 1951. The other three were stricken 1952.

Ex-German S-BOAT type *fast attack craft*

Armament:	1–40mm, 1–20mm, 2 MG, 2–533mm (21in) TT
Other particulars:	As German S-boats (*S 6* and *S 10* groups)

Class:

Blink (ex-*S 9*), *Brand* (ex-*S 10*), *Kjekk* (ex-*S 12*)

Launched 1934–35. All three were ceded to the Allies in 1947; *Brand* was transferred to Denmark in 1951, and the other two were discarded shortly afterwards. Norway also received *S 21*, *S 48*, *S 76*, *S 195* and *S 302*, and although the last pair carried the names *Kjekk* and *Blink* for a short time before transfer to Denmark in 1951, none was operational.

Ex-US 'ELCO' type *fast attack craft*

Armament:	1–40mm, 1–20mm, 4–12.7mm MG, 2–533mm (21in) TT
Other particulars:	As US 'Elco' type

Class:

Hai (P 956), *Hauk* (P 957), *Hval* (P 958), *Hvass* (P 959), *Sel* (P 950), *Sild* (P 951), *Skrei* (P 952), *Snar* (P 953), *Snögg* (P 954), *Springer* (P 955)

Ex-US 'Elco' type PT-boats *PT 602–PT 606*, *PT 608–PT 612*, launched in 1945. Four were transferred under MDAP on 16.3.51 and the remaining six later in the same year. In 1955 *Hauk*, *Hvass*, *Snar* and *Snögg* were renamed becoming *Laks*, *Delfin*, *Lyr* and *Knurr* respectively. *Skrei* was BU in 1960, *Delfin*, *Knurr* and *Sel* were stricken 1.12.61, *Lyr* on 1.3.62 *Sild* in Dec 62, and the remaining four (whose names had been transferred to the *Tjeld* class) in 1966.

RAPP class *fast attack craft*

Displacement:	72t standard
Dimensions:	87ft × 23ft × 5ft
	26.5m × 7.0m × 1.5m
Machinery:	2 shafts, 4 Packard petrol engines, 4800bhp = 41kts (32kts sea speed)
Armament:	1–40mm, 1–20mm, 4–533mm (21in) TT
Complement:	18

Class:

Rapp (P 351), *Rask* (P 352), *Kvikk* (P 353), *Kjapp* (P 354), *Snar* (P 355), *Snögg* (P 356)

Norwegian construction, built at Westermoens Baatbyggeri, Mandal. *Rapp* launched 7.5.52, completed 18.11.52; remaining five launched 1953–55 and completed 1953–56. Wooden hull construction. All stricken 1970.

NASTY *fast attack craft*

Displacement:	69t standard; 76t full load
Dimensions:	75ft pp, 80ft 4in oa × 24ft 6in × 6ft 9in
	22.9m, 24.5m × 7.5m × 2.1m
Machinery:	2 shafts, 2 Napier Deltic diesels, 5000bhp = 43kts
Armament:	2–40mm, 4–533mm (21in) TT
Complement:	22

Experimental boat, built at Westermoens Baatbyggeri, Mandal, as private venture, launched and completed 1958, used as prototype boat for *Tjeld* class. Wooden hull construction. Stricken 1967.

Tjeld as completed   Royal Norwegian Navy

TJELD class *fast attack craft*

Displacement:	70t standard; 76t full load
Dimensions:	75ft 6in pp, 80ft 4in oa × 24ft 6in × 6ft 9in
	23.0m × 24.5m × 7.5m × 2.1m
Machinery:	2 shafts, 2 Napier Deltic 18cyl turbo-charged diesels, 6200bhp = 45kts. Range 450nm/1600nm at 40kts/25kts
Armament:	1–40mm, 1–20mm, 4–533mm (21in) TT (or as gunboat 2–40mm, 2–533mm TT)
Complement:	22

Class:

First group – *Tjeld* (P 343), *Skarv* (P 344), *Teist* (P 345), *Jo* (P 346), *Lom* (P 347), *Stegg* (P 348), *Hauk* (P 349), *Falk* (P 350), *Ravn* (P 357), *Gribb* (P 388), *Geir* (P 389), *Erle* (P 390)

Second group – *Skrei* (P 380), *Hai* (P 381), *Sel* (P 382), *Hval* (P 383), *Laks* (P 384), *Knurr* (P 385), *Delfin* (P 386), *Lyr* (P 387)

All were built by Westermoens Baatbyggeri, Mandal. The first series was ordered in 1957, launched 1959–60, and commissioned during 1960–62. The second series was ordered under a new five-year programme in 1962, launched 1962–63 and commissioned 1963–66. They were developments of the *Nasty* design intended for series production. Two similar vessels went to West Germany (and eventually Turkey), 2 to the USA and 6 to Greece.

Skarv was stricken in 1978 and *Teist*, *Lom*, *Jo*, *Hauk*, *Falk* and *Sel* in 1979. The remainder were laid up in reserve, and by 1982 only 8 survived; these all are up for sale and are now known only by their pennant numbers – *P 343*, *P 348*, *P 349*, *P 357*, *P 380*, *P 381*, *P 387* and *P 388*.

STORM class *fast attack craft*

Displacement:	100t standard; 125t full load
Dimensions:	120ft oa × 20ft 6in × 5ft
	36.5m × 6.2m × 1.5m
Machinery:	2 shafts, 2 Maybach diesels, 7200bhp = 32kts. Range 550nm at 32kts
Armament:	6 Penguin SSM (6×1), 1–76mm, 1–40mm, DCT
Sensors:	Radar TM-909, WM-26
Complement:	19

Class:

Storm (P 960), *Blink* (P 961), *Glimt* (P 962), *Skjold** (P 963), *Trygg* (P 964), *Kjekk* (P 965), *Djerv** (P 966), *Skudd* (P 967), *Arg* (P 968), *Steil** (P 969), *Brann* (P 970), *Tross* (P 971), *Hvass** (P 972), *Traust* (P 973), *Brott* (P 974), *Odd** (P 975), *Pil* (P 976), *Brask* (P 977), *Rokk** (P 978), *Gnist* (P 979)

Terne 1980   Royal Norwegian Navy

In 1959 23 MGBs were voted under the next five-year programme, but the number was reduced to 20. Built at Bergens Mekaniske Verksteder (except those marked * by Westermoens, Mandal). A first *Storm* was built as a prototype, launched 8.2.63 and completed 31.5.63. This boat underwent many modifications during 1963–65 and was eventually scrapped. First series boat *Blink* launched 28.6.65 and completed 18.12.65. Last boat commissioned 1968. Being fitted with TVT–300 optronic tracker and laser rangefinder abaft the mast. All extant 1982.

SNOGG class *fast attack craft*

Displacement:	125t standard; 138t full load
Dimensions:	120ft × 20ft 6in × 5ft
	36.5m × 6.2m × 1.3m
Machinery:	2 shafts, 2 Maybach diesels, 7200bhp = 32kts. Range 550nm at 32kts
Armament:	4 Penguin SSM (4×1), 1–40mm, 4–533mm (4×1) TT, 2 DC racks
Sensors:	Radar TM-626
Complement:	19

Class:
Snögg (P 380, ex-*Lyr*), *Rapp* (P 981), *Snar* (P 982), *Rask* (P 983), *Kvikk* (P 984), *Hjapp* (P 985)

All built at Westermoens Baatbyggeri, Mandal, launched 1969–70, commissioned 1970–71. Generally similar to *Storm* class. Have PEAB TORI fire control system; TT fire T–61 wire-guided torpedoes. All extant 1982.

HAUK class *fast attack craft*

Displacement:	120t standard; 155t full load
Dimensions:	120ft × 20ft × 5ft
	36.5m × 6.2m × 3.6m
Machinery:	2 shafts, 2 Maybach diesels, 7300bhp = 35kts. Range 440nm at 34kts
Armament:	6 Penguin 2 SSM (6×1), 1–40mm, 1–20mm, 2–533mm TT
Sensors:	Radar TM-1226; sonar SQ3D/SF
Complement:	22

Class:
Hauk (P 986), *Orn* (P 987), *Terne* (P 988), *Tjeld* (P 989), *Skarv* (P 990), *Teist* (P 991), *Jo* (P 992), *Lom* (P 993), *Stegg* (P 994), *Falk* (P 995), *Ravn* (P 996), *Gribb* (P 997), *Geir* (P 998), *Erle* (P 999)

Ten boats ordered 12.6.75 from Bergens Mekaniske Verksteder, four (P 996–P 999) from Westamarine, Mandal (the new name for Westermoens Baatbyggeri). *Hauk* laid down May 1976, launched 21.2.77 and commissioned 17.8.77. *Erle*, the last boat, was due to commission on 10.12.80. The 40mm is a Bofors, the 20mm is by Rheinmetall, and they also carry 2–50mm rocket flare launchers. Fitted with MS1–80S fire control system, using the two Decca TM–1226 radars, a TVT–300 optronic tracker and an Ericsen laser rangefinder. All were in service 1982.

OTHER SMALL CRAFT

There are also the patrol and inspection boats *Tarva* (TSD 1) and *Welding* (OSD 1), launched 1974 at Fjellstrand Aluminium Yachts, Omastrand; commissioned 1.12.74 and 1.11.74 respectively. Principal particulars are: 27.5t; 53ft 6in × 17ft 4in × 3ft 10in, (*16.3m × 5.3m × 1.2m*); 1–12.7mm MG; 2 shafts, 2 General Motors diesels = 15kts; complement 4.

MINE WARFARE VESSELS

Ex-US LSM type *minelayers*

Particulars:	See Danish *Beskytteren* class			
No	**Name**	**Builder**	**Acquired**	**Fate**
N 45	VALE (ex-*LSM 492*)	Brown SB, Houston	Oct 52	To Turkey 1.10.60
N 46	VIDAR (ex-*LSM 493*)	Brown SB, Houston	Oct 52	To Turkey 1.10.60

Ex-US *LSM 1* class landing ships rebuilt as coastal minelayers in the USA during 1952, and transferred to Norway. On 1.10.60 they were returned to the US Navy and later turned over to Turkey.

Vale c1958   Royal Norwegian Navy

VARGSUND class *minelayers*

Displacement:	600t standard
Dimensions:	185ft 6in oa × 38ft 9in × 4ft 3in
	56.5m × 11.8m × 1.3m
Machinery:	2 shafts, 2 Paxman Ricardo diesels, 500bhp = 8kts. Oil 43t
Armament:	2–20mm AA
Complement:	20

Class:
Vargsund (N 35), *Reinöysünd* (N 36)

Ex-British LCTs, built c1945, converted to minelayers 1952. Stricken 1960.

Ex-US AUK class *coastal minelayers*

Displacement:	180t standard; 1250t full load
Dimensions:	215ft wl, 221ft 2in oa × 32ft 2in × 11ft
	65.5m, 67.4m × 9.8m × 3.4m
Machinery:	2 shafts, 2 GM diesels, 2070bhp = 16kts
Armament:	1–3in/50, 4–20mm, 2 Hedgehog ASW mortars, 3 DCT
Complement:	83

No	Name	Builder	Acquired	Fate
N 47	TYR (ex-*Sustain*, MMC 2)	American SB, Cleveland	1959	Stricken 1976
N 48	GOR (ex-*Strive*, MMC 1)	American SB, Cleveland	1959	Stricken 1976
N 49	BRAGE (ex-*Triumph*, MMC 3)	Associated SB, Seattle	1960	Stricken 1978
N 50	ULLER (ex-*Seer*, MMC 4)	American SB, Cleveland	1959	Stricken 1978

Originally US *Auk* class steel-hulled ocean minesweepers launched in 1941–43. *Gor* and *Tyr* were converted to coastal minelayers at Charleston N Yd in 1959 and *Brage* in 1960; *Uller* was similarly converted at Horten N Yd in Norway. All were transferred under MDAP, and were numbered AM (later MSF) 119, 117, 323 and 112 in the order of the above table. *Uller*'s armament was different: 1–3in/50, 1–40mm, 1 Terne ASW system, 1 DCT.

BORGEN *controlled minelayer*

Displacement:	282t standard
Dimensions:	102ft 6in oa × 26ft 3in × 11ft
	31.2m × 8.0m × 3.4m
Machinery:	2 shafts, 2 GM diesels, 660bhp = 9kts
Armament:	2–20mm AA, mines
Complement:	18

No	Name	Builder	Launched	Fate
N 51	BORGEN	Horten N Yd	29.4.60	Extant 1982

Coastal minelayer of Swedish 'Mul 12' type commissioned in 1961.

Vidar as completed

VIDAR class *coastal minelayers*

Displacement:	1150t standard; 1673t full load
Dimensions:	212ft 6in × 39ft 4in × 14ft 1in
	64.8m × 12m × 4m
Machinery:	2 shafts, 2 Wichmann 7AX diesels, 4200bhp = 15kts. Oil 247t
Armament:	2–40mm (2×1), 320–400 mines
Sensors:	Radar TM-1226; sonars SQ3D
Complement:	50

No	Name	Builder	Launched	Fate
N 52	VIDAR	Skaaluren SB, Rosendal	18.3.77	Extant 1982
N 53	VALE	Mjellem & Karlsen, Bergen	5.8.77	Extant 1982

Laid down 1.3.76 and 1.2.76 respectively; commissioned 21.10.77 and 10.2.78 respectively. Both were completed at Bergen. They are multi-role ships, capable of serving as minelayers (for which they have three decks with automated hoists between), torpedo-recovery vessels, transports, fishery protection vessels, or even limited ASW escorts (for which they have been fitted with 6–324mm Mk 32 ASW TT and 2 DC racks).

Ex-German 1940 type *coastal minesweepers*

Particulars:	As German 1940 type

Class:
M 261, M 272, M 302, M 306, M 321, M 322, M 323, M 326, M 361, M 362, M 364, M 365, M 436

Britain transferred 13 ex-German minesweepers to Norway in 1948. *M 321* and *M 326* were BU in 1951 and the remaining eleven during the following years.

US ADJUTANT type *coastal minesweepers*

Armament:	2–20mm
Sensors:	Radar RM-707; sonar UQS-1
Other particulars:	As US *Adjutant* class

Class:
Sauda (M 311, ex-*AMS 102*), *Sira* (M 312, ex-*MSC 132*), *Tana* (M 313, ex-*Roesleare*, ex-*MSC 103*), *Alta* (M 314, ex-*Arlon*, ex-*MSC 104*), *Ogna* (M 315), *Vosso* (M 316), *Glomma* (M 317, ex-*Bastogne*, ex-*MSC 151*), *Tista* (M 331), *Kvina* (M 332), *Utla* (M 334)

Sauda and *Sira* launched 1953 at East Boothbay, Maine, USA. *Alta*, *Glomma* and *Tana* were transferred in Mar 1966 from Belgian Navy in exchange for *Lagen* and *Namsen*. Five built in Norway; at Mandal, Risör (*Kvina* and *Utla*) and Rodendale (*Tista*), launched: *Ogna* 18.6.54, *Vosso* 16.5.54, *Tista* 1.6.54, *Kvina* 21.7.54 and *Utla* 2.3.55. In 1977 *Tana* was converted to a minehunter, with British Type 193M sonar, TM-1226 radar, and PAP 104 remote-controlled minehunters. All now have Rheinmetall 20mm guns.

Sira c1979   Royal Norwegian Navy

(For illustration see under United States)

Ex-US AGGRESSIVE class *ocean minesweepers*

Particulars:	As US *Aggressive* class

Class:
Lagen (M 950, ex*MSO 498*), *Namsen* (M 951, ex*MSO 498*)

Launched 13.8.54 and 15.10.54 at Bellington, USA, taken over 27.9.55 and 1.11.55 respectively. Transferred to Belgian Navy in 1966 in exchange for *Alta*, *Glomma* and *Tana* of *Sauda* (US *Adjutant*) class.

MISCELLANEOUS

HAAKON VII *training vessel*

Ex-US seaplane tender *Gardiner Bay*, launched 2.12.44. Taken over 17.5.58 and converted to training vessel for midshipmen (A 537). Displacement 1766t standard, 2800t full load. Rearmed with 1–5in (127mm), 8–40mm and 4–20mm. 2 diesels, 6080bhp = 18kts. Complement 215 plus 86 cadets and petty officer apprentices. Stricken 1974.

HORTEN *support ship*

Displacement:	2500t full load
Dimensions:	296ft pp, 285ft 5in oa × 42ft 7in × 23ft
	82.0m, 87.0m × 13.0m × 7.0m
Machinery:	2 shafts, 2 Wichmann diesels, 4200bhp = 16.5kts
Armament:	2–40mm (2×1), mines
Complement:	85

Horten (A 530) was built at Horten Werft, launched 12.8.77, and commissioned in April 1978. A general purpose logistical support and depot ship for submarines and fast attack craft, but has some limited offensive capability.

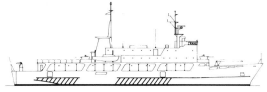

Horten as completed   *Nordkapp* as completed

NORGE *royal yacht*

Ex-*Philante*, launched at Camper & Nicholson, Gosport, England, 17.2.37. A gift from the Norwegian people to the late King Haakon VII after the Second World War. Naval pennant number A 533. Displacement 686t standard. Dimensions 250ft wl, 263ft oa × 28ft × 15ft 3in (*76.3m, 80.2m × 8.5m × 4.6m*). 8cyl diesels, 3000bhp = 17kts.

COAST GUARD

The Norwegian Coast Guard (Kystvakt) was set up in 1976 to protect Norway's burgeoning offshore interests, and to patrol the new 200nm Exclusive Economic Zone (EEZ). At first the service used ex-naval fishery protection vessels and chartered trawler-type merchant ships, but the new *Nordkapp* class patrol vessels would make useful warships, and therefore full details are included. The following Coast Guard vessels in service in 1982 might also be considered to have some naval value:

Andenes (W 303), *Senja* (W 304), *Nordkapp* (W 305): 400t standard; 183ft 9in × 31ft 3in × 16ft (*56.0m × 9.5m × 4.9m*), 16kts, 1–76mm, launched 1957 in the Netherlands, purchased 1965 and converted to patrol vessels. *Nordkapp* later A 531, *Senja* A 536. Stricken 1981.

Farm (W 301), *Heimdal* (W 302), 600t gross, 177ft 3in × 27ft × 16ft (*54.0m × 8.2m × 4.9m*), launched 1962, two diesels, 2700bhp = 16kts, 1–40mm, complement 29. Modernised in 1979–80. Ex-Navy.

Nornen (W 300), 1060t standard, 203ft 5in × 32ft × 15ft 9in (*62.0m × 10.0m × 4.8m*), 17kts, 1–76mm, launched and completed 1963 at Mjellem & Karlsen, Bergen. Ex-Navy. Modernised 1977.

NORDKAPP class *patrol vessels*

Displacement:	2700t standard; 3200t full load
Dimensions:	319ft 10in wl, 344ft 6in oa × 47ft 11in × 16ft 1in max *97.5m, 105.0m × 14.6m × 4.9m*
Machinery:	2 shafts, 4 Wichmann diesels, 14,400bhp = 23kts. Range 7500nm at 15kts (on 2 diesels)
Armament:	1–57mm, 4–20mm (4×1), 6–324mm Mk 32 TT (2×3), 1 DC rack (6 DCs), 1 helicopter
Sensors:	Radar TM-1226, RM-914, ASW-4, GLF-218; sonar SS-105
Complement:	55 peace; 76 war

No	Name	Builder	Launched	Fate
W 320	NORDKAPP	Bergens Mekaniske Verksteder	14.5.80	Extant 1982
W 321	SENJA	Horten Verft	16.3.81	Extant 1982
W 322	ANDENES	Haugesund Mekaniske Verksteder	21.3.81	Extant 1982

In 1977 the Naval Material Command requested two new types of vessel to patrol the EEZ, three of an ice-strengthened type and four of normal construction. However, the Coast Guard budget was cut and only the above three Type 320 ships were built. Only *Nordkapp* is strengthened for ice navigation. The first two were ordered in July 1978 and the third in November 1979. They are versatile ships capable of patrol, fire-fighting, anti-pollution work, meteorological reporting, and escort duties in wartime. For this last function they can be fitted with 6 Penguin 2 SSMs (6×1) and chaff launchers. The guns are Bofors (57mm) and Rheinmetall; they have a NAVKIS AIO system, and carry a Lynx helicopter.

Haakon VII as training ship   Royal Norwegian Navy

Senja as completed   Author's Collection

Portugal

Portugal's strategic position, and the fact that she eventually sided with the Allies during the Second World War, brought considerable benefits to her armed forces from the mid-1940s, in which the Navy shared. Her fragile economy would not have supported a naval re-equipment programme, but American aid started soon after the end of the war. In 1949, Portugal was a founder member of NATO and in 1951 she signed a treaty with the United States for establishing American bases in Portuguese territory, including the Azores. War-built ships were transferred, but from the 1950s a modest programme of new building commenced.

THE COLONIES
In the 1960s, Portugal still had an extensive overseas empire, and most of her warships, including a large number of small frigates and patrol vessels, were designed to patrol their waters. India invaded and annexed the colonies of Goa, Daman and Diu on the Indian subcontinent in December 1961, and the Portuguese Navy lost a frigate and two patrol boats in a futile effort to prevent this. In the face of widespread unrest in the African colonies where independence movements sprang up in Angola, Mozambique and Portuguese Guinea (now Guinea-Bissau), the Navy was hurriedly expanded to assist the other services. Large numbers of simply equipped small frigates, patrol boats and landing craft were built in a few years.

THE POST-COLONIAL ERA
The independence movements gradually won more and more territory. The end of Dr Salazar's dictatorship appeared to change none of Portugal's attitudes, but when his successor, Dr Caetano, was toppled by a military *coup* in April 1974, Portugal at last had leaders who were prepared to abandon the colonies and the drain they represented on the Portuguese economy and armed forces. The African colonies achieved their independence in 1974, 1975 and 1976, and most of the small craft built to serve in their waters were either transferred to Angola or Mozambique or scrapped.

PORTUGAL'S NAVY
A few medium sized frigates were built to American and French designs in the 1960s, but they are now ageing and urgently need updating. Otherwise, Portugal's remaining ships are mostly irrelevant to its needs, either as a member of NATO or as a small country with a stagnant economy. Those ships that could be were sold off, including a *Daphne* class submarine to Pakistan in 1975. The *Da Silva*, *Belo* and *Coutinho* classes are to be modernised, and this will go some way to solving the problem, though not so good as the more expensive solution of building new vessels. Portugal is capable of building small warships and in fact has built a number of her existing naval vessels, though most of them were designed abroad.

FLEET STRENGTH 1947

SUBMARINES

Name	Launched	Disp	Fate
Delfim class			
DELFIM	1.5.34	1092t	Discarded *c*1950
ESPARDARTE	30.5.34	1092t	Discarded *c*1950
GOLGINHO	30.5.34	1092t	Discarded *c*1950

These Vickers-built submarines were replaced by ex-British 'S' class boats in 1948.

DESTROYERS

Name	Launched	Disp (full load)	Fate
Douro class			
DAO	27.7.34	1563t	Discarded 29.11.60
DOURO	16.8.35	1563t	Discarded Dec 59
LIMA	29.5.33	1563t	Discarded 16.10.65
TEJO	4.5.35	1563t	Discarded 9.2.65
VOUGA	25.1.33	1563t	Discarded 3.6.67

They were refitted between 1946–49 in Britain. The machinery was overhauled, the aft funnel shortened, the original funnel casings replaced by aluminium ones to reduce topweight, and a tripod foremast installed. The AA armament was increased to 3–40mm (3×1) and 3–20mm (3×1) and radar and sonar was installed. They were again refitted in 1957 to enhance their ASW capabilities. Armament then consisted of 2–4.7in (120mm), 5–40mm (1×2, 3×1), 3–20mm, 1 Squid ASW mortar, 2 DC racks, 4–21in (533mm) TT

SLOOPS

Name	Launched	Disp	Fate
Albuquerque class			
ALFONSO DE ALBUQUERQUE	28.5.34	2440t	Sunk 18.12.61
BARTOLOMEU DIAS	10.10.34	2440t	Depot Ship Feb 67, discarded *c*1969
Vehlo class			
GONCALVES ZARCO	28.11.32	1414t	Discarded *c*1969
GONCIALO VEHLO	3.8.32	1414t	BU June 61
Nunes class			
PEDRO NUNES	17.3.34	1220t	Discarded 1976
JOAO DE LISBOA	21.5.36	1220t	Discarded 17.8.66

PORTUGAL

Albuquerque class
These first-class sloops were re-rated as frigates. *Albuquerque* was sunk by the Indian cruiser *Mysore* and Indian destroyers during the Indian invasion and annexation of Goa in December 1961. *Dias* was converted to a depot ship in February 1967 and renamed *Sao Cristavao*. All her armament except for 'A' and Y' position 4.7in (120mm) guns were removed.

Vehlo class
Second-class sloops. These were reclassed as frigates, as were the second-class sloops of the *Nunes* class.

Nunes class
Nunes was converted to a survey ship in 1956 and *Lisboa* in 1961. Her 20mm were replaced by 4–40mm guns (4×1).

GUNBOATS

Name	Launched	Disp	Fate
Zaire class			
DIO	Oct 29	397t	Discarded c 1970
ZAIRE (ex-*Goa*)	26.2.25	397t	Discarded c 1960
Faro class			
FARO	1927	295t	Discarded c 1960
LAGOS	1930	295t	Discarded c 1960
TETE	1918	100t	Discarded c 1975
Azevia class			
AZEVIA	1941–42	270t	Discarded 1975
BICUDA	1941–42	270t	Discarded 1976
CORVINA	1941–42	270t	Discarded 1975
DOURADA	1941–42	270t	Discarded 1975
ESPILHA	1941–42	270t	Discarded 1971
FATACA	1941–42	270t	Wrecked 22.1.49

Zaire class
Diu was used as a training ship from c1965.

Faro class
Faro and *Lagos* were employed as fishery protection vessels. *Tete* was a river gunboat on the River Zambesi. She was re-rated as a patrol boat in 1960.
　　The *Azevia* class were all used as fishery protection vessels. *Fataga* became a total loss after being wrecked on 22.1.49.

MAJOR SURFACE SHIPS

These two ex-British 'River' class frigates, launched in 1963, were purchased by Portugal in 1948 and transferred in May 1949. Both were refitted in 1959 when their ASW armament was modernised. The Hedgehog ASW mortar on the forecastle was removed and the 4in (102mm) gun moved farther forward. Two Squid ASW mortars (2×3) were then positioned side by side between the gun and the bridge. The DCT were

(For illustration see under Great Britain in 1922–46 volume)

Ex-British 'RIVER' class *frigates*

Particulars:　　As British *River* class

No	Name	Builder	Acquired	Fate
F 331	DIOGO GOMES (ex-*Awe*)	Fleming & Ferguson	1948	Discarded 20.4.69
F 332	NUNO TRISTAO (ex-*Avon*)	Charles Hill	1948	Discarded c1972

also removed. The armament then consisted of 2–4in (2×1), 6–40mm, 2 Squid ASW, 2 DC racks.

Formoe was originally to have been renamed *Zaire* and *Reynolds, Zambeze*, but when the two ex-USN 'WGT' type DEs (launched 1944) were transferred under MDAP on 7.2.57 they were actually renamed *Cao* and *Real* respectively. Both had their 3–21in (533mm) TT (3×1) removed, leaving an armament of 2–5in/38 (2×1), 10–40mm (1×4, 3×2), 1 Hedgehog, 8 DCT, 2 DC racks. They were rated as frigates by the Portuguese.

(For illustration see under United States in 1922–46 volume)

Ex-US JOHN C BUTLER class *destroyer escorts*

Particulars:　　As US *John C Butler* class (WGT type)

No	Name	Builder	Acquired	Fate
F 333	DIOGO CAO (ex-*Formoe*)	Federal	7.2.57	Discarded 19.11.68
F 334	CORTE REAL (ex-*McCoy Reynolds*)	Federal	7.2.57	Discarded 21.10.68

Ex-British 'Bay' class AA frigates, launched in 1944–45. *Cabral* and *Pereira* were purchased in April 1959 and transferred to Portugal on 11.5.59, and *De Almeida* and *Da Gama* were purchased in May 1961 and transferred after a refit on 3.8.61. A half-sister, *Alfonso de Albuquerque*, ex-*Dalrymple*, ex-*Luce Bay*, built by Wm Pickersgill, launched 12.4.45 and completed in 1949 as an unarmed survey ship, was purchased by Portugal in April 1966. She is employed as a survey ship and was extant in 1982.

(For illustration see under Great Britain in 1922–46 volume)

Ex-British 'BAY' class *frigates*

Particulars:　　As British *Bay* class

No	Name	Builder	Acquired	Fate
F 336	ALVARES CABRAL (ex-*Burghead Bay*)	Hill	April 59	Discarded 1971
F 479	D FRANCISCO DE ALMEIDA (ex-*Morecambe Bay*)	Pickersgill	May 61	Discarded 1970
F 478	VASCO DA GAMA (ex-*Mounts Bay*)	Pickersgill	May 61	Discarded 1971
F 337	PACHECO PEREIRA (ex-*Bigbury Bay*)	Hall Russell	April 59	Discarded 1970

(For illustration see under Venezuelan *Almirante Clemente* class in Part II of this volume)

Pedro Escobar had the same basic hull and machinery as the Italian-designed Venezuelan *Almirante Clemente* class, but had a considerably lighter armament to reduce topweight. She was modernised in 1968–69 to improve her AA and ASW armament, and was rearmed with 4–3in (76mm) (2×2), 2 Squid ASW mortars (2×3) and 6–12.7in (324mm) TT (2×3). She had MLT-3A and MLA-1B radar and SQS-29 sonar fitted, and this armament made her equivalent to the *Da Silva* class frigates. *Pedro Escobar* was built to a NATO order.

PEDRO ESCOBAR *frigate*

Displacement:	1250t standard; 1600ft full load
Dimensions:	306ft 9in wl, 321ft 6in oa × 35ft 6in × 10ft
	93.5m, 98.0m × 10.9m × 3.1m
Machinery:	2-shaft geared steam turbines, 2 boilers, 24,000shp = 32kts. Range 2800nm at 13.5kts
Armament:	2–76mm/50 DP (2×1), 2–40mm (1×2), 3–533mm (21in) TT (1×3). See notes
Complement:	165

No	Name	Builder	Laid down	Launched	Comp	Fate
F 335	PEDRO ESCOBAR	Castellammare	7.1.55	25.9.55	July 57	Discarded 1975

These three ships are built to a slightly modified version of the US *Dealey* class DE design. The ships are fitted for prolonged service in tropical waters and they have 2–14.75in (375mm) Bofors ASW rocket launchers (2×4) in 'B' position in place of Weapon Alfa, plus 6–12.75in (324mm) Mk 32 ASW TT (2×3). The complement is 166 and they are fitted with MLA-1B search, Type 978 tactical, SPG-34 fire control and RM-316P navigational radars and SQS-30 (*Da Silva*), SQS-31 (*Coutinho*), SQS-32 (*Correa*) search, SQA-10A VDS and DUBA-3A attack sonar. They were built in Portugal under MDAP. All three

US DEALEY type *frigates*

| Particulars: | As US *Dealey* class |

No	Name	Builder	Laid down	Launched	Comp	Fate
F 472	ALMIRANTE PEREIRA DA SILVA	Lisnave	14.6.62	2.12.63	20.12.66	Extant 1982
F 473	ALMIRANTE GAGO COUTINHO	Lisnave	2.12.63	13.8.65	29.11.67	Extant 1982
F 474	ALMIRANTE MAGALHAES CORREA	Viana do Castelo	30.8.63	26.4.65	4.11.68	Extant 1982

were to be modernised, but new ships will probably be built instead (see below).

The *Belo* class are very similar to the French *Rivières*, but are fitted for tropical service and have 2–40mm/70 in place of the *Rivières'* 2–30mm (2×1). The *Belo*s have a complement of 200 and have DRBV-22A search, DRBV-50 tactical, DRBC-31D fire control and RM-316 navigational radars, with SQS-17A search and DUBA-3A attack sonars. All four are to be modernised, and fitted to carry a helicopter.

French COMMANDANT RIVIERE type *frigates*

| Particulars: | As French *Commandant Rivière* class |

No	Name	Builder	Laid down	Launched	Comp	Fate
F 480	COMANDANTE JOAO BELO	AC de Nantes	6.9.65	22.3.66	1.7.67	Extant 1982
F 481	COMANDANTE HERMENGILDO CAPELO	AC de Nantes	13.5.66	29.11.66	26.4.68	Extant 1982
F 482	COMANDANTE ROBERTO IVENS	AC de Nantes	13.12.66	11.8.67	23.11.68	Extant 1982
F 483	COMANDANTE SACADURA CABRAL	AC de Nantes	10.8.67	15.3.68	25.7.69	Extant 1982

Comandante João Belo as completed

Navarret Collection

PORTUGAL

João Coutinho as completed

Baptiste de Andrada 1979

The *Joao Coutinho* class were designed by Blohm and Voss, Hamburg and built by them and by Bazan, Spain. They are relatively cheap and sparsely equipped light frigates, which could be acquired by Portugal in sufficient numbers to replace the old second-class sloops, corvettes, and gunboats. They can carry 34 Marines, and their chief function until 1975 was patrolling off Portugal's colonies. There is provision for a light helicopter to land aft. The class is due to be modernised.

The *De Andrada* class utilise the same hull and machinery as the *J Coutinho*s, but have a more sophisticated armament and sensors. They have a helicopter platform but no hangar. After the withdrawal from the colonies, all four were to be sold to Colombia in 1977, but the deal was not completed. Neither class is particularly well equipped with weapons or sensors, and are really only suitable for coastal patrols and fishery protection service.

JOAO COUTINHO and DE ANDRADA classes *frigates*

Displacement:	1252t standard; 1401t full load
Dimensions:	265ft 10in pp, 277ft 8in oa × 33ft 10in × 10ft 10in
	81m, 84.6m × 10.3m × 3.3m
Machinery:	2 shafts, 2 OEW-Pielstick diesels, 10,560bhp = 24.4kts. Range 5000nm at 18kts
Armament:	*J Coutinho* class 2–3in /50(76mm)(1×2), 2–40mm/70(1×2), 1 Hedgehog ASW mortar, 2 DCT, 20 DC in racks
	De Andrada class 1–3.9in(100mm), 2–40mm/70(2×1), 6–324mm(12.75in) TT (2×3), 1 helicopter
Sensors:	Radar *J Coutinho* class MLA-1B, TM-626, SPG-50
	De Andrada class AWS-2, TM-626, Pollux
	Sonar *J Coutinho* class QCU-2, *De Andrada* class Diodon
Complement:	*J Coutinho* class 93, *De Andrada* class 113

No	Name	Builder	Laid down	Launched	Comp	Fate
J Coutinho class						
F 475	JOAO COUTINHO	Blohm & Voss, Hamburg	Sept 68	2.5.69	7.3.70	Extant 1982
F 476	JACINTO CANDIDO	Blohm & Voss, Hamburg	Apr 68	16.6.69	10.6.70	Extant 1982
F 477	GENERAL PEREIRA D'ECA	Blohm & Voss, Hamburg	Oct 68	26.7.69	10.10.70	Extant 1982
F 484	AUGUSTO DE CASTILHO	Bazan	Aug 68	5.7.69	14.11.70	Extant 1982
F 485	HONORIO BARRETO	Bazan	July 68	11.4.70	15.4.71	Extant 1982
F 471	ANTONIO ENES	Bazan	Apr 68	16.8.69	18.6.71	Extant 1982
De Andrada class						
F 486	BAPTISTE DE ANDRADA	Bazan	1972	Mar 73	19.11.74	Extant 1982
F 487	JOAO ROBY	Bazan	1972	3.6.73	18.3.75	Extant 1982
F 488	ALFONSO CERQUEIRA	Bazan	1973	6.10.73	26.6.75	Extant 1982
F 489	OLIVEIRA E CARMO	Bazan	1972	Feb 74	Feb 76	Extant 1982

Netherlands 'STANDARD' type *frigates*

A decision has finally been made regarding the construction of three new frigates, financed by various NATO countries. The ships are to be based on the Dutch *Kortenaer* class hull, modified for Portuguese requirements. Orders for the first (to be built in the Netherlands) and a further two (to be built in Portugal) were expected during 1982.

SUBMARINES

These ex-British 'S' class submarines, built in 1943–45, were all purchased in 1948. The light AA guns (1–20mm, 3–0.303in (7.7mm)) were landed in 1961. The 'S' class boats were replaced by the *Daphnes*.

Ex-British 'S' class *patrol submarines*

Particulars:	As British 'S' class (1942/43 programmes)

No	Name	Builder	Acquired	Fate
S 160	NARVAL (ex-*Spur*)	Cammell Laird	1948	Discarded 1.10.69
S 161	NAUTILO (ex-*Saga*)	Cammell Laird	1948	Discarded 25.1.69
S 162	NEPTUNO (ex-*Spearhead*)	Cammell Laird	1948	Discarded 1.9.67

Albacora as completed

These French-designed *Daphne* type submarines were ordered in 1964 and are slightly modified to suit Portuguese requirements. They are fitted for operating in tropical waters, have a complement of 50 and DRUA-31 radar and DUUA-1 active and DSUV passive sonar. *Cachalote* was purchased by Pakistan in December 1975 and renamed *Ghazi*.

French DAPHNE type *patrol submarines*

Particulars:	As French *Daphne* class					
No	**Name**	**Builder**	**Laid down**	**Launched**	**Comp**	**Fate**
S 163	ALBACORA	Dubigeon	6.9.65	15.10.66	1.10.67	Extant 1982
S 164	BARRACUDA	Dubigeon	19.10.65	24.4.67	4.5.68	Extant 1982
S 165	CACHALOTE	Dubigeon	27.10.66	16.2.68	25.1.69	To Pakistan Dec 75
S 166	DELFIM	Dubigeon	12.5.67	23.9.68	1.10.69	Extant 1981

AMPHIBIOUS WARFARE VESSELS

LANDING CRAFT

Name	Launched	Disp (full load)	Fate
LCT type			
ALFANGE (LDG 101)	1964	635t	To Angola 1975
ARIETE (LDG 102)	1964	635t	To Mozambique? 1975
BACAMARTE (LDG 103)	1964	635t	Discarded 1976
CIMITARRA (LDG 104)	1965	635t	To Mozambique 1975
MONTANTE (LDG 105)	1965	635t	Discarded 1976
BOMBARDA (LDG 201)	1969	635t	Extant 1982
ALABARDA (LDG 202)	1970	635t	Extant 1982
LCM type			
LDM 101–121	1963–72	50t	3 extant 1982
LDM 201–205	1963–65	50t	None extant 1982
LDM 301–313	1964–67	50t	None extant 1982
LDM 401–424	1964–67	56t	8 extant 1982

LCT type
The LCT were based on the British LCT (4) Type. The last two differ slightly from the first five. They have Decca RM-316 radar. Built by Mondego S Yd.

LCM type
The LCM are based on the USN LCM type. The four series differ slightly from one another; all built by Mondego S Yd. Most were discarded in 1975–76; *LDM 119–LDM 121* and *LDM 406, LDM 418, LDM 420–LDM 424* were the only craft remaining in 1982

Other minor landing craft
A number of 12t assault landing craft designated LD (later LDP) were built at Mondego from 1961 onwards in the three series *LDP 101–LDP 109, LDP 201–LDP 217, LDP 301–LDP 304*. Most were discarded in 1975, leaving only *LDP 216* in service in 1982.

SMALL SURFACE COMBATANTS

(For illustration see under countries of origin in this and 1922–46 volume)

Ex-British BANGOR class *corvettes*

Particulars:	As British *Bangor* class			
No	**Name**	**Builder**	**Acquired**	**Fate**
F 470	CACHEU (ex-*Comandante Almeida Carvalho*, ex-*Fort York*, ex-*Mingan*)	Dufferin, Toronto	1950	Discarded 1971
A 525	ALMIRANTE LACERDA (ex-*Caraquet*)	N Vancouver	1946	Discarded 1975

The *Bangor* class fleet minesweepers *Caraquet* and *Fort York* (ex-*Mingan*) were built in Canada in 1941 and served in the Canadian Navy before being sold to the Portuguese Navy on 29.6.46 and 26.9.50 respectively and renamed *Almirante Lacerda* (A 525) and *Comandante Almeida Carvalho* (A 527). Both were originally employed as survey ships, but in 1965 *Carvalho* was renamed *Cacheu* and reclassified as a corvette. Both ships were armed with 1–3in (76mm) and 2–20mm.

Ex-British 'ISLES' class *patrol vessels*

Particulars:	As British 'Isles' class

Four British 'Isles' and 'Tree' class minesweeping trawlers were lent to Portugal from October 1943 to July 1945, *Bruray* as *P 1*, *Mangrove* as *P 2*, *Hayling* as *P 3* and *Whalsay* as *P 4*. They were later purchased by Portugal: *Bruray* on 11.2.46 as *Sao Miguel*, *Mangrove* on 11.2.46 as *Faial*, *Hayling* on 11.6.46 as *Terceira* and *Whalsay* on 11.6.46 as *Santa Maria*. *Saltarelo* ('Dance' class) was purchased by Portugal on 4.8.46 and renamed *Salvador Correia*, and *Ruskholm* was purchased on 2.9.49 and renamed *Baldaque da Silva*. The latter was used first as a patrol vessel, then as a minesweeper and then as a survey ship. The others were used mainly as patrol vessels, *Correia* being stationed in Angola. *Sao Miguel* was discarded in 1956, *Terceira* in 1957, *Correia* in 1961, *Faial* in 1967 and *Santa Maria* in 1968. When the first *Correia* was discarded in 1961, *Da Silva* was renamed *Salvador Correia* and took the preceeding ship's place in Angola. She was discarded in the early 1970s. They were all armed with 1–3in (76mm) and 2–20mm. *Correia* (ex-*Da Silva*)'s 3in (76mm) was removed in 1964.

Ex-US PC type *patrol vessels*

Particulars:	As US PC type

Class:
Principe (P 581, ex-*Flores*, ex-*PC 812*), *Madeira* (P 582, ex-*PC 811*), *Santiago* (P 583, ex-*PC 1257*), *Sal* (P 584, ex-*PC 809*), *Sao Tome* (P 585, ex-*PC 1256*), *Sao Vicente* (P 586, ex-*PC 1259*)

Six ex USN PCs were purchased by Portugal in 1948 under MDAP. They were originally employed mainly for air-sea rescue patrols off the Portuguese, Azores and Madeira coasts. In 1957 they were rearmed to bring them up to the standards of the new *Le Fougueux* type. Their 3in (76mm) and 2–20mm guns were removed and the new armament was 1–40mm, 3–20mm (3×1), 1 Hedgehog ASW mortar and 4 DCT. *Santiago* was discarded in July 1967 and the the remainder were discarded between 1968–69.

French LE FOUGUEUX type *patrol vessels*

Particulars:	As French *Le Fougueux* class

Class (no, launched):
Dubigeon – *Maio* (P 587, ex-*Funchal*, 27.9.54)
Normand – *Porto Santo* (P 588, 9.2.55), *Sao Nicolau* (P 589, 7.6.55)
Viano do Castelo – *Brava* (P 590, 2.5.56), *Fago* (P 591, 2.5.56)
Mondego – *Boavista* (P 592, 10.7.56)
Alfeite D Yd – *Santo Antao* (P 593, 8.6.56), *Santa Luzia* (P 594, 17.1.57)

ARGOS class *patrol vessels*

Displacement:	180t standard; 210t full load
Dimensions:	131ft 3in pp, 136ft 8in oa × 20ft 6in × 7ft 40.0m, 41.7m × 6.2m × 2.1m
Machinery:	2 shafts, 2 Maybach diesels, 1200bhp = 17kts. Oil 16t
Armament:	2–40mm (2×1)
Sensors:	Radar ?
Complement:	24

Class:
Argos (P 372), *Cassiopeia* (P 373), *Dragao* (P 374), *Escorpiao* (P 375), *Hidra* (P 376), *Lira* (P 361), *Orion* (P 362), *Pegaso* (P 379), *Centauro* (P 1130), *Sagitario* (P 1134)

PORTUGAL

Six *Argos* class were built at Alfeite and four at Viano do Castelo between June 1963 and September 1965. They were intended for use in the Portuguese colonies. *Centauro*, *Escorpião*, *Lira*, *Orion* and *Pegaso* were transferred to Angola in 1975, with *Argos* and *Dragão* for spares, while *Cassiopea* was discarded in 1975 and *Hidra* and *Sagitario* in 1976.

CACINE class *patrol vessel*

Displacement:	292t standard; 310t full load
Dimensions:	144ft 5in × 25ft 2in × 7ft 3in
	44.0m × 7.7m × 2.2m
Machinery:	2 shafts, 2 MTU diesels, 4400bhp = 20kts. Range 4400nm at 12kts
Armament:	2–40mm (2×1), 1–37mm RL (1×32)
Sensors:	Radar KH-975
Complement:	33

Class:
Cacine (P 1140), *Cunene* (P 1141), *Mandovi* (P 1142), *Rovuma* (P 1143), *Quanza* (P 1144), *Geba* (P 1145), *Zaire* (P 1146), *Zambesi* (P 1147), *Limpopo* (P 1160), *Save* (P 1161)

The first four ships were built to this design at Alfeite D Yd from 1967–69. The next six were built at Mondego, from 1968–71 and *Limpopo* and *Save* in 1973. They replace the earlier PC and *Le Fougueux* type patrol vessels. All were extant in 1982.

COASTAL PATROL BOATS

Name	Fate	Name	Fate
Fairmile 'B' type: launched 1942–44, 85.6t full load			
ALTAIR (L 1)	BU 1955	DENEB (L 4)	Discarded 1959
BELATRIX (L 2)	Discarded c 1959	ESPIGA (L 5)	Discarded Nov 59
CANOPUS (L 3)	Discarded Sep 59	FORMALHAUT (L 6)	Discarded 1959
Albatroz class: launched 1974–75, 45t full load			
ALBATROZ (P 1162)	Extant 1982	AGUIA (P 1165)	Extant 1982
ACOR (P 1163)	Extant 1982	CONDOR (P 1166)	Extant 1982
ANDORHINA (P 1164)	Extant 1982	CISNE (P 1167)	Extant 1982
Dom Aleixo class: launched 1967, 67.7t full load			
DOM ALEIXO (P 1148)	Extant 1982	DOM JEREMIAS (P 1149)	Extant 1982
Alvor class: launched 1966–67, 35.7t full load			
ALVOR (P 1156)	Discarded 1975	ALJELUR (P 1158)	Discarded 1975
ALBUFEIRA (P 1157)	Discarded 1975		
Jupiter class: launched 1944–65, 49t full load			
JUPITER (P 1132)	See notes	SATURNO (P 1136)	See notes
MARTE (P 1134)	To Angola 1975	URANO (P 1137)	See notes
MERCURIO (P 1135)	See notes	VENUS (P 1133)	To Angola 1975
Belatrix class: launched 1961–62, 29t full load			
ALDERBARAN	Discarded 1975	FORMALHAUT (P 367)	Survey ship 1975
ALTAIR (P 377)	To Angola 1975	POLLUX (P 368)	To Angola 1975
ARCTURUS	Discarded 1975	PROCION (P 1153)	Discarded 1975
BELATRIX (P 363)	Discarded 1975	RIGEL (P 378)	To Angola 1975
CANOPUS (P 364)	Discarded 1975	SIRIUS	To Mozambique 1975
DENEB (P 365)	Discarded 1975	VEGA	To Mozambique 1975
ESPIGA (P 366)	To Angola 1975		
Algol class: launched 1964, 24t full load			
ALGOL (P 1138)	Discarded c1975		
Castor class: launched 1964, 22t full load			
CASTOR (P 580)	Discarded 1976		
Antares class: launched 1959, 18t full load			
ANTARES (P 360)	To Mozambique 1975	SIRIUS	Sunk Dec 61
REGULUS (P 369)	Discarded 1975	VEGA	Sunk Dec 61
Rio Minho class: launched 1957, 14t full load			
RIO MINHO (P 370)	Extant 1982		

Fairmile 'B' type
The six Fairmile 'B' type motor launches were purchased from Britain in 1946. They were disarmed and used as air–sea rescue launches. A large deckhouse was built aft.

Albatroz class
Six were built at Alfeite in 1974–75 and eight more have been built since. They have RM–316P radar, and are armed with 1–20mm and 2–0.5in (12.7mm) (1×2). Eight more units are reported.

Dom Aleixo class
These are armed with 1–20mm. *Dom Jeremias* is in use as a survey craft.

Alvor class
These were all built at Alfeite, and were armed with either 1–20mm or 2 MG.

Jupiter class
These were armed with 1–20mm and were built by Mondego. Two were transferred to Angola; of the remainder, three went to Mozambique and one was discarded, but it is not clear which.

Belatrix class
All were built in Germany. They are armed with 1–20mm.

Algol was built by Argibay, Lisbon, and armed with 2 MG.

Castor was built by *Mondego* and armed with 1–20mm.

Antares class
Designed by James Taylor, Shoreham, who built *Antares* and the glass-fibre hulls of the other three. *Sirius* and *Vega* were sunk in action with Indian forces during the invasion and annexation of Goa in 1961.

Rio Minho patrols the River Minho on the Spanish-Portuguese border.

MINE WARFARE VESSELS

(For illustration see under United States)

US AGILE type *ocean minesweepers*

Particulars:	As US *Agile* class

No	Name	Builder	Launched	Fate
M 418	CORVO	Burger Boats	28.7.54	Discarded 1973
M 417	GRACIOSO	Burger Boats	19.11.53	Discarded 1973
M 416	PICO	Bellingham	18.6.54	Discarded 1973
M 415	SAO JORGE	Bellingham	30.4.54	Discarded 1973

USN *Agile* type MSOs built in the USA for Portugal under MDAP. While building they were assigned the USN designations MSO 487, 486, 479 and 478 respectively. They were all laid down in 1953 and commissioned between 24.4.55 and 23.11.55.

(For illustration see under Great Britain)

British 'TON' type *coastal minesweepers*

Particulars:	As British 'Ton' class

Class:
Sao Roque (M 401), *Ribeira Grande* (M 402), *Lagoa* (M 403), *Rosario* (M 404)

Four 'Ton' class coastal minesweepers were built in the CUF Shipyard, 1954–56. *Lagoa* and *Sao Roque* were funded by the USA under MDAP, and *Ribeira Grande* and *Rosairo* were paid for by Portugal. They had been ordered in 1954. Their 1–40mm gun was removed in 1972, leaving them with 2–20mm. All were extant in 1982, but are now used as patrol vessels.

(For illustration see under United States)

Ex-US ADJUTANT class *coastal minesweepers*

Particulars:	As US *Adjutant* class

Class:
Ponta Delgada (M 405), *Horta* (M 406), *Angra do Heroismo* (M 407), *Vila Porto* (M 408), *Santa Cruz* (M 409), *Velas* (M 410), *Lajes* (M 411), *Sao Pedro* (M 412)

Eight USN *Redwing* type MSC were built in the USA 1951–53 and transferred under MDAP to Portugal 1953–55. *Ponta Delgada* (ex-*Adjutant*, AMS 60), *Santa Cruz* (ex-AMS 92) and *Angra do Heroismo* (ex-AMS 62) were discarded in 1973, *Santa Cruz* (ex-AMS 92) and *Lajes* (ex-AMS 146) were discarded in 1975 and *Horta* (ex-AMS 61), *Vila do Porto* (ex-AMS 91) and *Velas* (ex-AMS 145) were discarded in 1976.

Spain

The year 1947 saw Spain's fortunes at a low ebb. The Civil War had cost more than half a million lives, with hundreds of thousands more forced into exile. Recovery was hampered by the great material destruction, particularly to transport, and by the almost immediate onset of the Second World War. Franco was able to keep the devastated and impoverished country neutral between 1939 and 1945, although his sympathies were with the Axis Powers, which had contributed so largely to his victory in 1938–39, and his Blue Division was formed to fight on the Eastern Front (1941–43). When in 1943 Axis defeat became a certainty, he shifted to a policy of strict neutrality which earned him little credit, and no reward, from the victors. Spain was excluded from the United Nations in 1945 and ostracised by the Western Democracies, while the Communist Bloc, which recognised the defunct Republic, remained implacable foes. Although VE and VJ Days were not followed by a blockade of Spain (or even the invasion which many on the left would have liked), her economic and political isolation brought grim years of near famine, rural misery and guerilla activity.

Franco, however, was not destined to be overthrown by his enemies without or within; the start of the Cold War was Madrid's opportunity and led gradually to the establishment of normal relations with the West. Internally, the regime relaxed and slightly released its grip, with the Falange virtually reduced to impotence, control of education returned to the Church, a fundamental law on personal freedoms and the promise of a return to constitutional monarchy at a future date. The state controls and stagnant economic nationalism of the corporate state were replaced by a normal capitalist system, and rapidly growing foreign investment. The 1953 Military Aid agreement with the United States gave Franco extensive military and financial aid in return for four US air and naval bases; with this accolade, Spain returned to international respectability.

The remaining Franco years (1953–75) were a time of political stagnation, as the many forces moving towards change marked time and waited for the old Caudillo's death. His mastery of the army and the rubber-stamp parliament, nominated without political parties or normal elections, guaranteed that there would be no change in the leadership or the regime in his lifetime. The economic growth and prosperity of the 1950s ensured that the bulk of the population had no wish for change, although the high growth rate brought the usual associated stresses: a wage-price spiral, inflation and labour problems. Basque separatism, harshly crushed in 1938–39, revived and developed a ruthless terrorist element.

Franco's death in 1975 was the signal for rapid political changes. The monarchy, considered an important element of continuity and stability, was restored and the formation of political parties allowed, while a new constitution, free elections and a proper parliament brought Spain into line with Western Europe. The changes were achieved smoothly and peacefully, diehard generals in the army preferring to protest and retire. In 1982 the fledgling democracy was still fragile and experiencing growth pains; elements of the army remained restless, disliking change and mistrusting the first socialist government in Spain for 46 years. Economic expansion had long since been stopped by the rise in oil prices and the world recession, while the Basques were only partly satisfied by their new autonomy.

In external relations, Spain's return to the Western camp from 1948 and subsequent close relationship with the United States as a staunch anti-Communist ally have been maintained, but membership of NATO did not follow until 1982. Unlike neighbouring Portugal, she did not cling to her colonies, those remaining after the 1898 débâcle being given up peacefully during the later Franco years. The Spanish Protectorate over part of Morocco was relinquished in 1956 (and the Ifni enclave was ceded to Morocco in 1969), Equatorial Guinea was turned over to what very rapidly became a brutal African dictatorship in 1968 and the Spanish Sahara was ignominiously surrendered to Moroccan pressure in late 1975. In giving up her Moroccan protectorate, however, Spain insisted on keeping the coastal cities of Ceuta and Melilla, Spanish since the sixteenth century, despite periodic Moroccan demands for the cession of both them and the Canary Islands, a short distance off the Moroccan coast. Meanwhile, Spanish claims to Gibraltar, in British hands since 1704, have been pressed with equal insistance and constancy. The land frontier with Spain was closed completely between 1969 and 1982, and a satisfactory solution of the problem is still remote.

NAVAL DEVELOPMENTS 1947–82

The progress of the Spanish Navy between 1947 and 1982 must be related to this politico-economic background. The Navy of 1947 was very much the Navy of 1939, the World War having made little difference to the fleet except to propel it almost a decade further into obsolescence. The light cruisers of the *Alfonso* class had undergone minor face-lifts, and the older *Mendez Nunez* a more substantial reconstruction as an anti-aircraft cruiser, but in general the major units had outdated AA and fire-control systems and were without radar and sonar, besides having none of the wartime 'A's and 'A's characteristic of units involved in hostilities. Ships authorised in the 1920s and 1930s but not begun until just before the Civil War, were still on the stocks, construction having been suspended between 1936 and 1939, and again between 1939 and 1944. A modest start to construction was allowed in 1944, when the completion of two destroyers and three submarines and the building of eight AA escorts was authorised.

A much more ambitious programme was announced in 1945: nine destroyers, nine large torpedo-boats, six corvettes, six submarines, six motor torpedo-boats and twelve patrol vessels were to be put in hand to replace older units and tonnage worn out in the Civil War. This programme, however, was delayed for many years because of limited funds and fluctuations in the availability of what could be allocated. Six destroyers, six submarines and ten patrol vessels were cancelled; the designs were distinctly old-fashioned (essentially pre-Second World War) and most of the ships which survived the financial stringencies were still fitting out when the 10-year 1953 Agreement with the United States marked the beginning of US assistance under the Mutual Defense Assistance Program, and a new era for the Spanish Navy.

The effect of this agreement and its continuations from 1963 were to give Spain access to recent developments in ship systems design and weapon technology. Naval Estimates more than doubled between 1954 and 1961, and personnel increased from 36,000 to 42,000 (the figure for 1945 was only 26,000). The acquisition of modern or renovated US warships started almost at once; twelve new coastal minesweepers were

107

transferred between 1954 and 1959, and five *Fletcher* class destroyers between 1957 and 1960. About thirty Spanish ships were modernised between 1959 and 1963, with new anti-aircraft guns, anti-submarine weapons, radar and other electronic equipment (some while still fitting out to their original designs): two *Alava* class destroyers, nine *Audaz* class fast frigates, two *Pizarro* class frigates, two *Jupiter* class frigate-minelayers, five *Atrevida* class corvettes and seven *Almanzora* class minesweepers, plus two submarines streamlined.

Similar plans announced for four old *Churruca* class destroyers were not implemented because their useful lives after modernisation would have been too short and, instead, a new construction programme of four destroyers, four escorts and twelve patrol vessels was put forward. Orders were not placed immediately, but negotiations were started with Britain for the construction of four *Leander* class frigates and possibly *Oberon* class submarines (Spain was anxious to obtain experience of non-American techniques and practices, and Britain had supplied radar equipment for the new destroyer *Oquendo*). Unfavourable UK Press and Parliamentary comments on these proposals (and on the Spanish regime) killed the negotiations (1964), and the orders went to the United States and France. Agreements were signed in 1966 for the construction in Spain of five modified *Knox* class frigates and two *Daphne* class submarines, with three more proposed. The strength envisaged at this time for the Spanish Navy in 1975 was 2 aircraft carriers, 2 cruisers, 8 destroyers, 12 frigates, 8 submarines, 60 mine-sweepers and 100 auxiliaries with 27 anti-submarine patrol aircraft and 48 helicopters.

A major reinforcement for the fleet arrived in 1967, when the light aircraft carrier *Dedalo*, ex-USS *Cabot*, was transferred. The first Spanish carrier (her namesake of the 1920s, an ex-merchantman fitted for transporting balloons and seaplanes, was not a front-line ship), she initially operated anti-submarine helicopters only, but an anti-ship capability was developed from 1973 with the order of Harrier AV-8 VSTOL aircraft (Matadors) from the US Marines; two of the first five were delivered in 1976 and the order of ten was complete by 1981. Smaller ships were also acquired. The United States agreed in August 1970 to supply two submarines, five destroyers, four ocean mine-sweepers, three tank landing and one dock landing ships (replacing an ammunition ship, while an oiler was not transferred), and the last of these were transferred in October 1973. Under a further Agreement in 1976, the United States was to provide four more ocean minesweepers and a repair ship, but these units had not yet been handed over in 1982.

Meanwhile, in January 1973, a Spanish new construction programme was announced, consisting of one light cruiser, three guided missile destroyers, ten corvettes, two *Agosta* class submarines, some PF type craft, twelve patrol craft for fishery protection, seven auxiliaries and several landing craft. For financial reasons, part of this programme, including the cruiser, the guided missile destroyers, two corvettes and the PF craft, was deferred until 1977–78 and was then ordered in modified form; the cruiser as a light aircraft carrier of the US Sea Control Ship type, and the destroyers as US 'FFG 7' class frigates.

The ultimate target strength of the fleet is two task groups, each consisting of one light carrier, one cruiser and four missile frigates, and four escort groups, each of two missile and two *Descubierta* class frigates. To achieve this, the next (1983–90) phase of the construction programme, as first announced, proposed the building of a second sea control ship, two cruisers, eight more missile frigates (either FFG or enlarged *Descubierta* type), two Tripartite minehunters, besides auxiliaries, ten more Matadors, six maritime patrol and four anti-submarine aircraft. Once again, however, financial considerations have intervened, and the new programme currently provides for two destroyers, seven frigates, the minehunters and a support ship, together with auxiliaries and additional aircraft.

In technical matters, the Spanish Navy attaches great importance to attaining self-sufficiency in all aspects of ship design and construction, but the limited development of the defence industries has meant the building of factories and plant for manufacturing foreign equipment under licence. Taking the *Descubierta* class of light frigates as examples, the basic ship characteristics were obtained by 'stretching' a German design for Portugal, the machinery is German in origin, the gun armament Italian and Swedish, the missile equipment American and the radar and fire control systems Dutch. The highly successful end-product is an excellent example of cooperation by the international armaments industry, but hardly a monument to Spanish self-sufficiency. More recently, however, Spain has itself originated an advanced weapon system, the Meroka CIWS, consisting of two non-rotating six-barrelled Oerlikon 20mm R TG guns, with Lockheed Electronics fire control incorporating Doppler radar and stabilised optical sights. Since being set up in 1947 the nationalised Empresa Nacional Bazán has built all of Spain's locally constructed warships – frigates at the Ferrol yard, surface ships and submarines at Cartagena, and smaller craft at La Carraca, Cadiz.

Operationally, the functions of the Navy include protecting national territory and interests – remembering Spain's highly strategic location – and projecting the power and prestige of the state. Between 1947 and 1982 warships participated in colonial defence on several occasions. The Ifni enclave, attacked sporadically by Moroccan irregulars, was the scene of cooperation with the army and air force, including shore bombardments, in 1957, 1958, 1962, 1964 and 1965. In an ostentatious display of force during one of these clashes, a squadron consisting of the cruisers *Canarias*, *Miguel de Cervantes* and *Mendez Nunez*, with an escort of destroyers and other warships, entered Moroccan territorial waters off Agadir and anchored 100 yards from the harbour entrance. In 1961 *Canarias* was sent further south, to support the administration in troubled Fernando Po and Rio Muni. When these territories became independent, *Canarias* returned to cover the evacuation of the remaining Spanish settlers. In 1969 and 1970 Spanish claims to Gibraltar were pointedly expressed by sending the carrier *Dedalo* and escorts to anchor in the Bay of Algeciras near the Rock. The British retorts were equally traditional: in 1969 *Eagle* and *Hermes* were ordered to reach Gibraltar slightly earlier. At present the main units of the fleet are based at Ferrol, except for the *Descubierta* class frigates at Cartagena. The older FRAM II destroyers and the submarines operate in the Mediterranean. There are also bases at Cadiz (La Carraca and Rota), Puntales (for amphibious ships), Tarifa (for small craft), Port Mahon on Minorca and Las Palmas in the Canary Islands.

In the past, Spain's Navy often had a poor reputation for efficiency, upkeep and fighting spirit. 'The Spanish Fleet you cannot see, because it is not yet in sight,' Sheridan's eighteenth-century comment reflected foreign opinion, and the miserable performance of Montojo's and Cervera's decrepit crocks in the Spanish-American War did nothing to change this view. Rapid improvements have, however, taken place in the present century, particularly during the past twenty years, and the Spanish Navy of 1982 is a balanced, well-trained, carefully maintained and up-to-date force.

FLEET STRENGTH 1947

CRUISERS

No	Name	Launched	Disp (full load)	Fate
Eugenia class				
–	NAVARRA (ex-*Republica*, ex-*Reina Victoria Eugenia*)	21.4.20	6500t	Stricken 1956
Nuñez class				
C 01	MENDEZ NUNEZ	27.7.22	6045t	Stricken Dec 63
Alfonso class				
C 11	GALICIA (ex-*Libertad*, ex-*Principe Alfonso*)	23.1.25	9900t	Stricken 2.2.70
C 12	ALMIRANTE CERVERA	16.10.25	9660t	Stricken 1966
C 13	MIGUEL DE CERVANTES	19.5.28	9900t	Hulked 1963
Canarias class				
C 21	CANARIAS	28.5.31	13,500t	Stricken 17.12.75

Nuñez class
During the 1950s the number of 20mm AA guns was altered to 16 (4×4) and later to 23 (4×4, 7×1). In the mid-1950s she received 2 DCT and 1 DC rack. Allocated pennant number C 01 in 1961. In the 1960s she served as an accom-

modation hulk for minesweeper crews at Las Palmas, and the forward 120mm guns were probably removed. Finally used as an accommodation hulk at Cartagena.

Alfonso class
Reconstructed from 1940 onwards: *Galicia* rearmed Jul 44, *Cervantes* Jul 45. Both reached 31.5kts in 1946. *Galicia* and *Cervantes* 8–90mm (4×2) replaced c1952 by 8–37mm AA (4×2) in addition to former 8–37mm AA (4×2). In 1957 (?1960) 12 *Cervera* or 6 TT *Galicia* and *Cervantes* were removed. In late 1950s *Galicia* received a radar scanner just abaft the main director on the bridge on a small lattice tower. In *Cervera* 4–105mm AA were replaced in late 1950s by additional 8–37mm AA (4×2) in lieu of planned US 76mm guns. In 1961 they were allocated the new pennant numbers in the table above.

Canarias class
In 1948–49 the recently installed foremast received a light bipod bracket forward. In October 1952–February 1953 she was refitted in Ferrol. The after four pairs of 37mm AA guns gave way to 4–40mm/70 AA Bofors (4×1). This change produced the final array of armament that would serve *Canarias* for the rest of her career: 8–203mm/50 DP (4×2), 8–120mm/45 DP (8×1), 4–40mm/70 AA (4×1), 4–37mm/70 AA (2×2), 1 or 2–20mm AA, 2 DCT and 1 DC rack. The broad trunked funnel was replaced by two vertical funnels, a return to the original plan which had never been carried out. The fore part of the bridge was enclosed and the wings extended. Navigational radar was installed on the fore top. The plan to mount an aircraft catapult, so long postponed, was finally dropped as useless. By the end of the 1950s, *Canarias* had a sturdy tripod foremast fitted to carry a suite of radar and other antennas. A few years later she got a light bipod support to the mainmast for yet another radar antenna. All this was to be temporary, for in the 1960s the Spanish Navy planned to make up for a belated entry into the electronics age with a thorough modernisation of the flagship. Preliminary plans called for guided missile armament, as other nations were doing with gun-armed cruisers, and US 127mm/38 guns or 76mm guns to replace the old 120mm. The US was to foot the bill. Despite the soundness of her hull and machinery, *Canarias* was clearly a vessel past her prime, and a joint US-Spanish evaluation concluded that a full modernisation was not practicable. Newer units of the Spanish Navy could perform almost any mission more efficiently and more cheaply. All she had in her favour was roominess and prestige, assets which kept her active beyond her normal years. She was allocated the pennant number C 21 in 1961.

Instead, a limited modernisation was completed in 1969. A roomy CIC was built into the bridge structure, complemented by an enlarged command bridge. A larger radar cabin was fitted aft and whip antennas graced the funnel and bridge. Radars included a Decca 12 navigation set, a US SG-6B surface search, and an Italian Marconi MLA-1B air search. Later she added a Marconi surface search set as well. Her weaponry would have had a limited use in any conflict, but she was at least a viable command ship for modern operations.

Preservation as a floating museum was impossible (lack of funds) and the ship was sold on 14.9.77 and broken up in 1978. Over her 38 years of service she had steamed 650,000nm and was the last Washington cruiser to retire! The 'B' 203mm mounting was preserved at the Escuela Naval Militar in Marin and one of the 120mm guns is on the esplanade of La Luz Castle in Las Palmas as a memorial.

DESTROYERS

No	Name	Launched	Disp (full load)	Fate
Alsedo class				
–	ALSEDO	26.10.22	1145t	Stricken 1957
–	JUAN LAZAGA	Mar 24	1145t	Stricken 1961
–	VELASCO	June 23	1145t	Stricken 1957
Churruca class – 1st Group				
D 11 (11)	SANCHEZ BARCAIZTEGUI	24.7.26	2087t	Stricken 1965
D 12 (12)	JOSE LUIS DIEZ	25.8.28	2087t	Stricken 1966
–	(32) LEPANTO	7.11.328	2087t	Stricken Aug 57
–	(34) ALCALA GALIANO	12.4.30	2087t	Stricken 1957
–	(42) ALMIRANTE VALDES	8.9.31	2087t	Stricken 1957
D 13 (33)	CHURRUCA	June 29	2087t	Stricken 1964
Churruca class – 2nd Group				
D 14 (13)	ALMIRANTE ANTEQUERA	29.12.30	2175t	Stricken 1969
D 15 (31)	ALMIRANTE MIRANDA	20.6.31	2175t	Stricken 2.3.70
D 16 (22)	GRAVINA	24.12.31	2175t	Stricken 1964
D 17 (24)	ESCANO	28.6.32	2175t	Stricken 1964
D 18 (43)	ULLOA	24.7.33	2175t	Stricken 1964
–	(14) JORGE JUAN	28.3.33	2175t	Stricken 1959
–	(41) CISCAR	26.10.33	2175t	Lost 17.10.57
Alava class				
D 23 (23)	ALAVA	19.6.47	2170t	Stricken 1978
D 21 (21)	LINIERS	1.5.46	2170t	Stricken 1982
Ex-Italian Poerio class				
–	HUESCA (ex-*Alessandro Poerio*)	4.8.14	1012t	Stricken 1953
–	TERUEL (ex-*Guglielmo Pepe*)	17.9.14	1012t	Stricken 1947
Ex-Italian Aquila class				
–	CEUTA (ex-*Falco*)	16.8.19	1730t	Stricken 1949
–	MELILLA (ex-*Aquila*)	27.6.19	1705t	Stricken 1950

Churruca class (1st and 2nd groups)
Armament of all surviving ships modified in the early 1940s to increase AA fire: 4–120mm/45 (4×1), 1–76mm/40 AA (only on 2nd group), 4–37mm AA (2×2), 4–20mm AA, 6–533mm TT and 4 DCT. Later some of 37mm and 20mm guns were removed. Originally had initials painted on bows, but allocated pennant numbers c1953. In 1961 the new 'D' pennant numbers quoted above were introduced. *Ciscar* ran aground in fog and broke her back off Ferrol and was discarded in 1958.

Alava after modernisation

Navarret Collection

SPAIN

Modernization of 4 *Churruca* class destroyers with new AA guns, ASW armament and new electronics, which was to be carried out under MDAP and planned for late 1950s and early 1960s, was later cancelled.

Alava class
Commissioned 21.12.50 and 27.1.51 respectively. Allocated pennant numbers 23 and 21 in *c* 1952–53, and D 52 and D 51 after modernisation. As modernised 1960–62: 3–76mm/50 AA Mk 22 on Mk 34 mounts (3×1), 3–40mm/70 AA SP48 (3×1), 2 side-launching racks for 6 ASW torpedoes, 2 Hedgehogs, 8 DCT, 2 DC racks. Refitted with lattice foremast and caps on after funnels. Forecastle lengthened aft *c* 8m. Classified as ASW or fast frigates, with a displacement of 1842t standard and 2287t full load (31,500shp = 29kts max and oil 370/?540t). Completed modernisation 17.1.62 (*Alava*) and 18.9.62. Air search MLA-1B radar, one SG-6B surface search set, Decca TM-626 navigational and 2 Mk 63 fire control. One hull-mounted sonar SQS-30A. *Liniers* was used for training midshipmen at the Naval Academy until 1982.

Ex-Italian (acquired during 1938–39)
Probably never had initials on bows. *Huesca* used as TS in 1950s.

GUNBOATS AND MINELAYERS

No	Name	Launched	Disp (full load)	Fate
Castillo class gunboats				
–	CANOVAS DEL CASTILLO	21.1.22	1314t	Stricken 1959
–	CANALEJAS	1.12.22	1314t	Stricken 1953
–	DATO	1923	1314t	Stricken 1954
Durango type gunboat				
–	CALVO SOTELO (ex-Mexican Zacatecas)	27.8.34	2000t	Stricken 1957
Jupiter class gunboat-minelayers				
F 11 (16)	JUPITER	14.9.35	2600t	Stricken 1974
F 01 (39)	MARTE	19.6.36	2600t	Stricken 1972
F 02 (17)	NEPTUNO	19.12.37	2600t	Stricken 1970
F 12 (38)	VULCANO	12.10.35	2600t	Stricken 1977
Eolo class gunboat-minelayers				
F 21 (28)	EOLO	30.8.39	1900t	Stricken 1972
F 22 (29)	TRITON	24.2.40	1900t	Stricken 1972
Pizarro class gunboats				
F 32 (18)	HERNAN CORTES	3.8.44	2246t	Stricken 2.12.71
F 34 (37)	MARTIN ALONSO PINZON	3.8.44	2246t	Stricken 1968
F 31	PIZARRO	3.8.44	2246t	Stricken 1968
F 33	VASCO NUNEZ DE BALBOA	3.8.44	2246t	Stricken 1972
F 42 (27)	LEGASPI	8.8.44	2246t	Stricken 1978
F 35 (26)	MAGALLANES	8.8.44	2246t	Stricken 1972
F 36 (36)	SARMIENTO DE GAMBOA	8.8.44	2246t	Stricken 1973
F 41 (19)	VINCENTE YANEZ PINZON	8.8.44	2246t	Stricken 1982

Castillo class
Dato sunk in 1936 by *Jaime I* but refloated and reconstructed at Cadiz. *Canovas del Castillo* was rated as *canonero* until 1958, when she was re-rated as *fragata*.

Durango type
Two of four 102mm guns removed ('B' and 'X' positions) and after superstructure reduced in late 1940s. Disarmed from 1952.

Jupiter class
All four allocated 'F' pennant numbers in 1961. *Jupiter* and *Vulcano* were modernised 1959–61 and in the latter year all were reclassified as frigates. The modernisation of *Jupiter* (with lattice foremast and SPS-6 search and tactical radar) was completed on 28.10.60, and of *Vulcano* on 28.2.61. Both ships: 4–76mm/50 AA Mk 26 (4×1), 4–40mm/70 AA (4×1), 2 Hedgehogs, 8 DCT, 2 DC racks, 254 (first) or 238 (later ship) mines. From the late 1950s *Marte* (*Neptune* in brackets) were armed with: 4–120mm, 2(0)–76mm AA, 3(4)–37mm AA, 2(3)–20mm AA, 2 DCT and 264 mines. Modernised ships have air search MLA-1B and tactical SG-6B radars. *Neptune* was employed as a training ship for midshipmen (51 cadets).

Eolo class
Dual-purpose frigates or gunboats and minelayers. Allocated 'F' pennant number in 1961. Armed with 4–105mm (not 102mm) AA Krupp Model 1933 (4×1), 4–37mm AA (2×2; not 4×1), 4–13mm AA (probably 2×2), 170 (*Triton* 180) mines, 2 DCT. In 1960s probably fitted with 2 fixed TT for ASW torpedoes. Removed from the effective list on 2.2.72 and 2.3.72 respectively and were scrapped.

Pizarro class
Some (for example *Pizarro, Vasco Nunez de Balboa, Vicente Yanez Pinzon*) were armed originally with 2–105mm (2×1) in 'A' and 'X' positions instead of 6–120mm AA. Later all eight armed with 6–120mm AA (3×2), 8–37mm AA

(4×2), 6–20mm AA (2×2, 2×1), 4 DCT and 30 mines. In 1958 were officially re-rated as frigates, and allocated 'F' pennant number in 1961. *Legaspi* and *Vicente Yañez Pinzon* as modernised: 2–127mm/38 DP (2×1), 4–40mm/70 AA (4×1), 2 side-launching ASW torpedo racks (6 torpedoes), 2 Hedgehogs, 8 DCT, 2 DC racks. Completed modernisation 14.1.60 and 25.3.60 respectively. Received lattice foremast, SPS-5B surface search radar, MLA-1B air search radar and Decca TM-626 navigational radar.

Hernan Cortes and *Sarmiento de Gamboa* (for disposal 1971) were not modernised. Since *c* 1981 *Vicente Yañez Pinzon* has been classified as *patrullero de altura* with new pennant number PA 41.

SUBMARINES

Name	Launched	Disp (surface)	Fate
'C' class			
C 2	4.5.28	916t	Discarded 1952
'General' class (ex-Italian)			
GENERAL MOLA (ex-*Evangelista Torricelli*)	27.5.34	880t	Stricken 1959
GENERAL SANJURJO (ex-*Archimede*)	1.10.33	880t	Stricken 1959
Type VIIC (ex-German)			
G 7 (ex-*U 573*)	17.4.41	757t	Stricken 2.5.70
'D' class			
D 1	11.5.44	1065t	Stricken 1965
D 2	21.12.44	1065t	Stricken 1971
D 3	20.2.52	1065t	Stricken 1971

Proposals announced in 1945 to build submarines *G 1–G 6*, generally similar to *G 7*, were abandoned *c* 1960.

'General' class (ex-Italian)
Wore the pennant numbers C 5 and C 3 respectively from the early 1950s; the after 100mm gun was removed at about the same time.

Type VIIC (ex-German)
Allocated the pennant number S 01 in 1961; 20mm gun later removed.

'D' class
The three 'D' class boats were completed on 18.3.47, 2.4.51 and 20.2.54 respectively. They were given the pennant numbers S 11, S 21 and S 22 in 1961.

D 1 was not modernised but the gun was removed in the early 1960s. The other two completed 2-year reconstructions on 10.12.63 and 14.3.63 respectively, in which the hull and conning tower were streamlined, and the deck gun and after TT removed.

MINESWEEPERS

No	Name	Launched	Disp (full load)	Fate
Bidasoa class				
M 01	BIDASOA	15.9.43	775t	Stricken 1972
–	GUADALETE	18.10.44	775t	Foundered 25.3.54
M 03	LEREZ	21.12.44	775t	Stricken 1971
M 02	NERVION	15.4.44	775t	Stricken 1972
M 05	SEGURA	15.5.45	775t	Stricken 1972
M 04	TAMBRE	18.10.44	775t	Stricken 1972
M 06	TER	15.4.45	775t	Stricken 1972

Guadalete was lost in a storm off Gibraltar while employed as a coast guard vessel. In 1961 their original pennant numbers (DM 1–DM 7 respectively) were changed to those noted above.

OTHER VESSELS
LT 11, 12 and *14*, the three surviving ex-German S-boats of the *S 2* type sold to Spain during the Civil War, were discarded in the 1940s. The motor torpedo-boat *LT 17* (ex-Italian *Napoli*, MAS 100), transferred in 1937, was stricken in 1951. *LT 21–LT 26* (the ex-German S-boats *S 73, S 78, S 124–S 126* and *S 128*, sold to Spain in 1943) were stricken between 1955 and 1958. The First World War-built 177t torpedo-boats Nos *14* and *17* were BU in 1952 after service as minelayers and training craft. There was also a large number of small patrol boats and motor launches, for fishery protection, customs and coast guard work.

MAJOR SURFACE SHIPS

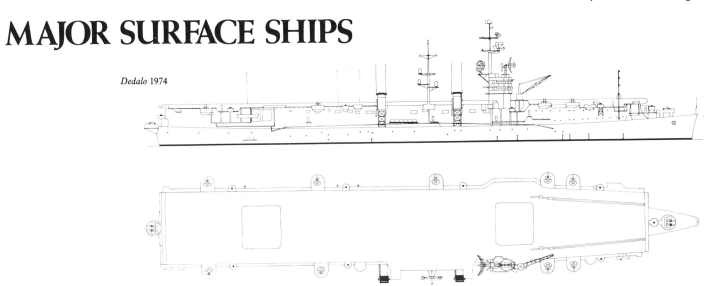

Dedalo 1974

USN *Independence* class light aircraft carrier, transferred to Spain under MDAP on 30 August 1967 and purchased outright in 1973. The transfer of *Thetis Bay* (LPH 6) was originally contemplated. Extensively refitted and modernised before transfer, with strengthened decks and lifts, new electronic equipment and funnels 1 and 3 removed. Hangar capacity 20 aircraft. Best recent speed reported as 24kts. Will be replaced by *Principe de Asturias*.

DEDALO *light aircraft carrier*

Displacement:	13,000t standard; 16,416t full load
Dimensions:	600ft wl, 623ft oa × 71ft 6in wl, 109ft 2in oa × 26ft *182.9m, 189.9m × 21.8m, 33.3m × 7.9m*
Machinery:	4-shaft General Electric geared turbines, 4 Babcock & Wilcox boilers, 100,000shp = 31kts. Oil 1800t. Range 7500nm at 15kts
Armour:	Belt 5in on 0.63in STS, bulkheads 5in, armour deck over belt 2in
Armament:	26–40mm/60 AA (2×4, 9×2), 7 VSTOL aircraft, 20 helicopters
Sensors:	Radar SPS-6, SPS-8, SPS-10, SPS-40, Mk 28 and Mk 29, Tacan
Complement:	1112 (excluding aircrew)

No	Name	Builder	Laid down	Launched	Comp	Fate
R 01	DEDALO (ex-*Cabot*)	New York SB	13.3.42	4.4.43	24.7.43	Extant 1982

Dedalo c1978 Spanish Navy

Designed by Gibbs and Cox, New York, as an updated sea control ship type (this type was proposed for the USN in FY 75, but never funded by Congress). Replacement for *Dedalo* expected to complete in 1984–85. Will have ski-jump at bows for more effective operation of AV–8 Matador aircraft (Harriers). The design has been offered for export as an economical replacement for the postwar light fleet carriers.

PRINCIPE DE ASTURIAS *light aircraft carrier*

Displacement:	14,700t full load
Dimensions:	640ft oa × 81ft × 29ft 11in *195.1m × 24.7m × 9.1m*
Machinery:	1 shaft, 2 LM2500 gas turbines, 46,000shp = 26kts. Range 7500nm at 20kts
Armament:	4–20mm Meroka CIWS, 17 VSTOL aircraft and helicopters
Sensors:	Radar SPN-35A, SPS-52C, SPS-55, Tacan; sonar ?
Complement:	793

No	Name	Builder	Laid down	Launched	Comp	Fate
R 11	PRINCIPE DE ASTURIAS	Ferrol	8.10.79	22.5.82		Fitting out 1982

A model of the US Sea Control Ship design 1973 USN

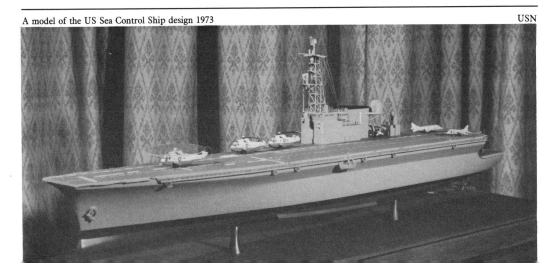

Rayo as reconstructed

Navarret Collection

Design based on the pre-war French *Le Fier* class of large torpedo-boats or light destroyers, as modified by the Germans. *Audaz*, *Meteoro*, *Osado* and *Rayo* completed with the quoted armament, although the 21in TT were apparently omitted, and were reconstructed as fast ASW frigates between 1959 and 1963, when particulars became: 1227t standard, 1548t full load, 31.6kts, 2–3in/50 AA (2×1), 2–40mm/70 AA, 2 Hedgehogs, 8 DC mortars, 2 DC racks, 2 side-launching racks for ASW torpedoes; the other five units were delivered with these data Reported as unstable on first trials. *Ariete* grounded on the Galician coast and became a total loss.

AUDAZ class *destroyers*

Displacement:	1106t standard; 1474t full load
Dimensions:	295ft 3in pp, 308ft 2in oa × 30ft 9in × 10ft
	90.0m, 93.9m × 9.4m × 3.0m
Machinery:	2-shaft Rateau-Bretagne geared turbines, 3 3-drum boilers, 30,800shp = 33kts. Oil 290t. Range 3800nm at 14kts
Armament:	3–4.1in/45 DP (3×1), 4–37mm AA, 8–20mm AA, 6–21in TT (3×2)
Sensors:	Radar MLA-18, SPS-5B, SPG-34; sonar QHBa
Complement:	145

No	Name	Builder	Laid down	Launched	Comp	Fate
D 36	ARIETE	Ferrol	3.8.45	24.2.55	7.2.61	Wrecked 25.2.66
D 31	AUDAZ	Ferrol	26.9.45	24.1.51	30.6.53	Stricken 1974
D 34	FUROR	Ferrol	3.8.45	24.2.55	9.9.60	Stricken 1974
D 38	INTREPIDO	Ferrol	14.7.45	15.2.61	25.3.65	Stricken 1982
D 33	METEORO (ex-*Atrevido*)	Ferrol	3.8.45	4.9.51	30.11.55	Stricken 1975
D 32	OSADO	Ferrol	3.8.45	4.9.51	26.1.55	Stricken 1972
D 35	RAYO	Ferrol	3.8.45	4.9.51	26.1.56	Stricken 1974
D 39	RELAMPAGIO	Ferrol	14.7.45	26.9.61	7.7.65	Stricken 1975
D 37	TEMERARIO	Ferrol	14.7.45	29.3.60	16.3.64	Stricken 1975

Nine units of this class, based on the pre-war French *Le Hardi* class, were ordered in 1947–48, but six, *Blas de Lezo*, *Blasco de Garay*, *Bonifaz*, *Gelmirez*, *Langara* and *Recalde*, were cancelled in 1953. The 8–4.1in guns (4×2), 7–21in torpedo tubes (1×3, 2×2) and 2 DC throwers originally planned were replaced by the 4.7in guns and ASW weapons in the Table while the ships were building. Trials of *Oquendo* showed a dangerous lack of stability, so she was taken in hand for ballasting and reduction of top weight. This work was completed on 22.4.63, and revised particulars were: 2582t standard, 3005t full load, 12ft 8in (*3.8m*) draught, 32.4kts, with armament reduced by the loss of 'X' turret (2–4.7in) and the 20mm AA. British radars and fire-control equipment were installed. *Roger de Lauria* and *Enseneda* were dismantled and completed to a much altered and enlarged design (see below).

OQUENDO class *destroyers*

Displacement:	2050t standard; 2765t full load
Dimensions:	363ft 6in pp, 382ft 1in oa × 36ft 5in × 11ft 10in mean
	110.8m, 116.5m × 11.1m × 3.6m
Machinery:	2-shaft Rateau-Bretagne geared turbines, 3 3-drum boilers, 60,000shp = 39kts. Oil 659t. Range 5000nm at 15kts
Armament:	6–4.7in/50 DP (3×2), 6–40mm/70 AA (6×1), 4–20mm AA, 2 Hedgehogs, 2 side-launching racks for ASW torpedoes
Sensors:	Radar Types 262, 275, 293, SNW-10; sonar QHBa
Complement:	267

No	Name	Builder	Laid down	Launched	Comp	Fate
D 41	OQUENDO	Ferrol	15.6.51	5.9.56	13.9.60	Stricken 1978
D 42	ROGER DE LAURIA	Ferrol	4.9.51	12.11.58	(30.5.69)	See notes
D 43	MARQUES DE LA ENSENEDA	Ferrol	4.9.51	15.7.59	(10.9.70)	See notes

Roger de Lauria as completed

Navarret Collection

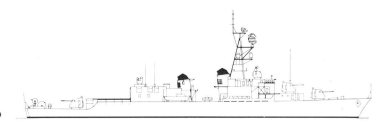

Roger de Lauria 1979

Launched as units two and three of the *Oquendo* class (above) but completed at Cartagena to an enlarged and modernised design; dates of relaunching after hulls were lengthened and widened are given in the Table. Full US weapon and electronic fit, and generally to USN *Gearing* class FRAM II standards. Best recent speeds reported as 28kts because of boiler problems. Repairs of *Enseneda*, damaged by a terrorist attack in 1981, are due to include modernisation with SAM and Meroka 20mm CIWS.

ROGER DE LAURIA class *destroyers*

Displacement:	3012t standard; 3785t full load
Dimensions:	391ft 6in oa × 42ft 8in × 18ft 4in
	119.3m × 13.0m × 5.6m
Machinery:	2-shaft Rateau-Bretagne geared turbines, 3 3-drum boilers, 60,000shp = 31kts. Oil 700t. Range 4500nm at 15kts
Armament:	6–5in/38 DP (3×2), 6–12.75in TT (Mk 44 ASW torpedoes; 2×3), 2–21in TT (Mk 37 ASW torpedoes), 1 helicopter
Sensors:	Radar SPS-10, SPS-40, RM-426, Mk 25 and Mk 35; sonars SPS-32C, SQS-10
Complement:	318

No	Name	Builder	Laid down	Launched	Comp	Fate
D 42	ROGER DE LAURIA	Ferrol/Cartagena	(4.9.51)	29.8.67	30.5.69	Stricken 1982
D 43	MARQUES DE LA ENSENEDA	Ferrol/Cartagena	(4.9.51)	2.3.68	10.9.70	Extant 1982

Three guided missile destroyers (projected under the January 1973 Programme) were in an advanced state of planning during the 1970s, but never laid down (commencement date probably 1974). Likely details are: SSM and SAM systems, 127mm DP OTO Melara guns, ASW helicopters, COGOG Propulsion giving a speed of 34kts.

Projected guided missile destroyers

Particulars:	Never published

(For illustration see under United States)

Built 1941–44 and transferred under MDAP and purchased outright in 1972. *Galiano* and *Jorge Juan* are of later *Fletcher* class.

Ex-US FLETCHER class *destroyers*

Armament:	4–5in/38 (4×1) (*Lepanto*, *Ferrandiz* 5–5in/38), 6–3in/50 Mk 33 (2×3) (*Lepanto*, *Ferrandiz* 6–40mm/60 AA, 6–20mm/70 AA), 3–21in TT (1×3, not in *Lepanto*, *Ferrandiz*), 6–12.75in Mk 32 ASW TT (2×3), 2 Hedgehogs, 1 DC rack (*Lepanto* 2 DC racks)
Sensors:	Radar SPG-34, SPS-6C, SPS-10 Mk 35; sonar SQS-4 or SQS-29
Complement:	290
Other particulars:	As US *Fletcher* class

No	Name	Builder	Acquired	Fate
D 24	ALCALA GALIANO (ex-*Jarvis*)	Settle-Tacoma	3.11.60	Extant 1982
D 22	ALMIRANTE FERRANDIZ (ex-*David W Taylor*)	Gulf SB	15.5.57	Extant 1982
D 223	ALMIRANTE VALDES (ex-*Converse*)	Bath Iron Wks	1.7.59	Extant 1982
D 25	JORGE JUAN (ex-*McGowan*)	Federal, Kearny	1.12.60	Extant 1982
D 21	LEPANTO (ex-*Capps*)	Gulf SB	15.5.57	Extant 1982

(For illustration see under United States)

Built in 1944–45 and transferred under MDAP and purchased outright on 17.5.78; all FRAM I modernisations; *Blas de Lezo* has both gun turrets forward and no ASROC, other turrets in 'A' and 'Y' positions.

Ex-US GEARING class *destroyers*

Armament:	4–5in/38 (2×2), 1 ASROC ASW system, 6–12.75in ASW TT (2×3), 1 helicopter (see notes)
Sensors:	Radar SPS-10, SPS-37 or SPS-40, Mk 25 or 28; sonar SQS-23
Complement:	274
Other particulars:	As US *Gearing* class (FRAM I type)

No	Name	Builder	Acquired	Fate
D 65	BLAS DE LEZO (ex-*Noa*)	Bath Iron Wks	31.10.73	Extant 1982
D 61	CHURRUCA (ex-*Eugene A Green*)	Federal, Kearny	31.8.72	Extant 1982
D 62	GRAVINA (ex-*Furse*)	Consolidated, Orange	31.8.72	Extant 1982
D 64	LANGARA (ex-*Leary*)	Consolidated, Orange	31.10.73	Extant 1982
D 63	MENDEZ NUNEZ (ex-*O'Hare*)	Consolidated, Orange	31.10.73	Extant 1982

SPAIN

Design very similar to the US Navy's *Knox* class, but with Tartar SAM system instead of the LAMPS helicopter and BPDMS. Hulls and machinery were fabricated in Spain, but the USN supplied weapons and sensors. All torpedo tubes fitted internally and fixed, the 12.75in being inclined at 45°, while the 21in are in the stern. Due for modernisation, which will include fitting of Harpoon SSM and Meroka 20mm CIWS.

BALEARES class *frigates*

Displacement:	3015t standard; 4177t full load
Dimensions:	415ft pp, 438ft oa × 46ft 9in × 24ft 7in (max over sonar)
	126.5m, 133.5m × 14.25m × 7.5m
Machinery:	1-shaft Westinghouse geared turbines, 2 V2M boilers, 35,000shp = 28kts. Range 4500nm at 20kts
Armament:	1–5in/54 Mk 42, 1 Tartar Mk 22 SAM (16 Standard SM1-MR missiles), 1 ASROC ASW system, 4–12.75in TT (Mk 44 ASW torpedoes), 2–21in TT (Mk 37 ASW torpedoes)
Sensors:	Radar SPS-10, SPS-52A, SPG-51C, SPG-53B; sonars SQS-23, SQS-35V VDS
Complement:	256

No	Name	Builder	Laid down	Launched	Comp	Fate
F 72	ANDALUCIA	Ferrol	2.7.69	30.3.71	23.5.74	Extant 1982
F 74	ASTURIAS	Ferrol	30.3.71	13.5.72	2.12.75	Extant 1982
F 71	BALEARES	Ferrol	31.10.68	20.8.70	24.9.73	Extant 1982
F 73	CATALUNA	Ferrol	20.8.70	3.11.71	16.1.75	Extant 1982
F 75	EXTREMADURA	Ferrol	3.11.71	21.11.72	10.11.76	Extant 1982

Baleares as completed   Spanish Navy

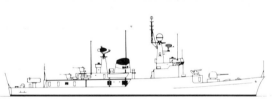

Descubierta as completed

Enlarged Portuguese *Baptista de Andrade* class, with heavier armament and more powerful machinery, and based on Blohm & Voss's original *João Coutinho* class. Four ships were ordered in December 1973, and four more in May 1976. A powerful and economic design, with attractive export possibilities. Two 4-cell Harpoon SSM launchers to be fitted amidships, and the Meroka 20mm CIWS will replace 1–40mm gun.

An improved *Descubierta* design has been prepared, displacing 1879t full load and with length oa of about 100m. The weapon fit is similar, but rearranged to make space for a helicopter and hangar, and gas turbines will give a speed of 30+ knots.

DESCUBIERTA class *frigates*

Displacement:	1233t standard; 1522t full load
Dimensions:	278ft 10in pp, 291ft 7in oa × 34ft 1in × 12ft 6in
	85.0m, 88.9m, 10.4m × 3.8m
Machinery:	2 shafts, 4 MTU-Bazan 16V956 TB 91 diesels, 16,000bhp = 25.5kts. Range 6100nm at 18kts
Armament:	1–3in/62 OTO Melara, 2–40mm/70 Breda Bofors (2×1), 1 Sea Sparrow SAM (1×8), 1–375mm Bofors ASW mortar (1×2), 6–12.75in ASW TT (2×3)
Sensors:	Radar DA-95/2, ZW-06, WM-22/41 or WM-25; sonar DE-1160B
Complement:	116

No	Name	Builder	Laid down	Launched	Comp	Fate
F 35	CAZADORA	Ferrol	14.12.77	17.10.78	20.7.81	Extant 1982
F 37	CENTINELA	Ferrol	31.10.78	6.10.79	June 82	Extant 1982
F 31	DESCUBIERTA	Cartagena	16.11.74	8.7.75	18.11.78	Extant 1982
F 32	DIANA	Cartagena	8.7.75	26.1.76	30.6.79	Extant 1982
F 34	INFANTA CRISTINA	Cartagena	14.9.76	25.4.77	24.11.80	Extant 1982
F 33	INFANTA ELENA	Cartagena	26.1.76	14.9.76	12.4.80	Extant 1982
F 38	SERVIOLA	Ferrol	28.2.79	20.12.79	Oct 82	Extant 1982
F 36	VENCEDORA	Ferrol	1.5.78	24.4.79	27.3.82	Extant 1982

(For illustration see under United States)

Ordered June 1977, but construction has been delayed because of precedence given to *Principe de Asturias* and slow delivery of US Mk 13 missile launchers. Will carry 20mm Meroka CIWS. The above names are not officially confirmed, and the dates refer to the schedule as foreseen in 1982.

US OLIVER HAZARD PERRY type *frigates*

Particulars:	As US *Oliver Hazard Perry* (FFG 7) class

No	Name	Builder	Laid down	Launched	Comp	Fate
F 81	NAVARRA	Ferrol	1983	1984–85	1986	On order 1982
F 82	MURCIA	Ferrol	1983	1985	1986	On order 1982
F 83	LEON	Ferrol	1984	1985	1987	On order 1982

Atrevida 1976

Atrevida and *Descubierta* were completed with the above armament, but the former was modernised for ASW duties in 1959–60, when particulars became: 997t standard, 1135t full load, 9ft (*2.7m*) draught, 1–3in/50 DP, 3–40mm/70 AA, 2 Hedgehogs, 8 DC mortars, 2 DC racks; the four later units were delivered with these data. Rated as corvettes although given 'F' pennant numbers. The four survivors were refitted in 1979 for offshore patrol and fishery protection duties.

ATREVIDA class *corvettes*

Displacement:	912t standard; 1022t full load
Dimensions:	223ft 1in pp, 247ft 8in oa × 33ft 6in × 8ft 8in
	68.0m, 75.5m × 10.2m × 2.6m
Machinery:	2 shafts, Sulzer diesels, 3000bhp = 18.5kts. Oil 100t. Range 8000nm at 10kts
Armament:	1–4.1in/45 DP, 2–37mm AA, 12–20mm AA, 4 DCT, 20 mines
Sensors:	Radar SPS-5B; sonar QHBa
Complement:	132

No	Name	Builder	Laid down	Launched	Comp	Fate
F 61	ATREVIDA	Cartagena	26.6.50	2.12.52	19.8.54	Extant 1982
F 51	DESCUBIERTA	Cartagena	26.6.50	9.6.52	1.2.55	Stricken 1978
F 63	DIANA	Cartagena	27.7.53	29.4.55	13.5.60	Stricken 1973
F 64	NAUTILUS	Cadiz	27.7.53	23.8.56	15.12.59	Extant 1982
F 62	PRINCESA	Cartagena	18.3.53	31.3.56	3.10.59	Extant 1982
F 65	VILLA DE BILBAO	Cadiz	18.3.53	19.2.58	2.7.60	Extant 1982
	(ex-*Favorita*)					

SUBMARINES

The construction of four new submarines *G 1*–*G 4* (*G 5* and *G 6* were also projected) ordered in 1945 under the 1943 Programme for construction at Cartagena. They were to have been generally similar to *G 7* (ex-German *U 573*), but the plan was abandoned, although some may have been laid down. Ex-US submarines were expected to be acquired under MDAP in their place.

'G' class *submarines*

Displacement:	766t normal; 930t submerged
Dimensions:	220ft 2in × 20ft 7in × 14ft 2in–15ft 9in
	67.1m × 6.3m × 4.3m–4.8m
Machinery:	2-shaft diesels plus electric motors, 3000bhp/750shp = 17.5kts/8kts. Oil 120t (132m³). Range 9000nm/6500nm at 10kts/12kts
Armament:	5–533mm TT (4 bow, 1 stern), 1–88mm AA, 1–20mm AA
Complement:	44

Class (fate):
SA 41 (stricken 1971), *SA 42* (stricken 1971).
Launched in 1957 and originally rated as experimental submarines, known as *Foca I* (F I) and *Foca II* (F II) respectively; re-rated as assault submarines and numbered as above in 1963. Built at Cartagena and based on the German 'Seehund' type.

FOCA class *midget submarines*

Displacement:	16t surfaced; 20t submerged
Dimensions:	45ft 5in oa × 6ft × 5ft
	13.9m × 1.8m × 1.5m
Machinery:	1-shaft Pegaso diesel plus Siemens electric motor, 160bhp/110shp = 9.2kts/12kts. Range 700nm at 7kts
Armament:	2–21in TT
Complement:	3

Class (fate):
SA 51 (stricken 1977), *SA 52* (stricken 1977).
Launched in 1958 and originally rated as experimental submarines, known as *Tiburon I* and *Tiburon II* respectively; re-rated as assault submarines and numbered as above in 1963. Built at Cartagena.

TIBURON class *midget submarines*

Displacement:	78t surfaced; 81t submerged
Dimensions:	70ft 6in oa × 9ft × 9ft
	21.5m × 2.7m × 2.7m
Machinery:	1-shaft Pegaso diesels plus electric motors, 4000bhp/400shp = 10kts/14.5kts
Armament:	2–21in TT
Complement:	5

Originally built 1943–44 and transferred in 1959 after modernisation. Further modernised in 1964–65, when armament became 6–21in TT and 4 TT for ASW torpedoes; can carry 22 torpedoes. Although due for deletion in 1975, this boat was retained in service until 1982, because of machinery defects in *Monturiol* (below). Name abbreviated to *A G Reyes*.

(For illustration see under United States)

Ex-US BALAO class *submarine*

Particulars:	As US *Balao* class (Fleet Snorkel type)

No	Name	Builder	Acquired	Fate
S 31	ALMIRANTE GARCIA DE LOS REYES (ex-*E 1*, ex-*Kraken*,)	Manitowoc	24.10.59	Stricken 1982

Narval (outboard) alongside *Narciso Monturiol* 16.8.80   MG Photographic

Built as *Balao* class submarines in 1943–44, but extensively modernised in 1953–54. Transferred in 1971 (S 32), 1972 (S 33, 34) and 1974 (S 35). S 33 laid up with mechanical defects in 1975; when deleted in 1977 her name was transferred to S 35.

Ex-US BALAO class *submarines*

Particulars: As US *Balao* class (GUPPY IIA type)

No	Name	Builder	Acquired	Fate
S 34	COSME GARCIA (ex-*Bang*)	Portsmouth N Yd	1.10.72	Extant 1982
S 32	ISAAC PERAL (ex-*Ronquil*)	Portsmouth N Yd	1.7.71	Stricken 1982
S 33	NARCISO MONTURIOL (ex-*Picuda*, ex-*Obispo*)	Portsmouth N Yd	1.10.72	Stricken 1977
S 35	NARCISO MONTURIOL (ex-*Jallao*)	Manitowoc	26.6.74	Extant 1982

(For illustration see under France)

Two ordered in December 1966, and a second pair in March 1970, and a fifth was originally envisaged. Built with extensive French assistance, under Agreement of July 1966. To be modernised to the same standard as the French boats of this class (DUUA-2 active sonar, DUUX-2 passive ranging sonar).

French DAPHNE type *submarines*

Particulars: As French *Daphne* class

No	Name	Builder	Laid down	Launched	Comp	Fate
S 61	DELFIN	Cartagena	13.8.68	25.3.72	3.5.73	Extant 1982
S 62	TONINA	Cartagena	1969	3.10.72	10.7.73	Extant 1982
S 63	MARSOPA	Cartagena	19.3.71	15.3.74	12.4.75	Extant 1982
S 64	NARVAL	Cartagena	1972	14.12.74	22.11.75	Extant 1982

(For illustration see under France)

Two ordered in May 1975, and a second pair in June 1977. Built with some French assistance, and may carry submarine Exocet (SM39) SSM.

French AGOSTA type *submarines*

Particulars: As French *Agosta* class

No	Name	Builder	Laid down	Launched	Comp	Fate
S 71	GALERNA	Cartagena	5.9.77	5.12.80	1982	Extant 1982
S 72	SIROCO	Cartagena	1978	1982		Building 1982
S 73	MISTRAL	Cartagena	30.5.80			Building 1982
S 74	TRAMONTANA	Cartagena				On order 1982

AMPHIBIOUS WARFARE VESSELS

(For illustration see under countries of origin in this and 1922–46 volume)

Ex-US CABILDO class *dock landing ship*

Particulars: As US *Cabildo* class

No	Name	Builder	Acquired	Fate
L 31	GALICIA (ex-*San Marcos*)	Philadelphia N Yd	1.7.71	Extant 1982

Originally built in 1944–45, transferred 1971 and purchased outright in 1974. Reported that 2 twin 40mm are being replaced by 2 single 76mm (ex-destroyers). In service 1982.

Ex-US TERREBONNE PARISH class *tank landing ships*

Particulars: As US *Terrebonne Parish* class

No	Name	Builder	Acquired	Fate
L 11	VELASCO (ex-*Terrebonne Parish*)	Bath Iron Wks	29.10.71	Extant 1982
L 12	MARTIN ALVAREZ (ex-*Wexford County*)	Christy Corp	29.10.71	Extant 1982
L 13	CONDE DE VENADITO (ex-*Tom Green County*)	Bath Iron Wks	5.1.72	Extant 1982

Originally built 1952–53; all transferred in 1971–72 and purchased outright on 5.8.76. In service 1982.

Ex-US HASKELL class *attack transport*

Particulars:	As US *Haskell* class			

No	Name	Builder	Acquired	Fate
TA 11	ARAGON (ex-*Noble*)	USA	19.12.64	Extant 1982

Built in 1944–45; transferred in 1964. Name transferred to new transport in 1980 and ship laid up.

Ex-US ANDROMEDA class *attack cargo ship*

Particulars:	As US *Andromeda* class			

No	Náme	Builder	Acquired	Fate
TA 21	CASTILLA (ex-*Achernar*)	USA	2.2.65	Extant 1982

Launched 1943; transferred in 1965. Name transferred to new transport in 1980 and ship laid up.

Ex-US PAUL REVERE class *amphibious transports*

Particulars:	As US *Paul Revere* class			

No	Name	Builder	Acquired	Fate
L 21	CASTILLA (ex-*Paul Revere*, ex-*Diamond Mariner*)	New York SB	17.1.80	Extant 1982
L 22	ARAGON (ex-*Francis Marion*, ex-*Prairie Mariner*)	New York SB	11.7.80	Extant 1982

Originally C4-S-1 cargo vessels, launched in 1953–54; for conversion notes, see under United States. Both purchased by Spain in 1980.

OTHER AMPHIBIOUS WARFARE CRAFT

Three US medium landing ships were transferred in 1960 and given Spanish numbers (*LSM 1*, ex-*LSM 329*; *LSM 2*, ex-*LSM 331*; *LSM 3*, ex-*LSM 343*). *LSM 3* was stricken in 1974 and the other two were hulked as accommodation ships in 1976.

The three Spanish-built tank landing craft (*LCT 6–8*, ex-*BDK 6–8*) of the French EDIC type, built 1965–66, were in service in 1982 (665t, 1–20mm, 2–12.7mm, 9.5kts). The earlier Spanish-built tank landing craft *LCT 3–5* (ex-*BDK 3–5*, ex-*K3–5*), built 1958–59, of the British LCT(4) type, were also in service in 1982 (602t, 2–20mm, 8.5kts). The ex-British *BDK 1* and *BDK 2* (ex-*Foca*, K 1 and *Morsa*, K 2) of the LCT(4) type were discarded in 1978 and 1981 respectively.

Also in service in 1982 were a total of 2 LCUs, 22 LCM(6)s, 6 LCM(8)s, 22 LCP(L)s, 1 LCP(R) and 70 LCVPs.

SMALL SURFACE COMBATANTS

German S-BOAT type *fast attack craft*

Displacement:	100t standard; 116t full load
Dimensions:	114ft 2in oa × 16ft 9in × 4ft 7in
	34.8m × 5.1m × 1.4m
Machinery:	3 shafts, Mercedes-Benz diesels, 7500bhp = 40kts. Oil 20t. Range 650–800nm at 30kts
Armament:	2–20mm AA, 4 MG, 2–21in TT
Sensors:	Radar RM-914 (some boats)
Complement:	22

Class (fate):
LT 27 (stricken 1963), *LT 28* (stricken 1963), *LT 29* (stricken 1963), *LT 30* (stricken 1977), *LT 31* (stricken 1977), *LT 32* (stricken *c*1978).

All built by La Carraca, Cadiz, in 1952–56, to the Lürssen S-boat design of 1944. *LT 27–29* completed 1953, *LT 30* 1954, *LT 31* and *32* 1957.

LAZAGA class *fast attack craft*

Displacement:	275t standard; 399t full load
Dimensions:	178ft 6in wl, 190ft 7in oa × 24ft 11in × 9ft 2in
	54.4m, 58.1m × 7.6m × 2.8m
Machinery:	2 shafts, MTU-Bazán MAI5 TB 91 diesels, 8000bhp = 30kts. Range 2260nm/4200nm at 27kts/17kts
Armament:	1–76mm/62 OTO Melara compact, 1–40mm/70 Breda Bofors, 2–20mm Oerlikon GK 204, 6–12.75in Mk 32 ASW TT, DC racks
Sensors:	Radar WM-22; sonar ? ELAC
Complement:	34

Class:
Lazaga (PC 01), *Alsedo* (PC 02), *Cadarso* (PC 03), *Villamil* (PC 04), *Bonifaz* (PC 05), *Recalde* (PC 06)
Ordered in 1972, to the basic Lürssen T 57 design, the first unit being built by Lürssen, Vegesack and the remainder by Bazán, La Carraca, between 1974 and 1977. For fishery protection in peacetime, but being relieved in these duties by the new *Anaga* class. To be fitted with Harpoon SSM; ASW weapons not installed in all units. All were in service in 1982.

Cormoran class
A modified version of the *Lazaga* type (with more speed, shorter range and armed with Exocet SSMs) is reported to be under consideration. Morocco has ordered four of this *Cormoran* type, but the Spanish Navy was still uncommitted in 1982.

BARCELO class *fast attack craft*

Displacement:	134ft full load
Dimensions:	118ft 9in oa × 19ft × 8ft 2in
	36.2m × 5.8m × 2.5m
Machinery:	2 shafts, MTU-Bazán MD-16V TB 90 diesels, 5760bhp = 36kts. Range 600nm/1200nm at 33.5kts/16kts
Armament:	1–40mm/70 Breda Bofors, 2–20mm Oerlikon GAM 204, 2–12.7mm, 2–21in TT
Sensors:	Radar Raytheon 1620/6
Complement:	40

Class:
Barcelo (PC 11), *Laya* (PC 12), *Javier Quiroga* (PC 13), *Ordoñez* (PC 14), *Acevedo* (PC 15), *Candido Perez* (PC 16).
Ordered in 1973, the first unit being built by Lürssen, Vegesack, and the remainder by Bazán, La Carraca, between 1975 and 1977. For fishery protection in peacetime TT are not fitted. All were in service 1982.

Ex-US PC type *patrol vessel*

Armament:	1–3in DP, 1–40mm
Other particulars:	As US PC type

No	Name	Builder	Acquired	Fate
–	JAVIER QUIROGA (ex-*PC 1211*)	Lüders Marine	1956	Stricken 1971

Built in 1943; transferred to Spain in 1956. Rearmed with 2–37mm AA *c*1965.

ANAGA class *large patrol craft*

Displacement:	296.5t full load
Dimensions:	145ft 7in oa × 21ft 7in × 8ft 2in
	44.4m × 6.6m × 2.5m
Machinery:	1 shaft, MTU diesel, 4300bhp = 22kts. Range 4000nm at 15kts
Armament:	1–76mm/62 OTO Melara compact, 2–20mm Mk 10
Sensors:	Navigational radar only
Complement:	25

Class:
Anaga (PVZ 21), *Togomago* (PVZ 22), *Marola* (PVZ 23), *Monro* (PVZ 24), *Grosa* (PVZ 25), *Medas* (PVZ 26), *Izaro* (PVZ 27), *Tabarca* (PVZ 28), *Deva* (PVZ 29), *Bergantin* (PVZ 210).
All ordered from Bazán, La Carraca in 1978 and completed between 1980 and 1982. Specially designed for fishery protection and EEZ patrol service, relieving the *Lazaga* class.

OTHER LIGHT CRAFT

In addition to the above, the following light craft are included:
The patrol vessels *Pegaso* and *Procyon*, built at Cartagena between 1947 and 1951 and rated as coast guard vessels, were attached to the Naval School and used as training ships *c*1970 (503t full load, 1–3in AA, 2–20mm, 12kts. 3in gun removed in late 1960s). These were the only units built of the twelve *Rigel* class coast guard vessels projected in 1945.

The patrol vessels *Centinela* and *Serviola*, completed at Ferrol in 1953 and rated as fishery protection vessels, were transferred to Mauritania in 1977 (282t full load, 2–37mm, 12kts).

The trawler-type patrol vessels *Cies* and *Salvora*, purchased in 1952 and rated as fishery protection vessels, were stricken in 1973 and in service in 1982 respectively (270t full load, 1–20mm, 12kts).

The large patrol craft *Candido Perez* (*W 11*, ex-*SC 679*), a former US submarine-chaser of the Second World War. This '110ft' wooden-hulled type transferred in 1956, was stricken in 1974 (138t full load, 1–40mm, 3–20mm, 2 DCT, 2 Mousetraps, 15.6kts).

Some seventy coastal and inshore patrol craft were also in service in 1982. With the exception of an old ex-tug, they were all of the motor launch type; the most recent were the four boats of the *PVZ 31* class (*PVZ 31–34*, 85t, 2–20mm, 25kts).

MINE WARFARE VESSELS

GUADIARO class *minesweepers*

Displacement:	671t standard; 770t full load
Dimensions:	243ft 10in oa × 33ft 6in × 12ft 3in max
	74.3m × 10.2m × 3.7m
Machinery:	2-shaft triple expansion plus auxiliary turbine, 2 Yarrow boilers, 2400ihp = 16kts. Range 1000nm at 6kts
Armament:	1–3.5in, 1–37mm AA, 2–20mm AA
Sensors:	Radar TM-626 or RM-914; sonar UQS-1
Complement:	79

No	Name	Builder	Launched	Fate
M 14	ALMANZORA	Cartagena	27.7.53	Stricken 1977
M 17	EO	Cadiz	22.9.53	Stricken 1978
M 13	EUME	Cartagena	27.7.53	Stricken 1977
M 16	GUADALHORCE	Cartagena	18.2.53	Stricken 1978
M 11	GUADIARO	Cartagena	26.6.50	Stricken 1977
M 15	NAVIA	Cadiz	28.7.53	Stricken 1979
M 12	TINTO	Cartagena	26.6.50	Stricken 1976

Based on the German 1940 type minesweepers, and very similar to the earlier *Bidasoa* class. The auxiliary turbine utilised the exhaust steam from the reciprocating engines. Modernised 1959–61 with removal of the 3.5in and 37mm guns. Used as patrol craft in their final years.

Ex-US AMS type *coastal minesweepers*

Particulars:	As US AMS type

Class (no, former Spanish no, ex-US name/no):
Duero (M 23, M 28, ex-*Spoonbill*, MSC 202), *Ebro* (M 22, M 26, ex-*MSC 269*), *Genil* (M 25, M 31, ex-*MSC 279*), *Jucar* (M 21, M 23, ex-*AMS 220*), *Llobregat* (–, M 22, ex-*AMS 123*), *Mino* (PVZ 53, M 25, ex-*AMS 266*), *Nalon* (PVZ 51, M 21, ex-*AMS 139*), *Odiel* (M 26, M 32, ex-*MSC 288*), Sil (PVZ 55, M 29, ex-*Redwing*, MSC 200), *Tajo* (M 24, M 30, ex-*MSC 287*), *Turia* (PVZ 54, M 27, ex-*AMS 130*), *Ulla* (PVZ 52, M 24, ex-*AMS 265*).

Wooden-hulled minesweepers of the *Adjutant*, *Redwing* and *MSC 268* classes, launched 1953–58 and transferred in 1954 (M 21, M 22), 1955 (M 27), 1956 (M 23–25), 1958 (M 26) and 1959 (other five). *Llobregat* was discarded in 1980 after a fire, five were transferred to patrol duties in 1980 and given PVZ numbers (all extant 1982), and six were in service as minesweepers with new M numbers in 1982. They have Decca TM-626 or RM-914 tactical radar and UQS-1D sonar.

Ex-US AGGRESSIVE class *ocean minesweepers*

Particulars:	As US *Aggressive* class

No	Name	Builder	Acquired	Fate
M 41	GUADALETE (ex-*Dynamic*)	Colbert, Stockton	1.7.71	Extant 1982
M 42	GUADALMEDINA (ex-*Pivot*)	Wilmington BW	1.7.71	Extant 1982
M 43	GUADALQUIVIR (ex-*Persistant*)	Tacoma	1.7.71	Extant 1982
M 44	GUADIANA (ex-*Vigor*)	Burgess, Manitowoc	4.4.72	Extant 1982

Built in 1952–55; transferred under MDAP in 1971 and 1972. All purchased 1974. Have SQQ-14 VDS and therefore mine classification capability, but no PAP or diving facilities. *Guadalete* transferred to patrol duties in 1980, and was renumbered PVZ 41.

Turkey

In 1946 the USSR tried to make Turkey revise their mutual border, and also attempted to change the Straits agreements to enable Soviet ships to leave the Black Sea more easily. It was not surprising, therefore, that Turkey signed an aid treaty with the United States in 1947, and that she later joined NATO (with Greece) in 1952. Turkey's main problems during the last three decades, however, have not been with the USSR but with Greece. She has also suffered considerable internal unrest including a number of military *coups*, some of which have been successful.

PROBLEMS WITH GREECE

There have been problems with Greece both over the Greek islands in the Aegean and in Cyprus, where the Turks are in a minority of one third. Over Cyprus there has been continuous Greek pressure for *Enosis* (union with Greece), and after Cyprus became independent in 1960 the troubles escalated. In 1964 Turkey and Greece intervened militarily in Cyprus and had to be separated by the United Nations' peacekeeping force, and in 1975 Turkey mounted an amphibious invasion of Cyprus. The only casualty the Turkish Navy suffered was the destroyer *Kocatepe*, sunk in mistake for a Greek ship by the Turkish Air Force. An unlooked for side-effect of this invasion for the Turkish armed forces was the imposition of an arms embargo by the US Congress in 1975. This has only just been lifted.

THE TURKISH NAVY

Considerable numbers of ex-British and ex-USN vessels were transferred to Turkey to bolster her position in NATO, and even though there was a partial *rapprochement* with the USSR in 1964, Turkey has maintained its ties with the West. The Turkish economy is not strong, and Turkey could not build her own ships without Western financial and technical assistance. During the past decade, an attempt has been made to standardise ship types and create a new fleet, but lack of money and the effects of the US arms embargo, combined with the desire for a large fleet, has meant that Turkey has taken any warships she can obtain – even reactivating vessels acquired solely for cannibalization. The large number of narrow channels and small islands in the Aegean, combined with recent disputes with Greece over the new EEZ, have led to an emphasis on small craft and mine warfare ships. However, there is also a large (though ancient) force of destroyers and of submarines (some of which are new-built). The Turkish Navy's most urgent current need is for some modern frigates. A source of confusion with Turkish warships is the habit of giving a replacement vessel the same name as the earlier ship. This is particularly the case with submarines.

FLEET STRENGTH 1947

SUBMARINES

Name	Launched	Disp	Fate
Birindci Inonu class			
BIRINDCI INONU	1.2.27	620t	Discarded c 1950
IKINDCI INONU	12.3.27	620t	Discarded c 1927
Dumlupinar class			
DUMLUPINAR	4.3.31	1150t	Discarded c 1950
Sakarya class			
SAKARYA	2.2.31	940t	Discarded c 1950
Gur class			
GUR	1932	960t	Discarded c 1950
'Ay' class			
SALDIRAY	23.7.38	1210t	Discarded 1957
YILDIRAY	26.8.39		Discarded 1957
Oruc Reis class			
BURAC REIS	19.10.40	861t	Discarded 1957
MURAT REIS	20.7.40	861t	Discarded 1957
ORUC REIS	19.7.40	861t	Discarded 1957

The *Birindci Inönü* class were German-designed, Dutch-built coastal submarines. *Dumlupinar* and *Sakarya* were built in Italy and resembled contemporary Italian submarines. *Gur* was built to German designs in Spain. The 'Ay' class were modified versions of the German *IXA* design. Sister *Atilay* was lost by accident on 14.7.42.

The *Oruc Reis* class were reduced versions of the British 'S' class. They were taken over by the RN and became *P 614*, *P 612* and *P 611* respectively. *Murat* and *Oruc* were delivered to Turkey in 1942 and *Burac* in 1945. Sister *Ulac Ali Reis* was sunk as *P 615* on 18.4.43.

MINELAYERS

Name	Launched	Disp	Fate
ATAK	1938	500t	Discarded early 1960s
Sivrihisar class			
SIVRIHISAR	1940	350t	Discarded 1960
TORGUD REIS			Discarded 1960

Atak and the *Sivrihisar* class carried 40 mines.

COASTAL MINESWEEPERS

Name	Launched	Disp	Fate
Kavak class			
KAVAK	1937	32t	Discarded 1950s
CANAK	1937	32t	Discarded 1950

COASTAL FORCES

Name	Launched	Disp	Fate
MTB class (launched 1942,70t)			
MTB 1–10			Discarded 1950s
Fairmile 'B' type (launched 1940–42, 86t)			
AB 1–8			Discarded 1970–73
HDML type (launched 1940–44, 54t)			
LSB 1–8			Discarded 1960s

TURKEY

MTB 1–10 were armed with 2–21in (533mm) TT (2×1).

Fairmile 'B' type motor launches were transferred from Britain in 1944–45. *AB 1–8* were RN *ML 386, ML 584, ML 836, ML 837, ML 838, ML 842, ML 862* and *ML 863* respectively. HDML type harbour defence motor launches were also transferred from Britain in 1944–45.

BATTLECRUISER

Name	Launched	Disp	Fate
YAVUZ SULTAN SELIM (ex-*Goeben*)	23.3.11	22,980t	BU 1971

Yavuz was immobile at Izmir from 1948. She was decommissioned in 1960 and several attempts were made to preserve her.

DESTROYERS

Name	Launched	Disp	Fate
Kocatepe class			
KOCATEPE	19.3.31	1630t	Discarded *c* 1950
APATEPE	7.2.31	1650t	Discarded *c* 1950
Tinaztepe class			
TINAZTEPE	27.7.31	1610t	Discarded 1957
ZAFER	27.7.31	1610t	Discarded 1957
Gayret class			
DEMIRHISAR	1941	1880t	Discarded 1960
MUAVENET	24.2.41	1880t	Discarded 1960
SULTANHISAR	1941	1880t	Discarded 1960
'O' class			
GAYRET (ex-*Oribi*)	14.1.41	2430t	Discarded 1965

The *Kocatepe* and *Tinaztepe* classes were built in Italy, based on contemporary Italian destroyer designs.

The *Gayret* class was based on British 'H' class destroyers. *Muavenet* served in the RN as *Inconstant* before being delivered to Turkey in 1945. Her sister, *Gayret*, was never delivered to Turkey, having been lost as *Ithuriel* on 28.11.42. She was replaced by the British 'O' class destroyer *Oribi*, which was transferred to Turkey on 18.6.46 and renamed *Gayret*.

MAJOR SURFACE SHIPS

(For illustration see under countries of origin in this and 1922–46 volume)

All were ex-USN *Gleaves* class destroyers. They were modernised in the USA 1957–58, and were fitted with a tripod foremast and an enclosed bridge. *Gelibolu* and *Giresun* had their 'X' position 5in (127mm) and their AA guns replaced by 4–3in (76mm). Although *Gemlik* was discarded in 1974, her hulk remained in use as a tender to the Turkish Navy's Engineering School until 1981.

Ex-US GLEAVES class *destroyers*

Particulars:	As US *Gleaves* class			

No	Name	Builder	Acquired	Fate
D 344	GAZIANTEP (ex-*Lansdowne*)	Federal, Kearny	1970	Discarded 1973
D 346	GELIBOLU (ex-*Buchanan*)	Federal, Kearny	29.4.49	Discarded 1976
D 347	GEMLIK (ex-*Lardner*)	Federal, Kearny	1950	Stricken 1981
D 345	GIRESUN (ex-*McCalla*)	Federal, Kearny	29.4.49	Discarded 1973

Ex-British 'M' class destroyers transferred to Turkey after refitting in 1958–59. During the refit the aft 4–21in (533mm) TT (1×4) and the AA guns were removed, and a new deckhouse and AA and ASW armament were installed. In Turkish service they were armed with 6–4.7in (120mm) (3×2), 6–40mm (1×2, 4×1), 1 Squid ASW mortar (1×3) and 4–21in (533mm) TT (1×4). *Piyale* was fitted as flotilla leader.

Ex-British 'M' class *destroyers*

Particulars:	As British 'M' class			

No	Name	Builder	Acquired	Fate
D 348	ALP ARSLAN (ex-*Marne*)	Scotts	29.6.59	Discarded early 1970s
D 350	KILIC ALI PASHA (ex-*Matchless*)	Stephen	29.6.54	Discarded early 1970s
D 349	MARESAL FEVZI CAKMAK (ex-*Meteor*)	Vickers-Armstrong, Tyne	29.6.59	Discarded early 1970s
D 351	PIYALE PASA (ex-*Milne*)	Stephen	29.6.59	Discarded early 1970s

All are standard ex-US *Fletcher* class destroyers except *Icel*, which has a modified bridge; the latter is now serving as a harbour training ship at Gölcük.

Ex-US FLETCHER class *destroyers*

Particulars:	As US *Fletcher* class			

No	Name	Builder	Acquired	Fate
D 344	ICEL (ex-*Preston*)	Bethlehem, San Pedro	15.11.69	Stricken 1981
D 343	ISKENDERUN (ex-*Boyd*)	Bethlehem, San Pedro	1.10.69	Stricken 1981
D 340	ISTANBUL (ex-*Clarence K Bronson*)	Federal, Kearny	14.1.67	Extant 1982
D 341	IZMIR (ex-*Van Valkenburgh*)	Gulf SB	28.2.67	Extant 1982
D 342	IZMIT (ex-*Cogswell*)	Bath Iron Wks	1.10.69	Stricken 1980

Zafer is an ex-US *Allen M Sumner* class destroyer. She was given a FRAM II modernisation by the USN, but was then used as a trials ship for planar passive sonar arrays. She was purchased by Turkey on 15.2.72. *Muavenet* was completed as a *Robert H Smith* class (modified *Allen M Sumner* type) minelayer. She was modernised before being transferred to Turkey on 22.10.71, but she has no ASW equipment. *Zafer* was fitted

Ex-US ALLEN M SUMNER class *destroyers*

Particulars:	As US *Allen M Sumner* class (FRAM II type)			

No	Name	Builder	Acquired	Fate
DM 357	MUAVENET (ex-*Gwin*)	Bethlehem, San Pedro	22.10.71	Extant 1982
D 356	ZAFER (ex-*Hugh Purvis*)	Federal, Kearny	15.2.72	Extant 1982

with 4–40mm (2×2) between the funnels in 1977 and a 3in (76mm) on the helicopter flight deck in 1979.

Muavenet's armament has not been altered and she retains rails for 80 mines.

These are all ex-US *Gearing* class destroyers, originally launched 1944–45. *Adatepe* was purchased on 15.2.73, two years after first transfer. The first *Kocatepe* was sunk in error by Turkish Air Force jets which mistook the destroyer for an identical ex-US Greek *Gearing* trying to interfere with the Turkish amphibious landings on Cyprus. Ex-US *Norris*, which had been purchased for cannibalization for spares on 7.7.74, was hastily refitted, renamed *Kocatepe*, and commissioned in the Turkish Navy on 24.7.75. Ex-US *Meredith* was purchased for spares on 7.12.79, but she has been refitted and is joining the Turkish fleet. Two more ex-US *Gearings*, ex-US *Robert H McCard* and ex-US *Fiske*, were transferred to Turkey on 5.6.80 under a leasing agreement, and commissioned on 30.7.81.

In addition to their 4–5in/38 DP (2×2), the FRAM II vessels, *Kocatepe* (ex-*Norris*) and *Tinaztepe* have

GEARING class *destroyers*

Particulars:	As US *Gearing* class (FRAM I and II types)			
No	Name	Builder	Acquired	Fate
D 353	ADATEPE (ex-*Forrest Royal*)	Bethlehem, Staten Is	27.3.71	Extant 1982
D 351	MARESAL FEVZI CAKMAK (ex-*Charles H Roan*)	Bethlehem, Quincy	29.9.73	Extant 1982
D 352	GAYRET (ex-*Eversole*)	Todd-Pacific, Seattle	11.7.73	Extant 1982
D 354	KOCATEPE (i, ex-*Harwood*)	Bethlehem, San Pedro	17.12.71	Sunk 22.7.74
D 354	KOCATEPE (ii, ex-*Norris*)	Bethlehem, San Pedro	7.7.74	Extant 1982
D 355	TINAZTEPE (ex-*Keppler*)	Bethlehem, San Francisco	30.6.72	Extant 1982
D 347	SAVASTEPE (ex-*Meredith*)	Consolidated, Orange	7.12.79	Extant 1982
D 349	KILIC ALI PASA (ex-*Robert H McCard*)	Consolidated, Orange	5.6.80	Extant 1982
D 350	PIYALE PASA (ex-*Figue*)	Bath Iron Wks	2.6.80	Extant 1982

4–40mm (2×2) between the funnels, and 2–40mm (2×1) on what was the DASH flight deck aft (replaced by a 35mm twin Oerlikon mount on *Kocatepe* in 1979); for ASW they have a trainable Hedgehog forward and 6–324mm Mk 32 TT, plus a DC rack.

The remaining vessels are FRAM I types. *Adatepe*, *Cakmak* and *Gayret* have been refitted with a light AA armament of 2–40mm (1×2) forward, and 2–35mm (1×2) aft; the others have only 2–40mm. ASW weapons consist of an 8-tube ASROC launcher

(not in *Savastepe*), 6–324mm Mk 32 TT, plus a DC rack. Harpoon missiles may be added to all ex-*Gearings* in the near future. It has been reported that two further *Gearings* were scheduled for transfer to Turkey during 1982.

The *Carpenter* class was a specialized ASW version of the *Gearing* and was completed in 1949. The present armament is 2–5in/38 DP, ASROC (1×8, plus 6 reloads) and 6–324mm MK 32 TT, but additional weapons may be fitted in Turkish service. *Robert A Owens* of this class was reported due for transfer on 16.2.82.

Ex-US CARPENTER class *destroyer*

Particulars:	As US *Carpenter* class (FRAM I type)			
No	Name	Builder	Acquired	Fate
D 347 ANITEPE (ex-*Carpenter*)		Consolidated, Orange	20.2.81	Extant 1982

Peyk 1976

These were the first major warships built in Turkey since before the First World War, and are based on the USN *Claud Jones* class frigate design. They have a slightly different hull, however, a more powerful armament, different machinery and one large funnel. There is a helicopter pad at the break of the forecastle aft, but no hangar.

BERK class *frigates*

Displacement:	1450 standard; 1950 full load
Dimensions:	312ft 4in oa × 39ft 10in × 18ft 1in 95.2m × 38.8m × 18.1m
Machinery:	1 shaft, 4 Fiat diesels, 24,000bhp = 25kts
Armament:	4–3in/50 (2×2), 6–324mm TT (2×3), 2 Hedgehog
Sensors:	Radar SPS-40, SPS-10, SPG-4; sonar SQS-11
Complement:	?

No	Name	Builder	Laid down	Launched	Comp	Fate
D 358	BERK	Gölcük N Yd	9.3.67	25.6.71	12.7.72	Extant 1982
D 359	PEYK	Gölcük N Yd	18.1.68	7.6.72	24.7.75	Extant 1982

Four West German-designed MEKO 200 type frigates were reported to have been ordered in mid-1982, one for construction by Blohm & Voss and the other three in Turkey. Provisional particulars are: 2000t standard,

West German MEKO 200 type *frigates*

Particulars:	Not yet published

2-shaft diesels = 27kts, 8 Harpoon SSM (2×4), 1 NATO Sea Sparrow SAM (1×8), 1–5in/54 Mk 45, 1–20mm Phalanx CIWS, 6–324mm (12.75in) Mk 32 TT, 1 helicopter.

SUBMARINES

They were all US *Balao* class submarines, built in 1943–44. The ones transferred in 1948 were more or less unmodified, but *Canakkale* and subsequent boats were semi- or fully steamlined, and most of them were brought up to the fully streamlined 'Fleet Snorkel' standard eventually. *Dumlupinar* was lost accidently in the Dardanelles on 4.4.53. *Turget* was purchased on 15.2.73 and *Hizir* in Aug 73, and they were cannibalized for spare parts after being discarded.

Ex-US BALAO class *submarines*

Particulars:	As US *Balao* class (unmodified and Fleet Snorkel types)			
No	Name	Builder	Acquired	Fate
S 330	BIRINCI INONU (ex-*Brill*)	Electric Boat	1948	Discarded 1973
S 333	CANAKKALE (ex-*Bumper*)	Electric Boat	1950	Discarded 1973
S 341	CERBE (ex-*Hammerhead*)	Manitowoc	7.8.54	Discarded 1973
S 335	DUMLUPINAR (ex-*Blower*)	Electric Boat	1950	Lost 4.4.53
S 334	GUR (ex-*Chub*)	Electric Boat	1948	Discarded 1974
S 344	HIZAR REIS (ex-*Mero*)	Electric Boat	20.4.60	Discarded 1977
S 331	IKINCI INONU (ex-*Blueback*)	Electric Boat	1948	Discarded 1973
S 343	PIRI REIS (ex-*Mapiro*)	Manitowoc	20.4.60	Discarded 1973
S 340	PREVEZE (ex-*Guitarro*)	Manitowoc	7.8.54	Discarded *c* 1970
S 332	SAKARYA (ex-*Boarfish*)	Electric Boat	1948	Discarded 1974
S 342	TURGET REIS (ex-*Bergall*)	Electric Boat	17.10.58	Discarded 1977

TURKEY

She was converted by the USN to GUPPY IA standard in the early 1950s, and was transferred to Turkey on 24.8.72. *Dumlupinar* was badly damaged in a collision on 1.9.76, and had to be beached. She was eventually repaired and put back into service.

Ex-US BALAO class *submarine*

Particulars:	As US *Balao* class (GUPPY IA type)			
No	**Name**	**Builder**	**Acquired**	**Fate**
S 339	DUMLUPINAR (ex-*Caiman*)	Electric Boat	24.8.72	Extant 1982

Murat and *Uluc Ali* had been used by the USN as ASW targets. All these *Balao* class submarines had been converted by the USN to GUPPY IIA standard.

Ex-US BALAO class *submarines*

Particulars:	As US *Balao* class (GUPPY IIA type)			
No	**Name**	**Builder**	**Acquired**	**Fate**
S 346	BIRINCI INONU (ex-*Thredfin*)	Portsmouth N Yd	15.8.73	Extant 1982
S 335	BURAK REIS (ex-*Seafox*)	Portsmouth N Yd	Dec 70	Extant 1982
S 340	CERBE (ex-*Trutta*)	Portsmouth N Yd	24.8.72	Extant 1982
S 336	MURAT REIS (ex-*Razorback*)	Portsmouth N Yd	17.11.70	Extant 1982
S 337	ORUC REIS (ex-*Pomfret*)	Portsmouth N Yd	3.5.72	Extant 1982
S 345	PREVEZE (ex-*Entemedor*)	Electric Boat	24.8.73	Extant 1982
S 338	ULUC ALI REIS (ex-*Thornback*)	Portsmouth N Yd	24.8.73	Extant 1982

The USN modernised these two war-built *Balao* class submarines to GUPPY III standards in 1962. Two more GUPPY IIIs – *Clamagore* and *Tiru* – were to have been transferred to Turkey, but this was prevented by the US Congress imposing an arms embargo on Turkey in 1975. Others may yet be transferred in the future.

Ex-US BALAO class *submarines*

Particulars:	As US *Balao* class (GUPPY III type)			
No	**Name**	**Builder**	**Acquired**	**Fate**
S 341	CANAKKALE (ex-*Cobbler*)	Electric Boat	21.11.73	Extant 1982
S 333	IKINCI INONU (ex-*Corporal*)	Electric Boat	21.11.73	Extant 1982

Tang was to have been sold to Iran, but following the Iranian revolution this was cancelled and she was leased to Turkey for five years.

Ex-US TANG class *submarine*

Particulars:	As US *Tang* class			
No	**Name**	**Builder**	**Acquired**	**Fate**
S 343	PIRI REIS (ex-*Tang*)	Portsmouth N Yd	29.2.80	Extant 1982

Similar to the Type 209 German-designed submarines serving in the Greek and several South American Navies. A single hull, medium-sized design capable of diving to more than 650ft (*200m*). Three have been built for Turkey in Germany and two more in Turkey with German technical assistance. More may well be built. *Yildray* is the first submarine to have been built in Turkey. *Saldiray* was completed in 1975, but not taken over until 15.1.77. They have Hollandse Signaal M8 torpedo fire control, and up to a total of twelve boats is planned.

ATILAY class *submarines*

Length: 183ft 9in oa *56m*
Other particulars: As Greek *Glavkos* class

No	Name	Builder	Laid down	Launched	Comp	Fate
S 347	ATILAY	Howardtswerke, Kiel	2.8.72	23.10.74	29.7.75	Extant 1982
S 348	SALDIRAY	Howaldtswerke, Kiel	2.1.73	14.2.75	21.10.75	Extant 1982
S 349	BATIRAY	Howaldtswerke, Kiel	11.6.75	26.10.77	20.7.78	Extant 1982
S 350	YILDIRAY	Gölcük N Yd	1.5.76	20.7.77	20.7.81	Extant 1982
S 351	TITIRAY	Gölcük N Yd	1977	?	?	Building

AMPHIBIOUS WARFARE VESSELS

Ex-US LST 511 class *tank landing ships*

Particulars:	As US LST type (*LST 511–1152* group)

Class:
Bayraktar (NL 120), *Sancaktar* (NL 121)

Bayraktar (ex-*Bottrop*, ex-*Saline County*, ex-*LST 1101*) and *Sancaktar* (ex-*Bochuum*, ex-*Rice County*, ex-*LST 1089*) were originally transferred from the USN to West Germany in 1961. There they were converted to minelayers. They were then transferred to Turkey on 13.12.72 and 12.12.72 respectively and converted back to LSTs in 1974–75. They were replaced in the mine warfare category once more in 1980.

Ex-US TERREBONNE PARISH class *tank landing ships*

Particulars:	As US *Terrebonne Parish* class

Class:
Ertugrul (L 401), *Serdar* (L 402)

Two ex-USN *Terrebonne Parish* class LSTs were transferred to Turkey, *Ertugrul* (ex-*Windham County*, ex-*LST 1170*) was transferred on 4.6.73 and *Serdar* (ex-*Westchester County*, ex-*LST 1167*) was transferred on 27.8.74. They are armed with 6–3in/50 (3×2).

CAKABEY class *tank landing ships*

Displacement:	1600t
Dimensions:	253ft 6in oa × 39ft 5in × 7ft 6in
	77.3m × 12.0m × 2.3m
Machinery:	3 shafts, 3 diesels, 4320bhp = 14kts
Armament:	4–40mm (2×1), 4–20mm (2×2)
Sensors:	?
Complement:	2

Class: *Cakabey* (NL 122), *Sarukabey* (NL 123)

Cakabey was built at Taskizak N Yd, in Turkey and launched on 30.6.77. Her design is based on th ▲ of the USN LSTs but she has a higher freeboard and a helicopter landing deck amidships and has a minelaying capacity (150 mines). She can transport 400 troops, 9 tanks and 10 jeeps; two LCVPs are carried under davits. The second ship which was launched on 30.7.81 is larger and two more are planned.

LANDING CRAFT

Name	Launched	Disp	Fate
Ex-British LCT (4) type C 101–106	1942	700t	Only *C 103* extant 1982; rest BU 1981–82
EDIC type C 107–138	1966–80	580–600t	Extant 1982
Ex-US LCU 501 class C 201–204	1943–44	320t	Extant 1982
Turkish LCU type C 205–216	1965–66	405t	Extant 1982
US LCM (8) type C 301–320	1965	113t	Extant 1982

C 101–C 106 were transferred on 25.9.67. They have been modernised. *C 107–C 137* are based on the French EDIC Type. *C 119–C 137* are slightly larger than the earlier vessels. *C 130* and *C 131* transferred to Libya in Jan 1980. *C 201–C 204* were transferred in Jun 67. *C 205–C 216* differ from US LCU by having the conning tower forward. They were built in Turkey. *C 301–C 320* were also built in Turkey to the US LSM (8) design. There are a number of other small landing craft.

SMALL SURFACE COMBATANTS

Ex-US AUK class *patrol vessels*

Particulars: As US *Auk* class

No	Name	Builder	Acquired	Fate
	CANDARLI (ex-*Frolic*)	Alameda	Mar 47	Extant 1982
M 507	CARDAK (ex-*Tourmaline*)	Gulf SB	Mar 47	Discarded 1974
	CARSAMBA (ex-*Tattoo*)	Associated	Mar 47	Extant 1982
M 505	CESME (ex-*Elfreda*)	Associated	Mar 47	Discarded 1974
M 509	EDINCIK (ex-*Grecian*)	Associated	Mar 47	Discarded 1974
M 512	EDREMIT (ex-*Chance*)	Associated	Mar 47	Discarded 1973
	ERDEMLI (ex-*Catherine*)	Associated	Mar 47	Discarded 1963
	EREGLI (ex-*Pique*)	Gulf SB	Mar 47	Discarded 1973

These eight ships were built in the United States as *Auk* class minesweeping escorts, and were transferred to the RN on completion under lease-land as the *Catherine* class. They were re-transferred to Turkey in Mar 47 and were employed mainly as escorts. By the late 1960s they were being used in auxiliary roles. *Candarli* (A 593) and *Carsamba* (A 594) were converted to survey ships, with a deckhouse between the funnels and only 2–40mm (2×1). The others were used either as command ships for light craft (*Cesme*, *Cardak* and *Edremit*), or training (*Edincik* and *Erdemli*) or support (*Eregli*) ships.

Ex-British BATHURST class *patrol vessels*

Particulars: As British *Bathurst* class

No	Name	Builder	Acquired	Fate
M 501	ALANYA (ex-*Broome*)	Sydney	Aug 46	Discarded 1975
M 502	AMASRA (ex-*Pirie*)	Broken Hill	Aug 46	Discarded 1975
	AYVALIK (ex-*Gawler*)	Broken Hill	Aug 46	Discarded 1963
M 500	AYVALIK (ex-*Antalya*, ex-*Geraldton*)	Brisbane	Aug 46	Discarded 1975
M 503	HAMIT NACI (ex-*Ayancik*, ex-*Launceston*)	Sydney	Aug 46	Discarded 1965

These Australian-built *Bathurst* class fleet minesweepers were transferred to Turkey in 1946. They were mainly used as escorts. *Antalya* took the original *Ayvalik*'s name when the latter was discarded in 1963. By the late 1960s the survivors were used as logistic support ships.

Ex-British BANGOR class *patrol vessels*

Particulars: As British *Bangor* class

No	Name	Builder	Acquired	Fate
P 121	BAFRA (ex-*Nipigon*)	Dufferin	29.11.57	Discarded early 1970s
P 129	BANDIRMA (ex-*Kenora*)	Port Arthur	29.11.57	Discarded early 1970s
P 130	BARTIN (ex-*Kentville*)	Port Arthur	29.11.57	Discarded early 1970s
P 122	BEYKOZ (ex-*Blairmore*)	Port Arthur	1958	Discarded early 1970s
P 123	BEYLERBEYI (ex-*Mahone*)	North Vancouver	1958	Discarded early 1970s
P 124	BIGA (ex-*Medicine Hat*)	Canadian Vickers	29.11.57	Discarded 1963
P 125	BODRUM (ex-*Fort William*)	Port Arthur	29.11.57	Discarded early 1970s
P 126	BORNOVA (ex-*Westmount*)	Dufferin	1958	Discarded early 1970s
P 127	BOZCAADA (ex-*Swift Current*)	Canadian Vickers	1958	Discarded early 1970s
P 128	BUYUKDERE (ex-*Sarnia*)	Dufferin	1958	Discarded early 1970s

All built in Canada as *Bangor* class fleet minesweepers, but re-rated as coastal escorts in 1953. They were transferred to Turkey in 1957 and early 1958, and sailed to Turkey on 19.5.58.

Norwegian NASTY type *fast attack craft*

Particulars: As Norwegian *Tjeld* class

Class:
Dogan (P 327), *Marti* (P 328)

Two ex-West German *Nasty* type (*Tjeld* class) MTBs, built by Boat Services, Norway, in 1959–60, were transferred to Turkey as part of the German-Turkish war reparations. *Dogan* (ex-*Hugin*) and *Marti* (ex-*Munin*) were discarded in 1973.

Ex-West German JAGUAR class *fast attack craft*

Particulars: As West German *Jaguar* class

Class:
Firtina (P 330), *Tufan* (P 331), *Kilic* (P 332), *Mizrak* (P 333), *Yildiz* (P 334), *Kalkan* (P 335), *Karayel* (P 336)

Seven ex-West German *Jaguar* class, which can be distinguished from the later *Kartals* by their shorter, stepped deckhouse, were transferred to Turkey between late 1975 and early 1976. These were *Firtina* (ex-*Pelikan*), *Kalkan* (ex-*Wolf*), *Karayel* (ex-*Pinguin*), *Kilic* (ex-*Löwe*), *Mizrak* (ex-*Hähner*), *Tufan* (ex-*Storch*) and *Yildiz* (ex-*Tiger*). In addition, ex-*Alk*, ex-*Fuchs* and ex-*Reiher* were transferred at the same time to provide spares. All were extant 1982, but *Firtina* was for disposal.

KARTAL class *fast attack craft*

Dimensions:	140ft 6in oa 42.8m
Armament:	4 Penguin 2 SSM (4×1), 2–40mm/70 (2×1), 2–21in TT. See notes

Other particulars: As West German *Jaguar* class

Dogan 1977   Lürssen

TURKEY

Class:

Denizkusu (P 321), *Atmaca* (P 322), *Sahin* (P 323), *Kartal* (P 324), *Melten* (P 325), *Pelikan* (P 326), *Albatros* (P 327), *Simsek* (P 328), *Kasirga* (P 329)

Nine *Kartal* class convertible patrol boats were built by Lürssen for Turkey between 1967–71. *Albatros, Atmaca, Denizkusu, Kartal, Kasirga, Melten, Pelikan, Sahin* and *Simsek* were almost identical with the West German *Jaguar* class when first built, but *Albatros, Melten, Pelikan* and *Simsek* were fitted with SSM in place of the aft pair of 21in (533mm) TT in 1975 and the other five may have been similarly fitted since. All were in service in 1982.

DOGAN class *fast attack craft*

Displacement:	353t normal; 434t full load
Dimensions:	190ft 6in × 25ft × 8ft 8in
	58.1m × 7.6m × 2.7m
Machinery:	4 shafts, 4 MTU 16V956 TB91 diesels, 18,000bhp = 36.5kts. Range 700nm/3000nm at 35kts/16kts
Armament:	8 Harpoon SSM (2×4), 1–76mm, 2–35mm (1×2), 2–7.62mm MG (2×1)
Sensors:	Radar 1226, WM28–41
Complement:	38

Class:

Dogan (P 340), *Marti* (P 341), *Tayfun* (P 342), *Volkan* (P 343), plus 1 unnamed

The first four of these steel-hulled boats were ordered 3.8.73, the designers (Lürssen) building the first at Vegesack (launched 16.6.76) with the remainder being built at the Taskizak Yard in Istanbul. They are very similar to the Israeli *Reshef* class. One a year has been commissioned between 1977 and 1980 and the construction of a further one per year is planned. The 76mm is the OTO Melara compact, with 300 rounds; the Oerlikon 35mm mounting carries 2750 rounds.

US PC type *patrol vessels*

Particulars:	As US PC type

Class:

Sultanhisar (P 111), *Demirhisar* (P 112), *Yarhisar* (P 113), *Akhisar* (P 114), *Sivrihisar* (P 115), *Kochisar* (P 116)

Six PC boats were built for Turkey in 1963–65 to the same design as the wartime PC Boats. All were built by Gunderson in the United States, except *Kochisar* which was built by Gölcük N Yd in Turkey. They are armed with 1–40mm, 4–20mm (2×2), 1 Hedgehog ASW mortar forward and 4 DCT. All were in service in 1982.

Ex-US PGM 71 class *patrol boats*

Particulars:	As US *PGM 71* class

Class:

AB 21 (P 1221), *AB 22* (P 1222), *AB 23* (P 1223), *AB 24* (P 1224)

AB 21–24 (ex-PGM 104–108) are four USN *PGM 71* type patrol boats built in the United States and taken over by Turkey on completion in 1967–68. Pennant numbers were originally P 117–P 120. They are armed with 1–40mm, 4–20mm (2×2), 4–12.7mm MG (2×2), 2 Mk 22 Mousetrap ASW, and 2 DC racks. All were in service in 1982.

Ex-US ASHEVILLE class *patrol vessels*

Particulars:	As US *Asheville* class

Class:

Yildrim (P 338), *Bora* (P 339)

Two ex-US *Asheville* class patrol vessels were transferred to Turkey, *Bora* (ex-*Surprise*) on 28.2.73 and *Yildrim* (ex-*Defiance*) on 11.6.73. Both were in service in 1982.

GIRNE *patrol boat*

Particulars:	As Spanish *Lazaga* class

Class:

Girne (P 140)

Girne was built at Taskizak, Istanbul in 1975–76. The PB 57 design by Lürssen, was based on the Spanish *Lazaga* class but with lighter armament. She was originally to have been armed with 1–40mm, 2–35mm (1×2), 1 Mousetrap ASW mortar and 4–21in (533mm) TT (4×1), but is now reported to carry either 3–40mm (1×2, 1×1) or 2–40mm (2×1) and 2–20mm (2×1). ASW weapons comprise 4 Mk 20 Mousetrap launchers, 2 DCT and 2 DC racks. She was to have been the first of a class, but she has not been successful in service, and no more have been built.

USCG 83ft Cutter type *patrol boat*

Particulars:	As US 83ft Coast Guard Cutter type

Class:

LS 9–LS 19

LS 9–12 are four US 83ft Coast Guard cutters built in the United States for Turkey in 1953. Pennant numbers were changed from P 339, P 308–P 310 to P 1209–P 1212. All were in service in 1982.

AB 25 class *patrol boats*

Displacement:	150t normal; 170t full load
Dimensions:	132ft × 21ft × 5ft 6in
	40.2m × 6.4m × 1.7m
Machinery:	2-shaft diesels, 4800bhp = 22kts.
Armament:	2–40mm (2×1) or 1–40mm, 1–20mm
Sensors:	?
Complement:	?

Class:

AB 25–AB 36 (P 1225–P 1236)

AB 25–36 were built at Taskizak between 1967–70 with French assistance. Some have Mousetrap ASW launchers and DC racks. All were in service in 1982, and several more have been constructed for the Turkish Gendarmerie.

MINE WARFARE VESSELS

NOTE

Turkey operates a number of LSTs in the dual minelaying/landing ship role (see under Amphibious Warfare Vessels). The destroyer *Muavenet* also retains minelaying capability (see under Major Surface Ships). Minesweepers transferred from the British, Canadian and US Navies were used principally as escorts and patrol vessels (see under Small Surface Combatants). There is also the 540t controlled mineplanter *Mehmetcik* (N 115), built by Higgins, New Orleans in 1958. She is normally unarmed.

Danish FALSTER class *minelayer*

Particulars:	As Danish *Falster* class

No	Name	Builder	Acquired	Fate
N 110	NUSRET	Frederikshaven N Yd	1964	Extant 1982

Laid down in 1962, *Nusret* was built in Denmark for Turkey under MDAP. She is almost identical with the Danish *Falster* class minelayers, but has no Sea Sparrow SAMs. Pennant number was N 108.

Ex-US LSM 1 class *coastal minelayers*

Particulars:	See Danish *Beskytteren* class

Class:

Mordogan (N 101), *Meric* (N 102), *Marmaris* (N 103), *Mersin* (N 104), *Mürefte* (N 104)

Marmaris (ex-*LSM 481*), *Meric* (ex-*LSM 490*) and *Mordogan* (ex-*LSM 484*) were built by the USN as LSM in 1945. They were rebuilt as coastal minelayers and transferred to Turkey in 1952. Two more were supplied to Norway as *Vidar* (ex-*LSM 494*) and *Vale* (ex-*LSM 492*). They were retransferred to Turkey on 1.11.60 and renamed *Mersin* and *Mürefte* respectively. Armament is now 6–40mm (3×2), 5–20mm (5×1), 400 mines. All five were in service in 1982.

US REDWING/ADJUTANT type *coastal minesweepers*

Particulars:	As US *Redwing* class and *Adjutant* class

Class:

Redwing early type – *Samsun* (M 510), *Sinop* (M 511), *Surmene* (M 512), *Seddul Bahr* (M 513)
Redwing later type – *Silifke* (M 514), *Saros* (M 515), *Sigacik* (M 516), *Sapanca* (M 517), *Sariyer* (M 518)
Adjutant type – *Seymen* (M 507), *Selcuk* (M 508), *Seyhan* (M 509)

Four US-built *Redwing* class coastal minesweepers were transferred to Turkey as they were completed in 1958–59 under MDAP: *Samsun* on 30.9.59, *Sinop* in Feb 59, *Surmene* on 27.3.59 and *Seddul Bahr* in May 59. Five more were built for Turkey between 1964–67: *Sigacik*, transferred in June 65, *Sapanca* on 26.7.65, *Silifke* in Sept 65, *Saros* in Feb 66 and *Sariyer* on 8.9.67. This later five were of the MSC 294 type, with a slightly larger hull, lower superstructure, taller funnels and different machinery. Three of the earlier *Adjutant* type were acquired in 1970. *Seyhan* (ex-*Renoncule*) and *Selcuk* (ex-*Pavot*) on 24.3.70, and *Seymen* (ex-Belgian *De Panne*) on 19.11.70. These were transferred from France and Belgium to Turkey via the United States. All twelve were in service in 1982.

Fethiye on trials 29.7.67　　　　　　　　　　　　　　　　　　　USN

Ex-Canadian 'BAY' class *coastal minesweeper*

Particulars:	As Canadian 'Bay' class

Class:

Trabzon (M 530), *Terme* (M 531), *Tirebolu* (M 532), *Tekirdag* (M 533)

Four Canadian 'Bay' type coastal minesweepers, all built in 1951–53, were transferred from Canada to Turkey under MDAP on 19.5.58. They werer *Tekirdag* (ex-*Ungava*), *Terme* (ex-*Trinity*), *Tirebolu* (ex-*Comax*), and *Trabzon* (ex-*Gaspé*). All four were in service in 1982.

French MERCURE class *coastal minesweepers*

Particulars:	As French *Mercure* class

Class:

Karamürsel (M 520), *Kerempe* (M 521), *Kilimli* (M 522), *Kozlu* (M 523), *Kusadasi* (M 524), *Kemer* (M 525)

Six ex-West German *Vegesack* class coastal minesweepers, built to the French *Mercure* class design between 1959–60, were transferred to Turkey; *Karamürsel* (ex-*Worms*), *Kerempe* (ex-*Detmold*), *Kilimli* (ex-*Siegen*), *Kozlu* (ex-*Hamelin*) and *Kusadasi* (ex-*Vegesack*) between late 1975–early 1976, and *Kemer* (ex-*Passau*) in 1979. All six were in service in 1982.

Ex-US YMS type *inshore minesweeper*

Particulars:	As USN YMS type

Eight ex-*YMS* type motor minesweepers were acquired by Turkey from the United States in 1947. *Kas* (ex-*YMS 79*) and *Kilimi* (ex-*YMS 289*) were discarded in 1963, *Kozlu* (ex-*YMS 348*) and *Kusadasi* (ex-*YMS 468*) in 1965 and *Kemer* (ex-*YMS 228*), *Kerempe* (ex-*YMS 239*), *Kirte* (ex-*YMS 307*) and *Karamürsel* (ex-*Küllük*, ex-*YMS 375*) in 1966.

US CAPE class *inshore minesweepers*

Particulars:	As USN 'Cape' class

Class:

Foca (M 500), *Fethiye* (M 501), *Fatsa* (M 502), *Finike* (M 503)

Four US 'Cape' class inshore minesweepers (*MSI 15–MSI 18*) were constructed under MDAP and were transferred to Turkey on completion between Aug and Dec 67. All four were in service in 1982.

United Kingdom

Although for the past 36 years Great Britain has not been at war with her neighbours, the years 1947–83 have been traumatic ones for the Royal Navy, and as full of change as any in its previous history. The rapid rundown after the end of the Second World War hit the RN harder than any of the other victors: not only was the British economy in a parlous state, but the colossal subsidies of the Lease-Lend Programme were suddenly withdrawn, and the urgent need to release manpower from the armed forces meant that large numbers of ships had to be laid up at short notice.

In 1948 a large-scale pruning of the Reserve Fleet removed all but five of the surviving battleships, all cruisers earlier than the *Southampton* class and all prewar destroyers. Almost every one of these ships was scrapped, but a handful found their way into other navies.

With more vessels than complements to man them, and a desperate shortage of merchant ships, there was no priority for new construction, but work on battleship design continued until as late as 1948. This was largely because of rumours about Russian capital ships, but there was a tacit admission that battleships were beyond the RN's means and were in any case of limited value. With less validity the same reasoning was applied to cruiser designs, for at this time Western strategic thought was dominated by fears of a nuclear holocaust. Many military writers and theorists believed that warships had no role to play since a future war would be decided by long-range bombers armed with nuclear weapons.

It was recognised by the more perceptive planners that the aircraft carrier could still play a major role, and so permission was given to continue work on two large and four intermediate hulls from the wartime programme. The very big *Malta* class had been cancelled before any work had been done on them, but the hulls chosen, the smaller 36,800t *Africa* class, were a better-balanced design, probably had more 'stretch' and were therefore more cost-effective, and had enclosed hangar space, a necessity for nuclear war.

The modernisation of the six armoured carriers was looked into, but it was found that the restricted hangar height ruled out the newest, the two *Implacable*s and the *Indomitable*. Of the other three, *Illustrious* and *Formidable* had suffered heavy war damage, leaving only *Victorious*. It

The British carrier force of the 1950s: *Eagle*, *Bulwark* and *Albion* 20.10.56

is interesting to note that before the survey, made in 1949, which settled her fate, modernisation plans had been drawn up for *Formidable*: she would have had a fully angled flight deck, some two years before the RAE Bedford Conference at which the angled deck is claimed to have been 'invented'. In fact, it was the intention to modernise all six carriers; *Victorious* was uniquely the prototype.

REFITS AND MODERNISATIONS

The Admiralty was well aware that the fire control and radar of current ships were obsolescent, and this, coupled with their strenuous war service, poor anti-corrosion protection and general lack of amenities, made major overhauls imperative. There was also the question of replacing out-of-date weaponry, and to correct the situation a series of major refits was put in hand in the early 1950s. The battleships were considered for conversion to missile ships, but, as in the United States, the cost was seen to be prohibitive and out of all proportion to any improvement in fighting value, so work on the battleships was confined to routine maintenance. Finally, the modernisation programme was cut back to one carrier and as many cruisers and destroyers as possible.

The *Southampton* and 'Colony' classes and the *Belfast* were all given partial modernisations between 1950 and 1960, but mounting costs and the growing age of the ships caused the programme to be cut back at the *Swiftsure*. It has been suggested that *Swiftsure* turned out to have been inadequately surveyed after sustaining severe damage in collision with the destroyer *Diamond* during the big NATO exercise 'Mainbrace' in 1953, and that by the time the extent of the damage became evident in 1960 the ship's modernisation had been almost completed; nothing could be done to remedy the situation and she was towed away to the scrapyard.

Apart from the 'Battle' class and later destroyers, virtually all the wartime 'Emergency' destroyers were unsuitable for modern warfare because of inadequate air defence and fire control. Current needs for fleet escorts were met by the big destroyers, but there were no fast escorts to cope with the new Soviet 'Whiskey' type submarines. The 'Emergency' destroyers were ideal for conversion and so the Type 15 frigate design by N G Holt, based on his *Whitby* design, was drawn up as a stopgap until the new frigate designs were ready. Despite the end of the Korean war, East-West tension remained high throughout the 1950s, and to make up numbers other simpler and cheaper conversions were also put in hand.

It is not often realised that corrosion was a major problem with war-built ships. Before the war, mill scale was removed by pickling in dilute acid; thin plating, particularly in destroyers, was galvanised. To save time, war-built ships did not receive either treatment, and by the end of the war were usually in a worse condition than older vessels.

NEW CONSTRUCTION

The major surface threat in the 1950s was seen as the Soviet *Sverdlov* class cruisers operating against Western trade. So seriously was this possibility taken that two new designs were drawn up to deal with it, a cruiser and a super-destroyer. The cruiser was intended to provide air cover with guided missiles and relied on rapid-firing 6in guns as its main armament, while a new rapid-firing single 5in gun was designed for the destroyers.

The cruiser would have displaced 18,000t (standard) and would have carried Seaslug missiles aft and automatic 6in guns forward. The destroyer, on the other hand, relied on three 5in guns for air defence, and when the project was finally dropped it was because she had no missile defence. The gun, derived from the British Army's land-mobile 5in, reached an advanced design stage, but was then stopped when the Ordnance Board recommended an end to 'gunnery solutions to AA defence' in 1958.

All that remained of this interesting design was the advanced steam machinery which was developed for the fast escort, stopped, and then cut down and married with the gas turbines for the 'County' class, the larger fleet escort which the Board, after much thought, opted for. The first two were ordered in 1955, followed by two further units in 1957. The more urgent need of frigates had meant that the first six Type 12 ships, intended as prototypes, had been ordered in 1951, followed by another twelve of slightly modified design in 1954. These frigates were intended to be cheap, and to be seen as such, but they were a great success and are still widely regarded as one of the finest escort designs

of the past 25 years in any navy; although not unduly complex, they were, however, costly to build. In 1952–55 a dozen even cheaper, 'utility' Type 14 ships were laid down to supplement the Type 12s, and a simpler destroyer conversion, the Type 16, was put in hand.

Two other new classes of frigates were ordered in 1951, a standard diesel-engined hull in two variants, one for anti-aircraft defence and the other for aircraft-direction. It had been intended to make up numbers in both categories with more conversions of destroyers, but these plans were shelved when a change of heart by the Staff indicated that it would be possible to go back to building general-purpose warships. This change of policy was influenced by new trends in technology, with more compact machinery and electronics on the way. Despite cutbacks and delays, however, the Korean War building programme had created an impressive escort force. By the end of 1958, 24 new frigates had been completed and 34 destroyers had been converted; in addition, 21 'C' class destroyers had received varying degrees of modernisation to improve their escort capability, and many of the slower 'Loch' class had been re-armed.

The other area in which the Royal Navy invested heavily was mine warfare. Having suffered considerable casualties from the mining of harbours and estuaries, and because of their much shallower coastal waters, the British were understandably more sensitive about this than the Americans and when it was learned during the Korean War that Russian magnetic mines were proving immune to degaussing measures it was realised that a large number of new minesweepers were needed to replace the steel-hulled *Algerines*. Between 1950 and 1958 some 120 coastal minesweepers were built, concurrently with 100 inshore types. The CMS design proved an outstanding success, robust and sufficiently seaworthy to be used on offshore patrol, but the IMS design proved too small to accommodate the generating power needed for the latest anti-acoustic and anti-magnetic sweeping devices. A further improvement was the introduction of 'minehunting', using a special sonar to detect and classify mines on the seabed so that they could be destroyed by a demolition charge. When this equipment had been perfected a number of coastal minesweepers were converted to minehunters and over the years the new technique has largely replaced or influenced traditional sweeping as the major method.

SUBMARINES

By 1945 the Royal Navy had built up a formidable submarine force and there was no intention of frittering away such hard-won expertise. Apart from the possibility of offensive use in wartime, an active force of submarines was ruled to be essential in training anti-submarine forces, and great attention was paid to German developments. After prolonged tests with some Type XXI boats and the Type XVIIB *Meteorite*, it was decided to build two experimental boats with Walter hydrogen peroxide turbine propulsion, and to modernise the 'A' class and the welded boats of the 'T' class along the lines of the Type XXI, with enlarged batteries and streamlined hulls.

The two peroxide boats proved expensive, but the lessons learned from them were incorporated in a new design of diesel-electric boats, the *Porpoise* class. This hull form was very successful and was repeated in the improved *Oberon* class, one of the most outstanding 'conventional' designs of the past 25 years. What put paid to peroxide propulsion was the successful adaptation of nuclear power, for this gave virtually unlimited thermal power without oxygen from any source. When the USS *Nautilus* proved such a triumph in 1955, the Royal Navy immediately decided to switch to nuclear propulsion.

Although the intention to 'go nuclear' was there even before the two peroxide boats were built, work on a prototype reactor, at Dounreay in Scotland, did not start until 1957, and it fell so far behind schedule that the Admiralty decided to buy a reactor from the United States for the first British boat, and to put the Dounreay type into two later classes. Since then a fourth class has been built and work has started on a fifth, making the RN one of only five navies operating nuclear-propelled ships.

For some years it was believed that no more diesel-electric 'submersibles' would be built, but the cost not only of building nuclear boats but also of manning them has forced the RN to return to a conventional design, the 2400-tonne SSK (submarine, hunter-killer) announced in 1979. These will carry a similar armament to the nuclear boats and will be in service by the late 1980s.

127

UNITED KINGDOM

In 1963 the momentous decision was taken to transfer responsibility for the British nuclear deterrent from the RAF to the RN, in the form of Polaris underwater-launched ballistic missiles. Five submarines were ordered in 1963–64, but the incoming Labour Government cancelled the fifth boat in February 1965 as a gesture of appeasement to its left wing. The entire project, including training the crews, building four submarines and providing base and support facilities, was carried through with great rapidity, making Polaris one of the few major British defence projects to keep within its financial limits and become operational on time.

In July 1980 it was announced that four new submarines would be built, armed with Trident II missiles. These will have a range of 4000 miles, well outside the range of Soviet anti-submarine forces, and will have eight independently targeted warheads instead of three. As before, the major components of the missile system will be bought from the United States, but many sub-systems will be provided by British sub-contractors.

A NEW GENERATION OF WARSHIPS

Although the 'electronic' component of ships had been growing rapidly since 1940, during the 1950s there were signs that the trend might be beginning to slow down to some extent because of the reduction in size of individual items of electronic equipment. This meant, for example, that the previous policy of building single-function escorts could be discarded. The unsophisticated 'Tribal' class showed that it was now possible to build a general-purpose frigate once more, and so in 1960 the decison was made to build the last three *Rothesay* class frigates to a totally recast design. The hull was identical, but it was now possible to include a light helicopter and a long-range surveillance radar, combining a high-level anti-submarine capability with a good measure of air warning and aircraft-direction.

It was now recognised that no small escort could do more than defend herself against air attack (point defence), and a new class of larger air-defence destroyers (DLGs) was planned to provide area defence for the new aircraft carriers that were scheduled. Known as the Type 82, four were planned as escorts for two carriers, armed with a new surface-to-air missile, but propelled by a combined steam and gas turbine plant as in the 'County' class. When the carrier programme was cancelled in 1966 the class was cut to one ship (to be used as a testbed for new weapons and machinery), but she was followed by a new class of smaller destroyers (DDGs), whose function would be AAW and not general-purpose.

The cancellation of the aircraft carriers in 1966 was a traumatic experience for the Royal Navy, involving the resignation of the First Sea Lord and the loss of its chief striking force. The carrier *Victorious* went quickly (after fire damage), followed later by the *Eagle*, and the responsibility for naval air strike was handed over to the RAF. All the other inter-service rivalry flared up, for it was felt by many supporters of naval air power that the RAF had unfairly (and inaccurately) convinced the Minister of Defence that the carriers were vulnerable to strikes from land-based inter-continental ballistic missiles. The Navy kept its helicopters, but was to hand over its Phantom and Buccaneer aircraft to the Air Force, with a contingent of RAF aircrew mixing with the surviving carriers' air groups so that shorebased RAF squadrons could take over the mission of protecting ships at sea.

As had been predicted by many, the scheme proved unworkable. The RAF was already over-stretched in providing for the air defence of the United Kingdom, and even if the aircraft earmarked for naval support were serviceable a few minutes' delay in take-off meant that they arrived on the scene too late. But even after both services realised that the situation could not continue, the politicians clung to their ruling that there could never be any more aircraft carriers. What was certain, however, was that the RN could not afford to build or operate a large fixed-wing aircraft carrier comparable to those in the US Navy. The original decision had been the right one, for the cost of the aircraft alone would have been crippling.

The answer would have to be found elsewhere. In 1967 serious consideration was given to a 'command cruiser' carrying six large ASW helicopters, similar to the French *Jeanne d'Arc*. Further studies showed that greater efficiency would be obtained with nine helicopters, but in an internal hangar; logically this led to a starboard island, lifts and a clear flight deck. But to avoid political disputes with the RAF and

the politicians, the euphemism 'through-deck cruiser' was coined, lest it be said that an aircraft carrier was under consideration. A further complication was the existence of the Harrier V/STOL aircraft, a naval version of which had been under development, and it was decided to make sure that the design of the new ship could accommodate the Sea Harrier if required. Thereafter the battle became purely political, and the Sea Harrier was not ordered until May 1975, more than two years after the ship had been laid down. In 1980 the first two squadrons were formed, giving the RN control over its own air power once more, and the debate now revolves around the aircraft to follow the Sea Harrier.

By the mid-1970s the growing strength of the Soviet Navy in nuclear submarines was focusing attention on the so-called GIUK (Greenland–Iceland–UK) Gap. This 'choke point', through which submarines from Murmansk must pass to attack targets in the North Atlantic, had already been 'bugged' with networks of passive acoustic sensors laid on the seabed to track the passage of hostile submarines. Known as SOSUS (Sound Surveillance System), the system needed big, weatherly anti-submarine ships to patrol the area and pounce on targets in areas defined by the SOSUS arrays. While the US Navy built the big *Spruance* class destroyers, the RN opted for 4000t frigates armed with two helicopters, surface missiles and a new point-defence missile capable of functioning against other missiles, and fitted with elaborate command, control and communications (C^3). The Sea Wolf missile had originally been conceived as an anti-aircraft point-defence weapon, but during development it had been tailored to meet the threat from underwater-launched missiles and sea-skimmers, and is currently the only anti-missile missile system in service.

Despite the return to a balanced navy, time was running out for the RN. The cost of warships was rising beyond control, and in particular the cost of protecting them against anti-ship missiles – for example, computer studies showed that a double-ended Sea Dart destroyer would be over 8000 tons and cost hundreds of millions. To make matters worse the overheads of the Royal Dockyards made the cost of half-life refits exorbitant: fitting Sea Wolf and Type 2016 sonar to a *Leander* class frigate cost more than £70m, and even a modest refit for a 'County' class DLG in 1981 cost £64m.

In June 1981 the axe fell, when the new Minister of Defence, John Nott, announced that the surface fleet would be cut back. One of the three support carriers would be laid up or sold, the escort-force would be cut to 50 ships, and no more half-life modernisations would be approved. The Type 22 programme would be cut short and replaced by a new utility escort known as Type 23, but to compensate, the nuclear hunter-killer programme would be accelerated and the Type 2400 diesel electric submarines would proceed. As things stood at the beginning of 1982, the old commando carrier *Bulwark* had been paid off, *Hermes* was to pay off shortly, *Invincible* was 'on offer' to the Australian Navy, and two DLGs and two *Leander* class frigates had been sold. All the older frigates and several of the *Leanders* were also to be sold. Such was the situation when the Falklands crisis intervened.

THE FALKLANDS CAMPAIGN

When Argentine forces occupied the Falkland Islands and South Georgia on 2 April 1982, the British Government immediately dispatched a task force to recapture the islands. Although the assembling and equipping of such a force around the carriers *Hermes* (flagship) and *Invincible* was a masterpiece of speed and efficiency (the carriers and several warships sailed and 5000 tons of military stores were loaded, all within 72 hours of the order to embark), the fighting around the Falklands showed that the Royal Navy was no longer adequately equipped for such operations. The fact that the Falklands are 8000 miles from Britain and that the nearest base was Ascension caused particular strain, but air attacks by Argentine shore-based aircraft showed that a small air group of less than 30 Sea Harriers was no substitute for a large carrier with high-performance aircraft.

The first blow came on 4 May, when the DDG *Sheffield* was hit by an air-launched Exocet missile from a Super Etendard strike aircraft. The missile failed to detonate, but it set the fuel tanks on fire and the ship had to be abandoned some hours later. She was taken in tow because the Navy hoped to have the damage examined by experts at South Georgia, but when the weather deteriorated on 10 May the burned-out hulk was scuttled. The strike against the Task Force was undoubtedly provoked by the loss of the old cruiser *General Belgrano*, which was torpedoed by the nuclear submarine *Conqueror* on 2 May. According to later claims by the British Government, the *Belgrano* and her Exocet-armed destroyers were the southernmost element of a three-pronged attack on the Task Force, and the submarine's CO was given permission to attack any hostile targets. Surprisingly the elderly Mk 8 torpedo was used, at a range of about 3000yds, rather than the long range Mk 24.

Once the amphibious assault had got under way at San Carlos on 21 May, fierce air battles became an almost daily occurrence, and bombing or rocket attacks accounted for the DDG *Coventry* and the frigates *Ardent* and *Antelope*. The Navy found that the lack of airborne early warning aircraft made the Sea Harriers' task much harder, and the older radars, 965 and 992Q, had great difficulty in tracking fast, low-flying air targets. The need for stronger close-range defence led to the use of troops and their GPMGs to provide AA fire, and ships still in the UK were hurriedly rearmed with twin 30mm and single 20mm guns, as well as additional chaff-launchers to give protection against guided missiles. The Vulcan Phalanx 20mm 'Gatling' was acquired from the United States and two were put on the flight deck of the new carrier *Illustrious*.

A large number of merchant ships were chartered or requisitioned, including the luxury liners *Canberra* and *Queen Elizabeth II*, with helicopter platforms, naval-standard communications and, in some cases, 20mm guns, added. The most elaborate conversions were the giant ro-ro/container ships *Atlantic Conveyor* and *Atlantic Causeway*. The former took RAF Harriers to the South Atlantic and then acted as a 'spare deck' for aircraft and helicopters in San Carlos Water, while the latter was given a hangar and four anti-submarine Sea King helicopters. The *Atlantic Conveyor*'s loss to an Exocet attack was a major setback to the timetable of Operation 'Corporate' for she carried a portable airstrip and refuelling equipment which were intended to permit the ground-support aircraft to operate away from the carriers. Although the land forces got safely ashore, the Navy's presence remained vital throughout, to move supplies and to provide cover against Argentine air strikes. A rash attempt by 5 Brigade to move without Sea Harrier cover led to the crippling of the LSLs *Sir Galahad* and *Sir Tristram* at Bluff Cove, arguably the worst moment of an otherwise brilliant campaign in which numerically inferior forces had repeatedly out-thought and out-fought the opposition.

Two days before the surrender on 24 June, the DLG *Glamorgan* was hit by a land-launched Exocet missile, which wrecked her hangar and killed 15 men, but by a near-miracle she escaped serious damage. The missile was detected on radar and correctly identified, giving her a vital 70 seconds to turn away and try to get out of range. As the Exocet was nearly out of fuel it did not strike with full force, and it seems that the warhead may have detonated only partially.

MINE WARFARE
The Soviet Navy's interest and expertise in mine warfare showed no sign of decreasing in the 1970s, and the replacements designed for the RN's ageing coastal minesweepers proved to be, ton for ton, among the most complex and expensive warships ever built. To reduce their magnetic signature virtually to nil, it was necessary to design non-magnetic diesels and build the hull of glass-reinforced plastic (GRP). GRP is expensive and difficult to fabricate on such a large scale, and the *Brecon* class are currently the world's largest ships built of this material. They are known as Mine Counter Measures Vessels (MCMVs) because they can accommodate both hunting and sweeping functions in one hull.

COMMONWEALTH NAVIES
The disappearance of the Empire weakened the links which bound the navies of Canada and Australia to that of Great Britain, and there was a steady drift away from a reliance on British equipment. The RCN was the first, purchasing USN weapons and electronics to make it easier to get spares in an emergency, and going as far as to design its own escort destroyers. The RAN, on the other hand, continued to build RN designs in its own shipyards for some years.

An attempt to follow the Canadian example in designing a special class of missile destroyer to meet Australian specifications came to nothing, and since 1962 standard US Navy designs have been bought. Co-operation with the RN continues, however, and the Ikara anti-submarine missile system and other equipment has been jointly developed. While South Africa remained in the Commonwealth the

Hermes, the flagship of the Falklands Task Force, on her return to Portsmouth, July 1982
C & S Taylor

UNITED KINGDOM

SAN relied totally on British *matériel*, but after 1961 political pressure to prevent them from buying military equipment forced the South Africans to turn elsewhere. Three French submarines were bought, but in 1979 even France had to bow to international opinion, and contracts for two more submarines and two frigates were cancelled.

The 'New Commonwealth' navies, principally India and Pakistan, fitted the traditional mould for a longer period because they lacked indigenous resources, but Pakistan turned increasingly to China for help and India to the Soviet Union. India also pursued a sensible policy of building up local resources to the point where British designs could be expanded and even equipped with Soviet weaponry.

WEAPONRY

The Royal Navy continued its policy of demanding high standards in its weapons and equipment, but the underlying economic weakness which had become particularly evident after 1918 largely frustrated this. Lack of money to buy equipment led to endless delays, some imposed by the Navy's bureaucratic machinery and others by the Treasury. In the end the result was always the same: equipment came into service far too late, making it obsolescent almost from the day it became operational. Other problems were caused by the temptation to allow too many committees to make alterations to specifications. Thus the Seaslug missile was made extraordinarily bulky on the advice of the Royal Aircraft Establishment, Farnborough, who did not believe reports that the American Terrier missile had its booster motor mounted in tandem. For political reasons it is almost impossible to purchase foreign equipment, but when it is bought the immediate temptation has been to 'Anglicise' it; this happened with the American Mk 56 fire control system, which after many years of painful development re-emerged as the MRS3.

The beam-riding Seaslug gave way eventually to the much superior semi-active homer Sea Dart, which followed American ideas more closely, and this weapon is currently being developed in a lightweight form capable of use against surface targets as well. The experience with lighter missiles has been happier, for the short-range Seacat was designed to replace the 40mm Bofors gun, and by being tailored specifically to one role it has emerged as a relatively cheap and cost-effective close-range defence system for ships down to frigates. Its replacement was to have been Sea Wolf, but during its lengthy and costly development new technology enabled the designers to give it a capability against sea-skimming missiles. A belated programme has produced a lighter version, which will at least enable it to be fitted to ships smaller than the 4000t *Broadsword* class.

The problem for the RN is that it has shrunk in size without losing its front-line commitments, and as a result its production runs are short. This pushes up cost and explains why so many good ideas have had to depend on export orders before they can go ahead. Originally it was hoped to persuade the Dutch to buy Sea Dart in exchange for a Signaal 3-D radar, and the Type 22 frigate was also begun as a joint venture.

Since 1947 British torpedoes have earned a poor reputation, most of it undeserved. Although the Mk 8 submarine torpedo was by far the most efficient and cost-effective torpedo used in the Second World War, it was hoped to replace it with faster and more accurate weapons, using wartime developments as well as ideas found in Germany in 1945. The most promising development was High-Test Peroxide (HTP), and this was used to drive the high-speed 'Fancy' or 21in Mk 12. This weapon had to be withdrawn after a propellant explosion sank the submarine *Sidon* in 1955, but was subsequently redeveloped by the Royal Swedish Navy into the Tp61, a remarkably safe and effective torpedo.

Several torpedoes were designed and then axed for financial reasons, notably the Pentane and the Mk 30 Mod 1. The desperate need of a light-weight homing torpedo for aircraft, helicopters and frigates led to the purchase of American Mk 43, Mk 44 and Mk 46 torpedoes, but the Mk 43 is obsolete and the other two are being replaced by the Stingray. Despite many problems, the Mk 24 Tigerfish came into service in the 1970s and is being followed after 1985 by the new heavyweight, Spearfish. The cancellation of the Undersea Guided Weapon (USGW) has forced the Navy to buy the USN's Sub-Harpoon to give its nuclear submarines a long-range anti-ship weapon, and this started trials in October 1981.

BRITISH NAVAL GUNS 1947–82*

Type	Remarks
20mm Oerlikon Mk 7A single	Obsolete in 1945, but brought back as close-range surface weapon in 1964
20mm Oerlikon twin	Obsolescent in 1945, but used in CMSs
30mm single	Naval Rarden, on trials 1980; may replace 20mm
40mm/60 Mk 3 single	Obsolete in 1945, but brought back as armament of OPVs 1977
40mm/60 Mk 4 twin	Hazemeyer tri-axially stabilised; obsolescent by 1945 and replaced by STAAG Mk 2 *c* 1950
40mm/60 STAAG Mk 2 twin	Radar-controlled automatic AA mounting, replaced Mk 4
40mm/60 Mk 5 twin	Utility mounting which proved more reliable than the STAAG; still in service 1980
40mm/60 Mk 6 6-barrelled	Heavy-duty multiple with auto-feed for capital ships and carriers; obsolete by mid-1960s
40mm/60 Mk 7 single	Power-mounted but hand-loaded; replaced by Mk 9 post-1950
40mm/60 Mk 8 single	Battery-driven version of Mk 7; not operational, re-engineered Mk 7
40mm/60 Mk 9 single	Replacement for Mk 7; still in service
40mm/70 Mks 10, 11, 12	Single, twin and sextuple mountings with L/70 Bofors and new ammunition; order for 350 barrels cancelled *c* 1957
6pdr (57mm) 7 cwt Mk 2	Coastal Forces power-mounting; obsolescent in 1945, but not withdrawn until 1950s
3in/50 Mk 22 twin	USN mounting provided with shields and modified Mk 63 radar fire control; *Victorious* only
3in/70 Mk 6 twin	British production model based on USN experimental mounting; intended for frigates, but used only in *Tiger* class cruisers and by RCN
3.3in CF Mk 2	Unsuccessful adaptation of Centurion tank's 20pdr, intended for *Brave* class
4in/45 Mk 5 HA single	Obsolete destroyer gun on high-angle mounting; obsolete in 1945, but still in service 1950s
4in/40 Mk 12 single	Submarine gun; in service to 1950s
4in/40 Mk 20 single	Submarine gun; in service to 1950s
4in/45 Mk 16 twin	Obsolescent, but continued in service to 1960s; some fitted with US Mk 63 radar on shield
4in/45 single	Vickers automatic type, developed from Army gun for East Coast Gunboat *c* 1950; cancelled, but sold to Chile
4.5in/45 Mk 5 single	Mk 4 gun, replacement for 4.7in Mk 9; adapted to RPC and still in service
4.5in/45 Mk 6 twin	Standard frigate and destroyer mounting of 1950s and 1960s, continued in place of 3in Mk 6 when that gun did not appear on time. Still in service
4.5in/25 8 cwt CF Mk 1	Adaptation of 95mm demolition howitzer to replace 57mm (6pdr) in Coastal Forces; obsolete by mid-1950s
4.5in/55 Mk 8	New surface bombardment gun for DDGs, DLGs and frigates, with modest performance but higher reliability; introduced in mid-1960s and still in production
5in/56 single Mk 2	Naval version of Army's 'Green Mace' intended as new DP gun for destroyers in early 1950s. Cancelled *c* 1957
5in/56 twin Mk 1	Twin version of same gun, intended for cruisers; design stage only
5.25in/50 QF Mk 1 twin	DP mounting in capital ships and AA cruisers; obsolescent by 1950s, but retained until 1968
6in/50 QF Mk 23 triple	Standard cruiser turret-mounting; obsolete by 1950s
6in/50 QF Mk 25 triple	Designed for *Neptune* class, but work ceased after 1946 in favour of Mk 26
6in/50 Mk 26 twin	Rapid-fire twin with 80° elevation, water-cooled; *Tiger* class
8in/50 Mk 8 twin	Obsolescent in 1945, but remained in service in old heavy cruisers until 1954
14in/46 Mk 7 quad and twin	*King George V* class
15in/42 Mk 1(N) twin	Original 1912 model with elevation increased to 30°, improved shell and supercharges; used in *Vanguard* with RPC
16in/45 Mk 1 triple	Obsolescent by 1945; *Nelson* only
16in/45 Mk 4 triple	Projected for 'Improved *Lion*' class but never got beyond design stage

*Roman numerals replaced by Arabic Mark numbers *c* 1948; new form used throughout for clarity

BRITISH TORPEDOES 1947–82

Torpedo	Weight (lb)	Explosive (lb)	Range (yds)/ at (kts)	Remarks
21in Mk 8	3353	750	5000/44½ or 7000/40	Introduced 1927, but in service in submarines until 1980s
21in Mk 9	3731	750	10,000/40 or 14,000/35	Surface version of Mk 8; in service until 1960s
21in Mk 11	?	750	?	Copy of German G7e; replaced 1950s by Mk 12, etc
21in Mk 12		c750	?	Code-named 'Fancy SR'. HTP version of Mk 8; withdrawn as unsafe 1959
21in Mk 20 (E)	1800	200	12,000/20	'Bidder', ASW single-speed for frigates; withdrawn 1950s
21in/Mk 20(S)	1800	200	12,000/20 8000/12	Two-speed submarine homer variant of Bidder; still in service in improved form
21in/Mk 21	?	c300	12,000/30	'Pentane'; dropped during development
21in Mk 22	1800	200	12,000/20	Cable-set version of Mk 20; cancelled
21in Mk 23	c2000	?	12,000/78	Wire-guided submarine type; replaced Mk 20 in 1970
21in Mk 23	c2000	c750	12,000/40	Tigerfish heavy-weight for submarines; Mod 0 superseded by Mod 1 1981
18in Mk 30	630	?	2500/19 or 8000/12	Ex-'Dealer B', air-dropped ASW homer withdrawn 1971 Mod 1 cancelled 1955
12.75in Mk 31	?	?		Cancelled 1971
10in Mk 43	?	c50	?	Mod 3, US air-dropped weapon; bought as interim replacement for Mk 30
12.75in UK Mk 44	?	75	5500/30	Electric ASW homer built under US licence for ASW aircraft and ships; brought into service late 1960s
12.75in Mk 46	?	90	12,000/40	Otto-fuel version of Mk 44; bought 1971 to replace Mk 30 Mod 0 and Mk 31
12.75in Stingray	?	c75		Replacement for Mk 44/46; entering service 1980
21in Spearfish	?	c750	c25,000/55	Successor to Mk 24; capable of fast-running at 3000ft. Runs on HAP-Otto fuel. Ordered late 1981, to be in service 1985

BRITISH RADARS 1947–82

Type	Band	Remarks
167	10cm	Submarine. Seaguard 'cheese', also fitted to periscope
242	IFF A–Band	
253	IFF A–Band	
262	3cm	Tracker for STAAG, CRBF, etc, with dish antenna; obsolescent
267	P/X–band	Surface search for submarines; also in 267MW and 267PW versions
274	10cm	Surface warning for capital ships and cruisers; obsolete by 1964
275	10cm	Tracker fitted to Mks 37, 6 and 6M fire control directors
277P	10cm	Height-finder introduced 1943; replaced mid-1950s by Type 277Q/278
277Q	10cm	Replacement for Type 277 in major surface ships
278	10cm	Solid-state replacement for 277, using same antenna ('County' class DLGs)
79/279	metric	Obsolete air warning set, but remained in active ships until 1948
79B/281	metric	Still in use until 1951
291	10cm	Air warning, dipole antenna for submarines
293P/Q	10cm	Surface/low-angle air search and target-indication
690	–	Electronic warfare (EW) set, introduced 1981
801	?	Projected surveillance radar; cancelled mid-1950s
901	5–7.5cm	Seaslug tracker
903/904	1.5–3.75cm	Tracker for MRS3, with dish antenna
909	3–3.75cm	Sea Dart tracker
910	3–3.75cm	Sea Wolf tracker
912	3–3.75cm	RN designation for Italian RTN–10X tracker
931	1.5cm	Auxiliary surface gunnery set to improve Type 274; not operational
932	K–Band	Canadian splash-spotting set
940	G–Band	Late Second World War IFF
960	Metric	Long-range air warning, introduced c1950; replaced by 965
961/962X/ 963	?	Early forms of Carrier Controlled Approach (CCA) radars
965	1.5/200MHz	Anglicised version of SPS–6B, in service 1961 onwards; in single 'bedstead' AKE–1 or double AKE–2 aerial. Being replaced by 1022 (966 is designation of 'cleaned up' version)
967/968	7.5–30cm	Sea Wolf surveillance, mounted back-to-back; in service 1978
973	?	Periscope-mounted ranging set for submarines
974	3cm	Decca 12 navigation set
975	1.5–3.75cm	Surface search set for small ships; Type 975ZW used for position-fixing in MCMVs
977	?	Shore-based radar, to detect aerial minelaying
978	3cm	Navigation radar for frigates
980–981 982–983	7.5–15cm	Formerly combined as WCB–1 for carriers, and used in Eagle; subsequently separated into height-finder and 'Hayrake' for carrier air warning
984	?	Comprehensive Display System (CDS), 3-D using massive 'searchlight' antenna; obsolete since 1966
985	?	Experimental fixed-array surveillance set under development about 1959, but later dropped
986/987	?	Projected successors to 982/983
988	?	Projected 'Broomstick' Anglo-Dutch 3–D set intended for Bristol class DLGs and CVA–01
992/992Q and R	10cm	Surface/low-level air search and target-indication, replacing 293 in large ships
993	10cm	Surface/low-level air search and target-indication, replacing 293 in small ships
994	10cm	Solid-state version of 993, using Plessey AWS–4 processing equipment
996	25cm?	Projected STIR to replace 965/966 and 992Q (in place of 1030); open to competition 1982–83
1000/1001	?	Submarine search set in 1950s and 1960s; replaced by 167
1002	?	Surface-search set used in Porpoise class submarines
1006	I–Band	Navigation, replacing 974; also exists in submarine version
1010	?	Alternative designation for Cossor Mk 10 IFF
1022	15–30cm	Interim Surveillance and Target-Indication Radar (STIR) using Signaal LW–08 processing with antenna for 1030; replacement for 965; at sea 1979
1030	25cm	STIR using back-to-back antennae; at sea 1980, but cancelled 1981

UNITED KINGDOM

Type	Band	Remark
AN/SPG–34		USN fire-control set used with 4in AA guns in *Fiji* class cruisers and RCN 'Tribals'
AN/SPS–6		USN air warning set fitted in *Fleetwood* and *Warrior*
AN/SPN–35		USN Carrier Controlled Approach (CCA) radar in carriers *Ark Royal* and *Melbourne*

BRITISH SONARS* 1947–82

Type	Remarks
129	10kc 'chinstrap' submarine search set
138	15kc 'dustbin' submarine search set
144	Standard escort set; introduced 1943, obsolete by 1950s
144Q	Depth-finding set, used to provide settings for Squid; replaced by 147
147	Attack set, linked direct to 144; replaced 144Q
162	Bottom search set; still in use 1982
165	Original experimental towed array; became 2038
170	Attack set used to control Squid and Limbo; replaced 147 in 1950s
174	Medium-range search set used in frigates from 1950; replaced by 177
177	Replacement for 174; obsolescent
182	Torpedo decoy
184	Medium-range search set, introduced in *Leander* class; still in service 1982
184M	Solid-state version of 184
185	Underwater telephone
186	Non-steerable VLF array, fixed around submarine ballast tanks
187	Submarine attack set; bow array, 2.5/10KHz
193	Minehunting; introduced in 1960s
193M	Solid-state version of 193
195	Helicopter 'dunking' set
196	Escape underwater telephone
197	Submarine passive ranging set, for detection of sonar
199	Variable-depth set; RN designation for Canadian SQS–505
719	H/F fast turning array for submarines
2001	Active/passive set for nuclear submarines; to be replaced by 2020
2007	Long-range passive ranging set for submarines; replaced 186
2016	Long-range passive search set for surface ships; in service 1979
2017/2018	Sonar and noise analysis sets for submarines
2020	Submarine version of 2016, for new nuclear submarines
2019	Joint Anglo-Dutch-French submarine Passive/Active Range and Intercept Sonar ('PARIS'), in all classes since 1978
2024	Towed array, developed initially with US, but later separately. At sea in 1981; for submarines only
2026	Successor to 2024
2038	Towed array for surface warships
2040	'Argonaute' set developed from French 'Eledone' and Dutch 'Octopus' sets; for Type 2400 submarines
AN/LIQC	USN-pattern underwater telephone; replaced by 185

*Known as Asdics until 1948, when USN term became standard

CODENAMES

AIO	Action Information Organisation
Ben	Early codename for 'Longshot'; later renamed 'Popsy'
Bidder	1945 torpedo project; 'Bidder–A' was an 18in homer which became 'Dealer–B' and ultimately the Mk 30
CAAIS	Computer-Aided Action Information System, developed by Ferranti for frigates in 1970s
CACS	Computer-Aided Command System, developed by Ferranti for later *Broadsword* class frigates
CDS	Comprehensive Display System for Type 984 radar
CF299	Project-number for Sea Dart GWS30 missile system
Chevaline	1970s programme to update warheads of British A–3 Polaris missiles
CLOS	Command to Line of Sight
CRBF	Close Range Blind Fire, designation for radar-controlled light fire control system developed in the 1950s
DACR	Multiple 6-barrelled 40mm Bofors gun-mounting projected in early 1950s; possibly the L/70 Mk 12
DCA	AIO system for submarines
DCB	Submarine fire control system for Mk 24 torpedoes
DCC	Fire control system for Type 2400 submarines
Dealer-B	Early name for 18in Mk 30 torpedo, under development 1945–59
Flyplane	Computer processing equipment associated with Mk 6M fire control system
GMS1	Guided Missile System No 1; original designation of Seaslug GWS1 missile system
Green Light	Project name for Seacat GWS20 system
Grog	Formerly 'Mackle', became the 21in Mk 23 torpedo in 1971
GWS20/21/ 22/23/24	Variants of Seacat short-range missile system
GWS25	Sea Wolf point-defence missile system
GWS30	Sea Dart area-defence missile
GWS31	Sea Dart Mk 2 (cancelled 1981)
Hot Shot	Later codename for 'Long Shot', ex-'Popsy', ex-'Ben'
Limbo	Project name for Mk 10 anti-submarine mortar
Long Shot	Early 1950s project to adapt an air-to-air missile (probably Fireflash) for surface-to-air defence; ex-'Popsy', ex-'Ben'
Lop/Gap	1944 beam-riding missile, later redesignated RTV and then Project 502, leading to Seaslug
LRS1	Long-range System No 1, a 1944 projected development of Type 901 radar for guns up to 5.25in; dropped 1949
Mackle	Original name for Mk 20 torpedo, started in early 1950s; renamed 'Grog' in 1956
MRS1	Medium-Range System No 1, a 7000yd AA fire control system based on Type 262 radar, first in STAAG mountings and then in CRBF systems
MRS3	Medium-Range System No 3, adaptation of US Navy's Mk 56 director to replace MRS1
MRS8	Medium-Range System No 8, a CRBF director with predictor units replaced by a computer, for controlling 4in and 40mm guns
NSR	Naval Staff Requirement, the specification which precedes construction of a warship for the RN
NST	Naval Staff Target, the outline specification which leads to a Staff Requirement
Ongar	Original codename for the Mk 24 Mk 1 Tigerfish torpedo
Orange Crop	Helicopter-borne electronic warfare system
Popsy	Ex-'Ben', became 'Long Shot'
Project 502	Early designation for Seaslug missile system
STD	Simple Tachymetric Director, optical sight for 40mm guns
STIR	Surveillance and Target-Indication Radar, developed into Type 1022 and Type 1030 radars
STWS	Ship's Torpedo Weapon System, British development of US Navy's Mk 32 torpedo-launcher
TCSS–3	Torpedo Control System for submarines; fitted in *Porpoise* class and older submarines
TCSS–5	Hybrid TCSS–3 system adapted to allow RCN *Oberon* class to fire Mk 37 torpedoes
TCSS–7	First umbilical-link set FCS in RN; fitted in *Oberon* class; replaced by TCSS–9
TCSS–9	Action information-handling system in *Oberon* class
TCSS–10	Update of TCSS–9 to allow *Oberon* class to handle Mk 24 Mod 1 torpedoes
TOM	Tachymetric One-Man Director
Type B	Improved 'Squid' anti-submarine mortar
Type D	Triple trainable anti-submarine mortar, later named 'Limbo'

FLEET STRENGTH 1947

BATTLESHIPS

Name	Launched	Disp (deep load)	Fate
Nelson class			
NELSON	3.9.25	44,054t	Sold Feb 48
King George V class			
KING GEORGE V	21.2.39	44,460t	BU 1957
DUKE OF YORK	28.2.40	44,790t	BU 1957
ANSON	24.2.40	45,360t	BU 1957
HOWE	9.4.40	44,510t	BU 1957
Vanguard class			
VANGUARD	30.11.44	51,420t	BU 1960

Nelson class
Because *Nelson* had been refitted in the United States at the end of 1944 she was in sufficiently good shape to serve in the postwar fleet, unlike her sister *Rodney*, which was in such poor repair by 1945 that she was laid up immediately. Apart from removal of the 20mm Oerlikons *Nelson* remained unaltered from the last days of the war.

According to Winston Churchill's memoirs, a major modernisation was discussed to enable *Nelson* to serve for several years in the postwar fleet, but no other details have survived. In any case she was too slow and there was no front-line role for battleships any more. After a brief spell as flagship of the Home Fleet at the end of 1945, she joined the Training Squadron at Portland in August 1946 as Flagship, RA Training Battleships for a year. She was sold in February 1948 and used as a bombing target in the Firth of Forth before scrapping commenced in March 1949.

King George V class
The four survivors were immediately stripped of their smaller light AA guns, but otherwise remained unaltered until scrapped. *King George V* and *Howe* had 64–2pdr pompoms (8×8), but *Duke of York* and *Anson* had an extra 4-barrelled pompom on each side of the bridge and on the forecastle deck.

King George V served as flagship of the Home Fleet in 1946 and then as a private ship until paid off into reserve in 1950. After a spell with the Training Squadron at Portland, *Anson* paid off in 1949, while *Howe* served as a harbour TS at Portsmouth from 1950 to 1951, after a year as Flagship, RA Training Battleships (1947). *Duke of York* served with the Home Fleet as flagship until 1949 and remained in commission as flagship of the Reserve Fleet until 1951. All four were eventually laid up in the Gareloch and schemes were discussed in the mid-1950s for converting them to missile ships, but the cost would have been prohibitive and in 1957 they were sold for scrapping.

Vanguard
Only two minor changes were made to the ship during her career: the removal of the 11–40mm single Bofors guns and the temporary replacement of the twin STAAG Bofors mounting on 'B' turret by an observation and saluting platform for the Royal Tour to South Africa early in 1947. She refitted at Devonport in 1947–48 and went to the Mediterranean in January 1949 for six months. She became a training ship at Portland, acting as temporary Home Fleet flagship during exercises. After a refit at Devonport in 1954 she paid off into reserve at Portsmouth, becoming the flagship of the Reserve Fleet and NATO HQ ship. She was sold for scrapping in 1960.

MONITORS

Name	Launched	Disp (deep load)	Fate
ROBERTS	1.2.41	9500t	BU 1965
ABERCROMBIE	31.3.42	9900t	BU 1954

Roberts was initially used as a turret drill ship at Devonport and later as an accommodation ship for the Reserve Fleet. Although removed from the Navy List in 1955 she lasted another ten years until sold for scrapping in 1965. Neither she nor *Abercrombie* underwent any further change apart from items stripped over the years. Although nominally a sister to *Roberts*, *Abercrombie* differed in several respects. In July 1946 she replaced the old *Erebus* as turret drill ship at Chatham, and subsequently served as an accommodation ship for the Nore Reserve Fleet. She was towed to Portsmouth in 1959 and sold for scrapping the following year.

AIRCRAFT CARRIERS

Name	Launched	Disp (deep load)	Fate
Illustrious class			
ILLUSTRIOUS (R 87)	5.4.39	31,630t	Sold 23.11.56
VICTORIOUS (R 38)	14.9.39	31,630t	Reconstructed (see notes)
FORMIDABLE (R 67)	17.8.39	31,630t	Sold 11.11.53
Modified Illustrious class			
INDOMITABLE (R 92)	26.3.40	29,730t	Sold 1955
Implacable class			
IMPLACABLE (R 86)	10.12.42	32,110t	BU 1955
INDEFATIGABLE (R 10)	8.12.42	32,800t	BU 1956
Unicorn			
UNICORN (R 72)	20.11.41	20,300t	BU 1959
Colossus class			
GLORY (R 62)	27.11.43	18,040t	BU 1961
OCEAN (R 68)	8.7.44	18,040t	BU 1962
VENERABLE (R 81)	30.12.43	18,040t	To Holland 1948
VENGEANCE (R 71)	23.2.44	18,040t	To Brazil 1956
THESEUS (R 64)	6.7.44	18,300t	BU 1962
TRIUMPH (R 16)	2.10.44	18,300t	Repair ship 1964
WARRIOR (ex-*Brave*) (R 31)	20.5.44	18,300t	To Argentina 1958
Perseus class			
PERSEUS (ex-*Edgar*) (R 51)	26.3.44	16,475t	BU 1958
PIONEER (ex-*Mars*) (R 76)	20.5.44	16,475t	BU 1954
Majestic class			
MAGNIFICENT (R 36)	16.11.44	19,550t	To Canada 1948
TERRIBLE (R 93)	30.9.44	19,550t	To Australia 1948
POWERFUL (R 95)	27.2.45	20,000t	To Canada 1952
MAJESTIC (R 77)	28.2.45	20,000t	To Australia 1949
HERCULES (R 49)	22.9.45	19,500t	To India 1957
LEVIATHAN (R 97)	7.6.45	17,780t	BU incomplete 1968

Illustrious class
All three ships had seen strenuous war duties and only *Victorious* was still serviceable. *Formidable* had suffered severe damage off Okinawa and was laid up on her return from trooping in 1947, while *Illustrious* had been in hand for repairs and a major overhaul since June 1945. When she recommissioned in mid-1946 she had a more powerful catapult and 30 per cent more aviation fuel, and the forward and after ends of her flight deck had been remodelled to extend its area. She then served for eight years as the trials and training carrier for the Home Fleet, occasionally embarking front-line squadrons for exercises. During this time she launched and landed the first jet aircraft, a modified Vampire. The armament of *Illustrious* was altered in 1946, the single 20mm guns being replaced by 21–40mm single Bofors, although the six 8-barrelled pompoms were retained.

Indomitable 1953 CPL

UNITED KINGDOM

In 1949 plans were drawn up for a full modernisation of *Formidable*, including an angled deck, but a survey revealed that her hull had suffered extensive strain and in 1950 she was towed to the Motherbank and lay there derelict until sold in 1953.

Victorious returned to the United Kingdom from Australia in October 1945, but two months later, after a short refit, she returned to the Far East to begin repatriation of British troops. When this was over in January 1947 she was paid off into reserve because of the rapid demobilisation of 'hostilities only' ratings, but recommissioned in October the same year. Until March 1950 she served as the Home Fleet training carrier, based at Portland, and was then paid off for modernisation. For details of this see under Major Surface Ships.

Modified Illustrious class
Indomitable returned to the United Kingdom in November 1945, having landed her aircraft to make room for repatriated personnel, and made two more trooping runs in 1946. From 1947 to 1950 she was refitted to the same standard as *Illustrious* and joined the Home Fleet for a three-year commission. During this period her close-range armament consisted of 40–2pdr pompoms (5×8), 24–40mm Bofors (24×1) and 4–3pdr saluting guns. Aircraft embarked included Fireflies, Sea Furies, Sea Hornets, Firebrands and the first ASR helicopters. In October 1953 she was reduced to reserve and laid up in the Clyde until October 1955 before being sold for scrapping.

Implacable class
Implacable served with the British Pacific Fleet (BPF) after the war's end and did not leave for the UK until April 1946. On her arrival in June she immediately recommissioned in the Home Fleet for deck-landing trials. Late in 1947 her air group was allocated, but teething troubles meant that she did not finally embark her 13 Sea Hornets and 12 Firebrands until March 1949. In the autumn of that year she embarked four Sea Vampires of the Jet Fighter Evaluation Unit and the following summer she operated 12 Barracudas in the ASW role, but only three months later, in Spetember 1950, she was paid off into reserve. After service from 1952 to 1954 as a training carrier she was sold for scrapping in 1955, having given only eight years of active service.

Indefatigable repatriated Allied ex-prisoners from Japan and then re-embarked her air group for a cruise to New Zealand. She left Sydney at the end of January 1946 for the UK, but made a trip to the Far East to repatriate troops before paying off into reserve. From 1950 she served as a training carrier, with the hangars converted to classrooms and messdecks, and with *Implacable* paid off for the last time in August 1954, being sold for scrapping in 1956. Although completed late in the war, neither she nor her sister were suitable for operating the new generation of large aircraft because of their lack of hangar height. As with *Victorious*, they could have been stripped to the hangar deck and reconstructed, but cost and time stifled the programme. As with earlier carriers the close-range AA armament was reduced in 1946, and as training carriers all 8-barrelled pompoms were removed as well. *Indefatigable* had a conspicuous box structure built at the after end of the flight deck and had the large D/F top removed from her foremast.

Unicorn
On her return from the Far East in January 1946, *Unicorn* was immediately put into reserve, but she recommissioned in the summer of 1949 to carry aircraft and spares for *Triumph* in the Fast East. After the outbreak of war in Korea in June 1950 her commission was extended, and she did not return to Devonport until November 1953. Shortly before her departure she bombarded land targets in North Korea with her 4in guns, a rare event for a carrier. Despite her short service life of only seven years she did not recommission again and was sold for scrapping in 1959. In June 1953 she had been re-rated as a ferry carrier.

Colossus class
Apart from the name-ship, which had been transferred to France as *Arromanches* in 1946, *Venerable* was sold to the Royal Netherlands Navy on 1 April 1948, replacing the escort carrier *Nairana* and taking the same name; *Karel Doorman*; *Warrior* had been lent to the Royal Canadian Navy on completion in 1946, but she was returned in 1948 when *Magnificent* was ready, and was recommissioned in the RN; and in 1952 *Vengeance* was lent to the Royal Australian Navy, pending completion of *Melbourne*.

Glory, Ocean, Theseus and *Triumph* served with great distinction in the Korean War in 1950–53, proving that they were among the most successful utility carrier designs ever built, but they were rapidly made obsolescent by the new generation of jet aircraft coming into service at the end of the 1950s. *Glory, Ocean* and *Theseus* were all scrapped 1961–62, *Vengeance* having already been sold to Brazil in 1957 and renamed *Minas Gerais*.

On her return from the RCN in 1948, *Warrior* was used for deck-landing trials and in 1948–49 she was fitted with a flexible landing deck to allow jet fighters fitted with a skid undercarriage to make 'soft' landings. This flexible deck consisted of a rubber sheet supported on air bags and extended from abaft the island to within 150ft of the stern. Abaft this 'carpet' the flight deck was built up to the same level with a light steel ramp rising to 2ft 6in high, with a single arrester wire. In 1952–53 the ship was modernised with a new enlarged bridge and a lattice foremast, and two years after that she was again refitted with a partial angle deck and stronger arrester gear to allow her to continue trials with the latest aircraft. Her ten arrester wires could stop a 15,500lb aircraft landing at 60kts and the single catapult could launch a 20,000lb aircraft at the same speed (she had originally been designed to take 14,000lb aircraft). She acted as HQ ship for the nuclear test programme at Christmas Island in the Pacific from February to October 1957 and on her return was offered for sale to Argentina. The deal was concluded in July 1958 and she sailed for Argentina three months

later, to be renamed *Independencia* at Puerto Belgrano. In RN service she had been armed with four twin 40mm Bofors and 20 singles, but these were reduced and when she entered Argentine service she had only eight single 40mm. With all the modifications her full load tonnage had risen to 19,600t and speed had dropped to 23kts.

After her return from Korea in 1953, *Triumph* was employed as a training ship for officer cadets, but under the 1956–57 Estimates funds were allocated to convert her to a heavy repair ship. This involved filling the hangar with machinery and workshops to enable her to carry out major maintenance work for escorts and helicopters on foreign stations, without the assistance of a naval dockyard. It was not a priority job, and with numerous delays the work finally cost £10.2 million and lasted seven years. She was laid up at Chatham in a high state of preservation, ready to provide emergency repair facilities if needed, but was stripped for disposal in 1981.

Perseus class
Laid down and launched as light fleet carriers of the *Colossus* class, these two ships were completed as aircraft maintenance ships in the light of Pacific Fleet requirements. This involved the provision of large-scale workshops and repair facilities for other carriers' aircraft. Unlike *Unicorn*, however, they could not operate aircraft as they had two heavy cranes and deckhouses on the flight deck. Armament consisted of 16–2pdr pompoms (4×4) and 2–20mm Oerlikons (2×1), but the latter were replaced by 40mm Bofors in 1946–47. Standard displacement was 26,265t and dimensions 633ft pp, 694ft 6in oa × 80ft 4in wl × 23ft max.

In 1950–51 *Perseus* was modified with a steel structure at the forward end of the flight deck carrying the prototype Mitchell steam catapult. These trials proved that the heaviest aircraft could now be launched, even when the carrier was not under way, by using steam from the ship's own boilers. Both ships were re-rated as Ferry Carriers in June 1953 together with *Unicorn*, but *Pioneer* was sold for scrapping the following year. *Perseus* remained in reserve for another four years before she too was scrapped.

Majestic class
Work on all six of this class was stopped after the end of hostilities, but when the Australian and Canadian Navies expressed interest in acquiring two, work restarted on *Terrible* and *Magnificent*. These were handed over in 1948 without modification of the original design, and the following year work also started on *Majestic* for the Australians, but to a greatly modified design. Then in 1952 the Canadians bought *Powerful* and she too underwent major reconstruction. Finally in 1957 the Indian Navy bought *Hercules*, leaving only *Leviathan* which was progressively cannibalised to provide spares for her sisters (for example her boilers were removed and sold to the Dutch to refit *Karel Doorman*).

For further details of transferred *Colossus* and *Majestic* class carriers, see under the recipient navy.

Campania
Sole survivor of three largely similar fast refrigerated cargo ships converted to escort carriers in 1942–44, she was the first British CVE to have an Action Information Organisation (AIO) and Type 277 height-finding radar. After a period in reserve she recommissioned as a ferry carrier and special transport, but was lent out for the Festival of Britain in 1951 and refitted by Cammell Laird. As a special exhibition ship she visited ports in the UK and Europe, her 515ft × 71ft hangar filled with exhibits and displays. She was returned to the Admiralty and after another short period in reserve recommissioned as a transport to take scientists and observers out to the Monte Bello Islands for the first British nuclear tests in 1952. On her return in December 1952 she was laid up and then sold for scrapping.

As a ferry carrier she could carry 90 aircraft. Her original armament was replaced by two twin Mk 5 Bofors mountings forward and two single Bofors aft, sponsored to port and starboard.

CRUISERS

Name	Launched	Disp (deep load)	Fate
Kent class			
CUMBERLAND (C 57)	16.3.26	13,540t	BU 1959
London class			
LONDON (C 69)	14.9.27	14,580t	BU 1954
DEVONSHIRE (C 39)	22.10.27	14,300t	
Norfolk class			
NORFOLK (C 78)	12.12.28	14,600t	BU 1950
Leander class			
ACHILLES (C 70)	1.9.32	9740t	To India 1948
Arethusa class			
AURORA (C 12)	20.8.36	7400t	To China 1948
Southampton class			
BIRMINGHAM (C 19)	1.9.36	12,190t	BU 1960
GLASGOW (C 21)	20.6.36	12,190t	BU 1958
NEWCASTLE (C 76)	23.1.36	12,190t	BU 1959
SHEFFIELD (C 24)	23.7.36	12,190t	BU 1967
Gloucester class			
LIVERPOOL (C 11)	24.3.37	12,330t	BU 1958
Edinburgh class			
BELFAST (C 35)	17.3.38	14,900t	Preserved 1971

Cumberland as trials ship 1958
CPL

Name	Launched	Disp (deep load)	Fate
Dido class			
ARGONAUT (C 61)	6.9.41	7515t	BU 1955
CLEOPATRA (C 33)	27.3.40	7515t	BU 1958
DIDO (C 37)	18.7.39	7515t	BU 1958
EURYALUS (C 42)	6.6.39	7515t	BU 1959
PHOEBE (C 43)	25.3.39	7515t	BU 1956
SIRIUS (C 82)	18.9.40	7515t	BU 1956
Fiji class			
BERMUDA (C 52)	11.9.41	11,090t	BU 1965
CEYLON (C 30)	30.7.42	11,090t	To Peru 1959
GAMBIA (C 48)	30.11.40	11,090	BU 1968
JAMAICA (C 44)	16.11.40	11,090t	BU 1960
KENYA (C 14)	18.8.39	11,090t	BU 1962
MAURITIUS (C 80)	19.7.39	11,090t	BU 1965
NEWFOUNDLAND (C 59)	19.12.41	11,125t	To Peru 1959
NIGERIA (C 60)	18.7.39	11,040t	To India 1957
Bellona class			
DIADEM (C 84)	26.8.42	7560t	To Pakistan 1956
ROYALIST (C 89)	30.5.42	7360t	To New Zealand 1954
Swiftsure class			
SWIFTSURE (C 08)	4.2.43	11,240t	BU 1962
Superb class			
SUPERB (C 25)	31.8.43	11,546t	BU 1960

Kent class
Cumberland was converted to a trials ship in 1949–51, with lattice masts, new directors and added accommodation. The original armament was entirely removed, but individual light weapons were added from time to time for trials. At first she carried one, then two single 4.5in Mk 4 guns and two STAAG 40mm Bofors mountings on the starboard side with a 'Battle' class Mk 37 director on the starboard bridge wing, but these were later removed. From 1953 she carried first the twin 3in/70 Mk 6 aft with an MRS3 director on the bridge and then the 6in Mk 26 twin automatic turret on 'B' barbette. At the end of the 1958 trials programme, which tested a new stabiliser design and the first pre-welling NR propellers, she was finally reduced to reserve and was sold the following year.

London class
London served in the Far East in 1947–49 and was damaged by Chinese shore batteries while trying to rescue the sloop *Amethyst* in 1949. The 20mm guns had been removed in 1945, but little else was done to alter her. *Devonshire* was rebuilt as a cadet TS in 1946–47, with only 'A' turret and the secondary battery retained. This was altered to two twin 4in AA mountings (port and starboard amidships), a quadruple 2pdr pompom, a single 40mm Bofors, three 20mm and four saluting guns. The original machinery remained unchanged, but only four boilers were used, giving a speed of 21kts max. In April 1947 she recommissioned as a sea-going training cruiser for officer cadets and finally paid off at the end of 1953.

Norfolk class
Norfolk became flagship of the East Indies Squadron postwar, but returned home to pay off in 1949.

Leander class
Achilles was bought by the newly independent Indian Navy and renamed INS *Delhi*. She was handed over on 5 July 1948, her sisters *Ajax* and *Leander* having been offered as well, but rejected on grounds of cost and lack of manpower.

Arethusa class
Aurora was transferred to China in 1948 and was renamed *Chungking*, but a year later she defected to the Communists. Renamed *Huang Ho* and finally (allegedly) *Pei Ching*, she was reported to have been sunk by bombing in Taku by Nationalist aircraft, but was then salved and recommissioned by late 1951. By the mid-1950s she was reported to be laid up as a hulk, and it is most unlikely that she ever again became operational.

Southampton class
In 1950–52 *Birmingham* and *Newcastle* were modernised, with new bridge-work, a lattice foremast and air conditioning to suit them for service in the Far East. To control the 4in AA they were given two Mk 6 high-angle directors at the corners of the former aircraft hangar. *Sheffield* was similarly modernised in 1956–57, but *Glasgow* remained very much as she had finished the war. All four ships were actively employed in the postwar fleet, but were considered to be too old to justify any major modernisation.

Gloucester class
Liverpool served for a few years in the Mediterranean, but never received any modernisation.

Edinburgh class
Belfast recommissioned for the Korean War and was then scheduled to receive full modernisation in 1955–56. This would have involved upright funnels, a new large bridge and a new secondary armament of Mk 11 40mm/77 Bofors guns, but it had to be shelved because of a lack of manpower at Portsmouth Dockyard. However, the ship was given a partial modernisation in 1956–59 during which she received a new *Tiger*-style bridge. Her secondary armament was unaltered, but the close-range AA was changed to six twin 40mm Mk 5 Bofors mountings, with directors (MRS8, externally similar to CRBF) controlling them in four groups. Although the original raked funnels remained, two upright lattice masts replaced the tripods, giving her an ungainly profile.

In 1963 the forward pair of 40mm mountings was removed, but very few other changes had been made by the time the ship was paid off. In that year she became flagship of the Reserve Fleet at Portsmouth and in 1971 was acquired by a charitable trust for conversion to a museum. She now lies in the River Thames below London Bridge.

Dido class
Although modern, these ships were regarded as too cramped and insufficiently stable to receive new equipment, and therefore the majority were used for a few years and then scrapped. *Dido* and *Sirius* retained the fifth 5.25in turret in 'Q' position, and *Phoebe* and *Cleopatra* had US-pattern quadruple 40mm Bofors mountings in 'Q' position and in the waist. *Phoebe* was the first to be scrapped, partly as a result of damage suffered in a collision in the Mediterranean and partly due to her very poor condition.

Fiji class
The main complaints against these ships were that their accommodation was very cramped (hence there was no space for additional equipment) and that their side armour was thin, but in spite of this several served on foreign stations as flagships. *Nigeria* was the only one to retain 'X' triple 6in turret after the war, but it was removed when she was bought by India in 1954. The survivors were all variously modified, some with covered bridges and others with new CRBF directors for their 4in guns, but only *Ceylon* and *Newfoundland* received a modernisation on the lines of that given to the *Southamptons* and to *Mysore* (the renamed *Nigeria*). *Newfoundland* was modernised at Devonport in 1955–56 with two lattice masts and Mk 6 high-angle directors, but *Ceylon* had only a lattice foremast and CRBF directors. Both were sold to Peru, *Newfoundland* becoming *Almirante Grau* on 30 December 1959 and her sister became *Coronel Bolognesi* on 9 February 1960.

UNITED KINGDOM

Bellona class
In 1954 *Royalist* was taken in hand for modernisation, and when at the end of 1955 *Bellona* returned to the UK her crew transferred to *Royalist* to take her back to New Zealand. The only other member of the class to be modernised was *Diadem*, which had a fairly extensive refit (new bridge, lattice masts) at Portsmouth in 1956–57 before being sold to Pakistan as *Babur*.

Swiftsure
Shortly after the war the Admiralty gave serious consideration to the problem of what to do with their latest cruisers. *Swiftsure*, *Ceylon* and *Newfoundland*, it was hoped, could have their triple 6in Mk 23 turrets replaced by two twin automatic 6in Mk 26 mountings, and their 4in Mk 19 mountings replaced by three twin 3in Mk 6. Lack of money and the slow production of new radars and gun mountings made the scheme a poor starter, but at the end of 1953 it was still hoped to begin *Swiftsure*'s modernisation in January 1956. Her refit started in February 1957 at Chatham, but in August 1959, with her new bridge structure and lattice masts in position, all work was halted; it was costing far too much to produce an obsolete ship.

Superb
Superb was under consideration for a similar modernisation to *Swiftsure*, bringing her up to *Tiger* standard. Work has to have begun in April 1957, but this was never done, leaving her erstwhile sisters to be completed to a radically different design (see Major Surface Ships).

CRUISER-MINELAYERS

Name	Launched	Disp (deep load)	Fate
Abdiel class			
MANXMAN (N 70)	5.9.40	4000t	BU 1971
Apollo class			
APOLLO (N 01)	5.4.43	4000t	BU 1962
ARIADNE (N 65)	16.2.43	4000t	BU 1964

Abdiel class
Manxman served in the postwar fleet, but principally as a flagship in the late 1940s and early 1950s. In 1955 she had the after twin 4in replaced by an extended deckhouse. In 1962–63 she was converted at Chatham to a parent ship for coastal minesweepers. To enable her to maintain and repair up to 16 minesweepers the capacious mine deck was converted to storerooms and offices. Half the boilers were removed, allowing the forward boiler room to be converted to accommodate extra generators and evaporators. The forward funnel was retained to carry ventilator trunking and the diesel exhausts. Her armament was reduced to 6–40mm Bofors, one twin Mk 5 on the centreline abaft the mainmast and four single Mk 7s sided amidships. On her return from her last commission in the Far East in 1968 she was used for a short while for sea training of engineer officers.

Apollo class
Like *Manxman*, *Apollo* was used for several years as a flagship, but in 1954 the after deckhouse was raised by one deck and so she retained the after twin 4in gun. *Ariadne* was laid up at Sheerness in 1946 and never recommissioned.

DESTROYERS

Name	Fate	Name	Fate
Napier class: launched 1940–41, 2540–2555t deep load			
NAPIER (D 297)	BU 1956	NOBLE (ex-*Piorun*, ex-*Nerissa*) (D 165)	BU 1955
NEPAL (D 125)	BU 1956	NORMAN (D 149)	BU 1958
NIZAM (D 38)	BU 1955		
Milne class: launched 1940–41, 2810–2840t deep load			
MARNE (D 135)	To Turkey 1959	MILNE (D 58)	To Turkey 1959
MATCHLESS (D 252)	To Turkey 1959	MUSKETEER (D 186)	BU 1955
METEOR (D 273)	To Turkey 1959		
Onslow and Pakenham classes: launched 1941–42, 2365–2430t deep load			
OBDURATE (D 139)	BU 1964	OPPORTUNE (D 180)	BU 1955
OBEDIENT (D 248)	BU 1962	ORWELL	Type 16 (see notes)
OFFA (D 29)	To Pakistan 1959	PALADIN	Type 16
ONSLAUGHT (D 04)	To Pakistan 1951	PETARD	Type 16
ONSLOW (D 17)	To Pakistan 1949		
Quilliam and Rotherham classes: launched 1941–42, 2425–2480t deep load			
RAIDER (D 15)	To India 1949	RELENTLESS	Type 15
REDOUBT (D 141)	To India 1949	ROCKET	Type 15
ROTHERHAM (D 209)	To India 1949	ROEBUCK	Type 15

Name	Fate	Name	Fate
RAPID	Type 15 (see notes)		
Saumarez, Troubridge, Grenville, Valentine and Kempenfelt classes: launched 1942–43, 2505–2545t deep load			
SAUMAREZ (D 12)	BU 1950	URCHIN	Type 15
SAVAGE (D 27)	BU 1962	URSA	Type 15
TROUBRIDGE	Type 15	VENUS	Type 15
TEAZER	Type 16	VERULAM	Type 15
TENACIOUS	Type 16	VIGILANT	Type 15
TERMAGANT	Type 16	VIRAGO	Type 15
TERPSICHORE	Type 16	VOLAGE	Type 15
TUMULT	Type 16	KEMPENFELT (ex-*Valentine*) (D 103)	To Yugoslavia 1956
TUSCAN	Type 16	WAGER (D 298)	To Yugoslavia 1956
TYRIAN	Type 16	WAKEFUL (ex-*Zebra*)	Type 15
GRENVILLE	Type 15	WESSEX (ex-*Zenith*)	To South Africa 1950
ULSTER	Type 15	WHELP (D 237)	To South Africa 1953
ULYSSES	Type 15	WHIRLWIND	Type 15
UNDAUNTED	Type 15	WIZARD	Type 15
UNDINE	Type 15	WRANGLER	Type 15
URANIA	Type 15		
Myngs and Cavendish classes: launched 1943–44, 2510–2575t deep load			
MYNGS (D 06)	To Egypt 1955	CAVENDISH (ex-*Sibyl*)	Modernised (see notes)
ZAMBESI (D 66)	BU 1959	CAESAR (ex-*Ranger*)	Modernised
ZEALOUS (D 39)	To Israel 1955	CAMBRIAN (ex-*Spitfire*)	Modernised
ZEBRA (ex-*Wakeful*) (D 81)	BU 1959	CAPRICE (ex-*Swallow*)	Modernised
ZENITH (ex-*Wessex*) (D 95)	To Egypt 1955	CARRON (ex-*Strenuous*)	Modernised
ZEPHYR (D 19)	BU 1958	CARYSFORT (ex-*Pique*)	Modernised
ZEST	Type 15	CASSANDRA (ex-*Tourmaline*)	Modernised
ZODIAC (D 54)	To Israel 1955	CAVALIER (ex-*Pellew*)	Modernised
Childers, Cossack and Cromwell classes: launched 1944–45, 2510–2535t deep load			
CHAPLET (D 52)	BU 1965	COMET (D 26)	BU 1962
CHARITY (D 29)	to Pakistan 1958	COMUS (D 20)	BU 1958
CHEQUERS (ex-*Champion*) (D 61)	BU 1966	CONCORD (ex-*Corso*) (D 03)	BU 1962
CHEVIOT (D 90)	BU 1962	CONSORT (D 76)	BU 1961
CHEVRON (D 51)	BU 1969	CONSTANCE (D 71)	BU 1956
CHIEFTAIN (D 36)	BU 1961	CONTEST (D 48)	BU 1960
CHILDERS (D 91)	BU 1963	COSSACK (D 57)	BU 1961
CHIVALROUS (D 21)	To Pakistan 1954	CREOLE (D 82)	to Pakistan 1958
COCKADE (D 34)	BU 1964	CRISPIN (ex-*Craccher*) (D 168)	To Pakistan 1958
'Battle' class (1st group): launched 1943–45, 3290–3300t deep load			
ARMADA (D 14)	BU 1965	LAGOS (D 44)	BU 1967
BARFLEUR (D 80)	BU 1966	ST JAMES (D 65)	BU 1961
CADIZ (D 79)	To Pakistan 1957	ST KITTS (D 18)	BU 1962
CAMPERDOWN (D 32)	BU 1970	SAINTES (D 84)	BU 1972
FINISTERRE (D 55)	BU 1967	SLUYS (D 60)	To Iran 1966
GABBARD (D 49)	To Pakistan 1957	SOLEBAY (D 70)	BU 1967
GRAVELINES (D 24)	BU 1961	TRAFALGAR (D 77)	BU 1970
HOGUE (D 74)	BU 1962	VIGO (D 231)	BU 1964
'Battle' class (2nd group): launched 1945–46, 3400–3420t deep load			
AGINCOURT	Radar-picket (see notes)	CORUNNA	Radar-picket
AISNE	Radar-picket	DUNKIRK (D 09)	BU 1965
ALAMEIN (D 17)	BU 1964	JUTLAND (ex-*Malplaquet*) (D 62)	BU 1965
BARROSA	Radar-picket	MATAPAN (D 43)	BU 1978
'Weapon' class: launched 1945–46, 2825t deep load			
BATTLEAXE	Radar-picket	CROSSBOW	Radar-picket
BROADSWORD	Radar-picket (see notes)	SCORPION (ex-*Tomahawk*, ex-*Centaur*)	Radar-picket

Napier class
All except *Nepal* had a lattice foremast by 1945 and were laid up in 1945–46. *Nepal* carried out sweeping trials from 1949 and was fitted with twin davits and a big sweep winch on the quarterdeck. All five vessels were considered for Type 16 or 18 frigate conversions (see below), but they were not worth the cost as they were more than half way through their hull-lives.

Milne class
All were laid up in 1946, but in 1951 *Musketeer* had a short refit to become an accommodation ship for coastal forces at Harwich. The remaining four were modernised and sold to Turkey: *Marne, Matchless, Meteor* and *Milne* became *Maresal Fevzi Cakmak, Kilic Ali Pasa, Piyale Pasa* and *Alp Arslan*. They had been under consideration for conversion to Type 62 aircraft direction frigates.

Onslow and Pakenham classes
Obedient and *Obdurate* retained their minelaying capability postwar. *Orwell, Paladin* and *Petard* were converted to Type 16 frigates in 1951–56 (see under Major Surface Ships). *Offa, Onslow* and *Onslaught* became the Pakistani *Tariq, Tippu Sultan* and *Tughril*.

Rotherham class
Apart from three sold to India, the remainder of the class were converted to frigates in 1949–53 (see under Major Surface Ships). *Raider, Rotherham* and *Redoubt* became the Indian *Rana, Rajput* and *Ranjit*.

Saumarez, Troubridge, Grenville, Valentine and Kempenfelt classes
Saumarez and *Volage* were mined by Albanian pirates in the Corfu channel in October 1946; the former was so badly damaged that she was laid up and scrapped four years later, but the latter had her bow rebuilt and rejoined the Mediterranean Fleet. There was a proposal to weld the wrecks together as HMS *Sausage*! Postwar, *Savage* was used for trials of propellers and shafts; these trials and those conducted later with *Teazer*, together with the associated R&D, gave the RN a 10-year lead in the design of quiet propellers. *Savage* was laid up in 1952 and although considered for conversion to a frigate she was put on the disposal list in 1958 and sold in 1962. *Wessex* and *Whelp* were sold to South Africa in 1950–53 and *Kempenfelt* and *Wager* to Yugoslavia in 1956; the remainder were converted to frigates between 1950 and 1956 (see under Major Surface Ships).

Myngs and Cavendish classes
Both classes were laid up shortly after the war, but from 1957 the *Cavendish* class received a major modernisation (see under Major Surface Ships). In 1955 four of the *Myngs* class were sold to Egypt and Israel; one of the survivors became a frigate and the others were scrapped. *Myngs* and *Zenith* became the Egyptian *El Fateh* and *El Qaher*, while *Zealous* and *Zodiac* became the Israeli *Elath* and *Yaffo*.

Childers, Cossack and Cromwell classes
Creole and *Crispin* had a prominent W/T cabin in place of 'B' gun, but the majority were refitted for ASW with 'Y' gun replaced by two Squid mortars and a handing room at the after end of the deckhouse. Light AA was modernised in all of them, a typical fit being a twin 40mm Mk 5 amidships, two single Mk 7s in the bridge wings and two more abaft the funnel. They retained the Mk 6 fire control and did not receive the same degree of modernisation as the *Cavendish* group. In 1954 *Charity* and *Chivalrous* were lent to Pakistan, followed by *Creole* and *Crispin* four years later. The rest of the class saw considerable service in home waters and on foreign stations in the late 1940s and 1950s. *Charity, Chivalrous, Creole* and *Crispin* became the Pakistani *Shah Jehan, Taimur, Alamgir* and *Jahangir*.

'Battle' class (1st group)
All ships fitted with the 4in starshell gun in 'Q' position had it replaced by two single 40mm AA guns, and the 40mm Mk 4 Hazemeyer twins were replaced by two STAAG Mk 2 mountings aft. In 1947 *Saintes* had her 4.5in Mk 4 BD mounting replaced temporarily by the Mk 6 twin, the prototype for the *Daring* class. In all ships the single 40mm on the quarterdeck was replaced by a Squid mortar on the starboard side. In the early 1960s the STAAGs were replaced by twin Mk 5s in *Camperdown* and *Saintes*. All the class were actively employed in the post-war fleet. *Finisterre* (and later *Vigo*) was used as a gunnery firing and training ship and had a square deckhouse added on the platform between the torpedo-tubes. In 1956 *Cadiz* and *Gabbard* were sold to Pakistan, becoming *Khaibar* and *Badr*, and in 1966 *Sluys* was sold to Iran, being renamed *Artemiz*. In 1959 *Hogue* was badly damaged in collision with the Indian cruiser *Mysore* off Ceylon. She was laid up disarmed at Singapore until 1961. The remainder were scrapped without receiving any further modernisation.

'Battle' class (2nd group)
Four were selected for conversion to radar-pickets in 1960–62 (see under Major Surface Ships) and *Alamein, Dunkirk* and *Jutland* were scrapped. *Matapan* was laid up immediately after completing trials in September 1947 and never commissioned until 1971, when she was taken in hand for a two-year conversion to a sonar trials ship.

'Weapon' class
All four ships served with the Fleet from 1948. In the mid-1950s *Scorpion* had her Squid mortars replaced by a single Limbo mortar of greater range and wider training arcs. She also had an experimental shield fitted to 'A' gun, but this was subsequently removed. In 1958–59 all four were converted to radar-pickets (see under Major Surface Ships).

Ex-GERMAN DESTROYERS
The *Leberecht Maass* class ships *H 97* (ex-*Richard Beitzen*) and *R 38* (ex-*Hans Lody*), and the *Z 23* class *Z 30* were all evaluated and cannibalised for technical information. *Z 30* was in very poor condition and was sent to Rosyth for structural experiments in February 1946; she arrived at Troon for scrapping in September 1948. *R 38* was renumbered *H 40* to release the pennant number for HMS *Crystal* in February 1946. She was used as an accommodation ship at Woolston from October 1946 until January 1949. *H 97* had to be beached after her bottom plating corroded, and she was put on the disposal list in January 1947. *Z 38*, later *Nonsuch*, was used for trials on the Clyde in 1945, then laid up at Portchester until renamed early in 1947. She recommissioned after repairs in September 1948 and was used for trials until November 1949.

SUBMARINES

Name	Fate	Name	Fate
'T' class (2nd group): launched 1942–44, 1327t/1575t			
TRESPASSER (S 12)	BU 1961	TAPIR (S 35)	To Netherlands 1948, streamlined (see notes)
TACTICIAN (S 14)	BU 1963	TAURUS (S 39)	To Netherlands 1948
'T' class (3rd group): launched 1942, 1327t/1575t			
TEMPLAR	BU 1960	TALLY HO (S 87)	BU 1967
TRUCULENT	Sunk in collision 12.1.50		
'T' class (4th group): launched 1942–43, 1319t/1571t			
THULE (S 25)	BU 1962	TOKEN	Streamlined
TUDOR (S 126)	BU 1963	TRADEWIND (S 29)	BU 1955
TIRELESS	Streamlined	TRENCHANT (S 31)	BU 1963
'T' class (5th group): launched 1943, 1319t/1571t			
TELEMACHUS (S 21)	BU 1961	THOROUGH (S 24)	BU 1961
'T' class (6th group): launched 1944–45, 1319t/1571t			
TIPTOE	Converted (see notes)	TALENT (ex-*Tasman*)	Streamlined
TRUMP	Converted	TEREDO	Streamlined
TACITURN	Converted	TABARD	Converted
'T' class (8th group): launched 1943–45, 1319t/1571t			
TOTEM	Converted	TURPIN	Converted
TRUNCHEON	Converted	THERMOPYLAE	Converted
'S' class (3rd group): launched 1941–45, 814–842t/990t			
SATYR (S 84)	To France 1952	SEA SCOUT (S 153)	BU 1965
SERAPH (S 89)	BU 1965	SELENE (S 154)	BU 1960
		SENESCHAL (S 75)	BU 1960
SIRDAR (S 76)	BU 1965	SENTINEL (S 56)	BU 1962
SPITEFUL	To France 1952	SAGA	To Portugal 1949
SPORTSMAN	To France 1951	SCORCHER (S 58)	BU 1962
STOIC	BU 1950	SIDON (S 59)	Sunk 16.6.59
SCYTHIAN (S 137)	BU 1960	SLEUTH (S 61)	BU 1958
SCOTSMAN (S 143)	BU 1964	SOLENT (S 62)	BU 1962
SEA DEVIL (S 44)	BU 1965	SPEARHEAD	To Portugal 1949
STATESMAN (S 46)	To France 1952	SPRINGER (S 64)	To Israel 1958
STURDY (S 48)	BU 1958	SPUR	To Portugal 1948
SUBTLE (S 51)	BU 1959	SANGUINE (S 66)	To Israel 1958
'U' class (2nd group): launched 1942–43, 646t/732t			
UNTIRING (ex-*Xifias*, ex-*P 59*)	BU 1957	UPSTART (ex-*Amfitriti*, ex-*Upstart*, ex-*P 65*)	Sunk as target 1957
Acheron class: launched 1944–47, 1385t/1620t			
ACHERON	Modernised (see notes)	ANDREW	Modernised
ALCIDE	Modernised	AUROCHS (S 26)	BU 1967
ALDERNEY	Modernised	AENEAS	Modernised
ALLIANCE	Modernised	AMPHION (ex-*Anchorite*)	Modernised
AMBUSH	Modernised	ALARIC	Modernised
AURIGA	Modernised	ASTUTE	Modernised
AFFRAY (S 20)	Sunk 16.4.51	ARTEMIS	Modernised
ANCHORITE (ex-*Amphion*)	Modernised	ARTFUL	Modernised
XE 1 class: launched 1942–45, 30.3t/33.6t			
XE 1	BU 1952	XE 9	BU 1952
XE 8	BU 1952	XE 12	BU 1952

UNITED KINGDOM

From 1951 a series of improvements was put in hand. Those with riveted hulls were limited in diving depth, and got the 'T' class 'Streamlined' conversion; this involved fitting new batteries, streamlining the conning tower into a new 'fin', and reshaping the bow casing to give higher speed. Both these boats and the unmodernised ones had the 'snort' (snorkel) mounted on the port side, hinged at deck level. The 20mm gun was removed from all, but several retained their 4in guns.

Tactician, *Telemachus* and *Thorough* were lent to the Royal Australian Navy in 1951 for ASW training, but remained under RN control. *Tapir* and *Taurus* became the Netherlands *Zeehund* and *Dolfijn* from June 1948 to June 1953 and then reverted to the RN; they were scrapped in 1966 and 1960 respectively. *Truculent* was run down by the Swedish tanker *Dvina* in the Thames Estuary on 12.1.50 and sank with heavy loss of life; she was salved two months later and scrapped.

The class differed widely in appearance, some retaining the deck gun and others having a streamlined fin and modified casing. The 6th group had welded hulls and so most underwent a full modernisation from 1951 (see under Submarines).

Seraph 1948   CPL

'S' class
This class was not scheduled for any major modernisation, but several boats underwent modification for trials. *Seraph* had light padding over her saddle tanks to protect her from practice torpedoes, while *Scotsman* was given a series of modifications, including the removal of her CT followed by a streamlined fin and casing to give her higher speed while carrying out sonar trials. Most had the deck gun removed, but the three sold to Portugal retained a 4in gun in a revolving shield, as in the early 'T' class.

The three Portuguese boats were transferred in 1948–49 and in 1951–52 four more were lent to France; Israel bought two in 1958. *Sidon* was lying alongside the depot ship *Maidstone* in Portland on 16.6.59 when a torpedo exploded and sank her. The cause was officially claimed to be a compressed air bottle, but many years later it was admitted that the real cause was high-test peroxide (HTP) in a Mk 12 'Fancy' torpedo.

Spur, *Saga* and *Spearhead* became the Portuguese *Narval*, *Nautilo* and *Neptune*; *Satyr*, *Spiteful*, *Sportsman* and *Statesman* became the French *Saphir*, *Sirène*, *Sibylle* and *Sultane* and *Sanguine* and *Springer* became the Israeli *Rahav* and *Tanin*.

'U' class
The rest of the class had all been disposed of, but in 1952 *Amfitriti* and *Xifias* were returned by the Royal Hellenic Navy and were reinstated in the RN under their original names. Both were used as bottom targets, one off Start Point and the other off the Isle of Wight.

Acheron class
As with the 'T' class all 20mm guns were removed shortly after the war and those boats with low bow casings had bow buoyancy tanks fitted. Subsequently the external bow tubes were blanked off. All except *Aurochs* underwent conversion from 1955 (see under Submarines).

XE class
No alteration was made to these midget submarines. *XE 9* was the last to be operational, being retained for training until the replacements came into service.

EX-GERMAN SUBMARINES
These comprised the Type VIIC: N 86 (ex-*U 249*), N 83 (ex-*U 1023*), N 65 (ex-*U 776*) and *U 953*; the Type VIIC/41–42: N 16 (ex-*U 1105*), N 19 (ex-*U 1171*) and *U 1108*; the Type XVIIB: *Meteorite* (ex-*N 25*, ex-*U 1407*); the Type XXI: N 41 (ex-*U 3017*) and *U 2518*; and the Type XXIII: *U 2348*. Most were 'cannibalised' to evaluate components, but the Type XXI and Type XVIIB

were run to evaluate their impact on ASW tactics and to gain experience for new designs. The fates of most are obscure, but it must be assumed that the majority were finally scuttled as bottom targets and then raised and scrapped c1948–49 (they disappear from the Navy List in 1948). *U 2518*) was given to France in 1947 and became the *Roland Morillot*.

Although the Type XXI was the most potent U-boat of all and the most influential on future designs, Allied scientists were fascinated by the possibilities of the Walter high-test peroxide turbine, in which an enriched oxidant called perhydrol was decomposed by a catalyst to produce steam and oxygen at 1765°F. This mixture was then burned with oil fuel at a lower temperature (986°F) to produce a gas which drove a conventional geared turbine. There were two drawbacks: the unpleasant nature of perhydrol, which is corrosive and unstable, and the limited range of only 114 miles.

Despite these drawbacks, the RN worked hard to get *Meteorite*, their Type XVIIB, going, but she was never regarded as more than '75 per cent safe'. She was commissioned as early as 25.9.45, but did not receive her name until 1947, presumably once she was running. She provided valuable experience for the *Explorer* class.

FRIGATES

Name	Fate	Name	Fate
'Hunt' class (Type 1): launched 1939–40, 1420–1450t deep load			
ATHERSTONE (F 05)	BU 1957	GARTH (F 120)	BU 1958
BLENCATHRA (F 24)	BU 1957	HAMBLEDON (F 137)	BU 1957
BROCKLESBY (F 142)	BU 1968	HOLDERNESS (F 148)	BU 1956
CATTISTOCK (F 135)	BU 1957	MENDIP (F 160)	To China 1948, to Egypt 1950
CLEVELAND (F 146)	Wrecked 28.6.57	MEYNELL (F 182)	To Ecuador 1954
COTSWOLD (F 154)	BU 1957	PYTCHLEY (F 192)	BU 1956
COTTESMORE (F 178)	To Egypt 1950	QUANTOCK (F 158)	To Ecuador 1954
EGLINTON (F 87)	BU 1956	SOUTHDOWN (F 25)	BU 1956
FERNIE (F 111)	BU 1956	WHADDON (F 145)	BU 1959
'Hunt' class (Type 2): launched 1940–42, 1580–1625t deep load			
AVON VALE (F 206)	BU 1958	FARNDALE (F 70)	BU 1962
BEAUFORT (F 14)	To Norway 1952	LAMERTON (F 88)	To India 1953
BEDALE (ex-*Slazak*, ex-*Bedale*) (F 126)	To India 1953	LEDBURY (F 190)	BU 1958
BICESTER (F 134)	BU 1956	MIDDLETON (F 174)	BU 1957
BLACKMORE (F 143)	To Denmark 1952	OAKLEY (ex-*Tickham*) (F 198)	To Germany 1958
BLANKNEY (F 130)	BU 1959	SILVERTON (ex-*Krakowiak*, ex-*Silverton*) (F 55)	BU 1959
CALPE (F 171)	To Denmark 1952	TETCOTT (F 199)	BU 1956
CHIDDINGFOLD (F 131)	To India 1953	WHEATLAND (F 22)	BU 1959
COWDRAY (F 152)	BU 1959	WILTON (F 128)	BU 1959
CROOME (F 162)	BU 1957	ZETLAND (F 59)	To Norway 1954
EXMOOR (ex-*Burton*) (F 08)	To Denmark 1953		
'Hunt' class (Type 3): launched 1941–43, 1545–1590t deep load			
ALBRIGHTON (F 112)	To Germany 1958	HAYDON (F 75)	BU 1958
BELVOIR (F 132)	BU 1957	MELBREAK (F 173)	BU 1956
BLEASDALE (F 150)	BU 1956	STEVENSTONE (F 16)	BU 1959
EASTON (F 109)	BU 1953	TALYBONT (F 118)	BU 1961
EGGESFORD (F 15)	To Germany 1958		
'Hunt' class (Type 4): launched 1942, 1700–1750t deep load			
BRECON (F 176)	BU 1962	BRISSENDEN (F 79)	BU 1965
Grimsby class: launched 1936, 1480–1510t deep load			
FLEETWOOD (F 47)	BU 1959		
Bittern class: launched 1936, 1790t deep load			
STORK (F 81)	BU 1958		
Egret class: launched 1938, 1790t deep load			
PELICAN (F 86)	BU 1958		
Black Swan class: launched 1939–42, 1770–1950t deep load			
BLACK SWAN (F 57)	BU 1956	WILD GOOSE (F 45)	BU 1956
ERNE (F 03)	BU 1965	WOODCOCK (F 90)	BU 1955
FLAMINGO (F 18)	To Germany 1959	WREN (F 28)	BU 1956
WHIMBREL	To Egypt 1949		

Name	Fate	Name	Fate

Modified Black Swan class: launched 1942–46, 1880–1950t deep load

Name	Fate	Name	Fate
ACTAEON (F 07)	To Germany 1958	MODESTE (F 42)	BU 1961
ALACRITY (F 60)	BU 1956	NEREIDE (F 64)	BU 1958
AMETHYST (F 116)	BU 1957	OPOSSUM (F 33)	BU 1960
CRANE (F 123)	BU 1965	PEACOCK (F 96)	BU 1958
CYGNET (F 38)	BU 1956	PHEASANT (F 49)	BU 1963
HART (F 58)	To Germany 1959	REDPOLE (F 69)	BU 1960
HIND (F 39)	BU 1958	SNIPE (F 20)	BU 1960
MAGPIE (F 82)	BU 1959	SPARROW (F 71)	BU 1958
MERMAID (F 30)	To Germany 1959	STARLING (F 66)	BU 1965

'Captain' class: launched 1943, 1823t deep load

HOTHAM (F 583)	BU 1956		

'River' class: launched 1941–43, 1920–2180t deep load

AVON (F 97)	To Portugal 1949	NITH (F 215)	To Egypt 1948
AWE (F 526)	To Portugal 1949	ODZANI (F 356)	BU 1957
BALLINDERRY (F 155)	BU 1961	PLYM (F 271)	Expended 3.10.52
CHELMER (F 221)	BU 1957	RIBBLE (ex-*Duddon*) (F 525)	BU 1957
DART (F 21)	BU 1957	ROTHER (F 224)	BU 1955
DERG (F 257)	BU 1960	SPEY (F 246)	To Egypt 1948
DOVEY (ex-*Lambourne*) (F 523)	BU 1955	SWALE (F 217)	BU 1955
ETTRICK (F 254)	BU 1953	TAFF (F 367)	BU 1957
EXE (F 92)	BU 1956	TAVY (F 272)	BU 1955
FAL (F 266)	To Burma 1948	TAY (F 232)	BU 1956
HALLADALE (F 417)	Sold 1949	TEES (F 293)	BU 1955
HELFORD (F 252)	BU 1956	TEST (ex-*RIN Neza*, ex-*Test*) (F 56)	BU 1955
HELMSDALE (F 253)	BU 1957	TEVIOT (F 222)	BU 1955
JED (F 235)	BU 1957	TOWY (F 294)	BU 1956
KALE (F 241)	BU 1957	USK (F 295)	To Egypt 1948
LOCHY (F 365)	BU 1956	WAVENEY (F 248)	BU 1957
MEON (L 369)	BU 1966	WEAR (F 230)	BU 1957
NENE (F 270)	BU 1955	WYE (F 371)	BU 1955
NESS (F 219)	BU 1956		

'Loch' class: launched 1943–45, 2260t deep load

LOCH ACHANALT (F 424)	To New Zealand 1948	LOCH KILLISPORT (F 628)	BU 1970
LOCH ACHRAY (F 426)	To New Zealand 1948	LOCH LOMOND (F 437)	BU 1968
LOCH ALVIE (F 428)	BU 1965	LOCH MORE (F 639)	BU 1963
LOCH ARKAIG (F 603)	BU 1960	LOCH MORLICH (F 517)	To New Zealand 1949
LOCH CRAGGIE (F 609)	BU 1963	LOCH QUOICH (F 434)	BU 1957
LOCH DUNVEGAN (F 425)	BU 1960	LOCH RUTHVEN (F 645)	BU 1966
LOCH ECK (F 422)	To New Zealand 1948	LOCH SCAVAIG (F 648)	BU 1959
LOCH FADA (F 390)	Sold 1968, but used for trials until 1976	LOCH SHIN (F 421)	To New Zealand 1948
LOCH FYNE (F 429)	BU 1970	LOCH TARBERT (F 431)	BU 1959
LOCH GLENDHU (F 619)	BU 1957	LOCH TRALAIG (F 655)	BU 1963
LOCH GORM (F 620)	Sold 1961	LOCH VEYATIE (F 658)	BU 1965
LOCH INSH (F 433)	To Malaysia 1964	DERBY HAVEN (ex-*Loch Assynt*)	To Iran 1949
LOCH KATRINE (F 625)	To New Zealand 1948	WOODBRIDGE HAVEN (ex-*Loch Torridon*) (F 654)	BU 1965
LOCH KILLIN (F 391)	BU 1960		

'Bay' class: launched 1944–45, 2420t deep load

BIGBURY BAY (ex-*Loch Carloway*) ((F 06)	To Portugal 1959	ST AUSTELL BAY (ex-*Loch Lyddoch*) (F 634)	BU 1959
BURGHEAD BAY (ex-*Loch Harport*) (F 622)	To Portugal 1959	ST BRIDES BAY (ex-*Loch Achilty*) (F 600)	BU 1962
CARDIGAN BAY (ex-*Loch Laxford*) (F 630)	BU 1962	START BAY (ex-*Loch Arklet*) (F 604)	BU 1958
CARNARVON BAY (ex-*Loch Maddy*) (F 636)	BU 1959	TREMADOC BAY (ex-*Loch Armish*) (F 605)	BU 1959
CAWSAND BAY (ex-*Loch Roan*) (F 644)	BU 1959	VERYAN BAY (ex-*Loch Swannay*) (F 651)	BU 1959
ENARD BAY (ex-*Loch Bracadale*) (F 35)	BU 1957	WHITESAND BAY (ex-*Loch Lubnaig*) (F 633)	BU 1956
LARGO BAY (ex-*Loch Fionn*) (F 423)	BU 1958	WIDEMOUTH BAY (ex-*Loch Frisa*) (F 615)	BU 1957
MORECAMBE BAY (ex-*Loch Heilen*) (F 624)	To Portugal 1961	WIGTOWN BAY (ex-*Loch Garasdale*) (F 616)	BU 1959
MOUNTS BAY (ex-*Loch Kilbirnie*) (F 627)	To Portugal 1961	ALERT (ex-*Dundrum Bay*, ex-*Loch Scamadale*) (F 647)	BU 1981
PADSTOW BAY (ex-*Loch Coulside*) (F 608)	BU 1959	SURPRISE (ex-*Gerrans Bay*, ex-*Loch Carron*) (F 436)	BU 1965
PORLOCK BAY (ex-*Loch Seaforth*, ex-*Loch Muick*) (F 650)	To Finland 1962		

Modified 'Flower' class: launched 1943–44, 1350–1370t deep load

ARABIS (F 85)	BU 1951	ARBUTUS (F 103)	BU 1951

'Castle' class: launched 1943–44, 1590–1630t deep load

ALLINGTON CASTLE (ex-*Amaryllis*) (F 89)	BU 1959	KENILWORTH CASTLE (F 420)	BU 1959
ALNWICK CASTLE (F 105)	BU 1958	KNARESBOROUGH CASTLE (F 389)	BU 1956
AMBERLEY CASTLE (F 286)	Weather ship 1960	LANCASTER CASTLE (F 691)	BU 1960
BAMBOROUGH CASTLE (F 12)	BU 1959	LAUNCESTON CASTLE (F 397)	BU 1959
BERKELEY CASTLE (F 387)	BU 1955	LEEDS CASTLE (F 384)	BU 1958
CAISTOR CASTLE (F 690)	BU 1956	MORPETH CASTLE (F 693)	BU 1960
CARISBROOKE CASTLE (F 379)	BU 1958	OAKHAM CASTLE (F 530)	Weather ship 1958
DUMBARTON CASTLE (F 388)	BU 1961	OXFORD CASTLE (F 692)	BU 1960
FARNHAM CASTLE (F 413)	BU 1960	PEVENSEY CASTLE (F 449)	Weather ship 1960
FLINT CASTLE (F 383)	BU 1958	PORTCHESTER CASTLE (F 362)	BU 1958
HADLEIGH CASTLE (F 355)	BU 1959	RUSHEN CASTLE (F 372)	BU 1960
HEDINGHAM CASTLE (ex-*Gorey Castle*) (F 386)	BU 1958	TINTAGEL CASTLE (F 399)	BU 1958

'Hunt' classes

These former escort destroyers were re-rated as anti-aircraft frigates in 1947, but very few saw postwar service in the RN, apart from training and occasional recommissioning (*eg Eglinton* in Exercise 'Sleeping Beauty'). *Brocklesby* was disarmed for service with AUWE at Portland, and from 1953 carried out trials with a large variable-depth sonar on the quarterdeck. *Mendip* served as the Chinese *Lin Fu* in 1948–49 and on her return was sold to Egypt as *Mohamed Ali el Kebir*, with *Ibrahim el Awal* (ex-*Cottesmore*); Denmark bought *Blackmore*, *Calpe* and *Exmoor* in 1952–53 and renamed them *Esbern Snare*, *Rolf Krake* and *Valdemar Sejr*; India was lent *Chiddingfold*, *Bedale* and *Lamerton* and renamed them *Ganga*, *Godavari* and *Gomati*; Norway received *Badsworth*, *Beaufort* and *Zetland*, renaming them *Arendal*, *Haugesund* and *Tromsö*; Ecuador received *Quantock* and *Meynell* as *Presidente Alfare* and *Presidente Velasco Ibarra*; and *Albrighton*, *Eggesford* and *Oakley* became *Raule*, *Brommy* and *Gneisenau* in the Federal German Navy in 1958.

UNITED KINGDOM

Grimsby class
The former sloop *Fleetwood* was disarmed in 1947 and fitted out as trials ship for the Admiralty Signal and Radar Establishment with a lattice foremast to carry extra arrays and deckhouses added forward and aft. In 1950 she was refitted and later had a lattice tower added aft.

Bittern and Egret classes
The ex-sloop *Stork* was laid up from 1946; *Pelican* served for short while postwar but was then laid up.

Black Swan class
These former sloops served postwar but were paid off in the early 1950s, *Erne* becoming the RNVR drillship *Wessex* in 1952. *Whimbrel* became the Egyptian *El Malek Farouq*, and *Flamingo* became the Federal German *Graf Spee*.

Modified Black Swan class
Most of this class saw considerable service on foreign stations from 1940s to the early 1960s. *Amethyst* was severely damaged by Chinese field artillery on the Yangtze in 1949, and like her sisters had the midships Mk 4 Hazemeyer Bofors gun replaced by Mk 5 mountings. Only *Pheasant* and *Redpole* retained the tripod foremast. In 1948–49 *Redpole* and *Starling* were disarmed and converted to tenders for navigational training. *Redpole* had a tripod foremast and a radar scanner on a short lattice mainmast while *Starling* had two tall lattice masts. Foreign sales of these ex-sloops were limited to *Actaeon*, *Hart* and *Mermaid*, which became the Federal German *Hipper*, *Scheer* and *Scharnhorst* in 1958–59.

'Captain' class
In theory all the Lease-Lend warships had to be returned to the United States immediately after the war, but inevitably some slipped through the net. The ex-*Buckley* class DE *Hotham* was a particular exception for she remained on the Navy List until 1956. Early in 1945 she had been stripped of fittings to allow her to be used as an emergency generating station for Singapore. When it turned out that she was not needed she was sent to Hong Kong as guardship, although subsequently she returned to Singapore. In 1951 she returned to the UK, and was then earmarked as trials ship for gas turbines. The machinery – twin-shaft EL60A turbines developing 6000shp each – was built by English Electric, but was never installed because more modern turbines became available. Finally the ship was nominally returned to the USN in 1956, but scrapped in the UK.

'River' class
Virtually all these frigates paid off in the postwar years and never recommissioned, as there were more than sufficient 'Lochs', 'Bays' and 'Castles' to meet peacetime needs. Those that were refitted had 40mm singles in place of the 20mm guns, and a Type 277 height-finder radar in place of the original Type 271 above the bridge. *Helmsdale* was disarmed for trials, and had two Squid DC mortars in 'B' position. *Meon* and *Waveney* were used for propeller silencing trials and as Landing Ships Headquarters, Small (LSH (S)), with armament reduced to three 40mm and four 20mm guns; the after deckhouse was enlarged to provide offices for Army and Royal Marines personnel. *Exe* was earmarked for a similar conversion, but this does not appear to have been undertaken. Scrapping of the survivors began in the mid-1950s, but the last did not go to the breakers until 1966.

'Loch' class
This class proved ideal for postwar duties, with modern sensors and weapons, and they survived to the mid-1960s. For service in the Persian Gulf nine were modernised in the early 1950s: *Loch Alvie*, *Loch Fada*, *Loch Fyne*, *Loch Insh*, *Loch Killisport*, *Loch Lomond*, *Loch Ruthven*, *Loch Tralaig* and *Loch Veyatie*. This involved replacing the single 4in Mk 5 HA gun with a twin 4in Mk 19 and updating the secondary armament and radars. The secondary armament now consisted of four single 40mm Mk 9 (in bridge wings and at the forecastle break) and a twin 40mm Mk 5 aft. The Type 277 height-finder aerial at the masthead was replaced by a Type 277Q. *Loch Insh* became the Malaysian *Hang Tuah* in 1964. *Loch Fada* was used to test Vertically Launched Sea Wolf in 1976.

Two ex-'Loch' class frigates were completed in 1945 as depot ships (2160t full load; 2–40mm Mk 5) for small minesweepers and coastal forces. *Derby Haven* became the Iranian *Babr* in 1949 but *Woodbridge Haven* was actively employed for most of her life.

'Bay' class
Although also used widely on peacetime duties this class did not prove quite as successful as the 'Lochs' because of their weak anti-submarine armament, and they were never given any form of major modernisation. *Porlock Bay* became the Finnish *Matti Kurki* in 1962; and *Burghead Bay*, *Morecambe Bay*, *Bigbury Bay* and *Mounts Bay* became the Portuguese *Alvares Cabral*, *Don Francesco de Almeida*, *Pacheco de Pereira* and *Vasco da Gama* in 1959–61.

Two ex-'Bay' class frigates were completed in 1946 as dispatch vessels and C in C's yachts on foreign stations. *Alert* and *Surprise* had a full load displacement of 2440t and were armed with 2–4in/45 Mk 16 (2×2), 2–40mm Mk 7 (2×1), 4–3pdr saluting. For the Coronation Naval Review on 15 June 1953 *Surprise* was converted to a temporary Royal Yacht, with the twin 4in gun replaced by a glassed-in saluting platform for HM The Queen. Greatly increased accommodation was provided aft, with a broad shelter deck extending from the break of the forecastle to the stern.

Modified 'Flower' class
These two ex-corvettes were returned by the Royal New Zealand Navy in 1948, and were retained on the Navy List for three years. They were thus the only survivors of the large number of corvettes operated by the RN from 1940 onwards. The remainder were disposed of in large numbers from 1946, some to be converted to whalecatchers and small coasters, but the majority to be scrapped.

'Castle' class
Like other escorts these vessels were absorbed into the frigate category in 1947. Many served with the Training Squadron at Portland, but the hulls were too small for any sort of modernisation, and they went for scrap from the mid-1950s. *Berkeley Castle* capsized in dry dock at Sheerness during the disastrous floods in February 1953 and was never repaired. The weather ships were lent to the Air Ministry with the 40mm Bofors guns and the Squid DC mortar cocooned, but never returned to naval service.

TRAWLERS

'Isles' class
Annet, *Bardsey*, *Bern*, *Caldy*, *Coll*, *Fetlar*, *Flatholm*, *Foulness*, *Gorregan*, *Graemsay*, *Erraid*, *Gateshead*, *Lindisfarne*, *Lundy*, *Neave*, *Orsay*, *Ronay*, *Sandray*, *Shillay*, *Skomer*, *Skye*, *Steepholm*, *Sursay*, *Switha*, *Tahay*, *Tiree*, *Tocogay*, *Trodday*, *Trondra*, *Vaceasay*, *Vallay*, *Wiay*.

Survivors of a large class of Admiralty trawlers. Many served postwar as danlayers, wreck dispersal vessels, experimental anti-submarine vessels, etc. They were scrapped 1957–67, apart from a few converted to tank-cleaning vessels.

MINESWEEPERS

Halcyon class: launched 1936–38, 1330t deep load
Franklin, *Scott*, *Seagull* and *Sharpshooter* reverted to surveying duties postwar, *Sharpshooter* being renamed *Shackleton* in 1953. They were scrapped between 1956 and 1965.

Algerine class: launched 1941–45, 1225–1325t deep load
Eighty-three of these successful sweepers were retained; many were transferred to other navies, and served as training ships. They were surplus to requirements after it was realised during the Korean War that steel-hulled sweepers could no longer rely on degaussing for protection against magnetic mines.

Cadmus, *Fancy*, *Liberty*, *Ready*, *Rosario* and *Spanker* became the Belgian *Georges Lecointe*, *A F Defour*, *Adrien de Gerlache*, *Jan van Haverbueke*, *De Moor* and *De Brouwer* (1949–53); *Hare* became the Nigerian *Nigeria* (1959); *Flying Fish* and *Pickle* became the Ceylonese *Vijaya* and *Parakrama* (1949–58); *Fly* became the Iranian *Palang* (1949); *Pelorus* and *Rosamund* became the South African *Pietermaritzburg* and *Bloemfontein* (1949); *Arcturus*, *Aries*, *Gozo*, *Lightfoot* and *Postillion* became the Royal Hellenic Navy's *Pyrpolitis*, *Armatolos*, *Polemistis*, *Navamachos* and *Machitis* (1947); *Mariner* became the Burmese *Yan Myo* (1958); and *Minstrel* became the Royal Thai Navy's *Phosampton* (1947).

COASTAL FORCES

Vosper 73ft type: 47t deep load
MTB 386, 392, 502, 523–527, 529, 530, 532, 533
These were renumbered as fast patrol boats in 1950, *MTB 386* and *392* becoming *FPB 1001* and *1002*, and *523–527*, *529*, *530*, *532* and *533* becoming *FPB 1023–1027*, *1029*, *1030*, *1032* and *1033*. *FPB 1030* sank after a collison with her sister *FPB 1032* off the Dutch coast on 28.3.50, while *FPB 1023* caught fire and blew up in Aarhus harbour, Denmark, on 17.5.53. Only *FPB 1002* survived (as a hulk) by 1956. The armament was mixed, some having a 6pdr forward, others twin 20mm. *FPB 1032* received an experimental 4.5in/25.

British Power Boat 71¾ft type: 53t deep load
MTB 470, 480, 496, 498, 505–509, 519, 521, 522, 596, 598
Nine were renamed in 1947: *Proud Fusilier* (ex-*MTB 505*), *Proud Grenadier* (ex-*MTB 506*), *Proud Guardsman* (ex-*MTB 507*), *Proud Highlander* (ex-*MTB 508*), *Proud Knight* (ex-*MTB 509*), *Proud Lancer* (ex-*MTB 519*), *Proud Legionary* (ex-*MTB 522*), *Proud Patriot* (ex-*MTB 596*) and *Proud Patroller* (ex-*MTB 598*), with 1000 added to their numbers. The others were all stricken by 1947, except *MTB 470*, *480*, *496* and *498*, which were renumbered as fast patrol boats *FPB 1570*, *1580*, *1596* and *1598*.

Camper & Nicholson Type: 102.5t deep load
MGB 2009
Ordered in 1941 and laid down in May 1942, was completed in 1945 for experimental purposes. She displaced 86.5t standard, was 117ft 3in oa × 19ft 1in × 4ft 4in max *35.7m × 5.8m × 1.3m* and was fitted with 3-shaft gas turbine/gasoline machinery (1 Gatric gas turbine plus 2 Packard engines, 5200shp = 34kts); she was unarmed and had a complement of 31. Renumbered *P 5559*, she ran a series of trials in 1947 before being sold c1948.

Fairmile 'D' type: 118t deep load
MTB 731, 750, 758, 759, 780, 790, 793, 794, 795
All were renumbered, *MTB 731*, *750*, *758*, *779*, *780*, *785*, *790* and *793–795*, becoming *FPB 3001*, *3002*, *5001*, *5003*, *5010*, *5013*, *5031*, *5032*, *5033* and *5035–5037*; *3001*, *3002*, *3050* and *3053* served as motor anti-submarine boats, (MA/SBs) the others as convertible MTBs/MGBs with four TT or two guns,

6pdrs in most, but 4.5in/25 in *5036*. Only *FPB 5001, 5035 and 5036* were still in service by 1958 and they were put on the disposal list shortly afterwards.

Modified Fairmile 'D' type: 118t deep load
MTB 5002, 5005, 5007, 5008, 5009, 5015, 5020
These craft had numbers in the same series as the ordinary 'D' type, and so were not renumbered, merely reclassified as FPBs. They were armed as convertible MTBs/MGBs, with 6pdr guns and 21in TT, although *5009* mounted two 4.5in/25. by 1958 only *FPB 5015* and *5020* survived, but they were soon put on the disposal list.

Fairmile 'F' type
MGB 2001
Prototype 'F' with four Bristol Hercules engines.

Fairmile 'B' Type Motor Launches: 85.6t deep load
ML 2154–2156, 2217, 2220, 2221, 2223, 2237, 2248, 2250, 2337, 2338, 2342, 2357, 2360, 2461, 2462, 2489, 2491, 2493, 2564, 2567, 2568, 2571, 2575–2577, 2581–2583, 2585, 2586, 2592, 2593, 2595, 2866, 2869, 2882, 2886, 2901, 2906, 2912, 2919, 2921; RML 495, 496, 498, 512, 515, 529
Most were scrapped or sold in the 1950s and only five were in service by 1958.

Habour Defence Motor Launches (HDML): 54t deep load
SDML 1001, 1053, 1081, 1085, 1091, 1301, 1323, 1326, 1329, 1393, 1411, 3328, 3501–3503, 3505–3508, 3510–3516, Meda (ex-SML 352, ex-ML 1301)
Most were scrapped in the 1950s, only nine remaining by 1958. Several served in the Far East as gunboats, with a power-operated 6pdr forward and a 20mm aft. Latterly they were re-rated as Seaward Defence MLs.

126ft Motor Minesweepers: 430t deep load
MMS 1002—1004, 1011, 1017, 1030, 1034, 1038, 1042, 1044, 1048, 1060, 1061, 1075, 1077, 1089, 1090
105ft Motor Minesweepers: 295t deep load
MMS 1501, 1505, 1532, 1534–1536, 1546, 1548, 1550, 1553, 1556, 1558, 1569, 1579, 1583, 1584, 1586, 1599, 1600, 1602–1606, 1609, 1610, 1635, 1644, 1667, 1672, 1681, 1685, 1717, 1724, 1728, 1733, 1736, 1761, 1763, 1771, 1772, 1775, 1783, 1785, 1786, 1788–1791, 1794
Both the 126ft and 105ft types were replaced by the 'Ton', 'Ham' and 'Ley' classes in the late 1950s, although four of the large type served for longer as degaussing vessels *DGV 401–404*.

EX-GERMAN MOTOR TORPEDO-BOATS

At the end of the Second World War about 34 ex-*Schnellboote* or 'E-Boats' were handed over. Most were scrapped, but three were retained for experimental purposes, *S 130, S 208* and *S 212*. These were renumbered *P 5230, P 5208* and *P 5212*. Displacing 105t normal load and 114ft 6in oa × 16ft 9in × 6ft mean *34.9in × 5.1m × 1.8m*, they were fitted with 3-shaft diesels (*P 5230* Mercedes-Benz, 7500bhp; *P 5212* 1 Mercedes Benz + 2 Napier Deltic, 9000bhp; *P 5208* 3 Napier Deltic, 9000bhp) giving 39kts. Oil was 20t and complement *c*15.

P 5212 operated in British waters until paid off for scrapping in 1956. The other two were employed on what were officially described as fishery protection duties under the British Flag Officer, Germany. What this actually involved was surveillance of the Soviet Navy in the Eastern Baltic. Both craft, unarmed and fitted with equipment for monitoring signals, observed manoeuvres, trusting to their big margin of speed to get away if detected. In 1957 these marine equivalents of the U-2 spy-plane were handed over to the newly-formed *Bundesmarine* in 1957 and renumbered *UW 10* and *UW 11*. They were rearmed for training duties with two TT and were finally scrapped in 1964–65.

STEAM GUNBOATS

Grey Seal class: launched 1941–42, 255t deep load
Grey Seal, Grey Fox, Grey Wolf, Grey Goose
Three of the survivors were sold and scrapped in 1948–49, but *Grey Goose* was selected to replace the frigate *Hotham* as the trials ship for the prototype Rolls-Royce RM60 gas turbine. She was taken in hand in 1952 and given two funnels with sharply raked tops. In 1954–55 she ran a series of intensive trials, paving the way for the successful 'marinising' of the G2 and Proteus for small craft and the G6 for large ships. When the trials were over in 1955 she was stripped and laid up.

AMPHIBIOUS WARFARE SHIPS

LST (3): launched 1944–45, 4980t deep load
Frederick Clover (LST 3001), Anzio (LST 3003), Tromsö (LST 3006), LST 3008, Reginald Kerr (LST 3009), Avenger (LST 3001), Ben Nevis (LST (Q) 1, ex-LST 3012), Ben Lomond (LST (Q)2, ex-LST 3013), (LST 3014), Battler (LST 3015), Dieppe (LST 3016), LST 3017, Vaagsö (LST 3019), Charles McLeod (LST 3021), Maxwell Brander (LST 3024), Bruizer (LST 3025), Charger (LST 3026), Lofoten (LST 3027), Snowden Smith (LST 3028), Chaser (LST 3029), LST 3031, LST 3033, LST 3035, Puncher (LST 3036), Evan Gibb (LST 3037), Fighter (LST 3038), LST 3040, LST 3041, Hunter (LST 3042), Messina (LST 3043), Narvik (LST 3044), LST 3501, Pursuer (LST 3504), Ravager (LST 3505), LST 3507, Scorcher (LST 3508), Humphrey Gale (LST 3509), Slinger (LST 3510), Reggio

(LST 3511), LST 3512, Salerno (LST 3513), Smiter (LST 3514), Stalker (LST 3515), Striker (LST 3516), St Nazaire (LST 3517), Suvla (LST 3518), LST 3519, Thruster (LST 3520), Tracker (LST 3522), Trouncer (LST 3523), Trumpeter (LST 3524), Walcheren (LST 3525), Zeebrugge (LST 3532), LST 3524
Numbered craft were all sold by 1950 or transferred – *3017, 3035, 3501* became the Australian *Tarakan, Labuan* and *Lae* in 1951 – and all vessels with generals' names (*Frederick Clover*, etc.) had been on charter to the War Department from 1946. *Avenger* became Indian *Magar* in 1951 and *Smiter* was wrecked off Lagos on 25.4.49. In 1956 *Tromsö, Attacker, Battler, Charger, 3033, Fighter, 3041 Hunter, Pursuer, 3507, Slinger, 3512, Nazaire, 3519, Thruster, Trouncer, Trumpeter, Walcheren* and *3524* were chartered commercially and renamed *Empire Gannet, Empire Cymric, Empire Puffin, Empire Nordic, Empire Shearwater, Empire Grebe, Empire Doric, Empire Curlew, Empire Tern, Empire Gaelic, Empire Kittiwake, Empire Celtic, Empire Skua, Empire Baltic, Empire Petrel, Empire Gull, Empire Fulmar, Empire Guillemot* and *Empire Cedric*. The rest were broken up from 1970 onwards. In 1964 *Lofoten* was converted to a helicopter support ship, with a flight deck to enable her to carry six Wessex ASW helicopters out to sea for deep-water training. Last in service was the RFA *Empire Gull*, scrapped in 1980.

LCM (7): launched 1943–44, 63t
Approximately 50, from *LCM 7007* to *7216*, survived in 1953. By 1967 only five were left, three serving as naval servicing boats (NSB) and stores carriers. Several had been re-engined.

LCT (8): launched 1945–47, 810t loaded
LCT 4001, 4002, 4025, 4037–4045, 4049, 4050, 4061–4064, 4073, 4074, 4085, 4086, 4097–4099, 4128, 4148, 4156, 4164, 4165
LCT 4001, 4002, 4037–4041, 4043, 4044, 4049, 4061, 4062, 4064, 4073—4074, 4085, 4086, 4097, 4099, 4128 and *4164* were renamed *Redoubt, Agheila, Rampart* (later *Akyab*), *Citadel, Parapet, Bastion, Abbeville, Counterguard, Portcullis, Audemer, Aachen, Sallyport, Ardennes, Antwerp, Agedabia, Arromanches, Andalnes, Buttress, Arezzo* and *Arakan* in 1956. Numbered craft were put on the disposal list in 1958–60. *Counterguard* became the Malaysian *Sri Langkawi* in 1965, *Buttress* was sold to France as *L 9061* in 1965 and *Bastion* was transferred to Zambia in 1966. The remainder were disposed of from 1965 onwards but in 1980 *Abbeville, Agheila* and *Audemer* were still being operated by the Royal Corps of Transport.

LCT (3): launched 1941–44, 640t loaded
LCT(E) 341, LCT(E) 413
341 was lent to the Royal Malaysian Navy as *Malaya (MRC 1401)*; *MRC 1413* (ex-*LCT(E) 413*) was scrapped.

LCT (4): launched 1942–45, 640t loaded
LCT 403 (ex-LCT 1220), 404, (ex-1231), 405 (ex-523), 406 (ex-941), 407 (ex-1186), 408 (ex-1202); MRC 1013, 1015, 1023, 1097, 1098, 1100, 1109, 1110, 1119, 1120, 1122
All were broken up in the 1960s

LCA: built 1940–44, 13½t
A total of 286, ranging from *LCA 1010* to *1992*, were on strength in 1947; all were scrapped in the 1960s.

LCH: built 1943, 5½t
LCH 243 was broken up *c*1955.

LCP(L): built 1942, 10¾t
The 10 survivors, ranging from *LCP(L) 519* to *561* and *501*, were scrapped in the 1960s.

MISCELLANEOUS VESSELS

The river gunboat *Locust* became an RNVR drill ship in 1951, and was subsequently broken up. The netlayer *Guardian* was scrapped in 1962, while *Protector* was employed as an Antarctic patrol ship 1955–68, being broken up in 1970.

The following minelayers were in service in 1947: *Plover* (BU 1968), *Blackbird* (ex-*Sheppey*) (sold 1949) *Dabchick* (ex-*Thorney*) (to Malaya 1954), *Stonechat* (BU 1967), *Redshank* (ex-*Turbot*) (BU 1957), *Ringdove* (sold 1951), *Linnet* (BU 1964), *Miner I* (ex-*M 1*) (*Minstrel* 1962), *Miner II* (ex-*M 2*) (*Gossamer* 1949, sunk as target 1970), *Miner III* (ex-*M 3*) (for disposal 1974), *Miner IV* (ex-*M 4*) (sold 1964), *Miner V* (ex-*M 5*) (PAS *Britannic* 1960), *Miner VI* (ex-*M 6*) (sold 1966), *Miner VII* (ex-*M 7*) (PAS *Steady* 1959) and *Miner VIII* (*Mindful* 1963, sold 1965), and the depot ships *Resource* (BU 1954), *Woolwich* (BU 1962), *Maidstone* (for disposal 1978), *Forth* (for disposal 1979), *Tyne* (for disposal 1973), *Adamant* (BU 1970) and the aircraft transports *Blackburn* (RNVR drill ship 1950), *Ripon* (sold 1959), *Roc* (sold 1959), *Seafox* (sold 1958) and *Walrus* (renamed *Skua* 1953, sold 1962.

NATO PENNANT NUMBERS
Carried from 1950 by ships in commission, the most important are noted after the relevant vessel in the lists above. However, the following landing ships and minesweepers were also allocated numbers:

UNITED KINGDOM

Amphibious warfare ships

L 101	ANZIO	L 119	REGGIO	M 88	CHEERFUL	M 387	CHAMELEON
L 102	ATTACKER	L 120	ZEEBRUGGE	M 163	SKYE	M 389	HARE
L 104	BEN NEVIS	L 121	SALERNO	M 216	ESPIEGLE	M 390	JEWEL
L 105	BEN LOMOND	L 123	SLINGER	M 221	ONYX	M 422	IMERSAY
L 106	BUCHAN NESS	L 125	ST NAZAIRE	M 225	RINALDO	M 424	SANDRAY
L 107	CHARGER	L 126	STALKER	M 276	LENNOX	M 426	SHILLAY
L 108	DIEPPE	L 127	BRUISER	M 277	ORESTES	M 427	SURSAY
L 109	FIGHTER	L 128	STRIKER	M 289	MELITA	M 428	JASEUR
L 110	KEREN	L 129	SUVLA	M 293	PICKLE	M 429	RONA
L 111	LOFOTEN	L 130	TRACKER	M 294	PINCHER	M 431	TRODDAY
L 112	MESSINA	L 132	CHASER	M 295	PLUCKY	M 432	VACEASAY
L 114	NARVIK	L 133	TROUNCER	M 298	RECRUIT	M 433	LAERTES
L 115	PUNCHER	L 134	TRUMPETER	M 299	RIFLEMAN	M 434	VALLAY
L 116	PURSUER	L 135	WALCHEREN	M 302	THISBE	M 435	MÆNAD
L 117	RAVAGER	L 180	HUNTER	M 303	TRUELOVE	M 436	MAGICIENNE
L 118	BATTLER			M 304	WATERWITCH	M 438	MANDATE
				M 307	HOUND	M 443	MARVEL
				M 325	PROVIDENCE	M 444	MICHAEL
				M 329	MOON	M 448	PYRRHUS
				M 333	SEABEAR	M 449	ROMOLA
				M 341	WIAY	M 450	ORSAY
				M 350	COQUETTE	M 452	TAHAY
				M 354	SERENE	M 454	MYRMIDON
				M 356	WELFARE	M 455	MYSTIC
				M 360	MARY ROSE	M 456	NERISSA
				M 367	STORMCLOUD	M 462	ORCADIA
				M 376	GOLDEN FLEECE	M 463	OSSORY
				M 377	LIONESS		

Minesweepers

M 01	ALBACORE	M 379	CORNFLOWER
M 11	BRAMBLE	M 380	MARINER
M 17	SKIPJACK	M 381	MARMION
M 29	COCKATRICE	M 382	SYLVIA
M 46	PLUTO	M 383	TANGANYIKA
M 49	COURIER	M 384	ROWENA
M 53	FIERCE	M 385	WAVE
M 81	TOCOGAY	M 386	WELCOME

MAJOR SURFACE SHIPS

Although officially cancelled in 1944 (all serious work was stopped following the sinking of *Tirpitz*), the *Lion* class were kept on the drawing-board as the Admiralty hoped to be able to restart two of them postwar. The design was completely modified in the light of wartime experience, the principal changes being, to broaden the

Modified LION class *battleship*

beam, to deepen the torpedo protection and replace the original 16in/45 Mk II gun with a projected Mk IV/45 gun. Little else is known about the design except that by the time work stopped (*c* 1950) the thickness of deck armour had risen to 12in. Displacement was 49,000t (standard), 56,500t (full load) and dimensions 810ft × 115ft × 34ft 3in mean (*264.9m × 35.1m × 10.4m*).

Centaur as completed

Four completed units of a projected class of eight 'intermediate fleet carriers' were retained for the postwar fleet. One was so delayed that she eventually formed a separate type, but the other three, redesigned to incorporate as many wartime lessons as possible, were launched in 1947–48 and completed in somewhat leisurely fashion six years later. Almost as soon as the vessels were completed they were taken in hand for modification. An 'interim' or 5½° angled deck was added and this necessitated the removal of three twin Bofors guns from the port side. After the Suez operations in 1956 the ships were given steam catapults and stronger arrester wires, and the six-barrelled Mk 6 Bofors mounting abaft the island was removed to provide deck space.

They proved too small to operate the new generation of aircraft coming into service in the late 1950s, and in 1959–60 *Bulwark* was converted to a commando carrier. This involved the removal of her arrester gear and catapults, the provision of four assault landing craft (LCAs) in davits aft and the modification of her accommodation to allow 733 Royal Marines to embark. With 8 helicopters in place of her former air group, she could land troops and vehicles ashore rapidly, and proved such a success that her sister *Albion* was similarly converted in 1961–62. *Albion*'s conversion was slightly more elaborate, and allowed her to embark 900 commandos. Plans to convert *Centaur*, however, were shelved because of rising costs, and she was paid off into reserve in 1966, to be scrapped six years later.

The air groups varied during their careers. At Suez, for example, *Albion* was flying Sea Venom and Sea Hawk fighters, Skyraider AEW aircraft and Sycamore helicopters. At the end of her career *Centaur* carried four Gannet AEW aircraft and eight Whirlwind helicopters in addition to her Sea Vixens and Scimitars.

In April 1976 *Bulwark* paid off into reserve, but as a contingency against late delivery of the *Invincible* class she was maintained in the best condition possible. A rumoured sale to Peru did not materialise and in 1980 she recommissioned to release *Hermes* from the amphibious role when the latter embarked her Sea Harrier squadron. Under the 1981 defence cuts, however, she was paid off and put on the disposal list.

Victorious was virtually rebuilt from 1950 to the end of 1957 to allow her to operate modern jet aircraft. During the process the hull was widened, deepened and lengthened and the machinery and boilers replaced, although it was only decided in 1955 to replace the boilers (!). Two steam catapults, an angled deck and mirror landing sights were provided, as well as a 3-D radar and faster lifts.

The major item of the reconstruction was the provision of a massive sponson on the port side for the 8¾° angled deck. This extended the flight

CENTAUR class *aircraft carriers*

Displacement:	22,000t standard; 27,000t full load
Dimensions:	737ft 9in oa × 123ft max × 27ft max
	224.8m × 37.5m × 8.2m
Machinery:	2-shaft geared steam turbines, 4 3–drum boilers, 78,000shp = 28kts
Armour:	Flight deck, hangar deck (amidships) and main deck (ends), 1in–2in, uptakes 1in
Armament:	32–40mm (2×6, 8×2, 4×1), 26 aircraft
Sensors:	Radar Types 982, 983, 275, 974
Complement:	1028/1102 + *c*300 air group

No	Name	Builder	Laid down	Launched	Comp	Fate
R 07	ALBION	Swan Hunter	23.3.44	6.5.47	26.5.54	BU 1972
R 08	BULWARK	Harland & Wolff	10.5.45	22.6.48	4.11.54	For disposal 1982
R 06	CENTAUR	Harland & Wolff	30.5.44	22.4.47	1.9.53	BU 1971

Albion and *Bulwark* (foreground) as commando carriers, Nov 1962   CPL

VICTORIOUS *aircraft carrier*

Displacement:	30,530t standard; 35,500t full load
Dimensions:	740ft pp, 781ft oa × 103ft 6in wl, 157ft fd × 31ft
	228.0m 238.0m × 31.5m, 47.8m × 9.5m
Machinery:	3-shaft Parsons geared steam turbines, 6 Foster Wheeler boilers, 110,000shp = 31kts
Armour:	Belt and hangar side 4½in, flight deck 3½in, hangar deck 2½in
Armament:	12–3in/50 Mk 33 (6×2), 6–40mm Mk 6 (1×6), 36 aircraft. See notes
Sensors:	Radar Types 984, 974, 293Q
Complement:	2400

No	Name	Yard	Reconstructed	Fate
R 38	VICTORIOUS	Portsmouth DYd	Oct 50–57	BU 1969

deck 35ft 6in outboard and was the first fully angled deck fitted in a British carrier. The new island was surmounted by a huge 'searchlight' array for the Type 984 3-D radar, the first to go to sea. Two parallel-track 145ft steam catapults were provided and because of the angled deck there were only four arrester wires, each with an average span of 80ft. A major internal improvement was to nearly double the generating capacity to 4200kW, but even this had to be increased to 5000kW in 1962–63. The former armament was completely replaced by six twin 3in/50 Mk 33 automatic gun mountings purchased from the US Navy, mounted one on each side forward and two on each side aft. In addition one 6-barrelled 40mm Mk 6 automatic mounting was positioned on the starboard side between the boat crane and the after 3in guns. Each gun mounting was controlled by its own CRBF (Close Range Blind Fire) director positioned alongside. During a May 1962–August 1963 refit two 3in mountings and the Mk 6 Bofors were removed to compensate for the weight added.

During the 1962–63 refit the flight deck was strengthened and an access gangway was provided outboard of the island. The 'flyco' on the inboard

Victorious 1.6.67   CPL

side of the island was extended and enlarged and the mirror sights were replaced by projector sights.

When she recommissioned on 14 January 1958, *Victorious* was the most modern British carrier, but although it had originally been hoped that she

would operate 54 aircraft, the rapid growth in size of the latter meant that she never carried more than 28 (plus 8 helicopters) and finally carried only 23 (8 Buccaneers, 8 Sea Vixens, 2 Gannets and 5 Wessex). In 1968 she suffered a minor fire while refitting,

and as the decision had already been taken to run down the carrier force she was summarily put on the disposal list and sold for scrapping the following year.

Originally intended to form one of a class of four 32,500t improved *Implacable*s, *Audacious* was quite far advanced at the end of the war and was therefore earmarked for completion more or less as designed. Her name was changed to *Eagle* in January 1946 because the original *Eagle* had just been cancelled. Her surviving sister *Ark Royal*, however, was held up to allow numerous improvements to be incorporated, and so the two ships differed in many details. A new legend was drawn up in 1946 for both ships, raising displacement to 36,970t (standard), 45,720t (deep).

Eagle's design followed closely the pattern of the wartime armoured carriers, with eight twin 4.5in DP gun mountings in quadrantal sponsons, but the close-range armament was the most modern available. Eight 6-barrelled 40mm Bofors Mk 6, each with its own CRBF fire control director, were mounted, four on the port

Eagle 1.11.57

EAGLE *aircraft carrier*

Displacement:	43,060t (finally nearly 45,000t) standard; 53,390t full load
Dimensions:	720ft pp, 803ft 9in (finally 811ft 9in) oa × 171ft fd, 112ft 8½in wl × 36ft *219.5m, 245.0m (247.4m) × 51.8m, 34.3m × 11.0m*
Machinery:	4-shaft geared steam turbines, 8 Admiralty 3-drum boilers, 152,000shp = 31½kts. Oil 5500t
Armour:	Waterline belt 4½in, flight deck 4in–1½in, hangar side 1½in, hangar deck 2½in–1in. See notes
Armament:	(1952) 16–4.5in/45 Mk 6 DP (8×2), 48–40mm/60 Mk 6 AA (8×6), 4–40mm/60 Mk 5 AA (2×2), 9–40mm/60 Mk 7 AA (9×1), 60 aircraft; (1964) 8–4.5in (4×2), 6 Seacat GWS22 SAM (6×4), 45 aircraft
Sensors:	Radar Types 960, 982, 983, 275, 262, 974 (later Types 984, 963, 965 (AKE-2))
Complement:	2750 (inc air group)

No	Name	Builder	Laid down	Launched	Comp	Fate
R 05	EAGLE (ex-*Audacious*)	Harland & Wolff	24.10.42	19.3.46	1.10.51	BU 1978

side, two on the starboard side and one at each end of the island. In addition there were nine single 40mm Mk 7 on the island and on the port side, and before completion two twin 40mm Mk 5 were added in a sponson under the overhang of the flight deck at the stern. This gave the pheno-

menal total of 12 radar directors controlling 16–4.5in and 48–40mm barrels, with a further 13–40mm barrels under local control.

As the only large modern carrier, *Eagle* was a major addition to the RN's strength when she started her builder's trials in October 1951. On

trials she made 30.53kts at 44,250t with 156,630shp and 29.6kts at deep load (49,950t). Endurance was calculated at 4500nm at 24kts. She took part in her first major operation, the NATO exercise 'Mainbrace', at the end of 1952, and then went to the Mediterranean. From June 1954 to

CPL

February 1955 she was under refit, emerging with a 5½° angled deck and the new mirror landing sight. Apart from realignment of the arrester wires and other flight deck fittings, the change necessitated the removal of one Mk 6 Bofors mounting from the port side; the three single Mk 7s were also removed from the port side of the island.

On 1 November 1956 *Eagle's* Sea Hawks, Wyverns and Sea Venoms began six days of attacks on Egyptian airfields and positions during the Anglo-French attempt to seize the Suez Canal. The air group flew 621 sorties in spite of having a defective catapult. On her return to Devonport she had a short refit and then returned to the Mediterranean, where she spent most of the remainder of the commission.

From mid-1959 to May 1964 she underwent complete rebuilding at

Devonport to bring her up to the standard of *Victorious*: a fully (8½°) angled deck, steam catapults and the long-range 3-D air warning Type 984 radar were fitted. The opportunity was taken to renew her boiler firebricks, for these had given constant trouble since completion. In addition she was given a short lattice foremast carrying a Type 965 (AKE-2) 'double bedstead' surveillance radar, and the forward 4.5in sponsons were removed to increase internal accommodation. The close-range armament was entirely replaced by six quadruple Seacat GWS22 SAM systems, four sponsoned port and starboard forward and aft, one right aft under the flight deck overhang and one on the starboard side between the island and the after sponson. A less obvious but important improvement was to boost the generating capacity to 8250kW, nearly double the original power,

while flight deck armour was reduced from 4in to 1½in.

With the growing size and complexity of aircraft, and as the after half of the lower hangar was now given over to workshops, the complement dropped to 35 fixed-wing aircraft and 10 helicopters, half the complement envisaged in 1942. In 1954 she had operated 59 aircraft, including Sea Hawks, Avengers, AEW Skyraiders and a Dragonfly helicopter; ten years later she had Sea Vixens, Scimitars and Gannets.

In 1964 the ship sailed for the Far East to help contain the Indonesian Confrontation by maintaining standing air patrols over the Malacca Strait. No sooner was this crisis over than she sailed for Aden to provide reinforcements and then had to provide air defence for Zambia against possible invasion from Rhodesia. The 'Beira Patrol', a blockade to prevent oil from

reaching Rhodesia, involved the identification of more than 700 ships and the covering of 200,000 square miles of sea each day, and it kept *Eagle* at sea for 71 days.

Although the most modern carrier, she fell victim to the 1966 decision to axe the RN's carriers, on the flimsy pretext that she would cost too much to convert to operate Phantoms; in fact she had already operated Phantoms and needed only minor modifications to her flight deck equipment. She was paid off at Portsmouth in January 1972 and was laid up at Devonport later the same year. Although *Eagle* was officially in fully maintained reserve, the difficulty of keeping *Ark Royal* running meant that she was progressively 'cannibalised', and she was finally towed away to the breakers in 1978.

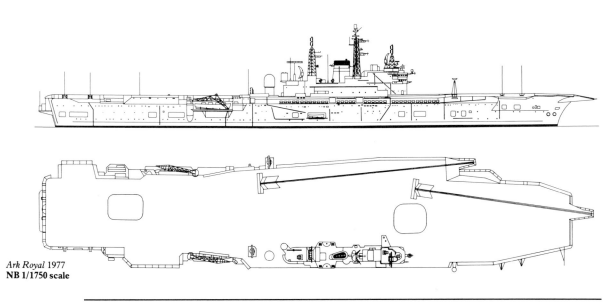

Ark Royal 1977
NB 1/1750 scale

Although often claimed to have been projected as HMS *Irresistible*, there is no official record of this name. The ship was in fact laid down 18 months after the previous *Ark Royal* was sunk, and there was every reason to reserve that name for a new carrier. She was not very far advanced at the end of the war and so the opportunity was taken to change the design considerably, but this made her completion more and more protracted, until she became the butt of comedians' jokes. She finally started trials in June 1954 and entered service in February 1955.

The most important alteration was to provide her with a deck-edge lift, as in US carriers. It was never a great success because it served the upper hangar only, and in any case the device was not really suited to the British type of closed hangar. The port forward 4.5in guns were never installed because the ship went to sea with a 5½° angled deck, and this also meant a smaller number of 40mm guns on the port side, as in *Eagle*. She had a tall lattice foremast, and a different island.

As with *Eagle* it proved difficult to accommodate two 210ft steam catapults on the foredeck, and so when these were intalled in 1967–70 an unusual disposition was adopted, with one on the port side forward and the other in the waist.

Ark Royal underwent many more

changes than *Eagle*. In 1956 the starboard 4.5in turrets were also removed, followed by the forward pairs (port and starboard) of the after group in 1964 and the rest in 1969. During the 1959 refit the side lift was removed to allow the hangar to be enlarged, and in 1961 a deck-landing projector sight was installed, with the 'Hilo' long-range guidance system and stronger steam catapults. Between March 1967 and February 1970 she underwent a major refit to allow the operation of Phantom F-4K interceptors and Buccaneer S2 strike aircraft. This involved removing the last of the 40mm guns; it was planned to replace them with four Seacat missile systems, but these were never installed.

The radar outfit always differed

from *Eagle's*. As built, *Ark Royal* had two Type 982 'hayrake' scanners and two Type 983 height-finders, with Type 262 fitted to the directors controlling the 40mm guns, and Type 275 controlling the 4.5in. In 1959 a 'double bedstead' Type 965M aerial was stepped on a short lattice mast forward of the mainmast; in 1967–70 a second 965M was added on a much taller lattice mainmast, and a large dome abaft the island, housing a Carrier Controlled Approach (CCA) radar of US origin, was fitted.

Although completed later than *Eagle*, the 'Ark' was never as mechanically reliable, and had the 1966 Defence Review not cancelled her replacement (CVA-02) she would have been scrapped first. In 1966 it was felt that she might last until 1972

without major repairs to her machinery, and the fact that she staggered on for another six years is testimony to the heroic efforts of her engineers. Although hard-worked she missed all the important actions except the Indonesian Confrontation, and had it not been for a 13-week TV serial called 'Sailor' she might never have endeared herself to the public in the way that she did. Despite efforts to raise money to preserve her the MoD steadfastly refused to sanction any unworthy scheme; in any case the sums talked of were wildly unrealistic, and the fight ended when she was towed away in the autumn of 1980. After she had been paid off at Devonport in December 1978 her name was given to the third of the *Invincible* class.

ARK ROYAL *aircraft carrier*

Displacement:	43,340t standard; 53,060t full load
Dimensions:	As *Eagle* except 164ft 6in fd 50.0m
Machinery:	As *Eagle*
Armour:	As *Eagle*
Armament:	(1955) 12–4.5in Mk 6 DP (6×2), 36–40mm Mk 6 AA (6×6), 4–40mm Mk 5 AA (2×2), 6–40mm Mk 7 AA (6×1), 50 aircraft; (1959) 8–4.5in (4×2), 28–40mm AA (4×6, 2×2), 48 aircraft; (1969) no guns, fitted for, but not with, 4 Seacat GWS22 SAM (4×4), 36 aircraft
Sensors:	Radars Types 960, 982, 983, 275, 262, 974; later Type 965 (AKE-2), SPN-35
Complement:	2637 (inc air group)

No	Name	Builder	Laid down	Launched	Comp	Fate
R 09	ARK ROYAL	Cammell Laird	3.5.43	3.5.50	25.2.55	BU 1980

Ark Royal 1961

CPL

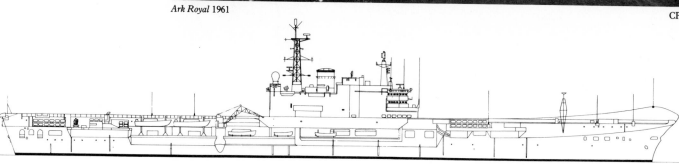

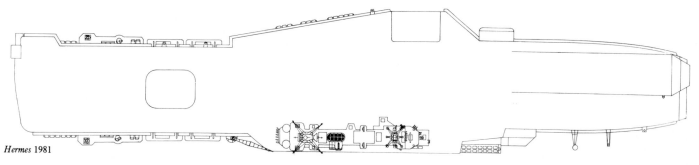

Hermes 1981

When the original order for *Hermes*, sixth of the *Centaur* class, was cancelled in October 1945, the name was given to *Elephant* of the same class; very little work was done on the hull, however, giving time for the specification to be revised. Thus, while the three *Centaur* class went ahead with their 'interim' standard of equipment, *Hermes* was radically redesigned to include a 6½° angled deck, a side lift and a Type 984 3-D long-range radar with Comprehensive Display System (CDS).

Although the deck-edge lift was unusual in British carriers (the first was still being installed in *Ark Royal*) it was dictated by the need to find space for the steam catapults at the forward end of the flight deck. Once the forward centreline lift was suppressed the side lift was needed to work aircraft, and it also provided a convenient extension to the angled deck area.

The appearance of the ship was very different from that of her former sisters, with a massive 'dustbin' scanner for the Type 984 radar over the island. The superstructure was considerably enlarged, but the armament was reduced to five twin 40mm Bofors

HERMES *aircraft carrier*

Displacement:	23,900t standard; 28,700t full load
Dimensions:	650ft pp, 744ft 4in oa × 160ft (increased from 144ft 6in in 1964–66) × 29ft mean *198.1m, 226.9m × 48.8m (44.1m) × 8.8m*
Machinery:	2-shaft geared steam turbines, 4 Admiralty 3-drum boilers, 76,000shp = 28kts. Oil 4200t
Armour:	Mantlets over magazines 40mm, reinforcing to flight deck 19mm
Armament:	10–40mm Mk 5 (5×2) (replaced 1964–66 by 2 Seacat GWS22 SAM (2×3)), 28 aircraft (as completed)
Sensors:	Radar Types 984, 982, 262, 974
Complement:	1830 + 270 air group (original)

No	Name	Builder	Laid down	Launched	Comp	Fate
R 12	HERMES (ex-*Elephant*)	Vickers-Armstrong, Barrow	21.6.44	16.2.53	18.11.59	Extant 1982

(two port, three starboard) controlled by MRS8 directors. In 1964–66 she was refitted and the Bofors were replaced by two quadruple Seacat close-range SAM defence systems, in the after port and starboard sponsons. Another improvement was the addition of the 'Alaska highway' outboard of the island. In 1971–73 the Type 984 scanner was replaced by a Type 965 'bedstead' and a massive array of deck-landing lights was provided on the foremast and bridge.

The main difficulty with *Hermes* was her size, for when she commissioned at the end of 1959 she could only operate 20 Sea Vixen, Scimitar and Buccaneer and eight Gannet ASW aircraft. After serving in the Atlantic, Mediterranean, Indian Ocean and Far East she had to be withdrawn from front-line service because she could not operate the new F-4K Phantom, which had replaced the Sea Vixen. In 1971 she paid off for conversion to a commando carrier, losing her arrester wires, catapults and 3-D radar. In 1977 she was re-rated as an ASW carrier, with Sea King helicopters in place of the Wes-

sex Mk Is, but she has now undergone conversion to operate a squadron of Sea Harrier STOVL aircraft. This conversion also includes the provision of a 7° ski-jump ramp, extending the full width of the flight deck.

In her new role *Hermes* bridges the gap until the second and third *Invincible* class carriers are complete, and will serve until at least 1984–85. Her last air group as an ASW carrier consisted of nine Sea Kings and four Wessex Mk 5s, but at the end of 1980 she embarked five Sea Harriers and nine Sea King Mk 2s. Although

Hermes as completed   CPL

threatened with premature scrapping under the 1981 defence cuts, she acted as flagship of the Falklands Task Force April–June 1982, during which time she embarked 20 Sea Harriers and 10 Sea Kings.

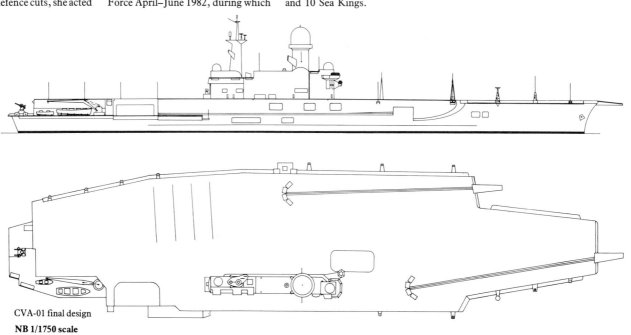

CVA-01 final design
NB 1/1750 scale

The story of the last class of fleet carriers designed for the RN is a harrowing one – although it must be said that the cancellation of the programme in 1966 was absolutely necessary, if only to save the Navy from getting the wrong carrier – and it will remain a classic example of how a design can be ruined by constraints.

The MoD needed two new fleet carriers to replace *Victorious* and *Eagle* in the early 1970s and their role was seen as providing strike power against airfields and hostile ships, and air defence for the fleet. It was hoped that the project would be backed by the RAF as well, using the planned joint RAF/FAA swing-wing 'strike fighter' as the principal unit of the air group. When that aircraft died stillborn the new carrier design (designated CVA-01 or Attack Carrier, as in the USN) hit its first problem. The second was purely political, for both Lord Mountbatten and his VCNS were certain that the Treasury and the 'bomber lobby' in the RAF would oppose a large carrier. This proved to be the case, and when it was pointed out that a carrier capable of accommodating the latest aircraft and catapults of the necessary length would displace over 60,000t, the politicians asked for the length of catapult to be reduced (!).

CVA-01 class *fleet aircraft carriers*

Displacement:	53,000t standard; c63,000t full load
Dimensions:	925ft oa × 184ft fd, 122ft wl
	281.9m × 56.1m, 37.2m
Machinery:	3-shaft geared steam turbines, 6 Foster Wheeler boilers, 135,000shp = 28kts
Armour:	Some deck and side armour and underwater protection
Armament:	Probably 1 Sea Dart GWS30 SAM (1×2), 4 Seacat GWS20/22 SAM (4×4), ?40 aircraft
Sensors:	New CDS, Types 903, 974, etc.
Complement:	2720

No	Name	Builder	Laid down	Launched	Comp	Fate
CVA 01	? INVINCIBLE					Cancelled 1966
CVA 02						Cancelled 1966

To cope with such ill-considered requests the designers cut the catapults from four to two and eliminated the deck park, reducing displacement to 55,000t, but there was still pressure to cut the size to 30,000t, half as big as the original target. Even though the design was changed to a 'furniture van' concept, with very light structure, no armour and only a novel form of underwater protection against torpedoes, it could not be reduced below 50,000t. Speed was restricted to 27–28kts, but after doubts were raised about putting so much power out through two shafts, the old 3-shaft system of the *Illustrious* class was re-adopted, so that one engine could be closed down for

maintenance and still leave enough power for Fleet speed.

The flight deck layout was unusual, offset to port, but angled at only 3½°. The passageway (known as the 'Alaska highway') fitted in the *Hermes* and other carriers was made even wider, allowing aircraft as well as vehicles to be moved forward and aft without disturbing the deck park. There were other novel features, such as doors at the after end of the hangar to allow engines to be run inside, and a new 'scissors' type of lift. It had been hoped to have two Anglo-Dutch 'Broomstick' radars housed in radomes forward and aft, but it was soon discovered that two radars of this type would have to be kept very far

apart – miles in fact! – to avoid mutual interference, and so one was dropped. Two BS6 catapults were planned, with water-spray type arrester gear.

Displacement had been kept to 50,000t, but when 2000t of armour were added, for political reasons the total continued to be referred to as 50,000t. Things gots worse. To fit all the requirements in such a small hull, many ingenious ideas were adopted. This was a recipe for disaster, as experience shows that only some 20–25 per cent novelty can be accepted in a design; more than this raises insoluble problems. With hindsight the biggest blunder was the political one of confusing size with cost, but given the Treasury's insis-

147

UNITED KINGDOM

tence that CVA-01 should not exceed the full load tonnage of *Eagle* there was very little that either Staff or Ship Department could do. Not for nothing did the project leader refer to the cancellation as the happiest day of his life. The design work was authorised in July 1963 and ended in February 1966 without an order being placed.

Official artist's impression of CVA-01   I A Sturton Collection

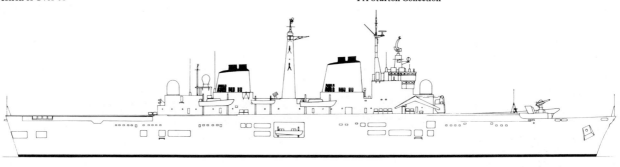

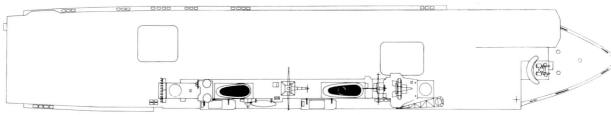

Invincible as completed

The death of the fleet carrier replacement programme in February 1966 did not mean the end of plans for air-capable ships. By 1967 an outline Staff Requirement had produced studies for a 12,500t command cruiser carrying six Sea King helicopters. The ship was designated CCH, or helicopter-carrying cruiser, and that is what she was: a derivative of the *Tiger* class, with a missile/gun armament forward and a large external hangar aft, as in the French *Jeanne d'Arc*.

Simple logic dictated that 'cleaning up' the superstructure and moving it to the starboard side would provide more deck space, although any attempt to do this was likely to be regarded by the politicians as a resurrection of the fleet carrier. But studies continued to show that increasing the air group to more than nine helicopters must lead to a 'through deck' or clear flight deck and island superstructure, if only to provide sufficient internal space for the hangar and workshops. Thus, despite the difficult climate, the design staff prepared designs for what were to be called 'through-deck cruisers' rising

INVINCIBLE class *support carriers*

Displacement:	16,000t standard; 19,500t full load*
Dimensions:	632ft pp, 677ft oa × 115ft fd, 90ft wl × 24ft full load
	192.2m, 206,6m × 35.0m, 27.5m × 7.3m
Machinery:	2-shaft COGOG: 4 Olympus gas turbines, 112,000shp = 28kts. Range 5000nm at 18kts. Fuel unknown
Armour:	None
Armament:	1 Sea Dart GWS30 SAM (1×2), 2 Phalanx CIWS (added 1982), 14 aircraft. See notes
Sensors:	Radars Types 1022, 909, 1006, etc; sonars Type 184M
Complement:	557 + 318 air group

No	Name	Builder	Laid down	Launched	Comp	Fate
R 05	INVINCIBLE	Vickers-Armstrong, Barrow	20.7.73	3.5.77	11.7.80	Extant 1982
R 06	ILLUSTRIOUS	Swan Hunter	7.10.76	1.12.78	20.6.82	Extant 1982
R 09	ARK ROYAL (ex-*Indomitable*)	Swan Hunter	14.12.78	2.6.81		Completing

*It has been suggested that these figures are intentionally misleading. If the standard displacement is 19,500t as suspected, her full load tonnage will be *c* 23,000t.

from 17,500t to 19,500t, and with the growth in size it became possible to consider the possibility of using short take-off/vertical landing (STOVL) strike aircraft. The RN had refused to accept the original P1154 STOVL fighter on the grounds that its lack of navigational radar and short endurance would give it a very low capabil-

ity at sea. But in the interim the designers of the successful subsonic Harrier had pressed ahead with a Sea Harrier equipped with a more powerful engine, more fuel and new avionics which would provide the pilot with computer-aided navigation and attack data. In effect, advances in electronics have made it possible to do away with

the observer while still reducing the pilot's work-load.

In May 1975 it was officially announced that the new TDC would carry Sea Harriers, although the capability had long since been designed into the ship to avoid subsequent delays; in service nine Sea Kings and five Sea Harriers are

Illustrious Aug 1982   C & S Taylor

embarked. The Sketch Design was ready at the end of 1970, but the order was not placed until April 1973. For a long time there was no mention of any sisters, but in May 1976 No 2 (*Illustrious*) was ordered, followed by No 3 in December 1978. The third ship was planned to be called *Indomitable*, but immediately after the old *Ark Royal* paid off it was announced that her name would go to the new ship.

There are many novel features in the design. First, it is the largest gas turbine-powered ship in the world, with four Rolls-Royce Olympus units coupled to two shafts. Second, the emphasis is on large internal volume to allow the maintenance of virtually all equipment by exchange; in other words, everything down to the gas turbines and operating consoles has to be removable. This had already been achieved in other gas turbine ships, but the *Invincible* design carries it much farther. Because of the lack of armour and the use of much light alloy, the volume of the hull is big for its tonnage.

Invincible is the first ship equipped with the new Type 1022 long-range

air warning radar and she also has a double-headed Sea Dart guided weapon-system, with Type 910 trackers at each end of the island and a twin-arm launcher on the centreline forward. The provision of Sea Dart had been criticised for an alleged reduction of the flying capability, but it must be remembered that the Sea Harrier is a subsonic strike aircraft, not a supersonic interceptor, and therefore the ship (and other vessels in company) needs a long-range, rapid-reaction defence against air attack.

While *Invincible* was under construction a very simple improvement was perfected which will revolutionise flying at sea. This is the 'ski-jump', a ramp which gives the Sea Harrier sufficient lift to enable it to take off using less fuel or carrying more payload. In *Invincible* and *Illustrious* it takes the form of a 47t light steel structure welded on to the port side of the flight deck, rising at an angle of 7° over the bow, but it has the effect of adding 1500lb of payload to the Sea Harrier; *Ark Royal* will have a steeper ramp to improve performance further.

The euphemism 'through-deck

cruiser' (CAH) was subsequently changed to 'command cruiser' which was a reasonable title: much of the cost of *Invincible* is accounted for by 'C³' (Communications, Command and Control), and above all she is a flagship, having effective control of submarines and surface ships. By the time that *Invincible* came into service, however, the term 'carrier' was back in favour, and she is now rated as a support carrier (CVS).

It remains to be seen what developments in STOVL aircraft will take place in the next decade or so, but the *Invincible* class promise to be very effective anti-submarine ships, taking the most potent ASW helicopters far out to sea, but able to protect them from attack by enemy bombers. Their principal role is clearly to patrol the Greenland-Iceland-UK Gap in support of ASW forces operating behind the SOSUS barrier. As the first Western ships designed to exploit fixed-wing STOVL aircraft they are having a marked influence on other navies.

Following the 1981 Defence Review the *Invincible* was offered to the Royal Australian Navy as a

replacement for *Melbourne*. The offer was accepted, subject to some modifications to fuel stowage, communications, etc, when the Falklands Crisis intervened. She sailed with *Hermes* on 5 April, but did not return until relieved by *Illustrious* late in August. During the campaign she embarked 9 Sea Harriers and 10 helicopters. *Illustrious* was rushed to completion with the addition of two 20mm Phalanx 'Gatling' guns (1 forward to starboard of Sea Dart, 1 right aft on starboard side of the flight deck – *Invincible* to be similarly fitted but a different system may be fitted in *Ark Royal*).

The *Neptune* design of 1944 was dropped at the end of the war, and in its place a new design was developed, known as the *Minotaur* class. Instead of the triple 6in Mk 25, the ships would have had five twin Mk 26 mountings, capable of rapid fire (12–15rpm) at 80° elevation. The layout would have been virtually an enormously expanded *Dido* with three turrets forward and two aft, but there would also have been a heavy secondary battery of 3in guns and TT. They would have been much inferior to the US *Worcesters* owing to their heavy electrical equipment.

The most important innovations were a flush weather deck and a 'staggered' machinery layout. The design was clearly influenced not only by war experience, but by the magnificent designs produced by the US Navy for the Pacific. Three main design stages were reached, following a Controller's meeting early in 1946. Each time the design was slightly reduced in size, but finally lack of money forced the Navy to abandon any idea of building a new cruiser class for the time being.

MINOTAUR class (1947 design) *cruisers*

Displacement:	14,300t standard; 17,260t deep load
Dimensions:	616ft wl × 74ft × 24ft mean
	187.7m × 22.5m × 7.3m
Machinery:	4-shaft geared steam turbines, 4 Admiralty 3-drum boilers, 120,000shp = 31½kts. Oil 2640t
Armour:	Side 3½in, deck 1½in, bulkheads 3½in–2in, turrets 4in
Armament?	10–6in/50 QF Mk 26 (5×2), 16–3in/70 Mk 6 (8×2), 16–21in TT (4×4)
Complement:	c1300

MINOTAUR class (1951 design) *cruisers*

Displacement:	15,280t standard; 17,940t deep load
Dimensions:	645ft wl × 75ft × ?26ft
	196.6m × 22.9m × 7.9m
Machinery:	4-shaft geared steam turbines, 4 boilers, 100,000shp = 31½kts. Oil 2300t
Armour:	Side 3¼in, deck over machinery 1½in (1in elsewhere), magazines 1¼in
Armament:	10–6in/50 QF Mk 26 (5×2), 8–3in/70 Mk 6 (4×2), 15 DC, 4–3pdr saluting (4×1)
Complement:	c1300

Although four ships, *Minotaur*, *Centurion*, *Edgar* and *Mars* had been planned in 1945, no contracts were placed.

A decision was deferred on the *Minotaur* class, allowing work to continue on refining the design. The last revision found is dated 1951, by which time the need for other types of warship was taking priority. It must be assumed that the project had died by 1952–53.

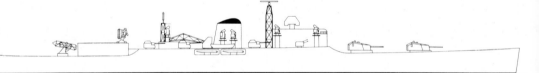

The 1960 medium cruiser design

In the years immediately after the war it was felt that a traditional cruiser with the ability to operate independently for long periods was still necessary to carry out the duties of trade protection and area anti-aircraft defence of fleets or convoys. However, it was also believed that such a ship had an offensive function as well, and these joint requirements led to a

1960 Medium Cruiser

Displacement:	12,250t standard; 14,750t deep load
Dimensions:	600ft wl × 70ft × 23ft
	182.9m × 21.3m × 7.0m
Machinery:	4-shaft geared steam turbines, 90,000shp = 31kts
Armament:	6–6in/50 Mk 26 (3×2), 8–3in/70 Mk 6 (4×2), 2 DACR mountings (2×6?), 8 TT (16 torpedoes)
Sensors:	Radar Types 984, 960, 992, gunnery sets; sonar not known
Complement:	?

The 1960 small cruiser design

series of design studies around 1948-49 for ships which could be in service in about 10 years' time, and were therefore referred to as '1960 cruisers'. They were to have some or all of the following features: surface gun armament; long and short range AA armament (with missiles is possible); speed, endurance and seakeeping; at least splinter protection to vitals; tor-

1960 Small Cruiser

Displacement:	10,500t standard; 13,000t deep load
Dimensions:	585ft wl × 68ft × 22ft
	178.3m × 20.7m × 6.7m
Machinery:	4-shaft geared steam turbines, 90,000shp = 31kts deep clean
Armament:	4–5in/56 DP (2×2), 6–3in/70 Mk 6 (3×2), 4 DACR mountings (4 × 6?), 16–21in QR TT (4×4)
Sensors:	Radars Types 960, 992, gunnery sets; sonar not known
Complement:	?

The 1960 missile-armed large cruiser design

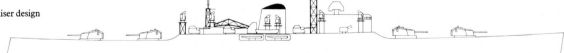

pedo, and ASW armament; aircraft direction capability; command and communications facilities. Radical solutions, such as nuclear propulsion, were deliberately excluded in order to meet the proposed schedule, which in turn was determined by the delivery of major new weapon systems – the twin 6in Mk 26 and 3in/70 in 1953, 5in/70 and a new close-range weapons (DACR) in 1957 and the Seaslug SAM in 1958. Conventional steam machin-

1960 Large Cruiser (Missile-Armed)

Displacement:	14,000t standard; 17,000t deep load
Dimensions:	630ft wl × 73ft × 22ft
	192.0m × 22.3m × 6.7m
Machinery:	4-shaft geared steam turbines, 95,000shp = 31kts
Armament:	4–5in/56 DP (2×2), 12–3in/70 Mk 6 (6×2), 2 DACR mountings (2×6?), 1 Seaslug SAM (1×2; 48 missiles)
Sensors:	Radar Types 960, 992, 901, gunnery sets; sonar not known
Complement:	*c* 900

The 1960 gun-armed large cruiser design

ery was adopted (improved *Daring* type), and the armament was arranged to obviate all physical fouling between guns (necessary because of high training speeds and automatic control).

Details of four variants are included here, although there is no evidence that the construction of any type was ever seriously planned.

1960 Large Cruiser (Gun-Armed)

Displacement:	14,500t standard; 17,500t deep load
Dimensions:	645ft wl × 74ft × 23ft
	195.6m × 22.6m × 7.0m
Machinery:	4-shaft geared steam turbines, 90,000shp = 31kts deep clean
Armament:	8–5in/56 (4×2), 12–3in/70 Mk 6 (6×2), 2 DACR mountings (2×6?), 16–21in QR TT (4×4)
Sensors:	Radar Types 960, 992, fire control sets; sonars not known
Complement:	900–950

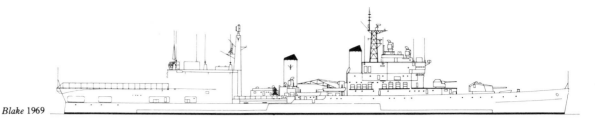

Blake 1969

Although the decision to complete the last three of the *Tiger* class to a new design was made by the Board of Admiralty in 1951 (a move strongly opposed by many), the dismantling of the old structure did not start until 1954. The new design had two twin 6in Mk 26 DP automatic mountings, one forward and one aft, with three twin 3in Mk 6 AA mountings in 'B' position and abreast the second funnel.

The internal fittings reflected the needs of a new generation of naval warfare: air conditioning throughout, a 200-line telephone exchange and a computer-aided Action Information Organisation (AIO). Each mounting had its own MRS3 fire-control set (bascially an Anglicised version of the US Navy's Mk 56 with a Type 903 dish scanner): there were two above the bridge, one aft and one on each side amidships. Radars included a Type 960 masthead dipole array for air warning (range 170 miles), Type 992 for surface search at the masthead (range 30 miles), and a Type 277Q height-finder on the mainmast (range 120 miles).

The armament was impressive, each water-cooled 6in barrel capable of delivering 20rpm. The 3in could theoretically deliver up to 120rpm; in practice 90rpm waš the best achieved.

Like most attempts to produce perfection, the *Tiger*s were too late, arriving on the scene just when the gun solution to AA defence was going out of fashion. Although fine, modern ships, there was little they could do other than engage smaller warships with gunfire or bombard shore positions. Their excellent command and communications facilities, however, still made them useful as task group flagships, and it was decided to give them more flexibility by replacing one 6in turret with a hangar and flight deck for four helicopters. This was approved, and in 1965–69 *Blake* was refitted at Portsmouth, followed by *Tiger* at Devonport in 1968–72. Lack of money prevented *Lion* from being taken in hand and she was put on the

TIGER class *cruisers*

Displacement:	9550t light load; 11,700t deep load. See notes
Dimensions:	538ft pp, 555ft 6in oa × 64ft × 23ft *163.8m, 169.3m × 19.5m × 7.0m*
Machinery:	4-shaft geared steam turbines, 4 Admiralty 3-drum boilers, 80,000shp = 31.5kts. Range 2100nm/6500nm at 31.5kts/13kts
Armour:	Belt 3½in–3¼in, bulkheads 2in–1½in, turrets 2in–1in, crowns to engine rooms and magazines 2in
Armament:	4–6in/50 Mk 26 (2×2), 6–3in/70 Mk 6 (3×2). See notes
Sensors:	Radar Types 960, 992Q, 277Q, 903. See notes
Complement:	880

No	Name	Builder	Laid down	Launched	Comp	Fate
C 20	TIGER (ex-*Bellerophon*)	John Brown	1.10.41	25.10.45	18.3.59	For disposal 1979
C 34	LION (ex-*Defence*)	Scotts	24.6.42	2.9.44	20.7.60	BU 1975
C 99	BLAKE (ex-*Tiger*, ex-*Blake*)	Fairfield	17.8.42	20.12.45	8.3.61	For disposal 1981

disposal list in 1975, but not before so much equipment had been 'cannibalised' that her sister was nicknamed 'Liger'. As reconstructed, displacement rose to 9975t standard, 12,080t deep load, and armament was now 2–6in Mk 26 (1×2), 2–3in Mk 6 (1×2), 2 Seacat GWS22 SAM systems (2×4) and 4 Wessex (later Sea King) helicopters. New sensors consisted of radar Types 965, 992Q, 278 and 903.

As refitted *Blake* had a particularly

ungainly profile, with a huge box hangar from mainmast to stern. The midships 3in turrets had to go, leaving her with the somewhat anomalous feature of two different calibres of gun in 'A' and 'B positions. When *Tiger* emerged in 1972 her funnels were considerably taller, with squared-off caps, and after another commission this improvement was given to *Blake* as well. Both ships proved useful in their new role, but their big crews

made them expensive to maintain, and when the manpower shortage hit the Royal Navy in the late 1970s they were prime candidates for the disposal list. In any case the recommissioning of *Hermes* and *Bulwark* had remedied the previous shortage of ASW helicopter ships, and so in 1979 *Tiger* was put on the disposal list, while *Blake* was laid up at Chatham in January 1980.

Lion as completed

CPL

Daring 1954

MoD

Defender 1969

Although similar big destroyers were built abroad, in 1953 the Admiralty decided that they should be rated as '*Daring* type ships' and manned as light cruisers, under a Captain, with bugle-calls instead of pipes, etc. These ships were divided into two groups: *Dainty*, *Daring*, *Defender* and *Delight* had a 220v DC electrical installation whereas the others had the new 440v AC system which was to become standard. Starting in 1963 the class was modernised, with all TT removed (the after bank had been removed in 1958–59), the STAAG Bofors mounting in the bridge wings removed and the Mk 6M director replaced by an MRS3 type. The DC group received two more twin Mk 5 mountings in place of the STAAG, but the others had Mk 7 singles in the bridge wings.

In 1963 *Decoy* was fitted with a quadruple Seacat short-range missile launcher abaft the second (visible) funnel, but although firing trials were successful it was decided not to refit the rest of the class, and the launcher was removed. The system was MRS8, a reworked CRBF director with new below-decks equipment.

DARING class *destroyers*

Displacement:	2830t standard; 3580t deep load	
Dimensions:	366ft pp, 390ft oa × 43ft × 13ft 7in mean deep load	
	111.6m, 118.8m × 13.1m × 4.1m	
Machinery:	2-shaft double-reduction geared turbines, 2 Foster Wheeler (*Daring, Delight, Decoy, Diana* Babcock & Wilcox) boilers, 54,000shp = 34.75kts. Oil 590t	
Armament:	6–4.5in/45 Mk 6 (3×2), 2 to 6–40mm/60 Mk 5 (1–3×2) (*Decoy, Diamond, Diana, Duchess* 2–40mm/60 Mk 9), 1 Squid	
Sensors:	Radar Types 903, 262, 293; sonar Types 170, 174/177	
Complement:	297–330	

No	Name	Builder	Laid down	Launched	Comp	Fate
D 108	DAINTY	White	17.12.45	16.8.50	26.2.53	BU 1972
D 05	DARING	Swan Hunter	29.9.45	10.8.49	8.3.52	BU 1971
D 106	DECOY (ex-*Dragon*)	Yarrow	22.9.46	19.3.49	28.4.53	To Peru 1970
D 114	DEFENDER (ex-*Dogstar*)	Stephen	22.3.49	27.7.50	5.12.52	BU 1972
D 119	DELIGHT (ex-*Disdain*, ex-*Ypres*)	Fairfield	5.9.46	21.12.50	9.10.53	BU 1971
D 35	DIAMOND	John Brown	15.3.49	14.6.50	21.2.52	Harbour TS 1970, BU 1981
D 126	DIANA (ex-*Druid*)	Yarrow	3.4.47	8.5.52	29.3.54	To Peru 1970
D 154	DUCHESS	Thornycroft	2.7.48	9.4.51	23.10.52	To Australia 1964

Diana and *Daring* were temporarily fitted with a steamlined after funnel casing a short while after completion, at the personal wish of Earl Mountbatten; it improved their looks, but restricted the arcs of fire of the aft twin Bofors and was removed after a few years. The ships served on all stations and gave good service, but as the design had already been stretched there was insufficient room for new sensors and weaponry. *Duchess* was transferred to the Royal Australian Navy in 1964 to replace *Voyager* and retained her name, and in 1970 *Decoy* and *Diana* were sold to Peru, becoming *Ferré* and *Palacios*.

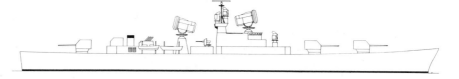

The 1953 destroyer design

To follow the *Daring* class it was proposed to build another class of large destroyers, but the Board of Admiralty's obsession with the threat from Soviet *Sverdlov* class cruisers (abetted by the usual exaggerated intelligence assessments) led to pressure to provide gunpower. After numerous studies an attempt was made to find commonality with the Army's Green Mace gun design. This was a massive mobile 5in/56 AA gun intended to use folding-fin, discarding-sabot (FFDS) ammunition and fire 96rpm. A constructor was lent to RARDE at Fort Halstead to study problems of adapting the installation to naval use.

Although the Naval Staff originally wanted a twin mounting for this class, a single mounting proved adequate. Even when scaled down from 96 to

1953 destroyer

Displacement:	*c*3000t standard; *c*3800t deep load	
Dimensions:	450ft pp × 47ft 3in × 12ft 8in	
	137.2m × 14.4m × 3.9m	
Machinery:	2-shaft geared steam turbines, 60,000shp = 38kts	
Armament:	3–5in/56 Mk 2 DP (3×1), 2–3in/50 AA (2×1), 1 Ruler, 1 Limbo Mk 10, 8–21in TT	
Sensors:	Radar Types 984 (2), 992, 903; sonars not known	
Complement:	?	

80rpm the rate of fire was calculated to be sufficient to overwhelm the *Sverdlov*'s dozen 6in guns. To enable the ship to close the range rapidly and make herself a difficult target she was intended to make 38kts.

The result, after many changes of design (64 different design stages are recorded), was a large and remarkably modern-looking warship, more reminiscent of the later USN CGs than their equivalents in the RN, the 'Counties'. They would have had two pyramidal 'macks', fixed TT in the superstructure and a 'Ruler' anti-torpedo system aft. But a growing belief by Mountbatten that guns could not cope with the air threat led to its being dropped in 1955 in favour of a DLG design.

The 1951 design shown is an intermediate stage, with two Type 984 3-D comprehensive display radars, a single 'mack' and three MRS3 directors. The 'Ruler' shown aft is an anti-torpedo system similar to Hedgehog, although with proximity rather than contact fuse, firing multiple charges to detonate in the path of a torpedo. What is also unusual is the pair of single 3in/50 US-pattern guns amidships.

Cavalier 25.7.79

MG Photographic

In 1953 the first of the class (*Carron*) was taken in hand for modernisation and by 1961 all eight had been recommissioned. The conversion enhanced the ships' capabilities as general-purpose escorts, with the latest Mk 6M fire control, remote power control (RPC) fitted to the guns, and the after TT replaced by a deckhouse with two Squid ASW mortars and a twin Mk 5 Bofors AA gun. *Caesar*, *Cambrian*, *Caprice* and *Cassandra* has an enclosed frigate-style bridge, which was left open on the others of the class. In 1966 *Caprice* and *Cavalier* received a quadruple Seacat GWS20 missile system in place of the Mk 5 Bofors, and this necessitated a big handing room on top of the original deckhouse. Shortly after recommissioning *Carron* was attached to the Dartmouth Training Squadron, with a large navigating bridge in place of 'B' gun. In 1960 she became a navigation tender attached to *Dryad* and had the rest of her armament removed.

Cavalier paid off in 1972, but avoided the breakers. Being the last RN 'conventional' destroyer, strenuous efforts were made to preserve her as a memorial. Finally she was acquired by the HMS *Cavalier* Trust in 1977 and is now open to the public at Southampton.

CAVENDISH class *destroyers*

Displacement:	1964–2053t light; 2675t deep load
Dimensions:	339ft 6in pp, 362ft 9in oa × 35ft 8in × 14ft 3in–14ft 6in mean deep load *103.5m, 110.6m × 10.9m ×4.3m–4.4m*
Machinery:	2-shaft Parsons geared turbines, 2 Admiralty 3-drum boilers, 40,000shp = 36.75kts. Range 2800nm at 20kts
Armament:	3–4.5in/45 Mk 4 on CPS mountings (3×1), 2–40mm Mk 5 AA (1×2), 2–40mm/60 Mk 9 (2×1), 2 Squid, 4–21in Mk 8 TT (1×4)
Sensors:	Radar Types 275, 293P or Q, 978/974, 944
Complement:	192 peace; 264 max

No	Name	Builder	Laid down	Launched	Comp	Fate
D 07	CAESAR	John Brown	3.4.43	14.2.44	5.10.44	Sold 1966, BU
D 15	CAVENDISH	John Brown	19.5.43	12.4.44	13.12.44	Sold 1967, BU
D 85	CAMBRIAN	Scotts	14.8.42	10.12.43	17.7.44	Sold 1970, BU
D 30	CARRON	Scotts	26.11.42	28.3.44	6.11.44	Sold 1967, BU
D 01	CAPRICE	Yarrow	28.9.42	16.9.43	5.4.44	Sold 1979, BU
D 10	CASSANDRA	Yarrow	30.1.43	29.11.43	28.7.44	Sold 1967, BU
D 25	CARYSFORT	White	12.5.43	25.7.44	20.2.45	Sold 1970, BU
D 73	CAVALIER	White	28.2.43	7.4.44	22.11.44	Preserved 1977

Broadsword 1962   CPL

Crossbow 1964

In 1958–59 all four vessels were converted to radar-pickets, with a tall lattice mast between the (visible) funnel and the foremast, carrying a Type 965 long-range radar array. The TT were removed and a continuous deckhouse ran aft as far as the original superstructure. The opportunity was taken to move *Battleaxe*'s and *Broadsword*'s twin Squid mortars and handing room from 'B' position back aft, and to resite the twin 4in gun forward; they were now identical with the other two ships in layout. The old Mk 6 director over the bridge was replaced by an MRS8 director.

On 1 August 1962 *Battleaxe* was badly damaged in a collision with the frigate *Ursa* in the Clyde and was laid up. The class were superseded by the 'Battle' conversions, with their more elaborate air-plotting facilities, and were put on the disposal list in 1966.

'WEAPON' class *radar-pickets*

Displacement:	2280t normal; 2935t full load
Dimensions:	341ft 6in pp, 365ft oa × 38ft × 14ft 8in mean deep load *104.1m, 111.2m × 11.6m × 4.5m*
Machinery:	2-shaft Parsons geared turbines, 2 Foster Wheeler boilers, 40,000shp = 34kts. Range 5000nm at 15kts
Armament:	4–4in Mk 16 AA (2×2), 4–40mm/60 STAAG Mk 2 AA (2×2), 2–40mm/60 Mk 9 AA (2×1), 2 Squid (*Scorpion* 1 Limbo Mk 10)
Sensors:	Radar Types 965 (AKE-1), 293, 262; sonar Types 170, 174/177
Complement:	234

No	Name	Builder	Laid down	Launched	Comp	Fate
D 118	BATTLEAXE	Yarrow	22.4.44	12.6.45	23.10.47	Sold 1964, BU
D 31	BROADSWORD	Yarrow	20.7.44	5.2.46	4.10.48	Sold 1968, BU
D 96	CROSSBOW	Thornycroft	26.8.44	20.12.45	4.3.48	BU 1972
D 64	SCORPION (ex-*Tomahawk*, ex-*Centaur*)	White	16.12.44	15.8.46	17.12.47	BU 1971

Agincourt Sept 1964   MG Photographic

In 1960 four of the second group were taken in hand for conversion to radar-pickets. This involved stepping a larger lattice foremast to carry the Type 965 radar array, with its 'double bedstead' AKE-2 antenna. The original AA and TT armament was removed and a new after superstructure built, with a short lattice mast carrying a Type 978 height-finder array. Abaft this was an MRS8 director and a quadruple Seacat missile launcher. The original Mk 37 fire control director was left and so was the Squid ASW mortar on the quarterdeck. Internally the ships were totally rebuilt to improve habitability and to provide a new AIO.

All four conversions were completed by the spring of 1962, but the ships were all on the disposal list in 1970. They were originally DC (direct current) ships and had to converted to AC (alternating current) to provide power for the new radars and the Seacat missile system.

'BATTLE' class *radar-pickets*

Displacement:	2780t standard; 3430t full load
Dimensions:	355ft pp, 379ft oa × 40ft 6in × 15ft 4in mean deep load
	108.2m, 115.5m × 12.3m × 4.7m
Machinery:	2-shaft Parsons geared turbines, 2 Admiralty 3-drum boilers, 50,000shp = 35.75kts. Range 4400nm at 15kts
Armament:	4–4.5in Mk 5 DP (2×2), 2–20mm (2×1), 1 Seacat GWS22 SAM (1×4), 1 Squid
Sensors:	Radar Types 965 (AKE-2), 293, 262 (Seacat), 278; sonar Types 174/177, 170
Complement:	268

No	Name	Builder	Laid down	Launched	Comp	Fate
D 86	AGINCOURT	Hawthorn Leslie	12.12.43	29.1.45	25.6.47	BU 1974
D 22	AISNE	Vickers-Armstrong, Tyne	26.8.43	12.5.45	20.3.47	BU 1970
D 68	BARROSA	John Brown	28.12.43	17.1.45	14.2.47	BU 1978
D 97	CORUNNA	Swan Hunter	12.4.44	29.4.45	6.6.47	BU 1975

Glamorgan 1976

The term 'destroyer' was applied to these ships to obtain Treasury approval, but they were later rated as DLGs, from the American term 'Destroyer Leader, Guided Missile', applied to the new generation of big fleet escorts. As in the USN ships, however, destroyer principles governed their design: there was no longitudinal subdivision and the ships had relatively light scantlings to keep down size and weight.

Like the *Whitby*s the design was volume-critical, and in particular it centred on the Seaslug missile system. Seaslug was a first-generation beam-rider, with its four booster-motors wrapped around the body. British guided weapons of the period relied on wrap-around boosters because it was feared (incorrectly) that end-on mounting of the booster would produce instability in the missile after launch.

Thus although the new DLG had ample vertical space between decks for upright stowage and loading through deck-hatches, she had to be given a horizontal 'tunnel' through the superstructure. The missiles are brought up from the forward magazine on a hoist and then travel through the tunnel, undergoing checkouts, fitting of wings, etc.,

'COUNTY' class *guided missile destroyers*

Displacement:	6200t normal; 6800t full load
Dimensions:	505ft pp, 521ft 6in oa × 54ft × 20ft 6in max
	153.9m, 158.9m × 16.4m × 6.3m
Machinery:	2-shaft COSAG: geared steam turbines, 2 Babcock & Wilcox boilers, plus 4 G6 gas turnines, 30,000shp + 30,000shp = 30kts. Range 3500nm at 28kts
Armament:	4–4.5in/45 Mk 6 (2×2), 1 Seaslug SAM (1×2), 2 Seacat GWS21 (later ships GWS22) SAM (2×4), 2–20mm (2×1), 1 helicopter. See notes
Sensors:	Radar Types 965 (AKE-1 or -2), 277/278, 992Q/993, 901, 903/904; sonar Types 170, 174/177 (replaced by 184)
Complement:	440–471

No	Name	Builder	Laid down	Launched	Comp	Fate
D 02	DEVONSHIRE	Cammell Laird	9.3.59	10.6.60	15.11.62	For disposal 1978
D 06	HAMPSHIRE	John Brown	26.3.59	16.3.61	15.3.63	Paid off 1976, BU
D 16	LONDON	Swan Hunter	26.2.60	7.12.61	14.11.63	To Pakistan 1982
D 12	KENT	Harland & Wolff	1.3.60	27.9.61	15.8.63	HS 1980
D 20	FIFE	Fairfield	31.5.62	9.7.64	21.6.66	Extant 1982
D 19	GLAMORGAN	Vickers-Armstrong, Tyne	13.9.62	9.7.64	13.10.66	Extant 1982
D 18	ANTRIM	Fairfield	20.1.66	10.10.67	14.7.70	Extant 1982
D 21	NORFOLK	Swan Hunter	15.3.66	16.11.67	7.3.70	To Chile 1982

Devonshire as completed   CPL

before being run out on to the launcher. This was a somewhat over-engineered, massive lattice-work affair weighing as much as a gun turret. Although the figure of 36 rounds is quoted, it is believed to be less in view of their bulk.

Four ships were voted under the 1955–56 and 1956–57 Estimates, followed by another four under the 1961–62 and 1964–65 Estimates. The second group had the slightly improved Seaslug Mk 2, externally identical, but having some capability against surface targets. They were also fitted with the 'double bedstead' AKE-2 version of the Type 965 long-range radar and had GWS22 directors controlling the Seacat missiles in place of GWS21. For the first time in a British warship, the design included provision for a medium helicopter, but arrangements for housing the Wessex – a hangar with a folding vertical door on the port side of the superstructure – were rather cumbersome.

The 'Counties' were, together with the 'Tribals', the first ships to have Combined Steam and Gas turbine (COSAG) machinery; main drive is supplied by twin HP and LP steam turbines and twin gas turbines are geared to the same shafts for boost. The system has the advantage of permitting the ship to get under way at short notice, as well as providing more power at high speed without excessive weight.

In 1972 *Norfolk* began a conversion to operate the new French Exocet surface-to-surface missile: four MM38 canisters were mounted in 'B' position, with special deflectors to avoid damage to the bridgework from the booster. She carried out firing trials in 1974, making her the first RN operational warship to fire an SSM. She was also refitted with a lighter tubular foremast carrying a Type 992Q radar scanner, a modification subsequently extended to *Antrim*, *Fife* and *Glamorgan* which also received Exocet. The older ships were refitted with GWS22 Seacat directors.

The limitations of the Seaslug missile system, inherent in the fact that it is a beam-rider, mean that these handsome ships are of diminishing value; furthermore, they are expensive to man and maintain, and so *Hampshire* was paid off in 1976 to be cannibalised. *Devonshire* was under consideration for sale to Egypt after conversion to carry six Lynx helicopters in the former missile loading space in the main deck, but this fell through in 1978 and she too went on the disposal list. *London* had been earmarked for conversion to a minelayer – again the Seaslug 'tunnel' would prove ideal – to meet the need for operations behind the SOSUS barriers in the Greenland-Iceland-UK (GIUK) Gap.

At the time of writing, however, the conversion has not been approved, and she will not be retained much longer. *Kent* was deleted in April 1980, but remained in service for harbour training. The later ships have good command facilities and were intended to last until the late 1980s,

until all three *Invincible* class carriers were in service, but under the 1981 defence cuts they will go earlier. Chile took over *Norfolk* on 6 April 1982 (renamed *Prat*) and Pakistan took over *London* in February 1982 (renamed *Babur*). *Antrim* and *Glamorgan* were damaged, one by

bombs, the other by bombs and an Exocet) in the Falklands.

Bristol 1979

BRISTOL class *guided missile destroyers*

Displacement:	6700t normal; 7700t full load
Dimensions:	490ft pp, 507ft oa × 55ft × 22ft 6in max
	149.3m, 154.3m × 16.8m × 6.8m
Machinery:	2-shaft COSAG: geared steam turbines, 2 Babcock & Wilcox boilers, plus 2 Olympus TMIA gas turbines, 30,000shp + 44,000shp = 30kts. Range 5000nm at 18kts
Armament:	1–4.5in/55 Mk 8, 1 Sea Dart GWS30 SAM system (1×2, 40 missiles), 1 Ikara ASW system (32 missiles), 1 Limbo Mk 10
Sensors:	Radar Types 909(2), 965 (AKE-2), 978, 1006, 992/993; sonar Types 184, 162
Complement:	407

No	Name	Builder	Laid down	Launched	Comp	Fate
D 23	BRISTOL	Swan Hunter	15.11.67	30.6.69	31.3.73	Extant 1982
	–					Cancelled 1967
	–					Cancelled 1967
	–					Cancelled 1967

The new carriers planned for the 1970s (see *CVA-01*) would need escorts to provide them with anti-aircraft and anti-submarine defence and so four new DLGs were planned to follow the 'County' class. Although rated as DLGs, for some reason they were given Type No 82 in the general-purpose frigate series (originally known as CF299 frigates). With the cancellation of *CVA-01* in 1966 it would have been logical to cancel them as well, and indeed the Board of Admiralty was willing to accept seven extra *Leander* class frigates in their place, but a trials ship had been promised for the Anglo-Dutch 'Broomstick' radar project in the hope that the Dutch would order the Olympus gas turbine. Finally, the class was cut back to one unit, the reason being that she could act as a trials ship for new weapons.

Although superficially resembling a 'cleaned-up' version of the 'County' class, the design incorporates another generation of equipment and ideas. For one thing, the Sea Dart missile system uses vertical stowage and a twin-arm zero-length launcher like USN systems, and for another, Sea Dart is a semi-active homing missile with a much greater capacity to handle multiple targets. Although the same type of COSAG machinery was adopted, much more attention was paid to providing good access to the gas turbines. The result was that the design changed from a single-funnel to a two-funnel configuration and finally to three funnels, the after uptakes being split into two separate funnels to allow the Olympus gas turbines to be lifted out. *Bristol* was thus the first RN ship to be designed around the new concept of upkeep by replacement, which reduces the time

Bristol 1974

spent on machinery overhauls. Although nearly 1000t bigger than the 'Counties', she needs 70 men fewer to run her.

She was also the first RN ship to go to sea with the Anglo-Australian Ikara ASW missile system, mounted in a 'zareba' forward of the bridge. The new 4.5in Mk 8 RARDE gun in a Vickers mounting replaced the old Mk 6 twin, but only one was provided, in 'A' position. Work had been proceeding on a joint Anglo-Dutch project to produce a Comprehensive Display System (CDS) radar for air warning, surveillance and aircraft direction, known as CF299, and it was to be mounted over the bridge, but the rising cost of research and development, combined with the belief that there would be no need for such a system because there would be no carrier-aircraft to direct, led to to Britain withdrawing from the scheme. At the same time, the Dutch were disenchanted with the spiralling cost (and volume) of the Sea Dart missile system; by mutual consent the

CDS was dropped, and *Bristol* went to sea with the less capable Type 965 (AKE-2).

Although sometimes criticised as being a 'white elephant' she is an extremely versatile ship, with sophisticated command and communications to back up her weapon systems. The only serious shortcoming is the lack of a helicopter hangar, omitted because she was originally intended to operate with carriers. Since completion she has been used for weapon and system trials, and as a result has never received the minor improvements given to other large ships.

The heart of *Bristol*'s weapon systems is the Action Data Automation Weapon System Mk 2 (ADAWS-2), which co-ordinates data from the radar and sonar plots, the inertial navigation system, and any other source, and processes it via a suite of digital computers. The information is displayed in the operations room to give a rapid picture of the threat; only the decision to fire remains to be given.

In 1973 the ship suffered serious, almost fatal, damage when her steam plant was virtually destroyed by fire. For a time it was feared that she would be scrapped, but she was able to complete the Ikara and Sea Dart trials programme running only on the two gas turbines. This helped to convince doubters about the wisdom of the change to all-gas turbine propulsion, and since then the steam plant has been repaired. She was intended to receive a big half-life modernisation in 1981 but under the defence review she will remain as she is until scrapped.

C & S Taylor

Southampton 1981

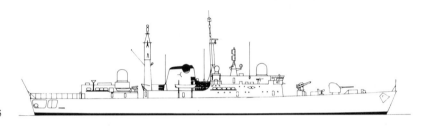

Sheffield 1975

The cancellation of *CVA-01* led to a new Staff Requirement for a smaller fleet escort capable of providing area defence. The result was the Type 42 guided missile destroyer (DDG), which achieved significant savings on cost and displacement by dropping the Ikara long-range ASW missile and Limbo mortar and adopting an all-gas turbine (COGOG) propulsion system, using Rolls-Royce Olympus turbines for main drive and Tynes for cruising.

Although lacking Ikara, the ASW capability was greatly improved over previous ships by providing a hangared Lynx light helicopter (armed with torpedoes and missiles). Unlike *Bristol* the forecastle deck extends right aft to form the helicopter flight deck, leaving a small covered quarterdeck below for handling mooring wires. Close-range ASW defence is provided by triple TT similar to the USN Mk 32, firing Mk 44 or Mk 46 weapons, but eventually to fire the new Stingray lightweight torpedo. Apart from having the Sea Dart twin-arm launcher forward (a lighter hand-operated version of the type in *Bristol*), the configuration is similar to *Bristol*: Type 909 Sea Dart trackers forward and aft and a Type 965 (AKE-2) air warning radar above the forward superstructure.

The appearance is quite different from previous DLGs, with a single wide funnel. *Sheffield* appeared with prominent 'Loxton Bends' on each side, an attempt to keep heat emission down, but this was not repeated in following ships. *Exeter* commissioned in 1980 with the new Type 1022 interim STIR radar in place of the double 965, and this set may be retro-fitted to the earlier ships. *Sheffield* did not receive her STWS TT, but the others carry them on small platforms abreast the mainmast.

The main weakness of the *Sheffield*

SHEFFIELD class *guided missile destroyers*

Displacement:	3850t normal; 4350t full load
Dimensions:	392ft wl, 410ft oa × 46ft × 19ft max *119.5m, 125.0m × 14.0m × 5.8m*
Machinery:	2-shaft COGOG: 2 Olympus TM3B gas turbines, 50,000shp = 30kts; 2 Tyne RMIA gas turbines, 8000shp = 18kts
Armament:	1–4.5in/55 Mk 8, 2–20mm (2×), 1 Sea Dart GWS30 SAM system (1×2, 22 missiles), 1 helicopter, 6–12.75in TT (2×3). See notes
Sensors:	Radar Types 909 (2), 965 (AKE-2) or 1022, 992Q/993, 1006; sonar Types 184M, 162
Complement:	299–312

No	Name	Builder	Laid down	Launched	Comp	Fate
D 80	SHEFFIELD	Vickers-Armstrong, Barrow	15.1.70	10.6.71	16.2.75	Sunk May 82
D 86	BIRMINGHAM	Cammell Laird	28.3.72	30.7.73	3.12.76	Extant 1982
D 108	CARDIFF	Vickers-Armstrong, Barrow	6.11.72	22.2.74	24.9.79	Extant 1982
D 118	COVENTRY	Cammell Laird	29.1.73	21.6.74	20.10.78	Sunk May 82
D 87	NEWCASTLE	Swan Hunter	21.2.73	24.4.75	23.3.78	Extant 1982
D 88	GLASGOW	Swan Hunter	16.4.74	14.4.76	24.5.79	Extant 1982
D 89	EXETER	Swan Hunter	22.7.76	25.4.78	19.9.80	Extant 1982
D 90	SOUTHAMPTON	Vosper Thornycroft	21.10.76	29.1.79	31.10.81	Extant 1982
D 91	NOTTINGHAM	Vosper Thornycroft	6.2.78	18.2.80	1982	Extant 1982
D 92	LIVERPOOL	Cammell Laird	5.7.78	25.9.80	9.7.82	Extant 1982

class lies in the constraints placed on dimensions during the design phase. As a result of Treasury pressure the Controller kept length and beam down, which results in cramped accommodation, a much smaller complement of missiles than in *Bristol*, and reduced endurance. The problem of endurance was shrugged aside on the grounds that the ships had no 'east of Suez' role and would always be within reach of a replenishment group around the coasts of north-western Europe, but the short forecastle affects their seaworthiness by making them very wet forward. This fault has been rectified in the improved vessels building (see below), but it places severe limits on what can be added to the existing ships.

With ten ships completed between

1975 and 1981 (less *Sheffield* and *Coventry*) they are the largest class of major ships built for the RN since 1967. During the Falklands Campaign the survivors were fitted with 4–30mm Oerlikons (2×2) and two single 20mm amidships, had their EW enhanced and US chaff systems added. In addition, the Lynx helicopter received the Sea Skua air-to-surface missile, rushed into service.

The high degree of automation has resulted in a reduction of 100 men over *Bristol*'s complement. The layout of the machinery compartments allows easy removal routes, and a complete change of gas turbine can be carried out by the ship herself: all that is needed is a sheltered anchorage and a crane capable of lifting the turbine in its module.

The building time has come down

from an average of five years to four. *Cardiff* was seriously delayed by a shortage of skilled manpower at Barrow-in-Furness and had to be towed to the Tyne in February 1976 for completion by Swan Hunter. *Liverpool* is the first to be built by the 'extrusion' method: large sections of hull are built separately and then moved on to the slipway. This enabled Cammell Laird to cut delivery time by a year.

Sheffield was disabled and set on fire by an Argentine AM39 Exocet missile on 4 May 1982; the wreck was scuttled 10 May. *Coventry* was sunk by bombs on 25 May.

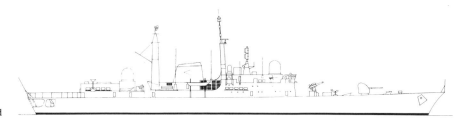

Manchester as completed

The shortcomings of the *Sheffield* class could easily be remedied by restoring the length cut off the original design and slightly increasing the beam, and in November 1978 an order was placed for the first of four 'stretched Type 42s'. In configuration they will be virtually identical with the later *Sheffield* class, with Type 1022 air warning radar. They will also have the later version of the STWS defence against submarines using the Stingray torpedo and will have four 30mm Oerlikons added. Because of the longer hull they are marginally faster than the *Sheffield* class.

'MANCHESTER' class *guided missile destroyers*

Displacement:	4750t normal; 5350t full load					
Dimensions:	434ft wl, 463ft oa × 49ft × 19ft max					
	132.3m, 141.1m × 14.9m × 5.8m					
Machinery:	As *Sheffield* class					
Armament:	As *Sheffield* class. See notes					
Sensors:	Radar as *Sheffield* class, but Type 1022, in place of 965					
Complement:	312					

No	Name	Builder	Laid down	Launched	Comp	Fate
D 95	MANCHESTER	Vickers-Armstrong, Barrow	19.5.78	27.11.80	1.11.82	Extant 1982
D 96	GLOUCESTER	Vosper Thornycroft	25.10.79	2.11.82		Fitting out
D 98	YORK	Swan Hunter	18.1.80	21.6.82		Fitting out
D 97	EDINBURGH	Cammell Laird	8.9.80			Building

The postwar frigate designs derived from studies carried out in 1944–45 by Herbert Pengelly and Ken Purvis. Wartime experience showed that escorts needed to be robust, with outer bottom plating at least 12lb (0.3in) thick and a strong forecastle deck. They should be easy to build and capable of being altered from the anti-submarine (ASW) to the anti-aircraft (AA) role at a late stage in building. Typical of a large number of studies was TSD 2001/45 for a 25kt 'sloop':

Displacement: 1400t standard
Endurance: 4500nm at 18kts (6 months out of dock)
Armament: ASW – 1 twin 4.5in Mk 6, 1 twin 20mm, 6 'Bidder' Mk 20(E)

The 1945 Frigate projects

torpedoes, 2 DC throwers; AA – 2 twin 4.5in or 3 twin 4in, 4 twin 20mm, 'Ben', 4 DC throwers
More detailed calculations for the ASW type suggested a ship 335ft × 43ft (*102.1m × 13.1m*) on 1650t standard, 2300t deep load.

By February 1946 an aircraft-direction (AD) frigate had evolved, equipped with Type 960, 277Q and 292Q radars and armed with a close-range AA missile known as 'Long-shot' (formerly 'Ben', then 'Popsy') or a twin 4.5in, four single Bofors and a Squid mortar. By the following August the requirements for 'Long-

shot' (later known as 'Hot Shot') had been dropped and there was even talk of dropping the 40mm gun as the Bofors was considered to be obsolete. Types 980 and 981 radars were specified for the AD version, and a Type 'D' mortar (Limbo) had replaced the Improved or 'B' Type Squid.

In March 1947 it was decided that the new frigates could not be given steam machinery as the British heavy engineering industry no longer had sufficient capacity and because it was doubtful whether sufficient skilled personnel could be recruited to run

advanced turbine machinery. Although the ASW design had to be steam-powered to get the required speed of 27kts, the ASW and AD versions were slower and could be given diesels.

A simple code was drawn up to distinguish the three streams of design: type-numbers 11–39 were allocated to ASW frigates, 41–59 to AA and 61–79 to AD. Although much modified (there have been at least two Types 18 and two Types 42 already), the system was still in use in 1982.

The original 1945 Frigate Concept called for a standard steam-engined hull capable of 25kts sea speed ('25kt sloop'), with two variants for ASW and AA. An AD variant appeared in February 1946. As the AA and AD

TYPE 11 class *frigates*

versions appeared there must at some stage have been a Type 11 ASW, but no trace has survived. As mention of it

stops so early in the post-1945 frigate papers, we must conclude that it was dropped as soon as news of the Soviet

'Whiskey' class became known, before any detailed design work was done.

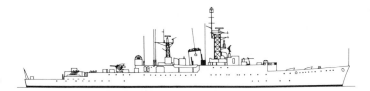

Relentless 1967

The urgent need of fast frigates to counter the new generation of fast Soviet 'Whiskey' class submarines could most readily be met by adapting the numerous 'Emergency' destroyer hulls. By the late 1940s these were totally unsuited to modern warfare, the majority having low-angle guns and primitive fire control. Accordingly in 1949 plans were drawn up to convert two prototypes, *Rocket* and *Relentless*.

The change was dramatic, with a new forecastle deck extending almost to the stern and a superstructure of riveted aluminium. A new type of enclosed bridge was provided at the forward end of the superstructure, directly ahead of the Operations Room, mainly in order to be close to the latter, but also to provide protection from the weather. The captain was provided with a periscope to permit him to con the ship from the Ops Room and even the lookouts were given transparent plastic domes at the bridge wings. The armament was light – a twin 4in Mk 16 with its own CRBF director aft and a twin Bofors above the bridge – but the ASW armament was nearly on a par with the as yet unbuilt Type 12, consisting of search and attack sonars of the latest type and two Squid mortars aft (replaced by an ASW mortar Mk 10 in later ships); *Rocket* and *Relentless* had the Mk 10 prototype. It was hoped to supplement this with eight 21in ASW homing torpedoes, but the failure of the 'Bidder' Mk 20 (E) torpedo caused the tubes to be removed from the few ships so fitted.

This Type 15 conversion ranks as one of the outstanding successes of the postwar period, wringing as much as an extra 25 years out of obsolescent hulls. They were regarded as expensive in their day, but the cut-price Type 16s which followed them were not nearly so effective. They proved weatherly and robust, and made up numbers of escorts at a time when new construction was coming into service very slowly. Endurance was reduced to 4750nm at 15kts (476t fuel).

Rocket and *Relentless* completed their conversion in 1952 and were followed by the others in 1952–57. Yards known to have been involved are: Portsmouth DYd – *Relentless* 1950–52, *Verulam* 1952, *Troubridge* (completed by White, 1955–57); Devonport DYd – *Rocket* 1950–52, *Roebuck* 1952–53, *Ulysses* 1952–53, *Venus* 1953, *Wizard* 1954; *Chatham* Chatham DYd – *Ulster* 1952–53, *Zest* 1954–56; *Grenville* 1953–54, *Virago* 1952; Scotts – *Wakeful* 1952–53; Palmers – *Whirlwind* 1952–53, *Ursa* 1952–54; Harland & Wolff, Belfast – *Wrangler* 1951–52; Harland & Wolff, Liverpool – *Urania* 1953–54; White – *Volage* 1952, *Undaunted* 1952–54; Barclay Curle – *Urchin* 1952–54; Stephens – *Rapid* 1952–53; Thornycroft – *Vigilant*; Yarrow – *Undine*. The main modification was to provide a new enclosed bridge above the Ops Room and in three of the ships (*Troubridge*, *Ulster*, *Zest*) the 40mm mount-

RAPID class *frigates*

Displacement:	2240t normal; 2850t full load
Dimensions:	339ft 6in pp, 358ft 3in oa × 35ft 8in × 13ft 10in–14ft 1in *103.5m, 109.2m × 10.9m × 4.2m–4.3m*
Machinery:	2-shaft Parsons geared turbines, 2 Admiralty 3-drum boilers, 40,000shp = 36.75kts. Range 3000nm at 20kts
Armament:	2–4in/45 QF Mk 16 AA (1×2), 2–40mm Mk 5 AA (1×2), 2–21in TT (2×1), 2 Squid Mk 4 (later ships Limbo Mk 10)
Sensors:	Radar Types 278, 262, 293; sonar Types 170, 174
Complement:	195

No	Name	Builder	Laid down	Launched	Comp	Fate
F 138	RAPID	Cammell Laird	16.6.41	16.7.42	20.2.43	For disposal 1979
F 185	RELENTLESS	John Brown	20.6.41	15.7.42	30.11.42	BU 1971
F 191	ROCKET	Scotts	14.3.41	28.10.42	4.8.43	BU 1967
F 195	ROEBUCK	Scotts	19.6.41	10.12.42	10.6.43	BU 1969
F 09	TROUBRIDGE	John Brown	10.11.41	23.9.42	8.3.43	BU 1970
F 197	GRENVILLE	Swan Hunter	1.11.41	12.10.42	27.5.43	For disposal 1979
F 83	ULSTER	Swan Hunter	12.11.41	9.11.42	30.6.43	BU 1980
F 17	ULYSSES	Cammell Laird	14.3.42	22.4.43	23.12.43	BU 1970
F 53	UNDAUNTED	Cammell Laird	8.9.42	19.7.43	3.3.44	Sunk as target 1978
F 141	UNDINE	Thornycroft	18.3.42	1.6.43	23.12.43	BU 1965
F 08	URANIA	Vickers-Armstrong, Barrow	18.6.42	19.5.43	18.1.44	BU 1971
F 196	URCHIN	Vickers-Armstrong, Barrow	26.3.62	8.3.43	24.9.43	BU 1967
F 200	URSA	Thornycroft	2.5.62	22.7.43	1.3.44	BU 1967
F 50	VENUS	Fairfield	12.1.42	23.2.43	28.8.43	BU 1972
F 29	VERULAM	Fairfield	26.1.42	22.4.43	10.12.43	BU 1972
F 93	VIGILANT	Swan Hunter	31.1.42	22.12.42	10.9.43	BU 1965
F 76	VIRAGO	Swan Hunter	16.2.42	4.2.43	5.11.43	BU 1965
F 41	VOLAGE	White	13.12.42	15.12.43	26.5.44	BU 1976
F 159	WAKEFUL (ex-*Zebra*)	Fairfield	3.6.42	10.6.43	17.2.44	BU 1971
F 187	WHIRLWIND	Hawthorn Leslie	31.7.42	20.8.43	20.7.44	Target 1974
F 42	WIZARD	Vickers-Armstrong, Barrow	14.9.42	29.9.43	30.3.44	BU 1967
F 157	WRANGLER	Vickers-Armstrong, Barrow	23.9.42	30.12.43	14.7.44	To South Africa 1956
F 102	ZEST	Thornycroft	21.7.42	14.10.43	20.7.44	BU 1970

ing was resited in an enbrasure at the forward end of 01 deck. *Wrangler* became the South African *Vrystaat* on transfer to that navy.

In their later years the survivors were used for training and some were disarmed. *Grenville* and *Undaunted* were fitted with helicopter platforms to test the new concept of using light helicopters to drop homing torpedoes against submarines.

Teazer 1957   CPL

Termagant as converted

The cost of the *Rapid* or Type 15 'full' conversion forced the Admiralty to order a Type 16 'limited' conversion. It had the virtue that it could be accomplished quickly because the original destroyer hull was retained, but capability was much lower. The twin 4in gun on 'B' position had to rely on a Simple Tachymetric Director (STD) above the bridge, and the main sensor was a single Type 293 surface/air search and target-indication radar at the masthead. To provide a surface capability (of dubious value), one quadruple set of TT was retained, and *Orwell* and *Paladin* retained their minelaying rails. Twin Squids and a handing room, as in the 'C' class destroyers were sited on the after superstructure. *Tenacious* completed her prototype conversion in 1952 and the rest were completed by 1956. Yards known to be involved were: Rosyth DYd – *Orwell* 1952, *Paladin*, *Tenacious*; Harland & Wolff, Belfast – *Petard* 1956; Thornycroft – *Terpsichore* 1952–53; Mountstuart – *Tuscan*, *Teazer*; Grayson Rollo – *Tumult*,

TENACIOUS class *frigates*

Displacement:	1793t normal; 2593t full load
Dimensions:	As *Rapid* class
Machinery:	As *Rapid* class; range 1700nm at 20kts (*Orwell*, *Paladin* and *Petard*)
Armament:	2–4in/45 Mk 19 AA (1×2), 2–40mm/60 Mk 5 AA (1×2), 3–40mm/60 Mk 9 AA (3×1), 4–21in TT (1×4), 2 Squid Mk 3
Sensors:	Radar Types 293, 974; sonar Types 170, 174P
Complement:	170–180

No	Name	Builder	Laid down	Launched	Comp	Fate
F 98	ORWELL	Thornycroft	16.5.40	2.4.42	7.10.43	BU 1965
F 169	PALADIN	John Brown	22.7.40	11.6.41	12.12.41	BU 1961
F 26	PETARD (ex-*Persistent*)	Vickers-Armstrong, Tyne	26.12.39	27.3.41	14.6.42	BU 1967
F 23	TEAZER	Cammell Laird	20.10.41	7.1.43	13.9.43	BU 1965
F 44	TENACOUS	Cammell Laird	3.12.41	24.3.43	30.10.43	BU 1965
F 189	TERMAGANT	Denny	25.11.41	22.3.43	18.10.43	BU 1965
F 19	TERPSICHORE	Denny	25.11.41	17.6.43	20.1.44	BU 1966
F 121	TUMULT	John Brown	16.11.61	9.11.42	2.4.43	BU 1965
F 156	TUSCAN	Swan Hunter	6.9.41	28.5.42	11.3.43	BU 1966
F 67	TYRIAN	Swan Hunter	15.10.41	27.7.42	8.4.43	BU 1965

Termagant; Harland & Wolff, Liverpool – *Tyrian*. Maximum draught was 16ft 1in and endurance 5225nm at 15kts (588t oil).

In the first ships the original destroyer bridge was retained, but *Teazer*, *Terpsichore* and *Tumult* were given a higher and narrow bridge, as in the new Type 12 frigates.

Type 17. Three separate designs received this designation. The first, *c*1950, was a 3rd Rate ASW frigate, intended as a less capable edition of the *Blackwood* (Type 14) but bigger to improve habitability. Armament would have been one Limbo Mk 10 mortar and one 40mm Bofors, on a length of 300ft (*91.4m*) and 10,000shp single-shaft steam machinery.

The second Type 17 was a 3000t ASW frigate design of the mid-1960s, and in the late 1960s a further design emerged. This was a large ASW ship displacing 6000t. No information has been released about these designs, but they were produced in answer to specific Staff Requirements.

From the Type 17 evolved the Common Hull Frigate, intended for mass production with optional ASW/AA armament. The hull was a derivative of the *Black Swan*, but with Y111 twin-shaft steam turbines. Armament would have been two twin 4in Mk 16, two twin 40mm Bofors Mk 5 and Squid, and the ASW version would have had Limbo Mk 10 plus two twin Bofors.

What was a very sound idea had to be dropped in 1954 because the concept of mass production in wartime was not feasible: war would last less than the four years needed to set up a production line.

Type 18. Again the designation covers more than one design. The first appears to have been a modified version of the *Rapid* (Type 15) destroyer conversion, with Limbo Mk 10 mortars positioned where the 21in TT were in *Rapid*. A second Type 18 was a 'T' class Type 16 with a modified bridge.

Type 19. The confrontation with Indonesia in 1964 led to a very unusual Staff Requirement: an escort capable of 40kts and having a propeller life long enough to get to Singa-

The frigate designs of the 1950s and 1960s

pore. The fighting qualities were to equal those of the *Whitby* frigate design. With hindsight one can only wonder what the utility of such a ship might have been, for even if such contradictory requirements could be reconciled the penalties paid in vibration and unreliability could have been enormous. It is said that the design team argued that the propellers' life expectation would be only 20 hours; the Admiralty Experiment Works at Haslar were less generous, allowing 20

minutes! Four Olympus gas turbines would have produced about 112,000shp on 4000t. Fortunately this product of diseased Staff thinking died under the 1966 Defence Review.

Type 20. Nothing is known about this project, but from its date (mid-1960s) it was possibly an early study for a *Leander* replacement.

Type 42. Better known as the East Coast Gunboat, this was a 1950 project for an AA frigate to defend coastal convoys. She would have carried

three single 4in of a new Vickers automatic type controlled by several MRS3 fire-control systems, on a displacement of 2000t. The 300ft hull would have been diesel-propelled at 25kts, and the gun was developed from an Army AA system (it was eventually installed in two Chilean destroyers).

Exmouth as converted 1969   CPL

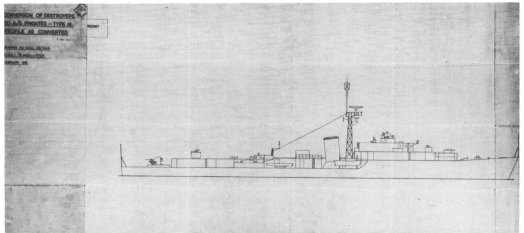

Official drawing of Type 18 ASW conversion 1951   NMM

The so-called 1945 Sloop studies had envisaged a 25kt ASW version of the standard hull, but the need for a Type 11 frigate very quickly disappeared with the postwar appearance of the fast submarine. If such a design existed it had a short life, for the Staff Requirements had raised the sea speed to 27kts, capable of being maintained in a seaway. Out of this emerged the Type 12 design, and the AA and AD, the downgraded, diesel-engined versions of the standard design.

The Type 12 hull-form was, and remains, one of the outstanding small warship designs of the century. A sharp 'V' form forward permitted the hull to be driven into a head sea without the 'panting' and 'slamming' which went with traditional destroyers, but amidships the hull widened to a deep square form. This acted against high smooth-water speed, but made for good sustained speed, ideal for pursuit of a submarine in rough weather. To reinforce this the big (12ft diameter) propellers were slow-running, making them quieter and more efficient, and a raised topgallant forecastle kept spray and green water off the bridge. Range was to be 4500nm at 12kts.

The armament was intended to be the twin 3in/70 Mk 6 AA gun, a 40mm STAAG, two ASW Mk 10 triple mortars and no fewer than twelve TT for launching homing torpedoes, eight fixed and two twin training tubes. The *Whitbys* were prototypes and so

WHITBY class *frigates*

Displacement:	2150t normal; 2560t full load
Dimensions:	360ft pp, 370ft oa × 41ft × 17ft max
	109.7m, 112.7m × 12.5m × 3.9m
Machinery:	2-shaft geared steam turbines, 2 Babcock & Wilcox boilers, 30,000shp = 29kts. Range 4500nm at 12kts
Armament:	2–4.5in/45 Mk 6 DP (1×2), 2–40mm STAAG Mk 2(1×2) (later 1–40mm Mk 7), 12–21in TT (2×2, 8×1), 2 Limbo Mk 10. See notes
Sensors:	Radar Types 275, 262, 293, 277, 974/978; sonar Types 162, 170, 174/177
Complement:	152–231

No	Name	Builder	Laid down	Launched	Comp	Fate
F 77	BLACKPOOL	Harland & Wolff	20.12.54	14.2.57	14.8.58	BU 1978
F 73	EASTBOURNE	Vickers-Armstrong, Tyne	13.1.54	29.12.55	9.1.58	HS 1977, for disposal 1979
F 63	SCARBOROUGH	Vickers-Armstrong, Tyne	11.9.53	4.4.55	10.5.57	BU 1977
F 65	TENBY	Cammell Laird	23.6.53	4.10.55	18.12.57	BU 1976
F 43	TORQUAY	Harland & Wolff	11.3.53	1.7.54	10.5.56	Extant 1982
F 36	WHITBY	Cammell Laird	30.9.52	2.7.54	10.7.56	BU 1979

went to sea with the existing, somewhat cumbersome 4.5in, although production vessels were scheduled for the 3in gun. The 21in Mk 20(E) torpedo (formerly 'Bidder') never became operational.

Because of the fine lines the armament and bridgework had to be far aft (this made for greater crew efficiency, but it did mean a crowded upper deck). In the first three ships (*Whitby, Torquay* and *Scarborough*) the funnel was a thin 'stovepipe' close to the lattice foremast (to resist atomic blast), and as the radar arrays suffered from smoke-corrosion (and to improve the

ship's appearance) *Eastbourne* was given a thicker, raked funnel with a special domed cap. It was liked, and was subsequently retro-fitted to all three.

The need to keep down weight meant that plating was very thin, with the result that all six ships had to be partially replated soon after completion. Only four vessels were fitted with TT and these were removed by the early 1960s. The STAAG was also removed and replaced by a single 40mm Mk 9. *Torquay, Eastbourne, Scarborough* and *Tenby* were altered for service in the Dartmouth Training

Squadron, with a large deckhouse aft for classrooms and offices. None of the class received any further modernisation: *Scarborough* and *Tenby* were temporarily transferred to Pakistan, but when the refit cost rose to £10 million each the deal was cancelled. *Blackpool* was on loan to New Zealand from 1966 to 1971. *Torquay* was recently used for navigation and direction training, and carried out trials of the first Computer Assisted Action Information System (CAAIS).

The high unit cost of the *Whitby* design – £3.5 million – led the Admiralty to consider cheaper vessels which could also be built more quickly: the result was the Type 14 (there was no Type 13), with the same ASW capability as the Type 12, but with only half the power and virtually every other capability eliminated. All were ordered in March 1951.

The result illustrates vividly the problems of building a 2nd Rate frigate, for although the *Blackwoods* achieved exactly what the Staff Requirement demanded – good ASW qualities at half the cost of the *Whitbys* – they were not popular in the Navy. Described as a utility design (as against the 'quality' Type 12) they were mocked as 'futility frigates', for their single-mission design made them inflexible for peacetime use. What was ignored was the fact that if hostilities had broken out with the Soviet Union in the late 1950s (as many Western defence planners envisaged) there would have been an extra dozen Type 14s and ten Type 16s. In ASW exercises the *Blackwoods* often proved superior to more sophisticated frigates, mainly because their

BLACKWOOD class *frigates*

Displacement:	1180t normal; 1535t deep load
Dimensions:	300ft pp, 310ft oa × 35ft × 15ft 6in max
	91.4m, 94.5m × 10.7m × 4.7m
Machinery:	1-shaft geared steam turbines, 2 Babcock & Wilcox boilers, 15,000shp = 27kts. Range 4500nm at 12kts
Armament:	3–40mm/60 Mk 9 (3×1), 2 Limbo Mk 10, 4–21in TT (2×2)
Sensors:	Radar Types 974, 291; sonar Types 174, 170, 162
Complement:	140

No	Name	Builder	Laid down	Launched	Comp	Fate
F 78	BLACKWOOD	Thornycroft	14.9.53	4.10.55	22.8.57	BU 1976
F 80	DUNCAN	Thornycroft	17.12.53	30.5.57	21.10.58	HS 1977
F 48	DUNDAS	White	17.10.52	25.9.53	9.3.56	For disposal 1979
F 84	EXMOUTH	White	24.3.54	16.11.55	20.12.57	BU 1979
F 51	GRAFTON	White	25.2.53	13.9.54	11.1.57	BU 1971
F 54	HARDY	Yarrow	4.2.53	25.11.53	15.12.55	HS 1971, BU 1979
F 85	KEPPEL	Yarrow	27.3.53	31.8.54	6.7.56	BU 1979
F 88	MALCOLM	Yarrow	1.2.54	18.10.55	12.12.57	BU 1978
F 91	MURRAY	Stephen	30.11.57	22.2.55	5.6.56	For disposal 1970
F 94	PALLISER	Stephen	15.3.55	10.5.56	13.12.57	For disposal 1979
F 62	PELLEW	Swan Hunter	5.11.53	29.9.54	26.7.56	For disposal 1971
F 97	RUSSELL	Swan Hunter	11.11.53	10.12.54	7.2.57	HS 1971

inflexibility permitted them to be left to continue their ASW training to a high level, whereas other frigates frequently had their training programmes interrupted.

With only half the machinery of the *Whitby* class the designers had to go for finer lines and less weight to reach 25kts, and so the short forecastle reappeared. Although later strengthened after experiencing exceptionally heavy weather off Iceland, they proved very seaworthy, and many gave good service in the Fishery Protection Squadron.

Blackwood, Exmouth, Malcolm and *Palliser* were completed with two twin 21in TT amidships to supplement the Mk 10 mortars, but the tubes were subsequently removed. After a few years in service the after 40mm gun was removed as well, mainly because it could not be used in heavy weather.

In 1966–68 *Exmouth* was re-engined with a Rolls-Royce Olympus gas turbine developing 23,200shp, backed up by two Proteus gas turbines for cruising (8500shp) geared to the same shaft. The ship was then put through an exhaustive series of tests, culminating in the adoption of the Olympus/Tyne combination as the future standard propulsion unit for the Royal Navy. There was no dramatic improvement in speed (maximum speed rose to 28kts, cruising speed of 22kts) because the hull could not absorb any great increase in power. The external configuration was unchanged apart from a new streamlined funnel, and fuel was slightly increased to compensate for higher consumption.

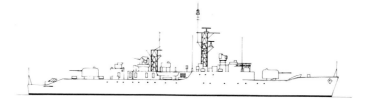

Puma as completed

For the remainder of the 1945 frigates it was decided to adopt diesel propulsion because it was felt that so many steam plants would over-stretch the capacity of British industry. The Type 41 AA frigate was intended to support the Type 12, along with its half-sister, the Type 61 AD version, and the first orders were placed in August 1951. The 41/61 in steam form was the basic design and the 12 was developed from it. The raised forecastle of the Type 12 was adopted in order to enable speed to be kept up in a head sea, but was somewhat shorter and therefore lacking in elegance. Another unattractive feature was the absence of a funnel, for the diesel exhaust-trunking was brought up inside both lattice masts. This proved unsuccessful as well as unsightly, and to prevent the corrosion of masthead equipment *Puma* had her mainmast plated. The improvement was retrofitted to the other ships.

By the standards of the day a most elaborate anti-aircraft defence was provided, with a Type 960 long-range air warning radar on the mainmast, a Mk 6M fire control system controlling two twin 4.5in automatic mountings backed up by a CRBF director aft, and a STAAG autonomous close-range 40mm mounting. The STAAG was not reliable, however; *Jaguar* entered service with a single 40mm gun in its place and the rest followed suit. *Jaguar* was the first to have the more effective Type 965 (AKE-1) long-range radar, but in time all four received it.

A fifth unit, *Panther*, was sold (before being laid down) to India as the *Brahmaputra*; a replacement was ordered, but subsequently cancelled.

LEOPARD class *frigates*

Displacement:	2300t normal; 2520t deep load
Dimensions:	330ft pp, 340ft oa × 40ft × 11ft 10in
	110.6m, 103.6m × 12.2m × 3.6m
Machinery:	2-shaft diesel: 8 ASR1 diesels, 14,400bhp = 25kts. Range 7500nm at 16kts
Armament:	4–4.5in/45 Mk 6 DP (2×2), 2–40mm/60 STAAG Mk 2 AA (1×2), 1 Squid
Sensors:	Radar Types 275, 960, 262, 974, 992Q (later Type 965 (AKE-1), 978, 993; sonars Types 170, 174, 162
Complement:	205

No	Name	Builder	Laid down	Launched	Comp	Fate
F 14	LEOPARD	Portsmouth DYd	25.3.53	23.5.55	30.9.58	BU 1977
F 27	LYNX	John Brown	13.8.53	12.1.55	14.3.57	To Bangladesh 1982
F 34	PUMA	Scotts	16.11.53	30.6.54	27.4.57	BU 1977
F 37	JAGUAR	Denny	2.11.53	20.7.57	12.12.59	To Bangladesh 1978
–	PANTHER (i)	John Brown	–	–	–	To India 1953
–	PANTHER (ii)	–	–	–	–	Cancelled 1957

In 1978 *Jaguar* was transferred to Bangladesh as *Ali Haider*, followed by *Lynx* in 1982 (renamed *Abu Bakr*). Although effective ships when built, the Admiralty Standard Range 1 diesel was not a great success.

Lynx 1977

C & S Taylor

Llandaff 1977

C & S Taylor

Salisbury as completed

On the same hull as the Type 41, the Type 61 design sacrificed the after 4.5in twin gun in favour of a much more comprehensive air warning radar outfit. The ships were thus a much more valuable addition to the fleet than the *Leopard* class, for with adequate radar coverage carrier aircraft provided much better defence against air attack than guns. This was recognised quite early, and the *Leopard* class was stopped at four units whereas the *Salisbury* class was to have been expanded to eight units. Furthermore, the survivors have received a more comprehensive modernisation.

The original STAAG Mk 2 was later replaced by 1–40mm Mk 9, and the fourth ship, *Lincoln*, was completed later, with a big deckhouse aft to take a GWS20 director and a quadruple Seacat missile launcher (a single 40mm gun was mounted initially). In 1962 *Salisbury* was refitted with a plated mainmast carrying a 'single bedstead' Type 965 antenna. In 1964 *Chichester* appeared with both masts plated, the mainmast carrying a 'dou-

SALISBURY class *frigates*

Displacement:	2170t normal; 2350t deep load					
Dimensions:	As *Leopard* class					
Machinery:	As *Leopard* class					
Armament:	2–4.5in/45 Mk 6 DP (1×2), 2–40mm/60 STAAG Mk 2 (1×2), 1 Squid					
Sensors:	Radar Types 275, 277, 960, 982, 293, 974 (later Type 965 (AKE-2)), 993, 978, etc.; sonar Types 170, 174, 162					
Complement:	207					

No	Name	Builder	Laid down	Launched	Comp	Fate
F 32	SALISBURY	Devonport DYd	23.1.52	25.6.53	27.2.57	HS 1980
F 59	CHICHESTER	Fairfield	26.6.53	21.6.55	16.5.58	BU 1982
F 61	LLANDAFF	Hawthorn Leslie	27.8.53	30.11.55	11.4.58	To Bangladesh 1976
F 99	LINCOLN	Fairfield	1.6.55	6.4.59	7.7.60	To Bangladesh 1982
–	COVENTRY	Vickers-Armstrong, Tyne	–	–	–	Cancelled 1961
–	EXETER	–	–	–	–	Cancelled 1957
–	GLOUCESTER	–	–	–	–	Cancelled 1957

ble bedstead' Type 965 array and Seacat GWS20; *Llandaff* was similarly fitted in 1966, followed by *Lincoln* in 1968 and *Salisbury* in 1970.

Two more of the class were cancelled under the 1957 Defence Review

and another (*Coventry*) was suspended. It was hoped to order her in 1961, but by then the more flexible *Leander* design was ready and so she was replaced by *Penelope*. *Llandaff* transferred to Bangladesh as *Umar*

Farooq in December 1978, followed by *Lincoln* (renamed ?) in 1982.

Mohawk as completed

Inspired by the work already done on the Common Hull Frigate (see Type 42 frigates), the Naval Staff drew up a project known as a Common Purpose Frigate (later called a Sloop) having a second-rate AA, ASW and AD capability; in effect this meant a reversion to general-purpose ships, an admission that the breakdown into single-purpose ships was wrong. The armament was to be two twin 4in Mk 16, a twin 40mm Mk 5, a Limbo Mk 10 mortar and eight ASW TT. The standard sonar and radars were to be provided, but a measure of aircraft-direction was to be provided by a USN SPS-6C long-range radar.

Several changes of armament were proposed: a twin 3in/70 Mk 6 and two Vickers single automatic 4in in turn, but these were rejected to avoid pushing up dimensions. Then it was decided to Anglicise the SPS-6C radar, and until the weight and dimensions of the new Type 965 radar aerial were known the lattice mast could not be designed; allowance was made for an aerial weighing 2½ times the manufacturers' 1956 estimate, and this turned out to be sufficient! The result was a very light mast which actually weighed less than the array it carried. Less difficulty was encountered with the fire control, for the Type 802 system was cancelled and replaced by the light MRS3, again Anglicised USN equipment, this time based on their Mk 56 director.

The designation 'sloop' was chosen deliberately because 'frigate' denoted

'TRIBAL' class *frigates*

Displacement:	2300t normal; 2700t deep load					
Dimensions:	350ft pp, 360ft oa × 42ft 3in × 13ft 3in max					
	106.7m, 109.7m × 12.9m × 4.0m					
Machinery:	1-shaft COSAG: geared steam turbine, 1 Babcock & Wilcox boiler, plus 1 AEI G6 gas turbine, 12,500shp + 7500shp = 27kts. Range 4500nm at 12kts					
Armament:	2–4.5in/45 Mk 5 (2×1), 2–40mm/60 Mk 7 or 2–20mm (2×1), 1 Limbo Mk 10, 1 helicopter					
Sensors:	Radar Types 965 (AKE-1), 993, 903, 974/978; sonar Types 170, 177, 162 (*Ashanti* and *Gurkha* also Type 199)					
Complement:	253					

No	Name	Builder	Laid down	Launched	Comp	Fate
F 117	ASHANTI	Yarrow	15.1.58	9.3.59	23.11.61	HS 1980
F 119	ESKIMO	White	22.10.58	20.3.61	21.2.63	Extant 1982
F 122	GURKHA	Thornycroft	3.11.58	11.7.60	13.2.63	Extant 1982
F 125	MOHAWK	Vickers-Armstrong, Barrow	23.12.60	5.4.62	29.11.63	BU 1982
F 131	NUBIAN	Portsmouth DYd	7.9.59	6.9.60	9.10.62	Extant 1982
F 133	TARTAR	Devonport DYd	22.10.59	19.9.60	26.2.62	Extant 1982
F 124	ZULU	Stephen	13.12.60	3.7.62	17.4.64	Extant 1982

a single-mission ship, and from the unused Type numbers over 80 came the later designation Type 81. Subsequently there was political pressure to show that the RN was capable of increasing its frigate force, and to bow to this whim the worthy designation of sloop was changed to frigate. There was a need to replace the nine 'Loch' class vessels in the Persian Gulf, and this became the prime mission for the new design. Several more attempts were made to upgrade the design, mainly to increase speed, but these were ruled out.

The most important innovation was the adoption of COSAG machinery,

half that of the *Kent* class, whose design was proceeding at the same time. *Ashanti* was thus in effect the test-bed for the new machinery and the weight saved could be used for a more effective armament. Air warning radar could be accommodated, and as the trials with light helicopters in Type 15 frigates had proved successful it was decided to try to incorporate a hangar for a Fairey Ultra Light helicopter. This hangar was ingenious, the lift forming both the roof of the hangar and the flight deck. When the helicopter (in fact a Wasp) is stowed the hangar is closed by portable roof-sections.

The adoption of COSAG machinery necessitated two funnels, the foremost serving the boiler room and the aftermost the gas turbine room. The ships were also unusual in having a tapering flush deck, giving good freeboard forward on a small displacement without sacrificing strength or covered access. On the displacement and cost-limits it was possible to provide only two single-loaded semi-automatic 4.5 Mk 5 guns (for shore bombardment) but provision was made for two Seacat (2×4) launchers, which replaced the 40mm weapons. As completed, only *Zulu* carried Seacat, with the prominent

Gurkha 1977   C & S Taylor

Plymouth 1976   C & S Taylor

GWS21 version of the CRBF directors on platforms abreast the second funnel; by 1977, however, the remainder had been fitted as well. Some had VDS.

Although successful ships, the 'Tribals' fell victim to the RN's 1979 manpower crisis, and all were paid off from the end of that year, *Gurkha*

being the first to be put on the disposal list; she recommissioned in 1982, however, in the wake of the Falklands Crisis, and some of her sisters will follow her back into service. They cannot take the newest sonars and weaponry so their active life must be short, but they might find foreign buyers.

Londonderry 1960

These were repeats of the *Whitby* design, ordered under the 1954–55 Programme, but 'tidied up' internally. The raked funnel fitted in *Torquay* was incorporated during construction, but there were few other external differences. The twelve TT were removed and only the early ships carried the STAAG 40mm mounting. In its place was put a large deckhouse to carry a Seacat GWS20 missile system, but for some years all ships carried a single 40mm Bofors gun.

The last three hulls were cancelled and completed to the *Leander* design, the success of which prompted a major modernisation of the *Rothesays*. The major improvement was the incorporation of a Wasp light helicopter (Mk 44/46 homing torpedoes), while the opportunity was taken to update the fire control by replacing the Mk 6M with the MRS3 system. The appearance was slightly changed by providing a new plated foremast and raising the funnel, but in other respects the layout remained the same. Armament was now 2–4.5in, 1 Seacat GWS20 SAM (1×4), 2–20mm, 1 Limbo Mk 10.

The class are nearing the end of their effective lives and are beginning to be downgraded to secondary roles. In 1978 *Falmouth* carried out trials of the winch gear for the new towed array sonar on the quarterdeck. From November 1975 to October 1979 *Londonderry* was reconstructed to serve as a trials ship for the Admiralty Surface Weapons Establishment (ASWE). This involves the removal of the 4.5in guns, altering the propulsion system to waterjets for quietness, and stepping a large, plated mizzenmast to carry the new Type 1030 STIR radar. In the autumn of 1980 she also took the 30mm Naval Rarden gun to sea.

The first *Hastings* (ordered February 1956) became the Royal New Zealand Navy's *Otago* in February 1957; another ship was ordered in her place, but completed as a *Leander*. The future of the *Rothesay* class was threatened by the June 1981 Defence Review, but now some may be

ROTHESAY class *frigates*

Displacement: 2150 (later 2380t) normal; 2560t (later 2800t) deep load
Dimensions: As *Whitby* class
Machinery: As *Whitby* class
Armament: As *Whitby* class. See notes
Sensors: Radar Types 975, 977, 293, 974, 262 (later 903), 994, 978; sonar Types 170, 174/177, 162
Complement: 200–235

No	Name	Builder	Laid down	Launched	Comp	Fate
F 107	ROTHESAY	Yarrow	6.11.56	9.12.57	23.4.60	Extant 1982
F 108	LONDONDERRY	White	15.11.56	20.5.58	18.10.61	Extant 1982
F 106	BRIGHTON	Yarrow	23.7.57	30.10.59	28.9.61	Extant 1982
F 113	FALMOUTH	Swan Hunter	23.11.57	15.12.59	25.7.61	Extant 1982
F 101	YARMOUTH	John Brown	29.11.57	23.3.59	26.3.60	Extant 1982
F 129	RHYL	Portsmouth DYd	29.1.58	23.4.59	31.30.60	Extant 1982
F 103	LOWESTOFT	Stephen	9.6.58	23.6.60	26.9.61	Extant 1982
F 115	BERWICK	Harland & Wolff	16.6.58	15.12.59	1.6.61	Extant 1982
F 126	PLYMOUTH	Devonport DYd	1.7.58	20.7.59	11.5.61	Extant 1982
–	WEYMOUTH	Harland & Wolff	10.4.59	–	–	Cancelled 1960
–	FOWEY	Cammell Laird	19.10.59	–	–	Cancelled 1960
–	HASTINGS (i)	Thornycroft	–	–	–	To New Zealand
–	HASTINGS (ii)	Yarrow	2.12.59	–	–	Cancelled 1960

retained. *Lowestoft* was fitted with Type 2038 towed array sonar in 1981–82.

Euryalus (Ikara conversion) 1977   C & S Taylor

Phoebe July 1982

C & S Taylor

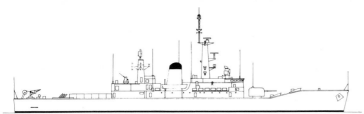

Euryalus as completed

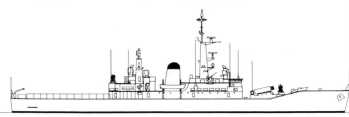

Cleopatra (Exocet conversion) 1977

LEANDER class *frigates*

Displacement:	2350t normal; 2860t deep load
Dimensions:	360ft pp, 372ft oa × 41ft × 18ft max *109.7m, 113.4m × 12.5m × 5.5m*
Machinery:	2-shaft geared steam turbines, 2 Babcock & Wilcox boilers, 30,000shp = 28½kts. Range 4000nm at 15kts
Armament:	2–4.5in/45 Mk 6 DP (1×2), 2–40mm/60 Mk 9 AA (2×1) (later 1 Seacat GWS22 SAM (1×4), 2–20mm (2×1) added), 1 Limbo, 1 helicopter
Sensors:	Radar Types 965 (AKE-1), 992Q, 903, 974/978; sonar Types 162, 184, 199
Complement:	251–263

No	Name	Builder	Laid down	Launched	Comp	Fate
F 109	LEANDER (ex-*Weymouth*)	Harland & Wolff	10.4.59	28.6.61	27.3.63	Extant 1982
F 114	AJAX (ex-*Fowey*)	Cammell Laird	19.10.59	16.8.62	11.12.63	Extant 1982
F 104	DIDO (ex-*Hastings (ii)*)	Yarrow	2.12.59	22.12.61	18.9.63	To New Zealand 1981
F 127	PENELOPE	Vickers-Armstrong, Tyne	14.3.61	17.8.62	1.11.63	Extant 1982
F 10	AURORA	John Brown	1.6.61	28.11.62	9.4.64	Extant 1982
F 15	EURYALUS	Scotts	2.11.61	6.6.63	16.9.64	Extant 1982
F 18	GALATEA	Swan Hunter	29.12.61	23.5.63	25.4.64	Extant 1982
F 38	ARETHUSA	White	17.9.62	5.11.63	29.9.65	Extant 1982
F 39	NAIAD	Yarrow	30.10.62	4.11.63	15.3.65	Extant 1982
F 42	PHOEBE	Stephen	3.6.63	8.7.64	15.4.66	Extant 1982
F 28	CLEOPATRA	Devonport DYd	19.6.63	25.3.64	1.3.66	Extant 1982
F 45	MINERVA	Vickers-Armstrong, Tyne	27.7.63	19.12.64	13.5.66	Extant 1982
F 40	SIRIUS	Portsmouth DYd	9.8.63	22.9.64	15.6.66	Extant 1982
F 52	JUNO	Thornycroft	16.7.64	24.11.65	18.7.67	Extant 1982
F 56	ARGONAUT	Hawthorn Leslie	27.11.64	8.2.66	17.8.67	Extant 1982
F 47	DANAE	Devonport DYd	16.1.65	21.10.65	10.10.67	Extant 1982

The advances made in the 'Tribal' class pointed the way to a return to the concept of a general-purpose escort instead of the prevailing idea of specialised escorts operating in a group. Work done on a revision of the Type 12 design for New Zealand, incorporating two helicopters and full air-conditioning, provided further impetus to studies by M K Purvis. The design which evolved managed to incorporate the long-range air warning radar and the helicopter of the 'Tribal' class, but with the armament, fire control and rough-weather capability of the *Whitby/Rothesay* design.

The secret was to replace the separate ballast tanks of the Type 12 with self-compensating fuel tanks, in which the fuel was displaced by sea water as it was consumed. As many heavy items as possible were moved lower down in the ship, increasing not only the margin of stability, but also the amount of space for the operations room, extra generating capacity and auxiliary machinery. The forecastle deck was extended right aft and a new superstructure deck was built above that, extending from the bridge back to the helicopter hangar. This transformed the appearance and as it was complemented by a well-balanced funnel the *Leander* set a new standard of good looks sadly lacking in some previous British designs. Building of the class was expedited by stopping work on the last three *Rothesays* at an early stage, and a further 13 ships were laid down under the 1960–64 Programmes.

The class are generally considered to be the finest escorts ever built for the Royal Navy and some of the best in the world. To increase the margin for future growth the next group of *Leanders* ordered was given 2ft more beam (see below).

The machinery of the original design was improved, providing a greater degree of automatic control: the first 10 have the Y-100 type and the rest Y-111. One of the benefits conferred by having advanced machinery control is the remarkable manoeuvrability and acceleration which is such a feature of the *Leanders*. During the 'Cod War' the *Leanders* proved that they could out-manoeuvre the Icelandic gunboats by changing speed.

All except *Diomede* received the Type 199 variable depth sonar (VDS) in a stern well, but this has now been removed. In some ships the well remains, but in others it has been plated in to provide extra accommodation.

While serving as a training ship *Diomede* had her 4.5in guns cocooned and the Type 965 radar removed. In 1966 *Penelope* was disarmed for trials in the Mediterranean. This involved removing her propellers and towing her at the end of a mile-long nylon hawser to measure flow noise and hull drag. She was later fitted with the prototype Sea Wolf GWS25 missile system, with the six-cell launcher on the quarterdeck, Types 967/968 radar on the mainmast and a Type 910 tracker on a deckhouse aft. The equipment was removed in 1979 and she went into dockyard hands for the Exocet conversion.

Although no longer bearing any relation to the *Whitby* design (apart from the hull-form), they are incorrectly referred to as Type 12 frigates.

Ikara conversions

Eight ships received the Batch 1 conversion, which involved replacing the 4.5in gun mounting with a 'zareba' containing an Ikara GWS40 ASW missile system and its magazine and loading gear below. The air warning radar was removed from the mainmast because the ships are intended to operate in mixed escort groups. The Seacat arrangement aft was improved, with the GWS22 director moved to the centreline, leaving room for two quadruple launchers to port and starboard.

Leander was recommissioned in December 1972 and was followed by *Ajax* (September 1973), *Galatea* (September 1974), *Naiad* (July 1975), *Aurora* and *Euryalus* (March 1976), *Arethusa* (April 1977) and *Dido* (October 1978). Displacement was now 2450t normal, 2960t deep load, and complement 257; sensors consisted of radar Types 994, 903 and 1006 and sonar Types 184, 162 and 170; 2–40mm/60 Mk 9 (2×1) and 6–12.75in TT (2×3) were fitted and 1 Wasp helicopter was carried.

Exocet conversions

Although twelve Ikara conversions were planned the programme was cut short at eight units, for the RN needed to improve its surface-strike capability. The eight Batch 2 ships were given four MM38 Exocet missiles in place of the 4.5in guns, and at the same time the helicopter hangar was enlarged to take the new Lynx, and the new STWS-1 torpedo defence was added; 2–40mm/60 Mk 9 (2×1) and 6–12.75in TT (2×3) are also carried. Unlike the Ikara conversions the Type 965 air warning radar (AKE-1) was retained; other sensors consist of radar Types 903, 1006 and 994 and sonar Types 184/184M and 162. *Cleopatra* was selected as the trials ship for the Type 165 towed array sonar, and conversion began in 1980.

The provision of self-compensating

fuel tanks did not prove successful, and as the Exocet missiles made relatively low demands on topweight it was possible to revert to separate ballast tanks. This eliminated problems with marine growths in fuel tanks and incidentally increased the usable fuel by nearly 50 per cent, providing a much-needed improvement in endurance: the original design called for

4000nm at 15kts, but the effective endurance was nowhere near this.

Apart from the four Exocets forward, the appearance was closer to the original profile than the Batch 1 ships. The Seacat arrangements on the after superstructure were altered to a centreline director and two launchers port and starboard, and a third launcher was positioned on the

centreline ahead of the Exocets. Displacement became 2790t normal and 3200t full load, and complement fell to 223.

Recommissioning dates were: *Cleopatra* November 1975, *Sirius* April 1977, *Phoebe* October 1977, *Minerva* March 1979, *Argonaut* March 1980, *Danae* September 1980 and *Penelope* 22.1.82. *Juno*'s Batch 2 con-

version has been cancelled and she is being disarmed as a TS at Rosyth. *Phoebe* was again refitted in 1981–82 when the Type 965 radar was removed, the Exocet ramps lowered and Type 2038 towed array sonar fitted. *Argonaut* was damaged by bombs during the Falklands fighting.

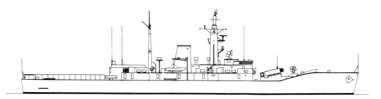

Andromeda (Sea Wolf conversion) 1981

To provide more fuel stowage and a better margin for future growth, the last ten of the *Leander* class were 'kippered' by adding 2ft to the beam. This reduced speed slightly, but improved stability and endurance, both items of greater fighting value. Although referred to in the RN as Type 12s or 'broad-beam *Leanders*', they form a separate class, with improved machinery, a difference enhanced by the radical reconstruction from 1977. The steady improvement in machinery stated in the original class continued, and these ships have the Y-136 plant. Speed has dropped by half a knot because of increased displacement, but the improved degree of automation made for more efficient use of the machinery.

As built the ten ships were identical with the *Leander* class in equipment, but the extra internal volume meant that they could be reconstructed to carry two important new systems: the long-range Type 2016 sonar and the Sea Wolf point-defence missile system, capable of destroying seaskimming missiles as well as supersonic aircraft. The two systems are inter-dependent because the Type 2016 is intended for detecting fast submarines in the GIUK Gap, far from the support of shore-based aircraft. The most likely opposition to be encountered is surface attack, against which Exocet missiles provide a long-range defence, and missile attack, either from bombers or from submarines. The Sea Wolf system is intended particularly to counter the 'pop-up' missile fired from Soviet 'Charlie' and 'Papa' class submarines. Other sensors now include radar Types 967, 968, 910, 294 and 1066 and sonar Type 162M. A Lynx helicopter armed with Sea Skua

'Broad beam LEANDER' class *frigates*

Displacement: 2500t (later 2790t) normal; 2962t (later 3300t) deep load
Dimensions: 360ft pp, 372ft oa × 43ft × 19ft max
109.7m, 113.4m × 13.1m × 5.5m
Other particulars: As *Leander* class

No	Name	Builder	Laid down	Launched	Comp	Fate
F 58	HERMIONE	Stephen	10.12.65	26.4.67	11.7.69	Extant 1982
F 57	ANDROMEDA	Portsmouth DYd	25.5.66	24.5.67	4.7.68	Extant 1982
F 60	JUPITER	Yarrow	3.10.66	4.9.67	13.8.69	Extant 1982
F 69	BACCHANTE	Vickers-Armstrong, Tyne	25.10.66	29.2.68	5.12.69	To New Zealand 1982
F 75	CHARYBDIS	Harland & Wolff	27.1.67	28.2.68	6.6.69	Extant 1982
F 71	SCYLLA	Devonport DYd	17.5.67	8.8.68	14.2.70	Extant 1982
F 12	ACHILLES	Yarrow	27.10.67	21.11.68	9.6.70	Extant 1982
F 16	DIOMEDE	Yarrow	30.1.68	15.4.69	2.4.71	Extant 1982
F 70	APOLLO	Yarrow	21.11.69	15.10.70	28.5.72	Extant 1982
F 72	ARIADNE	Yarrow	1.5.70	10.9.71	10.2.73	Extant 1982

ASMs or ASW torpedoes is carried.

The conversion is a tight fit, and it involves virtually gutting the ship internally and resiting bulkheads. Every spare ton of topweight has had to be reduced, by such expedients as cutting off the funnel-top and putting the 6–12.75in TT (2×3) a deck lower. The 6-cell Sea Wolf launcher is mounted forward of the bridge, with a heavy movable blast-shield to protect the four Exocet MM38 SSMs. A Mk 2 director, rather lighter than the original in the *Broadsword* class, is mounted over the bridge, with the back-to-back Type 967 and Type 968 surveillance radars at the masthead. As in the Exocet conversions the Limbo mortar was removed to allow for a larger flight deck and hangar. The generating capacity had to be increased over the 200kW in the Batch 2 *Leanders*, for five computers are required to handle the data (six if the ships get the new towed array sonar.)

Andromeda is the lead-ship, having gone into Devonport late in 1977; she recommissioned in November 1980, *Charybdis* in May 1982 and *Hermione* was due to complete early in 1983.

Following the 1981 defence cuts, the programme is to be reduced, leaving the remaining ships unconverted. They may be fitted with towed arrays instead.

Andromeda 1977   C & S Taylor

Mermaid as completed

Ordered by Ghana to serve as flagship and presidential yacht for President Nkrumah, but cancelled when a *coup* toppled him from power. She was launched without being named and completed fitting out in 1968, but without armament. Negotiations to sell her abroad failed and after being laid up at Scotstoun she was bought by the RN in April 1972 for conversion to a TS; refitting started at Chatham in October that year.

The design was based on the Type 41 or *Leopard* class, but without the

MERMAID *frigate*

Displacement: 2300t normal; 2520t deep load
Dimensions: 320ft pp, 339ft 3in oa × 40ft × 12ft
97.5m, 103.4m × 12.2m × 3.7m
Machinery: 2 shafts, 8 Admiralty Standard Range 1 diesels, 14,400bhp = 24kts. Range 4800nm at 18kts
Armament: 2–4in/45 Mk 16 AA (1×2), 4–40mm/60 Mk 9 (4×1), 1 Limbo Mk 10
Sensors: Radar ASW-1, 978; sonar 174, 170B
Complement: c235

No	Name	Builder	Laid down	Launched	Comp	Fate
F 76	MERMAID	Yarrow	1965	29.12.66	16.5.73	To Malaysia 1977

raised forecastle and with a flush fore-castle deck and a funnel. Although successful in RN service, she was an odd number in the inventory and was sold to Malaysia in May 1977 as *Hang Tuah*, replacing the previous ship of that name.

Alacrity 1977   C & S Taylor

Alacrity 1980

The Type 21 design had its origin in the need to replace the four diesel-engined frigates of the *Leopard* and *Salisbury* classes. At the same time private shipbuilders were lobbying for a chance to build a frigate for the RN without what they claimed to be ridiculously high standards imposed by the MoD's Ship Department at Bath. It was claimed that such a fri-gate would not only be cheaper (£3.5 million as against £5 million for a *Leander* at contemporary prices), but also a good export item. The Control-ler of the Navy backed this claim wholeheartedly, even to the point of trying to cut the Ship Department out of the design process.

The result was a wasted opportun-ity to bring private and official desig-ners together. Details of the design did not meet certain naval require-ments, the cost was £14.4 million for the first ship, and the vessels lack suf-ficient 'stretch' to take the next gener-ation of weapons (specifically the Type 2016 sonar, a long-range radar and the Sea Wolf missile). They are popular with the RN, however, par-ticularly because of their comfortable officers' accommodation (in contrast, the ratings' accommodation is below the standard in other RN ships) and because they handle easily. Unlike the Batch 3 *Leanders* they will not be modernised, apart from updating the fire control system.

From *Active* onwards, four MM38 Exocet SSMs have been fitted in 'B' position, toed inwards to allow the blast to vent outboard to port and starboard. The triple STWS-1 close-range torpedo defence has also been fitted since completion. The fire con-trol system was a new departure: as no suitable British light system existed, the RN bought the Italian Selenia RTN-10X radar tracker and com-bined it with the British Ferranti WSA-4 below-decks equipment, pro-viding control for both the 4.5in gun and the Seacat GWS24. Although there was talk of the design allowing the replacement of Seacat by Sea Wolf this was never possible because the ships were delivered overweight and did not have the margin of stability necessary for such a big system. A Lynx helicopter armed with Mk 44/46 torpedoes is carried.

The Royal Australian Navy contri-buted a large sum (believed to be

AMAZON class *frigates*

Displacement:	3100t normal; 3600t deep load
Dimensions:	360ft pp, 384ft oa × 41ft 9in × 19ft max *109.7m, 117.0m × 12.7m × 5.8m*
Machinery:	2-shaft COGOG: 2 Rolls-Royce Olympus TM3B gas turbines, 56,000shp = 30kts, 2 RM1A Tyne gas turbines, 8500shp = 17kts. Range 4000nm at 17kts
Armament:	4 MM38 Exocet SSM (except *Amazon* and *Antelope*), 1–4.5in/55 Mk 8, 2–20mm (2×1), 1 Seacat GWS24 SAM (1×4), 6–12.75in TT (2×3), 1 helicopter
Sensors:	Radar Types 992Q, 912, 978, sonar Types 184M, 162M
Complement:	175–192

No	Name	Builder	Laid down	Launched	Comp	Fate
F 169	AMAZON	Vosper Thornycroft	6.11.69	26.4.71	11.5.74	Extant 1982
F 170	ANTELOPE	Vosper Thornycroft	23.3.71	16.3.72	19.7.75	Sunk 24.5.82
F 171	ACTIVE	Vosper Thornycroft	23.7.71	23.11.72	17.6.77	Extant 1982
F 172	AMBUSCADE	Yarrow	1.9.71	18.1.73	5.9.75	Extant 1982
F 173	ARROW	Yarrow	28.9.72	5.2.74	29.7.76	Extant 1982
F 174	ALACRITY	Yarrow	5.3.73	18.9.74	2.7.77	Extant 1982
F 184	ARDENT	Yarrow	26.2.74	9.5.75	13.10.77	Sunk 22.5.82
F 185	AVENGER	Yarrow	30.10.74	20.11.75	15.4.78	Extant 1982

about 35 per cent) to the design costs, with the intention of building five ships in Australian yards; this project never came to fruition, however, and no export orders were ever won for this design. In 1980 it was confirmed that the class would not receive a mid-life modernisation, but specula-tion that they will be sold or scrapped in the next few years has been denied.

In 1977 in the Far East *Amazon* suffered a bad fire, and this drew

attention to the risk of building war-ships with all-aluminium superstruc-tures, a risk underlined by the Falk-lands War. The designers maintained that they could not have met the requirement to raise the weapon load without saving as much topweight as possible. To this their critics reply that the flimsiness of aluminium accentuates the vulnerability of mod-ern warships to relatively minor dam-age. Whatever the merits of the argu-

ment, after the construction of the *Amazon* class the British Naval Staff changed their minds about aluminium, and stipulated that future ships use steel only. During the Falk-lands conflict *Ardent* was badly dam-aged by air-launched unguided rock-ets on 21.5.82 and sank shortly after-wards; *Antelope* was hit by bombs on 23.5.82, and blew up on the following day while an explosives expert was trying to defuze an unexploded bomb.

Brilliant as completed   MoD

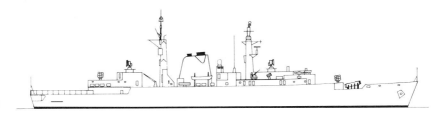

Battleaxe as completed

Originally conceived as a follow-on to the *Leander* class and intended to be built for the Royal Netherlands Navy as well, the Type 22 design was forced to grow to meet new threats and to accommodate new technology. The increasing inability of medium-range search sonars to cope with fast nuclear submarines led to the development of a new 'fleet' sonar, capable of long-range passive detection and use of convergence zones and 'bottom-bounce' techniques. The threat from SS-N-7 'pop-up' missiles dictated the development of the Sea Wolf anti-missile system, and finally the creation of the SOSUS barriers of underwater listening arrays in the GIUK Gap required a ship with a high degree of autonomy and seakeeping.

As a result the *Broadsword* hull has much more freeboard than the *Sheffield* class DDG, a double hangar to accommodate a second Lynx (a late addition), a double-headed Sea Wolf system, and a main armament restricted to four MM38 Exocet SSM. The hull is in fact an expansion of the original Type 12 design, intended to be driven in rough weather with little reduction in speed. The processing equipment needed for all this requires

BROADSWORD class *frigates*

Displacement:	4100t normal; 4600t deep load
Dimensions:	410pp, 430ft 6in oa × 48ft 6in × 19ft 10in max
	125.7m, 131.1m × 14.8m ×6.1m
Machinery:	2-shaft COGOG: 2 Rolls-Royce Olympus TM3B gas turbines, 56,000shp = 30kts; plus 2 Rolls-Royce Tyne RNM1A gas turbines, 8500shp = 18kts. Range 4500nm at 18kts
Armament:	4 MM38 Exocet SSM, 2 Sea Wolf GWS25 SAM system (2×6), 2–40mm/60 Mk 9 (2×1), 6–12.75in TT (2×3), 2 helicopters
Sensors:	Radar Types 967, 968, 910, 1006; sonar Types 2016, 162, 165
Complement:	223

No	Name	Builder	Laid down	Launched	Comp	Fate
F 88	BROADSWORD	Yarrow	7.2.75	12.5.76	3.5.79	Extant 1982
F 89	BATTLEAXE	Yarrow	4.2.76	12.5.77	28.3.80	Extant 1982
F 90	BRILLIANT	Yarrow	25.3.77	15.12.78	15.5.81	Extant 1982
F 91	BRAZEN	Yarrow	18.8.78	4.3.80	2.7.82	Extant 1982

no fewer than seven computers, but there is another reason for the spaciousness: experience has shown that maintenance is the biggest headache in a warship, and that the 'payload' has to be updated once or even twice in the lifetime of the 'platform' or hull. Thus the *Broadsword* design leaves additional space for future growth, in much the same way as the American *Spruance* design.

Although rated as frigates they are

bigger than the DDGs, and are magnificent ASW ships. The first two ships were not originally fitted with TTs. They are to be fitted with the new towed array sonar as soon as it comes into service. Large as they are, however, an improved ('stretched') version has already been started (see below). For the first time the lead-yard has received all subsequent orders, as it is now recognised that this saves a considerable amount of

time and money. *Broadsword* was damaged during the Falklands conflict, but both she and her sister *Brilliant* performed very well, the latter being the first to use Sea Wolf operationally when she shot down two Skyhawks on 12.5.82; she was also the first ship to use Sea Skua in anger.

Although an initial order of 12 *Broadsword*s was talked of, after four units had been ordered the decision was made to lengthen the subsequent ships in order to accommodate the Type 2038 towed array sonar. Orders for the first two of these improved *Broadsword*s were placed in April 1979, but there is some confusion because the 1979–80 Supply Estimates showed that FF-05 (*Boxer*'s designation) was started in February 1978, ie before *Brazen*. *Bloodhound* was renamed *London* at the request of the Lord Mayor of that city.

Four Type 22s were ordered to replace the Falklands losses, two more Batch 2 and yet another variant, Batch 3. The Batch 3 ships will be armed with a 4.5in Mk 8 gun forward, a close-in weapon system such as the Oerlikon-Contraves Seaguard quad 25mm and a new SSM, possibly a version of Sea Eagle, AM39 Exocet or

BROADSWORD (Batch 2) class *frigates*

Displacement:	4200t normal; 4800t deep load
Dimensions:	451ft pp, 487ft oa × 48ft 6in × 19ft 10in
	137.5m, 148m × 14.75m × 6.1m
Other particulars:	As *Broadsword* class (see notes)

No	Name	Builder	Laid down	Launched	Comp	Fate
F 92	BOXER	Yarrow	1.11.79	17.7.81		Fitting out
F 93	BEAVER	Yarrow	20.6.80	8.5.82		Fitting out
F 94	BRAVE	Yarrow				Building
F 95	LONDON (ex-*Bloodhound*)	Yarrow	2.4.82			Building
–		Swan Hunter				Ordered
–		Swan Hunter				Ordered
–		Yarrow				Ordered
–		Yarrow				Ordered
–		?				Projected

Harpoon. Fire control will be provided by two Laurence-Scott optical fire directors. *Brave*'s main drive propulsion will be two Marine Spey gas turbines, with Tynes for cruising.

Eight missiles will be carried and three CIWs.

Although the Type 22 is recognised as a highly efficient ASW platform, alarm at its high cost led to a call for a cheaper frigate, relying on the Type 2038 towed array sonar rather than the big Type 2016 and Lynx helicopters. Out of this has emerged the Type 23, but experience in the Falklands has led to the inclusion of lightweight Sea Wolf missiles and a helicopter.

The power plant will be two Rolls-Royce Marine Spey gas turbines

TYPE 23 *frigates*

Particulars:	Not yet published

for main drive and a single turbo-electric unit for silent running while using the towed array.

SUBMARINES

Thermopylae 1953

Eight boats of the *Taciturn* and *Tabard* groups were given conversions in 1951–56, following the 'S' class. The pressure hull was cut in two and lengthened by a 20ft (14ft in *Taciturn*, 12ft in *Thermopylae, Turpin* and *Totem*) section containing a second pair of electric motors, with clutches to convert them from direct drive to diesel electric, and fourth battery section containing 6560 type cells. This was to provide an underwater speed of 15kts, more than twice the previous normal speed. All guns, external TT and fittings were removed, the periscopes, snorkel radar and R/T masts were enclosed in a streamlined 'fin', and the bow and stern were reshaped. In *Tabard* and *Trump* the fin was fully enclosed, but the others had a small low-set bridge.

The torpedo armament, reduced by the removal of the five external tubes, was now four bow and two stern 21in. They were intended to receive the Mk 20(S) ('Bidder') electric passive homing torpedo, but received the wire-guided version, Mk 23 ('Grog') instead, and after the withdrawal of the Mk 12 ('Fancy'), the elderly Mk 8 was reintroduced to provide some

'T Conversion' type *patrol submarines*

Displacement:	1261–1460t normal; 1554–1588t/1734t
Dimensions:	285ft pp, 290ft 6in (*Tabard* group 293ft) oa × 26ft 7in × 16ft max *86.9m, 88.5m (89.5m) × 8.1m × 4.9m*
Machinery:	2-shaft diesel-electric: 4 supercharged ASR diesels, plus 4 electric motors, 2800bhp/6000shp = 14kts/15.4kts. Oil 200t
Armament:	6–21in TT (20 torpedoes) or 12 Mk 2 mines
Sensors:	Search and navigation radars; sonar Types 186, 187, 197
Complement:	68

No	Name	Builder	Laid down	Launched	Comp	Fate
Taciturn group						
S 34	TACITURN	Vickers-Armstrong, Barrow	9.3.43	7.6.44	7.10.44	BU 1971
S 55	THERMOPYLAE	Chatham DYd	26.10.43	27.6.45	5.12.45	BU 1970
S 54	TURPIN	Chatham DYd	24.5.43	5.8.44	18.12.44	To Israel 1965
S 52	TOTEM	Devonport DYd	22.10.42	28.9.43	9.1.45	To Israel 1964
Tabard group						
S 42	TABARD	Scotts	6.9.44	21.11.45	25.6.46	HS 1969, BU 1974
S 32	TIPTOE	Vickers-Armstrong, Barrow	10.11.42	25.2.44	13.6.44	BU 1975
S 33	TRUMP	Vickers-Armstrong, Barrow	31.12.42	25.3.44	9.7.44	BU 1971
S 53	TRUNCHEON	Devonport DYd	5.11.42	22.2.44	25.5.45	To Israel 1968

anti-surface capability, because the Mk 23 did not function particularly well against surface targets.

Turpin, Totem and *Truncheon* became the Israeli *Leviathan, Dakar* and *Dolphin*.

Explorer as completed

Although the RN was well aware of the importance of nuclear propulsion, there was an acute need of high-speed underwater targets to evaluate new ASW tactics, and as it was believed that the Soviet Navy was developing the Walter turbine, an order was placed in August 1947 for two improved versions of *Meteorite*. They were unarmed and purely experimental, and although much safer than the ex-U-boat they were unofficially known as 'Exploder' and 'Excruciator' because of their frequent minor mishaps. Diving depth was 550ft and surface endurance 500nm.

The nature of perhydrol meant that it had to be stored in plastic-lined tanks, open-topped to prevent the build-up of gas and to permit drenching with water in the event of spon-

EXPLORER class *experimental submarines*

Displacement:	776t standard; *c* 980t/1076t
Dimensions:	209ft 5in pp, 225ft oa × 15ft 8in × 18ft 2in *63.8m, 68.7m × 4.8m × 5.5m*
Machinery:	2-shaft Vickers hydrogen peroxide turbine, plus electric motor, 15,000shp/400bhp = 27kts/18¼kts. Fuel 39t perhydrol
Armament:	None
Complement:	41–49

No	Name	Builder	Laid down	Launched	Comp	Fate
S 30	EXPLORER	Vickers-Armstrong, Barrow	20.7.51	5.3.54	28.11.56	BU 1965
S 40	EXCALIBUR	Vickers-Armstrong, Barrow	13.2.52	25.2.55	22.3.58	BU 1964

taneous combustion. The slightest fragment of dust, rust or any other impurity was sufficient to start the release of oxygen, and a drop spilt would corrode metal, cloth or flesh. In view of the fact that both the

Americans and the Russians gave up their attempts to get HTP propulsion to work, the achievement of the RN was considerable, but there can have been few tears at the boats' paying-off.

In order to replace worn-out XE-craft, four midget submarines were ordered in September 1951 as *X 51–54*; in December 1954 they were given names. *Stickleback* was sold to the Royal Swedish Navy in July 1958 and renamed *Spiggen*, while *Sprat* was lent to the US Navy in the same year for short trials involving penetration of harbour defences. Although stricken in 1970 *Spiggen* was only laid up, and in 1977 she was returned to Great Britain for preservation. Diving depth was 300ft.

STICKLEBACK class *midget submarines*

Displacement:	32t standard; 35.32t/39.27t
Dimensions:	50ft 8in pp, 53ft 10½in oa × 6ft × 7ft 6in *15.4m, 16.4m × 1.8m × 2.3m*
Machinery:	1-shaft diesel-electric: 1 Perkins P6 6cyl diesel, plus 1 electric motor, 50bhp/44shp = 6.5kts/6kts. Oil 1.19t
Armament:	2 detachable 2t side-charges
Complement:	5

No	Name	Builder	Laid down	Launched	Comp	Fate
X 51	STICKLEBACK (ex-*X 51*)	Vickers-Armstrong, Barrow	?	1.10.54	?	Preserved 1977
X 52	SHRIMP (ex-*X 52*)	Vickers-Armstrong, Barrow	?	30.12.54	?	BU 1965
X 53	SPRAT (ex-*X 53*)	Vickers-Armstrong, Barrow	?	1.3.55	?	BU 1965
X 54	MINNOW (ex-*X 54*)	Vickers-Armstrong, Barrow	?	1955	?	BU 1965

Explorer 19.3.57   CPL

Sprat 25.6.57   CPL   *Tireless* as streamlined   MoD

Five riveted boats were given a partial modernisation on the lines of the 'T Conversions', with a streamlined casing and fin, guns removed, but no change in propulsion; they were a logical development of the 'S' class streamline. Although not so capable as the full conversions they were useful for ASW training because they were quieter and faster than before: in October 1952, trials between the prototype *Tireless* and the unconverted *Tudor* showed an increase of 1.4kts in submerged speed. Higher capacity 6560amp/hr batteries replaced the former 5350amp/hr type. The sensor suite is unknown, but photographs indicate earlier marks than fitted in the 'T Conversions'. The original Mk 8 torpedoes were replaced by Mks 20 and 23.

'T Streamline' type *patrol submarines*

Displacement:	1090t standard; 1424t/1571t
Dimensions:	265ft pp, 273ft 6in oa × 26ft 7in × 15ft 10in max
	80.8m, 83.4m × 8.1m × 4.8m
Machinery:	2-shaft diesel-electric: 2 ASR diesels, plus 2 electric motors, 2500bhp/1450shp = 15.25kts/9.5kts. Oil 209t
Armament:	6–21 TT (11 torpedoes)
Sensors:	See notes
Complement:	50

No	Name	Builder	Laid down	Launched	Comp	Fate
S 37	TALENT	Vickers-Armstrong, Barrow	21.3.44	13.2.45	26.7.45	BU 1970
S 28	TOKEN	Portsmouth DYd	6.11.41	19.3.43	15.12.45	BU 1970
S 77	TIRELESS	Portsmouth DYd	30.10.41	19.3.43	18.4.45	BU 1968
S 35	TAPIR	Vickers-Armstrong, Barrow	29.3.43	21.8.44	30.12.44	BU 1966
S 38	TEREDO	Vickers-Armstrong, Barrow	17.4.44	27.4.45	5.4.46	BU 1965

Andrew with deck gun, Mar 1974   C & S Taylor

Porpoise Oct 1966   CPL

Artemis 1967

Artful underwent modernisation in 1955–56, along the lines of the 'T Conversions', with enlarged batteries and rebuilt bow and stern and streamlined fin, etc but retaining the original motors. All except *Aurochs* had undergone a similar conversion by 1960. The Mk 8 torpedoes were subsequently replaced by Mk 23, and some boats could carry 26 Mk 5 mines. *Alliance* was put on concrete trestles at HMS *Dolphin*, Gosport, in 1979 as a permanent submarine memorial.

Before being scrapped *Aeneas* was lent to Vickers for trials with the SLAM (Submarine Launched Antiaircraft Missile). This is a TV-guided version of the Blowpipe missile, mounted in the fin and controlled from below, to provide a defence against helicopters. The system was not adopted by the RN and after the trials the boat was scrapped.

'A' class (modernised) *patrol submarines*

Displacement:	1120t standard; 1370t light; 1443t/1620t
Dimensions:	221ft pp, 282ft oa × 22ft 3in × 18ft 1½in max
	67.4m, 85.9m × 6.8m × 5.5m
Machinery:	2-shaft diesel-electric: 4 supercharged Vickers-Admiralty diesels, plus 2 electric motors, 4300bhp/1250shp = 19kts/15kts. Oil 213t
Armament:	6–21in TT (18 torpedoes) or 18 Mk 2 mines
Sensors:	As 'T Conversions'
Complement:	63

No	Name	Builder	Laid down	Launched	Comp	Fate
S 61	ACHERON	Chatham DYd	26.8.44	25.3.47	17.4.48	BU 1972
S 72	AENEAS	Cammell Laird	10.10.44	25.10.45	31.7.46	BU 1972
S 41	ALARIC	Cammell Laird	31.5.44	18.2.46	11.12.46	BU 1971
S 65	ALCIDE	Vickers-Armstrong, Barrow	1.2.45	12.4.45	18.10.46	BU 1972
S 66	ALDERNEY	Vickers-Armstrong, Barrow	6.2.45	25.6.45	10.12.46	BU 1972
S 67	ALLIANCE	Vickers-Armstrong, Barrow	13.3.45	26.7.45	14.5.45	Preserved 1979
S 68	AMBUSH	Vickers-Armstrong, Barrow	17.5.45	24.9.45	22.7.47	BU 1971
S 43	AMPHION (ex-*Anchorite*)	Vickers-Armstrong, Barrow	14.11.43	31.8.44	27.3.45	BU 1971
S 64	ANCHORITE (ex-*Amphion*)	Vickers-Armstrong, Barrow	19.7.45	22.1.46	18.11.47	BU 1970
S 63	ANDREW	Vickers-Armstrong, Barrow	13.8.45	6.4.46	16.3.48	BU 1977
S 49	ARTEMIS	Scotts	28.2.44	26.8.46	15.8.47	BU 1972
S 96	ARTFUL	Scotts	8.6.44	22.5.47	2.2.48	BU 1969
S 47	ASTUTE	Vickers-Armstrong, Barrow	4.4.44	30.1.45	30.6.45	BU 1970
S 69	AURIGA	Vickers-Armstrong, Barrow	7.6.44	29.3.45	12.1.46	BU 1971

Apart from the *Explorer* class these were the first British postwar submarines and they incorporated experience gained from wartime operations, trials with surrendered U-boats and the 'T Conversions'; the first batch was ordered in April 1951. They proved a great success (mainly because they were very quiet) and only started to go out of service because the 1975 Defence Review cut back the operational strength of the RN and because the new nuclear boats were making demands on manpower.

The two sets of batteries are linked in series to give 880v for short bursts of high speed. Being large boats they have a range of 9000nm on the surface, sufficient for world-wide deployment. Mk 8 and Mk 20 torpedoes are carried.

PORPOISE class *patrol submarines*

Displacement:	1565t normal; 1975t/2303t
Dimensions:	241ft pp, 290ft 3in oa × 26ft 6in × 18ft 3in
	73.4m, 88.5m × 8.1m × 5.6m
Machinery:	2-shaft diesel-electric: 2 ASR 1 16cyl diesels, plus 2 English Electric motors, 3680bhp/6000shp = 12kts/17kts. Oil 258t
Armament:	8–21in TT (6 fwd, 2 aft; 30 torpedoes)
Sensors:	Navigation and search radars; sonar Types 187, 2007, 2019
Complement:	71

No	Name	Builder	Laid down	Launched	Comp	Fate
S 01	PORPOISE	Vickers-Armstrong, Barrow	15.6.56	25.4.56	16.4.58	Extant 1982
S 02	RORQUAL	Vickers-Armstrong, Barrow	15.1.55	5.12.56	24.10.58	BU 1977
S 03	NARWHAL	Vickers-Armstrong, Barrow	15.3.56	25.10.57	4.5.59	For disposal 1982
S 04	GRAMPUS	Cammell Laird	16.4.55	30.5.57	19.12.58	BU 1980
S 05	FINWHALE	Cammell Laird	18.9.56	21.7.59	19.8.60	For disposal 1982
S 06	CACHALOT	Scotts	1.8.55	11.12.57	1.9.59	BU Feb 80
S 07	SEALION	Cammell Laird	5.6.58	31.12.59	25.7.61	Extant 1982
S 08	WALRUS	Scotts	12.2.58	22.9.59	8.2.61	Extant 1982

Although plans for a nuclear submarine had been in embryo as early as 1943, a Government directive to the Admiralty to wait until the land-based nuclear power stations were ready meant that nothing could be done until the mid-1950s. Delays with the British Dounreay reactor threatened to delay the programme even further, and so in 1958 the US Navy was asked to supply a Westinghouse S5W reactor of the same type as in the *Skipjack* class. This meant that the after end of *Dreadnought* is virtually an adaptation of that design to British industrial practice grafted on to British equip-

DREADNOUGHT *nuclear attack submarine*

Displacement:	3000t standard; 3500t/4000t
Dimensions:	265ft 9in pp × 32ft 3in × 26ft
	81.0m × 9.8m × 7.9m
Machinery:	1-shaft nuclear: 1 S5W reactor plus geared steam turbine, 15,000shp, plus diesel-electric auxiliary = 15kts/28kts
Armament:	6–21in TT (24 torpedoes)
Sensors:	Search and navigation radars; sonar Types 2001, 2007, 2019
Complement:	88

No	Name	Builder	Laid down	Launched	Comp	Fate
S 101	DREADNOUGHT	Vickers-Armstrong, Barrow	12.6.59	21.10.60	17.4.63	For disposal 1982

ment and weapon systems, although a considerable amount of information about advanced British design procedures was supplied to the USN in exchange.

The reactor was built by Rolls-Royce and the turbines by English Electric. She was fitted with Type 2001 sonar in the 'chin' position, Type 2007 for long-range passive detection and Type 2019 for ranging and interception. Because *Dreadnought* has one shaft and rudder, all the TT are forward. Early in 1982 it was announced that she had reached the end of her hull life and would be laid up after her reactor had been dismantled and the core removed.

Dreadnought on trials, Dec 1962 CPL

Otus 1969

Although outwardly identical with the *Porpoise* class, these boats bear the same relationship to them as the *Rothesay* class frigates did to the *Whitby* class: a number of detailed improvements were incorporated to make a considerable overall improvement in efficiency. *Orpheus* was given an aluminium casing, but later boats adopted glass-fibre laminate. The particular feature of this class is its quietness, with all equipment soundproofed, but in addition a higher grade of steel permits a greater diving depth than the *Porpoise* class (believed to exceed 1000ft). *Onyx* was bought on the stocks by the Royal Canadian Navy and launched as HMCS *Ojibwa* in 1964; a replacement was added to the programme.

When the Type 2400 submarines come into service towards the end of the 1980s this class will be disposed of, by which time they will be at the end of their hull lives. Being smaller and quieter than the nuclear boats, they play an important role in reconnaissance and surveillance.

OBERON class *patrol submarines*

Displacement:	1610t normal; 2030t/2410t
Dimensions:	As *Porpoise* class
Machinery:	As *Porpoise* class
Armament:	Originally as *Porpoise* class, but are being altered to fire Mk 24 Mod 1 torpedoes
Sensors:	Search and navigation radars; sonar Types 187, 2007, 2019
Complement:	64

No	Name	Builder	Laid down	Launched	Comp	Fate
S 09	OBERON	Chatham DYd	28.11.57	18.7.59	24.2.61	Extant 1982
S 10	ODIN	Cammell Laird	27.4.59	4.11.60	3.5.62	Extant 1982
S 11	ORPHEUS	Vickers-Armstrong, Barrow	16.4.59	17.11.59	25.11.60	Extant 1982
S 12	OLYMPUS	Vickers-Armstrong, Barrow	4.3.60	14.6.61	7.7.62	Extant 1982
S 13	OSIRIS	Vickers-Armstrong, Barrow	26.1.62	29.11.62	11.1.64	Extant 1982
S 14	ONSLAUGHT	Chatham DYd	8.4.59	24.9.60	14.8.62	Extant 1982
S 15	OTTER	Scotts	14.1.60	15.5.61	20.8.62	Extant 1982
S 16	ORACLE	Cammell Laird	26.4.60	26.9.61	14.2.63	Extant 1982
S 17	OCELOT	Chatham DYd	17.11.60	5.5.62	31.1.64	Extant 1982
S 18	OTUS	Scotts	31.5.61	17.10.62	5.10.63	Extant 1982
S 19	OPOSSUM	Cammell Laird	21.12.61	23.5.63	5.6.64	Extant 1982
–	ONYX (i)	Chatham DYd	27.9.62	–	–	To Canada 1963
S 20	OPPORTUNE	Scotts	26.10.62	14.2.64	28.12.64	Extant 1982
S 21	ONYX (ii)	Cammell Laird	16.11.64	18.8.66	25.11.67	Extant 1982

Valiant 1977

This class is a slightly enlarged edition of the *Dreadnought* to accommodate the bulkier British reactor developed at the Admiralty Reactor Test Establishment at Dounreay. The completion of *Valiant* was delayed by a year because of the priority given to the Polaris programme. As in the *Dreadnought*, conventional Laurence-Scott electric motors and a 112-cell battery provide emergency power, with a Paxman diesel generator. All TT are forward, and Mk 24 torpedoes have replaced the earlier Mks 8 and 23.

Courageous is the only one of the class to be refitted with the new Type 2020 long-range passive sonar, but the whole class will receive Sub-Harpoon missiles if the purchase goes ahead as planned. *Churchill* has already tested this weapon and she also evaluated the US Navy's Mk 48 Mod 3 torpedo, with the *Otus*. *Courageous* was the first to deploy Sub-Harpoon operationally, in 1981.

VALIANT class *nuclear attack submarines*

Displacement:	4000t normal; 4400t/4900t
Dimensions:	285ft pp × 33ft 3in × 27ft
	86.9m × 10.1m × 8.2m
Machinery:	1-shaft nuclear: 1 pressurised water-cooled reactor (PWR 1) plus geared steam turbine, 15,000shp, plus diesel-electric auxiliary = 20kts/28kts
Armament:	6–21in TT (26 torpedoes)
Sensors:	Search and navigation radars; sonar Types 2001, 2007, 183, 197, 2019
Complement:	103

No	Name	Builder	Laid down	Launched	Comp	Fate
S 102	VALIANT (ex-*Inflexible*)	Vickers-Armstrong, Barrow	22.1.62	3.12.63	18.7.66	Extant 1982
S 103	WARSPITE	Vickers-Armstrong, Barrow	10.12.63	25.9.65	18.4.67	Extant 1982
S 46	CHURCHILL	Vickers-Armstrong, Barrow	30.6.67	20.12.68	15.7.70	Extant 1982
S 48	CONQUEROR	Cammell Laird	5.12.67	28.8.69	9.11.71	Extant 1982
S 50	COURAGEOUS (ex-*Superb*)	Vickers-Armstrong, Barrow	15.6.68	7.3.70	16.10.71	Extant 1982

During the Falklands conflict the *Conqueror* sank the Argentine cruiser *General Belgrano* on 2.5.82 using two Mk 8 torpedoes.

Valiant as completed   CPL

Resolution as completed   MoD

Superb 1978   MoD

Renown 1969

RESOLUTION class *ballistic missile submarines*

Displacement:	7500t/8400t
Dimensions:	360ft pp, 425ft oa × 33ft × 30ft
	109.7m, 129.5m × 10.1m × 9.1m
Machinery:	1-shaft nuclear: 1 pressurised water-cooled reactor, plus geared steam turbine, *c* 20,000shp, plus Paxman auxiliary diesel, 4000bhp = 20kts/25kts
Armament:	16 Polaris A-3 UGM-27C SLBM, 6–21in TT
Sensors:	Radar Type 1006; sonar Types 2001, 2007, 183, 197, 2019
Complement:	?

No	Name	Builder	Laid down	Launched	Comp	Fate
S 22	RESOLUTION	Vickers-Armstrong, Barrow	26.2.64	15.9.66	2.10.67	Extant 1982
S 23	REPULSE	Vickers-Armstrong, Barrow	12.3.65	4.11.67	28.9.68	Extant 1982
S 26	RENOWN	Cammell Laird	25.6.64	25.2.67	15.11.68	Extant 1982
S 27	REVENGE	Cammell Laird	19.5.65	15.3.68	4.12.69	Extant 1982
–	RAMILLIES	–	–	–	–	Cancelled 1964

At the 1962 Nassau Conference, the momentous decision was taken to transfer responsibility for the United Kingdom's nuclear deterrent from the RAF to the RN, following the cancellation of the airborne Skybolt system. Instead the RN was to build five nuclear ballistic missile submarines (SSBNs) based broadly on the missile compartment of the US Navy's *Lafayette* class, with British equipment and machinery, but armed with missiles, tubes and fire control systems supplied from the United States.

A special Polaris Executive was set up to supervise the building of the boats and the creation of training and support facilities, and so successful was the collaboration between the administrative and technical sides that the first boat, *Resolution*, went on patrol as planned in 1968. With *Dreadnought* it was the only British post-1945 defence programme to remain within its financial budget. Only one problem was encountered: the figure of five boats was arrived at after a careful study of refit schedules, and when the new Labour Defence Minister, Denis Healey, cancelled the

order for the fifth boat as a gesture of appeasement, it became difficult to guarantee that one Polaris 'bomber' would remain on patrol at all times. Up to 1982, however, there has been no gap in the patrol.

Apart from the use of British equipment and design features from the *Valiant* class, the main departure from the *Lafayette* class is the rejec-

tion of diving planes on the fin. Although these are standard in USN submarines, British designers maintain that their advantages of better slow-speed control do not outweigh their disadvantages. These submarines will be replaced at the end of the 1980s by four new SSBNs armed with Trident missiles, but to improve the ability of the existing Polaris mis-

siles to penetrate defences a new warhead has been developed: codenamed 'Chevaline', it consists of three independently targeted re-entry warheads capable of hitting points 40km apart. The completion of this programme was announced in 1980, shortly before confirmation of the Trident purchase.

Superb 1977

Shorter and of fuller hull-form than previously, and designed to dive deeper. The fine bow-section means that only five tubes can be fitted, but in other respects the vessels are merely improved *Valiant*s. It is confirmed that reloading of torpedoes takes 15 seconds and that they are fitted with the Mk 24 Mod 1 and DCB fire control system. The class will receive Type 2020 sonar in place of Type 2001 as they are refitted, as well as Sub-Harpoon underwater-launched missiles. In this class the machinery is mounted on a raft to silence it.

SWIFTSURE class *nuclear attack submarines*

Displacement:	4000t normal; 4200t/4500t
Dimensions:	272ft pp × 32ft 4in × 27ft
	82.9m × 9.8m × 8.2m
Machinery:	1-shaft nuclear: 1 pressurised water-cooled reactor, plus 1 geared steam turbine, 15,000shp, plus 2 Paxman diesels, 4000bhp = 20kts/30kts
Armament:	5–21in TT (25 torpedoes)
Sensors:	Search and navigation radars; sonar Types 2001, 2007, 183, 2024
Complement:	97

No	Name	Builder	Laid down	Launched	Comp	Fate
S 126	SWIFTSURE	Vickers-Armstrong, Barrow	6.6.69	7.9.71	17.4.73	Extant 1982
S 108	SOVEREIGN	Vickers-Armstrong, Barrow	18.9.70	17.2.73	11.7.74	Extant 1982
S 109	SUPERB	Vickers-Armstrong, Barrow	16.3.73	30.11.74	13.11.76	Extant 1982
S 104	SCEPTRE	Vickers-Armstrong, Barrow	19.2.74	20.11.76	14.2.78	Extant 1982
S 111	SPARTAN	Vickers-Armstrong, Barrow	26.4.76	7.4.78	22.9.79	Extant 1982
S 112	SPLENDID (ex-*Severn*)	Vickers-Armstrong, Barrow	23.11.77	5.10.79	23.1.80	Extant 1982

The first of a new class of seven fleet nuclear submarines was ordered in September 1977, followed by a second in July 1978, third in July 1979 and the fourth and fifth in 1981 and 1982; two more are planned. They resemble the *Swiftsure* class, but with much more attention paid to silencing: PWR2 reactor, pump jet instead of a propeller, and anechoic tiling on hull.

TRAFALGAR class *nuclear attack submarines*

Displacement:	*c* 4000t normal
Dimensions:	Similar to *Swiftsure*
Machinery:	1-shaft nuclear: 1 PWR2 reactor, plus geared steam turbine and auxiliary diesel-electric = 20kts/28kts
Armament:	5–21in TT (25 torpedoes, Sub-Harpoon SSMs)
Sensors:	Sonar Type 2020, 2026, 2019
Complement:	?

No	Name	Builder	Laid down	Launched	Comp	Fate
S 113	TRAFALGAR	Vickers-Armstrong, Barrow	25.4.79	1.7.81		Fitting out
S 114	TURBULENT	Vickers-Armstrong, Barrow	8.5.80	1.12.82		Fitting out
S 115	TIRELESS	Vickers-Armstrong, Barrow	Aug 82			Building
S 116	TORBAY	Vickers-Armstrong, Barrow				Building
S 117	TALENT	Vickers-Armstrong, Barrow				Ordered
S 118	TACITURN	Vickers-Armstrong, Barrow				Projected
	–	Vickers-Armstrong, Barrow				Projected

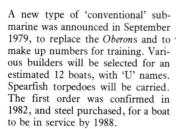

Upholder class design

A new type of 'conventional' submarine was announced in September 1979, to replace the *Oberon*s and to make up numbers for training. Various builders will be selected for an estimated 12 boats, with 'U' names. Spearfish torpedoes will be carried. The first order was confirmed in 1982, and steel purchased, for a boat to be in service by 1988.

UPHOLDER class *patrol submarines*

Displacement:	2117t/2352t
Dimensions:	229ft 8in oa × 25ft
	70.0m × 7.6m
Machinery:	1-shaft diesel-electric: Paxman diesels plus electric motors = *c*12kts/20kts. Range 8000nm at 10kts surfaced, 2500nm at 10kts submerged
Armament:	6–21in TT (18 torpedoes, Sub-Harpoon SSMs)
Sensors:	Sonar Types 2040, 2026, flank array, etc.
Complement:	44

No	Name	Builder	Laid Down	Launched	Comp	Fate
S	UPHOLDER	Vickers-Armstrong, Barrow				Ordered

In 1980 the MoD announced that it would build four submarines armed with the Trident UGM-93A, replacing the four Polaris-armed *Resolution*s towards the end of the decade. No details have been announced, but it is likely that they will have 16 Tridents each and all would have to be built by Vickers at Barrow because Cammell Laird no longer receive orders for

'TRIDENT' *ballistic missile submarines*

Particulars:	Not yet announced

nuclear submarines. As 'T' names have already been allocated to the *Trafalgar* class and 'U' names to the new conventional boats, they may revert to battleship names.

AMPHIBIOUS WARFARE VESSELS

Intrepid 1981

FEARLESS class *assault ships*

Displacement:	11,060t normal; 12,120t deep load; 16,950t ballasted
Dimensions:	500ft wl, 520ft oa × 80ft × 20ft 6in normal
	152.4m, 158.5m × 24.4m × 6.3m
Machinery:	2-shaft geared steam turbines, 2 boilers, 22,000shp = 21kts. Range 5000nm at 20kts
Armament:	2–40mm/60 Mk 9 Bofors (2×1), 4 Seacat GWS22 SAM (4×4)
Sensors:	Radar Types 978, 993
Complement:	580 + 400–700 troops

No	Name	Builder	Launched	Fate
L 10	FEARLESS	Harland & Wolff, Belfast	19.12.63	Extant 1982
L 11	INTREPID	John Brown, Clydebank	25.6.64	Extant 1982

To provide the Royal Marines with greater capability, two updated versions of the wartime dock landing ship were ordered in 1962. Although launched in surroundings of theatrical secrecy they were simply smaller versions of the contemporary *Raleigh* class building by the USN. The principal advantage over the existing LSTs was the seaworthiness, range and capacity, for they could accommodate 400 troops on board (700 for short periods) as well as, typically, 15 tanks and 27 vehicles. *Fearless* was laid down on 25.7.62 and completed on 25.11.65; *Intrepid* was laid down on 19.12.62 and completed on 11.3.67.

Despite being large and valuable ships the armament is light. Each ship carries four LCM(9) landing craft in davits amidships.

In 1976 a defence cutback caused *Intrepid* to be paid off into reserve and *Fearless* to be downgraded to the Dartmouth Training Squadron, but every effort was made to keep them available for an emergency. In 1979 *Intrepid* was brought forward from reserve to allow *Fearless* to be refitted. *Intrepid* had de-stored in late 1981 and was on offer to Argentina, but in April 1982 she was hurriedly recommissioned to join *Fearless* in the Falklands Task Force.

Fearless 1968   CPL

Sir Geraint 1977

SIR LANCELOT class *logistic landing ships*

Displacement:	3270t light; 5674t full load
Dimensions:	380ft wl, 412ft 1in oa × 59ft 8in × 13ft
	115.8m, 125.1m × 19.6m × 4.3m
Machinery:	2 shafts, 2 Mirrlees 10cyl diesels, 9400bhp (*Sir Lancelot* Denny-Sulzer diesels, 9520bhp) = 17kts. Range 8000nm at 15kts
Armament:	Fitted for 2–40mm (2×1), but not normally carried
Complement:	68 + 340–534 troops

No	Name	Builder	Launched	Fate
L 3029	SIR LANCELOT	Fairfield	25.6.63	Extant 1982
L 3004	SIR BEDIVERE	Hawthorn Leslie	20.7.66	Extant 1982
L 3005	SIR GALAHAD	Stephen	19.4.66	Bombed 8.6.82, scuttled
L 3505	SIR TRISTRAM	Hawthorn Leslie	12.12.66	Damaged 8.6.82
L 3027	SIR GERAINT	Stephen	26.1.67	Extant 1982
L 3036	SIR PERCIVAL	Hawthorn Leslie	4.10.67	Extant 1982

Sir Lancelot was the prototype of a class of six landing ships ordered by the Ministry of Transport for use by the Army. They were initially chartered to and operated by shipping companies, but were taken over by the Royal Fleet Auxiliary service in 1980. They can carry, and operate, helicopters, 16 main battle tanks, 34 mixed vehicles and up to 534 troops; they can also lay out pontoons. They were designed to mercantile specifications, to operate virtually as roll on/roll off ferries in support of the Army, and were never intended to take part in opposed landings – hence the generally lightweight construction and aluminium superstructure. *Sir Galahad* and *Sir Tristram* were bombed in Bluff Cove during the Falklands conflict; the former was so badly damaged that she was later towed out to sea and sunk with a Mk 8 torpedo, but *Sir Tristram* is still afloat and in use as an accommodation ship. One or two replacements may be built in Australia as an offset for the purchase of a new carrier.

LANDING CRAFT

Name	Fate	Name	Fate
Ardennes class: launched 1976–77, 1413t full load			
ARDENNES (L 4001)	Extant 1982	ARAKAN (L 4007)	Extant 1982
Avon class: launched 1961–67, 100t full load			
AVON (RPL 01)	For disposal 1982	LODDEN (RPL 11)	Extant 1982
BUDE (RPL 02)	Extant 1982	GLEN (RPL 07)	Extant 1982
CLYDE (RPL 03)	Extant 1982	HAMBLE (RPL 08)	Extant 1982
DART (RPL 04)	Extant 1982	ITCHEN (RPL 09)	Extant 1982
EDEN (RPL 05)	Extant 1982	KENNET (RPL 10)	Extant 1982
FORTH (RPL 06)	Extant 1982	MEDWAY (RPL 12)	Extant 1982
Arromanches class: launched 1981, c100t full load			
ARROMANCHES (L?)	Extant 1982	ANTWERP (L?)	Extant 1982
LCM(9) type: launched 1963–66, 176t full load			
L 700–L 711	Extant 1982	L 3507–L 3508	(See notes)
LCVP type: launched 1981, c14t			

Ardennes class
Operated by the Army's Royal Corps of Transport, more as ferries than as warships, although they are designed to replace the wartime LCT(8) type. They are unarmed, but can carry five 70t tanks or up to 24 standard 20ft containers, plus 34 troops. They were built by Brooke Marine.

Avon class
Also operated by the Royal Corps of Transport, they are officially Ramp Powered Lighters, hence the RPL pennant numbers. Built by White and Saunders-Roe, they are to be replaced by the *Arromanches* class.

Arromanches class
The first two were launched by Brooke Marine in 1981. Nine more are planned to replace the *Avon* class.

LCM(9) type
Vospers built the prototypes *L 3507* and *L 3508* in 1963, and the remainder were built by Dunstan, Brooke Marine or J Bolson in 1964–66. They are conventional LCM type craft and can carry 2 tanks or 100 tons of cargo. Four each of the *L 700* series are carried by *Fearless* and *Intrepid*. One was lost during the Falklands conflict.

LCVP type
The first of a new type was ordered on 8.2.80 from Fairey Allday Marine. Nine more were ordered in July 1980, to replace the remaining war-built LCVP(1), (2) and (3), of which 9, 8 and 9 respectively were still in service in 1982. They are redesignated LCSs of about 14t full load, and can carry 35 troops or two Land Rovers.

Other minor landing craft
In 1982 remaining minor landing craft were two ex-LCM(7)s, employed as naval servicing boats and three LCP(L)(3)s, plus a few Raiding Landing Craft (LCRs).

Ardennes July 1979   C & S Taylor

Two LCM (9)s from *Fearless*, July 1982   C & S Taylor

SMALL SURFACE COMBATANTS

'FORD' class *seaward defence boats*

Displacement:	120t normal; 160t deep load
Dimensions:	110ft pp, 117ft 3in oa × 20ft × 5ft
	33.5m, 35.7m × 6.1m × 1.5m
Machinery:	3 shafts, 2 12 cyl Paxman diesels plus 1 Foden, 1100/100bhp = 18kts/8kts
Armament:	1–40mm/60 Mk 7, 2 DCT
Sensors:	Radar Type 978; sonar Type 144
Complement:	19

Class:
Shalford (P 3101), *Aberford* (P 3102), *Axford* (P 3103), *Beckford* (P 3104), *Brayford* (P 3105), *Bryansford* (P 3106), *Camberford* (P 3107), *Desford* (P 3108), *Greatford* (P 3109), *Gifford* (P 3111), *Droxford* (P 3113), *Mayford* (P 3114), *Hinksford* (P 3115), *Ickford* (P 3116), *Dubford* (P 3119), *Glassford* (P 3120), *Kingsford* (P 3121), *Marlingford* (P 3122), *Tilford* (P 3123), *Montford* (P 3124)

Designed by W Holt as inshore ASW craft to replace the wartime HDMLs, with main drive diesels on wing shafts and a cruising diesel on the centre shaft. Appearance was distinctive, with two funnels side by side and a lattice mast. They were designed to carry a single-barrel Squid but this weapon did not materialise and so the lead-craft, *Shalford*, was fitted with a Squid triple DC mortar aft; the remainder had a standard armament of two depth-charge throwers and two racks. They were ordered April–May 1951 and built by various yards in 1950–57.

Foreign transfers: *Brayford* and *Glassford* (South African *Gelderland* and *Nautilus*, 1954–55); *Desford* (Ceylonese *Kotiya*, 1955); *Aberford* (Kenyan *Nyati*, 1964), and *Hinksford*, *Gifford* and *Dubford* (Nigerian *Benin*, *Bonny* and *Sapele*, 1966–68). Most of the class were put on the disposal list in 1966–67, but *Beckford* (renamed *Dee* in 1965) and *Droxford* (renamed *Dee* 1955–1965) were extant in 1982, serving as tenders to Liverpool and Glasgow University reserve units.

Droxford 1.4.81   MG Photographic

KINGFISHER class *patrol craft*

Displacement:	187t normal; 194t deep load
Dimensions:	110ft 11in wl, 120ft oa × 21ft 8in × 6ft 6in
	33.8m, 36.6m × 6.6m × 2.0m
Machinery:	2 shafts, 2 Paxman 16 YCJM diesels, 4000bhp = 25kts. Range 2000nm at 14kts
Armament:	1–40mm/60 Mk 9, 2–7.62mm MG
Complement:	19

No	Name	Builder	Launched	Fate
P 260	KINGFISHER	Richard Dunston	20.9.74	Extant 1982
P 261	CYGNET	Richard Dunston	26.10.74	Extant 1982
P 262	PETEREL	Richard Dunston	14.5.76	Extant 1982
P 263	SANDPIPER	Richard Dunston	20.1.77	Extant 1982

An unsuccessful attempt to adapt an RAF air–sea rescue design, the *Seal* type, these craft have proved unstable and suffer badly from vibration. Following problems with *Kingfisher*, the later craft were given a lighter mast and had no scuttles. Two were immediately relegated to RNR training tenders and all will be disarmed for service as inshore surveying craft.

JURA *offshore patrol vessel*

Displacement:	778t normal; 1285t deep load
Dimensions:	195ft 3in oa × 35ft × 14ft 4in
	59.5m × 10.7m × 4.4m
Machinery:	1 shaft, 2 British Polar SP11 2VS–F diesels, 4200bhp = 17kts
Armament:	1–40mm/60 Bofors Mk 3
Complement:	?

Under considerable political pressure to provide defence for offshore resources in the new 200-mile Exclusive Economic Zone (EEZ), the Royal Navy initiated studies of sea-keeping characteristics. These established criteria of length, beam, freeboard and subdivision, and thereafter commercial designs were sought which approximated to the parameters. The best answer appeared to be a pair of trawler-type fishery protection vessels, *Jura* and *Westra*, operated by the Scottish Department of Fisheries. *Jura* (P 296) was chartered in 1975 and armed with a 40mm gun. She proved successful and the design of the 'Island' class was adapted from it. When HMS *Jersey* became operational in January 1977, *Jura* was returned to her owners.

Orkney 1980

NB 1/750 scale

'ISLAND' class *offshore patrol vessels*

Displacement:	1000t normal; 1280t deep load
Dimensions:	176ft wl, 195ft 3in oa × 36ft × 14ft
	53.6m, 59.5m × 11.0m × 4.2m
Machinery:	1 shaft, 2 Ruston 12-RK 3 CM diesels, 4380bhp = 16kts. Range 11,000nm at 12kts
Armament:	1–40mm/60 Bofors Mk 3, 2–7.62mm MG
Sensors:	Radar Type 1006; sonar Simrad SU 'sidescan'
Complement:	35

No	Name	Builder	Launched	Fate
P 295	JERSEY	Hall Russell	18.3.76	Extant 1982
P 297	GUERNSEY	Hall Russell	17.2.77	Extant 1982
P 298	SHETLAND	Hall Russell	22.11.76	Extant 1982
P 299	ORKNEY	Hall Russell	29.6.76	Extant 1982
P 300	LINDISFARNE	Hall Russell	1.6.77	Extant 1982
P 277	ANGLESEY	Hall Russell	18.10.78	Extant 1982
P 278	ALDERNEY	Hall Russell	27.2.79	Extant 1982

To patrol fishing grounds and oilfields in the new 200-mile EEZ, the RN ordered five modified trawler-type vessels in February 1975. They were based on the Scottish Department of Fisheries' *Westra* and *Jura* (see above), giving time for studies for a more capable design. Although much criticised for their

UNITED KINGDOM

Speedy 1980   MoD

Leeds Castle as completed   MoD

low speed and weak armament they proved so successful that two more were ordered in October 1977, equipped with stabilisers but otherwise identical. The philosophy is quite simple: sea-keeping and endurance are the most important attributes, and weaponry is almost irrelevant. They are fitted to replenish at sea from naval oilers and have a sophisticated computer-aided navigation system. Stabilisers will be fitted to the first five.

SPEEDY *patrol hydrofoil*

Displacement:	117t
Dimensions:	(Foils up – hullborne) 101ft oa × 30ft × 6ft *30.8m × 9.1m × 1.8m* (Foils down) 90ft × 30ft × 17ft (hullborne), 7ft 10in *27.4m × 9.1m × 5.2m, 2.4m*
Machinery:	(Foilborne) twin waterjets, 2 Allison 501–K20A gas turbines, 6600shp = 43kts (50kts dash); 2 shafts, 2 GM 8U92 T1 diesels, 800bhp = 14kts (hullborne). Range 560nm/1500nm at 43kts/14kts
Armament:	2–7.62mm MG
Complement:	18

No	Name	Builder	Launched	Fate
P 296	SPEEDY	Boeing Marine, Seattle	9.7.79	For disposal 1982

The Royal Navy's first operational hydrofoil was ordered in June 1978 following an evaluation a year earlier of the commercial jetfoil *Flying Princess*. Boeing had already completed a design-study for the Japanese Maritime Self-Defence Force to adapt the jetfoil for the fishery protection role, and so the RN was able to acquire a hydrofoil at minimum cost (£6.2 million). Originally two 7.62mm machine-guns were to have been carried, but *Speedy* commissioned in June 1980 without armament. Her radar (Type 1006) and CANE computer-aided navigation system are similar to the 'Island' and 'Castle' classes, with which vessels she is working. She was also to have been used as a high-speed target, but in 1982 it was announced that she was up for sale.

'Castle' class design

'CASTLE' class *offshore patrol vessels*

Displacement:	1427t
Dimensions:	246ft wl, 265ft 9in oa × 37ft 9in × 11in 3in mean *75.0m, 81.0m × 11.5m × 3.4m*
Machinery:	2 shafts, 2 Paxman diesels, 2820bhp = 20kts. Range 10,000nm at 10kts
Armament:	1–40mm, 2–7.62mm MG
Sensors:	Radar Type 1006
Complement:	*c*40

No	Name	Builder	Launched	Fate
P 258	LEEDS CASTLE	Hall Russell	29.10.80	Extant 1982
P 265	DUMBARTON CASTLE	Hall Russell	3.6.81	Extant 1982

The need of a properly designed OPV led to Naval Staff Target 7040 being prepared. Experience with the 'Island' class showed that more length would make for greater crew efficiency on extended patrol and enable the ship to have

alternative roles. What has emerged is a substantial (but still cheap) ship which can be given a selection of weapons and sensors to meet customers' differing needs. In the RN version it was decided not to install a helicopter hangar, but to use the space instead to provide a bigger flight deck on which a Sea King can land and refuel if necessary. *Leeds Castle* was laid down in August 1979 and *Dumbarton Castle* in 1980, before they were officially ordered. The ultimate armament is undecided, but the main contenders are the new naval version of the 30mm Rarden tank gun and the 105mm Autonomous Patrol Gun developed from the L7 tank gun, and in wartime they could ship an OTO Melara 76mm/62 compact. They are capable of rapid conversion to minelayers or deep sweepers (EDATS). Two more may be ordered.

Both ships acted as dispatch vessels in the South Atlantic during the Falklands conflict, which is proof of their sea-keeping abilities.

PEACOCK class *patrol vessels*

Displacement:	*c*1100t
Dimensions:	204ft (oa) × 32.8ft × 18ft *62.2m × 10m × 5.5m*
Machinery:	2 shafts, 2 Crossley Pielstick 18PA6 V280 diesels, *c*8000bhp = 25kts
Armament:	1–76mm/62DP, 2–20mm
Complement:	42

No	Name	Builder	Launched	Fate
	PEACOCK	Hall Russell		Building
	PLOVER	Hall Russell		Building
	STARLING	Hall Russell		Building
	SWALLOW	Hall Russell		Building
	SWIFT	Hall Russell		Building

Jointly funded by RN (25 per cent) and the Hong Kong Government (75 per cent) to replace five elderly CMSs acting as gunboats. The design was prepared by Hall Russell and is a smaller edition of the 'Castle' class (OPV2), with heavier armament and higher speed.

First order placed June 1981 and keel of *Peacock* laid in Jan 1982. All are to be ready by 1984.

MTB 538 *fast attack craft*

Displacement:	36t normal; 45t deep load
Dimensions:	68ft pp, 74ft 2in oa × 20ft 3in × 6ft *20.7m, 22.6m × 6.2m × 1.8m*
Machinery:	3-shaft Packard petrol engines, 4050bhp = 40kts max
Armament:	2–20mm (1×2), 4–18in TT, or 1–4.5in/25 8cwt
Complement:	15

MTB 539 *fast attack craft*

Displacement:	43t normal; 50t deep load
Dimensions:	72ft pp, 75ft 3in oa × 19ft 9in × 5ft 6in *21.9m, 22.9m × 3.0m × 1.7m*
Machinery:	3-shaft Packard petrol engines, 4050bhp = 42kts
Armament:	As *MTB 538*
Complement:	16

These two vessels were planned at the end of the Second World War, but in 1946 the two firms involved, Vosper at Portsmouth and Saunders-Roe at Beaumaris, were given a free hand to develop their own ideas. In *538* (completed August 1948) Vosper developed an advanced, all-glued wood hull, but Saunders-Roe used aluminium alloy in *539*. Both boats were intended to serve as convertible MTBs/MGBs, with four TT or the 4.5in 8cwt short gun as main armament. On entering service they were re-rated as *FPB 1601* and *FPB 1602* respectively. Although they provided experience for the 'Gay' class they did not last long and were put on the sale list in 1956.

'GAY' class *fast attack craft*

Displacement:	50t standard; 65t deep load
Dimensions:	71ft 6in pp, 75ft 2in oa × 20ft 1in × 4ft 1in
	21.8m, 22.9m × 6.1m × 1.2m
Machinery:	2-shaft Packard petrol engines, 5000bhp = 40kts
Armament:	(As gunboats) 1–4.5in/25 8cwt, 1–40mm/60 Mk 7; (as torpedo-boats) 2–40mm/60 Mk 9 (2×1), 2–21in TT
Complement:	13

Class (no, builder, fate):
Gay Archer (FPB 1041, Vosper, sold 1963), *Gay Bombardier* (FPB 1042, Vosper, for sale 1963), *Gay Bowman* (FPB 1043, Vosper, sold 1963), *Gay Bruiser* (FPB 1044, Vosper, sold 1962), *Gay Carabineer* (FPB 1045, Thornycroft, for sale 1963), *Gay Cavalier* (FPB 1046, Taylor, sold 1963), *Gay Centurion* (FPB 1047, Thornycroft, sold 1962), *Gay Charger* (FPB 1048, Morgan Giles, for disposal 1958), *Gay Charioteer* (FPB 1049, Morgan Giles, for disposal 1959), *Gay Dragoon* (FPB 1050, Taylor, sold 1962), *Gay Fencer* (FPB 1051, McGruer, for disposal 1958), *Gay Forester* (FPB 1052, McGruer, sold 1962)

Short-hulled wooden convertible MTBs/MGBs, the last class with petrol engines, ordered between February and May 1951 and all completed in 1953. The design was developed from Vosper's *MTB 538* and was basically an interim one (after the 'Darks') since development of the Deltic diesel was being delayed. Pennant numbers later changed to 'P', although the number remained the same. Several hulls were used commercially after disposal and others were hulked.

Dark Adventurer as completed

NB 1/750 scale

'DARK' class *fast attack craft*

Displacement:	50t standard; 64t deep load
Dimensions:	67ft pp, 71ft 8in oa × 19ft 5in × 6ft 1in max
	20.4m, 21.8m × 5.9m × 1.8m
Machinery:	2-shaft Napier Deltic 16cyl diesels, 5000bhp = 40kts. Oil 8t
Armament:	(As gunboats) 1–4.5in/25 8cwt, 1–40mm/60 Mk 7; (as torpedo-boats) 1–40mm/60 Mk 7, 4–21in TT
Complement:	15

Class (no, builder, fate):
Dark Adventurer (FPB 1101, Saunders-Roe for sale 1964), *Dark Aggressor* (FPB 1102, Saunders-Roe, sold 1961), *Dark Antagonist* (FPB 1103, Saunders-Roe, for sale 1964), *Dark Attacker* (Saunders-Roe, cancelled), *Dark Avenger* (FPB 1105, Saunders-Roe, sold 1967), *Dark Battler* (Saunders-Roe, cancelled 1953), *Dark Biter* (FPB 1104, Saunders-Roe, sold 1967), *Dark Bowman* (Saunders-Roe, cancelled 1955), *Dark Buccaneer* (FPB 1108, Vosper, for sale 1964), *Dark Chaser* (Vosper, cancelled), *Dark Chieftain* (Vosper, cancelled), *Dark Clipper* (FPB 1109, Vosper, for sale 1964), *Dark Crusader* (Vosper, cancelled), *Dark Defender* (Thornycroft, cancelled), *Dark Explorer* (Thornycroft, cancelled), *Dark Fighter* (FPB 1113, Taylor, for sale 1964), *Dark Gladiador* (FPB 1114, Taylor, sunk as target 1975), *Dark Hero* (FPB 1115, McGruer, for sale 1965), *Dark Highwayman* (FPB 1110, Vosper, sold 1967), *Dark Horseman* (FPB 1116, McGruer, cancelled 1957), *Dark Hunter* (FPB 1117, Miller, sold 1962), *Dark Hussar* (FPB 1112, Thornycroft, for sale 1965), *Dark Intruder* (FPB 1118, Morgan Giles, ?), *Dark Invader* (FPB 1114, Morgan Giles, for sale 1964), *Dark Killer* (FPB 1115, Thornycroft, for sale 1964), *Dark Rover* (FPB 1107, Vosper, for sale 1964), *Dark Scout* (FPB 1106, Saunders-Roe, sold 1962)

The first diesel-engined FPBs built for the RN and the first to use the remarkable Deltic with an exceptionally good power-to-weight ratio (4.2hp per lb). They were built of alloy framing and wooden skin, apart from the all-aluminium *Dark Scout*. Conforming to previous practice, they were convertible MTBs/MGBs and could also lay six ground mines. They were ordered between December 1951 and January 1952.

The above-water exhaust caused problems and after a short while all the class were painted black. Flag superior later changed to 'P', although the numbers themselves remained unchanged. Although noisy and lively they were generally regarded as successful, but most were laid up in 1958 when Coastal Forces were disbanded, and all were either hulked or sold commercially by the mid-1960s.

Gay Bombadier as completed   CPL

'BOLD' class *fast attack craft*

Displacement:	130t standard; 150t deep load
Dimensions:	(*Bold Pathfinder*) 117ft pp, 122ft 8in oa × 20ft 5in × 6ft 7in
	35.7m, 37.4m × 6.2m × 2.0m
	(*Bold Pioneer*) 116ft 3in pp, 121ft oa × 25ft 6in × 6ft 10in
	35.4m, 36.9m × 7.8m × 2.1m
Machinery:	4-shaft gas turbine/diesel: 2 Metrovick G6 gas turbines plus 2 Metrovick diesels, 9000shp + 5000bhp = 43kts
Armament:	(As gunboat) 2–4.5in/25 8cwt (2×1), 1–40mm/60 Mk 9; (as torpedo-boat) 1–40mm/60 Mk 9, 4–21in TT
Complement:	20

Class (former no, builder, fate):
Bold Pathfinder (ex-*MTB 5720*, Vosper, sold 1964), *Bold Pioneer* (ex-*MTB 5701*, White, sold 1968)

Experimental prototypes built 1950–53 and serving as test-beds for development of the Gatric gas turbine first installed in *MGB 2009*, although they were initially fitted with ex-S-boat Mercedes diesels, which proved very unreliable. They were an earlier design than the 'Dark' and 'Gay' classes, but were bigger and more seaworthy. They were also very impressive, with twin funnels and a lattice foremast. They were both aluminium framed with a wooden shell, but *Bold Pathfinder* had a hull of round bilge form whereas *Bold Pioneer* had a hard chine hull, the object being to compare the two configurations. *Bold Pioneer* also tested the experimental 3.3in gun for the 'Brave' class (see below) but this was removed in 1958 when she was put on the disposal list. *Bold Pathfinder* was laid up in 1962.

(For illustration see under Greek *Astrapi*)

'BRAVE' class *fast attack craft*

Displacement:	89t standard; 114t deep load
Dimensions:	90ft pp, 98ft 10in oa × 25ft 6in × 7ft max
	27.4m, 30.1m × 7.8m × 1.8m
Machinery:	3 shafts, 3 Rolls-Royce Proteus gas turbines, 10,5000shp = 50kts. Fuel 25t
Armament:	1–40mm/60 Mk 9, 4–21in TT
Complement:	20

Class (no, builder, fate):
Brave Borderer (P 1011, Vosper, for disposal 1982), *Brave Swordsman* (P 1012, Vosper, preserved 1979).

The last operational fast patrol boats built for the RN, these had welded aluminium frames, a double mahogany skin and fibreglass sheathing below the waterline. They were built 1957–60. A feature of the design was the great beam (to accommodate the three engines), which with the hydraulic flap in the transom helped to maintain the trim.

Although the requirement for FPBs had officially lapsed with the demise of Coastal Forces they played a useful role as targets and in fishery patrol duties. They were originally intended to have the 3.3in CFS–2 (Coastal Forces System Mk 2) stabilised gun system, an adaptation of the Centurion tank's 20pdr. The prototype tested in *Bold Pioneer* had many teething troubles and when Coastal Forces were axed the development was not pursued. Although originally intended to have four TT they were given side-launching cradles to save weight.

Both were laid up in 1970, and in 1979 *Brave Swordsman* was presented to the Haydon-Baillie Collection.

TENACITY *patrol craft*

Displacement:	165t normal; 220t deep load
Dimensions:	144ft 6in oa × 26ft 6in × 7ft 9in *44.0m × 8.1m × 2.4m*
Machinery:	3-shaft CODOG: 3 Rolls-Royce Proteus gas turbines, 12,750shp = 39kts; 2 Paxman Ventura cruising diesels, 1200bhp = 16kts
Armament:	2–7.62mm MG. See notes
Sensors:	Navigation radar only
Complement:	32

An experimental private venture fast patrol boat built at Vosper Thornycroft's Camber yard in Portsmouth 1967–69. Designated P 276, she was not bought by the RN until January 1972, but was used for demonstrations and was twice chartered by the RN in 1971. Although designed for a heavy armament this was never fitted (the twin 35mm mounting and quad SSMs credited to her in *Jane's* being dummies), and when taken in to the RN she was given only two light machine-guns for fishery protection duties. The main alteration was the fitting of two davits for handling inflatable dinghies on the forecastle, but in 1978 she received a 40mm Bofors gun on the forecastle. She was reported to be for disposal in 1980.

Tenacity Apr 1974 C & S Taylor

Cutlass June 1979 C & S Taylor

SCIMITAR class *fast patrol boats*

Displacement:	80t normal; 102t deep load
Dimensions:	100ft pp, *c*106ft oa × 26ft 8in × 6ft 5in *30.5m, 32.3m × 8.1m × 1.9m*
Machinery:	2-shaft CODAG: 2 Rolls-Royce Proteus plus 2 Foden 6cyl diesels, 8500shp + 240bhp = 40kts
Armament:	None
Complement:	12

Class (no, builder, fate):
Cutlass (P 274, Vosper, for disposal 1982), *Sabre* (P 275, Vosper, for disposal 1982), *Scimitar* (P 271, Vosper, for disposal 1982)

Slightly smaller editions of the 'Brave' class, ordered in 1968 to serve as targets. The design permits installation of a third Proteus turbine and a light armament of missiles or guns if needed for the operational role, but so far they have been extremely useful simulating attacks by fast missile craft. In 1979 *Scimitar* was sent to Hong Kong, and in July 1980 *Sabre* lost her bow in a collision with a breakwater at Alderney. They have been placed in storage ashore since early 1981 and are unlikely to see further service.

MINE WARFARE VESSELS

Bossington 1957
NB 1/750 scale

'TON' class *coastal minesweepers*

Displacement:	360t normal; 425t deep load
Dimensions:	140ft pp, 152ft oa × 28ft 9in × 8ft 3in max *42.7m, 46.3m × 8.8m × 2.5m*
Machinery:	2 shafts, 2 12cyl Mirrlees or 18cyl Napier Deltic diesels, 2500bhp or 3000bhp = 15kts. Range 3000nm at 8kts
Armament:	1–40mm/60 Mk 7, 2–20mm (1×2)
Sensors:	Radar Type 978 (later Type 1006); sonar Type 193 (minehunters only)
Complement:	29 (minehunters 38)

No	Name	Builder	Launched	Fate
M 1101	CONISTON	Thornycroft	9.7.52	For disposal 1970
M 1102	ALCASTON	Thornycroft	5.1.53	To Australia 1961
M 1103	ALFRISTON	Thornycroft	29.4.53	Extant 1982
M 1104	ALVERTON	Camper & Nicholson	18.11.52	To Irish Naval Service 1971
M 1105	AMERTON	Camper & Nicholson	16.3.53	BU 1971
M 1106	APPLETON	Goole SB	4.9.52	For disposal 1970
M 1107	BEACHAMPTON	Goole SB	29.6.53	Extant 1982
M 1108	BEVINGTON	White	17.3.53	To Argentina 1967
M 1109	BICKINGTON	White	14.5.52	Extant 1982
M 1110	BILDESTON	Doig	9.6.52	Extant 1982
M 1111	EDDERTON	Doig	1.11.52	Survey ship *Myrmidon*

No	Name	Builder	Launched	Fate
M 1112	BOURSTON	Richards Iron Wks	6.10.52	BU 1975
M 1113	BRERETON	Richards Iron Wks	14.3.55	Extant 1982
M 1114	BRINTON	Cook, Welton & Gemmell	8.8.52	Extant 1982
M 1115	BRONINGTON	Cook, Welton & Gemmell	19.3.53	Extant 1982
M 1116	BURNASTON	Fleetlands	18.12.52	For disposal 1980
M 1117	BUTTINGTON	Fleetlands	11.6.53	For disposal 1970
M 1118	CALTON	Wivenhoe	24.10.53	For disposal 1967
M 1119	CARHAMPTON	Wivenhoe	21.7.55	For disposal 1967
M 1120	CAUNTON	Montrose	20.2.53	For disposal 1967
M 1121	CHEDISTON	Montrose	6.10.53	To Australia 1968
M 1122	CHILCOMPTON	Herd & McKenzie	23.10.53	Sold 1971
M 1123	CLARBESTON	Richards Iron Wks	18.2.54	For disposal 1968
M 1124	CRICHTON	Doig	17.3.53	Extant 1982
M 1125	CUXTON	Camper & Nicholson	9.11.53	Extant 1982
M 1126	DALWINTON	White	24.9.53	BU 1973
M 1127	DARLASTON	Cook, Welton & Gemmell	25.9.53	To Malaysia 1960
M 1128	DERRITON	Thornycroft	22.12.53	BU 1970
M 1129	OULSTON	Thornycroft	20.7.54	To Irish Naval Service 1971
M 1130	HIGHBURTON	Thornycroft	2.6.54	BU 1978
M 1131	HICKLETON	Thornycroft	26.1.55	To Argentina 1967
M 1132	HICKLETON	Thornycroft	26.1.55	To Irish Naval Service 1971
M 1133	BOSSINGTON (ex-*Embleton*)	Thornycroft	2.12.55	Extant 1982
M 1134	ESSINGTON	Camper & Nicholson	Sept 54	To Malaysia 1964

No	Name	Builder	Launched	Fate
M 1135	FENTON	Camper & Nicholson	Mar 55	For disposal 1967
M 1136	FITTLETON	White	3.2.54	Sunk in collision 1977, salved and BU
M 1137	FLOCKTON	White	3.6.54	For disposal 1968
M 1138	FLORISTON	Richards Iron Wks	26.1.55	For disposal 1967
M 1139	SOMERLEYTON (ex-*Gamston*)	Richards Iron Wks	1.7.54	To Australia 1961
M 1140	GAVINTON	Doig	27.7.53	Extant 1982
M 1141	GLASSERTON	Doig	3.12.53	Extant 1982
M 1142	HAZLETON	Cook, Welton & Gemmell	6.2.54	To South Africa 1955
M 1143	HEXTON	Cook, Welton & Gemmell	1954	To Malaysia 1963
M 1144	DUNKERTON	Goole SB	8.3.54	To South Africa 1955
M 1145	DUFTON	Goole SB	13.11.54	BU 1977
M 1146	HODGESTON	Fleetlands	6.4.54	Extant 1982
M 1147	HUBBERSTON	Camper & Nicholson	14.9.54	Extant 1982
M 1148	ILMINGTON	Camper & Nicholson	8.3.54	To Argentina 1967
M 1149	BADMINTON (ex-*Ilston*)	Camper & Nicholson	14.10.54	For disposal 1967
M 1150	INVERMORISTON	Dorset Yacht	2.6.54	For disposal 1971
M 1151	IVESTON	Philip	1.6.54	Extant 1982
M 1152	JACKTON	Philip	28.2.55	to Australia 1961
M 1153	KEDLESTON	Pickersgill	21.12.53	Extant 1982
M 1154	KELLINGTON	Pickersgill	12.10.54	Extant 1982
M 1155	MONKTON (ex-*Kelton*)	Herd & McKenzie	30.11.55	Extant 1982
M 1156	KEMERTON	Harland & Wolff	27.11.53	Sold 1971
M 1157	KIRKLISTON	Harland & Wolff	18.2.54	Extant 1982
M 1158	LALESTON	Harland & Wolff	18.5.54	Extant 1982
M 1159	LANTON	Harland & Wolff	30.7.54	For disposal 1967
M 1160	LETTERSTON	Harland & Wolff	26.10.54	For disposal 1970
M 1161	LEVERTON	Harland & Wolff	2.3.55	BU 1972
M 1162	KILDARTON (ex-*Liston*)	Harland & Wolff	23.5.55	For disposal 1968
M 1163	LULLINGTON	Harland & Wolff	31.8.55	To Malaysia 1966
M 1164	MADDISTON	Harland & Wolff	27.1.56	BU 1975
M 1165	MAXTON	Harland & Wolff	24.5.56	Extant 1982
M 1166	NURTON	Harland & Wolff	22.10.56	Extant 1982
M 1167	REPTON (ex-*Ossington*)	Harland & Wolff	1.5.57	For disposal 1970
M 1168	DILSTON (ex-*Pilston*)	Cook, Welton & Gemmell	15.11.54	To Malaysia 1964
M 1169	PENSTON	Cook, Welton & Gemmell	9.5.55	For disposal 1968
M 1170	PICTON	Cook, Welton & Gemmell	20.10.55	For disposal 1968
M 1171	ALDINGTON (ex-*Pittington*)	Camper & Nicholson	15.9.55	To Ghana 1964
M 1172	THANKERTON	Camper & Nicholson	4.9.56	To Malaysia 1966
M 1173	POLLINGTON	Camper & Nicholson	10.10.57	Extant 1982
M 1174	PUNCHESTON	Richards Iron Wks	20.11.56	BU 1975
M 1175	QUAINTON	Richards Iron Wks	10.10.57	BU 1979
M 1176	RENNINGTON	Richards Iron Wks	27.11.58	To Argentina 1967
M 1177	RODDINGTON	Fleetlands	24.2.55	BU 1972
M 1178	SANTON	Fleetlands	18.8.55	To Argentina 1967
M 1179	SEFTON	Fleetlands	15.9.54	For disposal 1967

No	Name	Builder	Launched	Fate
M 1180	SHAVINGTON	White	25.4.55	Extant 1982
M 1181	SHERATON	White	20.7.55	Extant 1982
M 1182	SHOULTON	Montrose	10.9.54	For disposal 1980
M 1183	SINGLETON	Montrose	18.11.55	To Australia 1961
M 1184	SULLINGTON	Doig	7.4.54	Survey ship *Mermaid*
M 1185	SWANSTON	Doig	1.7.54	To Australia 1954
M 1186	TARLTON	Doig	10.11.54	To Argentina 1967
M 1187	UPTON	Thornycroft	15.3.56	Extant 1982
M 1188	WALKERTON	Thornycroft	21.11.56	Extant 1982
M 1189	WASPERTON	White	28.2.56	Extant 1982
M 1190	WENNINGTON	Doig	6.4.55	To India 1956
M 1191	WHITTON	Fleetlands	30.1.56	to India 1956
M 1192	WILKIESTON	Cook, Welton & Gemmell	26.6.56	For sale 1972
M 1193	WOLVERTON	Montrose	22.10.56	Extant 1982
M 1194	WOOLASTON	Herd & McKenzie	6.3.58	For disposal 1974
M 1195	WOTTON	Philip	24.4.56	Extant 1982
M 1196	YARNTON	Pickersgill	26.3.56	Extant 1982
M 1197	OVERTON	Camper & Nicholson	28.1.56	To India 1956
M 1198	ASHTON (ex-*Cheriton*)	White	5.9.56	BU 1977
M 1199	BELTON	Doig	3.10.55	For disposal 1974
M 1200	SOBERTON	Fleetlands	20.11.56	Extant 1982
M 1201	DURWESTON	Dorset Yacht	18.8.55	to India 1956
M 1203	MARYTON	Montrose	3.4.58	For disposal 1968
M 1204	STUBBINGTON	Camper & Nicholson	8.8.56	Extant 1982
M 1205	WISTON	Wivenhoe	3.6.58	For disposal 1977
M 1206	FISKERTON	Doig	12.4.57	For disposal 1970
M 1207	CASTLETON	White	26.8.58	To South Africa 1959
M 1208	LEWISTON	Herd & McKenzie	3.11.59	Extant 1982
M 1209	SHAWTON	Fleetlands	24.9.57	BU 1977
M 1210	STRATTON	Dorset Yacht	29.7.57	To South Africa 1959
M 1211	HOUGHTON	Camper & Nicholson	22.11.57	For disposal 1970
M 1212	DUMBLETON	Harland & Wolff	8.11.57	To South Africa 1958
M 1213	OAKINGTON	Harland & Wolff	10.12.58	To South Africa 1959
M 1214	PACKINGTON	Harland & Wolff	3.7.58	To South Africa 1959
M 1215	CHILTON	Cook, Welton & Gemmell	15.7.57	to South Africa 1958
M 1216	CROFTON	Thornycroft	7.3.58	Extant 1982

During the Korean War it was learned that Russian magnetic influence mines could defeat degaussing, making the steel-hulled *Algerine* class 'fleet' sweepers obsolete and raising fears of a mining offensive against European ports. To counter this threat, in 1951 a massive programme of 118 coastal minesweepers was authorised, backed up by inshore sweepers for working in estuaries. The ships were launched between 1952 and 1959. The original plan was to name all coastal minesweepers after insects, with distinguishing colours for differing equipment fits, but eventually names of villages ending in 'ton' were adopted.

The design called for an aluminium-framed, wooden planked hull with non-magnetic fittings, capable of undertaking ocean passages, and the result was a sturdy craft which is still in service all over the world. Early vessels had Mirrlees diesels, but from *Highburton* onwards the more powerful Napier Deltic was fitted, and eventually the original 'Tons' were re-engined. Early members of the class had an open bridge and the lead-ship *Coniston* had no top to her funnel and a short lattice mast, but subsequent vessels had a double-finned funnel top and covered bridges were progressively introduced. The last major external change was to revert to a tripod mast, for a new radar.

In 1964 *Kirkliston* was converted to a 'minehunter', with LL sweep gear removed and a minehunting Type 193 sonar installed in the hull beneath the bridge. Active rudders were fitted to allow her to position herself over the mine, and four divers and two inflatable boats were carried to permit the mine to be blown up by hand. In *Shoulton* an auxiliary diesel-hydraulic pump-jet system was installed in 1965–66 to provide quieter propulsion. Another 15 were modified to minehunters, some with the Sperry Osborne Towed Acoustic Generator (TAG). Six were transferred to the RAN in 1961, four to the Indian Navy, one to

UNITED KINGDOM

Ghana, six to South Africa, six to Argentina in 1968 and three to the Republic of Ireland in 1971. Two, *Edderton* and *Sullington*, became the surveying vessels *Myrmidon* and *Mermaid*, while *Invermoriston* became an air–sea rescue vessel and *Laleston* was converted to a diving tender. The French, Canadians and Dutch were given the drawings to copy.

Many have served an RNVR/RNR tenders, reverting to their original names when replaced by others: *Thames* (*Alverton*, *Buttington*, *Woolaston*), *Venturer* (*Hodgeston*, *Buttington*), *Burnicia* (*Kedleston*), *Clyde* (*Amerton*, *Crichton*), *Humber* (*Bronington*), *Mersey* (*Amerton*, *Pollington*), *Solent* (*Warsash*, ex-*Crofton*), *Curzon* (*Bickington*, *Fittleton*), *Killiecrankie* (*Bickington*, *Derriton*), *St David* (*Crichton*), *Kilmorey* (*Alfriston*, *Kirkliston*), *Warsash* (*Alfriston*, *Boulston*, *Crofton*), *Montrose* (*Dalswinton*, *Nurton*, *Chediston*) and *Northumbria* (*Quainton*, *Hodgeston*).

Swanston, *Somerleyton*, *Singleton*, *Alcaston* and *Jackton* became the Australian *Gull*, *Hawk*, *Ibis*, *Snipe* and *Teal*; *Aldington* became the Ghanaian *Ejura*; *Whitton*, *Wennington*, *Durweston* and *Overton* became the Indian *Cannanore*, *Cuddalore*, *Kakinada* and *Karwar*; *Thankerton*, *Dilston*, *Essington*, *Hexton*, *Darlaston* and *Lullington* became the Malaysian *Brimchang*, *Jerai*, *Kinabulu*, *Ledang*, *Mahamiru* and *Tahan*; *Rennington*, *Santon*, *Ilmington*, *Hickleton*, *Tarlton* and *Bevington* became the Argentine *Chaco*, *Chubut*, *Formosa*, *Neuquem*, *Rio Negro* and *Tierra del Fuego*; and *Alverton*, *Blaxton* and *Oulston* became the Irish *Banba*, *Fola* and *Grainne*.

Late in 1971 *Beachampton*, *Monkton*, *Wasperton*, *Wolverton* and *Yarnton* were converted to coastal patrol craft, with 'P' numbers and a second 40mm/60 Mk 7 fitted abaft the funnel; all five were sent to Hong Kong. Minehunter conversions consisted of *Kirkliston*, *Shoulton*, *Bossington*, *Brereton*, *Bronington*, *Derriton*, *Glasserton*, *Highburton*, *Hubberston*, *Iveston*, *Kellington*, *Sheraton*, *Bilderston*, *Brinton*, *Gavinton*, *Kedleston*, *Maxton* and *Nurton*.

'HAM' class *inshore minesweepers*

Displacement:	120t normal; 159t deep load
Dimensions:	100ft pp, 106ft 6in–107ft 6in oa × 21ft–22ft × 5ft 6in–5ft 9in *30.5m, 32.5m–38m × 6.4m–6.7m × 1.5m–1.7m*
Machinery:	2 shafts, 2 Davey Paxman 12cyl diesels, 1100bhp = 14kts. Range 2350nm at 9kts
Armament:	1–40mm/60 Mk 7 or 1–20mm
Sensors:	Radar Type 978
Complement:	15

Class:
Inglesham (M 2601), *Altham* (M 2602), *Arlingham* (M 2603), *Asheldham* (M 2604), *Bassingham* (M 2605), *Bedham* (M 2606), *Bisham* (M 2607), *Blunham* (M 2608), *Bodenham* (M 2609), *Boreham* (M 2610), *Bottisham* (M 2611), *Brantingham* (M 2612), *Brigham* (M 2613), *Bucklesham* (M 2614), *Cardingham* (M 2615), *Chelsham* (M 2616), *Chillingham* (M 2617), *Cobham* (M 2618), *Darsham* (M 2619), *Davenham* (M 2620), *Dittisham* (M 2621), *Downham* (M 2622), *Edlingham* (M 2623), *Elsenham* (M 2624), *Etchingham* (M 2625), *Everyingham* (M 2626), *Felmersham* (M 2627), *Flintham* (M 2628),

Damersham (M 2629), *Fritham* (M 2630), *Glentham* (M 2631), *Greetham* (M 2632), *Halsham* (M 2633), *Harpham* (M 2634), *Haversham* (M 2635), *Lasham* (M 2636), *Hovingham* (M 2637), *Cranham* (M 2701), *Frettenham* (M 2702), *Isham* (M 2703), *Kingham* (M 2704), *Hildesham* (M 2705), *Ledsham* (M 2706), *Littlesham* (M 2707), *Ludham* (M 2708), *Mersham* (M 2709), *Mickleham* (M 2710), *Mileham* (M 2711), *Neasham* (M 2712), *Nettleham* (M 2713), *Ockham* (M 2714), *Ottringham* (M 2715), *Pagham* (M 2716), *Fordham* (M 2717, ex-*Pavenham*), *Petersham* (M 2718), *Pincham* (M 2719), *Powderham* (M 2720), *Pulham* (M 2721), *Rackham* (M 2722), *Reedham* (M 2723), *Rendlesham* (M 2724), *Riplingham* (M 2725), *Shipham* (M 2726), *Saxlingham* (M 2727), *Shrivenham* (M 2728), *Sidelsham* (M 2729), *Stedham* (M 2730), *Sparham* (M 2731), *Sulham* (M 2732), *Thakeham* (M 2733), *Tibenham* (M 2734), *Tongham* (M 2735), *Tresham* (M 2736), *Warningham* (M 2737), *Wexham* (M 2738), *Whippingham* (M 2739), *Wintringham* (M 2777), *Woldingham* (M 2778), *Wrentham* (M 2779), *Yaxham* (M 2780), *Portisham* (M 2781), *Popham* (M 2782), *Odiham* (M 2783), *Puttenham* (M 2784), *Birdham* (M 2785), *Rampisham* (M 2786), *Abbotsham* (M 2787), *Georgeham* (M 2788), *Malcham* (M 2789), *Thatcham* (M 2790), *Sandringham* (M 2791), *Polsham* (M 2792), *Thornham* (M 2793)

In parallel with the coastal minesweeper programme, 37 inshore sweepers were laid down, to operate in estuarine waters. J Samuel White acted as the lead-yard and as in the CMSs wooden and aluminium construction was adopted. A second series (mine disposal craft) followed, M 2701–M 2739, with 9in more beam and slightly deeper draught, while the third, all-wood series, M 2777–M 2793, were 1ft longer and 1ft beamier. *Reedham* was fitted with fin stabilisers and these were so successful that the rest of the class were similarly retro-fitted. Series 2 and Series 3 vessels had a prominent rubbing strake. All were ordered between September 1950 and November 1951.

Although sturdy and seaworthy craft they were found to be too small to cope with the latest electrical and acoustic sweep gear, as they lacked generating capacity. They were accordingly downgraded to subsidiary duties within a few years, serving as diving tenders, torpedo recovery vessels, degaussing vessels, etc. A number are still in service as auxiliary craft. *Bisham* and *Edlingham* were badly damaged by fire while laid up in reserve in 1955 and were scrapped in 1959.

Foreign transfers consisted of *Boreham*, *Felmersham*, *Bedham*, *Asheldham*, *Brantingham* and *Altham* (Malaysian *Jerong*, *Todak*, *Langa Suka*, *Sri Perlis*, *Temasek* and *Sri Johore*, 1958–59); *Greetham* and *Harpham* (Libyan *Zuara* and *Brak*, 1963); and *Bottisham*, *Chelsham* and *Halsham* (transferred to the RAN in 1965–66 and renumbered 5000–5002). Under MDAP *Frettenham*, *Wexham*, *Mersham*, *Isham*, *Kingham*, *Stedham*, *Rendlesham*, *Petersham*, *Mileham*, *Tibenham*, *Sparham*, *Whippingham*, *Sulham*, *Riplingham* and *Pincham* became the French M 771–776 and M 781–789 in 1954–55. *Littleham* and *Hildersham* became the Indian *Bassein* and *Bimlipatam* in 1955, *Ottringham* became the Ghanaian *Afadzato* in 1959.

'LEY' class *inshore minesweepers*

Displacement:	123t normal; 164t deep load
Dimensions:	100ft pp, 106ft 9in max, 21ft 9in × 5ft 6in *30.5m, 32.5m × 6.6m × 1.7m*
Machinery:	2 shafts, 2 8cyl Davey Paxman diesels, 7000bhp = 13kts. Oil 15t
Armament:	1–40mm/60 Mk 7 or 1–20mm
Sensors:	Radar Type 978
Complement:	15

Class:
Dingley (2001), *Aveley* (2002), *Brearley* (M 2003), *Brenchley* (M 2004), *Brinkley* (M 2005), *Broadley* (M 2006), *Broomley* (M 2007), *Burley* (M 2008), *Chailey* (M 2009), *Cradley* (M 2010), *Edgley* (M 2011)

Very similar to the 'Ham' class, composite-built with aluminium alloy framing and wooden planked hulls. The vessels were ordered between September 1950 and October 1951 but the programme was cut short with the cancellation of *Edgley*. They survived longer than the 'Ham' type because they were re-equipped for minehunting, minus sweep gear; *Iveley* and *Isis* (ex-*Cradley*) are still serving in this role. *Broadley* was scrapped in 1959 following severe damage while laid up in reserve four years earlier.

Pagham June 1977   MG Photographic

Isis June 1979   MG Photographic

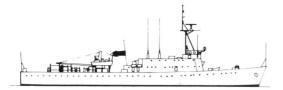

Abdiel 1970

ABDIEL *exercise minelayer*

Displacement:	1375t standard; 1460t full load
Dimensions:	265ft oa × 38ft 6in × 10ft
	80.8m × 11.7m × 3.0m
Machinery:	2 shafts, 2 16cyl Paxman Ventura diesels, 2690bhp = 16kts
Armament:	1–40mm/60 Mk 7, 44 mines
Sensors:	Radar Type 978
Complement:	98

No	Name	Builder	Launched	Fate
N 21	ABDIEL	Thornycroft	22.1.67	Extant 1982

Designed to lay exercise minefields and to support mine countermeasures forces, *Abdiel* was ordered in June 1965 and commissioned 17.10.67. She received a major refit in 1978.

WILTON *minesweeper/hunter*

Particulars:	As 'Ton' class

Wilton (M 1116) was the prototype Glass Reinforced Plastic (GRP) mine-sweeper/hunter, and the first of her kind in the world. To test the new non-magnetic material against wooden construction a copy of the 'Ton' class was built in GRP and equipped with machinery and gear stripped from *Derriton* before the latter was broken up. *Wilton* was laid down by Vosper Thornycroft 18.1.72 and is still in service. She is a great success, having weathered two collisions without serious damage.

Brecon as completed

BRECON class *mine countermeasures vessels*

Displacement:	615t normal, 725t deep load
Dimensions:	187ft wl, 197ft oa × 32ft 3in × 7ft 3in
	57.0m, 60.0m × 9.8m × 2.2m
Machinery:	2-shaft diesel: 2 Paxman 9–59K Deltic diesels, 3540bhp = 17kts (plus hydraulic drive, 8kts)
Armament:	1–40mm/60 Mk 7
Sensors:	Radar Type 1006; sonar 193M
Complement:	45

No	Name	Builder	Launched	Fate
M 29	BRECON	Vosper Thornycroft	21.6.78	Extant 1982
M 30	LEDBURY	Vosper Thornycroft	5.12.79	Extant 1982
M 31	CATTISTOCK	Vosper Thornycroft	22.1.81	Extant 1982
M 32	COTTESMORE	Yarrow	9.2.82	Fitting out
M 33	BROCKLESBY	Vosper Thornycroft	12.1.82	Extant 1982
M 34	MIDDLETON	Yarrow		Building
M 35	CHIDDINGFOLD	Vosper Thornycroft		Building
M 36	HURWORTH	Vosper Thornycroft		Building
M 37	DULVERTON	Vosper Thornycroft		Building
–		Vosper Thornycroft		Ordered 1982
–		Vosper Thornycroft		Ordered 1982

Concurrent with the building of *Wilton*, work began on a new generation of MCMVs or mine countermeasures vessels, a new term signifying that the vessels are capable of both sweeping and hunting. They are the largest GRP ships in the world, with Plessey Type 193M sonar, elaborate position-fixing gear, hydraulic drive and a bow-thruster to permit manoeuvring at slow speed. Every effort has been made to eliminate the magnetic 'signature' and to cut out radiated noise (including a near non-magnetic version of the Deltic diesel) but at the same time providing a ship capable of deep-sea passages. On a cost per ton basis, they rate as some of the most expensive warships every built, £24 million for *Brecon* and £15 million for the rest.

Two special GRP complexes have been built, one at Woolston and the other at Scotstoun, permitting two MCMVs to be built in each. An initial order for twelve may be followed by a further twelve.

Brecon and *Ledbury* swept two minefields at Port Stanley after the recapture of the Falklands.

Wilton 1977　　　　　　　　　　　　　　　　　　C & S Taylor

St David 5.10.82　　　　　　　　　　　　　　　　MG Photographic

VENTURER class *trawler-minesweepers*

Tonnage:	382t gross; 134t net
Dimensions:	120ft 9in wl × 29ft 3in × 12ft 10in
	36.8m × 8.9m × 3.9m
Machinery:	2 shafts, 2 Mirrlees-Blackstone EWSL8M(A) diesels, 2000bhp = 11kts. Oil 21,000gal
Armament:	Nil
Sensors:	Commercial navigational radar only
Complement:	24

Class (no, former name, builder, fate):
Venturer (M 08, ex-*Suffolk Harvester*, Cubow, Woolwich, extant 1982), *St David* (M 07, ex-*Suffolk Monarch*, Cubow, Woolwich, extant 1982).

To combat the threat from deep-laid mines (mainly to submarines) the RN chartered two commercial stern trawlers in 1977 and four more in 1978, using them with their original crews, but with naval mine warfare specialists on board. These 'Highland Fling' exercises showed that sweep wires could be operated at far greater depths than had been thought, and so a new concept of Extra-Deep Armed Team Sweeping (EDATS) came into being. Special depth-keeping gear allows the sweep wire to follow the contour of the sea-bed, and the depth is believed to be well over 1000ft. Explosive cutters are attached at 50-fathom (300ft) intervals.

In 1978 two trawlers (originally built in 1973) were chartered from Small and Co of Lowestoft for manning by RNR crews from the South Wales and Severn Divisions. In 1980 it was hoped to order twelve EDATS trawlers at a cost of £2.4 million each; a navy-designed EDATS sweeper had been mooted, and two or three commercial firms were asked to tender. Hall Russell, for example, submitted a version of their torpedo recovery vessel, but costs rose sharply, and as the RN wants the full twelve EDATS it seemed likely that more stern trawlers would be chartered. However, in September 1982 an order for four EDATS sweepers was placed with Richards, Lowestoft.

United States of America

The two primary themes of US naval development since 1945 have been the development of a capability to attack land targets, both coastal and deep inland; and anti-submarine warfare. These concerns contrast with the prewar and wartime primary naval function, the seizure of command of the sea by the destruction of the enemy surface fleet. In effect, the United States and her naval allies gained command of the world's oceans in 1945 by eliminating the German and Japanese navies, and from then on developed the means of exploiting that command. This included the freedom to land troops at great distances, to support massive operations overseas, and to attack enemy territory with naval aircraft. Not until the late 1970s did the growth of a large Soviet surface fleet begin to suggest that a future war would require a struggle for initial command of the surface of the sea. Submarines were a very different matter – they could not be fought offensively, at least not during and immediately after the Second World War. The success of wartime and postwar convoy ASW, however, depended upon the absence of an enemy surface fleet which could sweep away the escorts.

Thus the most probable future war, as envisaged after 1945, was a ground war against the Soviet Union, with naval forces protecting the resupply of Allied armies in Europe and in the Far East, and attacking around the Eurasian periphery. In addition, in the postwar breakup of the great colonial empires, the Soviets were able in several cases to use 'proxies' around their perimeter. In both Korea and Vietnam, it was the mobility of US naval strike forces which permitted the United States to respond in a timely manner. Indeed, it was often said of the Vietnam War that the US naval lifeline made the task of supplying US ground forces easier than that of supplying of the Viet Cong over a few hundred miles of the Ho Chih Minh Trail. Although North Vietnam had no serious capability to interdict that sea line of communications, the protection of such sea lanes has been a major preoccupation of the postwar US Navy.

THE US CARRIER FORCE

The value of resupply in a major war depends upon the expected length of that war. Studies carried out in about 1949 envisaged a lengthy conflict. Although nuclear weapons might be used, they would not be available in sufficient quantity to end the war, and therefore the war would probably resemble the Second World War, but fought with more modern weapons. Convoy escort, therefore, was a major consideration, and new convoy escorts such as the *Dealey* class were designed with mass production in mind. In view of inter-service rivalry with the newly independent Air Force, the Navy justified its desire to buy larger carriers on the basis of the submarine problem: their heavy attack planes would be able to destroy Soviet submarines at base. American war planning even included the mass production of ASW submarines (SSK), which would operate in the approaches to Soviet bases.

From 1952 onwards, the development of H-bombs seemed to indicate a rather different type of war, which might be concluded very rapidly with a series of massive nuclear strikes. By this time the infusion of funds from the Korean War mobilisation had largely healed the Navy-Air Force controversy over strategic missions, and the carrier force was assigned a strategic attack role in the general war plan. Heavy attack aircraft such as the North American AJ Savage and then the Douglas A3D Skywarrior had much the same role as the Air Force's B-47, and the Navy's attention turned largely to the development of fast attack carrier task forces. Such formations still had a sufficient margin of speed as to be almost immune to submarine attack. Although conventional ASW continued to be of great importance, the new mobilisation-design escorts were not built in very large numbers.

During the late 1940s and early 1950s the greatest threat to the fast carriers was air attack, and much of the large expenditure which could be assigned to the carrier task forces went on countermeasures. In 1945 the Soviets captured German air-to-surface missile technology, which had succeeded during the war in sinking several Allied warships, as well as the Italian battleship *Roma*. By 1946 there was a feeling that the prime threat of the future was the missile-equipped bomber, attacking by night or in bad weather, using radar. Ultimately there were two interconnected approaches to task force air defence. One was the carrier fighter. The carrier and her aircraft could be equipped for all-weather operation, and the efficacy of fighter control improved by equipping destroyers as radar pickets. For combat against high-performance bombers, which might be carrying nuclear weapons, the fighters were equipped first with unguided air-to-air rockets and then with missiles – Sidewinder, Sparrow and ultimately, the very long range Phoenix. The evolution of the naval fighter from a day fighter-bomber to an all-weather Fleet Air Defence interceptor was a very expensive one, with important financial consequences for the balance between aircraft and ship procurement budgets.

The other major element of fleet air defence was the missile-armed surface ship. The US Naval SAM Programme started with Project 'Bumblebee' in December 1944, and ultimately produced a family of three weapons (Terrier, Talos and Tartar, in order of appearance) which could arm anything, from a destroyer escort to a cruiser. Generally the radar and computer system associated with anti-aircraft missiles also suffices for fighter ocntrol, so that with the general availability of missile escort for fast carriers the specialised picket destroyers were phased out in the early 1960s. The SAM programme was huge, and it was considered extremely urgent. Hulls were relatively expensive, and the first US missile ships were all conversions of existing cruiser hulls, with the usual attendant inefficiencies. More compact missile systems went aboard destroyers and the enlarged destroyers (or fast task force escorts) which were then designated frigates, from the *Dewey* class onwards.

Of the several new technologies the Navy developed after 1945, shipboard anti-aircraft missiles appear in retrospect to have been the most expensive. The programme produced no really effective systems until about 1965, although by that time 11 existing ships had been converted, one nuclear cruiser built, and 21 missile frigates and 23 missile destroyers completed. Indeed, there was no question but that such a programme was needed. The problem was that even as the problems of the first generation were being solved, the postulated threat was far beyond that generation of systems, and entirely new systems (Typhon, which evolved into the present Aegis) were in hand. Cost escalation in new construction, particularly in the guided missile ships, led to a considerable curtailment of the shipbuilding programme in the late 1950s; for example, three planned missile cruiser conversions could not be carried out. The cost squeeze became particularly acute with the advent of Polaris, since funds for the new crash prog-

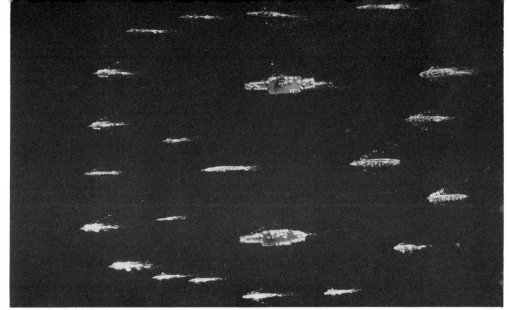

Saratoga and *Independence* at the centre of a Sixth Fleet carrier task force, March 1976.   USN

ramme had to come from a budget previously designed to cope only with ASW and with the carrier force.

The other major element of the carrier attack force was underway replenishment, or UNREP. Although a carrier might well be able to remain at sea for several months, her aviation fuel and ordnance would not support air operations for more than a few days at a time. Strike tactics therefore called for a run into a target area, followed by intense operations, then withdrawal to a safe area well out to sea and replenishment in preparation for another series of strikes. Such tactics were first used in 1945, and the continue to be important in 1982 except that the distance to which the task force must withdraw for safety is now much greater, given the reach of Soviet and Soviet-bloc bombers and coast defence vessels. UNREP modernisation was then an important element of the fast carrier programme from 1945 onwards, with the emphasis on reducing the period of vulnerability during replenishment. Ultimately the Navy adopted the concept of 'one-stop' replenishment, in which a single large auxiliary provided both fuel and ammunition simultaneously. Between 1964 and 1970, four large fast combat support ships (AOE), each rated at 26kts, were built. In principle they in turn would be supported by slower (20kt or 21kt) bulk stores carriers, combat stores ships (AFS), ammunition ships (AE) and fleet oilers (AO), the AOEs shuttling between such ships and the fast carriers.

Although the carriers have been the core of the surface Navy since 1945, their role and even their existence has been subject to almost continuous debate. The programme of heavy strategic carriers was cancelled with the *United States* in 1949, largely, it appears, because of Air Force objections. Even though the carrier programme was restored after the outbreak of the Korean War, the Air Force continued to argue throughout the 1950s that carriers were inherently inefficient, given the large investment in ships and aircraft required merely to protect them. After the authorisation of the large carrier *Enterprise*, the rising cost of new carrier construction led to the virtual suspension of the previous programme of annual authorisations, and to a debate between Navy advocates of nuclear power and a Secretary of Defence determined to economise by returning to oil fuel. Secretary of Defence McNamara also questioned the need for so large a carrier force, given the transfer of strategic attack functions to missiles. However, the demonstration of carrier utility in Vietnam convinced him, and by the end of his term he advocated a new nuclear carrier programme – which, however, was not to be completed for many years. Thus no carrier was authorised between 1973 (CVN 70, *Carl Vinson*) and 1979, when CVN 71 was approved despite Administration efforts to substitute a more limited ship, the abortive CVV. In 1982 the big carrier's future remained in doubt, but nevertheless Congress authorized two more large-deck carriers, CVN 72 and 73.

The rate of procurement has fallen sharply since the 1950s, in part because of escalating costs. With the *Forrestal* a 'one carrier per year' policy was laid down, culminating in *Enterprise* in FY58. Attempts to design a much less expensive nuclear carrier failed, and no new carrier was authorised until FY61 (CVA 66, *America*). A policy of buying a carrier every other year was then formulated; CVA 67, the *John F Kennedy* was authorised in FY63. However, the procurement of the next class of nuclear carriers (*Nimitz* type) was stretched out:

CVN 68 in FY67, CVN 69 in FY71 and CVN 70 in FY74. With the construction of CVN 71, there will be 13 modern large-deck carriers available, and the remaining two *Midways* of Second World War construction will probably be retired after 1985, after 40-year careers. This 13-ship force will include at least one *Forrestal* under extensive refit (SLEP, or Service Life Extension Program), and it has recently been attacked as inadequate: Admiral Thomas Hayward, the Chief of Naval Operations, has called for a total of 16 large-deck carriers, a need emphasised by the strain of maintaining carrier-based forces on station in the Indian Ocean.

In fact the planned size of the carrier force has varied considerably since the Korean War. For example, as of late 1950 the target was a total of 12 modern attack carriers (*Midways* and rebuilt *Essex*s) by June 1952. All would be able to launch nuclear-armed long-range attack aircraft, but 15 rather than nine *Essex* class carriers were rebuilt, so that with the introduction of the first two *Forrestals* the attack carrier force, including ships under reconstruction, was 18- to 20-strong for a short time in the late 1950s. After that, *Essex* class attack carriers were transferred to ASW duties as the new carriers joined, and the force objective settled to 15, a figure constant until the early 1970s, when the retirement of *Oriskany* and *Franklin D Roosevelt* cut it to its present size of 13. Generally three carriers are required to keep one on a forward station: one on station, one working up after overhaul, and one in overhaul. Thus 15 permitted the usual deployment of two in the Mediterranean and three in the Western Pacific, with virtually no leeway for contingencies, or for that matter, for the oft-discussed Indian Ocean Fleet. During the 1960s and 1970s there was some slack, to be sure, in the existence of nine *Essex* class ASW carriers capable of limited attack duty; one actually served in Vietnam in this role. However, the last of these ships was retired in 1974. An active 12-carrier force in practice means only two carriers forward-deployed in the two principal operating areas, unless time on station is drastically increased (to the detriment of morale and, importantly, re-enlistment) or overhauls are curtailed.

The size of the US carrier force in turn determines, to a considerable extent, the size of the surface Navy. High-quality missile escorts are bought to accompany fast carrier battle groups, and the slower ASW escort force is sized to protect the UNREP groups (as well as the amphibious assault force). To some extent even the attack submarine force is sized for fast carrier warfare, as current practice is to provide a nuclear submarine as part of the battle group, for distant ASW escort. In fact, the ideal ratio between escorts and carriers varies considerably, for example with developments in shipboard weapons and with the character of the threat: the balance between anti-air and anti-submarine within the battle group has changed considerably with the advent of a large Soviet nuclear attack submarine force, part of it now armed with short-range anti-ship missiles.

Despite a series of violent changes in the rationale for the carrier force, its development has been remarkably consistent since the Second World War. Perhaps the principal reason in the great flexibility of the carrier, given the variety of air groups it can support. The *United States* was designed in the late 1940s specifically for nuclear attack, but the great size required merely to support a heavy bomber made for great capacity for conventional ordnance and aviation fuel. Thus when the

183

UNITED STATES

Korean War demonstrated the value of carriers in conventional ground support, the Navy could argue that a new large carrier, which became the *Forrestal*, would be extremely effective in just that mission. Since the Second World War the carrier has been the only means by which the United States has been able to intervene abroad in the absence of friendly bases and base agreements. With the loss of many bases from the mid-1950s onwards, this has been an increasingly valuable capability, and it has been demonstrated many times.

Although the large carriers were originally designed for long-range nuclear attack, there was always considerable Navy sentiment against such a strategy. By the mid-1950s Navy long-range planners considered general nuclear war unlikely, in view of the probable development of the Soviet nuclear arsenal. They therefore adopted as a planning assumption the expectation that war in the mid and late 1960s – for which the Navy was buying prototype equipment and ships in the mid-1950s – would be limited, quite possibly involving Soviet proxies rather than the Soviet Union itself. The Fleet would have to fight around the Eurasian periphery, and its role would be a combination of tactical support of Marine amphibious operations and strikes at moderate range. Strategic attack, although a vital function, might well be shifted from carrier aircraft to missiles, particularly as surface-to-air missiles were beginning to limit the chances of survival of even advanced long-range bombers.

Such conclusions were particularly important because of their implications for carrier and aircraft design; in 1955 carriers were very large principally because they had to accommodate the 70,000lb supersonic A3D Skywarrior, and the Bureau of Aeronautics looked towards a 100,000lb supersonic bomber in ten years' time. However, if the Fleet's long-range attack mission were shifted to a missile such as Regulus, and much more modest demands placed on the attack aircraft, the carrier of the future might be much smaller and less expensive. In about 1956 this concept led to the design of the A2F Intruder, which became the A-6, a bomber which would survive by stealth rather than by high-speed, high-altitude penetration of enemy defences. It also appeared that fleet air defence would most efficiently be conducted by a low-performance fighter with very long range missiles, the F6D Missileer. In fact the change in carrier design never occurred, primarily because it transpired that large carriers were needed to support intensive ground attacks, even by relatively undemanding aircraft. In 1956 it still appeared that tactical nuclear weapons might be used quite freely, and that the total ordnance load of a carrier therefore would be small. Ten years later that was inconceivable, and a thousand tons of carrier ordnance lasted only a few days in Vietnam. Moreover, Missileer was replaced by a manned fighter of much higher performance, still carrying the very long range missile – the present F-14 Tomcat.

ANTI-SUBMARINE WARFARE

Throughout the 1950s the character of ASW began to shift, both as to tactics and as to rationale. There had always been a tension in ASW thinking between offensive (sub-hunting) and defensive (convoy) operations, with the use of submarine 'ambushers' in an intermediate position. During the Second World War offensive ASW was largely based on the success of codebreaking and on the means of detecting submarines at long range, either by high-frequency direction-finding (HF/DF) or by radar (against surfaced submarines and, at much shorter ranges, snorkels or even periscopes). In each case aircraft were extremely valuable because of their ability rapidly to close a fleeting contact, attacking before the submarine might escape. The German

development of fast submarines capable of extended underwater operation (Type XXI) materially reduced the effective detection range of existing airborne radars. A burst transmitter, 'Kurier', made shipborne HF/DF difficult if not impossible. Both developments fell into Soviet hands in 1945, and there could be no guarantee of success against Soviet codes in any future war. Although the Soviet submarine fleet actually in service in 1945–50 was composed of conventional submarines technically inferior to those the Germans had had in service in mid-war, it was clear that the Soviets had or would soon have the potential to produce a much more ominous fleet.

Thus during the first five years after victory the US Navy concentrated on efforts to overcome the new generation of fast submarines. Larger airborne radars were adopted to balance the much reduced radar cross-section presented by a snorkel, and sonobuoys were developed to permit a hunting aircraft some indication of the presence of a target. Indeed, forced back to convoy tactics, the Navy considered using aircraft to plant a sonobuoy barrier around a moving convoy, or helicopters to 'dunk' sonars ahead of it. Major efforts went into the development of larger ship-mounted sonars, culminating in the present SQS-26/53, which has a considerable impact on the design of ships carrying it. In the absence of any reliable means of detecting submarines at long range, the only effective tactic for the protection of shipping was convoy, a tactic extremely inefficient in terms of submarines killed per unit effort. Given the sophistication of the new submarines, the ASW ships would become more and more expensive, so that it might be expected that ultimately their procurement and maintenance would strangle the naval budget.

This issue was resolved by the advent of fixed underwater arrays. Fixed to the ocean bottom, SOSUS (Sound Surveillance System) hydrophones could detect submarines at a considerable distance, their effective range varying with the noisiness of the individual target, signal processing techniques and ocean sound conditions. SOSUS was first tested in 1954, and during the next decade the system was extended and its sensitivity improved. Offensive ASW tactics now became extremely attractive, with aircraft far more effective than surface ships in many cases, given their ability to reach a contact position more quickly. Generally the prosecution of a SOSUS contact was a somewhat extended process, as the original contact would be relatively imprecise and the attacker would therefore have to re-acquire the target. Thus very long range patrol aircraft such as the Lockheed Neptune (P-2) and Orion (P-3) became particularly important elements of the ASW team.

The specialist ASW carriers, originally intended to support convoy tactics, now were used to close mid-ocean gaps in patrol aircraft coverage, and the endurance of hunter-killer (HUK) task groups built around them had to be increased. By the late 1950s *Essex* class fleet carriers were operating in the ASW role as support carriers (CVS), screened by converted destroyers. In analogy to the development of the fast carrier UNREP force, smaller one-stop UNREP ships (AOR) were designed to support the HUK forces. However, as P-3 Orions replaced the P-2s, their increased range eliminated the mid-Atlantic gap in air cover, and the CVSs were reassigned to protect the fast carrier forces from an increasing Soviet submarine threat.

Offensive ASW was more than a matter of economics. From the late 1950s onwards the Soviets were known to possess strategic attack submarines, and Navy tasks expanded to include peacetime trailing and wartime destruction of these craft. It should perhaps be emphasized that this mission was by no means the oft-publicised one of

An ASW support group built around the *Yorktown*, 24.7.67   USN

instant destruction of all enemy strategic submarines upon the outbreak of war. Rather, given the fleeting and statistical character of SOSUS contacts, it was to eliminate these craft within a reasonable period after outbreak, assuming that the war would not begin with a surprise missile bombardment. This mission has received considerably less publicity in recent years, as advocates of theories of strategic stability have claimed that the very invulnerability of strategic submarines in some way guarantees that they will not be used. But the threat of US offensive ASW appears to be among the chief motivations of Soviet fleet development.

Submarines were another vital element of ASW strategy. They alone could occupy forward positions off Soviet submarine base areas, detecting and sinking enemy submarines as they emerged, and so reducing losses to what seemed, initially, to be almost undetectable craft. Such operations, however, would require hundreds of specialised killer submarines, figures as high as 250 frequently being cited in the late 1940s. To some extent the number could be made up by emergency conversions of existing fleet submarines, but such tactics were fundamentally unattractive, given the technology of the first postwar years.

Later, however, advances in submarine sonar technology made it possible to move the submarines back from Soviet coastal waters to such 'choke points' as the Greenland–Iceland–UK Gap, where more sophisticated craft in smaller numbers (but equipped with long-range weapons to match their sensors) could inflict severe losses as Soviet submarines made for the North Atlantic. From the *Thresher* class onwards the special SSK submarine ASW designation was dropped, and all new nuclear submarines were optimised for the ASW role, with very long range sonar and such weapons as the SUBROC ASW missile. The transformation was a fortunate one for the submarine force which, after a great triumph over Japan, faced an enemy with little essential seaborne traffic and no great pretensions towards conventional surface fleet development.

In principle, in a war lasting weeks or months, most Soviet submarines would be lost to a combination of the submarine barriers and the aircraft prosecuting SOSUS contacts. Surface ASW escorts, the most numerous and also the most expensive element of the net ASW system, would act primarily as a back-up, preserving shipping until the attrition enforced by the two primary systems had taken its toll. The consequences of this conceptual development first became apparent in the late 1960s, when the number of escorts on hand and in reserve fell well below the level required for a combination of convoy duty and the protection of fleet units. It would appear that this decline represented a conscious decision, apart from the severe economic forces acting against surface ship procurement at the time.

Convoy protection was not so important as the protection of naval formations because, it could be argued, there were so many merchant ships in Western service that even substantial losses early in a war could be sustained. High-value naval units such as attack carriers and amphibious ships were not nearly so expendable, and so required close escort even if the latter tactic was, on the whole, inefficient. Thus from the 1950s onwards the specialised ASW escorts began to have less the aspect of austere mobilisation ships and more that of high-quality units which might well on occasion replace destroyers. For example, their speed rose to permit them to combine tactically with CVS task groups, or with fast (and therefore valuable) merchant ships. The fast carrier escorts (frigates in then-current US naval terminology), which had been optimised for the anti-air defence of the carriers, received more powerful and more sophisticated ASW batteries. By the late 1960s the Major Fleet Escort study would show that the carrier task group required six ASW escorts, but that three missile anti-air ships would suffice. This was the genesis of the *Spruance*, a pure ASW ship which was fast enough to operate in the carrier screen. As early as 1960, new destroyer escorts were sometimes being described as destroyer replacements, capable of about 30kts at full power.

STRATEGIC MISSILE SUBMARINES

In 1959 a third major element was added to the Fleet – the Polaris submarine. Naval interest in missiles for strategic attack dated from immediately after the Second World War, when copies of German V1s were fired from surfaced submarines and experiments were conducted to develop a capsule in which a submarine might tow a V2

ballistic missile. A strategic attack cruise missile, Regulus, was designed and built, and several submarines were converted to carry 'Trounce' guidance equipment for it. However, the Regulus programme did not have nearly the impact on the fleet as a whole that Polaris had. To some extent, indeed, Regulus appeared to offer the possibility that the fleet would be able to conduct strategic attacks without heavy attack aircraft, a possibility recognised in the 1955 long-range study. Polaris offered something new, a survivable missile base which could reliably endure an enemy first strike. Moreover, Polaris was a separate system, linked to the remainder of the fleet only in the most tenuous way.

Polaris had two major impacts on the fleet. First, it permitted the release of the attack carriers from the strategic attack mission: the new long-range bomber, the A-5 Vigilante, was converted for reconnaissance. However, a Navy already reeling from cost escalation in the surface missile ships found it extremely difficult to pay simultaneously for Polaris (including a large nuclear submarine programme), the mass of new and sophisticated ASW ships, the reconstruction of the numerous wartime destroyers still in service, and large numbers of advanced naval aircraft: too many programmes coincided. Thus Polaris had a severe if indirect effect on the modernisation of the fleet, an effect which could only be reduced by the continued employment of obsolete warships.

AMPHIBIOUS WARFARE

Carriers were only one aspect of the new land-attack emphasis developed during and after the war. The other was amphibious assault, which before 1942 had been limited to a Marine Corps battalion on each coast, for what would now be called counterinsurgency. In 1945 it appeared that the day of large landings was over, given the vulnerability of concentrated shipping to nuclear attack. But the Marines and the Navy persisted, and from 1948 onwards set a goal of replacing the existing 10kt troop lift with an integrated 20kt amphibious force. Ideally many of the vast number of extemporised wartime types would be eliminated in favour of a small number of carefully designed specialised types. This ideal was met only in the late 1960s and even then only on a far smaller scale than had originally been envisaged.

In any case, one of the surprises of the Korean War was the continued utility of large-scale amphibious operations, demonstrated in the famous 'end-run' of Inchon. New amphibious ships were built during the 1950s, and the Marines began to develop a new technique of helicopter assault ('vertical envelopment'). It was intended specifically as a means of achieving tactical concentration at the objective without requiring a concentration of amphibious ships vulnerable to nuclear attack, and it led to the conversion and construction of specialised helicopter carriers. To some extent vertical envelopment was inspired, too, by the success of the extemporised British helicopter operation at Suez in 1956.

Vertical envelopment did not make earlier classes of amphibious ships obsolete, because the helicopters still could not move heavy equipment and supplies over a beach, and so the amphibious modernisation programme which began in the late 1950s included new dock landing ships and then a new class of fast LSTs, the latter finally realising the postwar goal of a 20kt amphibious force. The latest US amphibious ships, the *Tarawa* class LHAs, in effect combine the helicopter carrier with a dock landing ship capable of launching smaller landing craft which can actually move tanks and other vehicles over a beach.

Amphibious operations grew considerably more important in US naval planning as the United States and the Soviet Union approached strategic parity, at least to the extent that massive nuclear warfare grew increasingly unlikely. By the early 1960s the Navy's vision of future warfare, limited to proxy wars on the Eurasian periphery, was widely accepted, and the Kennedy Administration expected the most likely war to be a counter-insurgency. Both Vietnam and the short operation in the Dominican Republic fitted this pattern, and both came at a time of increasing investment in landing ships and craft. That investment seems, in retrospect, somewhat one-sided. By the mid-1960s the US amphibious force consisted not only of landing ships, but also of fire support vessels and mine warfare craft which could assure the security of the beach area. However, the fire support ships were all remnants of the large wartime building programmes, increasingly expensive to operate and with only a very limited remaining life. Mine craft were also proving expensive to operate, and their numbers were beginning to decline. To some limited extent the development of helicopter mine countermeasures appeared to solve the mine problem at the beach, but attempts to develop a new specialist fire support ship (LFS) failed, and a later decision to mount a single lightweight 8in gun aboard the new destroyers also proved abortive.

'LOW END' AND 'HIGH END' CAPABILITIES

These themes, carrier attack, ASW, the strategic submarine, and amphibious lift, largely describe the US Navy as it emerged from the postwar developmental period, and as it existed in 1982. By 1960 the new technology and the new ideas of the immediate postwar period had largely been assimilated and, in some cases, surpassed. Nuclear power was a reality for both submarines and surface ships, and long-range sonar was well along. Fixed systems and long-range aircraft had transformed the ASW problem and indeed had made it possible for the United States to wage an ASW war without the long period of mobilisation required in the past, given the balance between forces maintained in peacetime and wartime requirements. The new defensive missiles, although not yet satisfactory, did exist in considerable numbers, and, at least for the present, the fleet had a large number of missile escorts either in service or on order. The US Navy of 1960 was powerful and could look forward to increasing power and capability.

There was one major problem, and this problem has dominated US naval development since 1960: bloc obsolescence. By 1960 the fleet was ageing very rapidly: the great majority of its hulls were still of wartime construction, at least 15 years old. The vast force of more than 200 destroyers was already so badly worn that emergency measures were required, and many were rebuilt under the FRAM (Fleet Rehabilitation and Modernisation) programme which also applied to submarines and ASW carriers, and to some amphibious ships. It was intended to prolong service life by up to eight years, and thus to forestall the immense replacement programme which would ultimately be required. Even as large-scale replacement was being planned, however, the United States entered the Vietnam War. New naval construction was curtailed as limited funds went to operation and ammunition, while the war itself wore out the large remaining force of wartime destroyers and cruisers. The replacement programme planned in the late 1960s was ultimately reduced to 30 *Spruance* class destroyers, and a second and more austere project resulted in the *Perry* class frigates. In 1982 there appears to be little prospect of construction sufficient to bring the fleet back to the numerical levels of pre-Vietnam days, when as many as 900 ships were active, including (1964) 16 cruisers, 25 frigates (now rated as cruisers and missile destroyers), 21 missile destroyers, 179 all-gun destroyers and 40 ocean escorts.

One useful description of the procurement problems of the postwar Navy is to describe the fleet, in Admiral Zumwalt's terms, as a 'high-low' mix – a mixture of more and less capable ships. During the Second World War the 'high' end of the mix consisted of the new ships of the fast carrier task forces, the ships designed in about 1940 and built in such vast numbers in wartime. The 'low' end included both the ASW forces (destroyer escorts and old destroyers) and the amphibious and amphibious-support forces, including elderly battleships for shore bombardment. If the *Essex* class carriers represented the 'high' end, the escort carriers were the 'low' end. One important consequence of the strategic and technological shifts of 1945 was that the 'high' end of the wartime mix was swiftly shunted downwards to become the low-capability end of the postwar mix; the 'low' end of the wartime mix had so little capability that it was soon either discarded or laid up. Only the amphibious force maintained its place in the previous spectrum.

In effect the postwar programmes were devoted almost entirely to the 'high' end of the naval spectrum; quite naturally, they could not replace the vast number of 'low-end' ships remaining after the end of the war. However, it has proven extremely difficult for the Navy deliberately to design and build austere 'low-end' ships, given the 'high-end' character of almost the entire postwar programme. Moreover, the 'high-end' origins of the ships remaining in service postwar served to conceal from most observers their effective 'low-

end' status. Thus when Admiral Zumwalt tried to build a new 'low-end' in the *Perry* class, he was strongly opposed. *Perry* class frigates have been bought in some considerable numbers, but criticism of the austerity measures inherent in their design has increased their cost and brought new cries for a 'truly austere' ship, which may or may not materialise as the FFX.

The disappearance of the 'low end' had particularly severe consequences for the amphibious forces, which had long counted on 'low-end' ships such as surviving all-gun cruisers for fire support during opposed landings. The postwar Navy was above all a missile navy, designing some ships entirely without guns even as early as 1956. It certainly had no place for a new all-gun cruiser, especially as there was no important naval surface opponent in sight, at least until the 1970s. Moreover, there was considerable ambiguity concerning the amphibious forces and their need of gunfire support. Thus the LFS, first proposed about 1965 as a replacement for the rapidly ageing cruisers, was never really able to compete with the carrier escorts and the new ASW ships; all that the Marines could secure was a promise (since broken) that some of the new destroyers would mount a new lightweight 8in gun specifically for shore bombardment. Even this hope must have seemed dim, given the paucity of highly capable ASW escorts and the hazards of shore bombardment.

Thus, as of 1982, the issue of the mass replacement of the 'low-end' Second World War fleet has been resolved: there will be no mass replacements, unless the United States makes a sudden decision in favour of massive increases in defence spending. To be sure, there are always schemes for the emergency use of commercial shipping (eg 'Arapaho' for placing V/STOL fighters aboard large container ships), but there appear to be no serious plans for the expansion and simplification of any current building programmes: the *Perry* is not a mobilisation prototype like the *Dealey* of a quarter of a century earlier. On the other hand, the Navy does enjoy the support of an increasing variety of shore-based systems such as SOSUS, which may take the lack of numbers of small warships far more tolerable, particularly in an extended war of attrition at sea. Moreover, it can be argued that a modern war would quite likely end before the US production machine could be mobilised to produce a flood of escorts. In that case the Navy will have been proven correct in emphasising high unit capability.

AIRCRAFT CARRIER DESIGN

Since early in the Second World War, the carrier has been the principal instrument of US sea power, both for power projection against shore targets and for sea control (ASW and, during the war, anti-ship warfare). In 1945, with no prospective enemy fleet in sight, interest within the Navy shifted to carrier-based nuclear strikes, and a very large ship, the *United States*, was designed specifically to accommodate a new generation of long-range carrier bombers. At the same time existing ships were to be rebuilt to operate the new jet-propelled tactical aircraft: the *Essex* class carrier *Oriskany*, construction of which was suspended immediately after the war, became the prototype for a series of SCB-27A and SCB-27C carrier reconstructions, and the larger *Midway*s were later rebuilt as well. Meanwhile work proceeded on carrier ASW operations, using war-built escort and light fleet carriers at first. However, an unconverted *Essex* was tested in the ASW role in 1952, and as rebuilt *Essex*s joined the fleet their unconverted sisters were redesignated as ASW support carriers, or CVSs. Later the converted *Essex*s succeeded them, as new large attack carriers replaced them in the power projection role.

As for the *United States*, she fell victim to inter-service rivalry, because the Secretary of Defense, Louis Johnson, decided in favour of land-based (Air Force) strategic bombers. With the outbreak of the Korean War, however, it became more evident that carriers were valuable, and a new large-carrier design, which became the *Forrestal*, was begun in the autumn of 1950. She benefited greatly from two British inventions, the angled deck and the steam catapult, and she was the prototype for eight conventionally-powered attack carriers. For a time, it appeared that one would be authorised each year, this pace continuing from FY52 to FY58 (*Enterprise*), but the FY58 ship was so expensive that no carrier was approved in FY59 or in FY60; one problem was the issue of whether the next carrier should or should not be nuclear-powered. Conventional carriers were authorised in the FY61 and FY63 Budgets, in the latter case very much against the professional advice of the Chief of Naval Operations. In addition, rising carrier cost and the increased firepower of Soviet anti-carrier forces both made carrier construction far more controversial in the late 1960s and in the 1970s than in the 1950s.

Thus no carrier was authorised between FY63 and FY67, when the first of a new class of nuclear carriers, the *Nimitz*, was approved. At the time a class of three was to have been built on a single-contract basis; authorisations stretched out to FY70 for the second unit and FY73 for the third. After that the Carter Administration proclaimed the end of large carrier construction, seeking instead to build a 60,000t CVV or CTOL-V/STOL carrier. When Congress disagreed, President Carter went so far as to veto a Defense Bill to avoid the authorisation of an additional nuclear carrier. However, that ship was finally voted in the FY80 budget as CVN 71, and in 1981 Congress approved long-lead items for CVN 72, with CVN 73 planned by the Reagan Administration. Whether these plans will be carried out in their entirely remains a matter of some doubt, and there are still many who would like a new class of more austere carriers, at least to supplement the large ones.

The advent of V/STOL aircraft has made much smaller carriers attractive. As CNO, Admiral Zumwalt advocated the construction of a very austere V/STOL-helicopter ASW escort carrier, which he called the Sea Control Ship (SCS), and which was never approved by Congress. One of its political problems was that the carrier Navy saw it as an attempt to abandon the large-deck carrier with its high-capability conventional take-off air wing. Ultimately Spain purchased plans for the SCS, and is building it. Advanced SCS concepts continue to be investigated, as the Navy is still studying the carrier force of the next century – which must be laid down within the next decade. In 1982 there was still some considerable interest in the use of large amphibious ships (LPH and LHA) as V/STOL carriers; *Guam* served as the SCS concept trials ship. *Nassau* operated a squadron of Marine Harriers to argument a carrier group in the Mediterranean for a time in 1981. Reportedly this was in answer to Congressional insistence that the small carrier concept be examined; it led to the LHD dual purpose amphibious/sea control ship concept.

Given the long lead time inherent in building a large carrier, and the need of sea-based air power in a sudden crisis, several plans for ...eration have been proposed. One ...p is provided with a flat deck and ...s for V/STOL fighters. The ...oposed the reactivation of two *Homme Richard*, although Con-...problem is that these ships would ...e the full range of modern naval ...proposed for *Oriskany* consists

FLEET ESCORT CLASSES

Since the early 1950s the US Navy has used type designations such as 'cruiser' and 'destroyer', but in practice the distinction between fleet, *ie* fast task force escorts and convoy or ASW or 'ocean' escorts has been far more important: there are no longer traditional cruisers really suitable for independent operations, and the failure of the Strike Cruiser (CSGN) project suggests that such independent ships are not likely to be built in the near future either. The *Mitscher* class 'frigates' (or large destroyers) were the first specialised fast task force escorts, much of the addition in size compared with Second World War destroyers going into higher speed and better sea-keeping. In 1954 the Schindler Committee on the Long Range Shipbuilding and Conversion Program went to far as to recommend the elimination of the traditional destroyers in favour of a mixture of fast task force escorts (frigates), ASW ships (for ASW task force operations: DDC or 'corvettes' converted from existing destroyers), and extremely austere 'ocean escorts' which would fill in the numbers in convoy screens and perhaps in the ASW Task Force. Although new classes of cruisers were proposed from time to time, the only ship of that category to be built after 1945 was the nuclear *Long Beach*, designed originally as a nuclear missile frigate.

At the upper end of the size spectrum, 11 Second World War cruisers were converted to missile ships specifically to screen fast carrier forces. Their great size was dictated, first, by the availability of hulls of particular sizes exceeding the minimum required for conversion and, second, by the considerable size requirements of missiles such as Talos. By the mid-1960s however, it was clear that much smaller (large destroyer) hulls could accommodate much the same missile firepower, although not the same flag facilities or the same magazine stowage, at a much lower cost in manpower. Cruiser conversion ceased, and ships were withdrawn from service as their much smaller replacements were completed. From a functional point of view, then, there is little to choose between a *Cleveland* class Terrier cruiser such as the *Topeka* and the more destroyer-like *Leahy* or *Belknap*. This circumstance was explicitly recognised when most of the former frigates (DL) were reclassified as cruisers (CG) in 1975.

Even the distinction between those ships still classified as destroyers and the cruisers is at best a tenuous one. For example, in the mid-1960s there were projects for a new missile destroyer (DDG) to replace the *Charles F Adams* class; necessary additions for such systems as NTDS drove displacement up to almost 8000t. Only nuclear-powered versions of this ship were built, as the *California* class – and they are now designated as cruisers. The *Spruance* class are clearly cruiser-size specialist ASW ships, and their missile version (*Kidd* class) is difficult to distinguish from the *Virginia* class nuclear cruiser, at least in AAW capability. The *Spruances* are unique among fleet escorts built since the *Mitschers* in that they have no area AAW weapon. They reflect the growth of the Soviet fast submarine force, to the point at which it achieved a substantial capability even against fast-moving carrier forces. Given the relatively short range of ASW sensors, it is necessary almost to surround a moving force with ASW ships, whereas relatively fewer AAW launchers are needed. It was, then, decided in 1968 to build a mix of AAW-ASW fleet escorts and pure ASW escorts, the latter becoming the *Spruances*.

Thus the requirements for a ship to be considered as a fleet escort amount to high speed (at least 30kts in rough weather), long range, and good sea-keeping; the weapons and sensors do not always differ greatly from those of other categories. Even the speed limit may be relaxed in some cases to achieve affordable ships in sufficient numbers. Moreover, given the limited numbers of satisfactory escorts currently available, ocean escorts which marginally meet the speed requirement (such as *Garcia* and *Perry* class frigates) sometimes operate with fast carrier formations.

To an increasing extent fast attack submarines, particularly those of the *Los Angeles* class, operate as distant escorts for naval formations, in the 'direct support' role. They are excellent sonar platforms, and they can keep up with the force, generally operating some considerable distance ahead in the area from which a submarine would have to attack. For example, in some formulations the typical carrier battle group with a nuclear carrier includes two nuclear cruisers and a nuclear submarine.

The gun-armed cruisers left over from the Second World War programme clearly do not quite fit this account. They functioned as AAW/anti-surface escorts within carrier groups postwar, and in Korea and in Vietnam had an important shore bombardment role. Some were also refitted as flagships, losing some of their secondary guns in favour of electronics and accommodation. As a category, however, they died out as the Navy shifted more and more from guns to missiles, and as the threat to US naval forces came more and more to be an airborne or submarine-borne one: even the current Soviet surface fleet is likely to attack by missile rather than by surface gun. Thus, in 1982 the US cruiser force had been reduced to two large 8in ships which have been in reserve since 1960–61.

The missile cruisers were as important as air control platforms as they were as platforms for defensive weapons. In the Vietnam War, an NTDS ship operated on station in the Tonkin Gulf, controlling US aircraft operating over North Vietnam. The radar buoy in the Gulf defined a Positive Identification Radar Advisory Zone (PIRAZ), and the ship on PIRAZ duty was often responsible for successful interceptions by Air Force fighters. For example, one enlisted air controller aboard the cruiser *Chicago* was decorated for arranging the destruction of twelve MiGs. The track capacity of the NTDS system made it possible for US aircraft to operate successfully in an environment of neutral airliners as well as friendly and North Vietnamese fighters. Conventional radar could not have succeeded, since the neutral airliners would not have responded to IFF challenges.

UNITED STATES

The missiles deserve some mention. Early Terrier had a range of about 10nm, compared to about 50nm for Talos, but in the late 1950s Terrier and Talos ranges were both doubled, and the last production Terriers had a new engine which again doubled their range, to about 40nm. The much smaller Tartar underwent a similar evolution, from 7.5nm to 17.5nm in the Improved Tartar and then to about 25nm in TRIP (Tartar Reliability Improvements Program) and in the Standard Missile (SM-1). These Tartar and Terrier ranges are line-of-sight figures; in the new Aegis system command guidance permits the use of more energy-efficient trajectories, for range gains of, respectively, about 70 and over 100 per cent, for maximum ranges of about 42nm and 80nm: a Tartar-sized missile with Aegis guidance has Terrier range. Moreover, missile effectiveness depends upon fire control system capability and reliability: although some SPG-51D (Tartar-D) ships have fewer fire control channels than have earlier ships, these channels are available for a much greater proportion of the time.

The major recent development in missile systems is the integration of all of a ship's sensors to improve the probability of detection of an incoming weapon. This is possible because the new generation of naval radars, such as SPS-49 and updated versions of SPS-40, -48 and -52, automatically detect targets, which data they can automatically feed into a central computer for comparision with other radar data, and for correlation into track files. Given this data, the central computer can evaluate the degree of threat presented by each radar target, and can decide which target to engage. Systems of this type were developed from the late 1960s on in response to the threat of Soviet anti-ship missiles, under the New Threat Upgrade (NTU) programme; the central combat system integration computers are SYS-1 and -2. In addition, the combat system of the *Perry* class frigates (FFG 7 type) was designed along NTU lines, on the theory that it would have to counter pop-up missiles (such as the Soviet SSN-7) with inherently very short warning times. The NTU systems are being installed as this book goes to press.

OCEAN ESCORT TYPES

After the Second World War the former destroyer escort category was renamed 'ocean escorts'; functionally, this group also includes the long series of specialised ASW destroyer conversions, including the FRAM conversions of *Sumner* and *Gearing* class general-purpose destroyers. Originally it was expected that a new class of fast ASW ships would be complemented by a replacement for the coastal escorts (PC and PCE) of the Second World War; indeed, the *Dealeys* were conceived at first as a PC replacement, the DE replacement being capable of 30kts with greater endurance. The problem was that the new fast submarines (such as the German Type XXI, the Soviet 'Whiskey' and the US GUPPY and *Tang*) could outrun destroyer escorts and lesser craft in bad weather, for at least long enough to escape from sonar range. Thus a 5 to 6kt speed improvement over war-built types was desired (27kts for the coastal escort, 30 for the ocean-going type). With an enormous backlog of existing ASW craft, however, Congress was clearly unwilling to vote funds for new construction, particularly in the numbers needed by the Navy.

The first step, then, was a conversion programme: *Fletcher* class destroyers were to be converted to the new destroyer escorts (DDE). Indeed, it was hoped that all surviving *Fletchers* would be so modified, and most of them retained in reserve against an emergency. In practice, the reconstruction programme was halted after a short time in favour of increased expenditure on research as well as modest ASW improvement to the active general purpose destroyer force.

At the same time, *Gearing* class destroyers were modified or completed to ASW designs, essentially for experimental purposes, as part of a programme of carrier-destroyer hunter-killer groups. These latter were originally intended primarily to support convoys, but later evolved into specialised ASW task forces which prosecuted SOSUS contacts. Task force operation with converted *Essex* class carriers imposed a minimum speed limit of about 27kts, in itself a major influence on ASW escort development. The FRAM destroyers of the 1960s were in effect a mass-produced version of the DDE of a decade earlier, in that they represented an ASW modification of a general-purpose destroyer, all AAW capability (in effect) having been sacrificed. Although they were useful shore bombardment assets, and although they were considerably faster than the frigates which replaced

them, they were closer to frigates than to fleet escorts, and so are listed as ocean escorts.

Until the 1950s, the problem of the ocean escorts had been that they were not sufficiently capable of operating with carrier strike forces in peacetime, and indeed were rather expensive to maintain, in terms of the capability they possessed. However, very large numbers would be required upon mobilisation. The only possible solutions were specialised mass production design (in the cases of the *Dealey* and *Claud Jones* classes) and prototypes for the mass conversion of the remaining mothballed Second World War ships (as in the *Fletcher* DDE and in some ASW conversions of wartime destroyer escorts). In fact the solution chosen was to abandon most forms of convoy operation in favour of massive use of aircraft cued by long-range sensors such as SOSUS, with surface escorts reserved only for the most essential missions. The surface escorts could, in turn, be made far more sophisticated, to counter more and more submarines.

The evolution of the ocean escorts is symbolised by the evolution of their weapons. Until the mid-1950s average sonar range was about 1500yds; typical weapons were Hedgehog (approx 250–300yds) and Weapon Alfa (800yds), plus homing torpedoes. With the advent of the SQS-4 sonar, ranges of 5000–10,000yds became practicable, and long-range ASW weapons were developed: the RAT rocket-thrown torpedo (5000yds) and the DASH drone helicopter (up to about 15,000yds). FRAM II conversions generally provided a variable-length sonar in addition to SQS-4, for reliable operation even below the thermal layer; the primary stand-off weapons were DASH and a long ASW torpedo, Mk 37. FRAM I ships, as well as many new ships, had the larger SQS-23 sonar. With a reliable range generally given as 10,000yds; the associated weapons were ASROC (rocket-thrown torpedo or nuclear depth-charge) and the DASH drone. By the late 1950s there was another new sonar, SQS-26 (in transistorised form, SQS-53) with a reliable direct-path range probably exceeding 20,000yds, and theoretically capable of reaching the first convergence zone, at about 70,000yds. There was no associated weapon at first, although a longer-range ASROC (about 20,000yds) was proposed; but, the solution to convergence-zone attack turned out to be the manned LAMPS I helicopter. Finally, in the towed arrays, a beyond first convergence zone capability (passive, to be sure) is claimed. Prosecution requires a long-range helicopter, LAMPS III. One might suggest that confidence in the towed array is so great that its primary carrier, the *Perry* class frigate, has only a very short-range active sonar. With each advance in weaponry and sonar the minimum size of the platform to carry these devices has grown. For example, it was possible to fit SQS-4 into a Second World War destroyer escort, but not SQS-23. SQS-26 required very nearly a cruiser-size hull for high speed, the *Bronstein* class frigate representing a bare minimum.

Ocean escorts had a variety of designations. In the late 1940s a distinction was drawn between submarine-killers (DDK) and escorts (DDE) with somewhat less developed ASW capabilities; all later became DDE. In 1975, in line with most other navies, the United States redesignated its ocean escorts (DE) as frigates (FF), the missile-armed units becoming FFG (formerly DEG). The *Perry* class were briefly designated patrol frigates (PF), presumably as a way of distinguishing them from the unpopular but similar sized *Knox* class.

ATTACK SUBMARINE CLASSES

At the end of the Second World War the United States had a very large but somewhat confused submarine force, since its next potential adversayr presented few significant ship targets. During the next decade two divergent lines of development were pursued: submarine ASW and submarine strategic warfare. At first separate series of attack submarines loosely modelled on the new German Type XXI (*Tang* and her successors) and specialised ASW submarines (*Barracuda* class and fleet submarine conversions) were built; the latter emphasised long-range passive sonars over speed, as a means of detecting enemy high-performance submarines snorkelling en route to operational areas. To some extent, too, the construction of high-performance anti-ship submarines was justified as a means of maintaining the kind of technology needed to understand an adversary with a large modern submarine force; the first GUPPY conversions, for example, were pressed ahead in large part to provide realistic targets for the surface ASW force. They were also considered a mobilisation reserve against the need for large numbers of specialised ASW submarines.

The two major new items of submarine technology of the time were nuclear power and the new *Albacore* hull form, which promised much higher speed and manoeuvrability at fixed power levels. A third line of development, towards closed-cycle conventional power plants for high performance, was suspended, as was the development of advanced steam plants for radar-picket submarines. The latter did, however, lead to the pressure-fired boilers of the *Garcia* class frigates. It appears that nuclear power was initially pressed forward because of its obvious advantages for attack submarine operation, without much reference to US tactical requirements: the first nuclear submarines were anti-ship types. The *Tullibee* was an attempt to combine nuclear power with a long-range sonar; she had the relatively low speed of her conventional forebears, the contemporary *Skipjack* class adopting the high-speed *Albacore* hull form.

By about 1957, it had become clear that Soviet submarines would be the primary submarine targets. The next submarine class combined deeper diving depth and a very long-range sonar with a new long-range weapon, SUBROC, a ballistic rocket with a nuclear warhead; it also had the new high-speed hull form. It would appear that the BQQ-2 active-passive sonar of these *Thresher* class submarines could reach out to at least the first convergence zone, since SUBROC range is usually quoted as about 30–40nm. Since the new ships had the same power plant as the much smaller *Skipjack*s, they registered some loss of speed. With the appearance of the *Thresher*s with their great ASW capability, all submarines were reassigned the ASW mission, and the specialised ASW submarine designation (SSK) was cancelled. Submarine tactics continued along the lines familiar more than two decades later, with a technical emphasis on quietness and passive operation; most submarines would form ambush barriers across choke points such as the Greenland-Iceland-UK Gap.

Major attention was devoted to submarine noise reduction. The *Thresher*s were already very quiet, but during the 1960s two submarines were built to explore alternative means of silencing two major sources of noise: turbine reduction gearing (*Glenard P Lipscomb* had turbo-electric propulsion) and reactor pumps (*Narwhal* had a natural circulation reactor). Because these submarines were not completed until, respectively, 1969 and 1974, their operation could not contribute materially to the design of the next submarine class, the *Los Angeles*; essentially the *Los Angeles* is an attempt to recapture the speed lost in the transition from *Skipjack* to *Thresher*, at the cost of twice the installed power and a considerable increase in size. Almost certainly there have been advances in silencing as well, but nothing approaching what a major change in power plant (as in the experimental submarines) would accomplish. The chief virtue of high speed is that the submarine can operate in direct support (D/S) of fast carrier battle groups, patrolling ahead of them to destroy submarines in their path, or to vector carrier-based aircraft to attack such enemy submarines.

In the early 1970s an abortive successor to the *Los Angeles* class was designed. At that time a submarine-launched tactical missile (STAM) was in the early stages of development; it would have been a combination SUBROC and anti-ship missile with a torpedo warhead. Given the limited number of torpedo reloads carried by even a large attack submarine, it was to have had additional vertical launch tubes for its missiles. The length of the launch tube compartment contributed to the size of the submarine; in addition, it had further silencing and a higher maximum speed, all of which made for a submerged displacement of about 14,000t. As the *Los Angeles* class, of about only 6900t already strained Navy budgets, Admiral Zumwalt had the new type cancelled. Indeed, during the Carter Administration a new austere attack submarine, tentatively described as the F/A (Fleet Attack, but derisively named 'Fat Albert' by some) was proposed. It was never completely defined, and *Los Angeles* class construction continues until the early 1980s. However, the issue of limited weapon capacity was addressed: late units will be completed with twelve of the vertical launch tubes for Tomahawk or Harpoon anti-ship missiles, mounted between the pressure hull and the bow spherical sonar array.

STRATEGIC SUBMARINE CLASSES

Strategic attack was a major potential submarine function as early as 1945, when the United States captured German plans for a submarine-towed submersible barge containing a V2 rocket. At that time there was

already a programme for a US version of the German V1, which the Navy called Loon, and one was fired from the submarine *Cusk* on 18 February 1947. By this time a programme for air-breathing long-range weapons suited to submarine launch was well underway, resulting in the Regulus cruise missile, ultimately deployed aboard five specialised submarines (two conversions of fleet boats and three specially built submarines, one of them, *Halibut*, nuclear-powered). All operated in the deterrent role in the Pacific 1957–64, ultimately being replaced by the ballistic Polaris system; a supersonic follow-on cruise missile, Regulus II, was cancelled.

Thus most US strategic submarines have operated with ballistic missiles: Polaris, Poseidon, and the new Trident. Polaris itself was carried out as a crash programme, *George Washington* class submarines being conversions of *Skipjack* class hulls already under construction, with 130ft added abaft the fin. They were followed by the improved *Ethan Allen* class (which carried Polaris A-2 from the first) and then by the *Lafayette* class; the entire Fleet Ballistic Missile Program of 41 submarines was completed between 1959 and 1966. There followed a long hiatus, while development of new missiles (Poseidon) was not accompanied by any new submarine project. In 1967 there was a new strategic study (STRAT-X) advocating a new very long-range missile, initially envisaged as externally (and perhaps horizontally) carried, floating to the surface for firing. The new submarine would be very large but relatively inexpensive, capable of only very low speed and with a minimal crew. However, this ULMS (Undersea Long-range Missile System) concept gradually evolved into a Polaris-like submarine, with more missiles per submarine to obtain greater cost-effectiveness: the 24-tube *Ohio* is the result. Trident I missiles can also be retro-fitted to existing Poseidon-capable submarines.

There is some controversy over the choice of the *Ohio* design. The submarines themselves, by far the largest ever built in the West, have been seriously delayed in construction, and there are fears that their large size will make them vulnerable to non-acoustic detection. With the increase in the number of tubes per submarine, the total size of the sea-based force decreases, and the consequence of loss or accident to a single unit increases considerably. However, attempts to design a markedly less expensive ballistic missile submarine have not as yet been successful, and it appears that *Ohio* class construction will continue as the earlier missile submarines wear out.

RADAR-PICKETS

One of the major lessons of the Second World War was the immense value of early warning against air attack, whether against cities or against moving naval forces. Picket forces were extemporised, for example to protect the Fleet off Okinawa and to protect Britain from V1 attack in 1944–45; to some extent they were supplemented postwar by specialised radar-picket (airborne early warning) aircraft, the ancestors of the current E-2C Hawkeye and AWACS. Three main categories of seaborne radar-pickets developed postwar: tactical (surface) pickets, strategic pickets and picket submarines. The tactical units were direct descendants of the 24 radar-picket destroyers of 1945. Twelve more *Gearing* class destroyers were converted under the FY52 programme, and all Fleet Escorts were provided with height-finding radars and CICs suited to air (fighter) control. The reversion of all but four of the converted *Gearing* class destroyers to ASW roles under FRAM can be read as an indication of the increasing reliability of carrier-based radar-picket aircraft from the early 1960s onwards.

The next wave of radar-pickets was converted to serve the US Continental Air Defense System as a seaward barrier. Conversions began under the FY49 programme, their priority so that that the first each had two of the scarce SPS-6 radars. In the interests of endurance, nearly all were diesel-powered; the incomplete steam-powered *Vandiver* and *Wagner* appear to have been completed as pickets as mobilisation prototypes. The destroyer escort conversions were both expensive and relatively uncomfortable for lengthy stays on the picket line; in the mid-1950s sixteen Liberty Ship (merchant) hulls were converted, and provided with long-range radars and a CIC (YAGR1–16, FY55–58). There were even proposals for a follow-on armed picket force of radar/sonar/Talos or Terrier ships, perhaps based on 'Victory' hulls, and provisionally designated the PBG. However, with the fading of the bomber threat in the 1960s the DERs were transferred to surface patrol duties (largely Operation 'Market Time' blockade, off Vietnam) and the Libertys decommissioned and disposed of (April–September 1965).

Finally, there were submarine pickets. They were originally proposed as a result of the carnage on the picket line at Okinawa: a submarine could not match the radar suit of a destroyer, but it could submerge to avoid attack. Two submarines were converted (albeit without special radars) before VJ-Day, with four more under conversion; in 1946 the first two specialised conversions, *Spinax* and *Requin*, were carried out, under Project 'Migraine'. Ultimately twelve fleet submarines were converted, and three specialised submarine radar pickets built. All the diesel submarines had the basic defect of low speed and thus could not really accompany the fast task force; but the nuclear picket, *Triton*, for many years the largest submarine in the world, could.

Interest in submarine picket operations declined sharply towards the end of the 1950s, the converted submarines losing their radars and their special status in 1959. The two specially built diesel submarines reverted to attack status in 1961 and underwent FRAM modernisation in 1964. The immense *Triton* was also reclassified. A project to use her as a National Emergency Command Post Afloat (NECPA), natural in view of her large CIC, was dropped, and in 1982 she remained a white elephant, mothballed.

AMPHIBIOUS SHIP TYPES

In about 1948 a goal of a 20kt amphibious force was set, although there was no substantial new amphibious construction for the time being, given the mass of existing tonnage and considerable scepticism as to the viability of amphibious forces in a nuclear environment. The success at Inchon in 1950 (and, indeed, the entire Korean experience) showed that amphibious operations remained important, and the amphibious force was gradually replaced during the 1950s and 1960s. Meanwhile the maze of wartime types was rationalised, and the short-range non-transportable craft (LCI, LCS, LSM) discarded. In addition, the Marines added the 'vertical envelopment' concept and, with it, a series of totally new types and tactics.

Long-range amphibious operations during the Second World War required a combination of heavy-lift non-beaching ships and beaching craft to bring their equipment over the shore. The ships (except for dock landing ships, LSDs) could carry personnel-vehicle (LCVP) or small mechanized equipment (LCM) beaching craft; large tanks and vehicles required a larger beaching craft, the LCT, which postwar became the LSU and then the LCU (landing craft, utility). It could not be launched from a davit, and had therefore to be carried in a floodable well deck, as in an LSD. The non-beaching ships were attack (personnel) transports (APA, later LPA) and attack cargo ships (AKA, later LKA). There were in addition large beaching ships, LSTs, which could carry relatively less on their displacement than the AKAs, but which could carry very heavy equipment and could disgorge vehicles far more quickly, and which therefore remained valuable.

In the early 1950s the Marines concluded that amphibious operations under the threat of atomic attack required the dispersal of the amphibious fleet, which was impossible unless some means were found of moving troops and their equipment far more rapidly than had been possible with slow beaching craft. Their solution was the helicopter: although a helicopter could not carry very heavy equipment, it could concentrate troops very rapidly. In ship terms, carriers could be converted to carry troops and their helicopters beginning with the escort carrier *Thetis Bay*, which was followed by a series of early *Essex* class carriers (formerly CVSs) and then by the specialised *Iwo Jima* class. Their major defect was that they could not operate in bad weather, since they carried no landing craft. The solution was a combination of LPH and LSD with extra cargo space, the LHA, or amphibious assault ship, with a substantial well deck in addition to a large flight deck and hangar.

Perhaps the major technical problem faced by the 20kt programme was the LST, traditionally very slow because of its need to provide bow doors. The first attempt to design a fast LST called for a bow propeller and a stern ramp, but it was rejected in favour of a compromise, a 15–17.5kt conventional LST, 22 of which were built in the 1950s. However, twenty new 20kt *Newport* class LSTs were built under the FY65–67 programmes, with seven more planned for FY71 but deferred. They achieve a good hull form by using a ramp extended *over* their bows.

The other major classes developed less spectacularly. Shortly after the end of the War the Maritime Commission developed a new fast cargo ship, the 'Mariner', which, like its prewar predecessors, was well adapted to naval conversion: two became LPAs, and another became an LKA. Although several classes were developed to carry personnel, the cargo function was unique, and five more attack cargo ships (*Charleston* class) were built under the FY65 and FY66 programmes. Postwar LSDs were generally adaptations of the wartime LSD concept to higher speeds, with eight built in the 1950s (*Thomaston* class) and five more late in the 1960s (*Anchorage* class); in the 1980s a new LSD 41 class is to be built. Between the two LSD classes there was an attempt to combine LSD and attack transport roles in the LPD, a total of fifteen being built. However, with the advent of the LHA the LPD was abandoned.

Another major line of development was higher speed for the beaching craft. During the 1950s hydrofoil LCVPs were tested, but they were never adopted. There were also tests of very large amphibious tractors, similar in concept to the LVT; again, they were not adopted. In 1982 the principal new beaching craft concept is an air-cushion amphibious assault landing craft vehicle (LCAC); the LSD 41 well deck is to be sized to accommodate them.

PATROL CRAFT

Small fighting craft have had a very mixed career in the US Navy, generally being extemporised in wartime and discarded as soon as the immediate need of them ended. Very generally, small craft cost more to operate per ton than do larger ones, but they are much easier to build in numbers. Often they deteriorate rapidly because of their relatively flimsy construction. Moreover, in peacetime the Navy generally is far more concerned with its mid-ocean mission than with operations near its own or an enemy coast. Thus the large sub-chaser fleets of the First World War was almost completely discarded within a few years of the end of the war. After 1945 all but four of the hundreds of PT-boats were scrapped, although four postwar prototypes were built. As for the inshore ASW craft, most of them were also soon discarded, and repeated proposals for new PCE, PC, PCS, and SC designs produced no craft. On the other hand, the United States did build a variety of smaller combatants for its allies, including a series of motor gunboats (PGM).

Reasons for limited interest in coastal craft included very limited naval spending, most of it consumed by the rising cost of the new naval technology of the 1950s. There was no enemy fleet for a new generation of PTs to attack, and it appeared that small craft were grossly inadequate for any type of ASW, even off US ports. Thus interest in small combatants did not really begin to rise until the Kennedy Administration, which combined official interest in them with a pair of operational considerations: Cuba and Southeast Asia. The threat of Soviet-built small attack craft based in Cuba had a great effect on the US fleet of the time, leading to studies of the anti-ship efficacy of anti-aircraft missiles – and to the construction of the *Asheville* class motor gunboats. Once the United States found itself engaged in Vietnam, the coastal and river operations led to the construction of a great variety of small craft, some of which have been retained – albeit on an experimental basis.

The only other postwar small combatants were the hydrofoils, built at first as experiments in a new technology. Ultimately those experiments led to a proposal for a NATO-wide class of missile-armed hydrofoils (PHM), whose primary purpose would have been to deny the Soviets access to the narrow straits around Europe. Costs rose very steeply, however, and only the American programme of six craft survived at all. As in the 1950s, questions were soon raised as to their function in a fleet the main threats to which were Soviet air and submarine forces. At one point the hydrofoil advocates went so far as to propose lightweight fleet air defence systems (such as Sea Phoenix) for hydrofoil operation, but ultimately they reverted to single-system operation (Harpoon). At the time of writing it appears that the six *Pegasus* class hydrofoils will be the last US coastal combatants to be built for some time.

MINE WARFARE VESSELS

The postwar period saw, first, the decline of a massive war-built mine force, then its resuscitation under Cold War conditions and under the impetus of mine warfare in Korea, after which a second slow decline set in. One might well speculate that the low estate of mine warfare in the US Navy in 1982 is intimately connected with the limited prestige of offensive mining in a navy which has been quite successful at just that tactic in the past. One reason for the latter, some wags would say, is that it is not possible to win command of a mine; with the end of the specialised surface minelayers (which have been replaced by submarines and aircraft, neither of them dedicated to the mine mission) there are no major mine warfare commands afloat. The high cost of an active minesweeper force was also a major factor: the wooden hulls of non-magnetic sweepers were at best difficult to maintain, and reportedly the non-magnetic engines were a constant source of trouble. A Navy hard-pressed to maintain its most vital forces (for ocean ASW and for carrier attack) could not operate a large force of labour-intensive small craft. In some ways, then, the same forces which doomed the wartime PT force also doomed the mine force. In 1982, for example, there was a total of only 25 ocean sweepers (MSO), of which 22 were operated by the Naval Reserves, and 7 minesweeping boats. By way of comparison, at the end of the post-1945 rundown, there were 10 destroyer minelayers (4 active), 20 destroyer minesweepers (12 active), one large minelayer (in reserve), 123 ocean sweepers (10 active), and 57 coastal sweepers (27 active, 16 training reservists). In 1958, after a massive new construction programme, the former destroyers were gone and the minelayer remained in reserve; in addition there were 65 new ocean and 22 new coastal sweepers, all active, and 116 old steel ocean and 37 old coastal sweepers (1 ocean type active). There were also 33 minehunters (5 active), 52 minesweeping boats, and five mine support ships (all inactive).

There is a considerable difference between the position of the minesweeper in the US and allied navies. Allies of the USA are generally close enough to their potential enemies to be likely victims of large-scale mining campaigns. US analysts appear generally to have thought that extensive mining in their waters would be difficult at best, although the Soviet position in Cuba would seem to bring this view into question, at least with respect to southern ports. Thus the 1981 proposal for a new Mine Countermeasures Ship is sometimes justified on the basis of a Soviet deep-water mine threat to a most valuable US asset, the ballistic missile submarine. On the other hand, mines would always represent a major threat to amphibious operations, a point driven home by experience in Korea. Thus, at least from the mid-1950s onwards, minesweepers were always associated with the amphibious force for planning purposes. The postwar drive towards a 20kt amphibious force made development of efficient sweepers particularly difficult, since a relatively large hull would be required to combine very long range with such relatively high speed, yet large size was inimical to sweeping. For example, destroyer sweepers were withdrawn from Korea in favour of 220-footers because of their relative ineffectiveness.

On the other hand, the Soviet mine threat to West European ports was a major driving force in postwar US minesweeper development, as the United States sought to provide her European allies with the means to keep their ports open. It therefore designed and built (both at home and, under assistance programme, abroad) a coastal sweeper, a lineal successor to the wartime YMS. In effect this was a way to avoid the US manpower problem while still providing the initial capital outlay represented by the sweeper. Relatively few of these AMS or MSC were retained by the US Navy, whereas many of the larger AM or MSO (ocean sweepers), direct successors to the wartime 180-footer, were kept.

Mine development drove both programmes. Sweepers in service in 1945 could be defeated by the sensitive magnetic mines then entering service; non-magnetic construction was a major issue in postwar construction, with specified levels of magnetic signature from the earliest design phase. Where wooden construction had previously been adopted (in the wartime YMS) to make mass production easier, in postwar craft it was part of a careful programme of signature reduction. In both cases, large generators were required to power magnetic sweep gear; in some cases postwar that meant gas turbines. Pressure mines were a major problem. The US Navy developed a large towed countermeasure, XMAP, which was to simulate the pressure signature of a merchant ship, and postwar sweepers carried among their staff requirements the ability to tow it. Ultimately it proved insufficiently blast-resistant, and was abandoned, but the interest in unusual countermeasures continued, with experiments with blast-resistant Liberty ship hulls which could be operated (and propelled) entirely from above decks.

The problems associated with more sophisticated mines led to the development of minehunters, which might identify such devices one by one on the seabed for individual destruction. That is, the classical minesweeping technique of simulating a ship signature in order to neutralize mines in quantity (without destroying the simulator) was at least tentatively abandoned in favour of high-definition sonar and special mine-destruction devices. This programme began in 1945 with landing craft conversions: AMCU 1–6 were former tank landing craft, or LCT(6), and AMCU 7–11 were former infantry landing craft, LCIL; all were wartime conversions. AMCU 12–14, 44–50 (Harkness class) were YMS/PCS conversions; AMCU 15–42 (Accentor class) were LSIL conversions under the FY52 programme. In fact the conversions of AMCU 15, 23, 27, 31, 32, 36 and 40 were cancelled. Finally, a new-construction minehunter, the Bittern, was built as AMCU (later MHC) 43. All the existing AMCU were redesignated MHC (minehunter, coastal) on 7.2.55. Two sister ships, which would have become MHC 44 and 45, were not built. Finally, in Jan and Feb 1954, five auxiliary motor minesweepers (AMC, former YMS) were redesignated as minehunters (AMCU 46–50), although it does not appear that any modifications were made to them. Early in 1955, when it became apparent that MHC 44 and 45 would not be built, these hull numbers were applied to two more motor minesweepers, AMS 2 and 3.

The primary problem of the minesweepers was their identification with the amphibious force, which meant an ultimate goal of a 20kt mine force. That in turn suggested the development of small sweepers which could be carried to the objective area aboard large specialised or amphibious craft. Two approaches were tried. In one, small minesweeping boats (MSB) could be carried in the well decks of an LSD or on the deck of a cargo ship with heavy-lift booms. Alternatively, a 36-foot MSL could be carried in the davits of standard amphibious ships. In 1955 a specialised mother ship for such craft was planned, as a conversion of the wartime large minelayer/motorised transport (CM/LSV) hull. Two ships were converted in 1963–6; they could carry 20 MSL, two minesweeping helicopters, and spare gear (including that for MSLs), and could control as assault sweep. One LSD and one LST were also converted, but with lesser boat capacity and no helicopters.

The helicopters represented the next attempt at a fully mobile assault sweeping force. During the early 1960s a special helicopter-drawn sled, accommodating magnetic and other countermeasures, was developed; it could be towed by the standard CH-53 Marine helicopter, which was operated by a variety of fleet amphibious units, most of them capable of a sustained passage at 20 knots. Later even a minehunting sonar, AQS-14, was developed for helicopter towing. The Mk 105 sled was used in mine clearance operation off Hanoi in 1973, and nine years later represents the principal US distant mine countermeasures capability, although many in the Mine Force seem sceptical of its capabilities. Thus the return to some more conventional anti-mine force seems assured, although that has not been nearly as quick as might have been expected. The helicopters were always considered limited to fairly deep water, and in fact the MSBs were retained to provide a very shallow-water anti-mine force.

The run-down of new mine craft construction after the Korean War was extremely rapid. Thus the FY50 programme included only one XMAP anti-pressure-mine device, with another (and an ocean sweeper) authorised but deferred. In addition, the Army coastal controlled mineplanting function was turned over to the Navy, the latter receiving six coastal mineplanters, two local mineplanters (YMP), and four minesweeping boats (MCM, later MSB 1–4). Funds were released with the outbreak of the Korean War, however, and under the FY51 and three supplemental programmes a total of 19 ocean sweepers and 18 MSB were authorised; another 13 sweepers and 2 coastal sweepers were authorised but deferred, and the FY50 sweeper awarded. All of the deferred ocean and coastal sweepers were purchased under the FY52 programme, which included 17 more coastal sweepers, 30 MSHs, and the conversion of 31 craft to minehunters (AMCU, later MHC). FY53 included 9 ocean and 20 coastal sweepers (plus one ocean sweeper deferred), and FY54 included 4 ocean sweepers and the specialized minehunter Bittern. Small boat funds bought 4 MSL, coastal sweepers somewhat smaller than the MSB. By this time funds were beginning to tighten, as the carrier and guided missile programmes began very badly to overrun original estimates. Thus FY55 included only three ocean sweepers, and 2 MSI (replacements for the original postwar coastal sweeper) had to be deferred to FY56 before programme submission. The latter programme included no ocean sweepers at all, although 26 MSL were included among small boats authorised. No minecraft appeared in the FY57 programme; in FY58 two coastal craft were built to replace two transferred.

The threat of North Vietnamese riverine mines in Vietnam inspired the development of a variety of small craft, only the designations of which remained a few years later: drone minesweepers (MSD), river minesweepers (MSM), and patrol minesweepers (MSR). However, the minesweeping launches (MSL) remained, and there were headquarters ship conversions (MCS) under the FY63 and FY64 programmes. However, the reader might note that this latter programme was originally far larger, all of the *Terror* class hulls (except *Terror* herself) being redesignated in the MCS series as early as 1955. All were stricken 1 September 1961, but *Catskill* (MCS 1) and *Ozark* (MCS 2) were reinstated (and actually converted) 1 June 1964 and 1 October 1963, respectively. The LSD *Epping Forrest*, used as a mine escort tender, became MCS 7 on 30 November 1962. Similarly, the tank landing ship *Orleans Parish* was reclassified MCS 6 on 19 January 1959, reverting to LST status on 1 June 1965. It might be argued that these redesignations themselves reflected the new mine threat encountered in Vietnam: a coastal and riverine threat requiring countermeasures by small craft.

COAST GUARD CUTTERS

Although the US Coast Guard functions as a civilian organisation in peacetime, it is amalgamated with the Navy in wartime. Its cutters are therefore designed with secondary naval (generally escort) missions in mind, and in fact some of them operated in a naval role in Vietnam, the 'Cape' class coastal craft forming part of the riverine force. In addition, the Coast Guard did operate twelve ex-Navy destroyer escorts (as ocean weather ships) during the Korean War, and for much of the postwar period included an ASW weapon, Hedgehog, among the standard equipment of its cutters.

Primarily because of the size of its force in 1945, the Coast Guard received no major new units until the mid-1960s, when twelve long-endurance cutters (WHEC, formerly WPG) were laid down. They were to replace an existing force of *Owasco* and *Campbell* class cutters, the latest of which had been completed at the end of the Second World War; the Coast Guard of the postwar period had also operated a force of eighteen former small seaplane tenders transferred to it in 1947–48. Of these, seven were transferred to South Vietnam beginning in 1970, the others being decommissioned from 1968 onwards. The other major postwar re-equipment programmes were for smaller ships: the 210-foot *Reliance* class medium endurance cutter (WMEC, ex-WPC) and the newer 270-foot *Bear* class medium endurance cutters (WMEC). From a naval point of view, the other major postwar Coast Guard programme was the patrol boat (WPB), built in both the *Cape* (95-foot) and *Point* (82-foot) classes, the latter directly replacing a series of 83-footers which served prominently during the Second World War. The 95-foot WPB formed the basis for a US motor gunboat (PGM) design which was exported to many South American and Asian navies.

The extent to which Coast Guard designs are compatible with naval missions is shown by the series of studies of *Hamilton* (WHEC) class hulls as the basis for what became the *Perry* class FFG. In addition, the *Bear* class was proposed as a basis for an ASW-oriented corvette which the Carter Administration proposed as the FFX; all were to have been operated in peacetime by the Naval Reserves, a concept reminiscent of the origins of the Second World War PC. Among US warships of their size, the medium endurance cutters are unique in their very considerable helicopter capabilities, necessary for the Coast Guard sea rescue mission. Their armament is justified in peacetime by the need to maintain security in US coastal waters. They do not, therefore, have very powerful sonars, although the SQS-36/38 sonar of the *Hamilton*s matches the SQS-56 of the FFGs. With the advent of the towed array system, however, there is the possibility of greatly enhancing their wartime ASW capability at very low cost in peacetime capability. In that case the ability to operate large helicopters, particularly in rough weather, is a major asset.

For most of its existence the Coast Guard has been an arm of the Department of the Treasury; it is, indeed, descended from the Revenue Service (anti-smuggling). In recent years, however, it has emphasised its sea safety role and it became part of the new Department of Transportation on 1 April 1967.

MAJOR US NAVAL ELECTRONIC EQUIPMENT

US electronic equipment developed since 1945 has been designated in a tri-service series, in which the three prefix letters indicate, respectively, platform, equipment type, and function. They in turn are prefixed by 'AN/', indicating originally, 'Army-Navy', ie, multi-service. These letters are omitted for clarity here, so that, for example, AN/SPS-30 is referred to as SPS-30. The principal naval platform prefixes are 'B' (submarine), 'S' (surface ship), 'U' (land and sea: 'universal'), and 'W' (waterborne, ie, submarine and surface ship); 'A' indicates an aircraft system. Major type designators are 'L' (countermeasures), 'P' (radar), 'Q' (sonar), and 'Y' (computer system); major functions include 'G' (fire control), 'Q' (multi-role or specialised), 'R' (passive detection), 'S' (search), and 'Y' (multi-function electronically-scanned radar). For example, WLR-1 is the first 'waterborne' countermeasures receiver in the series; SPQ-5 is a special or multiple-function ship-borne radar, in this case a Terrier beam-guidance and tracking radar. (Full details can be found in the author's *Naval Radar*, published by Conway Maritime Press and Naval Institute Press in 1981.)

Type	Remarks
RADARS (Note surface-search sets are *not* included)	
BPS-2	Radar-picket submarine L-band air search radar, 1953
BPS-3	S-band height-finder for submarine radar-pickets
SPG-49	Talos guidance radar (target tracker) operating in conjunction with SPW-2, with one radar per missile launcher arm
SPG-51	Tartar tracking and illuminating radar
SPG-55	Terrier guidance radar, successor to SPQ-5
SPG-60	Fire control radar of Mark 86 Fire Control System, for gun and missile control
SPG-62	Slaved illuminator of the Aegis system, operating with SPY-1
SPQ-5	Terrier fire control radar, essentially a modified SPG-49
SPQ-9	Search and track radar of Mark 86 Fire Control System
SPS-2	Very large long-range air search radar for task force defense. Only aboard *Northampton* and missile cruiser *Little Rock*
SPS-6	First major postwar air search radar; L-band
SPS-8	Nodding height-finder with 'orange-peel' antenna; SPS-8B had a dish and formed a link to the later SPS-30
SPS-12	Postwar L-band air search radar, similar in general characteristics to SPS-6 but considered superior. The Canadian SPS-501 consists of an SPS-12 transmitter with a Dutch antenna
SPS-17	First major postwar P-band air search radar, a return to late-World War II concepts. SPS-17A had a much-enlarged antenna, for radar-pickets. These ideas were developed through SPS-28 (lightweight version for destroyers), SPS-29, SPS-37, and SPS-43. The latter two had large-antenna versions (SPS-37A, -43A) which were standard on US missile cruisers and carriers. Now being replaced by SPS-49
SPS-30	Nodding dish for height-finding and fighter control, aboard carriers and some missile cruisers
SPS-32/33	Hughes SCANFAR electronically-scanned combination of, respectively, search and three-dimensional radars. Aboard *Long Beach* and *Enterprise* only; replaced by conventional radars 1981, partly because of operational problems
SPS-39	Three-dimensional electronically-scanned (in elevation) radar for missile ships and area defense missile systems. SPS-52 is a modified version, using the same planar-array antenna as the improved SPS-39s. Lighter than, but inferior to, SPS-48. SPS-42 is a version specially adapted to interface with NTDS
SPS-40	UHF air search radar, in effect a replacement for SPS-6 series
SPS-48	Long range three-dimensional radar, with electronic scanning in elevation. Replaced SPS-30 in many carriers
SPS-49	Current long range two-dimensional air search radar, with stabilized mounting, adapted to current automated combat systems. It is replacing the SPS 29/37/43 series
SPS-58	Search radar for the Sea Sparrow Point Defense Missile System. Later versions were designated SPS-65, and in many cases used the same antenna as the standard SPS-10 surface search system. The Hughes Target Acquisition System Mark 23 performs much the same role but, presumably, at higher efficiency and at considerably greater cost
SPY-1	Aegis search and fire control radar
SYS-1, -2	Computer systems which integrate the search and fire control radars of an existing ship, for automatic target detection and tracking, threat assessment, and assignment of defensive weapons. Currently being installed aboard existing US missile-armed major warships

Type	Remarks
SONARS	
BQG-1, -4	PUFFS, submarine passive fire control sonar systems, consisting of hydrophones distributed along the length of the submarine for triangulation
BQR-2	Listening array for postwar submarines: 6ft circular array
BQR-4	Conformal array based on German GHG for ASW submarines: 10ft wide, 20ft long horseshoe
BQR-15	Towed array for ballistic missile submarine self-defence
BQQ-2	Integrated sonar system for *Thresher* and later submarines, now being upgraded to BQQ-5. It included a bow spherical sonar as well as a conformal array in the hull
BQQ-5	Replacement for BQQ-2, in *Los Angeles* class; includes a towed array
BQQ-6	Trident missile submarine sonar, similar to BQQ-5 but without any active element
SQR-14	Very long range towed array sonar, ITASS (Interim Towed Array Surveillance System)
SQR-15	Successor to SQR-14, for special surveillance ships (AGOS)
SQR-18	Interim Tactical Towed Array Surveillance System (TACTASS), widely deployed aboard frigates, towed from the SQS-35 'fish'
SQR-19	Planned successor to SQR-18
SQS-4	First major low-frequency sonar system, with a nominal range in its later versions of 5–8000yds. In FRAM II ships it was associated with the DASH ASW drone. There were many improved versions, their designations within a series depending on the frequency, between 8 and 12 kc: SQS 29–32 (RTD), SQS 39–42 (Improved reliability and maintainability); SQS 43–46 (VDS, operating off the same 'stack'), and SQS 49–52 (improved reliability and maintainability)
SQS-23	Lower frequency sonar (5 kc) with a nominal range of 10,000 yards, associated with ASROC. AQQ-23 was an active-passive system with a second transducer, usually in a second sonar dome. Many ships with SQS-23 are now being modified to a single-dome SQQ-23 configuration
SQS-26	The largest current US surface ship sonar, credited with very long range: about 20,000yds direct-path, as well as bottom-bounce and first convergence zone (about 35nm). SQS-53 is a transistorised version
SQS-35	Independent variable depth sonar (IVDS), a 'fish' operating from its own sonar 'stack'. Aboard many *Knox* class ocean escorts
SQS-36	Hull sonar developed from SQS-35; in Coast Guard ships. SQS-38 is a transistorised development
SQS-56	Hull sonar of the *Perry* class. Although often described as a transistorised SQS-23, it operates at a considerably higher frequency (8 kc) and is closer to a modernised SQS-36/38

Note: Some US electronic systems fall outside the AN series. The most important current ones are probably the Mk 23 Target Acquisition System, which is the search and acquisition radar associated with the Improved Point Defense Missile System, the Mark 92 Fire Control System (guns and missiles for the *Perry* class FFGs and gun fire control for the *Pegasus* class hydrofoils), and the radars associated with the Phalanx close-in weapon system

FLEET STRENGTH 1947

BATTLESHIPS

No	Name	Fate
Iowa class: launched 1942–44, 48,000t standard		
BB 61	IOWA	Active 1951–58, to recommission 1983
BB 62	NEW JERSEY	Active 1950–57, 1967–69, recommissioned 27.12.82
BB 63	MISSOURI	Active to 1954. TS 1950
BB 64	WISCONSIN	Active 1951–58

All four are to be recommissioned as cruise missile carriers, with secondary battery reduced to 12–5in, but 8 × 4 Harpoon, as well as 6 Phalanx Close-In Weapon Systems. Future plans call for greatly increased missile batteries and, perhaps, facilities for VSTOL aircraft. The main air search radar is an SPS-49 forward, with LAMPS data link antennas above it, and satellite antenna and SLQ-32 countermeasures just below the forward main battery director (Mark 13). *Iowa* is now being modernised at Avondale Shipyards in Louisiana, under a subcontract from Ingalls.

AIRCRAFT CARRIERS

New Jersey Sept 1982   USN

No	Name	Fate
Essex class: launched 1942–45, 27,100t standard		
CV 9	ESSEX	SCB-27A 1951, CVS 1960, FRAM FY62, decommissioned 1969
CV 10	YORKTOWN	SCB-27A 1953, CVS 1957, FRAM FY66, decommissioned 1970, memorial
CV 11	INTREPID	SCB-27C 1954, CVS 1962, FRAM FY65, decommissioned 1974, museum 1982
CV 12	HORNET	SCB-27A 1953, CVS 1958, FRAM FY65 decommissioned 1970
CV 14	TICONDEROGA	SCB-27C 1954, CVS 1969, decommissioned 1973
CV 15	RANDOLPH	SCB-27A 1953, CVS 1959, FRAM FY61, decommissioned 1969
CV 16	LEXINGTON	SCB-27C 1955, CVS 1962, active 1982 as training carrier
CV 18	WASP	SCB-27A 1951, CVS 1956, FRAM FY64, decommissioned 1972
CV 19	HANCOCK	SCB-27C 1954, decommissioned 1956
CV 20	BENNINGTON	SCB-27A 1952, CVS 1959, FRAM FY63, decommissioned 1970
CV 21	BOXER	CVS 1955, LPH 1959, FRAM FY63, decommissioned 1969
CV 31	BON HOMME RICHARD	SCB-27C 1955, decommissioned 1971
CV 32	LEYTE	CVS 1953, decommissioned 1959
CV 33	KEARSARGE	SCB-27A 1952, CVS 1958, decommissioned 1970
CV 34	ORISKANY	SCB-27A 1950, decommissioned 1976
CV 36	ANTIETAM	CVS 1953, decommissioned 1963; angled deck prototype
CV 37	PRINCETON	CVS 1953, LPH 1959, FRAM FY61, decommissioned 1970
CV 38	SHANGRI LA	SCB-27C 1955, CVS 1959, decommissioned 1971
CV 39	LAKE CHAMPLAIN	SCB-27A 1952, CVS 1957, decommissioned 1966
CV 40	TARAWA	CVS 1955, decommissioned 1960
CV 45	VALLEY FORGE	CVS 1953, LPH 1961, FRAM FY64, decommissioned 1970
CV 47	PHILIPPINE SEA	CVS 1955, decommissioned 1958
Midway class: launched 1945–46, 45,000t standard		
CVB 41	MIDWAY	Extant 1982

UNITED STATES

No	Name	Fate
CVB 42	FRANKLIN D ROOSEVELT	Decommissioned 1977, BU
CVB 43	CORAL SEA	Extant 1982 as reserve training carrier on West Coast
Independence class: launched 1943, 10,600t standard		
CVL 26	MONTEREY	Active 1950–56, stricken 1970
CVL 28	CABOT	ASW carrier, active 1948–45, stricken 1959, Spanish *Dedalo* 1967
CVL 29	BATAAN	ASW carrier, active 1950–54, stricken 1959
Saipan class: launched 1945, 14,500t standard		
CVL 48	SAIPAN	Decommissioned 1957, recommissioned 1966 as *Arlington* (AGMR 2), decommissioned 1970, stricken 1975
CVL 49	WRIGHT	Active to 1956, and 1963–70, stricken 1977
Bogue class: launched 1942–43, 9400t standard		
CVE 11	CARD	Active 1958–70, stricken 1970
CVE 13	CORE	Active 1958–69, stricken 1970
CVE 23	BRETON	Active 1958–71, stricken 1971
CVE 25	CROATAN	Active 1958–69, stricken 1970
Casablanca class: launched 1943–44, 8200t standard		
CVE 58	CORREGIDOR	Active 1951–58, stricken 1958, BU 1960
CVE 64	TRIPOLI	Active 1952–58; stricken 2959, BU 1960
CVE 86	SITKOH BAY	Active 1950–54, stricken 1960, BU 1961
CVE 88	CAPE ESPERANCE	Active 1950–59, stricken 1959, BU 1961
CVE 90	THETIS BAY	Active 1956–64, stricken 1964, BU 1966
CVE 92	WINDHAM BAY	Active 1951–59, stricken 1959, BU 1961
Commencement Bay class: launched 1944–45, 18,900t standard		
CVE 106	BLOCK ISLAND	Active 1951–54, stricken 1959, BU
CVE 107	GILBERT ISLANDS	Active 1951–55, *Annapolis* 1964–69, stricken 1976
CVE 108	KULA GULF	Active 1951–55, 1965–69, stricken 1970
CVE 110	SALERNO BAY	Active 1951–54, stricken 1961, BU
CVE 112	SIBONEY	Active 1950–56, stricken 1970, BU
CVE 114	RENDOVA	Active 1945–50, 1951–55, stricken 1971, BU
CVE 115	BAIROKO	Active 1945–55, stricken 1960, BU
CVE 116	BADOENG STRAIT	Active 1947–57, stricken 1970, BU 1972
CVE 118	SICILY	Active to 1954; stricken 1960, BU
CVE 119	POINT CRUZ	Active 1951–56, 1965–69, stricken 1970, BU 1971
CVE 120	MINDORO	Active 1945–55, stricken 1959, BU 1960
CVE 122	PALAU	Active 1946–54, stricken 1960, BU 1960

Essex Class
All SCB-27s were laid up 1947, reactivated for conversion, except for *Kearsarge*, which was active until conversion. All but CV 39 were fitted with enclosed bows and angled decks. Proposals to reactivate CV 34 and CV 31 failed in Congress in 1981–82. Full details of conversions are given below under Major Surface Ships.

Midway class
All remained active from commissioning onwards, except for SCB-110/110A and later reconstructions. In 1982 *Midway* was forward-deployed in Japan. Full details of conversions are given below under Major Surface Ships.

Saipan class
Saipan became a major communications relay ship and was recommissioned as *Arlington* in 1966 and served in Vietnamese waters. *Wright* became a NECPA command cruiser 1963 (see under Amphibious Warfare Vessels).

Bogue class
All four remaining escort carriers of this class served as aircraft transports until decommissioned.

Casablanca class
Thetis Bay was converted to a helicopter carrier (CVHA 1) at San Francisco N Yd Jun 55–Jul 56; she was reclassified LPH 6 on 28.5.59. Details were: 10,866t full load; 8–40mm (4×2), 20 helicopters (max), 1004 troops. The other escort carriers of this class served as aircraft transports for the whole of their postwar active lives.

Commencement Bay class
Gilbert Islands was converted to the major communications relay ship *Annapolis* (AGMR 1) 1962–63 and served until 1969. Details were: 11,473t standard, 22,500t full load; 8–3in/50 (4×2); complement 710. *Kula Gulf* and *Point Cruz* served as MSTS aircraft transports 1965–69.

CRUISERS

No	Name	Fate
Atlanta class: launched 1942–46, 6700t standard		
CL 95	OAKLAND	Decommissioned 1949, stricken 1959
CL 98	TUCSON	Decommissioned 1945, stricken 1966
CL 119	JUNEAU	Decommissioned 1955, stricken 1959

No	Name	Fate
CL 120	SPOKANE	Decommissioned 1950, stricken 1972
CL 121	FRESNO	Decommissioned 1949, stricken 1965
Cleveland class: launched 1943–45, 11,500t standard		
CL 65	PASADENA	Decommissioned 1950, stricken 1970
CL 66	SPRINGFIELD	Decommissioned 1950, reclassified CLG May 57
CL 67	TOPEKA	Decommissioned 1949, reclassified CLG May 57
CL 82	PROVIDENCE	Decommissioned 1959, reclassified CLG May 57
CL 83	MANCHESTER	Decommissioned 1956, stricken 1960
CL 87	DULUTH	Decommissioned 1949, stricken 1960
CL 90	ASTORIA	Decommissioned 1959, stricken 1969
CL 91	OKLAHOMA CITY	Decommissioned 1947, reclassified CLG May 57
CL 92	LITTLE ROCK	Decommissioned 1949, reclassified CLG May 1957
CL 93	GALVESTON	Never commissioned as CL, reclassified CLG May 57
CL 102	PORTSMOUTH	Decommissioned 1949, stricken 1970
CL 104	ATLANTA	Decommissioned 1949, expended in explosive tests 1965–70 as *IX-304*
CL 105	DAYTON	Decommissioned 1949, stricken 1961
CL 106	FARGO	Decommissioned 1950, stricken 1970
CL 107	HUNTINGTON	Decommissioned 1949, stricken 1961
Worcester class: launched 1947, 14,700t standard		
CL 144	WORCESTER	Decommissioned 1958, stricken 1970
CL 145	ROANOKE	Decommissioned 1958, stricken 1970
Baltimore class: launched 1942–45, 14,000t standard		
CA 68	BALTIMORE	Active to 1956, stricken 1971
CA 69	BOSTON	Decommissioned 1946, reclassified CAG 1 1.11.55
CA 70	CANBERRA	Decommissioned 1947, reclassified CAG 2 15.6.56
CA 71	QUINCY	Active 1952–54, stricken 1973
CA 72	PITTSBURG	Active 1951–56, stricken 1973
CA 73	SAINT PAUL	Active to 1971, stricken 1973
CA 74	COLUMBUS	Active to 1959, recommissioned as CG 12 1.12.62
CA 75	HELENA	Active to 1963, stricken 1974
CA 130	BREMERTON	Decommissioned 1948, active 1951–60, stricken 1973
CA 131	FALL RIVER	Decommissioned 1947, stricken 1971
CA 132	MACON	Decommissioned April 1950, recommissioned October, active until 1961, stricken 1969
CA 133	TOLEDO	Active to 1960, stricken 1974
CA 135	LOS ANGELES	Active 1951–63, stricken 1974
CA 136	CHICAGO	Decommissioned 1947, recommissioned as CG 11 2.5.64
CA 123	ALBANY	Active to 1958, recommissioned as CG 10 3.11.62
CA 124	ROCHESTER	Active to 1961, stricken 1974
Des Moines class: launched 1946–47, 17,200t standard		
CA 134	DES MOINES	Active to 1961, extant 1982
CA 132	SALEM	Active to 1959, extant 1982
CA 148	NEWPORT NEWS	Decommissioned 1975, stricken but retained as possible memorial ship

Cleveland class
Full details of the ships converted to missile cruisers (CLG) are given below under Major Surface Ships.

Baltimore class
Helena, Macon, Toledo and *Los Angeles* were equipped to fire Regulus cruise missiles. Full details of the ships converted to missile cruisers (CG) are given below under Major Surface Ships.

DESTROYERS

No	Name	Fate
Benson-Livermore class: launched 1941–42, 1800t standard		
DMS 19	ELLYSON	Japanese *Asakaze* 1954
DMS 20	HAMBLETON	Decommissioned 1955, stricken 1971
DMS 21	RODMAN	Taiwanese *Hsieng Yang* 1955
DMS 23	MACOMB	Japanese *Hatakaze* 1954
DMS 25	FITCH	Decommissioned 1956, stricken 1971
DMS 26	HOBSON	Lost in collision with *Wasp*, 26.4.52
DMS 33	CARMICK	Decommissioned 1954, stricken 1971
DMS 34	DOYLE	Decommissioned 1955, stricken 1971
DMS 35	ENDICOTT	Decommissioned 1955, stricken 1969
DMS 27	JEFFERS	Decommissioned 1955, stricken 1971

No	Name	Fate
DMS 38	THOMPSON	Decommissioned 1955, stricken 1971
DMS 30	GHERARDI	Decommissioned 1955, stricken 1971

Fletcher class: launched 1942–44, 2300t standard

No	Name	Fate
DD 445	FLETCHER	DDE 1949–69, stricken 1969, BU 1972
DD 446	RADFORD	DDE 1949–69, stricken 1969, BU
DD 447	JENKINS	DDE 1949–69, stricken 1969, BU
DD 449	NICHOLAS	DDE 1951–70, stricken 1970, BU
DD 450	O'BANNON	DDE 1951–70, stricken 1971, sold 1972
DD 465	SAUFLEY	DDE 1949–65, stricken 1966, target 1968
DD 466	WALLER	DDE 1950–69, stricken 1969, target 1970
DD 468	TAYLOR	DDE 1951–69, Italian *Lanciere* 1969, spares
DD 470	BACHE	DDE 1951–68, grounded, stricken 1968
DD 471	BEALE	DDE 1951–68, stricken 1968, target 1969
DD 498	PHILIP	DDE 1950–68, stricken 1968, sunk in storm 1972
DD 499	RENSHAW	DDE 1950–70, stricken 1970
DD 507	CONWAY	DDE 1950–69, stricken 1969, target
DD 508	CONY	DDE 1949–69, stricken 1969, target 1970
DD 510	EATON	DDE 1951–69, stricken 1969, target 1970
DD 517	WALKER	DDE 1950–69, Italian *Fante* 1969
DD 519	DALY*	Active 1951–60, stricken 1974
DD 520	ISHERWOOD*	Active 1951–61, Peruvian *Guise* 1961
DD 521	KIMBERLEY	Active 1951–54, Taiwanese *An Yang* 1967
DD 527	AMMEN*	Active 1951–60, stricken 1960
DD 528	MULLANY*	Active 1951–71, Taiwanese *Ching Yang* 1971
DD 530	TRATHAN*	Active 1951–65, stricken 1972, target
DD 531	HAZELWOOD	Active 1951–65, stricken 1974
DD 532	HEERMAN*	Active 1951–57, Argentinian *Brown* 1961
DD 534	McCORD	Active 1951–54, stricken 1971
DD 535	MILLER*	Active 1951–54, stricken 1972
DD 536	OWEN	Active 1951–58, stricken 1973
DD 537	THE SULLIVANS*	Activated for Korean War, stricken 1974
DD 538	STEPHEN POTTER	Active 1951–58, stricken 1974
DD 539	TINGEY	active 1951–53, stricken 1965, target 1966
DD 540	TWINING	Active (reserve TS and full service) to 1971, stricken 1971, Taiwanese *Kwei Yang*
DD 541	YARNALL	Active 1950–58, Taiwanese *Kuen Yang* 1968
DD 544	BOYD*	Active 1950–69, Turkish *Iskenderun* 1969
DD 545	BRADFORD	Active 1950–61, Greek *Thyella* 1962
DD 546	BROWN	Active 1950–62, Greek *Navarinon* 1962
DD 547	COWELL*	Active 1951–71, Argentinian *Almirante Storni* 1971
DD 556	HAILEY*	Active 1951–60, Brazilian *Pernambuco* 1961
DD 558	LAWS	Active 1951–64, stricken 1973
DD 561	PRITCHETT*	Active 1951–70, Italian *Geniere* 1970
DD 562	ROBINSON	Active 1951–64, stricken 1974
DD 563	ROSS	Active 1951–59, stricken 1974
DD 564	ROWE*	Active 1951–59, stricken 1974
DD 565	SMALLEY	Active 1951–57, stricken 1965
DD 566	STODDARD*	Active 1951–69, stricken 1975
DD 567	WATTS	Active 1951–69, stricken 1974
DD 568	WREN	Active 1951–63, stricken 1974
DD 576	MURRAY	DDE 1951–65, stricken 1965
DD 577	SPROSTON	DDE 1950–65, stricken 1968
DD 596	SHIELDS	Active (reserve TS and full service) to 1972, Brazilian *Maranhao* 1972
DD 629	ABBOT*	Active 1951–65, stricken 1974
DD 630	BRAINE*	Active 1951–71, Argentinian *Domecq Garcia* 1971
DD 631	ERBEN	Active 1951–58, Korean *Chung Mu* 1963
DD 642	HALE*	Active 1951–60, Colombian *Antioquia* 1961
DD 643	SIGOURNEY	Active 1951–1960, stricken
DD 644	STEMBEL*	Active 1951–58, Argentinian *Rosales* 1961
DD 650	CAPERTON*	Active 1951–60, stricken 1974
DD 651	COGSWELL*	Active 1951–69, Turkish *Izmit* 1969
DD 652	INGERSOLL*	Active 1951–70, stricken, target 1974
DD 653	KNAPP	Active 1951–57, stricken 1972
DD 654	BEARSS	Active 1951–74, stricken 1974
DD 655	JOHN HOOD*	Active 1951–74, stricken 1974
DD 656	VAN VALKENBURGH	Active 1951–53, Turkish *Izmir* 1967
DD 657	CHARLES J BADGER	Active 1951–57, to Chile for spares 1974
DD 658	COLAHAN	Active (reserve training and full service) to 1966, stricken, target 1966
DD 659	DASHIELL*	Active 1951–60, stricken 1974
DD 661	KIDD	Active 1951–64, stricken 1974
DD 666	BLACK*	Active 1951–69, stricken 1969
DD 667	CHAUNCEY	Active 1950–54, stricken 1972
DD 668	CLARENCE K BRONSON	Active 1951–60, Turkish *Istanbul* 1967
DD 669	COTTEN*	Active 1951–60, stricken 1974
DD 670	DORTCH*	Active 1951–57, Argentinian *Espora* 1961
DD 671	GATLING	Active 1951–60, stricken 1974
DD 672	HEALEY	Active 1951–58, stricken 1974
DD 673	HICKOX	Active 1951–57, Korean *Pusan* 1968
DD 674	HUNT*	Active 1951–63, stricken 1974
DD 675	LEWIS HANCOCK	Active 1951–57, Brazilian *Piaui* 1967
DD 676	MARSHALL	Active 1951–69, stricken 1969
DD 677	MC DERMUT*	Active 1950–63, stricken 1965
DD 678	MC GOWAN*	Active 1951–60, Spanish *Jorge Juan* 1960
DD 679	MC NAIR*	Active 1951–63, stricken 1974
DD 680	MELVIN	Active 1951–54, stricken 1974
DD 681	HOPEWELL*	Active 1951–70, stricken 1970, target 1972
DD 682	PORTERFIELD	active 1951–69, stricken 1975
DD 683	STOCKHAM	Active 1951–57, stricken 1974
DD 684	WEDDERBURN	Active (reserve and full service) to 1969, stricken 1969
DD 685	PICKING*	Active 1951–69, stricken 1975
DD 686	HALSEY POWELL	Active 1951–68, Korean *Seoul* 1968
DD 687	UHLMANN*	Active (reserve training and full service) to 1972, last active *Fletcher*, stricken 1972
DD 688	REMEY	Active 1951–53, stricken
DD 689	WADLEIGH*	Active 1951–62, Chilean *Blanco Encalada* 1962
DD 793	CASSIN YOUNG*	Active 1951–60, stricken 1974
DD 794	IRWIN*	Active 1951–58, Brazilian *Santa Catarina* 1968
DD 795	PRESTON*	Active 1951–69, Turkish *Icel* 1969
DD 796	BENHAM*	Active 1951–60, Peruvian *Villar* 1960
DD 797	CUSHING	Active 1951–60, Brazilian *Parana* 1961
DD 798	MONSSEN	Active 1951–57, stricken 1963
DD 799	JARVIS*	Active 1951–60, Spanish *Alcala Galiano* 1960
DD 800	PORTER	Active 1951–53, stricken 1972
DD 802	GREGORY	Active 1951–64, stricken 1966, non-operable training hulk *Indoctrinator* 1966–71 at San Diego, experimental hulk from 1971
DD 804	ROOKS*	Active 1951–62, Chilean *Cochrane* 1962

Allen M Sumner class: launched 1943–44, 2600t standard

No	Name	Fate
DD 692	ALLEN M SUMNER*	Decommissioned 1973, stricken, memorial
DD 693	MOALE*	Decommissioned 1973, stricken
DD 694	INGRAHAM*	Greek *Miaoulis* 1971
DD 696	ENGLISH	Taiwanese *Hui Yang* 1970
DD 697	CHARLES S SPERRY*	Stricken 1973, Chilean *Ministro Zenteno* 1974
DD 698	AULT*	Decommissioned briefly 1950, stricken 1973
DD 699	WALDRON*	Decommissioned briefly 1950, stricken 1973, Colombian *Santander* 1973
DD 700	HAYNESWORTH	Decommissioned briefly 1950 Taiwanese *Yuen Yang* 1970
DD 701	JOHN W WEEKS	Stricken 1970
DD 702	HANK	Argentinian *Segui* 1972
DD 703	WALLACE L LIND*	Korean *Dae Gu* 1973
DD 704	BORIE*	Argentinian *Bouchard* 1972
DD 705	COMPTON	Brazilian *Matto Grosso* 1972
DD 706	GAINARD	Stricken 1971
DD 707	SOLEY	Stricken 1970
DD 708	HARLAN R DICKSON	Stricken 1972
DD 709	HUGH PURVIS*	Turkish *Zafer* 1972
DD 722	BARTON	Active 1949–68, stricken 1968, target
DD 723	WALKE*	Active 1950–70, stricken 1974
DD 724	LAFFEY	Active 1951–75
DD 725	O'BRIEN*	Active 1950–72, target 1972
DD 727	DE HAVEN*	Active to 1971, Korean *Inchon* 1973
DD 728	MANSFIELD*	Active to 1971
DD 729	LYMAN K SWENSON*	Active to 1971
DD 730	COLLETT*	Active to 1970
DD 731	MADDOX	Active to 1972, Taiwanese *Po Yang* 1972
DD 732	J HYMAN	Stricken 1969
DD 734	PURDY	Stricken 1973
DD 736	THOMAS E FRASER	Active to 1955, minelayer DM 24, stricken 1970
DD 737	SHANNON	Active to 1955, minelayer DM 25, stricken 1970

No	Name	Fate
DD 738	HARRY F BAUER	Active to 1956, minelayer DM 26, stricken 1971
DD 744	BLUE*	Active 1949–71, stricken 1974
DD 745	BRUSH	Taiwanese *Hsiang Yang* 1969
DD 746	TAUSSIG*	Stricken 1970
DD 747	SAMUEL N MOORE	Taiwanese *Heng Yang* 1969
DD 748	HARRY E HUBBARD	Stricken 1969
DD 750	SHEA	Active to 1958, minelayer DM 30, stricken 1973
DD 752	ALFRED A CUNNINGHAM*	Active 1950–71, stricken 1974
DD 753	JOHN R PIERCE	Stricken 1973
DD 754	FRANK E EVANS*	Active 1950–69, sunk in collision with HMAS *Melbourne* 30.6.69
DD 755	JOHN A BOLE*	Decommissioned 1970
DD 756	BEATTY	Venezuelan *Carabobo* 1972
DD 757	PUTNAM*	Laid up 1949–50, stricken 1973
DD 758	STRONG*	Brazilian *Rio Grande de Norte* 1973
DD 759	LOFBERG*	Decommissioned 1971
DD 760	JOHN W THOMASON*	Decommissioned 1970
DD 761	BUCK*	Brazilian *Alacoas* 1973
DD 762	HENLEY	Briefly laid up 1950, stricken 1973
DD 770	LOWERY*	Active 1950–73, Brazilian *Espiritu Santo* 1973
DD 772	GWIN	Decommissioned 1958, minelayer DM 33, Turkish *Muavenet* 1971
DD 775	WILLARD KEITH	Active 1950–72, Colombian *Caldas* 1972
DD 776	JAMES C OWENS*	Briefly laid up 1950, decommissioned 1973, Brazilian *Sergipe* 1973
DD 777	ZELLARS*	Decommissioned 1971, Iranian *Barb* 1971
DD 778	MASSEY*	Decommissioned 1969, stricken 1972
DD 779	DOUGLAS H FOX*	Briefly laid up 1950, Chilean *Ministro Portales* 1974
DD 780	STORMES*	Briefly laid up 1950, decommissioned 1970, Iranian *Palang* 1973
DD 781	ROBERT K HUNTINGTON*	Stricken 1973, Venezuelan *Falcon* 1973
DD 857	BRISTOL	Taiwanese *Hwa Yang* 1969

Gearing class: launched 1944–46, 2600t standard

No	Name	Fate
DD 710	GEARING	FRAM I, stricken 1973
DD 711	EUGENE A GREENE	DDR 1952, FRAM I, Spanish *Churruca* 1972
DD 712	GYATT	DDG 1956, no FRAM, stricken 1969, target
DD 713	KENNETH D BAILEY	DDR 1953, FRAM II, stricken 1974
DD 714	WILLIAM R RUSH	DDR 1953, FRAM I, Korean *Kang Won* 1974
DD 715	WILLIAM W WOOD	DDR 1953, FRAM I, stricken 1976
DD 716	WILTSIE	FRAM I, Pakistani *Tariq* 1976
DD 717	THEODORE E CHANDLER	FRAM I, stricken 1975
DD 718	HAMNER	FRAM I, stricken 1979, Taiwanese *Chao Yang* 1981
DD 719	EPPERSON	DDE, FRAM I, Pakistani *Taimur* 1975
DD 742	FRANK KNOX	DDR 1945, FRAM II, Greek *Themistocles* 1971
DD 743	SOUTHERLAND	DDR 1945, FRAM I, for sale 1981
DD 763	WILLIAM C LANE	FRAM I, extant 1982 as TS
DD 764	LLOYD N THOMAS	DDE 1949, FRAM II, Taiwanese *Dang Yang* 1972
DD 765	KEPPLER	DDE 1949, FRAM II, Turkish *Tinaztepe* 1972
DD 782	ROWAN	FRAM I, Taiwanese *Chao Yang* 1977
DD 783	GURKE	FRAM I, Greek *Tombazis* 1977
DD 784	McKEAN	FRAM I, for sale 1981
DD 785	HENDERSON	FRAM I, Pakistani *Tughril* 1980
DD 786	RICHARD B ANDERSON	FRAM I, Taiwanese *Kai Yang* 1975
DD 787	JAMES E KYES	FRAM I, Taiwanese *Chien Yang* 1973
DD 788	HOLLISTER	FRAM I, stricken 1979
DD 789	EVERSOLE	FRAM I, Turkish *Gayret* 1973
DD 790	SHELTON	FRAM I, Taiwanese *Lao Yang* 1973
DD 805	CHEVALIER	DDR 1945, FRAM II, Korean *Chung Buk* 1975
DD 806	HIGBEE	DDR 1945, FRAM I, stricken 1979
DD 807	BENNER	DDR 1945, FRAM II, stricken 1974, target
DD 808	DENNIS J BUCKLEY	FRAM I, stricken 1973

No	Name	Fate
DD 817	CORRY	DDR 1954, FRAM I, stricken 1980, Greek *Kreizis* 1981
DD 818	NEW	FRAM I, Korean *Taejon* 1976
DD 819	HOLDER	FRAM I, Ecuadorian *Alfaro* 1978
DD 820	RICH	FRAM I, stricken 1977
DD 821	JOHNSTON	FRAM I, stricken 1980, Taiwanese (name?) 1981
DD 822	ROBERT H McCARD	FRAM I Striken 1980, Turkish *Kilic Ali Pasa* 1980
DD 823	SAMUEL B ROBERTS	FRAM I, stricken 1970
DD 824	BASILONE	DDE, FRAM I, stricken 1977
DD 825	CARPENTER	DDE, FRAM I, stricken 1980, Turkish *Anitepe* 1981
DD 826	AGERHOLM	FRAM I, stricken 1978, target
DD 827	ROBERT A OWENS	DDE, FRAM I, Turkish *Aleiptepe* 1982
DD 828	TIMMERMAN	Experimental destroyer (machinery), stricken 1958
DD 829	MYLES C FOX	DDR 1945, FRAM II, Greek *Apostolis* 1980
DD 830	EVERETT F LARSON	DDR 1945, FRAM II, Korean *Jeong Buk* 1975
DD 831	GOODRICH	DDR 1945, FRAM II, stricken 1974
DD 832	HANSON	DDR 1945, FRAM I, Taiwanese *Liao Yang* 1973
DD 833	HERBERT J THOMAS	DDR 1945, FRAM I, Taiwanese *Han Yang* 1974
DD 834	TURNER	DDR 1945, FRAM II, stricken 1969
DD 835	CHARLES P CECIL	DDR 1945, FRAM I, to Greece for spares 1980
DD 836	GEORGE K MACKENZIE	FRAM I, stricken 1976, target
DD 837	SARSFIELD	FRAM I, Taiwanese *Te Yang* 1976
DD 838	ERNEST G SMALL	DDR 1952, FRAM II, Taiwanese *Fu Yang* 1971
DD 839	POWER	FRAM I, Taiwanese *Shen Yang* 1976
DD 840	GLENNON	FRAM I, stricken 1976
DD 841	NOA	FRAM I, Spanish Blas de Lezo 1975
DD 842	FISKE	DDR 1952, FRAM I, stricken 1980, Turkish *Piyale Pasa* 1980
DD 843	WARRINGTON	FRAM I, stricken 1972
DD 844	PERRY	FRAM I, stricken 1973 (FRAM I prototype)
DD 845	BAUSSELL	FRAM I, stricken 1978
DD 846	OZBOURN	FRAM I, stricken 1975
DD 847	ROBERT L WILSON	FRAM I, stricken 1974
DD 848	WITEK	No FRAM, stricken 1968
DD 849	RICHARD E KRAUS	FRAM I, Korean *Kwang Ju* 1976
DD 850	JOSEPH P KENNEDY, JR	FRAM I, memorial 1973
DD 851	RUPERTUS	FRAM I, Greek *Kontouriotis* 1973
DD 852	LEONARD F MASON	FRAM I, Taiwanese *Lai Yang* 1976
DD 853	CHARLES H ROAN	FRAM I, Turkish *Cakmak* 1973
DD 858	FRED T BERRY	DDE 1949, FRAM II, stricken 1970
DD 859	NORRIS	DDE 1949, FRAM II, Turkish *Kocatepe* 1974
DD 860	McCAFFERY	DDE 1949, FRAM II, stricken 1973
DD 861	HARWOOD	DDE 1949, FRAM II, Turkish *Kocatepe* 1973, sunk in error by Turkish aircraft 7.7.74
DD 862	VOGELGESANG	FRAM I, Mexican *Quietźalcoatl* 1982
DD 863	STEINAKER	DDR 1953, FRAM I, Mexican *Netzahualcoyotl* 1982
DD 864	HAROLD J ELLISON	FRAM I, extant 1982 at TS
DD 865	CHARLES R WARE	FRAM I, stricken 1974
DD 866	CONE	FRAM I, extant 1982 as TS
DD 867	STRIBLING	FRAM I, stricken 1976
DD 868	BROWNSON	FRAM I, stricken 1976
DD 869	ARNOLD J ISBELL	FRAM I, Greek *Sachtouris* 1973
DD 870	FECHTELER	DDR 1953, stricken 1970
DD 871	DAMATO	FRAM I, stricken 1980, Pakistani *Tippu Sultan* 1980
DD 872	FORREST ROYAL	FRAM I, Turkish *Adatepe* 1973
DD 873	HAWKINS	DDR 1945, FRAM I, stricken 1979
DD 874	DUNCAN	DDR 1945, FRAM II, stricken 1973, target
DD 875	HENRY W TUCKER	DDR 1945, FRAM I, Brazilian *Marcilio Dias* 1973

No	Name	Fate
DD 876	ROGERS	DDR 1945, FRAM I, stricken 1980, South Korean *Jean Ju* 1981
DD 877	PERKINS	DDR 1945, FRAM II, Argentinian *Py* 1973
DD 878	VESOLE	DDR 1945, FRAM I, stricken 1976
DD 879	LEARY	DDR 1945, FRAM I, Spanish *Langara* 1975
DD 880	DYESS	DDR 1945, FRAM I, stricken 1980, Greek (name?)1981
DD 881	BORDELON	DDR 1945, FRAM I, stricken 1977
DD 882	FURSE	DDR 1945, FRAM I, Spanish *Gravina* 1972
DD 883	NEWMAN K PERRY	DDR 1945, FRAM I, stricken 1980, South Korean *Kyong Ki* 1981
DD 884	FLOYD B PARKS	FRAM I, stricken 1973
DD 885	JOHN R CRAIG	FRAM I, stricken 1979, target
DD 886	ORLECK	FRAM I, extant 1982 as TS
DD 887	BRINKLEY BASS	FRAM I, Brazilian *Marriz e Barros* 1973
DD 888	STICKELL	FRAM I, DDR 1953, Greek *Kanaris* 1973
DD 889	O'HARE	DDR 1953, FRAM I, Spanish *Mendez Nunez* 1975
DD 890	MEREDITH	FRAM I, Turkish *Savastepe* 1979

Benson-Livermore class
Only the minesweeper conversions listed remained in service.

Fletcher class
Other ships of the class were also transferred abroad, but since they were never active in the US Navy after 1947 they have not been listed. Ships of this class marked* were modified with 4–5in/38 (4×1), 6–3in/50 (3×2), 5–21in TT (1×5).

Allen M Sumner class
Unless otherwise noted, all ships listed were in continuous service until stricken or transferred. Ships of this class marked* received a FRAM II modernisation.

Gearing class
All ships remained active after 1945. The remaining ships in 1982 were serving in the Naval Reserve Force as training units and were expected to be sold in 1983–84.

DESTROYER ESCORTS

No	Name	Fate
Buckley class (TE type): launched 1943–44, 1400t standard		
DE 213	WILLIAM T POWELL	Active (training) to 1958 as DER conversion 1945, stricken 1965
DE 217	COOLBAUGH	Active to 1959, stricken 1972
DE 218	DARBY	Active 1950–58, then training, stricken 1968, target 1970
DE 219	J DOUGLAS BLACKWOOD	Active 1951–58, then training, active again during Berlin crisis 1961–62, stricken 1970, target
DE 634	WHITEHURST	Active 1950–62, stricken 1969
DE 644	VAMMEN	Active 1952–69, special ASW conversion
DE 667	WISEMAN	Active 1950–59, 1961–62, stricken 1973
DE 679	GREENWOOD	Active to 1958, then 1961–66, stricken 1967
DE 680	LOESER	Active 1951–68, stricken 1968
DE 696	SPANGLER	Active to 1958, stricken 1972
DE 697	GEORGE	Active to 1958, stricken 1969
DE 698	RABY	Active to 1953, stricken 1968
DE 699	MARSH	Active to 1958, then 1961–69, stricken 1971
DE 700	CURRIER	Active to 1960, stricken 1966
DE 704	CRONIN	DEC 1951–53, stricken 1970
DE 705	FRYBARGER	DEC 1950–54, stricken 1972
DE 791	MALOY	DEC 1950–54, stricken 1972
Rudderow class (TEV type): launched 1944, 1400t standard		
DE 583	GEORGE A JOHNSON	Active 1950–57, stricken 1965
DE 585	DANIEL A JOY	Active 1950–65, stricken 1966
DE 587	THOMAS F NICKEL	Active 1950–58, stricken 1972
DE 708	PARLE	Active 1951–62, then training, last active Second World War DE, stricken 1970, target
DE 684	DE LONG	Active 1951–69, stricken 1969
DE 685	COATES	Active 1951–70, stricken 1970
John C Butler class (WGT type): launched 1943–44, 1400t standard		
DE 255	SELLSTROM	DER 1956–60, stricken 1965

No	Name	Fate
DE 316	HARVESON	DER 1951–60, stricken 1966
DE 317	JOYCE	DER 1951–60, stricken 1972
DE 318	KIRKPATRICK	DER 1952–60, stricken 1974
DE 322	NEWELL	DER 1957–68, stricken 1968
DE 324	FALGOUT	CG service 1951–54, DER 1955–75, stricken 1975, target
DE 325	LOWE	CG service 1951–54, DER 1955–68, stricken 1968
DE 326	THOMAS J GARY	DER 1957–73, Tunisian *President Bourgiba* 1973
DE 327	BRISTER	DER 1956–68, stricken
DE 328	FINCH	CG service 1951–4, DER 1956–73, stricken 1974, target
DE 329	KRETCHMER	CG 1951–54, DER 1956–73, stricken 1973
DE 331	KOINER	CG 1951–54, DER 1955–68, stricken 1968
DE 332	PRICE	DER 1956–60, stricken
DE 333	STRICKLAND	DER 1952–60, stricken 1972
DE 334	FORSTER	CG 1951–4, DER 1956–71, Vietnamese *Tran Kanh Du*
DE 336	ROY O'HALE	DER 1957–63, stricken 1974
DE 339	JOHN C BUTLER	Active 1950–57, stricken 1970
DE 341	RAYMOND	Active 1951–58, stricken 1972
DE 351	MAURICE J MANUEL	Active 1951–57, stricken 1966, target
DE 352	NAIFEH	Active 1951–60, stricken 1966, target
DE 354	KENNETH M WILLETT	Active 1951–59, stricken 1972, target 1974
DE 357	GEORGE E DAVIS	Active 1951–4, stricken 1972
DE 359	WOODSON	Active 1951–52, stricken 1965
DE 360	JOHNNIE HUTCHINS	Active 1950–58, stricken 1972
DE 361	WALTON	Active 1951–68, stricken 1968, target 1969
DE 364	ROMBACH	Active to 1958, stricken 1972
DE 365	McGINTY	Active 1951–58, 1961–62, stricken 1968
DE 366	ALVIN C COCKRELL	Active 1951–68, stricken 1968, target 1969
DE 369	THADDEUS PARKER	Active 1951–67, stricken 1967
DE 406	EDMONDS	Active 1951–72, stricken
DE 414	LE RAY WILSON	Active 1951–59, stricken 1972
DE 416	MELVIN R NAWMAN	Active 1951–60, stricken 1972
DE 418	TABBERER	Active 1951–60, stricken 1972
DE 419	ROBERT F KELLER	Active 1950–59, 1961–62, stricken 1972
DE 421	CHESTER T O'BRIEN	Active 1951–59, stricken 1972
DE 422	DOUGLAS A MUNRO	Active 1951–60
DE 424	HAAS	Active 1951–58, sold 1967
DE 440	McCOY REYNOLDS	Active 1951–57, Portuguese *Corte Real*
DE 441	WILLIAM SEIVERLING	Active 1950–57, stricken 1972
DE 442	ULVERT M MOORE	Active 1951–58, stricken 1965, target 1966
DE 444	GOSS	Active 1951–58, stricken 1966
DE 445	GRADY	Active 1951–57, sold 1969
DE 446	CHARLES E BRANNON	Active 1950–60, sold 1969
DE 447	ALBERT T HARRIS	Active 1951–68, stricken 1968
DE 448	CROSS	Active 1951–58, stricken 1966
DE 449	HANNA	Active 1950–59, stricken 1972
DE 508	GILLIGAN	Active 1950–59, stricken 1972
DE 509	FORMOE	Active 1951–57, Portuguese *Diogo Cao*
DE 510	HEYLIGER	Active 1951–58, stricken 1966
DE 531	EDWARD H ALLEN	Active 1951–58, stricken 1972
DE 532	TWEEDY	Active 1952–69, ASW conversion, stricken 1969, target 1970
DE 534	SILVERSTEIN	Active 1951–59, stricken 1972
DE 535	LEWIS	Active 1952–60, ASW conversion, stricken 1966
DE 537	RIZZIE	Active 1951–58, stricken 1972
DE 538	OSBERG	Active 1951–57, stricken 1972
DE 539	WAGNER	Completed as DER 1955, decommissioned 1960, stricken 1974
DE 540	VANDIVER	Completed as DER 1955, decommissioned 1960, stricken 1974
Cannon class (DET type): launched 1943–44, 1200t standard		
DE 745	SNYDER	Active 1950–60, stricken 1972

UNITED STATES

Tweedy (ASW conversion) 1958   USN

No	Name	Fate
Edsall class (FMR type): launched 1942–43, 1250t standard		
DE 746	HEMMINGER	Active 1950–58, Thai *Pin Klao*
DE 748	TILLS	Active 1950–68, stricken 1968
DE 749	ROBERTS	Active 1950–64, stricken 1968
DE 750	McCLELLAND	Active 1950–60, stricken 1972
DE 765	EARL K OLSEN	Active 1950–58, stricken 1972
Edsall class (FMR type): launched 1942–43, 1250t standard		
DE 133	PILLSBURY	DER 1955–60, stricken 1965
DE 142	FESSENDEN	DER 1952–60, stricken 1966, target 1967
DE 145	HUSE	Active 1951–65, stricken 1973
DE 147	BLAIR	Active 1951–6, then DER 1957–72, stricken
DE 239	STURTEVANT	Active 1951–56, DER 1957–60, stricken 1972
DE 244	OTTERSTETTER	DER 1952–60, stricken 1974
DE 246	SNOWDEN	Active 1951–60, 1961–62, stricken 1968
DE 251	CAMP	DER 1956–71, Vietnamese *Tran Hung Dao*, escaped to Philippines 1975, became *Rajah Lakandula*
DE 252	HOWARD D CROW	Active 1951–68, stricken 1968
DE 382	RAMSDEN	CG 1951–4, DER 1957–60
DE 383	MILLS	DER 1957–70
DE 384	RHODES	DER 1955–63
DE 386	SAVAGE	DER 1955–69
DE 387	VANCE	CG 1951–54, DER 1956–69
DE 388	LANSING	CG 1951–54, DER 1956–65, stricken 1974
DE 389	DURANT	CG 1951–54, DER 1955–74, stricken
DE 390	CALCATERRA	DER 1955–73, stricken 1973
DE 391	CHAMBERS	CG 1951–54, DER 1955–60
DE 393	HAVERFIELD	DER 1955–69, stricken 1969
DE 397	WILHOITE	DER 1955–69, stricken 1969
DE 400	HISSEM	DER 1956–70, stricken 1975, target
DE 797	WEEDEN	Active 1950–58, stricken 1968
DE 800	JACK W WILKE	Active to 1960, stricken 1971, sold 1974

Active periods do not always include period of Naval Reserve Training. Ships were reactivated in 1961 for the Berlin Crisis.

FRIGATES

No	Name	Fate
Tacoma class: launched 1943, 1500t standard		
PF 3	TACOMA	Activated 1950, Korean *Taedong* 1951
PF 4	SAUSALITO	Activated 1950, Korean *Imchin* 1953
PF 5	HOQUIAM	Activated 1950, Korean *Naktong* 1951
PF 7	ALBUQUERQUE	Activated 1950, Japanese *Tochi* 1953
PF 8	EVERETT	Activated 1950, Japanese *Kiri* 1953
PF 21	BAYONNE	Activated 1950, Japanese *Buna* 1953
PF 22	GLOUCESTER	Activated 1950, Japanese *Tsuge* 1953
PF 27	NEWPORT	Activated 1950, Japanese *Kaede* 1953
PF 36	GLENDALE	Activated 1950, Thai *Tachin* 1951
PF 46	BISBEE	Activated 1950, Colombian *Capitan Tono* 1952
PF 47	GALLUP	Activated 1950, Thai *Prasae* 1951
PF 51	BURLINGTON	Activated 1950, decommissioned at Yokosuka 1952, Colombian *Almirante Bron* 1953
PF 70	EVANSVILLE	Activated 1950, Japanese *Keyaki* 1953

Second World War Patrol Frigates (PF) with reciprocating engines. All were stricken after the war, but some, returned by the Soviet Union, were in Japan at the outbreak of the Korean War and were re-acquired by the United States for local escort duties. Each ship was active for a year or more under the US flag, some operating during the Wonsan landings. Two frigates, PF 48 and PF 49, were lent to South Korea without US use in 1950.

Lansing (DER conversion) 16.11.63   USN

SUBMARINES

No	Name	Fate
Gato class: launched 1941–43, 1500t standard		
SS 214	GROUPER	Active to 1968, SSK conversion 1951, stricken 1968
SS 220	BARB	Active 1951–54, converted to GUPPY 1B and transferred to Italy as *Enrico Tazzoli* 1954
SS 222	BLUEFISH	Active 1952–53, stricken 1959
SS 229	FLYING FISH	Active to 1954, AGSS 1950, stricken 1958
SS 230	FINBACK	Decommissioned 1950, stricken 1958
SS 240	ANGLER	Active 1951–68, SSK 1953, stricken 1971
SS 241	BASHAW	Active to 1949, then 1951–69, SSK 1953, stricken 1969
SS 242	BLUEGILL	Active 1951–69, SSK 1953, stricken 1969, scuttled 1970
SS 243	BREAM	Active 1951–69, SSK 1953, stricken 1969, target
SS 244	CAVALLA	Active 1951–68, SSK 1953, stricken 1969, memorial
SS 246	CROAKER	Active 1951–68, SSK 1953, stricken 1971 memorial
SS 247	DACE	Active 1951–54, converted to GUPPY 1B for transfer to Italy as *Leonardo da Vinci* 1955
SS 267	POMPON	SSR 1951–60, stricken 1960
SS 269	RASHER	SSR 1951–67, stricken 1971
SS 270	RATON	SSR 1952–69, stricken 1969
SS 271	RAY	SSR 1951–58, stricken 1960
SS 272	REDFIN	SSR 1953–67, stricken 1970
SS 274	ROCK	SSR 1953–69, stricken 1969
SS 282	TUNNY	SSG 1953–65, APSS 1966–69, stricken 1969
Balao class: launched 1942–45, 1525t standard		
SS 285	BALAO	Active 1952–53, stricken 1963
SS 287	BOWFIN	Active 1951–54, then training, stricken 1971, memorial
SS 291	CREVALLE	Active 1951–55, 1957–62, stricken 1968
SS 298	LIONFISH	Active 1951–53, then training, stricken 1971, memorial
SS 299	MANTA	Active 1949–55, then training, stricken 1967, target
SS 302	SABALO	Active 1951–71, Fleet Snorkel 1952, stricken 1971
SS 303	SABLEFISH	Active to 1969, Fleet Snorkel 1951, stricken 1969
SS 307	TILEFISH	Active to 1959, Fleet Snorkel 1960 for Venezuela as *Carite*
SS 309	ASPRO	Active 1951–54, stricken 1962, target
SS 310	BATFISH	Active 1952–60, then training, stricken 1969, memorial
SS 311	ARCHERFISH	Active 1952–55, 1957–68, stricken 1969, target
SS 312	BURRFISH	SSR 1948–56, to Canada as *Grilse* 1961
SS 313	PERCH	SSP 1948–67, stricken 1971
SS 315	SEALION	SSP 1948–60, then training, stricken 1977 and test hulk

No	Name	Fate
SS 317	BARBERO	SSA 1948–50, SSG 1955–64, stricken 1964, target
SS 318	BAYA	Active 1948–72 as sonar test ship, stricken 1972, BU
SS 319	BECUNA	Active to 1969, GUPPY 1A 1951, stricken 1973, memorial
SS 320	BERGALL	Active to 1959, Fleet Snorkel 1952, to Turkey as *Turgut Reis* 1958
SS 322	BLACKFIN	Active 1951–72 as GUPPY 1A, stricken 1972, target
SS 323	CAIMAN	Active to 1972, GUPPY 1A 1951, to Turkey as *Dumlupinar* 1972
SS 324	BLENNY	Active to 1969, GUPPY 1A 1951, stricken 1973, target
SS 325	BLOWER	Active to 1950, then Fleet Snorkel for Turkey as *Dumlupinar*
SS 326	BLUEBACK	Active to 1948, then to Turkey as *Ikinci Inonu*
SS 327	BOARFISH	Active to 1948, then to Turkey as *Sakarya*
SS 329	CHUB	Active to 1948, then to Turkey as *Gur*
SS 330	BRILL	Active to 1948, then to Turkey as *Birinci Inonu*
SS 331	BUGARA	Active to 1970, Fleet Snorkel 1951, stricken 1971, foundered
SS 333	BUMPER	Active to 1950, then Fleet Snorkel for Turkey as *Canakkale*
SS 336	CAPITAINE	Active to 1950, then 1957–66, then Fleet Snorkel for Italy as *Alfredo Cappellini*
SS 337	CARBONERO	Active to 1970, SSG 1949, Fleet Snorkel 1952, stricken 1970, target
SS 339	CATFISH	Active to 1971, GUPPY II 1949, Argentine *Santa Fe* 1971
SS 338	CARP	Active to 1968, Fleet Snorkel 1952, stricken 1971
SS 340	ENTEMEDOR	Active to 1948, then 1950–72, GUPPY IIA 1952, Turkish *Preveze* 1973
SS 341	CHIVO	Active to 1971, GUPPY 1A 1951, Argentine *Santiago del Estero* 1971
SS 343	CLAMAGORE	Active to 1975, GUPPY II 1948, GUPPY III 1962, stricken 1975, memorial
SS 344	COBBLER	Active to 1973, GUPPY II 1949, GUPPY 1962, Turkish *Canakkale* 1973
SS 345	COCHINO	GUPPY II 1949, sunk 26.8.49 off Norway
SS 346	CORPORAL	Active to 1973, GUPPY II 1948, GUPPY III 1962, Turkish *Ikinci Inonu* 1973
SS 347	CUBERA	Active to 1972, GUPPY II 1948, Venezuelan *Tiburon* 1972
SS 348	CUSK	Active to 1969, missile test bed 1948, then Fleet Snorkel 1954, stricken 1969
SS 349	DIODON	Active to 1971, GUPPY II 1948, stricken 1971
SS 350	DOGFISH	Active to 1972, GUPPY II 1948, Brazilian *Guanabara* 1972
SS 351	GREENFISH	Active to 1973, GUPPY II 1948, GUPPY III 1961, Brazilian *Amazonas* 1973
SS 352	HALFBEAK	Active to 1971, GUPPY II 1948, stricken 1971
SS 362	GUAVINA	SSO 1950–59, then training, stricken 1967, target
SS 363	GUITARRO	Active 1952–53, then Fleet Snorkel for Turkey as *Preveze* 1954
SS 364	HAMMERHEAD	Active 1952–53, then Fleet Snorkel for Turkey as *Cerbe* 1954
SS 365	HARDHEAD	GUPPY IIA 1952–72, then Greek *Papanikolis*
SS 368	JALLAO	GUPPY IIA 1954–74, then to Spain as *S 35*
SS 377	MENHADEN	Active 1951–71, GUPPY IIA 1953, stricken 1973, target
SS 382	PICUDA	Active 1953–73, GUPPY IIA 1953, Spanish *Narciso Monturiol* 1973
SS 385	BANG	Active 1951–72, GUPPY IIA 1952, Spanish *Cosme Garcia* 1972–74
SS 391	POMFRET	Active 1952–71, GUPPY IIA 1953, Turkish *Oruc Reis* 1971
SS 392	STERLET	Active 1950–68, Fleet Snorkel 1952, stricken 1968, target
SS 393	QUEENFISH	Active to 1963, stricken, target
SS 394	RAZORBACK	Active to 1952, then GUPPY IIA 1954–70, Turkish *Murat Reis* 1970
SS 395	REDFISH	Active to 1968, stricken 1968, target
SS 396	RONQUIL	Active to 1952, GUPPY IIA 1953–71, Spanish *Isaac Peral* 1971
SS 397	SCABBARDFISH	Active to 1948, then Fleet Snorkel for Greece as *Trianna* 1965
SS 398	SEGUNDO	Active to 1970, Fleet Snorkel 1951, stricken 1970, target
SS 399	SEA CAT	Active to 1968, Fleet Snorkel 1952, stricken 1968

No	Name	Fate
SS 400	SEA DEVIL	Active to 1948, 1951–54, 1957–64, stricken 1964, target
SS 401	SEA FOX	GUPPY IIA 1953–70, Turkish *Burak Reis* 1970
SS 402	ATULE	GUPPY IA 1951–73, Peruvian *Pacocha* 1974
SS 404	SPIKEFISH	Active to 1963, stricken, target
SS 405	SEA OWL	Active to 1969, Fleet Snorkel 1951, stricken 1969
SS 406	SEA POACHER	Active to 1973, GUPPY IA 1952, Peruvian *La Pedrera* 1974
SS 407	SEA ROBIN	Active to 1970, GUPPY IA 1951, stricken 1970
SS 408	SENNET	Active to 1968, Fleet Snorkel 1952, stricken 1968
SS 409	PIPER	Active to 1967, Fleet Snorkel 1951, stricken 1970
SS 410	THREADFIN	Active 1953–72, GUPPY IIA 1953, Turkish *Birinci Inonu* 1973
SS 415	STICKLEBACK	Active 1951–58, GUPPY IIA 1953, sunk by ramming 30.5.58
SS 416	TIRU	Completed as GUPPY II 1948, GUPPY III 1959, decommissioned 1975, stricken

Tench class: launched 1944–46, 1570t standard

No	Name	Fate
SS 417	TENCH	Active 1950–70, GUPPY IA 1951, stricken 1973
SS 418	THORNBACK	Active 1953–71, GUPPY IIA 1953, Turkish *Uluc Ali Reis* 1972–3
SS 419	TIGRONE	SSR 1948–57, also active 1962–75 as AGSS, stricken 1975, target
SS 420	TIRANTE	GUPPY IIA 1952–73, stricken 1973
SS 421	TRUTTA	Active 1951–72, GUPPY IIA 1953, Turkish *Cerbe* 1972
SS 422	TORO	Active 1947–63, stricken 1963
SS 423	TORSK	Active to 1968, Fleet Snorkel 1952, memorial 1972
SS 424	QUILLBACK	GUPPY IIA 1953–73, stricken 1973
SS 425	TRUMPETFISH	Active to 1973, GUPPY II 1948, GUPPY II 1962, Brazilian *Goias* 1973
SS 426	TUSK	Active to 1973, GUPPY II 1948, Taiwanese *Hai Pao* 1973
SS 475	ARGONAUT	Active to 1968, Fleet Snorkel 1952, Canadian *Rainbow* 1968
SS 476	RUNNER	Active to 1970, Fleet Snorkel 1952, stricken 1971
SS 477	CONGER	Active to 1963, stricken 1963
SS 478	CUTLASS	Active to 1973, GUPPY II 1948, Taiwanese *Hai Shih* 1973
SS 479	DIABOLO	Active to 1964, Fleet Snorkel for Pakistan as *Ghazi* 1964
SS 480	MEDREGAL	Active to 1970, Fleet Snorkel 1952, stricken 1970
SS 481	REQUIN	SSR 1946–59, active to 1968, stricken 1971, memorial
SS 482	IREX	Prototype Fleet Snorkel conversion 1947, active to 1969, stricken
SS 483	SEA LEOPARD	Active to 1973, GUPPY II 1949, stricken 1973
SS 484	ODAX	Prototype GUPPY I 1947, GUPPY II 1951, active to 1972, Brazilian *Rio de Janeiro*
SS 485	SIRAGO	Active to 1972, GUPPY II 1949, stricken 1972
SS 486	POMODON	Active to 1970, GUPPY I 1947, GUPPY II 1951, stricken 1970
SS 487	REMORA	Active to 1973, GUPPY II 1947, GUPPY III 1962, Greek *Katsonis* 1973
SS 488	SARDA	Active to 1964, stricken, BU
SS 489	SPINAX	Completed as SSR, active to 1969, stricken 1969
SS 490	VOLADOR	Active to 1972, completed as GUPPY II 1958, GUPPY III 1963, to Italy as *Gianfranco Gazzana Priarogia* 1972
SS 522	AMBERJACK	Active to 1973, GUPPY II 1947, Brazilian *Ceara* 1973
SS 523	GRAMPUS	Active to 1972, completed as GUPPY II 1950, Brazilian *Rio Grande Do Sul* 1972
SS 524	PICKEREL	Completed as GUPPY II 1949, active to 1972, GUPPY III 1962, Italian *Primo Longobardo* 1972
SS 525	GRENADIER	Completed as GUPPY II 1951, active to 1973, Venezuelan *Picua* 1973

The SSA was a cargo submarine, the SSP were troop-carriers, and the SSO a submarine oiler. These and other conversions are covered in detail in the main tables below.

SSRs and SSKs reverted to fleet submarines about 1960; dates are *entire* active life of the submarine, *not* merely period of specialised service. Other units were very briefly reactivated before transfer abroad; they are not listed. Note, too, that units for Reserve Training Only are not listed; they were carried as 'In Service In Reserve'.

UNITED STATES

MINE WARFARE VESSELS

After the postwar rundown, only ten large minesweepers (AM 108, 109, 127, 277, 373, 384, 385, 286, 288 and 390) remained active on 1 January 1950. The following were recommissioned for the Korean War: AM 62, 100, 101, 104, 107, 110, 111, 112, 114, 117, 119, 122, 123, 126, 131, 220, 239, 249, 252, 255, 261, 275, 283, 296, 315, 316, 317, 318, 319, 320, 323, 341, 372, 374, 375, 376, 377, 378, 380, 382, 383, 387, 389

Similarly, of 57 motor minesweepers (AMS, formerly YMS) on the Navy List in 1950, only 27 were active. All inactive units were recommissioned for Korean War service.

PATROL CRAFT

Most of the wartime patrol craft were discarded after 1945. By 1950 there were 127 173ft PC (of which thirteen were active), as well as 29 180ft PCE and 16 wooden 136ft PCS. Four wartime motor torpedo-boats (PT) were retained for experimentation, awaiting the completion of the four experimental metal-hulled type ordered after 1945. As an indication of the decline of these craft, by 1958 only seven PC were active, together with seven PCE and one PCS; no PT were left.

AMPHIBIOUS CRAFT

Even after the postwar rundown, the Navy still owned 945 of the larger amphibious types in 1950. They included thirty attack cargo ships, 57 Victory type attack transports, 17 former C-3 type attack transports, 92 fast transports (APD), 21 landing ships dock (LSD), 6 LSV (which were never reactivated), 135 LST (of which 26 were active, with another 65 operating as auxiliaries (and two more of postwar construction), 161 LSM, 48 LSMR, 106 support landing ships (LSSL, formerly LCSL), 105 infantry landing ships (LSIL, formerly LCIL), and 129 utility landing ships (LSU, formerly LCT). In addition, the Maritime Commission reserve fleet included 36 discarded attack cargo ships (ten C2, twenty-six S4) and eighty attack transports (60 Victory, 15 S4, the two specially-built Doyens, and three older units). As part of the Korean War programme, all 30 AKA were recommissioned, and six more (AKA 3, 4, 96, 97, 99, and 103) were re-acquired from the Maritime Commission. To the 42 active APA were added 29 more; twelve APD were recommissioned in addition to 19 active units. All LSD were active by the end of 1951, as were 96 LST, 22 LSM,

and 17 LSMR. It does not appear that any LSI or LSSL were activated, and transfers abroad of LSSL began at this time. In addition, 32 LSIL were converted to Underwater Object Locators (AMCU), ten earlier units having been discarded (leaving one, AMCU-11).

FLAGSHIPS

Of fifteen ships completed as amphibious command ships, five remained active after the postwar rundown: AGC 7, 8, 11, 15 and 17. Two more, AGC 12 and 16, were reactivated for the Korean War, but another pair (AGC 8 and 15) laid up during the post-Korea rundown. The inactive units were all stricken in 1959–61, but the five active ones continued throughout the Vietnam War. *Eldorado* (AGC 11) was the last, decommissioned in 1973; her four sisters left service in 1969–71. Service was quite varied. For example, *Adirondack* (AGC 15) was flagship of the Operational Development Force in 1945–49 and as command ship for NATO forces in Southern Europe 1951–53. Others served as command ships in atomic tests and as headquarters ships moored abroad.

THE COAST GUARD

The active Coast Guard Force of the postwar period included thirteen *Owasco* (255ft) cutters, decommissioned in 1973–74 (except for *Sebago*, 1972, and *Iroquois*, 1965), six 'Secretary' class (327ft) cutters of prewar construction (four of which, *Bibb*, *Duane*, *Ingham* and *Campbell*, remain active as of this writing), three 250ft 'Lake' class cutters launched in 1938–41 (*Itasca*, active 1946–50, *Tampa*, 1947–54, and *Mocoma*, 1947–50), one 165ft 'A' class cutter (*Tahoma*, decommissioned 1953), eleven 165ft 'B' Class cutters (*Ariadne*, decommissioned 1968, *Atalanta*, 1950, *Aurora*, 1968, *Cyane*, 1950, *Daphne*, 1950, *Dione*, 1963, *Nemesis*, 1964, *Nike*, 1964, *Pandora*, 1959, *Perseus*, 1959, *Triton*, 1967) and twenty 125ft cutters. It is not clear which of the 230 83-footers remained active postwar.

Note In the tables which follow, all displacement figures are official; they do not represent the results of inclining experiments. Missile magazine capacities include ready-service rounds except where specified. Endurance figures represent design requirements, *not* service figures. Horsepower and speed of nuclear warships are generally classified, and the figures presented are published estimates unless otherwise stated.

MAJOR SURFACE SHIPS

United States design
NB 1/1750 scale

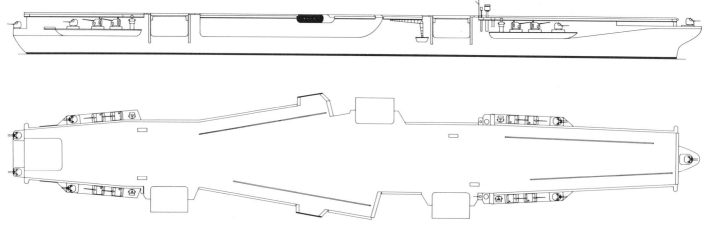

Although she was never completed, *United States* is significant in the course of US carrier development as the progenitor of the *Forrestals* and their successors. Unlike earlier carriers, she was designed specifically to operate a particular class of aircraft, in her case heavy attack planes intended for strategic nuclear operations. Indeed, the earliest proposals were for a carrier without any hangar at all, because the aircraft would be much too large to strike below. Only well into the design were non-strategic

UNITED STATES *aircraft carrier*

Displacement:	66,434ft standard; 78,946t trials; 83,249t full load
Dimensions:	1030ft wl, 1088ft oa × 125ft wl, 190ft ext × 34ft 6in at trials displacement
	314.0m, 331.7m × 38.1m, 57.9m × 10.5m
Machinery:	4-shaft geared turbines, 8 boilers, 280,000shp = 33kts. Range 12,000nm at 20kts
Armament:	8–5in/54, (8×1) 16–3in/70 (8×2), 20–20mm
Sensors:	Radar SPS-6, SPS-8
Complement:	4127

No	Name	Builder	Laid down	Fate
CVA 58	UNITED STATES	Newport News	18.4.49	Cancelled 23.4.49

roles considered, and indeed *United States* would have had smaller magazines than the later, multi-mission, *Forrestal*s. It appears that the hangar was originally included largely to house the fighter escorts for the heavy bombers. Much attention went into flight deck arrangement, the ship being intended to launch two bombers and two fighters simultaneously from a pair of bow catapults and a pair of waist catapults splayed out to each beam. Steam catapults had not yet been invented, and she was to have

had a new type of internal-combustion cylindrical catapult, which was also originally specified for the *Forrestal*s. A fully flush deck would have simplified flight operations, and her arrangement was to have been superficially similar to that of the later angled deck ships. However, the arrangement of arresting gear would have precluded the simultaneous launch and recovery operations which are the hallmark of the angled deck carrier. The *United States* was designed to carry 500,000gal (US) of Avgas (aviation fuel) and 2000t of aviation ordnance.

It appears that four ships in all were contemplated, and that later units might have had nuclear power. Certainly smoke disposal from a large flush deck carrier was considered a major and intractable issue. *United States* herself was laid down at Newport News on 19 April 1949, but the Air Force charged that the new carrier would merely duplicate its strategic mission, at a cost of $500 million (against a Navy estimate of $189 mil-

lion), and construction was stopped on 23 April, the funds being transferred to the Air Force for bombers. The ensuing fight resulted in one of the Navy's worst peacetime disasters; heavy attack aircraft were restricted to dimensions dictated by the wartime *Midway* class. The major postwar jet heavy attack bomber, the A-3 (A3D) was designed at this time. Only the Korean War brought back the Navy's carrier programme.

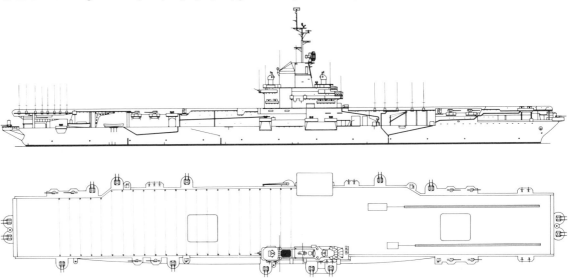

Oriskany 1950
NB 1/1750 scale

At the end of the Second World War the United States had what it considered an obsolescent carrier fleet: the 24 *Essex* class carriers then either completed or completing could not operate the coming generation of jet aircraft. A follow-on fleet carrier design, completed in 1946, was not built, and efforts were begun to adapt the existing hulls to the new conditions. The incomplete *Oriskany* was suspended pending completion of a new design, and most of the existing wartime ships were laid up in the postwar run-down. As completed, to a revised SCB-27A design in 1950, *Oriskany* lacked the flight deck gun mounts of her near-sisters. Her flight

ESSEX class (SCB-27A reconstruction) *aircraft carriers*

Displacement:	28,404t light; 40,600t full load
Dimensions:	819ft wl, 898ft 2in oa × 101ft 4in wl, 151ft 11in ext × 29ft 8in *249.7m, 273.8m × 30.9m, 46.3m × 9.1m*
Machinery:	4-shaft geared turbines, 8 boilers, 150,000shp = 30kts. Range 15,000nm at 15kts
Armament:	8–5in/38 (8×1), 28–3in/50 (14×2), approx 80 aircraft
Sensors:	Radar SPS-6, SC or SR, SPS-8 (SX at first) (SPS-6 was later replaced by SPS-12 and then by SPS-29; SPS-8 was later replaced by SPS-30); sonar SQS-23 (CVSs only)
Complement:	2905

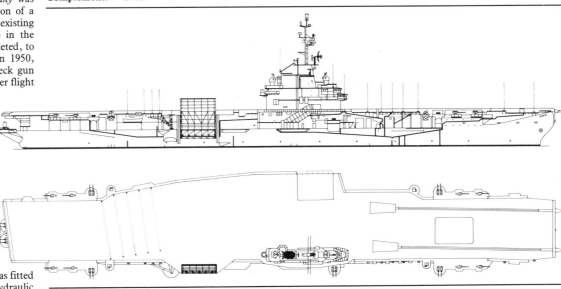

Shangri La 1957
NB 1/1750 scale

deck was stronger, and she was fitted with the most powerful hydraulic catapults available, H-8s. Four 5in/38 guns were mounted on the starboard side of her flight deck to supplement the four usually mounted to port. There were also important internal changes. For example, the ready rooms, which in standard *Essex* class carriers were in the gallery deck, were moved below the armoured hangar deck and an escalator fitted outboard of the island in these ships. There were also major revisions to the island structure itself, for better radar antenna coverage. The hull was blistered, but the blister was faired into

ESSEX class (SCB-27C reconstruction) *aircraft carriers*

Displacement:	30,580t light; 43,060t full load
Dimensions:	820ft wl, 894ft 6in oa × 103ft wl, 166ft 10in ext × 30ft 4in *250.0m, 272.7m × 31.4m, 50.9m × 9.2m*
Machinery:	4-shaft geared turbines, 8 boilers, 150,000shp = 29.1kts. Range 15,000nm at 15kts
Armament:	4–5in/38 (4×1)
Sensors:	Radar SPS-12, SPS-8 (ultimately SPS-37A, SPS-30), SR (later SPS-12)
Complement:	2585 (ship), 960 (air group)

For names of reconstructed ships and ultimate fates see under Fleet Strength 1947. Original data, including construction particulars, can be found in the 1922–1946 volume. The SCB-27C particulars given above refer to ships with angled decks, near the end of their operational lives. CV 11, 14 and 19 were originally converted with axial decks, 8–5in/38, 24–3in/50 (12×2) and open bows.

the hull all the way to the hangar deck level, so that it was not visible to a casual observer. Eight other ships were withdrawn from reserve for SCB-27A modernisation (CV 9, 10, 12, 15, 18, 20, 29 and 33.

A proposed austere SCB-27B conversion programme was dropped, and instead six ships were completed to SCB-27C standard, with a slightly wider blister, two steam catapults (C-11), and the after centreline elevator relocated to the after starboard deck-edge. As jet carriers they also had improved arresting gear. After three such conversions (CV 11, 14 and 19), three more ships (CV 16, 31 and 38) were given modified conversions incorporating angled decks and 'hurricane bows'. The first three SCB-27Cs were later brought up to this SCB-125 standard, as was *Oriskany* (SCB-125A). Of the SCB-27As, all but *Lake Champlain* were ultimately given angled decks and enclosed bows.

Thus a total of fifteen ships was modernised. The two carriers damaged late in the war, *Franklin* and *Bunker Hill*, were never reactivated, although they were both described during the late 1940s as being in excellent material condition, quite well suited to reconstruction. Of eight car-

Shangri La (after SCB-27C modernisation)   USN

riers active in 1945–48 (CV 21, 32, 33, 36, 37, 40, 45 and 47), only one (CV 33) was rebuilt. *Antietam* became test ship for the angled flight deck and then training carrier at Pensacola. *Boxer*, *Princeton* and *Valley Forge* became helicopter carriers (LPH); their unconverted sisters were the first *Essex*s to be withdrawn from service post-Korea, at the end of the 1950s. As reserve ships were converted to SCB-27A configuration,

active unmodernised ships were transferred to ASW duty under the CVS designation, replacing the Second World War escort and light fleet carriers previously used. Similarly, as the *Forrestal*s and the SCB-27C/125s entered service, SCB-27As were reduced to ASW service. The SCB-27C/125 conversions ultimately followed, although *Oriskany*, *Hancock* and *Bon Homme Richard* were still carried as attack carriers at the end of

the Vietnam War, and *Intrepid* operated off Vietnam as a 'light' attack carrier.

As modernised the SCB-27As carried 300,000gals (US) of Avgas (aviation fuel) and 725t of aviation ordnance (including 125t of nuclear weapons).

All of these ships lost their gun armament during their service, as topweight was needed for aviation-related items and also for radars. Typically the twin 3in/50 battery went first. Indeed, it appears that few of the SCB-27As had the full fourteen mounts, and that few of the 27Cs long retained their full complement of eleven. Ships generally ended their careers with only two 5in/38s, although some had as many as four. Aside from the enclosed bows, applied to all of the SCB-27s other than *Lake Champlain*, the most noticeable change during the careers of these ships was in their radars, the typical suit by the mid-1960s including both SPS-30 and the very large SPS-37A or -43A, the latter sponsoned out over the side of the island.

Eight ASW carriers were further modernised during the FRAM programme: CVS 9, 10, 11, 12, 15, 18, 20 and 33. Improvements included an SQS-23 bow sonar, a stem hawsepipe and bow anchor to clear it, and an improved and partially automated ASW-adapted CIC.

In 1981 the Reagan Administration proposed the reactivation and reconstruction of *Oriskany*, perhaps to be followed by *Bon Homme Richard* and *Shangri La*. Congress has so far proven unenthusiastic, partly because of severe restrictions on the range of aircraft these ships can operate. *Oriskany* has been the last in the class to operate as an attack carrier. However, the fighters and early warning aircraft these ships were capable of operating no longer exist in any numbers, and they would not be suitable for the new 'lightweight' F-18. It is sometimes argued, indeed, that in future the *Essex*s retained in reserve would be valuable primarily as helicopter carriers, if at all. The extent to which they have been cannibalised for spares is a matter of some dispute. At this time *Lexington* alone remains in commission, as a training carrier off Pensacola; she is scheduled to remain until the mid-1980s.

Independence 1962   USN

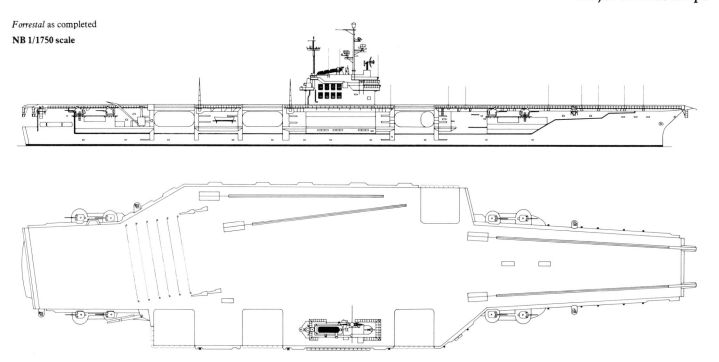

Forrestal as completed
NB 1/1750 scale

These four ships were a major fruit of the revival of naval shipbuilding during and after the Korean War. *Forrestal* was originally designed as a somewhat smaller version of the cancelled *United States*, Senator Vinson having decreed that he would approve any carrier short of 60,000t. Thus the design called for a flush (island-less) flight deck with four catapults, so that four aircraft could be launched simultaneously, with two in the bow and one angled out from each side in the waist. In order to launch heavy aircraft at high speed, the catapults were to be of a new explosive type, and the stowage of catapult charges was a major design problem. Compared to previous carriers, the sheer capacity of their magazines and aircraft fuel tanks was enormous: for example, *Forrestal* was credited with 1650t of aviation ordnance, 750,000gal Avgas and 789,000gal of JP-5 fuel (compared to 500,000gal for the limited-mission *United States* and 365,000gal for a *Midway*).

As redesigned with an angled flight deck, they have two catapults in the waist, to port, so that aircraft can be spotted simultaneously, although they must be launched in succession. In the first two ships the waist catapults were C-11s, as in the steam-catapult *Essex* class modernizations, whereas the two bow catapults were C-7s. However, all four catapults are C-7s in the last two ships, and in later carriers all four catapults are of the most powerful type. The original defensive battery of eight single 5in/54 rapid-fire guns was reduced, first, by the removal of the forward sponsons, which had reduced ship performance very greatly in heavy weather by generating spray. The four after guns were removed with the installation of the Sea Sparrow SAM (one forward, to starboard, and one aft, to port; 16 missiles). *Ranger* was the last to have her guns removed, losing two in 1977, and retaining her forward sponsons.

Major refits, under the Service Life Extension Program (SLEP) began with *Saratoga*, at the Philadelphia Naval Shipyard, in 1980. As in FRAM, all ship systems will be over-

FORRESTAL class *aircraft carriers*

Displacement:	61,163t standard; 78,509t full load
Dimensions:	990ft wl, 1039ft oa × 129ft 4in wl, 250ft ext × 33ft 10in
	301.8m, 316.8m × 39.4m, 76.2m × 10.3m
Machinery:	4-shaft geared turbines, 8 Babcock & Wilcox boilers, 280,000shp (260,000shp CVA 59) = 33kts. Oil approx 8570t. Range 12,000nm at 20kts
Armament:	8–5in/54 (8×1), approx 90 aircraft
Sensors:	Radar SPS-8, SPS-12 (later SPS-29, then -37A/43A in place of SPS-12, SPS-30 in place of SPS-8; SPS-58 for Sea Sparrow)
Complement:	2764 (ship), 1912 (air group)

No	Name	Builder	Laid down	Launched	Comp	Fate
CVA 59	FORRESTAL	Newport News	14.7.52	11.12.54	1.10.55	Extant 1982
CVA 60	SARATOGA	New York N Yd	16.12.52	8.10.54	14.4.56	Extant 1982
CVA 61	RANGER	Newport News	2.8.54	29.9.56	10.8.57	Extant 1982
CVA 62	INDEPENDENCE	New York N Yd	1.7.55	6.6.58	10.1.59	Extant 1982

hauled and new electronics fitted. SLEP will add Kevlar armour, longer catapults, and improved habitability, as well as SPS-48C and SPS-49 radars, an improved NTDS and a Tactical Flag Command Centre. The planned battery is three Sea Sparrow SAM launchers (Mk 29) and three Phalanx CIWS.

Franklin D Roosevelt (after SCB-110 modernisation) USN

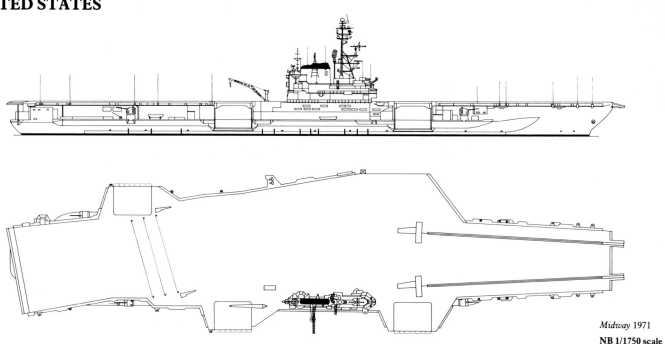

Midway 1971

NB 1/1750 scale

Of the US carriers surviving the Second World War, only the *Midway*s were capable, unmodified, of operating the first of the new generation of heavy attack aircraft, the AJ Savages. Indeed, *Coral Sea* flew off a Neptune land-based patrol bomber carrying a simulated nuclear bomb, to show that the Navy could indeed execute a nuclear mission with existing assets. Even so, by the late 1940s it was clear that some major reconstruction would be necessary, and the SCB-27 project which eventually led to wholesale modification of the smaller *Essex* class carriers was begun with the *Midway*s in mind. All three were modernised under the SCB-110 project, but because the modernisations were

MIDWAY class (SCB-110 reconstruction) *aircraft carriers*

Displacement:	42,710t light, 62,614t full load
Dimensions:	910ft wl, 977ft 2in oa × 121ft wl, 210ft ext × 34ft 6in
	277.4m, 297.9m × 36.9m × 64.0m × 10.5m
Machinery:	4-shaft geared turbines, 12 Babcock & Wilcox boilers, 212,000shp = 30.6kts. Range 15,000nm at 15kts
Armament:	10–5in/54 (10×1), 18–3in/50 (9×2)
Sensors:	Radar SPS-12, SPS-8 (later SPS-37A/43A, SPS-30; SPS-48 fitted about 1980)
Complement:	4060

For names of reconstructed ships and ultimate fates see under Fleet Strength 1947. Original data, including construction particulars, can be found in the 1922–1946 volume.

spread over a considerable period the three ships differed in detail, *Coral Sea* receiving SCB-110A. The first two ships received the two C-11 steam

Constellation 1962   USN

catapults, 'hurricane bow', and angled deck of SCB-27C, and their 5in and 3in batteries were considerably reduced. *Franklin D Roosevelt* was given a new tapered mast, *Midway* a lattice. *Coral Sea* received an additional C-11 in her waist. In each case, too, the after centreline elevator was replaced by an after starboard deck-edge unit and, as in the smaller carriers, elevators and flight decks were considerably strengthened.

By the mid-1960s it was clear that another round of reconstructions would be needed. Unlike the ageing *Essex*s, the *Midway*s seemed well-suited to current aircraft and were expected to serve well into the 1980s. *Midway* was the first, and the immense cost of her SCB-101.66 refit (February 1966 to January 1970 at Mare Island, for a total of $202 million) deterred the Navy from any similar modernisation of *Franklin D Roosevelt*. As the most modern, *Coral Sea* needed rather less in any case. *Midway* received C-13 catapults, an enlarged flight deck, and had her forward centreline elevator removed in favour of a second starboard deck-edge unit, her port deck-edge one replaced by a port deck-edge elevator further aft. NTDS was also fitted. *Franklin D Roosevelt* was given a far more austere refit ($46 million), her forward centreline elevator being replaced by a starboard deck-edge unit forward of her island. As she was in the worst material condition of the three, and the least suited for further service, she was stricken in 1977. *Coral Sea* had emerged from SCB-110A with both centreline elevators eliminated in favour of starboard deck-edge units, and she was not

heavily rebuilt; in 1982 she remained in active reserve, without a regularly assigned air group, partly for training activities on the West Coast. *Midway* was still an active unit of the Pacific Fleet in 1982.

The original very heavy gun batteries of these ships were rapidly drawn down in service, as both the value of the gun and its cost in space and weight were re-evaluated. It appears that some of their Mk 39 5in/54 mounts were ultimately mounted aboard Japanese destroyers built postwar with US aid. During the late 1940s the 5in batteries of *Midway* and *Franklin D Roosevelt* were reduced from 18 to 14 guns, and *Coral Sea* was completed with only 14. After SCB-110 *FDR* had only ten 5in/54, and by 1963 that number had been reduced to four; *Midway* was similar. *Coral Sea* had only six after SCB-110A, and only three after 1962. *Midway* retained three guns after her last reconstruction; *FDR* had four. All guns were later removed from *Midway* and *Coral Sea*; in 1982 the former had 2 Sea Sparrow SAM (2×8) and both had 3 Phalanx CIWS. The original provision for aviation stores was 1376t of ordnance, 356,000gal Avgas and 600,000gal of JP-5 fuel; ordnance was reduced to 1210t after SCB-101.66, but JP-5 was increased to 1,186,000gals JP-5 (no Avgas).

It appears that the surviving ships will remain in service at least until 1985, with forty-year careers. The only earlier very long careers were those of battleships, but the longest-lived of them, the *Arkansas*, lasted only about 34 years, from 1912 until 1946. The test battleship *Mississippi* lasted longer, from 1917 until 1956.

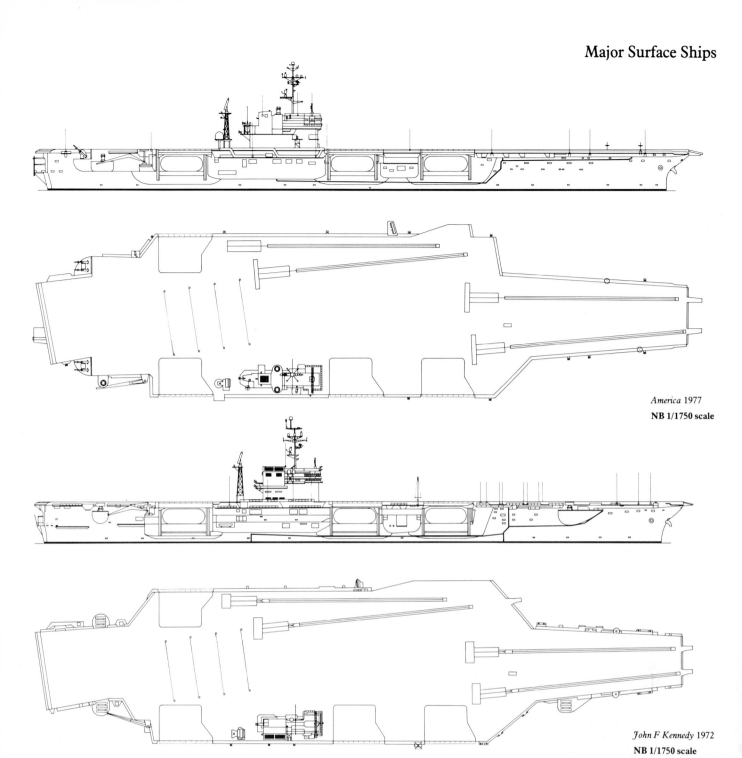

America 1977

NB 1/1750 scale

John F Kennedy 1972

NB 1/1750 scale

KITTY HAWK class *aircraft carriers*

Displacement:	60,005t light; 80,945t full load
Dimensions:	990ft wl, 1047ft 6in oa × 129ft 4in wl, 251ft 8in ext × 36ft
	301.8m, 319.4m × 39.4, 76.7m × 11.4m
Machinery:	4-shaft geared turbines, 8 Foster Wheeler boilers, 280,000shp = 33.6kts. Range 12,000nm at 20kts
Armament:	2 Terrier SAM (2×2, 40 missiles per launcher), 3 Sea Sparrow SAM (CVA 67 only, 3×8, no reloads), approx 90 aircraft
Sensors:	Radar SPS-37A, SPS-39, SPS-8B (CVA 63 and 64 only; CVA 66 SPS-30; no fighter control in CVA 67, which had SPS-48 in place of -39), SPS-43A (CVA 66 and CVA 67 as completed), SPG-55 (not CVA 67); sonar SQS-23 (CVA 66 only)
Complement:	3306 (ship), 1379 (air group) (CVA 66)

No	Name	Builder	Laid down	Launched	Comp	Fate
CVA 63	KITTY HAWK	New York SB	27.12.56	21.5.60	29.4.61	Extant 1982
CVA 64	CONSTELLATION	New York N Yd	14.9.59	8.10.60	27.10.61	Extant 1982
CVA 66	AMERICA	Newport News	9.1.61	1.2.64	23.1.65	Extant 1982
CVA 67	JOHN F KENNEDY	Newport News	22.10.64	27.5.67	7.9.68	Extant 1982

These ships actually form three sub-classes; all are improved *Forrestal*s. An entirely new carrier design for CVA 63 was foregone because of the imminence of the introduction of nuclear power, which, it was believed, would limit any new class to only two units. *Kitty Hawk* and *Constellation* differed from the *Forrestal*s in having their islands moved aft, so that two instead of one elevator are forward of them, for improved flight deck operations. They also have a lattice radar mast aft of the island structure, and were armed with Terrier missiles (two twin Mk 10 launching systems on the port and starboard quarters, with paired SPG-55 guidance radars on the island structure). *America* (CVA 66) is very similar, having been built in preference to an austere nuclear carrier in FY61; she received updated Terrier, compatible with the Standard Missile. *John F Kennedy* was built to a revised design, incorporating a new underwater protection system originally developed for the nuclear carriers, and, at first, without defensive weapons. Early in 1969 she was fitted

with three Sea Sparrow launchers, and her three half-sisters were similarly refitted. *Kennedy* has her funnel angled to starboard.

America was the first attack carrier with a special integrated CIC/airborne ASW control centre (ASCAC) and, in 1981, retained SM-1 missiles and SPG-55B radar directors, as well as

SPS-52 3-D radar instead of the more effective SPS-48 of her two sister ships. She is to receive three Sea Sparrows, as in her two sisters. All are to have three Phanlanx CIWS each. *Kennedy* is to have her BPDMS launchers replaced by the Mk 29 type associated with NATO Sea Sparrow; all use SPS-58 as a warning radar for

the point defence system.

America and *John F Kennedy* were fitted for SQS-23 sonar in bow domes, on the theory that in a spread-out fleet formation it would be impossible to maintain a tight sonar screen, so that the carrier might have to detect submarines leaking through; SQS-23 was also fitted to some ASW carriers.

UNITED STATES

Similar reasoning led to the installation of this sonar in *Cleveland* class missile cruisers. SQS-23 was not installed in CVA 67 to reduce cost; presumably the measure lost much of its value as submarine weapon ranges increased beyond torpedo range.

Aviation ordnance and fuel capacity is slightly greater than that of the *Forrestal* class, at 2150t and 1,950,000gal in the *Kennedy*. In 1979 a repeat *Kennedy* was proposed as an alternative to a non-nuclear CVV. Unlike the *Forrestals*, these ships have four C-13 catapults (one is a longer C-13-1 in CV 66 and 67). Their rearranged flight decks make it far easier and safer to launch and recover aircraft simultaneously.

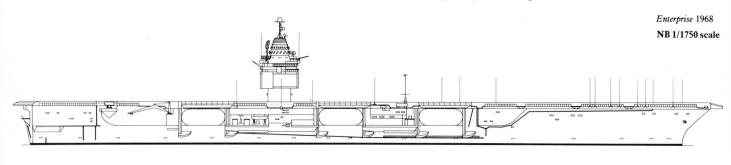

Enterprise 1968

NB 1/1750 scale

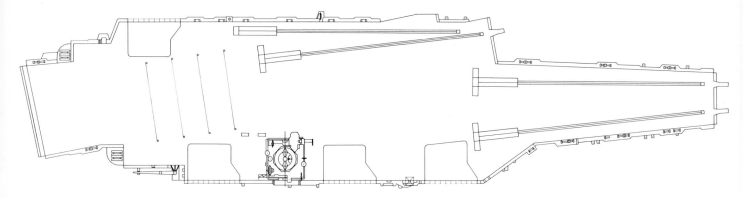

Probably the most spectacular warship of her time, *Enterprise* was the first US nuclear carrier. Her size was dictated by her power plant: although it was not much heavier than equivalent weights for a conventional ship, she still had to carry a large liquid load for underwater protection, and that load greatly increased her displacement. Since it could be used for aircraft fuel, it allowed her to operate an unusually large air group. Reportedly she can sustain twelve days of intense air operations without replenishment. Again, since she was already an outstandingly capable ship, she received other innovative equipment, such as electronically scanned main radars (SPS-32 and SPS-33), with a conventional radar (SPS-12 added in 1968) as back-up. Although space and weight for Terrier (as in CVA 63, 64 and 66) was provided, the missile was not fitted, in an effort to hold costs down; Sea Sparrow was fitted in 1967, with a

ENTERPRISE *aircraft carrier*

Displacement:	71,277ft light; 89,084t full load (as of 1968)
Dimensions:	1040ft wl, 1123ft 2in oa × 133ft wl, 255ft ext × 37ft 1in
	317.1m, 342.4m × 40.5m, 77.7m × 11.3m
Machinery:	4-shaft nuclear: 8 A2W reactors, 4 Westinghouse geared turbines, approx 280,000shp = 32kts
Armament:	None as built (3 Sea Sparrow SAM (3×8) fitted 1967), approx 90 aircraft
Sensors:	Radar SPS-32, SPS-33 (SPS-12 added in 1968)
Complement:	3325 (ship), 1891 (air group), 71 Marines

No	Name	Builder	Laid down	Launched	Comp	Fate
CVAN 65 ENTERPRISE		Newport News	4.2.58	24.9.60	25.11.61	Extant 1982

modified aircraft (F-4) fire control radar. *Enterprise* was refitted in 1980, and her massive fixed radars removed.

Her aviation fuel stowage is 2,720,000gal, reflecting the requirements of underwater protection rather than air group operations; in earlier ships aviation fuel stowage was balanced with ship endurance fuel

stowage in side protection spaces, and from time to time, it was proposed that ship boilers be modified to burn aviation fuel (JP-5). Aviation ordnance capacity is 2520t, compared to about 2000t in non-nuclear carriers. *Enterprise* has four C-13 steam catapults.

Like *Nimitz*, *Enterprise* has an integrated CIC/ASW command centre

(ASCAC). Since 1976 she has carried two British SCOT satellite communications antennae. As refitted, she has the standard carrier radar suit of SPS-48C and SPS-49, with SPS-65 (antenna common with SPS-10) for Sea Sparrow warning. She is to receive three Phalanx CIWS.

Enterprise 4.3.82

USN

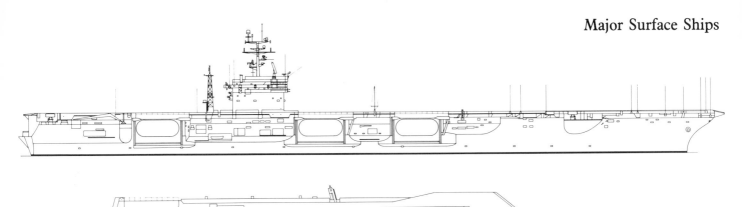

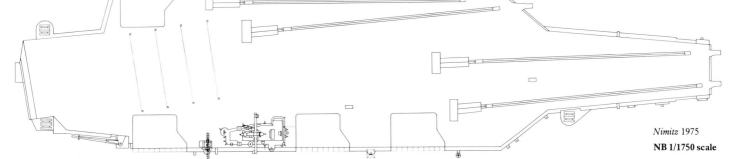

Nimitz 1975

NB 1/1750 scale

NIMITZ class *aircraft carriers*

Displacement:	73,973t light; 91,440t full load
Dimensions:	1040ft wl, 1088ft oa × 134ft wl, 257ft 6in ext × 36ft 8in
	317.1m, 331.7m × 40.8m, 78.5m × 11.2m
Machinery:	4-shaft nuclear: 2 A4W reactors, 4 geared turbines, approx 260,000shp = 30+kts
Armament:	3 Sea Sparrow SAM (3×8, no reloads), approx 90 aircraft
Sensors:	Radar SPS-43A, SPS-48 (later ships may have SPS-49 in place of SPS-43A)
Complement:	5621 (ship plus air group)

No	Name	Builder	Laid down	Launched	Comp	Fate
CVAN 68	NIMITZ	Newport News	22.6.68	13.5.72	3.5.75	Extant 1982
CVAN 69	DWIGHT D EISENHOWER	Newport News	14.8.70	11.10.75	18.10.77	Extant 1982
CVN 70	CARL VINSON	Newport News	11.10.75	15.3.80	13.3.82	Extant 1982
CVN 71	THEODORE ROOSEVELT	Newport News	31.10.81			Building
CVN 72						Authorised FY83
CVN 73						Authorised FY83

With these ships the US Navy returned to building nuclear carriers of *Enterprise* size. They incorporate a new two-reactor power plant, developed from a project for a single reactor destroyer/frigate plant, and so have even more internal space than the huge *Enterprise*; in addition they incorporate the more economical (in terms of space) torpedo protection system of the *Kennedy*. Their general arrangement and electronic suit also duplicate those of *Kennedy*, and they are armed with three Sea Sparrow launchers for self-defence. Approximate capacity is 2570t of aviation ordnance and 2,800,000gal of aviation fuel, in each case more than the *Enterprise*, of similar size, can accommodate. *Carl Vinson* will be completed with four Phalanx CIWS; the others will have three each. The Navy claims that these ships can take three times the damage which *Essex* class carriers survived in 1944-45, and (in order of completion) they are to receive Kevlar armour during 1982, 1987 and 1989 refits. CVN 71 is to be completed with Kevlar armour. They are described as carrying 90 per cent more aviation fuel and 50 per cent more aviation ordnance than a *Forrestal*; however, CVN 71 has been described as carrying only 1954t of ordnance (compared to the 2000t implied above). All have ASCAC (ASW Classification and Analysis Centre), permitting sharing of data between the carrier, ASW aircraft, and escorting ships.

CVN 72 and CVN 73 were included in the FY83 programme (as of Dec 82). The three ships can be distinguished by the presence of only a single bridle-catching boom in CVN 69 and 70. Current carrier aircraft employ a catapult attachment built into their landing gear, and so do not use the wire bridles of the past.

Dwight D Eisenhower 1977

USN

Medium Carrier Project (CVV) *aircraft carrier*

Displacement:	45,192t light; 59,794t full load
Dimensions:	860ft wl, 912ft oa × 126ft wl, 256ft 6in ext× 34ft 7in
	262.2m, 278.0m × 38.4m, 78.2m × 10.5m
Machinery:	2-shaft geared turbines, 6 boilers, 140,000shp = 27.8kts
Armament:	3 Phalanx CIWS, 50 aircraft (1191t avord, 2700t JP-5)
Sensors:	Radar SPS-48, SPS-49
Complement:	4024

The CVV was proposed by the Carter and Ford Administrations as a means of reducing the unit size and cost (and, incidentally, capability) of US attack carriers. It was ultimately defeated by the Navy and its Congressional allies. The concept originated in the Ford Administration as the Tentative Conceptual Baseline (T-CBL) for a new carrier to replace the

UNITED STATES

ageing *Franklin D Roosevelt*. The Chief of Naval Operations, Admiral Elmo Zumwalt, sought a reversal in the steady growth of warship costs. He was also responsible for an attempt to devise an inexpensive Aegis platform (DG/Aegis, which was abortive), for the Sea Control Ship, and for the limited-cost *Perry* class escort. Admiral Zumwalt's Project SIXTY advisory group, formed at the beginning of his term as CNO, initially examined a new 40,000t carrier, but ultimately chose to propose one of 50,000t to 60,000t. Secretary of Defense Laird issued a Programme Decision Memorandum for a $550 million (FY73 dollars) carrier on 21.9.72, studies beginning in Dec 1972. Although the product of these studies, the T-CBL, was not ordered, interest in such a ship continued, Secretary of Defense Schlesinger (who succeeded Laird) ordering a new round of studies in July 1975. They failed when the ship was redefined as nuclear at Navy request, and President Ford ultimately called for a repeat *Nimitz* rather than for a new

smaller ship. However, he did call for the construction of two smaller oil-fired carriers in FY79 and FY81. They were to be adapted for a new generation of VSTOL aircraft, and as such received a new designation, CVV. The incoming Carter Administration found the CVV idea attractive, at least in part as a means of reducing the cost of the shipbuilding programme.

The CVV employed half the power plant of a conventional steam carrier such as the *John F Kennedy*, and was criticised for its relatively low speed. For example, at full power (140,000shp) the T-CBL would make only 27.8kts, so that it would not be compatible with fast carriers. With her catapults in use, speed would fall much further, as a large percentage of available steam would have to be fed into the catapults. These problems would have been alleviated in the full CVV, which had two more boilers.

Cost-saving measures included a restriction to two shafts, two catapults, and only two elevators, all of which appeared to limit the sur-

Artist's impression of CVV design　　　　USN

vivability of the medium carrier. There were even proposals to forego a large fraction of the electronic installation of the CVV to save initial cost. For example, there would be no SPS-49 long-range air search radar; the SPS-48C three-dimensional radar would have to suffice, at least at first. Similarly, one of the two planned 2500kW ship service turbo-generators would have been deferred, as well as the liquid oxygen plant.

However, the CVV design incorporated a new and extremely robust form of magazine protection against cruise missile attack, as well as a new type of under-bottom protection. In this sense the proposed carrier was extremely non-austere. Presumably some of these ideas will eventually be incorporated in the full-deck carriers which have been authorised since the death of the CVV.

(For illustration of SCS model see under Spain)

Sea Control Ship Project (SCS) *aircraft carrier*

Displacement:	9773t light; 13,736t full load
Dimensions:	585ft wl, 610ft oa × 80ft × 21ft 7in *178.4m, 186.0 × 24.4m × 6.6m*
Machinery:	1 shaft, 2 LM 2500 gas turbines, 45,000shp = 26kts
Armament:	2 CIWS
Sensors:	Radar SPS-52
Complement:	700

The Sea Control Ship was a small helicopter carrier, part of Admiral Zumwalt's 'low-end' emphasis, and as such bitterly fought by much of the naval aviation community, as well as by advocates of nuclear power, led by Admiral H G Rickover. The concept appears to have originated in 1969 with a Long Range Objectives Group proposal for a new class of helicopter-carrying escorts (or DHK) to provide active-sonar screens for convoys and other naval formations. At the time, as now, US wartime ASW strategy was predicated on the capability of passive systems, most notably SOSUS, which were expected to guide P-3 aircraft to attack on Soviet submarines in an area-attrition campaign. It was feared that improvements in Soviet submarine silencing might neutralise SOSUS, and thus force the United States back to more conventional convoy tactics, which in turn would require much larger numbers of surface escorts. Studies as early as 1959 strongly suggested that, with the loss of the mass of the Second World War ships, these numbers would not be attainable in a crisis. Helicopters with active sonars might be an equalizer; the LRO study envisaged both escort carriers (initially converted *Commencement Bays*) and 30kt DHKs of 12,000t to 14,000t, each carrying twelve advanced ASW helicopters, as well as conventional destroyer weapons. There were to be a total of fourteen DHK and fifteen escort carriers. Within a few years passive tactical systems (such as the

towed array and many of the sonobuoys) were even more important than in 1969, but interest in small helicopter carriers survived.

As LAMPS became an important fixture of the surface escort ASW system, the small carrier became attractive as a maintenance base and hangar for helicopters operated by the escorts. That is, maintenance could be considered a major barrier to effective sustained helicopter operation. Admiral Zumwalt's programme called for a total of eight sea control ships, to support a total of eight convoys or underway replenishment groups (with their escorts). The SCS designation was adopted in May 1971 and a preliminary design was ready by Jan 1972. It showed a capability for intermediate-level maintenance, and was expected to cost $175 million in FY75 dollars (prototype; follow-on ships would cost $117 million each). At this time the prototype was to have been ordered in the FY75 programme, for completion in FY78, with three more in FY76, and two each in FY77 and FY78.

In theory, the helicopters of the SCS were to have localised and attacked submarines detected by the towed arrays streamed by the frigates, which (in 1971) were expected to have convergence zone range. In addition, VSTOL fighters aboard the SCS would be able to protect the convoy from aircraft at ranges of up to 100nm, backed up by the Standard missiles of the frigates. The SCS air group was set at eleven ASW and three early warning helicopters, plus three Harrier fighters: the carrier would maintain two ASW and one AEW helicopter continuously on station, with a ready fighter on deck alert. The concept was tested by the helicopter carrier *Guam*, which was modified between Oct 1971 and Jan 1972; major modifications included the provision of an ASW analysis centre and improved aircraft control, direction, and maintenance facilities. Tests, which continued until Apr 1974, were generally considered successful despite problems with the SH-3G helicopter. However, the evaluators questioned the viability of

the SCS, given the absence of both the advanced helicopter and the advanced VSTOL which she was intended to operate. Moreover, she had failed to maintain the two helicopters permanently on station – due, supporters of the SCS suggested, more to the deficiencies of the helicopters (and of the spares policy supporting them) than to basic problems. However, the SCS concept was dropped by Admiral Zumwalt's successor, Admiral Holloway, in favour of an alternative VSTOL support ship, or VSS.

Throughout the SCS design was optimized for minimum cost, the goal being to build eight ships for the cost of one nuclear carrier. Thus Admiral Zumwalt settled for a single shaft powerplant, and limited defensive weapons to two Phalanx close-in defensive guns. With the cancellation of the SCS project, the plans were sold to the Spanish Navy, and a modified version of the basic design is now (1983) being completed as the *Principe de Asturias* (see under Spain).

In 1975 the new CNO, Admiral Holloway, called for a new VSTOL carrier, which he hoped would assist in the planned transition to an all-VSTOL navy by early in the next century. Although theoretically not a direct replacement for the conventional carriers, the VSS was required to achieve speeds not far from those of such ships, and as such had to have

VSTOL Support Ship Project (VSS) *aircraft carrier*

Displacement:	20,116t light; 29,130t full load
Dimensions:	690ft wl, 717ft oa × 178ft oa × 25ft 4in *210.4m, 218.6m × 54.3m × 7.7m*
Machinery:	2 shafts, 4 LM 2500 gas turbines, 90,000shp = 30kts
Armament:	2 Phalanx CIWS, 8 Harpoon SSM (2×4)
Sensors:	Radar SPS-52
Complement:	959 ship, 628 aviation

two shafts. About fifty alternatives were examined in 1974–75, including large ships with catapults and arresting gear. However, the VSS design ultimately adopted was an enlarged SCS, which could operate sixteen SH-53, six LAMPS, and four Harriers. Four (compared to two in the SCS) LM 2500 gas turbines would

drive her at about 29kts. The design was reworked twice: first, to accommodate more advanced VSTOL aircraft, and then to achieve a measure of magazine protection; this last version, VSS III, is the one described in the table. In 1983 it is still sometimes used for comparison with more conventional carrier alternatives, although

design work effectively ended in 1978.

Congressional interest in such ships has continued. For example, in FY79 Congress almost funded the conversion of a helicopter carrier to an SCS; the Senate Armed Services Committee added $40 million for conversion, as well as $70 million for long-lead

items for a sixth LHA, which would more than replace the LPH withdrawn for the SCS conversion. It can be argued that the LHD (see under Amphibious Warfare Vessels) represents a reaction to this sentiment, in that it is to have a secondary sea control capability.

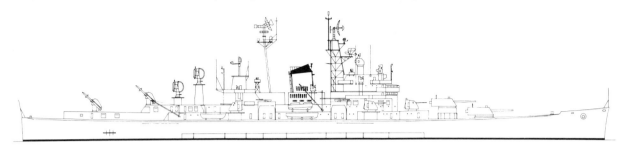

Canberra 1958

These two heavy cruisers were the first US anti-aircraft missile ships, rushed to completion to meet a very severe perceived threat. The first ship seriously considered for conversion was the older cruiser *Wichita*, which might have had three launchers, replacing all her heavy gun turrets. The Terrier missile itself was rushed into production; it began as a test vehicle in the Talos programme, and the conversion of *Boston* and *Canberra* was conceived as a first phase, an austere effort which might be followed by the removal of the two forward turrets if it proved successful. The conversions were in fact successful, but instead of giving the ships further refits, extra ships were converted. By 1966 the radar fit was CXRX, SPS-37A, SPS-30, two SPQ-5 (CAG 2). By the 1960s both were obsolete, and a project to modernise them was rejected as too expensive. They were reclassified as cruis-

BOSTON class *fleet escorts (missile cruiser conversions)*

Displacement:	13,589t light; 17,947t full load
Dimensions:	664ft wl, 673ft 5in oa × 69ft 8in × 24ft 11in
	202.4m, 205.3m × 21.25m × 7.6m
Machinery:	4-shaft geared turbines, 4 Babcock & Wilcox boilers, 120,000shp = 33kts. Range 7300nm at 20kts. Oil 1448t
Armament:	2 Terrier SAM (2×2, 72 missiles per launcher), 6–8in (2×3), 10–5in (5×2), 8–3in/50 (4×2)
Sensors:	Radar SPS-6, SPS-8, SPS-12, CXRX, two SPQ-5 (Mk 25 mod 7 in CAG 1)
Complement:	1544

No	Name	Yard	Recomm	Fate
CAG 1	BOSTON	New York SB	1.11.55	Decommissioned 1970, stricken
CAG 2	CANBERRA	New York SB	15.6.56	Decommissioned 1970, stricken

ers (CA) in May 1968 and relegated to shore bombardment duties; before de-activation, the missile launchers were removed, leaving them with two 8in triple turrets forward.

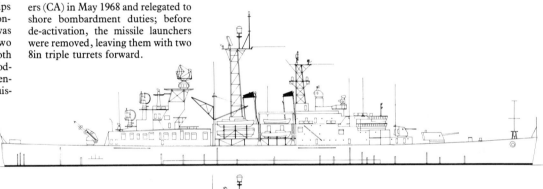

Little Rock 1960

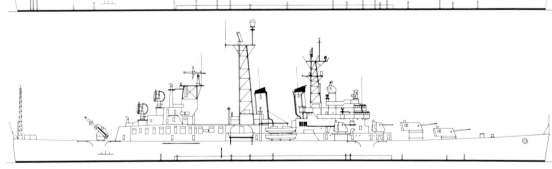

Galveston 1959

Six *Cleveland* class light cruiser hulls were withdrawn from reserve and converted to austere missile ships, the entire missile installation being above the weather deck aft, for either Talos (CLG 3–CLG 8) or Terrier (CLG 6–CLG 8), all being reclassified in May 1957. They were a solution to the problem of missile ship cost, as a series of specially built cruisers would have been far too expensive. Moreover, they were not double-enders as had originally been planned. In CLG 3 and CLG 8 the fore part of the ship, including two 6in turrets and three 5in/38 gunhouses, remained unaltered, except for the provision of a heavy new foremast to carry a long-range air search radar. In the other four, a new forward superstructure carried flag spaces, and only one 6in and one 5in mounting were retained.

CLEVELAND class *fleet escorts (missile cruiser conversions)*

Displacement:	11,066t light; 15,152t full load (CLG 5)
Dimensions:	600ft wl, 610ft oa × 65ft 8in × 25ft 8in
	182.9m, 186.0m × 20.0m × 7.8m
Machinery:	4-shaft geared turbines, 4 Babcock & Wilcox boilers, 100,000shp = 32kts. Range 8000nm at 15kts. Oil 2661t
Armament:	3–6in/47 (1×3), 2–5in/38 (1×2) (6–6in/47 (2×3), 6–5in/38 (3×2) in CLG 3 and CLG 8), 1 Talos SAM (1×2, 46 missiles, in CLG 3–CLG 5), 1 Terrier SAM (1×2, 120 missiles, in CLG 6–CLG 8)
Sensors:	Radar SPS-9 (SPS-17 in CLG 4), SPS-39, SPS-8B (CLG 3, CLG 5–CLG 8; SPS-2 in CLG 4), 2 SPQ-5 (CLG 6–CLG 8), 2 SPG-49/SPW-2 (CLG 3–CLG 5); sonar SQS-23. See notes
Complement:	1382

No	Name	Yard	Recomm	Fate
CLG 3	GALVESTON	Philadelphia N Yd	28.5.58	Decommissioned 1970
CLG 4	LITTLE ROCK	New York SB	3.6.60	Decommissioned 1976, memorial
CLG 5	OKLAHOMA CITY	Bethlehem	7.9.60	Decommissioned 1979
CLG 6	PROVIDENCE	Boston N Yd	17.9.59	Decommissioned 1973
CLG 7	SPRINGFIELD	Boston N Yd	2.7.60	Decommissioned 1973
CLG 8	TOPEKA	New York SB	26.3.60	Decommissioned 1969

UNITED STATES

All carried a lattice mast amidships for a three-dimensional electronically scanned radar, and a shorter one aft for a fighter-control height-finder; in some cases the two were interchanged. In each, too, a pair of guidance radars aft (SPG-49 for Talos, SPQ-5 for Terrier) controlled missiles fired by one twin-arm launcher. Flagships carried helicopters, with a landing pad on the quarterdeck, but had no hangars to stow them. By 1963 SPS-30 had replaced SPS-8B/SPS-2, and all ultimately had SPS-37A/43A rather than SPS-29. SPS-39 was removed from CLG 4 and 5 by 1967.

All these ships were refitted with SQS-23 hull sonars and with DASH drone control facilities in the early 1960s, as part of a programme to permit more open fleet formations (against nuclear attack): in such formations submarines would probably be able to penetrate the outer ASW screen, and each long-range sonar within that screen would be valuable.

Providence 1966   USN

Similar reasoning applied to the fleet carrier *America*. As first completed, the former *Clevelands* were considered top-heavy and had to be specially ballasted.

These ships were never entirely satisfactory, given their limited size. The two pure missile cruisers went first, decommissioned in 1969–70 and stricken in 1973. Fleet flagships were considered far more important, but the Terrier ships never received modernised fire control systems (with SPG-55 radars) because of the cost of conversion and the limited remaining life in their hulls; they were both withdrawn in 1973 and later stricken. The two Talos ships were the last to go, *Oklahoma City* ending her service with the Seventh Fleet in 1979.

Oklahoma City (as well as *Chicago* and *Long Beach*) used Talos anti-radar missiles (RGM-8H) to engage North Vietnamese radar sites during the Vietnam War. The number of such attacks has not been released, but it appears to have been small.

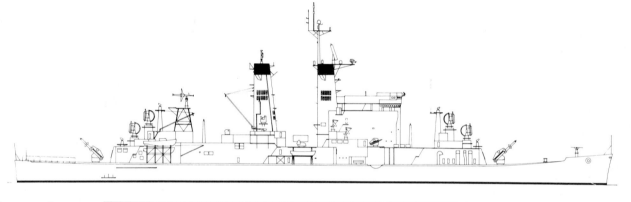

Albany 1970

These three ships were the most elaborate of the postwar US missile cruiser conversions, as well as the most futuristic in appearance. They alone received the kind of Talos launching system originally envisaged, extending its magazine deep into their hulls fore and aft (with 52 missiles at each end). Planned entirely without guns, they had a secondary battery of two twin Tartar launchers on their beams (84 missiles), as well as ASROC and the associated SQS-23 sonar system; in effect they were massive missile frigates. The high bridge was necessary to clear the paired SPG-49 missile control radars forward of it, and the unusual 'Mack' arrangement was chosen to reduce radar interference from the funnels. In addition, early planning called for the Regulus II surface-to-surface missile, but it was deleted at the design stage. However, plans for further conversions (which would have been CG 13–CG 15) did call for eight Polaris amidships. CG 10 and CG 11 were modernised with SPS-48 in place of SPS-39, and one SPS-30 was removed.

A pair of open 5in/38 guns was installed amidships at the insistence of the President, John F Kennedy, apparently after he had witnessed the failure of a demonstration of Terrier against a drone; the President may also have been impressed by the absence of any weapon suitable against a small torpedo-boat. Neither ASROC nor the Mk 32 TT have reloads.

Three further ships were to have been converted under the FY60 prog-

ALBANY class *fleet escorts (missile cruiser conversions)*

Displacement:	14,394t light; 18,777t full load
Dimensions:	664ft wl, 674ft 11in oa × 69ft 9in × 25ft 9in 202.4m, 205.8 × 21.3m × 7.9m
Machinery:	4-shaft geared turbines; 4 Babcock & Wilcox boilers, 120,000shp = 32kts. Range 7000nm at 15kts
Armament:	2 Talos SAM (2×2, 52 missiles each), 2 Tartar SAM (2×2, 42 missiles each), 2–5in/38 (2×1), 1 ASROC ASW system (1×8), 6–12.75in Mk 32 ASW TT (2×3)
Sensors:	Radar SPS-43A (in place of original SPS-29), 2 SPS-30, 4 SPG-49/SPW-2, 4 SPG-51; sonar SQS-23. See notes
Complement:	1266

No	Name	Yard	Recomm	Fate
CG 10	ALBANY	Boston N Yd	3.11.62	Decommissioned 1980
CG 11	CHICAGO	San Francisco N Yd	2.5.64	Decommissioned 1980
CG 12	COLUMBUS	Puget Sound N Yd	1.12.62	Decommissioned 1975

Albany 1968   USN

ramme as CG 13–CG 15, with a new SPG-56 missile control radar (SCB-173A rather than SCB-173); they were cancelled in favour of the new Typhon missile system, itself abandoned a few years later because of excessive cost. Only the last ship, *Chicago*, was completed with (a primitive) NTDS; *Albany* received a full NTDS system as part of an AAW modernisation (SCB-002) under the FY68 programme (Boston Naval Shipyard, Feb 1967–June 1969) at which time she was also fitted with SPS-48 radar in place of her earlier SPS-39, one of her

two SPS-30 fighter control radars being removed as weight compensation. Her Talos missile system was modernised with digital fire control. She was refitted in 1974–75 to serve as flagship of the Second Fleet and her remaining SPS-30 replaced by a satellite communications antenna. *Chicago* was modernised in Aug 1972–Aug 1973, albeit not on the same scale as *Albany*. Her NTDS was brought up to date, and she was fitted with an SLQ-26 Threat Reactive Anti-Ship Missile Defence system. *Albany* had already had the SLQ-19A ASMD sys-

tem fitted in 1970, after her SCB-002 modernization. *Columbus* alone was not modernised, and she was, therefore, the first of the class to be laid up, in May 1975. She was stricken in 1976. Her two sisters were decommissioned in 1980, their Talos missile system having been withdrawn from service to save money, even though initially they had been planned for retention through 1985. Normal practice would have been to strike them at this time, but in view of the international situation the Reagan Administration chose to retain them in reserve. Note,

however, that with Talos gone they are reduced to a Tartar missile battery.

Chicago served as primary air protection ship during the mining of Haiphong Harbour in 1972; she and other missile ships were assigned primary responsibility, with carrier fighters acting only as back-ups. When MiGs were detected heading for the low-flying mining aircraft, *Chicago* shot one down with Talos at a range of 48nm, and the others fled.

Intended at first as a nuclear frigate, this ship grew in the design stage to large cruiser size; indeed, she was the only cruiser (of traditional size) built as such by the US Navy after the war. She shared with *Enterprise* the futuristic fixed-array SPS-32/33 radar system, and has an SQS-23 long-range sonar in her bow, with the associated ASROC launcher amidships, as well as a pair of single 5in/38 guns, which were not part of the original design. She combined a pair of Terrier launchers forward (one with 40, one with 80 missiles) with Talos aft (52 missiles, as in the *Albany* class), and had a two-reactor power plant. Although *Long Beach* is a substantial ship at over 14,000t, she stands in contrast to much larger nuclear cruisers proposed in the mid-1950s, with four-shaft plants more closely approaching traditional cruiser power. Polaris or Regulus II was included in the original design, but neither was installed. The C1W reactors installed are reportedly very similar to the A2Ws of the *Enterprise*, presumably somewhat uprated, as total *Enterprise* power is reported as 280,000 shp.

The SPS-32/33 radar system was combined with one of the earliest NTDS installations. In 1968 a con-

LONG BEACH *fleet escort (missile cruiser)*

Displacement:	15,111t light; 16,602t full load
Dimensions:	690ft wl, 721ft 3in oa × 73ft 4in × 23ft 9in *210.4m, 219.9m × 22.3m × 7.3m*
Machinery:	2-shaft nuclear: 2 C1W reactors, 2 GE geared turbines, approx 80,000shp = *c* 30kts
Armament:	1 Talos (1×2, 52 missiles), 2 Terrier SAM (2×2, total 120 missiles), 2–5in/38 (2×1), 1 ASROC ASW system (1×8, 20 missiles), 6–12.75in Mk 32 TT (2×3). See notes
Sensors:	Radar SPS-32, SPS-33, 2 SPG-49/SPW-2, 4 SPG-55; sonar SQS-23. See notes
Complement:	1107

No	Name	Builder	Laid down	Launched	Comp	Fate
CGN 9 LONG BEACH		Bethlehem, Quincy	2.12.57	14.7.59	9.9.61	Extant 1982

ventional SPS-12 air search radar was added, partly because of maintenance difficulties with the fixed radars, and partly because the fixed sets did not have any integral IFF. A 1970 modernization provided integral IFF and digital Talos fire control, but the SPS-12 remained.

The Talos missile system was removed in 1979, leaving empty radar pedestals aft; 2×4 Harpoon launchers (with a total of eight missiles) were installed, and it appears that the former Talos magazine space, a considerable volume aft, is not being used. During her 1980 modernization, *Long Beach* received SPS-48 and SPS-49 in place of her SPS-32/33, but

the original square superstructure was retained, with 1.75in armour plate replacing the weight of the original panels. Two 20mm Phalanx CIWS have also been fitted. Her bow sonar has been modified to SQQ-23 configuration (improved passive operation) without the usual addition of a second sonar dome. A proposal for Aegis conversion (*ie* for the conversion of *Long Beach* to a prototype strike cruiser with an 8in gun forward) was rejected in 1977, reportedly out of concern that it would have jeopardised the Strike Cruiser programme itself.

In 1981 SM-2(ER) replaced the earlier SM-1(ER); the command

guidance of this system increases its range to match the performance of the earlier Talos. In addition, *Long Beach* retains flagship facilities (although she has not operated as a flagship) and will be fitted with extensive satellite facilities. During her next scheduled refit, 1984–85, she is to be fitted with a TFCC and with additional armour.

While operating in the Tonkin Gulf, *Long Beach* shot down two MiGs over North Vietnam at a range of about 65nm, in May and June 1968. At the time these were described as the first recorded combat uses of a naval SAM.

Long Beach 1979

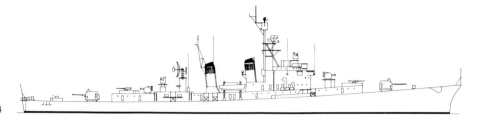

Mitscher 1954

MITSCHER class *fleet escorts (frigates)*

Displacement:	3331t light; 3642t standard; 4855t full load
Dimensions:	476ft wl, 490ft oa × 47ft 6in × 14ft 8in
	145.1m, 149.4m × 14.5m × 4.5m
Machinery:	2-shaft geared turbines, 4 Foster Wheeler boilers, 80,000shp = 36.5kts. Range 4500nm at 20kts. Oil 740t
Armament:	2–5in/54 (2×1), 4–3in/50 (2×2), 8–20mm (4×2), 4–21in TT, 2 Weapon Alfa ASW, 1 DC track, See notes
Sensors:	Radar SPS-6, SPS-8; sonar QHB, SQG-1 (sonar replaced by SQS-4 mid-1950s, SQS-23 in DLG conversions, with SPS-37 and SPS-48 plus two SPG-51; SQS-26 in the two remaining DLs). See notes

No	Name	Builder	Laid down	Launched	Comp	Fate
DL 2	MITSCHER	Bath Iron Wks	3.10.49	26.1.52	15.5.53	DDG 35 1968, stricken 1978
DL 3	JOHN S McCAIN	Bath Iron Wks	24.10.49	12.7.52	12.10.53	DDG 36, 1969, stricken 1978
DL 4	WILLIS A LEE	Bethlehem, Quincy	1.11.49	26.1.52	28.9.54	Decommissioned 1969, stricken 1972
DL 5	WILKINSON	Bethlehem, Quincy	1.2.50	23.4.52	29.7.54	Decommissioned 1969, stricken 1974

These four ships, laid down as DD 927–930, were originally designated 'destroyers', then 'frigates', in a new category which persisted until 1975. They owed their large size to the requirement for high speed, deeply loaded, in a seaway, and were originally designed in 1944-46 with conventional destroyer batteries, the only major innovation being the 5in/54 gun in a twin semi-automatic version. However, as the design developed it became clear that fast carrier escorts would require maximum anti-aircraft capability, including not only guns but also fighter-direction equipment (symbolised visually by the heavy stabilised SPS-8 height-finder). For a time, it appeared that the gun battery would consist entirely of the new 3in/70 twin automatic anti-aircraft gun, which was considered more effective than the new rapid-fire 5in/54 itself firing faster than the earlier twin type), but the latter was retained at the personal insistence of Admiral Nimitz, at least partly in view of the inability of the lighter weapon to deal with submarines forced to the surface. In fact the large CIC and the heavy radar were even more important; as early as 1945 it was clear that carrier fighters, controlled by the carrier and by radar-pickets such as the *Mitscher*s, would be the primary air defence of the fast carrier task force. Anti-submarine capability was secondary, as the high speed of the task force would in itself guarantee almost complete immunity. For example, in the design of the propel-

John S McCain 1977

lers and of the hull itself, high speed (to keep up with the task force) took priority over silencing. The primary ASW weapon was to be a guided torpedo, fired from a fixed tube, with a pair of rocket launchers (Weapon Alfa) as back-up.

High speed in a small ship meant a very compact machinery installation, and these four ships introduced the 1200lb plant to US service. All four were considered experimental, and gave considerable trouble in service, so that *Mitscher* and *John S McCain* had to be reboilered. Indeed, engine

trouble was sometimes given as the reason for the early retirement of the class. On trials, *Mitscher* made 34.84kts on 75,862shp at 4550t.

All were much modified in service. They were completed with open 3in/50s, as the enclosed 3in/70 was not yet ready. The latter were installed in 1957, and the original depth-charges as well as the after Weapon Alfa were surrendered as weight compensation, because the new mounting was much heavier than its original designed figure. In 1960 all four ships were fitted to operate the DASH

USN

drone helicopter, from a helipad which replaced the after 3in/70 mounting; *Wilkinson* landed the first DASH aboard at sea in August 1960. The DASH hangar was built above the torpedo room abaft No 2 funnel and the SPS-8 radar was re-sited to its top. The first two units were fitted with SQS-23 sonars, the last two with prototypes of the new SQS-26, in large bow domes which initially caused some problems. Of the forward 3in/70 and Weapon Alfa, the latter was soon landed in the two SQS-26 units. *Mitscher* abandoned her forward 3in/70 before her Weapon Alfa, but it appears that *John S McCain* retained both until her conversion as a DDG. In each case it was expected that ASROC would ultimately replace at least the forward Weapon Alfa.

As early as 1959 missile conversions were proposed, both Tartar and Terrier appearing feasible. The first two units were converted to Tartar-firing missile *destroyers* under the FY64 programme, but further conversions were abandoned in view of the ineffectiveness of the Tartar SAM system. Conversion entailed the replacement of the surviving superfiring weapons forward by ASROC (1×8, 16 missiles) with 6–12.75in TT and a single-arm Tartar launcher aft (40 missiles). The result was criticised as top heavy, and both ships were stricken after little more than a decade of service. The redesignation of the ships as DDG 35 and 36 rather than as DLG was indicative of the rapid growth in all classes of US warships. The two unconverted units were decommissioned in 1969.

All four were used to some extent as experimental ships. For example, *Mitscher* operated the first helicopter from a US destroyer in 1957, leading to the development of DASH.

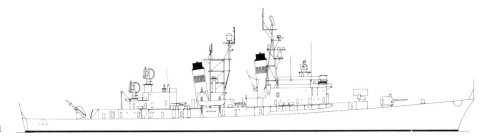

Dewey 1961

FARRAGUT class *fleet escorts (frigates)*

Displacement:	4167t light; 5648t full load
Dimensions:	490ft wl, 512ft 6in oa × 52ft 4in × 17ft 9in
	149.4m, 156.3m × 15.9m × 5.3m
Machinery:	2-shaft geared turbines, 4 Foster Wheeler boilers (Babcock & Wilcox in DLG 9–DLG 15) 85,000shp = 32kts. Range 5000nm at 20kts
Armament:	1–5in/54 RF, 1 Terrier SAM (1×2, 40 missiles), 1 ASROC ASW system (1×8), 6–12.75in Mk 32 ASW TT (2×3), 12 torpedoes
Sensors:	Radar SPS-29, SPS-37, 2 SPQ-5 (SPG-55 in DLG 7–DLG 13); sonar SQS-23
Complement:	360

No	Name	Builder	Laid down	Launched	Comp	Fate
DLG 6	FARRAGUT	Bethlehem, Quincy	3.6.57	18.7.58	10.12.60	Extant 1982
DLG 7	LUCE	Bethlehem, Quincy	1.10.57	11.12.58	20.5.61	Extant 1982
DLG 8	MACDONOUGH	Bethlehem, Quincy	15.4.58	9.7.59	4.11.61	Extant 1982
DLG 9	COONTZ	Puget Sound N Yd	1.3.57	6.12.58	15.7.60	Extant 1982
DLG 10	KING	Puget Sound N Yd	1.3.57	6.12.58	17.11.60	Extant 1982
DLG 11	MAHAN	Mare Island N Yd	31.7.57	7.10.59	25.8.60	Extant 1982
DLG 12	DAHLGREN	Philadelphia N Yd	1.3.58	16.3.60	8.4.61	Extant 1982
DLG 13	WILLIAM V PRATT	Philadelphia N Yd	1.3.58	16.3.60	4.11.61	Extant 1982
DLG 14	DEWEY	Bath Iron Wks	10.8.57	30.11.58	7.12.59	Extant 1982
DLG 15	PREBLE	Bath Iron Wks	16.12.57	23.5.59	9.5.60	Extant 1982

These were the first missile-armed fleet escorts designed and built as such, although the first three were originally to have been armed only with guns. They were designed on the recommendation of the Schindler Committee on the Long Range Ship-building Plan (1954), which argued for the construction of specialised Fast Task Force Escorts primarily for anti-aircraft screening, with submarine detection (for warning) but not destruction as an important secondary task. The resulting design called for four single rapid-fire 5in/54s as well as two twin 3in/50s; ASW weapons were limited to a single depth-charge track aft, a pair of fixed Hedgehogs (as in destroyers), and a quintuple torpedo tube intended primarily 'to embarrass enemy heavy units attempting to attack the carrier task force', as at Samar 1944.

Throughout the design, the installation of Terrier in place of the two after 5in/54s was carried as an alternative, and in 1955 the Chief of Naval Operations, Admiral Carney, personally decided that half of the FY56 ships were to be built as missile frigates. His successor, Admiral Burke, decided to accelerate the introduction of missiles into the fleet by ordering all six FY56 ships as missile ships. Meanwhile development of new anti-surface ship torpedoes was abandoned, and the planned quintuple trainable tubes, which were not compatible with existing long-range anti-submarine torpedoes, were dropped from the project. At about the same time, however, the advent of Soviet nuclear submarines, which were capable of attacking even fast task forces, made ASW a more important function of fast fleet escorts. Thus these ships were redesigned, first for the rocket-assisted torpedo (RAT) and then for ASROC, which replaced one of the two forward 5in/54s which had survived the transformation from all-gun to gun-and-missile frigates. At the same time their sonar was upgraded from the SQS-4 to the much larger SQS-23.

King and *Mahan* tested the prototype NTDS installations in 1961–62. Subsequently all ten ships were subject to extensive AAW modernisation. NTDS was installed and a new guidance radar for Terrier fitted (SPG-55B in lieu of SPQ-5A and SPG-55A in ships as built). Larger ship service turbo-generators were fitted to carry the increased electrical load. *Farragut* alone received reload stowage for her ASROC. Weight compensation included the removal of the two twin 3in/50s formerly carried. These refits were completed between 1969 and 1977, under the FY66–74 programmes (no awards in FY67 and FY73).

Harpoon quadruple launchers replaced the former twin 3in/50 mounts. *Coontz* tested the Vulcan Phalanx CIWS in 1973–4, before modernization, and in 1975 *King* carried two Vulcans. They now have two-dome SQQ-23A sonars, and are scheduled to receive SPS-49 radars in place of the former SPS-29C and SPS-37.

Mahan (DDG 42) was test ship for SM-2(ER) in 1979; this system allows a Terrier ship to engage several targets simultaneously, using a new Weapons Direction System Mk 14 and a new missile down-link. In addition, because it incorporates command guidance, the missile can fly a much longer-range energy-efficient trajectory; in effect the SM-2(ER) replaces the earlier Talos. In 1982 *Mahan* tested the New Threat Upgrade, which sharply reduces ship reaction time through the integration of shipboard radars (SPS-48E and SPS-49(V)5), NTDS, SYS-2, and the SM-2(ER) Block II missile. As of

early 1983, NTU/SM-2 Block II is scheduled for 10 Tartar and 21 Terrier ships: *Long Beach*, the *Leahy*, *Belknap*, *California* and *Virginia* class cruisers, and the *Kidd* class.

All were redesignated missile *destroyers* (DDG 37–46 in 1975, and are the only DDGs which fire the two-stage Terrier or Standard (Extended Range) missile.

Luce 1979   C & S Taylor

UNITED STATES

In these ships the guided missile was finally made paramount, with guns little more than an afterthought. The need for large numbers of missiles to protect the Fleet against a mounting air threat and the relatively slow rate of new construction led to a conscious decision that new missile ships be double-ended. It had previously been objected that missile mounts in the bow would be so subject to sea damage as to be useless; in the *Leahy* class special efforts were to protect the forward launcher, including the knuckling of the hull, which was uncharacteristic of previous US practice. The decision to adopt a forecastle type of hull reflects the explosive growth of space (rather than weight) requirements, a characteristic of modern warship development. As in the *Farraguts*, ASW was a distinctly secondary consideration, but the *Leahys* were designed to incorporate ASROC (without reloads) and had a bow dome for their SQS-23 sonars.

As in the case of earlier Terrier ships, the *Leahy* class suffered from limited effectiveness as built, and was subject to extensive modernisation. NTDS was fitted, with the improved

LEAHY class *fleet escorts (frigates)*

Displacement:	5146t light; 7590t full load
Dimensions:	510ft wl, 533ft oa × 53ft 4in × 19ft
	155.5m, 162.5m × 16.3m × 5.8m
Machinery:	2-shaft geared turbines, 4 Babcock & Wilcox boilers (Foster Wheeler in DLG 19–DLG 24), 85,000shp = 32kts. Range 8000nm at 20kts
Armament:	2 Terrier SAM (2×2, 40 missiles each launcher), 1 ASROC ASW system (1×8, no reloads), 4–3in/50 (2×2), 6–12.75in Mk 32 ASW TT (2×3, 12 torpedoes)
Sensors:	Radar SPS-37, SPS-39, 4 SPG-55; sonar SQS-23
Complement:	377

No	Name	Builder	Laid down	Launched	Comp	Fate
DLG 16	LEAHY	Bath Iron Wks	3.12.59	1.7.61	4.8.62	Extant 1982
DLG 17	HARRY E YARNELL	Bath Iron Wks	31.5.60	9.12.61	2.2.63	Extant 1982
DLG 18	WORDEN	Bath Iron Wks	19.9.60	2.6.62	3.8.63	Extant 1982
DLG 19	DALE	New York SB	6.9.60	28.7.62	23.11.63	Extant 1982
DLG 20	RICHMOND K TURNER	New York SB	9.1.61	6.4.63	13.6.64	Extant 1982
DLG 21	GRIDLEY	Puget Sound N Yd	15.7.60	31.7.61	25.5.63	Extant 1982
DLG 22	ENGLAND	Todd, Los Angeles	4.10.60	6.3.62	7.12.63	Extant 1982
DLG 23	HALSEY	Mare Island N Yd	26.8.60	15.1.62	20.7.63	Extant 1982
DLG 24	REEVES	Puget Sound N Yd	1.7.60	12.5.62	15.5.64	Extant 1982

SPG-55B guidance radar and a modernised fire control system capable of controlling the Standard Missile (SM-1). Refits were funded under the FY66 (DLG 16), FY67 (DLG 17, 18,

21, 22 and 24) and FY71 (DLG 19, originally under FY68- DLG 20 and DLG 23) budgets. Later all had their pair of twin 3in/50 removed for replacement by quadruple Harpoon

launchers; two Vulcan Phalanx (20mm Gatling guns) will be added, as will SM-2 capability.

All were redesignated CG (cruisers) rather than DLG in 1975.

Leahy 1979　　　　USN

Bainbridge 1980　　　　USN

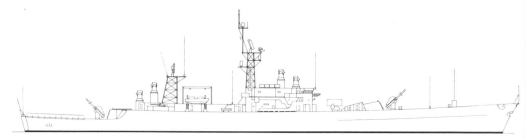

Bainbridge 1962

Bainbridge (DLG 25, CGN 25 from 1975) was essentially a nuclear-powered equivalent of the *Leahy* class, built as the prototype nuclear fast task force escort. At the time she represented the minimum platform for a two-reactor power plant which could be expected to attain destroyer speed; a fast submarine plant, such as that in the large *Triton*, was rejected because it weighed too much for the power it produced to propel a destroyer with a worthwhile payload at an acceptable speed. Destroyer nuclear propulsion was given high priority from about 1956 onwards because destroyer endurance, not carrier

BAINBRIDGE *fleet escort (frigate)*

Displacement:	7250t light; 7982t full load
Dimensions:	540ft wl, 565 ft oa × 56ft × 19ft 5in
	164.6m, 172.3m × 17.0m × 5.9m
Machinery:	2-shaft nuclear: 2 D2G reactors, 2 geared turbines, approx 60,000shp = *c*30kts
Armament:	2 Terrier SAM (2×2, 40 missiles each), 1 ASROC ASW system (1×8), 6–12.75in Mk 32 ASW TT (2×3) 4–3in/50 (2×2)
Sensors:	Radar SPS-37, SPS-39, 4 SPG-55; sonar SQS-23
Complement:	459

No	Name	Builder	Laid down	Launched	Comp	Fate
DLGN 25	BAINBRIDGE	Bethlehem, Quincy	15.5.59	15.4.61	6.10.62	Extant 1982

endurance, was a limiting factor in carrier task force operations.

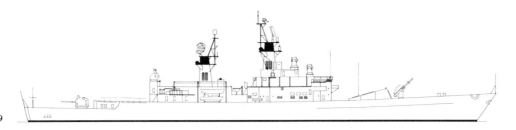

Sterett 1969

These ships suffered a somewhat tortured design history, originating as an attempt to produce a missile destroyer both less expensive than the *Adams* class and more effective in ASW, with the new SQS-26 sonar and endurance increased from under 4500nm to 6000nm; the result, even with a new austere missile system (12 rather than 40 Tartars were planned) was far more expensive than the original destroyer. Quite soon Terrier was substituted, as befitting so expensive a ship, and the existing *Leahy* class hull was adapted to the new design. However, its destroyer origin survived in the requirement for a single 5in/54 rapid-fire gun. Considerable economy in design was achieved by combining the Terrier and ASROC launchers; the system mounted in these ships can accommodate up to 60 Terriers, or it can accommodate 40 Terriers and up to 20 ASROCs. Increasing interest in ASW was also manifested in provision for the DASH ASW drone helicopter, and for Mk 48 torpedo tubes in the transom stern. They were redesignated 'cruisers' in 1975.

Wainwright (DLG 28) was the first to be completed with the Naval Tactical Data System integrated into her weapon control system; the two earlier ships later also received NTDS. *Belknap*, the name ship, was severely damaged by collison with the carrier *John F Kennedy* in the Mediterranean in November 1975, and was rebuilt at Philadelphia (1975–80); however, proposals to fit the new Aegis system were not accepted and she emerged only slightly modified. As of 1981 the modernisation programme called for eight Harpoon launchers (four to port firing forward, four to starboard firing aft) in place of the former 3in/50 secondary guns, and all are to receive a pair of Phalanx Close-In Weapon Systems. The Mk 25 torpedo tubes for long-range ASW torpedoes were removed from all ships of this class.

BELKNAP class *fleet escorts (frigates)*

Displacement:	5409t light; 7890t full load
Dimensions:	524ft wl, 547ft oa × 54ft 9in × 18ft 2in
	159.8m, 166.8m × 16.7m × 5.5m
Machinery:	2-shaft geared turbines, 4 Babcock & Wilcox boilers (Combustion Engineering in DLG 28–DLG 31, DLG 33), 85,000shp = 32kts. Range 7100nm at 20kts
Armament:	1 Terrier/ASROC SAM/ASW system (1×2, up to 20 ASROC of a total of 60 missiles), 1–5in/54 RF, 2–3in/50 (2×1), 6–12.75in Mk 32 ASW TT (2×3), 2–21in ASW TT (not fitted in some ships)
Sensors:	Radar SPS-43, SPS-48, 2 SPG-55; sonar SQS-26; NTDS in DLG 28–DLG 34
Complement:	388

No	Name	Builder	Laid down	Launched	Comp	Fate
DLG 26	BELKNAP	Bath Iron Wks	5.2.62	20.7.63	7.11.64	Extant 1982
DLG 27	JOSEPHUS DANIELS	Bath Iron Wks	23.4.62	2.12.63	8.5.65	Extant 1982
DLG 28	WAINWRIGHT	Bath Iron Wks	2.7.62	25.4.64	8.1.66	Extant 1982
DLG 29	JOUETT	Puget Sound N Yd	25.9.62	30.6.64	3.12.66	Extant 1982
DLG 30	HORNE	Mare Island N Yd	12.12.62	30.10.64	15.4.67	Extant 1982
DLG 31	STERETT	Puget Sound N Yd	25.9.62	30.6.65	8.4.67	Extant 1982
DLG 32	WILLIAM H STANDLEY	Bath Iron Wks	29.7.63	19.12.64	9.7.66	Extant 1982
DLG 33	FOX	Todd, San Pedro	15.1.63	21.11.64	28.5.66	Extant 1982
DLG 34	BIDDLE	Bath Iron Wks	9.12.63	2.7.65	21.1.67	Extant 1982

Fox was trials ship for the Tomahawk box launcher (1977) and all will be fitted with it from 1983. In addition, *Wainwright* has served as trials ships for SM-2(ER), which will also presumably be extended to all ships of this class; *Belknap*, *Jouett* and *Horne* had all been so fitted by the end of 1982.

Both *Sterett* and *Biddle* engaged and shot down North Vietnamese MiGs over the Gulf of Tonkin during 1972. The former was the first US ship to be attacked by the MiGs, on 19 April 1972, while covering *Oklahoma City* and *Higbee* in a shore bombardment. She shot down two MiGs and what was believed to have been a Styx missile, the first anti-ship missile to have been destroyed by another missile in combat. *Biddle* was attacked by five MiGs when on PIRAZ (Positive Identification and Radar Advisory Zone, or air control) duty in the Gulf of Tonkin on the night of 19 July 1972, shooting down two.

Belknap 1980   USN

Truxton 1968

Truxtun (DLGN 35) was essentially a nuclear version of the *Belknap* class, somewhat enlarged and rearranged to accommodate her power plant. The Nuclear Propulsion organisation had originally hoped to duplicate the earlier *Bainbridge*, but that was rejected in view of the need for the improved SQS-26 sonar.

This ship was designated 'cruiser' (CGN) rather than frigate (DLGN) in 1975.

TRUXTUN *fleet escort* (frigate)

Displacement:	8149t light; 8927t full load
Dimensions:	540ft wl, 564ft oa × 57ft 10in × 19ft 10in
	164.6m, 172.0 × 17.6m × 6.0m
Machinery:	2-shaft nuclear: 2 D2G reactors, 2 geared turbines, approx 60,000shp = *c* 30kts
Armament:	1 Terrier/ASROC SAM/ASW system (1×2, total 60 missiles), 1–5in/54 RF, 2–3in/50 (2×1), 6–12.75in Mk 32 ASW TT (2×3)
Sensors:	Radar SPS-40, SPS-48, 2 SPG-55; sonar SQS-26
Complement:	490

No	Name	Builder	Laid down	Launched	Comp	Fate
DLGN 35	TRUXTUN	New York SB	17.6.63	19.12.64	27.5.67	Extant 1982

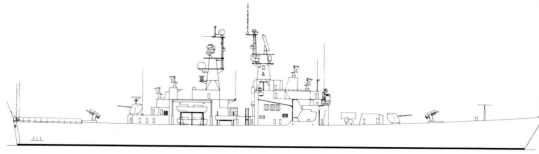

California 1977

These two ships were nuclear versions of the abortive conventionally-powered FY66 guided missile destroyer, built under the FY67 and FY68 programme, the first long lead time items having been bought under the FY66 programme. A third ship, partially funded in FY68, was built instead to a new design. Their construction was quite expensive, and by the late 1960s Secretary of Defense McNamara was unwilling to release funds for them; they were built as a result of Congressional pressure.

The design originally called for a pair of heavyweight Mk 42 5in/54 guns and two torpedo tubes for Mk 48 torpedoes, in the transom; the tubes were discarded and lightweight Mk 45 guns substituted. The missile battery was controlled by the new digital Tartar-D (SPG-51D) fire control system, and, compared to the *Bainbridge* and *Truxtun*, they had improved D2G reactors with about three times the core lifetime. A helicopter landing area was provided aft, but they had no hangar, as they were designed during the gap between DASH and LAMPS. The *California*s have been described as the first US nuclear surface ships intended for series production. They were redesignated 'cruisers' (CGN) in 1975.

CALIFORNIA class *fleet escorts (frigates)*

Displacement:	10,150t full load
Dimensions:	570ft wl, 596ft oa × 61ft × 20ft 6in
	173.8m, 181.7m × 18.6m × 6.3m
Machinery:	2-shaft nuclear: 2 D2G reactors, 2 geared turbines, approx 60,000shp = 30+kts
Armament:	2 Standard SAM (2×1, 40 missiles each), 1 ASROC ASW system (1×8, 24 missiles), 4–12.75in Mk 32 ASW TT (4×1 fixed, 16 torpedoes), 2–5in/54 (2×1)
Sensors:	Radar SPS-40, SPS-48, 2 SPG-51, SPG-60, SPQ-9; sonar SQS-26
Complement:	533

No	Name	Builder	Laid down	Launched	Comp	Fate
DLGN 36	CALIFORNIA	Newport News	23.1.70	22.9.71	16.2.74	Extant 1982
DLGN 37	SOUTH CAROLINA	Newport News	1.12.70	1.7.72	25.1.75	Extant 1982

California 1975   C & S Taylor

Redesignated cruisers in 1975, these ships were initially intended as nuclear counterparts to the *Spruance* DDG design (DXGN), although they were completed as slightly improved equivalents of the *California*s. Four were built under the FY70–75 budgets (with none in FY73 and FY74), but a fifth, longlead items for which had been approved under the FY75 programme, was stopped in FY76 because, without Aegis, she would be obsolete.

The original design called for a separate ASROC launcher and one Mk 13 missile launcher aft; however, it was argued that a nuclear frigate might well have to operate independently and therefore would need two missile launchers, to overcome limited magazine capacity as well as to assure the availability of at least one launcher. The adoption of the Mk 26 missile launcher eliminated the ASROC requirement, but these ships still have most of their battery aft (Mod 1, 44 weapons), together with both SPG-51D guidance radars; forward they have a single gun fire control system with one SPG-60 tracker-illuminator, providing a possible third missile-control channel. Typically they carry 50 SAM, 16 ASROC and 2 test rounds. A hangar below the quarterdeck can accommodate LAMPS helicopters, but its elevator reportedly leaks badly in wet weather, and the helicopter is not usually

embarked; this arrangement is often criticised.

Hopes that at least some ships of this class would be fitted with Aegis (then called ASMS) did not materialise, although a modified *Virginia* hull, CGN 42, was for a time a candidate successor to the Strike Cruiser.

These ships now (1982) carry their eight Harpoon missiles in cannisters firing athwartships, before the bridge. Two Phalanx are to be fitted, at the after end of the forward superstructure; SM-2 is to be installed, beginning in 1983; and they are to be fitted with Kevlar armour during FY82 to FY86 overhauls, with major modernisation scheduled to begin

with CGN 48 in FY87. Note that, although these ships carry modern ASW sensors, they are not scheduled to be fitted with either LAMPS III or with the towed array: they are primarily AAW ships. Part of the reason is that they are inherently relatively noisy, given the sound generated by the circulation pumps associated with their nuclear plants. Analogous sources of noise in nuclear submarines are sound-isolated.

VIRGINIA class *fleet escorts (frigates/cruisers)*

Displacement:	11,000t full load
Dimensions:	560ft wl, 585ft oa × 63ft × 21ft
	170.7m, 178.4 × 19.2m × 6.4m
Machinery:	2-shaft nuclear; 2 D2G reactors, 2 geared turbines, approx 60,000shp = 30+kts
Armament:	2 Standard SAM/ASW systems (2×2, 24 missiles forward, 44 inc ASROC aft), 2–5/54 (2×1), 6–12.75in Mk 32 ASW TT (2×3, 14 torpedoes), 1 helicopter
Sensors:	Radar SPS-40, SPS-55, 2 SPG-51, SPG-60, SPQ-9; sonar SQS-53
Complement:	519

No	Name	Builder	Laid down	Launched	Comp	Fate
DLGN 38	VIRGINIA	Newport News	19.8.72	14.12.74	11.9.76	Extant 1982
DLGN 39	TEXAS	Newport News	18.8.73	9.8.75	10.9.77	Extant 1982
CGN 40	MISSISSIPPI	Newport News	22.2.75	31.7.76	5.8.78	Extant 1982
CGN 41	ARKANSAS	Newport News	17.1.77	21.10.78	18.10.80	Extant 1982

Virginia 1976   USN

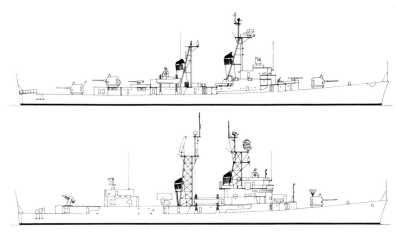

John Paul Jones as completed

Somers 1968

These were the only postwar general-purpose gun-armed destroyers, intended originally as a mobilisation version of the expensive *Mitscher* type (1950). However, when a Gibbs and Cox study showed that a simplification of the sophisticated construction of the earlier design would result in a 5000t ship, a new design was begun, concentrating more on anti-aircraft firepower than on ASW. In the end, even a trainable Hedgehog was given up, as it would have required extra length. It appears that the unusual gun arrangement, two aft and one forward, was adopted for dryness; in addition it was well suited for anti-aircraft defence. Given the high rate of fire of the automatic Mk 42 gun mounting in these ships, their battery was more than equivalent to that of the earlier *Gearing* class, although that was not evident at the time.

From DD 936 onwards the sheer line was raised 3ft at the bow for additional dryness; the first ships (FY53 group) were too far along to be modified. ASW weapons were fixed Hedgehogs and four long torpedo tubes, as well as a dropping system (succeeded by the familiar Mk 32 triple tubes) for lightweight torpedoes. However, the Bureau of Ordnance abandoned long torpedoes for surface ships in about 1956, and only the first two units were completed as planned.

By 1954 the state of destroyer and escort development was sufficiently confused to require special analysis, and a Committee of the Long Range Shipbuilding and Conversion Plan proposed the abandonment of general-purpose destroyer construction in favour of a combination of fast task force escorts (which became the *Farraguts*), fast ASW escorts (a proposed 'corvette' conversion of the *Bensons* and austere ocean escorts (destroyer escorts such as the *Dealeys*). In fact *Forrest Sherman* class construction was soon terminated in favour of a missile-armed equivalent, the *Charles F Adams* class, with 18 general-purpose escorts completed.

By 1959 all were scheduled for conversion to Tartar-armed missile destroyers, a single missile launcher aft replacing both 5in/54 guns there. However, Secretary of Defense Robert S McNamara sharply curtailed the conversion programme in view of high unit cost and the low effectiveness of the Tartar missile; only four were converted, as DDG 31–DDG 34. Of the others, all were to have had ASW modernisation (with one 5in/54 removed, SQS-23 and SQS-35 sonars, and ASROC), but

FORREST SHERMAN class *fleet escorts (destroyers)*

Displacement:	2734t light; 4916t full load
Dimensions:	407ft wl, 418ft 6in oa × 44ft 11in × 15ft
	124.1m, 127.6m × 13.7m × 4.6m
Machinery:	2-shaft geared turbines, 4 boilers, 70,000shp = 33kts. Range 4500nm at 20kts
Armament:	3–5in/54 (3×1), 4–3in/50 (2×2), 2 Hedgehog ASW mortars, 4–21in TT (4×1), 6–12.75in Mk 32 ASW TT (2×3)
Sensors:	Radar SPS-6; sonar SQS-4
Complement:	324

No	Name	Builder	Laid down	Launched	Comp	Fate
DD 931	FORREST SHERMAN	Bath Iron Wks	27.10.53	5.2.56	9.11.55	Extant 1982
DD 932	JOHN PAUL JONES	Bath Iron Wks	18.1.54	7.5.55	5.4.56	DDG 32 Sept 67, extant 1982
DD 933	BARRY	Bath Iron Wks	15.3.54	1.10.55	31.8.56	Extant 1982
DD 936	DECATUR	Bethlehem, Quincy	13.9.54	15.12.55	7.12.56	DDG 31 Apr 67, extant 1982
DD 937	DAVIS	Bethlehem, Quincy	1.2.55	28.3.56	28.2.57	Extant 1982
DD 938	JONAS INGRAM	Bethlehem, Quincy	15.6.55	8.7.56	19.7.57	Extant 1982
DD 940	MANLEY	Bath Iron Wks	10.2.55	12.4.56	1.2.57	Extant 1982
DD 941	DU PONT	Bath Iron Wks	11.5.55	8.9.56	1.7.57	Extant 1982
DD 942	BIGELOW	Bath Iron Wks	6.7.55	2.2.57	8.11.57	Extant 1982
DD 943	BLANDY	Bethlehem, Quincy	29.12.55	19.12.56	8.11.57	Extant 1982
DD 944	MULLINIX	Bethlehem, Quincy	5.4.56	18.3.57	7.3.58	Extant 1982
DD 945	HULL	Bath Iron Wks	12.9.56	10.8.57	3.7.58	Extant 1982
DD 946	EDSON	Bath Iron Wks	3.12.56	1.1.58	7.11.58	Extant 1982
DD 947	SOMERS	Bath Iron Wks	4.3.57	30.5.58	3.4.59	DDG 34 Feb 68, extant 1982
DD 948	MORTON	Ingalls	4.3.57	23.5.58	26.5.59	Extant 1982
DD 949	PARSONS	Ingalls	17.6.57	19.8.58	29.10.59	DDG 33 Nov 67, extant 1982
DD 950	RICHARD S EDWARDS	Puget Sound	20.12.56	24.9.57	5.2.59	Extant 1982
DD 951	TURNER JOY	Puget Sound N Yd	30.9.57	5.5.58	3.8.59	Extant 1982

six units (DD 931, 932, 944–946, 951) were dropped because of cost escalation; all received the large SQS-23, however. *Barry* was the test ship for the bow-mounted SQS-23, and *Hull* tested the Mk 71 8in/55 Major Caliber Lightweight Gun.

Bigelow was a test ship for Vulcan Phalanx. The DDG conversion carried 40 Tartar and 16 ASROC rounds, and the ASW conversions carried 20 ASROC; both had 6–12.75in Mk 32 TT (without reloads).

Edson was assigned to Naval

Reserve Training on 1 April 1977. During 1982 it was announced that the remainder of the class would be retired to offset the considerable cost of new construction. Reportedly the 1200psi plant was becoming a maintenance problem.

Barry (after ASW conversion) 1971

USN

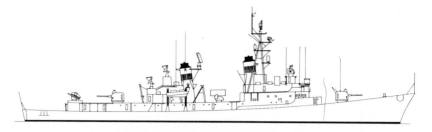

Charles F Adams 1962

These Tartar-armed missile destroyers were originally designed as modified versions of the *Forrest Sherman*: a design requirement of the Tartar missile system was that it could replace a single 5in mounting on a one-for-one basis. The twin 3in/50 nearest the missile launcher was to be replaced by a replenishment-at-sea area for missile replacement, the other by a twin ASW weapon launcher (for the RAT system then in development), and there was to have been a quintuple nest of torpedo tubes between the stacks. However, RAT was abandoned in favour of ASROC, whose eight-round 'pepperbox' replaced the originally contemplated long torpedo tubes; these ships also received the usual launching system for lightweight ASW torpedoes. Quite soon it became evident that the new destroyer would have to be lengthened considerably to accommodate the new SQS-23 sonar and an enlarged CIC (for missile control), and to balance off increased displacement without a loss of speed.

There were several modifications during the construction of the class. FY59 and later ships (DDG 15–DDG 24) had single- rather than twin-arm Tartar launchers for greater reliability; FY60 and FY61 units (DDG 20–DDG 24) had bow-mounted sonars, a change evident from the bow location of their anchors. Australia and West Germany both purchased near-sisters: the Australian DDG 25–DDG 27 had Ikara instead of ASROC amidships, and the West German DDG 28–DDG 30 had 'Macks'.

DDG production terminated with the FY61 programme largely because of the promise of the Typhon programme then in prospect; DDGs contemplated for the FY66–67 programmes were not built.

Some ships were refitted with 4-round ASROC reload magazines to starboard alongside the forward funnel. Programmes for modernisation were complicated by the very tight design of these ships. Thus a programme which was to have begun with DDG 3 in FY80 was abandoned under Congressional pressure when projected cost per ship rose to $221 million; it had already been cut to ten ships. Instead, DDG 15 to DDG 24 will be modernised as part of their regular refits, with work spread over two overhauls, for a total of two years per ship. The first was *Tattnall* (Philadelphia N Yd, begun Aug 1981); *Goldsborough* and *Benjamin Stoddert* have also been funded, as of early 1983. In the case of the *Tattnall*, the combat systems upgrade was carried out in the first overhaul period, with a hull and machinery (including sonar) upgrade scheduled for a second overhaul about two years later.

The major external changes evident are the installation of the Mk 86 gun/missile fire control system, which adds a third full missile control channel forward (the earlier SPG-53 had a secondary missile control capability); the installation of SLQ-32 and SLQ-20 countermeasures in place of the earlier ULQ-6B; and the installation of new radars (SPS-40C/D in place of the less reliable SPS-40B, SPS-52C in place of SPS-39, and LN-66 for navigation). More significantly, the ships are to be fitted with a three-computer NTDS and with an integrated combat system (SYS-1). Countermeasures capability is also increased by the installation of Super-Rapid Blooming Offboard Chaff (SRBOC). To service this increased electronic equipment, air conditioning compressor capacity increases from 140 to 225 tons, and ship service turbo-generator capacity is increased by 750kW. Modernised ships will have their SQS-23 systems upgraded to two-dome SQQ-23 configuration; several ships have already been so modified. In addition, all ships of this class will fire Harpoon from their Tartar launchers: 4 from Mk 11s, 6 from Mk 13s.

CHARLES F ADAMS class *fleet escorts (destroyers)*

Displacement:	3277t light; 4526t full load
Dimensions:	420ft wl, 437ft oa × 47ft × 15ft
	128m, 133.2m × 14.3m × 4.6m
Machinery:	2-shaft geared turbines, 4 boilers, 70,000shp = 33kts. Range 4500nm at 20kts
Armament:	2–5in/54 RF, 1 Tartar SAM (1×2, 42 missiles) (1×1, 40 missiles in DDG 15–DDG 24), 1 ASROC ASW system (1×8), 6–12.75in Mk 32 ASW TT (2×3)
Sensors:	Radar SPS-29 (SPS-40 in later units), SPS-39, 2 SPG-51; sonar SQQ-23A or SQS-23A (bow mounted in DDG 20–DDG 24)
Complement:	333–350

No	Name	Builder	Laid down	Launched	Comp	Fate
DDG 2	CHARLES F ADAMS	Bath Iron Wks	16.6.58	8.9.59	10.9.60	Extant 1982
DDG 3	JOHN KING	Bath Iron Wks	25.5.58	30.1.60	.4.2.61	Extant 1982
DDG 4	LAWRENCE	New York SB	27.10.58	27.2.60	6.1.62	Extant 1982
DDG 5	CLAUDE V RICKETTS (ex-*Biddle*)	New York SB	18.5.59	4.6.60	5.5.62	Extant 1982
DDG 6	BARNEY	New York SB	18.8.59	10.12.60	11.8.62	Extant 1982
DDG 7	HENRY B WILSON	Defoe	28.2.58	23.4.59	17.12.60	Extant 1982
DDG 8	LYNDE McCORMICK	Defoe, Bay City	4.4.58	9.9.60	3.6.61	Extant 1982
DDG 9	TOWERS	Todd-Pacific, Seattle	1.4.58	23.4.59	24.6.61	Extant 1982
DDG 10	SAMPSON	Bath Iron Wks	2.3.59	9.9.60	24.6.61	Extant 1982
DDG 11	SELLERS	Bath Iron Wks	3.8.59	9.9.60	28.10.61	Extant 1982
DDG 12	ROBINSON	Defoe, Bay City	23.4.59	27.4.60	9.12.61	Extant 1982
DDG 13	HOEL	Defoe, Bay City	1.6.59	4.8.60	16.6.62	Extant 1982
DDG 14	BUCHANAN	Todd-Pacific, Seattle	23.4.59	11.5.60	7.2.62	Extant 1982
DDG 15	BERKELEY	New York SB	1.6.60	29.7.61	15.12.62	Extant 1982
DDG 16	JOSEPH STRAUSS	New York SB	27.12.60	9.12.61	20.4.63	Extant 1982
DDG 17	CONYNGHAM	New York SB	1.5.61	19.5.62	13.7.63	Extant 1982
DDG 18	SEMMES	Avondale	18.8.60	20.5.61	10.12.62	Extant 1982
DDG 19	TATTNALL	Avondale	14.11.60	28.8.61	13.4.63	Extant 1982
DDG 20	GOLDSBOROUGH	Puget Sound N Yd	3.1.61	15.12.61.	9.11.63	Extant 1982
DDG 21	COCHRANE	Puget Sound N Yd	31.7.61	18.7.61	21.3.64	Extant 1982
DDG 22	BENJAMIN STODDERT	Puget Sound N Yd	11.6.62	8.1.63	12.9.64	Extant 1982
DDG 23	RICHARD E BYRD	Todd-Pacific, Seattle	12.4.61	6.2.62	7.3.64	Extant 1982
DDG 24	WADDELL	Todd-Pacific, Seattle	6.2.62	26.2.63	28.8.64	Extant 1982

Richard E Byrd 1977 C & S Taylor

These large destroyers were surely among the more controversial of recent US warships: designed by a private firm (Litton), they are usually described as too large and too poorly armed. In fact they were the direct consequence of an attempt to replace the mass of Second World War destroyers, which were nearing the end of their lives in the mid-1960s.

Initially, it was hoped that most of the ASW destroyers would be replaced by *Knox* class ocean escorts, and that the Navy would build a new class of missile destroyers to make up for the gap in such construction since the early 1960s, a gap caused largely by the failure of the Typhon system planned for FY63 and later units. Analysis suggested, first, that it would be wise to seek maximum commonality between the ASW and missile units, and second, that although each carrier would require six escorts, only three would need anti-aircraft missile capability. In addition, Secretary McNamara strongly espoused a project system in which preliminary design would be done by a contractor.

One of the benefits of a common hull was that, if the air threat were to increase in the future, ASW ships could easily be refitted to meet it. Ultimately, relatively few ships could be ordered, none of them for air defence. However, the *Spruance* remained an anti-aircraft design with its missiles, radars and some of its computers never installed. To some extent, too, its large size was mandated by the requirement for 30kts in rough weather, a requirement of carrier operations.

Plans to install single lightweight 8in/55 guns for amphibious fire support were cancelled in 1978, but the potential for major anti-aircraft upgrade remains. Indeed, Iran ordered six (later reduced to four) anti-aircraft versions of the *Spruance* class in 1973–74. With the Iranian Revolution, they were offered for sale, and all four were purchased as the *Kidd* class in July 1979, receiving DDG hull numbers in the *Spruance* series. As in the case of *Virginia* class cruisers, they have magazine stowage for 68 missiles, with two SPG-51D guidance radars plus an SPG-60. The greatly increased displacement of the *Kidd*s is due in part to the addition of armour. A thirty-first *Spruance*, DD 997, was authorised in FY78 with the proviso that it have increased helicopter facilities; however, it will be identical to the 30 ships already ordered, except for the provision of Kevlar armour and an SPS-49 air search radar. The Reagan Administration FY83–FY87 programme included three more ships of this type in FY86–FY87, out of a planned total of six.

On trials *Spruance* made about 32kts; the 1300t increase in the *Kidd*s cost about one knot.

SPRUANCE and KIDD classes *fleet escorts (destroyers)*

Displacement:	5826t light; 7800t full load (*Kidd* class 9200t full load)
Dimensions:	529ft wl, 563ft 4in oa × 55ft × 20ft 6in
	161.3m, 171.7m × 16.8m × 6.3m
Machinery:	2 shafts, 4 LM 2500 gas turbines, 80,000shp = 30kts. Range 6000nm at 20kts
Armament:	2–5in/54 (2×1), 1 Sea Sparrow SAM (1×8, 24 missiles), 1 ASROC ASW system (1×8, 24 missiles), 6–12.75in Mk 32 (2×3, 14 torpedoes), 1 helicopter
	Kidd class: as above except 2 Mk 26 launchers (2×2, typically 50 Standard SM-2 SAM, 16 ASROC and 2 test missiles) and 2–20mm Phalanx CIWS instead of Sea Sparrow and ASROC launchers
Sensors:	Radar SPS-40 (*Kidd* class SPS-48, 2 SPG-51), SPQ-9, SPG-60; sonar SQS-33
Complement:	296

No	Name	Builder	Laid down	Launched	Comp	Fate
Spruance class						
DD 963	SPRUANCE	Litton	17.11.72	10.11.73	20.9.75	Extant 1982
DD 964	PAUL F FOSTER	Litton	6.2.73	23.2.74	21.2.76	Extant 1982
DD 965	KINKAID	Litton	19.4.73	25.5.74	10.7.76	Extant 1982
DD 966	HEWITT	Litton	23.7.73	24.8.74	25.9.76	Extant 1982
DD 967	ELLIOTT	Litton	15.10.73	19.12.74	22.1.76	Extant 1982
DD 968	ARTHUR W RADFORD	Litton	14.1.74	1.3.75	16.4.77	Extant 1982
DD 969	PETERSON	Litton	29.4.74	21.6.75	9.7.77	Extant 1982
DD 970	CARON	Litton	1.7.74	24.6.75	1.10.77	Extant 1982
DD 971	DAVID R RAY	Litton	23.9.74	23.8.75	19.11.77	Extant 1982
DD 972	OLDENDORF	Litton	27.12.74	21.10.75	4.3.78	Extant 1982
DD 973	JOHN YOUNG	Litton	17.2.75	7.2.76	20.5.78	Extant 1982
DD 974	COMTE DE GRASSE	Litton	4.4.75	26.3.76	5.8.78	Extant 1982
DD 975	O'BRIEN	Litton	9.5.75	8.7.76	3.12.77	Extant 1982
DD 976	MERRILL	Litton	16.6.75	1.9.76	11.3.78	Extant 1982
DD 977	BRISCOE	Litton	21.7.75	15.12.76	3.6.78	Extant 1982
DD 978	STUMP	Litton	25.8.75	29.1.77	19.8.78	Extant 1982
DD 979	CONOLLY	Litton	29.9.75	19.2.77	14.10.78	Extant 1982
DD 980	MOOSBRUGGER	Litton	3.11.75	23.7.77	16.12.78	Extant 1982
DD 981	JOHN HANCOCK	Litton	16.1.76	29.10.77	10.3.79	Extant 1982
DD 982	NICHOLSON	Litton	20.2.76	11.11.77	12.5.79	Extant 1982
DD 983	JOHN RODGERS	Litton	12.8.76	25.2.78	14.7.79	Extant 1982
DD 984	LEFTWICH	Litton	12.11.76	8.4.78	25.8.79	Extant 1982
DD 985	CUSHING	Litton	2.2.77	17.6.78	22.9.79	Extant 1982
DD 986	HARRY W HILL	Litton	1.4.77	10.8.78	10.11.79	Extant 1982
DD 987	O'BANNON	Litton	24.6.77	25.9.78	1.12.79	Extant 1982
DD 988	THORN	Litton	29.8.77	14.11.78	12.1.80	Extant 1982
DD 989	DEYO	Litton	14.10.77	27.1.79	22.3.80	Extant 1982
DD 990	INGERSOLL	Litton	5.12.77	10.3.79	12.4.80	Extant 1982
DD 991	FIFE	Litton	6.3.78	1.5.79	31.5.80	Extant 1982
DD 992	FLETCHER	Litton	24.4.78	16.6.79	12.7.80	Extant 1982
Kidd class						
DDG 993	KIDD (ex-*Kouroush*)	Litton	26.6.78	11.8.79	27.6.81	Extant 1982
DDG 994	CALLAGHAN (ex-*Dargush*)	Litton	23.10.78	1.12.79	29.8.81	Extant 1982
DDG 995	SCOTT (ex-*Nader*)	Litton	12.2.79	1.3.80	24.10.81	Extant 1982
DDG 996	CHANDLER (ex-*Andushirvan*)	Litton	7.5.79	24.5.80	Mar 82	Extant 1982
DD 997	HAYLER	Litton	20.10.80	27.3.82	Nov 83	Extant 1982

Spruance as completed USN

UNITED STATES

Typhon was the follow-on missile system to the initial '3-T' systems. It was to have replaced both the medium-range Terrier and the long range Talos, with a combination of a Tartar-sized Medium Range weapon and a ramjet-powered Terrier-size Long Range missile. There were several proposals for ships to carry it, but the farthest advanced was the nuclear frigate described here; it is also the closest to the later Aegis ships. The nuclear frigate could be distinguished from alternative cruisers by its lack of flagship facilities; it was also much smaller because it followed frigate rather than cruiser design practice, and thus seemed a much better bargain from the point of view of getting Typhon to sea in significant quantity. Even so, it was extremely expensive, and late in 1963 Secretary of Defense Robert S McNamara cancelled the entire Typhon programme as far too ambitious and expensive. In particular, he was concerned that the existing '3-T' missiles, with much less ambitious planned performance, could not meet their goals, at least in terms of reliability. Money intended

TYPHON FRIGATES (DLGN) type *fleet escorts*

Displacement:	10,000t light; 12,000t full load
Dimensions:	650ft wl × 64ft × 21ft
	198.2m × 19.5m × 6.4m
Machinery:	2 shaft nuclear: 2 D2G reactors, approx 30kts
Armament:	1 Long Range Typhon SAM launcher (60 missiles, including up to 20 ASROC), 1 Medium Range Typhon SAM launcher (80 missiles), 1–5in/38, 2–21in TT (2×1), 6–12.75in Mk 32 ASW TT (2×3)
Sensors:	Radar SPS-49, SPG-59; sonar SQS-26/VDS
Complement:	743

Note data refers to SCB-240.65, the last Typhon DLGN design.

for Typhon was redirected to a 'Get-Well' programme for the existing ships, while a single SPG-59 radar was completed for the test ship *Norton Sound*.

Design problems peculiar to Typhon included the very high power drain of its SPG-59 tracking/search radar, which limited steaming endurance in non-nuclear Typhon ships, and the realisation, in the course of design, that command and control and sensors would far outweigh the missiles proper both in dollar cost and in ship impact. One reason for the provision of a conventional two-dimensional air search radar (SPS-49) was to permit operation without continuously running the big missile control set.

Alternative platforms considered during 1961–63 included a Typhon/fleet flagship conversion of the heavy cruiser *Newport News* in which only one turret (No 1) would have been retained, and in which the SPS-43 air search radar would have been wrapped around the SPG-59 tower.

The Typhon DLGN was close to the Aegis cruiser (CSGN/CGN 42) in concept and configuration. The latter, however, showed only a single

missile type, corresponding to the Medium Range Typhon: advances in missile design and in guidance considerably expanded that Medium Range. In addition, a high rate of fire was much more important in the Aegis cruiser, which was faced with a variety of short-range ('pop-up') threats. Thus a high rate of fire was much more important in the Aegis design, and the Mark 10 launcher, necessary for a long-range (booster-equipped) missile could not meet it, as the missiles had to be finned manually between the magazine and the launcher.

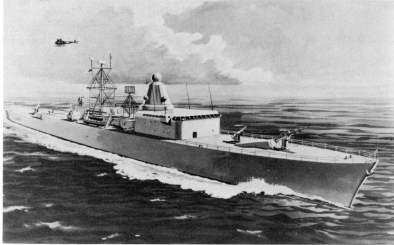

Artist's impression of a Typhon DLGN design, 1961   USN

Strike cruiser design, 1975   USN

The strike cruiser was an outgrowth of the US nuclear missile frigates/cruisers, rather than a follow-on to the *Long Beach*. It began in 1973 as a DLGN modified to accommodate the new Aegis missile system – which had been designed in the first place to fit the DLGN 38 class. However, Aegis was so capable a system that its opponents believed that an Aegis ship might be suitable for independent operations, and thus might revive the cruiser role dropped after the Second World War. At first this meant merely that the ship should have a substantial anti-ship capability, in the form of Harpoon and Tomahawk missile canisters. The initial CSGN design, held to minimum length to reduce displacement, could not make the 30kt speed considered essential for a carrier escort, and during 1975 its hull was lengthened and its D2G frigate power plant upgraded; the final CSGN design was considered fast enough. In this phase, a gun battery (incorporating the 8in lightweight gun) as well as passive protection (armour) unequalled in any postwar US surface combatant were added. It was a measure of the high cost of such protection that it had to be limited to

STRIKE CRUISER (CSGN) type *fleet escorts*

Displacement:	15,902t light; 17,172t full load
Dimensions:	666ft wl, 709ft 7in oa × 76ft 7in × 22ft 3in
	203.0m, 216.3m × 23.4m × 6.8m
Machinery:	2-shaft nuclear: 2 D2G reactors, approx 30kts
Armament:	2 Mk 26 Mod 2 missile launchers (2×2; 128 missiles, mix of SM-2 Medium Range and ASROC), 8 Harpoon SSM (2×4), 8 Tomahawk SSM (2×4), 1–8in/55, 6–12.75in Mk 32 ASW TT (2×3), 2 , LAMPS III helicopters or VTOL aircraft
Sensors:	Radar SPS-49, SPY-1; sonar SQS-53, Towed Array Sonar System
Complement:	?

armoured boxes surrounding the above-water magazines and computer spaces. In addition, the hull was large enough to accommodate some vital spaces below the waterline, and it was long enough to permit considerable separation between the two reactors of the power plant. The final Strike Cruiser design showed provision for VSTOL aircraft as well as missiles and guns, and at one point Reuven Leopold, the senior civilian ship designer, proposed a modified version incorporating a flight deck running the length of the ship.

As in the case of the Typhon frigate and cruiser, the sheer size and cost of the Aegis cruiser defeated it. Although two strike cruisers were

included in the Ford Administration's five-year programme, that Administration had to abandon the strike cruiser before it left office, substituting a 'cruiser' based on the existing CGN 39 (*California*) design. Even this was never built, although as of this writing a CGN 42 figures in the Reagan Administration Five-Year Shipbuilding Plan. The only other attempt to realise the strike cruiser concept, a proposed reconstruction of *Long Beach*, was also cancelled by the Ford Administration before it left office; in each case the non-nuclear *Ticonderoga* was perceived as a much more economical means of getting Aegis to sea fast enough in sufficient numbers.

The CSGN would have had major fleet flagship facilities, and was valued as such at a time when existing flagships were being stricken; in her absence, the Numbered Fleets are commanded from a variety of auxiliaries, including destroyer tenders and amphibious flagships. The flagship problem was so severe that in the mid- and late-1960s there was some considerable interest in building a new class of cruiser-size flagships with sufficient speed to keep up with major combatants, and with limited self-defensive capability, such as Tartar. This programme was dropped at the time in view of its high cost.

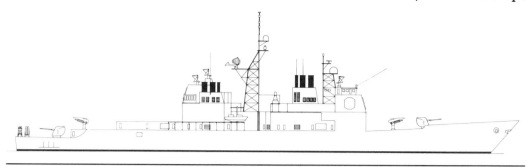

Ticonderoga design

This series, based on the *Spruance* hull form, is the result of a very lengthy evolution. The Aegis air defence system was originally designed for installation aboard a nuclear frigate (later redesignated cruiser) such as the *California*. However, when Admiral E M Zumwalt Jr became CNO he sought instead a minimum Aegis platform for construction in considerable numbers (DG/Aegis); for a time, it was to have been limited to $100 million in FY73 dollars and to 5000t, compared to $45 million and 3400t for what became the *Perry* class frigate. On that basis it would have been limited to a single Mk 22 launcher with 16 missiles, and DG had to be relaxed to 6000t and $125 million. On that basis there was to have been a single Mk 26 Mod 2 (64-missile) launcher, with cost rising to $200 million by early 1973. Advocates of a conventionally-powered Aegis platform rejected this design as making too little use of the power inherent in the missile control system; advocates of nuclear power rejected it as a means of killing off the nuclear ship programme. There was also some scepticism as to the accuracy of the cost estimates for DG/Aegis. Then the

TICONDEROGA class *fleet escorts (cruisers)*

Displacement:	6560t light; 8910t full load
Dimensions:	529ft wl, 563ft oa × 55ft × 31ft
	161.3m, 171.6m × 16.8m × 9.5m
Machinery:	2 shafts, 4 LM 2500 gas turbines, 80,000shp = 30kts. Range 6000nm at 20kts
Armament:	2 Mk 26 launchers (2×2, 68 Standard SM-1 SAM and 20 ASROC missiles), 8 Harpoon SSM (2×4), 6–12.75in Mk 32 ASW TT (2×3), 2–5in/54 (2×1), 2 LAMPS III helicopter
Sensors:	Radar SPY-1A, SPS-49, SPG-62; sonar SQS-53
Complement:	343

No	Name	Builder	Laid down	Launched	Comp	Fate
CG 47	TICONDEROGA	Litton	21.1.80	25.4.81	22.1.83	Extant 1982
CG 48	YORKTOWN	Litton	19.10.81	Feb 83		Building
CG 49		Litton				Ordered
CG 50		Litton				Ordered
CG 51		Bath Iron Wks				Ordered
CG 52		Litton				Ordered
CG 53		Litton				Ordered

Secretary of the Navy asked for studies of a new nuclear version, which eventually became the abortive Strike Cruiser (CSGN) of about 18,000t. Given the high cost of such a ship, the Secretary of Defense demanded a mix of nuclear and conventional Aegis ships, and the conventional study was based on the

largest existing destroyer-type hull, the *Spruance*.

The lead ship, *Ticonderoga*, was authorised under the FY78 programme, at the same time that the nuclear strike cruiser died a political death; it was so large and so important that it was redesignated a cruiser in January 1980. Compared to the strike

cruiser, it lacks an 8in gun and has only a limited capacity for surface-to-surface missiles, two quadruple canisters. From CG 52 they will have an enlarged missile capacity (122 as against 88) with vertical launchers, which will carry Harpoon and Tomahawk as well as the SM-2 anti-aircraft missile of the Aegis system.

Ticonderoga 1982

Artist's impression of DDG 51 design   USN

This DDG 51 class is planned as a complement to the Aegis cruisers, and as a replacement for the ageing missile destroyers. As this is written, the design remains somewhat unclear, even after several years of concept definition. The issue throughout has been the extent to which Aegis missile technology would have to be incorporated. In addition, the Naval Sea Systems Command has sought to incorporate a variety of new hull and machinery concepts, most of which

ARLEIGH BURKE class *fleet escorts (destroyers)*

have been rejected on cost grounds. Examples include turbo-electric propulsion, reversing gearing (to replace controllable-pitch propellers), and a regenerative type of gas turbine (RACER), which would have increased operating range. The chief proposed hull innovation was the large-waterplane-area hull patterned,

to some extent, on Soviet practices. This, combined with the desire for a steel superstructure, led to a new hull form, which is beamier and shorter than is usual. Some have suggested that, as a consequence, the ship may be unable to make the required 30kts on the 80,000shp of a *Spruance*; the reported power level is 100,000shp.

Initially gun armament was to have been limited to one OTO Melara 76mm gun. However, with the development of guided projectiles the 5in/54 became much more attractive. Indeed, Congress has insisted that the Seafire laser/optical 5in fire control system be made part of the DDG 51 project.

UNITED STATES

The USN's requirements as of February 1983 were for a ship of less than 8200t full load, 460ft × 61ft (*142.0m × 18.6m*), powered by 4 LM 2500 gas turbines, and armed with vertical launch systems fore and aft for a total of 90 weapons (SM-2 SAM, Tomahawk SSM, ASROC ASW), 1–5in/54, 2 Phalanx CIWS, 8 Harpoon SSM, (2 × 4), 6–12 75in ASW TT (2 × 3), and a flight deck (but no hangar) for a LAMPS III helicopter. The sensors were to consist of a down-rated Aegis system with SPY-1D radar, and SQS-53C and SQR-19 sonars. Complement was to be 336. However, these particulars are by no means fixed since a design contract was due to be placed at the end of February 1983; alternatives proposed include a modified *Spruance* hull and an up-rated *Kidd*.

The Reagan Administration programme calls for a prototype ship in FY85 and three in FY87 with a large number to follow. Target costs (in FY83 dollars) are 1.1 billion for the lead ship (compared with 3.3 billion for new CG 47s) and 700 million each for up to 60 follow-on ships.

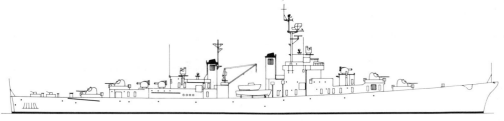

Norfolk 1954

NORFOLK *ocean escort (cruiser)*

Displacement:	4956t light; 5556t standard; 8315t full load
Dimensions:	520ft wl, 540ft oa × 53ft 6in × 19ft
	158.5m, 164.6m × 16.3m × 5.8m
Machinery:	2-shaft geared turbines, 4 Babcock & Wilcox boilers, 80,000shp = 33kts. Range 6000nm at 20kts. Oil 1230t
Armament:	8–3in/50 (4×2), 8–20mm (4×2), 8–21in TT (8×1), 4 Weapon Alfa ASW systems
Sensors:	Radar SPS-6; sonar QHB, SQG-1 (later SQS-4, then SQS-26)
Complement:	546

No	Name	Builder	Laid down	Launched	Comp	Fate
DL 1	NORFOLK	New York SB	1.9.49	29.12.51	4.3.53	Stricken 1973, BU

Laid down as an ASW cruiser (CLK), *Norfolk* was completed as the first of a new generation of large destroyers or 'destroyer leaders' (DL) or frigates (DL). She was designed specifically as a counter to the new generation of Soviet submarines, which were expected to match the performance of the German Type XXI (and which materialised as the Whiskey). However, given her great size and high cost she could not be duplicated, and a projected sister-ship, CLK 2, was never laid down. Hull design broadly followed that of the *Atlanta* class cruisers, and in details *Norfolk* reflected the experience of the Bikini nuclear tests. For example, special efforts were made to permit fallout to wash from her decks, and her bridgework was enclosed. ASW features included unusually large-diameter, slow-turning propellers for quietness, and her primary ASW weapon was the homing torpedo, fired from fixed tubes in her after superstructure. The visually more prominent Weapon A (automatic rocket launcher) was a closer-range secondary battery. Even her anti-aircraft battery was experimental, four twin 3in/70 having been specified (and four twin 3in/50 fitted at first).

In practice *Norfolk* was unique, serving with the Operational Test and Evaluation Force. She was test ship for ASROC and also for the SPS-26 electronically-scanned radar (the prototype of SPS-39). In 1959 conversion to a Terrier missile ship was proposed, as part of the same programme which produced the *Mitscher* and *Forrest Sherman* class missile destroyers (Tartar). *Norfolk* was dropped because of the high cost of conversion to what was perceived at the time as a relatively unreliable weapon, a consideration which curtailed the entire programme.

Norfolk 1965

FLETCHER class DDE conversions *ocean escorts (destroyers)*

Displacement:	2950t full load
Dimensions:	375ft 6in oa × 39ft 8in × 18ft (over sonar dome)
	114.8m × 12.1 × 5.5m
Machinery:	2-shaft geared turbines, 60,000shp = 35kts
Armament:	2–5in/38 (2×1), 4–3in/50 (2×2), 8–20mm (4×2), 1 Weapon Alfa ASW System, 1 trainable Hedgehog ASW mortar, 4–21in TT (4×1). See notes
Sensors:	Radar SPS-6; sonar QHB (later fitted with SQS-4)

For names of ships converted see under Fleet Strength 1947. Original particulars, including building dates, can be found in the 1922–1946 volume.

In 1946 at appeared that the Soviets would soon mass produce German-type fast submarines, both the 15kt Type XXI and the 25kt Walther U-boat, Type XXVI. To counter the latter, the destroyer escort would have to be upgraded to a type capable of 30kts in rough water, yet there was clearly no inclination to begin a new building programme. Instead, plans were prepared for conversions of existing *Fletcher* class destroyers, which were then being laid up. The programme ended at 18 units, after an internal Navy study showed that the Soviets had not yet built up their submarine fleet (1950) and that it would be best to conserve funds for

research against the day when large numbers of more advanced Soviet submarines appeared. In particular, the principal ahead-launched weapon of the late 1940s, Weapon Alfa, was not yet proved – and seemed not entirely satisfactory in service.

Those ships which were converted received Weapon Alfa and, ultimately, two fixed Hedgehogs, in place of No 2 gunhouse; Nos 3 and 4 5in guns were also removed, and four fixed torpedo tubes fitted. In some units a trainable Hedgehog replaced Weapon Alfa in No 2 position forward. All also received improved (scanning) sonar. Underwater fire control equipment and control spaces were also added. Again, in some units the standard quintuple trainable torpedo tube was retained, at first, as space and weight reservation against the installation of fixed tubes. Three units, DDE 446, DDE 447 and DDE 449, were modernised under the FRAM II programme, with provision for DASH and a variable-depth sonar aft.

Jenkins (after DDE conversion)

USN

At the end of the Second World War, a total of nine *Gearing* class fleet destroyers were delivered incomplete; four were completed as the prototypes of a new generation of specialised ASW ships. Two of them, *Carpenter* and *Robert A Owens*, were intended as experimental (and temporary) substitutes for the ASW cruiser (CLK) *Norfolk*, with a heavy battery of two Weapon Alfa and a trainable Hedgehog, as well as four fixed torpedo tubes – and a gun battery limited to two twin 3in/50s (later 3in/70s). Two others, *Basilone* and *Epperson*, were completed as prototype escort destroyers, retaining two of their three twin 5in/38 mounts, plus one Weapon Alfa and two Hedgehogs (originally trainable, abreast the forward funnel; later fixed, on the 01 level forward), and four fixed torpedo tubes.

Eleven other *Gearings* received limited ASW conversions as part of the formation of two postwar experimental Task Groups; in each case something comparable to *Basilone* was ultimately planned, but all that was done was the installation of a large trainable Hedgehog in place of No 2 5in mount, as well as the installation of a scanning sonar in place of the former searchlight type: DDE 818–DDE 820, DDE 847 and DDE 871 in 1947, and DDE 764, DDE 765 and DDE 858–DDE 861 under the FY50 programme. Two more ships, *Witek* and *Sarsfield*, had their No 2 gunhouses removed and were used for experiments; *Sarsfield* was a test ship for RAT, for example.

Although there were repeated proposals for DDE completion of the suspended destroyers, that was never done, and the DDE designation was dropped when all surviving *Gearing*

GEARING class DDE conversions *ocean escorts (destroyers)*

Displacement:	2182t light
Dimensions:	391ft oa × 40ft 10in × 14ft (full load)
	119.2m × 12.5m × 4.3m
Machinery:	2-shaft geared turbines, 60,000shp = 32kts
Armament:	4–3in/70 (2×2), 8–20mm (4×2), 2 Weapon Alfa ASW systems, 4–21in TT (4×1), 1 DC track
Sensors:	Radar SPS-6; sonar QHB (later SQS-4)

Data refers to *Carpenter*, the most extreme of the DDE conversions. For names of other ships converted see under Fleet Strength 1947. Original particulars, including building dates, can be found in the 1922–1946 volume

class destroyers received what amounted to an ASW conversion under the FRAM programme. It is only fair to note that in 1950 the Navy itself adopted a policy of ASW improvement to all active fleet destroyers, to match the threat of a Soviet undersea fleet rather less developed than had originally been expected. The outward mark of this programme was a pair of Hedgehogs on the 01 level forward; less obvious but just as important was the provision of improved sonar, first a scanning type (QHB), and then SQS-4.

Carpenter 1975

USN

Charles H Roan (after FRAM I conversion)

Ernest G Small (after FRAM II conversion, ex-DDR)

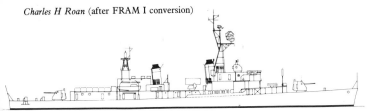

GEARING class FRAM I conversions *ocean escorts (destroyers)*

Displacement:	2406t light; 3493t full load (DD 717)
Dimensions:	383ft wl, 390ft 2in oa × 40ft 11in × 14ft 4in
	116.6m, 119.0m × 12.5m × 4.4m
Machinery:	2-shaft geared turbines, 4 Babcock & Wilcox boilers, 60,000shp = 32kts. Range 4000nm at 20kts. Oil 727t
Armament:	4–5in/38 (2×2), 1 ASROC ASW system (1×8, 17 missiles), DASH, 6–12.75in Mk 32 ASW TT (2×3)
Sensors:	Radar SPS-29, SPS-37 or SPS-40; sonar SQS-23
Complement:	310

For names of ships converted see under Fleet Strength 1947. Original particulars, including building dates, can be found in the 1922–1946 volume.

By 1958 the Second World War destroyers were beginning to wear out; FRAM was an attempt to extend their lives and so to put off the massive expenditure needed to replace them, in order to maintain the 200 or more operational destroyers required by the US fleet of that time. In fact, the Vietnam War further delayed replacement, and even cut the one replacement programme undertaken (*Spruance* class), while wearing out the rebuilt ships, so that FRAM *Gearings* remained in (reserve training) service in 1982, more than a decade after their scheduled demise.

FRAM I, the most extensive reconstruction programme, was limited to *Gearings* and was expected to extend their useful lives by eight years. All shipboard components were rehabilitated, and one 5in mount and all lesser guns removed; ASROC, DASH and triple ASW torpedo tubes were fitted, as well as the long-range SQS-23 hull sonar. The first eight conversions retained No 2 gunhouse and removed No 3, but it was argued that firepower should be better distributed, and most FRAM Is had 5in guns fore and aft. The only *Gearings* not converted to FRAM I standard were 16 FRAM II (six radar-pickets, four former radar-pickets and six former DDEs), the experimental *Witek*, and the former missile conversion *Gyatt*.

As converted, these ships retained little modern anti-aircraft capability, particularly in view of increasing aircraft speeds. *Higbee* was bombed and had her after 5in mount destroyed during a shore bombardment in the Gulf of Tonkin, 19 April 1972. Efforts were made to provide improved means of self-defence, and Sea Chapparal, which had been rejected as an alternative to Sea Sparrow, was tested aboard the *Floyd B Parks* in May 1972. Later that year, eight other FRAMs were fitted: *Anderson, Bausell, Gurke, Henderson, Mackenzie, Mason, Orleck* and *Tucker*. All missiles were removed as ships returned from South-East Asia the following year. Another special fit for Vietnam operations was Shrike-on-Board (SOB), in which Shrike anti-radar missiles were fitted on launch rails atop the ASROC box launcher amidships, as a means of countering North Vietnamese coast defence radars. No details of ships fitted are available, and the system was installed on an emergency basis.

John Willis 1971

Taussig 1967

USN

FRAM II was originally intended to extend the useful life of a destroyer by five years; it was applied primarily to *Sumner* class destroyers. All three 5in gun mountings were retained, but a new bridge was fitted, together with a new radar and ECM equipment. The existing SQS-4 sonar was retained but improved and relocated forward; it was supplemented by a variable-depth sonar operating from the same signal generator. Short (Mk 32) torpedo tubes were fitted but there was not enough space or weight for ASROC; instead these ships received the DASH drone and a pair of fixed long torpedo tubes (between their funnels) for Mk 37 torpedoes.

As applied to *Lloyd Thomas* (DDE 764, 765 and DDE 858–861) class escort destroyers, FRAM II involved the retention of the trainable Mk 15 Hedgehog forward, with

SUMNER class FRAM II conversions *ocean escorts (destroyers)*

Displacement:	2345t light; 3210t full load (DD 760)
Dimensions:	369ft wl, 376ft 6in oa × 40ft 10in × 14ft 1in
	112.5m, 114.8m × 12.5m × 4.3m
Machinery:	2-shaft geared turbines, 4 Babcock & Wilcox boilers, 60,000shp = 33.4kts. Range 3300nm at 20kts. Oil 497t
Armament:	6–5in/38 (3×2), 2 Hedgehog ASW mortars, 2–21in TT (2×1), 6–12.75in Mk 32 ASW (2×3), DASH
Sensors:	Radar SPS-29, SPS-37 or SPS-40; sonar SQS-4/RDT/VDS
Complement:	302

For names of ships converted see under Fleet Strength 1947. Original particulars, including building dates, can be found in the 1922–1946 volume.

DASH aft and a pair of long torpedo tubes amidships; they also received the new SQS-23 sonar. The six ships retained as radar-pickets (DDR) received limited ASW refits since they were primarily AAW ships: they retained their fixed Hedgehogs and received SQS-4 improvements and a variable-depth sonar, plus a new bridge and an enlarged CIC; new radars were also fitted. The former DDRs generally resembled *Sumner* class FRAM IIs, with long torpedo tubes and DASH, as well as all six 5in/38 guns.

The failure of DASH left these ships without a long-range ASW weapon. Ironically, it had been proposed at one time to omit ASROC from FRAM I ships in view of the potential of the drone helicopter, but the rocket had been retained for all-weather capability.

Cromwell 1970

The first postwar destroyer escorts, these ships were initially conceived as upgraded, versions of the wartime 22kt coastal escort (PC) with the additional firepower, sonar and speed required to counter the new generation of submarines. They were also designed with mobilisation in mind, hence the single screw for reduced pressure on the gear-cutting industry. *Dealey* herself was completed with the British Squid ASW mortar, but her sisters all had the US Weapon Alfa (Mk 108 rocket launcher).

They were fast and seaworthy, but were criticised as being underarmed. Under the FY62 and later programme, all but *Dealey*, *Courtney* and *Cromwell* were fitted with SQS-23 sonars, DASH hangars, and helicopter pads. Their after twin 3in/50 mounts were removed. Unconverted ships retained all of their guns and had variable-depth sonars complementing their hull SQS-4 series units, as in FRAM II destroyers. In 1967 four Pacific Fleet Units, DE 1023–DE 1026, had single Army-type Bofors guns fitted on their fantails, reportedly on the basis of local initiative. All ended their careers with the usual triple Mark 32 lightweight torpedo tubes, and Weapon Alfa was removed from most towards the end of their careers. No ships of this type served in Vietnam.

DEALEY class *ocean escorts (destroyer escorts)*

Displacement:	1314t light; 1877t full load
Dimensions:	308ft wl, 315ft oa × 36ft 8in × 11ft 10in
	93.9m, 96.0m × 11.2m × 3.6m
Machinery:	1-shaft geared turbine, 2 Foster Wheeler boilers, 20,000shp = 27kts. Range 6000nm at 12kts
Armament:	4–3in/50 (2×2), Weapon Alfa (2 Squid in DE 1006) ASW system
Sensors:	Radar SPS-6; sonar SQS-4
Complement:	173

No	Name	Builder	Laid down	Launched	Comp	Fate
DE 1006	DEALEY	Bath Iron Wks	15.10.52	8.11.53	8.6.54	Uruguayan *18 De Julio* 1972
DE 1014	CROMWELL	Bath Iron Wks	3.8.53	4.6.54	24.11.54	Stricken 1973
DE 1015	HAMMERBERG	Bath Iron Wks	12.11.53	20.8.54	28.2.55	Stricken 1973
DE 1021	COURTNEY	Defoe, Bay City	2.9.54	2.11.55	31.8.56	Stricken 1973
DE 1022	LESTER	Defoe, Bay City	2.9.54	5.1.56	14.6.57	Stricken 1973
DE 1023	EVANS	Puget Sound N Yd	19.9.55	14.9.55	14.6.57	Stricken 1973
DE 1024	BRIDGET	Puget Sound N Yd	19.9.55	24.4.56	24.10.57	Stricken 1973
DE 1025	BAUER	Bethlehem, San Francisco	1.12.56	4.6.57	22.11.57	Stricken 1973
DE 1026	HOOPER	Bethlehem, San Francisco	4.1.56	1.8.57	16.4.58	Stricken 1973
DE 1027	JOHN WILLIS	New York SB	5.7.55	4.2.56	21.2.57	Stricken 1972
DE 1028	VAN VOORHIS	New York SB	29.8.55	28.7.56	15.4.57	Stricken 1972
DE 1029	HARTLEY	New York SB	31.10.55	26.1.57	30.7.57	Colombian *Boyaca* 1972
DE 1030	JOSEPH K TAUSSIG	New York SB	31.1.56	9.3.57	10.9.57	Stricken 1972

Production of the same basic design by foreign navies attested to its basic value: five were built in Norway, and three in Portugal, in each case in somewhat modified form. However, reports circulating in the 1950s to the effect that postwar French frigates (which had US hull numbers because the United States paid for their construction) were modified *Dealey*s were not true.

John R Perry 1961

CLAUD JONES class *ocean escorts (destroyer escorts)*

Displacement:	1314t light; 1916t full load
Dimensions:	301ft wl, 312ft oa × 38ft × 12ft 11in
	91.8m, 95.1m × 11.6m × 3.9m
Machinery:	2 shafts, 4 diesels, 8700bhp = 21.5kts. Range 7000nm at 12kts
Armament:	2–3in/50 (2×1), 2 Hedgehog ASW mortars
Sensors:	Radar SPS-6; sonar SQS-4
Complement:	171

No	Name	Builder	Laid down	Launched	Comp	Fate
DE 1033	CLAUD JONES	Avondale	1.6.57	27.5.58	16.11.58	Indonesian *Mongindisi* 1974
DE 1034	JOHN R PERRY	Avondale	1.10.57	29.7.58	12.1.59	Indonesian *Samadikun* 1973
DE 1035	CHARLES BERRY	Avondale	3.9.57	17.3.59	25.11.60	Indonesian *Martadinata* 1974
DE 1036	McMORRIS	Avondale	1.10.57	26.5.59	4.3.60	Indonesian *Ngurah Rai* 1974

Given the relatively high cost of a *Dealey*, these were an attempt to produce a minimum ocean escort, consonant with ASW requirements and with mobilisation considerations. Diesel power (with two shafts) was therefore chosen, with speed limited to 22kts; weapons were reduced to a pair of fixed Hedgehogs, a lightweight ASW torpedo-dropping system and a single stern depth-charge track. The result was widely disliked, and a call for renewed construction of a more satisfactory escort led back to the *Bronstein*s and their successors. In 1961, the last pair, DE 1035 and DE 1036, received a Norwegian Terne III rocket-thrown depth-charge system as well as light-weight torpedo tubes. However, they were never considered really suitable for ASW, and spent their last years as electronic reconnaissance ships in the Pacific. Two modified versions of this design were built in Turkey (1967–74).

McCloy 1970

BRONSTEIN class *ocean escorts (destroyer escorts)*

Displacement:	1882t light; 2723t full load
Dimensions:	350ft wl, 372 ft oa × 41ft × 23ft
	106.7m, 113.4m × 12.5m × 7.0m
Machinery:	1 shaft geared turbine, 2 Foster Wheeler boilers, 20,000shp = 26kts. Range 4000nm at 15kts
Armament:	3–3in/50 (1×2, 1×1), 2–21in TT (2×1), 6–12.75in Mk 32 ASW TT (2×3), 1 ASROC ASW system (1×8), DASH
Sensors:	Radar SPS-40; sonar SQS-26
Complement:	191

No	Name	Builder	Laid down	Launched	Comp	Fate
DE 1037	BRONSTEIN	Avondale	16.5.61	31.3.62	16.6.63	Extant 1982
DE 1038	McCLOY	Avondale	15.9.61	9.6.62	21.10.63	Extant 1982

These ships, the progenitors of a long line of large US ASW escorts, were conceived as a reaction to the *Claud Jones* class, in effect a *Dealey* with the new SQS-26 sonar, ASROC and DASH, with one of the original four 3in/50 guns traded off for greater ASW effectiveness. One of the penalties was a loss of speed, so that the new escort was slower than the ASW Task Force with which she was to operate; the desire to regain speed (compared to the *Dealey* or even as compared to a 30kt submarine) led to the next series of ships. The after 3in/50 gun was later removed, to provide compensation for a variable-depth sonar; both ships were fitted with a towed array surveillance sonar in the mid-1970s, and *Bronstein* was later fitted with an SQR-15 towed array sonar system. Neither quite fitted the existing US ASW organisation, given their low speeds.

Garcia 1972   USN

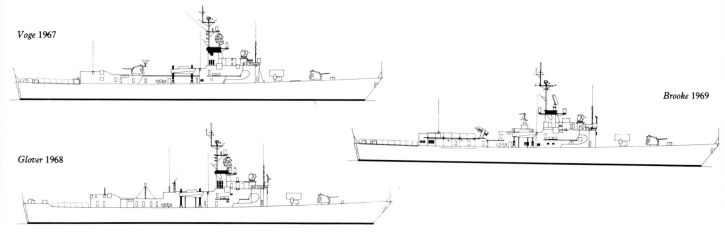

Voge 1967

Glover 1968

Brooke 1969

Bu 1959 there was interest in a 30kt successor to the *Bronsteins*; at the same time a new lightweight steam technology, the pressure-fired boiler, was maturing. At first BuShips proposed a conventionally powered 27kt destroyer escort for the FY61 programme, together with an experimental (and faster) pressure-fired ship. This gradually shifted to a requirement that at least one FY61 ship be pressure-fired (27kts), and ultimately to a choice to build an entire series of pressure-fired escorts, even before any one of the new power plants had gone to sea. Other demands at this time were for a replacement for existing Second World War destroyers: given its relatively high speed and good sonar, the pressure-fired escort was a natural candidate; it was therefore given 5in guns in place of the 3in/50s of earlier escorts. There were also calls from the Fleet for a missile battery, and the new ship was designed to accept a minimum Tartar battery in place of its after 5in gun. The result was actually capable of about 30kts on trials, and certainly exceeded mass production limits.

Ten ASW versions (*Garcia* class) and six missile versions (*Brooke* class) were built, as well as a modified research unit, *Glover* (AGDE 1), with a pumpjet propeller, a raised platform above the main deck aft, and no after 5in gun or missile launcher; she was redesignated FF 1098, an operational frigate, in October 1979. The Mk 24 or 25 torpedo tubes originally mounted in the sterns of these ships were removed with the end of the long torpedo programme; DASH facilities were enlarged to accommodate LAMPS. Production of the missile ships ended with the FY63 programme in view of their high cost and limited capability.

GARCIA and BROOKE classes *ocean escorts (destroyer escorts)*

Displacement:	2441t light; 3371 full load (*Brooke* 2710t, 3426t)
Dimensions:	390ft wl, 414ft oa × 44ft × 24ft
	118.9m, 126.2m × 13.4m × 7.3m
Machinery:	1-shaft geared turbine, 2 Foster Wheeler pressure-fired boilers, 35,000shp = 27kts. Range 4000nm at 20kts
Armament:	2–5in/38 (2×1) (*Brooke* class 1–5in/38, 1 Tartar SAM, 16 missiles), ASROC ASW system (1×8, 16 missiles, except DE 1040–1045, DEG 1–3), 2–21in TT (none in *Brooke* class), 6–12.75in Mk 32 ASW TT (2×3), DASH
Sensors:	Radar SPS-40 (*Brooke* SPS-39, SPG-51); sonar SQS-26
Complement:	209 (*Brooke* 228)

No	Name	Builder	Laid down	Launched	Comp	Fate
DE 1040	GARCIA	Bethlehem, San Francisco	16.10.62	31.10.63	21.12.64	Extant 1982
DE 1041	BRADLEY	Bethlehem, San Francisco	17.1.63	26.3.64	15.5.65	Extant 1982
DE 1043	EDWARD McDONNELL	Avondale	1.4.63	15.2.64	15.2.65	Extant 1982
DE 1044	BRUMBY	Avondale	1.8.63	6.6.64	5.8.65	Extant 1982
DE 1045	DAVIDSON	Avondale	20.9.63	2.10.64	7.12.65	Extant 1982
DE 1047	VOGE	Defoe, Bay City	21.11.63	4.2.65	25.11.66	Extant 1982
DE 1048	SAMPLE	Lockheed, Seattle	19.7.63	28.4.64	23.3.68	Extant 1982
DE 1049	KOELSCH	Defoe, Bay City	19.2.64	8.6.65	10.6.67	Extant 1982
DE 1050	ALBERT DAVID	Lockheed, Seattle	29.4.64	19.12.64	19.10.68	Extant 1982
DE 1051	O'CALLAHAN	Defoe, Bay City	19.2.64	20.10.65	3.7.67	Extant 1982
DEG 1	BROOKE	Lockheed, Seattle	10.12.62	19.7.63	12.3.66	Extant 1982
DEG 2	RAMSEY	Lockheed, Seattle	4.2.63	15.10.63	3.6.67	Extant 1982
DEG 3	SCHOFIELD	Lockheed, Seattle	15.4.63	7.12.63	11.5.68	Extant 1982
DEG 4	TALBOT	Bath Iron Wks	4.5.64	6.1.66	2.4.67	Extant 1982
DEG 5	RICHARD L PAGE	Bath Iron Wks	4.1.65	4.4.66	5.8.67	Extant 1982
DEG 6	JULIUS A FURER	Bath Iron Wks	12.7.65	22.7.66	11.11.67	Extant 1982
AGDE 1	GLOVER	Bath Iron Wks	Jul 63	17.4.65	Nov 65	Extant 1982

From DE 1047 onwards, these ships were fitted with the sloping bulkhead and ASROC reload magazine developed for the *Knox* class. All but DE 1048 and DE 1050 were refitted to operate the LAMPS helicopter between 1972 and 1975, the two remaining ships being employed to test towed array sonar systems. *Koelsch* and *Voge* were fitted with automated ASW combat systems. *Bradley* served as Sea Sparrow test ship in 1967–68. *Talbot* served as sea-going test ship for the *Perry* class combat system, with an OTO Melara 76mm gun temporarily replacing her 5in/38.

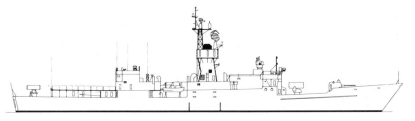

Bagley 1980

These large specialised ASW ships were the subject of considerable controversy, with their single screws and single 5in guns. They were direct descendants of the *Brooke* class, initially modified by 'work study' to reduce their complements and, without increase in hull size, to increase endurance by 500nm. In addition, it was hoped that electronic installations could be consolidated by the use of a series of 'bill-board' antennae spread around the crown of a tall 'Mack'. In

KNOX class *ocean escorts (destroyer escorts)*

Displacement:	3020t light; 4066t full load
Dimensions:	415ft wl, 438ft oa × 47ft × 25ft
	126.5m, 133.5m × 14.3m × 7.6m
Machinery:	1-shaft geared turbine, 2 boilers, 35,000shp = 27kts. Range 4500nm at 20kts
Armament:	1–5in/54, 1 Sea Sparrow SAM (1×8; DE 1052–1069, DE 1071–1083, 1971–75), 1 ASROC ASW system (1 × 8, 16 missiles), DASH (as completed; later fitted for LAMPS I helicopter), 2–21in TT (2×1, not fitted in most units), 4–12.75in Mk 32 ASW TT (2×2 fixed, 22 torpedoes)
Sensors:	Radar SPS-40; sonar SQS-26, SQS-35 (DE 1052, 1056, 1063–1071, 1073–1076, 1078–1097, installation begun 1972)
Complement:	224

practice, the Navy was moved to reject the new pressure-fired boilers, so that hull size had to grow to accommodate a more conventional installation, without loss of speed or endurance. In addition, with the rejection of further missile escort construction, the designers were left with a half-designed escort with only a single gun and with space aft which might be filled by a missile system – or by more DASH drones. In the end, the original single 5in/38 gun was replaced by a 5in/54 (in theory more than equivalent to the two 5in/38s of the *Garcia*) and space and weight was reserved aft for a short-range defensive missile, initially to have been Sea Mauler, but later Sea Sparrow. The generous hangar space originally provided aft made substitution of LAMPS for DASH relatively easy. SQS-35 VDS sonars were fitted to most units (DE, later FF, 1052, 1056, 1063–1071, 1073–1076 and 1078–1097), and their 'fish' later used to tow SQS-18 sonars. They were redesignated FF (frigates) in 1975.

From DE 1078 onwards, all were built by a single yard, Avondale, for economy. The last ten units, DE 1098–DE 1107, authorised in the FY68 programme, were not built. One had been planned as a gas turbine test ship (DE 1101). On the other hand, five missile-armed variants of the basic design were built in Spain (with US designations DEG 7–DEG 11). Thirty-one ships (DE 1052–1069 and DE 1070–1083) were fitted with the Sea Sparrow point defence missile system in 1971–75; however, a planned installation of Sea Chapparal in the remaining 14, was not carried out. Nor did these ships receive the pair of long torpedo tubes originally specified.

The *Knox* class were always criticised as too wet; in 1980 they began to receive raised bulwarks and spray strakes forward for improved sea-keeping.

No	Name	Builder	Laid down	Launched	Comp	Fate
DE 1052	KNOX	Todd	5.10.65	19.11.66	12.4.69	Extant 1982
DE 1053	ROARK	Todd, Seattle	2.2.66	24.4.67	22.11.69	Extant 1982
DE 1054	GRAY	Todd, Seattle	9.11.66	3.11.67	4.4.70	Extant 1982
DE 1055	HEPBURN	Todd, San Pedro	1.6.66	25.3.67	3.7.69	Extant 1982
DE 1056	CONNOLE	Avondale	23.3.67	20.7.68	30.8.69	Extant 1982
DE 1057	RATHBURNE	Lockheed, Seattle	8.1.68	2.5.69	16.5.70	Extant 1982
DE 1058	MEYERKORD	Todd, San Pedro	1.9.66	15.7.67	28.11.69	Extant 1982
DE 1059	W S SIMS	Avondale	10.4.67	4.1.69	3.1.70	Extant 1982
DE 1060	LANG	Todd, San Pedro	25.3.67	4.1.69	3.1.70	Extant 1982
DE 1061	PATTERSON	Avondale	12.10.67	3.5.69	14.3.70	Extant 1982
DE 1062	WHIPPLE	Todd, Seattle	24.4.67	12.4.68	22.8.70	Extant 1982
DE 1063	REASONER	Lockheed, Seattle	6.1.69	1.8.70	31.7.71	Extant 1982
DE 1064	LOCKWOOD	Todd, Seattle	3.11.67	5.9.68	5.12.70	Extant 1982
DE 1065	STEIN	Lockheed, Seattle	1.6.70	10.12.70	8.1.72	Extant 1982
DE 1066	MARVIN SHIELDS	Todd, Seattle	12.4.68	23.10.69	10.4.71	Extant 1982
DE 1067	FRANCIS HAMMOND	Todd, San Pedro	15.7.67	11.5.68	25.7.70	Extant 1982
DE 1068	VREELAND	Avondale	20.3.68	14.6.69	13.6.70	Extant 1982
DE 1069	BAGLEY	Lockheed, Seattle	22.9.70	24.4.71	6.5.72	Extant 1982
DE 1070	DOWNES	Todd, Seattle	5.9.68	13.12.69	28.8.71	Extant 1982
DE 1071	BADGER	Todd, San Pedro	17.2.68	7.12.68	1.12.70	Extant 1982
DE 1072	BLAKELY	Avondale	3.6.68	23.8.69	18.7.70	Extant 1982
DE 1073	ROBERT E PEARY	Lockheed, Seattle	20.12.70	23.6.71	23.9.72	Extant 1982
DE 1074	HAROLD E HOLT	Todd, Seattle	11.5.68	3.5.69	26.3.71	Extant 1982
DE 1075	TRIPPE	Avondale	29.7.68	1.11.69	19.9.70	Extant 1982
DE 1076	FANNING	Todd, San Pedro	7.12.68	24.1.70	23.7.71	Extant 1982
DE 1077	OUELLET	Avondale	15.1.69	17.1.70	12.12.70	Extant 1982
DE 1078	JOSEPH HEWES	Avondale	15.5.69	7.3.70	24.4.71	Extant 1982
DE 1079	BOWEN	Avondale	11.7.69	2.5.70	22.5.71	Extant 1982
DE 1080	PAUL	Avondale	12.9.69	20.6.70	14.8.71	Extant 1982
DE 1081	AYLWIN	Avondale	13.11.69	20.8.70	18.9.71	Extant 1982
DE 1082	ELMER MONTGOMERY	Avondale	23.1.70	21.11.70	30.10.71	Extant 1982
DE 1083	COOK	Avondale	20.3.70	23.1.71	18.12.71	Extant 1982
DE 1084	McCANDLESS	Avondale	4.6.70	20.3.71	18.3.72	Extant 1982
DE 1085	DONALD B BEARY	Avondale	24.7.70	22.5.71	22.7.72	Extant 1982
DE 1086	BREWTON	Avondale	2.10.70	24.7.71	8.7.72	Extant 1982
DE 1087	KIRK	Avondale	4.12.70	25.9.71	9.9.72	Extant 1982
DE 1088	BARBEY	Avondale	5.2.71	4.12.71	11.11.72	Extant 1982
DE 1089	JESSE L BROWN	Avondale	8.4.71	18.3.72	17.2.73	Extant 1982
DE 1090	AINSWORTH	Avondale	11.6.71	15.4.72	31.3.73	Extant 1982
DE 1091	MILLER	Avondale	6.8.71	3.6.72	30.6.73	Extant 1982
DE 1092	THOMAS C HART	Avondale	8.10.71	12.8.72	28.7.73	Extant 1982
DE 1093	CAPODANNO	Avondale	12.10.71	21.10.72	17.11.73	Extant 1982
DE 1094	PHARRIS	Avondale	11.2.72	16.12.72	26.1.74	Extant 1982
DE 1095	TRUETT	Avondale	27.4.72	3.2.73	1.6.74	Extant 1982
DE 1096	VALDEZ	Avondale	30.6.72	24.3.73	27.7.74	Extant 1982
DE 1097	MOINESTER	Avondale	25.8.72	12.5.73	2.11.74	Extant 1982

Downes 1971   USN

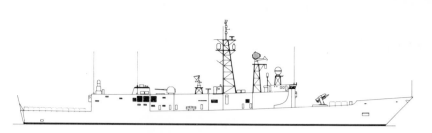

Oliver Hazard Perry as completed

These frigates, direct successors to the *Knox* class, suffer from much the same criticisms: a single screw and a single weapon (one Mk 13 missile launcher). However, they benefit from a considerable, if unappreciated, degree of redundancy. For example, the fire control system has two channels (two guidance radars, physically well separated). There is a pair of retractable 325hp motors to bring the ship home at 6kts if she loses her main power plant. Although the hull sonar is a short-range (direct path) SQS-56, the primary ASW sensor will be an SQR-19 towed array, its contacts prosecuted by the two LAMPS helicopters in a large hangar aft. All units will eventually have their helicopter pads enlarged to take the new LAMPS III helicopter.

The *Perry* class suffers from several ironies. It was first conceived after the truncation of the *Spruance* class failed to replace the FRAM destroyers; Admiral Zumwalt sought alternative weapon suits for AAW, ASW and anti-ship warfare in the hope of reducing unit costs. In fact, the primary anti-ship weapon, Harpoon, could be fired from the primary AAW launcher, the Mk 13. If the ASROC missile (which cannot be fired from the Mk 13) was foregone, helicopter delivery would provide an AAW-oriented frigate with a considerable ASW stand-off capability. Indeed, even though the *Perry* does not share the elaborate silencing of the *Spruance* (for example, it has a diesel ship service generator) or the long-range sonar of previous ocean escorts, it gains a very considerable detection capability in the form of the towed array. Ironically, the ASW frigate was originally rejected on the theory that large numbers of such ships with effective sonars already existed. The advent of the towed array/helicopter combination shows in the decision to double the number of helicopters, which had a considerable effect on the overall design. In the original one-helicopter version, the helipad was placed aft of amidships, in the most favourable position, with the hangar splitting the uptakes. However, two helicopters required a much wider hangar, and both it and the helipad had to be moved aft.

The Mk 92 fire control system is of Dutch origin and is employed, in a somewhat simpler form, in the *Pegasus* class hydrofoils. As installed in the *Perry* class, it is part of a combat system particularly adapted to combat 'pop-up' weapons such as the Soviet SSN-7 underwater-launched missile.

The OTO Melara 76mm gun was chosen as superior to a 5in/54 in air defence, and it is complemented by a Vulcan Phalanx close-in defence weapon.

Perry made over 31kts on trials. FFG 56–58 were authorised in FY82.

OLIVER HAZARD PERRY class *ocean escorts (frigates)*

Displacement:	2648t light; 3486t full load
Dimensions:	408ft wl, 445ft oa × 47ft 5in × 14ft 5in
	124.4m, 135.7m × 14.5m × 4.4m
Machinery:	1 shaft, 2 LM 2500 gas turbines, 40,000shp = 28.5kts. Range 4500nm at 20kts
Armament:	1–3in/62, 1 Standard SAM (40 SM-1 SAM or Harpoon SSM missiles), 6–12.75in Mk 32 ASW TT (2×3, 24 torpedoes), 2 LAMPS I or III helicopters
Sensors:	Radar SPS-49, Mk 92 fire control system; sonar SQS-56
Complement:	176

No	Name	Builder	Laid down	Launched	Comp	Fate
FFG 7	OLIVER HAZARD PERRY	Bath Iron Wks	6.12.75	25.9.76	30.11.71	Extant 1982
FFG 8	McINERNEY	Bath Iron Wks	16.1.78	4.11.78	15.12.79	Extant 1982
FFG 9	WADSWORTH	Todd, San Pedro	13.7.77	29.7.78	28.2.80	Extant 1982
FFG 10	DUNCAN	Todd, Seattle	29.4.77	1.3.78	24.5.80	Extant 1982
FFG 11	CLARK	Bath Iron Wks	17.7.78	24.3.79	17.5.80	Extant 1982
FFG 12	GEORGE PHILIP	Todd, San Pedro	14.12.77	16.12.78	18.11.80	Extant 1982
FFG 13	SAMUEL ELIOT MORRISON	Bath Iron Wks	4.12.78	14.7.79	11.10.80	Extant 1982
FFG 14	SIDES	Todd, San Pedro	7.8.78	19.5.79	30.5.81	Extant 1982
FFG 15	ESTOCIN	Bath Iron Wks	2.4.79	3.11.79	10.1.81	Extant 1982
FFG 16	CLIFTON SPRAGUE	Bath Iron Wks	30.7.79	16.2.80	21.3.81	Extant 1982
FFG 19	JOHN A MOORE	Todd, San Pedro	19.12.78	20.10.79	14.11.81	Extant 1982
FFG 20	ANTRIM	Bath Iron Wks	21.6.78	27.3.79	26.9.81	Extant 1982
FFG 21	FLATLEY	Bath Iron Wks	13.11.79	15.5.80	20.6.81	Extant 1982
FFG 22	FAHRION	Todd, Seattle	1.12.78	24.8.79	Jan 82	Extant 1982
FFG 23	LEWIS B PULLER	Todd, San Pedro	23.5.79	29.3.80	Jan 82	Extant 1982
FFG 24	JACK WILLIAMS	Bath Iron Wks	25.2.80	30.8.80	19.9.81	Extant 1982
FFG 25	COPELAND	Todd, San Pedro	24.10.79	26.7.80	7.8.82	Extant 1982
FFG 26	GALLERY	Bath Iron Wks	17.5.80	20.12.80	5.12.81	Extant 1982
FFG 27	MAHLON S TISDALE	Todd, San Pedro	19.3.80	7.2.81	13.11.82	Extant 1982
FFG 28	BOONE	Todd, Seattle	27.3.79	16.1.80	May 82	Extant 1982
FFG 29	STEPHEN W GROVES	Bath Iron Wks	16.9.80	22.9.80	Mar 82	Extant 1982
FFG 30	REID	Todd, San Pedro	8.10.80	27.6.81		Completing
FFG 31	STARK	Todd, Seattle	24.8.79	30.5.80	23.10.82	Extant 1982
FFG 32	JOHN L HALL	Bath Iron Wks	5.1.81	24.7.81	26.6.82	Extant 1982
FFG 33	JARRETT	Todd, San Pedro	11.2.81	17.10.81		Completing
FFG 34	AUBREY FITCH	Bath Iron Wks	10.4.81	17.10.81	9.10.82	Extant 1982
FFG 36	UNDERWOOD	Bath Iron Wks	30.7.81	6.2.81		Completing
FFG 37	CROMMELIN	Todd, Seatle	30.5.80	1.7.81		Completing
FFG 38	CURTS	Todd, San Pedro	1.7.81	6.3.82		Completing
FFG 39	DOYLE	Bath Iron Wks	16.11.81	22.5.82		Completing
FFG 40	HALYBURTON	Todd, Seattle	26.9.80	13.10.81		Completing
FFG 41	McCLUSKY	Todd, San Pedro	21.10.81	18.9.82		Completing
FFG 42	KLAKRING	Bath Iron Wks	Mar 82	18.9.82		Completing
FFG 43	THACH	Todd, San Pedro	Mar 82	18.12.82		Completing
FFG 45	DERWERT	Bath Iron Wks	June 82	30.12.82		Completing
FFG 46	RENTZ	Todd, San Pedro	18.9.82			Building
FFG 47	NICHOLAS	Bath Iron Wks	27.9.82			Building
FFG 48	VANDERGRIFT	Todd, Seattle	15.10.81	July 82		Completing
FFG 49	ROBERT E BRADLEY	Bath Iron Wks				On order
FFG 50	TAYLOR	Bath Iron Wks				On order
FFG 51		Todd, San Pedro	13.12.82			On order
FFG 52	CARR	Todd, Seattle	26.3.82			On order
FFG 53		Bath Iron Wks				On order
FFG 54		Todd, San Pedro				On order
FFG 55		Bath Iron Wks				On order

Oliver Hazard Perry 1977

USN

SUBMARINES

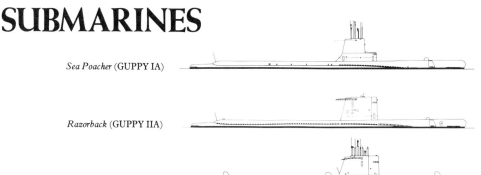

Sea Poacher (GUPPY IA)

Razorback (GUPPY IIA)

Clamagore (GUPPY III)

In 1945 the US Navy operated a very large force of conventional 'fleet submarines', which had been extremely successful in the war against Japan, but which had been rendered obsolete by the advent of the German Type XXI. Partly to modernise this force, and partly to provide fast submarines, comparable to Type XXIs, to train the postwar US ASW force, the Navy developed a conversion programme, Project 'GUPPY' (Greater Underwater Propulsive Power): submarines were provided with increased battery capacity (at the cost of four reload torpedoes, some fresh water tanks, and magazine space), and they were streamlined topside, their guns removed and their superstructures remodelled. Although snorkels were not fitted to the prototypes *Odax* and *Pomodon* (GUPPY I), all subsequent conversions had them. Trials with the first two units were extremely encouraging, *Pomodon* making 18.2kts submerged (half-hour battery rate). Streamlining made a very considerable difference, a snorkel GUPPY (Type II) requiring only about 44 per cent of the power of the fleet boat, submerged, at speeds up to 10kts at periscope depth.

Twelve Type II GUPPYs, equivalent to the original Type Is except for their snorkels, were approved in 1947; four of them were submarines which had been suspended incomplete in 1945. Their batteries were extremely advanced and rather expensive, with much shorter working lives than the Sargo II batteries adapted from those earlier US submarines, and in 1949 it was decided that further conversions would all incorporate the more conventional batteries, at a cost in underwater performance (*eg* 15 rather than 16kts at maximum power submerged). The FY51 programme thus included ten GUPPY IA conversions, as well as sixteen more austere 'Fleet Snorkel' conversions, in which the original Fleet Submarine superstructure was replaced by a GUPPY-type fin and a snorkel fitted, but the basic hull form was unchanged; some of these latter units even retained a 5in/25 deck gun. By this time the ASW training role had been eclipsed by a conventional attack submarine function. Two further GUPPY IA conversions were carried out for the Royal Netherlands Navy, *Hawkbill* and *Icefish*.

GUPPY conversions were designed to facilitate later conversions to an SSK. Visually, Fleet Snorkel submarines could be distinguished by their raked bow, where GUPPY bows were rounded; underwater they could not make much more than the 10kts of a fleet submarine, although they could snorkel at 6.5kts (compared to

GUPPY fleet submarine conversions (*attack submarines*)

Displacement:	GUPPY IA: 1830t surfaced; 2440t submerged GUPPY II 1870t surfaced; 2440t submerged GUPPY IIA 1848t surfaced; 2440t submerged GUPPY III 1975t surfaced; 2450t submerged
Dimensions:	307ft (GUPPY III 326ft 6in) × 27ft × 17ft *93.6m (99.5m) × 8.2m × 5.2m*
Machinery:	2-shaft diesels, 4610bhp (GUPPY IIA 3430bhp) = 18kts (surfaced) 9kts (snorkel, on one engine), 16kts (max submerged), 3.5kts (submerged cruise) in GUPPY II; 17.2kts, 6.2kts, 14.5kts, 6.2kts in GUPPY III
Armament:	10–21in TT (6 bow, 4 stern, 24 torpedoes)
Sensors:	BQR-2, BQS-2, JT or SQR-3 (BQG-4 PUFFS in many GUPPY III)
Complement:	82 (186 in GUPPY III)

For names of boats converted see under Fleet Strength 1947. Original particulars, including building dates, can be found in the 1922–46 volume. Note SSK were similar to GUPPY IIA, but had BQR-4 passive array in bow. Fleet Snorkel conversions were rated at 10kts underwater (half-hour rate) or 6.5kts snorkelling. In a very few cases, Fleet Snorkel submarines retained their single 5in/25 deck guns as initially converted; they could be distinguished from true GUPPY conversions by their ship-type bows (overall length 312ft) and could make only 3kts sustained underwater.

Sabalo (Fleet Snorkel) 1953   USN

7.5kts for a GUPPY IA, or 9kts for a GUPPY II. Finally, sixteen more fleet submarines were converted to GUPPY IIA under the FY52 programme, with improved sonar performance, one main engine being removed to allow the relocation of auxiliary machinery away from sonar transducers. Two of the GUPPY IIAs, *Thornback* and *Razorback*, were designed specifically as underwater targets, easily convertible back to standard GUPPY IIA configuration.

Under the FRAM programme, nine GUPPY II submarines were rebuilt to a GUPPY III configuration, lengthened 10ft to allow for a plotting room and a longer conning tower, with new fire control systems to permit them to fire Astor (Mk 45) nuclear ASW torpedoes. They also received a new plastic fin similar to that of the nuclear submarines. During the 1960s, too, US yards converted a number of the surviving fleet boats, as well as several which had already been transferred abroad, to the late 'Fleet Snorkel' configuration, with the new plastic fin. Indeed, Fleet Snorkels remained in service alongside GUPPYs as late as 1973. Many of these ships had the PUFFS (BQG-4) passive sonar system, with its characteristic trio of tall sonar domes.

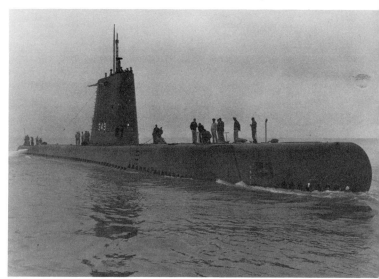

Diodon (GUPPY II) 1965   USN

Finally, the specialised SSK conversions should be mentioned: six fleet boats in FY52 after a prototype conversion in the FY50 programme. All were considered as mobilisation prototypes. In each case two of the four main engines were removed and a snorkel and streamlined fin was fitted; in the prototype, *Grouper*, the passive array was fitted around the forward side of the fin; in Type II (FY52) units, the BQR-4A array was wrapped around the bow, which was clearly blunter than in GUPPYs. There was extensive silencing and sound isolation to permit effective passive operation.

K 1 as completed
NB 1/750 scale

These three small diesel submarines were intended as prototypes of a mass produced ASW submarine, which would ambush enemy submarines as they emerged from their bases. The principal requirements were quietness, low cost and an effective passive sonar, the latter being carried in an enlarged bow sonar dome. They were later criticised as too small for habitability or for sea-keeping, and *Tullibee* was an attempt to update the ASW submarine (SSK) concept. In view of limited resources available for new construction during the early postwar period, an SSK conversion of fleet submarines was developed as a mobilisation measure, and the GUPPY submarine conversions were all designed to permit later modification to SSK standard.

BARRACUDA (ex-'K') class *attack submarines*

Displacement:	765t standard; 1160t submerged
Dimensions:	196ft 1in oa × 24ft 7in × 14ft 5in
	59.8m × 7.5m × 4.4m
Machinery:	2 shafts, 2 GM diesels plus GM electric motors, 1050shp = 13kts surfaced, 8.5kts submerged
Armament:	4–21in TT (2 bow, 2 stern)
Sensors:	Sonar BQR-4 (in bow dome)
Complement:	37

No	Name	Builder	Laid down	Launched	Comp	Fate
SST 3	BARRACUDA (ex-*K 1*)	Electric Boat	1.7.49	2.3.51	10.11.51	Stricken 1973
SS 551	BASS (ex-*K 2*)	Mare Island N Yd	23.2.50	2.5.51	11.1.52	Stricken 1965
SS 552	BONITA (ex-*K 3*)	Mare Island N Yd	17.3.50	21.6.51	11.2.52	Stricken 1965

All three were renamed with 'B' names in December 1955, and in 1959 they were withdrawn from the SSK role, *Barracuda* becoming the training submarine *T 1* (SST 3), her sisters the attack submarine SS 550 and SS 551. They were both stricken in April 1965, *Bonita* having been used as a target (with only superficial damage) in the 1958 nuclear test series. *Barracuda* was stricken on 1 October 1973, having been reclassified formally as an attack submarine on 1 August 1972. All three had their large bow arrays removed in 1959.

Trigger as completed

These ships, the US counterpart of the Soviet 'Whiskeys', were the US attempt to assimilate German Type XXI concepts. The first four also had a new compact radial ('pancake') diesel, which itself caused considerable problems in service, the four units being lengthened and re-engined with the more conventional power plants of the last pair (SS 563–SS 566, 4500bhp diesels and 5600shp electric motors, length 278ft (*84.8m*); all were later lengthened to 287ft (*87.5m*) and speed in this configuration was reported as being 16kts surfaced and submerged. Originally conceived almost as an experimental high-speed type (in opposition to the usual fleet boat), they became the basis for postwar development. Compared to wartime fleet submarines, they had much increased battery power for greater submerged speed. Compared to the GUPPY conversions, they benefited from a shorter hull form which in itself reduced resistance underwater. They also had streamlined superstructures, snorkels and improved sonars, although by no means in the SSK category; the new hull form reduced the torpedo tube battery to eight, with only two aft.

There were two competitive designs, SS 563 by Portsmouth Naval Shipyard and SS 564 by Electric Boat, both to the same basic Characteristics. The initial Ship Characteristics Board requirements included the potential for re-engining with a closed-cycle or nuclear power plant for an underwater speed of 25kts (17kt with a diesel-electric plant), and an increase in diving depth from the wartime 400ft to 700ft postwar. *Darter* was an improved version, with console controls; two planned sisters were completed instead as the strategic missile submarines *Grayback* and

TANG class *attack submarines*

Displacement:	1560t standard; 2260t full load
Dimensions:	269ft 2in oa × 27ft 2in (27ft 3in SS 564, 566, 568) × 17ft
	82.0m × 8.3m × 5.2m
Machinery:	2 shafts, FM 'pancake' diesels plus electric motors = 15.5kts/18.3kts (designed). See notes
Armament:	8–21in TT (6 bow, 2 stern)
Sensors:	Sonar BQS-4 (later BQG-4 in SS 565 and 567)
Complement:	83

No	Name	Builder	Laid down	Launched	Comp	Fate
SS 563	TANG	Portsmouth N Yd	18.4.49	19.6.51	25.10.52	Turkish *Piri Reis* 1980
SS 564	TRIGGER	Electric Boat	24.2.49	3.12.51	31.3.52	Italian *Livio Piomarta* 1974
SS 565	WAHOO	Portsmouth N Yd	24.10.49	16.10.51	30.5.52	Stricken 1980
SS 566	TROUT	Electric Boat	1.12.49	21.8.51	27.6.51	Stricken 1978
SS 567	GUDGEON	Portsmouth N Yd	20.5.50	11.5.62	21.11.52	Extant 1982
SS 568	HARDER	Electric Boat	20.6.50	14.6.51	19.8.52	Italian *Romeo Romei* 1973

Darter 1967

DARTER *attack submarine*

Displacement:	1872t surfaced; 2372t submerged
Dimensions:	268ft wl, 268ft 7in oa × 27ft 2in × 16ft 9in
	81.7m, 81.9m × 8.3m × 5.1m
Mahcinery:	2 shafts, 3 FM diesels plus electric motors, 3100bhp/4500shp = 19.5kts/14kts
Armament:	8–21in TT (6 bow, 2 stern)
Sensor:	Sonar BQS-4 (later BQG-4)
Complement:	83

No	Name	Builder	Laid down	Launched	Comp	Fate
SS 576	DARTER	Electric Boat	10.11.54	28.5.56	26.10.56	Decommissioned 1982

Growler. Tang, Wahoo and *Trout* were scheduled for transfer to Iran in 1982, 1980 and 1979 respectively, but the Iranian revolution intervened.

T 2 1955 **NB 1/750 scale**

SST 1 originally ordered as AGSS 570. Originally numbered simply *T 1* and *T 2*, they were named in 1956.

MACKEREL (T1) class *target submarines*

Displacement:	303t surfaced; 347t submerged
Dimensions:	131ft 2in oa × 13ft 6in × 12ft 2in
	40.0m × 4.1m × 3.7m
Machinery:	1 shaft, 2 GM diesels plus electric motors, 380bhp/1050shp = 8kts/9.5kts. Range 2000nm at 8kts
Armament:	1–21in TT (bow)
Complement:	18

No	Name	Builder	Laid down	Launched	Comp	Fate
SST 1	MACKEREL	Electric Boat	12.5.52	14.10.53	28.11.53	Stricken 31.1.73
SST 2	MARLIN	Portsmouth N Yd	1.4.52	17.7.53	9.10.53	Stricken 31.1.73

This project was inspired indirectly by the British X-Craft of the Second World War, one of which visited the USA specifically to provide design references. The original propulsion plant used hydrogen peroxide, this craft being the sole US fruit of the postwar Allied peroxide programme; (see the British *Explorer* class). She was built in 1954–55, but suffered an internal explosion in February 1958, which broke her into three pieces. Rebuilt at Philadelphia, she rejoined the Navy on 14 December 1960 as a special test craft at NSRDC, painted orange.

X 1 *midget submarine*

Displacement:	31t surfaced; 36t submerged
Dimensions:	49ft 2in × 7ft × 7ft
	15.0m × 2.1m × 2.1m
Machinery:	1 shaft, diesels plus electric motors, 30bhp = 15kts/12kts. Range over 500nm
Complement:	8 (4 minimum)

No	Name	Builder	Laid down	Launched	Comp	Fate
	X 1	Fairchild, Farmingdale	Jan 54	7.9.55	6.10.55	Stricken 16.2.73

Nautilus 1958

NAUTILUS attack submarine

Both built under the FY52 programme, these were the prototype US nuclear submarines, *Nautilus* being by far the more successful of the two. She was the world's first nuclear warship, with an S2W reactor and six torpedo tubes, all of them forward. *Seawolf* was designed around the S2G sodium-cooled reactor, intended as a back-up to the S2W, but abandoned because of operational problems and replaced by an S2Wa in 1959. From 1969 she has been used for research, with four bow thrusters above her pressure hull (two forward and two aft) for precise manoeuvring, and provision for a DSRV research vehicle to be mated to her aft. *Seawolf* also had the last conning tower in a US submarine, within her stepped fin as later submarines have only a bridge access trunk in their fin.

Displacement:	3533t surfaced; 4092t submerged
Dimensions:	319ft 6in wl, 323ft 9in oa × 27ft 8in × 21ft 9in
	97.4, 98.7 × 8.4m × 6.6m
Machinery:	2-shaft nuclear: 1 S2W reactor, approx 15,000shp = approx 23kts submerged
Armament:	6–21in TT (bow)
Sensors:	Sonar BQS-4
Complement:	105

No	Name	Builder	Laid down	Launched	Comp	Fate
SSN 571	NAUTILUS	Electric Boat	14.6.52	21.1.54	22.4.55	Museum 1982

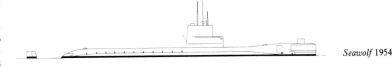

Seawolf 1954

SEAWOLF *attack submarine*

Displacement:	3741t surfaced; 4287t submerged
Dimensions:	337ft 6in × 27ft 8in × 22ft
	102.9m × 8.4m × 6.7m
Machinery:	2-shaft nuclear: 1 S2G reactor (later S2Wa), approx 15,000shp = approx 20kts submerged
Armament:	6–21in (bow)
Sensors:	Sonar BQR-4, BQS-4
Complement:	105

No	Name	Builder	Laid down	Launched	Comp	Fate
SSN 575	SEAWOLF	Electric Boat	15.9.53	21.7.55	30.3.57	Extant 1982

Seawolf (foreground)
and *Nautilus* as completed   USN

UNITED STATES

Swordfish 19.1.70   USN

Launch of *Albacore*   CPL

Skate as completed

These four attack boats were the first US approach to a 'production' nuclear submarine, considerably smaller than *Nautilus*, with about half her power (S3W in SSN 578 and SSN 583, S4W in SSN 579 and SSN 584); they corresponded approximately to the earlier *Tang* class in dimensions, although they were somewhat heavier. Production was abandoned in favour of the much faster *Skipjack* class, the transition occurring in the FY56 programme.

SKATE class *attack submarines*

Displacement:	2550t surfaced; 2848t submerged
Dimensions:	267ft 8in × 25ft × 20ft 7in
	81.6m × 7.6m × 6.3m
Machinery:	2-shaft nuclear: 1 S3W (S4W in SSN 579, 584), 6600shp = approx 20kts submerged
Armament:	8–21in TT (6 bow, 2 stern)
Sensors:	BQS-4
Complement:	84

No	Name	Builder	Laid down	Launched	Comp	Fate
SSN 578	SKATE	Electric Boat	21.7.55	16.5.57	23.12.57	Extant 1982
SSN 579	SWORDFISH	Portsmouth N Yd	25.1.56	27.8.57	15.9.58	Extant 1982
SSN 583	SARGO	Mare Island N Yd	21.2.56	10.10.57	1.10.58	Extant 1982
SSN 584	SEADRAGON	Portsmouth N Yd	20.6.56	16.8.58	5.12.59	Extant 1982

Although by no means a fighting ship, the experimental submarine *Albacore* deserves inclusion in this book by virtue of her pioneering work in submarine hull form design. She was the first US submarine designed entirely for underwater operation, with a hull form unsuited to surface operation. Conceived initially as a target for surface ASW forces, she was financed partly (as SCB 56 of FY50) by cancelling *Fletcher* class DDE conversions. Her outstanding internal feature was a massive battery capacity which permitted her to operate briefly at extremely high underwater speeds, initially about 27kts and later about 33kts. She was extensively modified during her operational career. Initially she was 203ft 9in long, with

ALBACORE *experimental submarine*

Displacement:	1500t standard; 1850t submerged
Dimensions:	210ft 6in oa × 27ft 4in × 18ft 6in
	64.2m × 8.3m × 5.6m
Machinery:	1 shaft, 2 GM, 2 diesels plus 1 electric motor, 1500bhp/15,000shp = 33kts (submerged in final configuration reportedly)
Complement:	52

No	Name	Builder	Laid down	Launched	Comp	Fate
AGSS 569	ALBACORE	Portsmouth N Yd	15.3.52	1.8.53	5.12.53	Stricken 1.5.80

conventional stern surfaces. However, Phase III modifications of August 1961 provided her with a new stern with X-form planes, a dorsal rudder, a new bow sonar dome, and dive brakes. Phase IV (December 1962–March 1965) included the installation of a new high-capacity silver-zinc battery and contraprops.

DOLPHIN
The other major experimental submarine in the standard numbering sequence is *Dolphin*, AGSS 555 of the FY61 programme (SCB 207), designed for deep diving, with a 15ft constant-diameter pressure hull. Her experimental torpedo tube was removed in 1970.

Blueback 1967

These submarines, the last US diesel-electric types built, adopted the streamlined hull form of the experimental *Albacore* to achieve high underwater speed, albeit for only relatively short periods. Stern torpedo tubes had to be eliminated because of the adoption of a single propeller shaft. As built, they had conventional bow diving planes, but they were later modified with planes in their fin structures. They were the first US submarines with all controls centralised in an 'attack center', a practice adopted for all later classes.

Unlike earlier diesel submarines, they were not refitted with PUFFs passive fire control gear, perhaps because the three large sonar domes

BARBEL class *attack submarines*

Displacement:	2146t surfaced; 2639t submerged
Dimensions:	218ft 8in wl, 219ft 2in oa × 29ft × 20ft 8in
	66.7m, 66.8m × 8.8m × 6.3m
Machinery:	1 shaft, 3 FM diesels plus 1 Westinghouse electric motor, 4800bhp/3150shp = 15kts/21kts
Armament:	6–21in TT (bow)
Sensors:	Sonar BQS-4
Complement:	77

No	Name	Builder	Laid down	Launched	Comp	Fate
SS 580	BARBEL	Portsmouth N Yd	18.5.56	19.7.58	17.1.59	Extant 1982
SS 581	BLUEBACK	Ingalls	15.4.57	16.5.59	15.10.59	Extant 1982
SS 582	BONEFISH	New York SB	3.6.57	22.11.58	9.7.59	Extant 1982

involved would have ruined streamlining. They differ from *Albacore*-shaped nuclear submarines in that they retain a substantial casing with a noticeable free-flooding slot running most of its length.

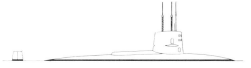

Scamp 1976

These six ships were essentially nuclear equivalent of the *Barbel*s, benefiting from the *Albacore* hull form and also introducing the S5W reactor and single-hull construction to US SSNs. They were the fastest submarines in US service until the appearance of the *Los Angeles* class, and they formed the basis of the *George Washington* class ballistic missile submarines. A single propeller shaft precluded the installation of stern torpedo tubes, so that they are limited to six bow tubes. Although they do not have the bow sonar or SUBROC of later US submarines, they continue to be highly regarded, and projects for *Skipjack* sonar improvement were considered during the 1960s. *Scorpion* of this class was lost with all hands in May 1968 south-west of the Azores.

SKIPJACK class *attack submarines*

Displacement:	3070t surfaced; 3500t submerged
Dimensions:	246ft wl, 251ft 9in oa × 31ft 8in × 25ft 3in
	75.0m, 76.8m × 9.7m × 7.7m
Machinery:	1-shaft nuclear: 1 S5W reactor, 15,000shp = approx 30kts submerged
Armament:	6–21in TT (bow; 24 torpedoes)
Sensors:	Sonar BQS-4
Complement:	85

No	Name	Builder	Laid down	Launched	Comp	Fate
SSN 585	SKIPJACK	Electric Boat	29.5.56	26.5.58	15.4.59	Extant 1982
SSN 588	SCAMP	Mare Island N Yd	23.1.59	8.10.60	5.6.61	Extant 1982
SSN 589	SCORPION	Electric Boat	20.8.58	19.12.59	27.6.60	Lost May 68
SSN 590	SCULPIN	Ingalls	3.2.58	31.3.60	1.6.61	Extant 1982
SSN 591	SHARK	Newport News	24.2.56	16.3.60	9.2.61	Extant 1982
SSN 592	SNOOK	Ingalls	7.4.58	31.10.60	24.10.61	Extant 1982

Tullibee 1960

Tullibee was an attempt to built a minimum nuclear submarine specifically for ASW; originally she was to have been even smaller than she turned out to be, and ultimately she was somewhat underpowered, with an S2C reactor reportedly producing only 2500shp, one-third of the *Skate* power plant. She was completed with the BQQ-2 sonar and quartet of hull-mounted torpedo tubes of the *Thresher*s, but was not fitted to fire SUBROC. She also had a prototype turbo-electric drive, for quietness. *Tullibee* was later fitted with three large sonar domes for a PUFFS (BQG-4) passive-ranging sonar system.

TULLIBEE *attack submarine*

Displacement:	2316t surfaced; 2607t submerged
Dimensions:	272ft 10in × 23ft 4in × 19ft 4in
	83.2m × 7.1m × 5.8m
Machinery:	1-shaft nuclear: 1 S2C reactor, 2500shp = approx 15kts submerged
Armament:	4–21in TT (amidships)
Sensors:	Sonar BQQ-2 (later BQG-4 as well)
Complement:	56

No	Name	Builder	Laid down	Launched	Comp	Fate
SSN 597	TULLIBEE	Electric Boat	26.5.58	27.4.60	9.11.60	Extant 1982

Permit as completed   USN

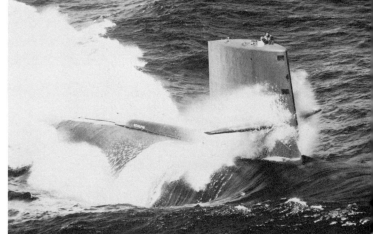

Sculpin 1961   CPL

Sturgeon 17.1.67   USN

Note SSN 612–615 are usually included in the *Permit* group, but share the dimensions of the *Sturgeon* class, and are therefore listed with it.

This is the largest class of submarines built by the United States since 1945; officially it was subdivided into *Permit* and *Sturgeon* classes; the original name-ship, *Thresher*, was lost on diving trials on 10 April 1963. They combine a stronger hull for deeper diving with an advanced long-range BQQ-2 sonar and its associated SUB-ROC missile; diving depth is reportedly 1300ft *(396.2m)*. Later units were lengthened to permit the installation of a BQQ-5 sonar in place of BQQ-2; the extra space is free flooding, and underwater displacement rises by about 300t (SSN 613–615 and most *Sturgeon* class submarines); ultimately all of these units will have BQQ-5. All will also ultimately receive the Mk 117 fire control system in place of their current Mk 113, providing facilities for Harpoon anti-ship missile control. However, since SUBROC is an analogue rather than a digital weapon, and Mk 117 is a fully digital fire control system, the long-range ASW capability (except as provided by the Mk 48 torpedo) is being lost. SSN 613–SSN 615 were, in effect, prototype *Sturgeon*s with heavier machinery, taller fins (20ft rather than 13.8ft or 15ft), improved safety features ('Subsafe' programme), and lengthened hulls (292ft 3in rather than 278ft 6in). SSN 678 and later units are 302ft long. SSN 666, 672 and others were modified to carry a DSRV (submarine rescue vehicle) aft, for launch and recovery while submerged.

As officially described in 1979, *Thresher* class design compromises included a low sail, inadequate numbers of periscopes and antennas, and limited electronics. The reduced sail height was specifically accepted to minimize the speed loss, given the fixed reactor power of the S5W. The SSN 637 class was considerably enlarged for a combination of quieting and additional electronics, as well as improved internal arrangements. Presumably the electronics was a combination of sonar signal processing and torpedo control, one control console being required for each wire-guided torpedo.

These submarines were intended primarily for ASW, with a large spherical sonar array filling their bows, and the torpedo battery, reduced to four tubes, moved aft to abreast the fin, firing diagonally from the hull. One advantage of this arrangement was that a large torpedo room could be provided, permitting a relatively easy choice of weapons for each tube. By the late 1960s, the submarine commander had a choice of long ASW torpedoes, nuclear torpedoes (Astor, or Mk 45, now retired), long anti-ship torpedoes, or SUBROC; now there are Harpoon (first tested in *Permit* in 1976) and, very soon, Tomahawk. Unfortunately total weapon capacity is quite small, figures as low as twenty torpedoes in stowage being reported, so that this variety of weapons is very much a mixed blessing. Indeed, one advantage of the adoption of the Mk 48 torpedo is that it can replace both long ASW and long anti-ship weapons, and

Permit 1970

THRESHER/PERMIT class *attack submarines*

Displacement:	3705t surfaced; 4311t submerged
Dimensions:	278ft 6in (296ft 9in SSN 605) × 31ft 8in × 25ft 2in
	84.9m (90.5m) × *9.7m* × *7.7m*
Machinery:	1-shaft nuclear: 1 S5W reactor, 15,000shp = approx 27kts submerged
Armament:	4–21in TT (amidships)
Sensors:	Sonar BQQ-2
Complement:	94.

No	Name	Builder	Laid down	Launched	Comp	Fate
SSN 593	THRESHER	Portsmouth N Yd		9.7.60		Lost 10.4.63
SSN 594	PERMIT	Mare Island N Yd	10.7.59	1.7.61	29.5.62	Extant 1982
SSN 595	PLUNGER	Mare Island N Yd	20.3.60	9.12.61	21.11.62	Extant 1982
SSN 596	BARB	Ingalls	9.11.59	12.2.62	24.8.63	Extant 1982
	(ex-*Pollack*)					
SSN 603	POLLACK	New York SB	14.3.60	17.3.62	26.5.64	Extant 1982
	(ex-*Barb*)					
SSN 604	HADDO	New York SB	9.9.60	18.8.62	16.12.64	Extant 1982
SSN 605	JACK	Portsmouth N Yd	16.9.60	24.4.63	31.3.67	Extant 1982
SSN 606	TINOSA	Portsmouth N Yd	24.11.59	9.12.61	17.10.64	Extant 1982
SSN 607	DACE	Ingalls	6.6.60	18.8.62	4.4.64	Extant 1982
SSN 612	GUARDFISH	New York SB	28.2.61	15.5.65	20.12.66	Extant 1982
SSN 621	HADDOCK	Ingalls	24.4.61	21.5.66	22.12.67	Extant 1982

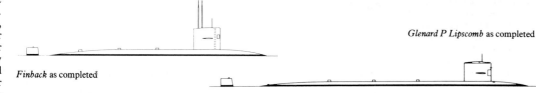

Glenard P Lipscomb as completed

Finback as completed

STURGEON class *attack submarines*

Displacement:	4246t surfaced; 4777t submerged
Dimensions:	292ft 3in (302ft from SSN 678) × 31ft 8in × 25ft 6in
	89.1m (92.1m) × *9.7m* × *7.8m*
Machinery:	1-shaft nuclear: 1 S5W reactor, 15,000shp = approx 26kts submerged
Armament:	4–21in TT (amidships)
Sensors:	Sonar BQQ-2
Complement:	99

No	Name	Builder	Laid down	Launched	Comp	Fate
SSN 613	FLASHER	Electric Boat	14.6.61	22.6.63	22.7.66	Extant 1982
SSN 614	GREENLING	Electric Boat	15.8.61	4.4.64	3.11.67	Extant 1982
SSN 615	GATO	Electric Boat	15.12.61	14.5.64	25.1.68	Extant 1982
SSN 637	STURGEON	Electric Boat	10.8.63	26.2.65	3.3.67	Extant 1982
SSN 638	WHALE	General Dynamics, Quincy	27.5.64	14.10.66	12.10.68	Extant 1982
SSN 639	TAUTOG	Ingalls	21.1.64	14.4.67	17.8.68	Extant 1982
SSN 646	GRAYLING	Portsmouth N Yd	12.5.64	22.6.67	11.10.69	Extant 1982
SSN 647	POGY	Ingalls	4.5.64	3.6.67	15.5.71	Extant 1982
SSN 648	ASPRO	Ingalls	23.11.64	29.11.67	20.2.69	Extant 1982
SSN 649	SUNFISH	General Dynamics, Quincy	15.1.65	14.10.66	15.3.69	Extant 1982
SSN 650	PARGO	Electric Boat	3.6.64	17.9.66	1.5.68	Extant 1982
SSN 651	QUEENFISH	Newport News	11.5.64	25.2.66	6.12.66	Extant 1982
SSN 652	PUFFER	Ingalls	8.2.65	30.3.68	9.8.69	Extant 1982
SSN 653	RAY	Newport News	1.4.65	21.6.66	12.4.67	Extant 1982
SSN 660	SAND LANCE	Portsmouth N Yd	15.1.65	11.11.69	25.9.71	Extant 1982
SSN 661	LAPON	Newport News	26.7.65	16.12.66	14.12.67	Extant 1982
SSN 662	GURNARD	Mare Island N Yd	22.12.64	20.5.67	6.12.68	Extant 1982
SSN 663	HAMMERHEAD	Newport News	29.11.65	14.4.67	28.6.67	Extant 1982
SSN 664	SEA DEVIL	Newport News	12.4.66	5.10.67	30.1.69	Extant 1982
SSN 665	GUITARRO	Mare Island N Yd	9.12.65	27.7.68	9.9.72	Extant 1982
SSN 666	HAWKBILL	Mare Island N Yd	12.9.66	12.4.69	4.2.71	Extant 1982
SSN 667	BERGALL	Electric Boat	16.4.66	17.2.68	13.6.69	Extant 1982
SSN 668	SPADEFISH	Newport News	21.12.66	15.5.68	14.8.69	Extant 1982
SSN 669	SEAHORSE	Electric Boat	13.8.66	15.6.68	19.9.69	Extant 1982
SSN 670	FINBACK	Newport News	26.6.67	7.12.68	4.2.70	Extant 1982
SSN 671	NARWHAL	Electric Boat	17.1.66	9.9.66	12.7.69	Extant 1982
SSN 672	PINTADO	Mare Island N Yd	27.10.67	16.8.69	11.9.71	Extant 1982
SSN 673	FLYING FISH	Electric Boat	30.6.67	17.5.69	29.4.70	Extant 1982
SSN 674	TREPANG	Electric Boat	28.10.67	27.9.69	14.8.70	Extant 1982
SSN 675	BLUEFISH	Electric Boat	13.3.68	10.1.70	8.1.71	Extant 1982
SSN 676	BILLFISH	Electric Boat	20.9.68	1.5.70	12.3.71	Extant 1982
SSN 677	DRUM	Mare Island N Yd	20.8.68	23.5.70	15.4.72	Extant 1982
SSN 678	ARCHERFISH	Electric Boat	19.6.69	16.1.71	24.12.71	Extant 1982
SSN 679	SILVERSIDES	Electric Boat	13.12.69	4.6.71	5.5.72	Extant 1982

the Mk 45 was discarded partly because it consumed valuable space but was unlikely to be used in action.

Since the power plant, the S5W, duplicated that of the earlier *Skipjack*, and the size of these submarines was much greater (by at least 800t), these ships were considerably slower, their speed reportedly about 26kts. There were three attempts within this class to improve propulsion. *Jack* has contraprops on her single screw, an arrangement never duplicated. *Narwhal* has a natural convection powerplant (S5G rather than S5W); and *Glenard P Lipscomb* has turbo-electric propulsion, both of the last two choices having been made for quietness.

No	Name	Builder	Laid down	Launched	Comp	Fate
SSN 680	WILLIAM H BATES (ex-*Redfish*)	Ingalls	4.8.69	11.12.71	5.5.73	Extant 1982
SSN 681	BATFISH	Electric Boat	9.2.70	9.10.71	1.9.72	Extant 1982
SSN 682	TUNNY	Ingalls	22.5.70	10.6.72	26.1.74	Extant 1982
SSN 683	PARCHE	Ingalls	10.12.70	13.1.73	17.8.74	Extant 1982
SSN 684	CAVALLA	Electric Boat	4.6.70	19.2.72	9.2.73	Extant 1982
SSN 685	GLENARD P LIPSCOMB	Electric Boat	5.6.71	4.8.73	21.12.74	Extant 1982
SSN 686	L MENDEL RIVERS	Newport News	26.6.71	2.6.73	1.2.75	Extant 1982
SSN 687	RICHARD B RUSSELL	Newport News	19.10.71	12.1.74	16.8.75	Extant 1982

Note SSN 671 and 685 are not properly part of this class, but were test vehicles for alternative propulsion: SSN 671 for a natural-circulation (S5G) reactor, SSN 685 for turbo-electric drive (for quietness) – at a considerable cost in size (5800t standard; 6480t submerged, 365ft (*111.2m*) long) and therefore of speed. SSN 671: 4450t standard; 5350t submerged, 314ft (*95.7m*) oa.

Los Angeles as completed

LOS ANGELES class *attack submarines*

Displacement:	6000t standard; 6900t submerged
Dimensions:	360ft × 33ft × 32ft 4in
	109.8m × 10.1m × 9.8m
Machinery:	1-shaft nuclear: 1 S6G reactor, approx 30,000shp = approx 31kts submerged
Armament:	4–21in TT (amidships; Tomahawk SSMs)
Sensors:	Sonar BQQ-5
Complement:	127

These submarines restore the speed advantage of the *Skipjack*s while retaining the sonar and weapon capability of the *Permit* class; the great increase in size (displacement submerged rising from 4650t in late *Sturgeon*s to 6900t in these units) is due largely to a doubling of installed power (S6G reactor) with little other improvement, except undoubtedly in silencing. They are reportedly about 5kts faster than the earlier submarines, with the improved BQQ-5 sonar system consisting of a spherical bow array, three hull-mounted hydrophones on each side, a conformal hydrophone array, and generally a towed array as well. Given the limited number of weapons carried, recent proposals call for the installation of vertical launch tubes for Tomahawk long-range missiles in the empty (free-flooding) space between the pressure hull and the bow sonar dome; twelve tubes can be accommodated. Units from SSN 719 onwards are to be completed with vertical launch tubes, and there are reports that earlier ones will be retrofitted; one such report refers to eight missiles each for *Permit* and *Los Angeles* class submarines. Harpoon missiles were carried from 1978 onwards.

Design work began in 1968 on a new 'mid-1970s' attack submarine, to incorporate both new sensor and propulsion technology and a new stand-off weapon (which would have replaced SUBROC and would have had both anti-ship and anti-submarine roles). In view of the limited internal weapon space available in the torpedo rooms of conventionally designed nuclear submarines, twenty vertical launch tubes would have been provided abaft the fin of the new submarine. Other improvements, such as greatly increased power and improved silencing, added size, so that by December 1972 the new submarine was being described as: 472ft × 40ft (*143.8m × 12.2m*) (as against 335ft × 33ft (*102.1m × 10.1m*) for a *Los Angeles*); displacing 13,700t submerged (as against 6630t estimated at that time). It would have cost about 80 per cent as much as a Trident missile submarine, then estimated at $500 million in FY73 dollars. Admiral Zumwalt cancelled it and its new missile in 1973, and a submarine-launched version of Harpoon was substituted. The SUBROC

No	Name	Builder	Laid down	Launched	Comp	Fate
SSN 688	LOS ANGELES	Newport News	8.1.72	6.4.74	13.11.76	Extant 1982
SSN 689	BATON ROUGE	Newport News	18.11.72	26.4.75	25.6.77	Extant 1982
SSN 690	PHILADELPHIA	Electric Boat	12.8.72	19.10.74	25.6.77	Extant 1982
SSN 691	MEMPHIS	Newport News	23.6.73	3.4.76	17.12.77	Extant 1982
SSN 692	OMAHA	Electric Boat	27.1.73	21.2.76	11.3.78	Extant 1982
SSN 693	CINCINATTI	Newport News	6.4.74	19.2.77	10.6.78	Extant 1982
SSN 694	GROTON	Electric Boat	3.8.73	9.10.76	8.7.78	Extant 1982
SSN 695	BIRMINGHAM	Newport News	26.4.75	29.10.77	20.12.78	Extant 1982
SSN 696	NEW YORK CITY	Electric Boat	15.12.73	18.6.77	10.3.79	Extant 1982
SSN 697	INDIANAPOLIS	Electric Boat	19.10.74	30.7.77	5.1.80	Extant 1982
SSN 698	BREMERTON	Electric Boat	8.5.76	22.7.78	28.3.81	Extant 1982
SSN 699	JACKSONVILLE	Electric Boat	21.2.76	18.11.78	16.5.81	Extant 1982
SSN 700	DALLAS	Electric Boat	9.10.76	28.4.79	18.7.81	Extant 1982
SSN 701	LA JOLLA	Electric Boat	16.10.76	11.8.79	24.10.81	Extant 1982
SSN 702	PHOENIX	Electric Boat	30.7.77	8.12.79	19.12.81	Extant 1982
SSN 703	BOSTON	Electric Boat	11.8.78	19.4.80	30.1.82	Extant 1982
SSN 704	BALTIMORE	Electric Boat	21.5.79	13.12.80	24.7.82	Extant 1982
SSN 705	CITY OF CORPUS CHRISTI	Electric Boat	4.9.79	25.4.81	14.12.82	Extant 1982
SSN 706	ALBUQUERQUE	Electric Boat	27.12.79	13.3.82		Completing
SSN 707	PORTSMOUTH	Electric Boat	8.5.80	July 82		Completing
SSN 708	MINNEAPOLIS-ST PAUL	Electric Boat	20.1.81	18.12.82		Completing
SSN 709		Electric Boat	24.7.81			Building
SSN 710		Electric Boat	1.4.82			Building
SSN 711	SAN FRANCISCO	Newport News	26.5.77	27.10.79	24.4.81	Extant 1982
SSN 712	ATLANTA	Newport News	17.8.78	16.8.80	6.3.82	Extant 1982
SSN 713	HOUSTON	Newport News	29.1.79	21.3.81	25.9.82	Extant 1982
SSN 714	NORFOLK	Newport News	1.8.79	31.10.81		Completing
SSN 715	BUFFALO	Newport News	25.1.80	8.5.82		Completing
SSN 716	SALT LAKE CITY	Newport News	26.8.80	16.10.82		Completing
SSN 717		Newport News	31.3.81			Building
SSN 718		Newport News	10.11.81			Building
SSN 719		Electric Boat	9.10.82			Building
SSN 720		Electric Boat				Ordered
SSN 721		Newport News				Ordered
SSN 722		Newport News				Ordered
SSN 723		Newport News				Ordered
SSN 724		Electric Boat				Ordered
SSN 725		Electric Boat				Ordered
SSN 750		Newport News				Ordered

replacement was delayed, and will appear later in the 1980s as the ASW Stand-Off Weapon (SOW).

In the late 1970s the Carter Administration proposed an austere 'fleet attack' submarine of about 5000t with the S5W reactor and six torpedo tubes, at three-quarters of the cost of a *Los Angeles*. It was criticised

as too slow, and derisively nicknamed 'Fat Albert', from its F/A designation, and the Reagan Administration rejected it entirely. Production of *Los Angeles* class fast attack submarines will probably continue, then, through the 1980s, despite delays in delivery. *Los Angeles* herself was authorized under the FY70 programme, laid

down in August 1972, and not delivered until November 1976; by way of contrast, some *Sturgeon*s were delivered in only three years. SSN 724 was authorised in FY81, SSN 725 and 742 in FY82, with 2 proposed in FY83, 3 in FY84 and 4 in end year from FY85 to FY87.

Cusk 12.9.48　　　　　　　　　　　　　　　　　　　　　　　　　　　　　　　USN

Los Angeles 1976　　　　　　　　　　USN　　*Grayback (as LPSS) 1975*　　　　　　　　USN

Two submarines, *Cusk* and *Carbonero*, were converted as part of the Loon (copied V1) programme, with launching ramps aft; later they were fitted with cylindrical hangars for two Loon missiles: *Carbonero* was originally only a control craft. Upon termination of the Loon programme in 1953, *Cusk* was converted to a Fleet Snorkel attack submarine, but *Carbonero* was retained for tests with Regulus. Two fleet submarines were converted as operational Regulus I carriers, *Barbero* (a former cargo-carrying submarine) and *Tunny*, a full conversion with a streamlined fin, as in the GUPPYs. She also received a snorkel, and one main engine was removed. By way of contrast, *Barbero*, converted in 1955, never received a streamlined fin; she was considered an interim measure against the availability of specially built submarines such as *Grayback*. Her earlier transport conversion had already cost her two main engines and the stern torpedo tubes; she was fitted

Fleet submarine conversions *strategic submarines*

Displacement:	1525t standard; 2400t submerged
Dimensions:	312ft oa × 27ft 4in 95.1m × 8.3m
Machinery:	2 shafts, diesel-electric (one main generator engine removed in SSG 282, two removed in SSG 317), 3430bhp (2305bhp in SSG 317)/2740shp (2305shp in SSG 317) = 17 (15) kts/9kts
Armament:	10–21in TT (6 bow, 4 stern; bow TT only in SSG 317)
Complement:	84

For names of boats converted see under Fleet Strength 1947. Original particulars, including building dates, can be found in the 1922–1946 volume.

with a snorkel and ultimately with a streamlined fin.

Carbonero reverted to SS status (from SSG) at the end of the Regulus I test programme in 1961, and the other two reverted in 1965; *Barbero* was stricken, and *Tunny* was converted to a transport submarine (her Regulus hangar proving useful for stowage) at Puget Sound in 1966. She thus joined *Perch* and *Sealion*, converted to submarine transports in

1948, and active in Korea and Vietnam; both had snorkels and Regulus-like LVT/jeep hangars abaft their superstructures, losing all of their torpedoes and two main engines. By way of contrast, *Barbero* was a pure cargo submarine, with cargo spaces in her former torpedo rooms, forward engine room, and some of the after battery compartment. She, too, received a snorkel. The other major submarine auxiliary conversion of the

early postwar period was *Guavina*, the oiler, carrying 160,000gal, with all but three torpedo tubes removed (and one forward restricted to discharging cargo) and a snorkel; she had a streamlined fin. She may have been intended to supply forward-deployed SSKs, on the wartime German 'milch cow' principle. In any case, her SSO classification was dropped for a time and then revived briefly in connection with the P6M seaplane programme.

Growler 1959

These two submarines were laid down as sisters to *Darter*, then cut in two and lengthened by 50ft *(15.2m)* (*Growler* is 4ft longer) to accommodate two cylindrical hangars for Regulus missiles; both were decommissioned in May 1964 when Regulus was retired. However, *Grayback* was converted to an amphibious transport (LPSS) at Mare Island (November 1967 to May 1969) and lengthened by 11ft 8in *(3.5m)*, and had her former missile hangars converted to 'lock out' swimmers and Swimmer Delivery Vehicles (SDV); her fin structure was raised and three large sonar domes for PUFFS passive sonar (BQG-4) added. She was reclassified as an attack submarine in 1975, apparently without any further changes. A similar planned conversion of her sister ship was cancelled in view of the high cost of the first conversion, and in 1982 she remains in reserve. As a commando ship, *Grayback* has a crew of 96 and can accommodate 10 officers and 75 enlisted men.

GRAYBACK *strategic submarine*

Displacement:	2287t light; 3638t submerged
Dimensions:	322ft 4in oa × 30ft × 17ft 4in 98.3m × 9.1m × 5.3m
Machinery:	2 shafts, 3 FM diesels, 2 electric motors, 4500bhp/5600shp = 15kts/12kts (designed; 20kts on surface unofficially reported 1978)
Armament:	4 Regulus I or Regulus II SSM, 8–21in TT (6 bow, 2 stern)
Sensors:	Sonar BQS-4 (BQG-4 later installed)
Complement:	84

No	Name	Builder	Laid down	Launched	Comp	Fate
SSG 574	GRAYBACK	Portsmouth N Yd	1.7.54	2.7.54	May 58	Extant 1982

GROWLER *strategic submarine*

Displacement:	2174t light; 3387t submerged
Dimensions:	317ft oa × 27ft 2in × 17ft 96.6m × 8.3m × 5.2m
Machinery:	2 shafts, 3 FM Diesels, 2 electric motors, 4600bhp/5600shp = 15kts/12kts
Armament:	4 Regulus I or 2 Regulus II SSM, 6–21in TT (4 bow, 2 stern)
Sensors:	Sonar BQS-4
Complement:	84

No	Name	Builder	Laid down	Launched	Comp	Fate
SSG 577	GROWLER	Portsmouth N Yd	15.2.55	5.4.57	15.12.58	Extant 1982

Robert E Lee 1966   USN

Halibut 1960

Halibut was the sole US nuclear-powered cruise-missile submarine, originally conceived as a near-sister to the *Grayback*s. She was completed with nuclear power and with enlarged missile hangars, for a total of two Regulus II or five Regulus I cruise missiles. The engineering plant was reportedly similar to that of the *Skipjack* class (S3W reactor), with two shafts. The FY58 programme originally included three larger Regulus II submarines, SSGN 594, 595 and 596, with another (SSGN 607) planned for FY59; all completed as *Permit* class attack submarines. This SCB-166A submarine would have carried four Regulus II (or eight Regulus I) in four separate missile hangars forward of the sail. *Halibut*'s hangars were removed after the end of the Regulus

HALIBUT *strategic submarine*

Displacement:	3846t surfaced; 4895t submerged
Dimensions:	350ft × 29ft 6in × 20ft 9in
	106.7m × 9.0m × 6.3m
Machinery:	2-shaft nuclear: 1 S3W reactor, approx 6600shp = 15kts/15.5kts
Armament:	2 Regulus II or 5 Regulus I SSM, 6–21in TT (4 bow, 2 stern)
Sensors:	Sonar BQS-4
Complement:	111

No	Name	Builder	Laid down	Launched	Comp	Fate
SSGN 587	HALIBUT	Mare Island N Yd	April 57	9.1.59	4.1.60	Decommissioned 1976

programme in 1965 (reclassified to SSN). She was employed in research from then until 1976, with a ducted bow thruster forward and facilities for a deep submergence vehicle (DSRV)

aft; all that was left of her missile equipment was a bulged structure on her foredeck. *Halibut* was decommissioned on 30 June 1976 and was in reserve in 1982.

George Washington 1960

The first US ballistic missile submarines, these vessels were converted from *Skipjack* class attack submarines under construction, by the addition of a 130ft (*39.6m*) missile section amidships; they have the S5W reactor and the six bow torpedo tubes of the earlier submarines, but reportedly with much reduced torpedo loads. All were converted from Polaris A-1 to A-3 missiles, but could not accommodate Poseidon; they were de-activated in 1980–81 to make way for the *Ohio* class.

Several alternative proposals for future use were made. For example, up to eight cruise missiles can be accommodated in a single Polaris tube. Beginning late in 1980, the missile sections of *Theodore Roosevelt* and *Abraham Lincoln* were physically removed, both units decommissioning on 28.2.81 at Bremerton, where they remain on the Navy List, in two pieces. Neither had made a missile patrol since 1978, and both required refuelling. The other three units were redesignated attack submarines

GEORGE WASHINGTON class *strategic submarines*

Displacement:	5959t surfaced; 6709t submerged
Dimensions:	373ft 6in wl, 381ft 8in oa × 33ft × 26ft 8in
	113.9m, 116.4m × 10.1m × 8.1m
Machinery:	1-shaft nuclear: 1 S5W reactor, approx 15,000shp = approx 20kts
Armament:	16 Polaris SLBM, 6–21in TT (bow)
Sensors:	Sonar BQS-4 (later BQR-19)
Complement:	112

No	Name	Builder	Laid down	Launched	Comp	Fate
SSBN 598	GEORGE WASHINGTON	Electric Boat	1.11.57	9.6.69	30.12.59	SSN 1981
SSBN 599	PATRICK HENRY	Electric Boat	27.5.58	22.9.59	9.4.60	SSN 1981
SSBN 600	THEODORE ROOSEVELT	Mare Island N Yd	20.5.58	3.10.59	13.2.61	Decommissioned 1981
SSBN 601	ROBERT E LEE	Newport News	25.8.58	18.12.59	16.9.60	SSN 1981
SSBN 602	ABRAHAM LINCOLN	Portsmouth N Yd	1.11.58	14.5.60	11.3.61	Decommissioned 1981

(SSN). The former missile tubes are to be filled with cement, and the missile fire control system removed. Note that, compared to *Skipjack* class attack submarines, they are quieter, but considerably slower, and have fewer torpedoes. They lack the bow

sonars of the later attack submarines, but do have towed array passive systems, fitted for self-protection; compared to later SSBNs, they lack advanced silencing, and cannot dive as deep.

Ethan Allan 1971

The first US ballistic missile submarines designed as such, these ships, like the *George Washington*s, could not be refitted with the Poseidon missile and as such are being retired as attack submarines. All were originally armed with Polaris, A-2, later refitted with A-3; they have towed array passive sonars for self-protection. They were, in effect, ballistic missile submarine versions of the *Thresher*s, sharing their deeper-diving hull material and superior silencing. Dates of redesignation to SSN: SSBN 608 (1.9.80), SSBN 609 (10.11.80), SSBN 610 (6.10.80), SSBN 611 (1.5.81), and SSBN 618 (11.3.81), in each case at the conclusion of final Polaris cruise. Physical changes began under the FY82 programme (SSBN 608, beginning January 1982): missile tubes were filled with concrete, and missile

ETHAN ALLEN class *strategic submarines*

Displacement:	6946t surfaced; 7884t submerged
Dimensions:	410ft 5in × 33ft × 27ft 7in
	125.1m × 10.1m × 8.4m
Machinery:	1-shaft nuclear: 1 S5W reactor, approx 15,000shp = approx 20kts
Armament:	16 Polaris SLBM, 4–21in TT (bow)
Sensors:	Sonar BQS-4, BQR-15, BQR-19
Complement:	110

No	Name	Builder	Laid down	Launched	Comp	Fate
SSBN 608	ETHAN ALLEN	Electric Boat	14.9.59	22.11.60	8.8.61	SSN 1982
SSBN 609	SAM HOUSTON	Newport News	28.12.59	2.2.61	6.3.62	SSN FY83
SSBN 610	THOMAS A EDISON	Electric Boat	15.3.60	15.6.61	10.3.62	SSN FY83
SSBN 611	JOHN MARSHALL	Newport News	4.4.60	15.7.61	21.5.62	SSN FY84
SSBN 618	THOMAS JEFFERSON	Newport News	3.2.61	24.2.62	4.1.63	SSN FY84

fire control system removed. SSBN 609 and 610 were converted under

FY83, and the others will be done under the FY84 programme. Propos-

als to install Tomahawk vertical launchers were abandoned.

Lafayette as completed

These are enlarged versions of the *Ethan Allen* class, all refitted with Poseidon missiles; the last twelve are being refitted with Trident I, *Francis Scott Key* being the first (first patrol 20 October 1979). *Daniel Webster* is unique in having bow, rather than fin, forward diving planes. Patrol endurance is 68 days, with 32-day refit periods between patrols, and a 16-month yard overhaul every six years; each ship has two crews.

The last twelve units, officially the *Banjamin Franklin* class, are quieter and have detail improvements. Four more were proposed in the FY65 programme but were not built.

LAFAYETTE class *strategic submarines*

Displacement:	7325t surfaced; 8251t submerged
Dimensions:	425ft × 33ft × 27ft 10in
	129.6m × 10.1m × 8.5m
Machinery:	1-shaft nuclear: 1 S5W reactor, 15,000shp = approx 20kts
Armament:	16 SLBM (see notes), 4–21in TT (bow)
Sensors:	Sonar BQS-4, BQR-7, BQR-15, BQR-19
Complement:	140

No	Name	Builder	Laid down	Launched	Comp	Fate
SSBN 616	LAFAYETTE	Electric Boat	17.1.61	8.5.62	23.4.63	Extant 1982
SSBN 617	ALEXANDER HAMILTON	Electric Boat	26.6.61	18.8.62	27.6.63	Extant 1982
SSBN 619	ANDREW JACKSON	Mare Island N Yd	26.4.61	15.9.62	3.7.73	Extant 1982
SSBN 620	JOHN ADAMS	Portsmouth N Yd	19.5.61	12.1.63	12.5.64	Extant 1982
SSBN 622	JAMES MONROE	Newport News	31.7.61	4.8.62	7.12.63	Extant 1982
SSBN 623	NATHAN HALE	Electric Boat	2.10.61	12.1.63	23.11.63	Extant 1982
SSBN 624	WOODROW WILSON	Mare Island N Yd	13.9.61	22.2.63	27.12.63	Extant 1982
SSBN 625	HENRY CLAY	Newport News	23.10.61	30.11.62	20.2.64	Extant 1982
SSBN 626	DANIEL WEBSTER	Electric Boat	23.12.61	27.4.63	9.4.64	Extant 1982
SSBN 627	JAMES MADISON	Newport News	5.3.62	15.3.63	28.7.64	Extant 1982
SSBN 628	TECUMSEH	Electric Boat	1.6.62	22.6.63	29.5.64	Extant 1982
SSBN 629	DANIEL BOONE	Mare Island N Yd	6.2.62	22.6.63	23.4.64	Extant 1982
SSBN 630	JOHN C CALHOUN	Newport News	4.6.62	22.6.63	15.9.64	Extant 1982
SSBN 631	ULYSSES S GRANT	Electric Boat	18.8.62	2.11.63	17.7.64	Extant 1982
SSBN 632	VON STEUBEN	Newport News	4.9.62	18.10.63	30.9.64	Extant 1982
SSBN 633	CASIMIR PULASKI	Electric Boat	12.1.63	1.2.64	14.8.64	Extant 1982
SSBN 634	STONEWALL JACKSON	Mare Island N Yd	4.7.62	30.11.63	26.8.64	Extant 1982
SSBN 635	SAM RAYBURN	Newport News	3.12.62	20.12.63	2.12.64	Extant 1982
SSBN 636	NATHANIEL GREENE	Portsmouth N Yd	21.5.62	12.5.64	19.12.64	Extant 1982
SSBN 640	BENJAMIN FRANKLIN	Electric Boat	25.5.63	5.12.64	22.10.65	Extant 1982
SSBN 641	SIMON BOLIVAR	Newport News	17.4.63	22.8.64	29.10.65	Extant 1982
SSBN 642	KAMEHAMEHA	Mare Island N Yd	2.5.63	16.1.65	10.12.65	Extant 1982
SSBN 643	GEORGE BANCROFT	Electric Boat	24.8.63	5.12.64	22.1.66	Extant 1982
SSBN 644	LEWIS AND CLARK	Newport News	29.7.63	21.11.64	22.12.65	Extant 1982
SSBN 645	JAMES K POLK	Electric Boat	23.11.63	22.5.65	16.4.66	Extant 1982
SSBN 654	GEORGE C MARSHALL	Newport News	2.3.64	21.5.65	29.4.66	Extant 1982
SSBN 655	HENRY L STIMSON	Electric Boat	4.4.64	13.11.65	20.8.66	Extant 1982
SSBN 656	GEORGE WASHINGTON CARVER	Newport News	24.8.64	14.8.65	15.6.66	Extant 1982
SSBN 657	FRANCIS SCOTT KEY	Electric Boat	5.12.64	23.4.66	3.12.66	Extant 1982
SSBN 658	MARIANO G VALLEJO	Mare Island N Yd	7.7.64	23.10.65	16.12.66	Extant 1982
SSBN 659	WILL RODGERS	Electric Boat	20.3.65	21.7.66	1.4.67	Extant 1982

Ohio as completed

These are by far the largest US submarines, although they will be overshadowed by the Soviet *Typhoon*s. They differ from earlier US strategic submarines in having 24 rather than 16 missiles, and incorporate a bow sonar (BQQ-6, similar to BQQ-5 but without active elements) and torpedo tubes set back from the bow, as in the newer attack submarines. The S8G reactor is reportedly a natural circulation type, presumably related to the S5G in the *Narwhal*. They are also reported to have turbo-electric drive, which would be another quieting feature. *Ohio* class submarines will operate 70-day patrols, with 25-day refit periods between patrols (shortened by the provision of special access trunks into the hull), with a 12 month refit every nine years, for an overall force availability of 66 per cent, compared to 55 per cent for Poseidon submarines. The entire programme has

OHIO class *strategic submarines*

Displacement:	16,000t surfaced; 18,700t submerged
Dimensions:	560ft × 42ft × 35ft 6in
	170.7m × 12.8m × 10.8m
Machinery:	1-shaft nuclear: 1 S8G reactor, 60,000shp (reported)
Armament:	24 SLBM, 4–21in TT (see notes)
Sensors:	Sonar BQQ-6
Complement:	133

No	Name	Builder	Laid down	Launched	Comp	Fate
SSBN 726	OHIO	Electric Boat	10.4.76	7.4.79	11.11.81	Extant 1982
SSBN 727	MICHIGAN	Electric Boat	4.4.77	26.4.80	11.9.82	Extant 1982
SSBN 728	FLORIDA	Electric Boat	9.6.77	14.11.81		Completing
SSBN 729	GEORGIA	Electric Boat	7.4.79	6.11.82		Completing
SSBN 730	RHODE ISLAND	Electric Boat	19.1.81			Building
SSBN 731	ALABAMA	Electric Boat	17.8.81			Building
SSBN 732		Electric Boat				Ordered
SSBN 733		Electric Boat				Ordered
SSBN 734		Electric Boat				Ordered

suffered from severe delays. *Ohio* did not run trials until June 1981, although delivery was originally scheduled for December 1977. One further ship is envisaged in each FY from 1983 to 1988.

Spinax 27.9.56   USN

Ohio on trials 1981   USN   *James Monroe* 1972   USN

A total of ten fleet submarines were
converted to radar-pickets under
three phases of the 'Migraine' programme. In the two prototypes, *Requin*
and *Spinax*, the after torpedo room
was used as a radar room and CIC,
radars being mounted on the hull casing aft and so usable only when the
submarine was surfaced. In Migraine
I (*Tigrone* and *Burrfish*, FY48–49), the
former crew's mess and galley were
used as a CIC, and the after torpedo
room used for berthing; two of the
forward torpedo tubes were also
removed, and the battery space
reduced by use of GUPPY-type batteries. In Migraine II (a reconstruction of the two original pickets) the
main air search radar (as in Migraine
I) was raised well above deck, so that
it could operate with the submarine
awash. A snorkel was fitted. Finally,
in Migraine III (FY51–53) six *Gato*
class fleet submarines (SS 267,
269–272, 274) were cut in half and a

Fleet submarine conversions *radar-pickets*

Displacement:	Migraine I: 1525t standard; 2410t submerged
	Migraine II: 1570t standard; 2410t submerged
	Migraine III: 1700t standard; 2308t normal
Dimensions:	312ft (Migraine III: 341ft) oa × 27ft 4in
	95.1m (104.1m) × 8.3m
Machinery:	2 shafts, diesels plus electric motors, 4610bhp/1750shp = 17kts/8kts. Range 12,000nm at 10kts
Armament:	1–40mm (not in Migraine III), 4–21in TT (6 in Migraine III; all bow)
Sensors:	Migraine I: Radar SS, SV-1, SV-2, BPS-2, YE-2
	Migraine II: Radar SS, SV, SV-2, SR-2, YE-3
	Migraine III: Radar BPS-2, BPS-3, BPS-4
Complement:	Migraine I: 82–90
	Migraine II: 82–85
	Migraine III: 95–108

For names of boats converted see under Fleet Strength 1947. Original particulars, including building dates, can be found
in the 1922–1946 volume.

new 24ft (*7.3m*) section added between the forward battery compartment and the control room for a CIC
and other electronics; the after torpedo room was converted for berthing

space. A streamlined fin with a snorkel was fitted.

All these pickets reverted to conve-
tional submarine status after 1959.

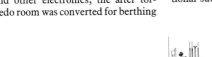

Sailfish 1958

These large diesel-electric submarines
were built to supplement the fleet
boat conversions of the 'Migraine'
programme, they remained unsatisfactory in that their surface speed did
not suffice to keep up with a carrier
task force. Throughout the early
1950s the Bureau of Ships continued
to work on more efficient powerplants
for radar-picket submarines,
pressure-fired steam plants showing
particular promise.

Both were reclassified as attack
submarines on 1 March 1961 and later
given FRAM refits. *Salmon* was temporarily reclassified as an auxiliary, as
test and evaluation submarine for the
DSRV programme (June 1968), but
reverted to attack submarine status

SAILFISH class *radar-pickets*

Displacement:	1900t standard; 318t submerged (surface displacement given as 2625t in 1978)
Dimensions:	350ft 6in oa × 29ft 1in × 16ft 4in
	106.9m × 8.9m × 5.0m
Machinery:	2 shafts, 4 FM diesels plus 2 electric motors, 6000bhp/8200shp = 19.5kts/10kts (given as 14kts after removal of radar equipment)
Armament:	6–21in TT (bow)
Sensors:	Radar BPS-2, BPS-3; sonar BQG-4 installed after deletion of radar-picket equipment)
Complement:	95

No	Name	Builder	Laid down	Launched	Comp	Fate
SSR 572	SAILFISH	Portsmouth N Yd	8.12.53	7.9.55	May 56	Stricken 1978
SSR 573	SALMON	Portsmouth N Yd	10.3.54	25.2.56	Dec 56	Stricken 1977

when that programme was delayed.
Both were ultimately fitted with
PUFFS passive fire control sonar, and

both were stricken under the FY78
programme (30 September 1978 and 1
October 1977, respectively).

239

Triton as completed

The construction of this very large nuclear submarine seemed to solve the problem of low surface speed in radar-pickets: with her two-reactor plant, she had a reported speed of 27kts on the surface (but only 20kt submerged). Design features included a very large fin into which air search antennas could retract, and a large CIC for air control. She was also the first US submarine with a three-deck hull. Commissioned in 1959, she was reclassified as an attack submarine on 1 March 1961, and decommissioned 3 May 1969 as too expensive to operate and too unwieldy to be an effective attack submarine. Proposals to use her as an alternative National Emergency Command Post Afloat (as in the cruiser *Northampton*)

were abandoned; she was the first nuclear-powered warship to be laid up.

TRITON *radar-picket*

Displacement:	5963t surfaced; 7773t submerged
Dimensions:	445ft wl, 447ft 6in oa × 36ft 11in × 23ft 6in
	135.7m, 136.4m × 11.3m × 7.2m
Machinery:	2-shaft nuclear: 2 S4G reactors, approx 34,000shp = 27kts surfaced, 20kts submerged
Armament:	6–21in TT (4 bow, 2 stern)
Sensors:	Radar BPS-2, SPS-26
Complement:	180

No	Name	Builder	Laid down	Launched	Comp	Fate
SSRN 586	TRITON	Electric Boat	29.5.56	17.8.58	10.11.59	Decommissioned 1969

AMPHIBIOUS WARFARE VESSELS

Northampton 1961

NORTHAMPTON *command ship*

Displacement:	12,429t light; 17,049t full load (1964)
Dimensions:	664ft wl, 677ft 2in oa × 69ft 9in × 24ft
	202.4m, 206.5m × 21.3m × 7.3m
Machinery:	4-shaft geared turbines, 4 Babcock & Wilcox boilers, 120,000shp = 32.8kts. Range 7000nm at 20kts. Oil 2969t
Armament:	4–5in/54 (4×1), 8–3in/50 (4×2; later 3in/70)
Sensors:	Radar SPS-2, SPS-3, SPS-6, SPS-8
Complement:	1635

No	Name	Builder	Launched	Fate
CLC 1	NORTHAMPTON	Bethlehem, Quincy	27.1.51	Stricken 1.12.77

Northampton 1963   USN

The US Navy first experimented with specialised command and control ships during the Second World War, when it converted a variety of merchant and Coast Guard hulls to Amphibious Command Ships or AGC. In 1946 the incomplete heavy cruiser *Northampton* (laid down on 31.8.44) was designated as a future AGC; she would have the speed and survivability lacking in the wartime ships. However, as her design progressed her function shifted more and more to that of flagship of a fast carrier force. This transition was only emphasised as the design of the new carriers (*United States* and then *Forrestal*) seemed to show no great capacity for the long-range air search radars then in prospect. That is, the fleet flagship would be valuable because she would be the ship with the long-range radar and therefore the ship controlling Fleet Air Defence. The *Northampton* was, then, designed around the requirements of the largest sea-based radar then in prospect, the massive SPS-2, and a very large Combat Information Centre (CIC) by means of which the Fleet's air defence resources could be concentrated and controlled. Even before she could be completed, proposals were made to complete the suspended battle cruiser *Hawaii* on similar lines, and they were abandoned only in 1954, and then on grounds of cost. Meanwhile the advent of the angled flight deck permitted the construction of conventional islands for the new generation of carriers, and the unique qualities of the radar-equipped fleet command ship lost some of their appeal.

Northampton, completed on 7.3.53, thus remained unique in the US Fleet. However, the need for specialised fleet flagships with command and control facilities beyond those available in a carrier is reflected in the decision to complete three of the six *Cleveland* class missile cruisers with enlarged command spaces, at the expense of one triple 6in turret and two twin 5in/38. One might also note the longevity of the flagship missile cruisers, as compared to their non-flagship half-sisters, which (from a missile point of view) had identical combat capabilities. Indeed, as the converted flagships neared the end of their service lives, efforts were made to design a new fleet flagship. It was argued that the numbered fleets (*eg* the Sixth in the Mediterranean and the Seventh in the Far East) required more elaborate flag facilities than could be accommodated aboard a carrier. The issue was no longer fleet air defence, which could be handled quite well enough, particularly as the primary radar platforms were now carrier aircraft. Rather, it was strategic planning at the highest levels: it was argued that, after a Soviet nuclear strike, commanders afloat might well be the most senior surviving national authorities, and thus responsible for retaliation. Nuclear strike planning in itself could be justified. At about the same time the increasing age of the amphibious flagships (AGC, later LCC) seemed to demand the construction of new ones, and there were proposals to amalgamate the two tasks. However, the fleet flag role demanded a high enough speed to remain with the fleet at sea, whereas the amphibious force was still designed for 20kts.

In fact only the amphibious flagships were built, as *Blue Ridge* and *Mount Whitney*. *Northampton* decommissioned in 1970.

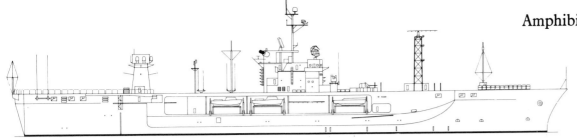

Blue Ridge as completed

BLUE RIDGE class *command ships*

Displacement:	19,290t full load
Dimensions:	620ft oa × 82ft wl, 108ft ext × 27ft
	189.0m × 25.0m, 32.9m × 8.2m
Machinery:	1-shaft geared turbines, 2 Foster Wheeler boilers, 22,000shp = 20kts
Armament:	2 Sea Sparrow SAM (2×8), 4–3in/50 (2×2)
Sensors:	Radar SPS-40, SPS-48 (plus extensive communications arrays)
Complement:	720 (plus 700 flag)

No	Name	Builder	Launched	Fate
AGC 19	BLUE RIDGE	Philadelphia N Yd	4.1.69	Extant 1982
AGC 20	MOUNT WHITNEY	Newport News	8.1.70	Extant 1982

These two ships, survivors of a planned class of six, are direct successors to the merchant hull conversions of the Second World War. Their design was determined by a combination of internal volume requirements (for accommodation and for command spaces) and communications requirements (for antenna performance). It is based on, but by no means identical with, the earlier helicopter carrier (LPH) design, with an additional deck level and with an entirely new (full width) superstructure. Special amphibious warfare features included extra control spaces for the amphibious commander. To some extent the decision not to build further LCCs was justified on the ground that the new LHA incorporated considerable command features on its own. In 1982 the two LCCs were being used as fleet flagships, replacing the cruisers formerly employed in that role. *Blue Ridge* replaced the cruiser *Oklahoma City* (Seventh Fleet) in October 1979. *Mount Whitney* is now flagship of Second Fleet, but also carries Commander Amphibious Group Two and Commander Fourth Marine Amphibious Brigade. In contrast to the helicopter carriers, these ships never carried their full designed battery of four twin 3in/50; only two were installed, and in 1974 a pair of octuple Sea Sparrows were added.

WRIGHT and ARLINGTON *command ships/communications ships*

Displacement:	14,500t standard; 19,600t full load
Dimensions:	664ft wl, 683ft 6in oa × 78ft 9in × 28ft
	202.4m, 208.4m × 23.6m × 8.5m
Machinery:	4-shaft geared turbines, 4 boilers, 120,000shp = 33kts
Armament:	8–40mm (3in/50 in AGMR 2; 4×2), 6 helicopters (CC 2 only)
Sensors:	Radar SPS-6B
Complement:	1317 (ship) plus 522 (flag; CC 2 only)

In 1961 the threat of Soviet ballistic missiles seemed increasingly acute, and it appeared that no fixed US national command centre would be secure in wartime. The Navy proposed the use of surface ships off the coasts. In an emergency, the President could be helicoptered to them, and they could communicate reliably with forces ashore by means of the newly developed troposcatter radio, which required a large dish antenna aboard ship. *Northampton* carried out the first tests, and served in the National Emergency Command Post Afloat (NECPA) role until her decommissioning in 1970. Under the FY62 programme the light carrier *Wright* (CC 2) was refitted for the same role, on the same 'antenna farm' basis as the amphibious command ships. She did retain her all-weather landing system, presumably to permit the Presidential helicopter to come aboard in any weather. Plans to convert her sister *Saipan* into a third NECPA ship were cancelled, and instead she became a major communications relay ship, *Arlington* (AGMR 2); a fourth NECPA ship was proposed but never reached the appropriation stage. Both NECPA ships were decommissioned in the spring of 1970. Presumably by that time improvements in the Soviet submarine force and, even more, in the number of Soviet submarines operational in the North Atlantic in peacetime, had reduced the value of the NECPA, and attention turned to an airborne command post NECPA. Proposals to use the very large radar-picket submarine *Triton* as an NECPA did not prove acceptable, perhaps in part because of the difficulty of moving personnel out to her, and the considerable limits on her own ability to communicate with the nuclear forces.

Iwo Jima 1963

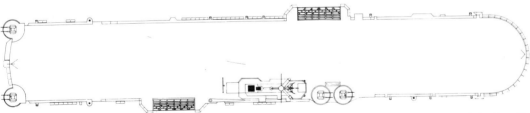

IWO JIMA class *helicopter carriers*

Displacement:	10,717t light; 18,004t full load
Dimensions:	556ft wl, 602ft 4in oa × 84ft 2in × 26ft 1in
	169.5m, 183.6m × 25.7m × 8.0m
Machinery:	1-shaft geared turbine, 2 Combustion Engineering boilers, 22,000shp = 23.5kts
Armament:	8–3in/50 (4×2). See notes
Sensors:	Radar SPS-40
Complement:	667 (plus 2057 troops)

No	Name	Builder	Launched	Fate
LPH 2	IWO JIMA	Puget Sound N Yd	17.9.60	Extant 1982
LPH 3	OKINAWA	Philadelphia N Yd	14.8.61	Extant 1982
LPH 7	GUADALCANAL	Philadelphia N Yd	16.3.63	Extant 1982
LPH 9	GUAM	Philadelphia N Yd	22.8.64	Extant 1982
LPH 10	TRIPOLI	Ingalls	31.7.65	Extant 1982
LPH 11	NEW ORLEANS	Philadelphia N Yd	3.2.68	Extant 1982
LPH 12	INCHON	Ingalls	24.5.69	Extant 1982

These ships were the culmination of a long Marine Corps development of vertical envelopment, or helicopter assault. The basic motivation was fear of nuclear bombardment of concentrations of landing craft off relatively restricted beaches; helicopters could approach from greater distances, preserving concentration of the assault troops at the beaches while permitting dispersal of assault shipping. Probably the single greatest defect of the LPH was its inability to operate landing craft. Thus it could not attack or support troops on the beach in rough weather, and its helicopters could not move heavy equipment over a beach. The *Iwo Jima* class helicopter carriers were designed in 1957 after studies of the conversion of alternative hulls, including some of the wartime fast battleships. In fact three *Essex* class ASW carriers (*Boxer*, *Princeton* and *Valley Forge*) were converted to become austere LPHs (LPH 4, LPH 5 and LPH 8) with cargo stowed on their former hangar decks. They retained their 5in batteries for shore bombardment, a capability not matched by the specially-built LPH (but in fact restored in the later LHA). The basic LPH design incorporated provision for conversion to an ASW helicopter carrier, and in this sense provided a full replacement for the CVS conversions. However, unlike the *Essex* class CVS, the *Iwo Jima* could not operate fixed-wing aircraft, since the design never incorporated either a catapult or arresting gear. Note that, at the time of design, there was no question of retiring the *Essex* class CVS.

The first special helicopter assault ship was the former escort carrier *Thetis Bay* (see under Fleet Strength 1947), converted at San Francisco between 1 June

UNITED STATES

1955 and 1 September 1956, and designated CVHA 1 before being redesignated LPH 2. A second CVE conversion under the FY57 programme, the *Block Island*, was cancelled; she would have been LPH 2. Both the CVE and the CVS conversions were deficient in having insufficient troop spaces and so were not considered true LPHs by the Marines. Even when troops could be accommodated, the subdivision of typical warships made that accommodation less than suitable. For example, the former fleet carrier *Princeton* had Marine spaces ranging in capacity from 4 to 157 men, and such division would destroy unit cohesion.

The *Iwo Jimas* solved this problem. Their troop spaces, accommodating 2000 troops, were air conditioned, and there were special vehicle stowage areas and special cargo facilities. Flight decks were 'spotted' to accommodate seven CH-46 or four CH-53 helicopters for take-off; the hangar can accommodate, respectively, 19 and 11 of these helicopters. When helicopters are heavily laden, they benefit from take-off runs, so that effective operation limits the number of helicopter 'spots'. *Inchon* (LPH 12) was unique in having davits to accommodate two LCVP landing craft.

In 1971 *Guam* was modified as a prototype Sea Control Ship; she was later refitted as an LPH. *Inchon* operated minesweeping helicopters in Operation Endsweep, the clearance of the ports of North Vietnam in 1973. Other units also served in the capacity of countermine mothership. Between 1970 and 1974 all had two of their four twin 3in/50 mounts replaced by Sea Sparrow (BPDMS; 2×8), one on the flight deck forward and one on the port quarter. In 1982 each ship was scheduled to receive 2 Phalanx CIWS.

A modified version of this design was offered to Australia as a replacement for the carrier *Melbourne*; it was considered the most likely candidate, in a competition which included the Spanish (formerly US) Sea Control Ship and the Italian *Garibaldi*. The original LPH steam turbine plant was to have been replaced by a pair of LM2500 gas turbines of twice the power. This plan was dropped when Britain offered *Invincible*. However, with the change in British naval policy following the Falklands War, the British offer was withdrawn, and as of this writing it remains to be seen whether the Australian competition is reopened.

Blue Ridge 1974   USN

Iwo Jima 1978   USN

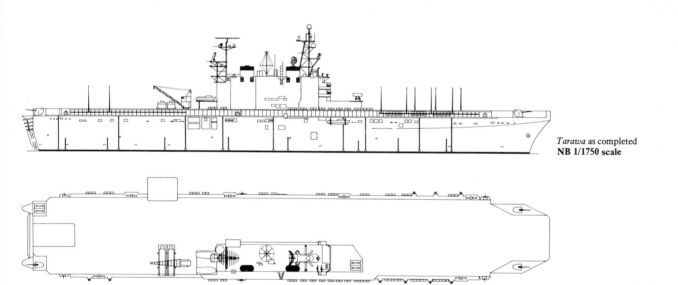

Tarawa as completed
NB 1/1750 scale

TARAWA class *assault ships*

Displacement:	25,588t light; 38,761t full load
Dimensions:	778ft wl, 820ft oa × 106ft 8in wl, 126ft ext × 25ft 9in *237.2m, 250.0m × 32.5m, 38.4m × 7.8m*
Machinery:	2-shaft geared turbines, 2 Combustion Engineering boilers, 70,000shp = 24kts. Range 10,000nm at 20kts
Armament:	2 Sea Sparrow SAM (2×8), 3–5in/54 (3×1), 6–20mm (6×1). See notes
Sensors:	Radar SPS-40, SPS-52, SPG-60, SPQ-9
Complement:	892 (plus 1903 troops)

No	Name	Builder	Launched	Fate
LHA 1 TARAWA		Litton	1.12.73	Extant 1982
LHA 2 SAIPAN		Litton	18.7.74	Extant 1982
LHA 3 BELLEAU WOOD		Litton	11.4.77	Extant 1982
LHA 4 NASSAU		Litton	21.1.78	Extant 1982
LHA 5 PELELIU		Litton	25.11.78	Extant 1982
(ex-*Da Nang*)				

These very large assault ships are the final evolution of the helicopter assault concept, combining the functions of LPH, LPD, and LKA. They have both a very large flight deck (with spots for 12 CH-46 Sea Knights or 9 CH-53 Sea Stallions), a full-length hangar deck (for, respectively, 30 and 19 such craft), space for a reinforced Marine battalion (about 1900 troops), considerable vehicle and cargo stowage, and a 268ft × 78ft (*81.7m × 23.8m*) well deck which can accommodate small craft up to LCU size. There is a complex automated cargo-handling system employing conveyors and elevators, and even a 5000sq ft training and acclimatisation room permitting troops to exercise in a controlled environment, so that they can adapt to the climate of their target area en route. Perhaps as importantly, they incorporate substantial command and control facilities, which make up for the shortfall in dedicated amphibious flagships (LCCs). Externally, the emblem of these facilities is the extensive electronic array above the island, including an austere three-dimensional radar (SPS-52) for limited fighter control in the operational area.

Conceived in 1965, the *Tarawas* were ordered under the Concept Definition Contract Formulation procedure which also produced the *Spruance* class destroyers and the abortive Forward Deployment Ships (FDL). Nine were originally planned, but on 20 January 1971 the Navy announced that LHA 6–LHA 9 would not be built. From time to time the LHA hull, which is about the same size as a Second World War *Essex* class fleet carrier, is proposed

Tarawa 1976

as the basis for a limited or VSTOL carrier, and in fact at one point Litton reportedly made such a proposal to the Australian government; later it was scaled down to an LPH derivative. There have also been Congressional attempts to convert an existing LHA to a light carrier, with an additional unit being built to replace it.

Typical small craft capacity is 4 *LCU 1610* class or 2 LCU and 3 LCM-8 or 17 LCM-6, plus 40 tracked landing craft (LVT) on the vehicle deck.

LHA 5 was originally to have been named *Da Nang*, but was renamed *Peleliu* on 15 February 1978, presumably in view of popular feelings about the Vietnam War and particularly about its conclusion. Sea Sparrow is to be replaced by Phalanx.

Current US shipbuilding plans call for the construction of an LHA derivative, the LHD, from FY84 onwards. Construction was originally planned for FY87, but was moved to FY84 to fill a perceived gap in Marine assault shipping. The current objective is an ability to project simultaneously the assault echelons of a Marine Amphibious Force (MAF) and a Marine Amphibious Brigade (MAB). The LHD class is to replace the *Iwo Jima* class in the 1990s, after five or six have been completed, so that in 1983 a total of about twelve ships is envisaged. The FY83–87 programme of February 1982 showed one in FY84 (at a lead-ship cost of $1328.1 million) and two more in FY87 (a total cost of $1200.9 million).

The LHD was originally to have been a new design, and Lockheed Shipbuilding proposed a ship based in part on its own LSD 41, to carry two LCAC or twelve conventional landing craft (LCM-6) on a displacement of about 40,000 tons. In mid-1981 this design was rejected in favour of a modified LHA. There were to be two major changes. First, unlike the LHA, the LHD is to be designed specifically to operate air-cushion landing craft, with an entirely redesigned well deck; it can accommodate three such craft, compared to only one in an LHA; on the other hand, vehicle area has been reduced from 31,200 to 22,000sq ft. In theory LCACs can be launched about fifty miles from the objective, so that the

LHD can (and should) remain well over the horizon throughout the operation. This is reflected in the LHD design by the omission of the 5in/54 shore-bombardment battery of the original LHA.

Unlike the original LHA, the LHD is to have a secondary sea control mission, and therefore is to incorporate maintenance facilities for at least twenty VSTOL (Harrier) and four to six ASW helicopters (LAMPS III). The flight deck is so long that no ski-jump will be required, although there have been unofficial reports that a steam catapult is planned for later installation. It would permit such ships to operate airborne early warning aircraft, which are needed if the fighters on board are to be properly controlled.

Artist's impression of the LHD design, 1983

Spiegel Grove 1968

THOMASTON class *dock landing ships*

Displacement:	6880t light, 11,270t full load (LSD 32–LSD 34, 12,150t)
Dimensions:	510ft oa × 84ft × 19ft *155.5m × 25.6m × 5.8m*
Machinery:	2-shaft steam turbines, 2 Babcock & Wilcox boilers, 24,000shp = 22.5kts. Range 10,000nm at 20kts
Armament:	16–3in/50 (8×2), 12–20mm (designed). See notes
Sensors:	Radar SPS-6
Complement:	404 (plus 341 troops)

Class (no, launched):
Thomaston (LSD 28, 9.2.54), *Plymouth Rock* (LSD 29, 7.5.54), *Fort Snelling* (LSD 30, 16.7.54), *Point Defiance* (LSD 31, 28.9.54), *Spiegel Grove* (LSD 32, 10.11.55), *Alamo* (LSD 33, 20.1.56), *Hermitage* (LSD 34, 17.6.56), *Monticello* (LSD 35, 10.8.56). All built by Ingalls.

These postwar LSDs were intended to provide a heavy landing craft capacity within the 20kt amphibious force; actually they could make 24kts. Their hull form was more refined, their well decks had a greater depth of water, their machinery (as in an LPD) was located entirely below the well deck rather than in the side walls, and they had mezzanine and super-decks (both portable) for cargo stowage and for helicopter operation. The 391ft × 48ft (*119.2m × 14.6m*)

well deck accommodates three LCU or 9 LCM-8 or 50 LVT. The helicopter deck is removable and there are no maintenance facilities; two 50t cranes can reach down to a mezzanine (vehicle stowage) or the well deck. Bows were strengthened for ice navigation, and the last two units were air conditioned. They can carry about 340 troops.

The *Thomaston*s were part of a general revitalisation of the amphibious force in the 1950s, traceable to Korean War experience: four were built under the FY52 programme, two under FY54 and two under FY55. Defensive armament was reduced to 6 twin 3in/50 during the 1960s and to 3 twin 3in/50 during the 1970s. All were extant in 1982.

POINT BARROW
One somewhat similar ship requires mention, the T-AKD (cargo ship dock) *Point Barrow*, in effect an unarmed LSD built to a Maritime Administration design (S2-ST-23A) specifically to support US radar stations in the Arctic. She operated with the Military Sea Transport Service (MSTS) until 1965, and then was used until 1970 to carry Saturn rockets and other space equipment from California to Cape Kennedy; she also carried some landing craft to Vietnam. After being laid up in 1971–72, she was returned to general cargo carrying, then again refitted 1974–76 to support the research submersible *Trieste* as AGDS 2, renamed *Point Loma*. The Military Sealift Command (successor to MSTS) also operates a variety of ships which, although unarmed in peacetime, could be used as assault transports in an emergency.

UNITED STATES

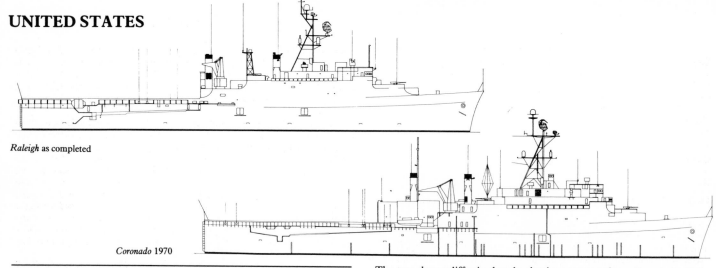

Raleigh as completed

Coronado 1970

RALEIGH class *dock landing ships*

Displacement:	8051t light; 13,745t full load
Dimensions:	500ft wl, 513ft 1in × 84ft × 20ft 6in
	152.4m, 156.4m × 25.6m × 6.3m
Machinery:	2 shaft geared turbines, 2 Babcock & Wilcox, 24,000shp = 21kts
Armament:	3in/50 (3×2)
Sensors:	Radar SPS-40
Complement:	501 (plus 932 troops)

Class (no, launched):
Raleigh (LPD 1, 17.3.62), *Vancouver* (LPD 2, 15.9.62), *La Salle* (LPD 3, 3.8.63). All built by New York N Yd, and were extant in 1982.

AUSTIN class *dock landing ships*

Displacement:	10,000t light; 16,900t full load
Dimensions:	570ft oa × 84ft × 23ft
	173.8m × 25.6m × 7.0m
Machinery:	2-shaft geared turbines, 2 Babcock & Wilcox, 24,000shp = 20kts
Armament:	8–3in/50 (4×2). See notes
Sensors:	Radar SPS-40
Complement:	410–447 (plus 930 troops in LPD 4–6, 840 in others)

Class (no, launched):
New York N Yd – *Austin* (LPD 4, 27.6.64), *Ogden* (LPD 5, 27.6.64), *Duluth* (LPD 6, 14.8.65)
Ingalls – *Cleveland* (LPD 7, 7.5.66), *Dubuque* (LPD 8, 6.8.66)
Lockheed, Seattle – *Denver* (LPD 9, 23.1.65), *Juneau* (LPD 10, 12.2.66), *Coronado* (LPD 11, 30.7.66), *Shreveport* (LPD 12, 25.10.66), *Nashville* (LPD 13, 7.10.67), *Trenton* (LPD 14, 3.8.68), *Ponce* (LPD 15, 20.5.70)

These ships were intended as successors to the Landing Ship Dock with much increased troop (930, 840 in flagships) and cargo (about 2500t) capacity and a smaller well deck (168ft × 50ft *51.2m × 15.2m*), accommodating one LCU and three LCM-6 or four LCM-8 or twenty LVT; in addition there is a large crane at the after end of the superstructure which can launch craft carried on the flight deck, typically two LCM-6 or four LCPL. The *Raleigh*s had no helicopter hangar or maintenance facilities, but ships after the *Austin* (LPD 4) have a hangar 58ft to 64ft (*17.7m–19.5m*) in length and 18ft 6in to 24ft (*5.6m–7.3m*) in width, extensible to about 80ft. The deck has two helicopter spots, but ships have deployed with up to six CH-46 embarked.

The two classes differ in that the *Austins* are somewhat enlarged. *La Salle* (LPD 3) was reclassified as a flagship (AGF 3) for the Middle East Force, undergoing conversion during 1972. She received a small helicopter hangar and covered assembly area on her flight deck, as well as a lattice mast for a satellite communications antenna, and admiral's accommodation, plus additional air conditioning. She is painted white to help reduce heating in the Indian Ocean. *La Salle* replaced a succession of small seaplane tenders (AVP) which had operated as Middle East flagships from the late 1940s onwards; *Valcour* (AVP 55) was reclassified as AGF 1 on 15 December 1965 and based at Bahrein, being replaced by *La Salle* in 1972. The LPD *Coronado* served as Middle East Flagship (AGF 11 vice LPD 11) while *La Salle* underwent a major refit from 1980 to 1982.

LPD 7–LPD 13 are fitted as amphibious squadron flagships and have an extra bridge level. A proposed LPD 16, to have been built under the FY66 programme, was deferred in favour of the LHA programme then cancelled in 1969. The other LPDs were built under the FY59 (prototype), FY60 (1), FY61 (1), FY62 (3), FY63 (4), FY64 (3) and FY65 (2) programmes.

In all of these ships, the original anti-aircraft battery of four twin 3in/50 mounts was reduced in the late 1970s, as these weapons were withdrawn from the anti-aircraft role. Thus in 1982 the *Austins* have only two such mounts and the *Raleigh*s have three; they are scheduled for replacement by Phalanx CIWS in the *Austins*. All were extant in 1982.

Coronado 28.4.70 USN

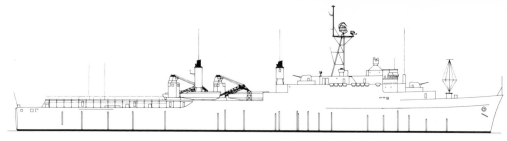

Anchorage 1969

ANCHORAGE class *dock landing ships*

Displacement:	8600t light; 13,700t full load
Dimensions:	553ft 4in oa × 84ft × 18ft 6in
	168.7m × 25.6m × 5.6m
Machinery:	2-shaft geared turbines, 2 boilers, 24,000shp = 20kts
Armament:	8–3in/50 (×2). See notes
Sensors:	Radar SPS-40
Complement:	397 (plus 376 troops)

Class (no, launched):
Ingalls – *Anchorage* (LSD 36, 5.5.68)
General Dynamics – *Portland* (LSD 37, 20.12.69), *Pensacola* (LSD 38, 11.7.70), *Mount Vernon* (LSD 39, 17.4.71), *Fort Fisher* (LSD 40, 22.4.72)

The construction of these ships showed, in effect, that the LPD could not quite combine all the capabilities required by the Amphibious Force. Five were built under the FY65 (one), FY66 (three) and FY67 (one) programme. Like their *Thomaston* class predecessors, they have a removable helicopter deck, no helicopter maintenance facilities, and limited troop space (375 men). The 430ft × 50ft well deck accommodates three LCU or nine LCM (8) or about 50 LVT. In common with other amphibious ships, they have had some of their original 3in/50 battery removed (one of four twin mounts) and are scheduled to be fitted with Phalanx CIWS. All were extant in 1982.

WHIDBEY ISLAND class *dock landing ships*

Displacement:	11,125t standard; 15,726t full load
Dimensions:	609ft 6in oa, 580ft wl × 84ft × 19ft 8in
	185.8m, 176.8m × 25.6m × 6.0m
Machinery:	2 shafts, 4 Colt/Pielstick diesels, 41,600bhp = 22kts
Armament:	2–20mm Phalanx CIWS, 2–20mm Mk 67
Sensors:	Radar SPS-67, SPS-40B, LN-66
Complement:	376 (plus 440 troops)

No	Name	Builder	Launched	Fate
LSD 41 WHIDBEY ISLAND		Lockheed, Seattle		Building
LSD 42		Lockheed, Seattle		Building

A new LSD 41 class was proposed to replace the eight *Thomastons*, but the Carter Administration deferred construction until Congress voted $41 million in long-lead items in FY80; the Administration then announced the construction of six ships in alternate years, beginning in FY81. LSD 41 is to have an enlarged well deck, 440ft × 50ft *(134.1m × 15.2m)*, adapted to carry 4 air cushion landing craft (LCAC) or 21 conventional LCM (6) landing craft; by way of comparision, the LHD will carry only three LCAC. The first of the class is to be completed in 1984; she was laid down on 4.8.81, followed by LSD 42 on 5.8.82. The Feb 1982 five-year shipbuilding plan (FY83–FY87) showed one ship each in FY83 and FY84, and two each in FY85, 86 and 87. The first of a new LPDX class is scheduled for construction in FY88.

TERREBONNE PARISH class *tank landing ships*

Displacement:	5777t full load
Dimensions:	384ft oa × 56ft × 16ft 1in
	117.1m × 17.1m × 4.9m
Machinery:	2 shafts, 4 diesels, 6000bhp = 15.5kts
Armament:	6–3in/50 (3×2)
Complement:	205 (plus 391 troops)

Class (no, launched):
Bath Iron Wks – *Terrebonne Parish* (LST 1156, 9.8.52), *Terrell County* (LST 1157, 6.12.52), *Tioga County* (LST 1158, 11.4.53), *Tom Green County* (LST 1159, 2.7.53), *Traverse County* (LST 1160, 3.10.53), Ingalls – *Vernon*

County (LST 1161, 25.11.52), *Wahkiakum County* (LST 1162, 23.1.53), *Waldo County* (LST 1163, 17.3.53), *Walworth County* (LST 1164, 18.5.53), *Washoe County* (LST 1165, 14.7.53), Christy – *Washtenaw County* (LST 1166, 22.11.52), *Westchester County* (LST 1167, 18.4.53, *Wexford County* (LST 1168, 28.11.53), *Whitfield County* (LST 1169, 22.8.53), *Windhem County* (LST 1170, 22.5.54).

Probably the greatest disappointment of the early postwar amphibious programme was the failure to develop a fast LST. Quite radical schemes were tried, including a design with bow propellers, which would turn its blunt stern to the beach, and one with a long false bow. Instead, a maximum speed of 15 knots was accepted, and these fifteen ships were modified versions of two experimental units (LST 1153 and 1154) laid down at the end of the Second World War, with diesel plants replacing the steam engines of the earlier ships. All had increased troop accommodation, greater tank and cargo capacity and improved discharge arrangements as compared to wartime LSTs. Thus they had a powered vehicle turntable, hydraulic bow doors, heavier ramps, and pontoon causeways. Their hull lines were also finer than those of earlier LSTs, and they had reversible pitch propellers.

The entire LST 1156 class was authorised (as SCB-9) under the FT52 programme, as part of the renaissance of the amphibious force after the demonstration of its continued value during the Korean War. Fates: LST 1166 converted to mine countermeasures craft (MMS 2) 1973, used to test sweeping of Hanoi/Haiphong, then stricken in 1973. LST 1156 to Spain 1971, LST 1159 and LST 1160 to Spain 1972, LST 1168 to Spain 1971; LST 1157 and LST 1169 to Greece 1977; LST 1161 to Venezuela 1973; LST 1167 to Turkey 1974; LST 1170 to Turkey 1973. The remaining ships were stricken and transferred to the Maritime Administration after brief service as MSC cargo carriers.

Of the two very similar steam-driven *Talbot County* (LST 1153) class, launched in 1946–47, *Tallahatchie County* (LST 1154) was converted to an advance aviation base ship (AVB) at the Charleston Navy Yard under the FY60 programme (completed 13 March 1962); she was fitted with a new aluminium superstructure, shops, briefing rooms, and even a portable aircraft control tower. She could support a 270-man aircraft squadron. She was stricken in 1970 and *Talbot County* shortly afterwards.

WAR-BUILT LSTs
Of earlier LSTs still in service postwar, six were converted to small craft tenders (AGP) (LSTs *782, 786, 821, 831, 838* and one other), although three were so designated. *LST 1069* served as a minecraft support ship (MCS 6).

Terrell County 1969

USN

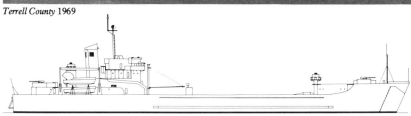

York County 1960

DE SOTO COUNTY class *tank landing ships*

Displacement:	3859t light; 7854t full load
Dimensions:	426ft wl, 442ft oa × 62ft × 13ft 5in
	129.9m, 134.8m × 18.9m × 4.1m
Machinery:	2 shafts, 6 FM diesels, 15,000bhp = 17.2kts
Armament:	6–3in/60 (3×2)
Complement:	185 (plus 634 troops)

Class (no, launched):
Avondale – *De Soto County* (LST 1171, 28.2.57), *Grant County* (LST 1174, 12.10.56)
Boston N Yd – *Suffolk County* (LST 1173, 5.9.56)
Newport News – *York County* (LST 1175, 5.3.57), *Graham County* (LST 1176, 19.9.57)

American SB – *Lorain County* (LST 1177, 22.6.57), *Wood County* (LST 1178, 14.12.57).

These SCB-119 LSTs of FY54 (prototype) and FT55 showed little speed improvement over their predecessors (17kts at more than double the power) but were designed for better sea keeping, and in particular for less pounding at high sustained speed. They were fully air conditioned, and two of them could carry as many troops as an APA plus an AKA, as well as more vehicles. They were designed to carry four landing craft in davits, a 175ft *(53.4m)* pontoon causeway on the side, and two powered pontoon barges and an LCU as deck cargo for side-launching. In addition, they could accept up to five helicopters landing on deck. LST 1172 was cancelled in 1955; all remaining LSTs were assigned 'County' and 'Parish' names that year.

Even at 17 knots, these ships could not operate effectively with the 20kt amphibious force, and they were discarded with the advent of the fast *Newport* class LSTs. *Graham County*, scheduled for decommissioning, was instead converted to a tender (AGP-1176) for *Asheville* class gunboats in the Mediterranean at Philadelphia Navy Yard, February–May 1972. Her bow doors were welded shut, the former tank deck becoming machine shops and store rooms. Boat booms were added to her sides, and steam generators fitted to provide steam to gunboats alongside. She was stricken 1977. *Wood County* was

scheduled for a similar conversion to support the *Pegasus* class PHMs (with designator AGHS), but the conversion was deferred in 1977 when the future of the PHM programme came into doubt. The following were transferred: LST 1174 to Brazil 1973, LST 1171 and 1175 to Italy 1972; LST 1173 and 1178 to Greece 1981; LST 1177 to Mexico 1982.

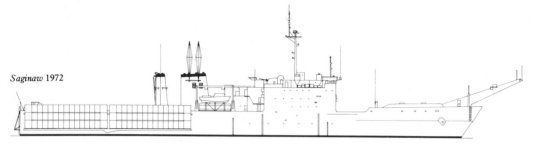

Saginaw 1972

NEWPORT class *tank landing ships*

Displacement:	8342t full load
Dimensions:	522ft 4in oa over hull, 562ft (over derrick arms) × 69ft 6in × 17ft 6in
	159.2m, 171.3m × 21.2m × 5.3m
Machinery:	2 shafts, Alco diesels (GM diesels in 1179–1181), 16,500bhp = 20kts. Range over 2500nm (reported cruising range)
Armament:	4–3in/50 (2×2). See notes
Complement:	218 approx (plus 385 troops)

Class (no, launched):
Philadelphia N Yd– *Newport* (LST 1179, 3.2.68), *Manitowoc* (LST 1180, 4.6.69), *Sumter* (LST 1181, 13.12.69), National Steel & Shipbuilding Co – *Fresno* (LST 1182, 28.9.68), *Peoria* (LST 1183, 27.11.68), *Frederick* (LST 1184, 8.3.69), *Schenectady* (LST 1185, 24.5.69), *Cayuga* (LST 1186, 12.7.69), *Tuscaloosa* (LST 1187, 6.9.69), *Saginaw* (LST 1188, 3.2.70), *San Bernardino* (LST 1189, 28.3.70), *Boulder* (LST 1190, 22.5.70), *Racine* (LST 1191, 15.8.70), *Spartanburg County* (LST 1192, 11.11.70), *Fairfax County* (LST 1193, 19.11.70), *La Moure County* (LST 1194, 13.2.71), *Barbour County* (LST 1195, 15.5.71), *Harlan County* (LST 1196, 24.9.71), *Barnstaple County* (LST 1197, 2.10.71), *Bristol County* (LST 1198, 4.12.71).

With these ships the Amphibious Force finally attained its goal of 20kts performance throughout. The many failures to design a fast LCT showed primarily that radical measures were required; in these ships there is a normal ship-shaped bow, but the upper portion splits and a long causeway is lowered through a gallows above; the bow ramp is 112ft (*34.1m*) long. There is also a stern ramp which permits unloading of LVTs into the water or into a landing craft or on to a pier. Above it is a helicopter deck; there is no hangar. Capacity is 385 troops and 500 tons of cargo; vehicles can be driven down to the lower deck via a ramp, or through the superstructure on to the helicopter deck aft. A 30ft turntable at each end of the tank deck permits vehicles to turn round without having to reverse. There are davits for up to four LCVP. Two Phalanx CIWS are due to be fitted during the 1980s.

The size and speed of the *Newport* class programme suggests the urgency of new amphibious construction in the late 1960s; one analyst has suggested that amphibious craft were one programme that Secretary of Defense McNamara's men strongly supported, as an essential element of the US force projection capability. Thus the prototype was ordered in FY65, followed by eight in FY66, and then by eleven in FY67. They were completed in 1969–72 and are all extant 1982.

With the advent of the LHAs, with their large well decks and vast cargo spaces, the rationale of the LSTs came into question, and as this is written the *Newport*s are perhaps the least valuable of the specialised amphibious ships. They may well become obsolescent as amphibious doctrine shifts to distant assault with air-cushion vehicles (LCAC), which can be launched from beyond the horizon, and whose range and speed add considerably to the element of surprise in an amphibious assault.

Francis Marion 1964   USN

TULARE and PAUL REVERE class *attack transports*

Displacement:	12,000t light; 16,800t full load (*Paul Revere* 10,709/16,838t)
Dimensions:	564ft oa × 76ft × 26ft
	172.0m × 23.2m × 7.9m
Machinery:	1-shaft geared turbines, 2 CE boilers (Foster Wheeler in *Paul Revere* class) 22,000shp = 22kts
Armament:	12/8–3in/50 (6×2; 4×2 in *Paul Revere* class)
Complement:	393 plus 319 troops (307 plus 1657 troops in *Paul Revere* class)

Class (no, launched):
Bethlehem, San Francisco – *Tulare* (AKA 112, 22.12.53)
New York SB – *Paul Revere* (APA 248, 13.2.54), *Francis Marion* (APA 249, 11.4.53).

These three ships, the only new AKA and APA construction of the 1950s, were conversions of Mariner cargo hulls (C4-S-1A). Of 35 'Mariners' built, the Navy acquired five in all, the other two being the Polaris missile firing ship *Observation Island* (YAG 57, then EAG 154) and the navigational test ship *Compass Island* (EAG 133), both associated with the Polaris programme. The two attack (personnel) transports, commissioned in 1958 and 1961 respectively, were fitted as amphibious squadron flagships or as troop commander or transport division flagships; they carried nine LCM-6, 12 LCVP, and 3 LCP(L), and could handle these craft and heavy vehicles with 10t, 30t and 60t cargo booms. In an early example of adaptation to helicopter operation, their helicopter decks were served by cargo elevators. In fact they were the last conventional attack personnel transports, as the transport function was next taken over by a combination of LPH (helicopter carriers) and LPD (landing ship docks with additional troop spaces). They could accommodate 1500 troops each. Both were sold to Spain in 1980.

Tulare was designed primarily for cargo, although she could carry 575 troops (and 300 vehicles), handling up to 27 landing craft with heavy-lift (60t) booms rigged from her quadrupod masts. Like the APAs, she had a helicopter platform. She was stricken on 1.8.81 and will be used as TS *Bay State* by Massachusetts Maritime Academy.

WAR-BUILT ATTACK TRANSPORTS
Although very extensive forces of attack transports and cargo ships were built up during the Second World War, they were largely dispersed postwar, many ships going to the Maritime Administration for lay-up and then disposal. Although some Maritime Administration reserve hulls remain in 1981, the shift in commercial shipping from break-bulk (as in an AKA) to containers sharply reduces the degree to which the merchant fleet (both reserve and active) can form a mobilisation reserve. That was not always true: both in FY52 (for Korea) and in FY62 (for Vietnam) six Maritime Reserve fleet AKAs were reacquired and reactivated. Note, however, that in FY65–66 it was necessary to design an entirely new ship as an attack (cargo) transport (*Charleston* class).

CHARLESTON class *assault cargo ships*

Displacement:	20,700t full load
Dimensions:	575ft 6in oa × 82ft × 25ft 6in
	175.5m × 25.0m × 7.8m
Machinery:	1-shaft geared turbine, 2 CE boilers, 22,000shp = 20kts
Armament:	8–3in/50 (4×2)
Complement:	334 (plus 226 troops)

Class (no, launched):
Charleston (LKA 113, 2.12.67), *Durham* (LKA 114, 29.7.68), *Mobile* (LKA 115, 19.10.68), *St Louis* (LKA 116, 4.1.69), *El Paso* (LKA 117, 17.5.69). All were built by Newport News.

The first assault cargo ships specifically designed for the role, these ships were built under the FY65 (4 units) and FY66 programme. They are considerably larger than the 'Mariner' and 'Victory' class conversions they succeed. Designations were changed from AKA to LKA in 1968–69. They carry nine LCM as deck cargo, launching them with two 78t capacity booms; there are also two 40t and eight 15t cranes. There is a helicopter pad aft, but no hangar. They carry 226 troops. One of two twin 3in/50 mounts originally fitted was removed in the late 1970s, with the Mk 56 director, as the 3in was removed from the anti-aircraft role. All were extant 1982.

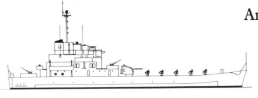
Carronade 1961

MINOR LANDING CRAFT

Production of Second World War type landing craft continued after 1945. The LCU (Landing Craft Utility) are the largest which can be carried by the various dock landing ships. The first postwar series was *LCU 1466–1609* (completed 1954–1957), of which 14 were completed in Japan for foreign service (*1594–1601* for Taiwan and *1602–1607* for Japan). *LCU 1610–1624* were completed in 1960 and *LCU 1627–1680* in 1967–1976 (*LCU 1637* was an all-aluminium prototype alternative design; *LCU 1625* was an *LCU 1466* fitted with vertical-axis propellers; and *LCU 1626* was transferred). These later craft have both bow and stern ramps, so that vehicles can drive through. Although these boats are not normally armed (they can be fitted with two 20mm), they are mentioned here as the lineal successors of the World War Two LCT, and as the predecessors of the LCAC. They were redesignated LSU from LCT in 1949, and LCU on 15.4.52. They will be replaced by air cushion landing craft (LCAC), which can operate over a far wider range of beaches than the LCU. They can carry 75t as opposed to 180t of the LCU, but at 50kts. A total of 107 is envisaged.

The next smaller type is the LCM, of which two types, LCM(6) and LCM(8) are in service. The former, a World War Two 56ft design, remained in production as late as FY75. LCM(8) was lengthened to 74ft to take an M60 tank or 65t of cargo (compared to 34t in the earlier type). About 300 LCM(8) were built for the Army up to 1967, and 217 were built for the Navy 1949–67. In addition, 626 LCM(6)s were delivered 1952–67. Post-1967 production: 218 LCM(6) (including 4 for Iran, 19 for Saudi Arabia), and 93 LCM(8) (including 6 for Spain).

At the low end of the scale were several 36ft craft: the ramped LCVP of Second World War design, built of wood or GRP, and the personnel-carrying LCPL, which had no ramp. The LCVP could carry 4t of cargo and both types could be carried in davits. A total of 1552 LCVP were built 1954–66: 349 with wooden hulls 1954–55, 910 wooden hulls in 1956, 27 plastic hulls (Mk 5) in 1956, 9 wooden hulls in 1964, and 257 plastic hulls (Mk 7) in 1967, and 32 since 1967. A total of 490 LCVP were converted into gunboats armed with 0.30cal MGs, for Vietnam service 1950–62.

The 10kt LCPL Mk 1 was originally intended to land troops, but with the appearance of the ramped LCVP it was used instead to control boat waves in amphibious assaults. A total of 103 Mk 1 were built in 1956. A total of 233 LCPL Mk 4 (with a cockpit) were built between 1957 and 1967; Mks 2, 3, and 5–10 were all experimental craft, and Mk 11 (194 built 1959–67) was a modified type with a tall windshield, roughly resembling a commercial motorboat. Both types could attain 19kts on a 300bhp diesel. The LCPL remains in production, with 154 built since 1968, and a contract pending in 1983 for another 42 (or up to 79).

CARRONADE *fire support ship*

Displacement:	1040t light; 1500t full load
Dimensions:	245ft × 39ft × 10ft
	74.7m × 11.9m × 3.0m
Machinery:	2-shaft diesels, 3100bhp = 15kts
Armament:	1–5in/38, 4–40mm (2×2), 8 rocket launchers
Complement:	139

Class (no, launched):
Carronade (IFS 1, 26.5.53). Built by Puget Sound B & D.

Carronade was a direct successor to the wartime rocket-firing landing ships and craft, built as a result of revived interest in amphibious warfare after Inchon. Design work actually began in 1948, and at one stage a converted DE was considered. Considerations included suitability for mass production and the desire to achieve 20kts (as in other ships of the amphibious convoy then contemplated); the two conflicted, since speeds above about 15kts proved very expensive. In addition, the conflict between a need for large numbers of rockets and the desire to hold down ship size was resolved by placing large numbers of rockets in magazines above the waterline, protected only by 30lb (3/4in) STS. Proposals for a mortar-locating radar, for counter-battery fire, were dropped, the ship being limited to conventional weapons and fire control systems.

Carronade was considered a peacetime luxury, and she was decommissioned in 1960. However, she and three LSMR were reactivated for Vietnam service in 1965, being stricken in 1973. At that time she was classified as an LFR.

SMALL SURFACE COMBATANTS

PT 812 type *fast attack craft*

Displacement:	67.9t light; 92.5t full load
Dimensions:	100ft wl, 105ft oa × 18ft 4in × 3ft 11in
	30.5m, 32.0m × 5.6m × 1.2m
Machinery:	4 shaft, 4 Packard gasoline engines, 10,000bhp = 38.2kts
Armament:	2–40mm (2×1), 4–20mm (2×2), 4 torpedoes
Complement:	17

Class (launched):
Electric Boat – *PT 809* (7.8.50)
Bath Iron Wks – *PT 810* (2.6.50)
Trumpy, Annapolis – *PT 811* (30.11.50)
Philadelphia N Yd – *PT 812* (1.2.51)

These four torpedo-boats were intended to embody wartime design lessons. All were aluminium; 809 was riveted, 810 riveted and welded, and 811 and 812 all-welded; each was designed to mount two single 40mm guns (one in 812), two twin 20mm, one 81mm mortar, one Mk 107 rocket launcher (812 only), four torpedo racks, and four depth-charge racks; speed was set at 46kts (43 for the somewhat longer 812). Although these figures represented a considerable advance on Second World War practice, they still did not make up for the lack of an operational requirement for such coastal craft. *PT 812* was modified as a gas turbine test bed in 1956, with two 4000shp gas turbines on her outboard shafts, and two 800bhp diesels (18kts with controllable-pitch propellers) inboard. *PT 810* and *811* were reactivated in 1963 as *PTF 1* and *PTF 2* in a new Fast Patrol Craft series, officially associated with 'unconventional operations' with SEAL (sea-air-land) teams. Reacquired officially on 21 December 1962, the two ex-PTs were based with six 'Nasty' class acquired from Norway at Subic Bay in the Philippines at the outset of the Vietnam War. *PTF 1* and *PTF 2* were stricken in 1965 and sunk as targets.

PT 812 was transferred to the Army in 1959, to South Korea in 1968. Returning to the USA in 1969 she was later reactivated as *Guardian* and employed until 1974 as an escort for the Presidential Yacht; she became a drone recovery craft (DR-1) in 1975. In that role she is gasoline powered, recovering aerial drones and controlling drone boats; she was named *Retriever* in 1975.

Norwegian NASTY type *fast attack craft*

Displacement:	80.4t
Dimensions:	80ft 4in oa × 24ft 7in × 3ft 10in
	24.5m × 7.5m × 1.2m
Machinery:	2 shafts, 2 Napier-Deltic diesels, 6200bhp = 38kts. Fuel 5800gal
Armament:	1–40mm, 2–20mm (2×1), 1–81mm mortar/0.50cal MG
Complement:	17

Class (completed):
Boatservice, Mandal – *PTF 3–PTF 16* (Dec 62–Sept 64)
Trumpy, Annapolis – *PTF 17–PTF 22* (1967–68)

These Norwegian-designed torpedo-boats were acquired by the US Navy for 'unconventional operations'. *PTF 3–PTF 16* were built by Boatservice A/B, Mandal, Norway, and the hulls were shipped to the United States for outfitting.

The first two were acquired in Dec 1962, *PTF 5–PTF 8* on 1 March 1964 and the remainder on 2 September 1964. *PTF 4* was sunk in 1964, *PTF 9*, *PTF 14*, *PTF 15* and *PTF 16* in 1966. *PTF 3* and *PTF 5–PTF 7* were leased to South Vietnam on 26 January 1966 and returned (and recommissioned) in 1970. Of this class, one unit (*PTF 13*) was disposed of in 1972; *PTF 3*, *PTF 6*, *PTF 7* and *PTF 12* in 1977; *PTF 18* and *PTF 19* in 1980, and the remainder were stricken in 1981.

PTF 17–PTF 22, built by John Trumpy and Sons, Annapolis, duplicated the Norwegian design, entering service in 1968 (*PTF 17–PTF 20*) and 1969 (*PTF 21*, *PTF 22*).

The Trumpy boats were built under the FY67 programme, the Norwegian units having been acquired under FY64.

Armament varied in all these craft; originally it was reported as two 40mm and two single 20mm, but the forward 40mm was later replaced by the combination 81mm mortar/0.50 cal machine-gun of many Vietnam-era combatants. However, as of 1976 *PTF 18* (and possibly others) retained both 40mm guns.

PTF 1 (ex-PT 810) 1963 USN

PTF 23 1970   USN

Grand Rapids 1970   USN

'OSPREY' type *fast attack craft*

Displacement:	80t light; 105t full load
Dimensions:	94ft 9in oa × 23ft 2in × 7ft
	28.8m × 7.0m × 2.1m
Machinery:	2 shafts, Napier-Deltic diesels, 6200bhp = 40kts
Armament:	1–40mm, 2–20mm (2×1), 1–81mm mortar/0.50 cal MG
Complement:	19

Class (completed)
Sewart Seacraft – *PTF 23—PFT 26* (1967-68)

Under FT67 the Navy bought four 'Ospreys' (*PFT 23–PFT 26*) from Sewart Seacraft of Berwick, Louisiana. They were a commercial, aluminium (rather than wooden) hulled design, sometimes described as improved versions of the *Nasty*. Although reportedly not completely sucessful, they were not sold until 1979. (*PTF 25* was experimentally fitted with gas turbines in 1978, stricken in 1980). They can be configured as torpedo-boats, minelayers, or submarine chasers.

CPIC type *patrol craft*

Displacement:	75t full load
Dimensions:	100ft oa × 18ft 6in × 6ft
	30.5m × 5.6m × 1.8m
Machinery:	3 shafts, Avco gas turbines , 6750shp (plus auxiliary Volvo diesels on outboard shafts, 500bhp) = over 40kts
Armament:	2–30mm (1×2). See notes
Complement:	11

Developed as a PTF successor, the Coastal Patrol and Interdiction Craft was built by Tacoma Boatbuilding in 1974 and turned over to the South Korean Navy. She was returned to the United States in 1980 for research. As in the PTFs, there are major weapon positions fore and aft of the bridge structure, as well as pintles for machine-guns along the sides, and guns, missiles, and torpedo tubes can be accommodated. As completed, the CPIC prototype was armed with an Emerson Electric twin 30mm cannon forward.

ASHEVILLE class *fast attack craft*

Displacement:	225t standard; 245t full load
Dimensions:	164ft 6in oa, 23ft 11in × 9ft 6in
	50.1m × 7.3m × 2.9m
Machinery:	2-shaft CODOG: 2 Cummins diesels, 1750bhp = 16kts, 1 GE gas turbine, 14,000shp = approx 38kts. Range 1700nm at 16kts
Armament:	1–3in/50, 1–40mm, 4–0.50cal MG. See notes
Complement:	28

Class (no, completed):
Tacoma Boatbuilding – *Asheville* (PG 84, 6.8.66), *Gallup* (PG 85, 22.10.66), *Antelope* (PG 86, 4.11.67), *Ready* (PG 87, 6.1.68;), *Crockett* (PG 88, 24.6.67), *Marathon* (PG 89, 11.5.68), *Canon* (PG 90, 26.7.68), *Tacoma* (PG 92, 14.7.69), *Chehalis* (PG 94, 11.8.69), *Benicia* (PG 96, 25.4.70), *Grand Rapids* (PG 98, Aug 70), *Douglas* (PG 100, Nov 70)
Petersen – *Defiance* (PG 95, 24.9.69), *Welch* (PG 93, 8.9.69), *Surprise* (PG 97, 17.10.69), *Beacon* (PG 99, 21.11.69), *Green Bay* (PG 101, 5.12.69)

These gas turbine 'motor gunboats' were a product of the Kennedy era, with its Presidential support for small craft and its fascination with Cuba. Originally a diesel design was proposed, a natural outgrowth of PGMs built for many US allies and suited for river and coastal operations. However, some within the Bureau of Ships noted that the advent of gas turbines for main propulsion made a much more advanced design possible, their high speed was a dubious advantage, but they did prove extremely useful in riverine warfare, in some cases sustaining considerable damage and in all cases displaying endurance well beyond design goals. They were completed in 1966–71, and their designation changed from PGM to PG in 1967.

The *Asheville* class were also used to test 'special warfare' coastal infiltration techniques, benefiting from their small radar cross-section and in many US and NATO exercises they simulated Soviet small missile craft (Osa and Komar types). In addition, after Vietnam, four units in the Mediterranean were assigned by the then CNO, Admiral Zumwalt, to a 'counter-tattletale' role, following Soviet warships to provide positive warning of any imminent Soviet missile attack on the Sixth Fleet. In this role they were armed with a surface-to-surface variant of the US Standard anti-aircraft missile, with two launchers aft and an additional pair of reloads forward of the launchers. Admiral Zumwalt later used this experience to justify the PHM programme. The ships concerned were PGM 86, 87, 98 and 100, after tests had been carried on aboard PGM 96.

Cavitation generally limited their maximum speed to something less than the design figure always quoted, although at the time it was stated that the provision of new propellers would have allowed them to reach design speed. In service they had a bad reputation for discomfort in a seaway, although they were good sea boats and could ride out very severe storms. Thus proponents of the PHM could argue that the *Ashevilles* had demonstrated the utility of small fast surface-attack craft and that hydrofoil design could overcome their bad riding characteristics.

PG 86 and 87 had the Dutch-developed Mk 87 fire control system, a close relative of the Mk 92 of the PHMs and FFGs, employing a computer and automatic aiming; the others all had the Second World War Mk 63 to control their 3in guns. Although up to 22 were planned, rising costs and the absence of a clear mission (particularly in the context of the costs of the Vietnam War) cut short the programme, and the absence of a rationale shows in the quick disposal of most of the class. Transfers were as follows: PG 96 to South Korea 1971; PG 95 and 97 to Turkey 1973; PG 85 and 90 (stricken 1976 and 1977) to Taiwan 1981; PG 99 and 101 to Colombia 1981. PG 86 and 88 to Environmental Protection Agency 1977; PG 100 to Naval Ship Research and Development Center 1979; PG 94 and 98 to Naval Ship Research and Development Center 1975 and 1977 as high-speed tugs *Athena I* and *Athena II*. In 1981 the two survivors were being retained to train Saudi personnel who are to man somewhat similar craft built in the United States for their Navy.

HIGH POINT *hydrofoil*

Displacement:	93.9t light; 119.7t full load
Dimensions:	110ft wl, 115ft 9in oa × 31ft 2in × 3ft 11in
	33.5m, 35.3m × 9.5m × 1.2m
Machinery:	2 Bristol-Siddeley gas turbines, 6800shp = 45kts; (hull-borne, 1 diesel 600bhp = 12kts)
Armament:	2–0.50cal MG (1×2), 1 DC rack, 4–12.75in TT (2×2), 4 Harpoon SSM (in 1973–74 tests)
Sensors:	Sonar for trials
Complement:	13

Class (no, launched):
High Point (PCH 1, 17.8.62). Built by J M Martinac.

Hydrofoils were the major exception to US Navy disinterest in fast patrol craft during the 1950s; they were so promising a technology that they could not be ignored. At that time the primary naval problems was ASW, and it was for ASW that the first large US hydrofoil, the *High Point* (PCH 1, SCB 202 of FY60), was designed. It was to function in a 'sprint and drift' mode, listening briefly between high speed dashes. Because it could not really hope to listen while moving at high speed, it would have to operate in pairs, one unit vectoring the other into an attack with homing torpedoes. A large hull sonar wold be retracted

High Point (foreground) and the experimental *Plainview* 1978   USN

Pegasus 1975   USN

in the hull at high speed, and extended during low-speed hull-borne operation. There was also an auxiliary sonar, either a variable-depth unit for deep operation, or a towed unit which might provide some limited capability even at speed. There were, in addition, exotic operational concepts, such as buoy-borne MAD for target classification during an attack.

Interest in such ASW hydrofoils dated from about January 1955, although it appears that there was information concerning Soviet experiments the previous year. In February 1956 the Office of Naval Research began operational evaluation of hydrofoil craft systems for ASW. Meanwhile, conventional coastal ASW craft (SC and PCS) were repeatedly included in proposed shipbuilding plans, but were always dropped due to their low priority. In January 1958, however, the CNO asked the Bureau of Ships to study the use of hydrofoil craft for harbour security, and that April the PCH was substituted for the usual combination of PCS and SC prototype in the FY60 budget. Probably largely because of its innovative character, the PCH did survive the FY60 pruning of the budget. Originally several follow-on craft were proposed. For example, an October 1958 proposal for the FY61 budget carried 3 PCH (as well as a variety of other doomed craft, such as a missile-armed barrier patrol ship, or PBG, five of which were to have been bought).

In fact, only one PCH was built, and it functioned as an experimental boat. Between August 1971 and July 1973 she was converted at Puget Sound as operational test and evaluation platform for the Harpoon missile system, with a quadruple missile cannister on the centreline aft and a new control system, including a steerable forward strut. She was lent to the Coast Guard (WMEH 1) in March 1975 and stricken in 1980.

FLAGSTAFF *hydrofoil*

Displacement:	56.8t
Dimensions:	74ft 5in oa × 21ft 5in × 13ft 6in (foils extended) 4ft 3in (retracted)
	22.7m × 6.5m × 4.1m, 1.3m
Machinery:	1 shaft, Rolls-Royce Tyne gas turbine, 3620shp = 48kts (hull-borne, 2 GM diesels, 300bhp, water-jet propulsion)
Armament:	1–40mm, 4–0.50cal MG (2×2), 1–81mm mortar
Complement:	13

Class (no, launched):
Flagstaff (PGH 1, 9.1.68)

TUCUMCARI *hydrofoil*

Displacement:	58t
Dimensions:	71ft 10in oa × 19ft 6in × 13ft 11in (foils extended) 4ft 6in (foil retracted)
	21.9m × 5.9m × 4.2m, 1.4m
Machinery:	Proteus gas turbine, water-jets, 3040shp = 40kts (auxiliary diesel for hull-borne operation, 160bhp)
Armament:	1–40mm, 4–20mm (2×2), 1–81mm mortar (replaced 1971 by another twin 20mm)
Complement:	13

Class (no, launched):
Tucumcari (PGH 2, 15.7.67)

By the early 1960s interest had shifted towards the fast gunboat role, and it appeared that a relatively small hydrofoil could duplicate many of the qualities of the larger *Asheville* class fast gunboat. Two competitive prototypes were built under the FY66 (SCB 252) programme; the Grumman *Flagstaff* and the Boeing *Tucumcari*. At one time a follow-on class of 34 hydrofoils was planned, with features borrowed from both. They differed largely in propulsion, Grumman using a geared propeller with the main lifting surface forward; Boeing, water-jets with the main foil surfaces aft. Both were tested in Vietnam, returning home in 1970. Originally armed with a 40mm gun forward, *Flagstaff* was tested with an Army 152mm tank-turret gun in 1971. She was loaned to the Coast Guard (WPGH 1) between November and December 1974, sustaining considerable damage in a collision with a whale; she was sold in 1978. *Tucumcari* ran aground on 16 November 1972, was damaged beyond economical repair, stricken, and her hulk used for fire tests by the Naval Ship Research and Development Laboratory.

PEGASUS class *hydrofoils*

Displacement:	231t full load
Dimensions:	131ft 6in (foils extended) × 23ft 2in × 6ft 2in (foils retracted)
	40.0m × 8.6m × 1.9m
Machinery:	CODOG (water-jet propulsion): 2 Mercedes-Benz diesels (1600bhp = 11kts), 1 GE gas turbine, 18,000shp = over 40kts on foils
Armament:	1–3in/62, 8 Harpoon SSM (2×4)
Sensors:	Radar SPS-63, Mk 92 fire control system (Mk 94 in PHM 1)
Complement:	22

Class (no, launched):
Pegasus (PHM 1, 9.11.74), *Hercules* (PHM 2, 13.4.82), *Taurus* (PHM 3, 8.5.81), *Aquila* (PHM 4, 16.9.81), *Aries* (PHM 5, Nov 81), *Gemini* (PHM 6, 17.2.82). All built by Boeing.

Although neither *Flagstaff* nor *Tucumcari* was reproduced, Boeing did use *Tucumcari* as the basis for the Italian *Sparviero* class missile boats. Israel ordered two 'Super *Flagstaffs*' with Harpoon missiles in 1978. Moreover, Boeing experience with *Tucumcari* presumably shows in the design of the next-generation missile hydrofoil *Pegasus*, PHM 1.

The missile hydrofoils were originally conceived by Admiral Zumwalt as successors to the missile-armed *Asheville* class 'tattletales', ie as a means of countering Soviet missile-armed surface craft, particularly in restricted waters. They had the important advantage of very high speed even in rough weather; it must have appeared that their small size would equate to low unit cost. The PHM programme was, for a time, a NATO-wide one, the Italian and West German governments participating in the design. Germany was to have built twelve. However, as costs rose only the United States, which planned 30, remained in the programme. Cynics suggested strongly that the PHM was a solution in search of a problem, and (with the programme reduced to six craft) PHM 2–PHM 6 were cancelled on 15 April 1977. However, they were reinstated that August at the request of Congress. PHM 2 is to be unarmed, and in 1981 it appeared unlikely that further units would be built. One of the more curious aspects of the PHM story was the attempt to find alternative missions, a Sea Phoenix variant for fleet air defence coming close to the formal proposal stage within the Department of Defense. All were extant in 1982.

PROJECTED HYDROFOILS
The hydrofoil story in the US Navy would be incomplete without mention of some paper projects for much larger types, sometimes designated DE(H) and occasionally Deepwater Escort Hydrofoil. Sketch designs for units as large as 1400 tons have been executed and construction proposed from time to time during the 1970s. Thus the DE(H) competed (apparently unsuccessfully) with the Surface Effect Ship as an Advanced Naval Vehicle; ultimately both died of immature technology and extreme unit cost.

'SWIFT' (PCF) type *patrol craft*

Displacement:	Mk 1: 42,500lb (19t)
	Mk 2: 43,035lb
Dimensions:	Mk 1: 50ft 2in × 13ft 1in × 3ft 6in
	15.3m × 4.0m × 1.1m
	Mk 2: 51ft 4in × 13ft 7in
	15.6m × 4.1m
Machinery:	2 shafts, 2 GM diesels, 860bhp = 28kts. Fuel 800 and 828gal, respectively
Armament:	2–0.50cal MG (1×2), 1–81mm mortar/0.50cal MG
Complement:	6

Class:
Approximately 125 were built from 1965 onwards, 104 transferred to South Vietnam. Others were transferred to the Philippines. In 1982 only two remained on the US Navy List.

The US Navy, which since 1945 had systematically abandoned coastal warfare, found itself operating a large fleet of very small craft in Vietnamese waters. This fleet was, moreover, extemporised very rapidly. The two principal wartime types were the 'Swift' or PCF and the 'Plastic' or PBR.

The 'Swift' was adapted from a standard commercial boat used to support oil drilling rigs in the Gulf of Mexico. All were built by Sewart Seacraft of Berwick,

A Mark II PCF 1968   USN

A PBR 1967   USN

A flotilla of ATCs and a Monitor (right foreground) 1967   USN

Louisiana, in 1965–66. The first 104 units were Mark 1, the remainder (of about 200 built), Mark II with less sheer, a broken deck line, and the pilot house set somewhat farther back from the bow. A typical armament was a twin 0.50cal machine-gun above the pilot house, with a combination 81mm mortar/0.50cal machine-gun mount aft. PCF denoted Patrol Craft, Fast, a typical rated speed being 28 knots.

PBR type *river patrol boats*

Displacement:	Mk 1: 6.5t
	Mk 2: 7.1t
Dimensions:	Mk 1: 31ft × 10ft 7in × 1ft 11in
	9.5m × 3.2m × 0.6m
	Mk 2: 31ft 11in × 11ft 8in × 2ft 7in
	9.7m × 3.6m × 0.8m
Machinery:	2 GM diesels, 432bhp, 2 water-jet pumps = 25kts. Fuel 160gal
Armament:	3–0.50cal MG (2×1, 1×1), 1–40mm grenade launcher, 1–60mm mortar (in some)
Complement:	4

Class:

Approximately 500 were built 1966–73, most transferred to South Vietnam and to Thailand. A total of 27 remained in US Navy service in 1982.

The Patrol Boat, River was smaller than the PCF, with an open-topped conning position, and had a fibreglass hull lined with plastic foam; it was propelled and steered by water-jets, for an extremely shallow draft (3ft compared to 4ft for a Swift). A typical battery consisted of a twin 0.50cal machine-gun forward, a single 0.30cal machine-gun aft, and an infantry-type 40mm grenade launcher. The somewhat larger Mark II typically had three 0.50s (one twin and one single) and a 60mm mortar; it had more powerful engines and enlarged mufflers. A total of 160 Mark I were built by United Boat Builders, Bellingham, Washington between December 1965 and April 1966. More than 500 PBR were built in 1966–1973, the great majority being transferred to South Vietnam. The PBRs were based afloat, LST 846, 821, 838 and 786 being converted to support them. In 1982 5 PCFs and 29 PBRs remain in service with the Naval Reserves, to preserve a core of riverine warfare expertise.

PB type *patrol boats*

Displacement:	Mk I: 26.9t light; 36.3t full load
	Mk III: 31.5t light; 41.3t full load
Dimensions:	Mk I: 65ft × 16ft × 4ft 10in
	19.8m × 4.9m × 1.5m
	Mk III: 64ft 11in × 18ft 1in × 5ft 10in
	19.8m × 5.5m × 1.8m
Machinery:	Mk I: 2 shafts, 2 GM diesels, 1635bhp = 26kts
	Mk III: 3 shafts, 3 GM diesels, 1800bhp = 26kts; range 450nm/26kts, 2000nm/cruising
Armament:	Mk I: 6–20mm (1×2, 4×1), or 0.50cal MG
	Mk III: 4–0.50cal MG (4×1); 4 Penguin SSM (fitted for evaluation 1981)
Complement:	Mk III: 5

Class:

2 Mk I built by Sewart Seacraft 1973; 17 Mk III built by Marinette Marine and Petersen; PB Mk II was not built.

The Patrol Boat (PB) was developed as a successor to the 'Swift'. Two Mark I were completed by Sewart Seacraft in 1972 and delivered in 1973. They have one twin and four single gun positions for 20mm or 0.50cal guns. An alternative Mark III design by Peterson Builders of Sturgeon Bay, Wisconsin won in competition with Mark I and was being procured, in 1982, for inshore warfare. Like the Swift, it is adapted from a Gulf of Mexico support boat. The pilot house is offset to starboard to provide maximum deck space, and the nominal armament of four 0.50cal machine-guns can be reinforced by heavier weapons on the main deck. For example, in 1981 the Norwegian Penguin III anti-ship missile was evaluated for them; it proved too heavy.

Assault Support Patrol Boat (ASPB) type *riverine craft*

Displacement:	26.1t full load
Dimensions:	50ft 2in × 15ft 3in over guards × 3ft 9in
	15.3m × 4.7m × 1.1m
Machinery:	2-shaft diesels, 850bhp = 14kts
Armament:	1– or 2–20mm (and 2–0.50cal, 1×2, in boats with 1–20mm), 2–0.30cal, 2–40mm grenade launchers, 1–81mm mortar/0.50cal MG (in some)
Complement:	5

Command and Control Boat (CCB) and Monitor type *riverine craft*

Displacement:	CCB: 167,000lb (74.5t)
	Monitor: 169,000lb
Dimensions:	60ft (oa) × 17ft 6in × 3ft 4in
	18.3m × 5.3m × 1.0m
Machinery:	2 diesels, 450bhp emergency, 330bhp continuous = 8.5kts (6kts sustained)
Armament:	1–40mm or 20mm, 1–20mm, 2–0.30cal MG, 1–81mm mortar (Monitor only)
Complement:	11

Riverine warfare required considerable numbers of escort craft to operate directly with the troop carriers. Both shallow-draft 'monitors' (MON) and Assault Support Patrol Boats (ASPB) were developed. The first monitors were converted from LCM(6) (landing craft) hulls, which formed the basis for many of the riverine craft. A typical battery was 1–40mm gun, 1–20mm, 2–0.50cal MGs and 1–81mm mortar (or 2–M10-8 flame throwers). Later units (Mk V) were built as such from the keel up, and had rounded bows without landing craft type bow doors. They used the same hull as the CCB command boats, with a twin 20mm bow turret, an 81mm mortar in a well, and a smaller turret on the superstructure for a 0.30cal MG. Total armament included 4–0.30s. Some had a 105mm howitzer in place of the bow turret and mortar well. Both types were armoured against shaped-charge rockets with characteristic armour slats like Venetian blinds. Numbers built are not available, but all survivors were handed to the South Vietnamese Navy in 1973. They included at least 22 converted LCM(6) – transferred 1964–67 – and 42 purpose-built monitors.

The ASPB (Assault Support Patrol Boat) was the only craft specially designed for the river war, described as the destroyer and minesweeper of that specialized fleet. It was equipped with a chain drag to counter command mines, and armed with a 20mm cannon, a twin 0.50cal MG, two Mk 18 grenade launchers, and an 81mm mortar. ASPBs generally led riverine operations, sweeping ahead of the assault formation; they were also used as escorts, patrol craft, and counter-ambush craft. One unusual feature was the underwater exhaust system, adopted for silencing. The ASPB was built in two Marks in 1967–68, with welded steel hulls, and capable of about 14kts (compared to 16 as designed). The ASPB hull was also used for minesweeping (as the MSR) and for CCB duties. At least 84 ASPB were transferred to the South Vietnamese Navy and the remainder discarded.

Troops were generally carried in converted LCM(6)s, ATCs (Armoured Troop Carriers), each carrying a platoon of about 40 men. Some were fitted with helicopter decks as ATC(H), serving as batallion aid stations. In addition, until the arrival of the specially designed ASPB, the ATCs were the minesweepers of the Riverine Force. Each was armed with 1–20mm cannon, 2–0.50cal MGs, and two Mk 18 grenade launchers. Postwar, a new 'mini-ATC' was developed, primarily for Special Forces-type operation, with an aluminium hull and ceramic radar, quiet engines (for 28kts), shallow draft (1ft), and space for up to seven pintle-mounted weapons. As of 1981, a total of eighteen had been delivered, one powered by gas turbines.

For command and control, the Riverine Navy had CCBs, converted from LCM(6)s and similar to the monitors except that a command module replaced the 81mm mortar of the latter; it was inserted between the after superstructure and the covered gun position in the bow. The latter could accommodate one 20 or 40mm gun, and there were typically several 0.30 and 0.50cal machine-guns.

MINE WARFARE VESSELS

AGILE/AGGRESSIVE class *ocean minesweepers*

Displacement:	637t light; 735t full load (MSO 488)
Dimensions:	165ft wl, 171ft 6in oa × 34ft × 13ft 1in *50.3m, 52.3m × 10.4m × 4.0m*
Machinery:	2 shafts, diesels, 1550bhp = 13kts. Range 2400nm at 12kts. See notes
Armament:	1–40mm
Sensors:	Sonar UQS-1
Complement:	70

Class (no):

Agile (MSO 421), *Aggressive* (MSO 422), *Avenge* (MSO 423), *Bold* (MSO 424), *Bulwark* (MSO 425), *Conflict* (MSO 426), *Constant* (MSO 427), *Dash* (MSO 428), *Detector* (MSO 429), *Direct* (MSO 430), *Dominant* (MSO 431), *Dynamic* (MSO 432), *Engage* (MSO 433), *Embattle* (MSO 434), *Endurance* (MSO 435), *Energy* (MSO 436), *Enhance* (MSO 437), *Esteem* (MSO 438), *Excel* (MSO 439), *Exploit* (MSO 440), *Exultant* (MSO 441), *Fearless* (MSO 442), *Fidelity* (MSO 443), *Firm* (MSO 444), *Force* (MSO 445), *Fortify* (MSO 446), *Guide* (MSO 447), *Illusive* (MSO 448), *Impervious* (MSO 449), *Implicit* (MSO 455), *Inflict* (MSO 456), *Loyalty* (MSO 457), *Lucid* (MSO 458), *Nimble* (MSO 459), *Notable* (MSO 460), *Observer* (MSO 461), *Pinnacle* (MSO 462), *Pivot* (MSO 463), *Pluck* (MSO 464), *Prestige* (MSO 465), *Prime* (MSO 466), *Reaper* (MSO 467), *Rival* (MSO 468), *Sagacity* (MSO 469), *Salute* (MSO 470), *Skill* (MSO 471), *Valor* (MSO 472), *Vigor* (MSO 473), *Vital* (MSO 474), *Conquest* (MSO 488), *Gallant* (MSO 489), *Leader* (MSO 490), *Persistant* (MSO 491), *Pledge* (MSO 492), *Stalwart* (MSO 493), *Sturdy* (MSO 494), *Swerve* (MSO 495), *Venture* (MSO 496), *Acme* (MSO 508), *Adroit* (MSO 509), *Advance* (MSO 510), *Affray* (MSO 511). They were launched between 4.10.52 and 18.12.56. MSO 450–454, 475–487, 498–507, 512–518 were built for other countries under MDAP (8 for France, 6 for Netherlands, 4 for Portugal, 4 for Belgium, 2 to Norway, and 2 to Italy).

ABILITY class *ocean minesweepers*

Displacement:	792t light; 934t full load
Dimensions:	182ft wl, 189ft 9in oa × 35ft 1in × 10ft *55.5m, 57.9m × 10.7m × 3.0m*
Machinery:	2 shafts, GM diesels, 2700bhp = 14.5kts
Armament:	1–40mm
Sensors:	Sonar UQS-1
Complement:	83

Class (no):

Ability (MSO 519), *Alacrity* (MSO 520), *Assurance* (MSO 521). Launched 1956–57.

Although minesweeper design continued after 1945, and although the prototype new ocean sweeper was authorised under the FY50 programme, construction on a large scale did not begin until the Korean War, with 10 units under the FY51 first supplemental budget, 18 under the second, and 15 under the third, another 5 being planned under the FY52 programme. The new sweeper was somewhat smaller than the 180ft Second World War type, and it was built of plywood for minimum magnetic signature. Two XMAP pressure sweeping caissons could be towed. Given problems in diesel engine procurement under what were then expected to be mobilisation conditions, designs were prepared for either a new Packard light-weight engine or for an existing GM commercial type. Reportedly the rapid development of the Packard (which

Embattle 12.6.63   USN

was also used in the new coastal sweepers) and its aircraft-type design led to many mechanical problems, which were not corrected for as much as eight years after its introduction. Given its unfortunate reputation, the Packard never saw large-scale commercial service, and the Navy suffered again as production ended and spares were largely unavailable. Of 93 ships to the SCB-45 A or *Agile* class design, 58 were retained by the US Navy, the others being transferred. They were all reclassified from AM to MSO in 1955.

Some writers split the *Agile* class into sub-classes. *Agile* and 36 sisters, transferred abroad had 3040shp Packard diesels. Of 53 *Aggressive* class sweepers (MSO 422 series, 2280bhp Packard diesels), 12 were transferred. Four *Dash* class (MSO 431 series, 1520bhp GM diesels) were improved *Agiles* with two rather than four engines.

The *Acme* (MSO 508) and *Ability* (MSO 519) classes were improved and slightly enlarged *Agiles* built under the FY54 and 55 programme, the latter designed as mine division flagships. Ultimately both series were fitted as flagships.

All of the new ocean sweepers were built of wood with bronze and stainless (non-magnetic) steel fittings, with automatic degaussing, to compensate for course changes, as well as electrical insulators in internal piping, lifelines, and stays. All also had a new mine-locating sonar, UQS-1, later replaced by SQQ-14, a variable-depth unit on a rigid retractable rod.

Originally all ocean sweepers in commission in the mid-1960s were to have been modernised; however, only 19 of the 64 ocean sweepers then in service began refits. Modernisation of five (MSO 460, 468, 470, 472 and 519) was cancelled 16.10.1970 and the hulks were scrapped. *Avenge* caught fire during modernisation and had to be scrapped, and another converted ship (MSO 445) burned and sank at sea on 24 April 1973 en route from Subic Bay to Guam. The modernization programme itself was abandoned with a shift of emphasis to minesweeping helicopters. Modernization was funded under the FY58 (MSO 433, 441–3, 445, 446, 449, 456) and FY69 (MSO 437, 438, 448, 488, 490) programmes.

Fire was a considerable hazard to the wooden sweepers, and at least six caught fire. In 1981, only 25 survived. Units fitted with SQQ-14 sonars have a massive external hoist forward of the bridge, in place of the single 40mm gun formerly mounted there. These units have a single 20mm gun forward; some appear to be entirely unarmed. In most cases, modernization provided an enlarged superstructure abaft the bridge.

Disposals: MSO 423, 469 stricken 1970: 460, 463 (to Spain), 468, 470, 472, 491 (to Spain) 1971; 426, 435, 436 (to Philippines), 440 (to Philippines), 447, 457, 473 (to Spain) 1972; 432 (to Spain) 1974; 422, 424, 425, 466, 467, 1975; 458, 459, 508, 410 1976; 421, 461, 462, 471, 474, 494, 495, 496, 1966; MSO 445 sunk 24.4.73. MSO 519 was stricken 1971. MSO 520 and 522 were reclassified as AG 520 and 521 in 1973, their sweeping gear removed, and SQS-15 towed array sonar system fitted for tests. This sonar was operationally tested in the 6th Fleet, 1970–73 by DE 1015, DE 1021, and DE 1022. The two towed array AGs were stricken in 1977. An improved MSO design (MSO 523 class) was planned for construction in the late 1960s as SCB-501 (FY66); it was to have combined MSO and MHC capabilities (940t, 184ft × 35ft at waterline). SCB-500.55 was the MSS-1 conversion, and SCB-502 was the MSO 422 class modernization.

AVENGER class *ocean minesweeper/minehunter*

Displacement:	1100t full load
Dimensions:	213ft oa × 38ft 4in × 10ft 2in *64.9m × 11.7m × 3.1m*
Machinery:	2 shafts, 4 L1616 diesels, 2400bhp = 13.5kts
Armament:	2–12.7mm MG (2×1)
Sensors:	Radar SPS-55; sonar SQQ-14
Complement:	80

No	Name	Builder	Launched	Fate
MCM 1	AVENGER	Peterson		Ordered 29.6.82

UNITED STATES

From the late 1960s onwards there were several projects for more or less sophisticated new minesweepers, as mine countermeasures technology became more and more elaborate. As of this writing it is primarily a matter of locating mines on the seabed, using high-definition sonar (currently SQQ-14), and then destroying mines one by one (minehunting). Success requires, among other things, a very high degree of navigational accuracy. Meanwhile, the function of the minesweepers has been a matter of some controversy. For example, with the appearance of deep-water ASW mines such as CAPTOR, there was a call for deep-water sweepers particularly adapted to keeping the approaches to ballistic submarine bases clear of Soviet mines. On the other hand, the Soviet fleet continues to threaten US ports and coastal waters with more conventional forms of mine warfare; and there is still the threat of mining to stop amphibious assaults – a threat which will abate somewhat as the United States shifts to air-cushion vehicles for such assaults.

A new programme for mine countermeasure (MCM) ship construction began in the 1970s, and the CNO approved a 1640t, 265ft, 18kt ship in Nov 1976. As of early 1977 nineteen were planned for construction in FY79–FY82. Its primary purpose would have been to counter deep-water ASW mines, and it was abandoned as too expensive. A new design, closely based on that of the existing ocean minesweeper (MSO), was substituted. The first unit, USS *Avenger* (MCM 1), was ordered on 29.6.82, under the FY82 programme. The next ships were moved from the FY84 to the FY83 programme in view of the 'the severity of the mining threat'. As of Feb 1982, the Reagan Administration FY83–87 shipbuilding programme showed four units in each of FY83 and FY84, and five in FY85.

The MCM was envisaged as the high end of a high-low mix of minesweepers, the lower end of which would consist of a combination of coastal minehunters (MSH) and mobilized civilian craft as well as minesweeping helicopters. As in the case of her predecessors, *Avenger*, which is to be completed in 1985, is to use a variable-depth sonar (SQQ-30, an improved SQQ-14) for minehunting. Deep mines will be neutralized by remote-control vehicles, operated from an automated CIC, which will plot mine locations with the assistance of a precise integrated navigation system (SSN-2, PINS). As of this writing, nine MCM were included in the FY82–FY85 programme, with a total of 20 to 30 planned for the 1980s.

As of this writing no MSH design has been drawn, although a 1982 account suggested that a GRP hull was favoured. As of Feb 1982, the Reagan Administration FY83–FY87 programme showed the prototype MSH for construction under the FY84 programme, at a planned cost of $73.1 million. With five follow-on ships in each of FY86 and FY87. The mobilization programme is intended to avoid the peacetime cost of maintaining very large sweeping forces. Instead, Naval Reserves will continue to provide an important element of the mine force. British experience with extemporized trawler minesweepers in the Falklands has inspired a Craft of Opportunity Program (COOP) to use suitable fishing and commercial vessels as wartime sweepers, manned by reservists. Three pilot units were formed in 1982.

An artist's impression of *Avenger* 1980   USN

Thrasher 1964   USN

BLUEBIRD ('ADJUTANT') class *coastal minesweepers*

Displacement:	360t light; 400t full load
Dimensions:	138ft wl, 145ft 5in oa × 26ft 6in × 7ft
	42.1m, 44.3m × 8.1m × 2.1m
Machinery:	2 shaft, 2 GM diesels, 1000bhp = 13kts. Range 2500nm at 10kts
Armament:	1–20mm
Sensors:	Sonar UQS-1
Complement:	39

Class (no):

Bluebird (MSC 121), *Cormorant* (MSC 222), *Falcon* (MSC 190), *Frigate Bird* (MSC 191), *Hummingbird* (MSC 192), *Jacana* (MSC 193), *Kingbird* (MSC 194), *Limpkin* (MSC 195), *Meadowlark* (MSC 196), *Parrot* (MSC 197), *Peacock* (MSC 198), *Phoebe* (MSC 199), *Redwing* (MSC 200), *Shrike* (MSC 201), *Spoonbill* (MSC 202), *Thrasher* (MSC 203), *Thrust* (MSC 204), *Vireo* (MSC 205), *Warbler* (MSC 206), *Whippoorwill* (MSC 207), *Widgeon* (MSC 208), *Woodpecker* (MSC 209), *Albatross* (MSC 289), *Gannet* (MSC 290).

These ships were essentially versions of the Second World War YMS, initially for transfer abroad under the MDAP programme, and initially designated AMS (later MSC, for coastal). The original design did not show XMAP capability, and 'improved magnetic signature, but because of cost and time considerations, the extreme measures taken in AM design will not be used'. Designs with both the new Packard (total 1200bhp) and a proven GM 8-268A (total 880bhp) diesel were prepared, the latter favoured for foreign customers. They were to be armed with a twin 20mm gun forward, compared to the 3in/50 of the YMS and to the single 40mm of the MSO. Of 159 units of the original *Bluebird* (SCB 69) class launched from 1953 onwards all but 20 were transferred. They are often called the *Adjutant* class. Many more units were built abroad with US assistance, primarily to British designs. Where the US MSCs had wooden frames, the British used aluminium. All had controllable-pitch propellers for agility in minefields. *Albatross* (MSC 289) and *Gannet* (MSC 290) were the last US sweepers authorised until the MCMs of the 1980s (which may not in fact be built) and were slightly enlarged *Bluebirds*. Of 25 units built, only two were retained in US service. They introduced gas turbine generators for magnetic sweeping and modified gear-handling equipment.

Of the US units, only MSC 203–209 had the original GM diesels; MSC 289–290 had updated GM units of about 1000bhp.

Note that US minesweeper (MSC) construction for transfer abroad continued after the end of construction for the US Navy. For example, MSC 201–2 were built for Iran, MSC 293–4 for Pakistan, 295, 296, 316, 320, 321 for South Korea, 297, 301, 303, 313 for Thailand; 298, 299, 308–310, 314, 317, 318 for Greece; 300, 302, 306, 307 for Taiwan; 304, 305, 311, 312, 315 for Turkey; and 322–325 for Saudi Arabia; most are rated in a separate MSC 284 class. *Albatross* (MSC 289), and *Gannet* (MSC 290) were intended for transfer to Spain under MDAP, but MSC 200 and 202 were substituted. Disposals: MSC 289 and 290 were stricken 1970, MSC 194 (collision) and MSC 197 in 1972. Six were transferred to Indonesia in 1971: MSC 190–193, 195, 196. MSC 203 and 207 transferred to Singapore 1975. MSC 208 stricken 1973, MSC 122 1974, MSC 121, 198, 199, 201 1975, MSC 204 1977. MSC 205 and 206 to Fiji 1975, MSC 209 to Fihi 1976.

(For illustration see under Turkey)

COVE class *inshore minesweepers*

Displacement:	197t light; 232t full load
Dimensions:	105ft wl; 110ft oa × 23ft × 8ft
	32.0m, 33.5m × 7.0m × 2.4m
Machinery:	1 shaft, 2 GM diesels, 595bhp = 12.5kts. Range 1000nm at 9kts
Armament:	1–0.50cal MG

Class (no):

Cove (MSI 1), *Cape* (MSI 2). Both were built by Bethlehem, Bellingham and launched in 1958.

These inshore sweepers (MSI) were intended to replace the MSCs. Design work began in 1955, one author describing them as an attempt to fill the gap in shallow-water capability left by the deficiencies of the minesweeping boats (MSB). They were to carry MSB-size magnetic sweep gear and MSC-size moored sweep gear on a hull capable of limited ocean passages, and of overseas passage in an emergency – essentially the requirements levied on the original YMS of the Second World War. The advent of gas turbine generators permitted them to incorporate the basic sweeping capability of the MSC 289 class in a much smaller hull. Of fourteen ships built, two were retained by the US Navy and the rest transferred (SCB 136 type). There were also five units of an improved *Cove* class (MSI 15 type), capable of minehunting as well as of sweeping. All were built in 1965–67 specifically for transfer abroad.

The two US Navy units were relegated to research status, and were being operated by the Applied Physics Laboratory of Johns Hopkins University (MSI 1) and the Naval Undersea Systems Center, San Diego (MSI 2).

Bittern 1958   USN

BITTERN *minehunter*

Displacement:	300t standard; 360t full load
Dimensions:	138ft wl, 144ft 6in oa × 28ft × 8ft
	42.1m, 44.1m × 8.5m × 2.4m
Machinerh:	2-shaft diesels, 1200bhp = 14kts
Armament:	1–40mm
Complement:	40

Class (no, launched):
Bittern (MHC 433, 1957). Built by Consolidated SB.

Bittern, built under the FY54 programme, was a prototype to succeed 31 YMS and LSI(L) conversions (then called underwater object locators, or AMCU) under the FY52 (SCB 73) programme. She had no mine destruction capability at all, and was intended rather to locate and plot mine locations, so that small boats or divers could destroy them. To that end she was extremely manoeuvrable, with controllable-pitch propellers and active rudders. Her hull duplicated that of the contemporary *Bluebird* class coastal sweeper.

Proposals for additional minehunter construction (to a somewhat enlarged *Bittern* design, designated SCB 109A rather than 109) never materialized. This was the fate of all the mine craft. For example, an October 1956 sketch list of the FY58 budget showed two ocean and two coastal minesweepers as well as an MSS conversion; but when the budget was cut all had to be deleted. The next April a tentative list for FY59 showed the minehunter, as well as repeat sweepers and an MSS conversion. However, in order of priority the MHC was set below one of three coastal sweepers, and indeed below prototype coastal ASW craft – which were not built. Probably the last budget appearance of the MHC was in early versions of the FY61 budget; as of October 1958 it called for an MSS (then denoted SCB 195), mine support ship (MSC, SCB 123), and a coastal minehunter. However, a FY62–66 shipbuilding programme prepared at about this time showed no new minecraft construction; and all Navy plans of this period were being severely cut by the advent of Polaris.

Bittern herself was decommissioned in September 1965 and leased to a commercial operator in July 1968. She was stricken on 1 February 1972 and broken up.

UNDERWATER LOCATION
Of a total of fifty Underwater Locators, AMCU 1–6 were LCT(6) reclassified on 10 March 1945; AMCU 7–11 were LCI(L) reclassified the same day. AMCU 12–14, MHC 44 and 45, and AMCU 46–50 were all former YMS (coastal minesweeper) hulls, converted under the 1952 programme. AMCU 15–42 were former LCI(L) converted at the same time. Only *Bittern* was a new design. It was intended to build two more, for which the numbers MHC 44 and 45 were allocated. Early in 1954 five YMS were reclassified as AMCU 46–50; when, early in 1955, the two new *Bittern*s were cancelled, AMS (ex-*YMS*) -2 and -3 were the MHC 44 and 45 designations. It is not clear whether these higher numbers actually represent conversions. In addition, the conversion of LSI(L) 1089 to a minehunter under the FY52 programme was cancelled in 1954.

MSB type *minesweeping boats*

Displacement:	42t full load
Dimensions:	57ft 3in oa × 15ft 10in × 4ft 4in
	17.5m × 4.8m × 1.3m
Machinerh:	2 diesels, 300bhp = 12kts. Oil 15.8t
Complement:	6

Mks 1 and 2 type *minesweeping launches*

Displacement:	23,100lb (10.3t) for magnetic sweep; 18,900lb for acoustic sweep; 17,600lb for sweep of moored mines (with, respectively, 680, 360 and 340gal of fuel)
Dimensions:	36ft oa × 11ft 7in × 3ft 8in
	11.0m × 3.5m × 1.1m
Machinery:	1 gas turbine, 200hp = 10kts (without sweep gear streamed). Range 100nm (with full power and full load)
Complement:	4

MSL Mk 4 type *minesweeping launchers*

Displacement:	22,900lb (10.2t) for magnetic sweep; 20,950lb for acoustic; 18,870lb for moored mines (with in each case, 360gal of fuel)
Dimensions:	36ft × 11ft 7in × 3ft 8in
	11.0m × 3.5m × 1.1m
Machinery:	1 non-magnetic diesel, 160bhp = 10kts. Range 100nm
Complement:	4

Korean War experience showed particularly dramatically how badly the United States needed a shallow-water sweeping capability. In October 1950, 2000 North Korean mines kept a large US fleet out of the otherwise unprotected port of Wonsan for 15 days, with only six sweepers available. There was already a fair amount of shallow-sweeping experience; during the Second World War 36ft LCVPs had been converted for moored sweeps in water less than five fathoms deep, and some were fitted with banks of storage batteries for magnetic sweeping. The Army built four shallow-water minesweeping boats (two at Norfolk and two at Mare Island) in 1945; they came into Navy hands when the Army transferred the mine-planting mission in 1949. The ex-Army craft became *MSB 1–4* and formed the design basis for the *MSB 5* series.

Two new classes of shallow-water craft were designed for assault sweeping; the 57ft MSB and the 36ft MSL, the latter about the size and weight of the LCVPs which were standard for amphibious force Welin davits. The MSB itself grew too heavy for easy handling, partly because plans to use an aluminium hull had to be rejected: eddy currents set up as the boat moved through the earth's magentic field could themselves generate a magnetic field. One unusual feature of the MSB design was an early use of gas turbines for its magnetic sweep generator. Of 50 ordered (MSB 5–54), one (MSC 24) was not built, and MSB 23 was destroyed by fire on 2 February 1955 and a plastic-hulled replacement was delivered in August 1956. MSB 29 was an experimental unit built by John Trumpy & Sons, Annapolis, to see how sea-kindly a small sweeper could be; at 82ft it was far too large for overseas transport, but for some years served as flagship of the MSB squadron based at Charleston, South Carolina.

The 36ft MSL could indeed fit an AKA davit. Early units were of wood, later ones of plastic. With a very limited size, they could be fitted for moored, magnetic, or acoustic sweeping. They had gas turbines for both propulsion and for magnetic sweeping power, and production continued at least into the 1960s. Surviving MSLs reportedly have diesel engines and a plastic hull; they have been stripped of sweeping gear and are employed as utility launches. Total production was 56 during 1946–66: Mk 1 were *MSL 1–4* (1946); Mk 2 were *MSL 5–29* (1948); Mk 3 *MSL 30* (1948); Mk 4 *MSL 31–56* (1966); Mk 5 comprised two Mk 1 and one Mk 2 converted to diesels (1967). The first two Mks were wooden, the rest plastic.

MINE COUNTERMEASURE DEVICES
The threat of pressure mines was so severe that ship-size explosive targets were considered essential. In theory, they would simulate ship signatures, and would survive the subsequent mine explosions. The cylindrical XMAP was described as 'a towed, unmanned minesweeping device for sweeping modern pressure, acoustic and magnetic minefields'; it was to be strong enough to withstand 50 explosions by 2000lb mines in 40 feet of water, which appeared to require the use of 10in steel. Length was about 250, beam 29, and draft 20ft, with a displacement of 3100 tons, and two could be operated either side by side or in tandem. XMAP design concepts were reflected in the powerful towing engines of early postwar minesweeper designs. However, the prototype was disappointing, and the programme was abandoned in about 1955. On 1 January 1955, XMAP-1 was described as 85.3 per cent complete.

The 'guinea-pig' or 'sperrbrecher' was an alternative concept. As first described in 1948, it was to check-sweep sterilized fields of US pressure-magnetic mines or 'in cases of very great emergency, when no other method of pressure sweeping is available, such vessels may be used to attempt to clear a channel of enemy mines in order that more important vessels may pass'. At a minimum, such ships were to be of 5000 gross tons and 10 knots, but larger and faster were considered better. Machinery would be controlled from the bridge, and degaussing coils or an emergency deck would be used to increase her magnetic field so as to explode magnetic mines, hopefully beyond their lethal range. Buoyancy material would be fitted to protect the 'guinea-pig' from sinking in the swept channel; lumber was an example of material which could be extemporised. The 'guinea-pig' was considered very much an emergency device and a last resort, but its development (which continued well into the 1960s) suggests just how difficult mineseeeping had become after 1945.

MSB 17 1966   USN

MSL 32 1968   USN

Washtenaw County as MSS 2 in 1973
USN

Three Liberty hulls were converted to specialised sweepers under the FY53 programme: two at Yokosuka (YAG 36 and 38), and one (*John L Sullivan*, YAG 37) at Norfolk. The two Japanese conversions may well have been 'guinea-pigs' to determine whether the US mining efforts of the Second World War had actually been neutralized; they were sold for scrap in 1960. YAG 37 was powered by four T34 turbo-props mounted on gunmounts on deck, all other machinery having been removed. After explosion tests in Chesapeake Bay in 1957–58 she was broken up.

The 'guinea-pig' concept continued with the MSS (special devices sweeper) originally proposed in the FY60 programme. It was to sweep 'by its own passage' moored, magnetic, acoustic, and pressure mines in depths safely navigable by ships of this size'. The pressure signature of a 20,000t ship was sought; by sweeping at high speed, it was hoped that the MSS would 'insure that vessels larger than the sweeper will be able safely to traverse the channel at speeds lower than that of the sweeper'. The YAG 37 experiments appeared to show that turbo-prop engines above deck would provide propulsion and steering without the threat of underwater damage. There was some hope that the ship's pressure signature could be increased by special pressure generators, and she was to be able to detonate acoustic and magnetic mines as far away as possible. Conversion of the Liberty Ship *Harry L Glucksman* was authorized under the FY56 programme. Her hull was strengthened and her former superstructure replaced by a shock-mounted pilot house forward; propulsion was by four outboard motors rather than by the turbo-props of YAG 37. Completed on 16 June 1969, she was placed in reserve on 15 March 1973; in service, she had a crew of one officer and eight enlisted men. MSS 2 was a much more austere LST conversion carried out to support the clearance of North Vietnamese waters (Operation End Sweep); the major changes were the filling of the tank deck with styrofoam and some shock absorbers. LST 1166 was reclassified as MSS 2 on 9 February 1973, and was used to check-sweep sterilized channels; she was stricken 30 August 1973. Presumably she was a good example of the emergency 'guinea-pig' concept of 1948.

RIVERINE MINESWEEPING DEVICES

The special requirements of the Vietnam War inspired the development of a considerable variety of small craft, only the designations of which remained a few years later: drone minesweepers (MSD), 70t river minesweepers (MSM), and 38t patrol minesweepers (MSR). The MSM were LCM(6) conversions, as were many of the other riverine craft. They retained their bow ramps, and were fitted with bar armour against shaped-charge rockets. Typical armament was 2-20mm (not in all), 1–0.50cal MG, and 2–40mm rocket grenade launchers. They were fitted to sweep contact and acoustic mines. The patrol minesweepers, which replaced the MSM, were ASPB conversions (the ASPB is described under Small Surface Combatants above). Some were equipped with projecting pipe frames, to explode contact mines. Others had 4–3.5in bazookas fitted to their twin 0.50cal MG mounts forward. The MSD were special, being part of the force required to keep the approaches to Saigon clear. Eight of them were introduced in Feb 1969 by Mine Division 113; they drag-swept the Long Tau Shipping Channel, linking Saigon to the South China Sea. In practice they were generally towed by larger sweepers to their operational area, then operated by radio control.

Many of these craft were transferred to the Vietnamese, and in 1982 many were in Vietnamese hands. Transfers included 8 MSD (transferred 1970), 8 MSR, and 8 MSM (transferred 1970).

There were also large-ship conversions employed specifically in Vietnam, the Mine Countermeasures Headquarters Ships (MCS). These were planned as early as 1955, at which time all of the *Terror* class hulls (except for *Terror* herself) were redesignated in the MCS series. They were stricken 1.9.61, but *Catskill* (MCS 1) and *Ozark* (MCS 2) were reinstated (and actually converted) 1.6.64–1.10.65, respectively, under the FY64 and FY63 programme. They were armed with 2–5in/38 (2×1), and operated 20 MSCs and 2 minesweepering helicopters. The tank landing ship *Orleans Parish* was redesignated MCS 6 on 19.1.59, reverting to LST status 1.6.65. The LSD *Epping Forrest*, used as a mine escort tender, became MCS 7 on 30.11.62.

A patrol minesweeper (MSR) with a minesweeping drone (MSD) in the foreground, 1969

USN

Catskill as MCS 1 in 1963   USN

THE COAST GUARD

HAMILTON class *coast guard cutters*

Displacement:	2716t standard; 3050t full load
Dimensions:	350ft wl, 378ft oa × 42ft 9in × 20ft
	106.7m, 115.2m × 13.0m × 6.1m
Machinery:	2-shaft CODOG: 2 FM diesels, 7200bhp, 2 P & W gas turbines, 28,000shp = 29kts. See notes
Armament:	1–5in/38, 2–81mm mortars, 2–0.50cal MG, 6–12.75in Mk 32 ASW TT (2×3), 1 helicopter. See notes
Sensors:	Radar SPS-29; sonar SQS-36 or SQS-38
Complement:	164

No	Name	Builder	Launched	Fate
WHEC 715	HAMILTON	Avondale	18.12.65	Extant 1982
WHEC 716	DALLAS	Avondale	1.10.66	Extant 1982
WHEC 717	MELLON	Avondale	11.2.67	Extant 1982
WHEC 718	CHASE	Avondale	20.5.67	Extant 1982
WHEC 719	BOUTWELL	Avondale	17.6.67	Extant 1982
WHEC 720	SHERMAN	Avondale	23.9.67	Extant 1982
WHEC 721	GALLATIN	Avondale	18.11.67	Extant 1982
WHEC 722	MORGENTHAU	Avondale	10.2.68	Extant 1982
WHEC 723	RUSH	Avondale	16.11.68	Extant 1982
WHEC 724	MUNROE	Avondale	5.12.70	Extant 1982
WHEC 725	JARVIS	Avondale	24.4.71	Extant 1982
WHEC 726	MIDGETT	Avondale	4.9.71	Extant 1982

These large high-endurance cutters were among the first US warships to be powered by gas turbines, Pratt & Whitney FT 4As in a CODOG (Combined Diesel or Gas turbine) system. Such propulsion was specifically justified by the combination of high endurance (14,000nm at 11 knots on diesels) and high maximum speed (29 knots on gas turbines, with a range of 2900nm), the latter to run out to the scene of a rescue. There is also a retractable bow manoeuvring unit, described as useful for some oceanographic work. The unusual twin-funnel arrangement can be traced to the desire to place the helicopter pad at the most favourable point in the ship from the point of view of ship motion, about three-quarters of the way aft. The price paid is the narrowness of the hangar, which can accommodate only one HH-52 turbo-shaft helicopter. In the *Perry* class, a very similar configuration was originally selected (albeit with one rather than two shafts), but the uptakes were amalgamated when the design was altered to accommodate two helicopters: the hangar had to be widened and the helicopter pad consequently moved right aft.

The design originally called for a Hedgehog superfiring over the single 5in/38 gun forward, but Hedgehogs were removed from those ships which had them; all have the standard pair of triple Mk 32 lightweight torpedo tubes controlled by a Mk 309 Panel. The 5in gun is now considered obsolete, and from time to time proposals are made for cutter modernisation, perhaps with an OTO Melara 76mm gun or with the lightweight 5in/54.

RELIANCE class *coast guard cutters*

Displacement:	950t standard; 1007t full load
Dimensions:	210ft 6in oa × 34ft × 10ft 6in
	64.2m × 10.4m × 3.2m
Machinery:	2 shafts, 2 Alco diesels, 5000bhp = 18kts; 5000nm at 13kts (WMEC 620–630, at 14kts). See notes
Armament:	1–3in/50. See notes
Sensors:	Sonar (see notes)
Complement:	61

Class (no, launched):
Todd – *Reliance* (WTR 615, 25.5.63), *Diligence* (WMEC 616, 20.7.63), *Vigilant* (WMEC 617, 24.12.63)
Christy, Sturgeon Bay – *Active* (WMEC 618, 31.7.65)
Coast Guard Yd – *Confidence* (WMEC 619, 8.5.65), *Venturous* (WMEC 625, 11.12.67), *Durable* (WMEC 628, 29.4.67), *Decisive* (WMEC 629, 14.12.67)
American SB – *Resolute* (WMEC 620, 30.4.66)), *Valiant* (WMEC 621, 14.1.67)), *Courageous* (WMEC 622, 18.5.67), *Steadfast* (WMEC 623, 24.6.67), *Dauntless* (WMEC 624, 21.10.67), *Dependable* (WMEC 626, 16.3.68), *Vigorous* (WMEC 627, 4.5.68), *Alert* (WMEC 630, 19.10.68)

These small cutters were designed to operate within about 500 miles of the US coast, with a 15 day endurance. The first five have CODAG Propulsion (two 1000shp gas turbines, plus two 1500bhp diesels). There is no stack, the diesels exhaust right aft. They can tow a 10,000t ship. Although they are too small for a hangar or maintenance facilities, they accommodate a landing pad large enough for the standard Coast Guard HH-52 or HH-3 helicopter. *Alert* was the first US ship fitted with the Canadian 'Beartrap' helicopter system, which provides greatly increased capability in rough water.

From a wartime point of view their armament is extremely limited, only one 3in/50 and two machine-guns; presumably the standard torpedo tubes would be added in wartime. There is no hull sonar in peacetime, but the design makes provision for a wartime installation of SQS-36/38.

Original plans called for the construction of thirty units, but only sixteen were built, all being launched between 1963 and 1968.

BEAR class *coast guard cutters*

Displacement:	1780t full load
Dimensions:	270ft × 38ft × 13ft 6in
	82.3m × 11.6m × 4.1m
Machinery:	2-shaft diesels, 7000bhp = 19.5kts
Armament:	1–3in/62
Sensors:	See notes
Complement:	95

Class (no, launched):
Tacoma Boatbuilding – *Bear* (WMEC 901, 25.9.80), *Tampa* (WMEC 902, 19.3.81), *Harriet Lane* (WMEC 903, 10.1.82), *Northland* (WMEC 904, Mar 82)
Derecktor Corp – *Spencer* (WMEC 905), *Seneca* (WMEC 906), *Escanaba* (WMEC 907), *Tahoma* (WMEC 908), and five others reported to be named *Legare, Argus, Eric, McCulloch* and *Ewing*, for completion up to 1987.

These 270ft medium endurance cutters were originally designed to replace the 'Secretary' class high endurance units, built before the Second World War. They have also been proposed as the basis for a Navy ASW-oriented corvette, which the Carter Administration tentatively designated FFX. That is, they can accommodate a large LAMPS III helicopter and, like the *Hamilton*s, have hangar space. They also have fantail space reserved for a van-mounted towed array, which can obtain contacts which the helicopter(s) can prosecute. Wartime improvements would also, presumably, include the SLQ-32 countermeasures set and the Phalanx CIWS and Harpoon SSMs. There is no peacetime ASW suit, and no hull sonar.

As in the case of the *Reliance* class, very large numbers were planned. However, in 1981 only thirteen had been announced, of which nine have been authorized (two in FY77, two in FY78, two in FY79, three in FY80, of which one was deferred by the Carter Administration).

In contrast to the *Reliance*, they carry the modern Mark 92 fire control system and the OTO Melara 76mm/62 gun, as in the FFGs and PHMs.

UNITED STATES

COAST GUARD PATROL BOATS

During the war in Vietnam, the Coast Guard boats formed part of the Riverine Force, and as such they are included here. There are two series, 82 and 95ft boats. The former were intended to replace a series of Second World War wooden craft. All are steel-hulled, and the 95-footers were fitted with 'Mousetrap' type rocket ASW weapons.

All Coast Guard small craft are numbered in series prefixed by the nominal hull length, *eg* CG 95315 is a 95-footer. The 95ft type was built in three series: A, 95300–95311, B, 95312–95320 in 1955–56, and C, 95321–95335, in 1958–59. Two were transferred to Haiti in 1956, two to Ethiopia in 1958, four to Thailand, one to Saudi Arabia, and nine to South Korea; some were new construction transferred under PGM designations, and indeed the 95-footer formed the basis for a PGM which the United States exported widely (built in 3 series: PGM 39 was a 100ft derivative; PGM 53 was identical to the B type; and the PGM 43 series was an austere variant of the B type). All the survivors received 'Cape' names in 1964. Of the three types, the 'C' type, specially adapted for search and rescue, has less armament, electronics, and displacement.

During the 1970s each carried a pair of 0.50cal machine-guns or a combination machine gun/81mm mortar. These weapons were later removed, and 'Cape' class cutters now have a pair of 40mm grenade launchers (Mk 64). Plans to scrap the 25 surviving units (several having been scrapped) in favour of thirty new WPBs were cancelled and the survivors were modernized in 1977–81 with new engines.

The 82ft cutters were built in four series: A, 82301–82317, built in 1960–61; B, 82318–82331, built in 1961; C, 82332–82370, built in 1962–63 and 1965–67; and D, 82371–82379, built in 1970. In 1965, 26 units were deployed with the Navy in Vietnam, armed with combination 0.50cal machine-gun/81mm mortars, replacing the original 20mm cannon. As a result 17 replacement cutters (plus nine already planned) were added to the programme in FY65 (82345–82350) and FY66 (82351–82370). All 26 in Vietnam were transferred to the Vietnamese Navy in 1969–70. 'Point' names were assigned in January 1964, later units being named as built, and classified as patrol craft rather than as patrol boats. Their high-speed diesels are controlled from the bridge; the heavier D series makes 22.6 rather than 23.7 knots and has reduced endurance (*eg* 1200/8kts as opposed to 1400nm to 1500nm at that speed in earlier craft). WPB 82314 had two gas turbines and controllable pitch propellers, for up to 27kts, but was later refitted with diesels. In all of these craft the original 20mm gun or combination mount had been removed by 1981, and armament reduced to a pair of 40mm grenade launchers (if that). They are described as well equipped for salvage and towing.

FORMER NAVY UNITS

In 1952 the Coast Guard took over twelve former diesel destroyer escorts (see under Fleet Strength 1947 for names and fates), largely for air-sea rescue in the Pacific.

In 1946–48 the Coast Guard took over eighteen former small seaplane tenders (WAVP 370–383 on loan and 384–387 on permanent transfer). They served as cutters into the 1970s: WAVP 370, *Casco*, 371 *Mackinac*, 372 *Humboldt*, 373 *Matagorda*, 374 *Absecon*, 375 *Chincoteague*, 376 *Coos Bay*, 377 *Rockaway*, 378 *Half Moon*, 379 *Unimak*, 380 *Yakutat*, 381 *Barataria*, 382 *Bering Strait*, 383 *Castle Rock*, 384 *Cook Inlet*, 385 *Dexter* (ex-*Biscayne*), 386 *McCulloch* (ex-*Wachappreague*), 387 *Gresham* (ex-*Willoughby*). Former Navy designations: AVP 12, 13, 21–25, 29, 26, 31–36, 11, 56, 57. *Dexter* was a former command ship (AGC 18), and *McCulloch* and *Gresham* were former MTB tenders (AGP 8 and AGP 9). In Coast Guard service these ships were armed with a single 5in/38 and two twin 40mm (one quadruple in 374, none in 385). Two twin 20mm were removed in 1957. ASW armament consisted of a Hedgehog (Mk 10) and four DC projectors. Triple 12.75in ASW torpedo tubes were fitted in the mid-1960s. They were used initially as weather ships, with a balloon hangar and launching deck aft. *Dexter* was fitted with four new FM diesels 1957, recommissioned Jul 1958 as West Coast Training ship, 1966. *Rockaway* was adapted as oceanographic ship, 1966. *Unimak* was adapted as East Coast training ship, 1966. She was redesignated as a training cutter (WTR) in 1969, serving as such until her decommissioning in 1975, and was recommissioned as a High Endurance Cutter (WHEC) to enforce the 200m offshore resource zone in 1977, the last of her class. *Gresham*, modified for ocean-station weather work, ultimately had her single 5in/38 removed. All were redesignated High Endurance Cutters (WHEC) in 1966. WHEC 376 returned to Navy 1967 and sunk as target; 371, 373, 385 returned 1968 and sunk as targets; 370 returned 1969 and sunk as target. WHEC 372 and 381 were stricken in 1970. WHEC 380 and 382 were transferred to South Vietnam 1.1.71, 383 and 394 on 21.12.71, and 374, 385 and 386 on 21.6.72. New names: *Pham Ngu Lao* (374), *Ly Thuong Kiet* (375), *Tran Nhat Quat* (380), *Tran Quang Khai* (383), *Tran Binh Trong* (383), *Tran Quoc Toan* (384), and *Ngo Kuyen* (386). In Vietnamese service, all ASW equipment was removed, and 2–81mm mortars replaced the former 40mm battery. Of these ships, the former WHEC 375, 382, 283 and 386 succeeded in fleeing to the Philippines in 1976, upon the fall of South Vietnam. They became the Philippine *Andres Bonifacio*, *Diego Silang*, *Francisco Dagohoy* and *Gregorio de Pillar*.

Mellon as completed   US Coast Guard

Bear as completed   US Coast Guard

Reliance 16.6.71   US Coast Guard

Cape Carter, one of the first series of 95ft patrol boats   US Coast Guard

West Germany

THE FIRST DECADE: 1945 to 1955

The unconditional surrender of Germany in 1945 brought to an end the history of the *Kriegsmarine*. Disposal of the surviving naval units posed a delicate problem. Stalin wanted one-third because the Soviet Union's naval forces were ill-equipped; the US was not interested in acquiring German fighting units, while Britain's chief interest lay with the U-boats which she wished to study and then destroy. Under the final terms of the contentious Potsdam Conference signed on 1 August 1945, the Soviet Union received one-third of all surviving warships; the remainder were distributed among the other Allied nations. The US and Great Britain proposed that all German merchant shipping be placed under the control of the Combined Shipping and Adjustment Board and The United Maritime Authority until the end of the war with Japan. A further US proposal was that all riverine and coastal vessels remain German property to assist in industrial regeneration. The USA feared that in the event of a complete breakdown of German postwar industry she would end up effectively paying war reparations to the Soviet Union indirectly via her Marshall Aid Plan.

Meanwhile there remained the problem of clearing the extensive minefields. The Berlin Declaration of June 1945 charged Germany with this task. In July the German Mine Sweeping Administration (GMSA) was formed; a force of 755 vessels, including 440 ex-*Kriegsmarine* minesweepers, manned by 16,000 German seamen under British command, which swept a total of 581,000 mines, 126,000 of which were German. By December 1947 the GMSA had been disbanded and replaced by the Minesweeping Unit of the Customs Inspection, Cuxhaven. This subordinate arm of the British Frontier Inspection Service (FIS) was supervised by the RN in the last of the mine clearance and was disbanded in June 1951.

In March 1951 the German Frontier Inspection Authority was created, and this included a naval frontier inspection unit which at first deployed vessels of the former minesweeping force, and included four patrol boats, three fast boats, ten war-built fishing vessels, one sailing boat, one tanker, one tug, two tenders and other small craft. The formation of this unit coincided with the establishment of the new Federal German Republic.

In July 1951 the US Navy helped to establish the Labour Service Unit (LSU) which had two sub-units: LSU(C) consisting of small boats of the Rhine and Weser River Patrols, and LSU(B) consisting of ex-GMSA and ex-Customs, Cuxhaven minesweepers plus other vessels. The total was six 1940 and 1943 type German minesweepers, 26 *R-Boote* (fast motor minesweepers), two tenders, three *S-Boote*, one submarine-chaser, three air-sea rescue boats, one salvage barge, one tanker, two accommodation ships and six patrol craft. LSU(C) consisted of 22 LCMs and 4 LCTs.

THE BIRTH OF THE FEDERAL GERMAN REPUBLIC

As early as 1946 the Germans had been allowed their own government; regional parliaments and local governments had been elected, and in January 1947 the US and British occupation zones had become linked economically. The Marshall Aid Plan provided the first funds for the re-establishment of the new Republic. In September 1948 a parliamentary council had been appointed to work out the constitution of a future Germany. In April 1949 the occupation zones of the three Western Allies, the United States, Great Britain and France, were linked economically and all three accepted the new constitution which came into force on 23 May 1949.

On 14 August 1949 the first German *Bundestag* (Parliament) was elected and in September Konrad Adenauer became the first Federal Chancellor of the German Federal Republic.

FIRST STEPS TO GERMAN REARMAMENT

As early as 1949 the first talks had been held between the High Commissioners and the Federal German Government concerning a German role in Western defence policy, in the light of the worsening international situation between the Soviet Union and her former allies. Steps towards this development had been the so-called 'Dunkirk Pact' of 1945 between Great Britain and France, which was followed in 1948 by the 'Brussels Contract', when The Netherlands, Belgium and Luxemburg joined together to form the 'Western European Union' under the stimulus of the Communist Party's seizing control of Czechoslovakia. The Communist blockade of Berlin in 1948–49 and the Communist rise to power in China led to the foundation of NATO.

With the advent of the Korean War, Sir Winston Churchill proposed the building of a 'European Defence Community' with German participation. The possibilities and consequences were examined by the so-called '*Amt Blank*' (literally, Blank Office, after the name of its chief) and it was decided that the basic prerequisites for such participation were changes to the Occupation Statute, a legal declaration that the World War was officially over, and an end to the dismantling of German industry. On 26 May 1952 the German Contract was signed and on the 27th, the Contract of the Western European Defence Union. The latter was rejected by the French National Assembly in 1952, but British initiatives brought about the signing of the Paris Contract in October 1954, so that on 5 May 1955 – ten years after the capitulation – Germany became a member of NATO and was now independent in all questions of internal and foreign politics.

THE NEW FEDERAL GERMAN NAVY

On 7 June 1955 the former '*Amt Blank*' became the new Federal Defence Ministry. Its first order dated 1 January 1956, initiated the so-called 'Programme 6000', consisting of a naval instruction division, with four officers, 24 NCOs and 140 ratings. In July 1956 the Frontier Inspection Authority was disbanded and all its vessels and some personnel were transferred to the new Navy which now numbered four patrol boats, two fast motor boats, ten coast guard boats, two tenders, one tanker, one tug, six MMS type boats and one training boat. LSU(B) and LSU(C) were also disbanded and their vessels with many crews were handed over: six minesweepers, 26 *R-Boote*, one submarine-chaser, nine patrol boats, three tugs, one accommodation ship, one tanker, one salvage barge, two tenders and other small craft.

To meet the first urgent requirements of the new Navy, many ships were purchased or taken on lease from abroad, and some war reparations ships were returned to Germany. These included six ex-British frigates, six Lease-Lend US destroyers, four purchased LSMs, two LSMRs, one LSD, seven LSTs and a number of minor vessels. In addition, five former 1935 type minesweepers were purchased from France.

In 1950 the Navy envisaged its requirements as: 12 torpedo-boats, 36 MTBs, 24 submarines, 12 escorts, 36 LSIs, 36 minehunters, 12 submarine-chasers, 36 patrol boats, 24 minesweepers, 114 naval aircraft.

PROPOSED GERMAN NAVAL BUILD-UP PRIOR TO GERMANY'S JOINING NATO

Type	Autumn 51	EDC plan*	Oct 54	Sep 55	End 1955
Mining vessels	3	2	2	2	2
Destroyers	12	–	12	12	18
Submarine-chasers	12 ⎫	18	18	6	– ⎫
Escorts	12 ⎭				10 ⎭
MTBs	36	60	36	40	40
Submarines (coastal)	24	–	12	12	12
Landing craft	36	36	30	12	–
Minesweepers (coastal)	24	24	16	24	54
Minesweepers (fast)	36	36	36	30	
Patrol vessels	36	10	10	10	–
Naval aircraft	204	54	54	58	58
Personnel	?	?	?	35,000	?

*plan of the European Defence Community
? no figure available

This first intake of ships was a hotch-potch of types and all the vessels were so outdated that they could never have been made fit for active service, but they did fulfil the vital training role. In 1955 the first naval building programme was defined and was sanctioned by the *Bundestag* in May 1956. The second programme was sanctioned in 1958 and the third programme, of 1960, was sanctioned in 1960–61. It envisaged the strength of the Federal German Navy as: 12 destroyers, 6 escorts (frigates), 40 MTBs, 12 submarines, 52 minesweepers, 2 training ships, 12 landing craft, 10 patrol boats, 120 auxiliaries, 58 naval aircraft.

In 1965 the *Bundestag* fixed the final strength of the Navy as: 6 destroyers (Type 119), 4 destroyers (Type 101), 6 frigates (Type 120), 50 MTBs (Types 140, 141 and 142; 40 built), 30 submarines (Types 201 and 205; 12 built), 20 patrol boats (Types 360, 361 and 362), 24 coastal minesweepers (Types 320 and 321), 30 fast minesweepers (Types 340 and 341), 13 tenders (Types 401, 402 and 403), 20 inshore/riverine minesweepers (Type 390; only 1 built), 6 landing craft (Type 502; none built), 12 tankers, 12 supply ships, 8 transports, 20 tugs and numerous small craft for trials and training, plus 2 large training ships. This was later increased by: 3 destroyers (Type 103), 20 MTBs (Type 148, replacing Type 140), 10 MTBs (Type 143, replacing Type 141).

By 31 August 1982 the Federal German Navy numbered 193 fighting ships, 80 auxiliaries, 162 naval aircraft and 38,000 personnel.

INTEGRATION WITH NATO

The Federal German Navy is now fully integrated with NATO's naval forces, her ships being able to fulfil all their duties within the NATO mandate. The *Hamburg* class destroyers and *Köln* class frigates, together with the new generation of *Bremen* class frigates, serve in turn with the Standing Naval Forces Atlantic (STANAVFORLANT). The *Lindau* class minesweepers/minehunters serve with the Standing Naval Forces Channel (STANAVFORCHAN). In addition, the Navy's ships take part in all bi- and multi-national NATO manoeuvres in order to maintain a standardised training level. The function of the Federal German Navy is to protect the frontiers of the Republic, and to defend the Baltic and North Sea entrances, in cooperation with NATO's naval, ground and air forces. Based on the doctrine of 'forward defence', the Navy's main operations theatre is the Baltic and the North Sea.

PROPULSION AND WEAPONS

With the exception of three older types of destroyer with steam propulsion, the Navy has followed the example of the *Kriegsmarine* and used diesel propulsion with CP propellers for all major units. The hulls of submarines and minesweepers are of non-magnetic materials.

Weapons are NATO standard, except in the older units which retain their original armament. The 100mm/55 and the 40mm/70 guns are to be found in almost all the NATO navies, as is the new 76mm/62 OTO Melara gun. All missiles except the French MM38 Exocet are of US Origin. All ships down to minesweepers can carry mines: in the major units minerails are fixed on deck; in the smaller ships part of the mine deck equipment is removable.

GERMAN SHIPYARDS

At the end of the war Germany's shipbuilding industry had been virtually destroyed and any remaining machinery was dismantled. The first objective was the rebuilding of the mercantile fleet. All warship construction was strictly prohibited; naval yards did not exist and it was, and is, not intended to re-start them. Today the German shipbuilding industry has a high international reputation, and domestic and foreign warship construction is a valuable part of it. Lürssenwerft has more than 100 years experience in the building of small fighting boats, and concentrates mainly on MTBs. As early as 1953–54 the yard received special permission to build *Plejad* class fast MTBs for the Swedish Navy. Apart from the German Navy's *Jaguar* type MTBs, the yard has produced more than fifty fast fighting craft for foreign navies, including improved *Jaguar* types and entirely new designs. Lürssen designs are built under licence in many countries.

During the 1950s Abeking & Rasmussen built a number of R-boat types for Indonesia and are building a similar type for Brazil, in addition to the *Schütze* type minesweepers. Their most recent design is the SAR 33 type, a hard-chine planing boat, to be built in large numbers under licence in Turkey.

Blohn & Voss entered the field of warship export with the MEKO 360 type frigates for Nigeria and the Argentine Republic. Argentina is now building the Blohm MEKO 140 A 16 type frigate under licence.

Howaldtswerke/Deutsche Werke, Kiel built the FS 1500 corvette, but are primarily engaged in building submarines. Under the manage-

Schleswig-Holstein Sept 1975

USN

D 182

ment of Professor Gabler, Ingenieurkontor Lübeck (IKL) designed the successful types built by Howaldtswerke and Nordseewerke, Emden (now Thyssen-Nordseewerke). Norway has ordered 15 Type 207, and Denmark has built 2 Type 205 under licence. More than 35 Type 209s have been built to foreign orders. After the lifting of the displacement limits on 21 July 1980, larger submarines have been built, such as the SSK Type 1500 for India and the Types TR 1700 and 1400 for Argentina.

A large number of small yards are building small patrol vessels to foreign orders.

MAJOR SURFACE SHIPS

During 1958–60 these six US *Fletcher* class destroyer were transferred under MDAP for a lease period of 5 years; they received no German names. Before being handed over they were modernised with new weapons, new electronics and additional German command systems. During later refits the bridge structure was altered.

In 1974 *Zerstörer 4* carried for trials purposes a containerised 76mm/62 OTO Melara gun. From 1973 the quintuple TT were removed from all ships.

Zerstörer 6 was sold for scrap and *Zerstörer 1* was sunk in the Mediterranean as a torpedo target. In 1976 the remaining ships were purchased by the Federal German Navy and handed over to the Greek Navy in 1981–82 as part of the military aid programme (see Greece).

Ex-US FLETCHER class *destroyers*

Armament:	4–5in/38 Mk XII (4×1), 6–3in/50 Mk XXII (3×2), 5–533mm (21in) TT (1×5), 2–533mm ASW TT (2×1), 2 Hedgehog
Sensors:	Radar SPS-6, SPS-10, Mk 25, Mk 36, Mk 35; sonar SQS-29
Other particulars:	As US *Fletcher* class

No	Name	Builder	Acquired	Fate
D 170	ZERSTORER 1 (ex-*Anthony*)	Bath Iron Wks	17.1.58	Sunk as target 16.5.79
D 171	ZERSTORER 2 (ex-*Ringold*)	Federal, Kearny	14.7.59	To Greece Sept 81
D 172	ZERSTORER 3 (ex-*Wadsworth*)	Bath Iron Wks	6.10.59	To Greece Oct 80
D 178	ZERSTORER 4 (ex-*Claxton*)	Federal, Kearny	15.12.59	To Greece Feb 81
D 179	ZERSTORER 5 (ex-*Dyson*)	Consolidated, Orange	23.2.60	To Greece Feb 82
D 180	ZERSTORER 6 (ex-*Charles Ausburne*)	Consolidated, Orange	12.4.60	Sold for BU Oct 68

Hamburg 1979

Originally the German Navy wanted 12 Type 101 destroyers and, in fact, ordered them in August 1957, but it transpired that they could not be built on the planned displacement of 2500t. So the Western European Union by a *post facto* decision raised the displacement to 6000t.

All four ships were modernised 1974–77: the boilers were modified to burn light oil, and the lattice mainmast was removed. The 'X' position 100mm was replaced by two MM38 Exocet twin launchers. In 1978 all ships received a closed bridge. During subsequent refits the superstructure and funnel caps were modified and the electronics were updated. The five TTs were replaced by 4 short ASW TTs. The data Table refers to the ships' 1982 state.

HAMBURG class *destroyers*

Displacement:	3340t standard; 4330t full load
Dimensions:	420ft wl, 438ft 9in oa × 44ft × 17ft 128m, 133.7m × 13.4m × 5.2m
Machinery:	2-shaft Wahodag turbines, 4 Wahodag boilers, 72,000shp (52,992kW) = 36kts. Oil 800t. Range 6000nm at 13kts
Armament:	3–100mm/55 (3×1), 4 MM38 Exocet SSM (2×2), 8–40mm/70 (4×2), 4–533mm ASW TT (4×1), 2–375mm ASW mortars (2×4)
Sensors:	Radar KH 14/9, DA-08, LW-04, SGR-103, M-45; sonar ELAC 1BV
Complement:	284

No	Name	Builder	Laid down	Launched	Comp	Fate
D 181	HAMBURG	Stülcken, Hamburg	29.1.59	26.3.60	23.3.64	Extant 1982
D 182	SCHLESWIG-HOLSTEIN	Stülcken, Hamburg	20.8.59	20.8.60	12.10.64	Extant 1982
D 183	BAYERN	Stülcken, Hamburg	14.9.60	14.8.62	6.7.65	Extant 1982
D 184	HESSEN	Stülcken, Hamburg	15.2.61	4.5.63	8.10.68	Extant 1982

Lütjens as completed   Navarret Collection

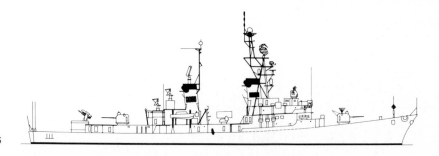

Lütjens 1975

These Type 103 destroyers are based on the USN family of 'Tartar guided-missile destroyers SCB 155' (*Charles F Adams* class Mod 14 – *Goldsborough*, DDG 20 and following vessels). They stemmed from a US/German agreement of 11.5.64; the USN ordered them 1.4.65 as DDG 28–DDG 30.

They differ from the original *Charles F Adams* class in having modified funnels with side exhausts, and different masts. Originally it was intended to build six ships in German shipyards, but three were ordered from Bath Iron Works, USA. At the end of the 1970s their boilers were modified to burn light oil; at the beginning of the 1980s their weapons and electronics were updated. See US section, *Charles F Adams* class.

LUTJENS class (US CHARLES F ADAMS type) *guided missile destroyers*

Displacement:	3370t standard; 4717t full load
Dimensions:	420ft 4in wl, 441ft 3in oa × 47ft 3in × 14ft 9in
	128.1m, 134.4m × 14.4m × 4.5m
Machinery:	2-shaft General Electric turbines, 4 boilers type D-V2M, 70,000shp (51,520kW) = 36kts. Oil 930t. Range 4500nm at 20kts
Armament:	1 Tartar Mk 13 (40 SM-1MR SAM and Harpoon SSM missiles), 2–5in/54 Mk XVI (US Mk 42; 2×1), 1 ASROC ASW (1×8), 6–324mm Mk 32 ASW TT
Sensors:	Radar SPS-40, SPS-10, SPS-52, KH 14/9, SPG-51C, SPG-53; sonar SQS-23
Complement:	333

No	Name	Builder	Laid down	Launched	Comp	Fate
D 185	LUTJENS	Bath Iron Wks	1.3.66	11.8.67	22.3.69	Extant 1982
D 186	MOLDERS	Bath Iron Wks	12.4.66	13.4.68	20.9.69	Extant 1982
D 187	ROMMEL	Bath Iron Wks	22.8.67	1.2.69	2.5.70	Extant 1982

These seven frigates belonged to the Royal Navy's *Black Swan*, modified *Black Swan* and 'Hunt' Types 2 and 3 classes, and all had seen service during the Second World War. They were purchased in 1957, renamed and designated Type 138. They were modernised in British yards and all except *Scheer* had their original armament when transferred. *Scharnhorst* and *Gneisenau* were later rebuilt: their bridges, masts and funnels were changed and they received NATO standardised weapons. During a refit *Scheer* received additional radar, and the armament of *Raule* and *Brommy* were changed; only *Raule* received an ASW component.

During their entire service with the German Navy they served as training ships: *Gneisenau* and *Scharnhorst* for gunnery, *Raule* and *Brommy* for underwater weapons, *Scheer* for radar, and *Hipper* and *Graf Spee* for cadet training. Towards the end of their active lives it was envisaged that *Hipper* and *Graf Spee* be converted to air–sea rescue/pilot vessels, but this was dropped because of the cost. All were sold for scrap except *Scharnhorst* which is serving as a training hulk for damage control. The acquisition dates relate to their commissioning in the German Navy.

Ex-British HUNT class *frigates*

Displacement:	1050t standard; 1610t full load (*Gneisenau*)
	1087t standard; 1490t full load (*Raule, Brommy*)
Dimensions:	272ft pp, 264ft 3in wl, 282ft 9in oa × 31ft 6in × 12ft 6in (*Gneisenau*)
	83.0m, 80.6m, 86.1m × 9.6m × 3.8m
	272ft wl, 281ft 6in oa × 31ft 6in × 10ft 3in (*Raule, Brommy*)
	83.0m, 85.9m × 9.6m × 3.1m
Machinery:	2-shaft Parsons turbines, 2 Admiralty boilers, 19,000shp (13,984kW) = 27kts. Oil 280t. Range 2000nm at 12kts (*Gneisenau*)
Armament:	6–4in/45 (3×2), 6–2pdr (1×4, 2×2); after conversion 1–100mm/55, 3–40mm/70 (1×2, 2×1) (*Gneisenau*)
	4–4in/45 (2×2), 5–2pdr (1×4, 1×1), 2–533mm TT, 2 Hedgehog; after conversion 1–40mm/70, 14–375mm ASW mortar (1×4), 2–533mm ASW TT (2×1) (*Raule, Brommy*)
Complement:	83 (*Gneisenau*), 170 (*Raule, Brommy*)

No	Name	Builder	Acquired	Fate
F 212	GNEISENAU (ex-*Oakley*)	Yarrow	18.10.58	Sold for BU 12.1.77
F 217	RAULE (ex-*Albrighton*)	John Brown	14.5.59	BU 1971
F 218	BROMMY (ex-*Eggesford*)	White	14.5.59	BU 1979

Ex-British BLACK SWAN class *frigates*

Displacement:	1470t (1580t *Scheer*) standard; 1925t full load
Dimensions:	283ft 3in wl, 299ft 9in oa × 40ft × 11ft 6in
	86.4m, 91.3m × 12.2m × 3.5m (Scharnhorst, Hipper)
	283ft 3in wl, 299ft 9in oa × 37ft 6in × 11ft
	86.4m, 91.3m × 11.4m × 3.4m (Graf Spee)
	322ft 4in oa × 41ft × 11ft 2in
	98.2m × 12.4m × 3.4m (Scheer)
Machinery:	2-shaft General Motors/Parsons turbines, 2 Admiralty (Foster Wheeler *Scharnhorst*) boilers, 4200shp (3091kW) = 18.2kts. Oil 440t, later 341t (*Scharnhorst*), 453t (*Hipper*), 460t (*Graf Spee*), 387t (*Scheer*). Range 3200nm (2783nm *Scheer*) at 12kts
Armament:	6–4in/45 (3×2), 12–20mm (6×2); after conversion 2–100/55 (2×1), 4–40mm/70 (2×1, 1×2) (*Scharnhorst*)
	6–40mm/70 (2×2, 2×1) (4–40mm/70 (2×2 *Scheer*), 2 Hedgehog (*Hipper, Graf Spee*)
Complement:	147 (*Scharnhorst*), 147 + 40 (*Hipper, Graf Spee*), 60 (*Scheer*)

No	Name	Builder	Acquired	Fate
F 213	SCHARNHORST (ex-*Mermaid*)	Denny	28.5.59	HS 1974
F 214	HIPPER (ex-*Actaeon*)	Thornycroft	10.1.59	BU 1967
F 215	GRAF SPEE (ex-*Flamingo*)	Yarrow	21.2.59	BU 1967
F 216	SCHEER (ex-*Hart*)	Stephen	21.5.59	BU 1971

Scheer as TS — Author   *Gneisenau* as gunnery TS — Author

Emden as completed

These Type 120 frigates were ordered in March 1957 having been designed in 1955–57 as 'Geleitboot 55' (Escort 55). They were the first German warships to receive CODAG propulsion. During numerous refits they received increased hull protection and stability, and updated electronics. The original two 533mm TT were subsequently replaced by four tubes for short 533mm ASW torpedoes. *Köln*, *Emden* and *Karlsruhe* are to be replaced within the next two years by Type 122 frigates of the same name.

KOLN class *frigates*

Displacement:	2090t standard; 2750t full load
Dimensions:	344ft 6in wl, 360ft 4in oa × 36ft 1in × 15ft 1in
	105.0m, 109.8m × 11.0m × 4.6m
Machinery:	2-shaft (CP propellers) CODAG: 4 MAN diesels, plus 2 Brown Boveri gas turbines, 12,000bhp + 24,000shp = 32kts. Oil 360t. Range 3450nm at 12kts
Armament:	2–100mm/55 (2×1), 6–40mm/70 (2×2, 2×1), 4–533mm ASW TT (4×1), 2–375mm ASW mortars (2×4)
Sensors:	Radar DA-02, SGR-103, KH 14/9, M44, M45; sonar PAE/CWE hull-mounted M/F set
Complement:	238

No	Name	Builder	Laid down	Launched	Comp	Fate
F 220	KOLN	Stülcken, Hamburg	21.12.57	6.12.58	15.4.61	For disposal 14.7.82
F 221	EMDEN	Stülcken, Hamburg	15.4.58	21.3.59	24.10.61	Extant 1982
F 222	AUGSBURG	Stülcken, Hamburg	29.10.58	15.8.59	7.4.62	Extant 1982
F 223	KARLSRUHE	Stülcken, Hamburg	15.12.58	24.10.59	15.12.62	Extant 1982
F 224	LUBECK	Stülcken, Hamburg	28.10.59	23.7.60	6.7.63	Extant 1982
F 225	BRAUNSCHWEIG	Stülcken, Hamburg	28.7.60	3.2.62	16.6.64	Extant 1982

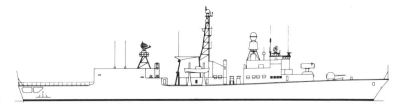

Bremen as completed

Preparatory work on the design of new fighting ships began with the institution of the new Navy in 1955–56, but until the 1960s all design was based on the knowledge and experience of wartime officers and civil servants who had re-enlisted. The German shipbuilding industry was faced with the problem of closing a ten-year gap in design experience. The design of the *Hamburg* and *Köln* classes was commendable given the short space of time in which it was produced, but like other contemporary designs they suffered from the WEU's displacement limit, which resulted in too many components for the displacement. This is why all the units of the first shipbuilding programme look so voluminous and have such high superstructures.

The role of Types 101 and 120 were very clearly defined: escorting convoys against submarines and aircraft, repelling of surface attack plus minelaying ability. At this time the submarine, the chief opponent, was diesel-powered, and the aircraft menace was represented by fighter-bombers. The weaponry of this first

BREMEN class *frigates*

Displacement:	3700t standard; 3800t full load
Dimensions:	399ft 7in wl, 420ft oa × 47ft 10in × 19ft 9in
	121.8m, 128.0m × 14.6m × 6.0m
Machinery:	2-shaft (CP propellers) CODOG: 2 GE LM 2500 gas turbines, 50,000shp (36,800kW) = 30kts, plus 2 MTU diesels, 10,400bhp (7654kW) = 18kts. Range 4000nm at 18kts
Armament:	1–76mm/62, 8 Harpoon SSM (2×4), 1 Sea Sparrow SAM (1×8), 4 Mk 32 ASW TT (2×2), 2 helicopters
Sensors:	Radar 3RM-20, LW-08, WM-25, HSA STIR; sonar SQS-21B(Z)
Complement:	189

No	Name	Builder	Laid down	Launched	Comp	Fate
F 207	BREMEN	Bremer Vulkan	9.7.79	27.9.79	7.5.82	Extant 1982
F 208	NIEDERSACHSEN	A G Weser	9.11.79	9.6.80	15.10.82	Extant 1982
F 209	RHEINLAND-PFALZ	Blohm & Voss	25.9.79	3.10.80		Building
F 210	EMDEN	Thyssen-Nordseewerke	23.6.79	17.12.80		Building
F 211	KOLN	Blohm & Voss	16.6.80	27.5.81		Building
F 212	KARLSRUHE	Howaldtswerke, Kiel	10.3.81	8.1.82		Building

generation of German surface combatants clearly matched requirements: panoramic aircraft-warning radars plus gun-directors for quick reaction. The 100mm turrets plus the 40mm produced the necessary gun component. The destroyer's propulsion consisted of conventional steam turbines, the frigates had diesels plus

gas turbines for dash speed. But the tremendous development in engineering technology, nuclear propulsion, new weapons and electronic guidance systems, made conventional warships of this first generation quickly obsolete.

During the 1960s preliminary studies for a follow-up type were pro-

duced. The first design was for an AA corvette of 1200t displacement, ten of which were envisaged. But the increasing submarine menace necessitated an ASW component which forced the displacement up to 2500t. Because of the restricted defence budget of the Federal German Republic at this time, the project was drop-

WEST GERMANY

ped and in place of the new AA/ASW corvettes both the *Lütjens* class destroyers and the ten boats of the *Zobel* class were modernised.

The next design stage was the 'Frigate 70' which was to have incorporated all the required components. Although the budgetary board had accepted on 23.1.69 and the defence board of the Bundestag had accepted this Type on 8.2.69, the orders were cancelled because the design stage had not been completed and the displacement had risen to 3600t while the building costs had soared.

So design studies started again from scratch by comparing various foreign frigate designs of which the Netherlands' 'Standard' frigate of the *Kortenaer* class turned out to be optimal. On 17.7.75, a 'Memorandum of Understanding' with the Netherlands was signed, followed by acceptance by the German Defence Board on 28.1.76.

On 26.11.77 six units were ordered, designated the Type 122. The general project responsibility lies with the Bremer Vulkan shipyard, the other units to be built by Blohm & Voss, Thyssen-Nordseewerke, AG Weser and HDW, Kiel. The final fitting out will be the job of Bremer Vulkan. The NATO Sea Sparrow system employs a Mk 21 launcher; 24 missiles are carried. The helicopters are WG–13 Lynx with DAQS–13D dipping sonar

Karlsruhe Nov 1979   C & S Taylor

and the Canadian Bear Trap system is fitted to the helicopter deck. The US RAM (Rolling Airframe Missile) point defence SAM is to be fitted atop the hangar in two 24-round launchers, when the system becomes operational. The urgent request to order six more units of this type, two of which were considered as extremely urgent, was dropped by the government. The six new frigates are to replace the Type 119 destroyers (*Fletchers*) and three units of the *Köln* class. Although the fighting potential of the Navy's surface combatants has risen, the number of destroyers and frigates decreases.

Bremen May 1982   Author

SUBMARINES

HAI class (ex-Type XXIII) *coastal submarines*

Displacement:	233.9t surfaced; 275t submerged
Dimensions:	118ft 6in oa × 9ft 9in × 12ft 3in
	36.1m ×3.0m × 3.7m
Machinery:	1-shaft diesel-electric: 1 Mercedes Benz diesel, plus 1 electric motor, 635shp (467kW) = 9.7kts/12.5kts. Oil 18t. Range 1350nm at 9kts surfaced
Complement:	17

No	Name	Builder	Acquired	Fate
S 170	HAI (ex-*U 2365*)	Deutsche Werft, Hamburg	15.8.57	Foundered 14.9.66
S 171	HECHT (ex-*U 2367*)	Deutsche Werft, Hamburg	1.10.57	BU 1969

Belonging to the Type 240, these boats were former *Kriegsmarine* submarines of the coastal Type XXIII. *U 2365* was commissioned on 2.3.45 and lost 8.5.45 after a bomb hit, while *U 2367* was commissioned 17.3.45 and sank after a collision on 5.5.45. In 1956 they were raised and recommissioned as *UW 20 Hai* and *UW 21 Hecht*. They were used as training boats, for the weapons school. Both received numerous modifications and subsequently received equipment envisaged for the new Type 201. They were enlarged, with a new conning tower and the old MWM diesels were replaced by Mercedes Benz. From now on they had – like the follow-up types – pure electric propulsion; the diesels were used solely for charging the batteries, the propellers were driven by electric motors only. *Hai* was lost during a storm in 1966.

Hai before 1960   Author

WILHELM BAUER (ex-Type XXI) *experimental submarine*

Displacement:	1620t surfaced; 1820t submerged
Dimensions:	247ft 5in wl, 251ft 6in oa × 21ft 7in × 22ft 6in
	75.4m, 76.7m × 6.6m × 6.8m
Machinery:	As Type 206. Range 11,000nm/490nm at 12kts/3kts submerged
Armament:	4–533mm TT
Complement:	57

This was the former *U 2540* of the *Kriegsmarine* built by Blohm & Voss: launched 13.1.45, commissioned 24.2.45 and lost near the Flensburg lightship on 3.5.45 after bomb hits. Raised 3.11.58, she was commissioned 1.9.60 after a total refit as *Wilhelm Bauer* (Y 888). Incorporated as the only Type 241 boat, she served for experimental purposes only, first with a naval crew, after her rebuilding at Blohm & Voss, and then with a civilian crew acting for the Trials Command 71 of the *Bundeswehr*. The data in the above Table relates to the submarine in her final guise, with a trials version of the Type 206 propulsion unit. She was never considered an operational unit and was decommissioned on 15.3.82.

Type 201 *coastal submarines*

Displacement:	395t surfaced; 433t submerged
Dimensions:	139ft wl, 142ft 9in oa × 15ft × 13ft
	42.4m, 43.5m × 4.6m × 4.0m
Machinery:	1-shaft electric drive: 2 Mercedes Benz diesels, plus 1 electric motor, 1200bhp/1500shp = 10kts/17.5kts. Range 3800nm at 10kts
Armament:	8–533mm TT (bow)
Complement:	21

No	Name	Builder	Launched	Fate
S 180	U 1 (i)	Howaldtswerke, Kiel	21.10.61	BU 1971
S 181	U 2 (i)	Howaldtswerke, Kiel	25.1.62	BU 1971 (?)
S 182	U 3	Howaldtswerke, Kiel	7.5.62	BU 1971

Friedrich Schürer on trials

Author

Originally consisting of 12 boats, this class of coastal submarines belonged to the Type 201 and was first designed as '*U-Boot 55*' by Ingenieurkontor Lübeck (IKL). The boats were to be section-built and were ordered in March 1959. In November 1958 it was decided that the hulls should be non-magnetic, but the material used quickly showed corrosive defects. In June 1962 *U 1* showed the first signs of structural weakness which quickly increased so that *U 1* and *U 2* had to be decommissioned. Later they were entirely rebuilt (see Type 205).

U 3 was first commissioned for the Royal Norwegian Navy as a training boat, as Norway wanted to have 15 boats of this type. Norway's coastal waters had no corrosive effect on the hull. In June 1964 the boat was handed back to Germany and was commissioned as a training boat. At the end of her service career she was used for shock-testing trials and scrapped in 1971. For test purposes *U 1* for a short time shipped an above-surface stern torpedo tube.

Type 202 *coastal submarines*

Displacement:	100t surfaced; 137t submerged
Dimensions:	72ft 3in wl, 75ft 9in oa × 11ft 3in × 9ft
	22.0m, 23.1m × 3.4m × 2.7m
Machinery:	1-shaft electric drive: 1 Mercedes Benz diesel, 330bhp (243kW) = 6kts/13kts. Range 400nm at 4kts dived
Armament:	2–533mm TT (bow)
Complement:	6

No	Name	Builder	Launched	Fate
S 172	HANS TECHEL	Atlaswerke, Bremen	15.3.65	BU after 1970
S 173	FRIEDRICH SCHURER	Atlaswerke, Bremen	10.11.65	BU after 1970

Type 202 were originally built in an endeavour to develop a Type on this displacement. They made extensive trials, first with naval crew, and later a civilian one. They were ordered in February 1959. *Friedrich Schürer* had a Kort jet on her vertical rudder. Hopes for them were not realised and they were soon decommissioned and scrapped.

U 12 1971

NB 1/750 scale

Type 205 *coastal submarines*

Displacement:	419t surfaced; 455t submerged
Dimensions:	141ft 3in pp, 144ft 5in (*U 1, 2, 9*) 143ft 9in (*U 10*) 150ft 4in (*U 11, 12*) oa × 15ft × 13ft 9in
	43.4, 44.0m (43.8m) (45.8m) × 4.5m × 4.2m
Sensors:	Radar Calypso; sonar SRS-M1H, GHG AN5039A1
Other particulars:	As Type 201

No	Name	Builder	Launched	Fate
S 183	U 4	Howaldtswerke, Kiel	25.8.62	BU 1977
S 184	U 5	Howaldtswerke, Kiel	20.11.62	BU 1977
S 185	U 6	Howaldtswerke, Kiel	30.1.63	BU 1977
S 186	U 7	Howaldtswerke, Kiel	10.4.63	BU 1976
S 187	U 8	Howaldtswerke, Kiel	19.6.63	BU 1977
S 188	U 9	Howaldtswerke, Kiel	20.10.66	Extant 1982
S 189	U 10	Howaldtswerke, Kiel	5.6.67	Extant 1982
S 190	U 11	Howaldtswerke, Kiel	9.2.68	Extant 1982
S 191	U 12	Howaldtswerke, Kiel	10.9.68	Extant 1982
S 180	U 1 (ii)	Howaldtswerke, Kiel	17.2.67	Extant 1982
S 181	U 2 (ii)	Howaldtswerke, Kiel	15.7.66	Extant 1982

With the exception of *U 1* (ii) and *U 2* (ii), all boats were originally to have been of the Type 201. The order was placed in March 1959 to the particulars of this class. Because of the corrosive defects in *U 1* and *U 2*. the hull of the following boats, *U 4*–*U 8* were covered with tin, and suffered severe operational restrictions. Construction of *U 9*–*U 12* was stopped until a newly developed non-magnetic steel could be produced. *U 1* and *U 2* were entirely re-hulled with this steel, their inner construction remaining intact. They can carry 16 mines in lieu of their 8 torpedoes. They differ from the Type 201 in having a totally enclosed conning tower whose shape differed to form four sub-types: *U 7* differing from *U 4*–*U 6*, *U 8* and from *U 9*–*U 12* and *U 1* and *U 2*, the latter having a distinctive sonar dome in the bow. *U 11* and *U 12* also had a different rudder arrangement. *U 4*–*U 8* belonged to the training group and were scrapped after decommissioning.

U 28 1976

NB 1/750 scale

Type 206 *coastal submarines*

Displacement:	456t surfaced; 500t submerged
Dimensions:	159ft 6in oa × 15ft × 14ft
	48.6m × 4.6m × 4.3m
Machinery:	As Type 201. Oil 23.5t
Armament:	8–533mm TT (16 torpedoes), 24 mines
Sensors:	Radar Calypso; sonar AN410A4, AN5039A1, DBQS-21D
Complement:	21

No	Name	Builder	Launched	Fate
S 192	U 13	Howaldtswerke, Kiel	28.9.71	Extant 1982
S 193	U 14	Rheinstahl-Nordseewerke, Emden (RNSW)	1.2.72	Extant 1982
S 194	U 15	Howaldtswerke, Kiel	15.6.72	Extant 1982
S 195	U 16	RNSW, Emden	29.8.72	Extant 1982
S 196	U 17	Howaldtswerke, Kiel	10.10.72	Extant 1982
S 197	U 18	RNSW, Emden	31.10.72	Extant 1982
S 198	U 19	Howaldtswerke, Kiel	15.12.72	Extant 1982
S 199	U 20	RNSW, Emden	16.1.73	Extant 1982
S 170	U 21	Howaldtswerke, Kiel	9.3.73	Extant 1982
S 171	U 22	RNSW, Emden	27.3.73	Extant 1982
S 172	U 23	RNSW, Emden	22.5.73	Extant 1982
S 173	U 24	RNSW, Emden	26.6.73	Extant 1982
S 174	U 25	Howaldtswerke, Kiel	23.5.73	Extant 1982
S 175	U 26	RNSW, Emden	20.11.73	Extant 1982
S 176	U 27	Howaldtswerke, Kiel	21.8.73	Extant 1982
S 177	U 28	RNSW, Emden	22.1.74	Extant 1982
S 178	U 29	Howaldtswerke, Kiel	5.11.73	Extant 1982
S 179	U 30	RNSW, Emden	26.3.74	Extant 1982

The Type 206 boats were designed by the IKL in 1964–65, *U 25*–*U 30* being the replacement units for the Type 205 boats *U 4*–*U 8*. In April 1969 the orders for *U 13*–*U 24* and in autumn 1970 those for *U 25*–*U 30* were placed. The general interior arrangement resembles that of the Types 201 and 205, the visual difference being a rounded bow with sonar dome. Improvements were the use of wire-guided torpedoes, decreased underwater noise, better steering and higher underwater manoeuvrability. Submerged range is 200nm at 5kts.

In addition to the 16 mines that can be carried in lieu of the torpedoes, this class can carry 24 extra mines in a pair of external GRP containers. This ingenious system was developed by IKL to allow the submarines to embark both torpedoes and mines simultaneously if required.

AMPHIBIOUS WARFARE VESSELS

Karpfen July 1978   Author

Ex-US LSM type *medium landing ships*

Displacement:	830t standard; 1080t full load
Dimensions:	196ft 6in wl, 203ft 7in oa (*Krokodil* after conversion 191ft 7in, 201ft 10in) × 34ft 6in × 8ft 3in *59.8m, 62.1m, (58.4m, 61.5m) × 10.5m × 2.5m*
Machinery:	2 shafts, 2 GMC diesels, 2800bhp (2061kW) = 12.5kts. Oil 195.8t. Range 2500nm at 12kts
Armament:	2–40mm/56 (1×2)
Complement:	50

No	Name	Builder	Acquired	Fate
L 750	KROKODIL (ex-*LSM 537*)	Brown SB, Houston	15.8.58	Sold 10.5.76
L 751	EIDECHSE (ex-*LSM 491*)	Brown SB, Houston	15.8.58	Sold 10.5.76
L 752	SALAMANDER (ex-*LSM 553*)	Charleston N Yd	15.8.58	Sold 22.5.70
L 753	VIPER (ex-*LSM 558*)	Charleston N Yd	15.8.58	Sold 22.5.70

Ex-US LSMR type *support landing ships*

Displacement:	994t standard; 1084t full load
Dimensions:	204ft 3in wl, 210ft 3in oa × 34ft 6in × 9ft 4in *62.2m, 64.1m × 10.5m × 2.8m*
Machinery:	2 shafts, 2 GMC diesels, 2800bhp (2061kW) = 12.5kts. Oil 164t. Range 2500nm at 12kts
Armament:	1–5in/38, 4–40mm/56 (2×2), 20–5in (127mm) rocket projectors (10×2), after conversion: 1–5in/38, 4–40mm/70 (2×2), 16–5in (127mm) rocket projectors (8×2)
Complement:	100

No	Name	Builder	Acquired	Fate
L 754	OTTER (ex-*Smyrna River*, LSMR 532)	Brown, SB Houston/ Charleston N Yd	15.8.58	Sold 8.9.71
L 755	NATTER (ex-*Thames River*, LSMR 534)	Brown, SB Houston/ Charleston N Yd	15.8.58	Sold 8.9.71

In 1958 the Federal German Navy bought four former LSMs and two former LSMRs from the USN, all built in 1944–45. The vessels were taken over 15.8.58 at Charleston, Va and commissioned 5.9.58. They were incorporated as the Types 550 (*Eidechse* and others) and 551 (*Otter, Natter*). During their service they remained unmodified, with the exception of the armament as shown in the particulars. *Krokodil* was designed as a command and hospital craft and therefore received a helicopter platform over the stern and a new hinged bow-ramp while the folding doors were removed. No other unit of this class was converted to this scheme. *Krokodil* was sold 10.5.76 and serves as a Pipeline Carrier for Pauses Shipping, as does *Eidechese*. *Salamander* was scrapped and *Viper* was sold to the Norvolk Lijen, Scheveningen, and renamed *Duchess of Holland*. In 1973 she was renamed *Oil Dragon*.

BUTT class *utility landing craft*

Displacement:	166t standard; 397t full load
Dimensions:	120ft 5in wl, 131ft 5in × 29ft × 7ft 3in *36.7m, 40.0m × 8.8m × 2.2m*
Machinery:	2 shafts, 2 MWM diesels, 1320shp (971kW) = 12kts. Oil 40t
Armament:	2–20mm Mk 20 (2×1)
Complement:	15

Class (no, launched):
Flunder (L 760, 6.1.66), *Karpfen* (L 761, 5.1.66), *Lachs* (L 762, 17.2.66), *Plötze* (L 763, 16.2.66), *Rochen* (L 764, 18.3.66), *Schlei* (L 765, 17.5.66), *Stör* (L 766, 18.5.66), *Tümmler* (L 767, 14.6.66), *Wels* (L 768, 15.6.66), *Zander* (L 769, 13.7.66), *Butt* (L 788, 28.3.65), *Brasse* (L 789, 28.3.65), *Barbe* (L 790, 26.11.65), *Delphin* (L 791, 25.11.65), *Dorsch* (L 792, 17.3.66), *Felchen* (L 793, 19.4.66), *Forelle* (L 794, 20.4.66), *Inger* (L 795, 14.7.66), *Makrele* (L 796, 22.8.66), *Muräne* (L 797, 23.8.66), *Renke* (L 798, 22.9.66), *Salm* (L 799, 23.9.66)

All built by Howaldtswerke, Hamburg. These multi-purpose landing craft of the type MZL 63, being an improved version of the US *LCU 1640* class, were ordered in 1964 and belong to the Type 520. Shortage of crews and changing concepts meant that most of them were transferred to the reserve immediately after delivery, laid up and cocooned. With the exception of *Renke* and *Salm* all were finally commissioned in 1973. Since 5.8.74 *Inger* has served as training boat for the Seamen Training Group.

All were refitted in the 1970s, receiving an enclosed bridge and a modern AA armament consisting of 2–20mm Rheinmetall guns. All were designed to carry minerails for the transport and laying of mines. Stern and stem are designed in such a manner that the boats can form a chain, so as to produce a massive floating bridge.

OTHER LANDING CRAFT
Apart from these 22 boats, there are 28 LCM type boats (*LCM 1–28*). Carrying a five-man crew they serve for transport and supply purposes, but are unarmed. Some of them have been laid up.

From 1959 to 1968 a former US LCT was in commission. This was *LCU 1* ex-*L 7981*, ex-*LCU 779* ex-*LSU 779* ex-*LCT 779*. With only one MG she had no fighting value and served as headquarters ship of ten LCAs of the beachmaster company. She was sold 19.9.1968.

SMALL SURFACE COMBATANTS

(For illustration see under France)

French LE FOUGUEUX type *submarine-chaser*

Particulars:	As French *Le Fougueux* class

Originally ordered by the USA as a part of a NATO order in France, where a whole series of this type was built, *UW 12* was built by Dubigeon, Nantes. Belonging to the *La Fougueux* class she was commissioned in 1955 by the USN together with a sister ship and was given the pennant number P 1618. Taken over by Germany in 1957, she was commissioned on 12.3.57 by the Navy, pennant number *UW 12* as Type 179 and was used as training boat for the underwater weapons school. She was decommissioned 15.9.67, sold to the Tunisian Navy which commissioned her on 16.7.70 as *Sakiet Sidi Youssef* (P 313).

The second boat, *P 1616*, was not taken over by the Navy, but went to Ethiopia under MDAP, where she was renamed *Belay Deress*. She was soon handed back to the USN who lent her to Italy 3.2.59. She was commissioned 3.12.59 under her new name *Vedetta* (F 597).

Najade 1964

THETIS class *corvettes*

Displacement:	599t standard; 732t full load
Dimensions:	215ft wl, 229ft oa × 27ft × 13ft 10in *65.5m, 69.8 × 8.2m × 4.2m*
Machinery:	2 shafts (CP propellers), 2 MAN diesels, 6000bhp (4416kW) = 24kts. Oil 78t. Range 2760nm at 15kts
Armament:	2–40mm/70 (1×2), 1–375mm ASW mortar (1×4), 4–533mm ASW TT
Sensors:	Radar KH 14/9, TRS-N; sonar ELAC 1BV
Complement:	68

No	Name	Builder	Launched	Fate
P 6052	THETIS	Rolandwerft, Bremen	22.3.60	Extant 1982
P 6053	HERMES	Rolandwerft, Bremen	9.8.60	Extant 1982
P 6054	NAJADE	Rolandwerft, Bremen	6.12.60	Extant 1982
P 6055	TRITON	Rolandwerft, Bremen	5.8.61	Extant 1982
P 6056	THESEUS	Rolandwerft, Bremen	20.3.62	Extant 1982

Originally designed in 1958–59 as 'Large B Type' torpedo-recovery vessels, their official designation until 1974 was fleet service craft, now they are referred to as the Type 420. It soon turned out that they were unable to fulfil their planned role in torpedo-recovery and they were used for various purposes, mainly as training units of the weapons school. During the 1970s they were modified and received a powerful ASW component. The crane amidships and the two boats were removed, the original 2–533mm TT for ASW torpedoes were replaced by 4–533mm TT. In addition they received the necessary sonar systems.

Najade differs from her sisters in having an enlarged bridge. Because they were three times reclassified their pennants changed: P 6111–6115, A 1430–1434, and finally P 6052–6056.

HANS BURKNER *corvette*

Displacement:	983t standard; 1347t full load
Dimensions:	265ft 3in oa × 30ft 10in × 9ft 3in
	81.0m × 9.4m × 2.8m
Machinery:	2 shafts, 4 MAN diesels, 13,600bhp (10,010kW) = 24kts. Range 2180nm at 15kts
Armament:	2–40mm/70 (1×2), 1–375mm ASW mortar (1×4), 2–533mm ASW TT
Complement:	60

No	Name	Builder	Launched	Fate
Y 879	HANS BURKNER	Atlaswerke, Bremen	16.7.61	Trials ship

Originally rated as a 'Large B Type' torpedo-recovery vessel, *Hans Burkner* was manned by the Navy who first commissioned her in May 1963. However she has been turned over to Trials Command 71 and operates under the pennant number A 1449 with a reduced civilian crew. All armament except the Bofors ASW mortar has been removed, and the ship serves as a trials ship for ASW equipment and underwater experiments.

SILBERMOWE class *fast attack craft*

Displacement:	109t standard; 155t full load (*Seeschwalbe* as *UW 9* 135.6t)
Dimensions:	111ft 9in wl, 116ft 9in ow × 17ft × 5ft 3in
	34.0m, 35.6m × 5.2m × 1.6m
Machinery:	3 shafts (*Seeschwalbe* CP propellers), 3 Mercedes Benz (*Seeschwalbe* Maybach) diesels, 9000bhp (6624kW) = 42kts. Oil 13t
Armament:	2–20mm (2×1), later 1–40mm/70 (*Eismöwe, Raubmöwe, Seeschwalbe* 2–40mm (2×2), 2–533mm TT (2×1)

No	Name	Builder	Launched	Fate
P 6052	SILBERMOWE (ex-*Silver Gull*)	Lürssen	21.1.55	To Greece Nov 68
P 6053	STURMMOWE (ex *Storm Gull*)	Lürssen	7.12.54	To Greece Nov 68
P 6054	WILDSCHWAN (ex-*Wildswan*)	Lürssen	23.3.55	To Greece Nov 68
P 6055	EISMOWE	Lürssen	15.9.55	To Greece Nov 68
P 6056	RAUBMOWE	Lürssen	27.10.55	To Greece Nov 68
P 6057	SEESCHWALBE	Lürssen	13.9.56	Sold 29.1.74

These boats were a modified repeat of the *Kriegsmarine*'s wartime S-boats. They were designated as Type 149. The first three were ordered in February 1952 by the then Federal Home Office for the Federal Frontier Guard. But the projected speed of 43kts was prohibited under the terms of the Potsdam Conference and construction was stopped by the British Military Security Department. From the spring of 1953 construction of these boats continued, but officially on behalf of the Royal Navy. On 3.5.55, after renewed negotiations, the Military Security Department gave permission for the construction of three more boats. The first three served with German crews under British command until their incorporation into the new Navy on 29.5.56. The fourth and fifth boats were commissioned by the Federal Frontier Guard (Naval) as *S 1* and *S 2* on 15.12.55 and 2.2.56 respectively. *S 1* and *S 2* were taken over by the Navy on 1.7.56 together with all the vessels of the Federal Frontier Guard (Naval). The last boat *Seeschwalbe* was commissioned on 23.4.57. The first five boats were transferred to the Greek Navy in November 1968 as military aid, but *Seeschwalbe* was deleted on 1.10.60 and became a training vessel *UW 9* (W 63). In 1964 she was rebuilt and served under her new name *Wilhelm Laudahn* (Y 839) for the Trials Command 73 especially carrying out trials of new engines with a civilian crew. She was frequently modified and rebuilt.

WARTIME S-BOATS
Also belonging to the Type 149 were three further units: *UW 10* (W 49) ex-*S 130*, *UW 11* (W 50) ex-*S 208* and the former *S 116*.

UW 10 was commissioned for the *Kriegsmarine* on 21.10.43 as *S 130*, taken by the British in 1945 and served in the Royal Navy as experimental craft *FPB 5130*. From 1948 she served, together with *Silbermöwe* and *Sturmmöwe*, as a fishery protection vessel, with a German crew. Commissioned 7.5.57 as *UW 10*, she served as a training boat for the underwater weapons school. On 15.8.63 she was reclassified as *EF 3* (Y 840) and served with a civilian crew for Trials Command 71.

UW 11 was commissioned by the *Kriegsmarine* on 28.9.44 as *S 208*, became a British prize in 1945 and served in the Royal Navy as experimental craft *MTB 5208*. From 1951 she served as a fishery protection vessel. Commissioned on 12.3.57 as *UW 11*, she too served as a training boat for the underwater weapons school. After its elimination she was used as a target boat.

S 116 was commissioned by the *Kriegsmarine* on 9.7.42. Little is known about her post-war fate. In 1952 she was purchased by the Federal Frontier Guard (Naval) to be used as a training hulk. In 1957 the Navy took over the hulk and used her for the damage control training group. She was destroyed by fire on 25.5.65.

While *S 116* remained unmodified, *UW 10* and *UW 11* were disarmed. During their service with the Royal Navy they had foreign engines. On their return they were re-engined with Mercedes Benz diesels. *EF 3* (ex-*UW 10*) has only her middle shaft remaining.

Elster 1982

NB 1/750 scale

JAGUAR class *fast attack craft*

Displacement:	183.6t (P 6068–P 6077 194.6t) standard; 210t (P 6068–P 6077 221t) full load
Dimensions:	130ft 7in wl, 139ft 10in oa × 23ft 4in × 7ft 6in (P 6068–P 6077 8ft)
	39.8m, 42.6m × 7.1m × 2.3m (2.4m)
Machinery:	4 shafts, 4 Mercedes Benz (P 6068–P 6077 4 Maybach) diesels, 12,000bhp (8832kW) = 43kts. Range 500nm/1000nm at 39kts/32kts
Armament:	2–40mm/70 (2×1), 4–533mm TT (4×1)
Complement:	39

No	Name	Builder	Launched	Fate
P 6058	ILTIS	Lürssen	15.8.57	Sold 3.6.78
P 6059	JAGUAR	Lürssen	12.6.57	To Turkey Feb 76
P 6060	LEOPARD	Lürssen	4.1.58	Sold 15.9.75
P 6061	LUCHS	Lürssen	2.11.57	Sold 27.10.75
P 6062	WOLF	Lürssen	21.9.57	To Turkey Nov 75
P 6063	TIGER	Kröger	21.4.58	To Turkey Jan 76
P 6064	PANTHER	Kröger	18.10.58	Sold 14.12.78
P 6065	LOWE	Lürssen	8.11.58	To Turkey Oct 75
P 6066	FUCHS	Lürssen	20.12.58	Sold 3.6.78
P 6067	MARDER	Lürssen	21.3.59	Sold 27.10.75
P 6068	SEEADLER	Lürssen	1.2.58	To Greece Mar 77
P 6069	ALBATROS	Lürssen	20.3.58	To Greece 1977
P 6070	KONDOR	Lürssen	17.5.58	To Greece Mar 77
P 6071	GREIF	Lürssen	28.6.58	To Greece Oct 76
P 6072	FALKE	Lürssen	30.8.58	To Greece Oct 76
P 6073	GEIER	Lürssen	1.10.58	To Greece Oct 76
P 6074	BUSSARD	Kröger	29.11.58	To Greece 1976
P 6075	HABICHT	Kröger	21.2.59	To Greece 1977
P 6076	SPERBER	Kröger	4.4.59	To Greece June 76
P 6077	KORMORAN	Kröger	16.7.59	To Greece May 77
P 6082	WEIHE	Lürssen	20.6.59	To France as target 1973
P 6083	KRANICH	Lürssen	15.8.59	Museum Bremerhaven, 1974
P 6084	ALK	Kröger	19.9.59	To Turkey 1976
P 6085	STORCH	Lürssen	16.11.59	To Turkey June 75
P 6086	PELIKAN	Kröger	12.12.59	To Turkey June 75
P 6087	HAHER	Lürssen	9.1.60	To Turkey Jan 76
P 6088	ELSTER	Lürssen	26.3.60	Sold 7.1.78
P 6089	REIHER	Lürssen	7.5.60	To Turkey Feb 76
P 6090	PINGUIN	Lürssen	4.7.60	To Turkey Aug 75
P 6091	DOMMEL	Lürssen	20.8.60	Sold 7.1.78

Designated 'Schnellboot 55' by Lürssenwerft, Vegesack, these composite-built units belonged to the Type 140/141. The only difference between the classes was in the choice of engine. This type was a further development of the well-known wartime 'S-boats' (E-boats) of the *Kriegsmarine*, but incorporating the latest advances.

The boats could carry mines, when the aft TTs were removed, the minerails being fixed on deck.

Originally *Iltis* carried 2–20mm/85, but later she received the standard 2–40mm/70. Experiments with *Pelikan* and *Geier*, to cover the hulls with a radar-absorbing coat of rubber and plastic were unsuccessful.

For experimental purposes *Pelikan* received a conical stub mast. *Geier* was rebuilt several times, receiving a conical stub mast and later a telescopic mast. Finally she received additional superstructure aft of the bridge for ABC warfare experiments. The Type 149 boat *Wilhelm Laudahn* (Y 839) ex-*Seeschwalbe* was modified to the same standards. *Kormoran* was used for trials of stern TTs which were later part of the armament of the 142 and 149 Types. After they had been stricken they were transferred as military aid in groups of ten each to the Greek and Turkish Navies. The others were sold for scrap. *Weihe* went to France as a 'fast target' and *Kranich* is exhibited at the German Maritime Museum in Bremerhaven.

WEST GERMANY

HUGIN class *fast attack craft*

Displacement:	648t standard; 755t full load
Dimensions:	75ft 6in wl, 80ft 5in oa × 24ft 8in × 3ft 8in 23.0m, 24.5m × 7.5m × 1.1m
Machinery:	2 shafts, 2 Napier-Deltic diesels, 6280bhp (4622kW) = 45kts. Oil 10t
Armament:	2–40mm/70 (2×1), 4–533mm TT (4×1)
Complement:	34

No	Name	Builder	Launched	Fate
P 6191	HUGIN	Batservice Verft, Mandal	26.3.60	To Turkey Aug 64
P 6192	MUNIN	Batservice Verft, Mandal	26.6.60	To Turkey Aug 64

Based on a private design study by the Norwegian shipbuilder who designed the prototype vessel *Nasty* for the Norwegian Navy. Later the *Tjeld* class was developed from this design. The Navy ordered two units (designated Type 152) in May 1959 to find out whether a cheap hard-chine planing boat would be of use in narrow coastal waters. Trials showed that the design did not match requirements and no more were ordered. The two existing boats were handed over to Turkey as military aid.

(For illustration see under Greek *Astrapi*)

PFEIL and STRAHL *fast attack craft*

Displacement:	75t standard; 85t full load (*Strahl* 96.5t; 101.6t)
Dimensions:	90ft 8in wl, 95ft oa × 24ft × 7ft (*Strahl* 97ft 2in, 99ft 2in × 23ft 10in × 6ft 10in) 27.6m, 29.0m × 7.3m × 2.1m (29.6m, 30.2m ×7.3m × 2.1m)
Machinery:	2-shaft CODOG: 2 Proteus gas turbines, 8500shp = 54kts; 2 diesels, 300bhp = ?kts. Oil 21t (*Strahl* 3-shaft Proteus gas turbines, 10,500shp = 55kts)
Armament:	2–40mm/70 (2×1), 2–533mm TT (2×1)
Complement:	22

No	Name	Builder	Launched	Fate
P 6193	PFEIL	Vosper	26.10.61	To Greece Jan 67
P 6194	STRAHL	Vosper	10.1.61	To Greece Jan 67

Both designated as the Type 153, these two hard-chine planing boats were ordered 22.8.60 as experimental units for comparative tests. *Strahl* was of the British *Brave* type, while *Pfeil* was of the improved *Ferocity* type. Both boats had their gas turbine exhausts situated in the stern. After trials they were handed over to the Greek Navy as military aid.

ZOBEL class *fast attack craft*

Displacement:	172.5t standard; 190t full load (after conversion: 212.5t standard; 219t full load)
Dimensions:	130ft 8in wl, 139ft 10in × 23ft 4in × 7ft 6in 39.8m, 42.6m × 7.1m × 2.3m
Machinery:	As Mercedes-engined *Jaguar* class (after conversion 38.5kts)
Armament:	As *Jaguar* class (after conversion 2–533mm TT)
Sensors:	Radar KH 14/9, M–20
Complement:	39

No	Name	Builder	Launched	Fate
P 6092	ZOBEL	Lürssen	28.1.61	Decommissioned 7.9.82
P 6093	WIESEL	Lürssen	14.3.61	Extant 1982
P 6094	DACHS	Lürssen	10.6.61	Extant 1982
P 6095	HERMELIN	Kröger	5.8.61	Extant 1982
P 6096	NERZ	Lürssen	5.9.61	Decommissioned 8.7.82
P 6097	PUMA	Kröger	26.10.61	Decommissioned 17.12.81
P 6098	GEPARD	Lürssen	14.4.62	Extant 1982
P 6099	HYANE	Kröger	31.3.62	Extant 1982
P 6100	FRETTCHEN	Lürssen	20.11.62	Extant 1982
P 6101	OZELOT	Lürssen	4.2.63	Extant 1982

The Lürssen-designed 'Schnellboot 60', now Type 142, is a modified version of the Type 140/141. They differ from the foregoing classes in having additional superstructure aft of the bridge, which was tested earlier in *Geier*, a more streamlined bridge and masts of a different shape. A further ten projected boats were not built.

Nerz was used for weapons trials in 1963–64 including the 'Tartar-Bullpup' guided missile system, which necessitated a spherical radome situated on a four-pod mast. The system was too heavy for these boats, the project was dropped, and continued with the British Seacat SAM instead. The Seacat missile was tried on a launch frame on the forward 40mm/70, but these experiments were also dropped.

At the end of the 1960s all the boats were substantially modernised, receiving a new mast with a spherical radome including a target indicating radar. The 4–533mm TT were removed and 2–533mm TT firing Seal wire-guided torpedoes were fitted in the stern. (See also the experiments with *Kormoran*, under *Jaguar* class). The 40mm/70 was now fully radar-directed. Since 1981 the boats have been successively decommissioned and are being replaced by the new Type 143A boats.

Tiger (S 41) as completed

NB 1/750 scale

S 41 class *fast attack craft*

Displacement:	234t standard; 263.7t full load
Dimensions:	144ft 5in pp, 150ft 8in wl, 154ft 3in oa × 23ft × 7ft 3in 44.0m, 46.0m, 47.0m × 7.0m × 2.2m
Machinery:	4 shafts, 4 MTU diesels, 12,000bhp (8832kW) = 38.5kts. Oil 33t. Range 570nm/1600nm at 30kts/15kts
Armament:	4 MM38 Exocet SSM (2×2), 1–76mm/62, 1–40mm/70
Sensors:	Radar 3RM20, Triton, Pollux
Complement:	30

No	Name	Builder	Launched	Fate
P 6141	TIGER (*S 41*)	CMN, Cherbourg	27.9.72	Extant 1982
P 6142	ILTIS (*S 42*)	CMN, Cherbourg	12.12.72	Extant 1982
P 6143	LUCHS (*S 43*)	CMN, Cherbourg	7.9.73	Extant 1982
P 6144	MARDER (*S 44*)	CMN, Cherbourg	5.5.73	Extant 1982
P 6145	LEOPARD (*S 45*)	CMN, Cherbourg	3.7.73	Extant 1982
P 6146	FUCHS (*S 46*)	CMN, Cherbourg	21.5.73	Extant 1982
P 6147	JAGUAR (*S 47*)	CMN, Cherbourg	20.9.73	Extant 1982
P 6148	LOWE (*S 48*)	CMN, Cherbourg	10.9.73	Extant 1982
P 6149	WOLF (*S 49*)	CMN, Cherbourg	11.1.74	Extant 1982
P 6150	PANTHER (*S 50*)	CMN, Cherbourg	10.12.73	Extant 1982
P 6151	HAHER (*S 51*)	CMN, Cherbourg	26.4.74	Extant 1982
P 6152	STORCH (*S 52*)	CMN, Cherbourg	25.3.74	Extant 1982
P 6153	PELIKAN (*S 53*)	CMN, Cherbourg	4.7.74	Extant 1982
P 6154	ELSTER (*S 54*)	CMN, Cherbourg	8.7.74	Extant 1982
P 6155	ALK (*S 55*)	CMN, Cherbourg	15.11.74	Extant 1982
P 6156	DOMMEL (*S 56*)	CMN, Cherbourg	30.10.74	Extant 1982
P 6157	WEIHE (*S 57*)	CMN, Cherbourg	13.2.75	Extant 1982
P 6158	PINGUIN (*S 58*)	CMN, Cherbourg	26.2.75	Extant 1982
P 6159	REIHER (*S 59*)	CMN, Cherbourg	15.5.75	Extant 1982
P 6160	KRANICH (*S 60*)	CMN, Cherbourg	26.5.75	Extant 1982

The steel-hulled Type 148 missile-firing attack craft are a modified French 'La Combattante II' type, which in turn is based on a Lürssen design. Orders were placed on 18.12.70, based on a German-French contract of 23.10.70. These boats were to replace the *Jaguar* class (Type 140). Under the project management of the Direction Technique des Constructions Navales (DTCN) of the French Ministry of Defence, the main shipyard employed was Constructions Mécaniques de Normandie (CMN).

S 46, S 48, S 50, S 52, S 54, S 56, S 58 and *S 60* were fitted out by Lürssen, the hulls having been brought from Cherbourg to Germany. In 1981 in addition to their numbers, the boats were given the traditional names of their forerunners.

Falke Apr 1975

S 61 class *fast attack craft*

Displacement:	380t standard; 393.7t full load
Dimensions:	178ft 6in pp, 188ft 9in oa × 26ft 3in × 8ft 3in
	54.4m, 57.5m × 8.0m × 2.5m
Machinery:	4 shafts, 4 MTU diesels, 16,000–18,000bhp
	(11,776–13,248kW) = 33–38kts. Oil 43t. Range
	600nm/1600nm at 30kts/16kts
Armament:	4 MM38 Exocet SSM (2×2), 2–76mm/62 (2×1), 2–533mm
	TT
Sensors:	Radar 3RM20, WM–27
Complement:	40

No	Name	Builder	Launched	Fate
P 6111	ALBATROS (*S 61*)	Lürssen	22.10.73	Extant 1982
P 6112	FALKE (*S 62*)	Lürssen	21.3.74	Extant 1982
P 6113	GEIER (*S 63*)	Lürssen	18.9.74	Extant 1982
P 6114	BUSSARD (*S 64*)	Lürssen	14.4.75	Extant 1982
P 6115	SPERBER (*S 65*)	Kröger	15.1.74	Extant 1982
P 6116	GREIF (*S 66*)	Lürssen	4.9.75	Extant 1982
P 6117	KONDOR (*S 67*)	Kröger	6.3.75	Extant 1982
P 6118	SEEADLER (*S 68*)	Lürssen	17.11.75	Extant 1982
P 6119	HABICHT (*S 69*)	Kröger	5.6.75	Extant 1982
P 6120	KORMORAN (*S 70*)	Lürssen	14.4.76	Extant 1982

The Type 143 were designed to replace the Type 141 (P 6068–6077). The design of the composite hulls is by Lürssen, the military requirements were defined in October 1966, the contract was signed 7.7.72 and the orders placed 13.7.72. The TT are aft-launching, and fire Seal wire-guided torpedoes. Since the end of 1982 the boats bear not only their original pennant numbers, but also the traditional names of their forerunners.

Type 143A design

NB 1/750 scale

S 71 class *fast attack craft*

Displacement:	As *S 61* class, but 397.5t full load
Dimensions:	189ft oa × 25ft 6in × 7ft 3in
	57.6m × 7.8m × 2.2m
Machinery:	As *S 61* class
Armament:	4 MM38 Exocet SSM (2×2, 1–76mm/62, RAM ASMD
	System (1×24)
Sensors:	As *S 61* class
Complement:	35

No	Name	Builder	Launched	Fate
P 6121	GEPARD (*S 71*)	Lürssen	25.9.81	Extant 1982
P 6122	PUMA (*S 72*)	Lürssen	8.2.82	Extant 1982
P 6123	HERMELIN (*S 73*)	Kröger	8.12.81	Extant 1982
P 6124	NERZ (*S 74*)	Lürssen	18.8.82	Extant 1982
P 6125	ZOBEL (*S 75*)	Kröger	30.6.82	Extant 1982
P 6126	FRETTCHEN (*S 76*)	Lürssen		Building

No	Name	Builder	Launched	Fate
P 6127	DACHS (*S 77*)	Kröger		Building
P 6128	OZELOT (*S 78*)	Lürssen		Building
P 6129	WIESEL (*S 79*)	Lürssen		Building
P 6130	HYANE (*S 80*)	Lürssen		Building

Officially designated Type 143A these boats were to replace the Type 142 and are still under construction. The general layout resembles Type 143, but has no stern TT. The US RAM point-defence is intended to be fitted in place of the Type 143s' after 76mm gun. The orders were placed 15.12.78.

Ex-KFK type *patrol craft*

Displacement:	110t standard; 112t full load
Dimensions:	67ft 6in–70ft 6in wl, 73ft 3in oa × 21ft × 9ft
	20.5m–21.5m, 22.3m × 6.4m × 2.7m
Machinery:	1 shaft, 1 Demag diesel, 150bhp (11kW) = 11kts. Oil 3.4t.
	Range 1200nm at 7kts
Armament:	1–20mm
Complement:	16

Class (no, builder, fate):
KW 1 (W 1, ex-*Vs 1441*, Burmester, Swinemünde, sold 12.12.68), *KW 2* (Y 828, ex-*M 3253*, Burmester, Swinemünde, 15.8.75, to Greece), *KW 3* (Y 829, ex-*K 561*, Burmester, Swinemünde, still in service), *KW 4* (W 4, ?, to Tanzania 30.9.64), *KW 5* (W 5, ?, to Tanzania 30.9.64), *KW 6* (Y 836, Eschler & Gabler, Lübeck, sold 1976), *KW 7* (W 7, ?, to Greece 22.12.67), *KW 8* (Y 831, ?, to Greece 15.8.75), *KW 9* (W 9, ?, to Tanzania 30.9.64), *KW 10* (W 10, ?, to Tanzania 30.9.64). All were commissioned 1.7.56.

These were former *Kriegsmarine* series-built naval fishing vessels (*Kriegsfisch-kutter*–KFKs) which were built in great numbers during the Second World War to serve as auxiliary patrol craft and reconnaissance units. The original design came from the Maierform GmbH and was developed with a view to their future peace-time usage as fishing vessels. With the exception of the three boats *KW 1*–*KW 3*, which had been part of the GMSA postwar, they were re-purchased by the Federal Frontier Guard (Naval) and modified to their needs. The modification was accepted by the Federal Home Office 21.9.51, the boats being commissioned as *W 13–W 19*.

When taken over by the new Navy the ten boats formed a harbour guard squadron. In 1963 they were decommissioned with the exception of *KW 2* and *KW 8*, which served as training boats for the Seamen Training School.

KW 3 was converted to a radio-control boat of the Wilhelmshaven naval arsenal, still serving with civilian crew. Four boats were sent as a gift to Tanzania and three to the Greek Navy. All the others were sold or scrapped.

KW 15 class *patrol craft*

Displacement:	51.4–51.6t standard; 71.5–77.8t full load
Dimensions:	84ft 10in–88ft 8in wl, 89ft–95ft 3in oa × 15ft–15ft 6in × 4ft 6in
	25.8m–27.0m, 27.1m–29.0m × 4.6m–4.7m × 1.4m
Machinery:	2 shafts, 2 Mercedes Benz diesels, 2000bhp (1472kW) = 25kts. Oil 7t
Armament:	1/2–20mm (1/2×1) or 4–20mm (2×2)
Complement:	17

Kondor Aug 1976 Author

Class (no, builder):

KW 15 (Y 827, Schweers, Weser), *KW 16* (Y 830, Lürssenwerft), *KW 17* (Y 845, Schürenstedt, Weser), *KW 18* (Y 832, Abeking & Rasmussen, Weser), *KW 19* (Y 833, Schweers, Weser), *KW 20* (Y 846, Lürssenwerft. All commissioned 30.11.56.

These six units of the Type 369 were former USN patrol boats, which served under the designation *USN 54–59* with the LSU's Weser River Patrol. They resembled the four patrol boats *P 1–P 4* of the Frontier Guard, which were commissioned 1.7.56 for the Navy as *KW 11–KW 14* and finally became the Type 909 air–sea rescue boats *FL 5–FL 8*.

They were launched in 1951–52 and commissioned with the USN in 1952–53. They were unarmed except during their Navy career as training boats.

KW 15, KW 16, KW 17 and *KW 20* were decommissioned in 1964 and transferred to the new inspection unit who commissioned them as *BG 1–BG 4*. After their return in 1971 they were disarmed like their sisters and commissioned as security vessels with civilian crews for the Territorial Command. Since the 1960s *KW 19* has served as a dispatch boat in the North Sea area with a civilian crew. She was decommissioned 22.12.1981.

MINE WARFARE VESSELS

BAMBERG class (ex-US LST type) *minelayers*

Displacement:	3640t standard; 4140t full load
Dimensions:	316ft wl, 332ft 8in oa × 51ft 10in × 9ft *96.3m, 101.4m × 15.8m × 2.7m*
Machinery:	2 shafts, 2 GMC diesels, 2650bhp (1950kW) = 11kts. Oil 600t. Range 15,000nm at 9kts
Armament:	6–40mm/56 (after conversion 6–40mm/70) (2×2, 2×1)
Complement:	60

No	Name	Builder	Acquired	Fate
N 120	BOCHUM (ex-*Rice County*)	American Bridge	1960	To Turkey 13.12.76
N 121	BOTTROP (ex-*Saline County*)	Missouri Valley	1960	To Turkey 12.12.76
A 1403	BAMBERG (ex-*Greer County*)	Jeffersonville	1960	Sold 15.7.70

In 1960 a total of seven US wartime LST type tank landing ships was purchased and in the summer of 1961 they arrived with German crews at Wilhelmshaven: *Rice County*, LST 1089; *Saline County*, LST 1101; *Greer County*, LST 799; *Montgomery County*, LST 1401; *Millard County*, LST 987; *Ulysses*, ARB 9, ex-*LST 967* and *Diomedes*, ARB 11, ex-*LST 1119*.

The last two were converted into the Type 726 maintenance ships *Odin* (A 512) and *Wotan* (A 513). The planned conversion of LST 987 and LST 1041 to maintenance ships was dropped and both were sold for scrapping.

The first three units arrived at Wilhelmshaven with the pennants A 1403 – A 1405 and were converted to Type 370 minelayers in 1962. During this conversion the bow ramp was removed and the bow doors welded up. Superstructure and interior equipment was adapted for the future use, six rails with launching ramps were fixed on the deck, the platform and lower deck also had minerails and two launching ramps with hatches. *Bochum* and *Bottrop* came into service on 9.4.64 and 6.2.64; they decommissioned on 14.4.71 and 28.9.71, were refitted and handed over to the Turkish Navy. The conversion of *Bamberg* was 60 per cent finished when this was stopped and the ship was sold for scrap.

Sachsenwald 1970

SACHSENWALD class *mine transports*

Displacement:	2962t standard; 3379t full load
Dimensions:	350ft 5in wl, 363ft 3in oa × 45ft 9in × 13ft 10in *106.8m, 110.7m × 13.9m × 4.2m*
Machinery:	2-shafts (CP propellers), 2 MTU diesels, 5600bhp (4122kW) = 17kts. Oil 250t
Armament:	4–40mm/70 (2×2), mines
Complement:	65

No	Name	Builder	Launched	Fate
A 1437	SACHSENWALD	Blohm & Voss, Hamburg	10.12.66	Extant 1982
A 1438	STEIGERWALD	Blohm & Voss, Hamburg	10.3.67	Extant 1982

KW 19 Sept 1977   Author

Projected under the auxiliary shipbuilding programme of 1959, both units were designed in 1963 and ordered in 1965. Officially, they were Type 762 mine transports, but they have full minelaying capabilities. All decks have minerails, the stern has four hatch-covered launching ramps and two rails on deck lead to the sideward launching positions. Their crane equipment enables them to supply other ships with mines.

Ex-1935 type *ocean minesweepers*

Displacement:	685t (*Wespe* 682t) standard; 878t (*Wespe* 874t) full load
Dimensions:	216ft 6in wl, 224ft 5in (*Wespe* 223ft 5in) oa × 28ft 6in × 8ft 6in *66.0m, 68.3m (68.1m) × 8.7m × 2.6m*
Machinery:	2-shaft reciprocating steam engines, 2 Wagner boilers, 3500shp (2576kW) = 18.3kts. Oil 155t. Range 1440nm at 9kts
Armament:	1956: 2–105mm/45 (2×1) 1958: 1–105mm/45, 1 Hedgehog 1960: 2–40mm/70 (2×1), 4–20mm (2×2), 1 Hedgehog
Complement:	100

No	Name	Builder	Acquired	Fate
F 207	BIENE (ex-*M 205*)	A G Neptun, Rostock	1956	BU 1974
F 208	BREMSE (ex-*M 253*)	Deutsche Werft, Hamburg	1956	BU 1976
F 209	BRUMMER (ex-*M 85*)	Lübecker Maschinenbaugesellschaft, Lübeck	1956	BU 1974
F 210	HUMMEL (ex-*M 81*)	Lübecker Maschinenbaugesellschaft, Lübeck	1956	BU 1976
F 211	WESPE (ex-*M 24*)	Flenderwerke, Lübeck	1956	Sunk as target 25.10.73

Designated Type 319 these minesweepers were former *Kriegsmarine* minesweepers of the 1935 type launched in 1940–41. Being a new design they had – in contrast to earlier minesweeper types – oil-burning high-pressure boilers and double-compound Lenz-type steam machinery.

After the war they became Allied prizes and were first used for GMSA duties. Later they were handed over to the French Navy to serve as minesweepers and fishery protection vessels under the following names: *Biene* as *Belfort* (M 606), *Bremse* as *Vimy* (M 608), *Brummer* as *Yser* (M 604), *Hummel* as *Laffaux* (M 607) and *Wespe* as *Ailette* (M 605).

Repurchased by Germany, the five were transferred to Wilhelmshaven in December 1956 and January 1957 and handed over to the Navy, and wore the following pennant numbers: *Biene* (Q 74), *Hummel* (Q 75) and *Wespe* (Q 76).

In February 1957 they recommissioned after being refitted, the armament was partially changed to new weapons and the interiors were refurbished to German standards. After that they formed the First Escort Squadron with an F pennant number, but only served as officer training ships.

In 1963 they were decommissioned and transferred to the Wilhelmshaven naval arsenal and modified to target ships, in which role they served for a short time. In 1966 *Biene* and *Brummer* went to the damage control training group as training hulks. In 1967 *Hummel* was handed over to the Trials Command 71 as a target ship and scrapped in 1976. *Wespe* was sunk in 1973 as a gunnery target by *Zerstörer 4*, while *Bremse* was scrapped in August 1976. During their service career they received standardised weapons and their funnel caps were changed repeatedly.

Ex-1940 and 1943 type *ocean minesweepers*

Displacement:	543t (*Seeschlange* 582t) standard; 775t (*Seeschlange* 821t) full load
Dimensions:	189ft (*Seepferd* 179ft 2in; *Seeschlange* 204ft 5in) wl, 204ft 5in (*Seepferd* 204ft; *Seeschlange* 207ft) oa × 28ft–29ft 3in × 8ft 6in–8ft 10in *57.6m (54.6m; 62.3m), 62.3m (62.2m; 63.1m) × 8.5m–9.0m × 2.6m–2.7m*
Machinery:	2-shaft triple expansion, 2 Navy (*Seeschlange* Navy-Wagner) boilers, 2700shp, (1987kW) = 17.2kts (*Seeschlange* 16.7kts). Coal 162t (*Seeschlange* 180t). Range 4000nm at 10kts
Armament:	1–3in (76.2mm), 4–40mm (2×2), 3–20mm (3×1)
Complement:	70

No	Name	Builder	Acquired	Fate
M 187	SEEHUND (ex-*M 388*)	Elsflether Werft	17.7.56	Sold for BU 7.9.73
M 188	SEEIGEL (ex-*M 460*)	Nederlandsche Dok Mij, Amsterdam	30.8.56	Sold 4.5.73
M 189	SEELOWE (ex-*M 441*)	P Smit, Rotterdam	17.7.56	BU 1969
M 190	SEEPFERD (ex-*M 294*)	Lindenauwerft, Memel	30.8.56	BU 1966
M 191	SEESCHLANGE (ex-*M 611*)	A G Neptun, Rostock	15.8.56	BU 1967
M 192	SEESTERN (ex-*M 278*)	Rickmerswerft, Wesermünde	15.8.56	BU 1966

Also designated Type 319, these were *Kriegsmarine* minesweepers of the 1940 and 1943 types, launched 1942–45. Designed in 1939–40 they showed a certain resemblance to the 1914–15 minesweeper designs of the Imperial German Navy. This type was the only *Bundesmarine* warship with coal-burning boilers and VTE engines. In 1945 they became Allied prizes and served with the GMSA. From 1951 on they belonged in disarmed status to the LSU(B) carrying the pennant numbers M 201–M 206. Before being handed over to the Federal German Navy they were refitted and then commissioned with letter codes, but in 1957 they received the standard NATO 'M' pennant numbers. After their decommissioning in 1960 they were partially modified to accommodation ships and received a block-shaped additional superstructure on the stern. Under the designation *WBM 1—IV* (abbr for *W*ohnboot *M*inensucher = accommodation boat minesweeper) they served as floating quarters for the crews of ships that were fitting out in the shipyards. *Seeigel* was modified once more and then served *Torpedoklarmachstelle II* (torpedo clearance establishment). All were scrapped between 1966 and 1973; *Seeigel* was sold in 1973.

LINDAU class *coastal minesweepers*

Displacement:	362t standard; 380t full load (after conversion 387t standard; 402t, as minehunter 465t, full load)
Dimensions:	137ft 9in (after conversion 142ft 9in) wl, 149ft 6in (first six 147ft 8in; after conversion all 154ft 6in) oa × 26ft 5in × 8ft 3in *42.0m (43.5m), 45.6m (45.0m; 47.1m) × 8.0m × 2.5m*
Machinery:	2 shafts (CP propellers), 2 Maybach diesels, 4000bhp (2944kW) = 17kts. Oil 42t. Range 1950m at 12kts
Armament:	1–40mm/70
Sensors:	Radar TRS-N or KM 1419; sonar DSQS-11 (DSQS-11A in Type 351; Type 193M in Type 331)
Complement:	45

Class (no, launched, fate):
Göttingen (M 1070, 1.4.57, 19.1.79 minehunter), *Koblenz* (M 1071, 6.5.57, 21.6.78 minehunter), *Lindau* (M 1072, 16.2.1957, 10.2.78 minehunter), *Schleswig* (M 1073, 2.10.57, 19.3.81 Troika), *Tübingen* (M 1074, 12.8.57, 20.3.78 minehunter), *Wetzlar* (M 1075, 24.6.57, 6.10.78 minehunter), *Paderborn* (M 1077, 4.2.57, 17.9.81 Troika), *Weilheim* (M 1076, 5.12.58, 17.11.78 minehunter), *Cuxhaven* (M 1078, 11.3.58, 6.6.79 minehunter), *Düren* (M 1079, 12.6.58, will become Troika), *Marburg* (M 1080, 4.8.58, 28.6.79 minehunter), *Konstanz* (M 1081, 30.9.58, 24.5.82 Troika), *Wolfsburg* (M 1082, 10.12.58, 4.3.82 Troika), *Ulm* (M 1083, 10.2.59, 11.11.81 Troika), *Flensburg* (M 1084, 7.4.59, 12.9.72 minehunter), *Minden* (M 1085, 9.6.59, 31.5.78 minehunter), *Fulda* (M 1086, 19.8.59, 1969 minehunter), *Völklingen* (M 1087, 20.10.59, 15.5.79 minehunter)

The Type 320 coastal minesweepers were built under the first naval programme and were a German version of the American-designed NATO standard AMS/MSC type. They were built of wood and non-magnetic materials. The first unit, *Lindau*, was the first ship to be built for the Federal German Navy. All were built by Burmester, Bremen. After completion of the first six boats it turned out that the extremely high bridge structure affected stability, so the next units were built with one deck less in the bridge; the first boats were modified to the same bridge. Another problem was the stern section, the boats having an upright transom stern, which resulted in insufficient working space on the poop, so the hulls were enlarged by 6m by the addition of a stern compartment. During the same refit all boats received a fixed bulwark from bow to stern, the hull plating in the midship-section was reinforced, an 18t lead keel and bilge keels were added. Aft of the funnel an ABC proofed space was erected and the original loading derricks abreast the funnel were replaced by cranes.

In 1968–69 *Fulda* was converted to a minehunter, as was *Flensburg* in 1970–72. Instead of the original sonar-equipment they received special minehunting sonar (Plessey Type 193M), the minesweeping equipment was removed as mines were now detected and deactivated by scuba-divers. The forecastle superstructure was extended aft. To improve manoeuvrability they were equipped with retractable Schottel-propellers in the transom (in fact, powerful electric outboard motors). This propulsion permits running at extremely slow speeds or manoeuvring on the spot. Between 1976 and 1979 a further ten boats were modified to similar standards with the exception of the Schottel-propulsion in place of which they received a special gearing on the shaft to produce the same manoeuvrability. On the quarterdeck they received a hydraulic telescope crane and two PAP 104 (*Poisson Auto Propulsé*) working in connection with the

Seehund 7, a 'Troika' drone — Author

Göttingen as a minehunter, Mar 1979 — Author

minehunting sonar Type 193M. Later, *Fulda* and *Flensburg* were also modified to the same standards, but retained their Schottel-propulsion. Now they are distinguished as the Types 331A (*Fulda, Flensburg*) and 331B (*Lindau, Tübingen, Minden, Koblenz, Göttingen, Cuxhaven, Weilheim, Marburg* and *Völklingen*).

From 1979 to 1983 the remaining six units (*Schleswig, Paderborn, Düren, Ulm, Konstanz* and *Wolfsburg*) were converted to control ships for the 'Troika' system, being designated Type 351. The Troika system consists of a radio control minesweeper of the Type 351 and three self-propelled drones. The drones are of the HFG-F 1 type and are named *Seehund 1–18*. All 18 *Seehunde* form a pool from which craft are drawn as necessary.

The system was introduced after a year of experiments and trials with *Niobe* (see below) and the prototype drones *Walross* and *Seekuh 1–3*.

Seehund 1–18 were designed by Blohm & Voss and built by MaK, Kiel. The drones have a boat-shaped hull, are fully non-magnetic and can be controlled both manually (during the passage) and by remote control (during the minehunting process). They also operate conventional sweep gear and can be used against acoustic mines. Their principal particulars are: 78ft 4in wl, 81ft 9in oa × 15ft 2in × 6ft (*23.9m, 25.0m × 4.6m × 1.8m*); 1-shaft Schottel propulsion, diesel-electric drive, 1 MWM diesel 320bhp (235.5kW) = 9.4kts. Range 520nm at 8.8kts. Complement 3.

VEGESACK class *coastal minesweepers*

Machinery:	2 shafts (CP propellers), 2 Mercedes Benz diesels, 1320bhp (972kW) = 14.5kts. Oil 34.8t. Range 5000nm at 12kts
Other particulars:	As French *Mercure*

Class (no, launched):
Vegesack (M 1250, 21.5.59), *Hamelin* (M 1251, 20.8.59), *Detmold* (M 1252, 17.11.59), *Worms* (M 1253, 30.1.60), *Siegen* (M 1254, 29.3.60), *Passau* (M 1255, 25.6.60)

These Type 321 coastal minesweepers were built at CMN, Cherbourg, as members of the *Mercure* class. This was a French version of the NATO standard AMS/MSC type built to German order. The wooden-hulled boats were built during the first naval building programme and replaced the obsolete Type 319 coal-burners.

The boats had a remarkably short service career: after their decommissioning they were in the reserve fleet from 1963 to 1974 and were only put into service for mobilisation exercises. After their deletion in December 1973 five units were handed over to the Turkish Navy as military aid during June–Oct 75. It was planned to convert *Passau* to an oceanography vessel; when this plan was dropped she also went to Turkey in 1978.

Herkules 1974
NB 1/750 scale

SCHUTZE class *inshore minesweepers*

Displacement:	241t standard; 266.5t full load
Dimensions:	144ft 9in wl, 155ft 9in oa × 22ft 10in × 7ft 6in *44.1m, 47.4m × 6.9m × 2.3m*
Machinery:	2 shafts (CP propellers), 2 Mercedes Benz diesels, 4500bhp (3312kW) = 25kts. Oil 26.4t. Range 1000nm at 18kts. See notes
Armament:	1–40mm/70 (as patrol boats 2–40mm/70)
Complement:	31

Class (no, launched):
Abeking & Rasmussen – *Mira* (M 1050, 16.12.59), *Castor* (M 1051, 12.7.62), *Krebs* (M 1052, 26.1.59), *Orion* (M 1053, 10.8.61), *Pollux* (M 1054, 15.9.60), *Sirius* (M 1055, 15.3.61), *Rigel* (M 1056, 2.4.62), *Regulus* (M 1057, 18.12.61), *Mars* (M 1058, 1.12.60), *Spica* (M 1059, 25.5.60), *Scorpion* (M 1060, 21.5.63), *Stier* (M 1061, 30.10.58), *Schütze* (M 1062, 20.5.58), *Waage* (M 1063, 9.4.59), *Algol* (M 1068, 23.1.63), *Wega* (M 1069, 10.10.62), *Steinbock* (M 1091, 25.8.58), *Fische* (M 1096, 14.7.59), *Gemma* (M 1097, 6.10.59), *Capella* (M 1098, 26.2.60)
Schürenstedt, Weser – *Deneb* (M 1064, 11.9.61), *Jupiter* (M 1065, 15.12.61), *Pluto* (M 1092, 9.8.60), *Widder* (M 1094, 12.3.59), *Uranus* (M 1009, 15.3.60)
Schlichting, Lübeck – *Pegasus* (M 1066, 3.1.62), *Altair* (M 1067, 20.4.61), *Perseus* (M 1090, 22.9.60), *Neptun* (M 1093, 9.6.60), *Herkules* (M 1095, 25.8.60)

These fast minesweepers of the Types 340/341, designed by Abeking & Rasmussen 1957–59, were built of wood and non-magnetic materials. They resemble the last R-boat type of the *Kriegsmarine* and at first were designated 'SM-boot 55'. They have subsidiary roles as coastal patrol craft and minelayers. As planned the boats were to have had Voith-Schneider propellers, but results with the first prototypes *Schütze* and *Krebs* were unsatisfactory and all boats were given two shafts and CP propellers. All boats from M 1060 onwards have 2 Maybach diesels of 4760bhp (3503kW) and are referred to as the Type 341.

In the mid-1960s the superstructure of some of the boats had to be renewed because of corrosion. *Schütze*'s hull was given an experimental radar-absorbing plastic coating, but it was unsuccessful as it tended to come loose at high speeds. The original derricks abreast the funnel were replaced by swivelling cranes. As commissioned, *Gemma*, *Pegasus*, *Waage*, *Deneb*, *Regulus* and *Altair* had no minesweeping gear, but 2–40mm/70 in singles were fitted in order to test the patrol boat role; later they were equipped to the general standard.

During their construction period, the pennants changed a number of times until they received those noted there. *Castor* carried out experiments with the Seacat SAM in 1968. For this purpose she got launching frames at the 40mm/70 and a director on the bridge. In 1964 *Stier* was relieved from the active squadron and was converted in 1966 to a mine clearance diver boat; she now belongs to the Type 732 under her new pennant Y 849. During the conversion the minesweeping gear was removed and replaced with a decompression chamber.

Mira was deleted 2.2.78 and attached to the Naval Technical College as a stationary training boat. On 18.1.73 *Algol* became an exercise hulk for the damage control training group. *Pegasus* was sold on 7.5.74 to the HDW shipyard, Kiel and served there as a security vessel for the Type 209 submarines building for foreign contractors. After deletion *Krebs* (22.6.76), *Orion* (3.6.79), *Steinbock* (5.11.76), *Uranus* (1973) and *Capella* (1976) were handed over to local sections of the German Naval League, to serve as floating clubrooms. All the others were in service in 1982.

Ex- R-BOAT type *inshore minesweepers*

Displacement:	*Capella* group 150t standard; 155t full load *Aldebaran* group 125t standard; 130t full load *UW 6* group 140t standard; 148t full load
Dimensions:	*Capella* group 126ft 8in wl, 134ft 9in oa × 18ft 10in × 5ft 3in *38.6m, 41.1m × 5.7m × 1.6m* *Aldebaran* group 120ft 9in wl, 127ft oa × 18ft 5in × 5ft *36.8m, 38.7m × 5.6m × 1.5m* *UW 6* group 120ft 9in wl, 130ft oa × 18ft 10in × 5ft 9in *36.8m, 39.7m × 5.7m × 1.7m*
Machinery:	2 Voith-Schneider propellers, 2 MAN diesels, 1800bhp (1325kW) = 18kts. Oil 11–18t. Range 900nm at 15kts (*UW 6* group: 2 shafts, 2 MWM diesels, 2800bhp (2061kW) = 24kts. Oil 14.7t. Range 1000nm at 15kts)
Armament:	1 or 2–20mm
Complement:	27–34

Class (no, commissioned, fate):
Capella group – *Capella*, ex-*R 133* (M 1050, 19.6.56, sold 1972), *Spica*, ex-*R 147* (M 1059, 31.7.56, sold 1970), *Castor*, ex-*R 138* (M 1051, 19.6.56, BU 15.6.78), *Mars*, ex-*R 136* (M 1052, 19.6.56, BU after 1966), *Orion*, ex-*R 132* (M 1053, 5.6.56, hulk DMB 20.6.68), *Pollux*, ex-*R 140* (M 1054, 19.6.56, sold 1970), *Regulus*, ex-*R 142* (M 1055, 31.7.56, BU 14.3.68), *Rigel*, ex-*R 135* (M 1056, 5.6.56, BU after 1966), *Saturn*, ex-*R 146* (M 1057, 31.7.56, sold 2.11.72), *Sirius*, ex-*R 144* (M 1058, 5.6.56, BU after 1970), *Spica*, ex-*R 147* (M 1059, 31.7.56, sold 1970), *Jupiter*, ex-*R 137* (M 1065, 31.7.56, hulk DMB 1969), *Merkur*, ex-*R 134* (M 1066, 5.6.56, sold 1.8.70), *UW 5*, ex-*R 150* (W 47, 11.12.56, sold 6.11.79)
Aldebaran group – *Aldebaran*, ex-*R 91* (M 1060, 16.11.56, sold 1.7.72), *Algol*, ex-*R 99* (M 1061, 30.10.56, hulk DMB 4.3.70), *Arkturus*, ex-*R 128* (M 1062, 16.11.56, BU 14.3.68), *Altair*, ex-*R 76* (M 1063, 30.11.56, sold 15.12.70), *Deneb*, ex-*R 127* (M 1064, 30.11.56, hulk DMB 20.6.68), *Wega*, ex-*R 67* (M 1069, 30.10.56, hulk DMN 1966), *Pegasus*, ex-*R 68* (M 1067, 16.11.56, sold 9.3.70), *Skorpion*, ex-*R 120* (M 1068, 16.11.56, hulk DMB 1.7.74), *UW 4*, ex-*R 101* (Y 870, 11.12.56, BU Mar 81)
UW 6 group – *UW 6*, ex-*R 408* (W 48, 11.12.56, BU 1977), *OT 1*, ex-*R 406* (W 52, 21.1.57, sold after 1959), *AT 1*, ex-*R 266* (W 61, 21.1.57, BU 1968), *AT 2*, ex-*R 407* (W 62, 21.1.57, target 1963)

These former *Kriegsmarine* R-boats were all built by Abeking & Rasmussen. They became Allied prizes after the war and saw service with the GMSA and the German Minesweeping Unit. After those forces were disbanded they were commissioned by the USN for the LSU(B), carrying the pennant numbers USN 130–USN 155.

Before being handed over to the new Federal German Navy they were substantially refitted; they commissioned from June 1956. While the first boats retained their old USN pennant numbers without the prefix USN, subsequent commissioned had a pennant number formed of a letter-group. From 1957 they received the NATO prefix 'M' and were designated Type 359. During their *Bundesmarine* career they were unaltered except for a lattice mast and some minor modifications to the training boats.

After decommissioning most served as accommodation boats carrying the designation WBR (abbr. for *Wohnboot Räumboot* = accommodation boat minesweeper) and formed the Type 730. After their final deletion *Orion*, *Deneb*, *Skorpion* and *Jupiter* became floating quarters for German Navy League local sections. *UW 4*, *UW 5*, *Algol*, *Altair*, *Merkur* and *Wega* were handed over to the Navy League, but have since been scrapped. Until 1972 *Saturn* was used as an exercise hulk for the damage control training group and *Aldebaran*, after minor modifications, served as a training boat for mine divers (pennant Y 850, Type 732). *UW 6* was used as a floating electric generator, *Stromer*, at the Naval Arsenal, Kiel. *Jupiter* became the training boat *OT 1* (ii) and *Regulus* the training boat *AT 1* (ii).

During the period 1946 to 1951 some boats were leased from the USN by private owners: *Arkturus* served as *Annegret*, *Wega* as *Hilligenlei* and *Rüstringen*, *UW 6* as *Hansa IV* and *OT 1* (i) as *Arngast*.

HANSA *inshore minesweeper*

Displacement:	155t standard; 175t full load
Dimensions:	111ft 8in, 115ft 5in oa × 21ft 10in × 6ft 5in *34.0m, 35.2m × 6.6m × 1.9m*
Machinery:	1 shaft, 1 Mercedes Benz diesel, 1000bhp (736kW) = 14kts. Oil 14t. Range 1500nm at 12kts
Armament:	1–40mm/70
Complement:	20

NIOBE *inshore minesweeper*

Displacement:	169.7t standard; 171t full load
Dimensions:	110ft 9in wl, 115ft 5in oa × 22ft 5in × 5ft 8in *33.8m, 35.2m × 6.8m × 1.7m*
Machinery:	2 shafts, 2 Mercedes Benz diesels, 2000bhp (1472kW) = 16kts. Oil 11t. Range 800nm at 12kts
Armament:	1–40mm/70
Complement:	20

Designed in 1955–56 as coast guard boats of the Types 361 and 360, they differed in the propulsion arrangement: *Hansa* had one shaft, *Niobe* two. Both were built by Krögerwerft and were launched on 18.11.57 and 8.8.57 respectively. These wooden boats were the first to use predominantly non-magnetic materials. In 1968 they were reclassified as riverine minesweepers, Types 392 and 391, their pennant number changing from a 'W' to 'M' prefix.

Since 1969 *Hansa* has served as a mine diver boat, pennant number Y 806, of the Type 732. During refit the minesweeping gear was removed and a cabin was erected on the quarterdeck.

Niobe was transferred as early as 1964 as a trials boat for the mine-warfare experimental department. In 1968 she was converted to a mine-warfare RC-control boat, the pennant prefix changing to 'Y'. In December she was modified yet again, changed her Type to 740, and served with a civilian crew at Trials Command 71. During modifications her minesweeping gear was removed and a hut was erected on the poop, and extensive electronic equipment was installed. The completely disarmed boat served for prototype trials and tests of the 'Troika' system using the towed-skid prototypes *Walross* and *Seekuh 1–3*. Particulars of the Troika prototypes are:
Walross: 84.7t full load; 88ft wl × 11ft 6in × 7ft (*26.8m × 3.5m × 2.1m*); 1 shaft Schottel propeller, diesel-electric drive, 290bhp (213.4kW) = 9kts. Oil 5.8t.
Seekuh: 90.1t full load (*Seekuh 1*); 78ft 2in wl, 88ft 8in oa × 11ft 8in × 7ft 4in (*23.8m, 27.0m × 3.5m × 2.2m*; *Seekuh 2, 3* 25ft (7.6m), wl, 1 shaft Schottel propeller, diesel-electric drive, 1 diesel 320bhp (235.5kW) = 9kts. Oil 6.2t.

ARIADNE class *inshore minesweepers*

Displacement:	199t–205t standard; 252t full load
Dimensions:	116ft 2in wl, 124ft 9in oa × 25ft 2in–26ft 4in × 7ft *35.3m, 38.0m × 7.6m–8.0m × 2.1m*
Machinery:	2 shafts, 2 Mercedes Benz diesels, 2000bhp (1472kW) = 14.5kts. Oil 16t. Range 830nm at 12kts
Armament:	1–40mm/70
Complement:	24

Class (no, launched):
Ariadne (M 2650, 23.4.60), *Freya* (M 2651, 25.6.60), *Vineta* (M 2652, 17.9.60),
Hertha (M 2653, 18.2.61), *Nymphe* (M 2654, 20.9.62), *Nixe* (M 2655, 3.12.62),
Amazone (M 2656, 27.2.63), *Gazelle* (M 2657, 14.8.63)

These wooden-hulled coast guard boats were designed in 1958–59 as 'KW
55–1', using mainly non-magnetic material in view of the successful outcome
with *Hansa* and *Niobe*. All units were built by Krögerwerft, and were commissioned with the pennant prefix 'W' and belonged to the Type 362.

From 1959 they were reclassified as riverine minesweepers of the 393 class
and pennant prefix was changed to 'M'. The eight units were built in two groups
which differed from each other in the shape of the main frame. From 1968 to
1974 they were in reserve with pennant prefix 'Y' although, with the exception
of *Gazelle*, they never carried it. In 1974 they were recommissioned as an active
minesweeping squadron. All were extant in 1982.

FRAUENLOB class inshore minesweepers

Displacement:	237.8t standard; 246.4t full load
Dimensions:	116ft 3in, 124ft 9in oa × 26ft 4in × 7ft *35.4m, 38.0m × 8.0m × 2.1m*
Machinery:	2 shafts, 2 Mercedes Benz diesels, 2000bhp (1472kW) = 14.5kts. Oil 13.3t. Range 993nm at 12kts
Armament:	1–40mm/L70
Complement:	24

Class (no, launched):
Frauenlob (M 2658, 26.2.65), *Nautilus* (M 2659, 19.5.65), *Gefion* (M 2660,
19.6.65), *Medusa* (M 2661, 25.1.66), *Undine* (M 2662, 16.5.66), *Minerva*
(M 2663, 25.8.66), *Diana* (M 2664, 13.12.66), *Loreley* (M 2665, 14.3.67),
Atlantis (M 2666, 20.6.67), *Acheron* (M 2667, 11.10.67)

These coast guard boats ('KW 60') of the Type 362 were reclassified in 1967
to riverine minesweepers of the Type 394. They resemble the previous *Ariadne*
class. The first seven boats commissioned with the pennant prefix 'W'; from
1968 they carried the prefix 'Y' and finally since 1974, 'M'.

HOLNIS *inshore minesweeper*

Displacement:	150t standard; 180.9t full load
Dimensions:	113ft 3in wl, 119ft 10in oa × 24ft 4in × 5ft 8in *34.5m, 41.7m × 7.4m × 1.7m*
Machinery:	2 shafts, 2 Mercedes Benz diesels, 2000bhp (1472kW) = 16.5kts. Oil 14.7t
Armament:	1–20mm (later removed)
Complement:	25

No	Name	Builder	Launched	Fate
Y 836	HOLNIS	Abeking & Rasmussen	20.5.65	Extant 1982

Another type of inshore riverine minesweeper was planned (Type 390), but only
the prototype unit, *Holnis*, was commissioned on 31.3.66. She was launched on
20.5.65 at Abeking & Rasmussen who were to have built the whole class, but the
project was cancelled.

After commissioning, *Holnis* carried the pennant prefix 'M'. In 1968 she was
converted to a communications trials boat. Guns and minesweeping gear were
removed and a hut was erected on the poop. She now belongs to the Type 740,
carries the pennant Y 836 and has a civilian crew.

Holnis after 1968

Author

Vineta Aug 1978
Author

MISCELLANEOUS

Donau Sept 1974
Author

RHEIN (Type 401) class *support ships*

Displacement:	2370t standard; 2740t–3016t full load
Dimensions:	304ft 6in wl, 322ft 2in oa × 38ft 10in × 17ft 2in *92.9m, 98.2m × 11.8m × 5.2m*
Machinery:	2 shafts (CP propellers), 6 MTU diesels, 11,400bhp (8390kW) = 22kts. Oil 330t
Armament:	2–100mm/55 (2×1), 4–40mm/L70 (2×2)
Sensors:	Radar KM 14/9, SGR-105, SGR-103, M45
Complement:	122

No	Name	Builder	Launched	Fate
A 58	RHEIN	Schlieker, Hamburg	10.12.59	Extant 1982
A 61	ELBE	Schlieker, Hamburg	5.5.60	Extant 1982
A 62	WESER	Elsflether Werft	11.6.60	To Greece 6.7.76
A 63	MAIN	Lindenauwerft, Kiel	23.7.60	Extant 1982
A 64	RUHR	Schlieker/Blohm & Voss, Hamburg	8.8.60	To Turkey 9.11.76
A 66	NECKAR	Lürssenwerft	26.6.61	Extant 1982
A 68	WERRA	Lindenauwerft, Kiel	26.3.63	Extant 1982
A 69	DONAU	Schlichting, Lübeck-Travemünde	26.11.60	Extant 1982

MOSEL (Type 402) class *support ships*

Displacement:	2330t standard; 3010t full load
Dimensions:	304ft 6in wl, 323ft 4in oa × 38ft 10in × 17ft 2in *92.9m, 98.5m × 11.8m × 5.2m*
Machinery:	2-shafts diesel-electric: 6 MTU diesels, 12,000bhp (8832kW) = 22.5kts. Oil 441t. Range 2500nm at 16kts
Complement:	99
Other particulars:	As *Rhein* class

No	Name	Builder	Launched	Fate
A 54	ISAR	Blohm & Voss, Hamburg	14.7.62	To Turkey 30.9.82
A 65	SAAR	Norderwerft, Hamburg	11.3.61	Extant 1982
A 67	MOSEL	Schlieker/Blohm & Voss, Hamburg	15.12.60	Extant 1982

271

WEST GERMANY

Saar 1971

LAHN (Type 403) class *support ships*

Displacement:	2633t standard; 2886 full load	
Dimensions:	292ft pp, 304ft 6in wl, 327ft oa × 38ft 10in × 17ft 2in	
	89.0m, 92.8m, 99.7m × 11.8m × 5.2m	
Machinery:	as *Mosel* class, but oil 452t	
Armament:	4–40mm/70 (2×2)	
Sensors:	Radar SGR-103	
Complement:	114	

No	Name	Builder	Launched	Fate
A 55	LAHN	Flenderwerke, Lübeck	21.11.61	Extant 1982
A 56	LECH	Flenderwerke, Lübeck	4.5.62	Extant 1982

Under the first building programme a total of 11 tenders (depot ships) was ordered, to a design produced in 1957–59. They were designed primarily to act as support vessels for particular types of warship. Officially, therefore, they are not fighting units, but considering their displacement, speed and armament they are real multi-role ships which can serve as command ships for their squadron, as accommodation ships (capacity for an additional 200 men), as escorts, minelayers and so on.

The tenders are sub-divided into three classes: Type 401 fast attack craft tenders, Type 402 fast minesweeper tenders, Type 403 submarine tenders. The Type 401 has pure diesel propulsion while the Types 402 and 403 have diesel-electric propulsion. The tenders of the Types 401 and 402 have identical armament, while the Type 403 has only 40mm guns.

Not all the tenders were actually allocated to flotillas; for example, *Weser*, *Ruhr* and *Donau* served as cadet training ships for a short time during the 1960s.

Because of the serious shortage of manpower, *Isar*, *Weser*, *Ruhr*, *Lech* and *Donau* were placed in reserve from 1968 to 1971. *Donau* was recommissioned in 1970 and *Lech* in 1975, while *Weser* was handed over to the Greek Navy, and *Ruhr* and *Isar* to the Turkish Navy as military aid.

NEUSTADT class *patrol craft*

Displacement:	191.4t standard; 218t full load
Dimensions:	118ft wl, 129ft oa × 23ft × 7ft 2in
	36.0m, 39.3m ×7.0m × 2.1m
Machinery:	3 shafts, (1 shaft for cruising, 1 MWM diesel 685bhp/504kW, 2 shafts, 2 MTU diesels 6000bhp/4416kW for high speed) = 9kts and 30kts. Oil 15.5t. Range 450nm at 27kts
Armament:	2–40mm/70 (2×1)
Complement:	23

Class (no, launched):

Neustadt (BG 11, 27.2.69), *Bad Bramstedt* (BG 12, 2.4.69), *Uelzen* (BG 13, 25.7.69), *Duderstadt* (BG 14, 3.6.69), *Eschwege* (BG 15, 16.9.69), *Alsfeld* (BG 16, 11.11.69), *Bayreuth* (BG 17, 9.1.70), *Rosenheim* (BG 18, 12.3.70)

The so-called Federal Frontier Guard (*Bundesgrenzschutz*) was instituted on 15 February 1951 and was taken over by the newly-created Navy (*Bundeswehr*) on 1 July 1956. Its personnel could choose to enter the service or remain as civil servants. The entire function of the Federal Frontier Guard (Naval) ('Bundesgrenzschutz/See') was assumed by the Navy when the former unit was disbanded.

The duties of the Federal Frontier Guard are: prevention of illegal entrants, passport control and security of the border. The strength of the Federal Frontier Guard was originally fixed by the Allied High Commissioners at 10,000 men, including 500 naval personnel. The unit is subordinated to the Federal Ministry of Home Affairs.

In 1963, because of continual border incidents, but also in order to release the Navy from frontier control duties – especially on the German Democratic Republic's border – the Ministry of Home Affairs and the Federal Ministry of Defence agreed to re-institute a small naval frontier inspection unit. As a first step four former Type 369 coast guard boats were handed over to the Guard in 1964. Meanwhile the first order for new boats had been given and on 27 February 1969 the first new vessel was launched. The Type consisted of eight boats designed and built by Lürssen. In contrast to the usual grey paint, they have a blue hull and white superstructure.

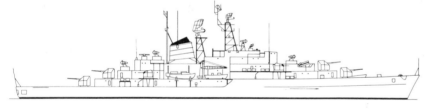

Deutschland 1963

DEUTSCHLAND *training ship*

Displacement:	4880t standard; 5684t full load
Dimensions:	426ft 6in wl, 453ft 6in oa × 52ft 9in × 16ft 8in
	130.0m, 138.2m × 16.1m × 5.1m
Machinery:	3-shaft (CP propellers), Wahodag steam turbines, 2 Wahodag boilers, plus 4 MTU diesels, 16,000shp (11,776kW) = 22kts. Fuel and diesel oil 643t. Range 3800nm at 12kts
Armament:	4–100mm/55 (4×1), 6–40mm/70 (2×2, 2×1), 2–533mm TT (stern), 4–533mm ASW TT (4×1), 2–375mm ASW mortars (2×4)
Sensors:	Radar LW-08, SGR-114, SGR-105, SGR-103, M-45; sonar ELAC 1BV
Complement:	172

No	Name	Builder	Launched	Fate
A 59	DEUTSCHLAND	Nobiskneg, Rendsburg	5.11.60	Extant 1982

The training ship *Deutschland* is of the Type 440 and is not strictly a fighting unit although she was designed in 1957–58 as a multi-purpose ship in case of war for troop transport, hospital, escort and minelaying duties. The extraordinary displacement required special permission from the WEU, and limits to speed and armament were imposed.

Deutschland serves as a cadet training ship only and for this reason she has a number of unique features, in combination not found in any other ship. The propulsion is mixed: the central shaft is steam-turbine driven, the outer shafts by two different types of diesel: one Maybach and one Mercedes Benz. In 1981 this was rationalised to Mercedes diesels because of maintenance costs. The armament includes all German Navy types except missiles.

In addition to a nucleus crew of 172 men, a further 250 cadets can be taken on board.

The stern TTs were removed in the mid-1970s.

Deutschland as completed

Navarret Collection

Australia

Before the Second World War the Royal Australian Navy had been the largest of the Commonwealth navies, but difficulties in supplying material from Great Britain after 1941 slowed down expansion by comparison with Canada. In 1946, however, there was still an impressive line-up of cruisers, destroyers and escorts.

Postwar building policy tended to follow RN lines at first, with copies of the latest destroyer designs being built locally, but in 1962, for the first time, guided missile destroyers were bought from the United States, marking a growing reliance on American technology rather than European, to avoid the shortage of spares which had plagued the RAN in 1942–45. There was still close liaison with the RN on design work, however, first on the Type 21 frigate programme and then for the DDL programme in 1966–73, but for political reasons the options were not taken up and once again US ships were purchased.

The RAN retains its fixed-wing aviation element and will build a replacement for HMAS *Melbourne* in the 1980s. Every available option has been looked at, but the commitment to American equipment makes it likely that the new carrier will come from the United States as well. Although the former insistence on building the hulls in Australia has proved impossible to sustain, every effort is made to generate work in Australia, either by developing systems or by offset agreements to make components. In conjunction with the RN an anti-submarine missile-system, Ikara, was developed in the late 1950s and early 1960s. When European and American sonars proved unable to cope with the temperature range and sound-propagation found in the South-West Pacific, the RAN went ahead with its own sonar, Mulloka.

In recent years the RAN has concentrated its efforts on providing forces capable of backing up US forces in the Pacific rather than trying to specialise in ASW or minesweeping. With an immense coastline to watch it has built a number of small patrol craft, but as tension with Indonesia has subsided, a number of the older craft were transferred both to that country and to the newly-independent Papua New Guinea. At present the main commitment is to the replacing of the heterogeneous fleet of destroyers and frigates of the 1950s and 1960s by US frigates. Some of the later ships of this programme will be built in Australia, marking a return to self-sufficiency.

FLEET STRENGTH 1947

CRUISERS

Name	Launched	Disp (deep load)	Fate
Kent class			
AUSTRALIA	17.3.27	14,910t	BU 1955
London class			
SHROPSHIRE	5.7.28	14,580t	BU 1955
Amphion class			
HOBART (ex-*Apollo*) (C 02)	9.10.34	9420t	BU 1962

Kent class
Australia served as the RAN flagship for several years. Following repairs to the kamikaze damage in January 1945 she had 'X' turret removed and had a modern RN-pattern director control tower on the bridge, fitted with Type 284 radar. A high-angle DCT with Type 285 radar was fitted on the centreline, forward of the mainmast. She was unusual in that her 4in guns were mounted one deck lower.

London class
Shropshire lost her 20mm guns, but was otherwise unaltered after 1945. She differed from *Australia* in having two high-angle DCTs fitted, one on the bridge and one abaft the funnels. She was laid up in 1948.

Amphion class
Hobart completed battle-damage repairs at the end of 1944, but was laid up postwar. She received an extensive refit at the Newcastle State DYd in 1953–56 for service as a training ship, but was then laid up once more. For this role she was given a lattice foremast, but had all TT and secondary guns removed.

DESTROYERS

Name	Fate	Name	Fate
'Tribal' class: launched 1940–44, 2710t deep load			
ARUNTA (D 130)	Foundered 13.2.69	WARRAMUNGA (D 123)	BU 1963
BATAAN	BU 1958		
Quilliam class: launched 1941–42, 2480t deep load			
QUADRANT	Type 15 (See notes)	QUIBERON	Type 15
QUALITY	BU 1958	QUICKMATCH	Type 15
QUEENSBOROUGH	Type 15		

'Tribal' class
In 1952–53 *Arunta* was modernised for ASW work, followed by *Warramunga* in 1953–54. This involved stepping a lattice mast and extending the after deckhouse from abaft the TT to the former 'Y' mounting. The original 4.7in guns were left in position forward as well as the original fire control, but a twin 4in Mk 16 AA gun, a twin Mk 5 and two Mk 7 Bofors guns were added on the deckhouse, with a Squid triple ASW mortar on the quarterdeck. *Bataan* was scheduled to be similarly modernised, but the cost of the other two ships was so high that her refit was cancelled in 1957. *Arunta* foundered in tow en route to Japan for scrapping.

Quilliam class
The transfer from the RN was made permanent in June 1950 and the vessels were then scheduled to undergo conversion to ASW frigates along the lines of the Type 15 frigates in the RN (see Major Surface Ships). As with the destroyers, however, costs rose beyond the original £A400,000 planned and in 1957 *Quality*'s conversion was cancelled and she was put on the disposal list.

FRIGATES

Name	Fate	Name	Fate
Grimsby class: launched 1936 and 1940, 1510t deep load			
SWAN (F 74)	Sold 1964	WARREGO (F 312)	BU 1966
'River' class: launched 1943–45, 2200t deep load			
BARCOO (F 174)	BU 1972	GASCOYNE (F 354)	BU 1972
BARWON (F 402)	BU 1962	HAWKESBURY (F 363)	BU 1962
BURDEKIN (F 376)	BU 1962	LACHLAN (F 364)	To New Zealand 1949
DIAMANTINA (F 377)	Paid off 1979	MACQUARIE (ex-*Culgoa*) (F 532)	BU 1962
Modified 'River' class: launched 1944, 2187t deep load			
CONDAMINE (F 698)	BU 1962	MURCHISON (F 442)	BU 1962
CULGOA (ex-*Macquarie*) (F 408)	BU 1972	SHOALHAVEN (F 535)	BU 1962

AUSTRALIA

Grimsby class
Swan was used for training cadets from 1955 and *Warrego* was employed as a survey ship. Both these former sloops had their armament reduced to 2–4in AA (1×2) and 1–40mm Bofors guns forward, and extra deckhouses were added aft.

'River' class
Originally similar to RN and RCN 'River' class but with different armament. *Barcoo*, *Hawkesbury* and *Macquarie* had the twin 4in Mk 16 in 'A' position, with two Squid DC mortars in 'B' position and a single 40mm Bofors gun on the Squid handing room (*Barcoo* and *Hawkesbury* only). From the early 1950s *Barcoo* was used on survey duties; she was replaced in 1959 by *Diamantina* and *Gascoyne*.

Modified 'River' class
The armament was modified to approximate to RN 'Bay' class AA frigates, with a twin 4in Mk 16 (2×2) forward and aft, 3–40mm Bofors (3×1) and two twin 20mm guns. To limit topweight the guns were mounted in 'A' and Y' positions. All four had lattice masts by 1955.

MINESWEEPERS

Name	Fate	Name	Fate
Bathurst class: launched 1940–43, *c*790t			
ARARAT (M 34)	Sold 1961	HORSHAM (M 235)	BU 1956
BENALLA (M 323)	BU 1958	INVERELL (M 233)	To New Zealand 1952
BOWEN (M 285)	BU 1956	JUNEE (M 362)	Sold 1958
BUNBURY (M 241)	BU 1962	KAPUNDA (M 218)	BU 1962
BUNDABERG (M 231)	BU 1962	KATOOMBA	BU 1957
CASTLEMAINE (M 244)	HS *c* 1956	KIAMA (M 353)	To New Zealand 1952
COLAC (M 05)	HS 1962	LATROBE (M 234)	BU 1956
COOTAMUNDRA (M 186)	For disposal 1973	LITHGOW (M 206)	BU 1956
COWRA (M 351)	BU 1962	MILDURA (M 207)	HS *c* 1956
DELORAINE (M 252)	BU 1956	PARKES (M 361)	Sold 1957
DUBBO (M 251)	BU 1958	ROCKHAMPTON (M 203)	BU 1962

Name	Fate	Name	Fate
ECHUCA (M 252)	To New Zealand 1952	SHEPPARTON (M 248)	BU 1958
FREMANTLE (M 246)	BU 1962	STAWELL (M 348)	To New Zealand 1952
GLADSTONE (M 324)	Sold 1956	STRAHAN (M 363)	BU 1962
GLENELG (M 236)	BU 1957	TOWNSVILLE (M 205)	Sold 1956
GYMPIE (M 238)	BU 1962	WAGGA (M 183)	Sold 1962

Bathurst class
Based on the *Bangor* class, but in fact a new design, sometimes described as 'corvette-type' fleet sweepers. Although obsolete many continued to serve as sea-going and static training ships. *Echuca*, *Inverall*, *Kiama* and *Stawell* were transferred to the RNZN in 1952 and retained their names.

TANK LANDING SHIPS

Name	Fate	Name	Fate
Ex-British LST (3) type: launched 1944–45, 3065t full load			
LAE (ex-*LST 3035*)	Sold 9.11.55	*LST 3008*	Sold 4.6.50
LABUAN (ex-*LST 3501*)	Sold 9.11.55	*LST 3014*	Sold 4.6.50
TARAKAN (ex-*LST 3017*)	Sold 12.3.54	*LST 3022*	Sold 4.6.50

Six vessels transferred after brief service in the Royal Navy; commissioned into the RAN on 1.7.46. They served principally as transport and supply vessels.

MOTOR LAUNCHES
Of the 35 Fairmile 'B' type MLs that were built in Australian during the war, 33 survived, but they were rapidly decommissioned and sold at the end of hostilities.

Of the HDML type, 9 were built in Australia, 3 in Britain and 16 in the USA, and all survived. In 1950 *HDML 1323*, *1326*, *1328* and *1329* were lent to the RN for use in Hong Kong, and on their return to Australia in 1958 were transferred to the Philippines. By 1952 only *HDML 1321*, *1322*, *1324*, *1325* and *1327* remained in the RAN, and they were rated as seaward defence motor launches (SDMLs) and from 1959 as seaward defence boats. *SDML 1322* was stricken in 1953, *SDB 1327* in 1966, *SDB 1321* in 1972, leaving *SDB 1324* (as TS *Nepean*) and *SDB 1325* extant in 1982.

Sydney (nearest) and *Melbourne* with a fleet oiler and a Type 12 frigate, 24.3.66

Courtesy Ross Gillett

MAJOR SURFACE SHIPS

HMS *Terrible*, the only aircraft carrier built in one of HM dockyards, was laid down on 10.4.43, launched on 30.4.44 and completed for the RAN on 5.2.49. She saw considerable active service in the Korean War alongside her British sisters, operating Sea Furies and Fireflies (normal complement 12 of each, plus 2 Sea Otter amphibious). A major modernisation was cancelled in 1954, and from May of 1953 she took on flying training duties. In 1962–63 she was relegated to a fast military transport, and her defensive armament was reduced to 4–40mm. In this role she carried vehicles stowed on deck and the hangar was used for troop accommodation, and from 1969 six LCPUs were carried under davits. She was put on the

SYDNEY *aircraft carrier*

Displacement:	14,000t standard; 17,780t deep load
Dimensions:	630ft pp, 695ft oa × 80ft × 23ft mean deep load
	192.0m, 211.8m × 24.4m × 7.0m
Machinery:	2-shaft Parsons geared turbines, 4 Admiralty 3-drum boilers, 40,000shp = 25kts. Oil 3000t
Armament:	24–40mm Bofors, 26 aircrafts
Complement:	1300

No	Name	Builder	Acquired	Fate
R 17	SYDNEY (ex-*Terrible*)	Devonport DYd	1948	BU 1975

disposal list in 1973 and sold for scrapping on 30.10.75.

NOTE

The British *Colossus* class light fleet carrier *Vengeance* was lent to Australia from 1952–55. Taken over by the

RAN on 13.11.52, the ship saw active service until defence cuts in late 1954 reduced the ship to a training role. She was intended as a stop-gap until the commissioning of *Melbourne* and was returned to the RN in June 1955.

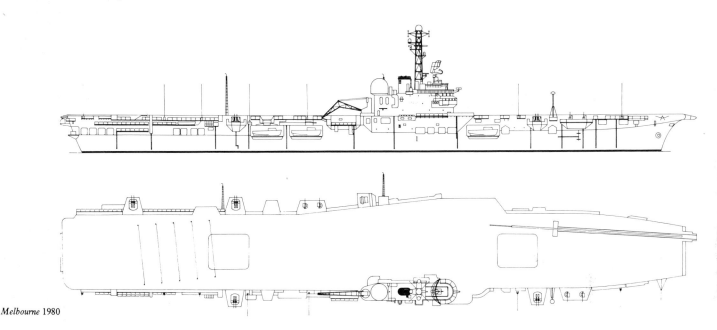

Melbourne 1980

Work was resumed on this vessel in 1949 after her purchase by the Australian government, and the opportunity was taken to incorporate as many new ideas as possible, including a steam catapult, a 6° angled deck and mirror landing sights. However, apart from a lattice mast and whip aerials she looked similar to the original *Majestic*s.

A greatly enhanced radar suite was incorporated, including no fewer than three Type 277Q height-finding sets. The armament was reduced slightly to 25–40mm. She recommissioned at the yard of her builders on 28 October 1955 and embarked an air group of 8 Sea Venom fighters, 12 Gannet antisubmarine aircraft (replaced in the early 1960s by Wessex helicopters) and 2 Sycamore helicopters; from 1963–67 this was reduced to 4 Sea Venoms, 6 Gannets and 10 Wessexes.

After several years' service as Flagship of the RAN she was taken in hand for modification to allow her to operate A–4 Skyhawk fighter-bombers (Dec 67–Nov 68). This involved new radar and communications and strengthening of the decks,

MELBOURNE *aircraft carrier*

Displacement:	16,000t standard; 19,966t full load
Dimensions:	701ft 6in oa, 650ft wl × 80ft 3in × 25ft 6in
	213.8m, 198.1m × 24.4m × 7.8m
Machinery:	2-shaft geared steam turbines, 4 Admiralty 3-drum boilers, 42,000shp = 23kts. Range 6200nm/12,000nm at 23kts/14kts
Armour:	Mantlets over torpedo warheads
Armament:	12–40mm/60 Bofors Mk 5 and Mk 7 (4×2, 4×1), 24 aircraft
Sensors:	Radar LW-02, Types 293, 978, SPN-35. See notes
Complement:	1417 (inc 347 air group) as flagship

No	Name	Builder	Acquired	Fate
R 21	MELBOURNE (ex-*Majestic*)	Vickers-Armstrong, Barrow	1949	Extant 1982

lifts, catapult and arrester gear. This time she received a mixture of Dutch and US radars, although the British Type 293 surface search set and Type 978 navigation sets were retained. The most obvious external changes were the addition of the Signaal LW-02 air surveillance scanner over the bridge, the dome covering the SPN–35 carrier-controlled approach scanner abaft the funnel and a TACAN aerial and various ECM pods on the lattice mast. In addition the funnel was fitted with an inconspicu-

ous cap to divert smoke from the radar arrays.

The air group now consisted of 4 A-4G Skyhawks and 6 S–2E Tracker ASW aircraft and 10 Wessexes, but from 1972 onwards she carried 8 Skyhawks, 6 Trackers and 10 Wessexes. Sea King Mk 50 ASW helicopters have replaced the Wessexes and some of the Trackers (the composition of her air group changes to meet requirements.)

In 1971 the catapult was rebuilt, with a bridle-catcher extension at the

forward end of the flight deck, and the deck was strengthened once more. She was refitted again in November 1972–July 1973, and after a further refit in 1976 it was announced that the ship will serve until 1985. Her replacement is now a matter of urgency as no shipyard can deliver a carrier in less than five years; the order was announced in September 1980 but the final selection of a design has still to be made. In the meantime *Melbourne* paid off into 'Contingent Reserve', 30.6.82.

AUSTRALIA

In 1980, the Australian Minister of Defence announced that a replacement for HMAS *Melbourne* would be ordered in 1981, but no announcement was made about type of ship or aircraft to be carried. It is known that British variants of the *Invincible* have been looked at, the Italian *Giuseppe Garibaldi* and the Spanish Sea Control

'MELBOURNE Replacement' *aircraft carrier*

Ship, and a derivative of the *Tarawa* class LHA produced by Litton Industries. However, the British government offered *Invincible* to Australia following the 1981 Defence Review, and the sale was agreed early in 1982.

The offer was withdrawn following the Falklands conflict, and at the end of 1982 the position was unclear. An *Invincible* class ship may be built for Australia.

Two ships were ordered for the RAN to a slightly enlarged (Batch 3) version of the Royal Navy's 1943 'Battle' design (eight more for the RN were cancelled in 1945). They were able to accommodate an extra 40mm STAAG mounting amidships, but had the Mk 6 fire control system of the original 1942 'Battle' design. *Tobruk*'s 4.5in guns were imported, but *Anzac*'s were built under licence in Australia; unlike their RN sisters, they had twin Mk 6 mountings as fitted to the *Darings*. In 1966 *Anzac* was converted to a training ship, with 'B' gun replaced by a classroom. Both ships had capped funnels, unlike the RN 'Battles'.

British Modified 'BATTLE' type *destroyers*

Displacement:	2400t normal; 3500t deep load
Dimensions:	355ft pp, 379ft oa × 41ft × 13ft 6in
	108.2m, 115.5m × 12.5m × 4.1m
Machinery:	As British 'Battle' class
Armament:	4–4.5in/45 Mk 6 (2×2), 6–40mm/60 STAAG Mk 2 (3×2), 6–40mm/60 Mk 7 (6×1), 10–21in TT (2×5), 1 Squid ASW mortar
Sensors:	Radars Types 275, 262, 293; sonar Types 170, 174
Complement:	332

No	Name	Builder	Laid down	Launched	Comp	Fate
D 37	TOBRUK	Cockatoo I DYd	5.8.46	20.12.47	8.5.50	BU 1972
D 59	ANZAC	Williamstown DYd	23.9.46	20.8.48	14.3.51	BU 1975

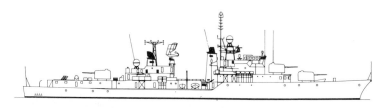

Vendetta 1977

Four modified *Daring* class destroyers were ordered in December 1946, but work did not start until 1949, with material imported from Great Britain. In general the original layout was followed, but the after bank of TT was suppressed and 'X' turret was moved forward to allow a Limbo mortar to be mounted on the centreline. *Waterhen* was cancelled in 1954. As completed, *Voyager* was very similar to the British *Daring*, but *Vampire* and *Vendetta* were given two CRBF directors on the centreline forward and aft of the funnel and two twin 40mm Mk 5 Bofors mountings sided.

Voyager was sunk on 10 February 1964 in collision with the carrier *Melbourne*, and HMS *Duchess* was transferred from the RN on loan; she was bought outright in 1972 and paid off in 1977. In 1969–73 *Vampire* and *Vendetta* underwent complete rebuilding, with Dutch Signaal WM22 fire control forward and aft, an enclosed bridge and an early-warning LW–02 radar array on a stump mast forward of the second funnel. The original lattice foremast was removed, so that a new capped funnel was now visible. *Duchess* was not refitted to the same extent, but had a new after funnel and a large deckhouse aft for classrooms in place of the twin 4.5in mounting and Squid.

Duchess and *Vendetta* were put on the disposal list in 1979, but in 1980 *Vampire* joined a new training squadron, and she was still serving in 1982.

British DARING type *destroyers*

Displacement:	2800t normal; 3600t deep load
Armament:	6–4.5in/45 Mk 6 (3×2), 4–40mm STAAG Mk 2 (2×2), 2–40mm Mk 5 (1×2) (*Vampire* and *Vendetta* 4–40mm Mk 5 (2×2), 2–40mm Mk 7 (2×1)), 5–21in TT, 1 Limbo Mk 10 ASW mortar
Sensors:	Radar Types 275, 262, 293; sonar Types 170, 174/177
Complement:	320
Other particulars:	As British *Daring* class

No	Name	Builder	Laid down	Launched	Comp	Fate
D 04	VOYAGER	Cockatoo I DYd	10.10.49	1.5.52	12.2.57	Sunk 10.2.64
D 08	VENDETTA	Williamstown DYd	4.7.49	3.5.54	26.11.58	For disposal 1979
D 11	VAMPIRE	Cockatoo I DYd	1.7.52	27.10.56	23.6.59	Extant 1982
–	WATERHEN	Williamstown DYd	Dec 52	–	–	Cancelled 1954
D 154	DUCHESS	Thornycroft		acquired 1964		For disposal 1979

Vendetta as completed

Courtesy Ross Gillett

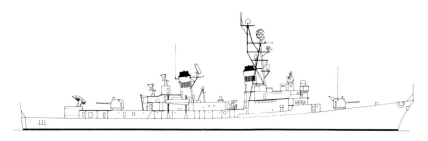

Brisbane 1978

Two *Charles F Adams* type guided missile destroyers (DDGs) were ordered from the United States in January 1962 and a third was ordered exactly a year later. They were virtually identical with the original class apart from having Ikara in place of ASROC; this necessitated building a deckhouse between the funnels housing the Ikara magazine, with two single-arm launchers port and starboard at the forward end. Between 1974 and 1979 all three were modernised, with Standard SM–1 missiles (40 carried) in place of Tartar and gun mountings converted to Mod 10. Although not yet announced, it is likely that they will also receive Harpoon SSMs in the near future.

US CHARLES F ADAMS type *guided missile destroyers*

Armament:	2–5in/54 Mk 42 (2×1), 1 Tartar RIM–24 (later Standard SM–1A RIM–66B) SAM system, 6–12.75in (324mm) Mk 32 ASW TT (2×3), 2 Ikara ASW systems (2×1)
Sensors:	Radar SPS-40, SPS-10, SPS-52B, SPG-51C, SPG-53A, Type 978; sonar SQS-23F
Other particulars:	As US *Charles F Adams* class

No	Name	Builder	Laid down	Launched	Comp	Fate
D 38	PERTH (ex-*DDG 25*)	Defoe SB	21.9.62	26.9.63	17.7.65	Extant 1982
D 39	HOBART (ex-*DDG 26*)	Defoe SB	26.10.62	9.1.64	18.12.65	Extant 1982
D 41	BRISBANE (ex-*DDG 27*)	Defoe SB	15.2.65	5.5.66	16.12.67	Extant 1982

Perth 12.12.80 Ross Gillett

Courtesy Ross Gillett

Official artist's impression of 1966 destroyer design

In 1966 the RAN and RN began a joint study of a 'light destroyer' (DDL) with good air defence and a limited ASW/surface role. The joint study broke up because the RAN had no intention of departing from its policy of buying US weaponry, but the resulting ship strongly resembled the Royal Navy's contemporary Type 42 DDG. The machinery was the same, and the dimensions very similar (slightly longer and beamier), but a double hangar for two Lynx helicopters was provided and six SSMs. It was also hoped to fit the new Mulloka sonar, designed for Australian requirements. The extra beam would have given a rather better fuel supply, and the ships had a designed endurance of 6000nm at 18kts.

1966 Light Destroyer Project

Displacement:	4200t normal; *c*5000t deep load
Dimensions:	425ft wl × 48ft × *c*22ft 129.5m, 14.6m × 6.7m
Machinery:	2-shaft COGOG: 2 Rolls-Royce Olympus plus 2 Tyne, 50,000shp = 30kts. Range 6000nm at 18kts
Armament:	1–5in/54 Mk 42 DP, 4–35mm Emerlec-30 (2×2), 6–12.75in (324mm) Mk 32 TT (2×3), 1 Standard SM–1A RIM–66A SAM system, 6 SSMs, 2 helicopters
Complement:	210

The detailed design work was entrusted to Y-ARD Australia in 1970 and it was hoped to lay the first keel in June 1975, followed by the others at two-yearly intervals. All three would have been built at Williamstown DYd. The first was to be ready in 1980 and the last in 1984, at an estimated cost of \$A118 million (£59.2 million) at 1972 prices; this figure included design and support costs as well as construction. The ships would have looked very similar to the *Sheffield* class, but with a single-arm Tartar launcher at the forward end of the hangar, a single missile-tracker radar abaft the funnel and a single plated mast.

The new Labour Government which came to power in 1973 deferred a decision on the DDLs and cancelled them outright in 1974, choosing American frigates instead.

AUSTRALIA

The wartime transfer of the five ships of the *Quilliam* class was made permanent in June 1950 and work began on conversion to the same standard as the RN's Type 15 frigates. The work was done by Williamstown DYd (*Quadrant* April 1950–July 1953), and Cookatoo Island (*Queenborough* May 1950–December 1954, *Quickmatch* April 1951–September 1955, and *Quiberon* November 1950–December 1957), but *Quality* was not converted and was scrapped in 1958. They differed little from the British ships apart from having a round-fronted bridge with the twin 40mm Bofors ahead of

QUADRANT class *frigates*

Particulars:	As British *Rapid* class					
No	Name	Builder	Laid down	Launched	Comp	Fate
F 01	QUADRANT	Hawthorn Leslie	24.9.40	28.2.42	26.11.42	BU 1963
F 02	QUEENBOROUGH	Swan Hunter	6.11.40	16.1.42	10.12.42	BU 1975
F 03	QUIBERON	White	14.10.40	31.1.42	22.7.42	BU 1972
F 04	QUICKMATCH	White	6.2.41	11.4.42	30.9.42	BU 1972

it. *Quadrant* had two Squid ASW mortars (2×3), whereas the other three were fitted with Mk 10 Limbo (2×3).

In August 1950 plans for six Type 12 frigates were announced, but subsequently the number was cut to four; No 5 and No 6 were later reordered to a modified design. They incorporated all the improvements of the RN *Rothesay* class, and in addition had MRS3 fire control and Dutch Signaal LW–02 air warning radar. The second pair had the forecastle deck extended aft to the stern, providing additional accommodation. *Stuart* was the first to be fitted with the Ikara ASW system, which replaced one of the Limbo Mk 10 mortars aft, and *Derwent* was the first RAN ship to receive the Seacat GWS22 missile system in lieu of the twin 40mm Bofors. All were subsequently fitted with both systems; approximately 24 of each missile are carried.

YARRA class *frigates*

Particulars:	(As Built) as British *Whitby* and *Rothesay* classes					
No	Name	Builder	Laid down	Launched	Comp	Fate
F 45	YARRA	Williamstown DYd	9.4.57	30.9.58	Jul 61	Extant 1982
F 46	PARRAMATTA	Cockatoo I DYd	3.1.57	31.1.57	4.7.61	Extant 1982
F 49	DERWENT	Williamstown DYd	16.6.59	17.6.61	Apr 64	Extant 1982
F 48	STUART	Cockatoo I DYd	20.3.59	8.4.61	27.6.63	Extant 1982
–	No 5	Williamstown DYd	–	–	–	Cancelled 1956
–	No 6	Cockatoo I DYd	–	–	–	Cancelled 1956

Yarra ran trials with the new Mulloka sonar in 1975–76 in place of her Type 177M, and then paid off for a half-life modernisation in which the Mk 10 mortar was removed and replaced with a helicopter flight deck. She is also due to receive SPS–55 in lieu of Type 293 radar and Signaal M22

fire control for the Seacat missiles. The other three are being given a more extensive modernisation, with similarly improved electronics and sonar, but with 6–12.75in (324mm) Mk 32 ASW TT replacing the Mk 10 mortar, and improvements to the boilers and to general standards of

habitability. *Parramatta*'s refit extended from June 77 to August 81, *Stuart* was taken in hand in March 79 (for completion mid-1983), and work on *Derwent* began in July 81. *Yarra* is now expected to pay off in 1986.

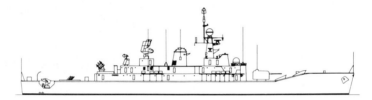

Swan as completed

The two cancelled *Yarra* class were re-ordered nine years later to a modified design which incorporated many features of the RN *Leander* class. The forecastle deck was extended right aft and a new continuous two-decked superstructure and streamlined funnel replaced the former light superstructure. The air warning radar antenna was mounted on a new stump mainmast, but no provision was made for a helicopter hangar.

The two ships are likely to have a new radar and sonar outfit at their half-life modernisation, with SPS–55 in place of Type 293 radar. The Mulloka sonar will replace the elderly RN

SWAN class *frigates*

Armament:	2–4.5in/45 Mk 6 (1×2), 1 Ikara ASW system, 1 Seacat M22 SAM (1×4), 1 Limbo Mk 10 ASW mortar
Sensors:	Radar LW-02, M-22, Type 293, Type 903; sonar Types 162, 170, 177M, 185
Complement:	247
Other particulars:	As British *Rothesay* class

No	Name	Builder	Laid down	Launched	Comp	Fate
F 53	TORRENS	Cockatoo I DYd	12.8.65	28.9.68	19.1.71	Extant 1982
F 50	SWAN	Williamstown DYd	16.8.65	16.12.67	20.1.70	Extant 1982

Type 177M now installed, and triple Mk 32 TT will replace the obsolete Mk 10 mortar.

Following the cancellation of the DDL project in 1974, the Department of Defence ordered two of the new *Oliver Hazard Perry* (PF 109, later FFG 7) class frigates. Orders were placed in February 1976 for FFG 17–18 out of the USN's programme, and FFG 35 was ordered in November 1977. The growing need of replacements for the *Daring* class led to an order for FFG 48 in April 1980 and in September the same year the Defence Minister announced that the replacements for the six 'River' class DEs (the *Yarra* and *Swan* classes) would also be members of this class. They are likely to be ordered at yearly intervals, for completion from 1984 to 1989.

US OLIVER HAZARD PERRY type *guided missile frigates*

Particulars:	As US *Oliver Hazard Perry* class					
No	Name	Builder	Laid down	Launched	Comp	Fate
F 01	ADELAIDE (ex-FFG 17)	Todd, Seattle	29.7.77	21.6.78	15.11.80	Extant 1982
F 02	CANBERRA (ex-FFG 18)	Todd, Seattle	1.3.78	1.12.78	21.3.81	Extant 1982
F 03	SYDNEY (ex-FFG 35)	Todd, Seattle	21.1.80	26.9.80		Fitting out
F 04	DARWIN (ex-FFG 48)	Todd, Seattle	3.7.81	31.3.82		Fitting out
	No 5	Williamstown DYd				Projected
	No 6	Williamstown DYd				Projected
	No 7					Projected
	No 8					Projected
	No 9					Projected
	No 10					Projected

SUBMARINES

Oberon class, built 1964–78. The first four boats are being refitted with USN-pattern periscopes and weapons, Sub-Harpoon missiles and Mk 48 torpedoes. The principal elements are a Singer/Librascope SFCS Mk 1 digital fire control system and a Krupp Atlas CSU3–41 active/passive sonar (active transducer in fin, passive array in the new bow sonardome). The refit programme is: *Oxley* Oct 77–Feb 80; *Otway* Jan 79–early 81; *Ovens* March 80–mid-82; *Orion* Nov 81–early 84.

British OBERON Type *patrol submarines*

Sensors: Radar Type 1006; sonar Types 187C, 197, 2007, Micropuffs
Other particulars: As British *Oberon* class

No	Name	Builder	Laid down	Launched	Comp	Fate
S 27	OXLEY	Scotts	2.7.64	24.9.65	27.3.67	Extant 1982
S 59	OTWAY	Scotts	29.6.65	29.11.66	22.4.68	Extant 1982
S 70	OVENS	Scotts	17.6.66	5.12.67	18.4.69	Extant 1982
S 60	ONSLOW	Scotts	26.5.67	29.8.68	22.12.69	Extant 1982
S 61	ORION	Scotts	6.10.72	16.9.74	15.6.77	Extant 1982
S 62	OTAMA	Scotts	28.5.73	2.12.75	27.4.78	Extant 1982

AMPHIBIOUS WARFARE VESSELS

TOBRUK *tank landing ship*

Displacement:	3400t normal; 5800t full load
Dimensions:	417ft × 60ft × 16ft
	127.1m × 18.3m × 4.9m
Machinery:	2 shafts, 2 Mirrlees Blackstone KDM8 diesels, 9600bhp = 17kts
Armament:	2–40mm
Sensors:	Radar KH 1006, RM 916
Complement:	70 (plus 350–500 troops)

No	Name	Builder	Launched	Fate
L 50	TOBRUK	Carrington Slipways	1.3.80	Extant 1982

Tobruk as completed   Courtesy Ross Gillett

A modified version of the British *Sir Bedivere* class LSLs, but rated as an amphibious heavy lift ship, *Tobruk* was laid down on 7.2.78 and commissioned on 23.4.81. She can operate Wessex helicopters, can carry pontoons and has a powerful heavy lift system. Two LCVPs are carried in davits.

BALIKPAPAN *utility landing craft*

Displacement:	310t light; 503t full load
Dimensions:	146ft × 33ft × 6ft 6in
	44.5m × 10.1m × 2.0m
Machinery:	2 shafts, 2 GM diesels, 675bhp = 10kts. Range 3000nm at 10kts
Armament:	2 MGs
Sensors:	Radar RM 916
Complement:	16

Class:
Balikpapan (L 126), *Brunei* (L 127), *Labuan* (L 128), *Tarakan* (L 129), *Wewak* (L 130), *Salamaua* (L 131), *Buna* (L 132), *Betano* (L 133)
   All were built by Walkers, Maryborough in 1971–72, they are rated as heavy landing craft (LCH) and can carry 3 tanks. They were originally built for the Army. *Salamaua* and *Buna* were transferred to Papua New Guinea in 1974, and the remainder were in service in 1982.

Wewak 25.8.80   Ross Gillett

SMALL SURFACE COMBATANTS

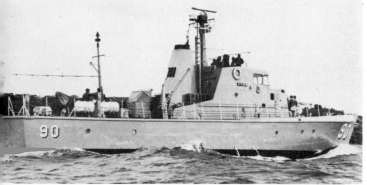

Attack 9.4.79   Ross Gillett

Fremantle as completed   Courtesy Ross Gillett

ATTACK class *patrol craft*

Displacement:	100t normal; 125t deep load
Dimensions:	107ft 6in oa × 20ft × 7ft 3in
	32.8m, 6.1m × 2.1m
Machinery:	2 shafts, 2 Paxman YJCM diesels, 3500bhp = 24kts max. Range 1220nm at 13kts
Armament:	1–40mm/60 Mk 7, 2–.5in MG (2×1)
Sensors:	Radar RM 916
Complement:	19

Class: *Acute* (P 81), *Adroit* (P 82), *Advance* (P 83), *Aitape* (P 84), *Samarai* (P 85), *Archer* (P 86), *Ardent* (P 87), *Arrow* (P 88), *Assail* (P 89), *Attack* (P 90), *Aware* (P 91), *Ladava* (P 92), *Lae* (P 93), *Madang* (P 94), *Bandolier* (P 95), *Barbette* (P 97), *Barricade* (P 98), *Bombard* (P 99), *Buccaneer* (P 100), *Bayonet* (P 101)

A total of 20 33m patrol boats were ordered in November 1965 for coastal patrol work; five – *Aitape*, *Samarai*, *Ladava*, *Lae* and *Madang* – were to be employed in New Guinea, the others in Australian home waters. P 81–82, P 85, P 89–92, P 94, P 98, P 100 were built by Evans Deakin, the rest by Walker's, Maryborough. In 1973–74 *Bandolier* and *Archer* were transferred to Indonesia and renamed *Sibarau* and *Silinan*, and in 1975 the five boats in New Guinea waters were transferred to the newly formed Papua New Guinea Defence Force. *Arrow* sank at her moorings in Darwin on 25.12.74 during Hurricane 'Tracy', but *Attack*, although damaged, proved capable of repair.

FREMANTLE class *patrol craft*

Displacement:	240t normal; c275t deep load
Dimensions:	137ft 10in oa × 23ft 5in × 6ft 11in
	42.0m, 7.1m × 1.9m
Machinery:	3 shafts, 2 MTU 16V538 TB91 diesels, plus Dorman cruising diesel, 6000bhp = 30kts. Range 1450nm/4800nm at 28kts/8kts
Armament:	1–40mm/60 Mk 7
Sensors:	Radar Decca 1226
Complement:	22

Class: *Fremantle* (P 203), *Warrnambool* (P 204), *Townsville* (P 205), *Woolongong* (P 206), *Launceston* (P 209), *Cessnock* (P 210), *Bendigo* (P 211), *Gawler* (P 212), *Geraldton* (P 213), *Dubbo* (P 214), *Geelong* (P 215), *Gladstone* (P 216), *Bunbury* (P 217), *Bauarat* (P 218), *Mildura* (P 219), *Armidale* (P 220), *Bundaberg* (P 221), *Pirie* (P 222)

Replacements for the *Attack* class, built to Brooke Marine's PCF–420 design. The lead-ship, *Fremantle*, was laid down at Lowestoft in 1977 and commissioned in March 1979; the remainder are being built by North Queensland Engineers and Agents at Cairns, and six were in service by the end of 1982. A further five are projected and the last of the class are expected to be laid down by 1985.

MINE WARFARE VESSELS

Ex-British 'TON' class *coastal minesweepers*

Particulars:	As British 'Ton' class

Class (former name, fate):
Curlew (ex-*Chediston*, extant 1982), *Gull* (ex-*Swanston*, sold 1975), *Hawk* (ex-*Somerleyton*, sold 1975), *Ibis* (ex-*Singleton*, extant 1982), *Snipe* (ex-*Alceston*, extant 1982), *Teal* (ex-*Jackton*, sold 1978)

Six CMSs bought from the Royal Navy in 1961 and modified to suit RAN requirements, with air-conditioning, re-engining with Deltics and fitting with stabilisers. *Curlew* and *Snipe* were converted to minehunters in 1967–70. For builders and pennant numbers see under United Kingdom.

New Zealand

Unlike Australia, New Zealand does not have the industrial base to consider building her own major warships, and therefore has remained dependant upon the United Kingdom for naval equipment. Few ships have been built for the New Zealand Navy since 1947 and these have been little-modified versions of standard RN designs – initially the *Rothesay* type, and then the *Leanders*. Basic maintenance is undertaken locally, but major refits are carried out in the UK (as, for example, with the recently acquired *Dido*). However, attempts have been made to provide Auckland Dockyard with experience of gas turbine maintenance, firstly with the proposal for the installation of Tynes in *Taranaki*, and more recently with the report that one of the newly purchased *Leanders* may be re-engined with Speys.

The two *Rothesays* are now due for replacement and at one time New Zealand was considered a potential market for the British Type 24 frigate design (since abandoned following the failure to secure any orders). However, it has been decided to make do with ex-British *Leanders*, two of which were purchased in October 1981. In 1982 the only vessels under construction were four new small craft ordered from the Whangarei Engineering Co of Auckland. These are to replace the aged HMDLs in the training role and will be completed over a period of three years.

Taupo as completed   Courtesy Ross Gillett

FLEET STRENGTH 1947

CRUISERS

Name	Launched	Disp (deep load)	Fate
BLACK PRINCE (C 81)	27.8.42	7410t	BU 1962
BELLONA (C 63)	29.9.42	7410t	BU 1959

In 1946 these two ships replaced *Gambia* and *Achilles*, on loan to the RNZN. *Black Prince* became the flagship while *Bellona* was used for harbour training at Auckland before being returned to the RN in April 1956. *Black Prince* left RNZN service in November 1961.

Other vessels in service with the RNZN in 1947 included the modified 'Flower' class corvettes *Arabis* and *Arbutus*; these were returned to the RN in 1950 and scrapped the following year. The 'Bird' class ASW and MS trawlers *Kiwi* and *Tui* were both laid up in 1946, but *Tui* later recommissioned for oceanographic service, not paying off until 1967. *Kiwi* was sold in 1963. The 'Castle' class trawlers *Hinau* and *Rimu* were sold in 1955 and the 'Isles' class *Inchkeith*, *Killegray*, *Sanda* and *Scarba* were all for disposal in 1958.

There were also the British HDML type motor launches *SDML 3551—3556* and *3562—3567*. Five were given names in the mid-1950s: *Mako* (ex-*SDML 3551*), *Paea* ex-*SDML 3552*), *Viti* (ex-*SDML 3555*), *Takapu* (ex-*SDML 3556*) and *Tarapunga* ex-*SDML 3566*). The remainder were named *c*1960. In the above order the names were *Tamaki*, *Irirangi*, *Olphert*, *Pegasus*, *Toroa*, *Wakefield*, *Manga* and *Viti* was renamed *Ngpona*. They were given pennant numbers prefixed with 'P', but retained the old numbers. They were used for survey duties, fishery protection and training. Some were again renamed in about 1970, and were stricken as follows: *Maroro* 1972, *Kahawai*, *Mako*, *Parore* and *Tamure* 1975, and *Manga* 1980. In 1982 the remaining vessels were *Paea*, *Kupara* (ex-*Pegasus*), *Kowa* (ex-*Toroa*), *Kahawai* (ex-*Takapu*) and *Mako* (ex-*Tarapunga*). Four replacement craft were called for in October 1981.

MAJOR SURFACE SHIPS

Royalist was modernised at Devonport DYd in 1954–56, with her former close-range armament replaced by three twin 40mm STAAG Mk 2 automatic AA mountings (one in 'Q' position and two abreast the second funnel) and TT removed. The bridge was rebuilt, lattice masts replaced and tripods and Mk 6M directors were installed forward and aft. With Flyplane predictors she now had one of the most effective AA defence systems of any British-built cruiser, and she replaced *Bellona* when that ship returned to Britain to pay off at the end of 1955. She damaged her boiler tubes when her feedwater became contaminated with seawater, and paid off prematurely in July 1966. She was returned to the RN and scrapped.

Ex-British Modified DIDO class *cruiser*

Displacement:	5950t standard; 7410t deep load
Dimensions:	485ft pp, 512ft oa × 50ft 6in × 17ft 11in mean deep load *147.8m, 156.1m × 15.4m × 5.5m*
Machinery:	4-shaft Parsons geared turbines, 4 Admiralty 3-drum boilers, 62,000shp = 32kts. Oil 1100t
Armour:	Side 3in, bulkheads 1in
Armament:	8–5.25in/50 QF Mk 1 (4×2), 8–40mm (3×2, 2×1), 6–21in TT (2×3)
Complement:	530

No	Name	Builder	Acquired	Fate
C 89	ROYALIST	Scotts	1954	BU 1968

Acquired from the Royal Navy. Virtually no change was made to them during their RNZN service.

Ex-British LOCH class *frigates*

Displacement:	1435t standard; 2260t deep load
Dimensions:	307ft × 38ft 7in × 12ft 4in mean deep load
	93.6m × 11.8m × 3.8m
Machinery:	2-shaft VTE, 2 Admiralty 3-drum boilers, 5500ihp = 19.5kts. Oil 724t
Armament:	1–4in/45 QF Mk V HA, 4–2pdr pompom (1×4), 2 Squid ASW mortars
Complement:	114

No	Name	Builder	Acquired	Fate
F 422	HAWEA (ex-*Loch Eck*)	Smiths Dock	1.10.48	BU 1965
F 426	KANIERE (ex-*Loch Achray*)	Smiths Dock	7.7.68	Sold for BU 1966
F 424	PUKAKI (ex-*Loch Achanalt*)	Robb	3.9.48	BU 1965
F 625	ROTOITI (ex-*Loch Katrine*)	Robb	7.7.49	Sold for BU 1966
F 421	TAUPO (ex-*Loch Shin*)	Swan Hunter	3.9.48	Sold for BU 1961
F 517	TUTIRA (ex-*Loch Morlich*)	Swan Hunter	1.4.49	Sold for BU 1961

Otago was ordered in February 1956 for the RN, but in February 1957 the contract was taken over by the RNZN, and a second ship was ordered at the same time. Apart from internal modifications they were identical with RN ships, and received quadruple Seacat GWS22 SAM systems. They also carried 6–12.75in (324mm) Mk 32 ASW TT (2×3). In 1978–79 *Taranaki* was converted to a training ship, minus Seacat and Limbo mortars, with a single 40mm Mk 7 on the after superstructure. The Type 277 radar has been removed from *Otago*. In 1980 it was announced that *Taranaki* would be converted to a training ship/offshore resources pro-

British ROTHESAY type *frigates*

Particulars:	As British *Rothesay* class

No	Name	Builder	Laid down	Launched	Comp	Fate
F 111	OTAGO (ex-*Hastings*)	Thornycroft	5.9.57	11.12.58	22.6.60	Extant 1982
F 148	TARANAKI	J S White	27.6.58	19.8.59	28.3.61	Extant 1982

tection vessel. For this purpose she would retain the 4.5in guns forward but would be re-engined, with twin-shaft Rolls-Royce Tyne gas turbines in place of the steam turbines. This interesting project was dropped after the British Defence Review in June 1981, when *Leander* class frigates

became available at a cheap price. Both ships are expected to be withdrawn in 1984 when the new *Leander*s are fully operational.

NOTE
The *Whitby* class frigate *Blackpool* was lent by the RN for five years from

June 1966 until HMNZS *Canterbury* was complete. She returned to Great Britain in 1971 and her ship's company turned over to the new frigate. For full details see under Major Surface Ships, United Kingdom.

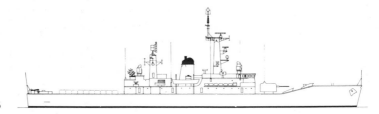

Canterbury 1976

In June 1963 one of the new *Leander* class was ordered from the RN, but when a second frigate was approved five years later the modified or 'broad-beam' version was ordered (August 1968). They are similar to the RN ships apart from a modified funnel cap and USN-pattern Mk 32 TT abaft the boats port and starboard. The hangar has recently been enlarged to handle a Lynx, although in 1980 a Wasp was still embarked.

In October 1981 it was announced that the Ikara-armed *Leander*, HMS *Dido*, and the broad-beam *Bacchante*

British LEANDER type *frigates*

Particulars:	As British *Leander* class

No	Name	Builder	Laid down	Launched	Comp	Fate
F 55	WAIKATO	Harland & Wolff	10.1.64	18.2.65	16.9.66	Extant 1982
F 148	CANTERBURY	Yarrow	12.4.69	6.5.70	22.10.71	Extant 1982
F 69	WELLINGTON (ex-*Bacchante*)	Vickers-Armstrong, Tyne	Acquired Oct 81			Extant 1982
F 104	SALISBURY (ex-*Dido*)	Yarrow	Acquired Oct 81			Refitting

would be purchased from the Royal Navy in 1981–82. HMNZS *Wellington* (ex-*Bacchante*) sailed to New Zea-

land on 11.10.82, but *Salisbury* (ex-*Dido*) will be under refit until July 1983.

SMALL SURFACE COMBATANTS

Ex-Australian BATHURST class *minesweepers*

Displacement:	650–790t standard
Dimensions:	186ft 2in oa × 31ft 2in × 9ft 10in mean deep load
	56.7in × 9.5m × 3.0m
Machinery:	2-shaft VTE, 2 3-drum boilers, 1550–2000ihp = 15–16kts. Oil 124–153t
Armament:	1–4in/45, 1–40mm
Complement:	80–90

Class (fate):
Echuca (BU 1967), *Inverell* (for disposal 1976, BU 1979), *Kiamia* (for disposal 1976, BU 1979), *Stawell* (BU 1968).

Acquired from the RAN in 1952. Despite their age they replaced the 'Loch' class on training duties in 1965–66, with sweep gear removed and the 4in gun replaced by a 40mm. For pennant numbers see under Australia.

PUKAKI class *patrol craft*

Displacement:	105t standard; 135ft full load
Dimensions:	107ft × 20ft × 11ft 10in
	32.8m × 6.1m × 3.6m
Machinery:	2 shafts, 2 Paxman YCJM diesels, 3000bhp = 25kts. Range 2500nm at 12kts
Armament:	2–12.7mm MG (1×2), 1–81mm mortar/12.7mm MG
Sensors:	Radar Decca 916
Complement:	21

Class (no, launched):

Pukaki (P 3568, 1.3.74), *Rotoiti* (P 3569, 8.3.74), *Taupo* (P 3570, 25.7.74), *Hawea* (P 3571, 9.9.74)

All built by Brooke Marine, Lowestoft, UK; all extant 1982

Japan

The Imperial Japanese Navy was crushed by the Second World War. The few surviving major ships, most of them badly battered, were scrapped, scuttled, or sunk by atomic bomb tests. A few of the minor fighting ships found their way into the new Navy, but not many. The devastating defeat created an anti-military attitude in Japan that would dominate military policy until the early 1980s. It has been said that the German armed forces in 1939 were the Prussian Army, the *Kaiser*'s Navy, and the Nazis' Air Force. The post-war Japanese Navy was not a rejuvenation of the old, but rather a new creation.

The Maritime Safety Agency (MSA) created on 1 May 1948 was Japan's initial postwar maritime force. US Coast Guard personnel played a key role in the creation of the MSA, and, therefore, it is not surprising that its missions and material closely parallel those of its American counterpart. The MSA is responsible for fisheries patrol, search and rescue, aids to navigation, pollution protection, traffic supervision, and the interdiction of illegal goods. Initially, the MSA was composed of 155 patrol ships, 53 minesweepers, 20 hydrographic ships and 52 lighthouse tenders. During the war, the US Navy had sown tens of thousands of mines in Japanese waters, which meant that a large minesweeping fleet was needed. The MSA acquired this fleet from the old Imperial Navy and miscellaneous government agencies. The vessels, almost without exception, were in very poor condition. From its inception, the MSA has been a bureau within the Ministry of Transportation and would serve as a supplement to naval forces in time of war.

As Cold War tensions increased, it became clear that Japan required more than a Coast Guard. In 1952 a Coastal Safety Force was created within the MSA. The minesweepers, now 43, plus 35 miscellaneous craft, were transferred to the new sub-organisation. At the end of 1954, the Coastal Safety Force was separated from the MSA and became the Maritime Self Defence Force (MSDF) which, in reality, is the new Japanese Navy. Because of the anti-military feeling in Japan, there was no mention of the new navy in the press or in official circles until about 1980. Steadfastly for 35 years, the Japanese maritime force had been referred to as the Maritime Self Defence Force, even though by the late 1970s it had become one of the ten most powerful navies in the world.

In 1954 the MSDF consisted of 115 ships totalling 58,293t. Initially the ships were patrol frigates and minor amphibious craft (employed as gunboats) on loan from the United States. From the early 1960s as new ships were acquired, the MSDF began to assume its organisational character. On 1 September 1961 the MSDF was reorganised, incorporating naval air under one command. In May 1962 the First Transport Unit was created and in July the Sea Training Group was organised. In March 1963 the Commander of the force was moved from afloat to a shore site, and this improved command and control. In February 1965 the First Submarine Group was established, thus providing a predominantly ASW fleet with more realistic training potential.

Currently, the MSDF has three major divisions. First, there are five regional commands headquartered at Yokosuka, Kure, Sasebo, Maizuru and Ominato. Each regional command is responsible for the defence of its area plus the support of ships within its region. The second division provides unit support. This includes a variety of missions, but primarily it provides training for personnel, services, rear support, schools, hospitals, supply centres, oceanographic services, signal corps and research and development. The third division is the high seas fleet, the primary responsibility of which is the protection of the sea lanes. If need arose, the fleet would provide escorts and aircraft

in support of regional commanders. Upon orders from the Director-General of the Defence Agency, all regional units and training units would come under the command of the MSDF Fleet Commander.

Japanese warship acquisitions have gone through three overlapping phases since the war. First (1954–59), Japan acquired second-hand warships directly from the United States. Japan's shipbuilding industry lay in ruins as the result of strategic bombing and naval bombardment – and yet Japan was a maritime nation and had immediate need of a substantial maritime force. Units of the *Gleaves* class (DDs), *Tacoma* class (PFs), and the LSSL class are illustrative of the 'acquisition era'.

Second (1960–75), Japan built warships dependent upon foreign technology. These ships tended to be of conservative design; they had American weapons, and their sensors were of American manufacture or were Japanese copies built under licence. A few traits of the Old Imperial Japanese Navy also appeared. For example, in the *Ayanami* class, reload torpedoes for the 21in TT are carried in racks on deck. There was also a great deal of power plant experimentation: sister-ships were completed with competing systems. Examples of this era are the units of the *Harukaze* class, *Oyashio* and *Akebono*.

The present era (1976 onwards) marks the introduction of indigenous equipment. In electronics, Japan has re-established its independence, and Japanese naval radars are no longer copies of American equipment. In 1968 the experimental Type 0 fire control system was installed in *Harusame*. This system is easily recognised by the fact that the radar antenna and the target designation transmitter are housed separately. The production-line successor, Type 1, was first installed in *Natsugumo* in 1968 and has spread throughout the fleet, while Type 2, capable of controlling multiple weapons, including missiles simultaneously, was installed on *Murakumo* in the mid-1970s. Japanese warships are also equipped with a unique indigenous infra-red communications device. The MSDF has not yet established its independence in guns and missiles, and since the war, the Japanese Navy has been dependent upon American ordnance, although in 1976 the Italian OTO Melara 76mm gun was introduced into the fleet.

American submarines inflicted staggering losses on the Japanese Navy and merchant marine during the war. William 'Bull' Halsey wrote: 'If I had to give credit to the instruments and machines that won us the war in the Pacific, I would rank them in this order: submarines first, radars second, planes third, bulldozers fourth.' There were many on the Japanese side who would agree with that evaluation. Since its inception, the priorities of the new Japanese Navy have been; first, anti-submarine warfare and, a very distant second and third, anti-air and anti-surface warfare.

From its rebirth until the late 1970s, the new Navy was obsessed with anti-submarine warfare. Strong evidence, both positive and negative, supports this. First, to the great credit of Japan, their Navy had at least limited success with DASH. The DASH ASW system employed drone helicopters to deliver torpedo attacks on suspected targets. Developed in the United States during the 1950s, the system had been a failure. Second, the Japanese made Weapon Alfa work: Weapon Alfa is an ASW rocket mortar, not successfully employed in US service. Third, Japanese escorts are 'armed to the teeth' with a variety of ASW weapons. The *Chitose* class, for example, carry two triple Mk 32 torpedo tubes and an eight-cell ASROC launcher on only 1500t standard displacement, while the large destroyer *Takatsuki* carries ASROC (with reloads), the Mk 32 tubes, one four-tube Bofors ASW launcher, and DASH. The DASH facilities will probably be replaced by a light helicopter in the mid-1980s. Even the Japanese torpedo-boats are ASW oriented: they are equipped with dipping sonars and sonobuoys, and the PT boat can be armed with ASW torpedoes.

Negative evidence of the dominance of ASW to the Japanese is also present. The Navy has yet to deploy a true surface-to-surface missile. Moreover, the mainstay of Japanese ordnance is the US Mk 33 3in gun – an obsolescent weapon. True, the Japanese have introduced the 76mm OTO Melara into the fleet, but it will be years before it is present in substantial numbers. The Navy did not have its first anti-air missile ship until 1965 nor its second until ten years later.

The character of the Navy, or Maritime Self Defence Force, up to the early 1980s has been that of a fleet dedicated to ASW warfare. Protecting the sea lanes from submarine attack was perceived to be the overriding mission. The early 1980s may be a watershed. International events have seemingly changed the Japanese public's attitude toward increasing the nation's military capabilities, and the post-war, anti-military stigma may be at an end. The most important of these international events were the announced withdrawal of US forces from South Korea, the termination of the defence treaty with Taiwan by the United States, the establishment of US political ties with mainland China, the increased Soviet naval pressures in the Pacific, the shifting of US carriers from the Pacific to the Indian Ocean, and the volatile Middle East situation. Japan has no domestic oil and receives much of her imports from that area. All these factors have caused the Japanese to reassess the adequacies of their military capabilities. During the 1980s the MSDF will become more balanced between anti-submarine, anti-air and anti-surface capabilities. New weapon and sensor systems will be introduced more rapidly than in the past. The numerical size of the fleet will probably not increase greatly; but the power of the fleet will grow significantly as relatively small, conservatively designed ships are replaced by some of the world's best-designed warships.

JAPANESE DESIGNATIONS

Until recently Japan has employed mainly US equipment, but with new designations when licence-built or when Japanese modifications have been incorporated. Because Japan does not export military equipment, however, information is not readily available. The following designations have been reported: radar – OPS-1 (for US SPS-10), OPS-2 (US SPS-6 or SPS-12), OPS-9 (British Type 978), OPS-11 (an indigenous design based on SPS-40), OPS-15 (SPS-6), OPS-16 (SPS-12), OPS-17 (SPS-5B); sonar – OQS-1/2 (US SQS-4/29 series), OQS-3 (SQS-23), OQS-4 and OQS-101 (indigenous low-frequency designs), ZQS-2 (British Type 193M). The US Mk 32 ASW triple TT is referred to as the Type 68 in the latest ships.

POSTWAR DISPOSAL OF MAJOR WARSHIPS OF THE IMPERIAL JAPANESE NAVY

BATTLESHIPS

Name	Launched	Disp (normal)	Fate
ISE	2.11.16	31,260t	Sunk 28.7.45, BU 1946
HYUGA	27.1.17	31,260t	Sunk 24.7.45, BU 1952
NAGATO	9.11.19	33,800t	Sunk as target 29.7.46
MUTSU	31.5.20	33,800t BU 1970	Sunk 8.6.43,
HARUNA	14.12.13	27,613t	Sunk 28.7.45, BU 1946

Nagato was used as a target for the Bikini atomic tests.

AIRCRAFT CARRIERS

Name	Launched	Disp (normal)	Fate
HOSHO	13.11.21	9630t	BU 30.4.47
RYUHO	28.11.42	15,300t	BU 1946
JUNYO	26.6.41	26,949t	BU 1947
AMAGI	15.10.43	20,450t	Sunk 24.7.45, BU 1947
KATSURAGI	19.1.44	20,200t	BU 1947
KASAGI	19.10.44	20,400t	BU 1947
ASO	1.11.44	20,100t	BU 1947
IKOMA	17.11.44	20,450t	BU 1947
IBUKI	21.5.43	14,800t	BU 1947

Hosho and *Katsuragi* were used for repatriation before being broken up. The last four units were scrapped incomplete.

CRUISERS

Name	Launched	Disp (normal)	Fate
MYOKO	16.4.27	12,374t	Scuttled 8.7.46
TAKAO	12.5.30	12,986t	Scuttled 27.10.46
TONE	21.11.37	13,890t	Sunk 24.7.45, BU 1948
KITAKAMI	3.7.20	5500t	BU 31.3.47
KATORI	25.9.39	6280t	BU 15.6.47
SAKAWA	9.4.44	6652t*	Sunk 2.7.46

*Full load displacement

Myoko and *Takao* were scuttled in the Malacca Straits by the Royal Navy.

Kitakami and *Katori* were employed on repatriation duties before being scrapped. *Sakawa* was used at Bikini.

MAJOR SURFACE SHIPS

Ex-US GLEAVES class *destroyers*

Both these ships (launched 1941) were transferred under MDAP and were the first destroyers to serve in the MSDF. During their lengthy stay with the MSDF, new electronics were added and the forward superfiring 5in gun was removed to compensate the added torpedo weight. Both ships were returned to the United States in 1969 but were later transferred to Taiwan, *Hatakaze* as *Hsien Yang* and

Asakaze for spares. See under United States and Taiwan for further details.

Particulars: As US *Gleaves* class

No	Name	Builder	Acquired	Fate
DD 181	ASAKAZE (ex-*Ellyson*)	Federal, Kearny	19.10.54	Returned USA 1969
DD 182	HATAKAZE (ex-*Macomb*)	Bath Iron Wks	19.10.54	Returned USA 1969

Ex-US FLETCHER class *destroyers*

Both launched 6.10.43; towed to Japan 1959. Both ships had been reconstructed by March 1963. Changes included improved bridges, larger CICs, new radars and a tripod mast. No 3 5in mounting was removed from both ships to compensate added topside weight, while No 2 5in mounting was removed from *Ariake* and replaced by Weapon Alfa. See under United States for full details.

Particulars: As US *Fletcher* class

No	Name	Builder	Acquired	Fate
DD 183	ARIAKE (ex-*Heywood L Edwards*)	Boston N Yd	10.3.59	Deleted 1974, BU 1976
DD 184	YUGURE (ex-*Richard P Leary*)	Boston N Yd	10.3.59	Deleted 1974

Harukaze as completed   Navarret Collection

Uranami c 1960   Navarret Collection

Harukaze as completed

The *Harukaze* class was authorised under the 1953 fiscal year programme as 'A type' high-speed escort vessels. The class were conservative in size and armament, and electric welding was extensively used in hull construction. As with the destroyer escorts built under the 1953 programme, different propulsion plants were used for study purposes. All weapons and electronics were US produced. In March 1959 both units were fitted with ASW torpedo launchers. In the mid-1970s, *Yukikaze*'s after mast, 5in mounting, K-guns, and DC rack were removed and a towed passive sonar array was installed. They were transferred to Fleet Training and Development Command as Special Use Auxiliaries ASU 7002 and ASU 7003. *Yukikaze* now mounts 1–5in/38 and 4–40mm only, in order to carry out trials with a towed passive sonar array.

HARUKAZE class ('A type') *destroyers*

Displacement:	1700t standard; 2340t full load
Dimensions:	347ft 9in wl, 348ft 9in oa × 34ft 5in × 12ft 2in max
	106.0m, 106.3m × 10.5m × 3.7m
Machinery:	*Harukaze:* 2-shaft Mitsubishi/Escher Weiss geared turbines, 2 Hitachi/Babcock boilers, 30,000shp = 30kts. Oil 557t
	Yukikaze: 2-shaft Westinghouse geared turbines, 2 Combustion Engineering boilers, 30,000shp = 30kts. Oil 557t. Range 6000nm at 18kts
Armament:	3–5in/38 (3×1), 8–40mm (2×4), 2 Hedgehog, 8 K-guns, 1 DC rack
Sensors:	Radar SPS-5, SPS-6; sonar SQS-29
Complement:	240

No	Name	Builder	Laid down	Launched	Comp	Fate
DD 101	HARUKAZE	Mitsubishi Zosen, Nagasaki	15.12.54	20.9.55	26.4.56	TS 27.3.81
DD 102	YUKIKAZE	Shin-Mitsubishi, Jyuko, Kobe	17.10.54	20.8.55	31.7.56	TS 27.3.81

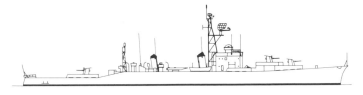

Ayanami as completed

The *Ayanami* class were designed principally for ASW warfare and originally designated DDKs. Four ships were built under the 1955 programme, one under the 1957 and two under the 1958 programmes. The 3in guns are US Mk 33s but the shields are uniquely Japanese. Later units of the class have a bulwark aft of the hull break. Reload torpedoes for the 21in tubes are carried in racks on deck, which was standard practice in Japanese destroyers during the war. *Ayanami* was equipped with eight wash-down systems for removing radio-active fallout. The units built under the 1957 and 1958 programmes were equipped with ECM, an improved sonar, and improved air conditioning. VDS was mounted in *Ayanami* (1965), *Isonami* (1966), and *Takanami* (1967). These three units had their original ASW torpedo system, the Mk 32 torpedo thrown overboard by the Mk 8 'Poor Boy' launcher, replaced by Mk 32 TT at the same time. *Isonami* and *Shikinami* had their 21in TT mount replaced by a deckhouse when converted to TS. The electronics are largely Japanese versions of US sets (OPS-1 is US SPS-6, and OPS-2 is SPS-12, for example).

AYANAMI class *destroyers*

Displacement:	1720t standard; 2500t full load
Dimensions:	357ft 7in wl × 35ft 2in × 12ft 2in light
	109.0m × 10.7m × 3.7m
Machinery:	2-shaft Mitsubishi/Escher Weiss turbines, 2 Mitsubishi-Nagasaki CE type boilers, 35,000shp = 32kts. Range 6000nm at 18kts
Armament:	6–3in (3×2), 4–21in TT (1×4), 2 ASW torpedo racks, 2 Hedgehog, 2 Y-guns
Sensors:	Radar OPS-1, OPS-15 (DD 103–106, OPS-2); sonar OQS-12 or 14 (DD 103, 104, 110, also OQA-1 VDS)
Complement:	220

No	Name	Builder	Laid down	Launched	Comp	Fate
DD 103	AYANAMI	Mitsubishi Zosen, Nagasaki	20.11.56	1.6.57	12.2.58	Extant 1982
DD 104	ISONAMI	Shin-Mitsubishi Jyuko, Kobe	14.12.56	30.9.57	14.3.58	TS 1975
DD 105	URANAMI	Kawasaki Jyuko, Tokyo	1.2.57	29.8.57	27.2.58	Extant 1982
DD 106	SHIKINAMI	Mitsui Zosen, Tamano	14.12.56	25.9.57	15.3.58	TS 1976
DD 110	TAKANAMI	Mitsui Zosen, Tamano	8.11.58	8.8.59	30.1.60	Extant 1982
DD 111	ONAMI	Ishikawajima Jyuko, Kobe	20.3.59	13.2.60	29.8.60	Extant 1982
DD 112	MAKINAMI	Iino Jyuko, Maizuru	20.3.59	25.4.60	28.10.60	Extant 1982

Murasame 1959

The *Murasame* class were designed principally for AAW and originally were designated DDAs. Two ships were built under the 1956 programme and the other under the 1957 programme. The 5in guns mounted in this class were Mk 39s removed from the US *Midway* class aircraft carriers, the only ships then fitted with this gun; this 5in/54 was to have been the successor to the ubiquitous 5in/38. Actually, their rate of fire was disappointing, making them less than the ideal AA weapon. The handling rooms and magazines for these guns required additional space, thus making the *Murasame*s much more crowded ships than the *Ayanami*s. Weapons constitute 18 per cent of the weight of the *Murasame* class unit. The ASW weapons have been removed from *Harusame* but all are now fitted with 6–12.75in Mk 32 ASW TT.

MURASAME class *destroyers*

Displacement:	1838t (*Harusame* 1800t, *Yudachi* 1840t) standard
Dimensions:	360ft 9in wl × 36ft × 12ft 2in light
	110.0m × 11.0m × 3.7m
Machinery:	*Harusame*: 2-shaft Ishikawajima geared turbines, 2 Ishikawajima Foster Wheeler boilers, 35,000shp = 32kts
	Murasame: 2-shaft Mitsubishi Escher Weiss geared turbines, 2 Mitsubishi CE type boilers, 35,000shp = 32kts
	Yudachi: 2-shaft Kanpon-Ishikawajima geared turbines, 2 Ishikawajima FW-D type boilers, 35,000shp = 32kts. Range 6000nm at 18kts
Armament:	3–5in/54 (3×1), 4–3in/50 (2×2), 2 ASW torpedo racks, 1 Hedgehog, 2 Y-guns, 1 DC rack
Sensors:	Radar OPS-1, OPS-15; sonar SQS-29 (DD 109, also OQA-1 VDS)
Complement:	220

No	Name	Builder	Laid down	Launched	Comp	Fate
DD 107	MURASAME	Mitzubishi Zosen, Nagasaki	16.12.57	31.7.58	31.3.59	Extant 1982
DD 108	YUDACHI	Ishikawajima Jyuko, Tokyo	16.12.57	31.7.58	16.3.59	Extant 1982
DD 109	HARUSAME	Uraga Dock, Yokosuka	17.6.58	18.6.59	15.12.59	Extant 1982

The *Akizuki* class were built under the 1957 US Military Aid Programme and carried the 5in/54 as in the *Murasame*s. They featured a long forecastle hull and were designed as flotilla leaders. Weapon Alfa, an ASW mortar developed in the United States, proved to be unsatisfactory. Weapons and ASW sensors were modernised on *Teruzuki* in 1976–77 and on *Akizuki* in 1977–78, with a 375mm Bofors ASW mortar replacing Weapon Alfa and 6–12.75in Mk 32 ASW TT replacing the original launchers; VDS was added and SQS-29 sonar was replaced with SQS-23.

AKIZUKI class *destroyers*

Displacement:	2388t standard; 2890t normal
Dimensions:	387ft 2in oa, 377ft 2in pp × 39ft 4in × 13ft 1in light
	118.0m, 115.0m × 12.0m × 4.0m
Machinery:	*Akizuki*: 2-shaft Mitsubishi Escher Weiss geared turbines, 4 Mitsubishi CE type type boilers, 45,000shp = 32kts
	Teruzuki: 2-shaft Westinghouse geared turbines, 4 Mitsubishi/CE type boilers, 45,000shp = 32kts
Armament:	3–5in/50 (3×1), 4–3in/50 (2×2), 1 Weapon Alfa, 2 Hedgehog, 2 Y-guns, 2 ASW torpedo, 4–21in TT (1×4, 8 torpedoes)
Sensors:	Radar OPS-1, OPS-15; sonar SQS-23, OQA-1 VDS
Complement:	330

No	Name	Builder	Laid down	Launched	Comp	Fate
DD 161	AKIZUKI	Mitsubishi Zosen, Nagasaki	31.7.58	26.6.59	13.2.60	Extant 1982
DD 162	TERUZUKI	Shin-Mitsubishi, Jyuko, Kobe	15.8.58	24.6.59	29.2.60	Extant 1982

Murasame on trials
Navarret Collection

Akizuki 25.9.63
CPL

Amatsukaze on trials | Navarret Collection | Akigumo as completed | Author's Collection

Amatsukaze as completed

Amatsukaze was the first guided missile ship built in Japan. She required a little over two years to build, a remarkably short time. The Tartar (Standard) system was applied from the United States. Her flush deck design gives a clean appearance, and because of her clean quarterdeck many publications mistakenly credit her with the capacity to handle a helicopter. She was refitted in 1967 when the Mk 32 TT and the SPS-52 radar were installed. A further refit with OTO Melara 76mm compact mountings and improved fire control has also been discussed.

AMATSUKAZE *guided missile destroyer*

Displacement:	3050t standard; 4000t full load
Dimensions:	429ft 9in pp × 43ft 11in × 13ft 9in max *131.0m × 13.4m × 4.2m*
Machinery:	2-shaft Ishikawajima/GE geared turbines, 2 Ishikawajima/Foster Wheeler boilers, 60,000shp = 33kts. Oil 900t. Range 7000nm at 18kts
Armament:	1 Mk 13 launcher (40 Standard MR-1(MR) missiles), 4–3in/50 (2×2), 1 ASROC ASW system (1×8), 2 Hedgehog, 6–12.75in Mk 32 ASW TT (2×3)
Sensors:	Radar OPS-17, SPS-29, SPS-52, SPG-51, SPG-34; sonar SQS-23
Complement:	290

No	Name	Builder	Laid down	Launched	Comp	Fate
DDG 163	AMATSUKAZE	Mitsubishi, Nagasaki	29.11.62	5.10.63	15.2.65	Extant 1982

Asagumo 1974

YAMAGUMO class *destroyers*

The *Yamagumo* class carry an impressive ASW armament, and being diesel-powered, the ships have a small complement for their size and potential. Originally, *Yuugumo* was to have been the lead ship of a new class. The fact that this last unit was laid down 12 years after the first reflects well upon the success of the design. They were authorised as follows: *Yamagumo* – 1962 Programme; *Makigumo* – 1963; *Asagumo* – 1964; *Aokumo* – 1965; *Akigumo* – 1967; *Yuugomo* – 1967. *Yamagumo* and *Makigumo* have a raised stern, which houses a VDS; the other units received the VDS during construction and, therefore, have a flat stern. The installation of OTO Melara 76mm mountings to replace the US Mk33s has been discussed.

Displacement:	2100t standard; 2700t full load
Dimensions:	376ft 11in pp × 38ft 9in × 13ft 2in max *114.9m × 11.8m × 4.0m*
Machinery:	2 shafts, 6 Mitsubishi (Mitsui in DDK 113 and 114) diesels, 26,500bhp = 27kts. Range 7000nm at 20kts
Armament:	4–3in/50 (2×2), 1 ASROC ASW system (1×8), 1–375mm ASW rocket launcher (1×4), 6–12.75in Mk 32 ASW TT (2×3)
Sensors:	Radar OPS-11, OPS-17; sonar SQS-23 (OQS-3 in DDK 119–121), SQS-35(J) VDS (not in DDK 115)
Complement:	210

No	Name	Builder	Laid down	Launched	Comp	Fate
DDK 113	YAMAGUMO	Mitsui, Tamano	23.3.64	27.2.65	29.1.66	Extant 1982
DDK 114	MAKIGUMO	Uraga, Yokosuka	10.6.64	26.7.65	19.3.66	Extant 1982
DDK 115	ASAGUMO	Maizuru Jyuko, Maizuru	24.6.65	25.11.66	29.8.67	Extant 1982
DDK 119	AOKUMO	Sumitomo, Uraga	2.10.70	30.3.72	25.11.72	Extant 1982
DDK 120	AKIGUMO	Sumitomo, Uraga	7.7.72	23.10.73	24.7.74	Extant 1982
DDK 121	YUUGUMO	Sumitomo, Uraga	4.2.76	21.5.77	24.3.78	Extant 1982

Nagatsuki 1976
USN

Takatsuki as completed

The *Takatsuki* class have a typical 'American' appearance because of their 5in guns and ASROC. The ships were designed for the US ASW DASH system (3 drones), which proved to be unsuccessful and was removed in 1977. *Mochizuki* and *Nagatsuki* have a knuckle in the hull sides forward. *Kikuzuki* is the only unit fitted with fin stabilisers. VDS has been mounted in *Takatsuki* (1970), *Kikutsuki* (1972), *Mochizuki* (1972) and *Nagatsuki* (1972). All units are fitted with gravity davits and telescopic high-line equipment. A substantial modernisation programme is due to be completed by 1985, whereby ships of the class will have the after 5in/54 and disused DASH hangar replaced by Sea Sparrow SAM (1×8, Mk 29 launcher), 8 Harpoon SSM (2×4), provision for 2 Phalanx CIWS, improved electronics and the addition of the American SQS-18A TACTASS towed array sonar.

TAKATSUKI class *destroyers*

Displacement:	3100t standard; 4500t full load
Dimensions:	446ft 2in oa × 43ft 11in × 14ft 5in max
	136.0m × 13.4m × 4.4m
Machinery:	2-shaft Mitsubishi geared turbines, 2 Mitsubishi/CE boilers, 60,000shp = 32kts. Range 7000nm at 20kts
Armament:	2–5in (2×1), 1 ASROC ASW system (1×8), 1–375mm ASW rocket launcher (1×4), 6–12.75in Mk 32 ASW TT (2×3), 3 DASH (now removed)
Sensors:	Radar OPS-11B, OPS-17; sonar SQS-23 (OQS-3 in DD 166 and 167), SQS-35(J) VDS (not in DD 166)
Complement:	270

No	Name	Builder	Laid down	Launched	Comp	Fate
DD 164	TAKATSUKI	Ishikawajima	8.10.64	7.1.66	15.3.67	Extant 1982
DD 165	KIKUZUKI	Mitsubishi	15.3.66	25.3.67	27.3.68	Extant 1982
DD 166	MOCHIZUKI	Ishikawajima Jyuko, Tokyo	25.11.66	15.3.68	25.3.69	Extant 1982
DD 167	NAGATSUKI	Mitsubishi Jyuko, Nagasaki	2.3.68	19.3.69	12.2.70	Extant 1982

Murakumo 1979

This class paralleled the *Yamagumo* class, substituting DASH for ASROC; the DASH system was a failure and is no longer carried. In 1978 *Murakumo* was fitted with 1–76mm OTO Melara compact, and an ASROC ASW system; the ASROC was placed on what had been the flight deck for DASH and a 76mm OTO Melara gun replaced the aft 3in mount. The other units will probably be refitted with ASROC and all three will carry 2–76mm mounts (2×1) in place of the present US 3in Mk 32s.

MINEGUMO class *destroyers*

Displacement:	2100t standard; 2750t full load
Dimensions:	376ft 11in pp × 38ft 9in × 12ft 6in max
	114.9m × 11.8m × 3.8m
Machinery:	2 shafts, 6 Mitsubishi IZUEV 30/40 diesels, 26,500bhp = 27kts. Range 7000nm at 20kts
Armament:	4–3in/50 (2×2), 1–375mm ASW rocket launcher (1×4), 6–12.75in Mk 32 ASW TT (2×3). See notes
Sensors:	Radar OPS-11, OPS-17, SPG-34; sonar OQS-3 (plus SQS-35(J) VDS in DDK 118)
Complement:	205

No	Name	Builder	Laid down	Launched	Comp	Fate
DDK 116	MINEGUMO	Mitsui, Tamano	14.3.67	16.12.67	21.8.68	Extant 1982
DDK 117	NATSUGUMO	Uraga, Yokosuka	26.6.67	25.7.68	25.4.69	Extant 1982
DDK 118	MURAKUMO	Maizuru, H I	19.10.68	15.11.69	21.8.70	Extant 1982

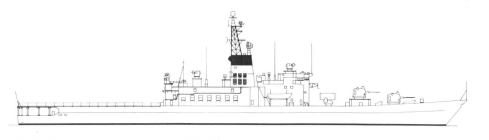

Haruna as completed

The *Haruna* class and the follow-on *Shirane* are the only destroyer-size ships in the world which carry three large ASW (HSS-2) helicopters. They have a strong ASW armament but are weak against air and surface targets, although they may be fitted with a short-range SAM system during their next major refit. These units have very large bridge areas (100m²). The funnel is located somewhat off-centre towards the port side of the ship, thus permitting space for the third helicopter in the hangar. Fin stabilisers are installed at the bilge keel, and the 'bear trap' landing system is installed. Modernisation, to include Sea Sparrow SAM, Phalanx CIWS, Harpoon SSM, and SQS-35 VDS, is planned for the near future.

HARUNA class *helicopter destroyers*

Displacement:	4700t standard; 6300t full load
Dimensions:	501ft 11in pp × 57ft 5in × 16ft 8in max
	153.0m × 17.5m × 5.1m
Machinery:	2-shaft geared turbines, 2 boilers, 70,000shp = 32kts
Armament:	2–5in/54 (2×1), 1 ASROC ASW system (1×8), 6–12.75in Mk 32 ASW TT (2×3), 3 helicopters
Sensors:	Radar OPS-11, OPS-17; sonar OQS-3
Complement:	340

No	Name	Builder	Laid down	Launched	Comp	Fate
DDH 141	HARUNA	Mitsubishi, Nagasaki	19.3.70	Dec 71	22.3.73	Extant 1982
DDH 142	HIEI	Ishikawajima-Harima, Tokyo	8.3.72	13.8.73	27.12.74	Extant 1982

Hiei 1974

Author's Collection

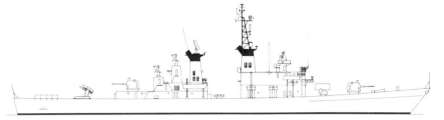

Tachikaze as completed

The *Tachikaze* class will greatly improve the MSDF's anti-aircraft capabilities. The first two carry fire control systems manufactured in the United States, but the third unit will probably complete with indigenous systems. The propulsion plant is identical with that fitted in the *Haruna* class. *Tachikaze* is due to receive a Phalanx CIWS and improved electronics, and all will receive satellite communications equipment.

TACHIKAZE class *guided missile destroyers*

Displacement:	3850t standard; 4800t full load
Dimensions:	469ft 2in pp × 46ft 10in × 15ft 1in max
	143.0m × 14.3m × 4.6m
Machinery:	2-shaft geared turbines, 2 boilers, 70,000shp = 32kts
Armament:	1 Standard SAM (1×1 Mk 13 launcher, SM-1(MR) missiles), 2–5in/54 (2×1), 1 ASROC ASW system (1×8), 6–12.75in Mk 32 ASW TT (3×3)
Sensors:	Radar OPS-11, SPS-52B, SPG-51C; sonar OQS-3 (OQS-4 in DDG 170)
Complement:	277

No	Name	Builder	Laid down	Launched	Comp	Fate
DDG 168 TACHIKAZE		Mitsubishi, Nagasaki	19.6.73	12.12.74	26.3.76	Extant 1982
DDG 169 ASAKAZE		Mitsubishi, Nagasaki	27.5.76	15.10.77	27.3.79	Extant 1982
DDG 170 SAWAKAZE		Mitsubishi, Nagasaki	14.9.79	4.6.81	Feb 82	Extant 1982

Tachikaze 1978   MSDF

Shirane 1980   MSDF

Shirane as completed

SHIRANE class *helicopter destroyers*

Displacement:	5200t standard; 6800t full load
Dimensions:	521ft pp × 57ft 5in × 17ft 5in max
	158.8m × 17.5m × 5.3m
Machinery:	2-shaft geared turbines, 2 boilers, 70,000shp = 32kts
Armament:	1 Sea Sparrow SAM (8×1), 2–5in/54 (2×1), 1 ASROC ASW system (1×8), 6–12.75in Mk 32 ASW TT (2×3), 3 helicopters
Sensors:	Radar OPS-12, OPS-28; sonar OQS-101, SQS-35(J) VDS, SQR-18A towed array
Complement:	370

These two units are improved *Haruna* type with better AAW capabilities. HSS-2B helicopters are carried. Both have received the American SQR-18A TACTASS towed passive sonar array, and 2–20mm Phalanx CIWS (2×1), and are due to be fitted with Harpoon SSM. The 'Masker' bubble-generating underwater noise reduction system is reported to have been added.

No	Name	Builder	Laid down	Launched	Comp	Fate
DDH 143 SHIRANE		Ishikawajima, Tokyo	25.2.77	18.9.78	17.3.80	Extant 1982
DDH 144 KURAMA		Ishikawajima, Tokyo	1977	20.9.79	27.3.81	Extant 1982

JAPAN

These units will be multi-purpose destroyers with a balanced anti-air, surface and sub-surface capability. Two further ships were funded in the 1981 programme. Two 20mm Phalanx CIWS (2×1) are due to be fitted to all ships of the class.

HATSUYUKI class *guided missile destroyers*

Displacement:	2950t standard; 3700t full load
Dimensions:	432ft 4in pp × 44ft 11in × 14ft 3in max *131.7m × 13.7m × 4.3m*
Machinery:	2-shaft COGOG (CP propellers): 2 Kawasaki Rolls-Royce Olympus TM-3B gas turbines, 56,780shp = 30kts; 2 Tyne RM-1C gas turbines, 10,860shp = ?kts
Armament:	8 Harpoon SSM (2×4), 1 Sea Sparrow SAM (1×8), 1–76mm OTO Melara compact, 1 ASROC ASW system (1×8), 6–12.75in Mk 32 ASW TT (2×3), 1 helicopter
Sensors:	Radar OPS-18, OPS-14B; sonar OQS-4
Complement:	190

No	Name	Builder	Laid down	Launched	Comp	Fate
DDG 122	HATSUYUKI	Sumitomo, Uraga	14.3.74	7.11.80	Mar 82	Extant 1982
DDG 123	SHIRAYUKI	Hitachi, Maizuru	3.12.79	4.8.81		Fitting out
DDG 124	MINEYUKI	Mitsubishi, Nagasaki	Apr 81	Oct 82		Fitting out
DDG 125	SAWAYUKI	Ishikawajima-Harima, Tokyo	Apr 81	Aug 82		Fitting out
DDG 126	HAMAYUKI	Mitsui, Tamano	4.2.81	June 82		Fitting out
DDG 127		Ishikawajima-Harima, Tokyo				Ordered
DDG 128		Sumitomo, Uraga				Ordered

A new type of DDG ordered under the 1981 programme. Although they can operate a H55-2B helicopter, no hangar is provided.

New type *guided missile destroyer*

Displacement:	4500t normal
Dimensions:	469ft × 51ft 3in × 19ft *143m × 15.6m × 5.8m*
Machinery:	2-shaft COGAG: 2 Olympus TM 38, plus 2 Spey SMIA gas turbines, 72,000shp = 32kts
Armament:	2–5in/54 (2×1), 1 Standard SAM (1×1, 40 SM-1 (MR) missiles), 8 Harpoon SSM (2×4), 1 ASROC ASW system (1×8), 6–12.75in Mk 32 ASW TT (2×3), 1 helicopter
Sensors:	Radar SPS-52C, OPS-28, OPS-11, SPG-51C; sonar OQS-4

No	Name	Builder	Laid down	Launched	Comp	Fate
DD 171		Mitsubishi, Nagasaki	1982			Building

(For illustration see under United States in 1922–46 volume)

Launched 1943 and transferred on loan in 1953. They are named after trees, as were IJN destroyers. *Keyaki* had a deckhouse added abaft the mainmast and served as a flotilla flagship; *Kaede* received a similar deckhouse. All ships were technically returned on 28.8.62, but were immediately transferred outright to the Japanese government the same day. *Kusu* was converted to a drone target carrier in 1964. The following units were reclassified from escort vessels to training ships (moored): *Buna* (1.2.65), *Kashi* (1.4.65), *Momi* (1.4.65), *Tochi* (1.4.65), *Ume* (1.4.65), *Kaede* (31.3.66), *Maki* (31.3.66), *Matsu* (31.3.66), *Nara* (31.3.66), *Sakura* (31.3.66). *Tsuge* was discarded in 1968; *Nire* and *Shii* were returned to the USA on 31.3.70; and *Kiri*, *Keyaki* and *Sugi* were decommissioned 31.3.70.

Ex-US TACOMA class *frigates*

Particulars:	As US *Tacoma* class

No	Name	Builder	Acquired	Fate
PF 281	KUSU (ex-*Ogden*)	Consolidated, San Pedro	1953	Deleted 1972
PF 282	NARA (ex-*Machias*)	Froemming	1953	Deleted 1972
PF 283	KASHI (ex-*Pasco*)	Kaiser, Richmond	1953	Deleted 1972
PF 284	MOMI (ex-*Poughkeepsie*)	Butler	1953	Deleted 1972
PF 285	SUGI (ex-*Coronado*)	Consolidated, San Pedro	Jan 53	Decommissioned 31.3.70
PF 286	MATSU (ex-*Bath*)	Froemming	Dec 53	Deleted 1972
PF 287	NIRE (ex-*Sandusky*)	Froemming	1953	Returned 31.3.70
PF 288	KAYA (ex-*San Pedro*)	Consolidated, San Pedro	1953	Deleted 1972
PF 289	UME (ex-*Allentown*)	Froemming	Apr 53	Deleted 1972
PF 290	SAKURA (ex-*Carson City*)	Consolidated, San Pedro	Apr 53	Deleted 1972
PF 291	KIRI (ex-*Everett*)	Kaiser, Richmond	Mar 53	Decommissioned 31.3.70
PF 292	TSUGE (ex-*Gloucester*)	Butler	1953	Deleted 1958
PF 293	KAEDE (ex-*Newport*)	Butler	1953	HS 31.3.68
PF 294	BUNA (ex-*Bayonne*)	American SB	1953	Deleted 1972
PF 295	KEYAKI (ex-*Evansville*)	Letham D Smith	Oct 53	Decommissioned 31.3.70
PF 296	TOCHI (ex-*Albuquerque*)	Kaiser, Richmond	1953	Deleted 1972
PF 297	SHII (ex-*Long Beach*)	Consolidated, San Pedro	1953	Returned 31.3.70
PF 298	MAKI (ex-*Charlottesville*)	Butler	Jan 53	Deleted 1972

(For illustration see under United States in 1922–46 volume)

Originally built in 1953, both ships were transferred on 14.6.55 under MDAP and returned to the United States in 1975.

Ex-US CANNON class *frigates*

Particulars:	As US *Cannon* class (DET type)

No	Name	Builder	Acquired	Fate
DE 262	ASAHI (ex-*Amick*)	Federal, Newark	14.6.55	Returned 1975
DE 263	HATSHUI (ex-*Atherton*)	Federal, Newark	14.6.55	Returned 1975

Nashi was one of the numerous *Tachibana* class, an emergency ship design constructed at the close of the Second World War. Launched 17.1.45, she was sunk by aircraft off Hatakiri Point, Inland Sea,but in 1955 was raised and purchased by the MSDF. She was reconstructed at Kure Zosen, completing 12.5.56. She was renamed *Wakaba* and commissioned 30.5.56. Used for training 1956–57, she was converted 10.9.57–26.3.58 to a radar-picket, receiving a lattice foremast and a tripod mainmast, and a large air search radar mounted atop her

WAKABA *escort*

Displacement:	1530t standard
Dimensions:	321ft 6in pp × 30ft 7in × 11ft max
	98.0m × 9.4m × 3.4m
Machinery:	2-shaft geared turbines, 2 Kampon boilers, 14,000shp = 27kts. Range 4680nm at 16kts
Armament:	2–3in/50 (1×2), 1 Hedgehog, 6 K-guns, DC racks
Complement:	206

No	Name	Builder	Acquired	Fate
DE 261	WAKABA (ex-*Nashi*)	Kawasaki, Kobe	30.5.56	Discarded 1972

bridge. She was reclassified as an experimental ship in 1968.

Akebono was authorised under the 1953 Programme as one of three 'B type' escort vessels. She was built with geared turbines and her near-sisters, *Ikazuchi* and *Inazuma* with diesels. There were many differences between the two designs, the most noticeable being *Akebono*'s twin funnels in contrast to the one funnel of the near-sisters. All weapons and electronics were US produced. In March 1959 her original gun armament was removed and she was fitted with 2–3in quick-firing guns. Four K-guns and a DC rack were also removed.

AKEBONO ('B type') *escort*

Displacement:	1075ft standard; 1350t full load
Dimensions:	301ft pp × 27ft 9in × 10ft 11in max
	91.8m × 8.5m × 3.4m
Machinery:	2-shaft Ishikawajima geared turbines, 2 Ishikawajima/Foster Wheeler boilers, 18,000shp = 28kts
Armament:	2–3in/50 (2×1), 4–40mm (2×2), 1 Hedgehog, 8 K-guns, 1 DC rack. See notes
Complement:	193

No	Name	Builder	Laid down	Launched	Comp	Fate
DE 201	AKEBONO	Ishikawajima Jyuko, Kobe	10.12.54	30.10.55	20.3.56	Discarded 1976

Inazuma as completed

Both units were authorised under the 1953 Programme as two further 'B type' escort vessels, powered by diesels. The *Ikazuchi* class had one funnel whereas *Akebono* had two – a prominent recognition difference. All weapons and electronics were US produced. The original 2–3in guns and 1–40mm gun were removed in 1959 and replaced by 2–3in quick-firing guns. Four K-guns and 1 DC rack were also removed. Due to projected vibrations from the diesels, mild steel plates were used and an aluminum alloy was employed in the superstructure.

IKAZUCHI class ('B type') *escorts*

Displacement:	1080t standard
Dimensions:	287ft 1in pp, 288ft 9in oa × 28ft 6in × 10ft 3in max
	87.5m, 88.0m × 8.7m × 3.1m
Machinery:	2 shafts, 2 Mitsubishi diesels, 12,000bhp = 25kts
Armament:	2–3in/50 (2×1), 4–40mm (2×2), 1 Hedgehog, 8 K-guns, 1 DC rack
Complement:	145

No	Name	Builder	Laid down	Launched	Comp	Fate
DE 202	IKAZUCHI	Kawasaki Jyuko, Kobe	18.12.54	6.9.55	29.5.56	Discarded 1976
DE 203	INAZUMA	Mitsui Zosen, Tamano	25.12.54	4.8.55	1.4.56	Discarded 1976

Mogami as completed

Two ships were constructed under the 1959 and two under the 1961 programme. Weapons and machinery varied considerably throughout these units (*Isuzu* and *Mogami* had Weapon Alfa instead of a rocket launcher, and no DCT) and they served as test platforms. VDS was mounted on *Mogami* in 1966 and *Kitakami* in 1968. All have different machinery, but *Isuzu* has only two engines, and consequently a smaller funnel.

ISUZU class *escorts*

Displacement:	1490t standard; 1700t full load
Dimensions:	308ft 5in wl, 318ft 3in oa × 34ft 1in × 11ft 6in max
	94.0m, 97.0m × 10.4m × 3.5m
Machinery:	2 shafts, 4 diesels, 16,000bhp = 26kts
Armament:	4–3in/50 (2×2), 4–21in TT (1×4), 1–375mm ASW rocket launcher (1×4), 6–12.75in Mk 32 ASW TT (3×2), 1 DCT, 1 DC rack. See notes
Sensors:	Radar OPS-1, OPS-16; sonar OQS-12 or OQS-14 (OQA-1 VDS in DE 212 and 213)
Complement:	183

No	Name	Builder	Laid down	Launched	Comp	Fate
DE 211	ISUZU	Mitsui Zosen, Tamano	16.4.60	17.1.61	29.7.61	Extant 1982
DE 212	MOGAMI	Misubishi Zosen, Nagasaki	4.8.60	7.3.61	28.9.61	Extant 1982
DE 213	KITAKAMI	Ishikawajima-Harima, Tokyo	7.6.62	21.6.63	1.2.64	Extant 1982
DE 214	OHI	Maizuru Jyuko, Maizuru	10.6.62	15.6.63	1.2.64	Extant 1982

Kitakami as completed   Navarret Collection

Yoshino as completed   Author's Collection

Chikugo as completed

Chikugo units are the smallest ships in the world to be armed with ASROC, and most units are equipped with VDS. Particular attention has been given to reduce vibration and noise. Because of the large superstructure area for ships of this size, they were given greater beam to improve stability. Early units are 1470t standard; from *Teshio* onwards they are 1530t. The Mitsui diesels are fitted to DE 216, DE 220, DE 222 and DE 224.

CHIKUGO class *escorts*

Displacement:	1470–1530t standard; 1700–1800t full load
Dimensions:	305ft 2in pp × 35ft 6in × 11ft 6in max *93.0m × 10.8m × 3.5m*
Machinery:	2 shafts, 4 Mitsubishi-Burmeister & Wain UEV 30/40 or Mitsui 28VBC-38 diesels, 16,000bhp = 28kts. Range 10,700nm/12,000nm at 12kts/9kts
Armament:	2–3in/50 (1×2), 2–40mm (1×2), 1 ASROC ASW system (1×8), 6–12.75in Mk 32 ASW TT (2×3)
Sensors:	Radar OPS-16, OPS-14; sonar OQS-3 (plus SQS-35(J) VDS in most ships)
Complement:	165

No	Name	Builder	Laid down	Launched	Comp	Fate
DE 215	CHIKUGO	Mitsui, Tamano	9.12.68	13.1.70	31.7.70	Extant 1982
DE 216	AYASE	Ishikawajima, Tokyo	5.12.69	16.9.70	20.7.71	Extant 1982
DE 217	MIKUMO	Mitsui, Tamano	17.3.70	16.2.71	26.8.71	Extant 1982
DE 218	TOKACHI	Mitsui, Tamano	11.12.70	25.11.71	17.5.72	Extant 1982
DE 219	IWASE	Mitsui, Tamano	6.8.71	29.6.72	12.12.72	Extant 1982
DE 220	CHITOSE	Hitachi, Maizuru	7.10.71	25.1.73	21.8.73	Extant 1982
DE 221	NIYODO	Mitsui, Tamano	20.9.72	28.8.73	8.2.74	Extant 1982
DE 222	TESHIO	Mitachi, Maizuru	11.7.73	29.5.74	10.1.75	Extant 1982
DE 223	YOSHINO	Mitsui, Tamano	28.9.73	22.8.74	6.2.75	Extant 1982
DE 224	KUMANO	Hitachi, Maizuru	29.5.74	24.2.75	19.11.75	Extant 1982
DE 225	NOSHIRO	Mitsui, Tamano	27.1.76	23.12.76	31.8.77	Extant 1982

Ishikari during trials

Two units of the *Ishikari* class were originally authorised, one in 1977–78 and the second in 1979–80, but only one was built. As many as twenty were planned. This design is smaller and less sophisticated than the preceding *Chikugo* class, but too much seems to have been attempted on the displacement – hence the curtailment of the programme, and the evolution of the *Yubari* design (see below).

ISHIKARI *guided missile frigates*

Displacement:	1200t standard: 1450t full load
Dimensions:	277ft 3in × 32ft 9in × 11ft 6in *84.5m × 10.0m × 3.5m*
Machinery:	2-shaft CODOG (CP propellers): 1 Kawasaki/Rolls-Royce Olympus TM-3B gas turbine, 28,390shp = 25kts; 1 Mitsubishi diesel, 5000bhp = 19kts
Armament:	8 Harpoon SSM (2×4), 1–76mm OTO Melara compact, 1–375mm ASW rocket launcher (1×4), 6–12.75in Mk 32 ASW TT (2×3)
Sensors:	Radar OPS-28; sonar?
Complement:	90

No	Name	Builder	Laid down	Launched	Comp	Fate
DE 226	ISHIKARI	Mitsui, Tamano	17.5.79	18.3.80	30.3.81	Extant 1982

Ishikari 1981
MSDF

An improved and enlarged *Ishikari*, with the addition of a Phalanx CIWS. A second ship was ordered under the FY80–81 programme, but no further ships have been requested to date.

YUBARI class *guided missile frigates*

Displacement:	1400t standard; 1690t full load
Dimensions:	298ft 6in × 35ft 5in × 11ft 6in
	91.0m × 10.8m × 3.5m
Machinery:	2-shaft CODOG: 1 Kawasaki/Rolls-Royce Olympus TM-3B gas turbine, 28,400shp = 25kts; 1 Mitsubishi diesel, 4650bhp = ?kts
Armament:	8 Harpoon SSM (2×4), 1–76mm/62 OTO Melara compact, 1–20mm Phalanx CIWS, 1–375mm ASW rocket launcher (1×4), 6–12.75in Mk 32 ASW TT
Sensors:	Radar OPS-28; sonar ?
Complement:	98

No	Name	Builder	Laid down	Launched	Comp	Fate
DE 227	YUBARI	Sumitomo, Uraga	Feb 81	Feb 82		Fitting out
DE 228						Ordered

SUBMARINES

The US *Gato* class submarine *Mingo* (launched 30.11.42) was transferred in August 1955 under MDAP. Her crew was trained at the US Submarine Bay, New London, Connecticut. *Kuroshio* was used primarily as a training boat until decommissioned on 31.3.66.

Ex-US GATO class *submarine*

Particulars:	As US *Gato* class

No	Name	Builder	Acquired	Fate
SS 501	KUROSHIO (ex-*Mingo*)	Electric Boat	15.8.55	Decommissioned 31.3.66

Oyashio was built under the 1956 programme and was the first submarine built in Japan since the war. Although equipped with a snorkel, she was a very conservative design. She had a whale-shaped hull with an internal frame and her 480 main storage batteries were arranged in four groups within two rooms. The diving planes were housed inside the hull, between the internal and external frames. She served as a TS from 1.4.75.

OYASHIO *submarine*

Displacement:	1139t surfaced; 1420t submerged
Dimensions:	258ft 6in pp × 22ft 11in × 15ft max
	78.8m × 7.0m × 4.6m
Machinery:	2-shaft, 2 diesels plus 2 electric motors, 2700bhp/5960shp = 13kts/19kts. Range 10,000nm at 10kts
Armament:	4–21in TT (bow)
Complement:	65

No	Name	Builder	Laid down	Launched	Comp	Fate
SS 511	OYASHIO	Kawasaki Jyuko, Kobe	25.12.57	25.5.59	30.6.60	Discarded 30.9.76

Constructed under the 1959 programme, these boats and their near-sisters, the *Natsushio* class, were small and limited in capability. They were air-conditioned and had good habitability and a large safety factor. They were modelled after the US *Barracuda* and were somewhat shorter and thicker than *Oyashio*. In order to reduce hull resistance, an effort was made to produce a perfect double hull; external framing was used in order to improve internal space. Attention was paid to improving underwater manoeuvrability, and a 'joystick' was installed for steering. The class used a water pressure system for launching torpedoes, thus eliminating the emission of air bubbles. The main storage batteries were water-cooled.

HAYASHIO class *submarines*

Displacement:	650t surfaced; 800t submerged
Dimensions:	193ft 6in oa × 21ft 4in × 13ft 6in max
	59.0m × 6.5m × 4.1m
Machinery:	2-shafts, 2 diesels plus 2 electric motors, 1350bhp/1700shp = 12kts/15kts
Armament:	3–21in TT (bow)
Complement:	43

No	Name	Builder	Laid down	Launched	Comp	Fate
SS 521	HAYASHIO	Shin-Mitsubishi Jyuko, Kobe	6.6.60	31.7.61	30.6.62	Stricken 1979
SS 522	WAKASHIO	Kawasaki Jyuko, Kobe	7.6.60	28.6.61	10.8.62	Stricken 23.3.79

Oyashio at launch 25.5.59
CPL

Hayashio as completed

Yushio 1981   MSDF

The *Natsushio* class was authorised in 1961 and, like their near-sisters, the *Hayashios*, were small and limited in capability. They were air-conditioned and had good habitability and a large safety factor.

NATSUSHIO class *submarines*

Displacement:	690t surfaced; 850t submerged
Dimensions:	200ft 1in pp × 21ft 2in × 13ft 6in max
	61.0m × 6.5m × 4.1m
Machinery:	2-shafts, 2 diesels plus 2 electric motors, 1350bhp/1700shp = 12kts/15kts
Armament:	3–21in TT (bow)
Complement:	43

No	Name	Builder	Laid down	Launched	Comp	Fate
SS 523	NATSUSHIO	Shin-Mitsubishi Jyuko, Kobe	5.12.61	18.9.62	30.6.63	Stricken 20.3.78
SS 524	FUYUSHIO	Kawasaki Jyuko, Kobe	6.12.61	14.12.62	31.1.64	Stricken 20.6.78

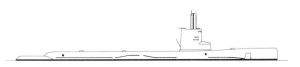

Asashio as completed

These boats are often cited as two distinct classes with the lead unit being segregated out, since she has a different shaped bow and less sophisticated sonar. These were the first fleet submarines constructed by the Japanese since the Second World War, being double the displacement of the *Hayashio* and *Natsushio* classes, and were specially equipped to serve as 'targets' in ASW exercises. The bow TT are US Mk 54 and the aft tubes are for 'swim out' torpedoes.

OSHIO class *submarines*

Displacement:	1650t (*Oshio* 1600t) standard; 2150t (*Oshio* 2100t) submerged
Dimensions:	288ft 8in pp × 26ft 11in × 16ft (*Oshio* 15ft 5in)
	88.0m × 8.2m × 4.9m (4.7m)
Machinery:	2 shafts, 2 Kawasaki-MAN diesels plus 2 electric motors, 2300bhp/6300shp = 14kts/18kts
Armament:	8–21in TT (6 bow, 2 stern)
Complement:	80

No	Name	Builder	Laid down	Launched	Comp	Fate
SS 561	OSHIO	Mitsubishi Jyuko, Kobe	29.6.63	30.4.64	31.3.65	For disposal Feb 1982
SS 562	ASASHIO	Kawasaki Jyuko, Kobe	10.10.64	27.11.65	13.10.66	Extant 1982
SS 563	HARUSHIO	Mitsubishi Jyuko, Kobe	12.10.65	25.2.67	21.12.67	Extant 1982
SS 564	MICHISHIO	Kawasaki Jyuko, Kobe	26.7.66	5.12.67	29.8.68	Extant 1982
SS 565	ARASHIO	Mitsubishi Jyuko, Kobe	5.7.67	24.10.68	25.7.69	Extant 1982

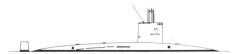

Uzushio as completed

The first teardrop-hull submarines produced by Japan. These boats have double hulls, a bow sonar array, and torpedo tubes amidships; NS-63 high-tensile steel was used in the hull shell in order to permit greater diving depth (200m). The class is equipped with a separate emergency blowing system which enables the submarine to surface rapidly. A three-dimensional automatic steering system, consisting of a combination of automatic depth-maintenance system and automatic direction-maintenance system is installed.

UZUSHIO class *submarines*

Displacement:	1850t surfaced; 3600t submerged
Dimensions:	236ft 3in pp × 32ft 6in × 24ft 7in max
	72.0m × 9.9m × 7.5m
Machinery:	1 shaft, 2 Kawasaki-MAN V8/V24–30 diesels plus 2 electric motors, 3600bhp/7200shp = 12kts/20kts
Armament:	6–21in TT (amidships)
Complement:	80

No	Name	Builder	Laid down	Launched	Comp	Fate
SS 566	UZUSHIO	Kawasaki, Kobe	25.9.68	11.3.70	21.1.71	Extant 1982
SS 567	MAKISHIO	Mitsubishi, Kobe	21.6.69	27.1.71	2.2.72	Extant 1982
SS 568	ISOSHIO	Kawasaki, Kobe	9.7.70	18.3.72	25.11.72	Extant 1982
SS 569	NARUSHIO	Mitsubishi, Kobe	8.5.71	22.11.72	28.9.73	Extant 1982
SS 570	JUROSHIO	Kawasaki, Kobe	5.7.72	22.2.74	27.11.74	Extant 1982
SS 571	TAKASHIO	Kawasaki, Kobe	6.7.73	30.6.75	30.1.76	Extant 1982
SS 572	YAESHIO	Kawasaki, Kobe	14.4.75	19.5.77	7.3.78	Extant 1982

A development of the *Uzushio* class, with a deeper diving capability and improved electronics. Later boats (from SS 577) may be fitted with Sub-Harpoon missiles. One more unit is expected to be ordered.

YUSHIO class *submarines*

Displacement:	2200t surfaced
Dimensions:	249ft 4in pp × 32ft 6in × 24ft 7in max
	76.0m × 9.9m × 7.5m
Machinery:	1 shaft, 2 Kawasaki-MAN V8/V24 diesels, plus electric motors, 3400bhp/7200shp = 13kts/20kts
Armament:	6–21in TT (amidships)
Complement:	80

No	Name	Builder	Laid down	Launched	Comp	Fate
SS 573	YUSHIO	Mitsubishi, Kobe	3.12.76	29.3.79	26.2.80	Extant 1982
SS 574	MOCHISHIO	Kawasaki, Kobe	28.4.78	12.3.80	5.3.81	Extant 1982
SS 575	SETOSHIO	Kawasaki, Kobe	17.4.79	12.2.81	3.3.82	Extant 1982
SS 576	OKISHIO	Kawasaki, Kobe	17.4.80	Jul 82		Fitting out
SS 577	NADASHIO	Mitsubishi, Kobe	10.4.81			Building
SS 578		Kawasaki, Kobe	Apr 82			Building
SS 579						Ordered

AMPHIBIOUS WARFARE VESSELS

Ex-US LSSL type *large support ships/gunboats*

Particulars:	As US LSSL class

Class:

Ajisai (ex-*LSSL 88*), *Akane* (ex-*LSSL 100*), *Aio* (ex-*LSSL 98*), *Ayame* (ex-*LSSL 115*), *Azami* (ex-*LSSL 27*), *Bara* (ex-*LSSL 78*), *Botan* (ex-*LSSL 129*), *Ezogiku* (ex-*LSSL 24*), *Fuji* (ex-*LSSL 75*), *Fuyo* (ex-*LSSL 110*), *Hagi* (ex-*LSSL 130*), *Hamagiku* (ex-*LSSL 87*), *Hamayu* (ex-*LSSL 68*), *Hasu* (ex-*LSSL 89*), *Himawari* (ex-*LSSL 102*), *Himeyuri* (ex-*LSSL 20*), *Hinagiku* (ex-*LSSL 83*), *Hiiragi* (ex-*LSSL 114*), *Isogiku* (ex-*LSSL 106*), *Iwagiku* (ex-*LSSL 120*), *Kaido* (ex-*LSSL 76*), *Kanna* (ex-*LSSL 109*), *Karukaya* (ex-*LSSL 67*), *Keito* (ex-*LSSL 60*), *Keshi* (ex-*LSSL 114*), *Kiku* (ex-*LSSL 57*), *Kikyo* (ex-*LSSL 119*), *Nogiku* (ex-*LSSL 22*), *Oniyuri* (ex-*LSSL 13*), *Ran* (ex-*LSSL 104*), *Renge* (ex-*LSSL 126*), *Rindo* (ex-*LSSL 79*), *Sasayuri* (ex-*LSSL 52*), *Sawagiku* (ex-*LSSL 84*), *Sekichiku* (ex-*LSSL 12*), *Shida* (ex-*LSSL 90*), *Shiragiku* (ex-*LSSL 72*), *Shobu* (ex-*LSSL 96*), *Suiren* (ex-*LSSL 94*), *Sumire* (ex-*LSSL 14*), *Susuki* (ex-*LSSL 58*), *Suzuran* (ex-*LSSL 25*), *Tsuta* (ex-*LSSL 85*), *Tsutsuji* (ex-*LSSL 101*), *Yagaruma* (ex-*LSSL 103*), *Yamabuki* (ex-*LSSL 116*), *Yamagiku* (ex-*LSSL 82*), *Yamayuki* (ex-*LSSL 18*), *Yuri* (ex-*LSSL 104*)

Wartime built fire support ships, originally rated as LCS(3)Ls; rocket launchers were removed before all were transferred in 1953. They are named after flowers, are armed with either 1–3in/50 and 4–40mm, or 3 twin 40mm, and all were disposed of between 1957 and 1961. See under United States in 1922–46 volume for full details.

Ex-US LSM type *medium landing ship*

Particulars:	As US LSM type

Class:

Yorikutei (LSM 3001)

The US *LSM 125* was transferred to the French Navy in 1954 for use in Vietnam, and later passed on to Japan (in 1958). She was deleted in 1974.

Ex-US LST type *tank landing ship*

Particulars:	As US LST type

Class (no, former name and no):

Oosumi (LST 4001, ex-*Daggett County*, LST 689), *Shimokita* (LST 4002, ex-*Hillsdale County*, LST 835), *Shiretoko* (LST 4003, ex-*Nansemond County*, LST 1064)

US wartime built LSTs transferred under MDAP and commissioned 1.4.61. The first two were deleted in 1974 and 1975 respectively, and the last was returned to the USA in 1976 for transfer to the Phillipines.

ATSUMI class *tank landing ships*

Displacement:	1550 standard; 2400t full load
Dimensions:	292ft × 42ft 8in × 8ft 10in
	89.0m × 13.0m × 2.7m
Machinery:	2 shafts, 2 Kawasaki/MAN diesels, 440bhp = 13kts. Range 4300nm at 12kts
Armament:	4–40mm (2×2)
Sensors:	Radar OPS-9
Complement:	100

Class (no, launched):

Atsumi (LST 4101, 13.6.72), *Motobu* (LST 4102, 3.8.73), *Nemuro* (LST 4103, 16.6.77)

Atsumi is only 1480t standard and is a knot faster. All were built by Sasebo. Troop capacity is 120 plus 20 vehicles; they carry 2 LCVPs in davits and can carry an LCM on deck. All three were in service in 1982.

MIURA class *tank landing ships*

Displacement:	2000t standard; 3200t full load
Dimensions:	308ft 4in pp, 321ft 6in oa × 45ft 11in × 9ft 10in
	94.0m, 98.0m × 14.0m × 3.0m
Machinery:	2 shafts, 2 Kawasaki/MAN diesels, 4400bhp = 14kts. Range 4300nm at 12kts
Armament:	2–3in/50 (1×2), 2–40mm (1×2)
Sensors:	Radar OPS-14, OPS-16
Complement:	18

Class (no, launched):

Miura (LST 4151, 13.8.74), *Ojika* (LST 4152, 2.9.75), *Satsuma* (LST 4153, 12.5.76)

All were built by Ishikawajima Harima, Tokyo. They can carry 180 troops and 1800t cargo; 2 LCVPs are slung under davits, and a travelling gantry handles 2 LCMs carried on the foredeck. The US Mk 33 3in mounting is forward and the 40mm mounting is aft. *Satsuma* has run trials with a 76mm OTO Melara compact in place of the 3in mount. All were in service in 1982.

YURA class *utility landing craft*

Displacement:	500t standard; 590t full load
Dimensions:	190ft 4in × 31ft 3in × 5ft 8in
	58.0m × 9.5m × 1.7m
Machinery:	2 shafts, 2 Fuji diesels, 3000bhp = 12kts
Armament:	1–20mm Gatling
Complement:	32

Class (no, launched):

Yura (LSU 4171, 10.8.80), *Noto* (LSU 4172, 1.11.80)

Both built by Sasebo Heavy Industries and completed 27.3.81. They are small LSTs with a bow door and ramp. Both were in service in 1982.

Nemuro as completed   MSDF

MINOR LANDING CRAFT

Japan also operated 6 ex-US LCUs (*LCU 2001–2006*), 42 ex-US LCMs (*LCM 1001–1042*), and 8 LCVPs. The last 13 LCMs were transferred under MDAP in 1961, the remainder having been taken over on 2.6.55. Most were deleted in the 1970s.

In 1982 the Japanese Navy had 15 locally-built 24t craft of the US LCM(6) design, plus 22 Japanese-built GRP hulled LCVPs (13t). These craft are primarily for service aboard the LSTs.

SMALL SURFACE COMBATANTS

KAMOME class *submarine-chasers*

Displacement:	330t (*Kari, Kiji, Taka, Washi* 310t) standard
Dimensions:	177ft 2in pp × 21ft 4in × 6ft 7in max *54.0m × 6.5m × 2.0m*
Machinery:	2 shafts, Mitsui/Burmeister & Wain (*Kari, Kiji, Taka, Kawasaki* MAN) diesels, 4000bhp = 21kts. Oil 21.5t. Range 2000nm at 12kts
Armament:	2–40mm (2×2), 1 Hedgehog, 2 K-guns (not in PC 305–307), 2 DC racks
Complement:	60

Class (no, launched):
Uraga, Yokosuka – *Kamome* (PC 305, 3.9.56), *Misago* (PC 307, 1.11.56)
Fujimagata, Osaka – *Kari* (PC 301, 26.9.56), *Taka* (PC 303, 17.11.56)
Iino, Maizuru – *Kiji* (PC 302, 11.9.56), *Washi* (PC 304, 12.11.56)
Kure – *Tsubame* (PC 306, 10.10.56)

All authorised under the 1954 programme, laid down between December 1955 and March 1956, and completed January–March 1957. In effect they were up-dated versions of the wartime US PC concept. All were scrapped 1977–78.

HAYABUSA *submarine-chaser*

Displacement:	370t standard
Dimensions:	190ft 3in × 25ft 7in × 6ft 6in max *58.0m × 7.8m × 2.0m*
Machinery:	3-shaft, CODAG: 2 Burmeister & Wain diesels, 4000bhp, plus 1 gas turbine, 6000shp = 26kts
Armament:	2–40mm (1×2), 1 Hedgehog, 2 DCT, 2 DC racks
Complement:	80

Built by Mitsubishi, Nagasaki, laid down 23.5.56, launched 20.11.56 and completed 10.6.57. Authorised under the 1954 programme, *Hayabusa* (PC 308) had a unique machinery arrangement with a gas turbine on the centre shaft. She was converted to a yacht (ASY 91) at Yokohama Yacht Co in 1977–78, when she was disarmed and new enlarged superstructure added. Painted white overall, she was in service in 1982.

UMITAKA class *submarine-chasers*

Displacement:	440t standard; 480t full load
Dimensions:	196ft 9in pp × 23ft 3in × 7ft 9in max *60.0m × 7.1m × 2.4m*
Machinery:	2 shafts, Mitsui/Burmeister & Wain diesels, 4000bhp = 21kts. Range 3000nm at 12kts
Armament:	2–40mm (1×2), 1 Hedgehog, 2 DCT, 2 DC racks
Sensors:	Radar OPS-35; sonar SQS-11A
Complement:	80

Class (no, launched):
Ootaka (PC 309, 3.9.59), *Umitaka* (PC 310, 25.7.59)

Both were authorised under the 1957 programme, *Ootaka* being built by Kure and *Umitaka* by Kawasaki, Kobe. They were later fitted with 2 Mk 3 launchers for Mk 32 torpedoes in place of the DCT. They were transferred to training duties in 1980 and 1981 respectively, and renumbered ASU 86 and 88.

MIZUTORI class *submarine-chasers*

Displacement:	420t–450t standard; 450–480t full load
Dimensions:	196ft 9in pp × 23ft 3in × 7ft 8in max *60.0m × 7.1m × 2.4m*
Machinery:	2 shafts, 2 MAN diesels, 3800bhp = 20kts. Oil 24.5t. Range 3000nm at 12kts
Armament:	2–40mm (2×2), 1 Hedgehog, 1 DC rack, 2 ASW torpedo racks
Sensors:	Radar OPS-35 or -36; sonar SQS-11A
Complement:	70

Class (no, launched):
Kawasaki, Kobe – *Mizutori* (PC 311, 22.9.59)
Fujinagata, Osaka – *Yamadori* (PC 312, 22.10.59), *Kasasagi* (PC 304, 31.5.60), *Kumataka* (PC 318, 21.10.63)
Kure – *Ootori* (PC 313, 27.5.60), *Wakataka* (PC 317, 13.11.62)
Sasebo – *Hatsukai* (PC 315, 24.6.60), *Umidori* (PC 316, 15.10.62), *Shiratori* (PC 319, 8.10.64), *Hiyodoro* (PC 320, 29.9.65)

The first two were authorised in the 1958 programme, with three in 1959, two in 1961 and one each in 1962, 1963 and 1964. Most have been reclassified as auxiliaries (ASU) and given a training role: PC 311, 312 and 314 on 27.3.81; PC 313, 315, 317 and 318 by Mar 1982. The remaining three are expected to be similarly reclassified during 1983.

TYPE 1 *fast patrol craft*

Displacement:	70t standard
Dimensions:	85ft 4in pp × 22ft 4in × 3ft 7in max *26.0m × 6.8m × 1.1m*
Machinery:	2 shafts, 2 diesels, 14,000bhp = 31kts
Armament:	1–40mm, 2–21in TT (2×1)
Complement:	18

Class:
Hitachi Zosen – *No 1, No 2*
Mitsubishi Zosen – *No 3, No 4*
Azuma Zosen – *No 5, No 6*

All units were authorised in the 1953 programme. Nos *801–806* were assigned on 1.9.57. These boats had an ASW capability, sonar domes being installed on the hull bottoms, but at high speeds the sonars offered considerable resistance. All units were deleted 1971–72.

TYPE 7 *fast patrol craft*

Displacement:	104t standard
Dimensions:	109ft 5in pp × 24ft 7in × 3ft 11in max *34.1m × 7.5m × 1.2m*
Machinery:	3 shafts, 3 Mitsubishi diesels, 6000bhp = 33kts
Armament:	2–40mm (2×1), 4–21in TT (4×1)
Complement:	24

Class (launched):
Mitsubishi Zosen – *No 7* (2.2.57), *No 8* (20.7.57)

Authorised under the 1954 programme, laid down August 1956 and launched 31.10.57 and 15.11.57 respectively. Numbers *807* and *808* were assigned 1.9.57. This class was fitted with an improved sonar dome which offered less resistance at high speed than the type used in the Type 1. From January 68 until December 72, *No 7* was fitted with an Ishikawajima-Harima T64 marine gas turbine for test purposes. Both units were deleted in 1973.

No 9 *fast patrol craft*

Displacement:	64t standard
Dimensions:	71ft 4in oa × 19ft 9in × 6ft max *21.7m × 6.2m × 1.8m*
Machinery:	2 shafts, 2 Napier Deltic diesels, 5000bhp = 40kts
Armament:	1–40mm, 2–21in TT (2×1)
Complement:	15

Type 9 craft, built by Saunders-Roe, Beaumaris, GB, delivered 29.7.57 and accepted 2.9.57. Similar to the British 'Dark' class. Number *809* was assigned 1.9.57. Deleted 1972.

No 10 *fast patrol craft*

Displacement:	120t standard
Dimensions:	105ft pp × 27ft 8in × 3ft 10in max *32.0m × 8.5m × 1.2m*
Machinery:	3 shafts, 3 diesels, 9000bhp = 40kts
Armament:	2–40mm (2×1), 4–21in TT (4×1)
Complement:	20

Type 10 craft, built by Mitsubishi, Shimonoseki, laid down 30.1.62, launched 28.7.61 and completed 25.5.62. Authorised under the 1960 programme; Number *810* was assigned. This boat was built as a test platform for the follow-on, mass produced Type 11 and was fitted with dipping sonar and sonobuoys. Deleted 1975.

PT 13 as completed   MSDF

TYPE 11 *fast patrol craft*

Displacement:	110t standard; 125t full load
Dimensions:	116ft 6in pp × 30ft 3in × 3ft 11in max
	25.5m × 9.2m × 1.2m
Machinery:	3-shaft CODAG: 2 Mitsubishi diesels plus 2 Ihi gas turbines, 11,000shp = 40kts
Armament:	2–40mm (2×1), 4–21in TT (4×1)
Sensors:	Radar OPS-13
Complement:	28

Class (no, laid down, commissioned):
PT 11 (811, 17.3.70, 27.3.71), *PT 12* (812, 22.4.71, 28.3.72), *PT 13* (813, 28.3.72, 16.12.72), *PT 14* (814, 23.3.73, 15.2.74), *PT 15* (815, 23.4.74, 10.7.75)

All were built by Mitsubishi, Shimonoseki and were in service in 1982.

OTHER SMALL CRAFT

Fifteen 18t patrol boats were transferred to Japan under MDAP in 1958, and numbered *Shokai* (patrol boat) *1–7* and *11–18*. They were deleted in the early 1970s.

Nine new 18t boats, *PB 19–PB 27*, were built by Ishikawajima, Yokohama, between 1971 and 1973. They are GRP-hulled craft, capable of 20kts, and armed with 1–20mm. All were in service in 1982.

MINE WARFARE VESSELS

ERIMO *minelayer/minesweeper*

Displacement:	630t standard; 670t full load
Dimensions:	210ft × 26ft × 8ft
	64.0m × 7.9m × 2.4m
Machinery:	2 shafts, diesels, 2500bhp = 18kts
Armament:	1–40mm, 2–20mm (2×1), 1 Hedgehog, 2 K-guns, 2 DC racks
Complement:	80

Erimo (AMC 491) was built by Uraga Dock, and launched 12.7.55. She was designed as a multi-purpose minesweeper, minelayer and submarine-chaser. She was converted to an Explosive Ordnance Disposal tender (for mine clearance divers) in 1975–76, with an armament of 2–40mm (1×2), 2–20mm (2×1) and a single Mk10 Hedgehog. Minelaying capability has also been retained, and she was still in service in 1982, with the number YAS 69.

TSUGARU *minelayer/cable layer*

Displacement:	950t standard
Dimensions:	216ft 4in × 34ft 2in × 11ft
	66.0m × 10.4m × 3.4m
Machinery:	2 shafts, diesels, 3200bhp = 16kts
Armament:	1–3in/50, 2–20mm (2/1), 4 K-guns, 40 mines
Sensors:	Radar OPS-16
Complement:	100

Tsugaru (ARC 481) was built by Yokohama Shipyard and launched 19.7.55; she was designed as a dual purpose coastal minelayer and cable layer. She was lengthened and widened to 338ft × 47ft 11in (*103.0m × 14.6m*) by Nippon Kokan, Tsurumi in 1969–70 and converted to a specialised cable ship (ASU 7001), retaining only 2–20mm guns. As such she was still in service in 1982.

HAYASE *mine warfare support ship/minelayer*

Displacement:	2000t standard; 3050t full load
Dimensions:	324ft 9in × 42ft 8in × 12ft 6in
	99.0m × 13.0m × 3.8m
Machinery:	2 shafts, 4 Kawasaki/MAN diesels, 6400bhp = 18kts
Armament:	2–3in/50 (1×2), 2–20mm (2×1), 6–12.75in Mk 32 ASW TT (2×3), 200 mines
Sensors:	Radar OPS-17; sonar SQS-11A
Complement:	85

No	Name	Builder	Launched	Fate
MST 46	HAYASE	Ishikawajima, Harima	21.6.71	Extant 1982

A multi-role mine warfare ship, with 5 rails for minelaying, a platform aft for landing a minesweeping helicopter, and the facilities to support mine counter-measures operations. Originally fitted with OPS-14 air search radar. The design has been developed into the *Souya* type (see below).

Souya 1971

SOUYA *minelayer*

Displacement:	2150t standard; 3250t full load
Dimensions:	324ft 9in × 49ft 3in × 13ft 9in
	99.0m × 15.0m × 4.2m
Sensors:	Radar OPS-14, OPS-16; sonar SQS-11A
Other particulars:	As *Hayase*

No	Name	Builder	Launched	Fate
MMC 951	SOUYA	Hitachi Maizuru	31.3.71	Extant 1982

Laid down on 9.7.70 and commissioned on 30.9.71, *Souya* has 6 mine rails (4 in the stern, and 2 externally). She is also equipped to operate a minesweeping helicopter, although there is no hangar.

Ex- US ALBATROSS class *coastal minesweepers*

Particulars:	As US YMS type

Class (no, former no):
Etajima (MSC 656, ex-*AMS 10*), *Moroshima* (MSC 663, ex-*YMS 372*), *Ninoshima* (MSC 662, ex-*YMS 376*), *Nuwajima* (MSC 657, ex-*AMS 18*), *Ogishima* (MSC 659, ex-*AMS 32*), *Ujishima* (MSC 655, ex-*AMS 5*), *Yakushima* (MSC 658, ex-*AMS 28*), *Yugeshima* (MSC 660, ex-*AMS 36*), *Yurishima* (MSC 661, ex-*AMS 40*)

Belonging to the wartime YMS type (renamed the *Albatross* class postwar), they were transferred under MDAP in 1955 (except *Moroshima* and *Ninoshima* in 1959). They had short careers in the JMSDF, most being deleted in 1957, although *Etajima* and *Ujishima* served until 1966, and *Yakushima* was returned to the USA in 1970.

Ex-US AMS/MSC type *coastal minesweepers*

Particulars:	As US AMS/MSC type

Class (no, former no, acquired):
Yashima (MSC 651, ex-*AMS 144*, 16.12.54), *Hashima* (MSC 652, ex-*AMS 95*, 3.6.55), *Tsushima* (MSC 653, ex-*AMS 255*, 18.7.56), *Toshima* (MSC 654, ex-*MSC 258*, 18.7.56)

Belonging to the numerous US-built AMS type (reclassified MSC in Feb 1955), they were transferred on completion to Japan. MSC 651 and 652 were reclassified as auxiliaries in 1971, and the other two shortly afterwards. MSC 682 was deleted in 1976 and the remainder in about 1978.

YASHIRO *coastal minesweeper*

Displacement:	230t standard; 255t full load
Dimensions:	118ft pp × 22ft 8in × 6ft 2in
	36.0m × 6.9m × 1.9m
Machinery:	2 shafts, diesels, 1200bhp = 13kts
Armament:	1–20mm

Yashiro (MSC 601) was built by Nippon Kokan, Tsurumi and launched 26.3.56. She was transferred to an auxiliary role as a diving tender (YAS 58) and was deleted in 1981.

ATADA class *class minesweepers*

Displacement:	240t standard; 260t full load
Dimensions:	118ft pp, 123ft 4in oa × 21ft × 6ft 9in
	36.0m, 37.6m × 6.4m × 2.1m
Machinery:	2 shafts, 2 diesels, 1200bhp = 13kts
Armament:	1–20mm

Class (no, launched):
Atada (MSC 601, 12.3.56), *Itsuki* (MSC 602, 11.3.56)

Both built of wood and lightweight metals by Hitachi, Kanagawa. Both were transferred to auxiliary roles as gunnery tenders (YAS 56 and 57) and were deleted in 1981.

JAPAN

Katsura 1979   MSDF

Ninoshima as completed   Hitachi Zosen

KASADO class *minehunters/minesweepers*

Displacement:	330t standard; 360t full load
Dimensions:	150ft × 27ft 6in × 7ft 6in
	45.7m × 8.4m × 2.3m
Machinery:	2 shafts, 2 Mitsubishi diesels, 1200bhp = 14kts
Armament:	1–20mm
Sensors:	Radar OPS-9; sonar ZQS-9
Complement:	43

Class (no, launched):
Amani (MSC 623, 31.10.66), *Chiburi* (MSC 620, 29.11.63), *Habushi* (MSC 609, 19.6.59), *Hario* (MSC 618, 10.12.62), *Hirado* (MSC 613, 3.10.60), *Hotaka* (MSC 616, 23.10.61), *Ibuki* (MSC 628, 2.12.67), *Kanawa* (MSC 606, 22.4.59), *Karato* (MSC 617, 11.12.62), *Kasado* (MSC 604, 19.3.58), *Katsura* (MSC 629, 18.9.67), *Koozo* (MSC 609, 12.11.59), *Koshiki* (MSC 615, 9.11.61), *Kudako* (MSC 622, 8.12.64), *Mikura* (MSC 612, 14.3.60), *Minase* (MSC 627, 10.1.67), *Mutsure* (MSC 619, 16.12.63), *Ootsu* (MSC 621, 5.11.64), *Rebun* (MSC 624, 7.12.65), *Rishiri* (MSC 623, 22.11.65), *Sakito* (MSC 607, 22.4.59), *Shikine* (MSC 613, 22.7.60), *Shisaka* (MSC 605, 20.3.58), *Tatara* (MSC 610, 14.1.60), *Tsukumi* (MSC 611, 12.1.60), *Urume* (MSC 626, 12.11.66)

Wooden coastal minesweepers, similar to many other classes in Western navies. The even-numbered vessels were built by Hitachi, Kanagawa, and the remainder by Nippon Kokan, Tsurumi. In 1982 only MSC 625–629 still served in their original role, the remainder having been transferred to auxiliary roles: MSC 612 and 613 became tenders to the gunnery school; MSC 621 and 609 became MCM support ships (MST 474 and 473) and 609 was deleted in 1981; MSC 604 (deleted 31.3.83, 608, 610, 614 and 618 became hydrographic ships; and the rest were reclassified YAS, most serving as mine clearance diver support ships. MSC 615 was deleted in 1981.

TAKAMI class *minehunters/minesweepers*

Displacement:	380t standard
Dimensions:	170ft 7in × 28ft 10in × 7ft 10in
	52.0m × 8.8m × 2.3m
Machinery:	2 shafts, 2 Mitsubishi diesels, 1440bhp = 14kts
Armament:	1–20mm
Sensors:	Radar OPS-9; sonar ZQS-2
Complement:	45–47

Class (no, launched):
Takami (MSC 630, 15.7.69), *Iou* (MSC 631, 12.8.69), *Mikaye* (MSC 632,

3.6.70), *Utone* (MSC 633, 6.4.70), *Awaji* (MSC 634, 11.12.70), *Toushi* (MSC 635, 13.12.70), *Tewi* (MSC 636, Oct 71), *Murotsu* (MSC 637, Oct 71), *Tashiro* (MSC 638, 2.4.73), *Miyato* (MSC 639, 3.4.73), *Takane* (MSC 640, 8.3.74), *Muzuki* (MSC 641, 5.4.74), *Yokose* (MSC 642, 21.7.75), *Sakate* (MSC 643, 5.8.75), *Oumi* (MSC 644, 28.5.76), *Fukue* (MSC 645, 12.7.76), *Okitsu* (MSC 646, 4.3.77), *Hashira* (MSC 647, 8.11.77), *Iwai* (MSC 648, 8.11.77)

Wooden minesweepers (developed from the *Kasado* class) which also carry divers for mine clearance duties. The electronics are largely Japanese-produced versions of British equipment. The even-numbered vessels were built by Nippon Kokan, Tsurumi, and the remainder by Hitachi, Kanagawa. *Miyato* was deleted on 31.3.82, but the rest were in service at the end of 1982.

HATSUSHIMA class *minehunters/minesweepers*

Displacement:	440t standard
Dimensions:	180ft 5in × 30ft 10in × 7ft 10in
	55.0m × 9.4m × 2.4m
Machinery:	2 shafts, 2 Mitsubishi diesels, 1440bhp = 14kts
Armament:	1–20mm
Sensors:	Radar OPS-9; sonar ZQS-2B
Complement:	45

Class (no, launched):
Nippon Kokan, Tsurumi – *Hatsushima* (MSC 649, 30.10.78), *Miyajima* (MSC 651, 18.9.79), *Nenoshima* (MSC 652, 25.7.80), *Yakushima* (MSC 656, June 82)
Hitachi, Kanagawa – *Ninoshima* (MSC 650, 9.8.79), *Ukishima* (MSC 653, 11.7.80), *Oshima* (MSC 654, 17.6.81), *Narushima* (MSC 657, Jun 82). Two further units are planned, but the contracts had not been placed when this section went to press.

Enlarged versions of the *Takami* type, and also wooden hulled. Besides conventional sweep gear, they carry Type 54 minehunting drones. *Ukishima* is carrying out trials with a 20mm JM61-MB Gatling-type gun.

MSB type *inshore minesweepers*

Class:
MSB 707–MSB 712

Six wooden-hulled boats were built by Hitachi, Kanagawa (odd numbers) and Nippon Kokan, Tsurumi in 1973–75. They are 74ft craft of 58t full load and during minesweeping operations they are supported by the *Ootsu*. They were in service in 1982.

MISCELLANEOUS

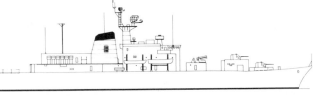

Katori 1970

AZUMA *training support ship*

Displacement:	1950t standard; 2400t full load
Dimensions:	308ft 5in pp, 321ft 6in oa × 42ft 7in × 12ft 6in max
	94.0m, 98.0m × 13.0m × 3.8m
Machinery:	2-shaft Kawasaki/MAN V8V 23/30 ATL diesels, 4000bhp = 18kts
Armament:	1–30/50in, 2 Mk 4 ASW torpedo racks
Sensors:	Radar OPS-15, SPS-40; sonar SQS-11A
Complement:	185

Laid down 13.7.68, launched 14.4.69 and completed 21.10.69 by Hitachi, Maizuru. A multi-purpose support ship, *Azuma* carries drones for anti-aircraft practice. In service in 1982.

KATORI *training ship*

Displacement:	3372t standard; 4100t full load
Dimensions:	400ft 3in pp, 418ft 2in oa × 49ft 1in × 14ft 4in max
	122.0m, 127.5m × 15.0m × 4.3m
Machinery:	2-shaft sets of Ishikawajima geared turbines, 20,000shp = 25kts
Armament:	4–3in/50in (2×2), 1 ASW rocket launcher (1×4), 6–12.75in Mk 32 ASW TT (3×2), 1 helicopter
Sensors:	Radar SPS-12, OPS-15; sonar OQS-3
Complement:	460 (inc trainees)

Katori was built by Ishikawajima Harima Tokyo, laid down 8.12.67, launched 19.11.68 and completed 10.9.68. She is capable of serving as a training ship in peacetime and as an escort command ship in wartime. She was ordered under the 1966 programme. In service 1982.